D1595342

My Life before the World War
1860–1917

AMERICAN WARRIORS

Throughout the nation's history, numerous men and women of all ranks and branches of the U.S. military have served their country with honor and distinction. During times of war and peace, there are individuals whose exemplary achievements embody the highest standards of the U.S. armed forces. The aim of the American Warriors series is to examine the unique historical contributions of these individuals, whose legacies serve as enduring examples for soldiers and citizens alike. The series will promote a deeper and more comprehensive understanding of the U.S. armed forces.

SERIES EDITOR: ROGER CIRILLO

An AUSA Book

MY LIFE
BEFORE THE
WORLD WAR,
1860–1917

A Memoir

General of the Armies
John J. Pershing

Edited and with an Introduction by

John T. Greenwood

UNIVERSITY PRESS OF KENTUCKY

Published by The University Press of Kentucky
serving Bellarmine University, Berea College, Centre College of Kentucky,
Eastern Kentucky University, The Filson Historical Society, Georgetown
College, Kentucky Historical Society, Kentucky State University, Morehead State
University, Murray State University, Northern Kentucky University, Transylvania
University, University of Kentucky, University of Louisville, and Western
Kentucky University.

Editorial and Sales Offices: The University Press of Kentucky
663 South Limestone Street, Lexington, Kentucky 40508-4008
www.kentuckypress.com

17 16 15 14 13   5 4 3 2 1

Library of Congress Cataloging-in-Publication Data

Pershing, John J. (John Joseph), 1860-1948.
 My life before the World War, 1860-1917 : a memoir / General of the Armies
John J. Pershing ; edited and with an introduction by John T. Greenwood.
     pages cm. — (American warriors)
 Includes bibliographical references and index.
 ISBN 978-0-8131-4197-8 (hardcover : alk. paper) — ISBN 978-0-8131-4198-5 (epub) —
 ISBN 978-0-8131-4199-2 (pdf)
 1. Pershing, John J. (John Joseph), 1860-1948. 2. Generals—United States—
Biography. 3. Indians of North America—Wars—1866-1895. 4. Spanish-
American War, 1898—Campaigns—Cuba. 5. Philippines—History—1898-1946.
6. United States. Army—History—Punitive Expedition into Mexico, 1916.
I. Greenwood, John T. II. Title.
 E181.P495 2013
 355.3'31092—dc23
 [B]   2013008899

This book is printed on acid-free paper meeting the requirements of the
American National Standard for Permanence in Paper for Printed Library
Materials.

Manufactured in the United States of America.

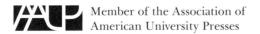 Member of the Association of
American University Presses

Contents

List of Maps and Illustrations   vii
Editor's Note   ix
Introduction   1

1. Ancestry and Boyhood   11

2. Youth—Its Happy Days and Others   24

3. West Point—Its Grind and Its Pleasures: 1881–July 1886   36

4. The Army—With the Sixth Cavalry in New Mexico:
   September 1886–November 1890   53

5. The Sioux Campaign and Commanding Indian Scouts:
   November 1890–August 1891   69

6. New Assignments, New Challenges, New Friends:
   September 1891–April 1898   81

7. The Spanish-American War to the San Juan Heights:
   April–30 June 1898   98

8. The Spanish-American War—Victory in Cuba and Its
   Consequences: 1 July–20 August 1898   112

9. The Division of Customs and Insular Affairs and My First
   Assignment to the Philippines: August 1898–November 1899   126

10. Duty in the Philippines—Manila, Mindanao, and Iligan:
    November 1899–April 1902   137

11. Dealing with the Hostile Moros around Lake Lanao:
    April–September 1902   155

12. Military Operations against the Lake Lanao Moros and the
    Routine of Governing: September–December 1902   174

13. Finishing the Campaign against the Lake Lanao Moros: January–May 1903   190

14. Return to the United States, Duty with the General Staff, and Romance and Marriage: June 1903–January 1905   206

15. Off to See a Modern War as the Military Attaché in Tokyo and Observer with the Imperial Japanese Army: February 1905–December 1906   217

16. Brigade Commander, Fort McKinley, Philippines: January 1907–August 1908   246

17. A Long Journey Home, Taft's Inauguration, Sick Leave, New Orders, and a Son Arrives: August 1908–October 1909   257

18. My Return to Mindanao: November 1909–December 1913   271

19. Disarming and Taming the Moros: September 1911–June 1913   287

20. The Last Military Governor of the Moro Province: 11 November 1909–14 December 1913   303

21. Diplomatic Missions, Our Return to the United States, and Commanding the Eighth Brigade at the Presidio of San Francisco: June 1911–April 1914   317

22. On the Mexican Border with the Eighth Brigade: April 1914–March 1916   327

23. The Expedition into Mexico: March 1916–February 1917   339

Epilogue   363

Appendices A–J   367
Biographical Appendix   465
Acknowledgments   609
Notes   611
Bibliography   681
Index   703

Maps and Illustrations

Maps

Trooper Pershing's New Mexico   55
Wounded Knee Campaign and Fort Niobrara   73
Montana   89
San Juan Battlefield   113
The Philippines   139
Lake Lanao Area   158
Russo-Japanese Theater of War   219
Mindanao and the Sulu Archipelago   273
Island of Jolo   290
Area of the Mexican Punitive Expedition 1916–1917   340

Illustrations

Pershing's boyhood schoolhouse, Laclede, Missouri   22
Pershing's boyhood home, Laclede, Missouri   27
Congressional nomination for the U.S. Military Academy   37
Pershing as Cadet First Captain, U.S. Military Academy   47
Second Lieutenant Pershing at Fort Wingate   57
"The Three Green P's" at Fort Stanton   61
Officers of the 6th Cavalry Regiment at Pine Ridge   76
Troop B, Ogallala Indian Scouts   79
Pershing and University of Nebraska cadet officers   83
Officers of the 10th Cavalry Regiment   90
Pershing as a captain   104
Commanding General and staff, Department of Mindanao and Jolo,
    Zamboanga   141
Datto Grande of Makadar   165
Brigadier General Samuel S. Sumner meeting with sultans   168
Datto Pandi-in of Dansalan, Lanao, Mindanao   172
Pershing with Moro *dattos* and sultans at Marahui   182

Pershing with the Rajamunda of Marahui 183
Camp Vicars, Lake Lanao, Mindanao 185
Captain Pershing, 15th Cavalry 188
Inspecting the Hospital Corps detachment, Camp Vicars 189
Welcoming Brigadier General Sumner and Rear Admiral Robley D. Evans 191
Observing the 15th Cavalry and the 27th Infantry leave on Bacolod expedition 195
Fort Bacolod's defensive earthworks 197
Mrs. Helen Frances "Frankie" (Warren) Pershing 215
Mukden street scene 227
Lieutenant General Kuroki 228
Foreign military observers at the Imperial Tombs 230
Imperial Palace and Tombs, Mukden, Manchuria 230
Captain Max Hoffmann 231
Wire entanglements at Fort Erlangshan, Port Arthur 232
Umezawa Brigade's memorial service and commemoration 233
Lieutenant Colonel Edward J. McClernand 234
Manchurian village where Pershing resided in 1905 234
Pershing's accommodations 234
Manchurian hut 235
Pershing's horse 235
Japanese artillery in action 236
Japanese infantry firing at Russian troops 236
Russian forward defenses, as seen from the Japanese defensive lines 236
The Japanese line north of Tiehling, Manchuria 237
Japanese machine gun 237
Brigadier General Pershing, 1906 243
Pershing with Francis Warren 270
Quarters at Pettit Barracks, Zamboanga 272
The Pershings in the Philippines 275
Aerial view of Bud Dajo, Jolo Island 293
Brigadier General Pershing in dress uniform, ca. 1912 320
Frankie Pershing and her children, 1914 324
Moraga Street residence destroyed by fire 325
Alvaro Obregón and Pancho Villa in El Paso, Texas 337
Pershing in Casas Grandes, Mexico 343
Pershing and staff, Casas Grandes, Mexico 345

Editor's Note

The Editing of This Manuscript

I worked carefully in the Papers of John J. Pershing in the Library of Congress's Manuscript Division in Washington, D.C., to review and select the most refined versions of the various chapters of the unpublished Pershing memoir that exist. These chapters were gathered together at some unknown date and titled the "Autobiography of General of the Armies John J. Pershing."[1] The first four chapters of the "Autobiography" are the versions of the June 1936 draft as retyped in December 1937, while the remaining chapters are versions from June–August 1936 as later edited and revised by Pershing himself. I then scanned, converted to Microsoft Word format, and edited these chapters. During the editing process, I frequently had to consult earlier drafts of the chapters when questions arose about the extensive revisions in the text or for purposes of clarification of unclear or incomplete passages.

The editing included the annotating in each chapter of the places and events that required a fuller identification for the reader's information. In his lifetime, Pershing came to know literally thousands of very important political, civilian, and military leaders from around the world, and many of them he met during his prewar career. Indeed, his personal contacts with many of these leaders were critical to his later assignments, promotions, and career. I decided that knowledge of who these people were was critically important to a fuller understanding of Pershing's own story, but all of them could not be included without making the manuscript much too lengthy. Thus, I compiled an alphabetical Biographical Appendix that includes only those individuals who I could identify as being important in Pershing's life and career. I have excluded those persons who any reader can easily obtain information on, such as former presidents and well-known American military figures. I also excluded those historical figures Pershing mentions in passing and foreign persons except those with whom Pershing had a significant relationship, such as his fellow observers in Manchuria during 1905. I have tried to identify more fully those U.S. Army officers with whom Pershing served and who in many cases were not insignificant at the time but who today are largely unknown. He knew each of them to some degree or another, and he would not have mentioned them had they not had some place in his life's story. Because he thought them important enough to mention in his memoir, I have thought them important enough to identify for the reader.

During his editing, Pershing occasionally omitted material within quoted documents and replaced it with ellipses. In some of these cases I elected to reinsert the full wording of the original source because I believed that the complete original text enhanced the reader's understanding of what Pershing was discussing. Those reinsertions are indicated with square brackets followed by a † symbol. All other bracketed corrections or clarifications that I have added for the reader's benefit are enclosed in square brackets alone. Because the manuscript that I used was never submitted for publication, it was never professionally reviewed and edited. A number of shortcomings remained in the text that probably would have been resolved had that editorial process taken place. Pershing frequently did not complete his stories, either intentionally or not, thus leaving incomplete accounts throughout. In some instances he and his team simply did not dig deeply enough into an issue, which they may have considered not to have been significant enough to merit additional work or which they simply never got back to. A number of times Pershing simply inserted blank spaces or question marks to indicate where more research was required to add the correct information to the text. Using documents in Pershing's papers or readily available to researchers, I have tried to answer questions such as these.

The manuscript also contained some factual errors because a thorough editorial review never took place and none of those who worked on the manuscript were professional historians. When found, I have corrected many of these in annotations rather than in the text because in some cases an extended explanation was required. Pershing also was not overly concerned about the dating of events in his narrative or inclined to provide dates that would allow the reader to place events in context. Where possible, I have added dates from documents in Pershing's papers so that the narrative has a better chronological and contextual cohesion and flow. Obvious typographical errors were corrected and punctuation was adjusted where necessary to improve readability, but Pershing's basic intent was never altered. After spending many hours reviewing the various drafts of these chapters, I have great empathy for Pershing and those who assisted him and can easily understand how these errors crept into the manuscript.

The original manuscript in the working files bore only the general title of "memoirs" until the various chapters were pulled together at some later date and named "The Autobiography of General of the Armies John J. Pershing." In the manuscript's most refined version, only chapters 1–9 were even given titles. Thus, I have titled the manuscript *My Life before the World War, 1860-1917: A Memoir.* I believe this title accurately reflects the scope and content of the original manuscript that is in the Pershing Papers. Of the twenty-four chapters in the book, twenty-three pertain to Pershing's life and career from 1860 to early 1917, and the epilogue is simply a very brief review of the years 1917 to 1935. I have also retitled all but the first two chapters to reflect more fully their actual content. In each of the revised chapter titles, except the epilogue, I have added the dates of the subject matter that is covered within the chapter to provide the reader with a better guide to its contents.

None of the draft chapters in the original manuscript had subheadings to facilitate the reader's journey through them. I thought that it was best to provide subheadings at points where Pershing made shifts in subject matter.

Appendices

In writing his memoir, Pershing relied heavily on the large collection of personal papers he had accumulated over the length of his army career. Because certain of these many documents were particularly critical sources in the telling of his story, I have selected ten of them for inclusion in this volume. These cover the period from the Spanish-American War (1898) through the fight at Carrizal (21 June 1916) during the Mexican Expedition. Eight of the documents pertain specifically to Pershing's two tours of duty on Mindanao with the Moros. Six official reports on his work with the Moros—one while at Iligan (April 1902) and five on the expeditions against them while commanding at Camp Vicars (June 1902–May 1903)—cover his activities during the period when he rose to prominence in the army and made his reputation. Copies of these reports are in his papers, and they were also published in the *Annual Reports of the War Department* for 1902 and

1903. The two other reports, on the Bud Dajo (1911) and Bud Bagsak campaigns (1913), exist only in his papers and in U.S. Army records in the National Archives and Records Administration (NARA). The final two documents are the speech he made about his experiences in the Cuban campaign on 27 November 1898 at his parents' church in Chicago, Illinois, and his memorandum on the fight with Mexican government forces at Carrizal on 21 June 1916.

Introduction

General of the Armies John J. Pershing is clearly a seminal figure not only in the history of the United States and its army, but also of the world in the early twentieth century. Major biographies of Pershing have relied heavily both on his published two-volume autobiographical account *My Experiences in the World War* (New York: Frederick A. Stokes, 1931) and on his unpublished "Autobiography of General of the Armies John J. Pershing" that rests in his papers.[1] While his published memoir is readily available to any interested readers or researchers, those wishing to dig into his unpublished account must travel to Washington and spend considerable time at the Manuscript Division's reading room. This edited version of General Pershing's autobiographical memoir of his years prior to the U.S. entrance into World War I in April 1917 and his appointment to head the American Expeditionary Forces (AEF) in France is intended to provide this invaluable document and its unequaled perspective on John J. Pershing to a wider audience.

The Writing of the Memoir

After Pershing completed his tour as U.S. Army chief of staff on 13 September 1924 and retired from the army, he still had his consuming work as chairman of the American Battle Monuments Commission (ABMC) and his many official activities as general of the armies to keep him busy, along with his on-again, off-again work on his personal memoir. President Calvin Coolidge then asked him late in 1924 to head a diplomatic effort to resolve the Tacna-Arica dispute between Peru and Chile that had festered since 1883. He accepted this mission but finally had to give it up due to ill health after spending six months in Arica (August 1925–January 1926). Once recovered, Pershing again seriously resumed work on an autobiography that emphasized his wartime role. He solicited information and stories from colleagues he had known in his earlier years as he drafted his account. In late October 1926, he wrote to Judge

1

Charles B. Elliott, whom he had known from his days as commander of the Department of Mindanao and governor of the Moro Province in the Philippines (1909–1913), seeking information on their trip to Hong Kong to celebrate the coronation of King George V in 1912 because he had now reached that point in his writing. Elliott's detailed reply of 17 November provided some colorful stories, which Pershing later incorporated into his memoir (see chapter 21).[2] However, Pershing's vision of a larger autobiographical account of his life centered on the World War soon gave way to the realization that simply writing his story of the war years would be an enormous undertaking.

With his focus now fixed on the war years alone, Pershing toiled for the next four years to complete and heavily revise his *My Experiences in the World War,* which appeared in two volumes in 1931. He could now return to his original idea of an autobiographical volume that would tell his life's story up to the time of his selection to head the American army in France. He wanted to provide those details of his personal and military life from his childhood in Laclede, Missouri, through the Mexican Expedition (March 1916–February 1917) to fill in some of what he considered to be blank spaces in his story. At first Pershing intended to conclude this memoir with several chapters on his World War I years and thus produce a more complete, balanced account of his entire life.

Pershing apparently returned to work on this memoir sometime during or after 1931 with the assistance of members of his office staff at Headquarters, General of the Armies: George E. Adamson,[3] Ralph A. Curtin,[4] and Charles B. Shaw.[5] As general of the armies, Pershing was always on active duty and was authorized a personal staff to assist him in his official duties. Adamson had first served Pershing in the Mexican Expedition as a civilian army field clerk and accompanied him to France in May 1917 in the same capacity. Shaw had also accompanied Pershing's party to Europe on board the SS *Baltic*[6] as an acting army field clerk and remained with him at General Headquarters, AEF, at Chaumont, France, throughout the war and thereafter. Curtin joined the staff at Chaumont during the war and also remained with Pershing following the Armistice. It appears that Shaw was Pershing's closest advisor, researcher, cowriter, and editorial assistant throughout the years that the general worked on the manuscript. He had previously worked closely with Pershing to revise completely the manuscript of *My Experiences in the World War,* especially during some arduous weeks the two spent at Greenbrier Resort in White Sulphur Springs, West Virginia.[7]

Pershing apparently used a process similar to that which he had adopted for completing *My Experiences in the World War,* although no man-uscript routing slips like those used for the first book have shown up for the second.[8] He wrote out the initial new drafts in longhand, using pencil or ink pen. Pershing possessed a great memory (which he read-ily attributed to his mother) and was a good writer, so he was able to get the basics of his story down on paper. Shaw had the drafts typed up, and Pershing, Shaw, Curtin, and Adamson then reviewed and commented on them. Shaw and Curtin had the tremendous advantage in their endeavors of having full access to the extensive files Pershing had collected during his career, dating back to the U.S. Military Academy and his first assign-ment with the 6th Cavalry. Pershing also had kept personal diaries and field notebooks from as early as his days at West Point. These provided a ready source of important personal and historical information, especially on his field operations against the Moros in the Philippines, with which to flesh out the story and add important details. From the 1890s on, Per-shing had carried on correspondence with numerous important leaders of the U.S. Army and War Department as well as with his many military, political, and civilian friends and acquaintances. During his years in the Philippines he was careful to keep his superiors fully informed of his plans, actions, and operations. He kept or later obtained copies of virtu-ally all of the reports, messages, letters, and newspaper clippings about him and his activities. For his years in the Philippines (1899–1903, 1907–1908, 1909–1913), this documentation accounts for nine full boxes in his personal papers in the Manuscript Division, while another four hold his files from the Russo-Japanese War and Tokyo period (1905–1906). Two more boxes contain Mexican Expedition reports, messages, and corre-spondence. Beyond this is all of his personal correspondence, which is filed alphabetically in 211 boxes.

Pershing's personal schedule of spending many of the spring, sum-mer, and early fall months each year from 1926 to 1939 in Paris certainly did not make the work of Shaw and Curtin any easier. In France he continued his duties as chairman of the American Battle Monuments Commission overseeing the design and building of the American mili-tary cemeteries in Europe. When not in France, Pershing usually spent at least some of the winter months each year in Tucson, Arizona, mostly at the El Conquistador Hotel, to escape the Washington weather. Thus, the time he actually worked directly with Shaw on his memoir was lim-ited to several months a year. On his leisurely voyages across the Atlan-tic, however, Pershing often wrote drafts in pencil, at least one of which remains on the stationery of the United States Lines, and reviewed the revised chapters that were then returned through the ABMC's Paris office.[9] During the mid-1930s this meant a lot of mailing of revised drafts back and forth, necessarily slowing the progress toward completion and publication.

Although an initial draft of the manuscript was completed within about a year or so, probably in late 1932 or early 1933, it is not certain exactly when it was finished because I could not locate any dated copy in Pershing's papers at the Library of Congress. An unfortunate aspect of working with these various drafts is that none of the early ones is dated, so it is most difficult to follow the sequence of the revisions. I believe that Shaw must have had these drafts organized for easy use because Pershing himself was a precise, well-organized person. Over the years that original structure has been lost in various reorganizations of Pershing's office files and in the Library of Congress's processing or reboxing of the papers after it received them. A second draft was definitely completed sometime in 1933, for Shaw and Curtin were working on it persistently with Pershing as of September of that year.

Pershing methodically worked over each draft chapter as Shaw returned it to him. The draft chapters now resting in the boxes of Pershing's papers show an incredible attention to the details of the story and the quality of the written narrative. The constant interaction and exchanges among all of the reviewers further refined and broadened the manuscript. Pershing often simply crossed out entire paragraphs and pages, scribbled his penciled comments in his distinctive handwriting, directed additional research, or requested that more information be located to fill in what he thought was missing. His deep and personal involvement in this exhausting process was never lacking, and he often directed a check of his papers for this or that bit of information. As he reviewed and revised the drafts, he frequently sent long interrogatories to Adamson and Shaw. These were often redirected to the War Department and its General Staff, and no one there ever refused General of the Armies Jack Pershing anything he requested. The archived boxes pertaining to his memoir project are filled with the War Department's responses to these many inquiries. Often they were extremely detailed—for example, Pershing wanted to know the names of all of the officers who served with him in the 6th and 10th Cavalry Regiments or at various posts like Fort Stanton, Fort Bayard; he wanted the names of all those who had served in command positions in the Mexican Expedition; he needed a compilation of telegrams between Major General Frederick Funston and himself and Funston and the War Department during his time in Mexico; and so on. Responses to all of these were forthcoming within a short time.[10] The materials accumulated by Shaw, Curtin, and Adamson grew quite extensive, eventually accounting for six boxes of invaluable primary and secondary source documents in the Pershing Papers in the Library of Congress (boxes 368–373).

Considerable evidence of Pershing's personal attention to this ongoing work remains throughout his personal papers. He continued to review his own notebooks and diaries for additional information even while spending his winters in Arizona. Frank Vandiver, in volume 1 of his *Black Jack: The Life and Times of John J. Pershing*, tells the story of Pershing's adventures in Vladivostok on 24 August 1908 (see chapter 17). He cites in a footnote Pershing's comment "slightly overdrawn" from the margin of Frankie Pershing's entry in their notebook "Notes on Leave 1908 up to Paris—Vladivostock, Moscow, & Berlin, Brussels, Paris" and gives it a date of March 1924. However, Vandiver was ten years off on his footnote because Pershing's comment was actually dated 7 March 1934 and read "Slightly overdrawn. JJP Tucson, March 7, 1934," which clearly indicates that Pershing was then carefully reviewing his own documents as he drafted his memoir.[11] In addition, he filled the first one-third of a 1934 memo book with jottings on various stories he wanted to add, notes of items to be reviewed and checked, and other personal details, all obviously intended for inclusion in his autobiography.[12]

Apparently Pershing was not happy with the 1933 draft, which was ready in corrected, retyped versions beginning in January 1934 and a more complete version in March. As Shaw continued working away at revisions in the late spring of 1934, Pershing hired Frederick Moore,[13] an author, professional writer, and correspondent, to redo and expand the existing manuscript. In June 1934, Moore headed to Paris, where he met with Pershing and worked with him extensively. Upon returning to Washington, he then spent a number of months in Pershing's offices while completing a thoroughly revised manuscript that was completed in twenty-eight chapters by late that year.[14]

While Moore worked with Pershing in Paris and then back in Washington, Shaw continued his efforts on the earlier manuscript of March 1934 as well as on the early drafts of Moore's chapters. After reviewing the new drafts, Pershing parted ways with Moore in a meeting on 11 January 1935 in his Washington office. Pershing's longtime secretary, Captain George E. Adamson, in a 12 January letter informed Moore that Pershing was "terminating your employment as of this date" based on their conversation of the previous day.[15] Adamson enclosed a check for

$625 "in payment for services rendered," which brought to $3,300 the amount that Pershing had paid Moore for the work he had done during 1934.[16] Moore wrote to Pershing a pleading letter on 12 January 1935 seeking to continue working on the manuscript.[17] Pershing simply wrote back on the 16th effectively ending their business relationship: "I have your note of a couple of days ago and can fully appreciate your feelings in the matter. But I think I have taken the wise course for the present and will have to stand by the decision. You will recall our conversation and it is not necessary to repeat it here."[18]

After this, the majority of the work on the "memoirs," as they were by this point labeled in his papers in the Manuscript Division of the Library of Congress, fell to Pershing, Shaw, Curtin, and Adamson. Moore's short involvement definitely enlivened the pace of work on the memoir that now continued at a high tempo throughout 1935 and 1936. As early as 4 February 1935, Shaw submitted rewrites of Moore's chapters 18 through 23, which he had consolidated into three chapters now numbered 18 to 20, to Pershing for his review and comments.[19] On 5 March he followed with copies of chapters 9 to 17.[20] Pershing reviewed the chapters meticulously, provided extensive written comments on each draft, suggested revisions and deletions, and requested additional information and research on numerous other points. Writing from his apartment at the Hotel de Crillon in Paris on 5 June, Pershing returned all the chapters he had received except for the last two, which would be sent "as soon as possible." He told Shaw: "In the work you two are doing please keep away from the formal style as much as you can." He added in a note to Shaw: "I am sending all of the chapters 17, 18, 19—yours, & mine and Mr. Moore's. Hope you can find your way out of the mess—*Yours* & *mine* as finished however are *not* half bad."[21] Shaw then melded Moore's work with his earlier versions, incorporated Pershing's input, and produced a clean, typed copy of a new hybrid version that became the "1934–35" manuscript.

Frequently Adamson, Curtin, and Shaw sent inquiries to Pershing's former associates asking for personal stories of their time with "the General."[22] As the pace of work quickened in 1935, Adamson sent copies of Shaw's newly revised chapters on the Spanish-American War, Mindanao and Jolo, and the Mexican Expedition to retired brigadier generals Henry H. Whitney, James A. Ryan, and Malvern Hill Barnum and active duty colonels James L. Collins and W. W. Gordon, all of whom were closely associated with Pershing during these years.[23] Whitney replied on 2 July that his initial impression of chapters 18–20 on the

Philippines "left a very pleasant and satisfactory impression, on account of their simplicity and clarity of expression and of the unique and historically interesting subject matter with which they are jammed full."[24] Brigadier General James Ryan replying on 10 September commented that the coverage of the Mexican Expedition was excellent but added a few personal stories from his perspective as a troop commander with the 13th Cavalry.[25] Brigadier General Malvern Hill Barnum, who had served with Pershing at the San Juan Heights in Cuba in 1898, added some coloring details for the Santiago Campaign, including that the reference to his being "slightly" wounded "should be omitted" because he "was shot through the right hip, the bullet coming out near the spine."[26] Shaw accordingly upgraded Barnum's wounding from "slightly" to "severely" in the revised manuscript.[27] Colonel Gordon sent a number of pages of his detailed comments on the Philippines and Mexico on 12 October 1935, and Collins provided his comments in letters to Pershing on 4 January 1936 and Adamson on 7 January.[28]

While Adamson was soliciting these additional comments on the manuscript, Shaw worked away at the revisions. On 1 July he sent the two revised Moore chapters on the World War, which he admitted "are poor and inadequate, but they are *first drafts* only." Admitting his own inadequacies as a writer, Shaw told the general, "with me it is a question of feeling my way along without really knowing where I am going."[29] On 12 August, Shaw forwarded copies of chapters 22 and 23 and brought Pershing up to date on the chapters that were then out for review and comment to Whitney, Ryan, Barnum, Gordon, and Collins.[30]

In 1935–1936 Shaw continued the difficult and time-consuming task of incorporating what was acceptable from Moore's drafts of twenty-eight chapters into the current concept that he and Pershing were working on, which dropped the two thin wartime chapters, consolidated others, and focused entirely on Pershing's pre–World War life and career. The manuscript now numbered twenty-three chapters, including an epilogue that summarized his years from the end of the Mexican Expedition in February 1917 to his seventy-fifth year in 1935.[31]

During the entire drafting and revision process, Shaw, Curtin, and Adamson were no less rigorous than Pershing in their reviews, often asking for more personal details from him. In reviewing a draft of the chapters on the Spanish-American War, Shaw concluded they were "too impersonal" and too much like history. "In other words," he noted on the draft, "there is not enough about the General in it." On the same draft he wrote that the account of the San Juan Heights should be from the general's personal point of view: "It was the General's first real battle and I would like to know his reactions, what he did, what he saw, what he thought, how he felt, and all that sort of thing."[32]

Much like a cross-examining prosecuting attorney, Shaw peppered Pershing with pointed questions about his activities at the San Juan Heights on 1 July 1898, trying to nail down details that were missing in the manuscript. He noted that Pershing's duty as regimental quartermaster in the 10th Cavalry meant he should have been "in the rear handling supply questions," so "it would be especially worthwhile to explain why the General was up at the front instead." Shaw noted that "the General should tell just what his duties were on that day, and throughout should say more about his own personal job." While Shaw wanted Pershing to tell his "personal part in the operations," he did not intend that Pershing "should go out of his way to criticize."[33]

Pershing concurred with Shaw's criticism, and wrote in an undated memo from Tucson (perhaps in the winter of 1935–1936 or the winter of 1936–1937) to George Adamson and Charles Shaw, "Study manuscript to see if there's anything we might add to make more interesting. It all seems flat and stale in places. . . . Please suggest topics to be touched on and indicate the places where they should go."[34] Commenting on the general's comments, Shaw told Adamson: "I agree that the manuscript *seems* flat and stale in places, but I wonder sometimes if this may not be at least partially due to the fact that all of us have been so close to it for so long. We here in the office have known practically everything of a personal nature that is in the book for years, and when we read it now it seems old and uninteresting. The reaction of a complete outsider might be a better test of the book's interest, provided he would give an honest opinion."[35]

Shaw went on to recommend that "the story could be greatly improved" by adding more personal details, anecdotes, and experiences and reinserting some of the more personal stories that Pershing had deleted earlier. Hence, he reinserted these stories "for further consideration because I think they are just the sort of thing that the book is entirely too lacking in." He told Adamson that official records were not going to produce these stories and that "further additions should be personal material that can be had only from the General's memory." Adamson approved Shaw's approach.[36]

From June through August 1936, Shaw completed another revision and delivered these revised chapters to Pershing. In January 1937, from the El Conquistador Hotel in Tucson, Arizona, Pershing penned a detailed three-page memo to Shaw. He noted ten specific items that he wanted Shaw to research pertaining to his service with the 6th Cavalry on the frontier.[37] Shaw sent all of the information he could find on 8 February.[38]

Pershing continued to review and annotate the draft chapters as Shaw sent them from January through November 1937. The general was then still traveling back and forth between Washington and Paris, where he spent many months each year, but his declining health now led him to spend more of the winter months in Tucson, where the climate was far more pleasant that time of the year. His comments, while still quite extensive, were now far less than those he had so readily showered on the earlier drafts, which probably reflected the continued refinement of the manuscript after some years of intense work. Of his continuing personal involvement there can be little doubt. On the 1936 draft of chapter 17 covering the period from August 1908 to October 1909, Pershing simply wrote: "I am not satisfied with this chapter."[39] He continued to add and delete material as he reviewed the drafts.

Shaw had Pershing's final edits of 1937 added to the manuscript, which entered retyping in December of that year. Only the first four chapters were apparently retyped and then reviewed by Pershing before all work ceased on the memoir when the general fell seriously ill with renal failure and uremic poisoning in February–March 1938. Pershing's deteriorating health thereafter effectively ended any further work on the manuscript.

Frederick Moore once again approached Pershing about working on the still unpublished manuscript after visiting him at Walter Reed Army Hospital in November 1939. Writing on 5 November, Moore accepted Pershing's concept of focusing the manuscript on "your recollections up to the time of the World War."[40] Moore said he desired no payment, but believed that he could get the book published and very much desired to see a good story come to fruition.[41]

Replying to Moore on 6 December, Pershing noted that he appreciated Moore's suggestions on the manuscript. However, he was nowhere near as positive about the work's "possibilities" as Moore, and said that "it seems to me to need a great deal that I alone could give it, and I intend to work on it as soon as possible."[42] Pershing's health had been in steady decline since early 1938, and he did no additional work on the manuscript so far as I can discover.

All of the known drafts of Pershing's memoir are now in his personal papers in the Library of Congress's Manuscript Division. The earliest drafts begin in box 373 and continue in tight-packed folders through box 380. Five additional folders labeled "last drafts" in box 385 of the Pershing Papers contained the latest versions of the twenty-three chapters and epilogue. While chapters 1–9 were apparently retyped in December 1937, there is no evidence that Pershing ever reviewed more than the first four. None of the remaining chapters from the 1936 revision was retyped.[43] Supporting this is the fact that only the first nine chapters of the manuscript even have tentative chapter titles; the remaining chapters were never given titles, although this was discussed between the general and Shaw in some detail at one time.[44] Eventually these drafts were combined into what was called "The Autobiography of General of the Armies John J. Pershing," and six copies were placed in his papers in boxes 429–431 in a late accession in the 1970s. Essentially, these chapters were the versions of 1936 and 1937, still carrying Pershing's final editorial notes and revisions on many of the pages.

In this final 1937 version Pershing never mentioned the tragic deaths of his wife, Helen Frances "Frankie," and their three daughters in their home at the Presidio of San Francisco on the night of 26–27 August 1915. In the concluding paragraph in chapter 21 of the 1934–1935 draft that was based on Frederick Moore's version, Pershing mentions that when he was ordered to the Mexican border in April 1914 he thought it best to leave the family at the Presidio because of the unsettled situation along the border. The last sentences then read: "Life seemed to be safer and better for them in San Francisco. But on the night of August 26, 1915, the house took fire and only our son was saved." However, Pershing struck out most of that paragraph, leaving only: "I was with the family in San Francisco only a short time, being ordered to the Mexican border in April, 1914, and the family, after remaining in our Presidio home for awhile, went to Cheyenne, Wyoming." He then apparently wrote some six lines in pencil, but these were then so thoroughly erased that very few words can be deciphered. The fact that he provides no mention of this tragic event is a measure of just how much the loss of his wife and daughters still so deeply hurt him twenty years later.[45]

The unpublished manuscript and all of its supporting documentation were donated to the Manuscript Division of the Library of Congress in 1952, with all rights granted to the people of the United States. Since then, the various versions of Pershing's unpublished memoir have been available to researchers and have come to form the backbone of biographical accounts of his years before the World War.

1

Ancestry and Boyhood

Ancestry

It is a matter of no little pride that my forebears were made of the fiber, mental as well as physical, found in the common people that form the backbone of this country. Originally of upstanding, though humble, European stock, we like to think they brought to America a worthwhile heritage of human traditions and achievements. They boasted no royal ancestry, but, like millions of other Americans, both the men and women were great in their simple, honest, wholesome way; and in that way they played their part in the history of the nation. Those of the early days had to meet the hardships and face the dangers of pioneer life, and with others of their kind left their mark upon the times. As the frontiers moved westward, each generation of my kinsfolk, on both my father's and my mother's side, had its men and women among the pioneers. They were found in the columns that settled the Western Reserve,[1] in the trains that carried civilization to Indiana, Illinois, Missouri, and other states of the middle west, and among the early settlers of Oregon and California. From Pennsylvania and from North Carolina to the Pacific their log cabins have dotted those territories that later became states. In earlier times they carried firearms to defend themselves against Indians and outlaws and to procure game for food. There were Pershings on my father's side and Thompsons and Brothertons on my mother's side in the ranks of the Colonial forces, in the Indian wars, in the war with Mexico, and in the Civil War. Though mainly tillers of the soil, many have been businessmen and a due proportion have entered the professions. Their story is so typically American that I venture to think a brief outline of it is warranted.

Going back about two centuries, we find the first Pershing, Frederick [originally Pfirsching, Pfoershing, or Pfershing before it was Anglicized (Americanized)],[2] arriving at Philadelphia [in 1749] as an immigrant from Alsace, after a three months voyage from Amsterdam. Speaking the little English he knew with a distinctly foreign accent, his native and secondary language being French and German respectively, he had spent five months en route from his native province. According to the custom commonly in vogue at the time, he came as a "redemptioner" because of lack of money, and later paid for his voyage in manual labor, thus saving the little money he had for use after his arrival.

In the overcrowded ships carrying immigrants in those days the passengers slept in hammocks or on the decks and generally provided their own food. The poor sanitary arrangements and the lack of medical attention caused excessive mortality during the voyage. The perils of the voyage across the Atlantic in the small sailing vessels of the time indicate the quality of the men and women who voluntarily braved them. But, they were buoyed by the hope of religious and political liberty in the new world of opportunity. The *Jacob,* on which Frederick Pershing came over, carried 249 passengers, 107 of whom were adult males and the others women and children. The members of that branch of the family to which he belonged were descendants of those Huguenots who, driven out of France by persecution, had scattered throughout the Palatinate [west bank of the Rhine River].[3] Upon arrival in Philadelphia he took the oath of allegiance to Britain required of all alien newcomers, and in 1765 he was naturalized as a British subject. In 1750, at the age of twenty-six, he was married in Hamilton Bann township, York County, to Maria Elizabeth Weygandt. The sixth of their nine children, Daniel, born 1769, was my great-grandfather. Daniel, who married Christena Milliron, had twelve children, of whom the seventh, Joseph M., born in 1810, was my grandfather. Joseph married Elizabeth Davis, and my father, John Fletcher, born in 1834 in Westmoreland County [Pennsylvania], was their oldest child.

As soon as he was old enough, my father had to do most of the work on the farm, due to his father's poor health. It was he who usually made the plans for plowing and carried them out. Though deprived of the opportunity of attending school for any length of time because of constant work on the farm, his desire for learning led him to study nights and at every other opportunity. In early manhood he became an ardent student of theology and later read law. Favored with a robust constitution, further developed by hard labor as a boy and youth, he grew to be an exceptionally powerful and vigorous man. Upon approaching maturity he left the farm management to the younger members of the family and struck out for himself. His first job was in a logging camp on the Ohio River, and soon after we find him piloting a raft of lumber down the Ohio and Mississippi rivers to New Orleans. I used to have many a thrill upon hearing him tell of his experiences on this adventure. In several accidents he barely escaped with his life. To me as a child, the journey of this youth down the long tortuous rivers was comparable to the historic voyage of the French LaSalle [René-Robert Cavelier, sieur de La Salle] nearly two hundred years before. That my father was not inspired by the dream of empire that filled the imagination of the great explorer as he floated down the "Father of Waters" failed to diminish in my mind the importance of his achievement.

Returning up the Mississippi in 1857, father, having decided to remain in the West, engaged in business as a produce broker in St. Louis as a member of the firm of Stone and Pershing. Being of French ancestry, it seems natural that he should have cast his lot in that part of the country that had attracted early explorers and traders of the same origin. The city has grown from the frontier trading post of 1764, established by the French explorer Laclede [Pierre Laclède Liguest], to a flourishing center of [160,733 in 1860] inhabitants.[4] But, seeking something more profitable, after a time he entered into a contract for the construction of a section of the railway [Hannibal & St. Joseph Railroad] then being built from St. Louis northwestward through St. Charles and Macon—a line which has long since become a part of the Burlington System [then the Chicago, Burlington, & Quincy Railroad and today the Burlington Northern Santa Fe (BNSF) Railroad]. It was while on this work near Warrenton, Missouri, that he met Miss Anne Elizabeth Thompson, to whom he was married on March 22, 1859. In speaking of that important event in their lives, I have heard both mother and father say that theirs was a case of love at first sight. I can testify that it was also enduring.

Mother's family were Southerners from Revolutionary times and some of them migrated in 1820 (?) [sic] from North Carolina to Tennessee and settled in Blount County, near Maryville, where she was born in 1835. Two years later her father took the family, not by rail, for there were no railroads, but by covered wagon, to Warren County, Missouri, where several other members of his wife's family of Brothertons were already located and where he settled on a farm and established a sawmill near Truxton. There were seven children, of whom my mother was the eldest. During those earlier years in Missouri life was very primitive. It is difficult to imagine how they got along without many things that were common even to the next generation, such as matches, farm machinery, sewing machines, the telegraph, and steam transportation. Mother used to tell how it was necessary occasionally to go to some neighbor a mile or so away to borrow burning coals with which to start the kitchen fire.

The family was distinctly southern and mother inherited the manners, the habits of speech, and the attitude of the South. A very vivid impression remains in my mind of the home when at the age of six or seven I visited my grandparents with mother. A charming picture of my grandparents, their home, the garden, and the large farm still lingers in my mind. One of the joys of that visit was to be carried about the place and down to the sawmill on the old gentleman's shoulder. The members of the family as they grew up did not agree in politics. One of my uncles, "Colonel" L. A. Thompson, mother's brother, the idol of the family, joined the Northern army and served under [Ulysses S.] Grant at the siege of Vicksburg, where he was seriously wounded. Another uncle, his elder brother, was a country doctor. When the war came his sympathies were with the Confederacy, and although never a soldier he gave freely of his services to that cause at every opportunity.

Laclede, Missouri, during the Civil War

After the completion of his construction contract father became foreman of a section of the Hannibal and St. Joseph Railroad west of Laclede, and there I was born, September 13, 1860.[5] There were nine children in our family, four boys and five girls, three of whom died in infancy, two girls and one boy.[6]

The times were stirring immediately preceding the Civil War, especially in that part of Missouri. My impressions of them come from hearing the tales of many of the participants. It was felt that the clash of opposing views held by the industrial North and the cotton-growing South on the slavery question was leading inevitably toward civil war. When the question of the admission of Kansas to the Union was before the country the struggle for the ascendency between the pros and antis led often to violence. Missouri, having been settled largely by people from Kentucky, Tennessee, and Virginia, had been stirred to the depths on the slavery question. Although bounded on the north and east by free states, there was a strong sentiment in Missouri in favor of the admission of Kansas only as a slave state. Abolitionists throughout the country were determined that this should not happen, and under their organized effort emigrants from the northern states poured into that territory to swell the numbers opposed to slavery. These conditions produced the "Bleeding Kansas"[7] of that day. In the northern counties of Missouri there was a slight majority of those who were anti-slavery in their sympathies. Slave-holding Missourians, however, and many others, especially of the border-ruffian type,[8] who owned no Negroes but believed in slavery, invaded Kansas Territory and without warrant voted in local elections. In retaliation, Kansas "Jayhawkers"[9] came into Missouri and carried off Negroes and otherwise avenged themselves. The struggle eventually became so intense that it lost the dignity of a direct issue between free-soilism and slavery and became a vicious, cruel, unprincipled, often hand-to-hand contest between man and man. Public officials were killed in cold blood and towns were sacked and burned. Kansans and Missourians ambushed and shot one another, hanged one another to trees and to barn rafters, and perpetrated unspeakable crimes against each other.

The spirit of lawlessness became prevalent throughout north Missouri. Robbery and murder committed by opposing factions were commonplace events. This state of affairs continued during the Civil War. Men on furlough returning to their homes in the north or going back to rejoin their regiments were often harassed en route, and they usually retaliated in kind. As a boy I used to hear alternately both Unionists and Southern sympathizers air their views or relate their experiences. Many were the stories of outrages committed by each side during those terrible years.

In his younger days father was tolerant toward slavery, but he said that while what he saw in the South impressed him unfavorably it was Lincoln's arguments in his debate with Douglas that turned him against it completely. He became an outspoken opponent of slavery—an attitude which, of course, alienated most of his Southern friends. While the Stars and Stripes hoisted over the section house brought prolonged cheers from the trainloads of troops that frequently passed over the railway, some of the neighbors objected to this display of the flag and sent a committee to tell father that to save trouble he had better take it down. They said, in fact, that if he refused they would have to come around and take it down themselves. But mother had made that flag with her own hands and it represented what both of them stood for. To this demand father replied in no uncertain terms and warned the committee that he would shoot any man who attempted to take it down. That was the last he heard of the matter. During this period father made many friends among Unionists in the nearby towns, but more especially in Laclede, named in honor of the great French explorer. He became a Mason there in October, 1860, and having decided to go into business for himself bought the small general store of John Lomax, in Laclede, moving there in October, 1861. When the war between the states began he was appointed sutler[10] of the Eighteenth Regiment of Missouri Volunteers, but gave up this post in March, 1862, to occupy the same position in the First Regiment, serving for nearly a year.

My earliest recollection takes me back to a day in June, 1864, when a band of about thirty southern "bushwhackers,"[11] so-called, under [Clifton D.] Holtzclaw rode into town, fired a few shots to terrify the people, and proceeded to sack the place. Father was postmaster and his store, the largest in town, naturally came in for considerable looting. Our residence was in the same block, five doors away, and both the store and the house were located on the north side of the public square. Here, just across the street and directly in front of the house, all male citizens who could be located were rounded up by Holtzclaw's men. Some members of the band entered father's store as he quietly left by the back way and went home through the alley. A couple of the raiders had just been to the front door of our house and demanded that father come out. Mother had told them he was not there but that if they did not believe her they might make a search. They had hardly left when father entered by the back door. He brought with him his double-barreled shotgun, and went at once to the front window with the intention of firing on the raiders in the square; but mother, instantly grasping the situation, threw her arms around his neck and begged him not to be so rash. One of the citizens of the town recently discharged from the army, David Crowder, who fired from a window in Earl's Hall in the next block, had already been killed, although mother did not know this at the time, and another prominent citizen, Squire John H. Jones, had been shot down because he refused to halt when ordered. The citizens were herded in the square and Holtzclaw made a short speech to them in which he claimed that this visit was made in retaliation for outrages committed upon his friends around Keytesville—about thirty miles to the south. There were, he said, some abolitionists in Laclede who ought to be hung and that if he had to visit the place again he would lay it in ruins. Meanwhile, several of his men were busy looting stores and cash drawers, including father's. They did not know, however, that as they rode into town two men had got away to Brookfield, five miles to the east, and notified the militia. Soon a special train bringing a detachment hove in sight and Holtzclaw and his men decamped. Naturally I have only a hazy recollection of seeing armed men in the square, but I clearly recall that I was badly scared for fear father would be killed and that mother made me and my small brother lie flat on the floor until the raiders disappeared.

After this raid a company of Home Guards was organized, consisting of all the able-bodied men of the town, and father became first lieutenant. The captain, Benjamin Hale, was wounded that autumn and father was elected captain. He continued as captain until the summer of 1865, when the services of the company were no longer needed and it was disbanded. The Home Guards were frequently called out to investigate rumors or to drive off roving bands. The company prepared for defense by throwing up breastworks on the southern edge of town and in the public square and these reminders of those turbulent times served years later as a playground for children.

The militia that served in that part of the state, with headquarters at Brookfield, gave protection to the people, at least gave them a feeling of security, but for several years after the war many stories, not always complimentary, were told at the expense of the militia officers. One story related that news had come to town of the approach from the south of a hostile detachment under the Confederate General Sterling Price. As this General had a reputation for severity, the possibility of an attack by a force under him was somewhat alarming. To meet the threat, some militia troops, commanded by a major who was a local doctor of prominence, hastened out from Brookfield to seize a bridge some ten miles away and contest the advance of the "Rebs." When the enemy came in sight their number seemed to be larger than the major had expected, and he immediately ordered a retreat. The men were reluctant to withdraw without firing a shot and hesitated to obey, some even protesting against retiring. But without listening to their arguments, the major became profane and repeating his command started the retreat himself. It was said that he out-distanced all those who accompanied him in his flight back to Brookfield. Those who refused to run away learned that the alleged enemy was only a group of men from an Iowa regiment returning to their homes on furlough. The major became so mortified over his action that he soon resigned his position.

Growing up in Laclede

The flotsam of war left in this borderland many good for nothing characters. There were almost as many of the worthless sort of whites as there were of freed slaves and from among them appeared not a few criminals and even desperadoes. These characters had an unwholesome influence upon the younger generation, and long after the war respect for the law and order continued at a low ebb. I need only cite such daring gangs as the James boys and the Younger brothers as proof of the degenerating contagion that existed in that part of the country. To make matters worse, the sensational press often made heroes of such men. The activities of these gangs usually took the form of bank robbery and horse stealing, but they stopped at nothing to save themselves from the clutches of the law. Laclede suffered its share from this general lawlessness and several youths of the town became members of a gang of horse thieves and finally landed in the state penitentiary.

For some years the town was known as "wild and woolly." It was not uncommon during the six or seven years following the war for rough characters to come to town on Saturdays, carouse at the two saloons, and then gallop through the streets yelling and firing their pistols in the traditional manner of the wild west. As a boy I saw such exhibitions. It is probable that many people seeking homes in the West immediately after the war gave Missouri a wide berth because of its reputation, although regardless of conditions the rich soil of the northern part of the state, coupled with the possibilities for business that the new country offered, attracted a large number of settlers from Illinois, Indiana, Ohio, and farther east. Many of the newcomers settled in and around Laclede, in Linn County, and the town became the merchandising center of a considerable territory, including several outlying smaller settlements. In addition to the general mercantile business which father conducted at the store, he sold agricultural implements and also had a lumber yard. Being postmaster was an advantage, as it drew people to the store, in one corner of which the post office was located. For a few years father's business was prosperous. He was a dominant character in the community, and while intensely interested in politics, he declined to become a candidate for the legislature, although urged to do so, and later he resisted efforts to persuade him to run for Congress.

Father and mother were very congenial and made a splendid team, so that the recollections of my childhood and youth are very happy ones. Mother was a capable woman and managed the home affairs with exceptional efficiency. The help, whether white or colored, was treated kindly, though their duties were clearly defined and they were required to do their work well. Mother was an expert at needlework and during the early years of married life made her own and her children's clothes.

I recall the pride with which I wore a suit of blue jeans that she made when I was about eighteen.

We were an unusually healthy lot of children, probably kept so by the application of a few homely remedies when necessary. In the fall, when malaria was prevalent, we were given an occasional toddy from the demijohn that was always kept in the closet. In the winter, when colds were troublesome, hot salt and vinegar was used as a gargle and externally we rubbed our throats with tallow, which we warmed in by the log fire before we went to bed with red flannel about our necks. In the spring came sassafras tea and a few doses of sulfur mixed with molasses. As children we all went barefoot in summer except on Sundays, but in winter we boys wore heavy woolen stockings and copper-toed boots that all boys wore and the girls wore high shoes.

My parents were God-fearing people and no Sunday passed that did not find the family attending either Sunday school or church, and usually both. The Saturday night or Sunday morning tub was always a prerequisite to preparation for that day, when bright and early we were all turned out in our best bib and tucker.[12] But it was not till later on that I began to think seriously about religious matters. Primarily I learned, mainly from my mother, that there were moral obligations that it was the duty of everyone to fulfill. As she was a devout Christian, few derelictions on our part escaped without her admonition. But above all it was her example and her character that shed the greatest influence for good not only upon her family but upon the community. However, in general the people were religious. Everybody who had any sort of standing in the community belonged to some church. They did not always live up to the tenets of their church, and those who did not were known as "backsliders." But they usually came back into the fold during the revivals held each winter, when they would express deep regret at their conduct, only to fall from grace again later on. But hypocrisy did not escape the observation of even the growing children. Sunday was observed by most people in almost Puritan fashion, no games of any sort being permitted. Such rules were, of course, irksome to spirited boys and girls and naturally were often broken, but our parents were liberal-minded and the consequences were not serious.

One Sunday afternoon when I was in my early teens the boys with whom my brother Jim and I played, in casting about for some diversion, conceived the idea of a raid on Hargreaves' peach orchard. Sneaking in the back way, we were plucking and eating the ripe peaches, at the same time stuffing our pockets full, when Hargreaves himself stepped out of his cornfield nearby. We broke and ran, but not before he had identified all of us. The next day we were a badly scared group of boys as rumors reached our ears that we were to be arrested for theft. Well! We just hadn't regarded it as serious as that, so a council was hurriedly called and I was elected emissary to visit Hargreaves and apologize. With a meekness that I can never forget, I told him how sorry we were, and with the promise not to repeat the offense he let us off.

Father took the lead in building the First Methodist Church in Laclede and felt considerable pride in the achievement. Our home was the rendezvous of Methodist preachers and elders, especially around regular quarterly meeting time. One dear old pastor who lived on a farm a few miles to the west had the assignment at Laclede for one year and when in town he stayed at our house. He was addressed as Brother Sidebottom by the members of the Church, but was called "Old Side" for short behind his back. He was very devout, but he both chewed and smoked natural leaf tobacco and had a fund of good stories. When with us he always presided at family prayers, held a few minutes before bedtime. During my childhood evening prayers was a fixed custom in the family. In later years when old Brother Sidebottom happened to be in town he always used to call and on such occasions usually rounded us up for prayers. We children loved him and respected him above all others who came to our home, but we were not always as reverent as we should have been. One Saturday he came to town on horseback and while paying his usual visit my eldest sister, then about eight or nine years of age, who had got hold of some circus handbills somewhere, slipped out to the barn and pasted them all over his horse. Mother was very much embarrassed, but "Old Side" thought it was a good joke, and laughed with the rest of us.

Both mother and father were fond of reading, but their time for this was limited. In our library, besides the Bible and Commentaries, were such old classics as *Pilgrim's Progress,* Shakespeare, Sir Walter Scott, Poe and Byron, *Aesop's Fables,* and *Robinson Crusoe,* besides the lives of Daniel Boone and Davy Crockett. In my youth Shakespeare delighted me and I used to learn and dramatically recite for the family and at school long passages from his works. *McGuffey's Readers*[13] contained a collection of literary gems, and several of those from the fifth and sixth readers became the favorite medium for the display of dramatic talent as we grew up to them. But there was another class of reading, not found in the home library, which I could not or did not resist. This consisted mainly of Beadle's "dime novels,"[14] which, like other boys, I read surreptitiously, often even in school when I was supposed to be studying. I became so absorbed in the hairbreadth escapes of the heroes of these blood-curdling tales that once or twice I failed to notice the teacher prowling about the room and was caught with a novel hidden behind my history or geography.

Education

When I went to school for the first time it was to a young lady teacher, Miss Sally Crowder, whose father, as we have seen, had been killed in the Holtzclaw raid. Although mother had taught me to spell up to words of two syllables, the school was the next thing to a nursery and the young teacher had her hands full looking after the group of youngsters entrusted to her care. The tuition paid her was a dollar and a half a month for each child, though she earned [deserved] several times that much. Shortly after the close of the war a Congregational minister by the name of Seward and his family came from the East. He bought a small piece of land at the edge of town and built a house that was rather pretentious for those days. I remember him as a devout, quiet man, with charming manners, highly respected in the community. There were three daughters in the family and all became teachers, the eldest, Miss Ella, being my second. Father Seward, as everybody called him, often came to talk to us children and sometimes opened the school in the morning by reading a chapter from the Bible, followed by prayer. Miss Ella was gentle and kind and we were all devoted to her. The son, Llewellen, and I some years later got into a fight, as boys will or did in those days, and I picked up a snowball that had been frozen into ice and hit him with it on the head. He ran home and fell into a faint, and his family never forgave me.

It was in this school that I made my first effort at public speaking. It was on Friday afternoon and the verses assigned to me were something about as serious as Mary and the Little Lamb. Mother had dressed me up in my best clothes, to which a blue bow tie gave a fancy touch, and had come with other proud parents to the exercises. My name was first to be called, and when I found myself standing on the platform with all eyes turned toward me I was completely stage-struck. The words had entirely left me. After a dreadful pause, mother, who sat well up in front, came to the rescue, whispering the first line loud enough for me to hear. I got through the first verse but fright again seized me at the beginning of the second, and again mother had to prompt me. My embarrassment was so

Pershing's boyhood schoolhouse in Laclede, Missouri. (Library of Congress, Prints and Publications Division, Pershing Collection, Lot 8850)

painful that the memory left with me was lasting, and often to this day when I get up to speak the latent memory of that first experience comes over me with distinctly unpleasant effects. I have rarely been entirely at ease before an audience on any formal occasion.

In the public school, which came next, children of all ages were huddled together in the small, one-room schoolhouse, and we had a succession of men teachers. In those days the "rod" was used liberally, and at the beginning of each week a fresh bundle of switches was usually to be seen standing in the corner. One or two of the teachers used the switches entirely too freely to manage the rather tough element among the elder boys. I have seen many a boy yanked into the middle of the room and get a whipping that raised welts on his body. I, myself, did not escape occasional punishment. These unruly boys were generally brought up without home discipline. Most of the whites among the newcomers who settled in Laclede and vicinity were good, honest people, but there were also some undesirables. Then, as a result of the war a rather lawless element had drifted into the community, and Laclede had its share of what the colored people called "po' white trash." The children of such parents, when they went to school at all, gave much trouble to the teachers, and as a rule they turned out badly. Fighting among the older boys was a common pastime and every boy had his share of it. I was usually able to hold my own but more than once returned home with a black eye. Yet I was always encouraged by father to stand up for myself. He often said to me, in effect, "John, my boy, you should not pick a fight, but do not allow other boys to impose upon you."

2

Youth—Its Happy Days and Others

Holidays

The Fourth of July was the gala day of the year. It was usually celebrated by a parade, followed by a picnic during the day, with fireworks at night. At noon the national salute was fired by the local blacksmith. A small quantity of powder was placed between two anvils, one on top of the other, and touched off with the red hot end of a long iron bar heated in his forge. It sounded like artillery and gave all the youngsters a great thrill. People from the country round about swarmed into Laclede for these celebrations. Led by the Union veterans of the war, all the boys and girls, large and small, under charge of their Sunday school teachers, and the grown-ups who elected to march, including the colored men who had been soldiers, formed in procession and to the music of the fife and drum paraded to Glovers Grove. On one Fourth of July, when I was nine years old, father was grand marshal. Wearing a frock coat and red sash and riding the family horse, old Selim, decked out with a flat saddle of the padded and quilted variety, with bridle to match, he seemed to us one of the highest dignitaries in the land. Every boy who was strong enough wanted the honor of carrying the flag. On one occasion the choice fell to me and while there was no happier boy in that procession at the start, the day was hot and the road dusty, and my enthusiasm began to wane long before we reached the grove of beautiful hickory trees a mile or so west of the town. The speakers and distinguished visitors sat on a platform and the audience on plank seats. One of the ministers opened the meeting with prayer, and, though weary from the march, I bravely held the flag through the whole program. The speakers dwelt on the greatness of the nation under Washington, Lincoln, and Grant, and warmly praised the veterans who had fought to preserve the Union. It was the wartime songs such as "John Brown's Body," "Marching Through Georgia," and "Union Forever" that stirred our blood. After the speeches the people scattered through the grove and the lunch baskets were opened for the picnic. The pleasure that marked such celebrations was evidence of the return to normal existence that had been so violently disturbed by four years of civil war.

Camp meetings were also held at Glovers Grove every summer for a number of years by the Methodists of that section, who assembled there in considerable numbers. Some lived in tents and others, among them our family, built rough shacks and made rustic chairs and tables and installed cooking outfits. Ministers from a distance came to assist the local clergy, and the religious instruction through the Sunday school and through sermons and lectures gave these meetings a unique place in the life of the people. For us children they provided a glorious outing of days and sometimes weeks.

My first business venture was in connection with one of these camp meetings. My brother Jim and I persuaded father to let us establish a refreshment stand, for which he advanced the necessary capital. Standing behind the counter in the small shack built of rough lumber, the shelves filled with candies, peanuts, and such things, we were ready on the opening day. Stimulated by the hope of gain, we worked hard at our small enterprise, against considerable experienced competition, but we found when the meeting was over that we had barely come out even. Our supplies were all gone, it is true, but not all had been sold, and the conclusion of the family was that Jim and I had eaten up the profits.

Hunting and Handling Guns

When we were large enough to shoot, my brother and I consulted the local gunsmith, Mr. James, and had him bore out two of the several rifles left behind by the army and turn them into shotguns. My preference, however, was the double-barreled shotgun that father had kept near him during the war and which he had given to me. Ducks, geese, prairie chickens, quail, and rabbits were plentiful in season, and when we could find time, usually on Saturdays, we had good sport, but we often returned home without any game. Along the creeks both east and west of town we found wild turkeys and squirrels in the woods, and once in a while scared up a deer in the tall prairie grass. Occasionally a group of young men and boys would organize a moonlight coon hunt, which we considered great fun, especially if the baying hounds succeeded in running a coon up a tree, when the tree would be cut down and the coon captured and killed by the dogs. To youngsters like us there was an eerie character about such adventures, and in imagination we could see wild animals of enormous size in the darkness of the woods and sometimes even things that looked like ghosts—such as we used to hear the darkies talk about as they gathered around the kitchen fire in the evening after supper. After the spring rise in the creeks and rivers, fishing expeditions were organized to seine the shallow ponds for fish marooned by the receding waters. We usually caught more fish in one day by that means than during the whole season with our lines, often returning with enough for ourselves and for distribution among the neighbors.

Another diversion that we and other boys about our age used to indulge in as often as we could without creating suspicion was to slip away to our favorite swimming hole on hot afternoons in summer. It was a beautiful pool in Turkey Creek. It was thought a good joke surreptitiously to tie knots in the other fellow's clothes while he lingered in the water.

I was especially keen about firearms and took it upon myself to keep those about the house in good condition. One day I found two old army revolvers, very rusty. Having cleaned them up and oiled and loaded them, I put on the caps and was carefully turning the cylinder of one to see if it worked perfectly. It did. The hammer slipped out of my grasp and there was a deafening explosion, with the result that a forty-five caliber bullet went tearing through the outside railing of mother's best mahogany bed. One of my sisters who was looking on screamed at the top of her voice and mother came running in, thinking she had been shot. Thereafter I was forbidden to play with loaded revolvers.

New Home, Household Chores, and Riding

Soon after the war my parents moved from the house near the public square to one several blocks away, and later, as the family increased, father bought another residence that was known as the Degraw house. This, while not a pretentious place, was then about the best in town. The yard was surrounded by a picket fence, which like the building, was in prosperous days always kept freshly painted white. It was essentially a New England type of house, with high gables, a porch, and a bay window. A large garden, bordered with fruit trees and shrubs, furnished

The Pershing family occupied three homes while they resided in Laclede, Missouri. The home pictured here was the final residence of the family. Except for his time at school in Kirksville, Pershing lived here with his parents and siblings from the age of twelve until he left home for the U.S. Military Academy in 1882. Today, the former Pershing residence is the General John J. Pershing Boyhood Home State Historic Site, a part of the Missouri State Parks system. (Library of Congress, Prints and Publications Division, Pershing Collection, Lot 8835)

an abundance of vegetables and fruit. Beyond the garden were the stables for horses and cows, with a barn lot where we could play the wildest games without protests from the grown folks that we would destroy shrubs or break windows.

As children we helped plant and cultivate the vegetable garden, and one of our delights was to watch for the first ripe strawberries, currants, cherries, or grapes, when we would carry the news in triumph to the household. We took special joy in watching for the early asparagus and rhubarb to appear. The cabbage and tomato plants were grown in glass-covered hotbeds ready to set out in the garden as soon as the frost was out of the ground.

An old colored cook, Martha Robinson, one of the family stand-bys and the favorite of us children, was always in the kitchen except when busy with her rapidly increasing brood of pickaninnies,[1] several of whom, about our own ages, became our frequent playmates. Martha was celebrated among her people for her cooking, and to us there was no one quite her equal. Her husband, a fine, upstanding man, was jani-tor at the white folks' church, into which, after years of loyal service, he and she were taken as members.

As soon as old enough to sit in a saddle I was permitted to ride my mother's horse, old Selim. He was a beautiful bay, with flowing mane and tail; father had bought him especially for her. In her younger days mother was a superb horsewoman, and I can still see her trim figure in her riding habit as she sat proudly on this horse and galloped across the open fields adjacent to town. Of course, to ride in anything but a side saddle was then unknown for a woman. Selim was naturally gentle and came to be regarded as a member of the family. All the children learned to ride him and often three or four got on him at a time in playing circus.

The Family Farm and Business

Father, although a trained farmer, also had instincts for business. As the possibilities of wealth from farming in that part of Missouri became known, there was an increasing demand for land, and he was not slow to see the opportunity for profit in its purchase and sale to settlers. New-comers had been locating in north Missouri in large numbers since the war, generally arriving in prairie schooners, as the covered wagons were called. Long trains of wagons also passed through our town going still farther west. Although the gold rush was long since over, wagon covers often bore the legend "Pikes Peak or Bust." A year or so later many came back with an added legend, "Busted by Gad." Prairie lands could be bought at first for from five to ten dollars an acre, but a boom advanced prices as high as twenty-five and even thirty dollars. At one time father owned forty quarter sections,[2] but it was not all paid for, much to his sorrow when the depression came. Among his holdings were two 160-acre farms near town, which he had enclosed with a post and rail fence and began to break. He bought several yoke of splendid oxen, which in teams of four or six pulled great breaking plows through the virgin turf in preparation for planting. These farms were opened in 1869, and from that time on for four or five years we prospered. Our stable grew to include teams of horses and mules, and we had all sorts of agricultural implements, including a threshing machine, which, after threshing our own wheat and oats, was sent around and did that of other farmers during the summer and fall. It was easy to pay for machinery in those years, with wheat at two dollars a bushel. This price was reached during the Franco-Prussian War [1870–1871] but was soon to recede to a point where it was no longer so profitable.

Although I remember the presidential campaign of 1868, when large posters about town bore the names of Grant and [Schuyler] Colfax, it was not until '72 that political campaigns aroused any special interest in my mind. Then the names of Grant and [Henry] Wilson emblazoned the town and rallies were frequent. Boys usually adopted the political party of their fathers, much as they did their religious creeds. Father was a Republican, hence I was also. To hold the Negro vote for the Republicans in Grant's second campaign, a colored spellbinder was imported to talk to the people of his race. He was a fluent speaker and in one of his speeches he referred to the slogan of the Democrats, which was, "Amnesty and Reform," saying it ought to be changed to read, "I am nasty and ought to reform." That and similar references caught his listeners and I think all the Negroes that year voted the straight Republican ticket.

County candidates usually went around campaigning in a body. In one of their visits they all made speeches except the candidate for sheriff. He got up and simply said, "I have no doubt that my opponent would make a good sheriff, but my wife thinks I would make a better one," and sat down. There was a great deal said in the campaign by Republicans about how they had saved the Union and how the Democrats had tried to destroy it. I rarely missed a political meeting. Carl Schurz and B. Graty Brown [Benjamin Gratz Brown] built up a considerable following as Liberal Republicans in opposition to the Regulars, the latter being elected as governor on the liberal ticket [in 1870].

As the farm began to produce, additional cows besides the two or three that had furnished milk and butter for the family were included. We raised hogs for hams and bacon, which we cured and afterwards smoked with hickory wood. We also had fine stock for sale as pigs and a few sheep for the market. At the first the management was in the hands of an overseer, who directed the labor, which was largely colored. These laborers, including women at planting time, were a happy lot only a few years out of bondage and well trained to work. As they wielded the hoe in planting and cultivating the corn, or the scythe and pitchfork in harvesting the hay and grain, the merry laughter and song of the groups made their labor seem like play.

From weeding and hoeing the garden came what seemed to me a series of important events as I was promoted from one job to another on the farm. The first was riding the near horse of the lead team that helped to pull the reaper around the fields of ripe wheat, oats, and barley. Then I learned to handle horses and harness, break colts, milk cows, take care of young calves, and fatten hogs. In the fall we boys helped the men butcher animals and make the trimmings into sausage. My next promotion was to plow, harrow, and sow the crops in the spring, cultivate them during the summer, and help harvest them when the time came. Thus at an early age my brother and I were able in many respects to take the place of farm hands.

But we were not entirely above temptation even after our experience in Hargreaves' peach orchard. On the farm next to ours on the east the owner had selected a choice spot for his melon patch and it was near enough so that Jim and I when plowing corn on that side of the field could look over the rail fence and see the growing watermelons. Finally one day when we thought the melons about ripe and when nobody appeared to be within sight we sneaked across, half crouching, and came away with a couple apiece. Just as we were enjoying them under the shade of a tree, father, making the rounds, came upon us with the luscious evidence of guilt in our hands. We expected something more drastic than the impressive talk he delivered on the sacredness of private property and the enormity of our offense, but so far as we were concerned that did more good than a dozen lickings.

During this time of prosperity the future looked bright and father and mother had hopes of sending all us children eventually to college. Farming was profitable and business at the store was flourishing. One day I overheard the head clerk say that father was regarded as one of the wealthiest men in the county. For a time I could picture myself as a student at college and then at law school. Apparently there was not a cloud in the business sky. Money was plentiful; prices of commodities were increasing; wages were good; and people were spending freely and incurring new financial obligations without hesitation.

The Depression of 1873 and Its Aftermath

Then came the depression of 1873,[3] with disaster to businessmen, farmers, and owners of homes, and we shared in the calamity. Father had acquired some of his lands at advanced prices and most of them had to be sold to meet the indebtedness. He could not collect all that was due him nor pay all that he owed. It finally became necessary for him to sacrifice the store, one of the cultivated farms, many of the animals, and much of the machinery. All he could save even temporarily was our home and one of the 160-acre farms. I was not told at once of his difficulties but was old enough to make deductions from the economies that had to be imposed and from bits of conversation overheard that something was seriously wrong.

One day father confided to me what had happened, saying how much he was in debt and that he was practically broke. He said that the hope he and mother had long cherished of sending me to the state university would have to be given up and that for the time being I would have to take my place as a full and regular hand on the farm. It was the first time he had ever told me in detail anything of his affairs and consequently I was brought more or less abruptly face to face with the realities of life. The revelation made a deep impression on me, but while realizing the serious effect of the collapse, I felt at the same time a certain pride that the responsibilities of manhood had been thrust upon me, and I was ambitious to meet them. The more I thought about the new conditions, the more evident it became that whatever success I should attain in life would depend upon my own efforts. The situation was such that temporarily our house was turned into a hotel, but this did not pay and father a year or so later, as his situation filled him with anxiety, taught a colored school for a while and then obtained employment as a traveling salesman for a St. Joseph clothing firm, and charge of the farm was left completely in my hands.

Hiring as little help as possible, my younger brother and I plowed and harrowed, planted and cultivated the crops, and harvested them. But luck was not with us. In 1875 there came a plague of grasshoppers which caused serious loss. At almost the same time a severe drought occurred. Everybody prayed for rain and meetings were held in the churches for the purpose, but the hot south winds withered the growing corn until even with belated rains much of it produced only nubbins [small or underdeveloped ears of corn]. Nevertheless, in the autumn of the year we had forty acres of beautiful timothy [a species of grass grown for hay], and, working the press myself, I baled a carload of choice hay and shipped it to St. Louis, counting on making a substantial profit. Much to my surprise, when the returns came in we found that the hay did not bring enough to pay the freight. During these hard times we had to do without many things we had been accustomed to. However, we were more fortunate than many other families, for we had plenty to eat from the garden and farm, and there was no depression in the morale of the family. We had been taught to work and all of us accepted the situation as one to be met courageously and without complaint. I do not cite our case as exceptional but as typical of the attitude of people in general toward the adverse conditions that confronted them. People living on farms or even on small plots were far better off during those times than those who worked for wages. Fewer people would be on the dole today if more of them owned a small patch of ground they could cultivate. Besides, there is a charm about association with growing things that is uplifting and ennobling. One who has not had the joy of producing something from the soil has missed a valuable experience. These years were really worthwhile for me, difficult as they were. I learned more of the practical side of life than during any similar period.

Many amusing recollections come to my mind as I write of those days, but they cannot all be recorded. One of them, however, forces itself upon me. We had one horse that would balk when he was not carefully handled. Once when bringing in a load of hay he took the notion. My brother was driving and father and I were walking. Father did his best to start old Jeff but he would not budge, even under the whip. We waited awhile and again tried all the expedients we knew, until all patience seemed exhausted. When we were about to unhitch the team and give it up Jim spoke up and said he had heard one of the neighbors say that if you sang the Doxology[4] to a balky horse he would go. After father recovered from his amusement he began the tune and Jim and I joined in, and, believe it or not, the old horse started and the team went along as though nothing had happened, and he never balked again.

Meanwhile life went on much the same as it does in most small towns, nor was it without wholesome diversion. Everybody knew everyone else, but society followed church lines rather closely and entertainments were generally church affairs. The older well-to-do families set the example of conduct and frowned upon anything that did not conform to their high ideals. In winter there were spelling contests and singing schools, usually promoted by Dan and Jake Slingerland, both industrious farmers, which created much interest. All members of our family were musical and one of my happiest memories takes me back to those evenings when we gathered around the piano and sang the popular songs of the day and old melodies of an earlier period. Another diversion was sleighing. When the snow was deep enough and lay on the ground for any length of time sleighing parties were popular among the young people and no one was ever deterred by the cold, which was often intense.

I was, of course, quite young to manage a farm. Though I had the confidence and determination of youth and did as well as most farmers, the time came when the farm had to go to pay the mortgage. One winter I took a job as janitor at the public school, but when it became evident that we could not save the farm I had to look for other employment. As a part of fate, the new conditions were later the cause of the complete change that came in plans for my future.

Teaching School

After assuming charge of the farm I was kept out of school in the earlier months of the term each year to gather the corn and to chop and haul the winter's wood from the small patch of timber on the farm and to split rails occasionally, but that was all a part of the game. Even when not in school I had managed to keep abreast of my classes by study at home and managed to acquire a fair knowledge of the common branches. With such equipment I decided to take an examination before the county superintendent of schools for a certificate to teach. Armed with this and one or two letters from former instructors, I applied for a position as teacher in the Prairie Mound district in Chariton County, about ten miles south of Laclede.[5] I first called on Mr. Samuel A. Henley, one of the directors, who had been a lieutenant during the Civil War and was an old friend of the family. I was eighteen years old, but he thought I looked too young and gave me little encouragement. At our second interview he said the directors had agreed to give me a trial. He then told me that the previous teacher had been compelled to resign because unable to maintain discipline and warned me that some of the older boys were hard to manage.

The school term began in November, 1878, and lasted four months. I boarded with the Henleys at two dollars and a half a week. Their two daughters, about my own age, were pupils at the school, in which there were about forty-five boys and girls ranging in age from six to twenty-one. The curriculum included everything from the first reader up through elementary geometry and algebra. Among the pupils were several bright boys and girls ready to match their wits with the teacher's, and it was necessary for me to be prepared to explain the whys and wherefores of many things, especially in mathematics. I encouraged athletics and, being active myself, used to join the boys in their games. My experience in teaching was most valuable and there is no doubt that I learned more than any of my pupils, especially in the practical lessons of managing others.

About the second week after I took charge, a group of boys—the same group who had forced my predecessor to resign—proceeded to try me out. The leader, who was older than I, played some prank on a smaller boy that could not be overlooked and I directed him to remain behind after the others were dismissed. Instead of staying in his seat as the others rose to file out, he too rose to go. The whole school saw defiance in this act and expected trouble. "Wilson," I said—"Tug" Wilson was his name—"I am here to run this school and you must obey my orders." Stepping down from the platform I went up to him and told him that if he didn't take his seat I would give him a thrashing then and there. Seeing that I meant to settle matters on the spot, he obeyed. These unruly boys had been supported by their parents in their previous acts of insubordination and the former teacher had appealed to the school board. It was not my intention to do this, and my determination to deal with them directly and forcefully brought an end to the trouble.

Kirksville Normal School

My salary was thirty-five dollars a month, but out of it I saved enough money to go to the Kirksville Normal School[6] for the spring term. There my time was devoted especially to methods of teaching and discipline. Kirksville then had about five thousand inhabitants, and the students included many from the town. The school was one of the three state institutions for training teachers and was under the presidency of a prominent educator, Doctor Joseph Baldwin. Several of the professors were outstanding men, such as [William P.] Nason in English, Davis in mathematics, and Paden in Latin, but all were earnest and generally efficient. The students in the main were serious-minded and were there to get the greatest possible benefit in the shortest time. The atmosphere was conducive to study and as a result I returned to Prairie Mound in the fall for a second term far better qualified to teach.

In the spring of 1880 I was once more at Kirksville, this time accompanied by my brother Jim. To me school teaching seemed to offer the best chance available as a source of revenue to pay for further basic training. This calling I had in view only for the time being, as I aspired ultimately to become a lawyer. As a small boy the splendid biceps of the local blacksmith had impressed me as the sparks flew from his anvil while he fashioned his iron into horseshoes. That was my first chosen profession, and years later in the cavalry I learned to shoe a horse and taught the art to the men of my troop. Then came the desire to be a carpenter and build something, but after several trips with father to Linneus, the county seat, where I listened to the learned Alex Mullins expound the law as father's attorney, these earlier ideas passed into limbo. I had already, in the little spare time available while teaching, read some of the *Commentaries* of [Sir William] Blackstone and [James] Kent and longed for the opportunity to study them under professional supervision. But all I could save was with a view to having a full year at the Normal School. It was for this purpose that I went to Kirksville again in September of the following year, 1881, this time happily having my sister Elizabeth as companion and fellow-student, my brother having decided to go to work.

3

West Point—Its Grind and Its Pleasures

1881–July 1886

Pursuing an Appointment to the U.S. Military Academy

My sister and I had just got well started with our studies at Kirksville when, one Saturday morning, while visiting her room reading the weekly newspaper from home, my eye happened to light on the notice of a competitive examination to be held in two weeks from that date at Trenton, Missouri, some sixty miles west, for the selection of a boy from our congressional district for appointment to the Military Academy at West Point. The appointment was to be made by the Honorable Joseph H. Burrows, who had been a clergyman before entering politics and had been elected to Congress on the "Greenback"[1] ticket. The idea of entering the country's service had never before entered my mind. In fact, I had at one time been offered, and had declined, an appointment to the Naval Academy at Annapolis. It was the chance to get an education that appealed to me most now. I read the notice to "Sister," as we always called her, then a girl of seventeen, asking what she thought. To my satisfaction, she approved, and then and there I decided to make the effort.

Obtaining permission to be absent temporarily from my classes, I worked diligently at the studies in which we were to be examined, and on the appointed day appeared before the examiners. In Trenton I found sixteen[2] other applicants who had come to the city in much the way I had, with only hazy notions of what West Point was like but all eager to go. Before a board of educators whom few of us had ever seen, we stood in competition. I had known one of them—Professor C. W. Bigger, of

Gainsville Mo.
Oct 24th., 1881.

To the Secretary of War:

I nominate John W. Pershing, *of* Laclede, *in the County of* Linn *and State of* Missouri *for appointment as a*

CADET OF THE UNITED STATES MILITARY ACADEMY,

from the Tenth *Congressional District of that State. He has been an actual bona-fide resident of the District for over* Five *years, and is believed by me, upon due inquiry, to be qualified for appointment, according to law, in every respect. His age is* Twenty one *years and* just *months.*

Joseph. H. Burrows
Selected by Competitive exam-ination by first class Board

Alex. W. Chapman of Chariton county was the 2nd best as reported to me

[NOTE.—It selected by competitive examination, the Representative is requested to add a memorandum to that effect.]

Rep. Joseph H. Burrows nominated Pershing for an appointment to the U.S. Military Academy on 24 October 1881, after he won a competitive examination ahead of Alexander W. Chapman. Notice that Pershing's middle initial was entered incorrectly as W. and then changed to the correct J. for Joseph. (LC/Pershing Papers, Box 384)

Linneus. The examinations in all subjects were written and when they were finished how well or poorly any of us had done we did not know until two of us, a boy named A. W. Chapman and I, were called up for an oral test. Then it was clear that the choice lay between us. The test was in the analysis of a sentence. His analysis was incorrect and mine correct. It was not only, however, because of my success in the examination that I was selected. One of the examiners afterward told me that my physique was taken into account. Fortunately my father and mother had passed on to me a measure of the rugged constitution of the family and my work on the farm had developed my frame and muscles.

I had not yet entered West Point by any means, as the real entrance examinations were to be taken at the Academy. But I was now ready to break the news at home and took the first train out of Trenton for Laclede. When I walked in, mother was greatly surprised. I expected her to be pleased at hearing what I had done, but she was not. "But, John," she said, "you are not going into the army, are you?" To her a soldier's life was not a desirable one and she did not want a son of hers in the army. I told her that going to West Point did not necessarily mean that I would remain in the army, pointing out that it was a chance to get an education. She was skeptical about the undertaking, but did not long demur; and in later years she became distinctly proud of having a son serving with the colors and followed my career with the utmost interest.

I had till the following June to prepare for the examinations at the Academy and set out for New York sometime in January, 1882, with many good wishes from friends in our little town. Going for the first time beyond the limits of our state, I was eager to see Chicago and New York City and spent a day in each. My tours of these cities were made in the horse-drawn street cars of the period and on the top of omnibuses. The views of the ocean-like Lake Michigan and the city of Chicago, the Brooklyn Bridge, then nearing completion, the tall buildings of New York, and the throngs of people on Broadway all seemed impressive then.

I entered a preparatory school at Highland Falls conducted by Colonel Caleb Huse, a graduate of West Point, who had served in the Confederate Army, principally in connection with a mission to England. The Colonel gave his pupils an excellent groundwork in the studies taught and a touch of the discipline required at West Point. The time at this school was not all spent over our books, but we organized excursions to various points of interest in the picturesque Catskills and we knew most of the lore of West Point and a lot of the surrounding country before we entered. We candidates visited the Military Academy but seldom, as it was wiser for candidates not to make themselves known as such. One of my visits happened to be on the day that the statue of Colonel Sylvanus Thayer, "Father of the Academy," was dedicated, and I was thrilled to recognize General Grant among the eminent men present. The General sat quietly on the platform, taking part in the ceremonies only as a guest. His unassuming manner seemed to add to his greatness. A little over three years later, when I was a cadet captain, the corps was taken across the Hudson to Garrisons, where we stood at attention with bowed heads as the funeral train bearing his remains passed by. I regarded him then and do now as the greatest general our country has produced.

Entering the Military Academy: Beast Barracks

Early in June the candidates reported to the Adjutant's office in the old administration building. We were a motley crowd but we represented, like all other classes, a cross section of the country's youth—dapper city boys and crude country lads, some in frock coats and broad-brimmed hats, others in natty straw hats and clothes in the latest fashion. The first important official we were to meet was the cadet officer in charge of candidates in that portion of the barracks set apart for us and referred to by the older cadets as "Beast Barracks." This was our first introduction to the military discipline of the Academy. Each of us in turn was told how to stand at attention, how to address the older cadets, how to enter and leave an office, and so on, all of which is doubtless still vivid in the minds of all who have had the experience. We were then assigned to temporary quarters and marched off to the commissary in groups to draw our mattresses, bedding, wash bowls, and other necessities, which we had to carry back to equip our barren rooms. At odd times we were subjected to a course of more or less absurd questioning by the older cadets, especially by those who had just finished their first year, as if to offset what they had endured.

When the candidates had all arrived, a hundred and forty-four of us, the examinations began.[3] My four months of coaching under a man who knew his business was put to the test, but I was among the one hundred and four who succeeded in passing. We became the Fourth Class—known officially as "new cadets" but called "plebes" by the others. But even as a "plebe" I was proud and happy, for I was now a student at the institution that had trained such soldiers as Grant, Lee, Sherman, Jackson, Sheridan, and other great figures of the Civil War. And for the next four years every minute of our time was to be accounted for. The hours devoted to study, recitation, drill, meals, sleep, and recreation were strictly prescribed. For the average cadet the course of study was heavy, but outdoor work on the drill ground provided the necessary physical exertion to keep us fit physically. While West Point is a place of exacting standards and acid tests, no advantage of birth, wealth, influence or favoritism exists, and each cadet stands upon his own pair of feet.

The class was divided into squads of eight or ten for drill, each under the direction of a "yearling" (Third Class) corporal. Upper-classmen also came at odd hours informally to visit our rooms, but this was mainly for their own amusement. It seemed foolish that we should stand at attention when one of these casual visitors entered the room and answer the ludicrous questions they asked, but whatever the theory was, it amounted to a mild form of hazing. We were addressed as mister this or that and in speaking to a cadet officially we were required to refer to ourselves in the third person. The formula was, "Mr. Blank reports so and so."

What seemed the most absurd was that we were required, by regulation, to depress our toes at each step and to carry our hands palms to the front, little fingers at the seam of the trousers, arms rigid. Above all, we had to hold ourselves strictly erect. This was not easy for those, including myself, who had already allowed themselves to become somewhat stoop-shouldered, but it soon corrected that fault. A more awkward looking creature could hardly be imagined than a plebe braced up in fulfillment of such requirements. But regardless of how one looked or felt, the system was well calculated to teach the proper carriage of the body and use of the legs. These requirements were enforced during the first summer, in ranks and out.

Cleanliness of person and quarters was imperative and during waking hours everything in our rooms had to be kept in prescribed order. Bedding had to be neatly piled and extra shoes well polished and lined up at the foot of the bed. Gloves, handkerchiefs, collars, shirts, and underclothing were kept carefully folded in open shelves. All this to teach order and system.

After about three weeks of preliminary training we moved into camp—located on the plain near an old fortification of revolutionary days, now razed to allow greater space for the camp. As in barracks, strict regulations were enforced regarding the manner of arranging things in tents. We had a joint clothes rack of canvas swung from the tent pole for clothing and a wooden locker for smaller things. The company streets were swept twice a day and thorough policing was required in every part of the camp, the plebe doing most of the work.

After morning parade, held only in camp, it was the custom to stack arms on the color line, which separated parade from the body of the encampment, and the colors were furled and placed in the center of the line, supported by two stacks. Three sentinels, selected for their smart appearance at morning guard mounting, walked that line in turn until it was broken, about four in the afternoon. Each cadet who crossed the line, which all had to do when entering or leaving camp, was required to salute the colors, and the sentinel was bound to report any failure to do so. Before long the more proficient plebes were detailed for guard duty and I happened to be in the first group. From among them three were chosen for the color line and I was fortunate enough to be one of the three. No one could forget his first tour of guard duty. All went well during the day, but at night the color line became part of the guard line surrounding camp and shortly after I was posted what looked like ghosts began to appear. There was no provision in the regulations that I knew of for the disposition of apparitions, but I challenged the first one with the usual formula of "Who comes there?" whereupon this ghost stopped in his tracks. Rising to the occasion, I called out, "Who stands there?" Another and still one more came into view and each was halted in turn. Then the first spook sat down on a camp stool it was carrying, when my challenge was altered to "Who sits there?" By that time the officer of the guard heard the commotion and at his approach the apparitions disappeared among the tents.

It was in camp that the fun for the older cadets, especially the year-lings, really began. Being just out of plebedom themselves, with the tribulations of the past year fresh in their minds, they became the pests and started playing pranks on the friendless plebes. Fifty years ago we made our beds of blankets spread on the tent floor and an exasperating joke for the plebe was to be dragged suddenly out of his tent after taps, bedding and all, into the middle of the company street. That was just cause for a fight but no one could find out who the culprits were. A few senior classmen required of plebes a kind of fagging, which consisted usually of carrying water and piling bedding for them. None of the so-called hazing that summer was vicious and most of it was amusing even to the plebes themselves. One instance will suffice. If an upper-classman happened to find in a plebe's home paper a notice of his appointment saying how soldierly or how handsome a cadet he would make, that was unfortunate for the plebe, as more than likely he would have to learn it by heart and recite it with appropriate gestures whenever called upon. The notice about me in the home paper never reached West Point.

We were kept constantly busy during that first summer, attending one military exercise after another both morning and afternoon. Rifles had to be cleaned and polished, lock, stock, and barrel, and the same with equipment and uniforms. But we made remarkable progress, it seemed to me, and even before our return to barracks in the latter part of August we were put into the battalion and marched to meals with the other classes. The end of plebe camp came before we could realize it. Moving into barracks was easily accomplished. Each cadet simply rolled up his bedding and bundled up his clothing in a sheet and carried them across the plain to the room assigned to him and his chosen roommate. The last fagging a plebe ever did was to help carry some upper-classman's bedding into barracks.

While in plebe camp the approaching academic work was a subject of anxious conjecture. Judging from the chaff by yearlings, it was evident that the most important hurdle would be mathematics. Thus we looked forward to our return to barracks and the beginning of study with different feelings, some with confidence and others with anxiety. There was one cadet in my class who, having been a "professor" in a western school, anticipated the academic year with supreme confidence. One night after he and I had come off post and were resting in one of the guard tents he indicated that there was no doubt in his mind that he would stand at the head of the class. Such degree of confidence as I had would warrant no more optimistic prediction than that I would be able to get through the year. When the studies began we were assigned alphabetically to sections for recitation, each of about ten men under an officer-instructor, and at the end of three weeks we were rearranged by being transferred up or down according to our marks. At this first readjustment the "professor" was sent to the last section in mathematics and did so poorly that in January he was dropped. Colonel [Edgar Wales] Bass, the professor of mathematics, had the gift of finding out by a question or two whether a cadet understood his lesson. He was very strict, though kindly, in requiring cadets to study. No cadet could get by otherwise.

Plebe Year

The men who fell into the last section—the "Immortals"—found it difficult either to pull up again or to pass their semi-annual examination. A greater number of cadets were found deficient in mathematics than in any other study, especially at the first examination in January. Most of them worked hard and deserved a better fate. The trouble was that they were unprepared for the swift progress through the mathematical course made necessary to cover the scope of the work laid out for the four-year term. Among those who had to go in that fatal January was my own roommate [William M. Wright], who simply could not get hold of geometry. He later entered the service by civilian appointment a year ahead of the class, but with our unanimous approval, and passing up through all the grades became a major general in the A.E.F. [American Expeditionary Forces], and a most efficient one.

In addition to the regular academic course of mathematics and English, with French the last half-year, an hour and a half each day was devoted to practical training outdoors when the weather permitted. During the winter months the Fourth Class had instruction in dancing, some fencing, and some work in the old gymnasium. Then this latter was not followed systematically and was of little benefit, but this was changed some years later, much to the improvement in physical development of cadets.

In the middle of the year the class was organized for the purpose of acting on matters of class interest and a president, secretary, and treasurer were elected. Much to my surprise, I received the honor of being named its first president. I had not the remotest idea that I was being considered, but could not help being highly gratified. I still hold the office.

At the end of our plebe year several more men found to be below requirements in studies or discipline were dropped. At that time cadets had to rely entirely upon themselves, with little if any personal assistance from the instructors. In principle this system was faulty, as there were many cadets who could probably have done well with some help over the more difficult places. In those days, however, cadets usually refrained from asking questions for fear it would affect their marks. I understand that they may now consult their instructors privately and receive reasonable assistance when necessary. It should not, however, be lost sight of that in all cases the best interests of the service must be considered paramount. The instructors were graduates of the Academy selected generally because of high standing as cadets. This plan worked well except in French. Few officers actually spoke the language, with the result that cadets rarely attained a practical facility in its use. Although I had studied some Latin, French was difficult for me, and I had to neglect other studies to ensure even a fair standing in it.

There is no such thing as cutting recitations at the Academy. Such a practice, though permissible to a greater or less extent in most colleges, would be regarded at West Point as not at all in keeping with the high standards required in academic work nor with the strict conception of duty so characteristic of the institution.

A group of us who lived in the old seventh division of barracks took turns in running a light after taps, which was sounded at ten o'clock, at which time we were supposed to be in bed. To do this it was necessary to darken the window, which was done by fastening a blanket over it. One night when the group was gathered in my room we heard the officer in charge coming up the iron stairs. All of the fellows got away safely except one, who crawled under my roommate's bed. I turned out the light, pulled down the blanket, and jumped into bed with my clothes on and pretended to be asleep, but the officer had evidently caught a glimpse of the light and I found my name on the delinquency list the next day, while the cadet who thought he was safe under the bed was "skinned" for absence from his own quarters. The punishment I got was confinement to my room for several days during recreation hours. But one evening I forgot to remain in confinement and for this breach was put in arrest and had to serve extra tours of duty by walking post three Saturday afternoons in the area of barracks. Though I "ran" a light many times thereafter, I was more careful in arranging the blanket.

Third Class Year

The number of cadets in the corps during my four years at the Academy averaged about three hundred and fifty, and we were organized as a battalion of four companies. The corporals came from the Third Class (Sophomores), the sergeants from the Second Class (Juniors), and the commissioned officers from the First Class (Seniors). After the graduation of the then First Class, we of '86 became yearlings. I happened to be one of the forty corporals appointed and became acting first sergeant of Company D during the absence on furlough of the Second Class.

During this second summer the duty of training the new cadets of the Class of '87 and of otherwise introducing them into the mysteries of military life fell to the new corporals, and needless to say we did our part in relieving any tendency toward monotony. We had our fun, but as I look back after the lapse of years I do not remember that there was anything done by my class that was seriously objectionable. Most of the jokes were witty and often amusing even to the plebe involved. If by chance an upper-classman overstepped the limits of what was considered permissible, the cadet himself had the right to demand satisfaction. This meant that the offender had either to apologize or fight. If the cadet against whom the offense was committed was no match for the offender, then a member of his class more nearly equal was chosen to fight for him. The sense of fair play was general and misconduct by an upper-classman brought down upon his head the indignation even of his own classmates. Fights were not frequent, and if they took place in the summer they were usually held in time-honored old Fort Clinton; if in winter they were held in one of the large tower rooms in barracks. Although presumably arranged with great secrecy and held surreptitiously, most of the cadets knew about them. If either or both the principals bore marks of the encounter next day, the officers also knew; but no questions were ever asked. It was then a part of the code and in some respects had its good points.

The Superintendent of the Academy was Colonel (and Brevet[4] Major General) Wesley Merritt, of the Cavalry, whose distinguished career in the Civil War and on the frontier gave him high prestige. He was a fine type of officer, then in his early fifties, and a strict disciplinarian. The Commandant of Cadets was Lieutenant Colonel H. C. [Henry C.] Hasbrouck, of the Artillery, who also had an excellent war record. These two officers were exceptionally well-fitted for the positions they held; their example of soldierly bearing and manliness had a stimulating effect upon the entire corps, and the cadets had sincere respect for them.

Included among General Merritt's friends were Grant, Sherman, Sheridan, and other great soldiers of the Civil War, several of whom came to visit West Point during my cadet days. I remember especially the stately figure of General Sherman as he took his daily walk about the post and how we used to consider it an especial honor to salute him.

When we became yearlings we were given our first opportunity to attend cadet hops, which were held twice or three times a week. Many young ladies visited West Point during the summer and that added much to our pleasure. Then there was Flirtation Walk, which we were permitted to enjoy. Its traditions are older than West Point itself, and judging from my own memories of that picturesque and romantic promenade I cannot imagine any graduate who can think of those days without some emotion. All cadets except plebes were permitted to attend Saturday night hops during the academic year. They were also attended by the officers and ladies of the post and frequently by visitors. Such occasions were delightful diversions for many of us, but some in the class formed a bachelor's club. They generally affected disdain for that sort of thing, but were usually the first after graduation to get married. Some of my most cherished friends, both men and women, were among those whom I met while a cadet.

At the end of the second summer there was a readjustment in the list of cadet officers and noncommissioned officers, and to my surprise I was appointed senior corporal. The course of study the second year was a continuation of mathematics, particularly in the higher branches, and French, which continued to be my bugbear. Riding twice a week began with the second year, and those of us who had ridden before got much pleasure out of it beside the amusement of seeing the beginners frequently fall off their horses into the tanbark. The method of riding with long stirrups was faulty, but it has been vastly improved since then through the development of horsemanship at the Cavalry School[5] at Fort Riley [Kansas]. Our cavalry today is unsurpassed for horsemanship by that of any other army.

Cadets of the two upper classes who had few enough demerits were permitted at Christmas time to take three days' leave, but there were few whose records entitled them to the privilege. At the end of the second year, when corporals generally became sergeants, I was made senior first sergeant and assigned to Company A. My class then went on furlough until August 28. By the end of the second year the class had begun to find itself and the ties of association in a common aim and purpose had welded its membership into a compact whole. This was our first vacation since entering two years before and we were a happy lot to be at liberty after this period of rigid military life. Of all the greetings received upon my return home, that extended by an old colored woman is the one I recall most distinctly. She was very religious and also very loud. When she saw me as she passed up the street she called out, "Land o' mercy, Johnny, I sho' is glad to see you. The Lord has been mighty good to you, boy, to bring you back here to your mother," and I have to confess sharing her joy. But the time passed all too quickly and I was back at West Point without knowing where the summer had gone.

Second Class Year

It was then the custom for the First Class to give the Second Class a royal welcome when it returned from furlough. When we came back most of us took the old *Mary Powell* up the river. After climbing the hill to the library we formed line on the south end of the cavalry plain and at the same time the First Class formed just outside of camp. The lines then rushed toward each other cheering, the men tossing hats into the air and otherwise behaving in hilarious fashion. We then all went into camp

During his four years at the U.S. Military Academy, Pershing was elected president of his Class of 1886 each year. His senior (First Class) year, the Academy's military leadership selected him as Cadet First Captain, the top leadership position for cadets at the Academy. (Library of Congress, Prints and Publications Division, Pershing Collection, Lot 8835)

together. It was gratifying after an absence of three months to receive such a welcome and the gesture made for good relations between the two classes. This picturesque custom exists no longer.

The third-year course embraced physics, chemistry, and drawing, while the practical work included tactics and a continuation of horsemanship. Professor [Peter Smith] Michie was at the head of the physics department and Professor [Samuel E.] Tillman that of chemistry. While not forgetting others, these two professors especially will be remembered as men of high character who, by their human sympathy and understanding, won the affection of the cadets and left an indelible impression for good upon the whole institution.

Cadets, especially men of the First Class, were invited from time to time to spend an evening or to dine with the families of officers, and on these occasions the officers seldom appeared.

There are a few days at West Point that seem to stand out in my memory. One was when the tactical officer[6] of the company called me in front of his tent one evening during yearling camp and said, "Mr. Pershing, I wish you would be more careful. I thought I saw a plebe leave a bucket of water in front of your tent, but I am not sure. Do not let it happen again." As it was forbidden to have plebes do that sort of thing, I was very grateful that the "Tac" was not sure of what he had seen. Another was when I received a perfect mark for a recitation in physics in an oral examination. General W. S. [William S.] Rosecrans, of Civil War fame, who was a member of the Visiting Board that year, sat beside Professor Michie and Lieutenant Arthur Murray, the instructor, and took part in testing my knowledge of the subject. The examination was held in the old library and when it was finished, feeling certain that I had "made a max," as we used to say, I fairly floated back to my room. One other day was when, upon the graduation of the Class of 1885, I found myself the senior cadet captain of the corps [First Captain].

First Class Year—First Captain

The morale of the corps of cadets is largely determined by the attitude and the conduct of the First Class. If the men of that class have a high regard for discipline and frown upon unbecoming behavior, the other classes follow the example; if there is laxity in the First Class, or if they are complaining or careless in dress, such faults are reflected in the classes below. So that much responsibility rests upon the First Class to maintain the high traditions of the institution. Without vanity, it can be recorded that a very keen sense of duty prevailed in my class from the beginning.

Among the famous men who visited West Point in my time was Mark Twain, who occasionally came to lecture to the Corps. One of his visits occurred during my senior year, and being a fellow Missourian I obtained permission for him to visit barracks after church the next morning, which was Sunday. Several of my classmates came to my room to meet him and he delighted us for an hour with stories from *Innocents Abroad, Tom Sawyer,* and other of his writings. The great humorist was much admired by the cadets and was always given a hearty welcome.

Attendance at Church was compulsory and each Sunday morning the Corps was assembled in dress uniform and marched to worship. The service followed the Episcopal form and was held in the charming old chapel that stood on a line with the barracks, facing the old cavalry plain. It was removed to the cemetery stone by stone after the present chapel was built. Cadets who were Catholics were permitted to attend the church of that faith at Highland Falls, to which they were marched each Sunday by the senior cadet among them.

First Class men were given greater freedom socially than the others. They could leave camp at their own discretion when off duty and were allowed to visit on the post without special permission. There was never much reason in keeping young men of the First Class in leading strings when they were so soon to become officers, although so-called privileges in general have been extended since my day and the seniors are now given somewhat greater opportunity to mingle with officers and their families and with the outside world.

Our studies during the final year included engineering, law, history, ordnance, and gunnery, with Spanish crammed into the last half-year. The practical training in field engineering embraced pontoon and spar bridge building and other work of that nature. I did little better in Spanish than in French and the memory of it has always caused me chagrin. Toward the end of the year, Professor [George L.] Andrews, the head of the language department, called me aside one day in the Academic Building and told me that I must do better in Spanish. I had just been transferred down two sections and was apparently headed for the "Immortals." But even without the Professor's warning, I had no idea of allowing this to happen, and by dint of some extra work on the subject succeeded in regaining all I had lost and something to spare.

Granting that the essential aim of the training at the Academy is to develop leadership, as much opportunity as possible should be given cadets to exercise command. Too little opportunity in this respect was afforded the average cadet in ranks when I was there. None but the cadet officers of the First Class were given command, even of a company, except for one day during the year. Another deficiency was that of the interior economy of the company in the army. No instruction was given except in rare instances when the tactical officer on his own initiative took up the subject. There were no tactical studies then, even of an elementary character, approximating those prescribed in the courses at the service schools, especially that at Fort Benning [Georgia] [the Infantry School]. Without any idea of this important subject a young graduate would be seriously handicapped if his regiment were sent immediately into the field. More practical knowledge of the principles of minor tactics ought, in my opinion, to be included in the West Point curriculum instead of leaving it until the graduate has the rare opportunity of attending the service schools. It is important also because West Point is the model of all other military schools in the country and graduates from these schools are probably equally deficient in a practical knowledge of this kind.

It was with mingled feelings of pleasure and regret that we contemplated graduation. While happy at the thought of being free after four years of stiff discipline and anxious to try our pinions [wings] in service, yet we were about to leave intimate association covering the period of our transformation from awkward youth to the estate of trained officers, with a well-defined career before us. Whatever may have been the opinion of individual cadets regarding life at West Point, I am sure that none failed to appreciate that the experience was beneficial.

In my opinion West Point is the outstanding military school of its kind as a builder of character. The high efficiency of the corps is maintained not only through the exceptional conditions of service but through the inspiring influence of the traditions that surround the institution. Cadets who enter it with the purpose of following a military career yield the hope of wealth and consecrate themselves to the service of country as completely as young men studying to take Holy orders consecrate their lives to the service of the Church. To the cadet who enters in this spirit there is a romance to the life that raises him above the petty trials and annoyances of its arduous requirements and gives him a sense of buoyant exaltation.

The high standards fixed by Colonel Thayer at West Point have been maintained to the present day. In all performance of duty a strict code of honor is constantly invoked. By the end of four years the sentiment has entered into the very fiber of the young man's being, becoming for him an unconscious reaction. The academic motto, "Duty—Honor—Country," well expresses the three elements that go to form the officer's simple philosophy of life.

My conception of the importance of the national military academy is that it should be the fountain head of our military system, not only educating young men sufficiently to enable them to take their places in civil life along with graduates from our best universities, but at the same time teaching them those basic principles of the military profession that will equip them as leaders of men in the event of war. That our armies will be needed again admits of no doubt, and the spirit that has made them superior on many a battlefield should be carefully fostered at West Point.

Graduation Day,[7] which at times had seemed far away, finally came. As we took our places in ranks for the last time a very pronounced lump arose in my throat. I had not realized that I was going to feel so deeply sentimental about it. I listened to the speech by General Sherman before he delivered our diplomas without remembering much that he said.[8] The life had been so fascinating, so gripping, that it took a very positive exercise of the will to shake off the spell, but uppermost, of course, was the thought that greater things in a new and broader military life possibly lay somewhere ahead.

Choosing the Cavalry

Previous to graduation each cadet had to decide upon the arm of service he wished to enter. To which of the different branches he would be assigned depended largely upon his class standing. The engineers were generally the first choice, although only ten or twelve of those who stood highest in my class were recommended for that branch. The next most popular preference lay between the artillery and cavalry, while the infantry, though not the least important, was usually the last. I was included among those recommended for any of the last three and indicated cavalry as my preference.

I considered myself fortunate to get a rather high choice among the regiments of cavalry and chose the Sixth, mainly for the reason that it was then active in the Southwest against the Apache Indians. This regiment had an exceptional war record. Organized in 1861, shortly after the outbreak of the Civil War, its first contacts with the enemy occurred in the vicinity of Yorktown, Virginia, and it had acquitted itself with great gallantry in that and subsequent engagements. It carried the scars of many actions, including Antietam, Fredericksburg, Gettysburg, the Wilderness, Cold Harbor, Appomattox Courthouse, and the siege of Yorktown. The regimental history during the years following the war contained incidents little less thrilling in service in Texas, Indian Territory, Kansas, Colorado, and Arizona. Its record, its prestige, and its esprit de corps were such as to fire the imagination of any young graduate eager to follow the cavalry guidons.[9]

It was my intention to join the regiment at once upon graduation, but by that time the end of the Geronimo campaign appeared to be near, and I decided to take advantage of the graduation furlough to visit my family and friends. After spending a few days in New York and Washington, I went to Lincoln, Nebraska, to which place the family had moved. My mother had now become fully reconciled to the thought of my entering the army.

4

The Army—With the Sixth Cavalry in New Mexico

September 1886–November 1890

Settlement of the Western United States

The flood of immigration which, in the late '60s and the '70s, had poured into the West had aroused anew the fear and resentment of the Indians. They saw the game which had been their main food supply from time immemorial fast disappearing before the advance of the white man. They looked upon the wanton destruction of the vast herds of buffalo, elk, and deer that roamed the western plains as a calamity. The hunting grounds allotted to them by the government in solemn treaties were being overrun by white settlers and gold seekers. And yet the Indian was in no sense making use of the vast empire except as a hunting ground. The Indian was not developing the country and so he had to give way to a race that would develop it. The change of ownership, however, might have been effected with little, if any, bloodshed had the settlers recognized certain rights of the Indian, but they were not all peace-loving, fair-dealing men. There were lawless and worthless characters among them. It was the old story of prospectors and ranchmen encroaching upon the Indians' reservations. To make it worse, the unscrupulous among them sold him liquor and weapons, regardless of any realization of the consequences. It is small wonder that the Indian frequently went on the warpath. It then became the duty of the army to punish him, yet the soldiers cherished a sincere sympathy for him and detested those who exploited and mistreated him.

Beginning with the earlier days of the development of the great West, it was necessary to protect law-abiding settlers not only from attack by the Indians but also from the "bad men" among our own people, and this task required the presence of troops in the newly-opened territories as the frontiers advanced. Their duty was not confined to guarding pioneers and railway construction forces but often included the support of courts of justice, the supervision of elections, and the protection of revenue collectors. The army often interceded in favor of the Indian when he suffered through mistreatment by corrupt government officials placed over him. Its record of service in the cause of good government in those romantic though tragic years is something of which it can be justly proud. Only through its vigilance and its courage could law and order have been established and maintained.

With the Sixth Cavalry at Fort Bayard, New Mexico

The Sixth Cavalry had been in the Southwest since 1875, and, usually in detachments of one or two troops, had participated in the frequent campaigns against the most warlike of Indian tribes, the Apaches. Several of the Indian leaders had achieved national fame for their daring and for their skill in evading the troops, the most notorious of these being Geronimo. In 1885 this chief led a band, including such locally known sub-chiefs as Nana, Mangus, Nachez, and Chihuahua, in flight from their reservation, raiding the country through the Mogollon Mountains and the Black Range in New Mexico and crossing into old Mexico without being apprehended, although at least two thousand men of the cavalry were in the field against them. The trail ran from the border over one hundred miles inland to the Sierra Madre Mountains, and the troops followed them into Mexico and drove them back into the States, but again they escaped. In November, 1885, a small band of these renegades under Josanie suddenly returned, successfully evading the cordon of troops and Indian scouts, and conducted through southern Arizona and New Mexico one of the most daring raids known in Indian warfare. Within a little over a month they traveled not less than 1,000 miles, leaving a trail of blood and ashes, with thirty-eight murders to their credit, returning to the main body with a loss to themselves of only one man. A well-organized campaign of operations was planned for the following year. The infantry were placed in small groups at important mountain passes, springs, and water holes, while the cavalry did the scouting. Finding the net being closely drawn around them, over a hundred of the renegades, in March, 1886, accepted the proposal of General [George]

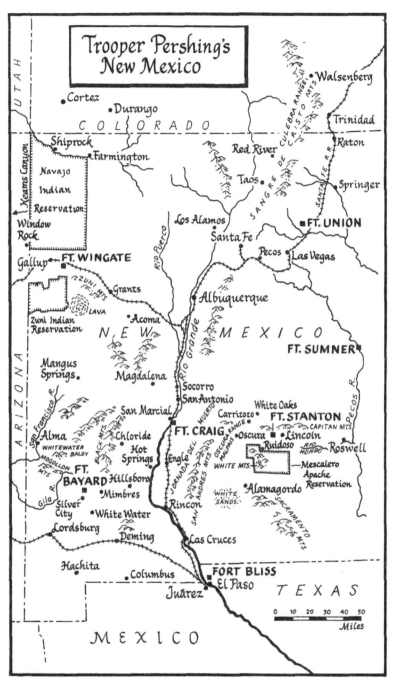

Trooper Pershing's New Mexico (Vandiver, *Black Jack,* vol. 1, p. 52).

Crook, in whom they had great confidence, and agreed to return from Mexico to their reservation. But while on the way back Geronimo and Nachez, with thirty-six followers, broke away again. They were pursued into Mexico by Captain [Henry W.] Lawton, of the Fourth Cavalry, and persuaded to return, negotiations being opened by a brave officer of the Sixth personally known to the Indians, Lieutenant Charles B. Gatewood, who entered the hostile camp at risk of his life accompanied only by two friendly Indians.

This brief review of conditions and events, now almost forgotten, is written mainly to show the tremendous appeal that service with the cavalry made to a young officer. I naturally hoped to take part in this campaign, but it was almost ended before I graduated, so, following the usual custom, I went on leave until September 30, when I joined the Sixth Cavalry at Fort Bayard, New Mexico. This was a typical western post, built of adobe brick, and nine miles from Silver City, then in the heyday of its prosperity as a mining town. The headquarters and six troops of the regiment and two companies of the Thirteenth Infantry were stationed there, with Colonel Eugene A. Carr, Brevet Major General, a cavalry leader of high standing and reputation, in command. I shall always remember his kindly manner when I reported to him for duty. Also of the Sixth was Captain Adna R. Chaffee, already held in high esteem by his fellow officers and men. He was later to distinguish himself as commander of our expeditionary forces in China in the Boxer Rebellion[1] of 1900, and later still as Chief of Staff in Washington. I had known several of the younger officers as cadets, and they were ready with advice during the rather trying experience through which every young officer had to pass before he learned the ways of the service.

My initial field duty came in October, when a force under Captain H. M. [Henry M.] Kendall, consisting of two troops, including my own, Troop L, was sent to scout the Mogollon Mountains to intercept Mangus and his band, the last of the hostile Apaches not accounted for. The details of preparation of the troop were left to me, and with the assistance of the first sergeant and the other noncommissioned officers, many with years of experience, everything, including ten days' rations, was made ready to be loaded on the pack train on the morning of our departure. We were up before daybreak for an early breakfast, mules were packed, and horses saddled; but when the command was formed I was amazed at the condition and appearance of several of the men. It was evident that the prospect of taking the field had led a number, including the excellent first sergeant, to patronize the bar at the Post

Second Lieutenant Pershing at Fort Wingate, New Mexico, in the late 1880s. In July 1886, Pershing was commissioned a second lieutenant in the 6th Cavalry Regiment and assigned to Fort Bayard, New Mexico. He later served with the 6th Cavalry at Forts Stanton and Wingate in the state. Apparently, the negative was reversed; the number on the saddle blanket should be "6" for 6th Cavalry Regiment. (Library of Congress, Prints and Publications Division, Pershing Collection, Lot 8835. LC-USZ62-17939)

Trader's rather too liberally. Moreover, the variety of uniforms, including hats and leggings, fell far below standard. This spectacle was not in accord with my conception of how troops of the Regular Army should appear, whether in field or garrison. But in those days considerable latitude was permitted in matters of dress. The personnel of the troop consisted of a fine group of seasoned soldiers and once over the effects of indulgence they were entirely reliable and efficient.

With the first lieutenant in nominal command of the troop, the command rode through Silver City and followed a route that led into the picturesque Mogollon Mountains and up the colorful San Francisco River to northern New Mexico. Our first camp was at Mangus Springs, and, as was the practice, the horses and mules were herded for the night to graze. At the beginning of a march the animals are usually somewhat restless, and during the night the herd took fright at some unusual noise, possibly the howl of a wandering coyote, and stampeded. The herd guard fortunately kept with them, but it was nearly noon the next day before they could be rounded up and returned. As stampedes were often started by lurking Indians, it was a somewhat embarrassing situation in which to find ourselves—cavalrymen afoot in such a wild country with not a horse in sight. After that, for a few days the horses were hobbled when turned loose to graze. Within a short time we learned that Chief Mangus' band had reached the reservation in Arizona, and we marched leisurely back to the post.

The first piece of individual work I had in the field was in charge of a detachment with instructions to establish a line of heliograph[2] stations between Fort Bayard and Fort Stanton [New Mexico], a distance of some hundred and seventy-five miles to the east as the crow flies but considerably more as the horse travels. Although the heliograph is now no longer much used, it was valuable in those days as a quick means of communication in a region of almost continual sunshine. Advantageous sites on hill or mountain tops for relay stations as convenient as possible to available roads were selected and through communication between the two posts was fully established. But there has never since been any occasion to use the line.

The remainder of the winter was spent in the ordinary duties, with a reasonable amount of reading and study. The mornings were devoted to horsemanship, troop drills, tactical training, and other outdoor work, usually under the junior officers, and the afternoons to various forms of recreation, including horseback rides across country. The ceremony of mounting guard in the morning and dress parade in the evening afforded some diversion and helped to maintain the morale and military appearance of the command. The Sixth Cavalry's excellent band gave a concert daily and played for the weekly hops, to which people from Silver City were frequently invited. From time to time the young folks of the post, including a group of young lady guests, initiated other forms of amusement, such as parties, private theatricals, and visits to nearby points of interest. Speaking of the band, I am reminded that the Colonel did not have much of an ear for music. On one of the programs at an afternoon concert the Adjutant, Lieutenant L. A. [Louis A.] Craig, father of General Malin Craig, had listed the air, "Hard Times." Most of us enjoyed it as being somewhat reminiscent of our own earlier experience, but the Colonel did not like the title. After hearing it through he directed that it be left off the program in the future. But it was one of Craig's favorites and some time later he put it on under the title of "Other Days," and the Colonel never knew the difference.

Back home I used occasionally to play euchre and seven-up on rainy days in the barn loft with other boys, but never played cards at West Point and did not learn poker until after joining at Bayard. There was usually a game running of evenings at the Officers' Club, where they played for moderate stakes, but I did no more than look on once in a while, until on one occasion one of the officers at the table was called out and asked me to take his place while he was away. I protested because of ignorance of the game, but he insisted. When he returned after an hour or so it was found that my luck had won him a considerable sum. After that I played occasionally but found myself getting interested in it to such an extent that it seemed best to drop that form of amusement, and I have rarely played since.

The winter passed quickly into spring and then came the target season, when the men were instructed in marksmanship, a most important feature in the training of the soldier. Having become familiar with the use of both rifle and shotgun in hunting as a boy and having made something of a record in target practice as a cadet, I became an enthusiastic rifleman and soon qualified as an expert. When the department competition came in August, 1887, at Fort Wingate [New Mexico], I was selected as one of the representatives of the regiment. While proficiency in the use of the rifle is as necessary as ever, the machine gun using rifle ammunition has become indispensable. The value of this weapon was fully demonstrated in the Russo-Japanese War [1904–1905], and the Germans made full use of it early in the World War. The other nations soon followed suit, but our army had failed to adopt a suitable type of gun until after we had entered the war, thus compelling us to purchase them abroad. Although I urged haste in their manufacture, none was supplied by our own factories until late in the war.

While at Wingate a small party of officers, including Lieutenant R. L. [Robert Lee] Bullard and myself, had a very interesting trip to the Zuni Indian Reservation, about forty miles to the south. The Zunis, known as Pueblo Indians, had long been a peaceful people. They lived in adobe pueblos (villages) of closely grouped apartment-like houses high up on the mesa, engaged in farming the lowlands, and owned considerable numbers of cattle and horses. Game was plentiful in the mountains south of Wingate. Our first camp on the trip was near Zuni and during the night there was a light fall of snow. When we awoke in the morning we found fresh tracks of a large bear and a cub at the entrance to our tent. We grabbed our rifles and hastened to follow the trail of the two bears but soon found they had too much the start of us.

Duty at Fort Stanton, New Mexico

During my absence Troop L was transferred to Fort Stanton, then under command of Lieutenant Colonel A. P. [Albert P.] Morrow. The post was garrisoned by two troops of the Sixth Cavalry and two companies of the Thirteenth Infantry. As a precaution against depredations by the Mescalero Apache Indians it was located near their reservation, one hundred miles east of Carthage, New Mexico, the nearest station, on the Santa Fe line.[3] To the north were the Capitan Mountains, where large game was plentiful, while to the south in the White Mountains numerous streams abounded in trout. Those officers and men disposed to hunt and fish could obtain occasional leaves of a few days for this purpose, and I took advantage of every opportunity to go.

The social side of life at the new post was somewhat less formal than at Bayard, as the garrison was small enough to be almost like one family. I shared quarters with two other second lieutenants, [Julius A.] Penn of the infantry, and [Richard B.] Paddock, of the Sixth Cavalry, both [since] deceased. Some wag at the post rather aptly dubbed us the "three green P's." Andre W. Brewster, the other second lieutenant of infantry, eventually became my inspector general in the A.E.F. in France. Baseball was the principal sport of the men, while the younger officers took to tennis. The small stream that ran though the post provided plenty of water for irrigation and each troop took pride in an excellent garden, which added a variety of vegetables to the regular ration. The post trader's store kept all sorts of merchandise and supplies and maintained a canteen for the troops and a club room for the officers. My sisters May and Grace, then students at the University [of Nebraska] at Lincoln, Nebraska, spent a month with me at Stanton, and we passed many happy hours with the younger set both on the post and on jaunts into the surrounding country. Later Grace married Paddock, but their life together did not continue many years for he died during the winter following the Boxer campaign in China [9 March 1901], and she, the most talented of our family, passed away three years later [25 April 1904].

"The Three Green P's" at the Chinaman's Hut, Fort Stanton, New Mexico, on 23 November 1887. Standing, left to right: Second Lieutenant Julius A. Penn Jr., Miss B. Rogers, Second Lieutenant Richard B. Paddock, Miss Flora Bishop, Second Lieutenant John J. Pershing, and Miss Virginia Rogers. Seated, left to right: Miss Dow, First Lieutenant Thomas Cruse, and "the Chinaman." Penn was a USMA classmate of Pershing's (1886) and retired as a brigadier general in 1924; Paddock married Pershing's sister, Grace; and Cruse (USMA 1879), who received a Medal of Honor while serving in Arizona with the 6th Cavalry in July 1882, retired as a brigadier general in the Quartermaster Corps in 1918. (Library of Congress, Prints and Publications Division, Pershing Collection, Lot 8835. LC-USZ62-28338)

The town of Lincoln [New Mexico], nine miles away, distinctly of the frontier type, was a sort of rendezvous for the happy-go-lucky cowboys of that section. Besides the cattle men and traders, most of the people in both the town and surrounding country were Mexicans. Some of us youngsters occasionally found pleasure in attending Mexican "bailes" to dance with the well-chaperoned and graceful senoritas of the elite families of the town. Lincoln was the scene of many encounters with outlaws, and the successive county sheriffs had difficulty in maintaining law and order. Included in the long list of desperate characters who had terrorized that region was the notorious "Billy the Kid." After committing several cold-blooded murders he was himself killed in a night encounter by Sheriff Pat Garrett, who had traced him to his hiding place at old Fort Sumner, some ninety miles northeast of Fort Stanton. But this was before my time, and while the West was by no means entirely law-abiding, it was making definite advances in that direction.

In the fall of '87 General Nelson A. Miles, the Department Commander, organized a series of maneuvers designed to develop skill in following Indian and outlaw trails, to familiarize both cavalry and infantry with the country, and to teach the cavalry to march long distances without injury to the animals. At a number of posts a troop was designated as a raiding party, with a definite objective, usually the capture of some distant post, and another troop was sent in pursuit. At Stanton First Lieutenant George L. Scott's Troop D was directed to play the part of raider and capture Fort Bayard and my troop was to pursue. The raiders were given eighteen hours' start and were permitted to use every device to throw their pursuers off the trail. After the first eighteen hours the raider could march only between noon and midnight, while the pursuer was not limited as to hours.

It was not difficult to follow Scott's trail except in crossing the Malpais, an ancient stream of lava of unknown origin some thirty miles long and in places five miles wide, where he left no trail. But thinking he would cross the Rio Grande at San Antonio bridge, I made a bee line for a pass in the Oscuro Mountains which lay in the direct route and upon reaching it found that he had camped there. Watering our horses and mules, we continued across the "Jornado del Muerte" (Journey of Death), a treeless plateau about forty-five miles wide and a hundred and fifty long, and that night made a dry camp. This plain was semi-arid but well covered with luxuriant grass, which served the animals for both food and water. As we rode along we saw several herds of antelope, but they scampered swiftly away and we did not get a shot. Reaching the Rio Grande bridge at noon on the third day, we saw Scott just leaving the town and overtook him a few miles farther west. My men were overjoyed, as there was considerable rivalry between the two troops.

After resting together at San Antonio for several days my troop became the raiding party and Scott's the pursuing. We had made good progress toward Bayard, having skirted the breaks of the Rio Grande, thence across country without trails, and made our second camp in the

Black Range. The Apaches had raided through that country not so long before and the inhabitants were still always on the lookout for them. As I was having my field breakfast of bacon, bread, and coffee, a local prospector strolled into camp, and, surprised at the presence of troops, inquired whether the Indians were on the warpath again. We said "No," but just at that moment Scott's troop hove in sight and let out a war whoop, whereupon the prospector exclaimed, "Good God! Captain, the Indians are on you," and grabbing his hat from his head took to his heels. Scott had returned the compliment, overtaking me in camp, so honors were even.

These maneuvers were fine sport and both officers and men took the liveliest interest in them. Several of the troops made exceptional rides, and there was every reason to be proud of the cavalry. The exercises offered a healthful outing for men and animals and put both in fine condition. They were also highly instructive in just what cavalry was expected to know in those days. On one occasion, I marched my troop one hundred and thirty miles in forty hours, including seven hours in camp the first night and three the second, and yet every horse and mule finished in good condition.

Leave in Lincoln, Nebraska

In the fall of 1888 I took a short leave of absence, most of which was spent with my family in Lincoln, Nebraska. While there I met several prominent citizens of the state and a number of university professors, and it was on this visit that the idea was suggested that I should apply for appointment as military instructor at the university. I also met the famous Colonel [William F.] Cody, better known as "Buffalo Bill," one of the most picturesque frontiersmen of the late '60s and the '70s, when great herds of buffalo roamed the plains. Bill wore a buckskin suit, a big sombrero, and a prominent goatee, as he did in his "Wild West Show" when, riding his beautiful gray, he introduced to the audience the "Rough Riders of the World." In a moment of relaxation he related many incidents of buffalo hunting and of his service with the Fifth Cavalry in Kansas and Nebraska and gave vivid accounts of some of his Indian fights. The average listener would be inclined to doubt the accuracy of a man who seemed to boast so much about himself, but General Carr told me later that "Buffalo Bill" had really been in a number of Indian fights with the Fifth Cavalry and had been highly valuable as a scout. As Cody lived at North Platte, Nebraska, he became successively an aide to most of the different governors of the period. He was at that time on the staff of Governor [John M.] Thayer, and later he and I with several others were aides on the staff of Governor [Lorenzo] Crounse. Although we all held the state rank of colonel, it always appeared to me a silly practice for a state governor to surround himself with a top-heavy group of so-called military aides.

Duty at Fort Wingate, New Mexico

Shortly after the expiration of my leave I was ordered to Fort Wingate, then the station of headquarters and five troops of the regiment, one company of Navajo Indian Scouts, and two companies of the Ninth Infantry. I was assigned to Troop A under Captain Kendall again and had command during his absence from March to June. The troop had usually stood lowest in the regiment in target practice, mainly because the men had not been given the necessary individual instruction. But with it they became intensely interested, and, although the rivalry among the organizations was keen, the troop led the regiment that year. There was an air of gaiety at this station, including riding parties, excursions, hunting, dancing, and all that sort of thing, which, together with the serious work of training, made it more desirable than any other post at which I had served.

During my stay an incident occurred at Zuni which, in the eyes of those peaceful Pueblo Indians, did no credit to the white man. One day a report came to General Carr that three white men had tried to steal a herd of horses from the Zunis and in a running fight had killed three Indians. The men had retreated to a log ranch house where they were being besieged by the Indians. General Carr sent me to the scene with ten men of my troop to investigate and do what was necessary. I found the Indians, a hundred or more, greatly excited and determined to take the thieves dead or alive. They had completely surrounded the house and from a distance were keeping up a fusillade against it. It was not easy to persuade them to let me arrest the men, and for a while it seemed that a fight would result from any attempt to deprive them of their vengeance. Nor, after the Indians finally gave in, was it easy to induce these thoroughly scared prisoners to give up their arms. I had to go into the cabin, which they had barricaded, and personally demand it before they submitted to unconditional surrender. I then put them on a buckboard and, placing my troopers advantageously on either side, rode back through the lines of threatening Indians and on to the post, where the culprits were confined in the guard house. A few days later one of them escaped and the other two were delivered to the civil authorities, who soon discharged them without punishment, presumably for lack of evidence against them.

Journey to the Grand Canyon of the Colorado

During the summer Lieutenant John M. Stotsenburg, who, with a detachment, was making surveys to discover possible sites for irrigation reservoirs, and I undertook a trip across country to the Grand Canyon, a distance by trail of about two hundred miles.[4] We hired Indian ponies for ourselves, took three pack mules and a packer, and engaged an Indian graduate of the Carlisle, Pennsylvania, Indian School to serve as guide and cook.

From the agency at Fort Defiance [New Mexico], we went first to a village of Moqui Indians (now known as Hopis), the snake dancers, one of the Pueblo tribes, who lived in fixed habitations. These were curiously built, much like those of the Zunis, of adobe, rising above one another, story after story, each upper structure reached from the one below by ladders. As usual, the village was on the flat top of a butte some three hundred feet high, thus originally located for defense against other tribes. The heights could be scaled only by a steep, narrow, time-worn trail, which could be easily guarded. The farms were in the lowlands. Everything the Moquis made and everything they harvested, as well as their animals, mostly burros, with some horses and a few head of cattle, were kept on top of the mesa for safety. Another place of interest at which we stopped was Kearns Canyon, a trading center where Indians from all the section went for barter. On the fourth day we came to the small Mormon settlement of Tuba City [Arizona], where the leading Elder hospitably put us up for the night.

Here we practiced a piece of economy that might have cost us dearly. On account of the scarcity of water in the hot, dry season, we needed a guide familiar with the water holes the rest of the way. But as those at Tuba City asked more than we were willing to pay we set off alone, leaving the Indian behind in search of a fresh mount. We learned that there was but one water hole between the Little Colorado [River] and the Grand Canyon. We crossed the Little Colorado before noon just above where it enters the box canyon through which it flows until it empties into the larger river. The heat of the tableland of northeastern Arizona at this season was intense, and Stotsenburg's pony soon gave out. He went on afoot and our packer and I, after some delay, followed with the animals. At the forks of the trail some distance farther along, the left fork seemed to me to lead toward the Grand Canyon, but I saw that he had taken the other one. When I overtook him he insisted he was right, so we continued.

The trail soon began to grow fainter and at sunset we found ourselves on the brink of the box canyon of the Little Colorado, with the stream a sheer two thousand feet below. It was clearly necessary that we should find the other trail and the water hole without delay. Changing our saddles from the worn out ponies to the two pack mules, we started off cross-country, thinking to cut the trail we had missed. For some hours we had no great difficulty picking our way across the trackless plateau, but when the moon went down there was nothing we could do but tether the animals and rest until daylight. When we woke the mules were gone and the packer, who had strayed from us the night before, was still missing. We ate some hard bread, moistened our mouths with the remaining drop of water in our canteens, discarded everything we were carrying but my carbine and ammunition, and took a new direction on foot. It was not till afternoon, when our lips were parched and we were suffering considerably from the heat, that we found the trail again. Stotsenburg was evidently very much fatigued. We calculated we were about twenty miles from the crossing of the Little Colorado of the day before and had no idea where the water hole was. We had not gone far from this point when, happily, we met our Carlisle Indian. With a supply of water in his large-sized canteen he was a welcome friend indeed. We drew not only upon that but he then and there made some coffee and fried some bacon for us. With Indian instinct, he thought the water hole must be near and within an hour located a stagnant pool in a depression in the rocks a few hundred yards away. We then rode out to find the animals and equipment we had abandoned the day before and returned late in the evening entirely successful. Making a shrewd guess that our packer would be coming back over the trail, he went to the nearest point to sleep and toward morning was awakened by the packer. The efficient packer had brought in one of our mules as well as his own. We stayed at the water hole that day and on the next completed our journey. If one should follow the automobile road that has replaced the trails over which we traveled, he could hardly believe this story, but the difficulties under the circumstances were very real to us.

The first house we had seen since leaving Tuba City was the log cabin of John Hance, near the rim of the Canyon at the point still known as Hance's Place. He had been a mule driver with the Sixth Cavalry in Arizona under Stotsenburg and of course greeted us most cordially. We feasted that evening quite royally on venison brought in by a Walapai [Hualapai] Indian whom we had passed on the mesa. In appearance this man was a character out of some fable or legend of ancient times. The breast of his buckskin hunting shirt was painted white, in contrast with his brown-red skin, and he wore a huge pair of antlers on his head to deceive the game he patiently stalked.

Next morning, rested and fit again, we were out early to see and enjoy the most wonderful piece of natural scenery of its kind on earth. At Hance's ranch the gorge was about six miles wide and nearly six thousand feet deep. The river, at the bottom, looked like a silver thread among the many-colored, picturesque strata of the chasm. We seemed to have come to the edge of the earth. The impression of awe created in my mind at this first view has never been equaled. Since that day I have seen the highest peaks of the Rockies, stately, snowcapped Fujiyama in Japan, and the towering masses of the Andes and the Alps, but never have I witnessed a sight so marvelous as the Grand Canyon of the Colorado. Nowadays the ease with which the Canyon may be visited has made it quite an old story to the traveling public.

On our return trip we sent our Indian guide ahead to hire relays of ponies, and with three different mounts the last day we made the final stretch of seventy-five miles between sunrise and sunset on July 3, reaching Defiance for the celebration next day.

Forts Wingate and Stanton

General Carr was fond of hunting and was especially interested in hunting bear, which were plentiful in the mountains south of Wingate. In talking with him one day I mentioned a family who lived near Stanton, did a lot of bear hunting, and kept a special breed of dog for that purpose. He at once commissioned me to get him one, and on my return to Stanton I selected what the bear hunters said was a "wonder" and had it carefully crated and shipped to the General. Not long thereafter I received a letter from the Adjutant telling me that the General had organized a hunt, invited some of the staff to go with him, promised them good sport with the new dog, and a feast of bear meat. The party soon spied a bear and brought the dog forward. But when it got sight of the animal, at bay and standing on its hind legs, the dog turned tail and fled back to the post. I had spent fifty dollars of the General's money for a cur like this and of course it was a long time before I heard the last of it.

The following summer (1890) each regiment of Cavalry was reduced by two troops, L and M, and the men, horses, and property distributed among the other ten troops. It was a sad day when Troop L, which I had rejoined at Ft. Stanton in September 1889, an organization with a fine record and high esprit de corps, had to be broken up, and I was loath to have this duty to perform, for I had become warmly attached to this splendid body of men. My new assignment took me again to Troop A, stationed at Wingate.

In the latter part of October the Department Commander, Brigadier General [Alexander McDowell] McCook, came to Wingate accompanied by the United States Commissioner of Indian Affairs, Thomas J. Morgan, on the way to visit the Navajo and Moqui Indian reservations. The General's aide and son-in-law was Lieutenant Chauncey B. Baker, a classmate of mine now deceased. The party was provided with a four-mule ambulance, and I was sent in charge of their small cavalry escort. At Kearns Canyon a large number of Navajos and Moquis [Hopis] were assembled to welcome the General and the Commissioner, the squaws in their finery, especially blankets of their own design, color, and weaving, and the young bucks in their war paint and feathers. Many had come on ponies, generally riding bareback. In the afternoon they held horse races, foot races, and wrestling matches, which we went out to see. The Indians would run a winning horse in a succession of races until he was finally worn out and beaten. We mingled with the throng and at length they challenged us to enter one of our party in a wrestling match. Baker, who thought to play a joke on me, whispered that I was a great wrestler. But I was not to be bantered into tackling one of their champions at a sport I knew little about and suggested that a foot race would suit me better. A hundred yard course was stepped off, and I, stripped down to almost as little as the Indian wore, started off at the crack of the pistol against an Indian said to be the fleetest in the tribe. The race was rather even for the first fifty yards, then I began gradually to draw away from him and in the end came out two paces ahead. The Indians were as much surprised as we were. But I had been something of a success as a boy at the shorter distances, while the Moquis are noted especially for being long-winded. Moqui messengers often made as much as sixty miles and back in twenty-four hours. There had been considerable betting between the Indians and our troopers on this match, and the latter gleefully gathered in a number of blankets, bows and arrows, and other Indian paraphernalia, which, however, I persuaded them to give back. The Moquis wanted another race, but I discreetly declined to take another chance.

5

The Sioux Campaign and Commanding Indian Scouts

November 1890–August 1891

Although our troops were always ready for field service, nothing unusual during the four years following the Geronimo campaign had occurred to suggest serious trouble with the Indians. An occasional Indian scare or the arrest of white cattle thieves or a practice maneuver gave us field service at intervals and added zest to the routine of training and post duty. I loved the service and the country, with its barren plains and rugged mountains. The various assignments that had fallen to my lot had furnished some practical and profitable experience.

Renewed Troubles with the Sioux Indians— The Ghost Dance Rising

The settlement of the great west continued with increasing volume after the Civil War and was vigorously opposed by the Indians. But their warriors were no match for the well-trained and well-armed white soldiers called upon to protect settlers, and although they were forced to yield their claims to large areas of farming and grazing lands, they still had a visible food supply in the millions of buffalo that roamed the plains. But this proved to be temporary, as the apparently inexhaustible herds began to disappear before the reckless onslaught of white hunters. Buffalo hunting became the sport of frontiersmen, and Indians also took part, killing the animals for their hides alone, which they used to cover their tepees and to spread on the dirt floors. The army purchased hides by wholesale and made them into overcoats, the last of which were issued to the cavalry in the Sioux campaign.

It was not in the Indian's nature to remain humbly quiescent and see their food supply disappear, and soon they began again to show their independence of spirit under the daring leadership of such men as Sitting Bull, already famous as a medicine man and war chief, and Red Cloud, until they could point to the Custer battle of 1876 as evidence of their prowess. After the subjugation of the Sioux and Cheyennes in 1879, they had been dismounted, their war ponies sold, and the proceeds returned to them largely in farm stock and implements to encourage them to peaceful and self-supporting pursuits. But such plans had been tried before, and the Indians had never turned extensively to farming.

The old frontier days were passing, the West was yielding to the already steady increase of settlers. The mining industry was rapidly growing; gold was discovered in the Black Hills [southwestern South Dakota]. Cattle and sheep ranches were covering available grazing lands, agriculture was spreading fast across the rich prairie lands, and irrigation was turning arid lands into farms of agricultural products and fruits. The Indians keenly felt the effects of the changes, of which they were not a part but mere observers. Their natural and time-honored activities were thus more and more circumscribed, and the cumulative effect of these developments gave them much concern.

For a year, however, reports, at first only vague rumors, had been coming in of uneasiness among the Sioux and Cheyennes of the plains country; a rebellious spirit seemed to be spreading among them; and the movement seemed about to reach a climax in the fall of 1890.

Confined to restricted areas from which the buffalo and other game that has furnished the bulk of their food had disappeared, they could not at once change the habits of generations and become self-sustaining. Much of the land allotted to them in recent years was unproductive, and their actual existence depended in large measure on the food supplies, principally beef, furnished by the government. But eventually the government failed miserably to meet its obligation in this regard. That the Indians were not receiving sufficient food on their reservations was declared not only by the Indians themselves; it was attested by missionaries, traders, and even by some in the Indian service [Bureau of Indian Affairs, Department of the Interior] in position to know.

No doubt the method of selecting personnel for that service was partially to blame. Politics had entered; civilian agents placed over the Indians were frequently changed and appointments of men without experience or other qualifications were often made for political reasons. Some were downright rascals and too often government supplies and funds were misappropriated. Nor were all the contractors honest men. The story used to be told of one who, after inspection, drove his cattle around again from behind a hill and passed them in front of the inspector to be counted a second time. Whether true or not, such stories indicated the belief held in and about Indian reservations that there was both inefficiency and dishonesty in the management of the Indians.

In 1889 the drought and widespread failure of crops in the plains country caused the loss to the Indians of this small addition to their food supply, and when the government topped it off by reducing its allotments the Indians were in desperate straits. Small wonder that they were ready to listen to the incitations of fanatical people living on the western slopes of the Rocky Mountains—some of them white men, according to report. These agitators professed to be prophets of God, and claimed that the Messiah had returned to the earth and would purge the land of the wicked and return it to the good, including both white and red men alike. Secret emissaries were dispatched to all the Indian tribes in the Northwest summoning them to send representatives to a conference at a given place near Pyramid Lake, in Nevada, in November, 1889. Unknown to the government, delegations from the Sioux, Cheyennes, Gros Ventres, Utes, Snakes, Piegans, Bannocks, Paiutes, and others, some traveling as much as fourteen hundred miles through sections of the country they had never visited before, joined in the extraordinary conclave.

Before them appeared a man impersonating Christ, who was said to be able to speak all languages. It was said that there were several men masquerading in the same robes, disguised as the one person. This alleged Savior made the most extravagant promises of restoring life to thousands of dead warriors and of destroying their living enemies. He taught them what was termed the Ghost Dance—that was performed in a light shirt-like garment or hunter's frock, which, after being blessed, was declared to be bullet-proof.

After this conclave the situation among the Cheyennes and Sioux, aggravated by the continuance of the drought in 1890, grew steadily more threatening. The frenzy of ghost dancing increased and in the fall of that year the fanatical wave swept over the reservations until the civil authorities practically lost control. From his camp on the Standing Rock Reservation Chief Sitting Bull, the famous war chief and medicine man of the Sioux, dispatched messengers in all directions, even into Canada, calling on the tribes to prepare for war in the spring of 1891.

Usually when the Indians went on the warpath they chose the spring, as then the weather was warmer and the grazing for their ponies more plentiful. But Short Bull, who aspired to leadership, proclaimed in a passionate harangue that he would hasten the day for the general uprising and with Kicking Bear and some three thousand followers from the Pine Ridge and Rosebud agencies left the confines of their reservations and fled to the Bad Lands of South Dakota. Big Foot, in his camp on the Belle Fourche River, was also in a hostile mood, while on the Cheyenne River Reservation [Chief] Hump, one of the most dangerous leaders of the Cheyennes, assumed a threatening attitude. Judging from events, the greatest Indian war our country had ever experienced seemed imminent and the government, becoming alarmed, directed the army to take charge. On November 23 telegraphic orders came for the Sixth Cavalry to prepare to move north by rail. In a moment the quiet of Fort Wingate was shattered and the post hummed with activity as men, horses, and equipment were made ready.

The Sixth Cavalry Moves to South Dakota for Action against the Sioux

The responsibility of directing the campaign fell to General Nelson A. Miles, then commanding the Department [Division] of the Missouri. General Miles was greatly admired by the army. He was a fine soldier with large experience in fighting Indians but at the same time with understanding sympathy for them. Even before the task was turned over to the army he had made representations to authorities in Washington in their behalf. After his assignment he went in person to the capital and obtained authority to provision the tribes from army stores as a practical military measure. The provisioning of those remaining on the reservations was started at once, even before the rounding up of the hostile Indians was begun, and without doubt was an important factor in keeping many of them in a friendly mood.

General Miles' plan of campaign envisaged the arrest or overpowering of the hostile groups before they could concentrate, and in an effort to remove Sitting Bull from the scene he sent "Buffalo Bill" to Standing Rock to induce him to surrender, but Cody was unable to get in communication with him. The commanding officer at Fort Yates was then directed to effect Sitting Bull's arrest. A detachment of Indian police was sent to the chief's camp and had placed him under arrest when one of his followers shot the leader of the police in the leg and the latter

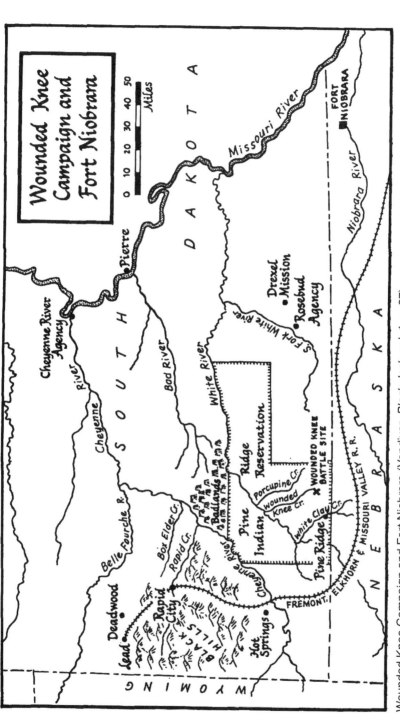

Wounded Knee Campaign and Fort Niobrara (Vandiver, *Black Jack*, vol. 1, p. 87).

thereupon shot Sitting Bull dead [15 December 1890]. In the fight that followed six of the police were killed before the hostiles fled. The death of Sitting Bull and the defeat of his followers had a subduing effect on the Standing Rock Indians.

The next step was to hold Hump in check if possible. For nearly seven years after the uprising in the '70s, Captain E. P. [Ezra P.] Ewers, of the Fifth Infantry, had been in charge of Hump and had won his confidence. General Miles therefore sent him in an effort to dissuade Hump from joining the hostiles. Ewers was then stationed in Texas but came to South Dakota at once and, accompanied only by Lieutenant H. C. [Henry C.] Hale, rode sixty miles through hostile country to Hump's camp. Hump agreed to keep the peace and by his example and subsequent influence with other chiefs rendered valuable service to the army.

To isolate and force back to the Pine Ridge Reservation the bands of Short Bull and Kicking Bear, a strong cordon of troops was thrown around the Bad Lands, while other troops guarded Big Foot's band and the various reservations. The Sixth Cavalry arrived at Rapid City, S.D., on December 9, where we were issued heavy winter outfits, including buffalo skin overcoats, fur caps, fur-lined gloves, and arctic overshoes. To be transferred after several years in the mild climate of Arizona and New Mexico to the rigors of the cold northwest in winter was a radical change, but we were hardy and accustomed to outdoor service.

We formed a part of the cordon around the Bad Lands and were designated to patrol the Cheyenne River country, the squadrons being distributed along that river in positions between the hostiles and the scattered white settlers. For the next few weeks we were almost constantly in the saddle, patrolling and scouting in every direction.

On December 20 our squadron [commander], Major Emil Adam, was ordered to White River, on the opposite side of the Bad Lands, and camped the night of the twenty-fourth at Porcupine Creek. That Christmas Eve was intensely cold, and we spent it huddling close to the fires. Christmas Day we were in the saddle again, and at James' ranch, near Kane Creek, a messenger from General Carr brought word that Big Foot had escaped from the Eighth Cavalry under Colonel E. V. [Edwin V.] Sumner and with his band was headed south. We were directed to be on the lookout and to arrest him, if possible. The following day I spent with a small outpost on a prominent peak overlooking the country but saw no sign of Indians. A much-used trail passed down Porcupine Creek, and I suggested to Major Adam that Big Foot would probably come that way. He, however, did not think it likely, and we took position on another trail a few miles to the west. I mention the incident only because of the interesting speculation it brings as to what might have happened had we covered the Porcupine Creek trail. As it turned out, this was the route taken by Big Foot's band, which was captured on the trail on the twenty-eighth by Major [Samuel M.] Whitside's squadron of the Seventh Cavalry.

Wounded Knee and Its Aftermath

Whitside was at once reinforced by additional troops of the regiment under Colonel [James W.] Forsyth, who assumed command. Camp was made that night on Wounded Knee Creek and the following day Colonel Forsyth undertook to disarm the Indians. Not satisfied with the progress being made, he ordered his troops to search the wigwams. While this was going on one of the Indians drew his rifle from under his blanket and shot a soldier. This precipitated the most serious clash of the entire campaign. Thirty officers and men and two hundred Indians, including women and children, were killed. This came like a thunderbolt, as the troops thought by that time that the campaign was going to be ended peaceably. The fight was similarly a great surprise to the Indians.

As a result, there were other clashes with the Indians of minor military importance, but our regiment participated in only one. On New Year's Day Captain [John B.] Kerr's troop on reconnaissance detached from the regiment was attacked while crossing White River and partially surrounded by superior numbers. General Carr rushed Major [Tullius C.] Tupper's squadron to Kerr's assistance and followed with the remainder of the regiment, but the Indians retired at Tupper's approach, and we got up only in time to see them disappear. There was constant fear that some isolated unit would be surprised and wiped out by overwhelming numbers.

The affair at Wounded Knee Creek threatened complete disaster to General Miles' plan of campaign. Short Bull and Kicking Bear had broken camp in the Bad Lands on the twenty-seventh and started for Pine Ridge and were on the verge of surrender, but on hearing of the Big Foot fight they turned back and resumed a hostile attitude. At the Agency the news caused general alarm among the Indians and many left to join Short Bull and Kicking Bear. For the next two weeks it was a question of guarding the hostile camps while General Miles parleyed with them. Urged by him to fulfill its obligations, the government at Washington acted promptly and took additional measures for the supply of the Indians. This, with the display of force and the appointment as agents of

Officers of the 6th Cavalry Regiment who served at Pine Ridge during the Wounded Knee Sioux uprising, photographed in 1891 (perhaps in January). Lieutenant Pershing is the seventh officer from the right in the rear row. (Library of Congress, Prints and Publications Division, Pershing Collection, Lot 8835. LC-USZ62-88606)

army officers in whom they had confidence, brought their opposition to an end and on January 15 and 16 they moved into the Agency and gave up their arms. Thus in a few weeks after the army had actually taken the field peace was restored. With one or two minor exceptions, this brought to a final conclusion a long series of combats with the Indians which had gone on intermittently ever since the first colonists landed on the New England and Virginia shores. A situation that might easily have resulted in protracted and bitter warfare, in which thousands of lives might have been lost, was brought to a quick and satisfactory conclusion because of experienced and judicious military handling. It was an exemplary lesson in what might well be called preventive action.

For Troop A it had been a period of arduous service, in the saddle almost daily, during weather that was generally below freezing and often below zero. We had all allowed our beards to grow, not as personal adornment but as a protection against the weather, and the result was a grim-looking group that assembled at Pine Ridge with the other regiments after the surrender. The officers and men were hardy and vigorous, and we formed a more efficient cavalry command than when we started if not than there was in that expedition. When I speak of appetites, I do not exaggerate in using the word enormous, at least in my own case. My tin mess plate was about the size and shape of a large pie plate, and the cook soon learned that anything less than that heaping full either of bacon and beans or their equivalent for breakfast, with a quart of steaming coffee and a due proportion of hard bread, would bring an immediate complaint. At noon we usually stopped only long enough to eat a moderate-sized lunch stowed away in our saddle pockets. Then in the evening camp the principal meal of the day was even more substantial, with components of beef and potatoes or something equally sustaining. I regret to say that I could not now eat in four days what I did then in one. That accounted for an increase of twenty pounds over my usual one hundred and ninety. The outdoor life proved invigorating to both officers and men.

When the artillery, cavalry, and infantry were all assembled at Pine Ridge, General Miles held a grand review during a snowstorm before sending us to our various stations. Although not a large assembly relatively, it was the largest that most of us had ever seen but small enough luckily to give a rare opportunity to get acquainted with the army. It occurred to me that the Indians must have been thankful that they were wise enough to surrender without fighting.

Assigned to Fort Niobrara, Nebraska

After the review, held on January 24 [1891], the troops were sent to their various stations. My troop, with three others of the Sixth, under command of Major T. C. Tupper, marched overland to our new post, Fort Niobrara, Nebraska, just south of the Rosebud Reservation in South Dakota. On the way the command was overtaken at Crookston by a terrific blizzard. As we approached this small station the sky became darkly overcast and a cold wind blew from the northwest carrying a few flakes of snow, warning us of what was to come. Fortunately we were near a camping place, as the troops had barely time to unsaddle, blanket the horses, tie them to an improvised picket line, feed them, and pitch tents before the storm swept down upon us with full violence. The conical tents, supposed to accommodate sixteen men each, were kept standing with difficulty during the night. It was almost impossible to keep the fires burning in the Sibley stoves[1]—small conical sheet iron heaters with stove pipes extending through the top of the tent. But for our substantial winter clothing there would probably have been many casualties. Cooking was impossible, though the cooks did manage to make coffee. By the next morning the snow had drifted and packed on some of the picket lines until it was three feet above ground, and these lines had to be dug out to release the horses, whose heads were held down nearly to a level with their feet. As men could go but a few yards from the tents without becoming bewildered, we remained at Crookston all that day. For practically the whole distance from there to Niobrara we had to spur our horses through enormous drifts, the different troops alternating in the lead. When we got to the post we found the barracks and quarters almost hidden by the heavy snowbanks.

Commanding the Sioux Indian Scouts

My stay at Niobrara was only long enough to refit, as I was at once ordered back to the Pine Ridge Agency to command a company of Sioux Indian Scouts. This was my first experience commanding men of other than my own race and color. Four companies of fifty men each had been enlisted for a period of six months, ostensibly for the purpose of preserving order on the reservation but really to give them something to do for which they would receive pay. The enlistment afforded an opportunity to discipline the Indians, teach them something of loyalty to the government, and win their confidence. They were mounted, each man furnishing his own horse. Their pay was the same as that of the regular cavalry, with an allowance of forty cents per day for a horse. The names on my muster roll alone told a story. Here is a partial list of names translated into English: Thunder Bull, Chief White Crow, Comes-from-Scout, Bear Nose, Running Shield, Red Feather, Big Charger, Black Fox, Broken Leg, Crow-on-Head, Eagle Chief, Has-White-Face-Horse, Yellow Bull, Ghost Bear, Iron Cloud, White Hawk, Wounded Horse, and Kills Alone.

The weather was very cold that winter and little could be done until spring in the way of outdoor drill. At first it was difficult, as the exercises had to be carried on through an interpreter. As the Indians learned to understand the commands in English their proficiency rapidly increased, and they soon took the greatest pride in their work. They were sent out frequently as individuals or groups among their people to learn the situation and to encourage the other Indians to visit the camp. My first sergeant, Thunder Bull, was a cousin of Chief Red Cloud, who had led the Fetterman massacre[2] in December, 1866, and had been in the Custer battle. The venerable chief, now very friendly, came to camp

Pershing (standing in the back row, far right) with Troop B, Ogallala Indian Scouts, 30 June 1891. After the Wounded Knee campaign, Lieutenant Pershing was assigned to command Troop B, which was stationed at Pine Ridge Reservation in South Dakota. (Library of Congress, Prints and Publications Division, Pershing Collection, Lot 8835. LC-USZ62-28335)

once in a while to pay us a visit. Though he had fought against white men most of his life, he became in his age deeply interested in the peaceful progress of the younger generation of his people toward civilization.

Although some of the scouts had learned to drink and once in a while became unruly, they were generally well-behaved. When they gave trouble the noncommissioned officers would exercise their authority effectively without instructions from me. These noncommissioned officers were selected from among those who had the highest tribal rank, and their prestige was an important factor in discipline. I often took the troop on marches to various points on the reservation for an outing and for instruction. But field work was second nature to them; they would send out advance guards and flankers and cover the main body perfectly, cautiously approaching the crest of a ridge as if actually in hostile country. On one occasion I took the troop to Wounded Knee to police the battlefield. While there more than one Indian with a "bad heart," as it was described, usually a relative of someone who had been killed in that unfortunate fight, was seen prowling about wrapped heavily in a blanket seeking revenge on some white man. But the noncommissioned officers never failed to keep an eye on him to see that he did not approach me or my tent. Whenever I left the tent one of the scouts, without my orders, would follow closely as a bodyguard.

The Sioux were fond of dancing, and it was easy to get up a dance by providing a feast. These diversions took place in a crude, circular structure where they held their tribal councils. The walls were formed of upright timbers of suitable size set in the ground and covered with a conical-shaped roof which was thatched. The dancers would appear for the occasion wearing only a loin cloth, moccasins on their feet, and feathers in their hair, with their faces and bodies painted in weird designs. In the center was a fire over which hung a pot of meat. Usually two or three of the older chiefs would open the entertainment by stepping into the arena and reciting a narrative of some victory the Sioux had won over other tribes, especially the Shawnees, their particular enemies. These recitals having stirred their blood, the younger men would string into the ring and, to the accompaniment of tom-toms and war songs, would follow in pantomime the trail of an imaginary enemy, stopping the while as though looking for his tracks, round and round the fire with their peculiar dance steps, weaving back and forth, uttering their shrill hi-yas, and becoming more furious in their contortions, until they ran him down and slew him. The pot of meat marked the end of the trail, when the leader jabbed an arrow into the boiling pot and drew out a chunk of meat. Then all joined in the feast, crowding around the pot and similarly capturing a portion of the beef and sometimes dog that it contained.

Another festive occasion was ration day. The issue of beef was usually on the hoof. Often cattle were turned loose and the Indians would ride bareback into the herd, cutting out a steer and killing it as they had in their buffalo hunts of former days. Groups of individuals or families usually banded together to divide up an animal.

The scouts exerted an excellent influence among the rest of the tribe, and their employment by the government helped greatly to restore contentment. We encouraged them to induce their people to plant crops and gave them leave of absence from time to time so that they might help their families.

I found much that was fine in Indian character. Once a red man gave his confidence he was entirely trustworthy. While he liked nothing better than to talk of his own experiences and those of his tribe, especially in war, he was eager to learn more of the ways of the white man. It was a sad day when their term of enlistment expired and these companies had to be broken up. It would have been an excellent idea to have formed one or two permanent regiments of them, as we had with the Negroes. Nothing would have done more to teach them loyalty to the government nor have gone further to bring them to civilized ways.

6

New Assignments, New Challenges, New Friends

September 1891–April 1898

When service with the Indian Scouts came to an end in August, I returned to Fort Niobrara, and in a few days received notice of my detail as military instructor at the University of Nebraska. That the suggestion had been made by members of the faculty and by state officials during the visit to my family at Lincoln two years before that I should return sometime as military instructor gave me assurance that my assignment would be looked upon with favor. The position appealed to me as affording greater opportunity for intellectual improvement through association with both the college faculty and the townspeople than continuous service at some isolated frontier post. As there seemed to be no immediate prospect of further active duty in the field, I made official application for the detail. Upon reporting in September the change brought but one regret, which was that the family meanwhile had moved to Chicago.

Commandant of Cadets, University of Nebraska, Lincoln

Service in the cadet corps, though required of all male students, had never been popular. The training had been erroneously regarded by many students as of no particular value. Some of the professors opposed it and others were indifferent; about half the faculty thought it beneficial to both students and to the university. Among the latter was the new Chancellor, Doctor James H. Canfield, an unusually able, far-seeing, vigorous man, with a delightful personality. He had received military training during the closing days of the Civil War and was outspoken in its favor. He saw its advantages as a means of inculcating a sense of loyalty and responsibility among the students at the university. He realized, and said so, that it promoted mental discipline as well as physical improvement. He had no fear, like some of its opponents, of making militarists of the young men and fully agreed with me that the training possessed high educational value. This encouraging support from the top increased my enthusiasm and enabled me from the start to insist on higher efficiency in the corps. Moreover, it influenced many who were indifferent.

During the autumn and spring, outdoor elementary training was given on the campus, where there was then ample space; and in the winter we used Grant Hall, an armory built at state expense through the efforts of one of my predecessors, Lieutenant E. S. [Edgar S.] Dudley, Coast Artillery, a veteran of the Civil War. The work consisted of what is known as close order drill of the various units from squad to company, exercises in the mechanism of extended order training for actual combat, and elementary instruction in target practice.

The cadets were required to provide their own uniforms, but for lack of funds for this purpose many willing boys had to be excused from military work. Some of them were paying their own way through college by selling newspapers, serving as waiters in restaurants, cleaning offices, or doing whatever odd jobs they could get. Among them were some of the best students in the university. As I had done much the same sort of thing in my earlier days, these students had my entire sympathy, but whenever at all possible I insisted upon the student's attendance.

There was a small element who took the position that the training was not compulsory. I contended otherwise. The Supreme Court has since held that military training, in all land-grant colleges, such as the State University at Lincoln [University of Nebraska], is compulsory.[1] This has cleared up the question and authorities, if they fulfill their obligations to the government, must insist on all male students taking the military course.

At the end of the first year, subject to the approval of the faculty, I reorganized the corps, instituting the system prevailing at West Point of taking corporals from the sophomore class, sergeants from the juniors, and officers from the seniors. This system gave the different grades the prestige of class seniority. Many of the details of training and discipline were left to these cadet officers and noncommissioned officers, who were thus given useful experience in leadership which could be obtained in no other course at the university.

Captain John J. Pershing (second from right, front row) with unidentified student officers of the cadet battalion, University of Nebraska, Lincoln, where he served from September 1891 to September 1895 (photograph is not dated). (Library of Congress, Prints and Publications Division, Pershing Collection, Lot 8854)

Green, awkward country boys were transformed within a few months into smart-looking, alert young men. In the military course precision, promptness, and a respectful attitude toward authority were emphasized as first principles of good citizenship. In the immediate result of the corps' development the conduct, bearing, and personal appearance of the student body showed marked change. Many boys who had been excused the first year found it desirable the next year to join the corps even at considerable sacrifice. It was noticeable that the students who attained high rank in the corps usually stood well in their regular college work. When the question of reorganization came before the faculty, the Chancellor emphatically expressed his satisfaction with the results attained and even remarked that certain professors might well take military training with advantage to themselves.

In June 1892 a triennial competition among the "crack" military companies of the country was to be held at Omaha, and the cadets were so elated over their progress by spring and so confident they could win that they wanted to enter a company. Of course, this meant much extra work for all of us, but after weighing the pros and cons, I decided to take advantage of their enthusiasm and prepare a selected company. After a few preliminary tests the required forty-five men were chosen from over a hundred volunteers for intensive training. A special uniform was adopted and the rather old arms and equipment put into the best possible condition. The company was commanded by a cadet captain, who had to be given special training for his task. The entire university became interested in the project. It was a great day for the military department and the university as a whole when the competition took place and the Chancellor and many professors and students were on hand at Omaha. In the "Grand National" class the company failed to win by a very slight margin, but easily won the first prize in the "Maiden" class. The enthusiasm of the faculty and students knew no bounds, the Chancellor himself scrambling over an eight-foot fence and joining the rush towards the company, who were literally carried off the parade ground. The award was a piece of plate and a cash prize of $1,500. The money was distributed among the cadets who had taken part, and to many their share was most welcome. Needless to say, the result gave such an impetus to military training that the following year a much larger percentage of boys registered for the course than ever before.[2]

Many amusing things happened in my service at the university. In one of them the joke was on me. The state was celebrating the twenty-fifth anniversary of its admission to the Union. There was a big parade of troops in Lincoln, and the cadet battalion led the procession. Of course, it was necessary for me to be mounted. I hired a horse which the livery stable keeper—a Missourian—said was afraid of nothing and perfectly trained for that sort of thing. While the cadets were forming I mounted the horse, and just as I got into the saddle my saber dangled against his flank. Thereupon the horse gave an exhibition of bucking in front of the battalion that would have done credit to any wild west show. Although the bridle broke and one stirrup came off, I rode him until he was tired out. It was entirely impromptu, and I had to draw heavily on my earlier experience to keep from being thrown. The cadets roundly applauded the show, which, together with the fact that the horse pranced through the whole parade, seemed partly to compensate them for the long and tedious march of the day. The cadet battalion made a fine appearance and distinctly reminded me of my cadet days when, during my senior year, it was my duty to march the corps to the mess hall and back three times each day.

During the summer of 1893 I took advantage of my vacation to obtain an appointment as an officer of the Columbian Guard[3] at the World's Fair at Chicago. The officers of that organization were nearly all of the Regular Army. The service, which carried a small stipend, offered a rare opportunity to see the exhibits of that great exposition.

During my second and third years at Lincoln I taught mathematics two hours a day. This was not only a pleasure, but it enabled me somewhat to augment my meager income. Among the students in my classes were Dorothy Canfield [Fisher] and Willa Cather, but I doubt that the study of mathematics gave either one of them a taste for literature. Several boys who took studies under me went to West Point [George T. Patterson, Ernest D. Scott, Evan H. Humphrey, and Halsey E. Yates] and Annapolis [not identified] and all have had successful careers. One became a general officer.[4] I also studied law while at Lincoln, graduating with the class of 1893, and was admitted to practice in the District Courts and the Supreme Court of the State of Nebraska, later being admitted to practice before the Supreme Court of the United States.

At that time service in our small army seemed to offer few advantages beyond routine promotion. While Congress was lavish in its payments of pensions to ex-soldiers, it was penurious in its appropriations for the maintenance of the army. Our people have never been able to learn that an ounce of prevention is worth a pound of cure. Of course, no one in those days could see what the future held in store for the United States. The war with Spain was not dreamed of; anyone at that time would have been considered ridiculous who predicted that the country would annex a chain of islands extending across the Pacific, including Asiatic possessions; and one would have been called mad who expressed the probability of our participating in a war in Europe. In fact, the belief was general that we were not likely to have any more war. The strength of the army was so reduced—2,100 officers and 25,000 enlisted men—that it was no larger than was needed as a national police force available for possible domestic disturbance. The future outlook for advancement for a young officer was not encouraging, and it looked as though I would not even reach the grade of captain for about fifteen years more and would probably retire with the rank of major. This prospect led me to seek an appointment in one of the staff corps, but I was glad later that my efforts failed. Because of the gloomy outlook it seemed best for me to plan to resign and enter the legal profession. My mind turned in that direction especially while in Lincoln, where many men about my age with whom I came in contact were already successful in that or other professions, some of whom were then or later became national figures. Several times I was about to take the step, but each time the prospect of interesting service intervened, until finally I gave up the thought altogether.

Of those whom I knew at Lincoln the outstanding figure was William Jennings Bryan. He was then a member of Congress, but retained a law office at Lincoln which contained a good library, generously placed at the disposal of aspiring law students. Charles G. Dawes, also located there, was another man of promise, though he was then only a struggling young lawyer with an inclination towards business and finance. He was not a "silver-tongued orator" able to sway masses of constituents, like Bryan, nor was he apparently ambitious in this direction. Though totally different in character and politics, both these men have occupied high places in the nation's council. I knew Bryan slightly and often borrowed books from his library. But I knew Dawes better, as we frequently met socially and more often at Don Cameron's lunch counter, where food was good and, what was more to the point, the price low. It was generally believed then by his friends that Dawes would be successful in the financial world, and possibly in the political world as well. In 1896, having moved to Evanston, Illinois, he became Secretary of the Republican National Committee and was later appointed Comptroller of the Currency by President [William] McKinley. Another prominent young lawyer and one of my closest friends, Charles E. Magoon, later became law officer of the Bureau of Insular Affairs and, through his association with Mr. Elihu Root, was appointed Governor of Panama and became Governor of Cuba while Mr. [William Howard] Taft was Secretary of War.

While I was in Lincoln, Mr. Bryan became a candidate for a second term in Congress. The Republicans selected as his opponent a judge of local distinction, Allan W. Field. Mr. Bryan at once challenged him for a joint debate on the issues between the two parties, Mr. Bryan then being a pronounced advocate of free trade. Judge Field, who was not a ready speaker, favored the tariff principles of his party. The greatest interest was aroused throughout the district, and the Republicans felt that while their candidate had made a poor showing in the first two contests he would at the third and last debate, to be held at Lincoln, have the issues well in hand. They turned out en masse to hear the speakers, and the crowd was clearly sympathetic toward Judge Field. But Mr. Bryan's superior powers of oratory so far overshadowed his opponent that the audience turned almost completely to his view and the election easily went to Mr. Bryan.[5] It was not the reasoning that won, it was the oratory. Mr. Bryan was not considered a very good lawyer and no one, I am sure, ever dreamed that four years later he would carry the democratic convention off its feet on the silver question and by his cross of gold speech[6] and himself receive the nomination for the presidency.

Among the students who were in the cadet corps in my day there have been a governor [George L. Sheldon], a senator [not identified], a secretary of war [George H. Dern], several members of Congress [only Ernest M. Pollard identified], and officers of the army and navy [in addition to those already identified above who attended the USMA, William H. Oury, Charles W. Weeks, William H. Hayward, Leroy Vernon Patch, Charles B. Robbins], members of scientific services and professional men [Professor Edward C. Elliott, Dr. Charles A. Elliot, Professor William L. Westermann]. When the Spanish-American War came, many former cadets volunteered in Nebraska's quota of troops, one regiment of which [the 1st Nebraska Volunteer Infantry Regiment], under Colonel J. M. Stotsenburg (one of my successors as military instructor and my companion on the trip to the Grand Canyon), served with distinction in the Philippines, where he was killed in battle. His successor as regimental commander was Colonel F. D. [Frank D.] Eager, a cadet captain of high standing in my day, and now one of Lincoln's most distinguished citizens.

The regular tour of duty for a military instructor was then three years, but at the end of that time the Chancellor asked that my detail be extended another year, and, much to my surprise, the War Department granted the request. It is a highly satisfactory thing to work among those who want you with them and to be responsible for the training of the splendid type of men who go to our universities. My association with them and with the professors was a valuable contrast to that of routine life in the army. The psychology of the citizen as a cadet was that of the citizen soldier. Under training by one who understands him, he can be quickly developed into a loyal and efficient fighting man. It would be an excellent thing if every officer in the army could have contact in this way with the youth which forms our citizenship in peace and our armies in war. It would broaden the officer's outlook and better fit him for his duties in the army, especially in time of war. My four years at Lincoln, mingling socially with the people of the university and the city, formed one of the most delightful and profitable periods of my life. It was because of my acquaintance there and the fact that it had become the residence of two of my sisters that I was led to purchase a house and make my home there after my return from the World War.

With the 10th Cavalry Regiment in Montana

With my next assignment came still another experience—a further test of my capacity to handle men of different race and character. Service with Negro troops was not especially sought after, but my promotion to the grade of first lieutenant in 1892 brought assignment to the Tenth Cavalry,[7] and upon completion of my tour at Lincoln, in 1895, I joined the regiment at Fort Assinniboine, Montana. The captain of Troop D, to which I was assigned, was away on recruiting duty and the command fell to me. It was a radical change to go from the command of a corps of cadets of the caliber from which are drawn the leaders of the nation to a company of Regulars composed of citizens who have always had only limited advantages and restricted ambitions. My attitude toward the Negro was that of one brought up among them. I had always felt kindly and sympathetic toward them and knew that fairness and due consideration of their welfare would make the same appeal to them as to any other body of men. Most men, of whatever race, creed, or color, want to do the proper thing, and they respect the man above them whose motive is the same. I therefore had no more trouble with the Negroes than with any other troops I ever commanded. Colored troops like the glamour of army life and nothing pleased them better than to be on parade and march to the music of a military band.

The autumn, especially delightful in the Northwest, was occupied by the usual program of training. Service with colored troops demands much greater effort on the part of officers than that with white troops. The Negro troopers had their limitations and required more supervision and more careful attention to the details of instruction. As to paperwork, such as reports and returns, a much greater responsibility devolved upon the officers. After winter set in the weather was usually too cold for outdoor work, although there were milder days due to the Chinook winds, which melted the snow as if by magic. We had only daily horse exercise outdoors, and that was generally conducted with the men in buffalo overcoats and the animals protected by heavy blankets, and even this had to be suspended in the coldest weather, which at one time registered 60° below zero. A few of us younger officers took up fencing and broad sword in order more efficiently to teach the troops the use of the saber. There were the usual post gaieties, private theatricals, and dances for officers and their families, as well as those for enlisted men. Just before the holidays Lieutenants Letcher Hardeman, [Samuel D.] Rockenbach, and I, with four or five expert rifle shots from the com-

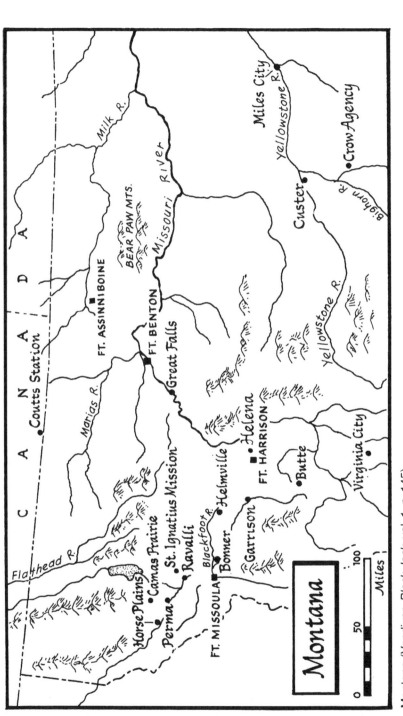

Montana (Vandiver, *Black Jack*, vol. 1, p. 145).

After leaving the University of Nebraska, Pershing joined his regiment at Fort Assin-niboine, Montana. In this undated photograph, he is seated on the porch, second from the right. He served with the 10th Cavalry at Fort Assinniboine from October 1895 until June 1897, except for a stretch of temporary duty as aide-de-camp to Major General Nelson A. Miles, commanding general of the army, from December 1896 to May 1897. (Library of Congress, Prints and Publications Division, Pershing Collection. Lot 8850)

mand, went deer hunting on the Missouri River, near the mouth of the Yellowstone, where whitetail deer were plentiful in the canebrake of the bottomland. We had exceptional sport and returned with eight or ten deer for distribution to the garrison at Christmas. On one occasion Hardeman and I were watching a clearing toward which the deer were being driven when a fine buck appeared on the opposite side, about one hundred yards away. Hardeman politely asked me to fire, but I said, "Let's both fire." As we could find but one bullet hole in the dead deer, it could never be determined who killed it, but I think that each of us secretly maintained the belief that his shot did the work.

The regiment had an interesting piece of service in the field while I was on duty with it. This was in rounding up during the summer of 1896 certain bands of Cree Indians, members of a tribe from Canada which had got into trouble with the authorities there and had fled across the border into the United States. It appears that during a conference at Duck Lake in 1881 between Canadian authorities and Cree chiefs in an attempt to settle what was known as the Riel Rebellion[8] one of the government representatives, a Catholic priest, had been killed, and the Indians, fearing the consequences, fled to Montana and North Dakota. They eventually became a great nuisance, as they continually committed thefts, especially of cattle, and efforts were made to get rid of them. Small bands had been captured from time to time and marched back across the border but had reentered as soon as our troops were out of sight. Finally, definite arrangements were made with the Canadian Government to receive and retain them, and several troops of the Tenth Cavalry, including mine, were detailed to round them up and return them.

I left Assinniboine on June 13 and upon reaching the Marias River, below Fort Benton, found it bank full and dangerous, but we wanted to reach Great Falls by the seventeenth and the crossing had to be attempted. Our two wagon beds were converted into ferry boats by covering the sides and bottoms with canvas tent flies. By the use of a cable made of lariats tied together and carried by boat to the opposite shore, upstream each trip, the current swung them back and forth, forming a sort of flying ferry. Supplies were crossed in this way, and we swam the horses and mules. It took us from daylight to dark to make this crossing, but it was a thorough test of what these black troopers could do.

When on detached duty in the field, where the usual methods of enforcing discipline were not available, it became necessary occasionally to resort to other means. There was one man in the troop, young, strong, and healthy, who had constantly avoided doing his part. He would put his shoulder to the wheel like the others but make no real effort. Whenever I was present he would hustle about as though he were the most energetic member of the troop. Here at the river where the men were loading the wagon bodies it was necessary for them to wade waist deep into the river, and I noticed that this shirk was careful not to get his feet wet. When I told him to get down into the water like the others, he made no move. Whereupon I gave him a punch with my fist that sent him toppling full-length into the stream. The First Sergeant remarked, "Lieutenant, that's what I've been wanting to do to him all day." I do not approve such methods in general, but there are times when an example is necessary. After that the men would get after any man who wasn't doing his part by saying, "You better git at it feller or 'Old Red' will knock you into the Marias River." The colored troops, like others, usually gave each officer a nickname by which they referred to him among themselves. Mine in that troop was "Old Red."

The first group of Crees, one hundred and seven men, women, and children, was captured near Great Falls. Having heard rumors that they were prepared to resist arrest, I marched the troop into their camp ready for action. This show of force, followed by my assurance that none who had not participated in the Duck Lake conspiracy would be punished by the Canadian Government, induced them to surrender. After we took them into custody a misguided American lawyer obtained a writ of habeas corpus requiring that I show cause why they should not be liberated. The court, however, dismissed the writ on receiving my answer that a state had no jurisdiction over Federal agents, but in the meantime the necessary rail transportation had been secured and the Indians, with their baggage and ponies, were already on their way back to Canada.

The next move was across the Rockies by the old Lewis and Clark trail—a picturesque march in summer—to Fort Missoula, Montana, then under command of Colonel Andrew Burt, 25th Infantry (Colored), who received us with every courtesy. From this base with part of the troop I proceeded to Camas Prairie, where another group of seventy with their mixed transportation and their herd of horses were captured. As the cheapest and most expeditious method of crossing the Flathead River, I arranged to entrain the troop at Perma and went from there by rail to Horse Plains. Upon arrival we hastily mounted and dashed out sixteen miles to Camas Prairie, where the Crees were surprised and surrounded too quickly for them to break camp and escape.

The distance back to Missoula was about one hundred miles. The crossing of the Flathead [River] by that nondescript outfit made a wonderful picture—naked Indians swimming horses barebacked, yelling, handling broncos that had never been roped, the black troopers manning an old ramshackle ferry to carry the women, children, property, and vehicles across the swollen river—all added rapidly and impressively to one's experience. We were a day and a half here at the crossing, but the task was accomplished with the loss of only a few Indian ponies.

In the meantime, my second lieutenant, L. J. [Lawrence J.] Fleming, who had been left at Missoula with the rest of the troop, had captured other groups of Crees in that vicinity, making a total of one hundred and forty-eight that started for the border on July 22. We followed up the Blackfoot River, over the Marysville divide, and along the eastern slope of the Rockies to the McLeod trail, thence to the Canadian line. Before we reached the border we had gathered up one hundred and ninety Indians in all of the primitive "blanket" type, old and young, men and women, warriors, squaws, and papooses. This trek would have made an epic story, so filled with episodes was this strange cavalcade of typical American aborigines. It was an odd procession of vehicles, a few serviceable, the rest creaking old wagons, worn out buggies, often breaking down, pack ponies, and a few travois. Then came the five hundred Indian ponies herded by the Indians themselves. In contrast, my troop of Negroes in blue field uniforms with campaign hats of that period were here and there urging and assisting along the slower units.

Coming again to the Marias River, where we camped, but at a point higher upstream, we had the misfortune to find ourselves suddenly flooded out by a rise of this stream in the middle of the night. For a while it was pandemonium; men were shouting, women screaming, children crying, dogs barking, and frightened horses neighing as they floundered in the flood. But due to the prompt action of the troop fortunately no lives were lost. It was a practical lesson in the wisdom of an old axiom of the frontier—never camp on the near side of a river that has to be crossed if you can help it. After waiting all the next day for the river to subside, we were able to proceed.

Much of the route up the Blackfoot River and across the Rockies afforded striking scenery. We climbed snow-capped mountains fringed with stately pines and camped beside beautiful streams. On the eastern slope we trudged along over barren wastes and made long marches to reach camp where water was available. We fought an outbreak of measles among the Indian children and had a death and a birth.

It was with a feeling of relief that I reached the Canadian line at Coutts Station on August 6. But to my surprise, because of the presence of measles, the Canadian police refused to receive the Indians. It was necessary to appeal by telegraph to General [John R.] Brooke, the Department Commander, to get over this piece of quibbling, but peremptory instructions soon came from Ottawa directing that our charges be received. Aside from this incident, the Canadian police were very courteous, and I formed a high opinion of their efficiency. My men were glad the job was done; we had been two months at it and were happy to turn our horses toward home.

Not long after our return to Fort Assinniboine, General Miles, then in command of the Army, arrived at the post to make an inspection and to have some shooting. He was accompanied by several officer and civilian friends, including the well-known painter of western life Frederic Remington. All the troops except mine were absent on maneuvers, so the pleasure of entertaining the General on a shooting expedition fell to me, assisted by Lieutenant Hardeman. We took him to Bear Paw Mountains, where prairie chickens were plentiful. The General was an excellent shot and frequently brought down two or even three birds out of a covey. We found him most companionable and considered ourselves fortunate to be with him under such conditions. Our bag of two days was sufficient to supply the General's party with all they would take and leave enough for a feast all around for the garrison.

As the Presidential campaign between McKinley and Bryan was in full blast, I obtained leave of absence shortly and went east, stopping at several points to get in touch with political activities. I visited Republican National Headquarters to see my friend Charles G. Dawes, then Secretary of the National Committee, and was introduced to Mark Hanna, the Chairman. While I was in Chicago, Bryan was there making a series of speeches advocating free silver and tariff reform. I stood on the corner of Michigan Avenue and Randolph Street one afternoon and saw the immense procession of Bryan followers go by. It was composed, it seemed to me, of all the riffraff of Chicago. While I was standing at this point someone threw a rotten egg from a high window at Bryan's carriage, a proceeding that aroused general indignation.

While in New York City I met Theodore Roosevelt for the first time, both of us being guests of A. D. [Avery D.] Andrews, a classmate of mine who had resigned and was then one of the three Police commissioners along with Mr. Roosevelt and Mr. Fred [Frederick D.] Grant, who was appointed a general in the army following the Spanish War. Having lived in the West, Roosevelt knew the life well, and having written *The Winning of the West*,[9] he knew the valuable part the army had played in that achievement. He spoke in high praise of the members of the police who had served in the army on the frontier. Here was a man, I thought, whose personality and vigor would carry him a long way. Marked by a decided individuality, whether as police commissioner, Rough Rider, or President, he was of the type one never forgets. It was a most enjoyable evening, of which he often spoke in later years. I had no idea then that his estimate of me would play such a part in my future.

Aide to Lieutenant General Nelson A. Miles, Commanding General of the U.S. Army

When I got to Washington I called on General Miles to pay my respects, as was then the custom, and much to my surprise before the expiration of my leave I was ordered to duty at his headquarters. It was not without personal satisfaction that I entered upon my first term of duty at the capital as acting aide to the commanding general. Several interesting subjects were assigned to me for study and recommendation, and on horseback rides when I accompanied him we had interesting discussions on the use of cavalry. But my duties were generally of a social character. I was frequently at their home and often escorted Mrs. Miles and her daughter, Miss Celia [Cecilia], in making calls and attending various functions. These included visits to the White House, where Mrs. Cleveland, a recent bride possessing beauty and charm, presided with graceful dignity. Later I had occasion to meet the President [Grover Cleveland], whom I admired greatly for his unflinching courage on public questions of the day, especially for his stand on the money question. While a cadet I had followed closely the presidential campaign of 1884 and was in favor of Cleveland's election.

It was never a practice of mine to "play politics," but I was guilty of doing so on one occasion about that time—if it is guilt to do what one can to get a good man appointed to an office where he is needed. Among the members of the expiring Congress when President Cleveland was succeeded by President McKinley was G. D. [George D.] Meiklejohn, of Nebraska, whom I had known when he was lieutenant governor of the state. He and I lived at the old Wellington Hotel, across the street from the Riggs Bank, now replaced by an office building, and often met and discussed public affairs. One evening as we were dining together it occurred to me that he would fill the position of Assistant Secretary of War very creditably, and I suggested that he try for it. The idea surprised him, as he said he knew nothing about military matters. I told him that the assistant secretary seldom did and that the appointment was generally only political. With some further discussion he consented to my seeing some of his friends about it. The following day I spoke to General Miles, and as he thought well of Meiklejohn, I went to see Senator John M. Thurston, of Nebraska. He was one of Nebraska's ablest lawyers and had been one of the first Republicans to advocate McKinley's nomination for the presidency. I had known him when his name was before the legislature for election and many of his friends were also mine. The Senator took the matter up at once with the new President and after some delay the appointment was made. Meiklejohn was very grateful for my interest in his appointment.

The men chosen for United States Senator in those days were far more likely to be well qualified than those elected by popular vote under the Seventeenth Amendment to the Constitution,[10] and they were more independent of political pressure. The members of the legislatures generally took pride in the men they sent to Washington to represent their states and were better able to judge of their qualifications than the average voter. I have heard it said that Theodore Roosevelt once remarked that one of his greatest errors was in advocating this amendment. But whether the former president said this or not, it is likely that it expressed his opinion.

Instructor in Tactics and Tactical Officer, U.S. Military Academy

In the spring of 1897, Lieutenant Colonel Samuel M. Mills, Jr., then Commandant of Cadets at West Point, came on a visit to Washington, and while there asked me how I would like a detail to the academy as instructor in tactics. I had twice before been asked to go there in the same capacity, but as the duty did not appeal to me I had not encouraged the appointment. At this time, however, as several friends of mine were on duty there, I told Colonel Mills I would be glad to accept and the assignment was made at his request.

The Superintendent when I arrived in June was Colonel Oswald H. Ernst, of the Engineer Corps, and the Commandant of Cadets was Lieutenant Colonel Otto H. Hein, Infantry, who had relieved Colonel Mills. In the eleven years since I had graduated several changes had been made, most of them in the right direction. One was a somewhat more liberal attitude in relations between officers and cadets. They were not so impersonal, though there was still room for improvement. Another was that a definite course in gymnastics has been introduced under the direction of Professor H. J. [Herman J.] Koehler, and this made decidedly for improvement in the physical development of the individual cadet. It was also advantageous to officers who wished to profit by it. There was no special attention given to physical training in my cadet days beyond the setting up exercises for plebes. There was a so-called gymnasium in the basement of the old academic building but no prescribed course under competent direction. The exercises were perfunctory and of no particular benefit. This was all changed under Koehler.

Cadets had also begun to play football with other colleges, and I think this was especially beneficial, not only to those who participated, but it brought the corps as a whole in contact with young men of other institutions. The cadets were not then permitted to play away from West Point, but this restriction soon came to an end. There had been no change in the human side of the cadet corps. The same delinquencies continued to occur as when I was a cadet. There was the same surreptitious violation of regulations against smoking and running lights after taps and slipping off to Highland Falls on a lark.

After my experience in the army I felt that practical instruction should begin early to include simple exercises in minor tactics in order better to prepare young graduates for active field service. It seemed to me that graduates of West Point should be given a course both theoretical and practical in the kind of service they would have as commanders of platoons and companies and even higher units in battle. I made some suggestions along this line to the Commandant, but he was not inclined to advance beyond a certain limited routine. Tactical officers under him had little encouragement to extend the scope of their instruction, which continued to remain somewhat monotonous for officers and cadets alike instead of being, as it should be, a stimulus for thought and study of the basic principles of combat and the development of leadership in their application.

7

The Spanish-American War to the San Juan Heights

April–30 June 1898

Events Leading to the War

Since 1895, the march of events in Cuba had been receiving more and more attention from the American people, who now, at the beginning of 1898, had reached a state of mind that strongly indicated the probability of intervention and consequent war with Spain.[1] The islands of Cuba and Puerto Rico were the last of the once widespread dominions of the Spanish Empire in the Western Hemisphere. The people of Cuba in particular were dissatisfied with their Spanish overlords and aspired to the freedom that other Spanish-American colonies had attained. There had been a rebellion in the island lasting from 1868 to 1878, but it had been effectively suppressed, and the one which began in 1895, it soon became apparent, was likely to meet with a similar fate without aid from the United States. The Cuban forces were only a poorly-armed, loosely-organized, inadequately-financed group of guerilla bands, while the Spanish army, in spite of all its defects, was incomparably larger and better equipped. The success of the rebellion depended on help from other sources, and the Cubans were doing everything possible to obtain it from us.

What was called the Cuban Junta was established in New York for the purpose of collecting funds, "running" arms to the *insurrectos,* and working up American sympathy; and a number of Americans, some of them adventurers, interested financiers, and sensational newspapermen, gave support to the movement. When the Spanish General, Weyler [Valeriano Weyler y Nicolau], established concentration camps where thousands of Cubans were imprisoned behind barbed wire, the details of their sufferings from hunger and mistreatment spread by the Junta and by our own press aroused American indignation beyond anything that had happened since the Civil War, and intervention was urged in many quarters. President McKinley was opposed to such extreme measures and struggled for many months to avoid it. But when, on the fateful night of February 15, 1898, the USS *Maine* was sunk in Havana Harbor with the loss of two hundred and sixty-six of its crew—which, justly or unjustly, was blamed on the Spaniards—war became inevitable. We now had, or assumed to have, not only a moral duty to perform in behalf of an oppressed people but our national honor to defend because of assault. "Remember the *Maine*" became the war cry of the American people.

While the report of the naval investigating committee found that the vessel had been sunk as a result of some unknown force applied from the outside, personally I have never been able to understand how, under the circumstances, the Spanish authorities could have been so lacking in common sense as to cause the destruction of an American naval vessel visiting in one of their harbors, nor do I see how this could have happened without discovery. It is difficult to conclude that the Spanish authorities deliberately brought about the explosion. However, it was generally believed that they were responsible and the sentiment in favor of action became too strong to be resisted.[2]

Outbreak of the War with Spain

To the American people the war was viewed as a righteous crusade undertaken not for any selfish reason but in behalf of an oppressed and suffering people struggling as we ourselves had done for independence. No thought or plan of territorial acquisition was voiced when we entered the arena. Yet the scheme to acquire Puerto Rico and the Philippines was definitely lodged in the minds of a few leaders who had the ear of the President, although he was at first loath to consider it. As to the people in general, the independence of Cuba was their sole object, and this was reflected in Congress, which expressed the national purpose in clear language with the declaration that the United States would not assume control over the island except for pacification and asserting the determination to leave the government to its people. Congress, in its resolutions of April 19, demanded the withdrawal of Spain and her military forces from Cuba. No self-respecting people like the Spaniards could submit to such a demand without fighting, and they accepted the challenge. Spain declared war on April 24 and our Congress made a similar declaration the following day.

Ultimate victory for the United States was a foregone conclusion. No one with ordinary information doubted the outcome once the well-known resources of our country in men and material were organized and made available. Our navy was distinctly superior to that of Spain, and especially so if it could have the advantage of fighting on its own side of the ocean. The Spanish themselves could not have had any illusions as to their eventual defeat. Nevertheless, the difficulties of campaigning in the tropics gave our War Department considerable anxiety.

Several attempts had been made before to wrest Cuba from Spanish control, notably by the British in 1741 and 1762. In both these campaigns the percentage of loss by disease was appalling. Similar defeats had been suffered by European forces in other parts of tropical America—not at the hands of armies but those of nature. In 1802 Napoleon sent 32,000 troops to Santo Domingo and 15,000 of them perished in two months. In the '80s [Ferdinand Marie] de Lesseps had tried to build a Panama canal, but disease destroyed his army of workmen. Yellow fever and other tropical diseases not only thinned the ranks of forces sent to the American tropics but left those who survived quite unfit for further duty. The evident difficulties of maintaining an unacclimated American army in Cuba for any length of time naturally were given every consideration. Medical men familiar with diseases peculiar to the tropics were sought and provision was made by Congress for the enlistment of five regiments of immunes, that is, immune from yellow fever.

Then there was the astonishing numerical inferiority of our army that must bear the immediate burden. Although between the years 1870 and 1898 the population of the United States had increased from thirty-eight million to seventy-three million, the army had actually decreased in size until it numbered but 2,100 officers and 25,000 enlisted men. War had been imminent for some months, but Congress had done almost nothing in the way of preparation until we were into it. On April 22 the President was given authority to call for volunteers, and the day after the formal declaration an increase in the Regular Army was authorized for a possible force of 62,500. President McKinley on April 23 called for 125,000 volunteers and on May 25 for an additional 75,000. But it was one thing to call for volunteers and quite another to organize and train them.

The utter failure to make provision for war until after we had entered upon it was shamelessly in keeping with the history of our country since its foundation. During the years following the Civil War, notwithstanding its lessons, the people had again fallen into their easy-going attitude. As in the past, it had been argued, and people believed it, as many do now, that there was no further danger of war. Pacifism was predominant. As the national debt had grown, partly as a result of pensions, retrenchment had been the political cry of both parties, and appropriations for defense had been constantly reduced. The people throughout the country were almost exclusively occupied with their own personal affairs to the neglect of such national considerations. Nobody listened to those who realized the wisdom of maintaining an adequate army and advocated it.

But even in the face of neglect, the miniature army had remained true to its traditions and was as highly trained as possible when we consider that it was scattered in small groups to garrison numerous posts throughout the country and that there were no postgraduate military schools until shortly before 1898 and no staff organized to undertake large operations. Under these conditions its record stood as a fine example of devotion in spite of the passive attitude of the government and people, and it was ready to serve to the best of its ability, both in the field and as a nucleus around which a greater structure composed mainly of volunteers could be built. The organization, equipment, and training of the relatively large numbers of men called to arms to meet the superior numbers that Spain actually had in the field was begun with enthusiasm.

The strength of the Spanish army at the outbreak of the war was over 300,000 men, of which 196,000 were in Cuba. The latter figure was not accurately known at the time but was variously estimated as high as 150,000. That our navy could prevent the arrival of Spanish reinforcements was well understood, but the army already in Cuba was a formidable force, assuming that even half of it could be concentrated against the invader. It was not known definitely where these troops were located on the island, although it was known that the city of Havana was well fortified and that the principal seaports, including Santiago, were fairly well prepared for defense. In any event, it was natural to suppose that our army would meet with strong resistance no matter where it should attempt a landing and that victory would not come easily or be quickly attained.

Feeling that war was a certainty and that an expeditionary force composed principally of units of the Regular Army would probably be the first to go, I applied on April 16 to be relieved from duty at West Point. My application was forwarded to Washington by the Superintendent recommending unfavorable action, and it was promptly returned disapproved by the Adjutant General, much to my disappointment and chagrin. It must have been the first application from among the officers on duty at the academy, as the Superintendent published it in orders, together with the War Department's endorsement of disapproval, and sent copies to all officers of the post.

Rejoining the Tenth Cavalry and Preparing for Movement to Cuba

At the same time that I filed this application I wrote to the commander of the Tenth Cavalry, Colonel Guy V. Henry, and told him of my wish to join the regiment. He at once requested my relief from West Point so that he could appoint me regimental quartermaster, but as the War Department seemed inclined to take no action I wrote to the Assistant Secretary of War, Meiklejohn, telling him of my application. Hearing nothing from him, I asked for three days' leave of absence and went to Washington to see him. It was difficult for him to get my point of view. He made several counter-suggestions, one of which was that I should accept a detail in the Judge Advocate's Department with the rank of captain. I told him that duty with troops was far more desirable at such a time and that was what I wanted and nothing else would do, even though it carried increased rank. Finally I said; "George, if it cannot be arranged for me to join an active regiment I shall resign and join some National Guard or volunteer unit that stands a chance of being sent to Cuba." With that, seeing that I was in earnest, he said he would relieve me the first time he became Acting Secretary of War. A short time afterward the Secretary of War was absent from Washington for a day or two and Meiklejohn, as Acting Secretary, directed that orders be issued sending me to my regiment. My action in going directly to Meiklejohn was not at all in keeping with accepted Army procedure then, and would not be today, but with our country at war I felt it excusable. The position of regimental quartermaster in wartimes was very onerous, and I was not keen for that sort of work, but preferred line duty. Still, I was at least in a fair way to get to the front.

About that time a piece of totally unexpected news emblazoned the front pages of every newspaper in the country. Even well-informed Americans were surprised and the nation got its first intimation that the war would not be limited to a military campaign in Cuba or naval fighting on the Atlantic. On the day before war was declared, Theodore Roosevelt, Assistant Secretary of the Navy, had cabled Admiral [George W.] Dewey at Hong Kong to proceed at once to the Philippines and capture or destroy the Spanish fleet in Manila Bay. Compliance with these instructions constituted the big news. Only a few Americans in the higher circles of the government who favored expansion and were urging it on the President had any idea that such a battle was expected until it had actually taken place. So the American people were given a surprise. A further sensational feature of the news was that our fleet had not lost a single ship or a single sailor.

We had not fought a battle overseas since 1812, and the sudden realization that one of our squadrons had won a decisive victory in Asiatic waters, on the other side of the globe, sent a thrill through the whole country. It required a study of their geographies before most people knew just where this sea fight had taken place. Only a few realized that this victory was to lead, first of all, to a campaign in the Orient for which we were poorly prepared, and fewer still comprehended that instead of remaining a strictly American power we were now, as a result of the Battle of Manila Bay, to become a world power with far-flung colonies and interests.

My regiment, along with several others, was in camp at Chickamauga Park, with Lieutenant Colonel Theodore A. Baldwin in command, when I joined on May 5. The people of the South had not seen much of the Regular Army since reconstruction days and were somewhat inclined to look askance at us. A friendly attitude, however, soon became the rule and very soon our officers were being entertained in private homes in most hospitable fashion. But their feeling toward the colored troops was different from that in the north and some of the men resented it. Barbers refused to serve our men, and at one shop farther south the proprietor put up a sign, "Niggers not wanted." One evening one of the recruits entered the shop and demanded a shave, which was refused with an insulting remark, whereupon the soldier stepped outside and, firing his pistol through the window, killed the barber. This incident was most regrettable, and fearing trouble the Colonel had the long roll sounded recalling all men to camp, and thereafter none was allowed into town without special permission. As most of the regiment soon left for Cuba, other possible clashes were avoided. The guilty man was later court-martialed and sentenced to death.

From the viewpoint of supply officer, I found little had been done

Pershing as a captain, around the time of the Spanish-American War. (Library of Congress, Prints and Publications Division, Bain News Service Collection)

to equip the regiment for field service. There was clothing to draw and issue and tentage, horses, mules, and wagon transportation and supplies of all sorts to obtain. As to field transportation, the Depot Quartermaster, Major D. E. [Daniel E.] McCarthy,[3] permitted me to select the necessary number of mules from the quartermaster corral, and these with the requisite harness and wagons for thirty-six four- and six-mule teams constituted our full allowance on a war footing. The task of assembling the harness and the wagons and the difficulty of breaking in green mules with inexperienced drivers, mostly Negroes, hired on the spot may easily be imagined. As we expected to move southward any day, it was necessary for me to work far into the night, and I scarcely got a wink of sleep. Before this transportation could be fully organized we were ordered to Lakeland, Florida, about twenty miles from Tampa, where, with other troops, we were to embark for Cuba. I shall never forget the difficulties we had when the regiment broke camp at Chickamauga on May 14. Although I had hurried at top speed to get the regimental train together, it was certainly a very inefficient outfit that turned out to haul baggage and supplies to Rossville, only seven miles away. Most of the mules were still unbroken and would have been hard to handle even with good drivers. As it was, there were several runaways, wagons were overturned, and property was scattered all the way to Rossville. But we managed eventually to reach the station and load the property, mules, and cavalry horses in time to depart as scheduled. The trip was slow and uneventful, and we were soon encamped in the pine woods beside a beautiful lake near Lakeland. Additional horses had to be drawn and one lot, while being brought to camp, stampeded, and thirteen of them were never found. Their cost was charged to me, and it was sometime after the war before I was relieved of paying for them out of my own pocket.

At Tampa the situation, from the lack of arrangements for handling the large influx of cars loaded with supplies, was little short of chaotic. It was difficult to get what we needed, especially additional clothing and equipment. Delay in receiving bills-of-lading through the small post office, lack of switching facilities, and the consequent congestion of freight cars all added to the confusion. The port had not been at all prepared to handle the amount of property or the numbers of men and animals that were concentrated there. No general plan of providing additional trackage or of improving the terminal facilities had been undertaken. It became necessary for regimental supply officers, using their own details, to break open cars in search of shipments. This lack of preparation was typical of all the ports where troops were concentrated.

Not only did this condition delay the equipment of our troops, but it resulted in confusion in loading transports with supplies to be carried along for the forces.

The effects of our unprepared condition were shown not only in ports of embarkation but were also seen in the generally unsanitary state of camps. This was especially true in Volunteer camps, mainly because of the ignorance of camp sanitation among medical officers and line officers as well. Even at Chickamauga the latrines were so badly located that the water supply became contaminated. Swarms of flies carried typhoid germs from filthy surroundings in the training camps during the summer, and on the whole there resulted such a serious epidemic of that disease, especially among the Volunteers, that it became a national scandal. The lesson was not lost on the army and every precaution was taken in our camps during the World War, both at home and abroad, with the result that our army made an exceptional record in preventing disease chargeable to unsanitary conditions.

The Tenth Cavalry was assigned to the 2nd Brigade (Brigadier General Samuel B. M. Young) of [Major General Joseph] Wheeler's Dismounted Cavalry Division, Fifth Corps. The other regiments of this brigade were the First Cavalry and the First Volunteer Cavalry, the latter popularly known as Roosevelt's "Rough Riders."[4] Colonel Leonard Wood commanded the latter and Lieutenant Colonel Charles D. Vielé the former. As trained infantry was needed for the fighting that was to be done, and the Regular Army had too little of it, the regiments of the cavalry division were sent to Cuba dismounted and all the work of obtaining horses and training them went for naught. One squadron of each regiment was to be left behind with the recruits, animals, tentage, and everything except the personal equipment of the officers and men. Colonel Baldwin directed me to remain behind to look after the property, but I succeeded in convincing him that my place was at the front with him.

The army was surprised when Major General William R. Shafter, a veteran of the Civil War, who had never commanded a force larger than a regiment in peace time, was placed in command of the expeditionary force. General Miles, Commanding General of the Army, an officer of large experience, would have been the choice of the army, but he was ignored, although later he was sent in charge of the bloodless expedition to capture Puerto Rico. The action of the administration was attributed, no doubt correctly, to a fear that Miles might become too strong politically after the war.[5]

The First and Tenth cavalry regiments were embarked on June 7 on the *Leona,* one of the coastwise ships that were to carry us to Cuba. Before putting the troops aboard, Colonel E. J. [Edward J.] McClernand, the Adjutant General of the expeditionary force, who had been a tactical officer at West Point when I was a cadet and who was the brains of the expeditionary headquarters, and I together made a careful inspection of the ship and found it in reasonably good shape. The hold had been thoroughly disinfected for occupancy and temporary bunks had been constructed or provision made for hammocks wherever space not used for cargo was available. Better arrangements might have been made with more time and would have been necessary for a long voyage, but everybody was so eager to go and so fearful of being left behind at the last moment that almost any conditions would have been accepted without grumbling. Docking space was limited at Tampa, and the transports had to take their turn in occupying one of the eight berths, so loading was very slow.

The convoy was ready and part of it was actually under way on the eighth, but because of rumors that two Spanish warships had been sighted in the vicinity of Nicolas Channel, between Cuba and Puerto Rico, through which the convoy must pass en route to Santiago, it did not sail until the fourteenth, after positive information had been received from Admiral [William T.] Sampson that none of the Spanish fleet had escaped from Santiago. In the convoy, which was escorted by two destroyers, there were for personnel and stores thirty-two coastwise vessels of various sizes and conditions, with two water tenders and three lighters. The force, with its auxiliaries, artillery, engineer, signal, and medical troops, numbered slightly under 17,000 officers and men—not a large army to send to an island where the enemy had ten times that strength. It was, in fact, a rather audacious undertaking that could easily have met with disaster.

The rate of speed of the convoy was necessarily slow because it was limited to that of the slowest ships. One night, through a misinterpretation of signals, the *Leona* was stopped, and we fell behind the rest of the convoy. When morning dawned there was not another ship in sight. Of course, there was little or no danger, as Spain had no submarines and everything else she had in the naval line on this side of the Atlantic was imprisoned in Santiago. Nevertheless, the brigade commander, General S. B. M. Young, who was on board, ordered the railing of the upper deck manned by troops ready to fire upon any Spanish ship that might appear—a precaution that seemed somewhat ludicrous to both officers and men. Although we had lagged three or four hours behind, we caught up with the rest of the convoy by the end of the day off Siboney, near our landing place.

The purpose of sending the Spanish fleet to Cuba is difficult to understand. Admiral Cervera [Pascal Cervera y Topete] had recklessly crossed the ocean without being molested, but he had entered Santiago harbor, where he was soon bottled up effectively by the American fleet under Admiral [Winfield S.] Schley, who was later joined by Admiral Sampson, then in command. This had determined at once the destination of our expedition. General Shafter was ordered to land near the port, reduce the city, and assist the navy in capturing the Spanish fleet. In prospect it was not as easy as it proved to be. Had the Spanish forces defending Santiago been equal in efficiency and determination to ours it could not have been accomplished without far greater cost. Speaking not of the details of the fighting on land or sea but of the whole war, it would seem that Spain waged it much as an inferior swordsman who had been challenged by a better man: she accepted the engagement and let the adversary shed a certain amount of her blood. In other words, she could not yield without fighting, even though aware of the outcome, and by so doing she at least saved her honor.

Landing and Initial Operations

Flanking Daiquiri, twenty miles east of Santiago, the landing place chosen by our army, was a rugged shore line and behind it lay a low ridge about one hundred and fifty feet high, rising into mountains farther inland. This afforded excellent positions for defense, of which the Spanish army took no advantage whatever. A limited force carefully placed and supported by artillery might have given us much trouble. As it was, our navy shelled the shore and the ridges to the east and west for an hour or more on June 23, eliciting, to our surprise, no response at all. There was no sign of the enemy and no opposition whatever was offered as the army proceeded to land.

Each soldier carried on his person not only his rifle and a hundred rounds of ammunition but also his blanket roll with shelter tent and poncho and three days' field rations. So laden, any man who fell into deep water was certain to be drowned. Happily, however, only two lives were lost.[6] Horses and mules were merely pushed overboard and left to swim ashore. Most of them did so, but some became frightened and, despite all efforts to stop them, swam out to sea. I was, of course, eager to get ashore with the regiment, but, being quartermaster, was left aboard ship, together with Lieutenant W. C. [William C.] Rivers, Quartermaster of the First Cavalry, and went with the *Leona,* which was accompanied by two other transports, to Aserraderos, to the west of Santiago, to bring Garcia and his "army" of insurgents, said to number about 3,000 in all, to join our forces.

This, incidentally, reminds me of "Mr. Dooley's" writings of that period. His "Alone in Cuba" portrayed Theodore Roosevelt as the spearhead, so to speak, of the American force that defeated the Spaniards. From "T. R.'s" ability and courage no one could make any detraction, but from the way in which the newspapers reported his actions the impression received by Mr. Dooley, allegedly an ordinary citizen, was that the Rough Riders were the only fighting force in the campaign. Mr. Dooley also hit off the Cuban insurgents accurately. He began his description of them by telling of the hundreds of thousands who were going to come rushing to our aid on landing and finished with how Garcia came alone to our assistance. As a matter of fact, we got little or no assistance from any band of Cuban *insurrectos.* Those we took aboard the *Leona* were a rag-tag, bob-tailed, poorly-armed, and hungry lot, in appearance anything but an effective fighting force. We had to give them food and all we could get out of the hold at the time was hard bread and sugar, which they ate ravenously.

Rivers and I did not get ashore until the twenty-fourth, the day of the first skirmish with the Spaniards at Las Guasimas. Late that afternoon I went forward to the scene, had supper at General Young's mess, and heard the story of what had taken place. On the afternoon and evening of the preceding day Wheeler had marched Young's brigade from Daiquiri and pushed on ahead of Lawton's division, hoping to overtake the Spanish troops that had deserted Siboney. Learning that they had taken position at Las Guasimas and were holding the heights over which our troops would have to pass, Wheeler decided to attack the next morning and gave Young directions accordingly. It was generally understood that he was largely influenced by his senior officers to push forward and be the first to engage the enemy. Whatever may have been the reason, it was exactly the thing to do.

The main road, narrow and eroded, passed from Siboney through a gap in the ridge at Las Guasimas, thence through Sevilla and Redonda to Santiago. To the left of the road was a trail running from Siboney to Las Guasimas, where it joined the main road. Young, on the morning of the twenty-fourth, took one squadron from the First Cavalry and one from the Tenth, to which were attached four Hotchkiss guns,[7] and moved up the main road; while Wood, with two squadrons of the Rough Riders and two automatic [Gatling] guns,[8] followed the trail to the left. An insurgent leader, Castillo, had agreed to assist in the attack with eight hundred of his men but did not put in an appearance until the fighting was over. Young located the Spaniards on Las Guasimas heights, where the road passes through the gap, and deployed his command. At 8 a.m., after waiting for Wood's column to make its way over the narrow trail through the rough jungle, he ordered his lines forward in the dense undergrowth, using his Hotchkiss guns against the Spaniards, who replied with rifle volleys. The terrain over which the advance was made appeared well-nigh impassable with nature's ready-made entanglements of wild tropical verdure obstructing the way. The position at Las Guasimas was held by nearly two thousand enemy troops, but under the attacks of the Regulars and Rough Riders their lines broke and retreated, leaving the defenses in the hands of our forces.

From the superficial point of view Las Guasimas was a minor engagement, as the Spanish commander, we now know, had received orders the day before not to attempt to hold the place but simply to delay the Americans and retire on Santiago. The Spanish position, however, was naturally very strong and the ease with which it was taken surprised our command. Without prejudice to later operations, Linares [Arsenio Linares y Pombo], the commander of the Santiago district, could have brought to Las Guasimas as reinforcements not only the sailors of Cervera's fleet but other troops from the west of the city. This road to Santiago was the only one available to the Americans and by holding the favorable ground at Las Guasimas the Spaniards could have caused considerable delay to the attacking force. Our men were fighting their way over narrow trails, through unknown tropical undergrowth, in a most enervating climate, and a serious check at this place might have been disastrous. On the other hand, the Spanish commander, by withdrawing, not only gave up an important position but undertook to defend a much longer and weaker line and yielded the possibility of bringing in any of his outlying troops. He lost an opportunity which an abler commander would have turned to his advantage.

Now that the army was ashore and the route to the fortifications of Santiago had been cleared, General Shafter could make further preparations with some deliberation instead of allowing any of his ambitious subordinates to rush forward precipitately and possibly commit the army to a faulty course of action. After Las Guasimas he gave instructions that advance units would under no circumstances bring on an engagement without positive orders to do so. There was now opportunity to make reconnaissance, find out the exact lay of the land, rest the troops, bring up supplies and transportation in limited amounts, and generally permit the command, especially division commanders, to become oriented. The American force, composed almost entirely of the Regular Army, seasoned by service and experience, constituted, for its size, as fine a body as any commander-in-chief could ask for. It was well-disciplined, eager, willing, and fully aware of its responsibilities. Such was the situation when General Shafter issued his orders for the attack to be made on July 1.

8

The Spanish-American War—Victory in Cuba and Its Consequences

1 July–20 August 1898

The Battle for the San Juan Heights, 1–3 July 1898

The morning of July 1 was ideal, the sky cloudless, the air soft and balmy. As the first rays of the sun tipped the stately palms that towered here and there above the jungle, all nature still lay in quiet repose. Our cavalry division had bivouacked near El Pozo, about two miles east of San Juan Hill. The camp was stirring at daybreak and our men were eager to enter what for most of them was to be their first battle. They stood about in small groups opposite their places in column, impatient for the order to advance. From the low ridge near the trail we could see the lines of the enemy's entrenchments and the blockhouses of the heights of San Juan. Beyond could be seen the successive lines of defense, and behind them arose the spires and towers of the city we were preparing to invest. To the northeast, overlooking all approaches, the stone fort and the smaller blockhouses of the enemy outpost at El Caney were outlined against the sky.

The plan was for us not to advance on San Juan Hill, probably the strongest point in the Spanish defenses on our front, until El Caney had been taken. At 6:30 the battery, which we knew was [Captain Allyn] Capron's, supporting Lawton's division at El Caney, began firing. It was said that Lawton hoped to capture the hill within an hour or two. But as the time passed it was evident that he was meeting greater resistance than

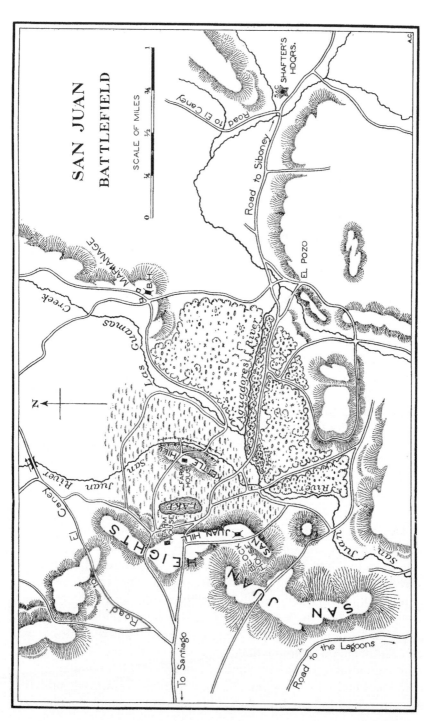

San Juan Battlefield (Herbert H. Sargent, *The Campaign of Santiago de Cuba*, vol. 2 [Chicago: A.C. McClurg and Company, 1907], map 10).

expected. About eight o'clock [Captain George S.] Grimes' battery at El Pozo opened fire, its position being clearly indicated by the smoke from the black powder they used. The Spanish batteries promptly replied. The artillery duel had been going on for some time when the cavalry division was directed to go forward along the El Pozo–Santiago road, cross the Aguadores River, and deploy to the right. The road was narrow and tortuous and was flanked by heavy jungle. The sun, now high in the sky, had become scorching. Our progress was slow and men soon began to drop out of ranks from the heat. An occasional bullet nipped a leaf above our heads, and our closed ranks began to suffer casualties. For some reason, there was delay ahead of us, and we halted for what seemed an hour. [Brigadier General Jacob Ford or J. Ford] Kent's division, which was immediately behind us, had orders to cross the San Juan River and deploy to the left. The leading regiment came up abreast of us in column of fours, although the road in places was hardly wide enough for one column.

The 1st brigade of the Cavalry Division and the leading regiment of the 2nd had crossed the Aguadores when down the road in which the Tenth Cavalry was crowded came an observation balloon, held at a height of about two hundred feet by a number of men at the ropes. Immediately the fire from the Spanish trenches was concentrated on the balloon, and the troops below came under a veritable hail of shot and shell. To heighten our indignation, Major [George McC.] Derby, in charge of the balloon, called down to us that the Spaniards were firing at us. The epithets that were hurled back at him were not very complimentary. The balloon was soon compelled to descend, much to the satisfaction of all below. Derby had, however, discovered a trail available for Kent's division, thus relieving some of the congestion on the road.

The regimental commander, Colonel Theodore A. Baldwin, Lieutenant M. H. [Malvern Hill] Barnum, the adjutant, and I were mounted, but as the firing became more severe we dismounted, tied our horses near the road, and left them. Approaching the Aguadores I ran ahead to find out the direction taken by the troops preceding us. I saw Lieutenant J. D. [John D.] Miley, General Shafter's aide, Colonel Leonard Wood, and several others on the opposite side of the river, standing under the shelter of the bank just above the ford. Some staff officer—I think it was Colonel McClernand—told me that we should move directly to our right, cross the Aguadores, and await further orders.

After the head of the column had crossed, we found that only the 1st Squadron had followed us. As I was recrossing to look for the 2nd

Squadron, there sat "Little Joe" Wheeler on horseback in the middle of the stream. As I saluted a fragment of shell struck the water in front of him. He remarked very casually that the shelling seemed quite lively. Knowing that [Samuel S.] Sumner, the next in rank, was in command of the cavalry division that day, I wondered why Wheeler was there. Later I learned that although on sick report he would not remain behind while his division was in action and simply had to come forward to be in the fight.

As I rejoined the regiment with the 2nd Squadron, I saw a surgeon of our brigade, an Americanized Cuban [probably Acting Assistant Surgeon Francisco Menocal],[1] standing in the water supporting two wounded colored troopers to keep them from drowning. About this time my colonel's son, Ted, a boy of twenty (19 yrs. 11 mo.), who had accompanied his father to Cuba, was severely wounded. Frank McCoy, then a second lieutenant, was also struck by a rifle bullet, and I stopped to help bandage his wound. A temporary dressing station for our regiment was established in the shelter of the river bank, where the wounded were then being taken.

For perhaps half an hour the regiment lay in the woods behind Las Guasimas Creek, which we then crossed before deploying in a partially open field. On our immediate front the terrain, covered with tall grass, was broken by masses of dense brush and crisscrossed by barbed wire fences. These were serious obstacles, though nothing like so formidable as those developed in the World War. Our men were under fire which they were unable to return as we confronted the intrenched heights which we were to take. When the order came to advance, the whole line, impatient to move forward, advanced rapidly against Kettle Hill, our regiment and the First Cavalry supporting the attack of the 1st Brigade reinforced by the Rough Riders.

In the underbrush and tall grass it was difficult to keep alignments, and the troops soon became very much mixed. But each officer or soldier next in rank took charge of the line or group immediately in his vicinity, halting to fire at each good opportunity. The men took cover only when ordered to do so and exposed themselves fearlessly in crossing the open spaces. On our left what seemed to be a flank attack gave us alarm, and I left the Colonel and hastened to where I could observe the place from which the firing seemed to come. Recognizing our own troops, I approached and found Lieutenant John Henry Parker manning his Gatling guns with only a limited crew, as many of his men lay about him either killed or wounded.

After wading the San Juan River, we were on the southern slope of Kettle Hill almost before we knew it. Some of our troops in the right wing of the regiment had pushed forward to aid the Rough Riders in the capture of this position, where white troops and black, Regulars and Volunteers, fought shoulder-to-shoulder. A large part of the regiment, however, had continued to the left of Kettle Hill. A group of men in blue, evidently from Kent's division, were hovering immediately under San Juan Hill, where the continuous fire of the courageous defenders held them in the dead angle. Pausing momentarily, the whole situation clearly in view, we went forward, moving to the left of the small pond behind Kettle Hill and charging with the Third and Sixth Cavalry and Kent's division against San Juan. The fire of the Spaniards, although somewhat lessened, was still severe as they tenaciously held their position, exposing themselves freely to return our fire. Near the crest of the hill there was a short halt, as the shells from our own batteries were bursting too close in front of us. As soon as this fire lifted the lines made the last dash and the hill was taken by storm.

In the elation that followed this achievement men cheered, shook hands with each other and threw their arms about each other, and generally behaved wildly quite regardless of rank. Many American and Spanish soldiers lay dead or wounded in front of and in the trenches. The wounded on both sides were cared for alike. A colored trooper gently raised the head of a Spanish lieutenant and gave him the last drop of water from his canteen. I assisted Lieutenant [Walter C.] Short, Sixth Cavalry, in bandaging slight wounds.

The captured position was at once organized for defense, and firing on the next Spanish position was begun. At dusk a group of officers including Colonel Wood, Captain H. P. [Henry P.] Kingsbury, Sixth Cavalry, and one or two others and myself sat below the crest of San Juan talking over the situation. I was surprised to hear Colonel Wood give it as his opinion that our lines should be withdrawn to another position, as he did not think we could hold the one we had captured. I took decided issue with that view, saying that I thought it would be a serious mistake. However, there were other officers who agreed with Colonel Wood. All the younger officers who heard this suggestion were decidedly opposed to it. Several officers of high rank did make such a recommendation to General Wheeler, but he disapproved it. There were many sound reasons against withdrawal: there was no apparent reason to question our ability to hold it; and there had been no indication of a counterattack. Moreover, El Caney had been captured that same afternoon, and Lawton's division of nine regiments and [Brigadier General John C.] Bates' brigade were expected to arrive during the night to reinforce and extend our lines. Retirement would have been very discouraging to the troops, who had taken the heights at considerable cost and now felt their superiority. It would have given them the impression that the high command lacked courage. It would also have encouraged the enemy. Sumner and Wood did send word to Kent during the afternoon that the cavalry line was weak, and the latter sent the Thirteenth Infantry to support us.

The following day this question of withdrawal was again raised. Strong representations were made to Shafter that the lines should be withdrawn, and he called a conference of the general officers to discuss it. There was a difference of opinion and the conference broke up without reaching a decision. However, Shafter cabled the War Department that he was seriously considering a retirement of about five miles to a new position on the high ground between the San Juan River and Siboney. The War Department replied at once that the effect on the country would be much better if he should not fall back, and Shafter's answer was: "I shall hold my present position." If he had followed his own judgment, it seems probable that Shafter would have withdrawn, and the opinion of the War Department embodied in General [Major General Henry C.] Corbin's telegram without doubt saved the army this humiliation. Excuses have been made for Shafter because he was very much overweight and was suffering from a lame leg, making it necessary for him to ride in a buckboard everywhere he went. He also suffered from the intense heat. No doubt his physical condition affected his judgment. But independent of that, the example of a fleshy old commanding general too ill to perform his duties properly was far from inspiring to the command.

Early in the evening of the first day I accompanied the stretcher-bearers under charge of Barnum carrying our Major Theodore J. Wint, who had been wounded, back to the field hospital at El Pozo.[2] As we passed over the now quiet landscape its peaceful aspect under the brilliant moon presented a striking contrast to the day of battle just closed. En route we passed General Bates' brigade moving to take its place in our lines. The hospital presented another contrast. Many of the wounded had not yet received attention, as they had been brought in faster than the surgeons could care for them and the lighter cases had been left lying about on stretchers or on the ground awaiting their turn. The surgeons were working as fast as they could with no better light than that of field lanterns. As a matter of fact, the number of medical officers and hospital corps men was entirely inadequate. Upon my return about midnight I was able to report to the Colonel that his son was doing well and that our wounded were being given all the care possible under the circumstances.

The following morning Barnum was severely wounded, and I became acting adjutant in addition to my other duties. Readjustments in the line were made and men were returned to their own units, having become badly mixed during the advance. We now had the First Cavalry on our right and the Rough Riders on our left. The first night the pack trains came up bringing ammunition, rations, and entrenching tools, and details worked all night constructing trenches, which were strengthened during the next two nights and most of them enlarged into standing trenches.

Service in and behind the front line in the sweltering heat and soaking rains which alternated every day became very onerous, and the sick list grew rapidly until the surrender on the seventeenth. There was no such thing as a troop mess. Each soldier prepared his bacon and hard bread individually. The supplies were meager for the first two or three days, until the blanket rolls left behind on July 1 could be brought up, but at first canned tomatoes or other vegetables were entirely lacking. A theoretical allotment of transportation to units was tried but failed, and thereafter it was held in the hands of the expedition Quartermaster, Captain [Edward H.] Plummer. I borrowed a four-mule wagon from him and succeeded with this in keeping the regiment fairly well supplied from Siboney. Other supply officers did likewise. Colonel John F. (Jack) Weston, the Chief Commissary, asked no questions about requisitions but told each quartermaster to back up his wagon and take all he could haul of the components he needed most. Returning over the trail one night with a load of supplies I heard a great commotion in the darkness ahead and on reaching the spot found Colonel Roosevelt and a detail of men trying to move their wagon, which had mired down to the hubs. He was urging his team forward with all the skill, including the forceful language, of a born mule-skinner.

On the various trips to Siboney I often stopped at the hospital to visit patients whom I knew and to chat with surgeons Major L. A. [Louis A.] La Garde, Captain M. W. [Merritte W.] Ireland, and Captain F. A. [Francis A.] Winter, who were friends of mine. Under these capable men the field hospital had grown by July 1 into the base hospital, then located in a vacant storehouse. Like everything else, medical supplies had been hurriedly loaded at Tampa without any particular reference to the order in which they would be needed. In spite of these handicaps and that of limited personnel, our medical officers and men did heroic work. As the days went by the list of the sick increased, and as fast as accommodations became available, those who could be moved were returned to the States.

On the morning of the third the sound of heavy firing came to our ears. It was not a surprise, as we had felt certain that a naval action must soon take place. As the firing receded it was evident that the Spanish ships had made an attempt to escape and that ours were in pursuit. Cervera, with desperate courage, had steamed out in column, as he was compelled to do owing to the partial obstruction of the entrance by the *Merrimac*—which had been sunk by Lieutenant [Richmond P.] Hobson and his crew with the object of closing the harbor. Steaming out in single file, each of Cervera's ships in its turn was exposed to overwhelming fire from the American fleet, with the result that they were either sunk, burned, or driven onto the beach.

After the surrender of the Spanish land forces I visited several of the Spanish hulks, and a more pathetic sight could hardly be imagined. The enemy clearly had been outclassed, ship for ship, by the American fleet. They lacked gun power and trained officers and men, to say nothing of their relatively low speed accentuated by the barnacled condition of the ships' bottoms. General [Ramón Blanco y Erenas] Blanco, as we afterwards learned, had succeeded in having their fleet kept in Cuba, though Cervera had strongly opposed it. Later Blanco advised its return to Spain, but it was too late. Now that the fleet was lost, hope for the Spanish cause was gone. While their army in Cuba, numbering 196,000 men, might have made an effort to continue the war, there was no chance of their obtaining either supplies or reinforcements, and the end would have been the same.

Siege of Santiago and Its Surrender

On the morning of July 3 General Shafter sent to General Toral [José Toral y Velázquez] a demand for the surrender of Santiago, threatening to shell the city if he did not comply. Toral, who had succeeded Linares as commander when the latter was wounded on the first, refused, and he at once made arrangements for the evacuation of foreigners, Cubans, and Spanish noncombatants.

It was a real procession that streamed out of the city through our lines on the road to El Caney during the following two days. Smart carriages drawn by well-groomed horses conveyed the consular officials, while primitive, creaking carts carried sick and infirm inhabitants and their poor belongings. The road was congested with vehicles, animals, and people on foot, old men and women hardly able to walk, young mothers with infants in arms, and toddling children, all laden with such of their belongings as they hoped to save.

When Shafter sent word on July 4 that the Spanish fleet was completely destroyed, Toral was still defiant. On July 8, however, he did offer to evacuate the city if permitted to retire to Holguin. Shafter referred the proposal to the War Department, recommending that it be accepted. But General Corbin again saw the situation more clearly than the commander in the field and in reply cited Shafter's own statements of his ability to hold, said reinforcements were under way, expressed great surprise at the proposal, and very properly disapproved. General Toral was then advised that his proposition was not acceptable, and Shafter sent him an ultimatum that unless he should surrender by 3 p.m. on the tenth hostilities would be resumed an hour later.

During this week of negotiations, though rains fell frequently and often made the trenches knee-deep in mud and water, our troops were engaged in strengthening and extending the lines. Reinforcements arriving from the States were put into position, some heavy guns were brought up, and Santiago was practically encircled. The Spaniards had likewise strengthened their positions, which were very strong and could not have been forced except at heavy cost. The firing began again on both sides at 4 p.m. on the tenth and continued until noon of the eleventh, when Shafter made his fifth demand for surrender. To this Toral acceded and final negotiations were begun.

At 9:30 a.m. on the seventeenth General Shafter and his staff, accompanied by the general officers and their staffs and escorted by one hundred cavalrymen, met General Toral and his staff with an escort of an equal number of men midway between the lines and the formal surrender took place. The two commanders then rode into Santiago together and in their presence at noon the Spanish flag was lowered and the Stars and Stripes raised over the Governor's Palace. The cavalry escort and the troops of the Ninth Infantry sent to occupy the city presented arms, cannon boomed a salute, and simultaneously along the line of trenches bands played the national air. A great cheer rose from the men as our flag broke out to the breeze. American and Spanish soldiers began at once to fraternize, and the relations between them from that time on were most friendly. A troop of Spanish cavalry had made camp just in front of our lines the evening before and in the captain's baggage were two kegs of rum, with which, in the cordial manner of Spanish camaraderie, he toasted a group of American cavalry officers, his late enemies but now become his friends.

Deteriorating Health of the V Army Corps and Return to the United States

The physical condition of the command had by this time reached a very low ebb. Drenched by the frequent tropical downpours, exposed by day to the blazing sun and by night to the chill of heavy dews, our unacclimated men were an easy prey to fevers. We were simply reliving the experience of other expeditions. I cannot give too high praise to that noble Roman, Clara Barton, and her associates of the Red Cross for their tender solicitude and untiring efforts in aiding and comforting our sick and wounded. They came as ministering angels to the suffering army at Santiago and also did much for the needy inhabitants. After consultation with Miss Barton, I donated a considerable quantity of our surplus rations, which she used to good advantage. Shortly after the surrender it was planned to withdraw to the hills four or five miles back of the city, but the men were scarcely able to reach the camp under the burden of their equipment. Within a short time approximately seventy-five percent of the command were either ill or convalescent and nothing but return to the States as soon as possible could prevent disaster. After our transports entered Santiago harbor we got supplies more easily, but it became increasingly difficult to find men who were physically able to help haul them to our camps. Most of the colored troops suffered fully as much as the white and came to look quite as woebegone. Because of the illness of officers after we went into the hill camp, I had fallen to the command of three troops of my regiment in addition to my other duties. But I, too, was soon to suffer with malaria, which caused a chill every day, followed by a raging fever.

It was about this time that the army began to receive frozen beef that had been treated with preservative. The quarters of beef often looked anything but fresh and this together with the taste due to the preservative led to complaints that "embalmed" beef was being issued. The investigation ordered by General Miles, who reiterated the charge, resulted in acrimonious correspondence between him and the Commissary General, Brigadier General Charles P. Eagan, which caused the latter to be tried by court-martial and suspended from rank and duty for six years.

As the War Department seemed inclined to postpone the movement of the troops back to the States, General Shafter assembled his division and brigade commanders and chief surgeons and obtained their opinions of the situation, which were unanimous that the army should return. The views of the surgeons and those of the general officers were handed to General Shafter in joint letters, which he forwarded to Washington by cable. The letter of the general officers, however, was deliberately given to the correspondents with the army. This was done even before it reached General Shafter and of course was cabled back and published all over the country before the official message was received by General Corbin. This letter became known as the Round Robin,[3] and it aroused the people of the country to a high pitch of excitement. The country had been surprised at the quick results of the campaign and felt that the army had done more than was really expected; it was now rapidly being decimated by illness, and there was every reason why it should be removed at once and replaced by fresh troops. If giving the Round Robin to the press was a violation by regulations—as it certainly was—the War Department, by delay even in expressing its purpose, could not be considered blameless. On August 4, the day the news was printed in the American press, the War Department directed the return of the expeditionary forces, and the movement began at once. The Tenth Cavalry sailed for Montauk Point, Long Island, on August 14 and arrived on August 20.

Unforeseen Consequences of the Victory: America Emerges as an International Power

As soon as Santiago surrendered, Spain, having saved her honor, sued for peace, and the negotiations were quickly got under way. We had entered the war to liberate Cuba, and we kept that promise. But for several reasons that was not all our government now decided to do. In the first place, determined to drive the Spaniards out of the Western Hemisphere, we demanded that Puerto Rico be ceded to us. But the far more dramatic and internationally important development in the peace negotiations was the purchase of the Philippines. The acquisition of this group of several hundred islands, with a combined area of 115,000 square miles and an estimated population of 6,500,000, mostly Asiatic peoples, with traditions and religions different from our own, and located over 5,000 miles away from our western seaboard, was a totally new policy for our country. Up to that time we had been a strictly American state, keeping hands off affairs in Asia as well as Europe. Now, however, under President McKinley and John Hay, his Secretary of State, seconded if not largely influenced by a coterie of imperialists of which Theodore Roosevelt and Henry Cabot Lodge were the most active, we assumed for the first time a conspicuous position in affairs far afield. In short, out of a war for the liberation of Cuba we emerged as an international power with possessions, interests, and policies on the other side of the world.

During the war the American people as a whole had been interested in the campaign in Cuba largely to the exclusion of other international affairs. They had paid little attention up to the time of the peace negotiations to what was going on in the remote Far East. But the year 1898 was a memorable one for China and Japan, events causing both of those countries serious alarm for the future. The four greatest powers in Europe were encroaching upon Chinese territory. Within the year Russia had moved down into Manchuria with military force and was threatening to take control of Korea; Germany had obtained a forced "lease" from China of Kiaochow Bay and was laying claims to a "sphere of influence" in the province of Shantung; Great Britain, to offset the Russian and German influences, had obtained a similar lease of the harbor of Weihaiwei[4] and looked upon the Yangtze valley as her special commercial sphere; and France had moved up to Kwanchowan [today Chang-Chiang]. Then immediately after our purchase of the Philippines, Germany bought the other Spanish possessions in the Pacific—the Caroline, Marshall, and Marianas islands. It is interesting to note that Spain alone was withdrawing not only from her last American possessions but also from the Orient, while America and Germany were taking her place, dividing the remnants of her once great empire between them.

The trade of China, in population the largest country in the world, was being boomed in Europe as a gigantic prize, and that lure was no less tempting to us. The greater powers of Europe were actively competing for the capture of this trade; each was planning territorial encroachments upon the colossus of the Orient. Though we held aloof from such designs on the mainland of China, the idea of accepting our "manifest destiny" and of not lowering the flag where it was once planted had taken possession of our people, and we did not hesitate to hold the Philippines. The price we paid Spain for these hundreds of islands was so small as to be almost nominal, only twenty million dollars, but even so the experiment was a costly one. We inherited an insurrection and problems that were new and strange and assumed a position that might at any time involve us in war—all to satisfy ambition to become a world power.

The theory of the imperialists was that these islands would become a base for our trade in the Orient and would enable us to get our share. Spain, it was argued, because of her own inertia, had failed properly to utilize her advantages, but we were an enterprising, progressive people and the islands in our hands would have a very different fate. This expectation has been realized. The Philippines have become vastly different in many ways, but not as a base for the China trade. Advocates of our expansion to the Orient failed to point out and perhaps to appreciate that the shortest route for our merchantmen crossing the Pacific from our western ports was the northern one, which took them first to Japan, then to China, later to Hong Kong, itself a great trade center, and last to the Philippines. Manila could not, therefore, prove the base we expected, as American traders would not be able to compete with Europeans if they added the cost and delay of sending goods by the longer, slower route and the charges of transshipping them at the Philippine base. But the fever of competition for the trade of China's teeming millions was difficult for any great power to resist, and, like the rest, we were captivated by the temptation.

China's trade was not enormous at the time, but it was widely believed that the "sleeping giant" of the East was about to awaken and, in the process of becoming a modern state, would become the purchaser of vast quantities of foreign goods. But the very movement of the Western Powers into the East, simultaneously, alarmed the Chinese into a reactionary attitude. Ignorant of the incapacity of her antiquated military forces to compete with western armies, the old Empress Dowager [Cixi, or Tz'u-hsi] gave her approval to the Boxer Uprising, and within two years (in 1900) these fanatics undertook to drive all foreigners, missionaries, and diplomatic representatives, as well as soldiers, "into the sea." The Boxers' failure when they met the allied armies of Europe, America, and Japan shook the confidence of the people in the ancient dynasty and was an important factor ten years later in bringing its downfall. When the Empire was proclaimed a Republic there followed a quick succession of civil struggles. Contests for power among her "warlords" followed in quick succession, which has left the country even today only a minor purchasing power.

The aggressions of the Western Powers in 1898 precipitated other wars in the East besides those in China. The Japanese also became alarmed for their security. However, the methods they employed to meet the danger were less precipitate and more intelligent than those of the Chinese. They began to prepare deliberately and systematically to fight the most menacing invader, the Russian, and in order to prevent either Germany or France from taking the side of the Czar they first sought and obtained the memorable alliance with Great Britain. That being accomplished in 1902, the historic series of Japanese notes to the Russian Government led inevitably to the war in 1904.

The field of the Far East, shortly after my return from Cuba, became my personal sphere of interest for a number of years.

9

The Division of Customs and Insular Affairs and My First Assignment to the Philippines

August 1898–November 1899

A day or so after our arrival, President McKinley visited Montauk Point and, accompanied by several general officers, made a casual inspection of the camp. I think much of his time was occupied by those who had political aspirations. I recall General Sumner's telling me that Theodore Roosevelt had said that he expected to find out the "old man's" attitude toward his candidacy for the governorship of New York, and later one of his intimate friends told that the President favored it.

Soon after reaching Montauk Point, I received notice of my appointment to the temporary grade of "Major and Ordnance Officer of Volunteers," with directions to proceed to Washington. Upon reporting, the Assistant Secretary, Mr. Meiklejohn, said he was planning to send an officer on a tour of inspection of a number of western posts that had not been garrisoned since the outbreak of the war. Seeing my physical condition and thinking the change would be beneficial, he selected me for this duty. Upon arrival in Chicago, where my parents then lived, the malaria in my system seemed to reach a serious stage. The family doctor pronounced my case rather alarming and finally said that I could not survive another chill. He gave me a heroic dose of quinine, which had the desired effect, at least temporarily. Making the tour with considerable leisure I gradually gained in strength, but for a year afterward I had chills with great regularity every other day despite all efforts to break them. Malaria was very prevalent in Missouri when I was a boy, but thanks to my father's custom of giving us whiskey and quinine every fall as a tonic I had escaped having it.

Division of Customs and Insular Affairs, War Department

On return to Washington I was for some months attached to the Assistant Secretary's office in connection with insular affairs. The administration of Cuba and the many newly acquired islands was military and fell under the supervision and direction of the War Department. The problems that arose involved readjustments in Government and the determination of policies to be followed in the complicated business of ruling peoples as distant from each other geographically as Puerto Rico and Mindanao and as different in character as West Indian Negroes are from Muhammadan Asiatics. Over the original code of laws of these peoples Spanish laws and custom had been superimposed. Our application of the rules of military occupation to the different alien groups frequently brought up questions which only the War Department could decide. The only precedents existing were the comparatively simple rulings made under the military occupation of California and New Mexico fifty years in the past, and it was necessary to decide nearly every question on its own merits. Such conditions, of course, had not been anticipated and there was no provision for administrative direction. Naturally, to find correct solutions required close study and often much research. A great deal of statistical data and other information also were constantly being asked for by Congress and by Americans interested in insular enterprises and commerce. Though the Department was by no means equipped to meet the emergency thrust upon it by the widespread acquisitions, it was the only branch of the government approximately prepared to cope with the work; it undertook the task and accomplished it with a highly praiseworthy record of achievement.

For a short while these matters were handled through the regular channels of the Department, but it soon became evident that a special bureau would be necessary. This bureau was organized in March, 1899, as the Division of Customs and Insular Affairs, and I was appointed its chief. Many questions could only be settled temporarily until the status of the new possessions could be determined by the Supreme Court. Meanwhile the patterns followed in general the old colonial forms. Legal advice upon which to base decisions of the Division was at first sought in the Attorney General's office, but it was not long before the necessity of having special legal counsel was obvious. To find a man qualified for this duty was by no means easy, but the Assistant Secretary and I agreed finally upon the selection of Judge Charles E. Magoon, an eminent Nebraska attorney whom we both knew personally. The Judge accepted the difficult position and showed exceptional legal ability in his opinions upon the questions that arose. When Mr. Elihu Root became Secretary of War he was so impressed by Magoon's opinions that he ordered them printed and later sent him to Panama as Governor. Upon our first intervention (1906–1909), Mr. Taft sent him to Cuba as Governor-General.[1] During my term of service in the Division, Major General John R. Brooke was Military Governor of Cuba for a period and later Brigadier General Leonard Wood; Brigadier General George W. Davis was Governor of Puerto Rico; and Major General Elwell S. Otis, of the Philippines.

In Cuba the problem was to establish a government for the people of the island which they were eventually to administer themselves. In working out the details Wood had the constant advice and counsel of the able Secretary of War, Mr. Root. In the Philippines the military government remained in control under various commanding generals until the institution of civil government under Mr. Taft, the first civil governor-general. Similarly the control of Puerto Rico was under the military and later was taken over by the civil government established by act of Congress.

The duties as chief of the Division of Customs and Insular Affairs were interesting and required close application; the associations were pleasant; and service in the War Department was a new experience. But duty in Washington did not at the time especially appeal to me, and when the insurrection of Filipinos—a term used to designate Christian civilized natives—broke out in the Philippines in January, 1899, I asked to be sent there. At the Assistant Secretary's request, however, I remained, but when General Otis called for additional staff officers the following summer, I made another application to be sent. In the meantime I had been mustered out as an Ordnance Officer of Volunteers but was later appointed to fill a vacancy that had occurred in the grade of Major and Adjutant General of Volunteers. This was an argument I used in seeking service in the field. But Meiklejohn again demurred, and both he and Magoon tried to dissuade me, holding out the alluring possibility of my being given, in the course of time, the rank of brigadier general as chief of the division. I realized that high rank might be attained by administrative service in Washington and I also realized the importance of such duties. I felt, nevertheless, that I was better fitted by training and disposition for service with troops, especially in the field, and I knew that my place in Washington could easily be filled by another officer or by a civil official. Therefore, I insisted on being relieved and my two friends yielded. Another reason for desiring to go to the Philippines was the possibilities for broad experience that the Islands seemed to offer as compared with the restricted character of the bureau work in Washington. New fields seemed to open before my mind regarding what might happen as a result of our new status as a World Power. And anyway, the problem of consolidation of our gains in the Orient was lure enough.

First Assignment and Trip to the Philippines

I was ordered to take passage on the hospital ship *Missouri,* which was then on the ways being refitted and made ready for the Philippines. The ship was to go via Suez, which afforded me the opportunity, by crossing the Atlantic in advance on a fast liner, to have a few weeks sightseeing in Europe before boarding it at Suez. I had never been abroad and went with the idea that the time might be profitably spent in seeing something of the civilization of older countries. Although I was on a pleasure trip, it proved in later years to be much more than that. It is difficult for the average man to understand the manners and customs or the genius of a foreign country unless he has been there, and even a brief visit may give one an inspiration to study and a basis of understanding on which it is easier to build. I took passage at my own expense on a British steamship bound for Liverpool.

Great Britain—Visiting London

We reached that port about the middle of September, when it was crowded with shipping from all parts of the world. Although there were other cities I was more anxious to see, I could not resist spending some extra time there in making a survey of its wonderful system of docks, little dreaming, however, that one day a knowledge of such things would be of practical use to me. As it was even then capable of accommodating almost any number of ships and was equipped with all modern facilities for handling large vessels and expeditiously loading and discharging immense cargoes of grain and material, my inspection of the system was most instructive.

After spending a day in historical Chester, I proceeded to London. My first duty on arrival was to call on our Ambassador, Mr. Joseph H. Choate. He received me most cordially and inquired especially about my mission. He was well informed on conditions in the Islands and was solicitous as to the progress being made in restoring order among the natives. My call was very pleasant and with only the impression left by that one meeting it was easy to agree with the general opinion that Mr. Choate was probably the most distinguished representative the United States has had at the Court of St. James in my day. The Britons whom I met spoke of him in the most complimentary terms. Someone then told me the story of Mr. Choate being at a large party when some distinguished guest about to depart stepped up to him, mistaking him for one of the servants, and said, "Please call me a cab." Mr. Choate promptly said, "You're a cab." The guest complained to the host and learned that it was Mr. Choate, who had taken advantage of the opportunity to make a joke of the incident, whereupon the complaining guest apologized profusely.

Our military attaché was Brigadier General S. S. Sumner, who had commanded the cavalry division in the battle of San Juan and was later to be my commanding general in the Philippines during the most stirring period of my first tour of duty there. Although I had known and admired General Sumner from the time I was on duty in Washington before the war with Spain, our friendship really began with my service under him in Mindanao. I kept up a desultory correspondence with him until he died in 1937, at the age of ninety-five.

Though the British were then in the midst of the Boer War,[2] London was going about its business quite unperturbed. The endless lines of horse-drawn busses and hansom cabs congested the narrow, tortuous streets. The speech of the educated man and woman seemed affected to my unaccustomed ear, the manners of the people of all sorts were noticeably polite. Except for the newsboys shouting their "extras" one would hardly have known from the outward appearance of the people that "thin red lines" of British "Tommies" were having no easy time running down the quick-moving, straight-shooting Boers. In conversation one heard constantly the names of Kitchener of Khartoum and Field Marshal Lord Roberts ("Bobs"), also of [Jan Christian] Smuts and Oom

Paul Kruger, and occasionally of the Kaiser [Wilhelm II of Germany], whose unfriendly utterances gave the British some uneasiness even then.

I explored London thoroughly, crowding my days and evenings there to the full. No one who has not traveled through the streets by the bus lines of thirty-eight years ago can fully appreciate London of that day. First on my list, of course, was Westminster Abbey, that tells the tale of the Empire's greatness. In its monuments can be read the inspiring story of Britain's rise to might and glory. I visited the Houses of Parliament, the finest buildings in the world of their kind. They seemed quite in keeping with the record of the two notable bodies which stand out as models among such assemblies. It was very pleasant to visit Parliament under quite different circumstances some twenty years later.

Notorious for imprisonments and executions of men and women who lost the favor of the Throne when it was all-powerful, it was the Tower of London that brought back most vividly stories I had read. Among the principal sights included in my hasty tour were Hampton Court, the sumptuous estate that Cardinal Wolsey created for himself while serving Henry VIII "more loyally than he served his God"; the Seven Dials,[3] whose infamy [Charles] Dickens brought to light; Scotland Yard, the headquarters of the most widely heralded detective service in the world. Then came the Bank of England, the Law Courts and Inns, where justice protects the pauper from even the Crown, and the palaces and the Mansion House, whence the Lord Mayor rides forth in his gilded medieval coach like a character out of children's fairy tales and in which twenty years later I was to ride when given the freedom of the City of London.

Paris

Paris, the playground of the world, city of art and music, the Mecca of American travelers, came next. With a thrill of anticipation I had allotted several days to my first sojourn here, where these lines are being written. Like everyone on his first visit, I was keen to see with my own eyes the Bastille, Notre Dame, the Madeleine, the Louvre, les Invalides, the Pantheon, the Opera, the Champs Elysees, the Bois de Boulogne, and Versailles. Each had its peculiar interest. Since then I have become more familiar with them and there attaches to most of them some incident of which I was a part. Unusual as it may seem in one with my training, what interested me most after this general survey on my first visit were the art galleries; in the Louvre and the Luxembourg I spent some time each day, fascinated by such a collection of the world's masterpieces of sculpture and painting. One thing that always impressed me was the manner in which the history of France is recorded in the names of Paris streets, plazas, and public buildings. The Place de la Concorde, the Rue du Quatre-Septembre, the Place Jeanne d'Arc, the Arc de Triomphe, the Avenue de la Grande Armee, and innumerable others, all speak of something memorable in France's past. Napoleon's Tomb was striking with its somber grandeur. The memory of that visit prompted me later, when speaking in New York City in 1925 on the anniversary of the inauguration of George Washington as our first President, to utter the following sentiment:

> A short time ago I stood by the tomb of Napoleon, the Corsican, whose irresistible magnetism, whose marvelous power of organization, and whose military successes once surprised the world. I contemplated the exceptional possibilities of service to mankind that opportunity presented to him, had not the taint of inordinate and imperious ambition led him to ignore the primary object of the French Revolution. In contrast, my mind recalled the consecrated devotion to humanity, and the extreme unselfishness of conduct that marked the career of Washington. And I would rather go down into history like the great patriot, Washington, with the love and admiration of succeeding generations, than to sit on the throne and wear the jeweled crown of the greatest monarch that ever ruled over any people.

My first meeting with Admiral [William S.] Sims, then a lieutenant, was on this visit to Paris, where he was our naval attaché. Sims' ideas of gunnery at sea were shortly afterward adopted by the navy, and they revolutionized its methods, bringing him high praise from Theodore Roosevelt when Assistant Secretary of the Navy and later.

Italy

From Paris I went to Italy, spending first a few days at Milan, where, of all the architectural achievements I had seen, the Cathedral seemed to my untrained eye the most striking in its stately dignity and the exquisite lacelike designs of its stonework. About the time I was in Milan a regiment of Bersaglieri,[4] strong, healthy young soldiers in dark uniform, with glistening black plumes in their alpine hats, had arrived for station and Sunday found them rambling over the cathedral.

Venice, the next city I visited, more than fulfilled my conception of it. None of the many descriptions and paintings of its canals, bridges, and palaces had given me a fair impression of its endless charm. The gondola ride passing along the Grand Canal from the station to the hotel, with the lights and shadows of the sunset, gave an air of mystery to the many magnificent buildings and brought me a feeling of complete restfulness. Saint Mark's and the pigeons, the Palace of the Doges, the Bridge of Sighs, the fishing boats with their patched sails of many colors, the gently gliding gondolas, the walled gardens into which one catches an occasional glimpse through beautiful grating, and the leisurely people, with their quaint costumes, the narrow streets, and the ancient shops, everything was enchanting. But my more serious reflections took me back to the days of Venice at the zenith of her power, when she carried her trade to every port of the then known world.

A very different type of city is Florence, with heavily walled houses and almost forbidding exteriors, yet with interiors that often impressed me as if they were enlargements of the inside of Portia's jewel box, decorated not only upon the walls but also on the ceilings and even, in some, on the floors. Here again the galleries, especially the Uffizi and the Pitti, where I spent many delightful hours, made a strong appeal.

At Rome, following the practice of hurried tourists, I employed a guide for the three days allotted to the Eternal City, where one could pass months and not begin to exhaust its treasures and wonders. To me the ruins of her past glory were the most appealing. In my mind's eye I could see the Colosseum filled with people turning thumbs down upon some wounded gladiator or gloating over the fate of the early Christian martyrs. Our explorations took us from the depths of the catacombs to the top of the Colosseum, to the Vatican, and the dome of St. Peter's.

At Naples I caught a glimpse of smoking Vesuvius and the site of Pompeii and Herculaneum and the entrancing group of little towns on the cliffs across the glorious bay. I sailed away at sunset on an Italian steamer that was taking a battalion of troops to one of the colonies, with the officers as my companions on the voyage. After leaving Messina we ran into one of the worst storms in the history of the Mediterranean. I thought myself immune to seasickness, but here I succumbed, and was told that the Italian officers were no better sailors than I. But storms always end and before we sailed into the ancient city of Alexandria the weather was clear and the sea as calm as an inland lake.

Egypt

And this was Egypt, in the Near East, only across the narrow Red Sea from Arabia, the desert land from which Muhammad started his campaign for the conquest of the world. It was a crusade of centuries that shook the foundations of empires of southern Europe and the Near East and spread the faith to the Malay Peninsula, thence by peaceful missionaries to the coast peoples of the southern Philippines, among which I was destined to serve for several years. Merely passing through Alexandria, I proceeded on to Cairo, and as the train sped toward the Egyptian capital the sails along the Nile appeared to belong to boats making their way across the land, so level are the rich alluvial lands bordering that great river. In visiting the Pyramids and the Sphinx I made part of the journey on the back of a camel and, assisted by two dragomen [interpreters or guides], climbed, like Mark Twain, to the top of Giza [the Great Pyramid of Giza] and ran furiously down holding tightly to one on each side of me.

The magnificent mosques of Cairo were filled with classes grouped in sitting posture around their white-robed teachers, reciting in sing-song fashion their lessons from the Koran. The British wisely refrained from meddling with the religious faith of the people but devoted themselves only to questions of government. Their success under Lord Cromer left a striking example for us to follow in the control of our own Muhammadan wards—an example which I studied with much benefit. Hastily concluding my visit, there remains with me impressions of ancient ruins, wailing walls, desert sunsets, veiled women and turbaned men, dignitaries in long robes and beggars in rags, great wealth and wretched poverty, swarms of flies and mosquitoes, diminutive underfed donkeys and stately long-striding camels—impressions that I shall not attempt to describe of Egypt and its mighty city in the sands.

Joining the *Missouri* and the Voyage to Manila

On the journey by rail from Cairo to Suez I got views at many points of the narrow but incalculably valuable waterway that stands as a monument to French engineering genius. The *Missouri* was in charge of Major W. H. [William H.] Arthur, of the Medical Corps, and on board there were several young officers, like myself bound for the Philippines. Again among my own people, we were soon sailing down the long, glassy Red Sea, with first a view of Egypt on one side and then of Arabia on the other. One day something went wrong in the engine room and we lay to for several hours, with the terrific heat pouring down from the cloudless sky. A school of sharks came about us looking for refuse and we rigged up fishing tackle consisting of a strong inch rope with a meat hook on the end well baited with a large piece of fresh beef. Hardly had we cast our cumbersome line overboard before one of the ravenous creatures started off with the bait. He did not get far, however, before we had him struggling, and with all hands at the line we landed him on deck.

Fortunately it was not the typhoon season and we had perfect weather crossing the Indian Ocean to Colombo, our only stop in India. Almost naked men, women, and children swam about the ship begging us to throw coins for them to dive after and which they never failed to recover. The people of Ceylon, though not large, are considered one of the most beautifully formed races in the world, and it was a delight to see their supple, richly-tanned bodies in graceful action.

On shore the palms and tropical verdure gave us a hint of what we should find in the Philippines. We spent a day in Ceylon, going on an excursion by rail forty miles up into flora of the temperate zone, to the quaint city of Kandy, one of the principal marts for tea, which we viewed in all stages of preparation for export. We were seeing the island that hangs in the ocean like a jewel from the point of greater India, so richly endowed by nature's magnificence with its dark people and their mysterious temples, where the elephant takes the place of the camel as the principal beast of burden. Colombo was our last port of call before we reached our destination, as we steamed through the Straits of Malacca and, without touching even at Singapore, proceeded directly to Manila, arriving there on Thanksgiving Day.

I went at once to see my younger brother, Lieutenant Ward B. Pershing, of the Fourth Cavalry, who was convalescing at Corregidor after a serious illness. He had been appointed in the army from Illinois at the outbreak of the Spanish War and had been sent to the Philippines the preceding June. He had campaigned with Lawton in Luzon in pursuit of [Emilio] Aguinaldo and other *insurrectos* and had suffered from the debilitating effects of the climate. He was most enthusiastic about his experiences and wanted very much to recover sufficiently to rejoin his troop, but his morale was higher than his physical strength and a little later he was sent back to the States.

Simply skirting the coastline of Asia brought to me a realization of its vastness, with its hordes of population. But these masses are not united and because of this the British are able to rule a population of three hundred millions in India. The Muhammadans fight among themselves in Arabia and remain nomads. The British employ one group of Indian people against another; the French use Algerian troops to fight Moroccans; the Chinese are so divided that it is safe to station European, American, and Japanese garrisons of a few hundred men in several of their principal cities, and it is a question of how soon it will fall a prey to some more aggressive nation.

10

Duty in the Philippines— Manila, Mindanao, and Iligan

November 1899–April 1902

There was something romantic in the thought of service in an oriental country inhabited by so many tribes in different stages of civilization beginning at the bottom with wild aborigines. It also offered a variety of opportunities not hitherto embraced in any service which the army had been called upon to perform. As usual [the army] greeted that call of duty with enthusiasm, and the able and devoted manner of its performance is already a matter of history.

The Philippines—Manila

Manila in those days still had the aspects of a medieval city. Its outstanding feature was the old walled city on the south bank of the Pasig River at its mouth. On the inland side a wide moat extended from the banks of the river to the shores of the bay. The total perimeter of the walls, less than three miles, was not great compared with those of the ancient cities of Spain, but set out here in the island fringe of Eastern Asia this miniature replica of a Spanish town of the days when soldiers fought in armor was impressive. Standing boldly at the point where the river runs into the bay was the imposing citadel known as Fort Santiago. Also inside the walled city were the principal government offices, barracks for the garrison, a magnificent cathedral, and picturesque old churches. Across the river and out beyond the moat the city proper had its active commercial quarter and the residences of foreigners and wealthy Filipinos. The city trailed off into suburbs up the Pasig [River] and out to Cavite on the bay shore. Manila was notably the largest city in the islands, having a population of nearly three hundred thousand, while the next in size was Cebu, with less than a quarter of that number. Most of the Filipinos lived in small towns and villages.

In the three and a half centuries of their occupation, the Spaniards, though they had not made loyal subjects of all the people, had impressed their character upon the islands in one remarkable way. This was in the conversion of the people to Christianity. Out of a population of a little over ten million, more than nine million were professing Christians. The Spanish priests who followed the conquering soldiers had caused the great bulk of the population to give up their faiths and adopt that which, though originally Eastern, had become the religion of the West. One reason for this notable achievement was probably the fact that the Spaniards, as in their Central and South American colonies, had mingled with the natives socially and had not withheld themselves from inter-marriage with them.

Into this civilization, definitely alien to our own, we Americans had come. Up to this time we were represented almost exclusively by the army. Few civil officials, missionaries, school teachers, and businessmen had yet arrived, and Americans out of uniform on the streets were the exception. Governor-General Otis lived at *Malacañan*, the palace of the Spanish Governor-General; the headquarters were in the *Ayuntamiento* [municipal council]; and the troops were quartered in the old Spanish barracks. The Oriente Hotel, then the only good hostelry in the city, was crowded with army and naval officers. On the roads in and about the city, in noticeable contrast with the pony *carromata,* a two-wheeled vehicle with a light roof, a few small two-pony carriages, and the *carabao* [water buffalo] carts of the Filipinos, were the big American cavalry horses and the mule teams. There were yet no motor cars in use.

The Philippine War

Few people realize the colossal task that confronted the army in the Philippines at that time. The problem involved the establishment of law and order in a thousand inhabited islands, making together a territory the size of Japan proper, situated in a hot, faraway region of the world to which our forces were not accustomed or acclimated. Washington had no trained personnel able to administer the affairs of the Islands and there was no department of the Government to which they naturally pertained. The job, therefore, fell to the army, which, besides its normal functions of maintaining law and order, found itself called upon to reconstitute the

The Philippines (Vandiver, *Black Jack*, vol. 1, p. 241).

functions of civil government, municipal, provincial, and insular, with its politics, diplomacy, finance, jurisprudence, and everything that goes with it. When the Spanish evacuated the various provinces following the ratification of the peace treaty, we had insufficient troops to move in immediately. As the Spanish moved out, the insurgents entered, seized control of the local government in many places, and soon proclaimed the Philippine Republic, under the presidency of Emilio Aguinaldo. It was essential to the welfare of the Islands that the independence movement be suppressed and American authority extended throughout the Archipelago. A peaceful settlement was earnestly sought, but the insurgents were determined, and what is known as the Philippine Insurrection [now also called the Philippine War or Philippine-American War] ensued.

The military task immediately before us was the suppression of this insurrection. For a period of nearly two years it entailed guerilla warfare in a country unknown to us, with its swamps and rivers and its hills and mountains, every foot of which was familiar to the inhabitants and their *insurrecto* troops. Our total force in the Islands reached a maximum of 75,000 in 1900, including ten special regiments of Infantry composed of officers and men who had served in the Spanish-American War, authorized for the emergency and sent to the Islands in the spring and summer of 1899.[1] It is not necessary here to go into the details of the army's accomplishment in the Islands between 1899 and 1901, but to the student it forms an epic in American history.

I had hoped upon arrival to have active field duty in the provinces, although at that time the insurgent forces had been widely scattered and the task of the army had become a matter of running down relatively small bands. Upon reporting to the Adjutant General, Colonel T. H. [Thomas H.] Barry, I was assigned to General Theodore Schwan as adjutant of an expedition to be made against the *insurrectos* in Cavite Province. As this plan was delayed for more than a month, with little prospect of its being carried out, I requested assignment to the [Military] District of Mindanao and Jolo. The Visaya Islands District was also without an adjutant general, but thinking that the Moro country would afford more interesting service, I asked for that.

Adjutant General of the Military District of Mindanao and Jolo

The voyage from Manila to Zamboanga, a distance of about six hundred miles to the south, which I made on a small Spanish steamer,

Commanding General and staff, 2 September 1900. Pershing served as the adjutant general of the Department of Mindanao and Jolo at Zamboanga from late December 1899 until he took over as district officer at Iligan on 1 November 1901. Left to right: Ben H. Randolph, inspector general; John J. Pershing, adjutant general; J. N. Morrison, judge advocate general; Theodore B. Hacker, chief commissary; William A. Kobbé, commanding general; Ferdinand W. Kobbé, aide-de-camp (standing behind his father); Richard W. Johnson, chief surgeon; Charles E. Stanton, chief paymaster; and Thomas Swobe, chief quartermaster. (Library of Congress, Prints and Publications Division, Pershing Collection, Lot 8854)

was enchanting. Passing through straits, often near the shores of various islands, the tropical flora presented every shade of green, from the bright tints of grassy hills to the darker hues of luxurious forests. Deep inlets offered protected harbors for the frail native sailboats that dotted the seas. The waters and skies of these eastern tropics were equally fascinating in line and color. We arrived at Zamboanga late in the evening on the last day of the year in time to participate in the festivities of New Year's Eve [31 December 1899].

The District included the islands of Mindanao and Paragua and the Sulu Archipelago, a chain of small islands beginning with Jolo, the largest, about seventy-five miles from the southern end of Mindanao, and extending southwest, including the Siassi group, next in the chain, and the Tawi-Tawi group, which is nearest to Borneo. Colonel J. S. [James S.] Pettit, Thirty-first Volunteer Infantry, was temporarily in command, the regular commander, Major General John C. Bates, being then in Luzon assisting in operations. Headquarters was located in the municipal building, the staff officers lived in the old Spanish customs house, and the troops were quartered in the former Spanish barracks, near old Fort del Pilar, erected by the Spaniards nearly three centuries before, which still remains as a model of medieval fortifications.

Zamboanga, located at the southern extremity of the island of Mindanao, on the Strait of Basilan, was an agreeable station, with a delightful climate. Its buildings consisted of a Catholic church, municipal building, customs house, Spanish barracks, several frame stores, and residences, although the latter, especially those of the natives, were usually of the fronds of *nipa,* a kind of palm that grows in swampy places. The frame of such houses was usually of bamboo lashed with strips of *bejuca,* a kind of vine that grows in tropical forests. Through the center of the town flowed a freshwater canal, which furnished water for all purposes. This stream was lined with coconut palms, while along the street leading through the old Spanish military post were wild almond trees, which attracted great flights of fruit bats from a neighboring island, their bodies as large as a medium-sized squirrel and wings often with a spread of three feet. Their chattering and scuffling as they fed on the almonds gave us many a sleepless night. Zamboanga was then a town, including the various outlying suburbs or barrios, of about twenty thousand inhabitants, most of whom were Filipinos, with two or three thousand Moros and a few Chinese. The Moros lived in the suburbs in *nipa* shacks usually built over the water's edge; they kept themselves quite apart from the Filipinos, with whom they had no contacts except for purposes of trade. They belonged to the proud and terrible faith of Muhammad, being the most eastern of the converts to the Prophet's creed; they regarded the others contemptuously as infidels. But, mainly inspired by fear, the dislike of the Christian Filipinos for the Moros was hardly less intense. The Chinese were neutral.

It was easy to distinguish the Chinese, Christians, and Muhammadans from one another; their dress, customs, and languages were markedly different. The Moros of the town were essentially fishermen, supplying the entire population daily with a choice variety of fresh food from the sea. At night their fishing boats, in which they carried *nipa* torches to lure the fish, which they speared from the prow, made a picturesque sight. They kept no pigs, but every Filipino family had at least one. The Filipinos lived in more pretentious *nipa* houses and were farmers, laborers, and often keepers of small shops. The Chinese were almost exclusively tradesmen and merchants. We Americans were a race apart, who, as the ruling class, mingled little with the others except officially.

Two or three days before my arrival an incident occurred which illustrates the frequent high-handedness of native officials. The local Filipino *Presidente,* or Mayor, Isodoro Midel, had been allowed to confine civilian prisoners in the garrison guardhouse and release them as he desired. Among those whom he had confined was an *insurrecto* leader who had committed various offenses, including murder, before the arrival of the Americans, a man considered dangerous to the community. One evening about ten o'clock Midel with several local policemen called at the guardhouse and asked for the prisoner. The officer of the day, having been specifically directed to do so by Colonel Pettit, complied with Midel's request. The latter, as it was learned later, took the prisoner outside the lines and shot him to death.

Midel was inclined to despotism, like the majority of Filipinos when given authority—and that sort of thing will develop again when the Americans leave the Philippines. Prior to the arrival of the Americans he had disposed of his chief rival for civil control by a ruse not uncommon in the past, particularly in China. He had some Chinese blood in his veins. By professions of friendship he won the confidence of his rival to the extent that the latter thought it safe to accept an invitation to pay him a visit. To welcome his guest Midel turned out the guard of native troops and then turned the rifles of the guard upon him.

Although the *Presidente*'s methods were drastic, he was of great assistance to the American authorities in the early days of the occupation, when they were not familiar with conditions. A firm hand and an understanding head were needed, and he supplied them. The Moro chief, *Datto* [tribal chief or leader, also spelled *dato* or *datu*] Mandy, a similarly keen half-Spaniard, cooperated with Midel in keeping good order between his people and the Filipinos.

The government of the district as a whole, however, presented a vastly more difficult problem. Here in Mindanao and Jolo the Spanish had made probably the least progress and three centuries of occupation left little that could be called modern outside of a few coast towns located at wide intervals. There were three distinct native elements to deal with: Christian Filipinos, Moros, and the native hill tribes. The Moros were divided into two principal groups, one exclusively occupying the Sulu

Archipelago, being subjects of the sultan of Sulu, and the other living on Mindanao, principally in the provinces of Iligan, Illana, Lanao, and Cotabato, with many minor sultans or *dattos* of their own. The Moros held all available agricultural lands in the vicinity of Lake Lanao and in the fertile Cotabato valley and had possession of the southern shores of Mindanao, including the best grazing lands. Being fighting people, with Muhammadan traditions, they were feared by all the others. The Filipinos occupied the northern and eastern coast towns of Mindanao, while the pagan or wild tribes generally inhabited the higher plateaus of the back country, subsisting on *camotes*, a kind of yam, and highland rice, with some dried fish which they obtained from the coast people.

The first American troops entered the district in May, 1899, and Mindanao had been occupied only since November. Two battalions of the Twenty-third Infantry were assigned to the Sulu Archipelago, with headquarters and four companies at Jolo and one company each at Siassi and Bangao. On Mindanao, besides one company of the Twenty-third at Cottabato and one at Cagayan, there was the Thirty-first Volunteer Infantry, with headquarters and four companies at Zamboanga, three companies at Cotabato, and one each at the other south coast towns of Parang, Davao, Pollok, Matti, and Baganga. In March, 1900, the Fortieth Volunteer Infantry arrived in the district, headquarters and four companies taking station at Cagayan, four companies at Iligan, two at Misamis, and one each at Dapitan and Surigao, all on the northern coast. In April, 1900, General Bates was relieved by Brigadier General William A. Kobbé and the district became the Department of Mindanao and Jolo, headquarters remaining at Zamboanga, and I continuing as adjutant general.

Adjutant General of the Department of Mindanao and Jolo

With so large a territory, the best that could be done at first was to occupy the more important towns. The control at each place was under the local commanding officer, with little interference by department headquarters. The officer in charge was more or less dictator in his particular subdistrict. There were few precedents and little knowledge of our new wards to guide us, and our first year of occupation was one of consolidation and acclimatization, so to speak, while establishing friendly relations and opening up new roads and trails here and there. For the latter purpose the government provided the District Commander with a limited amount of money in pesos (worth about fifty cents in our money) which he distributed to be expended under the direction of local commanders. Improved communications were meant to be valuable to the people in bringing their produce to the coast to market. The principal products were *abaca* (hemp) and copra (dried coconut) and wild rubber and wax gathered from the forests. The cultivation of rubber trees came later.

The usual duties of an adjutant general fell to my lot. In those days and under the circumstances the officer was an executive for the commanding general. Questions of supply of troops, construction of barracks and quarters, and transportation pertaining to the quartermaster came under the supervision of the adjutant general. We were content to leave questions of native control mainly to local commanders, but occasionally an important Moro personality came to Zamboanga for consultation. Otherwise there was little out of the ordinary until November, 1900, when a final drive throughout the Islands to put an end to the insurrection was ordered by the Division Commander, Major General Arthur MacArthur, and the Twenty-eighth Volunteer Infantry commanded by Colonel William E. Birkhimer was transferred to Mindanao to assist in the local campaign.

The insurrection had not spread widely through Mindanao but had been confined largely to the province of Cagayan, the most important band being under a leader named Capistrano. In the course of the year several attacks had been made on our garrisons and one or two small expeditions had moved against the insurgents, but sufficient troops to run them down had not been available until now. General Kobbé took command in person, proceeding to Cagayan and establishing headquarters there, with Captain S. A. [Sydney A.] Cloman as inspector general, Lieutenant [Ferdinand W.] Kobbé as aide, and myself as adjutant general. Upon the arrival of the Twenty-eighth early in December active pursuit was begun. Friendly natives furnished information of Capistrano's movements, and columns of troops were constantly on his trail and that of lesser leaders. The country was indescribably difficult, mountainous inland, heavily wooded here and there, and cut by rivers and precipitous ravines. As a rule the insurgents fought at long range, usually firing from covered heights or from ambush. When hard pressed they yielded one stronghold after another, often leaving quantities of supplies behind. One company of the Fortieth Regiment ran into an ambush and had ten casualties at the first volley and the insurgents escaped without a casualty, showing that the fighting was not entirely one-sided.

Among the most tireless officers in the pursuit was Colonel Birkhimer, who was held in high regard by General Kobbé. His arrival at headquarters, often at three or four o'clock in the morning, was announced by the clanking of his saber as he came up the stairs. Major J. F. [James F.] Case, of the Fortieth Infantry, was another very active officer.

Capistrano rejected all overtures for surrender, but after three months of pursuit, being driven into the interior and deprived of supplies, he was unable to hold out any longer. He surrendered on March 27, four days after the capture of Aguinaldo by General [Frederick] Funston in Luzon. Following his action, the other and smaller insurgent groups in the district, which had not already been captured, did likewise.

Problems with the Moros

The Moros had given trouble from the beginning, but not in organized groups like the insurgent Filipinos. They were simply continuing their usual lawlessness. Raids by people of one island or group on those of another were frequent, and the booty carried off sometimes included women and children. Moros had in the past conducted piratical raids as far north as the Visayas, but their special prey were the unfortunate hill tribes. The principal objects of theft locally were carabao, or water buffalo, wealth being largely estimated by the number a man possessed. These awkward, heavy, ox-like animals are useful not only to pull carts but also in the rice fields, where they are at home plodding through mud and water. The loss of carabao was a serious handicap to those who raised their own rice. Local military commanders were constantly called upon to investigate thefts of animals and also to determine rights of property in dispute and to arbitrate quarrels. The weaker groups and individuals often sought our protection.

There were then no restrictions regarding the possession of firearms or cutting weapons, and both were used in local quarrels between Moros and often against our soldiers, when caught unarmed. Such firearms as the Moros possessed were mostly weapons stolen from the Spaniards or occasionally from us or purchased in Borneo. The pride of the Moro, however, is in his *kris*, his *kampilan*, his *barong*, or his head knife, the four classes of cutting weapons with which he is most familiar. Many of these sidearms have been tested in tribal wars and handed down from generation to generation. Much as a Moro appreciates the value of money, he will not part with his cherished weapons, the greatest inheritance in his mind that his forefathers have bequeathed him. They sold many of their knives to Americans, but not these heirlooms. These keen-edged weapons of warfare were well-calculated to do effective work in hand-to-hand combats when wielded by a skillful fighter. It has been said by our predecessors [the Spanish] that some of the experts could with a single blow cut a human body in two, their favorite stroke being at the junction of the neck and shoulder diagonally down.

Among the many questions local commanders among the Moros had to contend with, the most difficult was that of Moros "going *juramentado*," particularly in Jolo. The word "*juramentado*" means one who has taken an oath. It grew out of the custom of several Muhammadans banding together to conduct a holy war against Christians. Going *juramentado* was in Jolo a religious rite practiced by individuals. This occurred so often that it was necessary to order that soldiers there should go armed at all times, and we had to impose restrictions against Moros entering the towns bearing arms. According to the Koran these men were supposed to warn their victims to become true believers, but the Jolo Moro going *juramentado* does so without warning, often lying in wait for his victim. There is a quotation from the Koran which reads in translation, "When you meet unbelievers cut off their heads until you have massacred them," and many followers of the Arabian prophet's faith have taken this injunction more or less literally, although it was probably meant to apply during a holy war. The promise of reward in the future life was often an inducement to fanaticism in the slaying of "infidels." They believed they would enter Paradise riding a white horse and that each Christian the Moro killed would be his slave in the future life; also that they would be rewarded by the possession in Paradise of beautiful virgins, as the Koran states, in recompense for their deeds. With such beliefs it is little wonder that they became the fiercest of warriors, unequalled for individual courage.

In Spanish days when a Moro decided to go *juramentado* he usually visited the *pandita* (priest), took an oath to kill a Christian, and received absolution. He then bathed, bound up his loins and torso tightly to prevent bleeding to death if wounded before accomplishing his purpose, and went forth to kill or be killed. In our day the preliminary ceremonies were generally dispensed with for fear of discovery. A Moro gone *juramentado* is a deadly menace, slashing with his *kris* any Christian that crosses his path; he is seldom stopped short of his own death, in fact, he expects to be killed.

Many tales of attacks by these fanatics were left by the Spaniards. An incident that occurred after our occupation of Sulu is worth recording as illustrating something of Moro character and the problems we had often to face. At Bongao, where Captain Sydney A. Cloman was in command, five soldiers of his company left the post on a hunting trip. Cloman, incidentally, had planned to accompany them but was prevented by illness from doing so. The party pitched camp near Bilimbing, on Tawi-Tawi Island, and after supper one evening four of the men were having a game of cards, while a number of Moros squatted behind them, apparently only interested spectators. The Moros had been with the party a day or so, had helped with the work, and seemed to be thoroughly friendly, so no apprehension was felt at their presence. Suddenly several whipped out their *krises* and attacked the unsuspecting card players, killing one instantly and severely wounding the others, one of whom died the following day. The fifth member of the party, who was in bathing at the time, escaped in the darkness. The story of the return of the party to Bongao, with only one unwounded man to handle the boat, is an epic of courage and fortitude. As soon as Cloman received word of what had happened he proceeded to Bilimbing with as many men as could be taken in the boats available, and, on threat of executing the village chiefs, the guilty Moros were surrendered. Persistent questioning of these men developed that they had never seen the hunting party before this visit to Bilimbing, were not seeking vengeance for any wrong, but simply had "infidels" in their power and decided to kill them. The guilty men were put to work under guard and the reports of the incident stated that they tried to escape and were killed by the guard. After that the Moros of the region would hardly make a move without first reporting to Cloman, even seeking his approval before marrying.[2]

Promotion to Captain but No Change in His Duties

The army legislation of February, 1901,[3] brought an increase of five regiments of cavalry, and with it came my promotion to the grade of captain in the regular service in my forty-first year. Fifteen years had been a long term as a lieutenant, especially as the period included a foreign war. The promotion took me to the First Cavalry, then in the States. But I was not anxious to return, feeling that service in the Islands presented greater opportunity. General Kobbé expected to remain in command of the department and wanted me to continue with him, saying that the thought of having a regular adjutant general "gave him the shivers." I arranged a transfer which took me to the Fifteenth Cavalry, then under orders for Philippine service, and so remained.

The Fifteenth Cavalry was one of the newly-organized regiments and soon began to arrive in the Islands. One troop came to Zamboanga.

When I asked the major of the squadron what kind of an outfit the troop was, he replied, "It has a hundred horses who never saw a soldier, a hundred soldiers who never saw a horse, and a bunch of officers who never saw either." While not literally true, it gave some idea of his difficulties in training a new outfit.

In the spring of 1901 General Kobbé visited several stations on a tour of inspection, taking with him Captain Cloman, Lieutenant Kobbé, his aide, and myself. Returning to Zamboanga, we were dining on deck one evening, and the conversation drifted into a discussion of stations in the Philippines. The General asked what my choice would be if given an opportunity to make a selection. I replied that it would be Iligan. He expressed some surprise that I should name such an isolated place and asked my reason. I said that in my opinion it would be necessary some day, perhaps soon, to bring the Moros living around Lake Lanao under control, that this would be the place from which any movement to get in touch with them should start, and that the officer then in command would have a rare opportunity for important service. Up to that time these Moros had been largely left to themselves, and we did not know much about them except that the Spaniards had made several attempts to bring them under subjugation but had largely failed. So far they had given us little trouble, although it was known that they seriously objected to American occupation. The General said no more about the matter, and I gave it no further thought.

As the term of enlistment of the ten [actually twenty-five] Volunteer regiments organized in 1899 for Philippine service expired at the end of June, 1901, they were returned to the States for discharge. General Kobbé was relieved by Brigadier General George W. Davis, who assumed command on August 31, the Volunteers were replaced by regiments of the Regular Army, and the regular regiment in Sulu was relieved by another. I was mustered out as adjutant general and reverted to my regular rank as captain of the line, Colonel S. W. [Samuel W.] Fountain taking my place. This meant almost a complete change of military personnel for the Department of Mindanao and Jolo. I was the only officer left at Zamboanga who had any experience whatever with the problems in the department, and General Davis appointed me as assistant to the adjutant general until the new arrivals could get their bearings.

In this capacity I was well occupied for some time explaining the situation here and there and what had been done and why. General Davis immediately put his keen mind to work on Moro questions, with the view especially of opening up the Lanao country, and I was constantly called in consultation with him. He soon reached the conclusion that we should begin a study on the ground and called me in one day in September and said, "Pershing, as you are the only man left here who knows anything about the Moros, I'm going to send you to Iligan. I'll give you two troops of your regiment and three companies of infantry. Do everything possible to get in touch with the Moros of central Mindanao and make friends of them."

Commanding the Iligan District, Mindanao

The prospect of being stationed for an indefinite term in a small native town rarely visited by an American out of uniform would seem to many like a term of exile. But this was just the place I wanted, especially as I was assigned a definite objective. I recalled my conversation with General Kobbé at the time of our visit to Iligan and wondered if he had spoken to General Davis of my desire for that station.

Upon arrival at Iligan [1 November 1901] I at once set the troops to work rebuilding the tumbledown barracks and generally preparing to make them comfortable. As soon as convenient I got in touch with the Lanao Moros—Malanaos, as they were called—and began to make overtures to some of their *dattos*.[4] An effective time to get acquainted with them was on market days held each Saturday, when at first a few from the surrounding country would come in bringing chickens, eggs, rice, *camotes*, once in awhile a fine steer, brassware—which they were experts at molding—baskets and vari-colored cloths of their own weaving and anything else they had to sell. The market became a picturesque sight. The increased garrison gave the Moros a greater outlet for their goods and the market space was enlarged especially for their benefit. I made it a practice to visit these gatherings frequently and go about among the people, inquiring in a friendly way about their crops, their carabaos, their government, and their leading men.

Receiving favorable reports from their people of the new conditions at Iligan, the *dattos* themselves soon began to come in for conferences. They liked to talk and wanted to speak with someone in authority, and in this they were given every encouragement. Before long the most important Moro on the north of the lake, Ahmai-Manibilang, former sultan of Madaya, who had abdicated in favor of his nephew but was still the power over his people, sent this nephew to see me. The former sultan and I exchanged letters, and I finally induced him to pay me a visit himself.

On the appointed day he came in great state, accompanied by a retinue of about thirty of his people. He was a tall, swarthy, well-built man,
past middle age, clean shaven, as most of them were. His jacket was of
many colors, his trousers tight-fitting, his turban smartly tied and set
jauntily to the side of his head. Like all Moros, he was barefoot. He rode
a fine-looking pony—a stallion—and for stirrups used a small rope knot-
ted at the ends which he grasped between the first two toes. On each side
of his horse a slave trotted along on foot, one carrying his gold-mounted
kris, the other his highly-polished brass box containing betel nut, *buya*
leaves, and lime—kept separate till the time for chewing, when, as was
their custom, he mixed them in proportions to suit his taste. Leading the
procession was a guard carrying a gun and behind this dignitary came
another. Then came minor chiefs, relatives, and more slaves, all in their
choicest finery. Even in this semi-savage setting the *datto* was a striking
looking man and proved to be very intelligent.

I took him to my quarters and gave directions that he should be
shown every attention. He remained for the night in the to him strange
surroundings, occupying one of my rooms, while his retinue were given
other quarters nearby. They prepared their own food, accepting only a
little of what we had to offer, careful to choose such edibles as could not
have been prepared with lard.

We had a conference of several hours, in which he plied me with
many questions. I went carefully into explanations of the American government's intentions, assuring him that there would be no interference
with his people's religion, and telling him that the sultan at Constantinople (Stamboul, as he knew it), the Vice-regent of Muhammad, to
whom the Moros professed spiritual allegiance, exchanged representatives with our President. I talked about trade and the value of new roads
to facilitate the transport of Moro products to market and of our solicitude for their welfare in general. They had held that the Moros became
again masters of the country when the Spaniards left, but he seemed
content to accept my explanation that we had taken the islands from the
Spaniards as a result of war and that the Moros would find us a different
and more friendly people. There were two knotty questions I succeeded
in keeping out of the discussion. They were slavery and the plurality of
wives. As to government, I announced to him that it would be my policy
to permit the *dattos* to govern their own people in their own way but that
the chiefs would be held personally responsible for any infringement of
the rights of others. The visit seemed to be a success. Manibilang took
his leave the following day in a very cordial frame of mind.

I wanted to return the ex-sultan's visit, but it was some time before he invited me. None of the chiefs had ever had an American in their homes and to do this unprecedented thing in the face of the existing prejudice and suspicion required, no doubt, many explanations and careful preparation. But in due time the invitation came, and I promptly accepted it. When I told my officers that I intended to go unarmed and without an escort, taking only Leon Fernandez, my Filipino interpreter, and a native servant, some doubted the wisdom of my going. But I had confidence in my friend and wanted to show it.

When the day came Manibilang sent his nephew with a number of his own men to conduct me. While nominally an escort of honor, it was really a guard to provide for my security. My host met me at the door of his home with warm salutations in the Moro manner and took me into the house—a massive frame structure built of hewn timbers, with plank floors and a high, steep roof, heavily thatched. The house and surroundings presented a homelike appearance and were noticeably clean—a Muhammadan characteristic but not usually found among the Moros. Only the wealthier of them had timber houses, the majority being made of *nipa* or grass attached to a bamboo framework.

At dinner my interpreter and I were served on chinaware, with knives, forks, and spoons. My surprise was probably shown on my face, judging from the delight of our host. The Moros did not as a rule use such utensils; their custom was to eat with their fingers, squatting around a container in the center of the circle, another Muhammadan custom, and I had expected to take my meals in that way. I have never tasted more delicious chicken, seasoned as it was with native herbs; and the rice, steaming hot, was cooked to perfection, the grains still whole, as few Americans at home ever see rice cooked. None of the women of the household sat with us, but the senior wife directed the serving with a quiet authority and in a subdued voice that the conditions made all the more noticeable. The Moros did not veil and seclude their woman like Muhammadans of the Near East.

The Koran limited to four the number of wives a man could have at one time, though it was a simple matter to divorce an old woman to make way for a young one. To repeat the words "I divorce thee" three times is considered sufficient. This procedure could be repeated indefinitely. Husband and wife often separated on mutual agreement, the wife returning to her people with all the presents she had acquired during her wedded life. If a husband found himself too poor to support all his wives, one or more could be returned to her former home. Wives were practically bought, an agreed amount being paid her parents. Thirteen years was considered marriageable age for girls. For a woman divorce was not so simple. If granted a divorce, she was forced to repay double the amount of her dowry and was forbidden to remarry within four months. The women dressed plainly, usually wearing a sort of loose drapery called a sarong, and, like the men, they went barefoot. They rarely went away from home, even to the market. A real spirit of affection seemed to exist in the families. The parents were very fond of their children and children of them. I do not recall ever having seen a Moro wife or child abused in any way. If cases of ill-treatment existed they were at least exceedingly rare. The affection of the father for his offspring is shown by the use of the word "Ahmai" before his name, meaning "the father of." Though usually smaller than the men, many of the women would be considered good looking were it not for the habit of filing their teeth and blackening them by chewing betel nut.

After dinner my host and I again discussed American-Moro relations, continuing until late in the evening, when an incident occurred that staggered me. He left the room for a few minutes, without explaining why, and returned with an attractive and youthful member of his harem, who he announced in an entirely matter-of-course way would be my companion for the night. I knew that Moro hospitality went to this extent among themselves but did not expect that it would include a foreign visitor, and my confusion was undoubtedly apparent. I did not want to impair in any way the friendly understanding I had laboriously built up and feared that declining might be misunderstood. This I explained in Spanish to Leon, asking him to put the rejection in the finest Moro phraseology at his command. Whereupon Manibilang sent the lady away in the same matter-of-course manner as he had brought her in.

The following day I was taken to several places along the lakeshore by *vinta*—a kind of canoe hewn out of a log and kept on an even keel by bamboo outriggers. The visits to other communities had evidently been arranged beforehand, for I seemed to be expected wherever we arrived and was well received. At one *rancheria*, it was market day and I had opportunity of speaking directly to a large group of the people. No sign of hostility was shown me anywhere, but it was often apparent that Manibilang was anxious that no untoward incident might occur. When I returned to Iligan, on the third day, his nephew, the sultan, accompanied me in person with a guard of his own all the way back.

From that time on Manibilang was not only a warm personal friend of mine but an earnest advocate of friendly relations between Americans and Moros. In the months to come he rendered much valuable assistance in dissuading other *dattos* from opposition. With the exception of two or three groups, the attitude of the north Lanao Moros in general, largely through his influence, became friendly. The word spread of the good business that could be done at Iligan and the security afforded Moros there, and the numbers of those who came to market steadily increased. I continued to welcome personally those of importance, especially on their first visit, and gave them to understand that I was interested in their welfare. The attitude of the other officers and the men was the same as mine.

11

Dealing with the Hostile Moros around Lake Lanao

April–September 1902

Although we had made good progress in winning over the Moros on the north side of Lake Lanao, the same thing could not be said regarding those on the south. In recent months detachments of troops sent out from Parang-parang to explore and survey the territory between there and the lake had met with opposition. An exploring party of seventeen cavalrymen under Lieutenant W. D. [William D.] Forsyth, Fifteenth Cavalry, had been ambushed [on 15 March 1902] and all its horses had been captured by the Moros;[1] individual soldiers had been waylaid and killed and their rifles stolen; and outposts had been frequently attacked. The situation was threatening. To let the culprits go unpunished was but to invite further defiance, and Colonel F. D. [Frank D.] Baldwin, Twenty-seventh [U.S.] Infantry, then in command with headquarters at Malabang, therefore obtained authority to conduct an expedition to the lake. This body of water is about twenty-three hundred feet above sea level and the intervening country is exceedingly rough.

The Lake Lanao Expedition of April–May 1902

While the troops were slowly advancing, building a temporary road as they went, the Commanding General of the Philippines Division, General A. R. Chaffee, in an effort if possible to avoid fighting, issued a proclamation in April, 1902 [on 13 April, while visiting Brigadier General Davis and Colonel Baldwin at Malabang, Mindanao], calling upon the

155

sultans and *dattos* in the southern lake region to return stolen property and surrender the guilty tribesmen, giving the chiefs a time limit of two weeks and holding them responsible for failure to comply. The appeal reassured the peaceful Moros and explained in detail our friendly attitude toward them.

General Chaffee sent me a copy of this proclamation, which I had translated and sent to the more influential sultans and *dattos* about the lake with a covering letter, of which the following is an example:

Iligan, April 18, 1902.

Letter to my friend, Ahmai-Manibilang, and to the Sultan of Madaya:

I have received a telegram from the military governor of the islands, in which he directs me to communicate to you and all Moros of Lanao, either personally or by letter, a proclamation issued by him in Malabang, April 13, and accordingly I am sending you a copy of this proclamation translated into your own language.

I have sent word to many, and have advised personally all the North Lanao Moros that I have seen recently of the action of certain Moros on the south side of the lake in opposing the American troops near Malabang and even killing American soldiers.

I have explained that we intended to punish the guilty datos, and all of my Moro friends have agreed that it should be done and that the Americans are right. I now write to you, my personal friend, what I have told many others. There is nothing else to do except to punish the sultans and datos referred to in the General's proclamation unless they accede to the demands made by the General; but I wish to reassure all of you that in punishing these bad Moros we have no intention whatever of molesting our true friends, and I wish you to communicate to all your people what I say and what is said in the General's proclamation.

If it is convenient I should like to visit the North Lake *rancherias* again and personally explain, more clearly than I can write it, this proclamation and the desire of the Americans for friendship and peace. I should like to go to see you on Monday (April 21) if you will send me word.

I am sending this letter with others by my old friend, Yanit, dato of Marahui, to whom I have explained the proclamation and this letter. With remembrances to your family and to that of your nephew, Ahmai-Sangacala, I hope to see you all again as soon as possible.

Your friend,
John J. Pershing,
Captain, Fifteenth Cavalry.

Several of the chiefs replied at once that they would be glad to see me but specifically requested that I bring no troops and that none be sent to the lake. In the meantime Colonel Baldwin's advance toward the southern shore of the lake caused all sorts of rumors and the Moros on the north were becoming very much excited. Many packed their household goods, ready to move away from their *rancherias,* and some sent their women and children to the *cottas* (forts), which they began hastily to strengthen.

I felt that more could be accomplished by personal contact than by writing to hold the friendship of the north shore Moros and prevent their uniting with those on the south should there be a clash. Thinking also that to show our confidence was a good way to win theirs, I went again to the lake unarmed and accompanied only by an interpreter. We arrived at Marahui on April 27 and the following day had a conference at Madaya, attended by the leading north lake Moros and many from other sections. I explained the meaning of General Chaffee's proclamation, corrected many false impressions and rumors, and gave assurances that those who were peaceful would not be molested. But I also made it clear that it was our intention to go where we pleased throughout the islands.

Most of the *dattos* accepted what I said, but some declared sullenly that they would fight the Americans if they came, and still others seemed to hold me personally responsible for what they called the invasion of their country by our troops. While at the house of a friendly *datto* in conference with a group of them, one fiery *datto* walked directly up to me in a threatening attitude and charged me with having deceived them. Jose Infanta, the interpreter, plainly showed his alarm. He, of course, realized what the *datto* was saying, though I could only judge its nature by the tone and manner until it was translated. Although I began to doubt

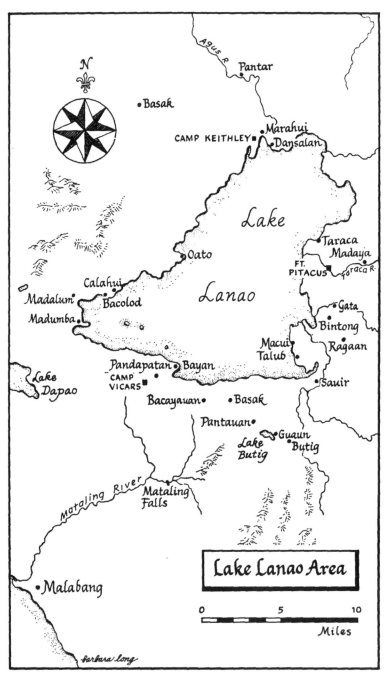

Lake Lanao Area (Vandiver, *Black Jack,* vol. 1, p. 289).

whether Jose and I were entirely safe, I warned him in Spanish, which the Moros could not understand, that any display of fear might be disastrous, but at this point Ahmai-Manibilang spoke up in my defense and the excited *datto* cooled down. Finally, nearly all of the *dattos* except some from the south of the lake expressed themselves as satisfied with my assurances, and I was able to return with the thought that something worthwhile had been accomplished.[2]

As was to be expected, General Chaffee's demands brought no results except defiance from the hostile Moros. Instead of complying, they strengthened and occupied their several *cottas* in Colonel Baldwin's line of march and even fired on his troops. There being no alternative, General Davis, who was present with Baldwin's column, ordered the advance continued. As the column approached a group of *cottas* near Pandapatan, the Moros abandoned two with little resistance, but at the third, Pandapatan itself, they made a determined stand. This *cotta* was typical of the better class of such defenses. Such *cottas* varied from one hundred to one hundred and fifty feet square, with earthen walls eight or ten feet thick, surrounded by a ditch from ten to fifteen feet deep whose sloping sides formed a sharp angle at the bottom. This ditch was set with a field of bamboo stakes, their sharpened ends pointing upward, ready to impale any attacker who might fall or be thrown into it. The parapets of these *cottas* were built by banking up earth on both sides of closely-planted bamboo trees, which thus formed a core to the parapet. The branches of bamboo usually became so interwoven as they grew that they formed an almost impenetrable barrier to an assaulting party. The entrance was skillfully concealed, and in many cases tunnels beneath the walls afforded means of escape. The loopholes in the parapets, where there were any, usually consisted of hollow bamboo tubes, which materially limited the field of fire of the defenders. Inside the walls the houses of the sultans and *dattos* were often built and arrangements made for storing provisions.

This fortification at Pandapatan was shelled by the mountain battery for an hour, no doubt with loss to the defenders. The Colonel then ordered it taken by direct assault. Our men made a valiant attack in the face of unexpected enemy fire at short range, with the result that fifty-one officers and men were killed or wounded and the attempt [also known as the Battle of Bayan, 2–3 May 1902] failed.[3] It was the first time our troops had engaged the Moros in a pitched battle, and they underestimated the defensive strength of the Moro stronghold. Without ladders they found it impossible to scale the high walls, and they were unable to reach the Moros with an effective rifle fire. The place was invested, and the next morning bamboo ladders were ready and another assault was to be made, but the Moros left in the fort surrendered without further fighting.

Assuming Responsibility for the Lake Lanao Moros

A day or so later [8 May] General Davis telegraphed me to come around by boat from Iligan to Malabang. On arrival I found General Chaffee—who was making a tour of southern stations on a naval vessel—just about to leave, and rode with him down to the landing, three miles distant. On the way he told me he was anxious to avoid more fighting if possible without losing prestige and said that, as I had been successful in handling the Moros on the north, he wanted me to join Colonel Baldwin on the south side of the lake and do what I could to pacify the Moros there. I asked him how he expected me to do that with a fiery colonel in command, and he replied that I would be placed in charge of Moro affairs and that orders would be given that no move should be made without my approval.[4] He was evidently much perturbed over the severe loss Colonel Baldwin's command had sustained and somewhat alarmed regarding the future. While at [Camp] Vicars[5] he had issued written instructions [13 May 1902] to General Davis of which the following is an extract: "Under no circumstances short of an attack by Moros will Colonel Baldwin or the members of his command resort to active hostilities or occupy or molest any fort or cota without authority from you. All punitive operations for redress or any other purpose must be conducted under and by virtue of your orders, and then only on full investigation as to the necessity of such action, when an immediate report will be made to the Division Commander."[6]

General Davis, as Department Commander, was equally anxious to prevent further clashes. He reiterated what General Chaffee had said and explained to Colonel Baldwin my status—which was somewhat unusual as it implied doubt by the latter's superiors regarding what might happen if matters were left wholly in his hands. Colonel Baldwin fully appreciated the implication and was very frank in his talk with me. His idea was that having once warned the Moros we should not hesitate to take action against any group that did not readily accept American sovereignty and submit to direct control. Moro character and religion and also their claim that the country was theirs made such a course impossible without excessive bloodshed. Patience in dealing with them was essential, lest in attempting to chastise one group we might provoke a religious war.[7]

Colonel Baldwin was a fine soldier with a long experience in handling Indians, but he was inclined to be impetuous. Fortunately, we had known each other well when I was on General Miles' staff. Occasionally we rode out to the heights on the lakeshore, from which we could look across the southwestern arm of the lake with field glasses and plainly see the Moros of Bacolod strengthening their *cotta*. He argued that such preparations in defiance of American authority should not be permitted. I contended that we should exhaust every means of winning them over peaceably, pointing out that we had the power at any time to punish them regardless of the kind of defenses they possessed. With forbearance I felt sure from experience that we could reduce the number of irreconcilable chiefs to a comparative few. The Colonel was reluctant to take this view but said that as I had been given the responsibility he would abide by my judgment, but he grew very impatient at the inaction.

Dealing with the Lake Lanao Moros

After the battle of Pandapatan the troops were withdrawn about a half mile to the south and a permanent camp, named Camp Vicars in honor of Lieutenant Thomas A. Vicars, killed in the battle, was established. Approaching the lake from Malabang, the Moro trails traversed very rough country, generally covered with timber, beneath which there was dense tropical undergrowth stimulated by excessive rainfall. With great difficulty, requiring expert engineering skill, a practicable route was found by Captain J. J. [Jay J.] Morrow and his company of engineers and a road was being constructed by troops under his supervision from Malabang to Mataling Falls, a distance of about fourteen miles. With greater difficulty, because the rise from the falls to the lake was much more rapid, it was being pushed through to Camp Vicars, seven miles farther. Before it was completed all our supplies were brought over the native trails by our own pack mule trains or by pony trains hired from friendly Moros. This was a mean task, not only because of continuous attacks by Moros but because we had come to Vicars in the rainy season, which lasts from May to September, and the road and trails were often well nigh impassable.

There was a heavy downpour almost every day and as tentage was lacking, the camp during the first couple of weeks, when the troops had only their shelter tents, was most uncomfortable. In the dry season, however, with our full allowance of tentage, living conditions were relatively much better than near the coast. Lake Lanao is triangular in shape and about fourteen miles long, and the same distance across. Camp Vicars was situated on a plateau some five hundred feet above the lake, so that the rise from Malabang to Vicars was an average of over one hundred twenty-five feet to the mile. The temperature at the higher altitude rarely fell below fifty-five degrees or rose above seventy-five except in the middle of the day. The lake lies in what is thought to be the immense crater of an extinct volcano that rose at the highest point on a neck of land nearly sixty miles wide. The landscape, with its graceful undulations, dotted with rice fields and rising from the shores of the lake to the low hills and the timbered mountains beyond, was always beautiful, especially in the rich southern lighting of the sky at early morning and evening.

The command at Vicars consisted of two troops of cavalry, one battery of artillery (light 2.9-inch guns carried on mule back), and four companies of infantry, about seven hundred men in all. It was the first American force that had ever been stationed on the lake. In bringing the supplies up from the seacoast at Malabang, the men with the pack trains never knew at what spot a party of Moros would dash out from the undergrowth or tall grass—high enough in places to hide a mounted man—and slash at them with their deadly *krises* or fire upon them from ambush. Individuals or groups from the unfriendly element constantly lurked along the trails and near Camp Vicars, seeking an opportunity of surprising lone soldiers, detachments, or pack trains, and the strictest precautions were necessary to prevent our troops being caught off their guard. It was not always possible to find out who the attackers were, and we could not indulge in wholesale punishment for the acts of such recalcitrants.

These Moros were keen to get their hands on an American rifle, and this was partly their object in attacking our troops. About twenty had already been stolen. We made particular effort to recover these guns, not only to prevent their being used against us but to demonstrate to all Moros that the possession of our rifles was likely to get them into trouble. A rifle stolen from two soldiers attacked near Malabang in March [30] was not traced for some months, when I received word from a friendly Moro [on 26 June 1902] that the sultan of Beibi had it. The following morning I set out at 2:30 with a small cavalry force, arriving at the sultan's house at 4:30 and surprising him before he was out of bed. After some parleying he came out and gave up the rifle, and I put him and two of his men under arrest and took them back to camp. The news spread quickly and within a few hours *Datto* Adta of Paigoay appeared before my tent with voluble explanations of what he declared was a misunderstanding. It was men from his *rancheria,* under the leadership of one called Bugulung, who had killed one of the soldiers [Private Lewis] and taken the rifle, and Bugulung had sold it to the sultan. Adta was profuse with attestations of friendship, but I told him that in his case mere words meant nothing, and that he now would have to prove he was my friend by bringing in the murderers. The next day [28 June 1902] he returned to camp with a party of slaves carrying the dead bodies of Bugulung and his brother Mamalampac, each lashed to a bamboo pole, and deposited them in front of my tent.[8]

After this Adta became my most trusted Moro confidant, often going for me on secret missions to various parts of the region to obtain information, and I always found his reports to be correct. He was a handsome, dashing-looking Malay, slender and swarthy, always well dressed in striking colors, his turban tied in jaunty fashion and a couple of *krises* stuck in his broad, thick sash.

Control over seventy-five thousand Muhammadan natives who were generally opposed to any government supervision involved many difficult questions. In dealing with a people extremely jealous of their semi-savage freedom and suspicious of the outside world—an attitude enhanced by contact with the Spanish—most careful and patient handling was required, with constant thought of the effect of each decision on the general situation. We were not dealing with any central government that could control these various chiefs, but were dealing with so many separate groups independent of all the others, each having its own arbitrary and often despotic chief. There were certain ties that gave them common aims and interests, such as religion, origin, habitation, and customs. But these did not affect the question of government.

The clash at Pandapatan was the most serious that had yet occurred and had left the Moros, particularly those on the south side of the lake, somewhat in doubt as to our intentions. To restore the confidence of well-disposed groups was a primary step, and I early arranged a series of conferences, beginning with those who were known to be friendly, including as many as possible from the north of the lake. Whenever any sultan or *datto* came to camp it was almost a state occasion. They brought a retinue according to their position as to wealth and heredity. Very few equaled the display made by Ahmai-Manibilang, but all came with a certain formality. They were received at the outpost and escorted to my tent, where I met them for conference. To confirm the mutual declarations of amity between any new visitor and ourselves, I always presented him formally with an American flag, which was thereafter carried as an evidence of good standing when they came to camp or went up and down the trail. Three days after my arrival at Vicars, accepting the invitation of *Datto* Grande, I visited his *rancheria* at Makadar, which was only a few miles away. On this occasion I went with an escort of infantry, as the same risk could not be taken with the Moros on the south as I had taken with my earlier friends north of the lake. I followed this with visits to the *rancherias* of several other peaceful *dattos* upon their invitation, with results that were generally favorable.

I must relate an incident that occurred on the way to Makadar. I was with the *datto* at the head of the column when we spied a wild boar on the trail at about a hundred yards. I took the rifle of one of the men and fired off hand. As the boar ran away, we all thought I had missed him, but we tracked him to a clump of bamboo, where he lay dead with a shot through the heart. I think my marksmanship established the impression that all Americans were dead shots, an impression not at all to our disadvantage.

Carefully written letters were sent to the distrustful chiefs advising them that we had their best interests at heart and inviting those who had not done so to visit us. In response to these invitations many came to the camp and others replied by letter expressing their desire to maintain good relations. But we had our suspicions that some, while pretending to be friendly, were really hostile. Several who were openly hostile wrote outspoken letters of defiance in reply to our overtures. One letter [from *Datto* Tanandundan and the sultan of Bacolod] read in part as follows: "we do not want you to live in Lanao, but want you to return to Malabang. You must follow our religion and our customs and in not doing so you will be to blame, for all the Dattos of the laguna will make war against you because we profess only one religion which is that of Stambul. This letter, burned in six places shows to you that it means war."[9]

One could only deplore their disregard or, more probably, their ignorance of possible consequences and continue patient efforts to gain their friendship. The best way to do that was by personal contact. Practically

Datto Grande of Makadar, in the traditional dress of a Moro *datto* of the Lake Lanao region, visiting Pershing at Camp Vicars in 1902. Pershing established a solid working relationship with *Datto* Grande, whose *rancheria* was near the camp and who often served as an intermediary with unfriendly Moro *dattos* and sultans. (Library of Congress, Prints and Publications Division, Pershing Collection, Lot 8850)

every day I held conferences with this or that group, pointing out the advantage that good relations with us would bring them. But it was not always easy to convince them of our altruistic motives. They had never known anything else, nor expected any other treatment than something entirely contrary. They doubted when we said that we wanted to build roads in order that their produce might be more easily taken to market. It was difficult for them to comprehend that we should voluntarily do things from benevolent reasons. At first they asked my authority for making statements or promises, but in time they came to regard me as representing the President and as having been sent to the lake especially to govern the Malanao district. They understood nothing but a one-man government, and the idea of dealing with different men representing the same power or authority, whatever their rank, was incomprehensible.

Often they would say in the early days, "Yes, we believe what you tell us, but what will your successor do? We will not know him nor have confidence in him as we have in you," and they were sometimes wise in having this doubt. I answered this by saying I would be at Lanao for a long time to come. Constant change of commanding officers at various stations was the weak point in the army system of control, and it was so only to a lesser degree in the civil administration that followed that of the army. Some said, "You Americans will want to make us eat pork," and it was only by continually reassuring them and demonstrating to them the contrary that they could be brought to think otherwise. They constantly reverted to the subject of religion. One day when it had been under prolonged discussion a sultan asked whether our God was the same as theirs. My reply was, "There is but one God and He must be the same." Whereupon he said, "Well, if that is so, we ought to be friends." I have often thought since, that if all civilized peoples could reach the same conclusion as this simple semi-savage most of the world problems of the present day would be solved.

Another old *datto* after numerous talks and much consideration finally capitulated, saying, "Hereafter the echo of my voice will always be for peace. As a *datto* I cannot lie. Let this be the beginning of our friendship and let it be agreed that the Moros will not covet anything the Americans have nor the Americans anything that the Moros have. I will be a friend of the Americans because you tell me that in America one can have any religion he desires. But do not bring hats here and make us wear them nor compel our women to wear skirts." He compared the average Moro to an untamed horse and said if one attempted to ride him at once he would probably buck, but if one went at him gently and gained his confidence he could be ridden without difficulty. This, of course, was exactly the procedure we were following. When they were willing to visit us, even though not entirely friendly, I usually succeeded in winning them over in the end. Once they openly expressed friendship they rarely changed.

Intimately connected with the question of religion was that of slavery. This was a subject on which it was wiser to be noncommittal for the time being. But slavery as it existed in Mindanao was not slavery in our sense of the term except in isolated instances. Very few cases of Moros treating their slaves as other than members of the household ever came to my notice; in fact, it was usually difficult to distinguish between slaves and other Moros, all living together as a family. From my observations I was of the opinion that few of the so-called slaves would leave their masters if given the opportunity. Children born of slaves were regarded as legitimate sons and daughters of the father, but could not inherit lands or titles. Another and even more serious question in its effect upon character was that of polygamy. As this Asiatic custom was recognized by the Koran, it was deemed unwise to meddle with it. At the same time, it was recognized that as an institution it had a debasing effect upon their mode of thought and their attitude toward a government whose people regarded its practice as immoral. It is a remarkable fact that where the custom has existed in the Near East or elsewhere a substantial political government has always been impossible.

On July 4 we held a large celebration at the camp and a general invitation was sent the Moros to come in and join the festivities. The exercises were opened with a parade, after which the troops put on a full program of the usual Fourth of July sports, in several of which the Moros participated. The tug of war caused the greatest enthusiasm among them as different *rancherias* were pitted against each other. Mixed foot races developed some fine sprinting, with honors about even. Exhibition dances were given by Moros in the use of spear and shield. Sultans and *dattos* were selected to act as judges of Moro events, for which special prizes in money were awarded. A beef was killed and the Moros were introduced to an old-fashioned barbecue feast, supplemented by rice and salmon, but no pork products were used, although a few Moros would eat bacon when no one was looking. The several hundred that spent the Fourth with us seemed highly delighted, and the day ended in a gale of friendly expressions as our guests departed. I had taken the precaution to post an armed man in each tent and a mounted detachment on the parade ground to provide against the possibility of some Moro going *juramentado*.

A few days later [9–11 July 1902] General Davis, who had been named to relieve General Chaffee as Division Commander when the latter's tour expired in the fall, came to camp with Brigadier General S. S. Sumner, his successor as commander of the Seventh Separate Brigade.[10] They spent a couple of days visiting, sightseeing, and discussing Moro problems.[11] General Davis, having initiated the extension of American authority over the Malanaos, always kept in close touch with developments. He never forgot the names of important Moros and frequently inquired about them and their attitude. It was most satisfactory to serve under a man of his ability, understanding, and interest, and whatever measure of success I may have had among those alien people was due largely to his support.[12]

Brigadier General Samuel S. Sumner, commanding general, Department of Mindanao and Jolo, meeting with the sultans of Bayan and Oato at Camp Vicars sometime in 1902. Captain Pershing, in his campaign hat, stands directly behind one of the seated sultans. (Library of Congress, Prints and Publications Division, Pershing Collection, Lot 8850. LC-USZ62-107906)

Commanding Camp Vicars and the Lake Lanao Region

As senior officer present, although only recently promoted to a captaincy, temporary command of the post had fallen to me upon the promotion of Colonel Baldwin to the rank of brigadier general [as of 30 June 1902]. It was my pleasant duty [on 9 July] to escort the distinguished visitors up the trail with my troop, then stationed at Vicars. As we rode along, General Sumner expressed satisfaction at his new assignment; he also gave me the gratifying news that I was to remain in command at Vicars. I was thus being given command of what was at the time probably the most important post in the Philippines. This was quite unusual in view of my rank, but was explained by General Davis in the following letter [19 February 1903] to The Adjutant General of the Army:

> The situation in one respect has been anomalous—the assignment of a captain to so large and important a command as that of Vicars—but it was in my opinion absolutely indispensable that the man to command on the spot should possess certain qualities not easy to find in one man: capacity for command, physical and mental vigor, infinite patience in dealing with these fanatical semi-savages, wise discretion, a zealous desire to accomplish the work set for him and knowledge of the Moro character.
>
> It was easy to find field officers possessing some of the characteristics and qualifications above mentioned, but there was no available officer of rank known to me in the 7th Separate Brigade whose endowments embraced all the requisites.
>
> Captain Pershing was the senior in his grade in the 15th Cavalry. He had made two visits to the Lake from his station at Iligan and had shown great tact and good judgment in dealing with the Malanaos. I ordered him to report to me at Vicars and when General Baldwin left, and as senior Captain present he succeeded to command and has been continued in it since by General Sumner.[13]

Several knotty questions were left for me to solve. One day in June [21] a party of Moros had attacked two soldiers on the trail to Malabang, wounding both and securing their rifles. In this instance we found out at once that the Moros were from Binidayan and were led by a *datto* named Tangul. The sultan was a powerful chieftain who had declared himself friendly. He acknowledged that the Moros who committed this offense were from his *rancheria* but pleaded that he was powerless to control them. I told him it was our policy to hold the sultans and *dattos* responsible for the acts of their people and that he must deliver to me the leader of these renegades. He failed to comply with this demand for some time, and I finally arrested him and took him to camp a prisoner [on 19 July 1902]. The two stolen rifles were delivered next day and in a few days several of his followers brought in the body of one of Tangul's party, reporting that it was Tangul himself. But this Moro whom they thought dead regained consciousness long enough to tell the true story. He said he was only one of the attacking party. In resisting arrest by his own people he had been mortally wounded and the Moros had then conceived the idea of palming him off on us as Tangul. I still insisted that the leader be brought in and offered to send troops to help take him if they would locate him.

Before this could be done, however, [on 14 August] the sultan, greatly humiliated by his arrest, went *juramentado,* struck the sergeant of the guard with a piece of bamboo taken from his bunk, grabbed the rifle of the sentry over him and was about to use it when the sergeant shot him with his revolver. Although it was evident that the sultan was mortally wounded, every effort was made by the surgeons to save his life, but without success. Before dying he confessed that he had gone *juramentado* and did not hold anyone to blame. His death was unfortunate and was much to be regretted, and I wanted to mollify the sorrow and the resentment of his people by showing their sultan some mark of respect. I therefore had an artillery salute fired in his honor as his followers bore the remains away from camp. They regarded this as a special distinction, and it greatly softened the grief of his people. But we never did get Tangul.[14]

Increasing Attacks by Hostile Moros

During the summer months there were several acts of violence committed along the trails, usually in attempts to capture arms, as only by the possession of such arms could they hope to fight us on equal terms. On several occasions individuals actually succeeded in crawling past the sentries in the darkness and stealing rifles from men in their tents asleep. They usually took advantage of rainy nights. One night a sentry saw in a flash of lightning a figure approaching the line of headquarters tents in a crouching position, and in the next flash he fired. The following morning the Moro was found dead with his heavy *kris* strapped to his wrist. In stealth of movement these warriors were more crafty than even

American Indians. The utmost vigilance was necessary at night and sentries dared not expose themselves but had to remain hidden as much as possible. Our field telegraph lines were constantly interfered with and the wire often for a distance of a mile carried away.

On the night of August 11 an outpost of four men [at the quartermaster corral] was surprised by a band from Bacolod, two men being killed [Sergeant Foley and Private Cary] and two [Private Christiansen and one other] wounded.[15] Thereafter the camp was fired into almost nightly. Occasionally one of our men in the interior of camp was hit, but none was killed. Although they attempted more than once to rush the camp, these attackers never succeeded in getting by our outposts without being discovered, when they promptly got a volley from one of the detachments always in readiness on the edge of camp for the purpose. . . . These night attacks were very disconcerting, but by increasing the number of outposts we succeeded frequently in surprising the attacking Moros and killing some of them in return.

The outposts, usually consisting of a noncommissioned officer and three men, had to be relocated each night to prevent their being spotted. In order that they might be able to fire upon any one approaching from any quarter but that of the camp, I directed that the officer or patrol making the rounds at night should go directly from camp to the outpost and back. One night the officer on his rounds attempted to make a shortcut, going straight from one post to the next. The corporal of this outpost together with the sentry on watch fired simultaneously at the officer's silhouette on the sky line, one bullet going through his sleeve. The following morning, after hearing the officer's report, I sent for the corporal. He was a short, stockily-built soldier, and was pale with anxiety over what might happen to him. "You know what you did last night, Corporal?" I asked formally. "Yes, sir; I have heard, sir," was his reply. "Well, I must compliment you on the way you carried out your orders," I said. "If the Lieutenant had been killed it would have been his own fault." News of the incident and my comment spread throughout the command and officers were thereafter more careful.

There were several bands of these raiders, the most troublesome being under the leadership of Sultan Uali, from Butig and vicinity; others were from Maciu and Bacolod. Frequently they came to the vicinity of camp and under protection of the woods nearby proceeded to make the night hideous by beating drums, firing in our direction, and yelling until dislodged by a few searching volleys of infantry fire. I had demanded that the sultans and *dattos* of those *rancherias* should restrain

Datto Pandi-in of Dansalan, Lanao, Mindanao, in 1945. On 2 September 1902, during the height of his troubles with various sultans around Lake Lanao, Pershing wrote letters of support and recognition for *dattos* who were friendly to the United States. The letters allowed the *dattos* to obtain supplies and support from U.S. Army posts. When the United States retook the Lanao area of Mindanao from the Japanese in the summer of 1945, *Datto* Pandi-in used his letter from Pershing to gain U.S. Army assistance for his people. Ironically, this photograph and one of the letters were forwarded to Pershing by Major General Franklin C. Sibert, commanding general of X Corps. Pershing had relieved Sibert's father, Brigadier General William L. Sibert, as commander of the 1st Division in France and returned him to the United States in 1918. (Library of Congress, Prints and Publications Division, Pershing Collection, Lot 8850)

the warlike element among them, but the replies received were defiant and our conciliatory efforts were treated with scorn. We continued to hope in vain that wiser counsels would prevail and that the example of friendlier groups might have some influence. The worst of it was that our failure to go out and punish the responsible chiefs was being mis-construed by friendly Moros, who could not understand why we took no action. But they were told that the time would come when those who had attacked us and annoyed us would have to pay the penalty. We were, how-ever, actually beginning to lose prestige, and further delay would in my opinion undo much of what had been accomplished. It was now Septem-ber and in the four months since May we had exhausted every possible means to win over the recalcitrants, and it was evident that they must be taught a summary lesson.

I put the whole situation before General Sumner, requesting author-ity to punish the guilty chiefs and their followers. He telegraphed the facts to General Chaffee, who had not yet relinquished command of the Division, and shortly after [on 5 September 1902] was directed to send out troops for the purpose. One of the columns sent was composed of my command.

12

Military Operations against the Lake Lanao Moros and the Routine of Governing

September–December 1902

The Continuing Problem with the Lake Lanao Moros

The task assigned to the army of suppressing insurrection and lawlessness had been accomplished throughout the archipelago except in this remote corner.[1] This was the only section left where any group of people still refused to recognize American sovereignty. Benevolent assimilation insofar as these groups were concerned had not succeeded. They had never submitted to the Spanish yoke and had rejected all overtures to accept American rule. No one could have been more considerate in dealing with them than my command had been. We had come with the olive branch and had been met with *kris* and *kampilan*, and it had been evident for some time that the use of force was inevitable. Every possible effort had been made to avoid this last resort, but we could no longer brook contempt for law and order. There was no doubt of our military superiority. Still, even after all the provocation they had given in preceding months, we wished to apply force with as little harshness as possible. The capture of their *cottas*, which they thought impregnable, would, in my opinion, require only patience in attack and could be accomplished with relatively small losses. The real danger lay in their cunning and treachery.

Hitherto we had refrained from any attempt to study or map the country about the lake, as we wished to avoid armed clashes that might interfere with peaceful negotiations. Our knowledge of the district had been limited to the little we had been able to gather from friendly Moros, and the necessarily inaccurate information they could give us was of small value. There was nowhere a road in the Moro country along which even a cart could pass, and the trails were narrow and in many places swampy and impassable for our animals. No material improvement could be accomplished without an acquaintance with the people and the region in which they lived. But the first requisite to progress of any sort was the suppression of lawlessness and the establishment of order. Our task, therefore, ran parallel to that of the early pioneer fighting his way into an unknown country himself, repeating the history of colonial advancement through the wilderness against [hostile natives].

General Sumner came to Vicars [on 10 September] to be in closer touch with operations and directed that several additional companies of infantry be moved up from Malabang for temporary service. He and I discussed the plan I had recommended, which was that we should move immediately and punish the sultans of Butig, Bayabao, and Maciu, whose *rancherias* were in the region adjacent to the southeastern shore of the lake, and then suspend operations to await the effect. We were not making war for war's sake, but to teach the lawless that outlawry did not pay.

Expedition to Lake Butig, Gauan, Bayabao, and Maciu, 18–22 September 1902

My command consisted of four companies of the Twenty-seventh Infantry, one troop Fifteenth Cavalry, and one battery of mountain artillery, with the necessary Medical contingent, an engineer officer, the usual staff, and a pack train of sixty mules to carry supplies.[2] Several friendly *dattos* wanted to accompany us with some of their fighting men to help clean out the hostile element, which, they said, was putting all Moros under more or less suspicion. It was inexpedient, however, for obvious reasons, to grant this request, although a number were taken along for their influence and for use as guides and messengers.

We left Vicars on September 18, very early, and at about daybreak reached Pantauan, where I established a temporary base. Leaving the mortar, the camp equipage, and the men's packs at Pantauan under guard, I proceeded with the rest of the column toward Gauan on Lake Butig—a small laguna southeast of Lake Lanao. Upon nearing this place we took the trail which followed a narrow wooded ridge and presently we saw several Moros armed with rifles retiring before us. Approaching the end of the ridge, a short distance away two *cottas* came in sight. One lay directly in our front blocking the trail and the other beyond Lake Butig at a distance of about three or four hundred yards. Lieutenant F. B. [Frank B.] Hawkins's Company C and Lieutenant C. G. [Charles G.] Bickham's Company F were promptly deployed and the battery placed in position. The artillery fire appeared greatly to surprise the Moros occupying the two *cottas,* and they soon abandoned both positions. Meanwhile, we received a fusillade from another *cotta* hidden by clumps of bamboo on a ridge to the left. Companies C and F were sent across the intervening swamp, the men wading in water up to their waists, and soon captured the *cotta.* We had run into a nest of *cottas,* and our position might have been difficult had the Moros been armed with modern weapons. A closer approach to Butig was blocked, as the swamp in which the trail apparently ended was then impassable, and with no time for repairs or to search for another route, we returned to Pantauan. A few days later [24–26 September] Butig was taken without opposition by a battalion composed of companies of the Tenth and Eleventh Infantry Regiments under Captain E. A. [Eli A.] Helmick.

The second day our objective was Bayabao, which lay to the northeast. Following a more northerly trail, the first opposition was offered by a band of about forty Moros, which was soon dispersed by Captain G. W. [George W.] Kirkpatrick's Troop L. Farther on, the *cotta* of the sultan fell into our hands. From their point of view it was a strong one, but it was not seriously defended. Not a white flag nor an American flag had been displayed so far, only red flags of war.

On our way back to Pantauan that evening appeared the first white flag we had seen. A local sultan, a man of much influence, came to meet us under its protection, and confessing that some of his men had participated in raids against us, said he would be glad to have them punished. But, he said, they had fled, of which he made certain no doubt before he reported the fact.

Giving up the base at Pantauan, I started on the third day for Maciu with the entire command. Near Sauir, on the southern shore of an inlet of Lake Lanao separating that *rancheria* from Maciu, we were fired on from several directions by considerable numbers of Moros in groups here and there, but at long range. Several large *vintas* filled with them were hurriedly crossing the arm of the lake carrying red flags, which indicated that they were probably going to reinforce others on our side of the inlet. A few shells from Captain W. S. [William S.] McNair's battery fired at eighteen hundred yards, one of which made a direct hit on one of the *vintas* carrying about twenty Moros, promptly stopped further attempts to cross. I sent my adjutant, Lieutenant C. S. [Claude S.] Fries, with Bickham and his Company F to develop the situation on the ridge to the east toward which these Moros seemed to be moving and from which a steady fusillade was coming. The company ran into a force strongly posted in a *cotta*, as suspected, and in business-like fashion after a brisk fight cleaned it out. In the meantime Lieutenant W. B. [William B.] Gracie's Company M, which had been sent toward Sauir, found that *cotta* abandoned, with cook fires still burning. Camp was at once established at this point and attention was turned to the problem of getting across or around the arm of the lake.

A brief reconnaissance disclosed an old trail, which, due to its swampy condition, was reported impassable without several days' labor. I then directed that bamboo rafts be tried and two were hastily constructed. Lieutenant [Kelton L.] Pepper and several men succeeded in reaching the Maciu shore, but only by wading the last three to four hundred yards, as the rafts could not be forced any closer because of the exceedingly heavy growth of tall grass and water lilies along the shore. The officers and men working with the rafts were in mud and water almost up to their necks, being all the while under fire from Moros, although our sharpshooters kept them at such a distance that we had no casualties. As this method of crossing proved to be impracticable, it was evident that we could reach Maciu only by land, either by the old trail, which we had partially explored, or by one altogether new, and that considerable time and full preparation for the necessary pioneer work would be required. I therefore abandoned further effort for the moment and returned to Camp Vicars [on 22 September], a distance of only a few miles, to make such preparation.

The officers and men of the command had been held on the leash for months under great provocation. There had been a number of casualties and still they had not been allowed to retaliate until now. Naturally, they were eager to even up old scores. A keener and more alert body of men could hardly be imagined. The thought of giving up caused much chagrin until I had the officers explain that we would resume the campaign a few days later.

During these three days eight *cottas* were captured and, with their contents, destroyed. From friendly sources it was learned that some thirty Moros were killed or wounded, with no casualties in our command, thus showing how greatly the Moros were outclassed. But each hostile group had to be taught this lesson. There had been little organized opposition to us, the greatest obstacle being the difficult terrain. It was not my intention to make direct assaults against any strongly held position if it could be avoided, and so far it had not been necessary. With our superior arms we could hold or force almost any number of Moros beyond the range of their weapons. There had been no thrilling hand-to-hand action so far, as the Moros had not pushed their resistance to that extent. Our sudden withdrawal no doubt led the Maciu Moros to believe they were protected by nature's defenses and that we would be unable to reach them. The fact that the Spaniards after several attempts had failed to do so strengthened this view.

Return to Maciu, 28 September–2 October 1902

When he understood what we had been up against, General Sumner was somewhat disappointed but entirely agreed with my notion and approved my plan to return at once to complete the task.[3] Fully equipped with axes for felling timber and with tools and implements for constructing boats or opening up trails, the command was ready for any emergency. With practically the same infantry and artillery organizations, slightly reduced, and with an additional troop of the Fifteenth Cavalry, and a detachment of Company F, Second Battalion of Engineers (First Lt. Earl I. Brown), and seventy-five pack mules, I left Vicars again on September 28, accompanied by a few friendly Moros. On the Maciu side of the inlet we found a newly-erected *cotta* covering the crossing, with the red flag flying above the parapet and Moros shouting defiance as we hove in sight. But we wasted no time on another attempt at crossing the arm of the lake.

Instead, a party of engineers under Captain J. J. Morrow was sent at once farther to investigate the trail. After a day of reconnaissance he estimated that two hundred men acting as pioneers could make the trail passable within two days. The work was started promptly at daybreak the next morning. In the afternoon while out on the trail Morrow reported that Lieutenant Pepper, in command of the detachment guarding the pioneers, had been sent in advance to drive off a party of Moros, evidently lurking about waiting for an opportunity to attack any isolated group. We heard some firing shortly after that, and taking Gracie with twenty men I went forward to inspect the trail myself. The combined detachments were fired on as they debouched from the timber, but the Moros were driven off with the loss of ten or twelve of their number.

Finding the work well along, we took the trail next day, continuing repairs on the worst places as we proceeded. There were still difficult spots where mules laden with supplies mired down and had to be lifted out or unpacked and their loads carried by the men. It was noon before we reached the scene of the skirmish the day before. In the meantime the advance guard under Gracie had encountered two *cottas* held by the fighting men of Sultan Ganduali. As we came up, two companies were deployed with McNair's mountain guns between them at a range under five hundred yards. Seeing several of their number killed or wounded as they exposed themselves, the rest of the defenders fled and disappeared in the tall *cogon* grass.

We did not pursue, but I sent a friendly Moro as courier with a letter from General Sumner to the two leaders, Ganduali and the sultan of Tauagan, asking them to treat with me. They read the letter but returned it, telling the courier to say that they would be waiting for us with two hundred warriors the following day at the *cotta* of the sultan of Maciu. The Moros were like Indians and other disunited peoples. Each group was vain of its own fighting ability and boastful of its bravery. When we defeated one *datto,* the others would decry the courage of his followers and assert that "if the Americans dare to come to our *rancheria* they will find we are different." Thus we were not fighting a large and united body of Moros as a political entity, but rather detached and independent hostile groups, and generally speaking each of them in turn had to learn its lesson.

We were on the march again the following morning over unknown terrain, with our advance scouts keenly on the lookout for a possible surprise, but there was no resistance serious enough to delay us until we reached a group of five *cottas* near the lake. Here in the principal one war flags were planted on the parapet, war drums were resounding, and the warriors were yelling to us to come on. Maciu Moros had made their stand, but of the two hundred said to be determined to fight to the death we estimated that probably half had by this time lost their nerve and run away. The usual dispositions were made with McNair's battery in front of the *cotta* at about four hundred yards, while [Lieutenant Sylvester Chouteau] Loring's Company G and Bickham's Company F, their right and left flanks respectively resting on the battery, extended the line toward the shore of the lake on each side of the *cotta* at such an angle that they would not be likely to fire into one another. The remaining troops were in reserve.

Under the fire of our sharpshooters and the battery, the defenders'

fire soon diminished in volume and our lines were gradually moved
closer. Through the din of gunfire, the yelling, and the beating of *agungs*
[gongs] by the defenders, the chanting of the *panditas* (priests) could be
heard from within the *cotta*. We set fire to the buildings in the deserted
cottas nearby, and the smoke and flames of the burning *nipa* rising high
gave a satanic setting to the scene. In the afternoon Lieutenant Loring
volunteered to make an attempt to fire the main *cotta* and if possible
locate the entrance. With great coolness and daring, he and ten men of
his company made their way to the walls with only one man wounded,
but found it impracticable to scale them without excessive loss.

As darkness came on, the lines were drawn in slightly and fires were
kept burning to reveal any attempts at a surprise attack on our lines or an
escape through the *cogon* grass on the side toward the lake. Until about
three o'clock in the morning the noise from the *cotta* continued, with
only sporadic firing. Then a few Moros in two daring rushes attempted
to break through the lines, and they came so suddenly some of them succeeded while others were stopped. The remaining effectives no doubt
took that moment to get away to the rear of the *cotta*, where the grass
was six or eight feet high. At daybreak our men entered the *cotta* without
resistance, as only a few dead and some wounded remained.

We found a few rifles, some knives of various sorts and sizes, and
two *lantacas*—old brass and bronze cannon probably of Chinese manufacture—also a great variety of household effects and large supplies of rice
and provisions, showing that serious preparations had been made for a
siege. But they could not have held out long, for, like most of the *cottas*, this one had no wells or springs and our force could have prevented
their fetching water from the lake. Inside the walls were three houses,
one a large frame building, evidently the residence of the sultan, the
others of *nipa*. The buildings were literally shot to pieces and the little
more than wreckage was put to the torch.

As I with other officers was examining the ground about the *cotta*, a
powerful, middle-aged Moro suddenly leaped out of hiding and slashed
one of our soldiers with a *kampilan*. He then rushed toward the line
where we were standing, a distance of thirty or forty yards, and despite
the fact that seven bullets were fired through or into his body before he
had gone more than a few steps he did not drop until almost upon us.
The man proved to be the sultan of Maciu himself, the last of a long line
who had always fought Christians. He had held out against us, I think,
purely as a matter of principle, and he vindicated his courage in his
death. As the troops in skirmish line continued the search, two or three

other Moros were flushed while waiting, *kris* in hand, for an opportunity to kill but were themselves killed before it came.

From careful examination of the *cotta* and the surroundings it was evident that a limited number of those who had stood out against us the day before escaped by stealth in the darkness, and it seemed probable also that others got away through some hidden passage. Fortunately, though somewhat surprising, we had only two men wounded. Only the Maciu Moros were disturbed on this expedition, but they and others banded with them were given a lesson they did not soon forget. As we had fulfilled our immediate mission, the command on October 2 returned to Camp Vicars.

As expected, one effect of the punishment we had given these troublesome Moros was that there were fewer attacks on Camp Vicars and along the trail. They had been surprised that our troops were able to overcome the most difficult kind of country, and they had paused to think it over. There were several extremely hostile chiefs, particularly Ahmai-Benaning of Gata and Ampuan-Agus of Taraca, who had led their bands of raiders against us, but they were still farther away, and it was decided to let them alone for awhile in the hope that given time to consider they might come to terms.

Relations with Friendly Moros: A Trip across Lake Lanao and Visits to Iligan and Marahui

Meanwhile, I conceived the notion that a visit to my old friends to the north might have a beneficial effect and undertook a trip across the lake by *vinta* to Madaya, a distance of fourteen miles. [Pershing left Camp Vicars on 26 November 1902.][4] Manibilang loaned me an old ten-oared barge abandoned by the Spaniards, capable of carrying twenty-five men, and other *dattos* rigged up four *vintas* that together would hold about thirty. Lieutenant A. W. [Arthur W.] Brown, Twenty-seventh Infantry, later to be Judge Advocate General of the Army, and Major L. C. [Lawrence C.] Carr, Surgeon, with a small command of fifty-three men selected for their soldierly qualities and good marksmanship, and two *dattos* and two sultans, each with a few followers, constituted this unique party. The extemporized fleet of galleys made a somewhat imposing array, though our soldiers at the oars showed only about the same amount of skill that the average sailor displays on horseback. The men took turns at rowing, but the "fleet" made only fair progress, being limited in speed to that of the slowest boat. Not all these *vintas* were seawor-

During Pershing's trip along northern Lake Lanao (26 November–2 December 1902) he stopped at Marahui on market day, 29 November 1902, to discuss American policies with a gathering of Moro *dattos* and sultans. Pershing is pictured in the foreground, wearing his campaign hat. (Library of Congress, Prints and Publications Division, Pershing Collection, Lot 8850)

thy, and when a stiff breeze arose on the lake the waves broke over their sides, and only the most persistent bailing could keep some of the shells afloat.

We were not molested by hostile Moros, but the friendlies came down to the shore in crowds at various *rancherias* and greeted us with shouts of welcome as we passed. At several of the larger places I had a salute of three volleys fired by a few men and in each case the compliment was returned by the firing of the largest *lantaca*—the Moros thus burning some of the powder that might otherwise have been used against us. Here and there American flags were shown and a variety of *agungs* filled the air with music by no means unpleasant to hear at a distance. At Madaya a royal welcome awaited us from my old friends. *Vintas* with gaily colored sails and streamers came out to escort us to the landing, where the chiefs and their people joined in the throng to meet us.

After a night's rest in camp we crossed the Agus River to Marahui.

Pershing meeting with the Rajamunda of Marahui, 30 November 1902. From left to right: Fernandez, Pershing's interpreter; an unidentified newspaperman; son of the Rajamunda of Marahui; the Rajamunda of Marahui; Captain Pershing; the sultan's slave, holding an umbrella over the Rajamunda, a sign of his rank; Captain James A. Ryan, Pershing's successor as district officer at Iligan; and Trumpeter Charles A. Pryor. The meeting took place during Pershing's trip along northern Lake Lanao (26 November–2 December 1902). (Library of Congress, Prints and Publications Division, Pershing Collection, Lot 8850. LC-USZ62-125493)

The large crowd attending market that day made the occasion propitious for a renewal of friendly assurances. Standing in the marketplace I spoke briefly, emphasizing the pleasure it gave me to be among them again and pointing out that the visit was made expressly to show that we did not forget our friends. They responded at once to this sentiment and an old crony of mine, the Rajamunda of Marahui, in a few polite phrases, greeted us warmly, saying that his house was mine as long as I cared to remain. In the course of his talk he said he was glad we intended to build a road from Iligan to the lake to replace the one originally built by the Spaniards which since '98 had been entirely destroyed by the excessive rainfall of the region, and he inquired whether a military post would be established at Marahui. This showed a definitely friendly attitude as well as an abiding interest in the welfare of his own people. Only a year before he had objected to American forces coming inland to the lake. Manibilang had asked me personally, and the Rajamunda repeated the request, to explain to my successor at Iligan that the disposition of the Moros on the north side of the lake towards us was still friendly. I was certain this was well known at Iligan but promised to comply with his request while at the coast with my detachment. I did say to the Colonel in command what was undoubtedly true, that the attitude of the Moros toward him was friendly but that their nature made them somewhat apprehensive. There was really little reason for Manibilang's fears, as Moro affairs were being ably handled by Captain J. A. [James A.] Ryan, Fifteenth Cavalry, who was in full sympathy with the people.

When, after a visit of two days, I came to assemble the detachment for the return trip it was found that the men had been somewhat too highly entertained by their comrades. This was easy to understand, as they had been on good behavior for several months, Camp Vicars being entirely "dry." With the combined efforts of Lieutenant Brown, assisted by Major Carr, our tireless Volunteer surgeon, then a man of sixty [Carr was actually only forty-seven at this time], and the more reliable noncommissioned officers, the detachment was finally rounded up, but the officers at Iligan who witnessed the behavior of my selected company seemed to think it a very good joke on me. Captain Ryan and his troop accompanied us partway on the twenty-mile hike back to Marahui, after which my men were again as able-bodied seamen as they had ever been, and we returned to Camp Vicars by *vinta* without mishap, and their brief spree was forgotten.

Visits of Lieutenant General Nelson A. Miles and Gifford Pinchot

In November I had a surprise that gave me much pleasure. It was the visit of General Miles, who was making a tour of the Philippines on the eve of his retirement as Commanding General of the Army. He was accompanied by Generals [Sumner], Baldwin and Jesse Lee, old friends of his of frontier days. The party was escorted from Malabang by one of my troops—a task which the cavalry disliked, as the rough and hilly road was a hard one for cavalry horses. I was glad to be the host of the Com-

Pershing commanded Camp Vicars, Lake Lanao, Mindanao, from June 1902 through May 1903. The headquarters is in the white conical tents in the background, and a battalion of the 27th Infantry occupied the pup tents in the foreground. (Library of Congress, Prints and Publications Division, Pershing Collection, Lot 8850. LC-USZ62-51584)

manding General again and welcomed him at this outlying station with the best the camp could offer. He reviewed the troops and made them a brief speech expressing his satisfaction at their appearance, referring to the command as being then on the new frontier and to the captain of cavalry in charge as one whom he had favorably known nearly twenty years before.[5]

A short time later we had a visit from a young forester by the name of Gifford Pinchot, who came with a letter of introduction from President Roosevelt. He brought with him an army man, Major George P. Ahern, another forester, and both were enthusiastic over the richness of the Philippine forests in rare hardwoods. As they were about to leave, Pinchot spied in the corner of my tent a Moro replica in carabao hide of a medieval Spanish armor of the days of the conquest. The Moros had several specimens of old Spanish armor which their ancestors had taken from the early invaders. The Moro copy was thick, heavy, and stiff enough to stand alone. Pinchot took a fancy to it, so I gave it to him, and I shall never forget the sight of this tall figure of a man, sitting high on a cavalry horse, starting back twenty miles to Malabang with this huge carabao hide armor tied to the pommel of his saddle. In later years I mentioned this incident to the then Governor Pinchot of Pennsylvania, and he told me he still had the armor.

Pests, Diseases, and Natural Disasters

During that year a plague of locusts appeared in the Lanao region and destroyed everything in their path until checked. The Moros stopped them by digging trenches or furrows ahead of the locusts to catch them before they began to migrate by flying. When the trenches were thick with them, they were burned with dry leaves or straw. The Moros turned out by whole villages to fight this plague and got off with small damage. But another plague that caused much loss was rinderpest[6] among the cattle and carabao. The only practical way then known to prevent its spread was to establish absolute isolation of infected areas, and that was very difficult because of lack of organization among the people. It had to be left to the Moros themselves after the methods had been explained to them, as we could not at the time go among them with impunity. There was yet another pest, and that was surra[7] among the horses and mules. A great many government animals at Camp Vicars and throughout the islands became infected, causing a large percentage of loss, as there was then no known remedy for the disease. We could only try to keep it from spreading by prompt isolation. Instructions on the subject were sent to all *rancherias,* as we had done in the case of rinderpest, and within a reasonable time it, too, disappeared.

The lake country being of volcanic origin, it was frequently subject to earthquakes. On August 21, 1902, we had the severest succession of shocks within the memory of the oldest inhabitant. It was so violent that all the log and frame structures in the camp, including the commissary storehouse and the bamboo and grass stables, were shaken down. Many of the timber residences of the Moros of the heavier type on the south side of the lake collapsed, and twelve people were killed at one *rancheria.* The first shock seemed to last several minutes. I was sitting at my field desk just at dusk when it came and was suddenly thrown over backwards. Getting up I rushed for the open, and as I went through the door of the tent the pole swung over like a pendulum and hit me a stiff blow on the side of the head. Outside a soldier was praying in a loud voice, saying, "Steady Lord, steady please, Lord," and everybody felt like making the same appeal. All the dogs in camp howled at the same time; horses neighed and several were thrown off their feet, as were many men. The ground moved in waves like an ocean ground swell rolling onto a beach and great gaps opened and closed. Meeting Lieutenant J. H. [John H.] Allen, Medical Corps, he and I stood together and held each other's shoulder to keep on our feet. As seems to be generally the case with earthquakes, lesser shocks followed for a day or so. On the whole it was a terrifying experience for us all.

The Philippine Islands were frequently in the path of typhoons, which now and then visited our part of Mindanao, and once in the early days leveled the entire camp to the ground. On one occasion during my first year at Zamboanga I was sent to Manila on a special mission for General Kobbé and on the return trip on our Spanish dispatch boat used for interisland communication we ran into a typhoon. To lighten the craft the captain ordered the cargo of supplies jettisoned, and all on board, three or four other officers besides myself and several soldiers, joined in to help the crew. Then, after a time of severe pitching and rolling, the engineer reported water in the engine room. We equipped ourselves with buckets and worked in shifts for several hours to prevent the seas that broke on deck from pouring down the engine room hatch. Finally the engineer came on deck, saying the engine room was being flooded and nothing more could be done. He refused to return to his post when ordered by the captain and had to be marched back at the point of the captain's revolver. It was impossible, of course, to sleep or to prepare food during this time, but we had soda crackers in plenty and also some whiskey to brace us against the chill weather. To a landsman at least it did not seem that the little vessel could long survive the terrific buffeting. On the morning of the second day we found ourselves only a few hundred yards away from a coral reef over which the seas were breaking with irresistible force and toward which we were slowly being driven. Our chances looked very slender indeed and all hands stood ready on the upper deck, each with a bamboo deck chair, prepared to go overboard and make for the quieter water toward shore. But almost miraculously the wind began to abate and, imperceptibly at first, we began to pull away. Finally, by steaming dead into the seas, we veered past the threatening reef. I have been in several typhoons since but not in so small a ship and never so close to disaster.

In December cholera, which had started in Manila, reached the lake, and the most rigorous precautions were at once taken to protect the command, while everything possible was done to help the natives combat this dread scourge of the Far East. The market at the camp was closed for a time and a dead-line established over which no Moro was per-

This photograph of Captain Pershing, 15th Cavalry, was probably taken sometime in 1903, when he commanded Camp Vicars on Lake Lanao. (Library of Congress, Prints and Publications Division, Pershing Collection. LC-USZ62-131533)

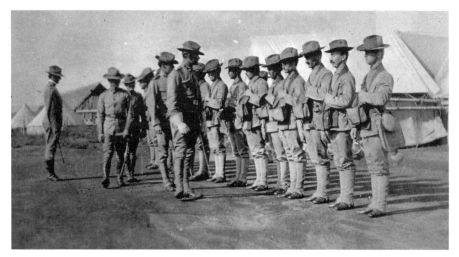

Pershing inspecting the Hospital Corps detachment at Camp Vicars (no date). (Library of Congress, Prints and Publications Division, Pershing Collection, Lot 8850. LC-USZ62-51578)

mitted to pass. I had letters of instruction prepared in the native language saying it was imperative to boil all water for drinking purposes and that only cooked food should be eaten and further warning the people against visiting infected regions. These bulletins were sent to all the principal *rancherias,* and insofar as possible medicines were furnished from our limited stores. Despite our efforts, however, the cholera spread, as the lake, from which many of the *rancherias* obtained drinking water, soon became contaminated in places and the people were not prompt in applying the rules we prescribed. They often brought their sick children to the camp limits to ask our doctors for help, some coming even from the still hostile groups. We responded as best we could to their heart-rending appeals, but it was seldom that our small medical staff could cure an advanced case of the disease. It was estimated that at least a thousand Moros died in the two or three months the epidemic was at its height, and we lost several soldiers.

During these trying months my conferences with the Moros continued, a meeting place having been fixed on a small hill near the camp. Almost daily some of them came with grievances for me to settle or just to have a talk. By this time I had picked up considerable of the Malay dialect and in these informal conferences was often able to meet alone without an interpreter.

13

Finishing the Campaign against the Lake Lanao Moros

January–May 1903

Continuing to Work with the Moros

Shortly after the New Year, 1903, the cholera having abated considerably, our self-imposed restrictions on visits were lifted and friendly marches to nearby *rancherias* were resumed.[1] Rather extended confidential negotiations had been carried on with some of the Moros, including those from Gata, a large *rancheria* of no small importance. I had been told by a representative from the sultan that they would be glad to have me visit them and after considerable discussion a date was fixed. At the appointed time, guided by a Gata Moro, I marched out with two or three companies of infantry and a mountain gun [an artillery battery, a troop of cavalry, and three companies of infantry], expecting a friendly reception. But, much to my surprise and chagrin, on coming in sight of the principal *cotta* we found the war flags flying and the warriors lining the parapets waving *kampilans*, rifles, and spears and yelling defiance. Thinking there was some mistake, I sent a messenger with a friendly message, but he returned with one very hostile. I was completely nonplused. It was plain that every man in the column wanted to accept the challenge and temptation to do so was very great. But in view of the serious negotiations that had taken place, I concluded that these Moros must be temporarily under the spell of a few hotheads. I, therefore, with considerable reluctance, made an about-face and marched the command back to Vicars without firing a shot.[2]

Rear Admiral Robley D. Evans (center), then Commander-in-Chief, Asiatic Station, toured the Philippines in 1902–1903. He spent several weeks in February 1903 visiting Brigadier General Samuel S. Sumner (right), commanding general, Department of Mindanao and Jolo, and various of his military posts. He and Sumner visited Pershing (left) at Camp Vicars, where he received a traditional Moro welcome—sniping through his tent. In 1910, he recalled his visit to Pershing and Camp Vicars in his *An Admiral's Log* (p. 232): "Captain Pershing, of the Cavalry, was in command of Fort Vickars [*sic*], and I can't imagine a man better fitted for the post. Young, active, and as tough as leather, he spoke the Moro tongue, and impressed all who saw him most favorably. He certainly won the stars that afterwards came to him." (Library of Congress, Prints and Publications Division, Bain News Service Collection)

In February, thinking to influence the sultan of Bacolod, I visited the sultan of Ganassi, a powerful and friendly Moro on the southwest shore of the lake, and camped near Madumba. Attempts to get into communication with the sultan of Bacolod, the construction of whose *cotta* Colonel Baldwin and I had watched from a distance, were in vain. He refused even to receive my Moro messengers and remained an opponent of American occupation.

With another important group of hostiles, however, the experience was quite different, culminating in the most unique ceremony in which I had ever participated. The Bayan Moros, who lived on the south shore below Camp Vicars, had harbored resentment towards us since their defeat the previous May by Colonel Baldwin at Pandapatan. Though there was a sultan of Bayan, their actual leader was an old *pandita* by the name of Sajiduciaman, a Muhammadan priest regarded with great reverence by the Moros. I succeeded twice through mutual friends among the Moros, mainly Ahmai-Manibilang, in persuading this venerable holy man to come to Camp Vicars and confer with me. The visits were formal, and we seriously discussed the future of the Moros. He expressed his desire to be on friendly terms with us but only on condition that we remain away from his *rancheria*. In other words, he would agree that his people would not molest us but insisted that we in turn should not send our soldiers among them. At the second conference I told him that we could not agree to any such conditions and that if my soldiers could not go to his *rancheria* I could no longer regard him as my friend. The result was that later he invited us to visit him, and it was arranged that I should take an escort of troops.

The appointed day arrived. As we descended to the main Bayan fortification, a *cotta* built high on a magnificent bluff nearer to and overlooking the lake, an unusual retinue of several hundred Moros and their slaves from surrounding *rancherias,* led by sultans and *dattos,* joined us, many of them with arms and all dressed as for some special occasion. Sajiduciaman came out from among his people to receive us, met me between the lines, and escorted us inside the fortress, where he resided in considerable state. The entrance through the outer works was by a narrow, winding causeway flanked on both sides with sharpened bamboo stakes. To reach the fort proper we had to climb a bamboo ladder standing against a rock that rose straight into the air. This *cotta,* a very strong one, was enclosed by graceful bamboo trees and the walls were built of stone with steps on their inner faces. Shelters of bamboo, earth, and corrugated iron covered the numerous old-style cannon and *lantacas*. As a medieval fortification the *cotta* was well designed and the construction unusual.

After showing me about the interior with great dignity, the patriarch brought me back to the gathering of Moros and American troops outside. I then had the troops stand at attention, present arms, and sound bugles as we raised the American flag. The artillery, using loaded shells, fired a salute of five guns, aiming out over the lake. Very few of these people had ever before seen modern artillery in action, and they looked on with awe and wonder at the firing and the effect of the distant explosion over the water. When this mark of respect—and incidentally power—was concluded, a conference was held near the shore, the people standing around in a circle, the chiefs and I in the center, squatting on our heels, the lines of American troops in the background. A treasured copy of the sacred Koran (of which there were not many among the Moros) was brought forth with solemnity and placed on a mat of native fiber in the center, the improvised lectern being presided over by an aged Muhammadan priest in gorgeous trousers of many colors and a robe of yellow silk. Above him a slave held a large red parasol, the symbol of Moslem authority. Beautifully engraved silver boxes containing betel nut for chewing were passed around the circle. Sajiduciaman then informed me with great formality that I had been elected a *datto* with equal rights and privileges of one to the manor born. This was the surprise of the occasion, as it was, I think, an honor no other American at that time had received. Each chief in turn gave a short address, which was orally translated for us into Spanish, and I made one which was turned into Moro. The ceremony concluded by the several participating chiefs placing their hands with me on the Koran and vowing friendship and allegiance to the United States. This gathering of brilliantly arrayed warriors and people of the East with khaki-uniformed troops from the West, in a setting of nature's magnificence, a glorious tropical sky overhead, the silvery lake shimmering below, the primeval forests and towering mountains in the background, was history made visible in most picturesque fashion. There was some tendency among Americans to regard this ceremony lightly, but to the Moros it was a very serious matter.

Expedition against Bacolod and the West Coast of Lake Lanao: 5–16 April 1903

The formal entry of Sajiduciaman into the circle of American friends had an excellent effect generally about the lake, but it did not change the warlike attitude of the Bacolod Moros and several others.[3] In December I had recommended that an expedition be sent along the west shore past Bacolod as far as Marahui, to be followed by another along the east. It seemed probable that marching an exploring expedition completely around the lake would be a demonstration that would finally bring the last of our opponents to terms. As no such march had ever been made, its effect upon the natives, I thought, would be conclusive. We felt certain that on the west the Bacolod people would attempt to stop our progress and on the east those of Taraca and vicinity would also try it. In my opinion there was no longer any basis for hope that these Moros would submit to our authority without being compelled to do so. In further correspondence with Generals Sumner and Davis, I had urged that these expeditions be made before the rainy season, when the trails would become impassable.[4] Early in April the authorization for an expedition along the west coast came to General Sumner in the following telegram from General Davis [on 30 March]:

> I want the west coast of Lake Lanao explored, and wish the commanding officer at Vicars to take this up before the rain sets in. All the datos on that coast are friendly and have invited the troops to visit them, save some of the principal Moros of the Bacolod rancherias, concerning whom reports indicate unfriendliness, but it is hoped that Captain Pershing, with his well-known tact and discretion, will be able to overcome this disposition, if it really exists, and that he will receive a friendly reception; but if the Bacolod Moros attempt to interfere with the survey and examination of the west shore of the lake, any opposition which they may offer must be overcome, as it is the purpose of the Government to visit all the centers of Moro population around the lake and establish the most friendly relations with all the native inhabitants. Requests have been made for medicine by some of the Bacolod Moros. If it is found that any are in need of medical aid it should be extended, if practicable. It will be very gratifying to me if this expedition can be accomplished without fighting or bloodshed. Full value will be paid for all supplies taken. If hostile Moro cottas bar the way they should be destroyed.[5]

On receiving orders from General Sumner I sent letters to all the *rancherias* in our line of march giving notice of our plan and again asserting our peaceful intentions, but also warning all concerned against any opposition.

The command consisted of myself, First Lieutenant C. S. Fries, Adjutant; Second Lieutenant T. W. [Thomas W.] Brown, Quartermaster; First Lieutenant E. D. [Ernest D.] Peek, Engineer; First Lieutenant R. U. [Robert U.] Patterson, Assistant Surgeon, Contract Surgeon H. [Hubert] Grieger, and four enlisted men of the Hospital Corps; Chap-

Pershing (left, with his hand on his hip) finally moved against the recalcitrant sultan of Bacolod in April 1903. Pictured here on 5 April, he observes troopers of the 15th Cavalry and men of the 27th Infantry as they depart for Fort Bacolod. (Library of Congress, Prints and Publications Division, Pershing Collection, Lot 8850. LC-USZ62-28333)

lain G. D. [George D.] Rice, Twenty-seventh Infantry; and three troops of the Fifteenth Cavalry, two batteries of Field Artillery with mountain guns and field mortars, and five companies, Twenty-seventh Infantry, with two interpreters and the necessary pack mule transportation. On account of the cholera, facilities for boiling water were provided and each man carried two canteens of boiled water.[6]

Leaving Camp Vicars on April 5, we camped that evening at Madumba near a beautiful spring, friendly Moros in the vicinity supplying us with wood for our cook fires. The hostile Bacolod Moros ran true to form. They attacked an outpost that night and seriously wounded two men of Troop A. On the morning of the sixth a large party of them came out to fight but retired when fired on and defied us from their flag-bedecked stronghold, which was located near the water's edge. The going was exceedingly difficult as we made our way first through swamp then over alternate ravines and ridges, and a downpour of rain in the afternoon made matters worse. It was late in the afternoon when we reached their *cotta* and the real battle of the west coast campaign was begun. For over a year they had been working to strengthen this *cotta*, and it was probably the strongest about the lake.

Reaching the ridge above the *cotta*, one company was deployed across it and one on each flank, extending toward the lake, with the artillery in the center. Although there was an exchange of a few shots, the tropical night had fallen over the scene before the right flank reached the lake. During the long eleven hours of darkness fires were kept burning in front of the lines, as at Maciu, to enable us to detect any movement outside the *cotta*. Officers and men took their turns at sleeping. All were tired enough to sleep soundly despite the excitement and incessant din of yelling and beating of *agungs* that came from the fort. There was little firing during the night, only occasionally the crack of a rifle when one of our men on guard on either side of the *cotta* thought he saw something in front of him. We learned afterward that several Moros escaped during the night. Firing was resumed early in the morning.

About nine o'clock firing from the *cotta* ceased and a white flag was displayed. Firing from our side was stopped immediately, and after we had raised the reply a delegation came out to ask for terms. The *Panandungan* [a retired sultan who was the chief counselor to the sultan] himself, accompanied by two *dattos,* came from the rear of the *cotta* carrying only their *krises,* and I with one officer and an interpreter met than midway between the lines. There were no formalities, and we proceeded with the discussion. He offered to surrender but with the understanding that his men should keep their arms and not be held as prisoners. Naturally, nothing but unconditional surrender could be accepted, although I gave him every assurance that the lives of his people would be protected. As this leader had refused to confer with me before the battle, he evidently did not trust us now. So the delegation returned to the fort, the white flags were hauled down, and firing began again.

Already our artillery had completely destroyed the embrasures and loopholes in the *cotta* walls, making it difficult for the defenders to fire effectively, as every man who showed even his head above the parapet became a target for our sharpshooters. The final assault could have been made then, but I delayed until the following day, hoping for surrender. Early the next morning the white flag went up again and once more firing ceased and the *Panandungan* came forth to meet me. He again, however, insisted on his terms, which again I refused, and he returned to the *cotta*. They chose to fight to the end, and I then gave orders for the assault.

In preparation for crossing the moat—a ditch about thirty-five feet

The Moros at Fort Bacolod prepared a strong *cotta* (fort), protected by a ditch that Pershing reported to be thirty feet wide at the top and at least thirty-five feet deep, and initially defended by about two hundred armed Moros. The soldiers first built bamboo ladders for crossing and scaling the ditch and filled it in with timber and brush before taking the fort on 8 April 1903. Most of the defenders fled the *cotta* during the night of 7–8 April, but some sixty Moros were found dead in the fort, including the leaders of the opposition to the American presence on Lake Lanao. (Library of Congress, Prints and Publications Division, Pershing Collection, Lot 8850)

deep and thirty feet wide, thickly set at the bottom with pointed bamboo spikes—we had felled a number of trees and constructed a bamboo bridge and several ladders. Under cover of fire from our lines the men of Company M and Troop A tumbled the trees and branches into the moat at one point and over the mass placed the foot bridge. The assaulting troops, Company C, Company M, and Troop A, dashed across and onto the parapet, and the remaining effective defenders rushed to the walls or along the berm to meet the attack. For a few minutes the fighting was hand-to-hand, *kampilan* and *kris* against rifle and bayonet. Three of our men were wounded, but the others made short work of the opposition. The Moros had made a gallant stand but were no match in skill or arms for our troops.

We remained in camp at Bacolod that night and the next morning moved on Calahui, located three miles to the northeast on a high point of land jutting into the lake. It presented the usual scene of war flags flying and knives flashing in the sunlight with which we had become familiar. But, exposed to the raking fire of our artillery from its location on higher ground, the Moros were in a hopeless position. I was not sorry when they showed that discretion which is the better part of valor and under cover of the bluff decamped by *vinta,* leaving their sultan and a few followers to come in and surrender.

The leading *dattos* of Tugayan and Oato *rancherias* farther north on the lakeshore came to camp on the tenth to assure me that there would be no further opposition to our progress. The Moros of that region, except a few individuals, had at last taken the lessons seriously to heart. The day was a succession of these picturesque demonstrations of long-delayed understanding, but it did not pass without untoward incident. In the afternoon Lieutenant [Ben] Lear, who with his troop had been sent in the day before with the wounded, was returning with a pack train load of supplies from Vicars when his advance guard was surprised. Four Moros, each choosing his man, sprang from behind large boulders with *kampilans* in hand and assaulted Lieutenant [Wiley P.] Mangum and the three troopers with him, mortally wounding one of them [Corporal Claude D. Reade] before the Moros could be killed. After Mangum's revolver had misfired three times he grappled with his assailant hand-to-hand and in the tussle killed him with blows from the pistol. Lieutenant Mangum's conduct was a fine example of the personal courage required to defend one's self single-handed against such an attack.

Meeting with no further opposition, we concluded the tour of the west side of the lake on the evening of the twelfth. Camp was pitched on the Agus River, opposite Pantar, near that of Major R. L. Bullard, who was in command of a battalion of the Twenty-eighth Infantry engaged at work in building a road from Iligan to the lake which had been recently begun. After a day's delay for rest and replenishment of supplies and a visit with Bullard and his officers, we started on the return journey. As we proceeded, we were met daily by groups of peaceful Moros, following their sultans, *dattos,* priests, and other leaders, announcing their loyalty. Some were friends who came to renew acquaintance, while others had hitherto been hostile. Practically all the important groups had heeded the warnings sent out, and the return march was made without serious opposition. Our casualties had been fifteen men wounded, one of whom had died. However, on this expedition the Moros had not been the only enemy we had to contend with. In spite of careful and repeated directions of the most rigid sort, some members of the command, in the heat of the day and under the strain of the march and the high pitch of excitement, had failed to drink only boiled water but had drunk from the lake or from apparently good springs, and nine enlisted men and four packers had contracted cholera, eight of whom did not recover.

The Expedition against Taraca and Fort Pitacus along Lake Lanao's Eastern Shore and the March around the Lake: 2–13 May 1903

We now had fairly accurate, firsthand knowledge of the country and the inhabitants on the north, south, and west of the lake.[7] The country and people on the east remained largely unknown, and it was General Davis' desire, following the success of the expedition just ended, that the circuit be completed. It was necessary that it be done soon, as delay until after the rains set in would make further exploration out of the question until fall. On May 2 we were on the march to the east, where there were a few *dattos* and sultans still unwilling to give up their centuries-old tradition of feudal independence and accept the authority of a government regarded as infidel. The command was composed about as before [in April].[8]

Marching by the familiar route leading around the arm of the lake, the column passed through Maciu, all quiet now, and crossed the Malaig River without opposition. On approaching Gata the afternoon of the third, friendly Moros came into camp and told us in apparent seriousness that the *cotta* of Ahmai-Benaning would be too strong for us and advised that we make a detour to avoid him. But before we came within range a delegation from Gata met us with friendly assurances. At the last moment, apparently saner judgment had prevailed over fanatical rashness, and my forbearance on the previous visit as related at the beginning of this chapter had been rewarded.

There was now but one other known enemy to oppose us, the *Datto* Ampuan Agaus of Taraca, whose *rancheria* was next in our path. The only route led directly across a low open flat. About midway we ran into a marsh and the command literally bogged down. Most of the pack mules, both of artillery and supply trains, had to be unpacked and their loads carried across by the troops. Meanwhile, we had to gather quantities of shrubs and grasses and build a causeway for the cavalry horses and the mules. Then, after passing several strong looking *cottas* floating white flags, we neared the *cotta* of Ampuan Agaus, and it was evident that we were in for a fight. Shots rather than emissaries of peace greeted us, and the fort was at once invested by Loring's Company G and [Charles E.] McCullough's Troop G, supported by [George G.] Gatley's battery. Our fire was entirely too strong and accurate to withstand, and on the morning of the fifth without ever coming to close quarters the disillusioned defenders ran up the white flag and twenty-nine Moros, including seven *dattos* and two *panditas*, surrendered.

At the beginning of the fight I had sent Lieutenants [George C.] Shaw and Gracie with their Companies C and M to clear the timber on both sides of the Taraca River, instructing them to go as far as Fort Pitacus, a mile away on the north bank. The timber on both sides of the stream was soon cleared of the enemy, and seven of their *cottas* destroyed. Fort Pitacus, with its war flags flying, was then approached by Shaw on the north bank and Gracie on the south. As only a light fire came from Pitacus, Shaw anticipated a quick capture and ordered a direct attack, leading the assault himself. He and two of his men scaled the wall and were surprised by a heavy fire from a large body of Moros inside. The two soldiers were shot down immediately. Shaw stood at the top of a bamboo ladder alone, emptying rifle after rifle quickly passed up to him by his men. How he escaped unharmed is a mystery. It was one of the most spectacular and heroic incidents that had ever come to my attention; I recommended him for the Medal of Honor, which he later received.

Lieutenant Gracie had immediately crossed the river and led his men in a similar assault on the south side, pouring a cross fire into the fort. The Moros within made attempts to dislodge the attackers, rushing to the top of the wall in places and trying to engage our men in hand-to-hand combat. But our troops were not to be driven back, and in brief time the defenders, having suffered heavily, surrendered. Among the number killed [ninety according to Pershing's report] were the sultan of Pitacus and two other important leaders. Twenty-three were taken prisoners and fifty-one rifles, sixteen *lantacas*, a cannon, and some swords and *kampilans* captured. On our part the loss was heavier than any we had yet suffered in a single engagement, with one man killed and six wounded.[9] The medical detachment at this point under Lieutenant R. U. Patterson, since Surgeon General of the Army [1931–1935], had their hands full and, as on previous occasions, rendered every service to our own wounded and also gave as much attention as possible to the Moro wounded.

After being made to bury the dead at Fort Pitacus, the prisoners were placed for the night in a conical tent with walls strongly pegged down and with a guard around it. My intention was to release them the following morning, prior to our departure. In the night a heavy rainstorm suddenly came up during which four prisoners escaped, one of whom was Ampuan Agaus, and four were killed trying to do so. The others were made to take the oath of allegiance in the usual manner, which they recognized as binding. Having no copy of the Koran on which to swear them, each man cut a piece of *bejuco* (a kind of wild vine) while taking his oath. They were then set free.

From Taraca to Ragayan the direct distance was less than ten miles, but the winding trails, the heavy undergrowth, and the boggy nature of the ground made our passage difficult. Though the spring rains had as yet only begun, it took us two days to cover the distance. While here and there shots were fired at us from long range, the people from all *rancherias* through which we passed were friendly. At Ragayan Captain J. A. Ryan, with Troop C of the Fifteenth Cavalry, had come to meet us. The sight of his command was a sign that our work was done. The following day General Sumner, beaming with congratulations, met us at Marahui.

The command certainly needed rest, and we spent two days at Marahui. Here my old friend Manibilang—who had now become a sage if not a prophet among his people for having been the first of the leaders to make terms with us—came to camp with a following of several *dattos* and *Pandita* [Imam] Nuzca, the head of the Muhammadan faith at Lake Lanao. The visit of this holy man was of signal importance; it was more than evidence, it was an announcement that at last the outpost stronghold of Islam in the east of Asia had capitulated.

Major Bullard had an amusing story to tell. He said that the Moros brought him daily news of our progress around the lake and that after the fight at Taraca an excited Moro had rushed into his camp and urged him quickly to raise the white flag, saying that Pershing and his warriors had all gone *juramentado* and were coming down the lake killing everybody they saw. Bullard said the man seemed astonished that he was not afraid of me.

The return journey to Camp Vicars was made by the west shore, the route taking us past the forts which we had captured and destroyed on the expedition of the month before. Above their ruins no war flag floated now and from their shattered parapets no bullet whizzed in our direction. Still the march was not entirely one of white or American flags and friendly greetings; here and there the outlaw bands again sent occasional shots towards us, and near Bacolod two of the cavalry flanking party were slightly wounded, Lieutenant [Francis A.] Ruggles and Sergeant Mohn, of Troop G. On the thirteenth, just eleven days after our departure, the column filed again into camp at Vicars.

About eight years later, when I was in command of the department, I visited a school on the east side of the lake near Taraca, where we had fought our final battle. Among the forty Moro children in the little wooden building was a particularly bright boy who attracted my attention, and I asked him his age. "I don't know exactly, sir," was the reply, "but I was about so big" (holding out his hand at about the height of a child of seven) "when you marched around the lake." The march around the lake had been an epoch-making event in the annals of Moro history.

On receiving the news in Washington the Secretary of War [Elihu Root] cabled General Davis, Commander of the Division of the Philippines, as follows [on 11 May 1903]: "I congratulate you and Brigadier-General Sumner on the work done at Mindanao. Express to Captain John J. Pershing and the officers and men under his command the thanks of the War Department for their able and effective accomplishment of a difficult and important task."

The officers and men of that command were a loyal and efficient lot. The men had been required to submit to annoyance, insult, and attack from the people whom they were there to serve. They had done so in silence, trusting the judgment of their superiors. When the time came for action they responded like trained athletes and acquitted themselves as expected, like the splendid soldiers they were. It is a great satisfaction after the passage of a third of a century to feel the glow of sentiment that comes over me as I write these lines.

On the Way Home: Relief and Transfer to Manila

Tropical service of nearly four years had begun to tell on my health, and although deeply interested in the problems that had been given me to solve, I was forced to the conclusion that a change was necessary and that I should return to the States for a period of rest and recuperation. My application to be relieved was promptly granted, and Lieutenant Colonel Alexander Rodgers, Fifteenth Cavalry, was sent to Camp Vicars to relieve me. It was not easy to part with my friends, either Moro or American, and they in turn showed as plainly their reluctance to see me go. But I hoped to see the Americans again in other places and promised the Moros that I would return for further service among them. I was glad to be able to tell them with conviction that Colonel Rodgers would be guided by the same principles of justice and consideration that they had learned to appreciate and expect during the period that I had been among them. The Colonel spent much time going over the situation with me, met many of the leading Moros, and made at once a favorable impression among them. It was a great satisfaction to have such an able soldier succeed me in this important and delicate duty, and his selection for the command was further evidence, I felt, of the determination of superior authority at Manila to make the work of the army in the Philippines exemplary.[10]

Returning to Manila [in early June 1903] was like coming back to civilization. I met many of my old friends again, both in the army and among civilians. One of them, Martin Egan, the Associated Press correspondent, I found temporarily laid up in the hospital. I was principally occupied with General Davis, discussing the future control of the Moros. To both the General and Governor Taft I had expressed the opinion definitely that these Muhammadan people, both on account of their militant religion and traditions and their retarded civilization, should remain for some time under military government. The organization of the Moro Province, principally the work of General Davis, was determined upon and the necessary steps were taken to make it effective. A few months later General Leonard Wood came to replace General Sumner as Department Commander [6 August 1903] and was appointed Governor of the Moro Province [25 July]. It was gratifying to have a man of his ability to initiate the new form of government General Davis had so wisely conceived.[11]

The results and observations of my year's duty at Camp Vicars were generally summed up in my report to General Sumner of May 15, 1903, as follows:

> The favorable results of these expeditions can hardly be estimated at this time but . . . it seems probable that there will be no more combined resistance in the future, nor is it believed that the Moros will again undertake to oppose us by the construction or defense of cottas. It is believed that our accomplishment of the entire circuit of the lake, overcoming as we did all hostile opposition with comparatively few casualties to ourselves, treating as friends all other Moros, visiting their rancherias without molesting them, taking no property for which we did not pay, and destroying nothing except unavoidably in battle has had and will have a far-reaching effect in permanently settling the Moro question of Lake Lanao. . . . The achievement has given to us an advan-

tage in their future control which the Moros will be as quick to realize as we are.

In view of the progress that has been made we are now in position to study carefully and work out along the lines of material progress the future of the Lanao Moros. Their government should, of course, for some time remain in charge of [under] the military, either directly or indirectly, thus naturally following the kind of rule to which they have been accustomed for generations. To handle the situation properly, all these Moros, being of one group, with the same dialect, customs, and habits of life, should be under the control of one head . . . who should know something of their language, their character, and their history, and to whom they can go for advice and for the settlement of many questions which heretofore have necessarily been left unsettled. As far as it is consistent with advancement . . . a government by the sultan or dato, as the case may be, should be disturbed as little as possible; that is, the people should be managed through the datos themselves, who . . . should therefore be held responsible for the proper control of the people of their several rancherias.

As between different rancherias . . . some sort of judicial tribunal appointed by or brought under the military governor could probably be successfully established. In fact, experience here (at Camp Vicars) has proved that in settling disputes between Moros of different rancherias . . . a board of arbitration consisting of friendly datos, agreeable to both parties . . . could be relied upon to satisfactorily adjust their differences. Due to their lack of confidence in each other, it would be difficult to . . . constitute a permanent board of this kind. . . . It is probable that by appealing to their reason slight changes in their laws could be made from time to time through the medium of these courts of equity. . . .

The Moro is of a peculiar make-up as to character, though the reason is plain when it is considered, first, that he is a (semi) savage; second, that he is a Malay; and, third, that he is a Muhammadan. The almost infinite combination of superstitions, prejudices, and suspicions blended into his character make him a difficult person to handle until fully understood. In order to control him other than by brute force one must first win his implicit confidence, nor is this as difficult as it would seem; but once accomplished one can accordingly by patient and continuous effort largely guide and direct his thoughts and actions. He is jealous of his religion, but he knows very little about its teachings. The observance of a few rites and ceremonies is about all that is required to satisfy him that he is a good Muhammadan. As long as he is undisturbed in the possession of his women and children and his slaves, there need be little fear from him. . . .

The number of people in the Lake Lanao region according to the recent census is estimated to be about 80,000. They have been unfortunate during the past year in losing a large number, probably 50 per cent, of their carabaos. For this reason it is expected that the acreage of crops this year will be considerably less than in previous years. People of Lake Lanao are practically self-sustaining, raising a great variety of agricultural products and fruit and manufacturing most of their own cloth and other articles of domestic use.

Naturally industrious and inhabiting a country capable of a high state of cultivation, there is no doubt but that the Moro can be induced to cultivate new products and introduce more modern methods in agriculture. His talent for creation is such as to warrant the belief that he is susceptible of training along the lines of industrial pursuits. . . . I would also recommend that the education of at least 10 bright boys of the upper class be undertaken to the extent of teaching them English in connection with work in some industrial school in the States.[12] [See Appendix C for the full report.]

14

Return to the United States, Duty with the General Staff, and Romance and Marriage

June 1903–January 1905

Return to the United States via Hong Kong, Shanghai, Japan, and Hawaii

My way home across the Pacific not only completed my first tour around the world but took me past a British colony and two Oriental countries upon which the eyes of the civilized world were then being fixed intently. The first stopping place was Hong Kong. This Far Eastern commercial port on the south coast of China, which the British had developed during the previous half century, was no doubt the sort of trading center which our imperialists had hoped might be developed in the Philippines when they prevailed upon the administration in 1898 to send Admiral Dewey there from Hong Kong. But the tremendous success that the British had made in transforming the Chinese fishing village into one of the world's great commercial bases was not to be ours in Manila, and for a very good reason. Hong Kong lies on the principal trade route for British shipping to the Far East, which goes through Suez to India, thence by the way of the Straits of Malacca and up the China coast to Japan, while on the other hand Manila is off the direct line for American transpacific passenger and cargo steamers, as it lies two days voyage south of Hong Kong. It is true that a considerable part of the trade that formerly went to Japan later came to us, but it is not demonstrable that our general commerce with the rest of the

Orient has grown because of our possession of the Philippines. Nor was that the main reason why President McKinley instructed the peace commissioners to hold the Philippines. The reason was that the American people, being obsessed with the idea of maintaining their new position as a world power, insisted on keeping the flag flying over territory once it was in our possession. Our people now have a distinct problem to face regarding the Philippines, and upon the wisdom of its solution probably hangs our future.

Having been face-to-face with the problem of governing an Asiatic people, I was particularly glad to get a firsthand impression of this British outpost in eastern Asia. This oriental port, with its magnificent landlocked harbor, had become a clean, well-governed city. Because of its liberal regulations, Chinese had flocked to it, deserting their own nearby port of Canton by the thousands, seeking to escape the oppressions of their own incompetent and unscrupulous officials, and they found here a refuge under a protecting though foreign administration. The difference in security of life and property compensated them for the distance between the island and the mainland cities.

While at Hong Kong I called on the Governor, merely to pay my respects, and visited the garrison of British troops at [Kowloon], across the bay. As to local government, I could not but contrast the British attitude of permanence with ours of uncertainty. They were in Hong Kong to stay; we were indefinite in both our attitude and our declarations. Although our motives have been above question, no fixed policy has been possible under the circumstances and Americans and Filipinos alike have looked upon everything we did as temporary. Our policy has veered this way and that according to which political party at home was in power and the trend of its thought at the time.

At Shanghai, the next port of call, just off the mouth of the mighty Yangtze River, there was an opportunity to observe the striking difference between Chinese and European capacity in government. Although the administration of the foreign-controlled settlements of this unique city was by no means perfect, it was incomparably superior to that of the Chinese. Neither the French Concession nor the International Settlement, in the government of the latter of which the United States participates, is free of defects. But this foreign-protected city had been for many years the principal refuge for Chinese who sought security of life and trade. It is difficult to realize that Shanghai was originally built on a mud flat which was at times covered by water. This land, thought to be worthless, was consigned by the Chinese Government contemptuously to foreigners as a trading post and gradually they had reclaimed it, and steadily it has grown to be a comparatively modern city. Into it during the course of its existence had came thousands of Chinese, not only tradesmen but officials, who deposited much of their wealth for safe keeping in its foreign banks. The importance of Shanghai to foreigners in the East is easily understood when one realizes that as far back as the Seventies [1870s] the city became the base of operations of [Charles George] "Chinese" Gordon, the remarkable British officer who saved the Manchu government from disaster at the hands of the Taiping rebels.[1] Likewise, it was clear how after the Boxer Rising in 1900 it had become a refuge of Chinese officials, good and bad. Fortunately, there was such a place as Shanghai when the Manchus were overthrown and the Republic proclaimed eleven years [later]. It then became a haven for American missionaries driven out of the interior by the succession of civil wars that followed the efforts of different Chinese military leaders to obtain control of the country.

But Shanghai had and still has its seamy side. There, numbers of unscrupulous British, French, Japanese, American, and other foreigners then, as now, plied nefarious trades and professions. It is common knowledge that there have been American as well as British and Japanese opium runners and illicit purveyors of arms in and out of the port. Many were the tales told me of the villainies of underworld Americans. And in the days when our consuls were often more political appointees the scandals of their behavior were numerous. A case as late as 1927 is recalled where one of our officials was convicted by our own government of taking bribes in the American Club from an American opium runner. Shanghai was an unholy port, and still is, but around about it, beginning in most places only across a narrow street hardly wider than an American alley, even a casual visitor would see that the Chinese city is a filthy settlement both physically and morally. Slavery and infanticide were not permitted in the foreign settlement, but in times of famine, outside the cordon of foreign police, it was said that children could be purchased for the price of a pair of shoes. Shanghai was and will remain a wonderful place to see, with its contrast of European and Chinese municipalities, with its harbor showing war and merchant vessels of many nationalities, and its cosmopolitan population from every corner of the globe. It was to me, however, a most depressing place, as it must be to the man who cannot close his eyes or harden his heart to the sufferings of humanity. In Shanghai, as in many other Far Eastern cities and districts, there arises the question whether it is better vigorously to "take up the white man's burden"[2] or follow the principle of vicarious independence for backward and ill-governed peoples.

Our next port of call, Nagasaki, took us among its unique race of people at an extraordinary period. The Japanese are as different from the Chinese as any two peoples in Europe, as different as the Turks from the English. Japan has been described as the clean country of the Orient, and with the custom of Japanese as a race to bathe every day they well deserve that reputation. Their public baths, which are ubiquitous, used to amuse foreigners, because men and women, old and young, all bathed together nude in large pools, springs or tanks. During a period of widespread unemployment, a practice was said to prevail which would not have taken place in Europe or even America; along with every rice ticket that was issued to the poor a bath ticket was given. The theory that rice-eating people are less aggressive than those who live largely on a meat diet does not always hold good. The northern Chinese, a heavy eater of meat, is physically a much larger man, though not more aggressive, than the Japanese, who consumes far more rice and an average of less than a pound of meat a year. No grazing lands were seen in traveling through Japan, and the reason is that they raise few cattle and almost no pigs, depending on the sea to provide their diet of fish. Their remarkable industry is shown by the terraced hillsides, on which rice is grown for a population that is half that of the United States, Japan proper only about the size of California and only about a fifth of it arable.

Comparing China and Japan, one finds a story almost biblical in its implications, where a favored son heavily endowed with land and resources has squandered his opportunities, while the poorly-endowed brother has made himself mighty. In China the soldier has always been regarded with contempt, as the Chinese soldier generally deserves to be; in Japan the old Samurai class has long been held in the highest esteem as men of honor and unselfishness. It is the soldier who has made Japan. Through his earnest and generally wise patriotism, to his influence is due the whole nation's development; to him more than any other group must go the credit for saving the nation from foreign encroachments. Particularly was this the case in the war with Russia—for which the Japanese were feverishly preparing at the time of my first visit. Little did I dream that I should return to Japan as military attaché and be with her armies in Manchuria.

A brief glance at what had previously transpired in the Orient will help us to understand Japan's position at this time. Eight years before, Russia (supported by Germany and France) had demanded that the Japanese hand back the base in South Manchuria [Port Arthur and the Kwantung Peninsula], which they had taken from China after their war with her. Three years later, in 1898, Russia had occupied all of Manchuria and was intriguing to take control of Korea, the peninsula that, as the Japanese said, extended like a dagger pointed at their heart. With wise foresight they had made an alliance with Great Britain in 1902 in order to block either Germany or France from giving assistance to Russia, and they were now preparing to fight their first great war with a European power. It was to be a life or death struggle, they said, and the determined character of their preparation was everywhere evident. From the men and women coaling our vessel or those plodding through the scanty rice fields on the terraced mountainsides to the bankers and the merchants, everyone spoke of the coming war and labored and sacrificed that they should win it. The hermit nation that we Americans had summoned from its feudal seclusion in 1854[3] was making ready to combat the power that had held the nations of Europe in dread for a century. It was a national, a mighty, and desperate effort.

Every available man was being trained for the contest and without any attempt to disguise the fact. It was amusing to see the short-legged Japanese recruits perched upon a high saddle learning to ride the tall horses such as they had never used before, animals recently imported from Australia and elsewhere, which they habitually rode with a rein in each hand. Many foreigners smiled not only at their efforts to get ready but also at their assurance of success. Most people outside of Japan believed that the armies of the colossal Power that spread across Europe and Asia would roll down upon the little people of this Land of the Rising Sun and crush them. But the Japanese knew from experience in fighting the Chinese that it is not the heaviest man that makes the best soldier, and they also knew what was notorious throughout the Orient, that too many of the Russian officers were grafters and that generally they spent more of their time in profligate living than in training their troops. The Japanese could estimate the difficulties that would have to be overcome by the Russians in sending their armies three thousand miles over a single-track railroad [the Trans-Siberian Railroad] and providing them with munitions and supplies. In military training the Japanese had closely followed German methods, while their navy was patterned after the British navy. From the time of opening the country down to the end of the coming war, the American people favored the island empire. We sold the Japanese their first naval vessels. Everywhere I was treated with the utmost courtesy—a characteristic of the Japanese but especially observed toward citizens of a friendly country at this particular period preceding the war. It was fortunate for them that they had at the time the friendship of both the great English-speaking nations.

To me, as probably to most visitors after the first glimpse, Japan seemed a veritable fairyland. The little people, their houses, palaces, temples, the scenery, and even their larger cities, like Tokyo and Yokohama, seemed to fit that conception. But practically no people are less like fairies. They are a strong, virile, aggressive race, with an ambition and a determination that will carry them very far in the contest of nations for power.

From Yokohama I crossed the Pacific on the steamship *Manchuria*, which touched at Honolulu. Here was another race who had become our wards—a happy, contented people who seemed the natural product of the mild, soft climate. Their music was suggestive of the balmy breeze that wafted it gently to the enchanted ear. The people were essentially different from the Filipinos or the Japanese. The difference politically between the situation in the Philippines and that in Hawaii lay in the fact that the Filipinos aspired to independence and had been fighting for it, while the Hawaiians had become a territory of their own free will. Hawaii, like Puerto Rico, had been given a territorial organization, but advancement to statehood had never been seriously considered for reasons that are obvious, especially to anyone who has visited either place. In the light of present world conditions, the Hawaiian Islands as an outpost in the Pacific are invaluable, and the statesmen of the time who made annexation possible performed a service to the country which will be more and more highly appreciated as time goes on. The same thing cannot be said of these same statesmen whose imperialistic ambition gave us the Philippines. At that time we had no naval base in the Hawaiian Islands nor had we built the Panama Canal. Both became necessary the minute we acquired possessions in the Far East. Still no thought of conflicting interests between ourselves and the Japanese had come to the American mind. It was not till after the defeat of Russia that some people began to think of such possibilities. If anyone thought misunderstanding probable, the Washington Treaty[4] must have allayed such misgivings. I never had any such feeling until after the passage of the Exclusion Act,[5] by which the Japanese were classed with the Chinese. Anyone knowing the Japanese psychology must have realized at the time of its enactment that if there ever was a piece of ill-advised legislation that was it. We avowedly wanted them as friends, and yet we slapped them in the face. The Japanese themselves would without doubt have undertaken to restrict immigration of their people by a gentleman's agreement, but no one had the good sense to propose it. Even now as I write this it would, in my opinion, be a fine gesture to repeal the Act and rely upon the proverbial friendship between the two countries to find a solution. The Hawaiian Islands were at the time not a naval outpost but a group of gem-like possessions recently acquired and only policed and garrisoned. Honolulu has a charm all its own and is such a delightful place that on looking back over my army career I regret that I never had station there.

Duty in Washington: The General Staff, Assignment to Tokyo, and Romance and Marriage

At San Francisco I had completed my tour around the world [arriving 30 July 1903]. It was good to be back in my own country after an absence of four years. I had not realized the pleasure I would feel. San Francisco was new to me, and yet it was my country and I was at home. I stopped over only a couple of days, met some army friends, and made a call on General Arthur MacArthur, then in command of the Department of California. The General's son [Douglas MacArthur], who had just graduated from West Point at the head of his class, was called into the office and introduced to me by his father, who added some complimentary phrases about me. I was favorably impressed by the manly, efficient appearance of the young second lieutenant. The father had rendered distinguished service during the Civil War and later had been Commanding General in the Philippines for a time during the Insurrection, and the son was to follow closely the career of his father and eventually become Chief of Staff of the Army.

Proceeding eastward across the Rocky Mountains for the first time, I stopped one day to visit my eldest sister and some of my old Lincoln friends, then went on to Chicago to see my family. The homecoming was saddened by the absence of my mother, who had passed away the year before [24 November 1902]. The news of her death had come to me by cablegram, the message being put into my hand by an orderly when my command at Vicars was formed and ready to march [26 November], and I was about to mount my horse and start on one of the expeditions in the Lake Lanao region. I had from her the finest heritage with which a parent can endow a child, a glorious memory.

Before leaving the Philippines I had received notice of my appointment as a member of our General Staff, just created, and it was in that capacity that I returned to Washington when my leave of absence expired [31 October 1903]. The advantages of a General Staff had been often discussed among officers, but its creation was hastened as a result of the army's experience in the war with Spain. The confusion from lack of cooperation among the various staff and supply departments and between the office of the Secretary of War and that of the Commanding General had been well-nigh disastrous. Under the practice which had grown up in the War Department, General Miles, as Commanding General, became almost a figurehead. The administration of the army staff and supply departments had been gradually withdrawn from the control of the Commanding General, and the chiefs of these departments, including the Adjutant General, had become part and parcel of the secretary's ménage. Instead of regarding the Commanding General as head of the army, these chiefs looked to the Secretary of War as their immediate military superior. When the Spanish War came on, the then secretary lacked the experience and ability to coordinate their activities.

Even before the war General Miles' recommendations had been, generally speaking, ignored, and when the war came the command of the expedition to Cuba was given to General Shafter. In any event, the War Department was left without efficient direction, and the result was utter confusion. It must be said, however, that the dominant character of Adjutant General Corbin enabled him to make decisions which fortunately prevailed. But when after the war the inefficiency and its causes were exposed, it became evident that a General Staff such as had long existed in other armies was necessary. Luckily President McKinley, who had been a soldier himself, realized its importance and acted accordingly. As he wanted the appointment of Secretary Alger's successor to come from New York, he inquired of his friends the name of the ablest lawyer in that city and was given that of Elihu Root, who was at once chosen.

Mr. Root found many difficult and important problems requiring solution, especially those pertaining to our insular affairs. But none was more vital than the reorganization of the army and the establishment of a General Staff. When he came to consider that question, he found competent officers to assist him, of whom Major William H. Carter, of the old Sixth Cavalry, then an adjutant general, was the real authority on the subject. The Secretary himself made a profound study of the proposal and later made his recommendations to Congress. The creation of a General Staff, of course, was no reflection on the ability of individual officers. The trouble was that the routine practice of administration had failed to coordinate the details of participation and responsibility. The mind of a modern army could not be that of a single man, but required assistants working together under one direction. That the efficiency and preparedness of modern armies were due to just such an organization was well known, and its value could not be called in question.

The size of the General Staff at the beginning was limited to forty officers detailed from the army at large. General Adna R. Chaffee, the second Chief of Staff [January 1904–January 1906], brought to the position a broad experience, but the task of perfecting the new organization was not easy. There is one point that should be very clearly emphasized: the change from the old system to the new placed the Secretary of War in immediate command of the military establishment as the representative of the President, with the Chief of Staff as his executive but with no authority in his own right except as commander of the War Department General Staff. The Chief of Staff could issue no general orders in his own name except to the War Department General Staff, but must issue them by direction of the Secretary of War. That was Mr. Root's intention plainly stated in so many words.

The General Staff did not meet at once with the full favor of the army. The chiefs of the staff and supply departments especially took exception to what they called usurpation of authority, and in several instances they had reason for complaint. Naturally, a full-fledged and competent General Staff could not be created by simply issuing the order and selecting the members. Experience under proper direction was necessary. The mere designation of members of the General Staff, including the chief, is no guarantee of their infallibility; in fact, the first General Staff could have been duplicated several times over from the commissioned personnel of the army, to its improvement in several instances.

A new arrangement of departments and divisions was adopted in January, 1904, and General S. S. Sumner, with headquarters at Oklahoma City, was placed in command of the Southwestern Division, which embraced the Departments of Texas and Colorado. I was sent to Oklahoma City on General Staff duty [January 1904] and for some time was acting chief of staff of the Division. In the spring I accompanied General Sumner on a tour of inspection to test the efficiency of the troops in minor tactics. While at Division headquarters with Captain John C. Oakes, General Staff, as assistant we worked out the details of the organization of a mobile army to consist of all the regular and National Guard troops within the Division. In the fall of 1904 [October], I was ordered to Washington to attend the [Army] War College, the class con-

On 26 January 1905, Pershing married Helen Frances "Frankie" Warren, the daughter of a powerful Republican senator from Wyoming, Francis Emory Warren. This photograph was taken in Tokyo in the fall of 1906, after Pershing's promotion to brigadier general. (Library of Congress, Prints and Publications Division, Bain News Service Collection [PRN 13 CN 1976: 136, Container 1])

sisting of nine officers. At that time, and for a number of years, the War College was an auxiliary to the General Staff and many problems were sent to it for solution. The duties were presumably in line with training for higher command.

In January, 1905, General Chaffee told us that Mr. Taft, the Secretary of War, was looking for someone to send to Tokyo as military attaché. I had not the remotest idea of receiving such an assignment but was keen to see something of the Russo-Japanese War, then entering its second year. Upon reporting to Mr. Taft, he asked me if I played bridge and told me that Lloyd Griscom, our Minister in Tokyo, wanted a bachelor who could play bridge with him. I had to say that my knowledge of the game was very meager. With one of his hearty laughs, the Secretary said, "well, I should like to send you anyway." I then had to divulge a secret. "But, Mr. Secretary," I said, "I am engaged to be married." Then he asked, "would you mind telling me the name of the young lady?" When I told him he congratulated me and said, "You are a very lucky dog," adding that even that would not make any difference. General Chaffee thought that by sailing from San Francisco not later than the middle of February I would be able to reach the front in Manchuria before the opening of the spring campaign.

I must now go back slightly more than a year, to an evening in Washington, 1903—to be exact, that of December 9. As always, the social diversions at the capital were somewhat distracting, and it was necessary to limit with firm resolution the number of invitations one accepted. Being fond of dancing, I could not often resist the weekly hops at Fort Myer, which were very popular with the younger set of official Washington. It was there, at the end of a pleasant evening, that I met Miss [Helen] Frances Warren, the daughter of the Senator from Wyoming [Francis E. Warren].

In the month that followed I saw her occasionally at dinners and dances here and there, and at each succeeding meeting the impression made upon me that first evening at Fort Myer grew stronger. And when, even that early, I thought that perhaps the attraction might be mutual, it gave me new courage. When my assignment to Oklahoma City came, I was loath to leave Washington, but that spring while on the tour of inspection with General Sumner I found opportunity to visit Miss Warren at Cheyenne. There we reached an understanding as to our future, but the engagement was not announced until after my conversation with Mr. Taft. President Roosevelt was told of it by Senator Warren, and I received from him a note of congratulations, in which he said that as soon as the announcement was made Mrs. Roosevelt and he would have us to lunch so that they might wish us well in person. He had this pleasure a few days later. Frances had set her heart on a wedding in June, but my orders to sail for Japan caused us to decide to be married at once—quietly with only the families and a few intimate friends present. But when we began to make out the list of guests, each one suggested another till finally we gave up hope of simplicity and plunged into an elaborate affair, including invitations to practically all of official Washington. Our wedding took place on January 26, 1905, at the Church of the Epiphany. In honor of Senator Warren, the upper house recessed for the occasion, and President and Mrs. Roosevelt were present.

15

Off to See a Modern War as the Military Attaché in Tokyo and Observer with the Imperial Japanese Army

February 1905–December 1906

Meeting with President Theodore Roosevelt

Before leaving Washington I went by appointment to the White House to pay my respects to President Roosevelt and was shown at once into his office by Mr. [George B.] Cortelyou, his private secretary. The President's office was then composed of two rather large rooms, one being a sort of alcove where his desk was located, the other and larger one being the reception room. He was standing in the corner to the left of the latter, talking in low tones but vigorously to Mr. Gifford Pinchot. In the opposite corner stood Senator [Albert J.] Beveridge, and on the other side of a long table near which I sat, two or three others were also waiting. When he finished talking with Mr. Pinchot, he passed across the room, speaking to each of us in turn, saying to me, "Pershing, I will see you presently." Seating himself at his desk, he resumed the conversation with his visitors. He had not more than started when Cortelyou again came in and told him that [John L.] Sullivan and [Jake] Kilrain had arrived by appointment, and he replied, "show them in." He then arose, squared his shoulders, and strode toward the door, buttoning his Prince Albert,[1] and said, "Ladies and Gentlemen, we will now receive John L. Sullivan and Jake Kilrain." In a moment the battle-scarred pugi-

217

lists, who were in town giving an exhibition of boxing, entered the presidential sanctum. "How do you do, John! How do you do, Jake," said T. R., giving each one a hearty handshake. "I am glad to see you." He put a hand on the shoulder of each of the fighters and said, "Say, I'm awfully sorry I couldn't see you two fight last night, but I was too busy to get away. When you come to Washington again, you'll let me know, won't you? I really would like to see you go at it for a couple of rounds; I'd even like to put the gloves on with you myself."[2]

John and Jake had no chance to say a word as the President continued, "You two are square fighters, you've always been. But they're not all square, John. We know them, don't we, John?" Then, before dismissing the fighters, he presented them to me, saying, "and here's another square fighter, one of our military men, Captain Pershing. Good luck to you, goodbye boys."Again he shook their hands, and the secretary ushered them out. He then turned toward the rest of us laughing, returned to his desk, and resumed his conference.

My turn came soon, and he sat down near me and began to talk about the war in the Orient. He spoke with a frankness that rather surprised me, indicating that at the proper time he would suggest that it [the war] be ended. Having met him two or three times since returning from the Philippines, I was struck more than ever with his virile personality and his strong mentality. No one could be long in his presence without feeling that he was exceptionally well qualified to be chief executive. He had been very sympathetic with the Japanese but did not think it expedient that they should go too far, and in the absence of such suggestion no one could tell how far that would be. The Japanese would certainly have carried on as long as they continued to win victories.

The Course of the Russo-Japanese War

Going somewhat ahead of my story, it may be recalled that shortly after the battle of Mukden[3] the President, according to the plan which he outlined to me, did propose to the belligerent governments that they consider ending hostilities. This proposal was readily accepted by Russia, largely because she was faced with internal revolution.[4] Japan accepted it mainly because of financial difficulties, but there were many delays and it required expert statesmanship on Mr. Roosevelt's part to bring their representatives together. The conference at Portsmouth [New Hampshire] resulted. The Japanese people expected a large indemnity, and they very generally resented the terms of the treaty, which provided

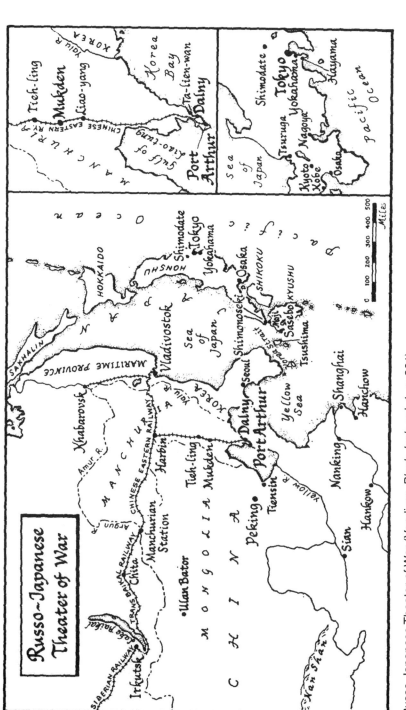

Russo-Japanese Theater of War (Vandiver, *Black Jack*, vol. 1, p. 361).

no indemnity but left the burden of their war costs upon them. Riotous demonstrations took place in Tokyo and other cities, and Americans were very unpopular for the time being. The elder statesmen of Japan, however, realized the value to their country of the President's intercession and most of them accepted the treaty philosophically. General Kodama [Gentaro], the Chief of Staff in Manchuria, in commenting on it, told me that the government was satisfied. He pointed out that they had not lost a battle, had driven the Russians out of Manchuria, and it was wiser to stop then without taking the chance of losing the next battle. It was evident that the question of supply was becoming more difficult for them and less so for the Russians. Yet after the war many Japanese army and navy officers continued to blame Mr. Roosevelt for the result. But the President showed when the Japanese annexed Korea that he recognized their legitimate interests. However, for a while the relations were not all that could be desired, but fortunately older and wiser heads among the Japanese were able to restrain their people from letting their irritations carry them off their feet.

At the time of my appointment to Tokyo, in the second year of the war, the battle of Mukden had not yet been fought and the outcome was at least uncertain. However, the Japanese navy had defeated Russia's fleet in the Pacific, and it seemed probable that it would deal similarly, as it did, with the one which Admiral [Zinovy Petrovich] Rozhdestvensky was soon to lead on its long voyage from the Baltic through Suez to the China seas [Battle of Tsushima, 27–28 May 1905]. On land the Japanese armies had doggedly captured the fortifications about Port Arthur, which had been widely regarded as impregnable, and forced its surrender [2 January 1905] from [Anatoly Mikhailovich] Stoessel. They had been persistently victorious, not having lost a single battle. They had displayed great skill in the use of modern arms, a thorough knowledge of strategy, exceptional discipline, with unquestioned courage and patriotism. They had shown their ability in adapting themselves to the technique of a profession in which heretofore only Occidentals had possessed special technical understanding and national cooperation. This nation, which had only recently emerged from medieval feudalism, had put the newest implements of modern warfare to test for the first time in a great struggle. They had so far defeated a country which Europe had held in awe since Napoleon's march to Moscow had created a general impression that it was invulnerable. The Japanese had surprised everybody and great praise was due them. But for several reasons their achievement was not as remarkable as it appeared to be.

They had fought probably the poorest of the great armies of Europe. While there were some able soldiers among the Russian leaders, the army lacked organization, discipline, and equipment. It had many defects and operated at great disadvantage. Behind it in St. Petersburg the government was disrupted with jealousies, rivalries, and demoralization, and threatened with revolution. Its long line of communications of more than three thousand miles was over a single-track railway across previously conquered territory bitterly cold in winter. The Russians had entered the war with a spirit dangerous to themselves. Having hitherto easily defeated and subdued all Eastern peoples in their marches of a century across Siberia, they had accepted the Japanese challenge arrogantly, contemptuous of their upstart island adversary. Among the officers there was a moral looseness in living, and in the ranks there was little heart for the contest. The aristocratic officers conducted themselves as if they were out on an imperial lark, and the peasant soldiers were not fighting in the defense of their homelands but waging an uninspiring war of conquest, while their families at home were in many cases all but starving.

But it should be noted that in spite of a general situation that appeared favorable to the Japanese, the observers with their armies freely predicted defeat for them in the next great battle, should there be another. And there was considerable ground for this conclusion. It was well known that teamwork in the Russian army had been faulty. In several instances they had failed to make use of their reserves and had unnecessarily permitted the Japanese to outnumber them at critical points of contact. With their experience and consequent better cooperation, it was believed that these mistakes would not be likely to occur in future. It must be said, however, that there was less desire on the part of the powers for a decisive victory by the Russians than by the Japanese.

Experiences as a Military Attaché and Observer

It was during the last months of the war—although we did not know that it would end so soon—that I was appointed military attaché at Tokyo.[5] My wife and I sailed from San Francisco on the *Korea,* aboard which were Major General and Mrs. Arthur MacArthur. The General, accompanied by his aide, Captain Parker West, was going to Manchuria as American observer. We got to Tokyo on March 5 and went to stay at the old Imperial Hotel, then the only foreign hostelry in the city. I reported at once to our Minister, Lloyd Griscom, and then went to call on the Minister of War, General Taraouchi [Terauchi Masatake], and the Chief of Staff, the venerable Field Marshal Yamagata [Aritomo]. I was received by the Assistant Chief of Staff, General Murata [Tsuneyoshi], and was sorry not to meet the old Marshal, who was ill at the time, for he was one of the last of the famous *Genro*,[6] the Elder Statesmen, who had unified and remade Japan. Before leaving Washington there had been some question about increasing the number of observers at the front, but, much to my satisfaction, Murata told me that it had been arranged.

A few days after our arrival the Minister of War gave a dinner in honor of General MacArthur, with whose distinguished service in the Philippines the Japanese were familiar. The dinner was charged high with excitement. It was a large affair given at the official residence, more than a hundred Japanese and foreign officers and ladies being present, the Japanese ladies wearing their beautiful native dress. Had the dinner been held the evening before, when the nation was hushed in an awe of fearful anticipation, it would probably have been subdued in tone and formal, with discussions of the war kept within general terms. But during the day tremendous news had come and the quiet in the streets was changing rapidly to riotous enthusiasm. We could hear the cheering and shouts of "Banzai" from the crowds in the thoroughfares. As we sat at dinner we were treated to the reading aloud of official dispatches arriving from the front. The tide had turned heavily in the battle of Mukden; what the Japanese Minister of War well knew might have been a disaster had been swung into a defeat of the Russian army. A tremendous relief had come to our hosts, the higher officers who understood, and they too shouted their "Banzais" and all but lost control of their emotions. We did not drink only the health of the Emperor [Meiji] and the President that evening. It is too frequently said by foreigners that the Japanese are inscrutable; they are human like the rest of us.

In accepting the detail as military attaché, I took it for granted that my duty was not to stay in Tokyo and play bridge with members of our Legation, as Secretary Taft had suggested, but to go to the front. Having been granted permission, I joined General MacArthur and Captain West when they started a day or so later. We left Mrs. MacArthur and my wife in the care of the ladies of the Legation and proceeded to Shimonoseki on a special car put at our disposal by the Japanese Government. On our way we visited the prison camp for Russians at Moji, a crude barracks inside a rough enclosure. The prisoners were comfortably clad and appeared well fed and in the warmer climate did not suffer from the cold. Though larger than the Japanese, they were not the stalwart men I expected to see.

With two British attachés, Colonel [William Henry] Birkbeck and Captain [Berkeley] Vincent, likewise on the way to Manchuria, we American officers sailed on a Japanese transport bound for Dalny, the port in Manchuria built by the Russians. Every possible attention was shown us. We were given the best staterooms on the vessel, foreign food was especially provided, and excellent attendants appointed to serve us. The ship was crowded with troops and animals. On arriving in the busy harbor after a two-day voyage, we dropped anchor in the midst of a flotilla of junks waiting to take the men and horses ashore. The debarkation was a novel sight, the men, fifteen at each hoist, being lifted over the side and lowered into the junks in great nets made of rope, and the horses going over in a sling one at a time.

There was a multitude of things to interest us when we got ashore two days later. Dalny was alive with activity. Since its capture from the Russians the year before, it had become the principal landing base of the Japanese army, as it was the seacoast terminus of the Russian railway running down through Manchuria [later known as the South Manchurian Railroad]. War vessels and merchantmen of many types and sizes crowded the harbor, with all sorts of small craft, from fast naval launches to one-oared Chinese sampans, plying to and fro among them. On shore the warehouses were insufficient for the army, and enormous stacks of supplies, all in perfect order and covered with tarpaulins, lined the waterfront. Long trains of carts, Chinese as well as Japanese, streamed through the streets. There was much hustling and bustling and consequently much noise, but no confusion. The capacity of the Japanese for organization had brought order out of what would otherwise have been Chinese chaos.

Here we observed a novel thing—the extraordinary willingness, even eagerness, of the Chinese to serve invaders of their land. Five years before they had flocked by scores of thousands out of China proper to help the Russians invade Manchuria. Now, for the same reason, gain, they were serving the Japanese. Many Chinese served as spies on both sides, even at the risk of certain death if caught. For ordinary labor either side could employ all the Chinese they were willing to pay. But this was nothing new. In China proper, British, French, German, American, and Japanese armies, whenever and wherever they had landed, had always employed Chinese in large numbers to assist them as laborers and informers. The Chinaman was not a fighter nor a patriot in the western or Japanese sense of these terms. Up to that time, he was an individualist willing to trade with an enemy if there was profit in it. And wherever a foreign army had gone in China, it found banners announcing the submission of the inhabitants. Our own troops have found paper flags with Chinese characters reading, in effect, "Loyal subjects of the Emperor of America." Imagine French laborers flocking to the aid of Germans invading their country!

Very little damage had been done to Dalny by the Russians when they evacuated, except to certain docks, and these the Japanese had been able to repair. The city's growth had not been the natural development of a commercial seaport but was artificial. It had been built according to fixed plans, with government money, and evidently at great expense, judging from the type and large number of brick structures, including barracks, administration and office buildings, pretentious residences, and even an opera house. It was nothing like the older cities, but everything looked new and modern. The Russians evidently intended and expected to remain.

The Japanese authorities took good care of us, assigning us to comfortable quarters, which were greatly overheated by coal stoves. Even we Americans felt uncomfortable, but the British officers, accustomed to cold houses in England, actually suffered in such quarters. With them I visited docks, storehouses, and the formerly Russian barracks, and together we looked up Mr. R. H. [Richard H.] Little, correspondent of the *Chicago Tribune,* who had been with the Russians and much to his regret had been captured by the Japanese at Mukden. Being new arrivals, we did not then know much the details of what had happened and were anxious to get information. Here was a man from the other side who might be able to throw light on the situation. The tall, lean young American seemed certain that the Russians had been caught napping and were much surprised by the quick Japanese advance.

In a car attached to a supply train, we were sent northward toward the front on March 16, and were soon passing Nanshan Hill,[7] where one of the early important battles had been fought. The successive lines of Russian trenches up the hillside were plainly visible from the car windows. It seemed surprising that the Russian position was so easily taken, but it was made clear when we learned that they had held back a large force that never got into the battle at all. En route we passed several trainloads of prisoners who, in spite of the cold, were being brought southward in open cars. Among them, curiously, were two American officers, Colonel Valery Havard, Medical Corps, and Major William Judson, Engineer Corps, who had also been captured at Mukden. They were treated with every consideration, of course, but were very crestfallen at having been caught. On arrival in Japan they were released and returned to the United States.[8]

Reaching Liaoyang on a cold St. Patrick's Day, the two Englishmen and I sallied forth to explore the old walled city. We found it a typical Chinese town, with narrow, congested streets, some hardly wide enough for two carts to pass, and all the pavements out of repair. The whole city reeked with filth, but here and there were spots of striking beauty. We visited the Japanese veterinary hospital outside the walls, where hundreds of sick and wounded horses were being treated. The sight was very depressing and the suffering of these faithful animals in war is harrowing to think about. But their destruction in Manchuria was negligible compared with that on the Western Front in France. Horses and mules, if they understood the significance, would rejoice whenever a mounted unit is mechanized. At Liaoyang I met for the first time the well-known correspondent Frederick Palmer, a man who has probably seen more different campaigns than any other American and who with the rank of major had charge of correspondents with the A.E.F. during the World War.

It will be recalled that for the battle of Liaoyang[9] the Japanese adopted a plan that would have been hazardous in the face of an alert opponent. Nozu's army and Oku's army made a frontal attack while Kuroki's army executed a wide movement to the east to reach the Russian left, but he met with strong resistance that was not overcome without severe losses.

Colonel Yoda, the Japanese commander at Liaoyang, accompanied us part of the way towards Mukden, pointing out the different battlefields of the previous year and explaining the campaign. As we approached the city there were many gruesome evidences of the recent battle. Over the great plains the bodies of many Russians still remained unburied; the fields were strewn with articles of uniform, rifles, equipment, shattered artillery, and broken-down transport, and the scattered villages were partially in ruins. But among the habitations were still the Chinese people, back already and at work again, reconstructing their hut-like houses with whatever they could find at hand, salvaging every little article or broken bit of anything that might be of use, and clearing the fields with a view to planting crops in one more of their ever-recurring efforts to survive.

The roads leading north and south were crowded with field transport trains—long columns, not of wagons drawn by four or six mules, but of Japanese army carts, each drawn by one small horse led by a soldier, and long lines of larger Chinese carts, no two alike, some drawn by as many as seven ponies, some by bullocks, and assisted often by coolies panting and grunting as they strained at the ropes no less desperately than the animals under lash. The Japanese engineers had not had time to put the roads in good condition or reconstruct the bridges the retreating army had destroyed, and men and animals had to pay the price in sweat and muscle. But we had not yet seen the worst of this congestion. The victorious army had advanced too rapidly for its supply service, and north of Mukden the streaming lines of slow-moving vehicles seemed endless. In places there was hardly space on the roads for those that were laden, going north, and those that were empty, coming south, had to plod their way through open fields.

Mukden, then the capital and greatest Manchurian city, had become in recent days the headquarters of the Commander-in-Chief, Field Marshal Prince Oyama [Iwao]. The armies were already well to the north. Here we stopped for a couple of days, comfortable quarters being allotted to us in one of the well-constructed Russian buildings. The first night we were there we were given a feast consisting of sardines, pâté-de-foie-gras, chicken and mushrooms, eggs, bacon, and coffee, after which all hands slept soundly. At Mukden I met Willard Straight, then correspondent of the Associated Press, and together we went on horseback for a survey of the terrain over which the retreating army had passed. The road to Teihling, as it wound through the hills, presented numerous ideal positions for rearguard action, and judging from the frequent lines of entrenchments we saw, the Russians had made good use of them.

At Mukden I parted company with General MacArthur and West and went a few miles out to the village of Chinchago to join the group of observers under charge of Colonel Saigo, attached to the First Army, General Kuroki's. I had expected to go at once to the front lines, but apparently our hosts had other plans. The Japanese army was new in handling officers from the West and as cautious in handling foreign observers as it was with newspaper correspondents. There was no lack of opportunity for routine observation of the army, but actual service at the front was what we all wanted, even though for the moment the activities consisted only of small operations here and there to improve positions. Those foreign observers who were on the other side had greater freedom. It was the first time in recent history that military observers and correspondents had not been left free of foot. In Greece and Turkey, in South America, and in Cuba, they had gone as far forward as they cared or dared. Being held back and restricted by the Japanese made many of the attachés resentful, but the attachés and correspondents had far less liberty in the World War.

Pershing photographed this street scene in Mukden with the Center Tower in the background (no date). (Editor's collection, JJP 112842)

General Fujii [Shigeta], Chief of Staff for General Kuroki, always granted our requests for information when it did not pertain to so-called military secrets, an excuse often used without rhyme or reason. Kuroki himself, a typical old Samurai, never failed to appear when we visited army headquarters and none of his staff outdid him in courtesy. The old commander was a quiet dignified gentleman of few words but iron determination. The Austrian military observer, who had been with the army the previous year, told me this tale of him: During the battle of Liaoyang success was largely dependent on the outcome of his flanking movement. In an attack on an important hill his lines were driven back with terrific loss. When told of this he continued to smoke his cigarette and calmly said, "Order them to attack again." They were repulsed a second time, and he repeated the order. This time the position was carried.

Among the other military observers with the First Army were the two Germans, Major [Günther von] Etzel and Captain [Carl Maximilian

Lieutenant General Kuroki commanded the Japanese First Army, to which Pershing was attached as an observer from May to September 1905. (Photograph by Pershing. Editor's collection, JJP 112816)

"Max"] Hoffmann, the Austrian Major Bela de Dani [Adalbert Dáni von Gyarmata], the French Colonel [Charles Pierre] Corvisart, and the Italian Major [Enrico] Caviglia. We were a friendly lot and often exchanged information and observations. We also had good times together, taking rides within our restricted sphere and entertaining each other. Each group of officers whose country's national day happened to come when we were together gave a banquet in honor of the occasion, and we all drank to the health of his sovereign or chief of state. These diversions could barely be called banquets. I am stretching the word considerably, for we were living in old Chinese farm houses, mud-walled structures which, after all our efforts, were anything but clean; our respective chefs were only imitators of the art of western cooking; and our supplies were by no means the best or most varied. Still, we were all in good health, leading active outdoor lives, and in fine spirit, and such occasions somewhat broke the monotony. Caviglia, who had a rich, grand opera voice, often sang and indeed frequently woke us early by singing some favorite opera while dressing. When the Great War came, nine years later, my companions of Manchuria days were quickly aligned on two opposing sides and each one held high rank. Hoffman, a jolly soul, succeeded [Erich] Ludendorff as Chief of Staff on the Russian front; Dani and Caviglia commanded corps and armies on opposite sides in Austria and Italy; and Etzel, commanding a division, and Corvisart, a corps, faced each other in August 1917 in the French attack astride the Meuse near Verdun, which I witnessed.[10]

As there was no prospect of an immediate battle, I returned to Tokyo the latter part of April for a short stay. My diary of April 25, written while at Oyama's headquarters en route, reads: "Dinner with Captain Tomako and Colonel _____. Latter remembered Perry visit and said all Japan was in arms. Old Samurai came to coast with swords and attempted to drive black ships[11] away. Hated foreigners, especially American, then. Now grateful. Text books teach that Japan should be grateful to America for awakening. Lives at Kyoto, has eleven children. Called on MacArthur." On my way, I stopped at Port Arthur and made a careful survey of the surrounding heights and the successive lines of Japanese trenches constructed as they approached step-by-step toward the lines of fortifications. These steep slopes were natural defenses made stronger by earthworks and manned by well-trained troops. To a casual observer it looked as though the positions should have been impregnable. Up to that time there had never been an attack against a better-prepared defensive position nor in modern war one more heroic and persistent than that of

Foreign military observers with the Japanese First Army visiting the Imperial Tombs in Mukden, Manchuria. Front row, left to right: Captain George H. Jardine, Great Britain; Major Payeur, France; Major Von Etzel, Germany; a Japanese escort officer; Lieutenant Colonel E. J. McClernand, United States; Major Caviglia, Italy; Captain Peter J. Hegardt, Sweden; and a Japanese escort officer. Back row: Japanese officer; Captain Max Hoffmann, Germany; and a Japanese officer. (Photograph by Pershing [no date]. Editor's collection, JJP 112824)

Gate at the entrance to the Imperial Palace and Tombs at Mukden, Manchuria. To keep the foreign observers busy, the Japanese escort officers took them to local tourist attractions such as the Ding Dynasty's Imperial Palace and Tombs, located in Mukden. In this photograph, Pershing caught two of his fellow foreign observers unlimbering their cameras. (Editor's collection, JJP 112861)

Captain Max Hoffmann of the German Army was an observer with the Japanese First Army while Pershing was attached to it. During World War I, Hoffmann was the operational genius behind the great German victories over the Russians in 1914 and 1915, which ultimately brought Field Marshal Hindenberg and General Ludendorff to control the entire German war effort in 1916. Pershing photographed him at the attachés' quarters near Mukden in the summer of 1905. (Editor's collection, JJP 112596)

the Japanese. The Russians had retired south to Port Arthur after their defeat at Nanshan Hill and had held on tenaciously in the hope of relief, but the Japanese had made that impossible by their control of the Liao-yang Peninsula south of Nanshan.

I went to the First Army again in May with Lieutenant Colonel E. J. McClernand and remained in Manchuria sharing a Chinese farmhouse with him until September. McClernand and I made several vain appeals for permission to go to the front, and I finally wrote an official letter addressed to our Adjutant General at Washington, saying among other things, that we were not allowed to see anything and might as well be somewhere else. Always keenly alive to criticism, the censor spotted this, as I hoped he would, and Major McClernand and I were allowed to go

Rudimentary smooth wire entanglements used in Russian defenses at Fort Erlang-shan, Port Arthur. Pershing took this photograph while visiting the battlefields around Port Arthur in late April 1905. The value of wire entanglements was a lesson learned in Manchuria, and thick ribbons of barbed wire entanglements were critical to the protection of defensive positions along the Western Front during World War I. (Editor's collection, JJP 112841)

to the front occasionally. On one occasion we joined a cavalry regiment on a reconnaissance in force. It was an interesting all-day ride, including a brisk skirmish with Russian cavalry, which was driven back; but there were no contacts between the opposing forces during that period that could be called a battle.

The ceremony to the dead in the battle of Liaoyang conducted by the Umezawa Brigade, McClernand and I witnessed. The ceremony was opened by four Buddhist priests, followed by General Umezawa [Michiharu] reading an address to the spirits, after which he burnt some incense at the alter and all officers in succession did the same thing. McClernand and I were offered the privilege of doing honor in the same way, and we gladly accepted. We were then taken through what they called a zoological garden, in which many different kinds of animals were represented in paper. A miniature of the battlefield had been laid out, with the positions of troops and installations shown. The bridge across the Gainan River was artistically decorated with arches at either end, and the wire entanglements were strung with blossoms.

It is intensely interesting as well as highly important for a soldier to know something of foreign armies, their methods, their equipment, and their psychology, and during my year and a half with the Japanese I had

On 5 September 1905, Pershing attended the Umezawa Brigade's memorial service and commemoration for soldiers lost during the Battle of Liaoyang in 1904. (Photograph by Pershing. Editor's collection, JJP 112873)

Lieutenant Colonel Edward J. McClernand, who was the senior American observer with the Japanese First Army during Pershing's time observing the Russo-Japanese War. (Photograph by Pershing. Editor's collection, JJP 112832)

Pershing and other foreign military observers attached to the Japanese First Army lived in this small Manchurian village during the summer of 1905. (Photograph by Pershing. Editor's collection, JJP 112881)

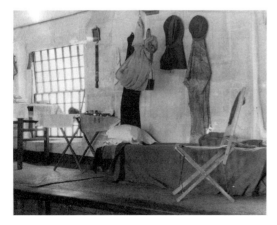

Pershing's accommodations in the Chinese house where he was billeted were very spartan. (Photograph by Pershing. Editor's collection, JJP 112804)

Pershing was a military attaché and observer with the Imperial Japanese Army in Manchuria for a number of months in 1905. In this rare, undated photograph, he stands in front of a Manchurian hut while on this duty. (Library of Congress, Prints and Photographs Division, Unprocessed Pershing Photographs [PRN 13 CN 1976: 136, Container 6])

A cavalryman and his horse were usually inseparable companions, as each depended on the other in battle. While Pershing had no photograph taken of himself with his own Kodak, he would not be a cavalryman if he did not take a photograph of his most trusted friend in the field, his horse. The Japanese provided the horse for Pershing's use while in Manchuria, and it remained there when he left in September 1905. (Photograph by Pershing. Editor's collection, JJP 112811)

Japanese artillery in action. (Photograph by Pershing. Editor's collection, JJP 112596)

Japanese infantry form a skirmish line while firing at Russian troops. (Photograph by Pershing. Editor's collection, JJP 112586)

Pershing photographed this view from the rear of the Japanese defensive lines, looking toward the Russian forward defenses on the distant ridges, during the summer of 1905. Both sides faced difficult terrain in Manchuria north of Mukden. (Editor's collection, JJP 112878)

A portion of the Japanese line north of Tiehling, Manchuria. Pershing took this photograph while visiting forward Japanese positions on 31 August 1905. (Editor's collection, JJP 112778)

All foreign observers were interested in the use of machine guns by both sides in Manchuria, and much effort was devoted to studying their technical and tactical aspects. Here, Pershing's photograph shows a Japanese machine gun fitted with a typical protective shield. (Editor's collection, JJP 112659)

opportunity to learn much of their army from personal contact. The willingness of their young men and their adaptability to training and discipline made it easy to mould them into a fighting force. Straggling was unknown in the Japanese army. It was looked upon as a disgrace to be absent from one's unit if possible to be present. Their officers as a whole were very earnest and their zeal and determination made it possible for them to master quickly the details of modern warfare. As a people it cannot be said that the Japanese are scientific, although they have produced several outstanding men in science. Neither are they mechanically-minded people as compared with those of the leading nations of the West. They are not a people of high or quick initiative, but it is a mistake to regard them as only imitators. They do their own thinking.

The Japanese displayed remarkable unity during the war with Russia, but frequently they have at times proved to be of many different opinions, and violent political contrasts have developed among them. Even in their army and navy there are factions and often the high commands are not able to control the minor officers.

This should cause no surprise when it is recalled that the Imperial household had long been relegated to obscurity and almost penury at Kyoto when, in the face of danger from western encroachments, the revolution of 1868 brought to an end the many rival feudal lordships and united the country. It was then deemed necessary to have a head of state, and because of the obscurity of the Emperor the country could agree upon his "restoration." But to revive the national spirit of loyalty to the Throne the reverence they had set aside for centuries had to be rekindled.

Duties as Military Attaché after the War and the Birth of His First Child

While I was in Manchuria an opportunity came for my wife to visit the Philippine Islands with a party of senators and congressmen that Mr. Taft, then Secretary of War, had organized and was taking on a tour of inspection.[12] Having been the first civil governor of the Philippines, he was personally interested in them and was anxious to have Congress understand the problems in order that it could legislate intelligently. There were a number of ladies in the party, including Alice Roosevelt [Longworth]. When the party reached Mindanao, Mrs. Pershing rode over the trail from Malabang to Camp Vicars on my private horse, which

I had left behind with the cavalry. At Lake Lanao she got something of a shock when two Moro children, a boy and a girl about twelve to fourteen years of age, came up and announced that I was their father. The boy was the son of *Datto* Ahmai Tampogao and the girl the daughter of the sultan of Ganassi, both of whom were particular friends of mine and who, according to Moro custom, had honored me by asking me to adopt these children, and I had become their honorary father.

Several members of the party, including Mr. Taft, went from the Philippines to China, visiting Peking [Beijing], which was then the capital, and my wife and her father, Senator Warren, and her brother, Fred [Frederick E.] Warren, accompanied them. They were received in audience in the Forbidden City by the famous old Empress Dowager—the last ruler but one of the illustrious line of conquerors who governed the enormous empire for nearly three centuries.

Among the social functions we attended in Japan was one of a very novel character. Outside of Tokyo is a specially-reserved park where numerous small lakes and much marshy ground make a veritable paradise for wild fowl. Several of these lakes are enclosed by high embankments and no one is permitted to molest the birds or hunt them in the ordinary way, and in consequence they lose their fear of men. Once a year the Imperial Household invites a number of Japanese and foreigners, including members of the Diplomatic Corps, to this park to what is called a hunt. The ducks are enticed by decoys into narrow openings and at the opportune moment they are flushed. As they rise the guests, who have remained hidden behind low embankments, try to catch them in huge hand nets, sort of enlarged butterfly nets. Ladies generally attended, and on the occasion when my wife and I were present the excited efforts of members of the party in making the captures resulted in some very humorous scenes in which the customary dignity of social functions was entirely lacking.

I traveled from one end of the country to the other, accompanied on some of my journeys by my wife. I went as far north as Hokkaido[13] and saw some of the people known as the Ainus, said to be the original inhabitants, who have been gradually pushed back by the descendants of the Malays, the ancestors of the present race of Japanese, until they now occupy the least desirable sections of the country. From here I visited Saghalien [Sakhalin], viewing some of the immense catches of salmon, which are largely used as fertilizer in Japan proper. Traveling by a Russian sleigh, I went to the limit of the newly-acquired Japanese section of the peninsula, passing through wonderful virgin forests, in which were located two or three isolated Russian villages. The *mujiks* [Russian peasants], evidently living in poverty, flocked around us, eager to learn when they were to be repatriated. On another occasion I visited Fukushima, one of the great naval bases, and frequently went to military stations to study training methods or attend local reviews and maneuvers.

Once, while at Sendai, a division headquarters, the Japanese soldier assigned to me as orderly—a bright young man who had become a convert to one of the many missionary churches—asked me to tell him my views of the Christian religion. "Sir," he asked, "do you believe in Christ and will you explain to me why?" The second part of the question was difficult to answer offhand, but after starting the story it became easier and my recital seemed to satisfy him. I had merely told him of the simple life of Christ, had repeated the two great commandments, and had said the Savior's example was the model for men to live by. Evidently the young Japanese had been bewildered by the many differences among Protestant denominations and between them and the Catholic. This set me to thinking over the misfortune of the disunion of Christianity, which the East cannot fail to perceive and question. But on the other hand, the people to whom we send missionaries cannot fail to appreciate their work and to realize the spirit behind it.

Of all the foreigners I met in the Orient, the medical missionaries impressed me as the finest group. At Mukden in the summer of 1905 thousands of Chinese assembled at the American mission hospitals for treatment by Doctors [Thomas C.] Fulton, [Dugald] Christie, [Frederick W. S.] O'Neill, and [John] Ross.[14] At Mukden during the cholera epidemic Chinese men, women, and children came by the hundreds, practically filling the vacant spaces within the mission compound, where they stoically waited sometimes for hours till their turns came for attention. There was no proselyting by these medical missionaries. By their example in treating the poorest without cost they taught Christianity to the rich as well. Among the Japanese some men and women of the highest standing have become Christians.

At the end of April, 1906, a grand triumphal review of troops was held before the Emperor. The troops that had participated in the war took part, including representative reduced battalions of all the divisions, together with the *Kobi* (second reserves), the skeletonized cavalry, artillery, and military trains. The Emperor, riding in a carriage drawn by two horses and followed by the Princes in carriages and by a large group of staff officers, all well mounted, drove along the front of the infantry line, thence along the cavalry and artillery fronts and back to the saluting point. The troops, in their new khaki uniforms recently adopted and also worn by the Emperor, marched past him in splendid fashion. At the end of the review an Imperial rescript was handed Marshal Oyama expressing pleasure at the martial spirit of the troops and enjoining him to exert further energies for their improvement. Marshal Oyama gave the Emperor a rescript in reply expressing his thanks and vowing to increase his efforts in response to the Imperial wishes.

The number of troops was variously estimated from thirty to forty thousand, and it was said to be about one sixteenth of the total force in Manchuria, which would make, using the smaller estimate, about one-half a million men. It was also said that the number on parade was about equal to one third the total number who lost their lives in the war.

Shortly afterward there was a grand review of the fleet by the Emperor in Yokohama harbor, which was also very impressive. Truly the Japanese have become a military people in the modern sense of the term.

There is no more striking view in the world than cone-shaped, snow-capped Fujiyama when seen in the morning sun, and it was this view that used to greet my wife and me each day of the delightful summer we spent on the seashore at Hayama. We lived in a rented Japanese bunga-low with sliding doors covered with translucent paper instead of glass. Near us on the beautiful bay lived Baron Kaneko [Kentaro], one of the early graduates of Harvard, who had been sent to Washington on a spe-cial mission during the war and knew President Roosevelt well. Later Kaneko was made a viscount and a permanent member of the Privy Council. He was a charming and excellent friend and has long been a highly-placed interpreter of the American people and government to those of his own country. When the moon shone and light breezes rus-tled through the pines and caused the temple bells to tinkle, my wife and I felt that peace was as near about us as we should ever find it on this earth.

But we left Hayama early, sooner than we wanted, returning to our home near the Legation in Tokyo because of an event to which we both looked forward hopefully. This was the birth, on September 8, 1906, of our first child, whom we named Helen, after her mother. The physician who attended my wife was Doctor Rudolf B. Teusler, that remarkable medical missionary of the Episcopal Church, who made St. Luke's Hos-pital in Tokyo a monument to Christianity and by his life and service promoted good will towards us Americans in the hearts of thousands of Japanese.

Promotion to Brigadier General, Return to the United States, and Another New Assignment

Another important event in the family occurred twelve days later. A cable came from Washington, signed by Adjutant General [Fred C.] Ainsworth, informing me that President Roosevelt had appointed me a brigadier general. The President had sent a message to Congress three years before objecting to the system of promotion in the army by seniority. His statement [from his *Third Annual Message to Congress*, 7 December 1903], which follows, is worth quoting not solely because of the reference to me:

> The only people who are contented with a system of promotion by seniority are those who are contented with the triumph of mediocrity over excellence. On the other hand, a system which encouraged the exercise of social or political favoritism in promotions would be even worse. But it would surely be easy to devise a method of promotion from grade to grade in which the opinion of higher officers of the service upon the candidates should be decisive upon the standing and promotion of the latter. Just such a system now obtains at West Point. The quality of each year's work determines the standing of that year's class, the man being dropped or graduated into the next class in the relative position which his military superiors decide to be warranted by his merit. In other words, ability, energy, fidelity and all other similar qualities determine the rank of a man year after year in West Point, and his standing in the army when he graduates from West Point; but from that time on, all effort to find which man is best or worst, and reward or punish him accordingly, is abandoned; no brilliancy, no amount of hard work, no eagerness in the performance of duty, can advance him, and no slackness or indifference that falls short of court-martial offense can retard him. Until this system is changed we cannot hope that our officers will be of as high grade as we have a right to expect, considering the material upon which we draw. [Here Pershing inserted a note: There is now a law which provides for the elimination of officers whose services are not satisfactory.] Moreover, when a man renders such service as Captain Pershing rendered last spring in the Moro campaign, it ought to be possible to reward him without at once jumping him to the grade of brigadier-general.

A youthful Jack Pershing in one of the few photographs of him without his usual mustache. This portrait of the newly promoted brigadier general in full dress-blue uniform was made in Tokyo sometime after his official promotion in September 1906, while he was still on duty as the U.S. military attaché. (Library of Congress, Prints and Photographs Division, Unprocessed Pershing Photographs [PRN 13 CN 1976: 136, Container 6])

My promotion advanced me over those captains senior to me and over all of the field officers in the army. This caused considerable comment and much criticism of the President and of me. The fact that Captain A. L. [Albert L.] Mills, Major Tasker H. Bliss, and Captain Leonard Wood had been similarly advanced did not mitigate the charges of favoritism that were made in my case off and on for several years. One of these, an article in the *Washington Herald,* was so bitter in attack, charging Senator Warren with being a party to my advancement, that he wrote to Mr. Roosevelt and enclosed a copy. The President's reply was in his characteristic style. It read:

November 18, 1910.
Dear Senator Warren:

It does not seem to me that the quotation in question is capable of misconstruction, whether taken apart from its context or not. Your son-in-law was promoted so strictly on his own merits that I had absolutely forgotten that he was your son-in-law until I received your letter. Even now, I cannot remember whether he was married to your daughter or engaged to her at the time he won the victory because of which I promoted him. My impression is that he was not yet married to her. In any event, the promotion was made purely on the merits, and unless I am mistaken you never spoke to me on the subject until I had announced that he was to be promoted. The article that you enclosed from the *Washington Herald* is a tissue of malicious falsehoods. It is not a case of a man writing under an erroneous impression, it is a case of a man being guilty of malicious and willful untruth.

Faithfully yours,
Theodore Roosevelt.

To promote a man *because* he marries a senator's daughter would be an infamy; and to refuse him promotion for the same reason would be an equal infamy.[15]

As a matter of fact, I did not meet Miss Warren until six months after the termination of the service for which I was promoted and after the President's message forecasting his action had been sent to Congress. The Adjutant General's cablegram informing me of the promotion contained also an order that neither my wife nor I welcomed. It instructed me to return to the United States without delay and upon arrival at San Francisco to report by telegraph for assignment to command the Second Army of Intervention in Cuba. We were sorry to leave beautiful Japan and the many warm friends we had made among both the Japanese and the little colony of Europeans and Americans, and we decided that my wife should remain a while longer, especially as she would be within reach of Dr. Teusler.

Upon arriving in San Francisco I learned that the intervention in Cuba had already taken place and that Brigadier General Thomas H. Barry had been put in command of our forces.[16] The dispatch of troops had come sooner than was expected, and I had got home too late. Temporarily I was given command of the Department of California. My stay there was very brief, however. [Pershing only commanded the Department from 2–8 and 18–20 November 1906.] I preferred a more active post, and as there was still important work to be done among the Moros in the southern Philippines, I asked the War Department to assign me there. This request was not granted until later, but I was ordered back to the Philippines. And only ten days after my arrival in San Francisco, I was again sailing out of the Golden Gate on the old *Korea*, once more on the way across the Pacific. I stopped in Japan long enough to assemble and ship our household effects, then sailed with my wife and daughter for Manila.[17]

16

Brigade Commander, Fort McKinley, Philippines

January 1907–August 1908

When I arrived in Manila for duty and throughout my term of service at Fort McKinley—from January, 1907, to August, 1908—Major General Leonard Wood was in command of the army in the Philippines. I had known him before the Spanish War when he was Attending Surgeon in Washington and physician for President McKinley's family, and had seen him often in Cuba when he was colonel of the "Rough Riders," and later after he was appointed Brigadier General of Volunteers. In fact, while we were still in the trenches he asked me if I would accept an appointment as aide-de-camp on his personal staff, but I preferred not to be tied down to that sort of duty. Moreover, I did not consider myself especially well fitted for it. General Wood was a fair-haired, well-built and athletic, muscular man, just my age, with a personality that won him many friends. He became a brigadier general in the Regular Army at forty. The army, however, had never become reconciled to the promotion of a captain in the Medical Corps with little military training to the rank of brigadier general of the line. But while General Wood was not a trained soldier, he had the good sense to select trained soldiers on his staff and also to permit those of the line who were trained to perform their duties without interference.

Commanding a Brigade and Fort McKinley

The commander of the Department of Luzon was Major General John F. (Jack) Weston, who had been promoted from the Subsistence Department for exceptional services in Cuba. He had seen line service before going to the staff but often spoke of himself as a grocer. He had a delightful sense of humor, and it was a pleasure to be in his company. Sometimes he indulged in jests at the expense of his superiors and others. For instance, in speaking of Major General Adolphus W. Greely, the distinguished Arctic explorer who, it will be remembered, ran out of rations, obliging the party to live on human flesh, Weston said, "Now, there's Greely, why he never had but one small command and he ate that." And of Major General Hugh L. Scott, who had mastered the Indian sign language, Weston would say, "Yes, but he learned it after all the Indians had forgotten it." He always referred to General Wood as "old Doc Wood." Once, when I applied for the return of an artillery officer to command the battery at Fort McKinley instead of an engineer officer who was assigned temporarily, General Wood disapproved and General Weston in returning the application could not refrain from making a joke of it. He added this facetious interrogation to the official reply he sent me: "If a doctor (Wood) can command a division, and a grocer (himself) can command a department, and a cavalry captain (myself) can command an infantry brigade, why can't a lieutenant of engineers command a battery of artillery?"

After the end of the insurrection it was decided wisely to concentrate the American forces in larger garrisons, leaving the more isolated stations to be held by native scouts [Philippine Scouts],[1] which were part of the army, and the police work to be performed by the native constabulary [Philippine Constabulary].[2] This had been done in both American and Filipino interests. In some cases there had been a good deal of demoralization among our American troops, both officers and men, when left in small units in remote stations, and it was considered better as far as possible to keep them together in larger groups, where they would have greater variety in training and more diversion. On the other hand, it had been found that the Filipinos could live well among their own people in small communities, where they were more at home as to language and temperament than our men. Under American officers, both Filipinos and Moros proved themselves valuable as constabulary and as soldiers. Military life appeals to them and having before them the good example of their American officers they usually perform their duties well.

The native constabulary had been developed to a high degree as a police force under such men as [Henry T.] Allen, [Harry H.] Bandholtz, and [James G.] Harbord, and the Scouts became fine soldiers under such leaders as [George B.] Duncan, [Samuel D.] Rockenbach, and Hanson E. Ely—all of whom, and several others with like experience, became general officers in the World War.[3]

There were three large posts on the Island of Luzon at that time where American troops were concentrated—Camp Stotsenburg, Camp McGrath, and Fort McKinley. The last was nearest to Manila, only six miles away up the Pasig River. Camps Stotsenburg and McGrath were cavalry regimental stations, while Fort McKinley was an infantry brigade post. Stationed here were two regiments of infantry, two squadrons or two-thirds of a regiment of cavalry, one battery of field artillery, one company of engineers, and a medical unit. This was the first experiment in our army of a brigade post, the only one we had anywhere. The command was known as a reinforced brigade.[4] I was glad, therefore, to have the assignment.

The command gave me the opportunity to put into practice something beyond the ordinary close order training, which is basically useful to teach men discipline, improve them physically, and make them alert and smart, but that sort of training alone is apt to pall on both officers and men. Troops rarely had the opportunity for practical field training, especially the higher units. So backward was our preparation in that regard that we were just beginning to have field training of a brigade as such for the first time. One of my first acts was to prepare an athletic field, for which General Wood, who was himself interested in sports, made a generous allowance of funds. We were thus able to provide increased diversion for the men by encouraging baseball, football, tennis, and other sports. The simpler exercises in field training opened the season and but little time was spent with more routine drill. Except for occasional freshening, such elementary instruction was, as it should be, confined to recruits. It is the thoroughness of the practical side of his training—with special attention to target practice, for which we built a splendid range—that determines the soldier's efficiency in battle.

Although there was no apparent danger of another war against a modern, well-equipped and -organized nation, it was and is always the duty of the head of the army and the local commanding officers to do everything within their power to have their forces prepared for such an emergency. Instead of being irksome, there is a romance about it all. The very thought of being ready to serve the country when it calls, the exhilaration of keeping physically fit, the stimulus of competition with one's fellows in trying to attain perfection in the things one would be expected to do, all add a zest to army life that takes it out of the humdrum if properly directed. I therefore proscribed a course of training covering all phases of action in the battle zone, starting with the individual and leading up through the different units to the brigade as a whole. No such advantage had hitherto been taken of the grouping together of the larger units from different branches of the Army. During the rainy season, that began about the middle of June, various classes in theoretical work were conducted in barracks and at the same time garrison training of troops was carried on when the weather permitted. Schools for officers included organization and tactics, map making, the solution of tactical problems, and the study of recent wars. Those for noncommissioned officers and privates embraced theoretical instruction in rifle and revolver firing, and horsemanship for the cavalry. Calisthenics and swimming formed a part of the practical work in this period. Selected groups were taught mule-packing, carpentry, clerical work, and baking, and for cavalry and artillery, horse-shoeing and veterinary studies. Every man in that command could do something useful and several of them could do many things beside being a well-trained soldier.

At the end of the rainy season, about the middle of November, practical field work began for all arms. Under the junior officers men were taught how to march with the least fatigue, to reconnoiter, and the technique of the attack. They also were taught to prepare defenses, aid the wounded, and especially to care for themselves when on campaign, particular attention being given to the instruction and development of efficient noncommissioned officers. They were grounded in squad leadership, and in the direction and control of musketry fire. Each arm had its special line of instruction. The captains conducted their companies, the majors their battalions, and the colonels their regiments through terrain exercises for such units, correcting defects and putting them through various tests. As brigade commander, the entire course was under my eye. The series of practical problems which I prepared and supervised and which were worked out on the ground, with tactical criticisms following each test, aroused the greatest interest on the part of both officers and men. One problem for the brigade involved the defense of Cavite Province against an army moving north on Manila.

It was amazing in the beginning to find a number of officers and noncommissioned officers with little conception of their duties and responsibilities in the conduct of actual operations. Many knew the mechanical details without being able to apply their knowledge practically.

Fort McKinley was an ideal place for training. The site was healthful, the water supply from artesian wells was the best in the islands, and the climate, though tropical, was from five to eight and even ten degrees cooler than that of Manila. There was an area nearby of about a hundred square miles available for all kinds of field training and maneuvers. It extended from the Pasig River on the north to the Zapote on the south and from Manila Bay on the west to the laguna on the east. Within these limits were low hills, ridges, ravines, streams, wooded and bare terrain and rice fields. The artillery could fire every day in the year over a different range, and other arms could find an infinite variety of ground for separate or combined exercises.

Where Fort McKinley stands was the scene of one of the battles between American troops and Filipino insurgents under Aguinaldo. One day we had a visit from the former *insurrecto* leader—a thin, mild-mannered man with a subdued voice, who on first acquaintance would have given few Americans the impression that he was the person of strong will, determination, and capacity for leadership that he had displayed. He stood on the veranda of our post club and pointed out to me and other officers the positions his troops had occupied when attacked by the American regiment under Colonel James F. Smith. A few days later Colonel Smith, then Governor-General, visited the post and from the same veranda pointed out the positions from which his command had advanced. The battle was not fought to a finish because the American troops, after becoming engaged, were withdrawn by order of General Otis, then in command of operations.

Being the "show" post in the Philippines and so near Manila, Fort McKinley had many visitors, including foreign military men who wanted to see what American troops were like. Among those who came was the general commanding the British forces at Hong Kong [Lieutenant General Sir Robert G. Broadwood], a group of officers from a visiting German naval vessel, Rear Admiral Yoshimatsu [Motaro], of the Japanese Navy, whom I had known during the war between Japan and Russia, and Colonel Caviglia, my Italian colleague in Manchuria. Among the many Americans were Governor-General Smith and the Secretary of War, Mr. Taft, and a frequent visitor as my guest was Commissioner W. Cameron Forbes, who later became Governor-General. The visit of the German naval officers reminds me of a dinner given on board the flagship of our Admiral [Joseph N.] Hemphill to the German admiral and his staff. When it came time for the toasts Admiral Hemphill arose and proposed the health of the German Emperor. We all rose and the band struck up, but instead of playing the *Wacht am Rhein* it played the *Marseillaise*, much to our admiral's chagrin.

Socially, Manila was most interesting. There were dinner parties, teas, and dances, those at Fort McKinley being very popular. Among the sports were polo, baseball, horse shows, and an annual carnival or fair promoted and managed by the Army. At these fairs native tribes from all parts of the Archipelago brought not only their native games but the products of their looms and their handiwork. The display of needlework by the native women of Luzon, and especially Manila, was extraordinary. Each year the most beautiful girl in native society was chosen as Queen of the Carnival. Generally speaking, the Americans lived very much to themselves and did not mix with the Filipinos, except officially. There was no such thing as an American hostess extending to Filipinos invitations to dinners, dances or garden parties where Americans were also invited. This was partly due to the differences in race, dress, and manners, but there was that innate prejudice that was never overcome. On certain occasions, such as receptions on holidays or to meet some distinguished personage, like the Secretary of War, the Governor-General or other high official would often include Filipinos among the guests. In the provinces there was more mingling with Filipinos, especially at dances. At Iligan, when there as a captain, I gave a large reception and dance at Christmas-time to which they were invited.

William Howard Taft's Visit, 1907

In due course of time the Act of Congress of July 1, 1902, providing for a census of the Islands, to be followed by the election of representatives to a popular assembly called the Philippine Assembly, had been carried out. The Assembly was to convene and organize in the fall of 1907 and Mr. Taft, then Secretary of War, upon whose insistence the above law was enacted, came to the Islands to inaugurate the first assembly [16 October 1907]. Mr. Taft thoroughly believed in the necessity of this step as an evidence of good faith in assisting the Philippine people in their preparation for self-government. But in the minds of many Americans in the Islands the wisdom of the move was doubtful. They felt that the Filipino participation in the government was being extended too rapidly. At a dinner given by the American Chamber of Commerce to Mr. Taft, after the address of welcome, Mr. Martin Egan, then editor of the *Manila Times,* spoke in the name of the American colony. He made a frank, clear-cut statement of the views of businessmen who had been induced to come to the Islands and make investments in the belief that American control would continue for a considerable time. They now felt that they were getting scant consideration in this long step toward Filipino rule. The Americans had already done much for the Filipinos. Our government had given them law and order such as they had never known before. Under the guidance of the [Philippine] Commission,[5] a special effort had been made to provide schools for the children, with good school buildings and hundreds of teachers, men and women, [who] had been brought from the States. Fair and honest taxation had reduced their burdens. With the funds so obtained, many beneficial public improvements had been undertaken. Sanitation in the cities was well under way, and throughout the principal islands many good roads had been built. Epidemics of disease had been largely brought under control. And the American government and business activity had given much labor and profit to the people. Americans in general then in the Islands, both businessmen and government officials and employees, entertained serious misgivings regarding the capacity of the Filipinos to carry on and govern themselves as an independent people, and a large proportion of Americans still believe it wiser for the United States to maintain control. This innovation was only another instance of the change in sentiment that was taking place among leaders at home. Theodore Roosevelt, under whose administration these things were being done, had been one of the early advocates of colonial expansion.[6]

Mr. Taft discussed the benefits to the people that should arise from the measure of self-government the Filipinos were being given, and it was evident that his program had already been determined. This was made perfectly clear when, in the course of his remarks, he announced that the Filipino Speaker of the Assembly would take rank in the Islands immediately after the Governor-General. This was a veritable bombshell thrown into the American camp. The Secretary got no applause for this statement. It signified that even the Vice-Governor and the Major General commanding the American Forces, to say nothing of the members of the Commission—in which was lodged powers of government—and their wives should in future follow after the Filipino Speaker and his wife in all public functions. This declaration was regarded by Americans as an advance that was quite radical and unnecessary in its concession to native sentiment. The Filipinos were, of course, elated with the decision.

During his visit to the Islands, I had the pleasure of entertaining Mr. Taft at Fort McKinley, but the dinner was given at the club as my wife was absent in Japan with our daughter. In preparing for the occasion I had a miniature White House of appropriate size made of thousands of small, snow-white flowers, a decoration for the dinner table of sixty plates. This was placed on the table with its main door facing Mr. Taft and caused him to remark that his actual entrance was still a long way off. At the reception that followed a demure little old lady, when it came her turn to be presented, said in low voice, "Mr. Secretary, I just came to pay my respects to the next President of the United States." The big man held on to the little lady's hand for a moment, smiled genially, and said in his rich, mellow voice, "Now, madam, don't you be putting notions like that in my head." It was generally believed at the time that the Secretary would be the next president, but the prospect did not affect him in any way. He was a friendly, plain-mannered, very human individual.

Prior to the reception, while he was dressing, I heard a loud call from his room, and going to his assistance found that his valet had forgotten the waistcoat of his white evening clothes. I scurried about to see if I could find one that could be expanded enough to fit him. The next largest man of the party was Frank Helm [Frank P. Helm Jr.], also a guest, then Chief of Inter-Island Transportation. But even his waistcoat, in order to meet the demands of the Secretary's girth, had to be split up the back and pinned to his shirt.

Mr. Taft's bulk was the source of jokes, usually told by himself. One of the stories told of him was that on a visit to Baguio, while he was Governor-General, he was so enthusiastic about the place that he was moved to send the following cablegram to Mr. Root, then Secretary of War: "Stood trip well. Rode horseback twenty-five miles to five-thousand foot altitude. Hope amoebic dysentery cured. Great province this. Only one hundred fifty miles from Manilla with air as bracing as Adirondacks or Murray Bay. Only pines and grass land. Temperature this hottest month in Philippines on my cottage porch at three in the afternoon sixty-eight. Fires are necessary at night."

Mr. Root cabled back: "How is the horse?"

Developing Baguio

Active service in tropical lowlands is very enervating to Americans and after a certain length of time a change to a cooler climate becomes urgent. The Spaniards had left accounts of a wonderful location for a resort in the mountains of Bengust Province called Baguio, about a hundred and fifty miles north of Manila. After careful investigation, Mr. Taft when Governor-General started the work of opening it up for the use of Americans. Being about five thousand feet in altitude, the climate of Baguio is delightful, the thermometer rarely rising above sixty-five degrees, which is about twenty degrees below the average of the lowlands. The site is located among rolling hills covered with pines and the air is bracing, but the rainfall is tremendous during the rainy season. At one time while I was there with my family it reached seventy-two inches in seventy-two hours, causing such a rise in the Bued River that the road built at great cost, which follows up the canyon through which that stream courses, was almost completely wrecked, the bridges being nearly all carried away. Nothing daunted, the Commission continued to carry out its plans. Besides the public buildings and residences erected by the civil government for official use, the army built a military post for the accommodation of its personnel needing recuperation [Camp John Hay]. Without such a resort, which I visited at various times, it would not have been possible for me and for many others to have served so long in the Islands.[7]

Observing the 1907 Imperial Japanese Army Maneuvers

In the fall of 1907, in response to an invitation from the Tokyo Government to send an observer to their annual maneuvers, I was designated and went once more to Japan. My wife and daughter were already there, having left the Philippines to escape the summer heat. My aide, Lieutenant C. S. [Claude S.] Fries, accompanied me, and we were joined at Tokyo by our military attaché, Colonel James A. Irons. There were about forty foreign officers present as observers. The maneuvers were held near Shimodate [15–18 November 1907], some seventy miles north of Tokyo. The arrangements for taking care of the observers were excellent. A school building was furnished and equipped completely for our accommodation. Each officer was provided with an attendant, a good horse, a rickshaw with a swift puller. We were grouped according to nationality and personally conducted by selected Japanese officers, each of whom spoke the language of those he had in charge.

Two army corps were arrayed against each other, and after some maneuvering the two corps confronting each other went into the mock battle in apparently dead earnest. There was no indication as yet of the open formations of successive lines that became necessary during the World War in attacking entrenched positions. The infantry made attacks against heavy artillery and machine-gun fire in rushes in close order, at the risk even then of tremendous loss—a procedure that was criticized by all foreign observers. Improvement in the cavalry was noticeable since 1905, due in part to the importation of better horses, which usually came from Australia. The riding of the Japanese had improved somewhat, though they were nothing like the horsemen of European or American cavalry. But this was to be expected, as horses had been rare animals in Japan half a century before, only the wealthier dignitaries possessing them.

The discipline of the Japanese troops was well-nigh perfect, implicit obedience being deep-rooted in both officers and men. The salute was never omitted and enlisted men of different ranks saluted one another formally. Their bearing showed fitness and physical stamina—for which they were noted in the war with Russia, where the infantrymen were able to keep up with the cavalry on the march.

The Japanese had not yet undertaken to manufacture their own arms and munitions, and their artillery was largely, if not all, from Krupp's works. Balloons were used advantageously for observation, but there were then no airplanes nor even auto-vehicles.

The maneuvers were intensely entertaining, as the Japanese, profiting by this war experience, had increased the proportion of artillery, had introduced the use of guns to accompany infantry in the attack, and had largely increased the number of machine guns. These were highly important points, indicating the trend of military thought more fully developed in the World War, especially in the use of large numbers of machine guns. Although these developments were reported, our army made no advance plans and at the beginning of the war we had not even adopted a type of machine gun. After we entered this was much to our disadvantage, as it was impossible to obtain them in sufficient numbers until late in the war, when increased numbers of an improved pattern of our own production were provided.

The contact of the opposing forces on the final day took place in the presence of the Emperor, who at the conclusion reviewed the troops. Such an occasion is a proud one for every Japanese soldier. After the review the Emperor entertained the Japanese officers of all ranks, about five thousand, at a lunch at Shimodate. The meal was served under a great canopy, but the number was so large that perhaps half were in the open, the Emperor being seated on a covered platform that was raised so that all could see him. During the luncheon the higher grades of Japanese officers went up in groups, according to rank, the highest first, and bowed before their sovereign, drinking to his health from their cups of sake. We foreigners were similarly presented and did the same thing.[8]

Return to Fort McKinley, Birth of Their Second Child, and Travel to the United States

Returning to Fort McKinley with my family, I spent another six months at training the brigade. During that time our second daughter was born at Baguio on March 25, 1908. We named her Anne, after my mother and Miss Anne Orr, one of my wife's dearest Wellesley friends and her maid of honor at our wedding. Miss Orr married Lieutenant W. O. [Walter O.] Boswell, who later became one of my aides, and much to our delight they were with us in Mindanao when I was in command of that Department.

Life at McKinley, with the large number of officers and their families, was in every way pleasant. The proximity to Manila brought the army in close touch with military headquarters and the civil end of this government and with the American element of the city's life.

After twenty months at McKinley, I obtained leave of absence and started back home with my wife and children for a vacation. We had never been across Siberia and both wanted to see that strange, enormous empire of the Tsar that lies across the top of Europe and Asia. We therefore took this route on our way back to Washington.

17

A Long Journey Home, Taft's Inauguration, Sick Leave, New Orders, and a Son Arrives

August 1908–October 1909

Travel across Russia to Moscow and St. Petersburg

The itinerary of our journey from Manila across Asia and Europe listed the names of places that alone stirred us with anticipation. It included not only the main Chinese and Japanese ports which lay on our route and which we had seen before but Vladivostok, Irkutsk, Omsk, Petropavlovsk, and Samara on the Trans-Siberian Railway and then Moscow and St. Petersburg and the capitals of Poland, Germany, and Belgium, then Paris and London. As we were traveling with two small children, it was necessary that we should have a capable and thoroughly reliable nurse. Such a person, fortunately, we found as we passed through Japan. This was Masa-san [her name was Ms. Minamioji], our amah, an educated woman and a trained nurse, who spoke English, a high-class typical Japanese, dainty, scrupulously cleanly, careful, patient, and courageous. Having her left us free to go about as we pleased, confident that the children were in safe hands.

On my first tour of the world I had traveled alone and had thoroughly enjoyed the sightseeing. Now, however, I looked forward with even keener pleasure to the plan we had agreed upon two years before, as I had for a companion my thoroughly congenial and equally interested wife. We stopped but a few days in Japan, only long enough to see the parks and temples of lovely Kyoto once more and to make final preparation for the long rail journey across Siberia. Then we set out for Tsuruga, the Japanese port from which the vessels sail across the Sea of Japan to Vladivostok, now the only Russian seaport on the Pacific.

Arriving there on the day of the departure of the Wagons Lits Express, we had but a glimpse of the place. It was not, however, one that a foreign traveler would go especially to see. Being an ice-locked port several months of the year, the Russian Government had not undertaken to make it as fine a city as Dalny—which the Japanese had taken from them. It was nevertheless distinctly Russian. The moment we descended the gangplank of our Japanese steamship we felt we were in the land of the Tsar. Here were the high-booted Russian soldiers, the bearded *mujiks* with tight-collared smocks, the tails hanging out of their belts, the long-robed, long-haired priests, and the droskies, drawn by high-yoked ponies, and towering over the city were the distinctive spires and domes of the Russian churches. Where the Tsar's soldier went, no matter how deep into Asia, there followed the Orthodox priest, and where the peasant huts began to group themselves around the official buildings, there arose at once the spires and domes.

In the days of the Tsar there was little trouble for foreigners entering Russia—unless they were Jews or persons suspected of relations with the revolutionists. When the customs officials came to my army revolver, I was under momentary suspicion of being an anarchist, but when that point was cleared up we were passed through the customs house without delay. We had shipped our trunks to Paris because of the high cost of transporting heavy baggage across Asia and Europe. This made it necessary for us to carry a greater amount of hand luggage than usual, and our valises and bags and the amah's belongings, with our extra heavy coats and shawls, piled high the extra droshky that hauled it to the station.

As our boat was late I had to drive by droshky at break-neck speed through the hilly streets to reach the bank before closing hour. Making a hasty calculation, I drew what seemed to be ample funds for the journey. But when all the extras and tips were paid I found myself, as the train started, with less than five rubles in my pocket. I am sure my wife thought me hopeless. However, on the way across from Tsuruga we had met two Danish naval officers, to whom I related my sad plight, and they very kindly helped me out with cash until we reached Moscow.

On the train we had a spacious compartment to ourselves connected with a similar one occupied by the children and their amah, with a common washroom between the two. Though the dining car was not as clean as on an American train, it was more spacious, the gauge of the tracks being somewhat wider than ours and the cars broader. It was used as the lounge car when meals were not being served. In some respects the train was noticeably more comfortable than any we had in our country at the time. But since that date great improvements have been made in our railways, while the revolution in Russia has, it is said, reversed the order there.

An incident occurred before we reached Harbin that illustrates the grafting propensities of the average Russian official of that period. As we approached Harbin the conductor-porter of our car came in with our tickets and said there had been a mistake in the amount charged and that we owed sixty dollars more. Having been warned, I accused him of trying to hold us up and threatened to report the matter at Harbin. Of course, that was the end of it.

The train stopped several times a day for half an hour or more and once, at Irkutsk, the halfway station, for several hours. We were thus able to get off at various stations and rest ourselves, see the strange people, and often purchase fresh milk for the two babies. At Irkutsk passengers and luggage were shifted to a similar [train] standing alongside. We took a drive about town and with that exception saw Siberia only from the car windows or the station platforms, but we got the impression we wanted of the vast north of Asia over which successive Tsars had been extending their conquests for more than a century. Every station, bridge, and tunnel had a guard of troops. Sometimes for a whole day we would travel over mountain and plain and pass only an occasional village with few scattered homes, and sometimes for hundreds of miles the only break in the forests was the line over which we were traveling. Never saw a soul except guards here and there or a handful of nondescripts hanging about some lonely station. But the timber had been cleared well back from the roadbed because of the danger of forest fires.

Efforts had been made by the Russian Government to induce people of the European provinces to migrate to Siberia, but comparatively few had done so. Except along the railway there were not many settlements of real Russians. North of the line there were adventurers, trappers, hunters, and buyers of furs, miners seeking gold and other ores, fishermen and lumbermen up the long rivers that flowed into the Arctic Ocean, and here and there a government village established for exiles; but otherwise in a territory approximately as large as North America there was not, according to statistics, as many as one white Russian to a square mile. What a conquest and what a failure to utilize it! For much of the country was no colder nor bleaker in winter than our own northern states or southern Canada. Only once or twice did we pass an emigrant train. Once we saw a prison car with barred doors and windows presumably taking exiles into the distant primitive land.

To us the journey was never monotonous, the scene never tiresome; there was always something of majestic beauty to look at. We were traveling along a vast plateau from which the rivers flow generally northward and southward. At one time there would be a plain of pastel colorings cut from the sky by a delicately-traced horizon, at another a somber forest with dark, mysterious depths; again a range of mountains with storm clouds massing over them, and almost every evening a fascinating sunset. We were crossing the heart of the widest of the continents. For half a day the train skirted the southern end of Lake Baikal, one of the longest inland bodies of water in the world. For days it passed through forests of silver birch and fir. It crossed the Tunguska, Yenisei, Ob, Irtysh, Ishim, Volga, and other great rivers, and passed through a hundred tunnels. And it stopped at places the names of which we had never heard before.

In the British Empire there are more different races of people than in Russia, but Great Britain is not geographically united while Russia is an unbroken stretch of territory in which there are some sixty different racial or national groups, and as their representatives gathered at the various stations we looked into the eyes of probably twenty. Beginning the journey we had seen Koreans, Chinese, and Manchus, and after entering Siberia we saw Mongols, including Tama priests in red or yellow robes, Buriat horsemen tending vast herds of cattle, fierce-eyed Turkomen, Muhammadans whose wives were veiled, Cossacks with curved scimitars at their sides, merchants from the Caucasus who possibly traded in opium, Tziganes in fantastic garments of many colors, and other peoples at whose race we could only guess. At Moscow there was a museum where we could see—and might have learned, had we had the time—what each of these peoples were. In the museum were one or more life-sized figures representing the different types of the Tsar's subjects, showing their differing features, colors of skin, hair, and eyes, fashions in beard and hair dressing, and designs and colors of costuming. The collection gave one an insight into the extent and racial complexity of the Eurasian Empire. "What does it matter," asked a Russian statesman cynically once, "whether we lose or gain ten provinces in war."

We spent a week at Moscow, stopping at the Hotel Metropole, which was then one of the finest in Europe, and going daily with a guide about this ancient center of the country. The first place we went to see was, of course, the Kremlin, the heart of that great city. I had never seen so impressive a mass of palaces and churches as these white walls enclosed, although my wife had been to Peking and had seen the red-walled enclosure of Manchu palaces and temples known as the Forbidden City.

In those days before the revolution anyone could pass through the eagle-topped portals in the battlemented walls, and we entered and gazed in wonder and admiration up at the clusters of enormous domes and bells, which seemed constantly to ring out their rich and mellow notes, and down from the terraces upon the river and out over the city—whose skyline is as unique as that of New York. We saw piles of cannon, eight hundred of them captured from Napoleon; we passed the spot where the Grand Duke Sergius was killed with a bomb two years before; we entered the Church of the Assumption where the Tsars were crowned; and finally went into the Palace, where thousands of treasures were open to view. There was gold and silver, it seemed, by the tons and precious stones by the hundred-weight, all wrought into handiwork by master craftsmen, sabres of the Tsars, many in Oriental patterns with highly-jeweled hilts, robes worn by Emperors and Empresses renowned for virtue or notorious for cruelty, and gifts from other sovereigns. We went into many of the gold-domed churches, massive, thick-walled structures whose building had engaged the skill of engineers, the genius of architects and the inspiration of artists. In these incense-laden sanctuaries we saw by the dim lights of candles—for their windows were not numerous—the profusion of sacred ikons framed in precious metals and often bedecked with precious stones.

Outside the Kremlin is what is now known as the Red Square, an open space about the size of a dozen city blocks, without a tree or even a blade of grass growing in it. Lenin's tomb did not stand in the Red Square then but the place was already notorious for the blood that had been shed upon its rough stone pavement. In it was the spot of former executions and the Cathedral of St. Basil—built for Ivan the Terrible by an Italian architect whose eyes were afterwards put out, so the story goes, in order that he should not build a finer one for another monarch.[1] But this cathedral is not fine; it is only bizarre. Because a man is a monarch he does not necessarily know or appreciate what is good in art. Before the revolution no workman entered the Square through the Troitsky Gate without doffing his cap and crossing himself at the shrine in its center.

In a religious procession of those Tsarist days we witnessed several golden banners carried by staggering and perspiring penitents who paid the priests for the privilege. Some of the banners were said to weigh five hundred pounds, and even when assisted by a friend on each side several penitents fell to the ground under the burden. We tried to obtain a photograph of this unique procession, but none had ever been permitted. But throughout history religious and political liberty have gone hand in hand. Dogmatic control by the church is possible only under an autocratic government. It would then have been difficult to believe, had anyone made the prediction, that within ten years the proletariat would rise and kill their Tsar, drive the priests out of the churches, and carve beside that reverenced gate the inscription that "Religion is an Opiate for the masses." Yet it was inevitable that some day the people would rise up and throw off the yoke of religious and political oppression.

We went one day to the Chateau Petrovsky, which the successive Tsars occupied for several days before they were crowned. This is where Napoleon lived while in occupation of Moscow. Another day we went to Sparrow Hill, the point from which the great soldier got his first view of the city—an inspiring sight for a conqueror to behold. At the Church of the Savior, built to commemorate the defeat of the French, we heard one of those famous Russian choirs of men and boys and saw one of the sumptuous services that were conducted in the Orthodox cathedrals, and incidentally saw an interesting opera based upon Napoleon's defeat at Moscow. We explored Moscow from the Kremlin through the bazaars to the outlying suburbs of squalor and misery and visited the foundling hospital established by Catherine the Great where a thousand noisy children, many of them still in their cradles, were being cared for.

Our purchases were limited to a few ikons and a samovar, having to ransack Moscow to get the right one. Nothing would do but that we should have a real Russian samovar from Moscow itself. We finally found and purchased a very striking one, and here my troubles began, for I struggled all the way from there to Washington to see that nothing happened to this precious treasure, and arrived with no greater damage to it than to have the faucet broken off.

Then we journeyed to St. Petersburg. The railway runs in a straight line for about five hundred miles, touching at no other city. The story goes that when the road was being projected the Tsar got weary of appeals to have it twist hither and yon to satisfy all the municipalities that wanted to profit by it, and, losing his temper one day, took the plan from his counselors and drew with a ruler the line that the road should follow.

We spent three days at St. Petersburg, but only two of them were good for sightseeing, as on the other it rained incessantly. We were glad, however, for the opportunity to rest, for sightseeing, while delightful, is also fatiguing business. Here we saw the Hermitage, the storehouse of treasures built on the site of the villa of Catherine the Great, and the Winter Palace at Tsarskoye Selo, as the royal family were in the city at the time. From the Palace we got a view of the city beyond the Neva, including the fortress in which General Stoessel was confined for surrendering Port Arthur to the Japanese. It is probably true that Stoessel did weaken before it was absolutely necessary, yet the fall of Port Arthur was inevitable. We intended to remain at the capital longer, but learning that two of the servants at our hotel had died of cholera the day before, we hurriedly left Russia proper and went to Warsaw. But, anyway, we had seen Moscow, which was even then a greater sight than St. Petersburg, and we had seen it thoroughly in the days when the Tsar was an autocrat.

Warsaw, Berlin, and Brussels

At Warsaw we were still at that time in Russia, as that part of Poland had fallen to the Tsar when that unfortunate country was parceled out by the neighboring powers.[2] We stopped at an excellent new and delightfully clean hotel, the Bristol, where the concierge got us a guide who said he had spent twenty years in the United States. There are some Europeans who prefer their own country even after long experience in ours; this man preferred to live in Poland even under the Tsar. But that was probably not the case with the thousands of Jews of Warsaw. We drove through the Israelite quarter, taking Masa-san and the children along. Here we saw such types as we had seen before only in pictures or on the stage, people of an ancient race still ancient in appearance. Even the children seemed to be of Old Testament lineage. As is generally the case with oppressed races, the Jews of Poland had clung steadfastly to their faith. They had not intermarried with gentiles and in physiognomy as well as costuming still bore outward and visible signs of an inward and spiritual difference. The bearded men in long robes and skull caps and the women in wide-out modest dresses, with their hair bound in colored cloths, were obviously different and apart from either the Russians or Poles. The bearing of this enduring stock—which had rejected both the great religions offered it, the Muhammadan and the Christian, and had suffered for centuries in consequence—was that of a downtrodden people. Old men and women were cringing in manner and boys and girls shy in speech and furtive in their glances. The suggestion was neither made to us nor came to our thoughts at the time that the Jews would soon play a prominent part in the Russian Revolution, one of them, [Leon] Trotsky, even becoming the commander of the Red Army. The World War wrought many changes in the thoughts of men as well as in the maps of empires.

Among the sights of Warsaw was the parliament building, said to be the oldest, and certainly one of the finest, in Europe. Another was the palace of the former Polish kings, then occupied by the Russian governor. Our guide took us to a tavern said to be three hundred years old, owned during all that time by the same family, still serving wine purporting to be of equally ancient vintage. But one cannot believe all one's guides declaim. We saw some riding by a troop of Cossacks, which was excellent but no better than our own cavalry does at Fort Myer outside of Washington. In Warsaw our supply of prunes for the children came to an end, and we had to forage for more. Fortunately we found a store so up-to-date that it had a shipment from California.

Berlin was our next stopping place and the Kaiserhof, then one of the best hotels in the city, our hostelry. As I particularly wished to see something of the German army, I at once got in touch with Colonel John Wisser, our military attaché. He took me the following day to call at the War Office, where I found, as I expected, every sign of smartness and efficiency. Through this visit I arranged to see an artillery regiment and barracks at Potsdam. The Colonel showed me the preparation they had made for quick transformation of the regiment's civilian reserves into fully-equipped soldiers ready to take their places in the ranks. I had never seen such perfect preparation. The complete outfit of every reservist was there in place, even "to the last button." As most of the troops were away on maneuvers, I did not see as much of the army as I would like. My interest, however, was only objective, that of a soldier in the most complete military machine that had ever been organized. It was only six years before the Great War, but no one could then foresee that our troops would fight against those of Germany on European battlefields.

The discipline of the German people was evident at every turn. All things seemed to be done in military fashion. The army, so to speak, was the nation. This was especially noticeable to one who had just come from Russia. There the army seemed a thing apart from the people; here it was a model which they were proud to emulate. In Russia there were murmurings of discontent and there had recently been a revolutionary outbreak which had included a mutiny in the Black Sea fleet [on the battleship *Potemkin* in Odessa in June–July 1905]; here the people were proud of their Kaiser, confident in his administration and apparently glad to perform what they believed to be his will. The men who ran the railroads and those who cleaned the streets went about the duties exactly as if under military direction. The nation was probably the best disciplined and most progressive in the world, and it is trite but possibly true to say that had it kept out of war it would have led the rest of the world in foreign trade in a very few years.

We went to parks, palaces, and museums by day, and in the evenings to theaters and operas or dinners with friends. Of the performance of *Salome*, with music by Richard Strauss, my wife noted in her diary, "a horrible thing, but music very thrilling in places." We heard *Tannhauser*, with Geraldine Farrar in the leading role. Of her my wife noted, "she made a charming Elizabeth and the audience cheered and cheered. The music was magnificent. One must hear [Richard] Wagner on his native heath."

Among the Americans we met in Berlin were Henry P. Fletcher, formerly a "Rough Rider," later a Volunteer in the Philippines, whom Theodore Roosevelt advised to enter the diplomatic service. Fletcher was then one of the secretaries at the Embassy; later he was Ambassador to Brussels and Rome. Joseph H. Grew, whom we met, was also in the Embassy at the time; later he became Under Secretary of State in Washington and Ambassador to Tokyo. At a dinner given us by Colonel and Mrs. Wisser, we met Consul General [Alexander M.] Thackara and his wife—who was a daughter of General Sherman [Eleanor]—Major and Mrs. [Herbert J.] Slocum, and Mr. and Mrs. Elmer Roberts, he being the Associated Press correspondent.

On leaving Berlin we went to Brussels for a few days especially to see the Grand Place,[3] which Victor Hugo described as the finest in the world. Certainly it is one of the finest, with its Gothic Town hall and church and the King's House. Belgium has a distinction thoroughly its own; in spite of the size of the country and its proximity to greater countries, it has, like other small European states, retained its individuality to a marked degree. That is one of the charms of Europe; while the continent, excluding Russia, is not territorially larger than the United States, each of the nationalities is distinctly different from the others. I could not let the opportunity go by and took occasion to go out from Brussels to see Waterloo. As the story of the movements of the Allied and French armies which brought them together on this great battlefield ran through my mind, Byron's stirring lines haunted me like an echo of schoolboy days, and, no doubt like many others before me, I found myself repeating half aloud the opening stanza. "There was a sound of revelry by night and Belgium's capital had gathered then her beauty and chivalry," and so on came to my tongue almost word for word.[4]

Paris, Tours, and London

We arrived in Paris at the time of one of those high political alarms that preceded the World War. Austria-Hungary had just annexed the provinces of Bosnia and Herzegovina, which she had been administering as a protectorate since the Berlin Conference that followed the Russo-Turkish War of thirty years before. The Dual Monarchy had now taken advantage of the weakened condition of the great Slav patron to the north and formally incorporated these south Slav provinces in her dominions. The Serbians and Montenegrins, who had long aspired to annex these contiguous sister provinces, at once mobilized their armies, and the effect throughout Europe gave evidence of the maze of political alliances and mutual and hostile interests that existed. From Russia immediately came diplomatic inquiries to France, her ally, and from France other inquiries went to England, with whom the Entente Cordiale[5] had recently been arranged. And on the other side of the scales that represented this European "balance of power," the diplomatists of the Triple Alliance[6] communicated with equal feverishness between Berlin, Vienna, and Rome. Coming so soon after the Casablanca dispute[7] between France and Germany, the French people began to fear grave consequences and crowds gathered eagerly around the bulletin boards and bought up quickly the special editions of the newspapers. But Russia was not ready to undertake another great war, France and Great Britain wanted none, and all three brought diplomatic pressure to bear on the Serbian states to dissuade them from any rash act, and the day of reckoning was postponed. But the situation continued tense long enough to keep me in France. General J. Franklin Bell, the Chief of Staff, sent me instructions by cable to be in readiness to serve as military observer, and in order to polish up my French I went to Tours for a course of study. The family came with me, and my wife and I studied together. And best of all, we took this opportunity to visit on weekends most of the beautiful chateaus of the Loire.

While we were at Tours Wilbur Wright was at the nearby town of Le Mans giving instruction to French officers to flying the airplane he had invented. The machine was a primitive one that had to be started by being catapulted down an inclined plane. I spent an interesting day with the inventor, and discussing military aviation with him found that he had a clear conception of what was soon to come to pass. There was no attempt to achieve great heights at that time, but within a year [Louis] Blériot had crossed the English Channel and another Frenchman the Alps.[8] But our own country was slower in taking advantage of the American invention. Other nations were wide awake to the possibilities of military aviation, and it is amazing to think that even two years after the World War began the American Army had only thirteen planes in commission, eight of which were used up by my command in Mexico in 1916. Before 1917 no steps whatever had been taken by us to get ready for the tremendous part we were to play in the war. If our people continue to wait until after war is actually upon us, the habit will some day prove disastrous.

At Tours there was a large military post and training ground. Having been a cavalry officer I was particularly interested in equitation, and through the kindness of Captain [William S.] Guignard, our military attaché, it was arranged for me to visit the celebrated cavalry school at Saumur—to which our War Department had begun to send young officers for a special course of training. One of the first to go was Lieutenant W. C. Short, who was there at the time of my visit. The results obtained at Saumur were so far superior to any in our army that I became a staunch advocate of the French system. Short introduced it at Fort Riley, and the officer who [preceded] him at Saumur [Guy V. Henry Jr., who succeeded Short at Fort Riley] aided in teaching it to the mounted army and throughout the service. Today as horsemen the officers of our cavalry have no superiors.[9]

When our stay at Tours came to an end we returned to Paris to finish our visit. While there I went to Metz and with a guide and maps went over the battlefield where the Germans captured Marshal Bazaine and his army in 1871. The visit was especially interesting to me not only as a soldier but because I remembered how as a ten-year-old boy I had eagerly read the dispatches about the Franco-Prussian War as they appeared in the *St. Louis Globe-Democrat*. It was the first great war that I was old enough to read about at the time it was being waged. The sight of the battlefield brought back to mind how the wiseacres of Laclede, my old hometown, used to gather in front of father's store and Dick Mitchell's drugstore next door and, whittling in Missouri fashion, hold forth on the strategy of the campaign—comparing the French and German generals to Grant and Lee. We spent the holidays in Paris and then went to London for a few days before sailing.

Back in Washington Again and William Howard Taft's Inauguration, 1909

It was good to be in Washington again among our many friends after four years of absence. We lived at the Willard Hotel to be near Senator Warren, who made that his home. Mr. Taft had been elected President and "T. R." had only till March to occupy the White House. His proposed expedition to Africa had been announced and the papers were publishing columns about the international preparations that were going on to aid and abet him in the adventure. No President of the United States, or of any other country, had ever done such a thing before and all the big game hunters in the world wanted to advise or assist him. In popular interest President Roosevelt was "stealing the thunder" of President Taft's inauguration.

It fell to my lot to take part in the latter in a social way; I was chosen a member of the Inaugural Ball Committee. In those days the ball was held in the old Pension Office because the hall in the building was the largest in Washington. It was then a very popular function and was attended by official Washington and by hundreds of visitors. Politicians of the new President's party and their wives came from every state in the Union to the inauguration and ball—one of the gratifications of the pilgrimage being that their names were telegraphed back to their hometown papers as "among the notables present." The preparations were elaborate and costly and the committee in charge worked for weeks in advance to make the gala evening a huge success. At our first meeting, held after a delightful luncheon with Mr. and Mrs. Larz Anderson at their mansion on Massachusetts Avenue, the various subcommittees, financial, business, political, et cetera were selected, and I was chosen to manage and lead the ball.

Some wag had suggested that each state be represented by two of its handsomest men. I do not recall that any Democrats were selected. Apparently masculine pulchritude and a sense of humor do not run strong together, for there was apparently no difficulty in persuading representatives to form the group. But just where they fitted into the scheme of things had not been decided. When the evening came and the guests began to arrive—in a deluge of rain—it dawned upon the committee that no special position had been allotted to America's handsomest.

These stars, who expected to form a galaxy of satellites around the new President, were about to go into eclipse when they made an appeal to me to save them from this humiliation. Happily the hall was not yet congested, and it occurred to me that the most conspicuous place to pose them would be about the fountain—an appropriate setting for a group of Apollos though it was unconventional to have them in evening clothes. In this position every one could see them, and they were especially conspicuous as the presidential party paraded around the fountain, and from their point of view the ball that threatened to be disastrous turned out a thorough success.

A Sojourn at the Army and Navy General Hospital

Five years' service in the tropics since the beginning of 1900 had not only run down my general health but had brought some anxiety as to the condition of my heart, and while abroad I visited Bad Nauheim in Germany. The heart specialist there was not too encouraging, and I returned to the States considerably alarmed. Immediately after inauguration, therefore, I went on sick leave and became finally a patient at the Army and Navy [General] Hospital in Hot Springs, Arkansas. Here I was given a thorough going-over by the staff under Colonel G. D. [George D.] Deshon, a classmate of mine at West Point who had resigned to practice medicine and later had been appointed to the Medical Corps. The examination covered several days and, feeling apprehensive, I finally asked Deshon to tell me the worst. "John," he said, "we have subjected you to every known test, and in my opinion and in that of my associates there isn't a damn thing the matter with you." But I had been too thoroughly scared to believe Deshon and when he continued, "Tomorrow morning two saddle horses will be ready at seven o'clock and we shall take a ride," I was, I freely confess, in a blue funk. Convinced in my own mind that my heart would not stand the exertion and that the chances were less than even that I should return alive, I had to drive myself to appear the next morning, and still was skeptical when after a short ride no untoward results followed. We had kept the horses at the walk and the exertion had been negligible. But as we continued to ride each morning, gradually increasing the distance and gait, my courage began to return, and when at the end of fifteen days I was galloping over the hills as I had when a lieutenant of cavalry fear had vanished entirely and I knew that once more, thanks to the army medical man, I was ready for active duty.[10]

A Return to the Philippines and a New Son

In October, therefore, I was again en route to the Philippine Islands, accompanied by my family and our Japanese amah. There were now five of us, our third having been born in June, in Cheyenne, Wyoming. This was our first boy, and we named him after my wife's father, Francis Warren.

Pershing with his son, Francis Warren (no date).
(Library of Congress, Prints and Photographs Division,
Bain News Service Collection. LC-DIG-ggbain-30224)

My Return to Mindanao

November 1909–December 1913

Commanding General, Department of Mindanao, and Governor of the Moro Province

The post to which I was now assigned was a dual one—that of Commanding General of the Department of Mindanao and Governor of the Moro Province, the military Department and the Province being practically the same geographically. This dual position offered unusual possibilities for constructive work among an alien and backward people. My first tour of duty in the southern islands had aroused my deep and sympathetic interest in their welfare, and from the time I left Camp Vicars, in 1903, I had hoped some day to return and have a further part in the establishment of law and order among them—a thing they had never known. At that time it was beyond the range of my imagination that my role could be more than a subordinate one, but my promotion in 1906 made me eligible for the high post to which I had just been assigned. I had let it be known that this was where I wanted to be above all other places and now, in 1909, the promise made to my Moro friends six years before that some day I would return for service among them had been redeemed. But before going into the details of my experience there, let me say a personal word about our life at Zamboanga, the little capital, situated at the extreme southern point of the Island of Mindanao.

Life at Zamboanga

The Governor's residence had been an old Spanish barracks. It was a spacious place, set close to the beach, facing the small parade ground

While he served as Commanding General, Department of Mindanao, and Governor of the Moro Province (December 1909–December 1913), Pershing and his family lived in these former Spanish quarters at Pettit Barracks, Zamboanga, Mindanao. (Library of Congress, Prints and Photographs Division, Pershing Collection, Lot 8854)

or plaza, around which the barracks and quarters of the garrison and department staff were grouped. The building, which was two-storied, had been altered from time to time by my predecessors and was further improved by me till it became a veritable palace. Most of the changes and additions were made with native hardwoods, which are noted for their beauty of grain, texture, and coloring. The windows were sliding panels into which translucent sea shells often used in the Islands had been set in lieu of panes of glass. The rooms were large and numerous and a broad second-floor veranda partially enclosed was soon filled with palms and other indigenous plants and profusely hung with a variety of rare and beautiful orchids. It overlooked the Straits of Basilan, from which came cool breezes to temper the tropical heat. It was the finest residence I ever occupied except the one in Paris owned by Ogden Mills Sr., and chateau of M. [Monsieur] Charles de Rouvre at Chaumont graciously put at my disposal by their owners for the duration. The lines and colors of the landscape, rich in many tones of verdure, would have

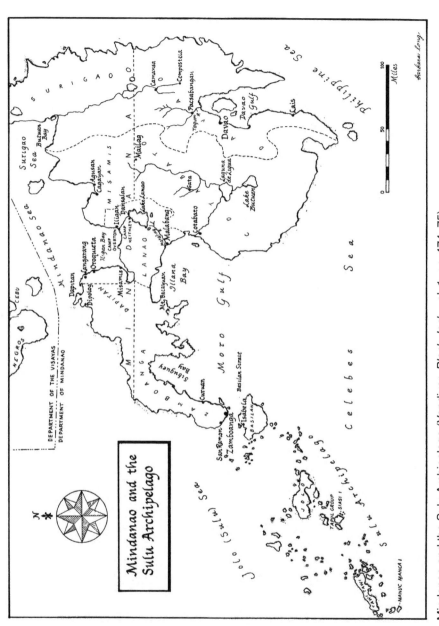

Mindanao and the Sulu Archipelago (Vandiver, *Black Jack*, vol. 1, pp. 474–75).

fascinated an artist, and the sky, especially at sunset over the water, presented a changing picture unsurpassed in nature.

Our staff of servants was curiously interracial. An American Negro, as black as ever came out of the Congo, was our coachman; a Filipino, one of the most efficient of his class, the houseboy; Masa-san, the Japanese amah or nursemaid, educated and refined; Ah Chong, the Chinese cook, than whom there was none better; and a white American trooper of the First Cavalry, my orderly [Private Frank Lanckton]. The Asiatic members of the household were sober, industrious, and reliable, but I cannot say as much for the others at all times. One afternoon when my wife and I were driving out to make a call, the erratic behavior of the horses caused me first to protest and then to notice that the driver was falling asleep on the box. When he dozed the reins would slacken and the horses would speed up, then he would awaken and bring them down. Finally, realizing that he had been drinking, I took him off the box and taking his place drove the carriage myself, much to the amusement of our hosts when we arrived at our destination. But he was faithful otherwise, besides being a field cook, and for that reason I kept him with me and later took him to Mexico in that capacity. The orderly had the same weakness but was better at "carrying" his liquor. When suspected and accused he would declare with pretense of offended innocence that he had not touched a drop, and it was some time before I could be sure otherwise. I never succeeded in reforming him, although I tried various methods, but because of his generally good deportment and his devotion, I bore with him for years.

At Zamboanga we led a life in the open air. The doors and windows of our house were always open in fair weather. When at home hardly a morning went by that we did not take a dip in the sea, which was but twenty paces away. When the tide was in we could dive off the end of our pier and when it was out could wade to deep water over good sea sands. My wife was an excellent swimmer and the children took to the water like ducklings. But I was never confident as a swimmer and often stood on shore in dismay when my wife would swim half a mile straight out into the sea.

Usually in the afternoons we went horseback riding, and here again Mrs. Pershing, having been raised in Wyoming and accustomed to horses, was very much at home. The children were taught as soon as they could sit a pony, our son before he was three years old. We had two Java thoroughbreds for the youngsters—not ponies but perfectly-proportioned small horses, one a sorrel and the other a roan. They were

The Pershing family, including John, Frankie, and their children, Anne, Helen (seated), and Francis Warren. This photograph was likely made while Pershing was commanding the Department of Mindanao and Governor of the Moro Province. Since Mary Margaret (their fourth child, who was born in May 1912) is not pictured and Francis Warren appears to be about two years old, the photograph probably dates to sometime in 1911. (Library of Congress, Prints and Publications Division, Lot 12362. LC-USZ62-107733)

as gentle and friendly as dogs, but we dare not let the children ride without a lead as they always wanted to gallop as fast as the animals could go. I had a spanking pair of horses for the carriage and four dapper mules for the Doherty wagon,[1] called an ambulance, which we frequently used on official occasions when the party was large.

I established a golf course and a polo field about three miles to the west for the diversion of those who enjoyed such sports, and I participated in both at every opportunity. It was because of our active lives that we were able to remain in the tropics longer than the usual period. Though I was stationed at Zamboanga for four years, we had no serious illness in the family except twice. Once when only a year old Warren had a severe case of dysentery and later Anne, at the age of four, also had a bad attack, both of which gave us considerable anxiety.

The fact that the station was quite active socially gave added zest to the life. We often had guests to luncheon or dinner, on occasions as many as ten or fifteen, and when some high official came on a tour of the Islands we might have twenty or thirty. The Americans in the community were mainly military men and their families connected with the department staff or with the garrison, which consisted usually of a regimental headquarters and one battalion of infantry. There were comparatively few civilians other than natives permanently located in the town, but merchant ships that came into harbor once or twice a week often brought transients. Those who came at intervals to visit Zamboanga and the Department or Province were Major General William P. Duvall, commander of the Philippines Division until early 1911 [28 December 1910]; and Major General Bell [13 January 1911–3 April 1914], his successor, and Governor-General Cameron Forbes. We had the pleasure of entertaining them each time they came and often held receptions in their honor.

Governor Forbes was fond of deep-sea fishing and of shooting. On one occasion I took him to the great swampy basin in the upper Cotabato valley on a duck hunt. The birds were so thick and unafraid that we could have got several at one shot as they sat in the water, but as sportsmen we waited to fire till they rose, and even then sometimes brought down an embarrassing number with one shell. Shooting from a dugout canoe managed by a Moro with one oar was ticklish business. On this trip in reaching too far to get a bird I had shot I went headlong, gun and all, into the water. Another time the Governor-General came to Bukidnon to settle a boundary dispute between officials of that Province and those of the Moro Province. As we approached the small native town of Tanculan we were met by a group of tribal warriors, one of whom danced in front of us with his spear and shield, making savage thrusts toward us as he leaped backward, pretending to combat our advance. It was their way of extending us a welcome. No sooner had we reached the public marketplace than we were challenged to a game of baseball, which we accepted. The Governor-General covered one base, Dean Worcester, the Secretary of the Interior, and I each another, while aides and secretaries took other positions, in the nine. The natives, although new at the game, played well and were somewhat surprised when they did not win.

Secretary of War Jacob M. Dickinson in [20–24 August 1910] came on a tour of inspection of the Province accompanied by a considerable party including Mr. and Mrs. Larz Anderson, and we led off with a large reception for him. At every center, as at Jolo and Lake Lanao, the leading Moros were assembled for conference. There was a great deal of agitation at this time among Filipinos in favor of independence. At Zamboanga [23 August] the assembly consisted of both Filipinos and Moros and several of the former spoke openly for independence. The Moros, led by *Datto* Mandi, spoke in opposition and asked that the Americans remain in control of the Islands.[2] He was followed by one old patriarch of a Moro, *Datto* [Sacaluran], who rose and said, "We want American rule and ask that the government be not turned over to the Filipino." He said, "I am an old man and had hoped to see no more fighting, but if the Americans leave we will not submit to the Filipinos, but I will lead my people again into battle."[3] At this there were loud protests from the Filipinos, which further exasperated the Moros, who were already in an ugly mood. It actually looked for a moment as though there might be a clash then and there, but Mr. Dickinson told them he had only come on a visit and could not discuss that question, and they all calmed down.[4]

Duties as Commander and Governor

But my four years in the Moro Province were by no means all pleasure and entertainment. We had much hard work to do and an endless succession of difficult problems to solve. It was the most active command I had held up to this time and new problems came up almost daily. In my dual role I had two offices, each independent of the other and in different buildings. When in Zamboanga, I usually spent the morning at one and the afternoon at the other. My Adjutant General, at first Major Frederick Perkins and later H. H. [Henry H.] Whitney, were both thoroughly efficient and fully conversant with the duties of that office, so that I was largely relieved of details. I was frequently off to various parts of the Province, by boat to the coastal stations and often went on foot into the interior.

The Province embraced hundreds of islands and was inhabited by perhaps as many radically different peoples as could be found in an equal area anywhere in the world. In territory it was about equal in square miles to [left blank in original] and had a population of a little over five hundred thousand. There were three main divisions among the inhabitants but many subdivisions. There were the Muhammadan Moros, under many different sultans and *dattos*; the pagans, divided into many unrelated tribes; and the Christian Filipinos. There was age-old hostility, not only among the three principal groups but among the subdivisions of each of the first two groups.

The largest element of population were the Moros, native Filipinos of Malay extraction both remote and recent, whose characteristics and ideas had been drastically changed by their conversion to the militant creed of Muhammad. They recognized the pretensions of the Sultan Abdul Hamid [Abdülhamid II] of Turkey to be the vice-regent of the Prophet on earth but were so cut off from contact with the distant Near East that few of them had heard of the overthrow of that ruler by the Young Turks[5] in 1908.

The numbers of the different peoples in the Province were approximately as follows:

Moros	325,000
Pagans or Wild Tribes	105,000
Christian Filipinos	85,000
Chinese	3,000
Americans and Europeans (civilians)	1,200
Japanese	1,000

According to ethnologists the Negritos, dwarf blacks with frizzly hair, were the earliest of the Filipinos. Their traditions date from a great deluge that covered the earth. Then came the Indo-Australians, but in any discussion of these early races we become involved in vague theories of a lost pacific continent and of apparently continuous waves of Polynesian and Indonesian migrations. The fierce Indonesians, a branch of the Malays whom we know as Moros, began their migrations in the first century. As we have seen, their *praos* [Malay sailing boat] sailed the seven seas; they conquered the coast towns, driving their brown predecessors into the interior with irresistible persistence. Then came the quiet teachers of Muhammadanism, the first missionary arriving from Arabia in 1380, and others continued the work they began.

The hill tribes, of East Indian blood, brought their worship of the Vedic gods,[6] which became the dominant religion in the Islands two thousand or more years ago. The tribes all have innate conceptions of their deities, and each names them in its own dialect and conducts its religious ceremonies according to its own traditions. When later migrations of the more advanced peoples settled along the coasts, these primitive inhabitants, unwilling to accept domination or assimilation, successively fell back into the hills for security and for freedom to continue their ancient worships and customs. Other languages and religions, in turn Buddhist, Muhammadan, and Christian, had made no headway among them, and they continued through the many centuries to follow the practices and superstitions of their early forefathers. A huge monster, they believed, caused the storms at sea; when he lay on the shore and shook himself it caused the earthquake; lightning was the glare of his eyes in anger; and thunder was his roar.

Each of these tribes had its own peculiar characteristics. The largest, the Subanos, numbered about thirty-five thousand and occupied the high interior of the Island of Mindanao. Unlike the Moros, they were neither polygamous nor warlike. They were a timid people who fled before danger, often deserting their habitations and settling on new lands, which had to be cleared of virgin forests for their farms. The Bagabos numbered about twenty-five thousand and lived on the west shore of the Gulf of Davao. They were the most advanced in the ways of civilization. They had horses and cattle, raised good crops, were industrious, and were the first who were willing to send their children to the schools the American Government established. They are the most picturesque of the hill tribes in their homemade, varicolored clothes. The Mandayans numbered about seventeen thousand and lived in the country north of the Gulf of Davao. They were the wildest and most savage. Their chiefs took rank according to the number of enemies they had slain. They often lived in trees to be out of range of the spears of adversaries. But they had one unusual virtue. Infidelity on the part of either man or woman was punished by death, and none could cohabit without marriage, which was compulsory. The Manobos, about ten thousand, lived in different sections of the Province. They were generally shiftless and indolent and subsisted largely on *camotes*, a kind of sweet potato, and wild forest products. Salt with them, as with most hill tribes, was a luxury, and Chinese traders made exorbitant profits in this commodity. Among the smaller tribes were the Tirurais, a poor and ignorant people who were an easy prey to others; the Atas, a strong, virile people of mixed negrito blood, who raided and killed at times for mere prestige; and the Yakans, long-haired inhabitants of the Island of Basilan, who punished adultery by tying the offenders together and throwing them into the sea. The wild tribes of the Province are found almost exclusively in the territory of Mindanao, while the Moros inhabit the Sulu Archipelago, the southern part of Zamboanga peninsula, the Lake Lanao country, and the extensive and fertile valley of the Cotabato River. The Christian Filipinos, Spanish Catholic converts who drifted south later, are the principal inhabitants of the larger coastal towns and vicinities.

It was a strange conglomeration of humanity for a small body of Americans, themselves different from these people in race, language, ideas, customs, and attainments, to attempt to govern. To bring them thoroughly under control, to terminate the warfare among then, to unify them and lead them into better ways of life was an undertaking never seriously attempted before. The Spaniards, after tentative efforts covering three hundred years, had not succeeded. The work required careful judgment and continual patience as well as force and readiness to use it. From one point of view much progress had already been made, but from another only a beginning. No single governor in his brief term of a few years in office could do more than advance the order a few steps. The first Governor was Major General Leonard Wood [25 July 1903–16 April 1906], and then came Brigadier General Tasker H. Bliss [16 April 1906–5 April 1909]. I succeeded the latter.[7]

The Moro Province had been delimited and constituted by the Philippines Commission in 1903. It included all of Mindanao south of the Eighth Parallel, the Sulu Archipelago, and other islands. It was divided into five districts. The organization provided for a governor, a secretary, a treasurer, and an attorney, all of whom were appointed by the Governor-General. These four Americans constituted the Legislative Council, which was empowered by the Organic Act to make laws, subject to the approval of the Philippines Commission. The Act conferred all essential authority for the enactment of constructive legislation and for the exercise of administrative direction of affairs. The Council, holding both legislative and executive powers, had largely a free hand. The Governor, as its head and with his control of military action, was almost a dictator. The Council raised revenue by taxation, which under its direction was expended on the construction of public works, the maintenance of schools, courts, police, and the support of the provincial government in general. The Province was dependent on its own revenues, which included customs duties collected at the ports and direct taxes levied on the people.

The military force in the Province at the beginning of my administration was a little over five thousand five hundred officers and men.[8] Of these about three thousand were American troops and the rest native scouts [Philippine Scouts].[9] The American forces were concentrated in the larger centers to be used only in serious emergencies, while the Scouts, considered a part of the army, occupied certain outlying stations. There were also several companies of Philippine native constabulary [Philippine Constabulary] in the Province under civil control. The five district governors under me were Americans. At first they were army or constabulary officers. Under those local governors came presidents of the Filipino towns and the head men of the Moro and tribal communities, who assisted in the maintenance of good government among their respective peoples.

In reviewing the six years since my departure from Vicars, it seemed to me that although much good work had been done, the military forces had been used at times unnecessarily. That force had to be used to a certain extent, and to the limit in dealing with the criminal elements, was unquestionable, but from time to time haste had been shown in the enforcement of laws and regulations that ran counter to age-old customs. Where patience and appeal would eventually have brought acquiescence, it had been demanded here and there arbitrarily, with regrettable results. In Lanao, the district I particularly knew, several of the friendships that I had made among the chiefs had been alienated. Shortly after taking command I made an inspection trip to all the larger posts of the Province. At several I had the head men called together to tell them of the government's intentions and to hear directly any suggestions they had to offer or complaints to make. I encouraged them to speak frankly and most of them did. Although serious in character, the meetings were always colorful, sometimes amusing.[10]

At Jolo the weak and repulsive sultan's greatest complaint was about the infidelity of one or two of his young wives. At Lanao my return after the six years' absence was something like that of the Prodigal Son; large crowds from all parts of the lake attended the meetings and hailed me like a far-traveled brother. An old friend, Ahmai-Tampugao, in greeting me on behalf of those present, said, "Since you left we have been like orphans, with no hope except in God on high, but now that you are returning we are, as I have said, very happy and glad to see you here among us." Had I been able to remain a week the time would have been filled with accounts of what had happened in my absence, for everyone wanted to tell me his story. Many of the chiefs had complaints to make of arbitrary and unjust treatment by the local government and in some cases no doubt with good reason, but no individual or group can be infallible and mistakes were made by all of us. However, I would say that as a general rule it was the depredations committed by the different tribes and peoples themselves that were basically responsible.

The Uprising at Boburan

In the first month of my incumbency, as if to welcome me, an uprising occurred among the Subanos [also now known as the Subanon people]. Aided by pagans and Christian outcasts and criminals, certain Moro chiefs from Lake Lanao gathered several thousands of the hill people of the Zamboanga District into an unknown and almost inaccessible portion of the country tributary to Dapitan. They accomplished this by resort to deception, false prophesy (telling the Subanos they must gather on Mount Boburan preparatory to ascending into Heaven just before the destruction of the earth by fire and water), and in many cases violence. The simple, pastoral Subanos were enticed or driven into camps, where they were under the control of these self-appointed leaders. The positions of defense they occupied were well-chosen and the men armed with cutting weapons. The Legislative Council offered a considerable reward for the apprehension of the leaders, but this brought no results. I thereupon ordered the constabulary force from Dapitan to the outskirts of the camp at Boburan to disperse the gathering. Led by their Moro chiefs, the Subanos attacked the constabulary and, after killing several, with heavier loss to themselves, scattered in the mountains. I then sent a company of Scouts to report to Major John P. Finley, Governor of Zamboanga District, who had been placed in immediate command, and after two months of difficult work peace was restored. Major Finley conducted his campaign with great patience and consideration, as the following from his report shows:

> [It was early manifest that][†] in order to secure the leaders and rescue the Subanos it was imperatively necessary to gain the confidence of the hill people. They must be made to understand and

appreciate the attitude of the government toward them and definitely the objects and plans of the troops assembled in their territory. They must know and be made to feel the friendship and reliance of the troops in protecting their interests and reestablishing their homes. Such confidence and trust could not be realized by the customary, rapid marching of troops through the theatre of operations.

Rapid, selfish and unsympathetic movements of troops among the hill people do not permit of harmonious and confidential contact with them.

Ample time was given the hill people to take a look at the troops and become convinced that this form of governmental power was friendly and really interested in their salvation and prosperity. After becoming thus convinced the good influences of the government spread with amazing rapidity among the Subanos. They returned to their farms by hundreds daily. They proffered their services to the government and declined remuneration. The important witnesses emerged from their hiding places and the apprehension of the leaders became a possibility. Thus the harmonious cooperation progressed to the end. The leaders were caught, the witnesses came forward from their hiding places to convict them, and the wandering Subanos reclaimed their homes and began life anew. [There was general rejoicing among them.]† 11

The Manobos Rampage

A year later the Manobos of the Sarangani Peninsula, in the District of Davao, went on a rampage. It was the custom of these pagans annually to celebrate the gathering of the harvest with great feasts. At such times their warlike inclinations mounted to a high pitch. The bravest men were the heroes of the hour. The test of bravery and prowess was the number of lives the hero had taken, and those who had participated in the greatest number of killings were looked upon with especial favor by their women. As a consequence each year about this time hostility against those toward whom they had a grievance often became active. In 1910 the Manobos had a bumper crop and the feasts aroused more than usual passion. Banded together in groups of fifty or one hundred they set out to exterminate their enemies, defying the constabulary. Several murders were committed by them in cold blood, including one American planter.

I immediately ordered two companies of Philippine Scouts, two companies of the Third Infantry, and a troop of the Second Cavalry to the scene and went myself to the district to direct operations through Major E. R. [Elvin R.] Heiberg, Philippine Scouts, who was placed in immediate command. The country was rugged and mountainous and probably the most difficult in the Islands. Columns were sent in pursuit of the hostile bands simultaneously from several points and the operations vigorously carried out until most of the individuals accused of crime were killed or captured and the bands broken up. After that many of those people who had never before visited the coast came down to cultivate the fertile valleys, declaring their intentions to abandon their nomadic habits. No effective action to punish them during these seasons of murderous rivalry had heretofore been taken.

Problems with Moro Outlaws and *Juramentado*

Such affairs as these, however, while bothersome and prominent in the news while they lasted, were not our most difficult military problem. It was the Moro outlaws who kept the Province in constant state of turmoil during previous administrations, and there was hardly a day after my arrival that a report did not come in of disturbance somewhere. Outlaw bands confined their activities generally to outlying districts, but *juramentados,* individuals ready to kill Americans at certain sacrifice of their own lives, appeared from time to time even in the towns. In the early spring of 1911 there were several such fanatical outbreaks. A particularly cruel case was that of the killing of Lieutenant W. H. [Walter H.] Rodney, of the Second Cavalry, one Sunday afternoon [16 April] in Jolo, close to the barracks. The Lieutenant was out walking with his little daughter, about five years old, when a Moro who passed him on the road suddenly drew his *barong,* turned, and killed him with several quick and vicious slashes from behind. There was a cockpit nearby where a large crowd of Christian Filipinos were assembled at their favorite Sunday sport. The cry went up *juramentado* and there was a scattering of people in every direction. The Moro, however, attacked none of them. He was after Americans. Going about his purpose calmly, he proceeded towards the nearby barracks. But the commanding officer, Colonel Frank West, had seen the attack and called out the guard, and before the man could kill anyone else he was shot dead in his tracks. These *juramentado* attacks were materially reduced in number by a practice the army had already adopted, one that Muhammadans held in abhorrence. The bodies were publicly buried in the same grave with a dead pig. It was not pleasant to have to take such measures, but the prospect of going to hell instead of heaven sometimes deterred the would-be assassins.[12]

In many parts of the Province, and particularly about Lake Lanao and in Jolo, such disorder prevailed that it was impossible to enforce the law without a large force of troops or constabulary. Life and property were safe nowhere in the interior of the Province. Especially in Jolo, owners of carabao, cattle, and horses had often to stand guard over them day and night, and their corrals for animals were almost as well fortified as the *cottas* in which the people took refuge when occasion required. The long list of murders and assassinations committed by Moros and pagans since the establishment of provincial government had brought discredit upon the Province and made it unsafe except in municipalities where the Filipino population predominated.

In most of the sub-provinces the local governors had no difficulty in engaging efficient and reliable interpreters. But in Jolo the authorities had depended upon two or three members of a family of Eurasians who spoke the language well but who for some reason, corruption or incompetence, never succeeded in bringing a single criminal to justice. I always thought they shielded guilty Moros for a price, as they became very well to do. It was not until the local governor[13] discovered a young Moro who had learned English under American rule and who was fearless enough to report truthfully the results of his investigations when any of these criminals were caught. Through him many guilty Moros were convicted by our courts. This Moro, Arolas Tulawie [Maas Arola Tulawi], became in manhood an important leader among his people.

I had instigated a vigorous campaign against the outlaws throughout the Province and in the two years ending June 30, 1911, ten different bands were rounded up, seventy-nine outlaws were captured, one hundred and twenty-six killed and ten surrendered. But even this did not stop the outlawry, which seemed to be a sort of second nature with many of them.

The Decision to Disarm the Moros and Non-Christians

It was the possession of arms by the criminal elements that nullified the most earnest efforts toward civil rule and left the peaceably inclined inhabitants at their mercy. To my mind, although many Americans opposed it, there was but one solution—the disarming of the Moros and other non-Christians. The problem had been left to the discretion of the provincial governors and hitherto none had considered it wise to make such an attempt. Shortly after becoming governor I discussed the question with Governor-General Forbes, who agreed with me that it should be done, provided it could be accomplished without too much difficulty. I did not decide to undertake it until convinced that there would be a continuance of the disorders until disarmament was accomplished and that it should be done even though the most drastic means might be necessary. I anticipated comparatively little trouble dealing with the scattered wild tribes but considerable with the Moros—who, though not fully united, had a bond of union in their religion. There were predictions made by both Americans and Moros that the attempt would bring about a Holy War—Muhammadan against "unbeliever"— a bloody thing to contemplate, but I did not believe it would have this effect. In fact, many of the *dattos* and sultans themselves favored the project provided all, good and bad alike, could be disarmed. The greatest fear was that the peaceful people, who would be the first to give up their weapons, would then be at the mercy of the lawless elements for the many months that it would takes the troops to run them down. We entered into it fully realizing that here and there force would have to be employed from the beginning but with the firm conviction that it was the only solution to the problem.

19

Disarming and Taming the Moros

September 1911–June 1913

Disarmament Program

It was a fortunate thing for several reasons that during the period of disarmament there was a man of the high moral courage and sound judgment of Cameron Forbes in the post of Governor-General of the Philippines. It was generally considered such a radical step that without his confidence the undertaking, difficult at best, could hardly have been accomplished. It was a period when either or both of us might have been subjected to uninformed criticism from home that would have seriously interfered with our work. A statesman is under constant suspicion of "playing politics" and a soldier of wanting to fight. But the Governor-General and I were agreed that without disarmament pacification of the Province was impossible. He wrote me, on February 4, 1913, when the situation was most tense, a letter that shows his attitude from the start. In it he said:

> [I am indeed sorry to come back to these waters and find trouble in your district. I had hoped that the thing would be done without bloodshed.]† I am not sure as to the effect of this in the United States at the present time. If it works out that it leads people to believe that the Islands are not ready for further concessions in the matter of participation in their own government we shall be charged with having brought it about for political reasons. If it tends to make the American people more anxious to pull out it

would be unfortunate in the other way. On the other hand, I am a great optimist and I dare say it will work out just right. At any rate, I think the proper thing is to do your duty and let the consequences take care of themselves. As I cabled you, I have every confidence in your skill in handling the situation. Of course drastic measures are occasionally necessary and I suppose they are now, and you will have my entire support in whatever you find it necessary to do within reason.[1]

After consultation with the Executive Council, I issued a Proclamation on September 8, 1911 [Executive Order No. 24], as Governor of the Moro Province, making unlawful the possession of firearms or the carrying of cutting or thrusting weapons by any person within the limits of the Province without permission of the Governor or unless otherwise authorized by law to possess and carry such weapons. Notice was spread throughout the Province that until December 1 compensation at fair values would be made for all weapons surrendered. Many arms were turned in promptly by the peaceably inclined, many old friends being among the first, but the hostile elements as soon as the Proclamation appeared began to group themselves and prepare for action. In effect they sent word that if we wanted their arms we would have to come and take them and that we would have to pay a high price in blood. Many of them, we learned, took the *juramentado* oath, the vow to kill as many Americans as possible regardless of their own fate.

More or less opposition was encountered in each of the five districts, but the hotbeds of disaffection were, as I had expected, the Moro centers of Jolo and Lanao. For years the people of the latter had been harassed by outlaw bands, whose disarmament, it went without saying, could be accomplished only by the energetic use of force. To add to the difficulties here, about the time the Proclamation was issued eight Moro Constabulary soldiers deserted and joined one or another of these bands, where, with their military training, they soon became leaders. I placed Colonel Lea Febiger, Sixth Infantry, in charge of disarmament in Lanao and for about a year detachments of his troops were almost constantly in pursuit of these renegades, often following them to the most remote hiding places. The services of Captains [Allen S.] Fletcher and [William J.] Ayers of the Scouts and Lieutenant [Oscar] Preuss of the Constabulary in this campaign were especially meritorious. It was arduous, dangerous work, but it was splendidly performed, resulting by December of the following year in the capture or surrender of practically all remaining arms, and leaving Lanao in a state of quiet and security that it had never known before.

In the District of Zamboanga the services of Lieutenant [Frank O.] Smith of the Scouts and Lieutenant [Samuel T.] Polk of the Constabulary in destroying the band of the outlaw Mapandi must be mentioned, as must those of Lieutenant [Benjamin E.] Grey, of the Eighth Infantry, in Cotabato District.

The Bud Dajo Campaign, Jolo Island

On the island of Jolo the use of force was not immediately invoked, but the Joloanos were given further opportunity to respond to the efforts of our civil officials for a peaceful submission to the terms of my Proclamation.[2] But well before December 1, the final date for the surrender of arms with payment, the loud boasts of leaders and numerous acts of hostility clearly indicated that force would be necessary. On November 26 I left for Jolo to direct operations.

The troops on Jolo were at once organized under the command of Colonel Frank West and placed in two camps established at convenient locations, one, under Colonel Henry Kirby, at Seit Lake, for the purpose of isolating the Moros in the eastern part of the island, and the other, under Colonel L. J. [Lawrence J.] Hearn, at Taglibi, eight miles east of the walled town of Jolo. The Moros of the Taglibi district had always been among the most violent opponents of American administration, and I did not believe many days would pass without an attack on Hearn's camp. To prevent a surprise, the jungle about it was cleared away for about two hundred yards, entrenchments dug and barbed wire strung. On the night of the twenty-eighth, just as the moon was going down, the attack came, the Moros repeatedly throwing themselves recklessly against our wire in attempts to enter the camp. But for the barbed wire protection, the fighting would have been hand-to-hand in the dark and our losses would probably have been heavy. As it was, we suffered no casualties, and I withheld any immediate retaliatory measures, hoping they might not be necessary. But as the savage attacks on our troops in and out of camp continued, I directed Colonel Hearn, on December 2, to send three columns out to police the jungle in the vicinity. About half a mile from camp the Moros opened fire but were driven from column to column and finally widely scattered.

Mrs. Pershing at this time was at Baguio with the children. Naturally she was concerned about me personally when off on an affair of this

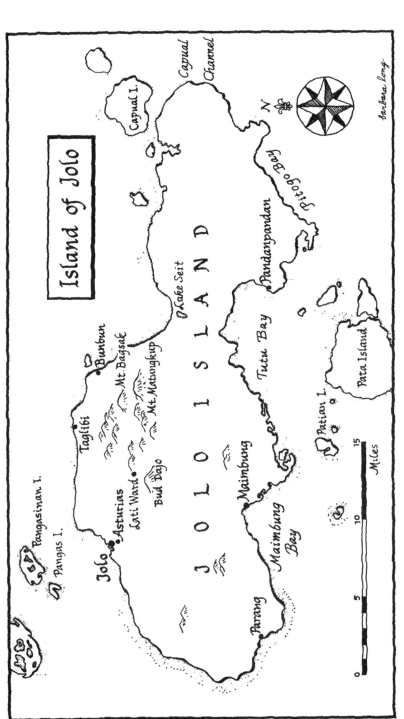

Island of Jolo (Vandiver, *Black Jack*, vol. 1, p. 562).

sort, and I made it a practice to write her a brief note each night of the day's happenings, scribbling it off on the leaves of a memorandum book I carried in my pocket.[3] The letters formed a sort of diary and in them I find many pertinent items. In that of December 2 I said:

> I would give anything to end this business without much fight-
> ing, but these Taglibi Moros seem vicious. They have shown their
> teeth and have even snapped at us. . . . [(Captain William O.)
> Reed thinks he can talk them around][†] but you can't talk a fellow
> around to much of anything if he is shooting at you all the time. I
> [stood this sort of thing for a year once and I][†] have always said it
> was an error to sit idly by and let these savages shoot you up with-
> out going after them, politics or no politics, and I do not intend
> to stand for it or permit it.[4]

Two days later five columns, starting simultaneously from equidis-
tant points along the Taglibi boundary and converging as they marched,
combed the district thoroughly. Little resistance was encountered except
by the column under Captain J. W. [John W.] Barker, which was attacked
by a group of *juramentados* who rushed him desperately. Two of his men
were killed and one wounded and one constabulary soldier killed, the
Moros losing fifteen killed. That afternoon an influential Moro came in
saying they had had enough and were ready to turn in their arms, and
although I suspected that it was only a ruse to gain time I postponed
further operations I had planned pending the outcome of negotiations.
I had been similarly deceived by the Moros several times before, but "I
want to give them all the chance in the world," I wrote my wife.[5]

I at once prepared a letter to the several hostile leaders of the district, had it translated into their language, and taken to them by friendly
Moros [6 December]. Couched in simple terms that they could readily
understand, it said:

> I write you this letter because I am sorry to know that you and
> your people refuse to do what the government has ordered. You
> do not give up your arms. Soldiers were sent to Taglibi so that you
> could come into camp and turn in your guns. When the soldiers
> went to camp at Taglibi, your Moros fired into camp and tried to
> kill the soldiers. Then the soldiers had to shoot all Moros who
> fired upon them. When the soldiers marched through the coun-
> try, the Moros again shot at them, so the soldiers had to kill several

others. I am sorry the soldiers had to kill any Moros. All Moros are the same to me as my children and no father wants to kill his own children. . . .

I do not want to punish you and your people any more. If you turn in your guns, no one will be arrested and your people may return to their homes to cultivate their fields. If your people need rice to eat, the government will give it to them. The soldiers did not destroy your houses nor any of your property.

If your leading men do not stop fighting, you will be responsible for the lives of many people under you who want to give up their guns. You will be responsible for the lives of your women and children. You have no right to lead all these people to follow you into a fight. You had better give up the guns and save your own lives and the lives of your people.

When you come to turn in your guns let me know if your people need rice. When you visit the camp at Taglibi to bring in your arms, carry a white flag. You can come to camp and leave again without any fear. You can come to Jolo if you want to and turn your guns in there. I want to see all of my people and speak to them so that we may forever be friends.[6]

But, as I feared, the negotiations failed. On December 14, at Zamboanga, where I had arrived only the day before hoping to get caught up on my work, I received word that several hundred of the Taglibi Moros had concentrated in the extinct volcanic crater on top of Bud (Mount) Dajo, a time-honored mountain near the center of the island with sacred traditions to which their forefathers had repaired when hard pressed by enemies. It had been the scene of a bloody battle between the Moros on one side and American and Filipino troops on the other some four years before. In that fight the government forces had had eighteen men killed and fifty-two wounded and the Moros had lost six hundred men, women, and children killed. It seemed strange that the Moros, in the face of such tremendous loss, should again risk a similar defeat. The striking difference in the losses on the two sides caused charges of "wanton slaughter" to be made in our newspapers in Manila and at home, and the Senate in Washington passed a resolution calling upon the Secretary of War for all reports of the engagement.[7]

It was practically impossible to avoid killing non-combatants when attacking fortifications because of the Moro custom of taking their families with them into these so-called *cottas,* but it was only humane to try to

Bud Dajo, Jolo Island. In December 1911, Pershing faced down rebellious Moros who were opposed to the disarmament policy and had fled to the forts on rugged Bud Dajo. Major Allen S. Fletcher, then serving with the U.S. Army in the Philippines, took this photograph from an airplane in April 1922 and sent it to Pershing. Fletcher served with the Philippine Constabulary in numerous operations on Mindanao and Jolo while Pershing was Governor of the Moro Province. (Library of Congress, Prints and Publications Division, Lot 8850)

limit their casualties as much as possible. The second Bud Dajo affair in point of numbers engaged on the respective sides was approximately the same as the first; the result, however, was different. Reports that came to us through friendly Moros stated that those at present on Bud Dajo had sworn to die fighting. I had no intention, however, of giving them the satisfaction of killing many of our men or of retaining their forbidden weapons indefinitely.

My letter to Mrs. Pershing, written en route to Jolo the night of the fourteenth, said: "I am very sorry these Moros are such fools—but this Dajo will not mean the slaughter of women and children, nor hasty assaults against *strong* entrenchments. I shall lose as few men and kill as few Moros as possible."[8] In this instance I thought Bud Dajo could be taken without a fight. One thing the Moro could not stand was a siege, and I planned to invest this stronghold and force its surrender with a minimum of bloodshed.

From information gained by a cavalry reconnaissance and that given us by friendly Moros, it was estimated that the hostiles probably numbered eight hundred, including women and children, but that they did not have more than two hundred and fifty firearms. Taking personal command, I ordered an immediate investment on the morning of December 17 and laid siege to the stronghold.

There were three trails known to us leading to the top of Bud Dajo, and at the foot of each I posted a strong force. They were connected up by a line of outposts placed around the base of the mountain, effectively sealing it, we thought, against ingress or egress of hostiles and cutting of the food supply of those on top. Patrols were then pushed up the sides and lateral trails were cut through the jungle to connect the most advanced posts, so that patrols were enabled completely to encircle the mountain. In doing this some sixteen or seventeen old trails were discovered, all of such were placed under guard. The ground was most difficult for operations. Here and there it was rocky and precipitous and in other places there was heavy tropical undergrowth, making the way beneath the thick stand of trees all but impassable. This had to be cut through, entailing hard work for days for many of our men. But successively five different tiers of investment were cut, the last, at an average distance of only about three hundred yards from the top, making escape even by individual men at night next to impossible. Nevertheless, during the intensely dark nights that prevailed, persistent efforts were made by Moros, both from the inside and outside, to break through our lines.

Friendly Moros had early been sent in to point out to the hostiles the hopelessness of their situation, surrounded by a superior force, but only after facing starvation and after discovering for themselves the impossibility of escape did they begin to surrender. Twenty came in on the nineteenth and daily from the twentieth to the twenty-third groups of fifty to two hundred. For a week all who came down, men as well as women and children, after being relieved of their arms, were set free. The people who surrendered were hungry, weary, frightened, pathetic looking individuals. Having been led to believe that our promises of good treatment were false, they gave up only in desperation. When the troops gave them food, the grown people seemed amazed and the children devoured it ravenously.

On Christmas Eve friendly emissaries reported that the crater was deserted and an occupying force was sent in. Knowing the Moros unaccounted for could not have escaped, it was evident that they must be hiding in the jungle waiting for our withdrawal or for the chance to attack under cover of darkness. I ordered special precautions taken and strengthened the line on that part of the front where they were believed to be. That night fierce attacks were made on the reenforced line but were everywhere repulsed and the next day, Christmas, forty-nine more Moros surrendered. The following day the mountainside between the rim of the crater and our outpost line was thoroughly searched, six being found and dying as they had vowed to do. That ended the Bud Dajo operation.

There was never a moment during the investment of Bud Dajo when the defenders would not have made a desperate fight if given the opportunity. They had expected our troops to storm their stronghold, but we made no attacks, and under the strain of expectation day and night, their nerves broke. Our only casualties were one officer [John W. Barker] and two enlisted men wounded, while the Moros lost but twelve killed and a few wounded, instead of perhaps hundreds of casualties on both sides that might have resulted from precipitous action.

I had brought my Negro driver along as cook and on returning to camp said to him, "Well, Johnson, you can pack up; we're going back to Zamboanga. It's all over."

"Yes, suh," he replied, "and widout much fuss neider."

We were back home again for the New Year.

The Bud Bagsak Campaign, Jolo Island

In the six months following Bud Dajo practically all arms in the possession of the Sulu Moros had been collected with the exception of those held by the followers of *Datto* Amil, in Lati Ward.[9] Once this group was disarmed our task would be finished, but they were the most stubborn, the most defiant, and the most difficult in the whole Province. By the fall of 1912 brigandage was rampant among them and action was imperative. At the first sign of any movement of troops, however, the entire group, estimated at from five to ten thousand, the large majority women and children, fled their homes and occupied their defenses on the top of Bud Bagsak. An attack under the circumstances would have resulted in the killing of hundreds of women and children. In an attempt to avoid this, if possible, negotiations were allowed to drag on for months. Successive delegations of friendly Moros were sent to talk with them, and Lieutenant W. W. [William W.] Gordon, the District Governor, went in person and at great risk to try to dissuade them from further fighting. Bishop [Charles H.] Brent, who always had a kindly interest in the Moros, wanted to make Amil a visit, but he was not known to this group of Moros and I feared it would cost him his life. Finally, however, in February, 1913, they accepted my proposition to withdraw our troops entirely from that district provided they would return to their farms and lay down their arms. I carried out my part of the agreement, but the Moros only partially fulfilled their promise. Many of the women and children and unarmed men did return to their homes and resume planting, but remained always ready at a minute's notice to flee again to Bagsak, where the leaders and most of the armed warriors maintained their position.

Governor-General Forbes, alarmed by the reports reaching Manila, cabled me on February 27 that: "Constant rumors from various sources indicate bad condition in Jolo growing worse, disaffected element murdering and pillaging Moros who have delivered up their arms and who are for self-defense joining them. It is my belief that there are times when as many men as are thought necessary should be sent in so as to absolutely smother any difficulty. I will support you in whatever action may be necessary for public order. Send me report as to conditions."[10]

I did not feel, however, that the time had yet come for unrestrained action and in my reply the following day explained that:

The nature of the Joloano Moro is such that he is not at all overawed or impressed by an overwhelming force. If he takes a notion to fight, he will fight regardless of the number of men brought against him. You cannot bluff him. There are already enough troops on the Island of Jolo to smother the defiant element, but conditions are such that if we attempt such a thing the loss of life among innocent women and children would be very great. It is estimated that there are only about three hundred arms altogether in the Island of Jolo and that these are assembled in Lati Ward on top of Mount Bagsak in fortified cottas. It is a common thing among these people to have the women and children follow them into these cottas so that we have there probably five or six times as many women and children as armed men. [This condition of affairs has sprung up very suddenly.][†] It is exactly what happened last year after the Bud Dajo campaign, but in as much as we did not care to have a big fight at that time I simply ignored it. The Moros afterwards came down from the mountains and proceeded to raise their crops.

We have been gathering up arms slowly with secret service men since that time and only recently have started in to make a general clean up. As soon as we began in Lati Ward in any force, these Moros again stampeded to Bagsac [Bagsak]. It could be very difficult to handle the situation by force without great loss of life among innocent people and I think the part of wisdom is to use every endeavor we can to segregate the innocent from the guilty. Our troops have instructions not to move in that part of the country for the present, but patrols will be kept up in the friendly districts where marauding is reported. . . .

I have visited Jolo frequently during the last month and am fully in touch with what is going on. According to the plans made several days ago, I shall go to Jolo tonight, taking with me Datto Mandi and a number of Zamboanga Moros who are friendly with many of the Jolo Moros openly opposing us. I shall remain in Jolo as long as necessary.

While I do not believe [now, nor have I ever believed at any time],[†] that the Moros who are openly opposing us will all yield without a fight, yet I am not prepared to rush in and attack them while they are surrounded by women and children [as I think most of the women and children can be induced to return to their homes.][†] The situation, as I stated at the beginning, is a difficult one, but every official concerned is striving his best. Coolness and patience are the requisites required. [I fully appreciate your confidence in my ability to handle it, and][†] you may rest assured that my best efforts are being put forth to carry out the purpose of our undertaking—Disarmament with as little disturbance and as little loss of life as possible.[ll]

By the end of May, however, the futility of further parleys was evident. Through dissimulation most of the noncombatants and some of the warriors had been held on their farms, but a considerable number of fighting men were still on Bagsak. The moment seemed opportune; an attack, if it could be made a complete surprise, would at least save the women and children and possibly many others. To eliminate so far as possible a leak, I confided only to the essential minimum my intention to take the field. I went so far as to direct the commanding officer at Jolo to stop all field operations and reconnaissances, so that even he thought negotiations were to be continued. I gave it out generally that I was going to visit my family, then recuperating at Marahui, and in the evening of June 9 sailed from Zamboanga on the transport *Wright*, accompanied only by my aide, Lieutenant J. L. [James L.] Collins, ostensibly for that purpose.

Out of sight of land our course was changed and at eleven o'clock that night we arrived at Isabela, Basilan, where Captain G. C. [George C.] Charlton's Fifty-first Company of Moro Scouts was embarked. At noon the following day the Fifty-second Company, Captain T. A. [Taylor A.] Nichols, and a medical detachment under Lieutenant G. P. [George P.] Stallman were taken aboard at Siassi. With lights out, we dropped anchor at Jolo at eight p.m., finding practically all the officers of the post in white, calling with their families on the newly-arrived commanding officer. Here we took aboard the *Wright* Company M of the Eighth Infantry, First Lieutenant Robert W. Adams, and a hospital corps detachment, First Lieutenant L. S. [Leonard S.] Hughes and First Lieutenant C. H. [Charles H.] Halliday. Major George C. Shaw, Philippine Scouts, his adjutant, First Lieutenant C. B. [Charles B.] Townsend, and three companies of his battalion, the Twenty-first Company, P.S., Captain R. S. [Robert S.] Dickson, Twenty-ninth Company, P.S., First Lieutenant G. H. [George H.] Wright, the Fortieth Company, P.S., First Lieutenant F. [Frank] Sperbeck, and the mountain gun detachments of First Lieutenant T. F. [Thomas F., Jr.] Van Natta and Second Lieutenant C. F. [Carl F.] McKinney were embarked on launches, the two guns and their ammunition being towed on barges behind. My aide, Lieutenant W. W. Gordon, accompanied Shaw's battalion. Captain Patrick Moylan, with the Twenty-fourth and Thirty-first Companies, P.S., was directed to march overland to the south slope of Bagsak, to arrive there about daybreak; and First Lieutenant J. T. [John T.] Sayles, with fifty men of Troop H, Eighth Cavalry, and pack train, was ordered overland to Bun Bun.

In order that what follows may be clearer, I shall digress a moment and give a brief description of the terrain over which the battle was fought. Bud Bagsak is about two thousand feet high, very precipitous, and for the most part heavily wooded. On the top was the crater of an extinct volcano, strongly fortified. In shape it resembled a huge horseshoe, warped on one side, about eight hundred yards wide between the heels and one thousand from heels to toe. The two heels, natural elevations of stone, rising perhaps two hundred feet above the rest, were occupied by the *cottas* Puyacabao and Bunga. A bald knoll, Languasan, and the *cotta* Pujagan represented the frog and its apex respectively and commanded the mouth of the crater. On the toe stood Bagsak *cotta*, the most formidable, and midway between it and Puyacabao, on the north or warped side, was the *cotta* Matunkup.

I planned to attack this mountain stronghold at daybreak the eleventh with three columns—the first, on the right of the line, consisting of

Company M, the Fortieth Company, P.S., and one mountain gun detachment, was to move against Languasan; the second, the Twenty-ninth Company, P.S., and Fifty-first and Fifty-second Moro Scouts and the second mountain gun, against Puyacabao and Matunkup; and the third, the Twenty-fourth and Thirty-first Philippine Scouts, coming overland, was to hold the south slope of Bagsak. The remainder of the force was to be held in reserve at Bun Bun.

Leaving Jolo at one o'clock on the morning of the eleventh, Bun Bun, twenty-five miles away, was reached at half past three. So quietly was the assembly and movement of this force of approximately twelve hundred men conducted that few, if any, outside the walls of Jolo knew of it. And so completely were the hostiles surprised that we had landed and were within a mile of their positions before the first resistance was encountered, although Bun Bun was three and one-half miles away. Luckily the women and children and even a number of men at work in the fields had been prevented from entering the stronghold. Probably not more than four hundred occupied the *cottas* we now faced.

In giving an account of this battle, it appears desirable to enter into some detail, as it was the last and also the greatest battle against the Moros. Shortly after seven o'clock our columns advancing from Bun Bun came under fire at a range of about twelve hundred yards. McKinney's mountain gun, with the first column, firing against Pujagan and Bunga, and Van Natta's, against Puyacabao, opened the battle on our side. Amil himself, the Moro leader, was in Puyacabao at this time, and, as we learned later, was wounded by a shell and retreated to Pujagan. There he died or was killed by another shot the following day. The Moros met us with their customary yells and beating of tom-toms, the bursting of our shrapnel among them adding to the din. Under the cover of the guns our two columns made their dispositions and advanced up the mountainside. Because of the location and elevation of Languasan, Puyacabao, and Matunkup with reference to each other, it was essential that they should all be taken early, otherwise the defenders by supporting each other would inflict heavy loss on our troops. I therefore sent Lieutenant Collins forward to coordinate the movements of these columns, with the result that within half an hour of each other these three positions fell into our hands.

Major Shaw's troops of the first column, mounting the bare slopes of Languasan, carried the crest at noon. This position commanded the mouth of the crater and as long as we held it the Moros could hope for no reenforcements from outside. They realized its importance too late and throughout the afternoon the fire of Bunga, Pujagan and Bagsak *cottas* was concentrated on Shaw's position on the knoll.

Charlton's Fifty-first Company of Scouts followed at once with the capture of Matunkup, Charlton leading his men up the sheer side of the mountain, cutting toe holds with their machetes and climbing the last hundred feet hand-over-hand on *bejuco* vines. This was a daring feat and only the covering fire from a platoon of the Twenty-ninth Company and Van Natta's gun prevented serious loss.

Outwitting the defenders of Puyacabao, that position was then taken by Nichols' Fifty-second Company without loss. Leaving a platoon to keep up the firing from the front, Nichols led the rest of his company into the wood. Cutting his way through the dense undergrowth, he emerged on Puyacabao ridge well above the *cotta*, and his advance down the ridge completely surprised the hostiles.

During the afternoon of the eleventh the two mountain guns were laboriously moved to the top of Languasan, and from there the following morning they shelled Pujagan at point-blank range. Under the hail of shell and rifle fire from the positions we had captured the day before, the Moros became desperate and small groups in successive lines led by Amil's son and *Datto* Jami, a notorious cattle thief, and other leaders assaulted Languasan with fanatical courage. Though hidden by the broken terrain until within fifty yards of our lines, none reached them alive. It was after one of these rushes that the gallant Captain Nichols, who had gone to Languasan for consultation, was killed, shot directly through the head.

A reconnaissance on the afternoon of the eleventh showed that an attack on Bagsak from the Matunkup side would be impracticable. Not only had the ground been cleared for some distance in front of the enemy's rifle pits but the ridge of approach narrowed so that deployment would have been impossible. Bud Bunga, however, offered a good position from which to shell Bagsak, but to reach it was no easy matter. Moylan's Twenty-fourth and Thirty-first Companies of Scouts, which had been brought around from the south slope of Bagsak, were given the task. Only two narrow hogbacks, with precipitous sides, led to the crest, two thousand feet above. Moylan divided his force into two detachments, which made their way up these hogbacks, the men pulling themselves up by hand, using the roots of trees or creepers, and after a brisk fight at the top, in which one man was killed with a *barong*, the position was taken.

Meanwhile, taking advantage of the diversion of attention to the fight on Bunga, Collins and I with an escort of ten men reconnoitered the Bagsak *cotta* to determine the best method of attacking it. Crawling on our hands and knees through the underbrush, we approached to within seventy-five yards of the position. We could see Moros on the parapet intently following the battle on Bunga, then at its height, and could hear them excitedly conversing among themselves.

With the fall of Bunga, all the surviving enemy were now concentrated in Bagsak *cotta*, the most formidable of the strong group. Here they were to make their last stand, but we did not make the final assault until after another day had been spent in preparation. To get our mountain gun to the top of Bud Bunga was a five-hour job on the fourteenth, requiring the dismantling of the piece and carrying or hauling the different parts up piecemeal. In the meantime, the Fifty-first and Fifty-second Companies, which I had selected for the assault, Moro against Moro, were marched around the base of the mountain to a favorable position on the southwest slope and about six hundred yards from the top of Bud Bagsak.

When day broke on the fifteenth a heavy fog encircled the Moro position like a halo. But slowly the outline of the crest began to appear through the mist, and at seven-thirty Van Natta's gun began its accurate fire from Bunga. At nine the assaulting lines moved forward, supported by the gun and the rifles of the Twenty-fourth and part of the Thirty-first Companies, almost to the first of the three lines of trenches protecting the *cotta*. From here over the remaining hundred yards of open ground Charlton had to make his way unsupported by artillery, as fire from the rear would have endangered his men.

Fighting for every foot of ground, our two companies advanced slowly along the narrow ridge. The first line of trenches was taken about eleven, but thereafter the resistance increased in viciousness and progress came practically to a standstill. The enemy held in force considerably higher ground and his trenches, extending completely across the ridge and protected by cleverly constructed bamboo fences, could hardly be flanked. We were, therefore, forced to a frontal attack. After Captain Nichols' death I had issued instructions that in this final attack the officers should direct operations through their sergeants and corporals. Without white leadership the Scouts began to hang back. Going forward and learning the situation, I reversed my order. For about half an hour I had our men hold their ground, with no attempt to advance. As I expected they would, the Moros then counterattacked, but were repulsed with heavy loss. Encouraged by this success and led by their officers, the Scouts were now ready to resume the advance. The line was extended by the right flank and soon reached the bamboo defenses, hacking and tearing them down under a shower of spears, barongs, rocks, cooking utensils, and every conceivable object hurled by the madly yelling hostiles. One Scout had a spear driven through his chest and a comrade put his foot on the prostrate body and pulled it out. With the destruction of the bamboo defenses an enfilading fire was poured into the remaining trenches and the *cotta*. Our front line was now less than twenty-five yards from the enemy and, their positions no longer tenable, the survivors made a last desperate charge, dying, as they had sworn to do, arms in hand. The capture of Bagsak entailed the severest fighting I had seen in the Philippines. I was gratified, of course, at our victory won, but conscious also of a deep admiration for the courage of the enemy. They had made a stand worthy of the best traditions of a warrior race.

Our total casualties in the five-day battle were one officer and fourteen men killed and twenty-five wounded. On the other hand the Moro losses, while not actually known, were probably between two and three hundred, as many had fled before the final assault was launched. With Amil's death and this defeat the opposition of the Jolo Moros en masse came finally to an end. There were a few arms still to be rounded up, but disarmament in general was at last an accomplished fact.[12]

In narrating this and other engagements I have not mentioned by any means all the officers and men whose work was invaluable and whose acts of daring were conspicuous. To do so would make the account unduly long. But in the records of the War Department in Washington their names are recorded. I recommended many for rewards and some received them. Those who were with me know what I thought and still think of them.[13]

20

The Last Military Governor of the Moro Province

11 November 1909–14 December 1913

In disarming the Moros a necessary preliminary step in the establishment of law and order had been taken. It ended the power of any disaffected leader to rally to his standard erstwhile armed warriors. It enabled us to devote attention to the more important work of civil administration. In the greater part of the province constructive achievement on the civil side went on unheralded, hand in hand with suppression of disorder. But without disarmament the civil administration could not have attained the success I am able to record, nor could I have recommended to Governor-General Forbes, as I did, that the Province be turned over to civil control at the end of my term.[1]

Governing the Moro Province

Prior to the coming of the Americans the various tribes of pagans and groups of Moros had been more or less in armed conflict against one another. Only in the few small towns along the coast had the Spaniards been able to maintain law and order. When I first went to Mindanao the people of the whole interior had little or no idea of law except what custom had established or the local head man willed, and in most places the strong rather than the just man ruled. The great majority of Moros and pagans were illiterate; only an occasional Moro was able to read or write. They used the Arabic in writing. The pagans had no written language. Famine was frequent when there should have been plenty; poverty the rule rather than the exception; communications nonexistent. Modern medicine was unknown; in cases of illness and in times of epidemic witchcraft and quackery were practiced and many deaths resulted needlessly. Here in fact existed, to a pathetic degree among the hill tribes, all the backwardness of the most primitive civilization.

These conditions it was our wish to improve. From Washington, through Manila, down to Zamboanga and beyond, our purpose was not one of selfish interest but of service to the peoples over whom we had assumed control. As I have said before, mistakes were made, of course, some of omission and some of commission, but it cannot be gainsaid that the work of the army in Mindanao and Jolo in more than a decade of control was of incalculable benefit to the population. Never before had any of them known the justice in government the army gave them. Never had they known such material progress and mental and physical betterment as the army brought to the Province.

Speaking now of my own administration, we imposed taxes, but these were far less onerous than the tribute that many of the groups had paid for centuries to bandit-like chiefs, and every possible peso went back into the Province for the benefit of the inhabitants. In 1913 administrative expenses were more than one hundred thousand pesos below those of 1910. We built roads where only trails had been and trails where no communications had existed, and made them safe to travel. We developed commercial intercourse throughout the interior, where even petty trading had formerly been conducted with difficulty and danger. We opened schools in villages which had not known what they were. We took medicine into regions where ordinary remedies were unknown. We promoted agriculture, encouraged industry, and made handicraft profitable. We introduced modern sanitation and demonstrated its value. We opened new territory and created homestead settlements. We drafted laws, established courts of justice, and made life generally secure. The full story would take a volume, but a few details will suffice to show the earnestness of our efforts.

Agricultural Developments

It required no superior ability to see that here in the Moro Province, munificently endowed by nature and the great majority of whose inhabitants were essentially of the soil, agriculture and kindred occupations must be developed as the chief source of life and prosperity. Furthermore, it is well known, a people profitably occupied in its own metier is generally a peaceful, contented people. In Jolo waters a few natives found profitable employment in diving for pearls, but the field was very limited. Notwithstanding the industrious habits of Moros as compared with wild tribes, they were often short of their staple crop of rice. From the beginning, therefore, agriculture in the broader sense of the word received our constant encouragement and assistance.

To divorce the wild tribes from their shiftless, semi-nomadic existence and establish them on the soil in permanent locations where they might benefit from the pride and industry that comes with ownership, and to give Moros living on farms inherited from their ancestors opportunity to gain legal title thereto and those owning no land opportunity to enter government land and acquire title thereto, a homestead project was inaugurated. Hundreds of Moros and pagans took advantage of it to secure legal title to plots of uncultivated government lands we opened up and to the farms heretofore merely passed down to them. The pagans particularly had practiced what was known as "Caingin" farming—cutting a clearing in the forest, raising a meager crop, and passing on each year to a new location. Thousands of acres of valuable forest lands had been denuded in this manner annually. Being prone to dispose of their lands carelessly, the Legislative Council enacted a law prohibiting such sale without the approval of the governor of the district in which located, and I recommended that this law remain on the statute books until the people of all classes should have learned to look out for their own interests. From Cebu we brought a hundred Filipino families and established them in an experimental rice colony in the Cotabato valley, a magnificent rice growing locality, under carefully worked out plans that made possible to each colonist the final ownership of his homestead. Such a thing a few short years before would have resulted in bloodshed. Thereafter the Cotabato Moros came forward with a request for permission to start a similar colony, and the Philippines Commission appropriated fifty thousand pesos for the experiment. In the Agusan valley of the District of Davao, Lieutenant R. A. [Robert A.] Gillmore, with a detachment of twenty men, won the confidence of the wild people. He laid out more than twenty towns, with an average population of three hundred and fifty. New houses were erected, streets graded, gardens and fields planted and sanitary rules enforced. On the east coast Captain Case, of the Constabulary, established several other towns.

Early in my administration San Ramon Farm, near Zamboanga, formerly the location of a Spanish penitentiary, was transferred from the Insular Government to the Moro Province, and we made of it not only a model prison architecturally designed for that climate but a station for experimental work in tropical agriculture and livestock breeding. At the same time the provincial prison at Calarian was transferred to

San Ramon Farm. Under the direction of an expert formerly with the Department of Agriculture, particular attention was given to the practical application of the principles of scientific agriculture, including small acreage with intensive cultivation, rotation of crops, fertilization, introduction of new food and forage crops, and the use of modern implements, and the elimination of pests, such as the coconut beetle. The prisoners were utilized for farm work, which gave them not only useful employment but a knowledge of crops and methods that would be beneficial to them after their release. Farming having been my first occupation as a boy back in Missouri, I was especially interested in San Ramon and often visited there to confer with our Dr. W. H. [Waller H.] Dade, whom I had appointed superintendent.

It was surprising to find that there in the province almost on the equator many products grown in the States did well, especially vegetables such as we used to raise in our garden when I was a youth. Fruits of the temperate zone could not be so successfully grown. There were no apples, peaches, or pears, but lemons, bananas, and coconuts were found wild. Mangos grew down there on trees often one hundred years old in places in the Province and the luscious mangosteen [similar to an orange] was also found in certain parts. Papayas, a kind of fruit similar in quality and shape to the muskmelon and containing vegetable pepsin and most delicious, were plentiful. In Lake Lanao and Jolo the natives raised a limited quantity of coffee of the first variety.

A number of medium-sized stallions from Australia were imported to improve native stock in the Province. In a short time the prison farm became highly valuable to the farmers and stock raisers of the Province. In 1911 a small agricultural school for boys of the wild tribes was started in the Davao District, and following its successful inauguration others were started in Cotabato and Lanao for Moro boys, all of which found great favor among the natives.

Trade and Markets

I have spoken of visiting native markets around Lake Lanao during my first tour of duty in Mindanao. Markets in the more thinly populated regions were established by the natives themselves, usually under a tree or on some open stretch of seashore, and had for years provided the Moros and tribesman their only opportunity to sell or trade their products. In general such markets afforded the illiterate and untutored savages no protection of their own interests, and they were often unmercifully cheated by unscrupulous traders, particularly Chinese. One of them, at a remote point on Dumanquilas Bay, was found to be bartering goods for carabao at over five hundred percent profit. In another instance rice was sold to famine sufferers at three hundred percent profit in trade. One trader paid a Manobo two and a half pesos in goods for a quantity of *biao* nut which he immediately resold in the tribesman's presence for eight and a half pesos cash.

An attempt to meet this situation had been made in the District of Zamboanga through the establishment before my arrival of a system of Moro Exchanges. The scheme had only a limited success because the management attempted to require the people to trade at a certain exchange. We replaced the exchanges by a system of Industrial Trading Stores empowered to buy and sell and engage in general mercantile business. Many of these stores were located at remote places throughout the Province where ordinary traders did not usually go and wherever it was found that extortion was practiced.

It was not intended that our stores would compete with honest traders and merchants, but we were anxious to see business expand. Goods were therefore sold to produce reasonable profits only and the volume of trade increased rapidly. However, we stood ready to hand over any of these stores to reliable traders and several were so transferred. The Legislative Council also enacted what was called the "Itinerant Traders Law," which prohibited any trader from entering the wild man's country without a license from the district governor.

So popular were the industrial stores that the requests for them became more numerous than we could meet. Frequently the natives expressed surprise at the high prices received for their farm and other products and often they came to trade from twenty-five and more miles away. At Zamboanga we had established a general sales house where some of the purchases from the outlying stores were put on sale to the troops and visitors to the city. Seldom an American came to Zamboanga who did not go away laden with souvenirs of native manufacture. In fact, the demand for silver, brass, and copper utensils and ornaments, native weapons and cloths became so great that we had difficulty in keeping the central store stocked.

Schools and Education

Schools had been introduced in the Province in the early days of American occupation. Each succeeding administration had devoted considerable attention to them, and my four years were, I felt, highly satisfactory in the further progress made. Although in the first year enrollment fell off slightly, due to the existence of cholera and turbulent conditions in several parts of the interior, in 1913 it had reached more than seven thousand five hundred, an increase of fifty percent. For this student body we had only a limited teaching force, including fifteen Americans, eighty-three Filipinos, seventeen Moros, and one Bagobo girl. Lack of teachers handicapped us particularly in the Moro districts. The Filipino teachers usually objected to assignment to Moro schools, an attitude easily understood, and the Moros on their part objected to Filipino teachers. In an effort to build up a corps of Moro teachers, the Legislative Council made a special appropriation annually for the appointment of Moro students, with the proviso that they should later accept positions in the teaching service.

Naturally there was much room for improvement in the qualifications of the native teachers, and with this in view a summer school for teachers was conducted at Zamboanga and the government gave the teachers free transportation by boat from any port in the Province. At the school, and in all the schools, emphasis was laid on domestic and industrial work, as there were greater opportunities of employment for the farmer and artisan than for one of higher learning. The importance of acquiring English was stressed and the improvement in this respect was marked. The salary of the native teacher averaged about thirty pesos, fifteen dollars, a month. This may seem small, but it was a living wage in Mindanao.

Prior to the coming of the Americans, few, if any, of the pagan tribes knew what a school was and the only teaching of the Moros was that given by the *panditas,* or priests. This was in the sayings of Muhammad as recorded in the Koran. Arabic script was taught for the writing of their native dialects, but knowledge of this was woefully limited. As the Moros began to see the advantages of our schools as compared with those of the *panditas,* they invariably asked for American teachers. In the meantime we recognized the *pandita* schools and exercised a measure of supervision over them while replacing them as fast as possible. In the last year of my administration we opened thirteen new Moro schools, and if funds and teachers had been available, twenty more could have been started, so great was the demand. This mark of progress was especially gratifying. There is no doubt that through the common schools the impetus could be given which, if accompanied by other civilizing influences, would eventually lead to the social elevation of both Moros and pagans. Throughout the Province, therefore, unremitting effort was exerted to extend through this medium useful lessons in morals and manners and to implant high ideals of personal conduct. The greatest credit should go to Charles R. Cameron, the Superintendent of schools of the Moro Province, for his intense interest and efficient administration of the provincial school system.

In Cotabato a school and dormitory for Moro girls was established by Mrs. [Edward (Anna)] Dworak, wife of the governor of the district [Edward Dworak]. Mrs. Dworak regarded the system of plural marriages, and particularly concubinage, as an abomination, and looked to enlightenment of the women to bring it to an end. It was difficult at first to overcome the objections of parents to sending their girls away from home, but before the school had been in existence six months we could have filled it to several times its capacity. Personal cleanliness, housekeeping, sowing, cooking, embroidering, and the speaking, reading, and writing of English were taught. Each girl on arrival was given a bath and a new white dress. This was an innovation among the Moros, who, though they fancied brilliant attire, were rather generally of the opinion that washing the face, hands, arms to the elbows, and feet to the ankles, as prescribed in the Koran, was sufficient. This was not so with the civilized Filipinos, who were fond of sea bathing and were relatively cleanly in their habits. Christianity as a religion could not be mentioned, but it was lived by the teachers and could not but influence to some degree the lives of these young girls.

Public Works

Public works were vigorously pushed and in the four years from the end of 1909 five hundred miles of new roads, partially graded, and trails were completed within the Province. In one of my conferences at Zamboanga with the leading men of the various districts who were attending the Zamboanga Fair (described in following pages) I asked a *datto* from the back country east of Lake Lanao, who had come down to the coast over the excellent road to Iligan thence by boat to Zamboanga, what he considered the most wonderful thing he had seen. He replied, "the fine road the Americans have built from Lanao to Iligan" (Camp Keithley to Camp Overton). I had been very insistent regarding the necessity for the building of this road. In that country a road, or even a good trail, was a blessing which Americans today, with their thousands of miles of wonderful highways, crisscrossing the continent, can hardly appreciate. Hundreds of days of labor without pay were given by Moros anxious to build roads through their part of the country. We also installed more than two hundred miles of telephone lines, bridged rivers, constructed wharves, municipal buildings, and schoolhouses. More than a million pesos were spent on public works alone, and it must be borne in mind that practically all had to be raised in the Province itself.

In my last year a scheme of public works was laid out which it was estimated would take five years to complete. It included a plan for the development of Zamboanga's port to make it one of the most important in the Islands; a combined district and municipal building for each district, where not already provided; provincial warehouses; school buildings, including a central high school at Zamboanga; municipal water systems; new wharves at Dapitan, Iligan, and Mati and the improvement of those at Jolo, Siassi, and Bongao; dredging of the mouths of navigable rivers; a complete road and trail system connecting important towns and districts; and the opening of new lands for settlement as demands might require. Some of these had been started before my departure.

Medical and Health Care

The provincial government also provided medical attention for the natives through the establishment of dispensaries. Heretofore the only recourse of the Moros when sick was to call in a priest, who usually repeated a formula over a glass of water, which the patient then drank. When ill they were eager to receive treatment and would soon accept with confidence any medicine that was given them. In the larger centers where troops were stationed they flocked to our dispensaries. Sometimes even avowed enemies came. The Board of Health, which was directed by Colonel Charles Richard, extended the service to lesser centers as fast as possible. Medicines were provided without cost to indigent persons and at nominal fees to others. By the last year of my term there were thirty-seven medical stations in operation. These were all, of course, small, but compared with the absence of any this was a tremendous advance. No labor that Americans performed was more effective in winning the appreciation and loyalty of the people once they realized its value. Frequently, seventy-five or more patients were treated in a day at some of these dispensaries, and in a single month Dr. J. H. [Josiah H.] Holland, of the army, treated without pay over five hundred cases at Cotabato. The doctors, outside of Zamboanga, were exclusively of the army Medical Corps and generally gave their services free.

In this work of charity we were glad to receive the assistance of philanthropic friends. At Zamboanga a concrete hospital costing twenty thousand pesos was built, the funds being raised by subscription there and in the States, while at Davao one of twenty beds was built and maintained by a group of New York gentlemen. Seven thousand four hundred and seventy-two patients received treatment at the latter in the first six months of 1913, two-thirds of them being people of the wild tribes. A free dispensary for sick children was started in Zamboanga by a society led by the American ladies of the community and organized for the purpose, and the provincial health officers generously gave their services without compensation. Originally intended to prepare milk for native babies not able to feed in the usual way, its work was soon extended to that of a general dispensary for children. The mothers were taught how to feed, bathe, and generally care for children. A pamphlet of instructions prepared by Captain F. W. [Frank W.] Weed was circulated in Spanish, Moro, and English. In 1909, before the dispensary was established, infant mortality in Zamboanga from beri-beri was two hundred and twenty, but in 1911, after its establishment, this was reduced to eighty-seven.

Malaria undoubtedly caused more deaths than any other disease, and the medical patrols we sent frequently to infested districts and remote settlements treated the people by fifties and hundreds. It required constant inspection, even in such municipalities as Zamboanga, to enforce sanitary regulations. The Moros particularly did not take naturally to cleanliness of surroundings; and often recourse to arrest and imprisonment was necessary, but we were determined to enforce these important regulations. Jolo became probably the cleanest and most sanitary town in the Archipelago. A general plan of vaccination against smallpox was undertaken, beginning with the centers of population and to extend gradually to the wild people of the interior. Scores of lepers were rounded up and transferred to the leper colony at Culion established by Governor-General Forbes. On one occasion, having no other transportation available, I put several lepers aboard an army transport, to the loudly expressed indignation of a Manila paper, and inquiry came to me from the Governor-General's office. But I had obtained assurances from our medical officers that our troops would not be endangered if the lepers were segregated and I myself had traveled on the same boat.

Zamboanga Fair

A lighter undertaking, but one that benefitted the Province tremendously, was the Zamboanga Fair, held in February, 1911. The purpose was two-fold: to promote a better understanding between the people of the Province and the government and among themselves, and to demonstrate the profitable return to themselves of industry. Other fairs had been held in the Islands and the annual carnival at Manila had become an institution, but the Zamboanga Fair outdid them all. This was not alone my opinion but that of many, including General Bell, Commanding General of the Philippines, who was present with Governor-General Forbes and who had visited the others. Our industrial exhibit was second to none, and nothing like the remarkable gathering of thousands of representatives of all the Moro and pagan tribes had ever been seen before. Heretofore at least suspicious of each other, if not in active warfare, here they mixed in the utmost harmony, in fact each delegation went to pay a friendly visit to all the others and not a single unpleasant incident occurred during the eight days the fair lasted.

The fair was opened with a parade and as the various delegations marched onto the grounds to the particularly appropriate tune of "Rings on her fingers and bells of her toes" played by the constabulary band it would have made the greatest "Wild West Show" look pale and tame. In it were delegations of probably forty different peoples, ranging from Americans whose normal habitats were New York's Fifth Avenue to pagans whose homes were in Davao forest trees. The procession was led by the band and a detachment of American troops with their flag and one of blue jackets from the naval vessels in the harbor. After these came Christian Filipino and Muhammadan Moro Scouts. Then, first among the representations of communities, came the delegation from the cosmopolitan district of Zamboanga. In its ranks were Chinese and Japanese merchants, Filipino schoolchildren, Moro warriors, Samal fishermen from surrounding waters, woman-faced Subano tribesmen from the hills, and long-haired Yakans from Basilan.

Headed in person by the sultan of Sulu [Sultan Jamalul-Kiram II]— of comic opera fame[2]—the Jolo Moros came next, they who had been the traders and pirates of the seas from Java to China when Manila was still a small Spanish town. Turbaned and fezzed, some in wide bell-shaped trousers and some with pants that fitted like ballet tights, all were brilliantly costumed, and most of them, as the disarming had not yet taken place, wore their time-honored cutting weapons proudly.

Then came the people of the Cotabato valley, among whom were the all-but-nude bodyguards of the American governor of the district. For this occasion these stocky, bronze-skinned men went back into turbans and gee strings and carried the long spears with which they had opposed American occupation. Also in this contingent came the Princess of Maguindanaw, borne in a purple-canopied palanquin by a body of her own men, surrounded by dancing girls and followed by slaves bringing along her many brass and silver ornaments. Less spectacular than this female potentate but of greater importance as a personage was *Datto* Piang, a man without heritage of royal blood but one who had shown his capacity as a leader in many ways and manifested his intelligence by accepting American authority without strife. The *datto*, son of a Chinese father and Moro mother, had become the chief of ten thousand loyal followers. Also from the Cotabato hills were the Tirurais, tribes folk laden down with jingling bracelets and anklets that made music where they went.

From Davao, land of the superstitious wild men, with twelve of the most colorful and distinctive tribes left in the present-day world, came the Bagobos, whose clothing was so fantastically beautiful that on returning home from the fair they left most of it behind in the possession of admiring American visitors. There were Bilanos in coats gorgeously decorated with sequins of shells; Manobos, bearing spears fifteen feet long; Dibabawans, with the "chanticleer" headdress said to have been created by them; the Mansakas, with ruffled trousers; the Tagacaolos, the Atas, the Guangas, the Calagans, the Mandayans, the Manguangas, and the Sangils, each distinguishable from all the others.

The contingent from Lake Lanao occupied a prominent place in the procession, though I have reserved mention of them to the last. They needed no urging to come a thousand strong to Zamboanga. As this body of "first class fighting men" passed the grandstand in which I stood with distinguished guests reviewing the procession they threw their turbans in the air and cheered till I could hardly keep back the tears. I had fought them but not without fair warning, and I had served them but not only as a duty. They had first thought of me as the leader of their enemies; now they regarded me as first among their friends. And I had a sincere affection for them.

To the thousand or more Americans present the sight of this extraordinary agglomeration of what might well be called the "Wild East" was a sight never to be forgotten. And likewise upon the minds of those of the natives who had never before seen us except as soldiers in their mountains the sights of Zamboanga made indelible impressions. They saw not only our women and children in costumes as strange to them as theirs to us, but our mounted troops (who gave an exhibition of daring horsemanship), our motorcars, and our unbelievable men-of-war, the cruisers *New York, New Orleans,* and *Albany,* then in the harbor, which they were given a chance to visit. But the thing at which they marveled most was the illumination of the fair. Some of them had never used in their huts a better light than a taper stuck in coconut oil and none better than a lamp purchased from a Chinese or Japanese trader. Here they saw by the pressing of a button a display of electric lights over an area several city blocks in dimension. The common exclamation of wonder was, "The Americans turn night into day."

There was much friendly rivalry among the different groups. Each of the five districts had its special day for display and on that day headed the parade. Discovering that Jolo had an exhibition superior to that of Cotabato, old *Datto* Piang rushed frantically about the town with five thousand pesos which he offered to spend in any way to improve the latter. When Zamboanga Day came *Datto* Mandi "put on" the greatest procession of Moros ever seen. The fair grounds were literally packed with them, all yelling like Indians. Every day there were sports of all kinds, dances, and band concerts, and every night a grand fireworks display. Whenever the Moros could beat the Filipinos in a race or other contest their supporters went as wild as American schoolboys in their cheers and demonstrations.

In the matter of business, too, the fair was as great a success as we had hoped. The exhibits, which consisted of characteristic products of the several districts, were all sold at good prices, and individually the people disposed of practically everything they brought to town. Americans and Filipinos went away laden with beautiful homespun cloths, magnificent pieces of hand-wrought metal, native costumes, headgear, and weapons of many sorts; and the Moros and tribes folk returned to their homes richer than they had ever been before.

Improving the System of Government in the Moro Province

Not long after the beginning of my term as Governor of the Moro Province an inherent weakness in the system of government became apparent to us. This was the appointment of army officers to the important administrative positions of governor and secretary of the districts. This is in no way a reflection on their ability; they were as fully capable of carrying on the work as any civilian could have been under the same conditions. The fault lay not in the officers but in the practice in the army of transferring them at short intervals from one place to another. No sooner would one become acquainted with his duties and his people than he was ordered elsewhere. In the work that had to be done among the natives, personality counted for much. The people were accustomed in their own communities to having rulers whom they knew and who knew them, but they could hardly get acquainted with a military governor or municipal *presidente* before a new one came to take his place. In only two or three instances were officers continued in their civil positions long enough to carry out well-digested plans for the management and development of their districts. I, therefore, in the last two years of my administration, replaced four of the five military district governors and three of the secretaries with civilians having no obligations to any other branch or arm of the government service.

And as the end of my own term approached, feeling that a solid foundation for the future had been laid and military control of the Province was no longer necessary, [on 1 November 1913] I recommended the appointment of a civilian governor. This recommendation conformed not only with the views of the newly appointed Governor-General [appointed 2 September 1913; arrived 6 October], Francis Burton Harrison, the appointee of President [Woodrow] Wilson, but also with those of General Bell, who endorsed my recommendation with the following addition [on 20 November 1913]: "His successor should be a man of all-round ability and moral courage, a man who can stand ignorant and unjust criticism without wavering, a man who will command universal respect from all good people in the Islands, both Americans and Filipinos, and preferably a man who has some knowledge of the organization, legal prerogatives, limitations and methods of administration of the Army."[3]

To succeed me I recommended Frank W. Carpenter, who had been in the Philippines a number of years and held several offices in which he had demonstrated good judgment and exceptional ability. Confident that Carpenter would prove an excellent administrator, I was highly pleased with his appointment. But on the score of our Government's general Philippines policy, I was distressed.

Unwise U.S. Government Policy
toward Philippine Independence

The new Governor-General came with instructions and ideas of granting quick "self-determination" to the Islands, which I was convinced was neither to the interest of the people nor ourselves. In 1898 we had assumed an imperial mission and fifteen years later were preparing to bring it to an end. The last act of President Wilson in office, in 1921, it will be remembered, was to propose to Congress the granting of independence to the Islands. We had not completed our work—nor have we done so since—and in my opinion the change of policy was a grave error. For the price of a block of ground in New York City, we had acquired a territory as large as Japan proper, which, had we maintained a fixed policy, could have been transformed into a permanently well-to-do insular possession which would have been far more profitable to our own people and to the people of the Islands than it has become or is likely to become under any system of independent self-government. Several very valuable products could have been developed in abundance. The capital was available and would have gone to the Islands freely had our Government given assurance of security. It began to go there soon after we took possession. But it soon became hesitant because of the altruistic policy adopted. This was a mistake. Things are not always what they seem. A real kindness to the people of the Philippines would have come from our continuance in authority and the development of the Islands with American capital. In particular I deplore the prospects of what will happen to the people of Mindanao Province under a government by Filipinos.

21

Diplomatic Missions, Our Return to the United States, and Commanding the Eighth Brigade at the Presidio of San Francisco

June 1911–April 1914

Hong Kong: Celebrating the Coronation of King George V

During this period in the Philippines I was twice sent by our Government on diplomatic missions to other Far Eastern lands, once to Hong Kong and once to Japan. The first was in 1911, on the occasion of the Corona-tion of King George V [22 June]. A special celebration of the event was being held in each of the colonies of the "Far-flung Empire," and I was delegated to join with the Honorable Charles B. Elliott, of Minneapo-lis, then [a member of the Philippines Commission and the Secretary of Commerce and Police] of the Islands, to represent the United States at the ceremonies in the nearby British possession. Mr. and Mrs. Elliott and my aide, Lieutenant [Innis] Palmer Swift, and I were invited by the Governor, Sir Frederick Lugard, to stop at the Government House and were his guests for several days.

Among the ceremonies was an impressive church service at which the minister read the exercises that were to take place in London; a review of troops of the picturesque garrison of the island at a beautiful place in the suburbs called "Happy Valley," which included a regiment of Sikhs from India with long hair and beards both done up in knots; and a Chinese fish procession in the Botanical Garden. The garden was decorated with Chinese lanterns, lit by candles, and the procession of paper fish, ten to fifteen feet long and of various shapes in proportion, winding around was a weird spectacle. In our travels about the city we rode in government chairs, each carried by four coolies dressed in white suits, short trousers, and pajama coats with the British coat of arms on the sleeves. Government chairs had the right of way, and all other chairs and the rickshaws cleared the road for them.

Each evening the city was illuminated by candles placed in every window throughout the city, and viewed from the harbor, from which we had a view from the Governor's launch, it was most impressive, the whole side of the hill on which lay Hong Kong being lit up by these tens of thousands of lights. There was one incident that gave us Americans at least considerable amusement. One evening when the many European ships and Chinese junks in harbor as well as the buildings of the city were aglow, the crowning feature of the illumination, standing out against the sky so that it could be seen far out at sea, lost one of its letters, causing it to read like a signal to the Navy—"Go Save the King."

Being particularly interested in colonial government, I could not fail to remark how fortunate it was for the Chinese people of the island to enjoy the blessings of able and honest administration. Their own country, within sight across the strait, was undergoing the agonies of civil war, resulting from the overthrow of the Manchu Dynasty and the attempts to form a republic, and thousands of people had fled to Hong Kong as a refuge. Among the refugees at one time was even the republican leader himself, Dr. Sun Yat-sen. It is a great testimony to British justice and liberty that political fugitives so often seek harbor on their shores.

On the return trip I narrowly escaped being carried to Australia. Being in a hurry to get back to Zamboanga, arrangements were made for a British boat to run in there. Through some oversight, however, I got away without a permit from the health authorities, who kicked up a row and cabled the authorities at Manila to put the boat in quarantine. The steamship people got wind of it and sent word to the steamer to head for Australia. But, fortunately, Judge Elliott was able to have the quarantine order rescinded. That was the nearest I ever came to a trip to the Antipodes.

Tokyo: The Emperor Meiji's Funeral

On August 12, 1912, the following cablegram from the War Department to General Bell, Commander of the Philippines Division, was transmitted to me: "Inform John J. Pershing that he has been designated by the President as military member of the Special Embassy which the Secretary of State is taking to Japan on the occasion of the Mikado's funeral. Direct him to report to American Ambassador, Tokio, not later than September 5. Inform him that the President desires Mrs. Pershing should accompany him as part of the Special Embassy."

There was an interesting bit of international politics behind the visit of the "Special Embassy" and a very unpleasant incident ahead of it. Before Mr. Taft became President, while he was on one of his visits to the Orient, he had given an address which was not favorably received in Japan. He had also appointed as Minister to China a gentleman who was openly critical of the Japanese. The appointment was announced but the Minister did not get to Peking, before the Secretary of State, Mr. Philander C. Knox, recalled him before he sailed from San Francisco.[1] On top of this, Mr. Knox's proposal in 1909 for the internationalization of the Manchurian railways had been misconstrued by the Japanese as interference in their affairs. The consequence was that they did not regard the Taft Administration as very friendly. Here was an opportunity, the occasion of the Emperor's funeral, not only for the United States Government to show the utmost respect but, by sending the Secretary of State in person, to reassure the Japanese of America's attitude regarding Far Eastern affairs.

The Special Embassy arrived in Tokyo and was received in true Japanese fashion, with the utmost courtesy. All the leading nations were represented by men of distinction—Germany by Prince Henry, the Kaiser's brother; Great Britain by Prince Arthur of Connaught; and Spain by Prince Alfonso. The official calls on the members of the Imperial Family and the visiting missions constituted a task of no small proportions. Mr. Knox assigned this duty to me, he himself making calls in person only on those senior to him in rank.

The funeral of the Mikado, held at midnight [13 September 1912], was most impressive. The remains lay in a catafalque in the form of a large cart with very high wheels, drawn by white oxen. An address, perhaps two, was delivered, the speaker standing some forty or fifty yards in the open in front of the cart. Then certain of the officials of the governments and the members of the royal family as individuals went forward from the

Brigadier General Pershing in his formal dress blue uniform and wearing his medals (left to right) for the Indian Campaign, Spanish Campaign (Cuba), and Philippine Campaign. This photograph was probably made in Yokohama, Japan, perhaps when he was in Tokyo for the funeral of Emperor Meiji in September 1912. The wear and tear of the years in Mindanao are clearly evident on his face (especially compared to his 1906 portrait), but his piercing gaze remains unchanged. (Library of Congress, Prints and Publications Division, Harris and Ewing Collection. LC-H261-6695)

pavilion especially built for the accommodation of the foreign representatives, another similar pavilion on the opposite side of the open parade in front of the catafalque being reserved for the family of the sovereign and the higher governmental officials. Each approached to a certain distance and bowed very solemnly, then backed away, faced about, and returned to the starting point. Much as in our military funerals, the Emperor's shoes were carried by a chamberlain immediately after the hearse.

Our mission, however, was humiliated by the appearance at the ceremonies of the regular Ambassador[2] plainly under the influence of liquor. Mr. Knox promptly did the proper thing; the next morning he relieved the offending emissary of his post and sent him home.

In the Special Embassy were Admiral Alfred Reynolds, representing the Navy, and Ransford S. Miller, the diplomatic service, who had been at the Embassy when I was military attaché. Miller was the man on whom the American mission depended for advice. He had spent his younger days in the East as a missionary and knew Japanese psychology perfectly. He was, moreover, a person of full knowledge, mature judgment, and extraordinary acumen. He was not a large or imposing-looking man, wore no splendid uniform, and had only the temporary rank of Minister Plenipotentiary, but he was one whose excellence of mind and character were in themselves commanding. No intelligent man who spoke with him for a quarter of an hour could fail to appreciate his exceptional qualities. The leading Japanese knew him well from long service among them, and the fact of their similar appreciation of his worth reminds me of Kipling's well-known verses on "East and West." Unfortunately, the first of those verses is the popular, often-quoted one; but the second is the greater, as surely the poet meant it to be. The first ends with this:

East is East and West is West,
And never the twain shall meet.

But the second says:

There is neither East nor West,
Border, nor breed nor birth,
When two strong men stand face to face
Though they come from the ends of the earth.

While we were in Tokyo a dramatic event peculiarly Japanese took place. This was the suicide at midnight, the hour of the funeral of the

Emperor, by the painful process of hara-kiri, of General Nogi [Mare-suke], the famous commander of the troops that took Port Arthur seven years before. The General had given his own two sons to his country and had served his Emperor and personal friend from boyhood. After the death of the Emperor he was said to have no further personal interest in life. And the General's wife in turn followed him, though her suicide took a less painful form. The two bodies were found on the mat floors in the simple little paper-windowed house in which this hero had lived very humbly. However deplorable a Westerner may regard self-destruction, the dignity of this man's modest existence and terrific death could not but hold one in awe. I recall General Nogi's stately figure as he appeared at official functions, such as the one given by the Emperor and Empress at cherry blossom time. He always went afoot when every-one else drove in carriages. Wherever he appeared he was the center of great enthusiasm.

Contrary to President Taft's wishes, my wife did not accompany me to Tokyo. She left Zamboanga with me fully intending to go, but when we got to Manila our second daughter, Anne, was not feeling well and was found by the doctor to be suffering from an attack of dysentery. This, we feared, might prove serious. My wife, therefore, remained behind. By the time my ship got to Hong Kong I found a cablegram awaiting me which was a great relief. It announced the diagnosis as amoebic, which I knew to be one of the less troublesome forms of the disease, and also reported that little Anne was recovering rapidly. Mrs. Pershing and the children arrived later, and we had a brief vacation at Hayama.

On May 19, 1912, the fourth and last addition came to our family. It was another girl and at the suggestion by Helen, then six, of the name Mary and by Anne, then four and a half, that of Margaret, we called her Mary Margaret. In the matter of birthplaces the family was a very mixed one, the first child having been born in Tokyo, the second at Baguio, and this one at Zamboanga, in the Moro Province; only our son, the third child, had been born in the United States.

On to the Next Command: The Eighth Brigade at the Presidio of San Francisco

It was with mingled feeling of relief and regret that we took our leave of the Philippines. I had had three terms of duty there, first as adju-tant general at Zamboanga and commanding officer at Camp Vicars, as a younger cavalry officer, then as a brigadier general with the brigade at Fort McKinley, and later as Commander of the Department and Governor of the Moro Province. My wife had been with me on the last two assignments. We had, therefore, made many friends in the Islands, whom we were sorry to leave. The people of Zamboanga turned out en masse in the plaza of the town and gave us a most touching farewell. But on the other hand my wife and I were both glad to be free of the anxiety lest one of the family contract one of the tropical ailments from which it is difficult to recover. Now, at last, after handing the administration over to civil officials, I felt that my work was done and we were free to return home to conditions that were safer and better. With us was Miss Mary Strong, the American whom my wife had brought to Zamboanga as governess. We sailed out of Manila Bay in December on the Army Transport *Sherman*.

The voyage before us was a long one, for the *Sherman* was not a fast vessel and had several ports of call to make. But we were not sorry for that, for in the past four years we had had too little time to ourselves, and we now looked forward with joy to the thirty days we would have together without responsibilities or cares other than those of the children. The entire passenger list was made up of army people, and it was a congenial group that sailed the Pacific, all happy to be homeward bound. On the whole the voyage was fine, and we were on deck most of the day, the children on their feet except at meal time or when my wife or Miss Strong was reading to them or telling them a story. I romped and played with them, getting as much fun out of it as they did. We spent Christmas Day out of sight of land, but the ship had a Christmas tree and of course turkey and plum pudding for dinner, and we had provided presents for the children. At Nagasaki we took them ashore and gave them rides in rickshaws. At Honolulu they were fascinated by the sight of the many native swimmers who came out to meet the ship and dive for coins thrown into the water from the deck, and ashore they each had to have a lei, one of the garlands of fresh flowers which are hung about the necks of visitors. General [Frederick] Funston, who was then in command, and Mrs. Funston entertained us at dinner one evening, as did the governor, Walter F. Frear. We sent a cablegram to Senator Warren, at Cheyenne, Wyoming, and he came to the coast to meet us and make the acquaintance of his latest grandchild.

I had been assigned by the War Department to the command of the Eighth Brigade, which was then stationed at the Presidio in San Francisco. My immediate superior there was Major General Arthur Murray, commander of the Department of California. He had been one

After the Pershings settled into the Presidio of San Francisco in early 1914, Frankie Pershing commissioned a portrait of herself and her four children. From left to right: Anne Orr, Helen, Mary Margaret, Frankie, and Francis Warren. Made on 7 February 1914, this picture may be the last formal photograph of Frankie with her children. (Library of Congress, Prints and Photographs Division, Unprocessed Pershing Photographs [PRN 13 CN 1976: 136, Container 6])

of my instructors at West Point, and it was a great pleasure to serve under this old friend. The residence assigned to us was the usual type to be found at army posts, by no means so commodious or attractive as our little "place" at Zamboanga. We could not afford here in San Francisco to have as many servants nor to entertain so freely as we had in the cheaper Philippines. But there were advantages—the better climate, school for the older children, theaters and concerts to attend, and other points of interest in that wonderful city almost entirely rebuilt since the fire of 1906. There was not the romance of the tropics around Zamboanga, but there were splendid city parks and beautiful country.

One of my happy memories of those brief months at San Francisco is of taking the children and their governess to the combined Buffalo Bill's Wild West Show and Floto Brothers' Circus. Unfortunately, my wife was laid up in the Letterman Hospital as the result of an accident caused by

Pershing's home on Moraga Street at the Presidio of San Francisco was destroyed on the night of 26–27 August 1915 by a fire which claimed the lives of Frankie, Helen, Anne, and Mary Margaret; his son Warren survived. Still suffering the anguish of their loss, Pershing never mentions the fire in the manuscript he completed twenty years later. For more information, see note 21.3. (Photograph from the *San Francisco Chronicle* library; Library of Congress, Prints and Publications Division, Historic American Building Survey)

a runaway automobile that came downhill from one of the cross streets and struck her carriage as she was returning from the city. The carriage was demolished and the team ran away, and my wife and the driver were thrown to the pavement. She was bruised quite seriously.

Old Colonel Cody, "Buffalo Bill," who still appeared in the arena among his "Rough Riders of the World," always remembered his army friends and sent me complimentary tickets for the "show." Among his Indian bareback riders were still several of the Sioux whom he had engaged as young men when I commanded a company of scouts on their reservation in Dakota. It reminded me of old times to see these Red Skins on the mock warpath again, and the children sat in wonder at this and other thrilling performances. But to them, who had spent most of their lives in the Philippines, everything in America was new, strange, and wonderful. In the menagerie the animals they liked best were the bears. This was probably because they remembered hearing from their favorite nursery books the story of the three bears. On leaving the big tent at the end of the performance we passed again through the zoo, the elder children under the guidance of the governess and the youngest in my arms. As we passed the bear's cage the baby waved her hand to him and said, as if speaking to an old friend, "Goodbye, Mr. Bear."

I was with the family in San Francisco only a short time, being ordered to the Mexican border in April, 1914, and the family, after remaining in our Presidio home for awhile, went to Cheyenne, Wyoming.[3]

22

On the Mexican Border with the Eighth Brigade

April 1914–March 1916

Service on the Mexican Border

At the time of my arrival in El Paso [27 April 1914] excitement on the border was running high. The people felt that this move meant intervention, which they believed was the only solution to their problems. Naturally, they received us with great cordiality. In the evening of the day after our arrival there was a large reception and ball at the leading club and invitations were extended to me and my staff and the senior regimental officers of the brigade. We thus had the opportunity to meet the prominent people of the city, whom we found most hospitable and charming, and many of whom became intimate friends. There was always the fullest cooperation between the townspeople and that part of the army that had the good fortune to be stationed there.

My headquarters was located at Fort Bliss and two regiments of the brigade, the Sixth and Sixteenth, were at El Paso and vicinity, and the other, the Twelfth Infantry, was at Nogales, Arizona. I promptly reported by letter to General Tasker H. Bliss, then commanding the Southern Department, saying that I was glad to have the opportunity of serving with him. The following reply, dated May 6, is quoted in part as showing something of the difficult situation:

> More than a year ago I recommended to the War Department that it at once strongly reinforce the troops along the border to enable us to thoroughly enforce the neutrality laws and the President's

Proclamation prohibiting the exportation of munitions of war. At that time, the revolution in North Mexico was deriving most of its strength in recruits, money and munitions of war from our side of the line. All the border towns in North Mexico were then held by Federal garrisons [Mexican] and the revolutionists were strengthening themselves by assistance from our side for the purpose of capturing these towns.

At that time it was the policy of our government to give no assistance whatever to the revolutionists, while it permitted the exportation of munitions of war to the Federals. At the same time, I was informed that nothing should be permitted to be done along the border on our side of the line that would result in dragging the United States into the Mexican controversy.

I represented to the War Department that if the troops along the border were not strengthened to absolutely seal it up against illegal exportation of munitions of war, the revolutionists would soon begin an attack on the border towns; that the resulting fighting would endanger life and property on our side of the line; that people of our towns would be thrown into a panic; and that, as a result, at any moment something might happen that would drag us into the very trouble that our government wanted to keep out of. . . .

And this is just what happened. The revolution grew until, according to the estimates of the Army War College, there was a combined force of fifty or sixty thousand well armed Mexicans in North Mexico. These people, on both sides, had become thoroughly seasoned in the kind of warfare that has been waged in Mexico for the past three years. [In some parts, the Constitutionalists held the field alone; in others there were more or less strong Federal garrisons, with the country at large in the hands of the Constitutionalists.]† Both sides combined (and the War Department plans have assumed that if it comes to a "show-down" between this county and Mexico, they would operate together) amount to fifty or sixty thousand men.[1]

My service on the border and in Mexico came at a time when the minds of men in responsible positions were much confused. Mexico was already in chaos when I arrived in Texas and within four months the war in Europe had begun. Apparently none of the world's greatest leaders, either civil or military, could see with perfect clarity or act with unerring judgment. Without exception, they all made mistakes. It was the beginning of the most tragic period that has come to the world since the business of waging war became that of nations rather than armies.

The Mexican Troubles and American Policy

When Mr. Wilson was inaugurated President of the United States, on March 4, 1913, the Mexican question was probably the most troublesome inherited by his administration. His policy with respect to that country has been loudly condemned by some and as highly praised by others, but none should fail to appreciate his humanitarian attitude toward a downtrodden people. At times I could not see eye-to-eye with the President, but scarcely had events passed into history before it became evident that he was right when, during the years 1914–1916, despite deliberate provocation and insistent clamor for intervention, he refused to change his friendly attitude toward Mexico. He declined to be moved either by insult from the nation whose people he desired to help or by the sentiment of those who foolishly advocated the seizure of Chihuahua as a solution of their difficulties or even by the insistence of those who favored intervention as a means of restoring security for American lives and property.

The situation in Mexico that confronted Mr. Wilson was exceptionally difficult. During the more than thirty years [José de la Cruz Porfirio] Díaz had ruled Mexico, he had maintained relatively peaceful conditions by force and the people were given no voice in their government, either municipal or national. That they continued to be held in a state of servility was largely because they were ignorant, inexperienced, the Indian strain being predominant, and incapable of self-government as more enlightened people knew it. Díaz became eighty years old in 1910 and with advancing years he naturally began to lose his firm hold on the reins of government. Intrigue against him had increased and when in that year Francisco Madero, a wealthy landowner and visionary, came forward with his fair ballot and free land scheme, popular imagination accepted it with avidity. The pathetic story of Mexico after the revolution is replete with lessons as well as interest. After Madero was imprisoned he was granted his release on bail by the aged President and fled to the United States, where he proceeded to organize and equip a revolutionary army which succeeded a year later in driving Díaz from the country and in the so-called election of Madero as head of the government. So began another of those periods of turmoil and strife of which we have seen so many in Latin American countries.

Our special concern in the Madero revolution and regime was the effect on American holdings in Mexico. Under Díaz foreign capital had been encouraged to enter the country, and to these outside interests, largely American, had been given the ownership or control of natural resources of great value, including millions of acres of land. The development of these "concessions" had contributed much of material prosperity and improvement in the country, as well as personal gain to national and local leaders, and in general there was probably little ground for the cry of "exploitation" raised by agitators. But once deprived of state protection, foreign interests began to suffer. Had Theodore Roosevelt been President he no doubt would have insisted upon adequate guarantees by the Mexican Government, but President Taft proposed the unpopular remedy that America should leave the country.

As is the case with many radical reformers, Madero, though honest and well-meaning, was too confiding. His mind was filled with vague and impractical theories, and it soon became evident that he was utterly unfitted to rule over a primitive people accustomed to government by men forceful in character, albeit for the most part unscrupulous. Madero had under him, however, at the head of his army, a forceful general determined to suppress opposition. This was Victoriano Huerta, a man largely of Indian blood, who had been trained under Díaz. Huerta supported Madero for about fifteen months, then, realizing the ultimate fate of the government under the type of leaders in whom Madero had placed his confidence, usurped authority himself. Probably fearing that Madero might repeat his former flight to the United States and reorganize an army there, Huerta apparently caused his assassination and that of [José María Pino] Suárez, the Vice President [on 22 February 1913]. Reports differ as to how they were slain, one saying they were strangled to death, though it was made to appear that they were shot by irresponsible soldiers while being taken to prison in a motorcar. The bodies, according to this report, had been propped up in the car as if still alive. The killing no doubt merited denunciation whether Huerta had a part in it or not. General Huerta was an able soldier and although known to Madero as untrustworthy he had been brought to Mexico City in the hope of converting him into a loyal supporter and had been given high command in the army. In the hour of Madero's greatest need, Huerta turned on his benefactor, forced his resignation, and himself assumed the title of Provisional President. Huerta was recognized by many American observers as well as other foreigners and Mexicans as the one person who could bring order out of the widespread chaos. If let alone he could probably have suppressed the revolutions of [Emiliano] Zapata in the south and of [Venustiano] Carranza and [Francisco "Pancho"] Villa in the north.

Soon after Mr. Wilson took office he refused to recognize the Huerta government on the ground that it was born of violence rather than the will of a free people expressed through a fair ballot. But Mexico was in no condition to have a constitutionally elected chief of state. It was not a country in which constitutional government was well established. The people had never known such an administration. Generally speaking, there was no such thing as the intelligent exercise of the electoral privilege. The masses had not yet achieved what advanced nations know as liberty and the right to choose their representatives. They had always been governed by local "Caciques,"[2] outstanding forceful men who had made themselves the rulers—as was the case in Europe in the middle ages and is still that in many countries, including the Philippines. What is known as "Caciquism" controlled votes without any reference to the judgment or knowledge of the individual. Mexico needed a strong and able man, and Huerta was that kind. With Madero out of the way, Huerta was probably the best man in the field both for Mexico and for the protection of foreign interests. Then there is the principle of non-interference—if we assume to right the wrongs in one foreign state, why should we not in another? The President went even further, however. He set out to eliminate Huerta. It is well known that Vera Cruz was occupied solely for this reason, though the excuse was refusal to salute the American flag.

On April 9, 1914, Mexican troops at Tampico without warrant arrested a paymaster and the crew of a small boat that had gone ashore from one of our naval vessels lying off that city. Our men were marched two blocks through the streets and then back to their boat and released. The local commander of the Mexican forces expressed regret verbally but refused to comply with Admiral [Henry T.] Mayo's demand for: "formal disavowal of and apology for the act, together with your assurance that the officer responsible for it will receive severe punishment. Also that you publicly hoist the American flag in a prominent position on shore and salute it with twenty-one guns, which salute will be duly returned by this ship. . . . Your answer to this communication should reach me and the called-for salute to be fired within twenty-four hours from 6 p.m. of this date."[3] In consequence, the port of Vera Cruz was occupied [on 21 April], closing it to the government as a source of customs revenue and for the importation of munitions of war. A much more serious insult to some of our naval men which occurred at another Mexican port [Mazatlán, on 18 June 1916] during the Carranza regime brought no such drastic reprisal.[4] On February 3, 1914, the embargo on arms to Huerta's adversaries was lifted.

It was during the excitement over the Tampico affair that my brigade was ordered to the border. The President's course soon brought retaliation in the form of increased violence against Americans in Mexico and along the border. Some were killed and millions of dollars worth of American property looted or destroyed. The situation was such that many Americans felt that, having intervened to such an extent, we should now complete the job and set up a government in Mexico that would serve the best interests of the Mexican people and ensure to our nationals their rights under existing treaties and international law. But the President, it became evident, had no intention of going that far. Apparently he reasoned that with the elimination of Huerta the revolutionary factions—the Carrancistas and Villistas in the north and the Zapatistas in the south—could then be brought together and working in harmony form a government that would establish order.

American opposition having made Huerta's position untenable, he was advised by the foreign diplomats to resign, which he did in July, 1914 [on the 15th]. This left the field at the mercy of the different factions. A month later [on 15 August] Carranza assumed the title of "First Chief" and took over direction of the government, with [Álvaro] Obregón friendly. Zapata, primarily a brigand, was little concerned with anything but loot and lust and has no important place in this story, but Villa, erstwhile ally of Carranza, split with the First Chief and conditions went from bad to worse. For several months our government took no action, hoping that the opposing factions might settle their differences. Meanwhile the numbers of outrages against American citizens in Mexico were mounting. But in June, 1915, it looked as though President Wilson had decided to intervene. He issued a proclamation [on 2 June] setting forth the deplorable state of affairs and calling upon the leaders of factions in Mexico to act together and act promptly for the relief and redemption of their prostrate country. He concluded with the threat that "if they cannot accommodate their differences and unite for this great purpose within a very short time, this Government will be constrained to decide what means should be employed by the United States in order to help Mexico save herself and serve her people."[5]

Many of our citizens interpreted this to mean intervention, but less than a month before [on 7 May 1915] the *Lusitania* had been sunk by a German submarine, with the loss of American lives, and it is doubtful, in view of the possibilities, if President Wilson really had any thought of doing so. It is evident that the President never at any time lost sight of the adverse effect our intervention would have on the other Latin American countries, and for that additional reason he hoped to avoid it. In calling a conference shortly thereafter of the diplomatic representatives in Washington of six Latin American countries—Argentina, Brazil, Chile, Bolivia, Uruguay, and Guatemala—to consider what should be done, he doubtless wished to ascertain definitely what their respective governments thought of the question of intervention. It was very clear that they opposed such a move, as the conferees decided to appeal to the leaders of the Mexican factions to meet and discuss a peaceful settlement of their differences and proferred their services as intermediaries. Villa and his supporters agreed to such a meeting, but Carranza did not. There appeared, however, to be a unity of purpose and authority among the Carrancistas which was entirely lacking among the others; Carranza was in control of approximately three-quarters of the country, and had given assurances that as soon as conditions in Mexico permitted, an election would be held to choose a constitutional government and that the lives and rights of foreigners would be protected and respected. All these things were in his favor, and the conferees thereupon recommended to their respective governments that he be recognized, though in September, at the very time Carranza claimed to dominate completely the regions in which they originated, attacks were made on Brownsville and several others towns in American territory and his adherents and soldiers were said to have openly participated in them. After these September raids strong notes of protest were sent him from Washington, and his further assurance was given that repetitions would be prevented. In view of this and the action by the conferees, President Wilson accepted the recommendation and on October 19, 1915, recognized Carranza.

The President's course was roundly criticized, but it is difficult to see how at the time he could have taken any other course short of intervention. Although Carranza turned out to be the worst sort of charlatan, none of his rivals could have been considered any better, and actual intervention would have been particularly unwise, especially in view of the European situation.

Conditions along the Border Deteriorate

While he was opposing Huerta, Villa had been in favor with our government and on his part had maintained an attitude of friendliness, no doubt with an eye to his own recognition. But when the recognition of Carranza came, followed at once by an embargo on the shipment of arms to his opponents, together with permission for his troops to pass through our territory by rail to operate against Villa, the latter turned bitterly against everything American.[6] Depredations against our nationals on both sides of the border at once rose to new heights in number and barbarity.

Carranza must have realized that he owed his position largely to President Wilson and for this reason alone might have been expected to make some effort to protect the lives and property of Americans in Mexico as well as to preserve good order along the border. But he did nothing of the kind. Less than a month later Mexican bandits again crossed the border, wrecked a train and killed several persons seven miles north of Brownsville, and within a few days made an attack on our troops stationed there. Outrages in Mexico itself continued unabated and bandit leaders well known as such to the authorities openly visited town after town in northern Mexico and roamed about apparently unmolested. Some of them were not only protected in outlawry but were even encouraged and aided by *de facto* authorities.[7] Conditions along the border were panicky as the apprehension of the people increased. Night and day our troops were on patrol, while inwardly we chafed at the orders to observe strict neutrality, as under no circumstances were our troops allowed to enter Mexican territory.

There was just one way to handle such a situation, insofar as protection of the border was concerned, in view of Carranza's attitude, and that was immediate and effective retaliation. We should have undertaken to guarantee the safety of our border towns ourselves. We should have informed the *de facto* government that with full regard for the sovereignty of the Mexican Republic any Mexican bandits or others invading American territory or attacking American citizens would be regarded as international outlaws and that we would hunt them down wherever they might take refuge and they would be made to answer to American authority for their crimes. I believe that such action would have materially changed Carranza's insolent attitude, and the bandits themselves would probably have given us a wide berth.

As it happened, no raids occurred along the section patrolled by my brigade, but we had to be just as much on the alert. I was determined that if any depredations were committed on that section of the border under my command the bandits would be pursued immediately into Mexican territory if necessary. It was during this period that a high official of the

War Department [unidentified] made an inspection trip along the border, and I asked him what would happen to an officer who disobeyed orders and crossed in pursuit of bandits. He replied that a court-martial would probably be the result. I told him that he might expect to have the opportunity to haul me before a court if anything of that sort occurred on my front. It was absurd to require troops to sit idly by and permit such things to happen. That summary action would have put a stop to raids on our side of the border was proved later.

Pancho Villa's Raid on Columbus, New Mexico, 9 March 1916

The crowning piece of barbarism occurred in January, 1916. A party of Americans set out by train to visit the Cusi mining property in the State of Chihuahua, where the mines had been looted time and again. Carranza authorities, with the full knowledge that Villa and his band were in the vicinity, had positively assured the party that the country was safe and that a guard on the train was not needed. On the tenth Villistas held up the train and eighteen of the Americans were taken off, stripped of their clothing and shot in cold blood. Once more promises were given, and it was claimed that one of the murderers was actually brought to justice, but the whole ghastly affair appeared as a mere piece of defiance on the part of the *de facto* government, whose troops must have known Villa's every move. A month after the massacre, unopposed if not assisted by *de facto* troops, Villa was on the march toward the border with the publicly-declared purpose of further vengeance. On our side of the line rumors had the notorious outlaw heading for a dozen different places. It would have been a simple matter for reliable scouts or small patrols to ascertain the truth or falsity of these rumors and to have accurately located the outlaw had our detachments not been forbidden to cross the line.

On the night of March 9, with a band variously estimated at from five to seven hundred mounted men, Villa crossed the border, swooped down upon the town of Columbus, New Mexico, surprised the regimental garrison of the Thirteenth Cavalry, looted stores, set fire to buildings, and killed eight American soldiers and eight civilians and wounded others. He was quickly driven from the town and, despite orders, followed some distance beyond the border by a squadron of cavalry under Major [Frank] Tompkins. But to Villa the vindictive excursion was costly, as he left sixty-seven of his men dead on American territory and lost in all nearly two hundred. Though the American command should not have permitted itself to be surprised, it deserves credit for its defense of the post and for its prompt pursuit even for a short distance.

In the face of this outrage there could be no longer delay in the government's action, which might well have been taken months before. President Wilson was not, however, swept off his feet by the indignant clamor of Americans. He still did not propose to become involved in war with Mexico. He issued a statement saying that adequate force would be sent in pursuit of Villa, but said "this can and will be done in entirely friendly aid of the constituted authorities in Mexico and with scrupulous respect for the sovereignty of that Republic."[8]

Designated to Command the Expedition into Mexico

Two days after the raid on Columbus I received a telegram from General Funston, who was in command of the Southern Department, saying that I had been designated to command the expedition. The War Department's instructions [Coded Message 883, 10 March 1916] to General Funston read as follows:

> You will promptly organize an adequate military force of troops under the command of Brigadier General Pershing and will direct him to proceed promptly across the border in pursuit of the Mexican band which attacked the town of Columbus and the troops there on the morning of the ninth instant. These troops will be withdrawn to American territory as soon as the de facto government in Mexico is able to relieve them of this work. In any event the work of these troops will be regarded as finished as soon as Villa band or bands are known to be broken up. [In carrying out these instructions you are authorized to employ whatever guides and interpreters necessary and][†] you are given general authority to employ such transportation including motor transportation, with necessary civilian personnel as may be required. The President desires his following instructions to be carefully adhered to and to be kept strictly confidential. You will instruct the commander of your troops on the border opposite the states of Chihuahua and Sonora, or, roughly, within the field of possible operations of Villa and not under the control of the forces of the de facto government, that they are authorized to use the same tactics of defense and pursuit in the event of

This 26 August 1914 photograph of Pershing welcoming Mexican generals Álvaro Obregón and Pancho Villa to El Paso, Texas, before escorting them to a Fort Bliss reception, first appeared in the *El Paso Morning Times* on 27 August. Obregón, the Mexican minister of war and navy, and Villa planned to meet with José Maria May-torena, the governor of Sonora, at Nogales, Sonora, Mexico, in an effort to resolve the growing trouble between Villa's anti-Carranza movement and Carranza's Constitutionalists. From left to right: Mexican general Francisco Serrano, Álvaro Obregón, Mexican general Ernesto Madero, Pancho Villa, Pershing, and First Lieutenant James Lawton Collins, Pershing's aide-de-camp. The iconic photograph was printed on postcards, one of which resides in LC/Pershing Papers, Box 384, and from which this image was made. (Library of Congress, Manuscript Division, Pershing Papers, Box 384)

similar raids across the border and into the U.S. by a band such as attacked Columbus yesterday. You are instructed to make all possible use of aeroplanes at San Antonio for observation. Telegraph for whatever reinforcements or material you need. Notify this office as to force selected and expedite movement.

McCain.[9]

I had once met on friendly terms the man I was now directed to pursue as an outlaw. This was in my first year on the border, shortly after Huerta's resignation. I invited him and Obregón, Carranza's chief military leader, to come and see me. They came across the river one afternoon in

August [26 August 1914], each accompanied by several staff officers, and I met them at the bridge and drove them by auto to my headquarters at Fort Bliss. Both were in uniform, Villa's a Norfolk jacket and long trousers, topped by a wide-brimmed felt hat, and Obregón's almost identical with our own. The latter, suave and cultured, was entirely at his ease, but the coarse, swarthy Villa was decidedly otherwise. He seemed suspicious and distrustful and his noticeably bulging coat indicated that he carried a brace of pistols beneath it. Both spoke with satisfaction of the part President Wilson had played in the downfall of Huerta, were gratified that he had refrained from intervention, and seemed then to be patriotically concerned about the welfare of their country and earnest in their desire to help it. A month later Villa was in rebellion against Carranza, and Obregón was at the head of the forces opposing him.[10]

23

The Expedition into Mexico

March 1916–February 1917

Problems Confronting Pershing's Expedition

The last time our troops had entered Mexico was in pursuit of the Apache Indian renegades who had left their reservations, committed a series of raids in Arizona and New Mexico, and had fled across the border and into the Sierra Madre mountains.[1] Our troops trailed them with the help of friendly Indians, but this was a different problem. Villa left a broad trail for a hundred miles and then the trail was lost, and we had to depend on information from generally unfriendly Mexicans. Although Villa was a public enemy, we were foreigners, there by agreement it is true, yet we were invaders and Villa was their countryman.[2]

The troops designated to form the expedition were widely scattered and had to be concentrated, some by rail and others by marching two or three days overland. I reached Columbus three days after the raid on the town and assumed direction of preparations, and another two or three days were lost while troops assembled before a start could be made. Two columns, one from Columbus and one from Hachita, were, according to General Funston's orders, to start from those points and unite at Ascención, but as that would be a loss of time I planned that they should meet at Colonia Dublán, one hundred miles from the border, which should for the time being serve as an advance base.[3]

The agreement reached after considerable telegraphic correspondence and some hesitation on Carranza's part was that each government would be permitted to send forces in pursuit of outlaws who had entered the territory of the other and that the two governments should cooperate to capture them. It was meaningless so far as any danger of

Area of the Mexican Punitive Expedition 1916–1917 (Vandiver, *Black Jack,* vol. 2, p. 615).

Mexican troops entering the United States was concerned, as no depredations were ever committed by Americans raiding the Mexican side of
the border.

When I sent word to the commanding officer of the Mexican troops
at Palomas, six miles south of Columbus, that we were about to cross the
line, he replied that he had received no orders to cooperate with us and
unless instructed to do so by his superiors would oppose us with force.
Here was a possibility of a fight right at the start. General Funston was
advised of the situation, and he reported it to Washington. It was then
that the hour of our moving was fixed for noon on the fifteenth, as Funston wired that he feared the President might change his mind if this
threat should cause delay. In fact, a telegram was sent from Washington
to Funston which directed that in event of refusal to tolerate our crossing the border we should await further orders. But these instructions
did not reach me until we were in Mexico. Fortunately, no resistance was
encountered in the crossing, as the Palomas commander evacuated the
morning of the fifteenth.

I notified Colonel G. A. [George A.] Dodd, who was in command
of the Hachita column of two regiments of cavalry, the Tenth and Seventh, to be ready to move that evening. The Columbus column was
composed of those troops that had arrived or were already there. After
seeing this column on its way unopposed I set out by motor to join Dodd
but en route my machine, a rented one, broke down and the departure was delayed till after midnight. It took us only two days to cover
the one hundred miles march and the evening of the second day found
us at Colonia Dublán, a few miles north of Casas Grandes. Columbus
was established as the base of supplies. The Columbus column, which
included the Thirteenth Cavalry, the Sixth and Sixteenth Regiments
of Infantry, and Battery C, Sixth Field Artillery, made the same relative rate of speed and joined three days later. This was excellent time
considering the wretched road. The army trucks plowed through the
long stretches of sand and caliche[4] with great difficulty. Here was a road
problem right at the beginning. The road soon became a series of ruts
that filled quickly with powdered dust that rose in clouds in dry weather,
and in wet weather turned to muck often hub deep, frequently requiring a whole day to get a stalled train over one of these stretches of quag-
mire. An engineer regiment was at once placed in charge and with the
assistance of line troops from time to time was kept constantly at work to
ensure even ordinary speed for the large numbers of trucks that became
necessary to supply the command. Supply would have been a compara-

tively easy matter had we been allowed the use of the railroad from El Paso to Dublán, but the cooperation of the Mexicans did not go that far and explicit orders from Washington forbade its use without permission of the *de facto* government.

Trying to Catch Pancho Villa

At this early stage of the pursuit it seemed that fortune might be favoring us. I had gone to Casas Grandes on the eighteenth and there obtained apparently reliable news that Villa and his band were in the vicinity of San Miguel de Babícora gathering supplies, recuperating their stock and seizing fresh mounts. San Miguel, as a study of the map revealed, lay fifty-five miles, only a long day's march, directly south of Colonia Dublán. If Villa should delay there another day or two there was clearly a possibility that if one column were sent to the east and one to the west of San Miguel to cut him off or strike his trail in those directions and a third, if time permitted, could intercept his retreat south we would have a chance of capturing him, but I was not sanguine of such early success. The least I thought probable was that one of these columns would discover his line of retreat and give us a clue to his intended movements as a basis of further operations. Even in this I was quite too optimistic, but at the moment we did not fully realize all the difficulties that would be thrown in our way.

It was with some hopefulness, however, that I gave the orders in accordance with this conception of the immediate problem. The east column, six hundred and seventy-six officers and men of the Seventh Cavalry under Colonel J. B. [James B.] Erwin, rode out of Colonia Dublán at 3:00 a.m. on the nineteenth, but the west column, two hundred and sixty-four officers and men of the Tenth Cavalry, commanded by Colonel W. C. [William C.] Brown, and the south, from the same regiment, two hundred and twelve strong, Major E. W. [Ellwood W.] Evans, were held up till afternoon. The Tenth Cavalry had already marched more than two hundred and fifty miles since March 10 and in order to save the strength of the horses and, as I thought, also to gain some time, arrangements were made with the local management at El Paso to use the railroad for part of the journey. The cars when they arrived needed some repairs, but once under way the obstructive tactics of railway employees caused irritating delays en route and Colonel Brown did not reach Rusio, his detraining point, only thirty miles away, until eight o'clock on the morning of the twentieth. The following day he arrived

Pershing at Casas Grandes, Mexico, during the Mexican Expedition, 20 April 1916. Pershing established his headquarters at Colonia Dublán in the vicinity of Casas Grandes during his operations in Mexico. (Library of Congress, Prints and Publications Division, Lot 9563-5. LC-USZ62-33567)

at San Miguel, only to learn that Villa had not been within miles of the place. Evans went on south and detrained at Musica. These columns were directed to cooperate to the fullest extent.

Of course, all concerned were disappointed, but it was only the first of a succession of moves based upon false information. There was no dearth of reports and rumors from Carrancista and native sources, but scarcely one, after being run down, was found to have any more basis of truth than the first. Before a week had passed it was perfectly clear that we were being intentionally deceived. I therefore telegraphed General Funston: "If this campaign should eventually prove successful it will be without the real assistance of any natives this side of line."[5] As General Bliss and other officers had warned the government, our entry into Mexico meant the unification of the opposing factions against us. It was like interfering in a family quarrel; they would fight each other when we were not about, but when we appeared frustration of our plans was the common objective. In the telegrams exchanged between our State Department and the Carranza Government, since then made available, the pretentions of friendship and willingness to cooperate on the part of the latter are seen to be couched in meaningless phrases, long drawn out, intended to make it appear that they were anxious to assist in running down outlaws such as Villa and his band when in fact they intended from the beginning to do nothing to aid but everything to obstruct. The actual attitude was something entirely at variance with the professions expressed in their diplomatic notes. It was shown in the instructions to their special agent in Washington for delivery to our Secretary of State, in which they denied the right of our government to send troops into Mexico and denied that any such permission had been granted. The action of the government, its troops, and the people generally from first to last was in accord with that view.

It was from the region in which we were now carrying on our activities that Villa had recruited most of the force with which he raided Columbus, and it was to be expected that the local natives should try to mislead us. Moreover, propaganda that the "Gringo" from the north was more to be feared than the worst outlaw was being used against us. As many of Villa's followers had deserted him and returned to their homes, they must have known something of the general direction he had taken and hence his approximate location, and through them these facts must have been known to the *de facto* military commanders. Although by proclamation the Mexican Secretary of War and Navy, Obregón, had called on all commanders to "act in accord with the military authorities of

Pershing and some of his staff at Casas Grandes, Mexico, on 20 April 1916. Left to right: Colonel Lucien G. Berry, inspector; Colonel De Rosey C. Cabell, chief of staff; Lieutenant Martin C. Schallenberger, aide-de-camp; Pershing; Lieutenant George S. Patton Jr., additional aide-de-camp; Major John L. Hines, adjutant; Major Jere B. Clayton, surgeon; and Captain Wilson B. Burtt, assistant to the chief of staff. (Library of Congress, Prints and Publications Division, Pershing Collection. Lot 9563-5. LC-USZ62-114561)

the American Army in order that the pursuit of these bandits may give the best results," they furnished us less cooperation and more deliberately false information than came from any other source.[6] They probably knew, at least most of them knew, being Mexicans, that the proclamation was merely a gesture.

As to the Americans in northern Mexico, it is not strange that those with interests in the country wanted intervention that would pacify the country. They were not anxious to have us succeed, as they feared, in view of past experience, that with the capture of Villa and the withdrawal of the expedition they would again be left to the mercy of other bandits and Carrancistas alike. Between the two there was no choice, one was as bad as the other in brutality, even to their own people. Both ravaged the country, robbing and raping and frequently killing defenseless inhabitants for no apparent reason. The ignorant and oppressed people had been led to expect similar treatment from us, but time quickly proved to them that American troops were different. Before long natives near the line of march began to sell food and forage to us freely, pathetically thankful to receive pay for produce that would otherwise have been confiscated by their own countrymen. The situation of the down-trodden population was deplorable and hopeless under the Carranza regime, and I wished heart and soul that I could help them. Intervention by the United States would have been a real service to Mexico. Many of the better class of patriotic Mexicans came to favor intervention and would willingly have assisted us, but, restricted as we were, we could not have protected them from the vengeance of Carranza's or Villa's followers, and they dared not risk it. But I am getting ahead of my story.

The country in which we were operating was wild and sparsely settled, with almost no means of communication, and in order to keep in touch with our columns as they moved south I followed closely with a small headquarters consisting of the Assistant Chief of Staff, one aide, two orderlies, and a cook, all of us in three Ford cars. Nevertheless there were anxious days when one column or another was completely out of reach, and we had no idea what might have happened to it. Illustrative of the difficulties of communication, on one occasion reports came to Colonia Dublán that a large force of Mexicans was moving from Sonora to attack our line of communications. Colonel [De Rosey C.] Cabell, Chief of Staff, who was in charge during my absences, took prompt action to meet the threat and twice daily until the reports were found groundless telegraphed me regarding the situation. But none of his messages ever reached me. The aeroplanes which had been sent for that purpose and which should have been invaluable for communication purposes were of little use. There were only eight antiquated machines available.[7] One of these was wrecked on the first flight from Columbus to Colonia Dublán and at the end of a month only two remained, and these were so unsafe that they were sent back to Columbus and decommissioned. The fault was not with the pilots and mechanics; under the direction of Captain Benjamin D. Foulois, the officers,[8] all of whom later won distinction in the World War, did tireless and heroic work in the effort to serve the expedition. The altitude of the plateau over which we operated was from seven thousand to nine thousand feet, and it was difficult for their machines to cope with the rarefied atmosphere and the violent wind currents of the height in which they had to fly. We were fortunate that none lost their lives, but they had many narrow escapes. Eventually new planes of an improved type were received, but even these were defective in many respects and were of the least service at the time they were needed the most. Niggardly appropriations for defense had made it impossible for the army to develop a suitable plane in advance.

Continuing Operations against Villa

The three columns had varied adverse experiences. Colonel Brown and Major Evans, who was with him part of the time, after following up several false rumors of Villa being here and there ran into a Carrencista command under Colonel Cano, who was loud in his expressions of a desire to cooperate. He led Brown to believe that Villa was at Oso Canyon and the latter was so fully convinced of that fact that he telegraphed me that he would attack Villa the next morning, the twenty-sixth. But Villa was found to be nowhere near there, and Brown in his chagrin reported that fact, adding "I fear that he (Cano) simply lied to me."[9]

Colonel Dodd, one of the older cavalry officers, appeared to me to be too far along in years to be very active. But when left behind, he came to me and asked for a chance, saying "General, I can outride any of them." I sent him to command the Seventh Cavalry column, with special instructions to coordinate the work of the several columns. Each was also kept advised as far as possible from my headquarters of the movements of all the others. On March 30 I was at San Gerónimo ranch, a few miles north of Bachineva, and that day a report came from Dodd that he had defeated a large band of Villistas at Guerrero the day before. The news of this success was very gratifying to me and heartening to the whole command. When Dodd reached Bachineva on the twenty-eighth he received confirmation of a report that Villa had fought with Carrancistas at Guerrero the day before and that he had been severely wounded and was still at that place, forty miles to the south, with five or six hundred men. Convinced that he was on the right track for once, Dodd did not hesitate but with his worn command started for Guerrero, pushing on throughout the night, not without misgivings, but finally coming out on the high bluff to the east of the town about seven o'clock on the morning of the twenty-ninth. But his satisfaction that the grueling ride had not been in vain was lessened by his disappointment at not reaching Guerrero at daybreak, but his Mexican guide, no doubt purposely, had led him over a circuitous route adding fifteen miles to the distance, giving him no opportunity to surround the town before his approach was discovered. Otherwise he would have had the outfit hemmed in and few could have escaped. Although the attack came as a surprise, the way was open for flight and the enemy took to their horses at the first appearance of Dodd's troops and fled in all directions, so that the fight had to be a running one, in which his tired horses were at a disadvantage. Nevertheless, thirty of Villa's men were known to have been killed, but, Dodd reported, "it must be remembered that four-fifths of the Villistas are Yaquis, who carry off their dead. Undoubtedly a much larger number than this was killed." One large body of Villistas escaped by a simple ruse that should not have succeeded. They carried the Mexican flag, marched along in an orderly manner, not firing, and our troops mistook them for Carrancistas and withheld their fire, and the group that might otherwise have been destroyed escaped. The same thing was tried by another group on the east side of the town, but there it did not work. After a ten-mile chase Dodd's horses were too weak to follow farther. Fortunately for Villa, he himself had left Guerrero the day before.[10]

Right here I must pay tribute to the energy and efficiency of the officers and men of these pursuing columns. Trail-weary though they were, scorched by the blazing midday sun and chilled by the cold night breezes, subsisting on the country and frequently hungry in consequence, they never lost heart but day after day doggedly stuck to their task. Dodd's column had been the first to have its perseverance rewarded, but all deserve equal praise. As a result of their combined efforts that section of Mexico had been thoroughly covered and no outlaws were left there.

Operations Leading to the Clash at Parral on 12 April 1916

Our difficulties, hitherto confined to misinformation, now took a more serious turn. Dodd's fine work at Guerrero altered the situation. Meanwhile, the line of communications and supply was being established and the principal points, such as Galeana, El Valle, and Namiquipa, garrisoned. With a view to taking up the pursuit with fresh troops, I had started at intervals four other columns from Colonia Dublán. These, in order, were Major Elmer Lindsley and two hundred and eighty-five officers and men of the Thirteenth Cavalry, March 20; Major Frank Tompkins with one hundred seventy officers and men of the Thirteenth Cavalry, March 21; Major Robert L. Howze and two hundred sixty-four officers and men of the Eleventh Cavalry, March 24; and Lieutenant Colonel Henry T. Allen, three hundred and one officers and men of the Eleventh Cavalry. Major Lindsley was sent to the west of the first three columns and the others moved over different routes south, ready to enter the more active advance operations when needed. Maintaining the principle of parallel columns converging near the Durango [State] line, Howze, to be on the west, was sent to Guerrero to take up the trail and be governed by circumstances. Brown's would be the eastern column and Tompkins' the central.

On April 4 Brown's column arrived at San Antonio, and there he received a message from the Carrancista General Cavazos informing him that American assistance in apprehending Villa was not desired. The next day, at San Borja [San Francisco de Borja], the General became more outspoken in the following message to Tompkins:

On the 3d of April I telegraphed you that I thought it prudent to suspend the advance of your troops until we both received orders on this subject from the Citizen Military Commander of the State [Carranza]. As I have just received knowledge that your forces are advancing in accordance with the itinerary which I have . . . prepared for the troops under my command, I would esteem it very much if you would suspend your advance until you receive the order to which I refer, by which means there can be avoided a conflict which may occur by reason of your advance.[11]

Tompkins went to see Cavazos, who told him Villa was dead and buried. He gave Tompkins a drink from his bottle, but permission to continue south was refused. To avoid a clash Tompkins wisely retired to Cieneguitá and on the sixth marched to Santa Rosalía.

The next to meet up with Cavazos was Howze, and the manner of the Mexican leader's approach is a fair indication of his judgment and ability. Howze had heard that the wounded bandit chief was being taken down the Sierra Puras Mountains to Durango and immediately took that direction. He had arrived in the neighborhood of San Borja on April 8 when Cavazos with a force of about three hundred men, yelling and with their rifles drawn, charged down on him. Howze immediately placed his command in an arroyo which afforded a splendid position, but he, himself, boldly rode out between the lines waving his hat and shouting in Spanish that his command were Americans. The charging Mexicans came within fifty yards before they stopped. A single shot would have precipitated a general fight in which the Mexicans would have suffered heavily. It was a perfectly stupid thing on Cavazos' part and might easily have cost him his life. Only the splendid control which Howze's officers exercised over their men and their good judgment in this delicate situation averted a tragic outcome.

This was a bitter pill, but we were not there to bring on a war and there was nothing to do but swallow it together with our pride and go on with the task assigned to us. Such incidents did not stop the pursuit of Villa and despite them the situation was decidedly in our favor. There were three columns now south of any considerable body of Villistas, while several others were combing the district in which they were hiding.

It was about this time that General Luis Herrera, who was known to be extremely hostile to Americans and whose father was *Presidenté* of Parral, came to pay me a visit at my headquarters at San Gerónimo. He was accompanied by fifteen or twenty staff officers well mounted and gaily caparisoned [that is, their horses were outfitted with ornamented covers and trappings] while my staff consisted of one officer, a clerk, an orderly, and a cook. We had no tentage and no equipment other than bare necessities and probably did not make much of an impression on our visitors. Herrera insisted that Villa was dead and that our continued presence in the district was unnecessary. I did not believe that Villa was dead and later on sent Lieutenant W. O. [William O.] Reed [previously one of Pershing's aides at Zamboanga], of the intelligence section, to locate the grave supposed to be his and exhume the body. Reed came back and reported that the supposed Villa was "just some little bit of a runt." On the death of Pablo López, one of his commanders, Villa had caused the report to be spread that it was himself who had died.[12] While Herrera pretended to be cooperating with me, his manner throughout this visit was distinctly surly.

Then, on April 12, came a crisis, but for which I believe the mission of the Expedition would soon have been accomplished. Let us note the positions of the different columns on that date. Dodd was at Miñaca and Lindsley at [probably San José de Barbícora, between Namiquipa and Madera], both having been alert and active as the other columns pushed southward. Howze, on the west, had struck Villa's trail and gone forward beyond Santa Cruz [de Villegas], south of San José [del Sitio], and Brown, on the east flank, had reached Media Ranch, near Sapien, both after considerable difficulty. Allen had reached Satevó, where I had gone by auto with my rolling headquarters to be in closer communication. In places these columns had been met in friendly manner, but generally it was otherwise, Brown having had a small fight at Agua Caliente with Villistas [on 1 April] and Howze having been fired on several times.

Tompkins' column, after passing through country infested by both Carrancistas and Villistas, was approaching Parral to resupply preparatory to taking up the chase again. At Conchos, or Valle de Zaragoza, where he camped the night of the tenth, a Carranza captain from Parral came into his camp, gave information about the government and Villa forces and told him [Tompkins] he could send word to General [Ismael] Lozano, commandant of the troops in the district, of Tompkins' approach so that he could be met, assigned a camp, and arrangements made for provisions. On arriving at Parral, Tompkins was not met, but with his advance guard he entered the town unmolested to interview Lozano. The General, with several of his officers, then led the command to a campsite, a veritable trap, surrounded by hills, which Tompkins, his suspicions having been aroused, declined to enter. As the rear guard left the edge of the town it was fired into. A few minutes later Carranza soldiers also opened fire from the hills; not till then did Tompkins reply. Seeing the soldiers and townspeople combined against him, he retired, deploying a troop at a time to hold in check the three hundred Carrancista and civilians following him. After withdrawing about sixteen miles to Santa Cruz de Villegas, Tompkins took up a strong defensive position, while the attackers, having suffered many casualties from Tompkins' marksmen, scattered in the hills, keeping up a fusillade until nightfall. It is probable that neither General Lozano nor the members of his staff knew of the treachery that had been planned, some of Tompkins' men in the rear guard having seen him use his saber on the crowd and one of his officers shoot down four of its members in an attempt to disperse them. It was reported by the *Presidenté* that the German Consul at Parral was instrumental in inciting the people. In any event there is no doubt that Germany would have been glad of a war between the United States and Mexico, although we did not then know the extent to which she was to go to bring about such a conflict.

Pershing's Recommendations to General Funston

General Funston called for my recommendations. Assuming that he wanted to know what should be done in case of an actual break, as there was no doubt that ample ground for aggressive action existed, I submitted a plan based entirely upon military considerations. From the moment our columns took the field the general attitude of the Carranza Government with few exceptions had been one of obstruction, changing more and more to open hostility the farther south we progressed.

Frequently our troops had been fired on by Carrancista soldiers masquerading as bandits. It was evident now that further penetration of our pursuing columns would lead to more serious clashes, but it was not my purpose to force the issue. If, on the contrary, it was to be forced upon us, as appeared to be the case, we would gain tremendously by striking the first blow. We had reached a point more than four hundred miles south of the border. A swift stroke at that moment would enable us to consolidate our favorable position in the north and give us a decided advantage in further military operations upon a large scale.[13]

My recommendation to Funston, in brief, was the immediate capture of the city and state of Chihuahua and the seizure of all railroads therein. He forwarded this to Washington and the Chief of Staff of the Army, General Scott, left for the border at once, "evidently coming for conference on Mexican situation," Funston wired me [on 19 April]. "Pending his arrival," the General continued, "there will undoubtedly be no action taken by War Department on any recommendation which you and I have taken."[14] Washington had to consider its course from the broad standpoint of the effect in the event of our going to war on the other side of the Atlantic and make the decision regarding further activities in Mexico accordingly. As I have already said, in my opinion President Wilson was right in not becoming too deeply involved on this side.

Consolidating the Expedition's Position at San Antonio and Deploying the Regiments

Fortunately, the dispositions and orders of the four columns operating in the region naturally brought them to the neighborhood of Parral about the same time. Soon after the fight there they had been united under command of Colonel Brown, making a force strong enough to have given a good account of itself under any circumstances likely to arise immediately. But to have retained troops in that advanced position while awaiting the outcome of negotiations would have required additional transportation and an extension of the line of communications more than one hundred and fifty miles from San Antonio over a difficult road through dangerous territory. Neither food nor forage was obtainable in the district, and troops and animals were already on reduced rations. Considering all the circumstances, withdrawal to San Antonio seemed advisable, especially as we would be in a more favorable position in case of extreme measures and would still be able to continue our search from there. So I ordered the retirement to that point.

Before the retirement to San Antonio was completed Funston telegraphed me that he was expecting orders from the War Department to withdraw to Casas Grandes, just south of Colonia Dublán, our starting point, there to await developments. In my opinion any such precipitate withdrawal would be a mistake. It would have meant giving up much of the moral and strategical advantage we had gained in a month of arduous campaigning, and it would have been considered by the Mexicans a positive defeat. I immediately wired back recommending that our troops should not retire farther north than San Antonio at that time, believing that in the territory thus left under our control and within easy reach active efforts should be continued to accomplish our mission. The following day, April 24, I was authorized to hold San Antonio and other points necessary in the further pursuit of the object of the expedition.

With considerable remaining hopefulness, I at once made new dispositions for the resumption of active pursuit of the scattered Villa forces within the State of Chihuahua, or for such other action as might seen advisable. The territory known to be infested by them, and in which Villa was believed to be somewhere in hiding, was divided into five districts, each to be patrolled by a regiment of cavalry, with the infantry and artillery well to the front in case their services should be required. The cavalry regiments were assigned to those districts where they had had the most service and with which the personnel was most familiar:

Namiquipa	10th Cavalry	Major Elwood W. Evans
Guerrero	7th Cavalry	Colonel George A. Dodd
Bustillos	13th Cavalry	Colonel Herbert J. Slocum
Satevó	5th Cavalry	Colonel Wilbur E. Wilder
San Borja	11th Cavalry	Colonel James Lockett

In the order establishing these districts all officers were again reminded that the expedition was operating within the limits of a friendly country whose peaceful inhabitants were to be treated with every consideration. Troops were also enjoined to continue cordial relations and cooperate as far as possible with the forces of the *de facto* government. But the order also said: "Experience so far has taught, however, that our troops are always in more or less danger of being attacked, not only by hostile followers of Villa, but even by others who profess friendship, and precautions must be taken accordingly. In case of an unprovoked attack, the officer in command will without hesitation take the most vigorous measures at his disposal to administer severe punishment on the offenders, bearing in mind that any other course is likely to be construed as a confession of weakness."[15]

Meanwhile Colonel Dodd, at Minaca, heard on the seventeenth that a force of Villistas had looted Yoquivo. Arriving at that place on the twentieth, he found them gone, and as Tomochic seemed their destination pushed on without delay. Reaching the outskirts of the town by a well-concealed trail, he entered at the gallop and took possession. The Villistas retired to the surrounding hills and a spirited engagement lasted until dark, between thirty and forty of the enemy being killed and Dodd having two killed and three wounded.

On the evening of May 4 it was reported to me at San Antonio that a force under Julio Acosta and Cruz Domingues, two Villista leaders, had attacked Ojos Azules, capturing seventy-seven of the garrison of eighty Carrancistas, and were then threatening Cusi [Cusihuiráchic]. Major Lopez, of the Carranza army, came in and asked me to send some troops to protect the town and accordingly Major Howze with fourteen officers and three hundred nineteen men of the Eleventh Cavalry were dispatched to Cusi with orders to proceed as circumstances might indicate. Reaching Cusi about midnight he learned that the bandits were in camp at Ojos Azules, where he arrived just after daybreak, completely surprised the Villistas, and in a two-hour running fight inflicted upon them a loss of sixty-one killed, with no casualties to his own command.

Withdrawal from San Antonio to Namiquipa and Consolidation at Colonia Dublán

After the Parral affair the Mexican government protested to Washington and the report became current among the people that the Americans were to be driven out of Mexico. Our government acted promptly in an effort to settle the disagreement, proposing a conference regarding the future activities of the expedition, and three weeks after the encounter Generals Scott and Funston met for the purpose with General Obregón at Juarez, on the Mexican side of the border opposite El Paso [28 April–11 May]. Obregón immediately demanded the withdrawal of my command and no argument would shake him from this position. His attitude became so threatening that, on the recommendation of Funston and Scott, President Wilson on May 9 called out 150,000 National Guard troops and ordered them to the border. There can be little doubt that this prompt action had its effect upon the Mexican mind, as there was less talk of war with us, and the Mexican Government became more inclined to listen to reason.[16] On the same day General Funston ordered the withdrawal of my command to Colonia Dublán, to start at once, stating that the necessity for concentration was considered imperative. Within two hours the order involving some forty different units in scattered localities was out and the movement started that afternoon.

It seemed that north of the border there was much anxiety for the safety of the expedition that was not entirely warranted. Any considerable body of Mexican troops assembled for the purpose of driving us out of the country would have been without intelligent leadership or organization. In fact, any army they could have mustered would have been little better than a rabble without training or discipline and not seriously to be feared. As yet no large bodies of troops had been reported near us and there was no evidence of an intention to attack us. Given an overwhelming preponderance of numbers and the advantage of position, the Mexicans undoubtedly would fight, but there never was a time in the history of the Mexican Expedition when they would have dared stand up to a formidable force. I telegraphed my views to Department headquarters, continuing the withdrawal, however, as ordered, and on the eleventh was directed to stop the movement at Namiquipa. As we withdrew from the advanced positions toward Namiquipa the *de facto* troops became more aggressive; our patrols frequently met those of the Mexican forces and avoided clashes only by the exercise on the part of our officers of the utmost discretion and forbearance. I shall never cease believing that but for this turn of affairs the arch-bandit would have been captured. To turn our backs upon the further possibilities was as great a disappointment to the command as it was to me. I remained at San Antonio and stood beside Colonel [John H.] Beacom, both of us with heavy hearts, as the flag was lowered and the last of the Sixth Infantry marched away, leaving a deserted post.

Any serious pursuit of the widely scattered Villistas was now out of the question, but troops continued local scouting. However, two important leaders were unexpectedly encountered by small detachments out on other business and paid the penalty. One of these, Colonel [Julio] Cárdenas, after a spirited close-range fight, was killed by my aide, Lieutenant G. S. [George S.] Patton, while out purchasing corn [on 14 May]. Patton had complied with his mission and with his detachment of six men went to Miguel to the home of Cárdenas and luckily found him. Patton brought Cárdenas' body and those of two of his companions strapped to the hoods of their three automobiles into camp, where Cárdenas was duly identified.[17] The other was Candelario Cervantes, who, with eight followers, [on 25 May] attacked a small detachment out sketching roads and hunting cattle. They killed Lance Corporal David Marksbury, the leader, but one of the men, Private George D. Hulett, Seventeenth Infantry, shot and killed Cervantes as he and his gang rode by firing at the detachment. Next to Villa himself Cervantes was undoubtedly the ablest of the band and his personal courage probably exceeded that of his chief. It was said that he had led the attack on Columbus while Villa stayed back with the horses, and that it was usually he who was at the front in any dangerous situation.

Events Leading to the Fight at Carrizal on 21 June 1916

For a month after withdrawal to Namiquipa we more or less marked time while relations between the two governments day by day drew more tense. Among the Mexican people war was believed inevitable. *De facto* troops were being assembled at points on the railroads to the east and west, threatening our lines of communications. The commanding general in the district of Ahumada had issued instructions for his forces to hold themselves in readiness to operate against us. Ten thousand men were reported in the vicinity of Ahumada and large numbers had moved from the south to the city of Chihuahua. We were told officially that these forces were being brought up to pursue Villa, but the Mexican people believed they were there for the purpose of driving us out of Mexico. The population began to hold themselves aloof from us and people who had been friendly became decidedly otherwise. Those whom we had employed as secret agents withdrew their assistance, and it became necessary to depend for information entirely upon the resources within the command. Constant reconnaissance in all directions became imperative to preclude surprise.

Then, on June 16, came the following telegram from General [J. B.] Trevino, the *de facto* commander at Chihuahua:

General Pershing.
Casas Grandes.

I have orders from my government to prevent, by the use of arms, new invasions of my country by American forces and also to prevent the American forces that are in this state from moving to the south, east or west of the places they now occupy. I communicate this to you for your knowledge for the reason

that your force will be attacked by the Mexican forces if these instructions are not heeded.
Courteously,

J. B. Trevino,
The General in Chief.

To this I replied:

General J. B. Trevino, Chihuahua, Mexico.

I am in receipt of your telegram advising me that your Government has directed you to prevent any movement to the east, south or west of the American forces now in Mexico, and that should such movement take place the American forces will be attacked by Mexican forces. In reply you are informed that my government has placed no such restrictions upon the movements of the American forces. I shall therefore use my own judgment as to when and in what direction I shall move my forces in pursuit of bandits or in seeking information regarding bandits. If under these circumstances the Mexican forces attack any of my columns the responsibility for the consequences will lie with the Mexican Government.

Respectfully yours,
John J. Pershing, General,
Commanding General American Forces.[18]

The local commanding officer of *de facto* troops delivered me a verbal message on the same day to the same effect, and in order to make my position quite clear I asked him to telegraph his superiors the following reply: "I do not take orders except from my own government."

Among the reconnoitering detachments that were sent out, Troop C of the Tenth Cavalry, under Captain C. T. [Charles T.] Boyd, was ordered in the direction of Ahumada to obtain information regarding the *de facto* troops and their movements. At the same time Captain L. S. [Lewis S.] Morey with Troop K of the Tenth was sent from Ojo Federico on the same mission. The two troops met at Santa Domingo ranch in the afternoon of June 20 and spent the night there. From the foreman of the ranch, an American who had recently been to Ahumada, the two captains got much reliable information. They there discussed going to Ahumada by way of Carrizal, a town some seven miles away. Morey opposed such a move because of the presence of Mexican troops at Carrizal and instructions to avoid an engagement. But Boyd insisted on passing through the town and, being senior officer, took the responsibility.

Arriving about a mile and quarter outside of Carrizal in the morning, he halted and shortly after was met between the lines by General [Felix] Gómez, the commander, and other officers of the garrison and told that their orders would not permit him to pass. Superior numbers of Mexican troops, said to be several hundred, were drawn up in battle formation in front of him; Troops C and K together could put only about seventy on the firing line. After two or three parleys Boyd ordered his troops to dismount and advance. The skirmish line was hardly formed when the Mexicans opened fire. Boyd and Lieutenant H. R. [Henry R.] Adair led Troop C in a dashing advance and drove the Mexicans from their first position. But Troop K did not go forward with them, which possibly caused the American defeat. The initial success was only temporary. In a short time both Boyd and Adair were killed and Morey wounded, leaving the troops without effective leadership. Ten of them were killed, ten wounded, and nineteen made prisoners. The rest succeeded in escaping and made their way slowly in scattered groups back toward Colonia Dublán. They were not followed, however, because the Mexicans had had a severe lesson. They had lost twelve officers, including their commander, General Gómez, and thirty-three enlisted men, while fifty-three had been wounded.

To this day Boyd's course at Carrizal has puzzled me. Before he started on this reconnaissance I told him personally, among other things, that Trevino had sent a threatening letter, that the Mexican situation was very tense, and that a clash with Mexican troops would probably bring on war and was to be avoided. He was told that he could probably obtain the information desired at Santa Domingo ranch, about sixty-five miles to the east of Colonia Dublán, and that at such a distance, should he clash with *de facto* troops, I would be unable immediately to support him. After our conversation I felt confidant that Boyd fully understood the importance and delicacy of his mission. No one could have been more surprised than I was to learn that he had become so seriously involved. Even had such instructions not been given Boyd it is difficult to comprehend why, after reaching the outskirts of Carrizal and talking with General Gómez and seeing the large number of Mexican troops moving into position in his front and toward his flanks, he should still have adhered to his determination to go on. He surely must have seen that he was greatly outnumbered and, if he thought there was going to be a fight, he could hardly have failed to foresee the dire consequences to his command in case of defeat. The only hypothesis ever advanced that seems at all plausible is that, for some reason or other, Boyd thought the Mexicans would not fight, or that, if they did, he could easily brush them aside.[19]

The news of the engagement was heralded throughout Mexico as a great victory. From Mexico City the report went to the United States and was published in the papers before I knew of the occurrence. I did not hear of it until the following day, when a telegram came from General George Bell at El Paso, followed at once by one from Funston asking why I had not reported. Confident that my instructions would be followed, I was amazed, and felt certain that Boyd must have been deliberately led into a trap. Here, it seemed, was an act of aggression that could be answered in only one way. Clearly the moment had come for military, not diplomatic, action, whether we wanted it or not. I immediately dispatched Major Howze with his squadron of cavalry to learn the facts. On the evening of the twenty-fourth Captain Morey with four soldiers and the American foreman of the ranch drove into his camp near San Louis ranch in a wagon. From them and others Howze got the story essentially as given above.

I also issued orders in preparation for an emergency and held the troops in readiness to march on short notice. I also recommended to Funston for a second time the seizure of Chihuahua and the Mexican Central Railroad. It was my purpose to move at once on Ahumada in accordance with earlier instructions that "If any part of your forces is attacked by an organized body of *de facto* government troops you will attempt to destroy all their forces within reach, taking care not to become too deeply involved or to expose your line of communications." I informed General Funston of my readiness to take the aggressive [move], but before making such a vital move it was necessary to ascertain all the facts. Major Howze returned in a day or so thereafter with full information regarding the engagement, from which it appeared that the responsibility could not be placed wholly on Mexican shoulders. I then wired General Funston that I should suspend the movement contemplated.

Aftermath of Carrizal—Sitting It Out
but Keeping the Troops Ready

Our government demanded the release of the prisoners and within ten days they were brought to the border and handed over. Otherwise the policy of peace with Mexico was maintained. Neither Washington nor Mexico City wanted war. The presence of a hundred and fifty thousand troops on our side of the border was evidently a factor in restraining Carranza. But his representatives at the long-protracted parley at Juarez persisted in their demand that we should be withdrawn. The conference having failed to reach agreement, our government proposed another, and after the exchange of many notes the new delegations [for the Joint American-Mexican Commission] met at New London, Connecticut, on September 6. Again the negotiations were long drawn out, lasting for months, until in January, 1917, President Wilson directed that my command be withdrawn from Mexico.

Shortly after the Carrizal affair the Mexican Expedition was concentrated principally at El Valle and Colonia Dublán and settled down to await the outcome of the diplomatic negotiations. The most disagreeable part of life in Mexico was the continual wind and dust storms. Against the latter, particularly, our tents provided little protection, but while on the move constantly there was nothing we could do about it. Now, however, it was not long before the troops had generally adopted the native custom of adobe houses. Their first efforts were rather primitive, and with few limitations in design at the start they turned out some bizarre dwellings. But with practice they became quite expert in making the "dobe" bricks and from the early designs the most suitable was selected as a standard pattern and soon the command was snugly housed. The adobe shacks not only withstood the rain and dust storms but were cool in summer and warm in winter.

From first to last there were in Mexico with the command five regiments of infantry, eight regiments of cavalry, one of field artillery, besides the engineers and detachments of the various staff corps, including the signal corps, aero squadron, the quartermaster truck trains, and the medical corps. The maximum strength of the command in Mexico was reached in May, when the number reached [approximately 12,000].[20]

The opportunity to train such a force after active operations had practically ceased was too favorable not to be utilized, particularly in view of the situation in Europe, and I instituted a thorough course of training for all arms from the company to the brigade, especially emphasizing combat exercises. Officers of the command known throughout the service as experts in musketry training were assembled at Colonia Dublán to aid in this most important fundamental and the machine-gun organizations were concentrated for a three-months course in that branch. The consensus of opinion among the officers was that never in the history of the army had such a thorough and comprehensive course of training been carried out. The experience during the months of our occupation was most valuable to both staff and line and the officers of the staff corps who were most efficient in Mexico formed the nucleus for that greater expansion in their special lines which was soon to take place in Europe.

Nor was the mental diversion of the troops overlooked. During periods of field inactivity it is desirable frequently to relieve officers and men from ordinary restraint of strict military duty. Such relief prevents discontent and despondency and promotes the morale and health of the command. All forms of athletics were encouraged and every available kind of entertainment provided, including moving pictures nightly at the large camps at El Valle and Colonia Dublán as soon an apparatus could be brought in. Each camp had its baseball league during warm weather and in the winter each regiment organized its football team. A polo field was laid out and the sport became a regular pastime.

At Christmas Miss Mabel Boardman, then at the head of the Red Cross, generously provided a gift box for practically every one of our soldiers. On Christmas Day there was a terrific storm which was a combination Montana blizzard and Sahara dust storm. From daylight till mid-afternoon it was impossible to see ten feet and the camp was almost a total wreck. It had been impossible to prepare the morning and noon meals, but after the storm ended the thick coat of dust and sand was washed off the turkeys and they were roasted and our Christmas dinner did for three meals. The mammoth Christmas tree, seventy feet high, which had been built by the engineers at Dublán could not be lighted till the next evening, when the headlights of all the motor cars in camp were turned on it with striking effect. A large star of Bethlehem was outlined on the ground and six thousand men of the command assembled around it. Carols were sung and prayers were offered. Then came Santa Claus, accompanied by a blare of trumpets and amid a shower of fireworks, and the Red Cross presents were distributed while the massed bands played the national anthem and familiar airs. The whole scene of this unique occasion was inspiring to a remarkable degree.

Withdrawal from Mexico

Late in January the order for withdrawal came, and on February 5 the entire Mexican Expedition was assembled at Palomas. With appropriate ceremony the flag was lowered and the command marched back home.

We had not captured Villa, to be sure, as we had hoped to do, but when active pursuit stopped we had broken up and scattered his band, which was our original mission. With the cooperation that we should have received from the Carranza forces few of the band that raided Columbus would have escaped us, and despite their opposition one hundred and thirty-five of the bandits had answered to us with their lives, eighty-five were known to have been wounded, and nineteen captured. The prisoners we captured were held in confinement by the army at Columbus while the State Department pondered their fate, and finally were released without further punishment. One wonders what our government would have done with Villa if we had captured him.

The Mexican Government lost a rare opportunity to rid the country of one of the most disturbing factors in its history. Although Villa again became active, Mexican outlaws had been taught the severe lesson that never again can they raid American towns or commit crimes on American soil without summary punishment.

Epilogue

For three months after the withdrawal of the Mexican Expedition from Mexico I remained on the border, at first in command of the El Paso District and then, on the death of General Funston, February 19, 1917, in command of the Southern Department. My promotion to major general in the previous September made me eligible for this post. Then, on April 6, came the declaration of war with the Imperial German Government. I have already written the story of my selection to command the American forces abroad and of my experiences in the world war up to the Armistice.[1]

After the Armistice there continued to be many difficult, sometimes irritating, situations to meet. There was the repatriation of the A.E.F. It was no easy task to return nearly two million men, yet by midsummer [1919] it had been practically completed. Marshal [Ferdinand] Foch proposed that while awaiting return our troops be put to work rehabilitating devastated areas, which I did not approve and would not permit. In the occupation of German territory the French made strong efforts to put us in a subservient role, and it required a determined stand to prevent this.

Shortly after the Armistice President Wilson came to France and on Thanksgiving Day visited my headquarters at Chaumont and reviewed the troops at Longres, nearby. It was a miserable day, cold and stormy, and I doubt if he enjoyed the trip, but, as a matter of fact, at no time did he display any particular interest in or desire to see our troops. I saw him myself only two or three times. He neither sought nor desired my views on the peace terms.

On September 1, 1919, I sailed for home on the *Leviathan* with my headquarters and the "Composite Regiment," composed of specially trained troops who had been selected to represent the A.E.F. in the great victory parades in London and Paris. Our trip up New York harbor was in decided contrast to that day in May, 1917, when with many of the men who now accompanied me, I slipped furtively down the bay in a tender from Governor's Island and secretly boarded the *Baltic* for the voyage to Europe. It was a tumultuous welcome that we received. Headquarters was established in the old Land Office Building in Washington [7th and E Streets, Northwest] and functioned there until [31 August 1920], when it was formally dissolved in orders and the A.E.F. ceased to exist.

Having [more than three] years to go before reaching the age of sixty-four, when retirement from active service is compulsory, I was then appointed Chief of Staff of the army [on 13 May 1921]. There was some question whether the position was commensurate with the rank of General, which had been conferred on me by Congress, but I was keen to have it. We had never had and had not then, a sound, up-to-date organization for national defense, and it seemed to me that I could in no better way repay my country for the trust it had placed in me and the signal honors it had conferred upon me than to devote the last years of my active service to the establishment of such a system.

My sixty-fourth birthday, September 13, 1924, was a sad day for me. I was loath to sever the ties of nearly forty years' service under the flag. My feelings were expressed in the following farewell message to the Army:

My Comrades:

No words seem adequate to express to you the conflicting emotions that I feel upon reaching the date which officially marks the termination of my active service. Our experiences together have been varied. We have withstood the same hardships and shared the same pleasures. We have faced discouragements and rejoiced over victories.

Today, the recollections that swiftly pass in review fill my heart with a deep sense of gratitude for the loyal service and warm appreciation of the sincere devotion to country of the patriotic officers and men with whom it has been my good fortune to be associated during the fleeting years of my army life. It is my proud privilege, in parting, to say of the men of all ranks who have borne arms under the flag that none have more earnestly wished peace, yet in defense of right none have ever been imbued with loftier purpose nor more completely consecrated to the maintenance of our ideals.

My esteem for them, and my admiration for their achievements continue to increase with the passing of time. The inspiration of their exalted conception of citizenship and their fulfillment of its obligations should ever assure the preservation of our institutions. The glorious example of their fidelity and courage will be remembered by those who come after us.

It is with an abiding confidence in our national forces, and with the assurance of my lasting interest in their welfare, that I bid you all an affectionate farewell.

Many a healthy, active man has broken rapidly without something to keep him mentally and physically occupied, and I am thankful that there has never been a day since my retirement that official and personal duties have not kept me busy.

The writing of my experiences in the world war was a matter of years. I had worked at it off and on beginning in 1920 and finally in 1930, after two years of intensive effort, completed the task.

Shortly after my retirement President [Calvin] Coolidge called me to the White House and asked me to go to Peru as a representative of the United States at the celebration of the centenary of the Battle of Ayacucho, where, in December, 1824, General [Antonio de] Sucre and a small army of patriots defeated the Spanish in the battle that finally freed the South American states from Spanish dominion. With the rank of Ambassador Extraordinary and Minister Plenipotentiary, I sailed from New York with Admiral [John H.] Dayton and Congressman F. C. [Frederick C.] Hicks and a small party on the battleship *Utah* late in November. Passing through the Panama Canal, we debarked at Callao, and after the celebration at Ayacucho made a sort of goodwill tour, in the course of which we encircled the continent of South America. I shall never forget the trip across the Andes and Lake Titicaca thence to Antofagasta, where we rejoined the *Utah* and those members of the party who had not cared for the overland trip or who had been obliged to turn back because of the rarefied atmosphere of the high altitudes. From Santiago, Chile, we journeyed overland to Buenos Aires while the *Utah* steamed on around Cape Horn. From Buenos Aires we continued northward, visiting Montevideo, São Paulo, Rio de Janeiro, Trinidad, Caracas, Havana, and thence to New York. It was on this trip that I crossed the equator for the first time and was initiated into the Royal Order of Shellbacks. The "tars" of the *Utah*, representing King Neptune and his court, were much easier on me, however, than on several other members of the party and those of the crew who were initiated at the same time.

In July, 1925, I returned to South America as President of the Tacna-Arica Plebiscitary Commission.[2] Over forty years before, Chile, in a war with Bolivia and Peru [the War of the Pacific, 1879–1883], had taken from the latter the provinces of Tacna and Arica. In the Treaty of Peace of Ancón in 1883 it was provided that at the expiration of ten years the inhabitants of the two provinces should decide by popular vote whether to remain under Chilean dominion or continue to form a part of Peru. But the two countries had never been able to agree on the form of the plebiscite. Finally, in March, 1925, President Coolidge, as arbitrator, decreed that a plebiscite should be held under the supervision of a plebiscitary commission of three, one each to be appointed by the contending governments and the third by the U. S. Government, the American member to be the president of the commission.

With a staff of legal and other experts, clerks, and aides, I sailed from Key West on the cruiser *Rochester* late in July and landed at Arica on August 2, 1925. Never had I labored with such a feeling of futility as I did in the ensuing five months in the attempt to ensure a vote that would be fair, especially to the Peruvians. When ill health forced my return to the States in January, 1926, I was convinced that such a thing never could be attained without a strong military force to carry it through. Major General William Lassiter, who succeeded me as President, continued the effort, but it was useless and in June, 1926, the proceedings of the Commission were terminated. In the end the dispute was settled by direct negotiations, both countries accepting the proposal of President [Herbert] Hoover that Tacna go to Peru and Arica to Chile.

I have had since the war and still hold one other presidential appointment, that of Chairman of the American Battle Monuments Commission.[3] Having commanded the American Expeditionary Forces, nothing has given me greater pleasure than to head the commission charged with the duty of erecting in Europe memorials to the achievements of our heroic troops. For me and for each member of the commission it has been a labor of devotion. On each of the American battlefields there stands a monument on a scale appropriate to the particular operation it commemorates. In each of the cemeteries where lie our immortal dead a beautiful chapel has been erected. At Tours, headquarters of the S.O.S. [Services of Supply],[4] a beautiful fountain commemorates the invaluable work of the men of that organization. At Brest and other naval bases the great accomplishments of the Navy have been recognized. The work is finished and now, with seventy-five milestones along the road of life behind me, my story is likewise ended.

Appendix A

An Address on the Campaign of Santiago

In the successful conduct of our recent war, America has again astonished the world.[1] In four months she has raised and recruited an army of a quarter of a million men, assembled and drilled them in various camps, transported them to distant lands, and, without one single reverse either on land or sea, has victoriously wrested from tyranny and misrule the island possessions of the proudest monarchy of Europe. Conceived and born amid revolution and by tradition the friend of the oppressed, she has stretched out her hand across the ocean to extend to ten millions of human souls the blessings of our own civil and religious liberties.

Fathers and mothers experienced a new sensation and made a new sacrifice when their sons, in response to the call of the President for volunteers, came to them and obtained consent to go to war. They came thrilled by the same patriotism that thrilled the heart of the volunteer in '61—the fathers, to extend freedom to a race of slaves at home, their sons to carry it to a race of worse than slaves abroad.

At the beginning of the war with Spain our government found itself in a deplorably unprepared condition. The admonition of George Washington, "in peace prepare for war," had gone unheeded for a third of a century. Congress had turned a deaf ear to the importunities of our military commanders. The staff departments of the army were only large enough to meet the ordinary necessities in times of peace of an army of twenty-five thousand men. They had not transported, even by rail, for over thirty years, a larger command than a regiment. The organization was crude and individual responsibilities were not clearly outlined. These staff departments had then to be increased by the appointment of inexperienced officers, but the unwieldy organization of the staff

367

corps still remained, and yet awaits the action of Congress. In the face of all this, every individual, both civil and military of staff and line seemingly did his best, and though, of course, mistakes were made, I should hate to attribute to any other than purest motives of patriotism. The work they undertook was enormous—arms, ammunition, commissaries, medical supplies, tentage, field transportation and all sorts of personal equipment had to be provided at once. Army officers, and all others understanding the difficulties of this great undertaking, under the conditions incident to an aggressive foreign war, can only be filled with wonder and admiration at the boundless resources of the nation. The wonder is it was done at all, the wonder is it was done so well.

That part of the war on land that was to be undertaken immediately was, of course, assigned to the Regular Army; regiments were assembled and recruited, and officers absent on special service reported for duty. The point of embarkation for the first army of invasion was Port Tampa, Florida, and here we find twenty-four regiments of the Regular Army—in fact, the Regular Army entire, except the heavy artillery, some light artillery and such few infantry and cavalry regiments as were deemed necessary to garrison the most exposed frontier posts, or were held for other duty. Assembled here, also, were three volunteer regiments—Roosevelt's Rough Riders, the Seventy-first New York and the Second Massachusetts, that had been selected to accompany the expedition to Santiago, or wherever it should be finally decided to send it. There was some delay in the embarkation, due to various causes, one of which was the inexperience of officers in transporting troops by water, and as a result of this inexperience and a lack of proper assignment and dependence upon officers so assigned, property and rations were loaded with but little system. Another cause of delay was the uncertainty as to whether or not the Spanish fleet was really confined in the harbor of Santiago. Certain it is that the transports were held in the harbor at Tampa for several days after they were ready to sail.

On the afternoon of June 14th the fleet steamed out after its naval escort, and a grander and more impressive sight the world has never seen. Fifty transports bearing an American army as splendid in the personnel of the officers and men of its line as ever invaded a foreign country; its officers and men trained in their profession; hardy from their years of frontier service; imbued with an eagerness for conflict born of patriotism and with a confidence in their strength inspired by a righteous cause, the army departed with that firm determination to win which, in itself, heralded victory. Ship after ship took her place in column amid the cheers of officers and men, with the music of regimental bands playing the uplifting strains of national airs, and many an eye dimmed with tears when good-bye was waved to dear old America as we started on this voyage which should carry freedom to a down-trodden people and our flag to foreign lands.

Our transports were either combined passenger and freight, or ordinary freight vessels hastily fitted up with stationary bunks, made of rough lumber and arranged in tiers on the lower decks, though with little room left for passage between the tiers, so that troops were really much crowded. In that southern climate the lower decks were very warm, but fortunately the weather was so pleasant that at all times, day or night, men could be permitted to remain on the upper decks.

On such a journey there is issued to enlisted men a travel ration, consisting of cooked corned beef in cans, canned tomatoes, hard bread, sugar and coffee, arrangements being usually made for cooking coffee about twice a day; on this journey fourteen days' rations were issued. The duties on shipboard consist of roll calls at reveille and retreat, a daily inspection of arms and quarters, guard mounting daily, a general police of the ship and such physical exercise as the commanding officer may deem practicable.

The voyage from Tampa to Santiago was without particular incident, and, except for the time occupied with the usual routine duties, officers and men had nothing to do except to lounge about the upper decks and cabins and smoke or sing, to enjoy the new and changing scenes of southern waters or to discuss the possibilities of the immediate future. There was among the officers a supreme confidence in our ultimate success. I remember, also, that it was the opinion among officers, and men as well, that one had better die fighting than to fall into Spanish hands, a prisoner; and the Spaniards had the same idea of us. We also had rather a contempt for their fighting qualities, but our opinion on both these subjects changed before the campaign was over.

Arriving in the vicinity of Santiago, some time was spent in deciding where to attempt a landing—the selection from a strategical standpoint depending, of course, upon the plan of campaign. Two plans were proposed; one an attack from the west, which it was said would involve, with the assistance of the navy, the capture of the outer defenses of the harbor of Santiago, after which it was thought the city would be easily reduced from the heights to the south and those to the west across the bay. This plan would require the use of heavy artillery at some stages of the advance, and the army was practically without siege artillery. It would have been difficult, also, to close the avenues of escape to the north and east. The other plan—the one which was adopted—ignored the existence of Morro Castle and the coast defenses, so far as a land attack was concerned, and contemplated an attack on the city from the rear—approaching from the east and north. This decided, a point of debarkation and one least likely to be occupied by the enemy in force was selected at Daiquiri, about thirteen miles east of Santiago.

There were no good maps of Cuba and very little was known of the coast or country about Santiago, or, for that matter, about any other part of the coast or country, simply because of its occupation, for the last four hundred years, by an unprogressive race of Spaniards. The main source of information, as to both the enemy and country, was the Cuban insurgents, and the information we obtained was often inaccurate and unreliable.

At Daiquiri the navy prepared the way for landing by bombarding the town and outlying blockhouses and driving out the Spanish troops, who, before leaving, set fire to the buildings of the town and the machine shops of the mines located there. There were no docks at Daiquiri except a small wooden affair, old and out of repair, and the vessels could get no nearer than about three hundred yards from shore, and then only in calm weather.

Before landing each officer and soldier was issued three days' field rations of raw bacon, hard-tack and coffee. The regiments selected to make the landing were loaded in the small boats from the naval vessels of the blockading squadron, drawn by steam launches—each launch hauling four or five boats. The First Regular Infantry, General Shafter's old regiment, was given the honor of leading and, by wading some distance in the surf, it succeeded in making a landing under protection of the guns of the naval vessels, meeting with practically no opposition from shore.

Nothing was taken ashore with the troops except what they carried on their backs, but the load was so heavy that to fall overboard in deep water meant to drown, though from the entire army but two men were lost. This plan of debarkation was the only one possible and it was tedious and dangerous. Men had often to drop from ten to fifteen feet from the freight porthole to the boat below, which is a very difficult task in a rolling sea; and yet, though dangerous, it was enjoyed by all as a sport—the many minor mishaps, such as being thrown down by the high waves while wading to shore, bringing forth shouts and peals of laughter from the troops.

On the morning of June 23d the 10th Cavalry, colored, my own regiment, together with the 1st Cavalry and Roosevelt's Rough Riders, three regiments which formed the second brigade of the cavalry division, were sent ashore, and moved out northwest, passing through Siboney, which later became the place of debarkation, to a point beyond the most advanced outposts toward Santiago. These troops, though belonging to the cavalry, were dismounted and in marching through marsh and bog along the single sunken road, overhung with boughs and vines, clad as they were in heavy clothing, they soon began to feel the wilting effects of a tropical sun; but every man had resolved for the honor of his country to make the best of the situation as a soldier and, whether working, marching or fighting, all behaved as though the success of the campaign depended upon their own individual efforts. It is to this resolution, which pervaded the army, that success was largely due.

During the day information was obtained, through insurgents, as to the location of a body of Spanish troops in force some three miles beyond Siboney. General Wheeler, the brave old ex-Confederate leader, who commanded our cavalry division, decided to attack this force on the following morning with the three regiments I have mentioned. It is at this battle that the Rough Riders are said to have been ambushed. This is not literally correct, for the battle had been planned the night before and the attack was made practically as planned; but, in their eagerness to get forward, the main body of the Rough Riders absorbed the advance guard, except a small portion of the advance, which was allowed by the Spaniards to pass through the lines and return without being fired upon, so that the whole line of Rough Riders came against the enemy before the latter opened fire. There is a trail leading from Siboney along the ridge of hills near the coast, which comes into the main road near the position occupied by the Spaniards, while the main road from Siboney inclines to the right and follows up the valley between this coast ridge and the mountain range farther inland. The part of the Spanish line attacked by the Rough Riders was at an angle across this trail, over which the Rough Riders moved, the right flank of this part of the Spanish line trending to the rear.

While the advance of the Rough Riders was in progress the First and Tenth Regiments were moving up the main road to the right, to the attack of the Spanish left, which lay across the main road at almost a right angle. These regular cavalry regiments attacked the Spanish left and drove them from their position in front and occupied it; the Tenth Cavalry having charged up the hill, scarcely firing a shot, and being nearest the Rough Riders opened a disastrous enfilading fire upon the Spanish right, and thus relieving the Rough Riders from the volleys that were being poured into them from that part of the Spanish line. This is in brief the story of how the Tenth Cavalry relieved the Rough Riders at La Guasima [Las Guasimas].

During the next week following this battle, the whole army had debarked and brigades and regiments marched to the front along this narrow road, passing and repassing each other, jovially chaffing an old acquaintance here and there, camping in open places on the deserted plantations, among the thorns and cacti along the roadside, long enough to build a shelter of palm leaves and fix a dry place to sleep, only to leave it the next day. In the meantime transports were being unloaded with much difficulty, owing to the absence of lighters. Horses and mules were simply thrown overboard by main force and towed ashore, if possible. Many got loose, became bewildered in the breakers, swam back to the transports or out to sea, and were drowned. A scant supply of rations was issued daily, and the problem became more difficult as the army advanced and the rainy season came on. Whole companies of our troops were put to work to make the road passable for wagons. Two batteries of artillery came by and were lustily cheered by the soldiers, who lined the road to witness the sight—a new one to many in the service. Everything indicated that preparations were being rapidly made for the coming battle; a package for first aid to wounded was issued to each officer and man.

On June 29th, a part of General Garcia's army of some four thousand Cubans, which had been brought by transports from the west of Santiago, was marched to the front, but they rendered little assistance, either in working or fighting, and most of them fled at the first explosion of a Spanish shell over El Pozo Hill on July 1st. However, some excuse is their's—ragged, some half-naked, barefooted, weary from hunger, laden with huge earthen water pots, heavy cooking utensils slung over their backs, armed with every conceivable obsolete pattern of gun—it is no wonder that they dared not face the deadly Mauser rifle; we, ourselves, had much less contempt for Spanish arms after we had met them face to face on the battlefield.

On June 30th the general order came to move forward, and every man felt that the final test of skill at arms would soon come. The Cavalry Division of six regiments, now under temporary command of General Sumner, camped in its tracks at midnight on El Pozo Hill, about three miles due east of Santiago, and awoke next morning to find itself in support of Grimes' battery, which was to open fire here on the left, with the idea of diverting the enemy's attention from the main battle, which was planned to be fought that day at El Caney.

The morning of July 1st was an ideally beautiful one; peace seemed to reign supreme; great quiet palms towered here and there above the low jungle; it was an oriental picture of a peaceful valley; there was a feeling that we had secretly invaded the Holy Land; a hush seemed to pervade all nature as though she held her bated breath in anticipation of the carnage that should that day strew those foreign fields with soldiers slain, and redden with their blood the very waters of her coursing streams.

The command had been aroused before daybreak and the men now stood about in little groups, opposite their places in line, anxiously awaiting the opening gun. From the ridge of the hill could be seen, half a mile beyond the river to the northwest, the dark lines of masked entrenchments and the mysterious blockhouses of the hills of San Juan. To the left of the first hill, holding a horse, stood one lone Spanish sentinel; farther to the west were plainly visible the successive tiers of the city's defenses, crowned at the top of the hill by the spires and towers of the apparently lifeless city of Santiago. Around to the northeast in the foothills, on an eminence overlooking all approaches, stood the stone fort and the smaller blockhouses surrounding the outpost El Caney.

As the sun's golden rays tinted the mountain tops and lighted the eastern horizon behind us, the stillness was broken—the suspense was over. Captain Capron's field guns had opened fire upon the stone fort at El Caney and the hills resounded with echoes; then followed the rattle of musketry of the attacking infantry; the battery in our front burst forth and the battle was on. The artillery duel began, and in company with foreign military attachés and correspondents, we all stood watching the effect of the shots as men witness any friendly athletic contest, eagerly trying to locate their smokeless batteries. A force of insurgents near the old sugar mill applauded at the explosion of each firing charge, apparently caring for little except the noise. The smoke hung heavily in front of our guns, preventing the accuracy of our aim, but locating us all too plainly for the enemy's gunners. A slug of iron now and then fell among the surrounding bushes or buried itself deep in the ground near us. Finally a projectile from an unseen Spanish gun disabled a Hotchkiss piece, wounded two cavalrymen and smashed into the old sugar mill in our rear, whereupon the terrorized insurgents fled and were not seen again near the fighting line until the battle was over. Thus the morning wore along.

A part of the plan was that the cavalry division and Kent's division of infantry should cross the San Juan River, connect with and, if necessary, assist the troops at El Caney, whose duty it was to carry that outpost early in the day of July 1st, then, on the following day, after preparing for further attack by the use of artillery, the whole line was to swing to the left to the attack of the San Juan Hills and the fortified ridge stretching in prolongation to the northwest. The movement of the cavalry division was accordingly begun. The road from El Pozo Hill leads in a northwesterly direction, follows along the river through the swampy jungle—tortuous and narrow, then crosses the river and passes toward and between the San Juan Hills and turns nearly west over the ridge into Santiago. The regiment moved slowly along this road under the scorching sun, and sweltered; a few men were overcome with heat; already, an occasional bullet nipped a leaf above our heads. Impatient at delay, the regiment and brigade finally swung past the waiting infantry and moved farther down the road. The Spaniards had evidently concluded that our plan was to march straight into the city that day, so that they soon began to dispute our progress by opening fire from the San Juan Hills and the trenches about the city upon the war balloon which had preceded us. So much has been said about this balloon that it hardly seems necessary to say more; why it was there, no one of the line could tell, as the only information its occupants furnished, so far as we knew, was that the Spaniards were firing upon us—information which, at that particular time, was entirely superfluous.

When the Tenth Cavalry arrived at the crossing of the San Juan River, the balloon had become lodged in the treetops above and the enemy had just begun to make a target of it—no doubt correctly supposing that our troops were moving along this road and were near at hand. A converging fire from all the works within range opened upon us, that was terrible in its effect; the Seventy-first New York, which lay in a sunken road near the ford, became demoralized and well-nigh stampeded; our mounted officers dismounted, the men stripped off at the roadside everything possible, and prepared for business.

We were posted for a time in the bed of the stream to the right, directly under the balloon, and stood in water to our waists, awaiting orders to deploy. Remaining there under this galling fire of exploding shrapnel and deadly Mauser volleys, the minutes seemed like hours. The Colonel's son, a civilian, a boy of nineteen, was seriously wounded in the side by a piece of shrapnel. General Wheeler and a part of his staff stood mounted in the middle of the stream. Just as I raised my hat to salute in passing up the stream to post the leading squadron of my regiment, a piece of bursting shell struck between his horse's legs and cov-

ered us both with water. Pursuant to orders, with myself as guide, the
Second Squadron climbed through wire fence and thicket to its position. A surgeon of our brigade, an Americanized Cuban, stood in the
water behind the bank in a bend of the river, supporting two wounded
colored troopers, to keep them from drowning. A temporary dressing
station was established behind a large tree near by. The regiment was
soon deployed as skirmishers in an opening across the river to the right
of the road, and our line of skirmishers being partly visible from the
enemy's position, their fire was turned upon us and we had to lie down
in the grass a few minutes for safety. Two officers of the regiment were
wounded here, and there were frequent calls for the surgeon; casualties
still occurred, but no order came to move forward. Whatever may have
been the intention as to the part to be played by the cavalry division on
that day, the officers present were not long in deciding the part their
command should play, and the advance began.

Each officer, or man next in rank, took charge of the line or group
immediately in his front or rear, and halting to fire at each good opportunity, taking reasonable advantage of cover, the entire command moved
forward as coolly as though the buzzing of bullets was the humming
of bees. White regiments, black regiments, Regulars and Rough Riders, representing the young manhood of the North and the South,
fought shoulder to shoulder, unmindful of race or color, unmindful of
whether commanded by an ex-Confederate or not, and mindful only of
their common duty as Americans. Through streams, tall grass, tropical
undergrowth, under barbed-wire fences and over wire entanglements,
regardless of casualties—on they go; up the hill to the right they gallantly
advance; with a cheer we appeared on the brow of the hill to find Spaniards retreating, only to take up a new position farther on, spitefully firing as they retired and stubbornly yielding their ground inch by inch.

Our line halted and lay down but momentarily to get a breath, and
in the face of continued volleys soon formed for attack on the blockhouses and entrenchments on the second hill. This attack was supported
by troops who had originally moved to the left toward this second hill,
and had worked their way in groups, slipping through the tall grass and
bushes, crawling when casualties came too often, courageously facing
a sleet of bullets, and now hung against the steep southern declivity,
ready to spring the few remaining yards into the teeth of the enemy.
The fire from the Spanish position had doubled in intensity—the pop-
ping of their rifles was a continuous roar. There was a moment's lull,
and our line moved forward to the charge across the valley separating

the two hills. Once begun, it continued dauntless and unchecked in its steady, dogged, persistent advance until, like a mighty resistless torrent, it dashed triumphant over the crest of the hill and firing a parting volley at the vanishing foe, planted the silken standards on the enemy's breastworks, and the Stars and Stripes over the blockhouse on San Juan Hill to stay.

This was a time for rejoicing; it was glorious. For the moment every other thought was forgotten but victory; men shook hands and congratulated each other; some hugged each other like children; rank was waived; their hearts were filled with a new joy. All wondered how they had done it; it was against all modern military theory that men should charge straight at a fortified and entrenched position, unshaken by artillery and defended by modern firearms in the hands of trained troops; and yet, here we were. Only American valor could have done it. I remember seeing a second lieutenant of the Sixth Cavalry lying wounded upon the grass at the top of the hill, and when I asked him if he was badly hurt, he replied: "I don't know, but we whipped them, any way, didn't we?" A brave man and like his comrades filled with only thoughts of victory.

But among these scenes of rejoicing there were others of sadness. Both American and Spanish troops lay dead and wounded around us; all were cared for alike. I saw a colored trooper stop at a trench filled with Spanish dead and wounded and gently raised the head of a wounded Spanish lieutenant and give to him the last drop of water from his own canteen. Their dead, of whom there were many, had fought bravely and we buried them in the trenches where they gallantly fell.

The losses of the day were heavy—the Tenth Cavalry losing half of its officers and twenty per cent of its men. We officers of the Tenth Cavalry could have taken our black heroes in our arms. They had again fought their way into our affections, as they here had fought their way into the hearts of the American people. Though we had won, it had cost us dearly; the field was strewn with brave fellows; the dressing stations were crowded with the day's victims. It was sad, indeed, as at night we checked up the losses of that terrible battle—gallant comrades, schoolfellows, chums, had there offered up their lives as a heroic sacrifice to humanity. "Their cherished names and their heroic deeds are ours to enshrine and ours to bless forever."

An attempt was made that evening to recapture the hill, but our defense was so strong that the attempt was futile, and the Spaniards retired to their first interior line of entrenchments—three hundred to five hundred yards away. The firing on both sides was kept up till dark and ceased only at intervals during the night. Over at El Caney the battle had raged with fury all day, but stubbornly as the Spaniards had held their positions, the fierce charges of the gallant Seventh and Twelfth Regiments of infantry were resistless. Soon after San Juan was ours El Caney fell. That night the troops engaged there were hurriedly brought forward to extend and strengthen our own line.

It was rumored that evening that some general officers considered our position untenable. "Our lines were too weak," they said, and it was proposed that the army withdraw to La Guasima [Las Guasimas], five miles in rear and there await reinforcements. The movement would have been as unpopular as the advance was popular; the very thought struck a false note—retreat! The line officer and soldier of the Regular Army did not understand the meaning of the word. No! Not while a man remained: right here lay Cuba; in holding this position lay the success of the expedition; to yield meant defeat and failure; they spoke boldly: "We can hold this line against the whole Spanish army." Possibly the temper of the army became known; in any event it was fortunate for the army and the country that these sentiments prevailed, and that they were permitted to hold the position they had so nobly won. Weak parts of the line were strengthened by new dispositions of troops; after dark lines of siege entrenchments were laid out; picks and shovels were bought up; companies to dig and others to guard them were designated; the night was spent in digging and men sprang to arms, only when interrupted by Spanish volleys or by annoying sharpshooters.

There was but little sleep that night; men forgot to eat and thought of water as a luxury; ambulances and even wagons were pressed into service and kept busy until dawn, gathering up the wounded; only a few of the dead were buried; pack trains carried ammunition, instead of commissaries. By morning the position was strengthened, so that our line was fairly well protected; reveille was sounded by Spanish small arms and artillery in chorus, but the signal had been anticipated and all men were in their places on the firing line. Daylight was barely breaking in the east, when both sides began where they had left off the night before and the firing all day was incessant. A few moments after the firing opened, a limber from one of the guns of the light battery near us got loose and it went tearing down the hill to the rear, for a quarter of a mile. Our artillery was silenced by the enemy's small arms, and compelled to take up a new position; Spanish shrapnel went screeching overhead and bursting beyond; the adjutant of my regiment was stricken by a hidden sharpshooter; the heat soon became intense and there was no shelter. Those men, not in the trenches, carried water nearly a mile for those who lay there fighting in the broiling sun. A soldier cooked bacon and coffee in the rear of the line, while a dozen others were waiting for his frying pan and his quart cup. A cannon ball plunged through the line at the top of the hill, and went rolling to the bottom of the valley; bullets spatted against the isolated trees or chugged into the soft earth, and covered us with dirt and fairly mowed the grass in front of the trenches. Now and then a man was hit while changing reliefs or carrying water to the fighting line. Thus the day went on, and the night and the succeeding day began. Then came the welcome truce; everybody drew a long breath and thanked God; it was possible once more to walk erect; however, the echoes of the last three days were slow to die away and at the breaking of a bough or the rustling of a leaf, there was a temptation to duck.

Officers and soldiers of both armies were glad, and stood in lines facing each other with a curiosity mingled with respect. Meanwhile, we were quietly locating the exact distance of this or that part of the opposing line, and no doubt the Spaniards were doing the same thing. We had taken a position giving us every advantage, and they could plainly see that our lines extended around on the right to Santiago Bay and on the left to the top of the ridge below the city. Our grasp was firm and unyielding; further resistance was useless. Cervera, the naval commander, appreciating this, had accepted the only chance of escape with his fleet, and had lost. At noon, on July 4th, the regiments were formed into line, and I had the pleasure of reading to my regiment a telegram from the President, extending the thanks and congratulations of the American people to the army in front of Santiago, for its gallantry and success. A message of congratulation and commendation from the Commanding General of the Army, stating that he was soon to arrive with reinforcements, was greeted with exultation.

The brave Linares, however, had already realized the hopelessness of his cause, but he would not surrender without permission from his home government. Therefore the city must be bombarded. Pacificos and other noncombatants were ordered out of the city, and were permitted to come within our lines. All day, along the hot, dusty road leading from Santiago to El Caney, passed the long, white line; frail, hungry women carried a bundle of clothing, a parcel of food or an infant, while weak and helpless children trailed wearily at the skirts of their wretched mothers. An old man tottered along on his cane, and behind him a puny lad helped an aged woman; old and young, women, children and decrepit men of every class, those refined and used to luxury, together with the ragged beggar, crowded each other in this narrow column. It was a pitiful sight; from daylight until dark the miserable procession trooped past. The suffering of the innocent is not the least of the horrors of war.

The days of truce and hostilities alternated; all roll calls were suspended except the sunset call—retreat on days of truce. At the evening call, we daily ceased our chatting, cooking or working, and groups or lines of officers and men stood with uncovered heads in respectful and reverent attention as the music of the "Star Spangled Banner" and the sight of the flag we had planted on the hill above us lifted us out of ourselves and carried us in thought to home and country; it was the soldier's silent "Ave Maria."

Duty in the trenches was not less arduous because of the few days of truce; all the available men were required to work at strengthening positions and building bombproof shelters; vigilance never relaxed until the capitulation. The rainy season had set in in earnest and the trenches were at times knee-deep with mud and water. The constant exposure to the heat and rain, together with the fearful strain of battle, began to have its effect upon even the strongest of us. Our sick list gradually grew and the dreaded yellow fever appeared in our ranks; the field hospitals, already overcrowded with wounded, were compelled to accommodate the increasing number of fever patients; medical supplies and food for the sick were lacking, and though many things were furnished by the Red Cross Society, there was yet a shortage.

Officers and men unite in saying that too much praise cannot be given those noble Christian women, Clara Barton and her associates, for their gentle care, their tender solicitude and for their untiring efforts in aiding and comforting our sick and wounded soldiers. They came as ministering angels to the suffering army at Santiago. Army chaplains, too, worked assiduously among the sick in camp and in the hospitals, and the friends of many a soldier who lies buried in that far-away tropical clime have to thank the army chaplain that the last sad religious rites were administered to their beloved here.

The supply departments exhausted every resource to feed the added burden of the insurgent army and the thousands of starving pacificos within our lines. Roads had become well-nigh impassable and swollen streams delayed transportation. The campaign must soon be forced to a conclusion.

Since July 3d, the firing from the Spanish trenches had become irregular, desultory and non-effective. Our artillery gunners now knew the range of every Spanish battery, and our men in the trenches—every one a trained marksman—knew the distance of every Spanish position. We had learned them so accurately that their soldiers could scarcely expose themselves long enough to take aim without being hit. A Spanish captain afterward told me that it was dangerous for them to stick up even a finger for fear of having it shot off; and yet the Spanish commander still held out.

On July 10th, the day set for the ultimatum of bombardment, the white flags of truce were again taken down and the men again climbed into the trenches. At four o'clock in the afternoon, at the signal of the first gun from our northern battery, the firing began and the battle raged with the same old fury as of those early July days; shells and bullets whistled violently for a few moments, but the enemy's fire gradually died away and was silenced. They realized their helplessness, and the battle was over.

On the morning of July 17th, the lines of both armies were drawn up to witness the formal surrender. General Toral, with an infantry escort, rode out from the city to meet General Shafter, who was escorted by a squadron of mounted cavalry. The formalities were courteous, though simple. Arms were presented by both commanders, and the Spanish general tendered his sword to our commander.

General Shafter, accompanied by all the general and staff officers, his escort of cavalry and one regiment of infantry, then entered the city.

Shortly before twelve o'clock our troops were again drawn up in line along the six miles of trenches, and stood at present arms. An officer ascended to the top of the Governor's palace, lowered the Spanish colors, and now held the Stars and Stripes, impatient to declare our victory to the world. Suddenly, at exactly twelve o'clock, the enthusiasm burst forth; cannon boomed the national salute, bands played the "Star Spangled Banner," hats were thrown into the air and ten thousand men burst their throats, joined in one grand American yell. We looked, and there just beyond the hill, outlined against a clear sky, over the Governor's palace in the captured city, floated our own beloved flag. The campaign was over. For us the war was ended.

Although our banners have been planted abroad, and a protocol has been signed conceding to us the victory, we are not yet ready to proclaim to the world that state of peace we all hope will come. We, as a nation, in the fulfillment of our manifest destiny, have risen in our strength to assert our position among nations, and in our wrath to rebuke a sister nation for her inhumanity. New responsibilities have arisen and we must meet them bravely and without hesitation. Although our prowess by land and sea is conceded abroad, our new condition requires us to stand ready at all times to enforce our demands. It is the duty of every soldier, as well as every citizen who has a true love of country at heart, to stand out against those who stir up strife or who bring us to scorn in the eyes of other nations. That firm support of those in authority, necessary to make us strong, should not be withheld until our new policy shall be fully determined and we are again at peace with all mankind.

Appendix B

Captain Pershing's Report on Moro Affairs

MAY, 1902.
The ADJUTANT-GENERAL, DIVISION OF THE PHILIPPINES,
Manila, P. I.
(Through military channels.)

SIR:

I have the honor to submit the following report respecting the execution of instructions received by me at Iligan, P. I., by cable April 16 in connection with the transmission of General Chaffee's message to the Moros on the north of Lake Lanao, and to inclose accordingly copies of all letters sent and received. Upon receipt of the proclamation I had a translation made and sent a copy to each of the following Moros: Ahmai-Manibilang, the sultans of Madaya, Bacolod, Toros, Marahui, Dansalan, Guimba, Marantao, and Taraca. With each copy I sent a personal letter of transmittal, referring to the friendship existing between us and to previous conversations I had held with most of them respecting our relations and our desire to remain at peace with them. These letters were delivered by one of the datos of Marahui. In reply I received a letter from Manibilang and one from the datos of Marahui jointly, which, as I have learned later, included some of the sultans to whom I had written.

When General Davis visited Iligan early in April he told me that it was the intention of the military authorities to punish certain datos on the south side of the lake for their depredations and for killing our men, and told me to do all I could to convince all Moros on the north side that we had no intention of molesting any of our friends. I did so by fully explaining the situation there and our purpose with respect to it to the leading Moros I met in Iligan, and invariably they replied that we had just cause for the position we had taken.

In view of the strained relations existing at this time on the south side, and to the difficulty in making them clearly understand by letter, as well as to disabuse their minds of certain rumors they had heard and believed, I thought it best to go to Lake Lanao, if possible, and have a conference with the leading Moros there, and I so wrote Manibilang and others. It was not until April 26, however, that their invitation came. I left the following day, and upon arriving at Marahui in the evening found them very much excited and frightened. All sorts of rumors were afloat among them about our designs; one to the effect that we were preparing 1,500 men at Iligan to move against them, and soon. Many had packed up their household goods ready to move and had sent their women and children to their forts and other rancherias.

The next day, Monday, April 28, was market day at Madaya, and we held a conference of about an hour and a half there during the market, all the leading North Lake Moros being present, as well as many Moros from other sections of the lake, including Linok, Bayan, Ganosi, Taraca, and Aremain. I explained the meaning of General Chaffee's proclamation, corrected many false rumors and impressions, and assured them that none who were friendly to us would be molested, but that it was firmly the intention of the Americans to go where they pleased throughout this island. The Moros are, as is well known, very jealous of their religion, and, like all Muhammadans, stand ready to defend their faith by force of arms. What I have always said to them was given authoritative force by what General Chaffee said on this subject in his proclamation. At the conclusion all, except some of those from the South Lake country, expressed themselves as satisfied that no general war was to be waged and that they could proceed unmolested in their religion and in the pursuit of their lawful and peaceful occupations.

To explain the relation Manibilang bears to the North Lake

Moros, it will be in place here to state that the part of Lake Lanao from Bacayauan, on the west coast, to Dalama, on the east coast of the lake, is called Bayabao, and is ruled over in a general way by the sultan of Aremain, recently deceased, and his family is intimately related to the family of Manibilang, formerly sultan of Madaya, and the latter seems to practically control this section. After stating that he and his people were relieved to hear what had been said, he told me he would go on Tuesday to Aremain and report the conference and felt sure that all the Moros of Bayabao would remain friendly. On May 9 the eldest son of the late sultan of Aremain, and the probable successor to the sultanate, came to Iligan, no doubt at Manibilang's suggestion, where he gave further assurances of friendship and good will and was presented with a flag. I am, therefore, still of the opinion that the Moros on the northern side of the lake will remain friendly and will not join the Moros on the south side against the Americans.

There will be noticed among the letters herewith, received from Lanao, one from the datos of Marahui requesting that no troops be sent there. This letter was written by Maciricampo and the conference included also some of the minor sultans on the north side. During my stay at Madaya, however, the subject of the occupation of Marahui by Americans came up in conversation, and I asked Manibilang why they objected. He said that so far as he and some others were concerned, they did not object, but that many of his people were still afraid, so the question up there seems to be one of gaining and holding their confidence. One Moro chieftain compared the average Moro to an untamed horse, and said if one attempted to ride him at once he would probably buck, but if one went at him gently and gained his confidence, he could be ridden without difficulty.

These letters, to which I have not particularly referred, are arranged consecutively and explain themselves.

Very respectfully,
JOHN J. PERSHING,
Captain, Fifteenth Cavalry.

Inclosures: Letter and copy of proclamation, marked "A"; letter to Ahmai-Manibilang, April 18, marked "B"; letter to Sultan of

Bacolod and others, April 18, marked "C"; letter from Ahmai-Manibilang, April 26, marked "D"; letter from Maciricampo, April 26, marked "E"; letter to Ahmai-Manibilang, May 1, marked "F"; letter to Ahmai-Manibilang, May 4, marked "G"; letter from Ahmai-Manibilang, May 6, marked "H."

A.

O. B., CEBU, CEBU, April 16, 1902.
Captain PERSHING.
(Through Commanding Officer, Iligan.)
Following communicated for your information, by command Brigadier-General Wade, Cebu, April 14, 1902:

SIR:

I inclose herewith a copy of communication or proclamation, sent to the datos whose names are mentioned in it, and several others of the principal datos of the lake.

This communication was translated into Moro and dispatched by runners. General Chaffee is very anxious to avoid a war with the Moros about Lake Lanao and wishes everything done that can be done to allay their suspicions and quiet their apprehensions as to our object in exploring their country; on the other hand, they must be made to understand that the sovereignty of the Government is complete and supreme, that assassination and robbery will not be tolerated, and such acts can only involve them in a war, the results of which will certainly be disastrous to them. As you have spent some time in Mindanao, and have been brought into contact with some of the datos of Lake Lanao, the General has sent you his proclamation, which he wishes carefully translated into Moro, and dispatched by trusty messengers to such datos as are accessible from your end of the lake.

With this proclamation you are authorized to send such assurances of your own as to the peaceful and kindly intentions of the Government toward the Moros in general as may serve to promote the object General Chaffee has in view. The nature of such communication can be easily determined from the subject-matter of the proclamation herewith. Instructions have been issued for the movement of a column of about 1,200 men from Malabang toward the lake, which will begin about the 25th of this month, for the purpose of punishing the datos concerned in the murder of our soldiers. It is thought that this information may be of importance to you in your correspondence with the Moros. It is, of course, desired that this movement be understood as directed against the offending datos only, and that there is no intention to molest anyone else, hoping by this intimation to prevent a combination, or, in other words, to separate the peaceful from the hostile datos, and thus prevent a general war. You will report in writing the execution of these instructions, and will submit to General Chaffee a copy of any correspondence you may have with the Moros.

Very respectfully,

J. P. SANGER, Chief of Staff.

B.

Letter to my friend, Ahmai-Manibilang, and to the Sultan of Madaya:

I have received a telegram from the military governor of the islands, in which he directs me to communicate to you and all Moros of Lanao, either personally or by letter, a proclamation issued by him in Malabang, April 13, and accordingly I am sending you a copy of this proclamation translated into your own language.

I have sent word to many, and have advised personally all the North Lanao Moros that I have seen recently of the action of certain Moros on the south side of the lake in opposing the American troops near Malabang and even killing American soldiers.

I have explained that we intended to punish the guilty datos, and all of my Moro friends have agreed that it should be done and that the Americans are right. I now write to you, my personal friend, what I have told many others. There is nothing else to do except to punish the sultans and datos referred to in the General's proclamation unless they accede to the demands made by the General; but I wish to reassure all of you that in punishing these bad Moros we have no intention whatever of molesting our true friends, and I wish you to communicate to all your people what I say and what is said in the General's proclamation.

If it is convenient I should like to visit the North Lake rancherias again and personally explain, more clearly than I can write it, this proclamation and the desire of the Americans for friendship and peace. I should like to go to see you on Monday (April 21) if you will send me word.

I am sending this letter with others by my old friend, Yanit, dato of Marahui, to whom I have explained the proclamation and this letter. With remembrances to your family and to that of your nephew, Ahmai-Sangacala, I hope to see you all again as soon as possible.

Your friend,
JOHN J. PERSHING
Captain, Fifteenth Cavalry.
Iligan, April 18, 1902.

C.

To my friends, the Sultans of Bacolod, Toros, Marantao, Dansalan, and Guimba:

I have sent to Ahmai-Manibilang a copy of a proclamation to the Moros of Lanao, issued at Malabang, April 13, by the military governor of the Philippines, and inclose herewith a copy for you also. On account of our friendship I request that you advise all Moros in neighboring rancherias of this proclamation and the friendship which the military governor feels toward all the Moros. I told you many of these things respecting the intentions of the Americans when I visited you. I desire to visit the lake again, as I can then explain personally, and more clearly than I can write it, all this proclamation means. I again assure you of my personal friendship and that of Americans in general for the Moros, and hope it may last for all time.

Your warm friend,
JOHN J. PERSHING,
Captain, Fifteenth Cavalry.
Iligan, April 18, 1902.

NOTE.—A copy of this letter was addressed to each of the above sultans, all of whom I had met, and practically the same was written to the sultan of Taraca, but I had never met him, and the letter was modified accordingly.

J. J. P.

D.

Letter from Ahmai-Manibilang, of Madaya, to my friend, Captain Pershing, Fifteenth Cavalry:

I am very much distressed, as I have heard that the Americans have arrived at Ganosi. Our women and children were frightened when they heard that the Americans had reached Lanao. I shall be very sorry if they come to Madaya, because you well know there are none here with bad intentions toward the Americans. The Spaniards always liked us because we never did them any harm, and they never molested us nor our rancherias. If it is true that we are friends, think before you do us any harm. Received at Iligan April 26, 1902.

NOTE.—In this letter Manibilang evidently refers particularly to the Moros of the rancheria of Madaya, for as a matter of fact the Spaniards were stubbornly opposed by the Moros in general on the north of Lake Lanao.

J. J. P.

E.

Letter from Maciricampo to his friend at Iligan, Captain Pershing:

God be praised.

I have to inform you that all the datos of Laguna de Lanao (Marahui and vicinity) have held a conference and all join in requesting you as commanding officer not to come here with troops. You may come without troops.

Your friend,
MACIRICAMPO OF MARAHUI.

Received April 26, 1902.

F.

To my friend, Ahmai-Manibilang, of Madaya:

I have just received a telegram from General Davis, dated the day before yesterday, sent to me at Sungut from Iligan. He is now near Ganosi with the troops, and says that many sultans and datos have come to his camp to visit him, including the sultan of Ganosi, Puatas, Gadungan, and Madumba, all of whom say they desire peace; and as the sultan of Madumba is now a friend of the Americans I think we can go to the other side of the lake by way of Madumba and Ganosi to meet the General, and if you can go advise me at once.

The General says if you are friendly with the sultan of Bayan that you should advise him to accede to his demands and avoid war and its consequences for his people. I write you hoping that you may influence these Moros who lack confidence in Americans to believe as you do respecting our desire for peace.

The General says further in his telegram that he does not intend to send the troops from Ganosi to the northern part of the lake. Advise all the people of Bayabao. May you live many years and your people always be at peace.

Your friend,
JOHN J. PERSHING,
Captain, Fifteenth Cavalry.
Pantar (or Sungut), May 1, 1902.

NOTE.—I was returning to Iligan when the above letter was written from Pantar (crossing of the Agus River), where I received a copy of a telegram from Major Pettit to Colonel Duggan, containing what is set forth herein.

G.

Letter to my friend, Ahmai-Manibilang, of Madaya:

I take pleasure in advising you that I have received a telegram from General Davis that he is at present with the troops on the banks of the lake at Bayan. In a fight at Bayan the sultan and Rajah Muda were killed; also the sultan of Pandapatan and all the principal men. The General says you and your people should not be frightened, as he does not intend to disturb the Moros on the northern part of the lake. He wishes that all the datos and principal men of Bayabao come to see him, and I wish to know when they will be ready to go with me across the lake. The General wishes to be at peace with you all.

Please transmit this notice to all your people, that they may understand and not be alarmed.

> Always, your friend,
> JOHN J. PERSHING,
> Captain, Fifteenth Cavalry.
> Iligan, May 14, 1902.

H.

Letter from your friend Ahmai-Manibilang to my friend Captain Pershing, Iligan:

I am very glad to know that the general has reached Onayan (Bayan), and has killed many datos who were opposed to him. When the general has dispatched all the bad Moros over there then you can go there with your friends, the datos of Bayabao, from here. Ahmai-Sangacala is not here, and it is difficult to reach Madumba.
Received at Iligan May 6, 1902.

NOTE.—I sent Ahmai-Sangacala across the lake with a message to General Davis on May 3, 1902, and to ascertain whether or not it would be safe to cross the lake.

Source: Appendix 8, "Captain Pershing's Report on Moro Affairs," May 1902, in Appendix G: Report of Brig. Gen. George W. Davis, commanding, Seventh Separate Brigade, to Annual Report of Maj. Gen. Adna R. Chafee, U.S. Army, command Division of the Philippines, in *Annual Reports of the War Department for the Fiscal Year Ending June 30, 1902*, vol. 9, *Report of the Lieutenant-General Commanding the Army and Department Commanders* (Washington, D.C.: GPO, 1902), pp. 556–59.

Appendix C

Captain John J. Pershing's Report of Activities at Camp Vicars, Mindanao, from 30 June 1902 to 15 May 1903

Camp Vicars, Mindanao, P. I., May 15, 1903.
Adjutant-General, Department of Mindanao
Zamboanga, P. I.

SIR: In compliance with telegraphic instructions, I have the honor to submit the following report covering the period from June 30, 1902, to the present date:

The command of Camp Vicars was relinquished by Gen. Frank Baldwin on June 30, 1902, and being the senior officer present I assumed the duties of commanding officer. At that time the command consisted of Troops A and L, Fifteenth Cavalry; the Twenty-fifth Battery of Field Artillery, and Companies F, G, and H of the Twenty-seventh Infantry; in all about 700 men. There have been some changes during the year. Company M relieved Company H on July 4, and Company C reported at Camp Vicars August 21.

Having been on duty at this station for practically a year, these troops have become thoroughly efficient by campaigning among and fighting against the hostile Moros of Lake Lanao. Having learned something of the Moro character, they have by fair and just treatment done much toward impressing upon the Moro mind the sincerity of our friendship. Partly through their influence many Moros have come to believe that American occupation will eventually have a beneficial effect upon the future of Lake Lanao Moros.

The rainy season in this region lasts from May until September, the months of July and August being the months of greatest rainfall.

On account of lack of tentage during the early occupation of this station the command was not properly protected from the heavy rains, and more or less sickness resulted. Up to the middle of October all the supplies were brought from Malabang by quartermaster's pack trains or by pony trains hired from the Moros, and of course supplies of all kinds were necessarily limited. In October the wagon road, for some time completed only to the Mataling River, was finished through to Vicars, and we were enabled to increase the variety of food and the supply of quartermaster stores.

So far as weather and field service would permit, daily instruction has been held by all organizations, and a practice march has been made on an average of at least once a week, except when the rainy season was at its height and during the prevalence of the cholera epidemic in the lake region. Serviceable sheds for cavalry and quartermasters animals were built during June and July by Moro labor. On the evening of August 21 a severe earthquake was felt about Lake Lanao, resulting in the destruction of the stables and the quartermaster and commissary storehouses. Several Moro houses about the lake were destroyed, and it is estimated that at least 50 Moros lost their lives. None of the old inhabitants remember an earthquake of equal severity. In rebuilding the stables they were placed south of camp on same ridge, thus giving a more concentrated as well as a more defensible position. In December a target range was constructed about a mile to the north, and during the three months following all organizations completed known distance firing.

The water supply at Camp Vicars has been obtained from a small spring which proved ample during the rainy season but insufficient for all purposes during the dry season, making it necessary to use water from a small stream about a mile southwest of camp, toward Tubaran, for bathing, for laundry purposes, and for the animals. Later a well sunk in the ravine below the spring has furnished enough water for bathing purposes. This water question is one that should be carefully investigated before final action is taken on the establishment of a permanent post at or in the vicinity of Camp Vicars, should the construction of a post at any time in the future be considered necessary. An estimate was made of the cost of keeping a command of this size under tentage for a year in this climate, and it was found that temporary buildings could be erected for about half the cost of the tentage. Their construction was authorized, and the work will probably be completed before the rainy season is well under way.

As to the construction of a permanent post, of course, circumstances depending to a great extent upon our relations with the Moros, must ultimately determine the course to be pursued. It is believed that troops will have to be kept on the south shore of the lake for some time to come, in the event of which there are several considerations which ought to govern in the selection of a permanent site. Other things being equal, that place should be selected which will bring to us and our market the greatest number of Moros. Their principal means of communication being by water, a site accessible to the lake would be most likely to attract them. Such a site would have an additional advantage, as regards supply, of being within reach by water from Marahui or such point on the north shore as may ultimately be selected for a permanent post there. For a site on the south shore it is believed that the second plateau at Bayan fulfills all conditions as well as any other, and its proximity to the lake eliminates the question of water supply.

Moro Affairs.

In order to more clearly understand the conditions as they exist in the lake region today, it should be borne in mind that there are three tribes or branches of Malanao Moros, viz, those of Bayabao, inhabiting the northern third of the lake, from Bucayauan, on the west shore, around to Dalama, on the northeast shore, with a center of population near Marahui; the Onayans, inhabiting the southern shore of the lake, from Madumba on the west to Sauir on the east, with a center of population at the former capital, Bayan; and the Maciu tribe, consisting of the remaining Moros about the lake except those inhabiting a few rancherias east of Maciu, among the foothills, who belong to the Bayabaos. Igacin Moros claim to be the most ancient, the Bayabaos and Onayans being offshoots, although not any of them are able to trace their ancestry back of the thirteenth century. It is probable that at one time each tribe had a sultan or leading dato whose rule over it was absolute, and while the lines separating these tribes are still more or less distinct, at present the head of each is practically such in name only, or at most, exercises a very limited control over it as a whole. Moros from the different tribes intermarry and have done so to such an extent in the past that it is often difficult for them to trace their ancestry to a particular tribe. The tribes have also disintegrated, so that in some 400 rancherias around the lake there are today about 150 sultans, all claiming to be of royal blood.

At the time of our occupation of Lake Lanao we found a considerable number of Moros opposing us either openly or secretly. Perhaps one-half of the Onayan Moros expressed their friendship soon after the battle of Bayan, and previous to this we had received assurances of friendship from most of the people constituting the Bayabao tribe, many of whom I had personally visited while stationed at Iligan.

All others in the Laguna may be considered as being opposed to us at that time. The Bacolod Moros on the west, some of the Macius on the east, and a number of the Onayan Moros, under the leadership of Sultan Uali of Butig, were openly hostile to us. With the small nucleus of friendly Moros to assist us, efforts were at once begun to influence others, at first those of the Onayan and Bayabao tribes, and later those of Maciu. Letters were written and friendly Moros were sent out to assure all of them that we had their best interests at heart, and inviting those who had not done so to visit us and become personally acquainted, in order, if possible, that mutual confidence might be established between us. They were told that our purpose was to avoid further war with them, if possible; that we did not want to kill their people nor destroy their property; that we desired them to bring their produce to our market; that we wished to employ them as laborers on the road and about camp; that we had no intention of disturbing their religion nor of changing their lawful customs, and that in coming among them we had no other idea than to make them our friends.

In response to these letters and invitations many visited us, and others replied by letter, expressing their desire to be on friendly terms with us. To all who came a welcome was given and every effort made to assure them that our motives were the best. A special invitation was sent inviting Moros to come and join us in celebrating the Fourth of July. About 700, from rancherias in the vicinity, accepted the invitation and seemed to enjoy both our sports and their own, for which special prizes were offered.

On June 21, 10 Moros, under the leadership of Dato Tangul, attacked 2 soldiers on the trail to Malabang, near Camp No. 10, wounding both of them and securing both their rifles. An investigation brought out the fact that these Moros were from Binidayan. The sultan had visited the camp after the battle of Bayan, had expressed his friendship, and had received pay for some growing rice destroyed during the Lake Lanao expedition. In conversation he acknowledged that the Moros who committed this offense were from his rancheria, but pleaded that he was powerless to control them. I told him it would be our policy to hold the sultans and datos responsible for the acts of their people and that he must deliver the leader of these offenders to us. As he failed to comply with this demand I arrested him and brought him to camp a prisoner.

The two stolen rifles were delivered next day, and in a few days several of his Moros brought in the body of one of Tangul's party, reporting that it was Tangul himself. This Moro whom they thought dead regained consciousness long enough to confess that he was a member of the party, but said that he was not Tangul, and that the Binidayan Moros were trying to deceive us. I still insisted that the leader be brought in, and offered to send troops to make the arrest if they would locate him. Before this could be done, however, the sultan went juramentado, struck the sergeant of the guard with a piece of bamboo, grabbed the gun of the sentry immediately over him and began to use it. Of course the guard was compelled to fire and the sultan fell mortally wounded. Every effort was made by the surgeons to save his life without avail. He made the statement that he had run amuck expecting to be killed by the guard and did not hold them to blame. His death in this manner was unfortunate and was to be regretted, but the whole affair served to impress upon the minds of all datos the position we had taken for the enforcement of law and order and caused positive action to be taken by many of them. The Moros of that rancheria assumed more or less of an unfriendly attitude, but they eventually presented themselves at camp under the new sultan, Mambao, and extended an invitation for us to visit their rancheria, which we did in February for the first time.

During the months of June and July there were several acts of violence committed along the trails by unfriendly Moros, usually in attempts to capture arms, and it may be stated in this connection that the one great desire of every Moro is to possess a modern rifle. Telegraph lines were constantly interfered with and the wire often for a distance of a mile was carried away. Camp Vicars itself, however, was not molested until the night of August 11, when one of the outposts was attacked by a band of 15 Moros from Bacolod. A sergeant and 1 man were killed and 2 men wounded. One Moro of the party was found dead afterwards and others were reported wounded. Night attacks were made on camp at intervals during August and September and several Moros were killed or wounded from time to time. These attacks were mainly under the leadership of Sultan Uali, who drew around him a crowd of renegade Moros from Butig and its subordinate rancherias in that section; and Moros from Maciu and Bacolod under different leaders also became offensive. To determine the correctness of reports regarding them I demanded explanations from the sultans and datos of those rancherias and in most cases received hostile replies. Our inactivity and failure to punish these offenders was misconstrued as cowardice on our part, and even friendly Moros could not understand why we took no action. I informed them that a time would come when they must pay the penalty and that they would learn sooner or later that Moros could not with impunity attack our soldiers and destroy our property. To put a stop to this marauding, it became necessary to punish the Moros responsible for it, and a campaign against them was ordered. The first campaign, September 18 to 22, was made against Sultan Uali, of Gauan and Butig, and Moros of the rancherias of Bayabao who had been active in their hostility against us.

The second campaign, September 29 to October 3, was made against Maciu Moros under Sultans Tauagan and Ganduali. An effort was made even after the campaign had begun to induce them to come in and surrender without fighting, but they refused and made stubborn resistance to our advance into their territory. The result was that their forts were destroyed, and all who opposed us were killed in battle or dislodged from their position in defeat. The immediate effect of this campaign was to put a stop to attacks on camps and on soldiers along trails, and since September, 1902, with one exception, there has been no further interference of this kind. It has been the experience with us, as with the Spaniards, that after the Moros of a particular rancheria have received a sound thrashing the lesson is remembered by them and its effect upon others has been beneficial. Their attacks on our troops and their attempts to stand against us have met with comparatively little success, while they seldom failed to secure arms from the Spaniards when they tried, at one time taking the Spaniards by surprise and securing thirty-seven Remingtons and ammunition. Even after reaching Marahui the Spaniards made little progress in exploring the Lanao region, and there is no record of their having made an expedition against any of the then hostile rancherias except one against Tugaya. Even with launches on the lake they secured no foothold on the eastern side, and were constantly annoyed and often attacked in their forts by large numbers of Moros from Pitacus, Taraca, and other rancherias from that side of the lake. Neither did they ever secure a foothold on the south side of the lake, nor did they progress along the western shore south of Tugaya.

After the campaign against Maciu it was decided to postpone further movements against other hostile Moros in the hope that they would profit by the experience of those who had encountered us. Letters were sent to the east lake and to Bacolod Moros, giving them every opportunity to come to friendly terms with us. They were told that even though previously hostile they might visit us without fear, and that we would welcome a change in their hostile attitude. Several Moros on the eastern side of the lake expressed a desire to be friends, including Raja Nurul Caquim, who controls a number of rancherias in that section, and who told his people that they must not interfere with Americans under penalty of severe punishment. Some of the Moros of Butig and Bayabao visited us, declaring that they wished no more war. Nothing of a friendly nature, however, was heard from Bacolod, who still held out against us and continued to send hostile notes.

Under escort of Amai-Manibilang and some of his people from Madaya, I crossed the lake in vintas with 50 men, in November, stopping at several towns along the route; visited Madaya and Marahui, and proceeded thence to Iligan and returned to Camp Vicars by the same route. We were shown every attention at Madaya and also at Marahui, where a large conference was held on market day, at which some 500 Moros from all sections were present. The assurances of friendship we received during this trip convinced me of the sincerity of the promises made one year previous by the Bayabao Moros. Moreover, it was plain that all Moros on the west shore of the lake, except those under the influence of Bacolod, had by this time become reconciled to our presence in the lake country.

In December cholera reached the lake, and has probably extended to all rancherias, our market was closed for a time, and a strict quarantine against Moros was established. I had letters of instructions prepared in Moro and sent to all the principal rancherias, explaining to them how to avoid the disease and offering to supply medicine in limited quantity to those who wished it. In some places the instructions were followed in the main, and it had the effect of holding the disease in check to a large extent. According to the best obtainable information, it is probable that about 1,500 people died of this disease.

After the battle of Bayan, in May, 1902, a relative of the former sultan, Dato Maguindanao, was unanimously elected sultan of that rancheria, and visited camp several times, expressing the friendship of his people. It soon became known, however, that Bayan harbored feelings of resentment toward us, and that they were strengthening their fort at Maliuanac preparatory to making another stand against us. The actual leader of these Moros was an old pandita by the name of Sajiduciaman. Knowing his friendship for Amai-Manibilang and one or two others, I summoned them to Camp Vicars to aid me in bringing him to see the folly of further resistance. In view of the proximity of Bayan and on account of the pandita's influence with other Moros, it was important that we should win him to our side without resort to force. An interview was finally arranged, at which he and I agreed to be personal friends, but he claimed to be unable to give any assurances as to the future actions of his people.

In January his followers began to interfere with the Moros employed by us, and the sultan was forced by them to return to Oato, his former home, thus confessing that he could not control them, and practically relinquishing his rights. As he is a man of little force of character, for whom the Moros have little respect, I made no effort to induce him to remain at Bayan. Again addressing Sajiduciaman directly, I told him that he must come to camp and explain to me the meaning of the attitude of his people. In the conference that followed he said that he desired to be on friendly terms with us, and that the Bayan Moros had committed no offense, but that they did not desire us to visit their rancherias. I told him that such friendship was of no value to us and that I should therefore not consider him as a friend. As a result a visit was arranged and made, and we were received with every manifestation of friendship. Since then there have been no complaints, and many Bayan Moros are to-day employed about Camp Vicars.

Toward the latter part of January reports indicated that cholera was abating to such an extent that, with caution, practice marches for short distances might he resumed. These marches were originally undertaken to convince the Moros that they need have no fear from the presence of our troops in their territory, and nearly every Onayan rancheria had been visited. With a command consisting of a battery of artillery, 1 troop of cavalry, and 3 companies of infantry a march was made to Gata, under the assurance that we would be received in a friendly spirit. Arriving in the vicinity, we were met by Amai Buncurang, whom I had previously sent with messages, who told us that cholera existed there and that they did not desire us to visit them. From this and from their general attitude it was evident that there was an unfriendly faction among them and that insistence upon a visit at that time would probably bring a clash. I reluctantly returned to Camp Vicars, passing through Maciu, where, at the crossing of the Malaig River, 5 Moros fired on the column, wounding 1 man. These Moros together with their cotta, were destroyed. In February, with a command of the same size, a visit was made to Madumba, on the west side of the lake, which was farther in that direction than we had yet been. While here I endeavored to communicate with the sultan and the panandungan [retired sultan and counselor to the current sultan] of Bacolod, but they refused to receive the Moro messengers. Their attitude was extremely hostile, war flags were flying over their fort, and they even went so far as to fire in the vicinity of our camp at night.

During the preceding months every possible effort had been made to convince these people of our friendly purposes and of our desire to avoid further bloodshed. Several datos visited Bacolod of their own accord, entertaining with me the hope that the disastrous results that must certainly come to the Bacolod people in case of a war with us might be averted; but the advice of these friendly datos was scorned. Among the Moros who have been of friendly assistance and who have used their influence with unfriendly Moros a few deserve especial mention in this report for their loyalty. Dato Grande, of Makadar, aided in securing the cavalry horses lost by Lieutenant Forsyth in March, 1902, all of which have been turned in or are accounted for, but one, so far as known, remaining in the bands of the Moros. Amai-Manibilang, of Madaya; the sultan of Ganasi; Dato Adta of Paiguay; Amai-Buncurung, of Oato, have made every effort to induce hostile Moros to become friends. Many Onayan Moros have furnished us with pack ponies and vintas for various expeditions.

In order to thoroughly explore the lake country and to convince all Moros of our benevolent intentions and to demonstrate to them that there was no truth in the stories they had heard that our purpose was conquest, it had been contemplated for some time to send an expedition completely around the lake. Cholera having abated to some extent and the dry season being nearly at an end, such an expedition was ordered to explore the west shore of the lake from Camp Vicars to Marahui and return. While the experience of the two attempted friendly visits recently undertaken indicated that there would probably be some opposition, the best information obtainable was to the effect that the Moros of Bacolod on the one side and of Taraca on the other side of the lake would be the only ones who would offer opposition of a determined character. The Moros of Bacolod had been strengthening their fort for a year and believed it to be impregnable.

In anticipation of the expedition around the lake a letter was written to all Moros, as follows:

"To all Moros in the Laguna de Lanao:

"The Americans have now been in the Laguna de Lanao nearly one year. During that time we have constructed a good road from Malabang to the lake. We have given employment to many Moros at good wages. We have purchased a great deal of Moro produce. We have established a good market at Bayan. We have not molested any Moros except some who attacked us. We have visited as friends all points on the south side of the lake from Ganassi to Gata. We have gone across the lake and visited many rancherias there. We have kept every promise we have made. We have not interfered with the customs, habits, government, or religion of any Moro. Therefore we have demonstrated to the Moros and to the whole world that we are not here to make war, nor to dispossess the inhabitants of Lanao of their lives, property, or anything that is theirs, but are here for the good of the Moros, as representatives of our great Government, of which all Moros are a part. All fair-minded Moros who know us have become our friends because they believe we are honest and that we can and will help the people in the Laguna. All sensible Moros in the Laguna want peace. Two or three datos refuse our friendship simply because, as they say, they do not like the Americans. To these datos I say they are obstructing the establishment of universal peace in the Laguna, and if they continue their opposition they must some day suffer the consequences of their stubborn ignorance."

The expedition consisting of the Camp Vicars command started on April 5, troops from Malabang having been sent to take their place in camp temporarily, and the following afternoon we arrived at Bacolod. It was evident that anything but fight was entirely out of the question and that they had planned a stubborn resistance. Outlying positions held by them were soon taken and their stronghold invested. After closing the avenues of escape, this fort was pounded by artillery and afterwards taken in a brilliant assault by infantry and dismounted cavalry of the command. One hundred and twenty Moros lost their lives in this battle, while the Americans sustained a small loss of 11 wounded. At Calahui, 3 miles farther on, some resistance was also met, but the fort at that place could not withstand the effect of our batteries, and the hundred defenders said to have been inside deserted their position, 23 of their number being killed or wounded. The expedition continued to Pantar, on the Agus River, and returned, meeting friendly receptions at all places along the entire route except the two above given.

The success of the Bacolod expedition warranted undertaking an expedition around the eastern side of the lake, and, as the season continued favorable, the necessary orders were given by General Sumner and the expedition got away May 2. Notice had been sent to all Moros in that section that we would not molest the persons nor the property of any who desired to be our friends, but that we would overcome any opposition offered in carrying out the purposes of exploration for which the expedition was ordered. Several Moros from the eastern part of the lake accompanied us and used their influence to persuade those who had declared hostility that opposition against us was useless. Among those who assisted us was the leading pandita or high priest of Lake Lanao, Imam Nuzca. He opposed resistance against us on religious grounds, and declared to the people that they would be punished in the hereafter for all such conduct, arguing that it was not supported by the teachings of the Koran and could not be upheld by any argument.

No opposition was encountered until we reached Taraca, where a group of cottas were flying red flags and making other hostile demonstrations. The battle of Taraca River was the result, in which, according to Moro accounts, some 250 Moros lost their lives and 10 cottas were destroyed, including the strong forts at Pitacus and Taraca, which were taken with great gallantry by our troops, and 36 cannon, 60 rifles, and 52 prisoners were captured.

With the exception of a few shots fired at long range soon after leaving Taraca, we were received in a friendly spirit along the route to Madaya. Even though the season was late and there had been no rains on the eastern side of the lake for three or four months, the flat rice country there was well-nigh impassable. It was found necessary to corduroy the trails in many places and to fill them with grass in others, in order to make them passable for our animals without their loads. Our transport trains had to be unpacked several times and the cargoes carried by hand across the marshes. The labor of the troops was indeed very trying, and in order to avoid possibly a worse experience it was determined to return to Camp Vicars by way of the less difficult trail along the west shore of the lake. As a result of the exploration of the trails around Lake Lanao it is suggested that plans be laid for the construction of a road around the lake at such time in the future as necessity for employing Moros may arise on account of any shortage of crops in the lake region.

The favorable results of these expeditions can hardly be estimated at this time, but reasoning from our own experience during the past year and from the experience of the Spaniards at Lake Lanao during several years, and comparing them, it seems probable that there will be no more combined resistance in the future, nor is it believed that the Moros will again undertake to oppose us by the construction or defense of cottas. It is believed that our accomplishment of the entire circuit of the lake, overcoming as we did all hostile opposition with comparatively few casualties to ourselves, treating as friends all other Moros, visiting their rancherias without molesting them, taking no property for which we did not pay, and destroying nothing except unavoidably in battle has had and will have a far-reaching effect in permanently settling the Moro question of Lake Lanao in so far as hostility is concerned, if, indeed, it does not result, under a wise administration, in the establishment of amicable relations that will lead to universal peace in this hitherto war-like region without any further use of force. The achievement has given to us an advantage in their future control which the Moro will be as quick to realize as we are.

In view of the progress that has been made we are now in position to study carefully and work out along the lines of material progress the future of the Lanao Moros. Their government should, of course, for some time remain in charge of the military, either directly or indirectly, thus naturally following the kind of rule to which they have been accustomed for generations. To handle the situation properly, all these Moros, being of one group, with the same dialect, customs, and habits of life, should be under the control of one head in whom they have confidence, who should know something of their language, their character, and their history, and to whom they can go for advice and for the settlement of many questions which heretofore have necessarily been left unsettled. As far as it is consistent with advancement, it is believed the government as we find it, a government by the sultan or dato, as the case may be, should be disturbed as little as possible; that is, the people should be managed through the datos themselves, who, being recognized as such in their authority, should therefore be held responsible for the proper control of the people of their several rancherias.

As between different rancherias, each of which is practically independent of every other, each having its own sultan or dato, who denies the right of every other sultan or dato to dictate to him, some sort of judicial tribunal appointed by or brought under the military governor could probably be successfully established. In fact, experience here has proved that in settling disputes between Moros of different rancherias and often those of the same rancherias a board of arbitration consisting of friendly datos, agreeable to both parties, selected by the military authority, could be relied upon to satisfactorily adjust their differences. Due to their lack of confidence in each other it would be difficult to select members to constitute a permanent board of this kind, nor would it be advisable at this time to do so. It is probable that by appealing to their reason slight changes in their laws could be made from time to time through the medium of these courts of equity and that it could be done without exciting their suspicions, although all growth along these lines must be gradual.

The Moro is of a peculiar make-up as to character, though the reason is plain when it is considered, first, that he is a savage; second, that he is a Malay, and, third, that he is a Muhammadan. The almost infinite combination of superstitions, prejudices, and suspicions blended into his character make him a difficult person to handle until fully understood. In order to control him other than by brute force one must first win his implicit confidence, nor is this as difficult as it would seem; but once accomplished one can accordingly by patient and continuous effort largely guide and direct his thoughts and actions. He is jealous of his religion, but he knows very little about its teachings. The observance of a few rites and ceremonies is about all that is required to satisfy him that he is a good Muhammadan. As long as he is undisturbed in the possession of his women and children and his slaves, there need be little fear from him. As a rule he treats his so-called slaves, who are really but serfs or vassals, as members of his family; but any interference with what he thinks his right regarding them had best be made gradually by the natural process of development, which must logically come by contact with and under the wise supervision of a civilized people.

The number of people in the Lake Lanao region according to the recent census is estimated to be about 80,000. They have been unfortunate during the past year in losing a large number, probably 50 per cent, of their carabaos. For this reason it is expected that the acreage of crops this year will be considerably less than in previous years. People of Lake Lanao are practically self-sustaining, raising a great variety of agricultural products and fruit and manufacturing most of their own cloth and other articles of domestic use.

Naturally industrious and inhabiting a country capable of a high state of cultivation, there is no doubt but that the Moro can be induced to cultivate new products and introduce more modern methods in agriculture. His talent for creation is such as to warrant the belief that he is susceptible of training along the lines of industrial pursuits. In my opinion it would be a good investment on the part of the Government to select a few of the leading Moros and take them on a visit to the United States, preferably during the World's Fair at St. Louis, and I would also recommend that the education of at least 10 bright boys of the upper class be undertaken to the extent of teaching them English in connection with work in some industrial school in the States.

JOHN J. PERSHING,
Captain, Fifteenth Cavalry Commanding.

Source: *Annual Report of the War Department, 1903,* vol. 3, in Appendix IV, *Occupation of the Lake Lanao Region,* Brig. Gen. Samuel S. Sumner, to Annual Report of Maj. Gen. George W. Davis, commanding, Division of the Philippines.

Appendix D

Report of Captain John J. Pershing, Fifteenth Cavalry, of an Expedition to the Southeast of Lake Lanao, 18–22 September 1902

CAMP VICARS, MINDANAO, P. I., *October 15, 1902.*
The ADJUTANT-GENERAL, DEPARTMENT OF MINDANAO,
Zamboanga, P. I.

SIR: I have the honor to submit the following report of an expedition under my command made against hostile Moros to the southeast of Lake Lanao, between September 18 and 22, 1902, pursuant to orders from the brigade commander, Brig. Gen. Samuel S. Sumner, U. S. Army, dated Camp Vicars, September 17, 1902, a copy of which is appended.

The command consisted of First Lieut. C. S. Fries, battalion adjutant, Twenty-seventh Infantry, adjutant; First Lieut. Charles Deems, jr., Artillery Corps, quartermaster and commissary; Capt. C. W. Hack, assistant surgeon, U. S. Volunteers; First Lieut. J. H. Allen, assistant surgeon, U. S. Army, with 6 enlisted men of the Hospital Corps; Troop L, Fifteenth Cavalry, Capt. G. W. Kirkpatrick in command, with Second Lieut. I. S. Martin, Fifteenth Cavalry, and 66 enlisted men; 2 Maxim-Nordenfelt guns and 1 3.6-inch field mortar of the Twenty-fifth Battery, Field Artillery, under command of Capt. W. S. McNair, with First Lieut. H. B. Clark and First Lieut. A. H. Sunderland and 90 enlisted men; and the following officers and companies of the Twenty-seventh Infantry: Company C, First Lieut. F. B. Hawkins in command, with Second Lieut. K. L. Pepper and 95 enlisted men; Company F, First Lieut. C. G. Bickham in command, with Second Lieut. A. W. Brown and 88 enlisted men; Company G, Second Lieut. S. C. Loring in command, with 81 enlisted men, and Company M, First Lieut. W. B. Gracie in command, with Second Lieut. H. E. Comstock and 101 enlisted men and a pack train of 60 mules carrying four days' rations for the command. Tomas Torres accompanied the command as interpreter. Maj. James S. Pettit, inspector-general, Seventh Separate Brigade, accompanied the command as a representative of the brigade commander, and First Lieut. A. A. Fries, Engineer Corps, as engineer officer, all as per appended copy of field return. The column left Camp Vicars at 1.30 a. m. the 18th instant, and arrived at Pantauan, about 10 miles to the southeast, at 6 a. m.

At Pantauan a base camp was established and the operations of the expedition were conducted from there. I was informed here by Amai-Pasandalan that Sultan Uali, of Gauan, and the sultan of Bayabao would not treat with me, but would resist our march toward their rancherias. Accordingly preparations were at once made to move to Gauan, and the pack animals, with rations, baggage, and blanket rolls, were left at Pantauan with Troop L, the mortar detachment of the Twenty-fifth Battery, Field Artillery, under First Lieut. A. H. Sunderland, and 50 men of Company M, under Second Lieut. H. E. Comstock, all under command of Captain Kirkpatrick.

With the remainder of the command I proceeded at once in the direction of Gauan on Lake Butig. On leaving Pantauan several armed Moros were seen at a distance, but no shots were fired on either side. The trail followed a narrow, wooded ridge, over which we cautiously proceeded, reaching Gauan, some 3 miles away, at about 8:30 a. m. The end of this ridge projected into a swamp, with Lake Butig on the south and southwest. The stronger of the two forts in sight was situated directly in our front, at the narrowest part of the ridge, completely closing the trail, and some 200 yards from the end of the ridge. This fort was first sighted as we debouched from the woods some 300 yards from it. Directly on our right and across the lake about the same distance was the other of the two Gauan forts that had up to this time been located. Companies C and F were moved into open ground to the front, and Company C was deployed to the left of the first fort, the line extending as far to the left front as possible and resting against a deep, narrow trench, leading from the fort toward the east. Company F was deployed facing the second fort.

The two guns of McNair's battery were unlimbered and posted on the right of Company F. Companies G and M remained in column of files on the trail, hidden from view to the front, but in a position to face the ridge on our left. Several armed Moros were seen to enter the two forts, and it was expected that the firing would come from them. On the contrary, however, the first firing came from a fringe of timber on the near slope of the ridge to our left. This fire was returned by the scouts of Companies G and M, and the battery opened on the fort across the lake, from which several Moros attempted to escape but were killed by the infantry. The battery was then turned on the first fort, which was shortly afterwards entered by Lieutenant Pepper and found to have been hastily abandoned. From the hills on the opposite side of the lake the Moros kept up a desultory fire with Krags and Remingtons. At a distance of some 500 yards to the west of the small fort and across the lake several armed Moros were observed, no doubt thinking they were beyond the range of our rifles; but a few well-directed volleys by Lieutenant Hawkins's scouts either destroyed or dispersed them. It should be added here, by way of explanation, that in each company of infantry 10 selected men were used as scouts. During this time the firing from the ridge on the left had continued at intervals, and my attention was called to a clump of bamboo at the extreme point of the ridge, some 500 yards to the east, and Captain McNair was directed to bring his guns to a more favorable point and to open fire upon it. After a half a dozen rounds from the battery Lieutenant Hawkins with Company C was sent across the swamp, through which the company waded to their waists, to attack and capture the position, thought to be another cotta or fort. He became engaged immediately upon arriving on the ridge, and Lieutenant Bickham with Company F was at once sent to his support.

After some thirty minutes the firing from the cotta ceased and it was entered by our men. Three dead Moros were found within and there were evidences of several having been wounded, the rest escaping by an opening in the wall near the extreme end of the ridge. This cotta was destroyed by fire, as were all others captured. Upon the return of Companies C and F an attempt was made to reach the Butig rancheria, which lay to the southeast beyond Lake Butig and the swamp leading from it to the Malaig River and behind a low intervening ridge, but at this time the swamp was impassable. I then returned with the command to the base camp at Pantauan, arriving about 4 p. m.

At 7 o'clock the next morning, with all of the command (except Company G, which, with the mortar detachment of the battery, was left as a camp guard), I started out to Bayabao, with Captain Kirkpatrick's Troop L in the advance. At about 2 miles from camp, on an open ridge covered with tall grass, the advance guard was attacked by a party of 40 Moros with firearms. Captain Kirkpatrick dismounted his troop and vigorously repelled the attack without any casualties, and moving forward at a double time he continued firing at the retreating Moros, several of whom ran into a wooded ravine on our right, the rest retiring into a cotta about a mile away. Approaching this cotta, from which a few shots were fired, the battery was placed in position at a range of about 400 yards, and Lieutenant Gracie with Company M was sent to the left to cut off any avenue of escape from that direction. Captain Kirkpatrick with Troop L, dismounted, and Lieutenant Bickham with Company F were sent to the right, both wings being directed to cover as far as possible any escape to the rear. In taking position the right wing encountered several Moros attempting to escape, all of whom were either killed or wounded.

The infantry being in position, fire was opened on the cotta with the battery. Lieutenant Gracie soon after entered the cotta and found it abandoned. This cotta was a very strong one, about 150 feet square, with walls of earth 10 feet thick, surrounded by a deep trench, with bamboo stakes protecting all approaches. It contained a large quantity of rice, in a large, substantial building. This building and contents of cotta were destroyed, as was another small cotta some 400 yards to the west. The command then took up the return march to camp at Pantauan, by way of the rancheria of Lumbayanagne, whose sultan came out to meet us and stated, after some hesitation, that several of the Moros of his rancheria were implicated in the attack on Matalling Falls on September 1, and that he would be glad to have them punished. He guided the column to the house of Dato Imam, who he said was the guilty dato, but Imam and his people had escaped. We reached camp about 5.30 p. m.

On September 20, with the entire command, I took up the march at 6.30 a. m. for Maciu, arriving at about 11 a. m. at the edge of the lake some 700 feet above Sauir, overlooking Talub, Maciu, and other rancherias on the alluvial peninsula at the southeast part of the lake. As directed by General Sumner, I was preparing to send a messenger with a letter to Sultans Ganduali and Tauagan, of Maciu, when the Moros opened fire upon us from the ridge to the east and from the cotta at Sauir, and from the adjacent wooded bluff below. From across the arm of the lake, lantaca and small-arm firing began, but with no effect.

I had had difficulty in obtaining any accurate information about trails and roads, as well as about the location of cottas, but it was evident that the Moros from Maciu had a fort somewhere near by on the south side of the arm of the lake, as many Moros were seen hurriedly crossing to this side in vintas. I directed Captain McNair to try his guns on them, and, if possible, stop reenforcements coming to this side. After three or four trial shots, a vinta was struck and sunk, and 7 Moros are said to have been killed or drowned. The distance at which the shot was fired was about 1,800 yards, and it made such an impression on the Moros that no further attempts were made by them to cross, and during the entire time thereafter vintas kept their distance.

I sent my adjutant, Lieutenant Fries, with Lieutenant Bickham and Company F, to proceed directly along the ridge toward the east and develop, if possible, any position the enemy might hold. They encountered a force strongly posted in a cotta that covered all approaches along the entire ridge, and, after a brisk engagement of twenty minutes, compelled the Moros to abandon the cotta. We were not again molested from that position that day.

Lieutenant Gracie, with Company M, was ordered at the same time to proceed toward Sauir to cover all trails leading in that direction and to overcome whatever opposition might be made to our passage to the cotta at Sauir. To support him McNair's battery was posted on the second bench below, overlooking the cotta at Sauir. Lieutenant Gracie advanced to Sauir, finding the cotta abandoned, with cook fires still burning. There was a large, well-constructed building within, containing rice, coffee, and cocoa, as well as all household furniture. The cotta and its contents were later ordered burned and the command went into camp at Sauir.

Upon our arrival at Sauir investigation of trails leading around the arm of the lake was immediately begun. It was found that the only trail which it is possible to pass at any time was, owing to its swampy condition, impassable at this time without several days' work, and it was determined to attempt to make the crossing of the arm of the lake by bamboo rafts, and the construction of two of them was at once begun. One of these rafts was practically completed on the same day and another was completed early the next morning.

Firing from the surrounding bluffs and from across the lake continued during the afternoon. The next day, September 21, Captain Kirkpatrick, with Troop L, Company G, under Lieutenant Loring, and one gun from the battery under Lieutenant Clark, was sent to examine the trails, if any, leading across or down the Malaig River. He found the same fort that Lieutenant Bickham had taken the day before again occupied by Moros, with whom he had a short engagement, driving them from and destroying their cotta. He then proceeded by a Moro trail leading to a village near the Malaig River, but failed to find any regular crossing of that river or any trail leading down it. He returned to camp the same evening.

Upon our arrival at Sauir, on the 20th, I sent a messenger to Sultans Ganduali and Tauagan, requesting them to visit camp and confer with me or to meet me at some point to be designated by them. The Moro messenger returned with a verbal message that they declined my invitation, but would meet me when we arrived at Maciu, and directed the messenger not to return with any more messages.

With the rafts an effort was made to cross the arm of the lake, and Lieutenant Pepper, who made the first attempt, succeeded with about 20 men in reaching a point from which, accompanied by several men, he waded with difficulty to a landing on the other side, some 800 yards distant from our side and some 400 yards from the farthest point he was able to reach with the raft, which could be forced no farther owing to the dense growth of water lilies that skirted the swampy edges of the lake as far as could be seen from our point of view. The raft from there could be gotten neither forward nor backward, until finally, with the aid of a picket rope, Lieutenant Pepper, assisted by Lieutenant Fries, of the engineers, and an additional number of men, succeeded in reaching our side again about noon. In the afternoon another attempt was made by a fresh detachment under these two officers, with results equally futile. During most of the afternoon the party at work with the raft was under fire from Moros on the other side, hidden in the grass, but scouts from our side prevented any close-range firing on the part of the Moros. Both the officers and men on this duty were most of the time in water and mud, oftentimes to their necks. From the day's experience the impracticability of making a crossing in this manner became evident, and the project was reluctantly abandoned. At one time, however, the success of the effort seemed so probable that I dispatched a messenger asking that two days' rations be sent us. My disappointment at the impossibility of making a successful passage at this time was very great and was keenly felt by the entire command.

On September 22 it was determined to return to Camp Vicars. Lieutenant Comstock, with 50 men of Company M, was sent as an escort to Lieutenant Fries, Engineer Corps, to ascertain if there was a trail farther up the Malaig River than any party had yet been. They left camp at 8 a. m. and joined the column about 12 o'clock, reporting no trails, having encountered a rough country approaching the river and swampy bottoms along its course, impassable at that time for animals. As the command moved out of camp at Sauir the Maciu Moros began to take courage, and congregated near the cottas of Tauagan and Ganduali, firing rifles and lantacas. As we came to the first bench or plateau above

Sanir these Maciu forts were plainly visible at a distance of about 3,000 yards. As much for practice as for results against the personnel of our opponents, Captain McNair was directed to try his guns and the mortar on them. The range proved too great for accurate firing, but it had the effect of dispersing all Moro gatherings in that vicinity, and sent them hurrying toward the north end of the peninsula. Several shots, however, apparently landed within one of the cottas. At 10 a. m. the return march was resumed, and Camp Vicars was reached at 7 p. m.

During this expedition, as learned since from friendly Moro sources, 30 Moros were killed and as many or more were wounded. Eight cottas were captured and with their contents destroyed. No other property was destroyed.

Although there were no individual acts that were particularly conspicuous above others, I can not speak too highly of the conduct of the officers and men of my command during this expedition. The discipline was well-nigh perfect. Such an implicit obedience to orders and such an intelligent and fearless execution of them is rarely seen. Wrought up by a defensive attitude for the preceding two months, they would have endured any privation or undergone any hardship to win.

Very respectfully,
JOHN J. PERSHING,
Captain, Fifteenth Cavalry, Commanding.

HEADQUARTERS SEVENTH SEPARATE BRIGADE
Camp Vicars, P. I., September 17, 1902

Field Order No. 9.

Capt. J. J. Pershing
Fifteenth Cavalry, Commanding Camp Vicars

You will proceed to the neighborhood of Butig with 4 companies of infantry, 1 troop of cavalry, and a platoon of artillery, with a sufficient number of pack animals to carry rations for four days. You will endeavor to communicate with Sultan Uali and the sultan of Butig and such other sultans and datos as you may meet in that country. You will explain to these leaders the desire of the Government to maintain friendly relations with the Moros and invite them to Camp Vicars for the purpose of coming to an amicable understanding. You will also inform Sultan Uali and the sultan of Butig that from their own statements and other reliable information we know they have been participants in attacks recently made on American soldiers. Make a demand on these leaders for any arms or other Government property in their possession. You are authorized, if necessary, to use force for this purpose against these leaders. You are also to use force against any leaders in that section who oppose your march or make any hostile demonstration against you. You are authorized to proceed from Butig to Maciu, carrying out those same general instructions. From Maciu you will return to Camp Vicars. Or you may return from Butig to Camp Vicars if circumstances make that course the more advisable. Two hundred rounds of ammunition will be carried per man. Strictest orders will be given to control the fire of the men in any engagement that takes place. No property will be taken, damaged, or destroyed outside of cottas captured in the execution of the above instructions.

By command of Brigadier-General Sumner:

L. C. ANDREWS,
Captain and Quartermaster, Fifteenth Cavalry,
Acting Assistant Adjutant-General.

Source: Appendix IV, *Occupation of the Lake Lanao Region,* Brig. Gen. Samuel S. Sumner, to Annual Report of Maj. Gen. George W. Davis, commanding, Division of the Philippines, in *ARWD, 1903,* Vol. 3: *Reports of Department and Division Commanders.*

Appendix E

Report of Captain John J. Pershing, Fifteenth Cavalry, of an Expedition against Hostile Moros of Maciu, 28 September–3 October 1902

POST OF CAMP VICARS, MINDANAO, P. I., *October 15, 1902.*

The ADJUTANT-GENERAL, DEPARTMENT OF MINDANAO.

Sir: I have the honor to submit the following report of an expedition against hostile Moros of Maciu, Lake Lanao, made between September 28 and October 2, inclusive, in compliance with Field Orders, No. 17, September 25, 1902, copy of which is appended hereto.

The command consisted of Maj. L. C. Carr, surgeon, U. S. Volunteers, First Lieut. J. H. Allen, assistant surgeon, U. S. Army, with 6 enlisted men of the Hospital Corps; First. Lieut. Claude S. Fries, battalion adjutant, Twenty-seventh Infantry, adjutant; Chaplain George D. Rice, Twenty-seventh Infantry; Capt. J. J. Morrow, Corps of Engineers, engineer officer; First Lieut. Earl Brown, Engineer Corps, commanding detachment of 20 enlisted men of Company F, Second Battalion, Corps of Engineers; Capt. J. W. L. Phillips, Twenty-seventh Infantry, commanding battalion of the Twenty-seventh Infantry, viz, Company C, First Lieut. F. B. Hawkins, Second Lieut. K. L. Pepper, and 76 enlisted men; Company F, First Lieut. C. G. Bickham, Second Lieut. A. W. Brown, and 72 enlisted men; Company M, First Lieut. W. B. Gracie, Second Lieut. H. E. Comstock, and 75 enlisted men; Twenty-fifth Battery, Field Artillery, Capt. W. S. McNair, Artillery Corps, First Lieuts. H. B. Clarke, Artillery Corps, and A. H. Sunderland, Artillery Corps, and 85 enlisted men; Troop A, Fifteenth Cavalry, Second Lieut. W. P. Mangum, jr., Fifteenth Cavalry, and 61 enlisted men; as per copy of field return . . . and a pack train of 75 mules, carrying four days' rations, one day's rations being carried in haversacks.

We left Camp Vicars at 8 a. m. on September 28, and, marching by way of Pantauan, arrived at Sauir at 3.30 p. m. . . . where the base camp was established. It was discovered that since the campaign some ten days previous the Moros of Maciu had erected at Talub, on the Macui side of the arm of the lake, a small earthwork, faced with stone, covering the landing that they evidently thought we intended to use, and upon the parapet they had hoisted their red flag of war. Upon arrival I immediately sent Captain Morrow, Engineer Corps, and 13 enlisted men of the engineers, with Company G, Twenty-seventh Infantry, under Lieutenant Loring, as an escort, to make a reconnaissance toward Maciu regarding trails leading in that direction. He returned about dark, reporting an old trail very swampy and obstructed by trees recently felled by the Moros, and that it would take 200 men at least two days to make it passable. Orders were accordingly issued for the work to begin at daylight, and two companies—F and G, Twenty-seventh Infantry—together with the engineers under Captain Morrow, were sent to work in the forenoon, the infantry companies being relieved at noon by Companies C and M. Lieutenant Brown, with a few men of the engineers, assisted by a detail from the Twenty-fifth Battery, constructed a catamaran of two large vintas that Dato Pedro, of Oato, and the Cabugatan of Oato had furnished. These vintas were of such a size that each would accommodate at least 20 soldiers, and the carrying capacity of the catamaran was about 35 men.

On the morning of the 29th the Moros from the fort opposite fired upon the cavalry as the horses were being watered. The firing was returned immediately by a gun of the battery previously posted for that purpose. After that the Moros kept up a fire from the opposite side during the day but did no damage, a party of sharpshooters being on the lookout for every Moro that exposed himself. Firing from the surrounding hills was also begun by the Moros during the morning, and at 1 o'clock p. m. I sent Captain McNair with 2 guns and Company F, under Lieutenant Bickham, to dislodge them. He encountered strong resistance to the southeast, the Moros being posted on the crest of the hill across the line of his advance, from which position they stood up in line and fired several volleys at him. The infantry soon drove them away and occupied the ridge as well as the cotta near by that had been taken by us on the previous expedition. Several Moros were killed in this skirmish, especially while they were escaping into the undergrowth and down the hillsides.

While I was out on the trail during the afternoon Captain Morrow reported having seen several Moros some distance to the front and that Lieutenant Pepper with 15 men of Company C had gone in that direction. Soon after, firing was heard from our front and with 20 additional men I, with Captain Morrow and Lieutenant Gracie, went hurriedly out along the trail, meeting Lieutenant Pepper and his detachment returning. I then ordered the whole detachment forward, Lieutenant Pepper's party in the advance, and as we debouched from the heavy timber to an open hillside in Maciu we were fired upon. Lieutenant Pepper and the advance returned the fire and the whole detachment closed on the Moros, killing 12 of them and capturing 1 Tower rifle.

I decided to occupy Maciu the following day, September 30, and to complete the trail as far as necessary as we went along. Accordingly an early start was made with the entire command, except the pack animals and a camp guard of 50 men of Company C under Lieutenant Pepper. Captain Morrow, Lieutenant Brown, and the engineer detachment hurried forward to repair the worst places in the trail. Lieutenant Gracie, with Company M, constituted the advance, followed by the battery, Company F, Company G, 26 men of Company C, and Troop A, under their respective company commanders, Troop A acting as rear guard. There was much difficulty in passing over the trail, which became very muddy with use and in places swampy to such an extent that all the battery mules and ammunition mules had to be unpacked, some of them several times, and their loads carried by the men, often as far as 200 yards. It was noon before we reached Maciu ridge, where the skirmish of the day before had occurred. In the meantime Lieutenant Gracie with Company M had encountered resistance, but had forced the Moros to return to their cottas, 2 in number, one being that of the defiant Sultan Ganduali. The command all up, I ordered Captain Phillips to post the leading company of his battalion on the right, facing the west, its right flank extending beyond the cotta that lay to our right front. In a similar manner Company F was sent to the left, covering the cotta to our left front. These two cottas were near the west end of the ridge, which sloped abruptly westward to the alluvial flat on which Maciu proper is located. McNair's four mountain guns were sent into position at 800 yards. The Moros were silenced within twenty minutes, and they deserted both cottas and attempted to escape. The two infantry companies, supported by Company G, advanced hurriedly past the cottas to the edge of the ridge and poured volley after volley into the retreating Moros. The Moro force probably numbered 150 in all, many of whom were known to be killed, and as learned since, a great number wounded. Two 3-inch muzzle-loading cast-iron cannon were captured and spiked. Both cottas and the houses within and their contents, household effects and rice, were then destroyed.

From here General Sumner's letter to Sultans Ganduali and Tauagan . . . was sent to them, and, pending their reply, the command was marched to Talub, opposite Sauir, and encamped for the night. The Moro messenger returned about dark, saying that they had read the letter, but refused to either keep it or answer it, sending word that 200 of them would be ready for us on the following day at the cotta of the Sultan-cabugatan [sultan and chief of police] of Maciu.

On the next morning, October 1, I moved out toward the supposed location of this cotta, Company G in the advance. When just west of Ganduali's cotta the advance guard was fired upon and developed what promised for a time to be the enemy in force. The battery was posted and the two leading infantry companies were deployed exactly the same as the day before, their flanks extending beyond the two cottas in our front, which were about 150 yards apart. There was no little resistance, however, and the command moved forward cautiously a mile farther, the leading company in skirmish line. Cries of defiance were heard at some distance off and were thought to come from a group of cottas near the lake. Upon reaching the principal one of the group, the battery was ordered into position in front of it, facing the lake, and at a distance of some 350 yards from the cotta. Captain Phillips was directed to place the leading company in position, with its right resting on the lake shore, and about 300 yards from the cotta. I placed Company F in a similar position on the right of the cotta. Company C was posted in front, on the right of and supporting the battery, while Company M and Troop A were held in reserve, with orders to protect the rear. As Company F was being placed in position, they cut off several Moros attempting to escape along the edge of the lake. All the troops being in position, McNair's battery was ordered to open fire. The Moros replied with a vigorous fire from the lantacas and small arms. Our sharpshooters and the battery soon brought their firing down to a minimum, for they found in short order that it was dangerous to expose themselves.

As the number of effective men within the cotta decreased, our lines were advanced from time to time until they were within about 150 yards on the flanks, and the battery and the line in front within about 100 yards of the cotta. The other cottas in this group, consisting of a small one on the left, a very small one in front, and two to the right and near the lake, were inside of our first lines, none of them, however, being occupied. The effective fire of the artillery and the infantry at these close ranges had a demoralizing effect upon the Moros, which they attempted to off-set by yells of defiance, by beating tom-toms, and by religious chants. Above all this, our interpreters and friendly Moros could distinguish the prayers of the panditas for their dead and wounded. At about 3 p. m. Lieutenant Loring suggested that he take some of his men of Company G and burn the buildings in the small cotta on the left, and he was directed to do so, as all buildings in other adjacent cottas had been burned. Afterwards Lieutenant Loring volunteered to make an attempt to set fire to the occupied cotta and, if possible, to locate the entrance. With 10 men he succeeded in reaching the walls of the cotta, but the fire set in some dead grass died out. One of his men, Private James Nolan, jr., Company G, Twenty-seventh Infantry, was wounded and had to be assisted to the rear. Lieutenant Loring found the walls to be at least 20 feet high from the bottom of the ditch and perpendicular, making it impracticable without unnecessary loss of life to scale them. During this time, Lieutenant Mangum, with Troop A, had driven some Moros out of, and had destroyed another group of cottas to the left and rear, from which he had been fired upon. At 3 p. m. the troop was sent to Talub, across from Sauir, the base camp, for rations, returning just after dark.

The Moros kept up constant firing at Company F's line from the rear that gave more or less annoyance, but as no casualties occurred to us I determined to do nothing more than to hold them off at a safe distance until we had settled with those in front of us.

I ordered the lines drawn closer after dark, so that the distance between the two extremities on the lake shore was only about 100 yards, and the outposts at these points were in sight of each other, and disposed Company M in a line of outposts covering our rear completely. Surrounding the cotta on all sides except the immediate front and immediate right there was a very rank growth of grass (cogon) 10 to 15 feet high, with deep narrow ditches running through it in all directions. I directed that fires be lighted between our lines and the cotta to overcome the darkness, although it was not thought possible for the Moros to escape. Continuous yelling and praying, with occasional firing, were kept up until about 3 a. m., when a party of Moros attempted to escape by rushing through our lines, first trying Company G, commanded in person by Captain Phillips, and then trying Company F, Lieutenant Bickham, but they were repulsed at both places, although one Moro succeeded in passing through G Company's line and was wounded as he ran away. Several Moros were killed in this attempt and others wounded. The next morning at daylight the cotta was discovered to be deserted. The lantacas, a great variety of household effects, were unearthed, and a large supply of rice and provisions were found in various places. There were three houses inside, one, large and substantial, from which the grass roof had been removed, probably as a precaution against fire. The interior of this cotta showed that the owner was of some distinction and evidently wealthy, as Moro wealth goes.

Of the 200 who were said to be determined to make a stand here probably half lost courage toward the last, and some of the remainder by the time we reached the cotta. Of those remaining there were many killed and wounded besides those we found, as we have since learned, and as was plainly to be seen on the inside of the cotta the next morning, the bamboo building being literally shot to pieces. This cotta had, as we know now, underground passage ways and caverns and escapes, and their dead and wounded are said to have been hidden therein, as was the case beyond a doubt. In all their forts they invariably provide a means of escape. There were certainly but three who escaped from this cotta during the night, the tracks of two of them being visible at the edge of the lake; then the one who broke through the line at night. I made a personal examination of every foot of the ground in company with other officers, and believe none others got away. After the cotta was burned a Moro juramentado sprang out of the grass in front of the angle formed by C and F companies' lines and attacked Private R. G. Macbeth, Company F, cutting him severely on the left arm with a campilan. This Moro, who afterwards proved to be the Sultan-cabugatan of Maciu, was killed, but was shot seven times before he fell. Company C and Troop A were sent through the tall grass in skirmish line, finding another Moro awaiting an opportunity to make a similar attack, but he was dispatched before he was able to do any damage.

Preparations were made to return, and the wounded were sent, under escort of the cavalry, direct to Talub, being taken to Sauir on the catamaran. As the command started back, I ordered Captain Phillips with two companies to make a detour to the north and destroy a group of cottas from which the volleys had been fired during the preceding day and night, and Lieutenant Mangum, Troop A, to destroy those in the direction of Talub, from all of which we had been fired upon. I took up the march toward Sauir, arriving there about 2 p. m. No Moros outside

Maciu were disturbed, but these were certainly given a severe lesson, and the next day the command returned to Camp Vicars.

I can not speak too highly of the conduct of the officers and men of my command during this expedition, and I desire especially to mention the officers and men of the Twenty-fifth Battery under Captain McNair for the manner in which they executed the difficult task of transporting the battery over the swampy country through which we were compelled to pass and for their fearlessness in pushing their guns almost under the walls of the Maciu forts. In their several capacities, the infantry and cavalry are equally deserving creditable mention for their splendid conduct, the infantry under Captain Phillips and Lieutenant Bickham especially, for holding back at night a charging band of desperate Moros.

For his personal daring and coolness in leading ten of his men under the walls of the cotta in an attempt to set fire to it and find an entrance and afterwards assisting to a place of safety one of his men, Private James Nolan, jr., who was wounded, I desire to particularly invite attention to the conduct of Second Lieutenant Loring, Twenty-seventh Infantry.

To the members of my staff, commissioned and noncommissioned, I desire to give especial credit for their efficient performance of duty during this campaign.

We were accompanied by several friendly Moros on this expedition, than whom none were of greater service than Dato Grande, of Makadar, and Dato Amai-Darimbang, of Oato, and their followers.

Very respectfully,
JOHN J. PERSHING,
Captain, Fifteenth Cavalry.

Camp Vicars, Mindanao,
September 25, 1902

Field Order No. 17.

Capt. J. J. Pershing
Fifteenth Cavalry, Commanding Camp Vicars, Mindanao

You will prepare your command for field service. Take 75 men in each company of infantry, one troop of cavalry, and three sections of artillery. Capt. J. J. Morrow, Corps of Engineers, will report to you for service on this expedition with 20 men from Company G, Battalion of Engineers. Take 200 rounds of ammunition per man. Leave this post tomorrow morning at 8 o'clock, with two days' rations carried in haversacks and three days' on pack train. You will proceed to Maciu, and if the sultans and datos in that community continue their hostile attitude and refuse to come to an amicable understanding you will capture their forts and damage them as much as possible. Endeavor to recapture the government stock now held by these people or force these sultans to surrender it. Your field of operations will be confined to the neighborhood of Maciu and be confined, if possible, to those datos and sultans who have expressed determination to resist the Government, and are actively engaged in such hostilities. On completion of this work you will return to this station. No property will be taken, damaged, or destroyed outside of cottas captured in the execution of the above instructions.

By command of Brigadier-General Sumner:

L. C. ANDREWS,
Captain and Quartermaster, Fifteenth Cavalry,
Acting Assistant Adjutant-General.

Source: Appendix IV, *Occupation of the Lake Lanao Region,* Brig. Gen. Samuel S. Sumner, to Annual Report of Maj. Gen. George W. Davis, commanding, Division of the Philippines, in *ARWD, 1903,* vol. 3, *Reports of Department and Division Commanders.*

Appendix F

Report of Captain John J. Pershing, Fifteenth Cavalry, of an Exploring Expedition from Camp Vicars to Marahui, along the West Shore of Lake Lanao, 5–16 April 1903

POST OF CAMP VICARS
Mindanao, P.I., May 15, 1903.

TO ADJUTANT-GENERAL, DEPARTMENT OF MINDANAO
Zamboanga, P. I.

Sir:

I have the honor to submit the following report of an expedition of exploration along the west shore of Lake Lanao from Camp Vicars to Marahui and return, made by troops under my command in accordance with instructions from department commander dated April 2, 1903, copy of which is appended hereto:

The command consisted of Capt. John J. Pershing, Fifteenth Cavalry, commanding; First Lieut. C. S. Fries, battalion adjutant, Twenty-seventh Infantry, adjutant: Second Lieut. T. W. Brown, battalion quartermaster and commissary, Twenty-seventh Infantry, quartermaster, commissary, and ordnance officer; Lieut. E. D. Peek, Engineer Corps, engineer officer; First. Lieut. R. U. Patterson, assistant surgeon, U. S. Army; Contract Surg. H. Greiger, U. S. Army, with 4 enlisted men of the Hospital Corps; Chaplain George D. Rice, Twenty-seventh Infantry; Troop L, Fifteenth Cavalry, Capt. G. W. Kirkpatrick, Fifteenth Cavalry, commanding, Second Lieut. Isaac S. Martin, and 50 enlisted; Troop G, Fifteenth Cavalry, First Lieut. Charles E. McCullough, Fifteenth Cavalry, commanding, with Second Lieut. F. A. Ruggles, Second Lieut. V. S. Foster, and 44 enlisted; 2 Vickers-Maxim mountain guns of the Twenty-fifth Battery, Field Artillery, under command of Capt. W. S. McNair, Artillery Corps, with First Lieut. Clarence Deems, jr., and 62 enlisted; two 3.6-inch field mortars of the Seventeenth Battery, Field Artillery, under command of Capt. G. G. Gatley, Artillery Corps, with Second Lieut. E. H. De Armond and 32 enlisted; Company M, Twenty-seventh Infantry, First Lieut. W. B. Gracie, Twenty-seventh Infantry, commanding, with Second Lieut. B. F. Miller and 75 enlisted; Company F, Twenty-seventh Infantry, First Lieut. A. W. Brown, Twenty-seventh Infantry, commanding, with Second Lieut. E. J. Moran and 71 enlisted; Company C, Twenty-seventh Infantry, First Lieut. G. C. Shaw, Twenty-seventh Infantry, commanding, with Second Lieut. Otis R. Cole and 70 enlisted; Company G, Twenty-seventh Infantry, Second Lieut. S. C. Loring, Twenty-seventh Infantry, commanding, and 68 enlisted; Company K, Twenty-seventh Infantry, 21 enlisted, attached to Companies C, F, and G, to bring their strength up to 75 each; interpreters Leon Fernandez and Tomas Torres; 4 large Moro vintas; 64 native pack ponies; and a quartermaster's pack train of 100 mules, carrying four days' rations. Lieut. Col. John L. Chamberlain, inspector-general, Department of Mindanao, accompanied the command unofficially, and Mr. J. Henry Savage Lander accompanied as a guest by authority of department commander.

The command was provided with ample facilities for boiling water, and each man was furnished an extra canteen. This was done as a precaution against cholera, which was prevalent among the Moros along the west coast of the lake.

Notice had previously been sent to all the principal rancherias on the west coast, and especially to Bacolod, as to the friendly purpose of this expedition, and all were cautioned that they must not molest us or oppose the march. The expedition started at 7 a. m., April 5, 1903, and went into camp at Madumba near a beautiful spring of water, friendly Moros in the vicinity furnishing an ample supply of wood. At about 1 a.m. that night several shots were fired at one of the outposts by Bacolod Moros, who had crept up in the grass to close range, and two enlisted men of Troop A, Fifteenth Cavalry, were wounded.

Resuming the march at early hour the next morning many war flags were seen displayed on the Bacolod stronghold, where opposition was expected, these Moros having been openly hostile and defiant for nearly a year. Some 2 miles west of Bacolod a large party of Moros had assembled on the lake shore and were brandishing their weapons and firing an occasional shot in our direction, but some well-directed volleys and two or three shots from one of the Maxim guns dispersed them. The country from Madumba to Bacolod is rough and the trails are difficult, so it was nearly 3 o'clock in the afternoon when the head of the column arrived in the vicinity of Bacolod, where the first real resistance was met, although a few shots had been fired from an insignificant fort at Linok, which was returned without delaying the column.

The plan was to attack Bacolod from the north, and to do this it was necessary to rather keep up in the hills, where we had to work our way very slowly. After a skirmish, in which several smaller outlying forts and parties of Moros were either destroyed or dislodged, the ridge on which Bacolod is located was cleared of hostile Moros and occupied. To reach this ridge we had to cross a deep defensive ditch that extended about 800 yards up the hill from the fort, the crossing being made at about 500 yards from the fort. The mortars were left in a commanding position about 2,000 yards from the fort, and opened fire soon after the advance from that point began. On reaching Bacolod hill about 4 o'clock a very heavy rain set in which considerably delayed the advance, especially of the artillery. The leading company was moved down Bacolod ridge toward the fort in skirmish line, and was received with a heavy fire of lantacas and small arms. Advancing to within 300 yards, one company was placed across the ridge and one moved to the right and another to the left, so as to partially envelop the fort. One section of the artillery having arrived, firing began in earnest on both sides. Instructions were given the two flank companies to gradually and carefully extend their flanks toward the lake, with a view of preventing the escape of Moros from the fort, and the remaining companies were ordered into camp on the ridge behind the firing line. The company forming the left wing succeeded in reaching the lake, thus opening up the trail for our water supply, but darkness came on rapidly, and it was impossible on account of the dense undergrowth and tall grass to conclude the reconnaissance on the right sufficiently to warrant the attempt to occupy that part of the line that night.

Desultory firing was kept up on both sides during the night, and at daybreak the morning of the 7th both flanks were extended to the lake. Lieut. A. W. Brown, with 25 men of Company F, was sent into the hills to the northeast to dislodge a party of Moros who had caused some annoyance by firing into camp. He successfully accomplished this mission, killing several and driving others toward Calahui, where he discovered another large fort with war flags flying. At about 9 o'clock a. m. the

Moros inside the fort ceased firing and hoisted a white flag, the Panandungan of Bacolod himself requesting terms of surrender. They were informed that nothing but unconditional surrender would be accepted, and that as prisoners their lives would be protected and that they would be well treated. They declined these terms, desiring to keep their arms and to remain in the fort. The effective work of the mountain artillery had already practically destroyed the embrasures and portholes on the north and east faces of the fort, and we soon reached a stage when all that remained to be done was to make the final assault. It was necessary, however, to remain at Bacolod until the following day, awaiting the arrival of supply pack trains sent to Vicars. Moreover, in order to avoid loss of life I was very desirous of forcing the Moros to surrender, and for these reasons concluded to delay the assault until the following day in the hope that they would finally give up. Fresh troops were sent to the firing line, which was strengthened at night, and the utmost precautions taken that none should escape from the fort and no reenforcements enter. Early the morning of the 8th the Panandungan again asked for and was granted a conference, which, however, resulted as before.

Material for filling the ditch was prepared at once, and detailed instructions were given to the officers of the assaulting lines, to be composed of Company C, Twenty-seventh Infantry, under Lieutenant Shaw; Troop L, Fifteenth Cavalry, dismounted, under Captain Kirkpatrick, and 1 Maxim gun, under Captain McNair. All in readiness, the infantry advanced toward the east face of the fort, and the cavalry, with the mountain gun between the two platoons, the north face. Under the protection of the fire of this line the ditch at the point of crossing, opposite the middle of the east face, was filled with fallen trees, and a bamboo bridge was thrown across by Company M, Twenty-seventh Infantry, and Troop A, Fifteenth Cavalry, under Lieutenants Gracie and Lear, respectively, Lieutenant Peek, Engineer Corps, immediately directing the work. Within twenty minutes this was accomplished without casualty, and men of Company C, Company M, and Troop A hurriedly crossed to the berm and sprang upon the parapet, encountering Moros in hand-to-hand combat, who rushed with campilans and krises from the berm galleries and interior of the fort to meet them. Three men were wounded almost instantly, but short work was made of the remaining Moros, who in all parts of the fort continued to fight desperately to the death. The plan of assault was executed in every detail. It was a brilliant action and one never to be forgotten by those who engaged, and the gallantry displayed by our troops has seldom been equaled.

It is said that there were in the beginning over 200 Moros in the fort, several of whom escaped the first day and night, and just before the assault the number was put at from 50 to 100. Sixty Moros were found dead in the fort and trenches among those killed being the Panandungan of Bacolod, the leader of opposition to the Americans; Dato Macasasa, Dato Tundia, Dato Antao, and several others of less importance. On account of the danger from cholera, a minute inspection of the interior was not deemed safe, and the fort was at once ordered burned. Many rifle barrels and kris blades were found in the ashes, together with 6 cannons and 7 lantacas, which were destroyed with gunpowder. Our casualties in the Bacolod fight previous to the attack on the fort proper were 5 men wounded, and in the final assault 3 wounded. According to conservative reports of friendly Moros, 60 Bacolod Moros were killed in the fighting in that vicinity in addition to those mentioned above, making 120 in all, besides some renegades from Taraca, Pindalunan, Binidayan, and other places.

The dimensions of Fort Bacolod included within the walls of the parapet were about 80 by 100 feet. The walls were 12 feet high, 15 feet thick at the base, and faced with stone on the outside. A berm 12 feet wide extended entirely around the fort, under which were constructed galleries, and both the fort and berm were covered with bamboo and earth. The fort proper and the galleries were used as a dwelling by the family of the Panandungan and many of his people. The parapet was loopholed for rifle fire, and contained embrasures for cannon and lantacas, and a series of bamboo loopholes extended entirely around the edge of the berm for rifle fire from the galleries.

The fort was surrounded by a ditch with a triangular cross section some 30 feet wide at the top and at least 35 feet deep, and a ditch of the same dimensions, protected by rifle pits, extended north from the northwest corner a distance of some 800 yards along the western slope of the ridge just below the military crest. From the general arrangement of the fort, and especially the position of the cannon and lantacas, they expected to be attacked from the south or southwest, and were undoubtedly surprised and accordingly placed at a disadvantage by our attack from the opposite direction. . . .

The command remained in camp at Bacolod during the night of the 9th, and preparations were made the next morning for moving toward Calahui, some 3 miles farther to the northeast. The sick and wounded and one of the mortars, under escort of Troop A, Fifteenth Cavalry, were sent back to Camp Vicars, and the command started for Calahui, keeping well up in the hills. At a distance of 2,000 yards the fort came in view with its war flags flying and its Moro krises and campilans flashing in the sunlight. This point was a good mortar position and mortar fire was opened. The rest of the column pushed forward as rapidly as possible toward a position above Calahui that appeared favorable for the Maxims and the infantry. On account of the lack of trails and the roughness of the country it was 4 o'clock in the afternoon when the two leading companies of infantry and the Maxim guns reached the point selected. Here the Moros began firing upon us with great vigor, but the command we had of the position was such that the interior of their fort could be raked with artillery, and it was soon evident that they not only could do but little, but that they could not remain long in the fort without great loss.

The fort was located on a point about 100 feet high that projected into the lake and was surrounded on three sides by water, the shores for some distance on both sides being covered with timber. Placing Company G across the ridge supporting the mountain guns, at a range of 700 yards, Lieutenant Gracie with Company M was ordered toward the fort, to move with his left flank touching the lake. He encountered some resistance in the heavy timber, but soon reached the vicinity of the fort and made a thorough reconnaissance of it. Returning after dark, he reported that many of the Moros had escaped by vinta, as many vintas were seen by him skirting the shore out of sight of our position. Upon his return about dark with the mortar, Captain Gatley reported having seen Moros escaping. As it was impossible to surround this fort, a firing line was held intact during the night, and strong outposts were posted about camp, which was established on the ridge.

Little firing was done during the night, and early next morning several Calahui Moros, under Dato Ampuan, came into camp and surrendered themselves, saying that all Moros had left the fort during the previous afternoon and night. In company with these Moros the fort was entered and afterwards destroyed. The Calahui Moros were required to take the oath of allegiance, which they did according to Moro custom, and were released. They reported that the fort was occupied the day before by about 250 Moros of Calahui and Taraca, 23 of whom were killed and several wounded. We had no casualties. Five cannon and lantacas were found inside the fort and destroyed.

As before stated, the fort at Calahui was located on a high point projecting into the lake and could be approached only from the land side and then only by crossing a wide triangular ditch some 40 feet deep. The walls were similar to those at Bacolod, although but one face was fortified. Against artillery from the position selected for the Maxim it was absolutely untenable. . . .

During the day the leading datos of Tugaya and several from Oato came into camp with assurances that there would be no more trouble at any of the remaining rancherias between Calahui and Marahui. In order to give the men a much-needed rest after the four days of constant engagement and to await the return of Troop A from Camp Vicars, the command was held in camp at Calahui during the remainder of that day and night. About 4 o'clock in the afternoon a messenger came in from Lieutenant Lear, stating that the advance guard of Troop A had been attacked by Bacolod Moros in the ravine just west of Bacolod ridge. Medical assistance was at once sent him, and the troop with the wounded reached camp at dark. Lieutenant Lear then reported that 4 Moros, armed with campilans, had sprung from behind some large boulders, each one attacking a member of the point of the advance guard, including Lieutenant Mangum. The 4 Moros were killed, but the 4 members of the advance guard were more or less severely wounded, of whom Corpl. Claude D. Reade died shortly after reaching camp.

The next day, the 11th, the sick and wounded were returned to Camp Vicars in vintas under charge of a guard commanded by Lieut. A. W. Brown. The command resumed the march under escort of many friendly Moros and went into camp for the night at Oato, where we were received with every manifestation of friendship and where every attention was shown us. While here I finally settled an old feud between the rancherias of Oato and Bucayanan that had been the cause of war between them in which several Moros had lost their lives.

On the 12th march was again resumed, and representatives from all the rancherias—including the principal rancherias, Bucayanan, Cauayan, Marantao, Bacolod (north), and Marahui—along the coast came out to meet us. The march was made without further incident to the Agus River, opposite Pantar. Here we remained in camp during the following day and obtained five days' rations and forage for the return trip.

The return march was begun on the morning of the 14th, and camp was made at Marahui. A delegation of Bayabao Moros visited camp, including sultans or their representatives from all the principal rancherias of that tribe, together with Pandita Imam Nuzca, a high priest, the head of the Muhammadan church in Lake Lanao, most of whom I had known and visited during my service at Iligan. On the 15th the command marched to Calahui without incident, and on the 18th, using the trails along the coast through Bacolod, reached Camp Vicars. Passing near Bacolod, Captain Kirkpatrick's troop, which had been thrown out on the right flank of the column as a precautionary measure, had a few shots fired at them from extremely long range.

As a result of this expedition of exploration it was definitely learned that all the Moros along the west shore of Lake Lanao were friendly to us except those of Bacolod and Calahui and a few about Linok. With these exceptions all gave us welcome or came out in large numbers to meet us where the road led us at any distance from their rancherias. Expressions of friendship had previously come from many of them during the trip from Camp Vicars across the lake in November and December. The Moros of Bacolod, however, had openly defied our authority for a year, and were supported by many who, while not openly hostile, were in sympathy with them. The destruction of their fort, thought by most Moros to be impregnable, and their losses in the battle destroyed their prestige forever, and will have a salutary and a lasting effect upon them and upon all the Moros in the Laguna. This effect will be strengthened by the fact that no property of any kind was destroyed except unavoidably, and that all Moros who expressed friendship were treated kindly. An accurate map of the west shore of the lake was made . . . and it was found that a wagon road could be constructed with little difficulty from Camp Vicars to Marahui, as the main trail follows the shore line only a part of the distance, or from Tugaya to Madumba, and even this could be avoided if found necessary.

The existence of cholera about the lake made the expedition extremely hazardous. The work necessary to carry and boil water increased the labor of the troops twofold, especially as camps could seldom be made near the lake and all springs and streams usually containing water during the rainy season were found dry at this time. Nine enlisted men contracted the disease during the expedition, 3 of whom recovered, while 4 civilian packers contracted it, 2 of whom recovered.

I cannot speak too highly of the conduct of the officers and men composing this expedition. Well disciplined and trained as they have been during the last year in campaigning among and fighting against these semi-savages, they were on the alert to take advantage of every opportunity to damage the enemy and at the same time to protect themselves against unnecessary losses. The arduous duty during the expedition was performed most willingly and without exception with good judgment. I desire especially to commend Capt. W. S. McNair and Lieut. Clarence Deems, jr., and the men of the Twenty-fifth Battery of Field Artillery under them for their services during this expedition, and especially during the fight at Bacolod; also Capt. G. W. Kirkpatrick and the officers and men of Troop L, Fifteenth Cavalry, and First Lieut. G. C. Shaw and the officers and men of Company C, Twenty-seventh Infantry, who deserve the greatest credit for their gallant conduct in the final assault on this Moro stronghold. Lieutenant Shaw led his company over the ditch and directed the movements of his men in the hand-to-hand encounter that took place against these fanatical Moros. The splendid services of First Lieut. R. U. Patterson, assistant surgeon, and the members of the medical and hospital corps under him are especially worthy of commendation. Lieutenant Mangum, Fifteenth Cavalry, displayed great personal courage, after his revolver had three times missed fire, in grappling with the individual Moro who was making for him, disarming the Moro and killing him by blows with his revolver. This report would be incomplete without mentioning the excellent services of Lieut. E. D. Peek, Engineer Corps, who directed the construction of the bridge across the ditch on the 8th of April, and of First Lieut. W. B. Gracie and the officers and men of Company M, Twenty-seventh Infantry, and of First Lieut. Ben Lear and the officers and men of Troop A, Fifteenth Cavalry, who performed this difficult work directly under the walls and fire from the fort. Chaplain George D. Rice, Twenty-seventh Infantry, who narrowly escaped losing his life in the assault on the fort at Bacolod, deserves especially to be mentioned for his untiring efforts in aiding the surgeons and caring for and comforting the sick and wounded. I shall forward recommendations in the cases of officers and enlisted men deserving special recognition for services during the expedition.

Very respectfully,
JOHN J. PERSHING,
Captain, Fifteenth Cavalry, Commanding.

HEADQUARTERS DEPARTMENT OF MINDANAO
Malabang, Mindanao, P. I., April 2, 1903.

Capt. John J. Pershing
Fifteenth Cavalry, Commanding Camp Vicars, Mindanao, P. I.

Sir:

You will proceed from Camp Vicars to explore the west shore of Lake Lanao as far as Marahui. From that point you will return to Camp Vicars. The object of this expedition is to gain information regarding the country, and to visit various Moro tribes inhabiting that section and endeavor to cultivate friendly relations. It is understood that most of the sultans and datos inhabiting the west coast of Lake Lanao are friendly to the United States; great care should be taken to strengthen this friendship.

Strict orders will be given your command not to molest or interfere with these Moros in any unauthorized manner. If they have anything to sell which is needed by the troops purchases will be made and paid for at once. No property will be destroyed unless unavoidable.

Indications point to opposition of your march on the part of Bacolod Moros and that they have constructed a large fort in their territory. If, on reaching the vicinity of Bacolod, you find these Moros unfriendly and determined to oppose your progress, you will take the necessary military measures to bring them into subjection.

Should any other Moros along your route make hostile demonstrations you are authorized to treat them in the same manner.

Have the country along the line of your march mapped as thoroughly as circumstances permit, particularly with regard to trails and the practicability of building a wagon road at some future day.

I inclose you herewith a copy of telegram from the division commander on which these directions are founded.

The troops composing this expedition will consist of 4 companies of infantry, 3 troops of cavalry, the Twenty-fifth Field Battery of artillery, and such men of the Seventeenth Field Battery as you deem advisable, and you will take 2 medical officers and the requisite complement of hospital corps men. In addition to the pack train at your post, you are authorized to employ such Moro transportation as you may deem advisable.

Owing to the prevalence of cholera in the country through which you will pass, the greatest possible care will be taken to protect the men against danger from this disease.

If the conditions around Bacolod make it necessary for you to return to Vicars from that point you are authorized to do so, but it is advisable to take advantage of the present dry season and continue the expedition as far as Marahui unless circumstances render it impracticable.

The command will be supplied with 200 rounds of ammunition per man and proper supply for field guns.

Very respectfully,
SAMUEL S. SUMNER,
Brigadier-General, U. S. Army, Commanding.

[Telegram]
MANILA, *March 30, 1903.*
SUMNER, *Zamboanga, Mindanao:*
(Forward to Malabang.)

I want the west coast of Lake Lanao explored, and wish the command-ing officer at Vicars to take this up before the rain sets in. All the datos on that coast are friendly and have invited the troops to visit them, save some of the principal Moros of the Bacolod rancherias, concern-ing whom reports indicate unfriendliness, but it is hoped that Captain Pershing, with his well-known tact and discretion, will be able to over-come this disposition, if it really exists, and that he will receive a friendly reception; but if the Bacolod Moros attempt to interfere with the survey and examination of the west shore of the lake, any opposition which they may offer must be overcome, as it is the purpose of the Government to visit all the centers of Moro population around the lake and establish the most friendly relations with all the native inhabitants. Requests have been made for medicine by some of the Bacolod Moros. If it is found that any are in need of medical aid it should be extended, if practicable. It will be very gratifying to me if this expedition can be accomplished without fighting or bloodshed. Full value will be paid for all supplies taken. If hostile Moro cottas bar the way they should be destroyed.

DAVIS.

Source: Appendix IV, *Occupation of the Lake Lanao Region*, Brig. Gen. Samuel S. Sumner, to Annual Report of Maj. Gen. George W. Davis, commanding, Division of the Philippines, in *ARWD, 1903*, vol. 3, *Reports of Department and Division Commanders.*

Appendix G

Report of Captain John J. Pershing, Fifteenth Cavalry, of an Exploring Expedition around Lake Lanao, 2–10 May 1903

POST OF CAMP VICARS
Mindanao, P.I., May 15, 1903.

TO ADJUTANT-GENERAL, DEPARTMENT OF MINDANAO
Zamboanga, P. I.

Sir:

I have the honor to submit the following report of an expedition of exploration made under my command around Lake Lanao between May 2 and 10, inclusive, pursuant to orders from department commander, Brig. Gen. Samuel S. Sumner, U. S. Army, dated Zamboanga, Mindanao, P. I., April 28, 1903, a copy of which is appended hereto.

The command consisted of Capt. John J. Pershing, Fifteenth Cavalry, commanding; Second Lieut. Victor S. Foster, Fifteenth Cavalry, acting adjutant; Second Lieut. William C. Gardenhire, Fifteenth Cavalry, acting quartermaster and commissary; Capt. W. F. Lewis, assistant surgeon, U. S. Army; First Lieut. R. U. Patterson, assistant surgeon, U. S. Army, and 7 enlisted men of the Hospital Corps; Troop A, Fifteenth Cavalry, Second Lieut. W. P. Mangum, jr., Fifteenth Cavalry, in command, with 40 enlisted men; Troop E, Fifteenth Cavalry, Capt. F. J. Koester, Fifteenth Cavalry, in command, with First Lieut. R. B. Going and 50 enlisted men; Troop G, Fifteenth Cavalry, First. Lieut. Charles

E. McCullough, Fifteenth Cavalry, in command, with Second Lieut. Francis A. Ruggles and 43 enlisted men; two Vickers-Maxim mountain guns and one 3.6-inch field mortar, all of the Seventeenth Battery Field Artillery, Capt. G. G. Gatley, Artillery Corps, in command, with Second Lieut. D. H. Currie, Second Lieut. E. H. De Armond, and 82 enlisted men; Lieut. Currie, in addition to his other duties, acting as engineer officer; Company C, Twenty-seventh Infantry, First Lieut. G. C. Shaw, Twenty-seventh Infantry, in command, and 58 enlisted men; Company D, Twenty-seventh Infantry, First Lieut. O. S. Eskridge, Twenty-seventh Infantry, in command, and 71 enlisted men; Company G, Twenty-seventh Infantry, Second Lieut. S. C. Loring, Twenty-seventh Infantry, in command, and 62 enlisted men; Company M, Twenty-seventh Infantry, First Lieut. W. B. Gracie, Twenty-seventh Infantry, in command, with Second Lieut. B. F. Miller and 63 enlisted men; Company F, Twenty-seventh Infantry, 38 enlisted men assigned to the infantry organizations; a pioneer detachment consisting of 5 enlisted men from each company of infantry.

Mr. Frank Helm, late ensign, U. S. Navy, joined the expedition after the battle of Taraca River and accompanied it around the lake to Camp Vicars; Contract Dental Surg. F. P. Stone, U. S. Army, on duty at Camp Vicars, was given permission to accompany the expedition as assistant to the surgeons; Lieutenant Williams, Marine Corps, accompanied as a guest; Leon Fernandez and Tomas Torres acted as interpreters, the latter in charge of Moro transportation; five days' rations and forage were carried on the quartermaster's pack train, consisting of 28 mules, and a native pack train, consisting of 115 ponies; several large vintas were employed to accompany the expedition, and were furnished by Dato Pedro of Oato, Dato Gamour of Tugaya, and the Cabugatan of Oato. Every available facility was provided for boiling water, as a precaution against cholera, and each man was issued an extra canteen.

As soon as it became known that this expedition was to be made, notice was sent either by letter or courier to all the leading Moros on the east shore of the lake, and their friendship and assistance solicited. They were assured that we would molest neither the persons nor the property of those who wished to be friends and would pay for all supplies furnished us, but that we would brook no interference or opposition. The expedition started at 7 o'clock a. m. May 2, and marching by the way of Pantauan arrived at Sauir at about 12:30 p. m., where camp was established. Two companies of infantry and the pioneer detachment were immediately sent out to repair the trail leading thence through the timber around the arm of the lake to Maciu, as this trail is unusually swampy in places and had been found obstructed on previous expeditions. The greater part of the work was completed during the afternoon, it being necessary to cover several muddy stretches with corduroy. One shot was fired from the Maciu side of the laguna during the night, but otherwise we were not disturbed.

On the morning of the 3d Dato Pedro, who was in charge of the vintas, arrived in camp as he had agreed. The Cabugatan of Ragayan and other datos of that rancheria and of Tupurug visited camp and offered their services as guides. Two companies of infantry were sent out at an early hour to finish work on the trail, and the command started at 7:30 a. m., marching through Maciu and across the Malaig River, keeping well to the east toward the foothills to avoid swampy rice lands. Reaching the vicinity of Gata, Dato Punilumabao and party met us and turned over one of the remaining Government horses lost by Lieutenant Forsyth in March, 1902. Moros from Gata and Minbailay reported that we would meet opposition at the fort of Amai-Benanning of Gata, and endeavored to dissuade us from passing through that rancheria. In order to give those Moros time to fully consider the matter I went into camp at Bansayan on the lake shore, in sight of and about 14 miles distant from their fort. Several delegations of Moros from the vicinity, carrying American or white flags, presented themselves and expressed their friendliness. From Bansayan the vintas were sent to Camp Vicars for rations and forage.

On the morning of the 4th the march was resumed directly toward Gata, but as we approached the fort a delegation came out to meet us and stated that they all desired to be friends. As the rear guard was crossing a small stream, just after leaving camp, two shots were fired by Moros concealed in the grass, and one man of Troop E was slightly wounded. The two Moros who did the firing were killed. From Gata we visited some of the rancherias under Rajah Nurul Caquim, one of the powerful datos of the east side of the lake, after which we crossed the Ragayan River and came out upon an open flat, some 3 miles wide, beyond which could be seen the hostile fort of Dato Ampuan-Agaus of Taraca, literally covered with war flags, situated in the edge of the timber that skirted the Taraca River. The line of march led directly across the flat, but midway we ran into a marsh about 100 yards wide that delayed the column two hours, as all the animals had to be unpacked and their loads carried this distance.

To reach the hostile fort the trail led us near and between two other strong forts that had been reported hostile, but, contrary to reports, several datos came out with white flags and said they wished to be considered friends, and that none of their people would oppose us or interfere with us. After passing these forts Moros were seen running from a strip of timber to our right toward Fort Taraca, and in a few minutes we were fired upon from the fort at about 600 yards. Company C, Twenty-seventh Infantry, was directed to form a skirmish line to the right and move to within 300 yards of the fort, and Company G to take a similar position on the left. The right and left flanks, respectively, of these two companies were ordered advanced so as to partially envelop the fort. The two Maxim guns and the field mortars were placed at a distance of 500 yards and opposite the interval left between these companies for that purpose. The firing became vigorous on both sides, the Moros using both lantacas and small arms. One platoon of Company D was sent toward the timber to the right as a protection to the troops not yet engaged and the animals. As Company D went into position they received the fire of a small cotta on the left, which was at once captured and destroyed.

Almost as soon as it arrived in position the right flank of the line, held by Company C, received a heavy fire from the woods along the Taraca River. Lieutenant Shaw, with that company, was ordered to enter the timber, cross the Taraca River if necessary, and drive out or destroy any opposing Moros and destroy any cottas from which he might be fired on. Troop G dismounted, took the place of Company C on the skirmish line, and the attack on the main fort continued, the artillery, which had been sent to a new and better position, firing with such effect that the defenders could do us little harm. Lieutenant Shaw made his way slowly and developed considerable resistance, so I reenforced him with Company M, under Lieutenant Gracie, and gave orders that in conjunction they should move down the river cautiously and reconnoiter a fort at Pitacus, said to be held by hostile Moros under the Sultan-cabugatan of Pitacus, on the north bank and near Fort Taraca, already engaged.

At the place from which the right flank was fired upon the river flows north, but a short distance farther on it changes direction and flows practically west past Fort Pitacus. Troop E was dismounted and sent to the river to support the infantry if necessary. The timber on both sides of the river was soon cleared of Moros and 7 of their cottas destroyed. Upon approaching Fort Pitacus two war flags were flying, although little resistance was made to the reconnoitering companies. Lieutenant Shaw, who was on the north bank of the river, first examined the fort and vicinity carefully and then ordered his men to scale the eastern wall. A large body of well-armed Moros was found inside, who delivered a heavy fire on the attacking party, but the latter held their ground. Lieutenant Gracie immediately crossed from the south bank and, scaling the south wall with his company, obtained a cross fire upon the Moros that soon demoralized them. Several hand-to-hand encounters occurred on the walls, and after a fight which lasted but a few minutes the Moros displayed a white flag and surrendered. Ninety Moros were found dead within the fort, 13 were wounded, and 28 were taken prisoners. Among the dead were the Sultan-cabugatan of Pitacus, the Sangupan of Lumasa, the Dato-cabugatan, the Cabugatan of Maciu, and the Mama of Maciu, the two former of whom were known on east side of the lake as being very bitter in their opposition to Americans. Fifty-one rifles and 16 lantacas and cannon and several krises and compilans were captured. In the assault 1 enlisted man was killed and 6 wounded, 1 of whom died the next day, shortly after reaching Camp Vicars.

The fort was a new one, situated in a small opening in the timber and apparently uncompleted. In construction it was like ordinary Moro forts, about 75 feet square, with walls about 12 feet high and about 12 feet thick at the base, and a ditch 10 feet deep. In the interior sheds of rough split lumber 2 or 3 inches thick were constructed against the north and south faces, intended as a protection against shrapnel and shell.

After the fall of Fort Pitacus Captain Koester with Troop E was ordered farther down the left bank of the river in rear of Fort Taraca, and after making a thorough reconnaissance took up a position closing all avenues of escape in that direction. Troop G was ordered to advance to within a short distance of the fort, so that the two troops combined were in a position not to be in danger from each other's fire, and so that they practically surrounded the fort. It was now growing dark, and leaving these two troops in position the remaining organizations were ordered into camp about 300 yards to the east of the fort and the same distance from the Taraca River. There was little firing at or from the fort until about 3 a. m., when it became evident that the Moros were attempting to escape. It was very dark at this hour and afterwards until daybreak, so that probably several Moros sneaked out, passing over the parapet at its lowest point, thence into the grass. A number were seen by the men of the investing cordon just outside the wall at different times, and there were evidences that some of them had been wounded. Friendly Moros afterwards learned that such was the case, and also that several were killed while escaping. At daylight a large white flag was floating over Fort Taraca, and 29 Moros, including Dato Ampuan-Agaus, 6 other datos, and 2 panditas (priests) of some importance called Dianal and the Cali of Maciu, surrendered themselves unconditionally. One dead and 1 wounded Moro were found inside. Prisoners reported that others who were wounded had been taken away. Twenty cannon and lantacas and 9 rifles, together with a number of krises and campilans, were captured. The fort was then destroyed by fire, and a few of the cannon and lantacas were broken up. After the battle friendly Moros reported that over 200 hostile Moros had lost their lives in the fighting that occurred in the forts and vicinity.

The vintas, having returned the night before with rations, were again sent to Vicars with the sick and wounded and such of the captured arms as could be easily carried, all under charge of Lieutenant Williams, Marine Corps, who desired to return. Many delegations of Moros visited camp during the day with assurances of friendship. The prisoners were required to bury the Moros killed at Pitacus, and medical assistance was given the wounded. The prisoners were held over night, for the effect it would have on other Moros, and for that purpose were put in a conical wall tent, with a strong guard around it. My intention being to release them the following morning, previous to our departure. A rain storm came up in the night, and in the extreme darkness four of them escaped and four others were killed in attempting to escape. The rest were released the next morning after taking the oath of allegiance, by cutting a piece of bejuco (a kind of vine).

The march was resumed, the trail leading across the Taraca River near Fort Pitacus, whence we soon debouched upon an extended alluvial flat, reaching some 8 miles from the shore toward the hills, and about 3 miles wide. For over half the distance across following a good trail, fair progress was made, but about the middle it became boggy beyond description and continued so for about three-quarters of a mile. Horses and mules were helpless to move. All hands were turned out, and with such scrubby brush and grass as could be obtained the trail was covered so that by leading the animals along it they managed with difficulty to pass over without their loads. It took five hours to go this distance, as all the animals had to be unloaded and their cargoes carried by the men.

There were a few long-range shots fired at the rear of the column about a mile from Taraca, but thereafter white flags and American flags were liberally displayed at various rancherias along the line of march during the day. Passing Mulundu, a report came in that the Moros of Muut had congregated at a certain cotta to oppose us, but upon our arrival there was no sign of hostility, although a shot or two were fired at the rear guard from long range from a small cotta in the vicinity, which was immediately taken and destroyed by the rear guard. About 1½ miles north of Dalama, whose sultan came out and acted as guide for us for some distance, we came to a wall of earth, which had been constructed by Maciu and Taraca Moros as an obstacle and for defense against troops from the north, extending from the edge of the lake up the hill some 400 yards and across the only trail along the shore at this point, where the foothills are very broken and reach the water's edge. A few minutes with pick and shovel enabled the command to pass easily. Camp was made at Bintong, on the only available spot near a small stream, but the site was so swampy that it was necessary during the night to remove animals from the established picket lines and lariat them without regard to order. At this camp occurred the only case of cholera that resulted fatally during the expedition.

The next day, the 7th, we came to the extensive flat alluvial country drained by the Remayn River, and made our way among the foothills when possible, crossing the marshy rice lands when necessary, covering trails with corduroy or with grass in many places, until, by dint of extremely hard work on the part of the men and animals from daylight on, we passed over the worst part of the road and reached camp at Ragayan, about 3 miles from Madaya, some time after dark. It was urgent that we should pass through this boggy country before any rain fell, as it was evident that any delay would almost, if not quite, hopelessly swamp us. Fortunately, the spring rains had not yet begun, and it was near the end of a very late dry season.

At Ragayan Capt. James A. Ryan, Fifteenth Cavalry, with Troop C, that regiment, met us and reported that all arrangements had been made for our rations and forage for the return trip. I had concluded to cross the Agus River at Madaya and to return to Camp Vicars by the more favorable west-shore trail. A good ford, though rocky, about 4 feet deep at the deepest place, just below the origin of the river, which was about 200 yards wide at this point, was used for the cavalry, artillery, and pack animals, while our Moro vintas were used on the lake for the infantry, the field guns, and the baggage, and by noon on the 8th the command was in camp again at Marahui.

General Sumner met us at Marahui, and after seeing the command safely over the Agus left in a short time for Pantar. The Sultan of Remayn, who had not previously visited any American camp or post, came in with Amai-Manibilang, of Madaya, accompanied by many datos, including Nuzca, the pandita or imam, who is at the head of the Muhammadan Church in Lake Lanao. The Sultan of Remayn expressed friendship for the Americans and reassured me as to the friendship of all the Moros of Bayabao, over whom he is the chief sultan.

On the 10th the return to Camp Vicars was begun, and nothing of consequence occurred during the day's march. Friendly Moros came out to meet us along the route, and upon arrival at Calahui, where we encamped, Dato Aliudan, with several of his people, visited me to pay their respects. The following day we marched through Calahui, Bacolod, Pindalunan, Corumatan, and Madullum along the shore. Troop G, under Lieutenant McCullough, was sent along the hill trail to act as a flanking party to the column. Between Calahui and Bacolod this troop was fired upon by hostile Moros, 9 in number, said to have been from Pindalunan, 5 of whom were killed and 4 wounded. Second Lieut. F. A. Ruggles and Sergeant Mohn were slightly wounded; otherwise the march was without incident.

The knowledge of the Lake Lanao country obtained on this expedition is invaluable. Heretofore the eastern part of Lake Lanao has been almost absolutely unknown, even Spanish records containing nothing of value relative to it. During the expedition we were able to make a good map, . . . examine the character of the country and the inhabitants, and form some idea of their numbers and resources. The tillable land on the east side of the lake between it and the foothills is capable, if properly cultivated, of maintaining at least 100,000 souls, and by using available land in the foothills a greater number could be maintained. To construct a wagon road for permanent use at all seasons of the year causeways would have to be built across the lowlands, the greater part of which are practically flooded during the rainy season, and substantial bridges would have to be thrown across the four larger rivers. Our humane purpose was impressed upon the people by contrasting this purpose with the opposite determination to severely punish all who interfered with us in the proper execution of a duty to the Government and to them, and while there are still a few who will retain feelings of resentment and revenge for a time there can be no doubt but that the effect will be lasting, and when considered in connection with our present knowledge of the country and the inhabitants it will give us an advantage in the future management of them which they, as a whole, will be as quick to recognize as we are.

The duty performed on other expeditions in which this command has participated during the past year has been arduous and the strain great, but on none of them have such discouragements or difficulties been met as on the expedition around the lake. It should be said also that on none of them have men behaved more splendidly while striving to prevent disease and to overcome natural obstacles, nor more gallantly in battle. I desire to make it of record that without the qualities, training, and discipline possessed by this command the successful accomplishment of the expedition and its objects would have been well-nigh impossible.

Among those to be especially commended for their services are First Lieuts. W. B. Gracie and G. C. Shaw, Twenty-seventh Infantry, and the officers and men under them for their action in the assault upon the fort of the Sultan-cabugatan of Pitacus. The attack and capture of the fort in this manner was the only way it could have been done, as previous preparation by artillery fire was impossible. The gallantry and courage with which it was accomplished can but excite the greatest admiration for the participants, and the small list of casualties on our part can only be attributed to the superiority of arms and judgment. Capt. G. G. Gatley, Seventeenth Battery Field Artillery, and the officers and men under him are deserving of praise for their patience and perseverance in moving their animals and guns over the difficult country on the east side of the lake, and no less arduous was the work of the cavalry and pack trains. First Lieut. C. E. McCullough, with Troop G, Fifteenth Cavalry, acted with promptness and effectiveness in repelling the attack by hostile Moros between Calahui and Bacolod on the 9th. The intelligent performance of their duties by the members of my staff, often attended by great personal danger, entitle them to high admiration. I shall, at an early date, submit recommendations covering all cases deserving special recognition.

The services of the Moros, with pack ponies, under Dato Grande, of Makadar, Dato Tampogao, of Tuburan, Dato Amai-Pasandalan, of Pantauan, and of the Moros with the vintas were invaluable; without their aid we should have been seriously embarrassed. Interpreters Leon Fernandez and Tomas Torres deserve consideration for the tireless and faithful manner in which they discharged their duties. I have already made suitable recommendation in their cases.

Very respectfully,
JOHN J. PERSHING,
Captain, Fifteenth Cavalry.

True copy of telegram forwarded by Adjutant-General, Department of Mindanao.

MANILA, *April 19, 1903.*
Brig. Gen. S. S. SUMNER,
Commanding Department of Mindanao, Zamboanga:

GENERAL: The favorable results which have been secured by the recent expedition from Vicars justify the conviction that the near future will be the best time to complete the exploration of the lake. We now have a good knowledge of the topography and inhabitants on the southwest and north shores of the lake. There remain only 20 miles on the east shore to close the gap. The Moro inhabitants have had abundant proofs of the beneficent purposes of the government and of the humanity of the Army, but there may still be a few disaffected ones.

In carrying out these objects of an occupation of the Lanao, I desire that there shall be a steady adherence to the policy of pacification and peaceable intercourse. If there should be any conflict, it must never be initiated by the troops. All Moros must learn that the troops may not be molested in passing along the roads and trails, and they must also learn that they cannot with impunity brandish their weapons and fly war flags in our faces.

The Moros have had abundant displays of our power and of their own impotence, and this has been specially emphasized at Bacolod. I trust there will be no more fighting and shall be specially glad if this work herein set out can be done without bloodshed.

Of course you will use the troops at Pantar should you deem such cooperation available.

The sooner this work is done the more likely will be an avoidance of bad weather.

GEO. W. DAVIS,
Major-General, U. S. Army,
Commanding Division of the Philippines.

[Telegram.]
ZAMBOANGA, *April 28, 1903.*
Capt. J. J. PERSHING,
Fifteenth Cavalry, Commanding Expedition around Lake Lanao:

You will proceed to carry out instructions contained in my letter of April 21 as soon as circumstances in your vicinity make it advisable, this in regard to the negotiations now going on between the east Lake Moros and the friendly Moros sent out by you. It is desired that the expedition of the east side of the lake be made without bloodshed if it can be accomplished, and sufficient time should be given the Moros to fully understand and appreciate your presence in their country. Regarding the military proposition, you will take such force as may be deemed advisable, taking care to have strength sufficient to overcome any opposition. I will direct the commanding officer at Malabang to send you two troops of cavalry and one of infantry and to advise with you as to departure from Malabang.

The interruption in the cable seriously prevents my keeping in direct communication with you or with it, and it is therefore impracticable to make any combined movements, as suggested by division commander, but I am going to Iligan in a few days and may send a force along the east shore from that place. If you can send a courier to Major Bullard notifying him of your date of departure, it would be advisable to do so, and you might also send the same notification to the commanding officer, Iligan, via Malabang, by wire.

The service by the latter route is uncertain, but works at times. You will send reply to this as soon as practicable, and the *Baltimore* will remain at Malabang for your reply. Let me know the date of your departure, if decided on. The orders heretofore given regarding the destruction of food or property will be strictly observed. Your own opinion that we should prove our friendship for this ignorant and superstitious people rather than engender a feeling of hatred and revenge accords with my views, and it is also in accord with the wishes of the division commander.

SUMNER, *Brigadier General.*

Source: Appendix IV, *Occupation of the Lake Lanao Region,* Brig. Gen. Samuel S. Sumner, to Annual Report of Maj. Gen. George W. Davis, commanding, Division of the Philippines, in *ARWD, 1903,* vol. 3, *Reports of Department and Division Commanders.*

Appendix H

Pershing's Report on the Bud Dajo Operation, 15–25 December 1911

HEADQUARTERS DEPARTMENT OF MINDANAO
ZAMBOANGA, P.I.

May 31, 1912.

The Adjutant General of the Army,
Washington, D. C.
(Through Military Channels).

Sir:

I have the honor to make the following report of operations against hostile Moros in the vicinity of Bud Dajo, Island of Jolo, from December 15th to 25th, 1911.

On December 14th, information was received from the Governor of the Sulu District to the effect that hostile Moros were occupying Bud Dajo in force. As there was some question as to the reliability of this report, the undersigned at once left for Jolo, accompanied by both his aides, Lieutenant W. O. Boswell, 21st Infantry, and Lieutenant I. P. Swift, 2nd Cavalry. Upon arrival the next morning, Colonel Frank West, 2nd Cavalry, at that time commanding all the military forces in the Island, verified the report regarding the occupation of Bud Dajo, stating that the number of Moros already within the crater was variously estimated at from 500 to 800, with from 150 to 250 rifles, besides cutting weapons, and that these Moros had already constructed rather formidable intrenchments.

On the morning of the 16th, a squadron of the 2nd Cavalry, under command of Captain Joseph S. Herron, 2nd Cavalry, was sent to make a reconnaissance in the vicinity of Bud Dajo, with special instructions to estimate, if possible, the strength of the hostiles occupying the crater and to thoroughly examine the country around the base of the mountain, with reference to camp sites. Upon his return, late on the afternoon of the 16th, he confirmed the report that Bud Dajo was occupied in considerable force. It was also reported from reliable Moro sources that the hostiles had not as yet provided themselves with all the supplies necessary for a prolonged siege. The undersigned assumed personal command of the operations, and ordered the immediate investment of the mountain.

On the 17th of December, the 29th, 30th, 34th Companies, Philippine Scouts, and Companies A, L, M, and the Machine Gun Platoon, 3rd Infantry, were embarked on the Cutter "Samar" and the launch "Geary," and brought from Camp Taglibi, about eight miles east of Jolo, for service in connection with operations around Bud Dajo. Companies B, C, and D, 3rd Infantry, and the 1st Company, Lanao Constabulary, under the command of Lieutenant Colonel Lawrence J. Hearn, 3rd Infantry, were ordered to march from Camp Taglibi to Tambang market near Bud Dajo.

Orders were issued for the abandonment of the Camp at Seit Lake, and the command, consisting of Companies E and I, 3rd Infantry, and Troops A, C and D, and Machine Gun Platoon, 2nd Cavalry, and the 46th Company, Philippine Scouts, all under command of Colonel Henry Kirby, 3rd Infantry, were concentrated at Augur Barracks.

The undersigned, with Captain Herron's troop of the 2nd Cavalry, personally inspected camp sites and trails near Bud Dajo and on December 18th ordered the following distribution of troops: Camp No. 3, situated at the foot of Lawton's trail, Colonel Henry Kirby, 3rd Infantry, with Headquarters, A, F, I, L, M, and Machine Gun Platoon, 3rd Infantry, the 25th, 30th, 34th and 52nd Companies, Philippine Scouts, and Battery A, 2nd Field Artillery: Camp No. 2, situated at the foot of Bundy's trail, Lieutenant Colonel Lawrence T. Hearn, 3rd Infantry, with the 1st Battalion, 3rd Infantry, and the 1st Lanao Constabulary; Camp No. 1, located at the foot of Koehler's trail, Captain William P. Jackson, 3rd Infantry, with Company K, 3rd Infantry, and the 45th and 46th Companies, Philippine Scouts. Troops B, D, I, K, L and M, 2nd Cavalry, were assigned to patrol duty and were distributed to various camps as became necessary.

As soon as these camps were occupied, a continuous system of patrols was established with instructions to reconnoiter, as far as possible, all trails leading up the mountain, without bringing on an engagement.

Each of the three camps was established at the foot of one of the only three that were then known. Outposts were placed around the base of the mountain to prevent all ingress or egress of hostile Moros. It was reported during the day that a few Moros had escaped on the night of the 17th.

The undersigned established Headquarters at Kirby's camp on the 19th. On the afternoon of that date, additional reconnoitering parties were pushed up the mountain side to examine all possible avenues of escape, and to explore every part of the mountain side through which it might be possible for Moros to pass or escape, with the object of making it impossible for any Moros to escape from Bud Dajo or for any supplies to be taken to the hostiles. Several Moros with supplies attempted to penetrate the line near Kirby's Camp at dawn on the 19th but were driven back with considerable loss by Kirby's outposts.

After the investment was completed, and it was assured that no Moros could get in or out, friendly Moros, under the leadership of Panglima Unga, were called upon to intercede in an effort to persuade the hostile Moros from the folly of attempting to hold Bud Dajo against the superiority of American forces that completely surrounded them. It was pointed out to them that eventually the end would be starvation or extermination, and that the question at issue was not of such serious importance at to warrant the continuance of an attitude of hostility.

Early reports that the food supply of the Moros on Bud Dajo was sufficient to last them but a short time were confirmed and orders for increased vigilance were given that escape might be made absolutely impossible, and an increase in the food supply unobtainable.

Beginning on the 19th, lateral trails were started through the jungles connecting the most advanced outposts. These were completed on the 21st, so that patrols were enabled to completely encircle the mountain at an average distance of 300 yards from the crater. So thoroughly was this work performed that reconnoitering parties discovered many old trails leading to the crater, bringing the number of possible routes of ascent and descent to nineteen or twenty. Notwithstanding the heavy guards covering these trails, Moros, both from the inside and outside, continued to make persistent efforts to break through the lines during the dark nights that prevailed, but without success. All advices from friendly Moros confirmed the opinion, formed after thorough personal reconnaissance daily, that all avenues of escape were closed. As there were troops enough present to maintain strict blockade, there could be no question of the eventual success of the plan.

On the 19th of December, twenty Moros surrendered. This gave encouragement to further efforts in this direction and between December 20th and 23rd, inclusive, hostiles surrendered daily in groups of from fifty to two hundred, including men, women and children. It is now known that there were about eight hundred people on Mount Dajo when the investment began.

On the 23rd, word was sent by friendly dattos that no further opportunity, after the 24th, would be offered Moros to surrender, except unconditionally. On the morning of the 24th, friendly emissaries returned from Dajo with the information that the crater was deserted and that the remaining hostiles, estimated at from sixty to one hundred, had gone, and that the evidence showed that they had left that morning very hastily. Major E. G. Peyton, Philippine Scouts, with two companies of native scouts was ordered to occupy the crater immediately, and to take extra precaution against a ruse, as it was suspected that the Moros had left with the intention of hiding in the jungle on the mountain side, until the troops should be withdrawn, or had planned to attack our lines in force under cover of darkness. The outpost line between Kirby's camp and the gulch was accordingly strengthened, as it was believed that the Moros were in front of this part of the line, and a strong line held along the crater, thus completely surrounding these hostiles who thought to escape. During the night of December 24th, desperate attacks were made upon the outposts along this part of the line, but the hostiles were repulsed at every point. Without food or water it was only a question of a short time before the surrender of these Moros could be expected.

On December 25th, one of the dattos who had surrendered a few days previous, requested permission to enter the jungle and endeavor to persuade the hostiles in hiding to come in and surrender. His request was approved, with the distinct understanding that they surrender unconditionally. He succeeded in bringing in, that afternoon, forty-six men, one woman, and one child, with several rifles and a large number of cutting weapons. The woman and child were turned loose and the men were sent under guard to Jolo, put aboard the Samar and sent to Calarian Prison.

It was learned from prisoners that several Moros were still hidden along the southwest side of the mountain. On the afternoon of December 26th, the 52nd Company, Philippine Scouts, formed a skirmish line, facing the south, along Lawton's trail, with the right resting against the rim of the crater and the left in touch with the line of outposts, under instructions to move around the mountain side, between the crater's rim and the outpost trail, and clear that section of hostile Moros. This movement occupied about three hours. Six Moros, determined to die, were found and dispatched. Orders were then issued for the withdrawal of the outposts, and the troops were temporarily rearranged in the three main camps preparatory to further operations. Casualties during these operations consisted of one officer of the army and two enlisted men of the scouts wounded, and twelve Moros killed and a few wounded.

It should be fully understood that there was never a moment during the investment of Bud Dajo when the Moros, including women, on top of the mountain would not have fought to the death had they been given the opportunity. They had gone there to make a last stand on this, their sacred mountain, and they were determined to die fighting. Their former experience on Bud Dajo did not deter them from taking this step, and it would not have deterred them from fighting to the death had an attempt been made to dislodge them by force. It was only by the greatest effort that their solid determination to fight it out could be broken. The fact is that they were completely surprised at the prompt and decisive action of the troops in cutting off supplies and preventing escape, and they were chagrined and disappointed in that they were not encouraged to die the death of Muhammadan fanatics.

In conclusion, it should be stated that the duty during the seven days investment was severe. A soldier can hardly be called upon to perform more arduous service than continuous outpost duty, under a tropical sun by day and torrential rains by night, especially if restrained from final aggressive action that leads to battle. The officers and men present during the investment of Bud Dajo performed every duty with efficiency and a splendid spirit prevailed among them throughout.

> Very respectfully,
> John J. Pershing,
> Brigadier General, U.S.A., Commanding.

Source: Library of Congress, Pershing Papers, Box 371, Folder: Governor of Moro Province (5).

Appendix I

Pershing's Report on the Bud Bagsak Operation

October 15, 1913.

From: Brigadier General John J. Pershing, U. S. Army
To: The Adjutant General of the Army
          (Through the Commanding General, Philippine Department)

Subject: Report of the Bud Bagsak operations.

1. Before entering into the details of the actual operations of the Bud Bagsak Campaign, it is considered essential to give here some of the principal events leading to this action. The disarmament of the Moros and Pagan tribes, as has been previously reported, was decided upon some eighteen months ago by the Civil Governor of the Moro Province, with the full knowledge that it would have to be enforced by the Army. This task had been generally completed throughout the Province, except in parts of Jolo. About five thousand arms had been gathered in from the Sulu Moros. It had seemed probable almost from the start that the outlaw element of that section of the Island of Jolo, known as Lati Ward, would give trouble before they would give up their arms. Under the leadership of Amil, those Moros who opposed the Government consisted of a force variously estimated at from five to ten thousand. Every move that was made by troops toward that part of the Island caused these people to assemble on the heights of Bud Bagsak. The final effort to finish the work of disarmament was begun December, 1912. No sooner had troops entered their duty elsewhere in the Island than the Lati Ward leaders gathered all their people to their Bud Bagsak stronghold.

To have attacked at this time would have meant the unavoidable killing of hundreds and perhaps thousands of women and children. There-

453

fore, every conceivable means was used to induce the recalcitrants to surrender their arms peaceably, but without success. It was finally proposed that, if they would return to their homes and comply with the Government's demands, the troops would be withdrawn. This was agreed to, and in the latter part of February the troops were ordered to retire from that part of the Island.

2. Most of the women and children did return to their homes and resume the cultivation of their neglected lands, but it was soon found in that they were held in readiness to return to the mountain at any time, and that most of the outlaws had not come down permanently. Unless these Moros could be persuaded to carry out their part of the agreement, it was evident that sooner or later there would be a clash. It was also very clear that to avoid the reassembling of the noncombatants on the mountain stronghold, it would be necessary to completely surprise its defenders. To accomplish this, the greatest secrecy was maintained, and some dissimulation was resorted to. The influence of every friendly Moro, including the Sultan of Sulu, and Datto Mandi from Zamboanga was tried again and again. Our officials who met with the armed representatives of these brigands in conference at Bun Bun were really led to the false hope of a peaceful ending, as some of the hostile Moros had consented to visit Jolo to discuss final conditions of surrender of arms. Their visit meant nothing, however, as toward the end of May the Moros openly declared that they would never lay down their arms. This final declaration, after three months of earnest effort to prevent fighting, ended further discussion, and the use of force became necessary.

3. Leaving Zamboanga on the Transport *Wright* on the evening of June 9th, accompanied by 2d Lieut. James L. Collins, 8th Cavalry, Aide-de-camp, ostensibly bound for Camp Overton, we arrived at Isabala, Basilan, at 11:00 p.m., the same night, and embarked Captain George C. Charlton's 51st Company of Moro Scouts. On the following day, June 10th, about noon, Captain Taylor A. Nichols' 52d Company of Moro Scouts, and 1st Lieut. George P. Stallman, Medical Reserve Corps, with Hospital Corps detachments, were embarked at Siasi and the transport sailed for Jolo, arriving at 8:00 p.m., with lights out. Orders were at once issued directing the movements of troops. Company M, 8th Infantry, 1st Lieut. Robert W. Adams, 7th Infantry, commanding, with 1st Lieut. Leonard S. Hughes, Medical Corps, and 1st Lieut. Charles H. Halliday, Medical Reserve Corps, and Hospital Corps detachment, went aboard the *Wright*; the 29th Company, Philippine Scouts, 1st Lieut. George H.

Wright, Philippine Scouts, commanding, and 1st Lieut. Thomas F. Van
Natta's Mountain Gun Detachment, on the launch *Jewell*; the 40th Company, Philippine Scouts, 1st Lieut. Frank Sperbeck, Philippine Scouts,
commanding, and 2d Lieut. Carl F. McKinney's Mountain Gun Detachment, on the launch *Geary*; and Major George C. Shaw, Philippine Scouts,
his adjutant, 1st Lieut. Charles B. Townsend, and 1st Lieut. William W.
Gordon, Aide-de-camp, and the 21st Company, Philippine Scouts, Captain Robert Dickson, Philippine Scouts, commanding, on the launch
New Orleans. The two mountain guns and their ammunition were towed
in barges behind the launches carrying their respective detachments.
Captain Patrick Moylan, Philippine Scouts, with the 24th and 31st Companies, Philippine Scouts, was ordered to march overland to the south
slope of Bagsak, to arrive there about daybreak; and 1st Lieut. John T.
Sayles, 8th Cavalry, with fifty men of Troop H, 8th Cavalry, and pack
train, was ordered to proceed overland to Bun Bun. Although no previous warning had been given the troops, this movement was conducted so
quietly that no one outside of the walls of Jolo knew of it.

4. The following instructions and orders were issued concerning this
expedition:

U.S. Army Transport *Wright*
At Sea, June 10, 1913

From: The Adjutant, Jolo Field Forces.
To   The Commanding Officers of Columns
Subject: Instructions regarding Field Operations

I am directed by the Commanding General, Jolo Field Forces, to fur-
nish you with the following information and instructions for your guidance in connection with the operations of the troops under your command.

GENERAL INSTRUCTIONS: (1) The object of this movement is to
disarm, with as little loss of life as possible, those hostile Moros who
have refused to give up their arms.

(2) The wanton destruction of life or property will be severely
punished.

(3) Co-operation of the different columns will be absolutely necessary to insure success.

(4) Great care must be exercised to prevent troops firing into each other.

(5) The expenditure of ammunition, especially of the mountain
guns, should be carefully watched and controlled.

(6) All Cottas captured should be destroyed, if time permits.

(7) The general plan of attack as previously explained, will be carried out unless circumstances fully warrant modifications.

SPECIAL INSTRUCTIONS: Ammunition—Each man will carry 270 rounds. Rations—One day's rations, to include breakfast June 12, will be carried in the haversack. Equipment—Axes, lanterns, shovels, bolos, and machetes, will be carried by each organization. Signalling—Each column should have at least 4 men with it who can signal. Field message blanks will be carried.

Such orders will be issued by Column Commanders as will insure the carrying out of the above instructions.

JAMES L. COLLINS
2d Lieut. 8th Cavalry, A.D.C.

———

HEADQUARTERS, JOLO FIELD FORCES,
Bun Bun, Jolo, P.I.,
11 June, 1913—1 a.m.
Field Orders, No. 1.

1. The enemy occupy BAGSAK ridge.
2. This forces will attack at daybreak.
3. (a) Column No. 1 consisting of Company M, 8th Infantry, 40th Company, Philippine Scouts, and Mountain Gun Detachment, will attack LANGUASAN.

(b) Column No. 2 consisting of 29th, 51st, and 52d Companies, Philippine Scouts, and Mountain Gun Detachment, will attack PUY-ACABAO and MATUNKUP.

(c) Column No. 3, consisting of 24th and 31st Companies, Philippine Scouts, will hold south slope of BAGSAK.

(d) The reserve, consisting of 21st Company, Philippine Scouts, and 30 men, Troop H, 8th Cavalry, will be at BUN BUN.

4. A dressing station will be established at BUN BUN.
5. Messages will reach detachment commander at BUN BUN.

BY THE ORDER OF BRIGADIER GENERAL PERSHING:

JAMES L. COLLINS
2d Lieut. 8th Cavalry, A.D.C.
Adjutant

Copies to Column Commanders and Officer in Charge of Mountain Guns.

———

5. Arriving at Bun Bun about 3:30 a.m., June 11th, the troops were all disembarked and the columns moved out for the attack at 5:15 a.m. Major Shaw commanded the right column (No. 1) and Captain Nichols the left column (No. 2). So complete was the surprise that no resistance was encountered until 1200 yards from the Moro position, although Bud Bagsak is three and a half miles from the beach at Bun Bun.

6. For an understanding of this action, a description of the mountain is necessary. Bud Bagsak resembles a huge warped horseshoe, with one heel at Puyacabao, and the other at Bunga at about the same elevation. The Cotta, known as Bagsak Cotta, would be the toe, about 200 feet higher than either heel. Matunkup is on the north or warped side of the shoe and about midway between Puyacabao and the Bagsak Cotta. Languasan is a bald knoll and Pujagan a strong cotta, both having about the same elevation and corresponding to the frog and apex of the frog, respectively. The dimensions of this crater are about 800 by 1000 yards and its average elevation slightly more than 2000 feet. The sides of the mountain are very precipitous and for the most part heavily wooded.

7. At 7:15 a.m., the enemy opened fire on our columns at a range of about 1200 yards. Lieut. McKinney's mountain gun, attached to the right wing, directed its fire on Pujagan and Bunga, while Lieut. Van Natta's gun, attached to the left wing, began shelling Puyacabao. Instructions were given in person by my Adjutant, Lieutenant Collins, as to the exact time for each column to move forward to the attack.

These orders were well executed: Languasan was reached and taken by the right column at 12:00 Noon, and the left column captured Matunkup and Puyacabao at 12:20 p.m. These last two Moro positions commanded the inside of the crater, and were considered impregnable by the Moros. To take Matunkup the 51st Company found it necessary to scale a sheer cliff hand-over-hand on bejuco vines for a hundred feet or more. To capture Puyacabao, Captain Nichols marched the 52d and 29th Companies through heavy timber and dense undergrowth over the steep sides of the rim of the crater above Puyacabao, coming up from the inside of the crater at a commanding point, and completely surprising the garrison. The advance of Major Shaw's column toward Languasan was in the open and under fire from Matunkup, Puyacabao, Pujagan and Bunga. Three men were killed, and 1st Lieut. Edwin H. Rackley, Philippine Scouts, and seven men of the 51st Company, were wounded in storming Matunkup and afterwards reconnoitering the Bagsak Cotta. Two men were killed and five wounded in the capture of Languasan.

8. The capture of Puyacabao and Matunkup rendered untenable sev-

eral strong cottas in the interior of the crater, while, as above stated, the possession of Languasan closed the mouth of the crater and prevented the entrance of friends and families of the defenders. After the capture of this latter position, the Moros realized its importance and concentrated upon it their fire from Bunga, Pujagan, and Bagsak Cotta in an effort to dislodge our troops entrenched on its bald top.

The afternoon of June 11th was spent in strengthening the positions already taken, and in reconnoitering the ground in the vicinity of the remaining cottas. The 24th and 31st Companies, Philippine Scouts, which, under the command of Captain Moylan, had been used as a retaining force on the south slope of Bagsak, were ordered to report to Major Shaw on Languasan at daybreak on June 12th. A desultory fire was kept up all the night of the 11th by the hostile Moros.

9. The continued action of the mountain gun at Languasan and the rifle fire from Languasan, Matunkup and Puyacabao, soon rendered the positions at Pujagan and vicinity intolerable. Unable to stand the strain, the hostiles began, on the 11th, to attack our Languasan trenches by successive waves. The topography between Pujagan and Languasan was such that just after leaving their cottas on Pujagan, about 200 yards distant, their advancing lines were not visible until within about 50 yards from our trenches. These successive rushes were led by Amil himself, by his son, and by the two principal leaders. It was on Languasan that the gallant Captain Nichols was killed on the morning of the 12th.

10. After a careful reconnaissance by Lieut. Gordon, it was found that Bud Bunga offered the best position from which to reach the Bagsak Cotta with the fire of the mountain gun. It was also found to be impossible to reach the cotta at Bagsak along the narrow rim of the crater from Matunkup without severe losses. On the morning of June 13th, Captain Moylan was sent with the 24th and 31st Companies, Philippine Scouts, and Lieut. Van Natta's gun detachment around to the right to occupy the position on Bunga from which the mountain gun could shell Bagsak Cotta. Bud Bunga was difficult to reach as it was only accessible by two hog-backs, with sheer precipitous sides. The mountain gun had to be taken apart and a whole company detailed to carry and haul it up the hill. The cotta on top of this hill was assaulted about 1:30 p.m., the casualties being one Scout soldier killed and one wounded.

11. On the morning of the 14th, at daybreak, the 51st and 52d Companies, Moro Scouts, and the Cavalry detachment, were sent to reconnoiter the rim of the crater between Bunga and Bagsak with a view to effecting a lodgment from which the final attack could be made upon this last and

strongest position, the Bagsak Cotta. These companies obtained a favorable position on the south slope of the hill and about 600 yards from the Cotta. The Moro position on the Bagsak slope consisted of a succession of standing trenches connected with each other and protected by heavy logs and earth.

12. Day broke on June 15th, with Bud Bagsak hidden by a heavy fog, and it was not until about 7:30 a.m., that the mist cleared. At that hour, the mountain gun on Bunga resumed its work of the previous day and prepared for the final infantry attack. At 9:00 a.m., Captain Charlton with the 51st and 52d Companies, Philippine Scouts, advanced. The attack was so effectively covered by the shrapnel fire from Lieut. Van Natta's gun on Bunga and the small arms fire of the 24th and 31st Companies, Philippine Scouts, in trenches on knoll south of Bagsak, that we had no casualties until the first trench was reached. The advance from the first trench up to the main position occupied some hours of fierce fighting. It was characterized by ferocious, fanatical counter attacks by groups of Moros. The resistance was very tenacious. Without decision, coolness, and control on the part of the officers, our losses would have been several times what they were. The actual losses in attacking Bagsak Cotta were 6 killed and 13 wounded.

13. A number of hostile Moros escaped, and most of the others could have escaped, especially from their final position, had they so desired. Many of those who got away have quietly returned to their homes, while others who persisted in crime have been hunted down. The total Moro losses are not known, but from Moro sources it is estimated that the number of defenders in these various positions was from three to five hundred.

14. Without exception the troops behaved splendidly throughout this action. Too much can hardly be said in praise of the gallantry of both the Moro and Philippine Scouts, under white leadership, in the final assault. In separate communications, I have forwarded approved recommendations for Medal of Honor in the case of 2d Lieut. Louis C. Mosher,[1] Philippine Scouts, and for Certificates of Merit in the cases of Corpl. Dimasangka and Private Bandira, 51st Company, Philippine Scouts, and Private Thomas Moseley, Hospital Corps. I also desire to recommend that the names of Captains Taylor A. Nichols, deceased, and Captain George C. Charlton and 1st Lieutenant Edwin H. Rackley, of Philippine Scouts, be mentioned in orders for distinguished gallantry in action in attack on Bud Bagsak on June 11, 1913. The 51st and 52d Companies, (Moro), Philippine Scouts, bore the brunt of the fighting on the last day

and the success of the movements on the first day was largely due to the brilliant leadership and distinguished gallantry of the officers of these two companies.

JOHN J. PERSHING

Source: Library of Congress, Pershing Papers, Box 371, Folder: Governor of Moro Province (5).

Appendix J

Pershing's Memorandum on the Carrizal Affair (Undated)

1. This report of the investigation made by Lieutenant Colonel George O. Cress, Inspector General's Department, of the encounter between Troops C and K, 10th Cavalry, under Captain William T. [Charles T.] Boyd, and Mexican troops of the de facto government, under Lieutenant Colonel Rivas, at Carrizal June 21, 1916, is very full and complete. Every phase of the occurrence has been covered and doubtful points cleared up as far as it seems possible to do so.

2. Attention should first be invited to the fact that this expedition having entered Mexico in pursuit of bandits, through the courtesy of the Mexican government, the de facto forces, in firing on our troops under these circumstances, committed a deliberate act of war. In declaring, through the military commander at Chihuahua, that the American forces were to be attacked under certain conditions, the Mexican government accentuated its own responsibility in the premises. So serious were the consequences believed to be that many did not think the de facto troops would risk committing such an overt act. Possibly this view may have had its effect upon Captain Boyd's mind, although there is no evidence to indicate that the thought ever occurred to him. Whether or not this be true, and regardless of Captain Boyd's attitude, the Mexican government itself was entirely responsible for the opposition offered to Captain Boyd's progress and, finally, for the culminating act of open hostility to the United States which started the fight at Carrizal.

3. With reference to Captain Boyd's action, I had known him a number of years, although not intimately, and considered him a capable and cautious officer who would faithfully carry out any orders he might receive. In giving him instructions regarding this reconnaissance, I told

him, among other things, that the Mexican situation was very tense, and that a clash with Mexican troops would probably bring on war and for this reason was to be avoided. I pointed out to him that the country to the east was uninhabited and that he might have to go as far as Santo Domingo Ranch, a distance of about sixty-five miles, to get reliable information regarding the Mexican forces. I told him that at such a distance, should he clash with de facto troops, it would be impossible for me to support him. After my conversation with him, I felt confident that Captain Boyd fully understood the importance and delicacy of his mission. No one could have been more surprised or chagrined than I was to learn that he had become so seriously involved.

4. Due to failure of our aeroplanes, and the impossibility of verifying through native or other reliable sources the reported presence in the vicinity of Ahumada of 8,000 to 10,000 de facto troops, who had threatened to move against our line of communications, there was no other recourse than to send cavalry to reconnoiter in that direction. The hostile de facto commands at Ahumada and Carrizal were in a very advantageous position from which to strike our line at either Dublan or El Valle before we could concentrate at either place to meet them, unless by obtaining timely information we could anticipate their intentions. Under similar circumstances it had been necessary on several previous occasions to send cavalry as far as ninety miles away.

5. In view of the detailed instructions given Captain Boyd, the reasons for his action remain more or less a mystery. His decision to push on through Carrizal can be explained only on the hypothesis that, for some reason or other, he thought the Mexican troops would not fight, or that if they did fight he could easily brush them aside. In this view he was probably largely influenced by Lieutenant Adair's opinion. But it is even more difficult to comprehend why, after reaching the outskirts of Carrizal and talking with General Gomez, and seeing the large number of Mexican troops moving into position in his front and toward his flanks, Captain Boyd should have still adhered to his determination to go on. He surely must have seen that he was outnumbered and, if he thought there was going to be a fight, he could hardly have failed to foresee the dire consequences to his command in case of defeat. As to his mission, Captain Boyd had already obtained at Santo Domingo Ranch the information sought. Captain Morey had pointed out that his own orders did not contemplate going to any place occupied by de facto troops.

6. Arriving immediately in front of the Mexican position, his own

command in an open plain, with mounted Mexican troops on his flanks within close range, it was a serious error to start a fight at all, but especially was it fatal to dismount to fight on foot under such disadvantage. Even though Captain Boyd had been directed to fight his way through to Ahumada, he would not have been in any way justified in deploying at such close range and engaging such a vastly superior force, occupying such a strong defensive position. But every circumstance, from the time he arrived at Santo Domingo Ranch, up to the time he gave the command to fight on foot, including the note he wrote while there reporting that he had been to Ahumada and was on his way back, point to the conclusion that in Captain Boyd's mind there was slight probability of a fight.

7. As to the conduct of the fight, there is little that can be said in approval. The deployment was made very near the enemy's lines without cover or protection of any sort, and, under the orders given, the two troops from the start advanced along divergent lines. The right flank under Captain Morey, soon left in the air, was partially surrounded and turned, and, Morey being wounded together with several others, that part of the line gave way, broke and scattered. Boyd's own troop, urged on by himself and the dashing Adair, pressed forward into the town, but was itself soon decimated, several of its numbers were captured, and the attack failed.

8. The troopers in charge of the lead horses were left, in the first instance, in an impossible position. Later, after the fight started, they were ordered further to the rear, receiving a rather heavy fire during this movement, and, having no responsible person in charge, the horses became stampeded and the horseholders never recovered anything like an organized formation. The scattered groups of horseholders, pursued by superior forces of Mexicans, could hardly be expected to assemble. Under the circumstances, unfortunate as they were, it is not believed that any disciplinary action is indicated as advisable. There is no reliable evidence obtainable to sustain charges against any individual or group of these men for their conduct.

9. Notwithstanding the disaster resulting from this encounter, it must be said to the credit of this little body of men that they fought well as long as their officers remained alive to lead them and for some time after. The Mexican casualties were forty-two killed and fifty-one wounded, and thirty-seven horses killed. If Captain Boyd's force could have maintained cohesion among its parts, the results would probably have been far different. Too much praise cannot be given Boyd, and

Adair for personal courage in their gallant fight against overwhelming odds in which both died, like the brave American soldiers they were.

John J. Pershing

Source: Library of Congress, Pershing Papers, Box 372, Folder: Punitive Expedition Reports (1).

Biographical Appendix

The biographical sketches of all graduates of the U.S. Military Academy are heavily based on their personal entries in the various volumes of the *Biographical Register of the Officers and Graduates of the U.S. Military Academy at West Point, New York, Since Its Establishment in 1802*, cited under the names of the individual editors. The works are commonly known as "Cullum's Registers" because Brevet Major General George W. Cullum compiled the initial volumes for the Association of Graduates (AOG) of the U.S. Military Academy. The first three volumes covered the period to January 1879 and were published that year. Beginning with the class of 1802, Cullum listed each graduate in their rank order of graduation and assigned a sequential number, the Cullum's number, by which the graduate was then listed in each succeeding volume and in any obituaries that were later published. Cullum then revised and updated the original volumes and in 1891 published three volumes according to graduation numbers through the Class of 1890. Each volume after this set was titled a "Supplement" and covered a decade. The last supplement to the *Biographical Register,* vol. 9, was published in 1955 and covered the years 1940–1950. Rather than annotate each biography with traditional note citations to volume and page for each USMA graduate, I have chosen to refer the reader to these volumes in the bibliography because most of the detailed biographical information was drawn from that person's entry in the respective volumes. Each graduate submitted the personal information contained in the individual entries, and thus the entries are considered to be the most accurate information available on their careers. Obituaries of graduates appeared regularly in the AOG's *Annual Reunion of the Association of Graduates* (1870–1916), *Annual Report of the Association of Graduates* (1917–1941), and *Assembly* (1942–present), although there is not an obituary for every graduate. Other sources used in drafting the biographical sketches, including these obituaries, are cited.

Henry R. Adair (13 April 1882–21 June 1916). Adair graduated from the U.S. Military Academy (USMA) in June 1904 and was commissioned in the 10th Cavalry. He served at Fort Robinson, Nebraska (1904–1907), and then in the Philippines at Fort McKinley until May 1909. He was with the 10th at Fort Ethan Allen, Vermont (1909–1911), before attending the Mounted Service School at Fort Riley, Kansas (1911–1912). He returned to Fort Ethan Allen until December 1913, when the 10th Cavalry was transferred to Fort Huachuca, Arizona, for duty on the Mexican border. Adair then completed the Mounted Service School course (1914–1915) before returning to duty with his troop in Arizona. He was with the 10th Cavalry as part of the Mexican Expedition and assigned to Troop C under Captain Charles T. Boyd (23 May) until he was killed in action at Carrizal, Chihuahua, Mexico, on 21 June. "Henry Rodney Adair,"

Forty-Eighth Annual Report of the Association of Graduates of the United States Military Academy at West Point, New York, June 12, 1917 (Saginaw, Mich.: Seemann and Peters, Printers and Binders, 1917), pp. 44–46.

Emil Adam (20 February 1831–17 January 1903). Born in Germany, Adam came to the United States as a child and grew up in Alton, Illinois. He served as an officer in the Illinois volunteer infantry from April 1861 until he was mustered out in July 1865 as a major, U.S. Volunteers (USV). Adam was appointed first lieutenant and captain in the 39th Infantry in 1867 and then joined the 5th Cavalry in Nebraska and in Arizona (1870–1872). He was frequently in action against the Indians in Arizona from 1872 to 1875, where he served under Colonel George Crook. He later participated in the Sioux campaign of 1876–1877, against the Nez Percé in 1877, and then against the Utes in 1879. He rose to major in June 1886 when assigned to the 6th Cavalry in New Mexico and commanded the post at Fort Stanton. Adam led his troops during the Pine Ridge expedition of November 1890–January 1891, including Pershing's troop. He retired at his own request in March 1893. Adam is also referred to erroneously in various official documents as "Emil Adams." U.S. War Department, The Adjutant General's Office (hereafter cited as TAGO), *Official Army Register for 1901* (Washington, D.C.: GPO, 1 December 1900) (hereafter cited as TAGO, *OAR,* and annual edition), pp. 285, 374; TAGO, *OAR, 1904,* p. 524; "Emil Adam (Major 6th Cav.)," in Major William H. Powell, *Powell's Records of Living Officers of the United States Army* (Philadelphia: L. R. Hamersly, 1890) (hereafter cited as *Powell's Records*), pp. 11–12; Dan L. Thrapp, *The Conquest of Apacheria* (Norman: Univ. of Oklahoma Press, 1967), pp. 121–23.

Robert W. Adams (28 April 1875–27 August 1918). Adams served as a private in the 21st Infantry and 2d Battalion of Engineers (September 1899–November 1901). He was commissioned a second lieutenant in the 13th Infantry in November 1901 and then transferred to the 8th Infantry in April 1902. He later served with the 2d Infantry (1904–1905) until he was promoted to first lieutenant with the 9th Infantry in August 1905. He transferred to the 7th Infantry in May 1913. On 2 March 1916 Adams was dropped from the rolls of the Army for being absent without leave for three months. As it turns out, Adams went to Canada where he enlisted in the Canadian Army and was sent to France. He served there until 27 August 1918 when he was killed in action. Heitman, *Historical Register*, vol. 1, p. 153; *Washington Times*, 6 March 1918, p. 4; *Washington Herald*, 8 April 1916, p. 8; TAGO, *OAR, 1915*, p. 335, and *OAR, 1918*, p. 1126; "Robert Walpole Adams," at Commonwealth War Graves Commission, http://www.cwgc.org/find-the-dead/casualty/249903/Adams, Robert Walpole.

Fred C. Ainsworth (11 September 1852–5 June 1934). Ainsworth completed his medical training at the University of the City of New York (now New York University) and received his M.D. in 1874. He joined the Army Medical Department in November and was stationed in Alaska and the Southwest. In 1886 he was placed in charge of the army Surgeon General's Record and Pension Division, which was then seriously mismanaged. He introduced a card-index filing system that completely revolutionized the division's organization and services. Because he cleaned up the lingering and politically troublesome Civil War pension mess, he soon became a great favorite of thousands of veterans and their families—and of many in Congress, who now had happy constituents. One of his primary projects during these years was the compilation and publication of the 128 volumes of *The War of the Rebellion: A Compilation of the Official Records of the Union and Confederate Armies* (1880–1901). In 1889 Ainsworth's division was transferred to the War Department and assumed some functions of the Adjutant General's Office, especially in the area of records and personnel management. He accepted a commission in the Regular line rather than continue in the Medical Department, and in May 1892 he was promoted to colonel and chief of the Record and Pension Office. He was promoted to brigadier general in 1899 and replaced Corbin as Army Adjutant General in April 1904 with the rank of major general. Like Corbin, Ainsworth exercised great influence in the War Department, at least partly due to his strong support in Congress. He was not in favor of the chief of staff and General Staff reforms of Root because it diminished the authority and power of his office. In 1910 he fought and lost a bitter contest with another former Army Medical Department physician turned line officer, Leonard Wood, for the post of chief of staff. His ongoing squabble with Wood brought the Secretary of War, Henry L. Stimson, to suspend Ainsworth from duty in February 1912 and charge him with insubordination. Ainsworth opted to retire on 16 February 1912 rather than face a court-martial. "Fred Crayton Ainsworth," *Who Was Who in American History–The Military* (Chicago: Marquis Who's Who, 1975) (hereafter cited as *Who Was Who–The Military*), p. 4; "Frederick Crayton Ainsworth," *Webster's American Military Biographies* (Springfield, Mass.: G. and C. Merriam, 1978), p. 2.

Henry T. Allen (13 April 1859–30 August 1930). Allen graduated from the USMA in June 1882 and was commissioned in the 2d Cavalry. He served in Montana, Washington, Alaska, and Idaho (1882–1888). He then served as military attaché in Russia (1888–1893) and Sweden (April–May 1893). He returned to regimental duty at Fort Riley, Kansas (1893–1895), before he was sent to Germany as military attaché (1895–1898). He rejoined the 2d Cavalry in June 1898 to command Troop D throughout the Santiago Campaign, but was evacuated to the United States ill with yellow fever and typhoid in July. In August 1899 he was appointed major, 43d U.S. Volunteer Infantry, and went to the Philippines. There his achievements on Samar (January–July 1900) and Leyte until July 1901 were such that he was then assigned to organize the Philippine Constabulary, the paramilitary national police force under the civilian governor-general. He was appointed brigadier general (a special Constabulary rank and not a military rank) and chief of the Constabulary in January 1903 and held that post until June 1907, when he returned to the United States. After service with the General Staff (1910–1914) he joined the 11th Cavalry (1914–1916) and served in the Mexican Expedition under Pershing (1916–1917). He commanded Fort Riley and a cavalry brigade and was promoted to brigadier general in May 1917. Promoted to major general, National Army (NA), in August 1917, Allen commanded the 90th Division in the United States and was with the AEF in France (August 1917–November 1918). He commanded the VIII Corps (1918–1919) and then the American Forces in Germany (1919–1923) during the occupation of the Rhineland. He was promoted to major general in July 1920 and retired on 23 April 1923. Allen published two books on his experience in the occupation: *My Rhineland Journal* (1923) and *The Rhineland Occupation* (1925). "Henry Tureman Allen," *Sixty-Second Annual Report of the Association of Graduates of the United States Military Academy at West Point, New*

York, June 10, 1931 (Chicago: R. R. Donnelley and Sons, 1931), pp. 183–92; "Henry Tureman Allen (1859–1930)," *Webster's American Military Biographies,* pp. 4–5; Heath Twitchell Jr., *Allen: The Biography of an Army Officer, 1859-1930* (New Brunswick, N.J.: Rutgers Univ. Press, 1974).

John H. Allen (20 October 1873–3 December 1940). Allen received his medical degree from Columbian University (now George Washington University) in Washington, D.C., in 1899. After serving as a contract surgeon early in 1901, he was commissioned in the Medical Corps on 29 June 1901. He served in the Philippines and on Mindanao. He was promoted to captain in June 1906 and major in January 1910. With America's entry into World War I, Allen was promoted to lieutenant colonel in May 1917 and assigned as camp surgeon at Camp Zachery Taylor, Kentucky, and division surgeon, 84th Division. He was appointed colonel, NA, in December 1917 and was discharged in January 1920. He served as an instructor with the Tennessee National Guard (1919–1922) and with the Illinois National Guard later. In June 1927 he was promoted to colonel. TAGO, *OAR, 1938,* p. 837; TAGO, *OAR, 1941,* p. 1257; "Medical Mobilization and the War," *Journal of the American Medical Association* (hereafter cited as *JAMA*) 69, no. 10 (8 September 1917), p. 832; "Eighty-Fourth Division, Camp Zachery Taylor, Louisville, Ky.," *JAMA* 70, no. 11 (16 March 1918), p. 785; "Lincoln Division (Eighty-Fourth), Camp Zachery Taylor, Louisville, Ky.," *JAMA* 70, no. 20 (18 May 1918), p. 1472.

Avery D. Andrews (4 April 1864–19 April 1959). Andrews graduated with Pershing from the USMA in 1886 and was commissioned in the 5th Artillery. On 27 September 1888 he married Mary Campbell Schofield, the daughter of Major General John M. Schofield, just appointed commanding general of the army in August 1888 upon Phil Sheridan's death and the former commander of the Division of the Atlantic. Andrews was on special duty at Headquarters, War Department, in Washington in 1889 before becoming aide-de-camp to Schofield (1889–1892). While serving as aide, Andrews completed law degrees at Columbian University (now George Washington University) in Washington in 1891 and at New York Law School in 1892. He resigned his commission in 1893 and practiced law in New York (1893–1895) prior to his appointment as a police commissioner in New York City under Theodore Roosevelt (1895–1898). During this time he also served in the New York State National Guard. He was appointed lieutenant colonel and quartermaster, USV, in May 1898 and was chief quartermaster of 1st Division, I Army Corps (May–July 1898) at Chickamauga Park, Georgia, and then served on the staff of Major General James H. Wilson (August 1898). When Roosevelt became governor of New York, Andrews acted as his chief of staff as well as state adjutant general with the rank of brigadier general, New York National Guard. In January 1900, he returned to his business pursuits as Roosevelt prepared to become vice president. After the American entrance into World War I, he was appointed colonel of engineers, NA, in October 1917 and sailed for France in November. He served as deputy director general of transportation for the AEF, as a member of the Inter-Allied Committee of the Supreme War Council, and as deputy chief of utilities for the AEF until July 1918, when he became deputy assistant chief of staff, G-4, Headquarters, Service of Supply. In late July he was assigned to the First Section, General Headquarters, AEF (GHQ AEF), and appointed assistant chief of staff, G-1 (Personnel), until April 1919. He was promoted to brigadier general, General Staff, in October 1918 and returned to the United States in May 1919 and was discharged, returning to New York City. In 1939 he published a book entitled *My Friend and Classmate, John J. Pershing with Notes from My War Diary* (Harrisburg, Pa.: Military Service Publishing Company, 1939). "Avery DeLano Andrews," *Assembly* 18, no. 3 (fall 1959), p. 70; "Avery DeLano Andrews," *Who Was Who in America*, vol. 3, *1951-1960* (Chicago: Marquis Who's Who, 1966) (hereafter cited as *Who Was Who*, volume and years covered), p. 28.

George L. Andrews (31 August 1828–4 April 1899). Andrews graduated from the USMA in 1851 and was commissioned in the Corps of Engineers. After serving three years under Colonel Sylvanus Thayer in construction of coastal fortifications in Boston harbor, he was transferred to West Point as assistant professor of civil and military engineering. He resigned in 1855 and worked as a civilian assistant engineer in the Corps of Engineers (1857–1860). On the outbreak of the Civil War, he was commissioned a lieutenant colonel in the 2d Massachusetts Volunteer Infantry and soon took command of it during the 1862 campaign in the Shenandoah Valley and then at Antietam on 17 September 1862. He was promoted to brigadier general, USV, in November 1862 and served as chief of staff to Major General Nathaniel P. Banks, commander, Department of the Gulf (1863–1864). After serving as U.S. Marshal for Massachusetts (1867–1871), in February 1871 President Grant appointed Andrews as professor of French at the Military Academy. In 1882 he became professor of modern languages and headed that department until he retired in August 1892. "George Leonard Andrews," *Twenty-Ninth Annual Reunion of the Association of Graduates, United States Military Academy, West Point, New York, June 9, 1898* (Saginaw, Mich.: Seemann and Peters, Printers and Binders, 1900), pp. 21–28.

William H. Arthur (1 August 1856–19 April 1936). Arthur received his medical education at the University of Maryland in Baltimore (M.D., 1877). He was appointed lieutenant and assistant surgeon, U.S. Army, in February 1881. He served in Wyoming, Utah, Arizona, and New Mexico (1881–1892), including Fort Bayard with Pershing (1888–1890). After the outbreak of the war with Spain, in June 1898 he was charged with converting a former freight and cattle ship, the *Missouri*, into an army hospital ship. He completed this arduous task in August and then commanded the *Missouri*, which carried sick soldiers from Cuba and Puerto Rico back to Montauk Point, Long Island, until February 1899. In 1899, the *Missouri* was refitted in Brooklyn, New York, and was then dispatched to Manila via the Suez Canal, and carried John Pershing among others to the Philippines. Having reached San Francisco with the *Missouri* in August 1900, Arthur was dispatched to the China Relief Expedition, where he served under Adna Chaffee as brigade surgeon at Tientsin. He then commanded the hospital at Beijing until he was reassigned to Manila, where he commanded the First Reserve Hospital (1900–1902). He was surgeon at the Soldiers' Home in Washington, D.C. (1902–1907), and then commanded the General Hospital at Washington Barracks (1907–1909). When that hospital closed and reopened as the new Walter Reed General Hospital in Takoma Park, Maryland, Arthur was appointed its first commander (1909–1911). Another tour in the Philippines followed as the department surgeon (1911–1914). Arthur was then commandant of the Army

Medical School in Washington (1915–1918). He was promoted to brigadier general, NA, in August 1917 and served until November 1918, when he was discharged and retired for age the next month. Arthur was returned to the rank of brigadier general by the act of 21 June 1930. Colonel Harold W. Jones, "Brigadier General William H. Arthur (1856–1936)," *Army Medical Bulletin*, no. 68 (July 1943), pp. 218–26; "William Hemple Arthur," *Who Was Who–The Military*, p. 16; TAGO, *OAR, 1916*, p. 41; TAGO, *OAR, 1931*, p. 764.

William J. Ayers (22 May 1873–12 April 1950). Ayers served as a private, corporal, sergeant, and first sergeant in the 6th Infantry (May 1894–May 1902) and then in the 6th and 18th Infantry Regiments (June 1902–March 1905). He was appointed a second lieutenant in the Philippine Scouts in March 1905, a first lieutenant in September 1908, and captain in September 1911. He resigned from the Scouts in January 1914 and was made a captain, retired, Philippine Scouts, in June 1916. He was later awarded a Purple Heart for wounds received in action. TAGO, *OAR, 1913*, p. 428; TAGO, *OAR, 1951*, vol. 1, p. 860.

Chauncey B. Baker (26 August 1860–18 October 1936). Baker graduated from the USMA with Pershing in 1886 and was commissioned in the 7th Infantry. He completed the Infantry and Cavalry School of Application (1887–1889) and was an assistant instructor at the school until June 1890, when he became aide-de-camp to Brigadier General Alexander McCook, former commander of Fort Leavenworth and the Infantry and Cavalry School and newly appointed commanding general of the Department of Arizona. Baker married McCook's daughter, Lucy, on 19 June 1889 and remained McCook's aide in Los Angeles (1890–1893) and also at the Department of Colorado until April 1895. He was chief quartermaster for the 2d Division, VII Corps, at Jacksonville, Florida, in 1898. He was chief quartermaster, Department of Cuba (1900–1902), and was then on duty at the Office of the Chief Quartermaster in Washington until 1906. He returned to Havana as chief quartermaster, Army of Cuban Pacification (1906–1909), and later served two more tours in the Office of the Quartermaster General (1912–1914, 1914–1916). He was promoted to colonel and quartermaster in May 1917 and was the senior member of the U.S. Military Commission sent to Great Britain, Belgium, and France (May–August 1917) upon America's entry into the war. In August he was made brigadier general, Quartermaster Corps, NA, and was chief of the Embarkation Service, Office of the Chief Quartermaster (1917–1918). He was then department quartermaster, Central Department, in Chicago (1918–1920) and corps area quartermaster, Sixth Corps Area (1920–1921). He retired as a colonel, U.S. Army, on 22 April 1921 and was promoted to brigadier general, U.S. Army, on the retired list on 21 June 1930. "Chauncey B. Baker," *Sixty-Eighth Annual Report of the Association of Graduates of the United States Military Academy at West Point, New York, June 11, 1937* (Newburgh, N.Y.: Moore Printing Company, 1937), pp. 128–31; "Chauncey Brooke Baker," in Henry Blaine Davis Jr., *Generals in Khaki* (Raleigh, N.C.: Pentland Press, 1998), p. 18.

Frank D. Baldwin (28 June 1842–22 April 1923). Baldwin grew up in Michigan and completed Hillsdale College but did not graduate because of the Civil War. He served as an officer in Michigan volunteer units and saw action in the Atlanta and Carolina campaigns under Sherman and was mustered out in June 1865. On 3 December 1891 he was awarded the first of his two Medals of Honor, this one for his heroism in the Battle of Peach Tree Creek, Georgia, on 20 July 1864. He joined the 19th Infantry in 1866 and moved to the 5th Infantry in 1869. He spent the next thirty years in that regiment, but his most important time was under Colonel Nelson A. Miles until Miles left the 5th in December 1880. Baldwin was very much one of Miles's men, and even his later assignments often found him serving with Miles. He distinguished himself in numerous campaigns against various Indian tribes on the frontier and especially with Miles in the Red River campaign (1874–1875) and the operations against the Sioux in the Yellowstone area (1876–1877). He remained with Miles in staff capacities in the Yellowstone District (1877–1880), all the while actively engaged in field operations in Wyoming and Montana. He later served under Miles at the Division of the Missouri and its successor, the Department of the Missouri (1891–1894), and as the Indian agent at Anadarko, Oklahoma (1894–1898). On 28 November 1894, he received his second Medal of Honor for his conspicuous gallantry in action and leadership in routing hostile Indians at McClellan's Creek, Texas, on 8 November 1874. He was appointed inspector general, III and I Army Corps, from May 1898 until he was sent to Cuba in early 1899 with I Army Corps as the inspector general for the Department of Mantanzas and Santa Clara. Baldwin was promoted to lieutenant colonel, 4th Infantry, in December 1899, and was sent to the Philippines, where he took command for active field operations. He was promoted to colonel and commander of the 27th Infantry Regiment on 26 July 1900. While commanding the 27th Infantry he led the first expedition against the Moros that successfully reached the south shore of Lake Lanao, Mindanao, and largely destroyed the Bayan Moros in the battle at Bayan on 2–3 May 1902. Promoted to brigadier general in June 1902, he commanded the Department of the Visayas in the Philippines (1902–1903) before returning to the United States to command the Department of Colorado (1903–1905), the Southwestern Division (1905–1906), and the Department of Colorado again until his retirement on 26 June 1906. TAGO, *OAR, 1901*, pp. 137, 358, 387; TAGO, *OAR, 1920*, p. 907; TAGO, *Medals of Honor Issued by the War Department up to and Including October 31, 1897* (Washington, D.C.: GPO, 1897) (hereafter cited as *Medals of Honor to October 31, 1897*), p. 16; *Annual Reports of the War Department for the Fiscal Year Ending June 30, 1899* (Washington, D.C.: GPO, 1899) (hereafter cited as *ARWD*, year, volume, and part), vol. 1, pp. 140, 428, 465, 499, 501; *ARWD, 1900*, vol. 1, p. 167; *ARWD, 1902*, vol. 9, pp. 177–78, 475–517, 567–73; "Frank Dwight Baldwin," *Who Was Who–The Military*, p. 26; Francis B. Heitman, *Historical Register and Dictionary of the United States Army from Its Organization, September 29, 1789, to March 2, 1903* (Washington, D.C.: GPO, 1903) (hereafter cited as Heitman, *Historical Register*, and volume), vol. 1, pp. 82, 87–88, 90, 127, 185–86; "Frank Dwight Baldwin," in *The National Cyclopaedia of American Biography*, vol. 14, supplement 1 (New York: James T. White, 1910), pp. 339–40; "Frank D. Baldwin," *Powell's Records*, pp. 35–36; "Memorandum: Military Geographical Divisions and Departments and Their Commanders, January 1, 1898, to December 31, 1905," addendum in Raphael P. Thian, *Notes Illustrating the Military Geography of the United States, 1813-1880* (Austin: Univ. of Texas Press, 1979) (hereafter cited as Thian, *Notes*), pp. 189–91, 199.

Theodore A. Baldwin (31 December 1839–1 September 1925). During the Civil War Baldwin served as a private and quartermaster sergeant in the 19th Infantry (May 1862–May 1865). He was commissioned a first lieutenant in May 1865 and remained in the army after the war. He was assigned to the 10th Cavalry in 1870 and served with it at various posts on the frontier. He was promoted to major with the 7th Cavalry in 1887, but returned to the 10th Cavalry as lieutenant colonel and battalion commander in 1896 and served with the regiment in Cuba in 1898. He was appointed brigadier general, USV, in October 1898 after assuming command of the dismounted cavalry division, V Corps, from Major General Joseph Wheeler. He was mustered out of the Volunteers in 1899 and was appointed colonel and commander, 7th Cavalry, in May. Baldwin was promoted to brigadier general on 19 April 1903 and retired the next day. TAGO, *OAR, 1916,* p. 545; "Theodore A. Baldwin (Major 7th Cav.)," *Powell's Records,* p. 36; "Theodore A. Baldwin," *Who Was Who–The Military,* p. 26.

Harry H. Bandholtz (18 December 1864–7 May 1925). Bandholtz graduated from the USMA in June 1890 and was commissioned in the 6th Infantry. He served in Cuba with the 7th Infantry at the battle of El Caney (1 July 1898) and at San Juan Heights. He later served in the Philippines (1900–1903). He was appointed colonel and assistant chief, Philippine Constabulary, under Henry Allen in April 1903 and commanded the 1st and 2d districts in Luzon (1903–1907). He succeeded Allen as brigadier general and chief of the Philippine Constabulary (1907–1913) and oversaw the end of most rebellious activities outside of the Moro areas. He commanded a battalion of the 30th Infantry and was on the Mexican border in June 1916. He was chief of staff, New York National Guard Division, on the border and then senior inspector of the New York National Guard in New York City (1916–1917). He was chief of staff, 27th Division (New York National Guard) (1917–1918) and was appointed brigadier general, NA, in December 1917. He commanded the 58th Infantry Brigade, 29th Division, in the United States (February–June 1918) and France, where it saw extensive action (June–September 1918). Bandholtz was appointed as provost marshal general, AEF (1918–1919). He was the U.S. military representative on the Allied military mission to Hungary in 1919 and U.S. commissioner in Hungary (1919–1920). He was assigned to the Office of the Chief of Staff from March 1920 until he was promoted to brigadier general in July and commanded the 13th Infantry Brigade at Fort Riley and Camp Meade, Maryland, until August 1921. He then commanded the Military District of Washington until he was promoted to major general, U.S. Army, and retired for disability on 4 November 1923. "Harry Hill Bandholtz," *Fifty-Ninth Annual Report of the Association of Graduates of the United States Military Academy at West Point, New York, June 8, 1928* (Saginaw, Mich.: Seemann and Peters, Printers and Binders, 1929), pp. 39–43.

John W. Barker (25 December 1872–14 May 1924). Barker graduated from the USMA in June 1894. He took part with the 3d Infantry in the Santiago Campaign in Cuba, including the battle for El Caney on 1 July 1898. He went to the Philippines with his regiment and served against the insurgents (1899–1902). He later completed the Army School of the Line (1908–1909) and then the Army War College (1909–1910). He was reassigned to the 3d Infantry and joined it in the Philippines in November 1911. He was involved in Pershing's campaigns against the Moros on Jolo Island and Mindanao (November 1911–January 1912) and was severely wounded in action at Mount Dajo, Mindanao, on 25 December 1911. After hospitalization, he rejoined his regiment at Madison Barracks, New York (1912–1914). A skilled French linguist with a French wife, Barker was assigned to serve with a French infantry regiment and study French infantry tactics, but the outbreak of the war in August 1914 found Barker in France with no assignment. He reported to the U.S. ambassador and was assigned as the U.S. military attaché and observer with the French Army (1914–1917). The French allowed Barker access to the front, which was very beneficial to U.S. interests. With the arrival of Pershing in June 1917, Barker was assigned to the AEF headquarters (1917–1918). He commanded the 165th Infantry, 42d Division, in operations against the Germans (January–May 1918). He was returned to the United States in June as a member of the General Staff Corps (1918–1919), serving as a brigadier general, NA, and then with the Adjutant General's Office (1919–1920). He retired at his own request as a lieutenant colonel in June 1920. He died in New York City on 14 May 1924. He was posthumously advanced to the rank of brigadier general, U.S. Army retired, by the Act of 21 June 1930. "John William Barker," *Sixty-first Annual Report of the Association of Graduates of the United States Military Academy at West Point, New York, June 11, 1930* (Newburgh, N.Y.: Moore Printing Company, 1930), pp. 239–42.

Malvern Hill Barnum (3 September 1863–18 February 1942). Major General Henry A. Barnum (24 September 1833–29 January 1892), USV, had a distinguished record of service as a regimental and corps commander in the Union army during the Civil War, including receiving a Medal of Honor (awarded July 1889) for his leadership at Lookout Mountain on 23 November 1863. When his son was born on 3 September 1863, then Colonel Barnum chose to name him after the Battle of Malvern Hill, Virginia, during the Seven Days' Battles of the Peninsular campaign, where he was severely wounded in the hip on 1 July. As a cadet at the USMA, Malvern Hill Barnum's nickname was naturally "P.T.," after the famous showman of the day. Barnum graduated with John Pershing in June 1886 and was commissioned in the 3d Cavalry. He was on frontier duty in Texas (1886–1891) before transferring to the 10th Cavalry in 1894 and serving as the regimental adjutant (1895–1898) under Guy V. Henry at Fort Assinniboine. He was with the 10th Cavalry in Cuba during the Santiago Campaign and was seriously wounded in the hip on 2 July at San Juan Hill. After recovering, he was assigned to the Military Academy (1899–1902). In 1905 he was sent to Fort McKinley, Luzon, as post quartermaster and also assigned as aide-de-camp to Major General John F. Weston, commanding the Department of Luzon and then the Philippines Division (1906–1908). He completed the Army War College in Washington, D.C. (1914–1915). He was then assigned to the 3d Cavalry at Fort Sam Houston, Texas (July–November 1915), where he was appointed chief of staff, Southern Department, under Frederick Funston and then John Pershing (1915–1917). On 31 October 1917, he was appointed brigadier general, NA, and assigned to command the African American 183d Infantry Brigade at Camp Grant, Illinois (1917–1918). He took the brigade to France, where it served as part of the 92d Division (June–December 1918). After the Armistice he was chief of the American Section, Permanent Inter-Allied Armistice Commission, at Spa, Belgium (1918–1919). He attended the Army War College (1919–1920). Promoted to brigadier general, U.S. Army, in 1923, he was assigned to Boston, Massachusetts, commanding the 18th Brigade (1923–1927). Barnum was promoted to major general, U.S. Army, on 23 June

1927 and retired by law on 3 September 1927. "Malvern-Hill Barnum," *Assembly* 1, no. 4 (January 1943), "In Memory" insert, pp. 9–10; "Henry A. Barnum" and "Malvern-Hill Barnum," *Who Was Who–The Military,* p. 30; Mark Mayo Boatner III, *The Civil War Dictionary,* rev. ed. (New York: Vintage Books, 1991), pp. 504–7; TAGO, *American Decorations: A List of Awards of the Congressional Medal of Honor, the Distinguished Service Cross, and the Distinguished Service Medal Awarded under Authority of the Congress of the United States, 1862-1926* (Washington, D.C.: GPO, 1927) (hereafter cited as TAGO, *American Decorations, 1862-1926),* p. 5; "Henry A. Barnum" and "Malvern Hill Barnum," *Who Was Who–The Military,* p. 30.

Thomas H. Barry (13 October 1855–30 December 1919). Barry graduated from the USMA in June 1877 and was commissioned in the 7th Cavalry. He served on frontier duty in the Dakotas until he transferred to the 1st Infantry in Texas in September 1880. Barry saw action in the Pine Ridge campaign in South Dakota (4 December 1890-4 March 1891). He was appointed adjutant general of Wesley Merritt's Philippine Expeditionary Forces (VIII Army Corps) and the Department of the Pacific in May 1898. In February 1900 he returned to Washington for duty in the War Department. He was promoted to brigadier general, USV, in June 1900 and was ordered back to the Philippines as chief of staff and adjutant general. After being diverted on temporary duty with the China Relief Expedition (July–October 1900), he finally reached the Philippines in November 1900 and was chief of staff, Military Division of the Philippines, until July 1901. Barry was chief of staff and adjutant general, Department of the East (1902–1903), until he was promoted to brigadier general, U.S. Army, in August 1903 and detailed to the first General Staff. He commanded the Department of the Gulf at Atlanta (1904–1905) and then was sent as an official military observer attached to the Russian Army in Manchuria (March–December 1905). Upon his return, Barry was assigned to the General Staff Corps and made president of the Army War College (1905–1907). He was also assistant to the chief of staff (1906–1907) before being assigned as commander, Army of Cuban Pacification (1907–1909). He was promoted to major general in April 1908. He commanded the Department of California (1909–1910) and was superintendent of the U.S. Military Academy (1910–1912) before commanding the Eastern Department (1912–1914) and the Philippine Department (1914–1916). He then commanded the Central Department in Chicago (1916–1917) before assuming command of Camp Grant, Illinois, and the 86th Division (1917–1918). He visited the AEF in France on a battlefield orientation tour (November 1917–February 1918), but upon his return was soon reassigned to command the Central Department (1918–1919) because he was found physically disqualified for frontline service in France. He was transferred to Governor's Island, New York, in January 1919 and commanded the Eastern Department until his retirement on 13 October 1919. "Thomas Henry Barry," *Fifty-first Annual Report of the Association of Graduates of the United States Military Academy at West Point, New York, June 14th, 1920* (Saginaw, Mich.: Seemann and Peters, Printers and Binders, 1920), pp. 108–11; "Thomas Henry Barry," *Who Was Who–The Military,* p. 32.

Edgar W. Bass (30 October 1843–6 November 1918). Born in Wisconsin, Bass entered the 8th Minnesota Volunteer Infantry in August 1862 and served on the northern frontier against the Sioux until discharged in June 1864 to accept an appointment to the U.S. Military Academy. He graduated in 1868 and was commissioned in the Corps of Engineers. He was detailed as acting assistant professor of natural and experimental philosophy in August 1869. After serving as a company commander and battalion adjutant at the Engineer School of Application at Willet's Point, New York (1875–1878), he was appointed professor (with the rank of colonel) of mathematics in April 1878 and served until he retired in October 1898. During his tenure, he reformed and modernized the mathematics curriculum and authored a number of works on mathematics. "Edgar Wales Bass," *Fiftieth Annual Report, Association of Graduates of the United States Military Academy at West Point, New York, June 10, 1919* (Saginaw, Mich.: Seemann and Peters, 1919), pp. 144–48.

John C. Bates (26 August 1842–4 February 1919). Bates was the son of Edward Bates (1793–1869), who served as attorney general (1861–1864) under President Abraham Lincoln. John Bates left Washington University in St. Louis to join the Union Army's 11th Infantry Regiment as a first lieutenant in May 1861. He was aide-de-camp to Major General George G. Meade (1863–1865) and remained in the army after the war, transferring to the 20th Infantry in 1866. He was promoted to major in the 6th Infantry in 1882 and transferred back to the 20th Infantry the same month. He became lieutenant colonel in the 13th Infantry in 1886 and rejoined the 20th Infantry in 1890 before he became colonel and commander of the 2d Infantry in April 1892. In May 1898, he was appointed brigadier general of volunteers and made commander of Bates' Independent Brigade (3d and 20th Infantry Regiments), forming a fourth brigade in Lawton's 2d Division of Shafter's V Army Corps. Bates commanded the base at Siboney, Cuba, after the landing but brought his brigade forward to join Lawton's attack on El Caney on 1 July. He was promoted to major general of volunteers on 8 July and took command of a new Provisional Division later that month. Bates was sent to the Philippines for duty under Major General Elwell S. Otis, then commanding VIII Army Corps. In July 1899 Otis sent him to the southern Philippines, where Bates negotiated an agreement in August with the Muslim sultan of Sulu, known thereafter as the "Bates Agreement," recognizing the rights of the Moros in exchange for U.S. sovereignty and stationing of troops on the Sulu Archipelago. This agreement preserved a relatively peaceful occupation of the Moro areas until it was unilaterally abrogated by the Leonard Wood and the United States in 1904. Otis appointed Bates as commander of the Military District of Mindanao and Jolo in October 1899. Henry Lawton's death in December 1899 brought Bates back to Luzon and Manila. Appointed a major general of volunteers in January 1900, he temporarily replaced Lawton as commander, 1st Division, and then assumed command of the Department of Southern Luzon (1900–1901). He was promoted to brigadier general, U.S. Army, in February 1901 and returned to the United States in April and commanded the Department of the Missouri (1901–1904). He was promoted to major general in July 1902 and commanded the Northern Division (1904–1905) until he was selected to succeed Adna R. Chaffee as War Department chief of staff. He was appointed assistant chief of staff in June 1905 and then took his new post in January 1906, with the rank of lieutenant general. He retired on 14 April 1906 at his own request. "John Coalter Bates (1842–1919)," in *Webster's American Military Biographies,* p. 27; "John C. Bates," *Powell's Records,* p. 47; Merrill E. Gates, ed., *Men of Mark in America: Ideals of American Life Told in Biographies of Eminent Living Americans,* vol.

1 (Washington, D.C.: Men of Mark Publishing Company, 1905) (hereafter cited as Gates, *Men of Mark*, and volume), pp. 131–32; Brian McAllister Linn, *The Philippine War, 1899-1902* (Lawrence: Univ. Press of Kansas, 2000), passim; "John Coalter Bates (1842–1919)" and "Bates's Independent Brigade," in *The Spanish-American War: A Historical Dictionary*, ed. Brad K. Berner, p. 37 (Lanham, Md.: Scarecrow Press, 1998); Robert A. Fulton, "Bates Mission 1899," Uncle Sam, the Moros, and the Moro Campaigns, http://www.morolandhistory.com; Robert A. Fulton, *Moroland: The History of Uncle Sam and the Moros, 1899-1920* (Bend, Oreg.: Tumalo Creek Press, 2009), pp. 41–57, 161–233; "John Coalter Bates," *Who Was Who–The Military*, pp. 34–35.

John H. Beacom (1 January 1857–17 September 1916). Beacom graduated from the USMA in June 1882 and was commissioned in the 18th Infantry. He served on the frontier in Montana and Dakota Territory (1882–1889) and then commanded Company I (Indian Company), 3d Infantry, until September 1894. While on leave of absence, he was attached to the headquarters, Japanese Second Army, during the Shantung campaign and surrender of Wei-hai-wei during the Sino-Japanese War (1894–1895). He was on garrison duty from 1895 to 1897 and was later an assistant instructor in tactics at the Military Academy (1897–1898). He was assigned to the II Army Corps and then VII Army Corps as assistant adjutant general, USV (May–June 1898). He was adjutant general, 3d Division, VII Army Corps (June–August 1898) and appointed lieutenant colonel, USV, and was adjutant general, Department of Santiago, under Leonard Wood (September 1898–March 1899). He was appointed lieutenant colonel with the 45th U.S. Volunteer Infantry Regiment in August 1899 and then transferred to the 42d in September. He commanded that regiment in the United States and Philippines until May 1901. He was Judge Advocate, Provost Guard, in Manila (June–August 1901) and in command of troops in Oriental Negros province until May 1902, when he returned to the United States. After he was military attaché at the U.S. embassy in London (1903–1907), he returned to the Philippines in command of the 1st Battalion, 6th Infantry, at Camp Keithley, Mindanao (1910–1912), part of the time commanding the regiment (April 1910–March 1911, November 1911–January 1912). After tours as an inspector general in the Philippine and Western Departments (1912–1913), he was later assigned to the 6th Infantry at El Paso on Mexican border duty until it was ordered to Columbus, New Mexico, on 13 March 1916. There he assumed command of the 1st Provisional Infantry Brigade under Pershing during the Mexican Expedition until 30 April. He then commanded the 8th Infantry Regiment after 1 May 1916. Upon receiving orders on 15 September to take over the Southern California District, he reported to Pershing at Colonia Dublán. While speaking with Pershing on 17 September, Beacom suffered a heart attack and died several hours later after suffering a second attack. "John H. Beacom," *Forty-Ninth Annual Report of the Association of Graduates of the United States Military Academy at West Point, New York, June 11, 1918* (Saginaw, Mich.: Seemann and Peters, Printers and Binders, 1918), pp. 43–44.

George Bell Jr. (23 January 1859–29 October 1926). Son of Brigadier General George Bell (USMA, 1853), Bell graduated from the USMA in June 1880 and was commissioned in the 3d Infantry. He served with the 3d Infantry in Montana (1880–1888) and Minnesota (1888–1892), where he began his study of law. He was professor of military science and tactics at Cornell University (1892–1896) and then returned to Minnesota until April 1898. During his time at Cornell he completed his law degree in June 1894 and was admitted to the New York bar in 1895. He commanded a company of the 3d Infantry in Cuba during the Santiago Campaign until 17 July 1898 and then commanded the 1st Battalion until 12 September. He went to the Philippines with the 1st Infantry and was engaged in active combat operations (1900–1903). He returned to the Philippines as a battalion commander with the 1st Infantry in 1906–1907 and then served as an inspector general with the Philippines Department (1907–1908), the Department of the Columbia (1908–1910), and the Department of California in San Francisco (1910–1911). He was assistant to the Inspector General, Western Division, San Francisco (1911–1912), and the Inspector General, Western Division (1912–1913). He was promoted to colonel in March 1913 and took command of the 16th Infantry at the Presidio of San Francisco (1913–1914) and then on the Mexican border at El Paso, Texas. He was promoted to brigadier general in July 1914 and later commanded infantry brigades along the Mexican border in Texas and Arizona until March 1916. He commanded the post at El Paso (1916–1917) and then the 2d Provisional Infantry Division (March–May 1917) and the El Paso District (June–August 1917). He was promoted to major general, NA, and sent to France for special duty (September–December 1917) before returning to command Camp Logan, Texas, and the 33d Division until April 1918. He took the 33d Division to France, where it achieved a solid combat record while serving with the British Expeditionary Force (May–September 1918) before joining the First U.S. Army for the Meuse-Argonne offensive to November 1918. After occupation duty in Luxembourg, the 33d Division returned to the United States in 1919 for demobilization at Camp Grant, Illinois, in June. Bell was transferred to command of the 6th Division (1919–1921). In June 1920 he was assigned as commander of the Central Department in Chicago (March–June 1920) and its successor, Sixth Corps Area, at Fort Sheridan, Illinois, until October 1922. He was promoted to major general in March 1921 and retired in November 1922. "George Bell, Jr.," *Sixty-First Annual Report of the Association of Graduates of the United States Military Academy at West Point, New York, June 11, 1930* (Newburgh, N.Y.: Moore Printing Company, 1930), pp. 139–48.

J. (James) Franklin Bell (9 January 1856–8 January 1919). Bell graduated from the USMA in June 1878. He served on frontier duty in the Dakotas (1878–1886) with the 7th Cavalry and then was professor of military science and tactics at Southern Illinois University (Carbondale) (1886–1889). During his time in Carbondale, he studied law and was admitted to the Illinois bar. He rejoined his regiment at Fort Riley (1889–1894) and was secretary of the newly opened Cavalry and Light Artillery School (1893–1894). When James W. Forsyth, commander of the 7th Cavalry, was promoted to brigadier general in November 1894, he selected Bell as his aide-de-camp upon being made commanding general, Department of California (1894–1897). With Forsyth's retirement, Bell returned to troop duty in Arizona and then briefly moved to the Department of the Columbia as judge advocate until he was assigned as chief, military information office (intelligence), Department of the Pacific, under Wesley Merritt and sailed for Manila in June 1898. He participated in military operations around Manila in August 1898 and on 10 August conducted a dangerous personal reconnaissance of hostile positions that made possible the successful attack on Manila on 12 August. He was posthumously awarded a Distinguished Service Cross (DSC) in 1925 for his heroism. He served with Arthur MacArthur's 2d Division, VIII Army Corps (March–June 1899) as chief engineer but mostly acting as chief scout, and was heavily engaged in combat operations. In July 1899 he was appointed to command of the 36th U.S. Volunteer Infantry as colonel, USV, and raised the regiment in the Philippines. He particularly distinguished himself at Porac, Luzon, on 9 September 1899, and was awarded a Medal of Honor on 11 December 1899. On 5 December 1899 he was appointed brigadier general, USV, and assumed command of the 4th Brigade, 2d Division, Division of the Pacific (January–July 1900). He was then Provost Marshal General of Manila until he was promoted to brigadier general, U.S. Army, on 19 February 1901. He then commanded the 1st District, Department of Northern Luzon, and the 3d Separate Brigade in operations against Filipino insurgents that largely destroyed their capacity for armed resistance (1901–1903). He returned to the United States and assumed the post of commandant, General Service School, Infantry and Cavalry School, Staff College, and Signal School at Fort Leavenworth (1903–1905). His contributions to the development of the Leavenworth schools and military professional education were most significant. He was then selected as chief of staff (April 1906–April 1910). During this time he actively organized and commanded the Army of Cuban Pacification (October–December 1906). He was promoted to major general in January 1907. After completing his tour as chief of staff, he was assigned to command the Philippines Division (1911–1914) and then returned to command the 2d Division at Texas City (1914–1915). Bell moved to San Francisco to command the Western Department (1915–1917). His next command was the Eastern Department at Governor's Island, New York (May–August 1917), and then he was given command of the 77th Division, NA, at Camp Upton, Yaphank, New York (September–November 1917). Bell went to France (December 1917–March 1918) to observe frontline combat methods before taking the division to join the AEF. He returned to the United States to command Camp Upton, New York, but a chronic illness prevented him from accompanying the division when it went to France. He commanded the Eastern Department once again from August 1918 until his death from a heart attack in New York City on 8 January 1919. "James Franklin Bell," *Fiftieth Annual Report of the Association of Graduates of the United States Military Academy at West Point, New York, June 10, 1919* (Saginaw, Mich.: Seemann and Peters, Printers and Binders, 1919), pp. 163–77; TAGO, *American Decorations, 1862-1926*, pp. 6, 157, 677; "James Franklin Bell (1856-1919)," *Webster's American Military Biographies*, p. 29.

Charles G. Bickham (12 August 1867–14 December 1944). Bickham grew up in Dayton, Ohio, and graduated from Princeton University in 1890. Along with his brothers, Abraham and Daniel, he edited the family's newspaper, the *Dayton Journal*, after his father's death in 1894. During the Spanish-American War he first served as a private in Company G, 3d Ohio Volunteer Infantry Regiment (May–July 1898), before he was commissioned a captain in the 9th U.S. Volunteer (Colored) Infantry. He served with the 9th in the United States (July–August 1898) and then at San Juan, Cuba, until it returned to the United States and was mustered out of service in May 1899. Bickham was appointed captain in the 28th U.S. Volunteer Infantry under Colonel Birkhimer in July 1899 and served with the 28th in the Philippines until mustered out on 1 May 1901. He was commissioned in the 27th Infantry Regiment under Colonel Frank Baldwin in June and once again returned to the Philippines, where he commanded Company F in operations in Mindanao. President Roosevelt awarded him a Medal of Honor in April 1904 for his heroism in rescuing a wounded soldier under heavy fire at Fort Pandapatan during the Battle of Bayan on 2 May 1902. Bickham remained in the army with the 27th Infantry but failed to pass examinations for promotion to captain in 1909 and 1910 and was honorably discharged from the army on 16 June 1910. He returned to Dayton, where he was again an editor of his family's newspaper. TAGO, *American Decorations, 1862-1926*, p. 8; TAGO, *OAR, 1910*, p. 369; TAGO, *OAR, 1911*, p. 582; *Princeton Alumni Weekly* 4, no. 2 (10 October 1903), p. 33; "Charles G. Bickham, 1891," Dayton Metro Library, http://www.flickr .com/photos/dmlhistory/5393790037.

William E. Birkhimer (1 March 1848–10 June 1914). Birkhimer enlisted in Company M, 4th Iowa Volunteer Cavalry, in March 1864 at the age of sixteen. He saw considerable action in Mississippi, Alabama, and Georgia before he was mustered out in 1865. He entered the Military Academy in September 1866 and graduated in June 1870 with a commission in the 3d Artillery. After completing the Artillery School at Fort Monroe, Virginia (1872–1873), he was assigned to the Military Academy as an instructor in engineering and artillery tactics (1874–1876). Later he was assigned as acting judge advocate for the Department of the Columbia (1886–1890), and during this assignment he obtained a law degree from the University of Oregon in 1889. Already a published author on the history of artillery and military laws, he published his work *Military Government and Militia Law* (Washington, D.C.: James J. Chapman, 1892; 3d edition, 1914). Birkhimer served as adjutant, 3d Artillery (1891–1895), and then was assigned to Light Battery C at Washington Barracks, D.C., and the Presidio of San Francisco (1895–1898). Promoted to captain in February 1898, he was with Battery L, 3d Artillery, and commanding the artillery post at Fort Baker, California, in June 1898 when his battery was selected for Merritt's expedition to the Philippines. He was given command of a battalion of the 3d Artillery (Batteries G and L) under William A. Kobbé and participated in operations against Manila and in its capture on 13 August. He was later appointed acting inspector general and judge advocate of the 1st Division (1899) and aide-de-camp to Henry Lawton when he commanded the division. While serving as Lawton's aide-de-camp, he was in the forefront of the combat at San Miguel de Mayumo on 13 May 1899 and on 15 July 1902 was awarded a Medal of Honor for his gallantry. He was appointed to command the 28th U.S. Volunteer Infantry Regiment when it was formed and appointed colonel, USV, on 5 July 1899. Apparently most at home in the field, Birkhimer was a courageous, tenacious, and skilled commander who was often not well liked by his subordinates and became increasingly more punitive in his tactics toward the Filipino insurrectionists and population as the war dragged on. Returning to the United States, he served as inspector of artillery in the Department of California (1901–1904) and the department's chief of staff (1904–1905). Increasingly beset with ill health, Birkhimer was promoted to brigadier general on 15 February 1906 and retired at his own request the next day. "William Edward Birkhimer," *Forty-Eighth Annual Report of the Association of Graduates of the United States Military Academy at West Point, New York, June 12, 1917*, pp. 74–83; Linn, *The Philippine War*, pp. 115, 286–87, 293.

Tasker H. Bliss (31 December 1853–9 November 1930). After completing two years at Bucknell University, Bliss attended the USMA, graduating in June 1875 with a commission in the 1st Artillery. He was an assistant instructor in French and in artillery tactics at the Military Academy (1876–1880). After attending the Artillery School of Practice at Fort Monroe, Virginia (1882–1885), he was an instructor at the Naval War College (1885–1888). His next assignment was at the War Department as aide-de-camp to the commanding general of the army, Major General John Schofield (1888–1895). He was on special duty at the office of the Secretary of War (1895–1897) and then served as military attaché in Madrid, Spain (March 1897–April 1898). He was appointed lieutenant colonel and chief commissary of subsistence, USV, for VI Army Corps in the United States (May–July 1898), but was eventually sent to Puerto Rico, where he served as chief of staff to Major General James H. Wilson, 1st Division, I Army Corps (July–September 1898). He was appointed collector of customs at Havana in December 1898 and chief, Cuban Customs Service, in January 1899. It was in this position at Havana that Bliss so clearly demonstrated his significant administrative skills. He was promoted to brigadier general, U.S. Army, in July 1902, appointed to the War College Board and the new General Staff, and served as president of the Army War College (1902–1905). Bliss was sent to the Philippines, where he commanded the Department of Luzon (1905–1906), the Department of Mindanao, while also acting as the governor of the Moro Province (1906–1908), and then the Philippine Division (1908–1909). Returning to the United States in June 1909, he once again served on the General Staff and as president of the Army War College (1909–1910). He commanded the Department of California (1910–1911), the Department of the East (1911–1913), and then the Southern Department at Fort Sam Houston, Texas (1913–1915) during a period of significant unrest along the Mexican border. Bliss was detailed to the General Staff as assistant chief of staff (1915–1916) and was promoted to major general on 20 November 1915. For much of this time he was acting chief of staff under Major General Hugh L. Scott. He was selected as chief of staff and appointed to that position on 22 September 1917. Promoted to full general on 6 October 1917, Bliss was retired due to age on 31 December 1917 and immediately recalled to active duty as chief of staff until May 1918 and sent to France in January 1918 as a member of the American Section, Supreme War Council (1918–1919) and later also as a member of the U.S. delegation to the Paris Peace Conference (1918–1919). After retirement, he was governor of the U.S. Soldiers' Home in Washington (1920–1927). He was promoted to full general, U.S. Army retired, on 21 June 1930. "Tasker Howard Bliss," in *Sixty-Second Annual Report of the Association of Graduates of the United States Military Academy at West Point, New York, June 10, 1931*, pp. 141–47; "Tasker Howard Bliss (1853–1930)," *Webster's American Military Biographies*, pp. 34–35; "Tasker Howard Bliss (1853–1930)," in *The United States in the First World War: An Encyclopedia*, ed. Anne Cipriano Venzon, pp. 94–96 (New York: Garland Publishing, 1995) (hereafter cited as Venzon, ed., *The United States in the First World War*); Frederick Palmer, *Bliss, Peacemaker: The Life and Letters of General Tasker H. Bliss* (New York: Dodd, Mead, 1934), passim.

Walter O. Boswell (19 December 1877–25 December 1952). Boswell was a cadet at the U.S. Military Academy from June 1898 to February 1900 when he resigned. In September 1900 he enlisted in Battery G, 1st Artillery (6th Company, Coast Artillery), and served as a private, corporal, and sergeant until July 1902, when he was commissioned a lieutenant in the 16th Infantry. He transferred to the 21st Infantry in March 1908 and served as Pershing's aide-de-camp in 1909–1911 and again in 1914–1915. He served as professor of military science and tactics at the University of Georgia (1915–1916). He was assigned to Headquarters, 1st Division, in France (1917–1918). After the war he was promoted to major in July 1920 and completed the School of the Line (1920–1921) and the General Staff School at Fort Leavenworth (1921–1922) and the Army War College (1922–1923). Assigned to the General Staff Corps (1923–1927), he served on the War Department General Staff (1923–1925). He was promoted to lieutenant colonel in October 1925 and served as executive officer of the 22d Infantry Regiment at Fort McPherson, Georgia (1929–1930), and retired as a lieutenant colonel in November 1930. He then joined his family's Boswell Cotton Company as vice president (1930–1950). Today the J. G. Boswell Company is an enormous cotton-growing and farming business in California and Arizona. In the 1950s the company sold 20,000 acres northwest of Phoenix, Arizona, to the Dell E. Webb Company, which then developed it into today's Sun City, Arizona. The Walter O. Boswell Memorial Hospital in Sun City was originally built with a contribution from the Boswell family and was named in his honor. Association of Graduates, U.S. Military Academy, *Register of Graduates and Former Cadets of the United States Military Academy, 2000* (West Point, N.Y.: Association of Graduates, USMA, 2000), Biographies, p. 4–80; TAGO, *OAR, 1916,* p. 403; TAGO, *OAR, 1931,* p. 776; "Banner Boswell celebrates 40th Anniversary" and "History," Banner Boswell Medical Center, http://www.bannerhealth.com.

Charles T. Boyd (29 October 1870–21 June 1916). Boyd graduated from the USMA in June 1896 and was commissioned in the 7th Cavalry. He served in Arizona and at the Presidio of San Francisco until July 1898, when he was sent to the Philippines with the VIII Army Corps. He was appointed major in the 37th U.S. Volunteer Infantry in the Philippines in July 1899 and served as regimental commander (1899–1900). He was discharged from volunteer service in March 1901 and transferred to the 4th Cavalry in May. He was again at the Presidio of San Francisco and then Jefferson Barracks, California (1901–1902), until he was appointed professor of military science and tactics at the University of Nevada, Reno (1902–1905). He was promoted to captain in the 10th Cavalry in January 1903. He was on leave in Manchuria observing Russian, Japanese, and Chinese forces during the opening months of the Russo-Japanese War (July–October 1904). He was appointed major in the Philippine Scouts and served with the 4th Battalion on Mindanao (May 1905–July 1906) and served as district governor of Cotabato, Mindanao, from January through October 1906. He then left the Scouts and returned to the 10th Cavalry in the United States, but soon returned with the 10th Cavalry to the Philippines and was assigned to Fort McKinley (1907–1909) when Pershing commanded the brigade and post. Upon returning to the United States, he served with the 10th at Fort Ethan Allen, Vermont (1909–1911), before completing the Army School of the Line at Fort Leavenworth (1911–1912). He commanded a troop at Fort Ethan Allen (1912–1913) and at Fort Huachuca, Arizona, on the Mexican border (1913–1915). He completed the Army Staff College (1915–1916) and was relieved to rejoin his regiment on the Mexican Expedition. He commanded Troop C, 10th Cavalry, in Mexico until he was killed in action against Mexican Army forces on 21 June 1916 at Carrizal, Chihuahua. Significant controversy still exists as to exactly what verbal orders Boyd had received from Pershing when they met on the evening of 17 June (Boyd was given no written orders) and why Boyd engaged Mexican forces at Carrizal on the 21st. "Charles Trumbull Boyd," *Forty-Eighth Annual Report of the Association of Graduates of the United States Military Academy at West Point, New York, June 12, 1917,* pp. 47–49; Joseph A. Stout Jr., *Border Conflict: Villistas, Carrancistas, and the Punitive Expedition, 1915-1920* (Fort Worth, Tex.: Texas Christian Univ. Press, 1999), pp. 84–88; Frank Tompkins, *Chasing Villa: The Story behind the Story of Pershing's Punitive Expedition into Mexico* (Harrisburg, Pa.: Military Service Publishing Company, 1934), pp. 207–12; Chris Emmett, *In the Path of Events with Colonel Martin Lalor Crimmons: Soldier, Naturalist, Historian* (Waco, Tex.: Jones and Morrison, 1959), pp. 307–10; H. B. Wharfield, "The Affair at Carrizal," *Montana: The Magazine of Western History* 18, no. 4 (autumn 1968), pp. 24–39.

Charles H. Brent (9 April 1862–27 March 1929). Brent was born and educated in Canada, receiving his divinity degree from Trinity College in Toronto in 1901. He became an Episcopal priest in 1887 and served in churches in Buffalo and Boston until he was elected bishop of the Philippine Islands in 1901. He served in the islands until 1918, when he became the bishop of western New York. Pershing brought him to France and made him head of the chaplain service in the AEF (1918-1919) as a major. "George Henry Brent," *Who Was Who in America,* vol. 1, *1897-1943,* p. 135.

Andre W. Brewster (9 December 1862–27 March 1942). Brewster was appointed a second lieutenant in the 10th Infantry in 1885. In the Spanish-American War he served as a major and assistant quartermaster of volunteers (1898–1899). Assigned to the 9th Infantry, he was sent to China in the China Relief Expedition in June 1900. While at Tientsin on 13 July 1900 he saved two men from drowning while under Boxer fire. For this act he received a Medal of Honor on 15 September 1903. He graduated from the Army War College in 1907. He was promoted to major with the 19th Infantry in 1909, but in December of that year he was detailed to the Inspector General's Department. In December 1913 he was promoted to lieutenant colonel of infantry and commanded the Puerto Rico regiment of infantry until October, when he was once again detailed as an inspector general. He was promoted to colonel in July 1916. When chosen to command American forces in France, Pershing selected Brewster as his staff inspector general. He accompanied the headquarters to France in May 1917 and was promoted to brigadier general, NA, in September. He was later the inspector general, GHQ AEF, in France, and was promoted to major general, NA, in November. He shaped the AEF's inspection program during the remainder of the war. Brewster returned to the United States in September 1919 and was again assigned to duty with the Inspector General's Department. He was promoted to brigadier general, U.S. Army, in 1920. He commanded the 5th Division until December 1922, when he was promoted to major general and assigned as commander of the First Corps Area with headquarters in Boston. Brewster retired in December 1925. TAGO, *OAR, 1901,* p. 158; TAGO, *OAR, 1941,* p. 985; *Who Was Who—The Military,* p. 65; Joseph W. A. Whitehorne, *The Inspectors General of the United States Army, 1903-1939* (Washington, D.C.: GPO, 1998), pp. 87, 106–272, passim; "Andre Walker Brewster," http://www.arlingtoncemetery.net/awbrewst.htm.

John R. Brooke (21 July 1838–5 September 1926). Brooke served as a captain in the 4th Pennsylvania Volunteer Infantry (April–July 1861) and was then appointed colonel of the 53d Pennsylvania Volunteer Infantry in November. He achieved a distinguished record in command of the 53d in the Army of the Potomac in northern Virginia until June 1864 and later as a brigade commander through the war's end. In 1866 he was commissioned a lieutenant colonel, 37th Infantry Regiment, and assigned to duty in New Mexico (1867–1869) before transferring to the 3d Infantry at Fort Dodge, Kansas, in 1869. Brooke saw duty in Colorado (1871–1873) and the Indian Territory (1873–1874) and then in Mississippi, Louisiana, and Alabama (1874–1877). He then moved to Montana with the 3d Infantry and was promoted to colonel and commander, 13th Infantry, in 1879 before transferring back to the 3d Infantry. He remained in command of the 3d Infantry until April 1888, when he was promoted to brigadier general and assigned to command the Department of the Platte at Omaha (1888–1895). During his tenure, he was in command of the campaign of 1890–1891 against the Sioux Indians at the Pine Ridge Agency until Nelson Miles took over control. After commanding the Department of Dakota (1895–1897), Brooke was promoted to major general in May 1897 and assumed command of the Department of the Missouri. In the Spanish-American War, he was assigned to command I Army Corps and the mobilization camp at Chickamauga Park, Georgia, until July 1898. He then was deputy commander of the military expedition to Puerto Rico under Nelson Miles (July–August 1898) and later replaced him as military governor (October–December 1898). Brooke next became the military governor of Cuba and commander of the Division of Cuba until falling out of favor with the new Secretary of War, Elihu Root, and Miles while also being undermined by his own subordinate, Leonard Wood, who then replaced Brooke in December 1899. After his return to the United States, he commanded the Department of the East until his retirement in 1902. TAGO, *OAR, 1901,* pp. 5, 347, 348; Russell Weigley, *History of the United States Army* (New York: Macmillan, 1967), pp. 318–19, 328; "Major General John R. Brooke," in M. Auge, *Lives of the Eminent Dead and Biographical Notices of Prominent Living Citizens of Montgomery County, PA* (Norristown, Pa.: Publisher by the author, 1879), pp. 418–26; *Powell's Records,* pp. 88–89; Major William H. Powell and Medical Director Edward Shippen, eds., *Officers of the Army and Navy (Regular) Who Served in the Civil War* (Philadelphia: L. R. Hamersly, 1892) [hereafter cited as *Officers of the Army and Navy (Regular)*], p. 56; "John Rutter Brooke," *Who Was Who–The Military,* p. 66.

Arthur W. Brown (9 November 1873–3 January 1958). Brown was educated at Cornell University and received his law degree in 1897. He enlisted in Battery A, 1st Utah Artillery, in May 1898 and served as private, corporal, and sergeant until August 1899. In December 1899, he was commissioned in the 4th Infantry in the Philippines and joined the regiment in January 1900. He transferred to the 27th Infantry in February 1902 and served on Mindanao under Charles Bickham in Company F and later commanded the company. In 1909 he became assistant to the judge advocate, Department of the Lakes, and then judge advocate of the 2d Division at Texas City, Texas. He remained in Texas as an acting judge advocate until he was promoted to major, judge advocate, in September 1916, and finally transferred to the Judge Advocate General's Department. He was promoted to lieutenant colonel, NA, in August 1917, and served as division judge advocate for the 78th Division in the United States and with the AEF in France. He was then a corps judge advocate, and finally judge advocate, First U.S. Army. Following the war he was assigned as judge advocate for the Panama Canal Department (1919–1922). He returned to the Judge Advocate General's Office in Washington for duty (1923–1927), during which he served with Pershing on the Tacna-Arica (Peru-Chile border) commission. He was judge advocate for Seventh Corps Area in Omaha (1927–1928) and promoted to colonel in December 1927. He then served as executive officer in the Judge Advocate General's Office (1929–1933) before being appointed judge advocate general of the army on 30 November 1933 and promoted to major general on 1 December. He served until he retired on 30 November 1937. TAGO, *OAR, 1916,* p. 463; TAGO, *OAR, 1938,* p. 863; "Arthur Winston Brown," *Who Was Who–The Military,* p. 67; "Cornellian Named Judge Advocate," *Cornell Alumni News* 36, no. 10 (November 30, 1933), p. 112.

Earl I. Brown (13 October 1874–25 June 1963). Brown graduated from the USMA in April 1898 and was commissioned in the Corps of Engineers. He was assigned to Company F, 2d Battalion of Engineers, at Willets Point, New York, until June 1901, and then in the Philippines (1901–1903). He was in charge of road construction on Panay (March–May 1902) and then in command of Company F on military road construction and in field operations against the Moros around Lake Lanao (May–October 1902) under Pershing. He served as chief engineer officer, Department of the Visayas (1902–1903) before returning to the United States. After commanding Company F (1904–1906) at Washington Barracks, he commanded it in Cuba during the Cuban Pacification (1906–1907) and then was in charge of river and harbor work in Wilmington, North Carolina (1907–1911), Galveston, Texas (1911–1912), and the Montgomery, Alabama, District (1912–1915). He served in the Panama Canal (1915–1917) and, upon promotion to colonel, NA, in August 1917, returned to the United States to take command of the 307th Engineer Regiment and become division engineer, 82d Division (August–October 1917). He then commanded the 317th Engineer Regiment, 92d Division, and was division engineer in the United States (1917–1918) and with the AEF in France (July 1918–January 1919). He was chief engineer of V Corps (January–February 1919) and commanded the 21st Engineer Regiment (March–June 1919) before returning to the United States to assume command of the Cincinnati Engineer District (1919–1921). He commanded river and harbor work at Wilmington, Delaware (1921–1927), and was then assigned as Corps Area Engineer, Eighth Corps Area, Fort Sam Houston, Texas (1927–1930). After serving as District Engineer in Philadelphia (1930–1933), Brown was Division Engineer, South Atlantic Division, at Norfolk (1934–1935) and Richmond, Virginia, until his retirement in August 1938. He was recalled to active duty as district engineer, Wilmington District (1940–1942).

Thomas W. Brown (25 October 1880–19 July 1957). Brown enlisted in Battery G, 6th Company, Coast Artillery Corps, in January 1900 and was commissioned in the 27th Infantry in April 1901. He served in the Philippines and on Mindanao with Pershing. He later served with the 27th from November 1905 until he transferred to the 17th Infantry in September 1915. During World War I he was assigned to the General Staff Corps (1917–1919). His assignments during the war are not known. He completed the Army School of the Line in 1921 and the General Staff School in 1922. After commanding the 35th Infantry Regiment, Hawaiian Division, at Schofield Barracks, Oahu (June–December 1924), he later commanded the 4th Infantry Regiment, 3d Division, at Fort George Wright, Washington (March–July 1928). Brown attended the Army War College (1928–1929). He was promoted to colonel in June 1932 and then commanded the 33d Infantry Regiment, Fort Clayton, Panama Canal Zone (1933–1935). He retired from active duty on 30 June 1942 and was recalled to serve from July 1942 to February 1944. TAGO, *OAR, 1916*, p. 385; TAGO, *OAR, 1941*, p. 105; TAGO, *OAR, 1950*, p. 667; *U.S. Army Register*, vol. 1, *U.S. Army Active and Retired Lists, 1958*, p. 1135; Lieutenant Colonel Steven E. Clay, U.S. Army (ret.), *U.S. Army Order of Battle 1919-1941*, vol. 1, *The Arms: Major Commands and Infantry Organizations, 1919-1941* (Fort Leavenworth, Kans.: Combat Studies Institute Press, U.S. Army Combined Arms Center, 2010) (hereafter cited as Clay, *U.S. Army Order of Battle*, vol. 1), pp. 360, 384, 386.

William Carey Brown (19 December 1854–8 May 1939). "Carey" Brown graduated from the USMA in June 1877 and was commissioned in the 2d Cavalry. He served on the frontier in Washington and Oregon. He was adjutant at the Military Academy (1885–1890) and then commanded Troop C, 1st Cavalry, in Montana and during the Sioux campaign (1890–1891). He commanded Troop E, 1st Cavalry, in Cuba during the Santiago Campaign. After returning from Cuba, he commanded Fort Washakie, Wyoming (1898–1899), and then was appointed major in the 45th U.S. Volunteer Infantry. He transferred to the 42d Infantry, which he helped organize and train before it went to the Philippines in December 1899. Brown was engaged in operations against the Filipino insurgents on Luzon. He mustered out of the 42d Infantry in June 1901 and commanded Fort Washakie again (1901–1902). He later returned to the Philippines with the 3d Cavalry (1904–1907). He served in Texas and New Mexico with the regiment (1908–1909) and then completed the Army War College (1909–1910). Brown commanded the 10th Cavalry and the post at Fort Huachuca, Arizona (1914–1916), and was responsible for patrolling the Mexican border. He led the 10th Cavalry during the Mexican Expedition until he was hospitalized and went on sick leave in May. He was then assigned to the Militia Bureau in Washington (August–December 1916) and held several other posts in the Eastern Department before going to France with the 42d Division (September–November 1917) and being assigned as inspector, Quartermaster Corps, at AEF headquarters (1917–1918). Brown was retired in December 1918 for age. By a Special Act of Congress on 28 February 1927, Brown was promoted to brigadier general on the retired list. "William Carey Brown," *Seventieth Annual Report of the Association of Graduates of the United States Military Academy at West Point, New York, June 10, 1939* (Newburgh, N.Y.: Moore Printing Company, 1939), pp. 115–20; George F. Brimlow, *Cavalryman Out of the West: Life of General William Carey Brown* (Caldwell, Idaho: Caxton Printers, 1944), passim.

Robert L. Bullard (5 January 1861–11 September 1947). Bullard graduated from the USMA in 1885 and was commissioned in the 10th Infantry. Stationed at Fort Union, New Mexico, he participated in the pursuit of Geronimo in 1885–1886. He then served at posts in New Mexico, Texas, Kansas, and Oklahoma until he was assigned as professor of military tactics at North Georgia Agricultural College (now

North Georgia College and State University) in Dahlonega (1895–1897). In June 1898 he served as a battalion commander in the Alabama Colored Volunteer Infantry (June–August) and commanded the 3d Alabama Colored Volunteer Infantry in the United States (August 1898–March 1899). In August 1899 he became colonel of the 39th U.S. Volunteer Infantry and commanded the unit in the Philippines with distinction until May 1901. Bullard transferred to the 28th Infantry in June 1902 and remained in the Philippines. He assumed command of the 3d Battalion, 28th Infantry, at Iligan, Mindanao, in September 1902 and was in charge of military road construction from Iligan to Lake Lanao during Pershing's time at Camp Vicars. He was then appointed the first governor of the Lanao District, Moro Province, under Leonard Wood (1903–1904) and involved in operations against hostile Moros. After extended sick leave, he returned to the 28th Infantry in 1905 and was promoted to lieutenant colonel in the 8th Infantry in 1906. He served in the Provisional Government during the Cuban pacification and occupation (1906–1909) before rejoining his regiment. He served with the 8th Infantry on the Mexican border (April–May 1911) and then attended the Army War College (1911–1912). Assigned to the 26th Infantry in August 1912, he remained with it through May 1917, seeing duty during the Mexican border troubles in 1916. He mobilized and commanded the 4th Brigade, 2d Division, in Texas (1913–1915). Soon after the United States entered the war, he took command of the 2d Brigade, 1st Division, for its movement to France in June–August 1917. Bullard was promoted to brigadier general, U.S. Army, in June 1917 and major general, NA, in August. Pershing placed Bullard in charge of the infantry officers' training schools in the AEF in August. He took command of the 1st Division in December 1917 and led it through its training and into the front lines in January 1918. He commanded the division through all of its early operations and the capture of Cantigny on 28 May 1918. On 14 July, Bullard took over III Corps, AEF, which he then led through the hard fighting in the Aisne-Marne (July–August) and Meuse-Argonne (September–November) offensives until 11 October 1918, when he assumed command of the Second U.S. Army. Promoted to temporary lieutenant general on 16 October 1918 and major general, U.S. Army, on 27 November, Bullard was readying the Second Army for operations in Lorraine against Metz when the Armistice went into effect on 11 November. He remained in command through the demobilization of the Second Army in April 1919 and returned to the United States in May. He commanded the Eastern Department (later designated Second Corps Area in 1920) at Governor's Island, New York, from November 1919 until his retirement in January 1925. He was promoted to lieutenant general, U.S. Army, on the retired list on 21 June 1930. He remained active in his retirement as president of the National Security League and as a writer. He published *Personalities and Reminiscences of the War* (1925), *American Soldiers also Fought* (1932), and *Fighting Generals: Illustrated Biographical Sketches of Seven Major Generals in World War I* (1944). "Robert Lee Bullard," *Assembly* 7, no. 2 (July 1948), "In Memory" insert, pp. 3–5; TAGO, *OAR, 1920*, p. 6; TAGO, *OAR, 1941*, p. 991; "Robert Lee Bullard," *Webster's American Military Biographies*, pp. 47–48. Allen R. Millett's *The General: Robert L. Bullard and Officership in the United States Army, 1881-1925* (Westport, Conn.: Greenwood Press, 1975) is the definitive biography.

Andrew S. Burt (21 November 1839–12 January 1915). Burt enlisted as a private in Company A, 6th Ohio Volunteer Infantry, in April 1861 and was commissioned in the 18th U.S. Infantry in May. After several staff assignments, he returned in September 1863 to command Company F, 18th Infantry, for the remainder of the war and into the postwar period. Burt remained with the 18th Infantry and saw action on the frontier as post commander at Fort Bridger, Wyoming, and Fort C. F. Smith, Montana (1867–1868), transferring to the 27th Infantry when the 18th Infantry was reorganized in December 1866. In 1869 he transferred to the 9th Infantry, serving at various posts in Wyoming and Nebraska. During the 1870s Burt was actively engaged in numerous expeditions against the Indians of the plains, including the 1876 Sioux expedition, in which he commanded a company at the Battle of the Rosebud (17 June 1876) under George Crook. Burt was promoted to major with the 8th Infantry in January 1883 and to lieutenant colonel with the 7th Infantry, commanding at Fort Laramie, Wyoming (1888–1890), and then at Rock Springs, Wyoming. In July 1892 he was promoted to colonel and commander of the 25th Infantry Regiment at Fort Missoula, Montana. He was appointed brigadier general, USV, during the Spanish-American War (May–December 1898) and commanded the 1st Brigade, 2d Division, VII Army Corps. Upon discharge from the USV, he returned to command the 25th Infantry and took the regiment to the Philippines in July 1899. He was in the Philippines until August 1901. He was promoted to brigadier general, U.S. Army, on 1 April 1902 and retired from active service on the 15th. TAGO, *OAR, 1901,* pp. 221, 356; "Andrew Sheridan Burt," *Who Was Who–The Military,* p. 77; Merrill J. Mattes, *Indians, Infants and Infantry: Andrew and Elizabeth Burt on the Frontier* (Lincoln: Univ. of Nebraska Press, 1988), passim.

De Rosey C. Cabell (7 July 1861–15 March 1924). Cabell graduated from the USMA in June 1884 and was commissioned in the 8th Cavalry. He served on frontier duty in Texas, Arizona, and New Mexico (1884–1888). He then moved with his regiment to the Dakotas and later served in the Sioux campaign of 1890–1891. With the war against Spain, he was appointed lieutenant colonel, 2d Arkansas Volunteer Infantry (1898–1899). He then commanded Troop M, 8th Cavalry, which was sent to China with the 6th Cavalry's contingent in the China Relief Expedition. Cabell's Troop M was the only cavalry in the U.S. column that retook Beijing and then garrisoned it (1900–1901). He served in the Philippines (1901–1903) and on regimental duty with the 2d Cavalry in Texas (1903–1907). He then commanded the 3d Squadron, 10th Cavalry, in 1911 and attended the Army Service Schools in 1912. After completing the Army War College in 1913, he was assigned to duty with the 11th Cavalry on the Mexican border. He was promoted to lieutenant colonel and assigned to the 10th Cavalry in 1914. Pershing chose Cabell as chief of staff for the Mexican Expedition (1916–1917), and he was responsible for organizing and controlling the logistical support of the forces in northern Mexico. He was promoted to colonel in July 1916 and commanded the 10th Cavalry at Fort Huachuca, Arizona (1917–1918). He was promoted to brigadier general, NA, in December 1917 and then commanded the 3d Cavalry Brigade at Douglas, Arizona (February–April 1918), the El Paso District (April–May 1918), and Nogales (Arizona) Subdistrict (May–September 1918). He was promoted to major general and commanding general, Southern Department, at Fort Sam Houston, Texas (1918–1919). In these posts, Cabell was responsible for the security of the U.S.-Mexican border at a very critical time when northern Mexico remained in turmoil. He commanded the 4th Cavalry on the Rio Grande River (1919–1920). He retired as a colonel in November 1920 and was promoted posthumously to major general, retired list, by the Act of 21 June 1930. "De Rosey Carroll Cabell," *Sixtieth Annual Report of the Association of Graduates of the United States Military Academy at West Point, New York, June 12, 1929* (Newburgh, N.Y.: Moore Printing Company, 1929), pp. 113–15; "De Rosey Carroll Cabell," in Davis, *Generals in Khaki*, pp. 64–65.

Charles R. Cameron (25 June 1875–?). Cameron graduated from Cornell University in 1898 and went to the Philippines, where he was a teacher on Panay before becoming superintendent of schools in the Moro Province. He was then superintendent of schools for the Department of Mindanao and Sulu and later secretary of the Department of Mindanao and Sulu and assistant to the departmental governor. While working for the department government, Cameron authored a volume entitled *Sulu Writing: An Explanation of the Sulu-Arabic Script as Employed in Writing in the Sulu Language of the Southern Philippines* (Zamboanga: Sulu Press, 1917). He was commissioned a captain in the Aviation Section, Army Signal Corps (1917–1918) and Army Air Service (1918–1919). After the war he joined the U.S. consular service, with assignments in Tacna, Peru (1919–1920), Pernambuco, Venezuela (1920–1923), Tokyo (1923–1925), and São Paulo, Brazil (1927–1929), before becoming U.S. consul general at São Paulo (1930–1933), Havana (1934–1935), Osaka (1937–1938), and Tokyo (1938–1941). *ARWD, 1915*, vol. 3, *Philippine Commission*, pp. 27, 397; "Charles Raymond Cameron," *Who Was Who–The Military*, p. 81; "Charles Raymond Cameron," The Political Graveyard, http://politicalgraveyard.com/geo/NY/phi-beta-kappa.html.

Allyn Capron (27 August 1846–18 September 1898). The son of Captain Erastus Allyn Capron (USMA, 1833), who was killed in action at Churubusco on 20 August 1847 during the war with Mexico, Capron graduated from the USMA in June 1867 and was commissioned in the 1st Artillery, his father's former unit. He served at a variety of coastal forts in the East, the South, and on the Gulf of Mexico (1867–1881). From 1886 to 1890, he served with the 1st Artillery on the West Coast at San Francisco and in Washington, during which time he was promoted to captain in December 1888 and took command of Light Battery E, 1st Artillery. With this field battery, he moved to the Light Artillery and Cavalry School of Application at Fort Riley, Kansas, late in 1890 and was then dispatched with elements of the 7th Cavalry to the Pine Ridge reservation in December 1890 with his four Hotchkiss guns. There he and his battery played a critical role at Wounded Knee (28–29 December) and then at Drexel Mission (30 December). After again serving at Fort Riley to September 1891, he commanded Light Battery E at Fort Sheridan, Illinois, and Washington Barracks, D.C., until April 1898, when he was ordered to take Light Battery E, 1st Artillery, known as "Capron's Battery," and its four 3.2-inch guns, to Tampa, Florida, for attachment to the V Army Corps for the Cuban expedition. In moving forward into action in Cuba, he passed the temporary grave of his son, Captain Allyn K. Capron (1871–24 June 1898), commander of Troop L, 1st U.S. Volunteer Cavalry, who was the first American officer killed in the war, on 24 June during the assault at Las Guasimas. Attached to support Lawton's division at El Caney on 1 July, Capron's battery had to close to within one thousand yards of the Spanish positions before its fire became effective. His battery later saw action on the San Juan Heights and during the ensuing siege of the city of Santiago. During his time at Santiago, Capron came down with typhoid fever and Army surgeons urged him to return to the United States, but he refused evacuation until his battery was evacuated. Upon reaching Camp Wikoff, Montauk Point, he requested sick leave and returned to his home at Fort Myer, Virginia, where he died on 18 September 1898. "Allyn Capron," *Thirtieth Annual Reunion of the Association of Graduates of the United States Military Academy at West Point, New York, June 7, 1899* (Saginaw, Mich.: Seemann and Peters, Printers and Binders, 1900), pp. 80–83; "Allyn K. Capron, Captain, United States Army" [*sic*], Arlington National Cemetery, http://www.arlingtoncemetery.net/allyncap.htm (this site incorrectly identifies Captain Allyn Capron as his son, Allyn K. Capron); "Allyn Kissam Capron, Captain, United States Army," Arlington National Cemetery, http://www .arlingtoncemetery.net/acapronj.htm; "Allyn K. Capron (d. 1898)" (also incorrectly identified) and "Allyn K. Capron, Jr. (1871–1898)" (he was not a junior), in Berner, ed., *The Spanish-American War,* p. 67; Heitman, *Historical Register,* vol. 1, p. 281.

Frank W. Carpenter (16 June 1871–28 February 1945). Carpenter enlisted in the army in 1889 and served as an enlisted man and an acting hospital steward. He left the army and was a civilian clerk at the headquarters of the Department of the Platte (later Missouri) in Omaha, Nebraska. In March 1899, Brigadier General Henry Lawton appointed him as his chief clerk and took him to the Philippines. Following Lawton's death in December 1899, Carpenter became secretary of Major General Elwell Otis, the military governor, and his successor, Arthur MacArthur. In 1903 he joined the civilian governor-general's office as an assistant in the Executive Bureau of the Philippine Commission. In February 1908 he became the executive secretary of the Philippine Commission and director of the Executive Bureau. His work in these positions was critical to establishing competent civilian administrations in the provincial and local governments throughout the Philippines. On 15 December 1913 he replaced Pershing as governor of the Moro Province, the first civilian governor in this post since American occupation began in 1898, and then became governor of the reorganized Department of Mindanao and Sulu in March 1914. In August 1916, Carpenter was appointed the first director of the Bureau of Non-Christian Tribes. In February 1920 he left this post to assume duties as the chairman of the Finance Commission in the Philippine government and retired due to ill health in 1923. After recuperating in Japan for several years, Carpenter began a large farming operation on Luzon that eventually failed and left him in dire financial condition. He returned to the United States and after 1937 lived in the U.S. Soldiers' Home in Washington, D.C. "Frank W. Carpenter," Arlington National Cemetery, http://www.arlingtoncemetery.net/fwcarpenter. htm; "Father: Gov. Frank W. Carpenter," Nonlinearhistorynut's Blog, http:// nonlinearhistorynut.wordpress.com/father-gov-frank-w-carpenter; "Frank Watson Carpenter," in Arthur S. Pier, *American Apostles in the Philippines* (Boston: Beacon Press, 1950), pp. 85–93; *ARWD, 1915,* vol. 3, *Philippine Commission,* pp. 60–61; Fulton, *Moroland,* pp. 466–83; C. W. Farwell, "The Biggest Man in the Philippines: Story of the Wonderful Work of Frank W. Carpenter as Department Governor of Mindanao and Sulu," *Current History* 13 (October 1920), pp. 20a–21.

Eugene A. Carr (20 March 1830–2 December 1910). Carr graduated from the U.S. Military Academy in 1850 and saw extensive duty on the plains and in the Southwest. At the outbreak of the Civil War, Carr commanded the post at Fort Washita, Indian Territory, and moved his troops into Missouri, where he was involved at Wilson's Creek (10 August 1861), which earned him a brevet as a lieutenant colonel and command of the 3d Illinois Volunteer Cavalry (August–September 1862). He commanded his regiment and a cavalry brigade and then the 4th Division at Pea Ridge (7–8 March 1862), during which he was wounded three times but remained on the field and in command. For his heroism at Pea Ridge, he was promoted to brigadier general of volunteers, and in January 1894 he was awarded a Medal of Honor. Reverting to his permanent rank of major after the war, Carr commanded a detachment of the 5th Cavalry during the difficult campaign against the Sioux and Cheyenne Indians in Kansas and Colorado (1868–1869). He then had various assignments until assuming command of the 5th Cavalry at Fort Hays, Kansas, in June 1876. He participated in the Sioux campaign of 1876 with the 5th Cavalry in the Big Horn and Yellowstone Expedition. Carr was assigned to command the 6th Cavalry at Fort Lowell, Arizona, in October 1879 and began his long years of operations against hostile Apache, Zuni, and Navaho tribes. He also commanded the posts at Forts Bayard and Wingate, New Mexico, and the District of New Mexico (1884–1890) before the 6th Cavalry was transferred to South Dakota in December 1890 for the Pine Ridge campaign (December 1890–January 1891). He then commanded Fort Niobrara, Nebraska (1891–1892), and retired in February 1893. Carr was known as one of the frontier army's great Indian fighters. "Eugene Asa Carr," *Forty-Second Annual Reunion of the Association of Graduates of the United States Military Academy at West Point, New York, June 12, 1911* (Saginaw, Mich.: Seemann and Peters, Printers and Binders, 1911), pp. 99–106. For a biography of Eugene A. Carr, see James T. King, *War Eagle: A Life of General Eugene A. Carr* (Lincoln: Univ. of Nebraska Press, 1963).

Lawrence C. Carr (10 March 1855–4 December 1921). Carr received his medical education at the Medical College of Ohio in Cincinnati (now the College of Medicine, University of Cincinnati) and was awarded his M.D. in 1877. He was appointed professor of obstetrics at the Cincinnati College of Medicine and Surgery in 1883. He was active in the medical department of the Ohio National Guard, advancing to the rank of major and surgeon by 1891. That year he became a founding member of the National Association of Military Surgeons of the National Guard of the United States, which was reorganized as the Association of Military Surgeons of the United States (AMSUS). In July 1898, he was appointed major and brigade surgeon, U.S. Volunteers. Sent to Santiago in September 1898, Carr took over control of the yellow fever hospital and sanitary and public health efforts to control that disease under Leonard Wood. He later served as the chief surgeon, Department of Santiago and Puerto Principe at Santiago, Cuba (April–October 1900) and then as medical inspector and chief sanitary officer and later chief surgeon for the Department of Eastern Cuba (1900–1901). After returning to the United States, he was recommissioned a major and brigade surgeon on 7 May 1901 and dispatched to the Philippines. There he was eventually assigned to Mindanao and served as Pershing's surgeon at Camp Vicars and on the expeditions of September–October 1902. He was discharged from the volunteer service in February 1903 and returned to Cincinnati. He resumed his practice and was a professor of obstetrics at his alma mater, the Medical College of Ohio. Heitman, *Historical Register,* vol. 1, p. 285; Otto Juettner, "Lawrence C. Carr," in *Daniel Drake and His Followers: Historical and Biographical Sketches* (Cincinnati: Harvey Publishing Company, 1909), p. 317; "The Public Service: Army Changes," *JAMA* 34, no. 16 (April 21, 1900), p. 1022, and vol. 35, no. 17 (October 17, 1900); "Deaths," *JAMA* 77, no. 27 (December 1921), p. 2141; *American Medicine* 2, no. 1 (July 6, 1901), p. 44; Mary C. Gillette, *The Army Medical Department, 1865-1917* (Washington, D.C.: U.S. Army Center of Military History, 1995), pp. 235-38; Edgar E. Hume, *The Golden Jubilee of the Association of Military Surgeons of the United States: A History of Its First Half-Century: 1891-1941* (Washington, D.C.: Association of Military Surgeons, 1941), pp. 19, 20, 214.

William Harding Carter (19 November 1851–24 May 1925). Carter graduated from the USMA in June 1873 and was commissioned in the 8th Infantry. He served on frontier duty in Wyoming, the Dakotas, Nebraska, and Arizona with the 8th and then with the 6th Cavalry after 1875. On 17 September 1891, he was awarded the Medal of Honor for his heroism against the Apaches at Cibicu Creek, Arizona, on 30 August 1881. He commanded Troop F, 6th Cavalry, at Fort Wingate, New Mexico (September–December 1890) and in the field during the Pine Ridge campaign (December 1890–February 1891). After tours of duty at Fort Niobrara, Nebraska (1891-1893), and as an instructor at the Infantry and Cavalry School (1893-1895), Carter was assigned to the Adjutant General's Department in June 1895. He was deeply involved under Henry Corbin in many aspects of the War Department's operations during the Spanish-American War and in preparing legislation for the creation of the U.S. Volunteer regiments (2 March 1899) and reorganization of the army (2 February 1901). In April 1902, he was promoted to staff colonel and made a member of the first War College Board (June 1902) before his promotion to brigadier general in July. He prepared the legislation establishing the War Department General Staff in 1903 and his concepts and work underpinned many of the reforms carried out by Secretary of War Elihu Root. He commanded the Department of the Visayas in the Philippines (1904-1905), the Department of the Lakes (1906-1908), the Department of Missouri (1908-1909), and the Philippines Department (1909-1910). Promoted to major general in November 1909, he returned to the United States and had a number of different assignments over the next several years, including developing the maneuver division at Fort Sam Houston (March–August 1911). He was relieved from the General Staff and assigned to command the Central Division (later Department) in Chicago (1912-1914) and also commanded the 2d Division at Texas City (1913-1914). He was next assigned to command the Hawaiian Department (1914-1915) and retired on 19 November 1915. He then worked for the Senate's Military Committee in preparing the National Defense Act of 1916. In the World War, he was recalled to active duty to command the Central Department (August 1917–March 1918) and was sent to France (March–July 1918). On 2 June 1918, he was retired after fifty years of service. Carter was a prolific writer on military affairs during his career, publishing important essays on the General Staff and preparedness as well as military histories, such as *Horses, Saddles and Bridles* (1895, 1906), *From Yorktown to Santiago with the Sixth Cavalry* (1900), *Old Army Sketches* (1906), *The American Army* (1915), and *The Life of Lieutenant General Chaffee* (1918). "William Harding Carter," in *Fifty-Seventh Annual Report of the Association of Graduates of the United States Military Academy at West Point, New York, June 11, 1926* (Saginaw, Mich.: Seemann and Peters, Printers and Binders,

1926), pp. 123–27; TAGO, *Medals of Honor to October 31, 1897*, p. 29; *American Decorations, 1862-1926*, pp. 17, 686; Ronald G. Machoian, *William Harding Carter and the American Army: A Soldier's Story* (Norman: Univ. of Oklahoma Press, 2006).

James F. Case (22 September 1868–?). Little is known about James F. Case except for the time of his service in the Philippines from 1898 to 1901 and then his later service in insular government. He was born in Wisconsin and was a civil engineer living in Portland, Oregon, and a member of the Oregon National Guard, commanding Company I, 1st Regiment of Oregon Infantry, when the war with Spain was declared. He was mustered in as a captain on 13 May 1898 and assigned to command Company F, 2d Oregon Volunteer Infantry, which was part of Brigadier General Thomas M. Anderson's first expedition of Merritt's VIII Army Corps that left San Francisco for Manila on 25 May 1898 and arrived on 30 June. Case played an important part in operations leading to the occupation of Manila in August and in the 2d Oregon's operations thereafter. He was assigned to the 1st Division headquarters as acting engineer officer (April–June 1899) and participated with Captain William Birkhimer in active operations in May. Case was given a brevet of major for his gallantry at Maasin bridge at San Isidro, Luzon, on 17 May 1899. Case was selected as a major in the 40th U.S. Volunteer Infantry that was then forming at Fort Riley, Kansas. He returned to the Philippines with the 40th in December 1899 and saw extensive service in the Philippines and northern Mindanao, during which he and Pershing became acquainted. The 40th returned to San Francisco on 24 June 1901 and Case was apparently mustered out of service. There is no evidence that he ever served in the Regular Army thereafter, but he did return to the Philippines and served in the city of Manila and insular government. In February 1903 he was appointed engineer in charge of the preliminary work for the new Manila water and sewer system, and he then became city engineer for Manila in September 1903. In April 1905 he was appointed chief engineer for the Department of Sewer and Waterworks Construction, and he completed the new system early in 1909. Governor-General James F. Smith then appointed Case director of the Bureau of Public Works, Department of Commerce and Police, Philippine Government. Case resigned that post in May 1910 and left the Philippines for good. Thereafter he worked as a civil and consulting engineer in a number of different countries, apparently dying sometime in the late 1920s in New York. "James F. Case," in Heitman, *Historical Register*, vol. 2, p. 198; Brigadier General C. U. Gantenbein, ed., *The Official Records of the Oregon Volunteers in the Spanish War and Philippine Insurrection* (Salem, Oreg.: W. H. Leeds, State Printer, 1902), passim, especially p. 216; *ARWD, 1900*, vol. 1, pt. 3, p. 372; *ARWD, 1901*, vol. 1, pt. 3, pp. 29, 32; *ARWD, 1903*, vol. 5: *Report of the Philippine Commission*, p. 546; *ARWD, 1909*, vol. 7, *The Philippine Commission*, pp. 67–68, 97–98, 141; U.S. War Department, Bureau of Insular Affairs, *Fifth Annual Report of the Philippine Commission, 1904* (Washington, D.C.: GPO, 1905), pt. 1, pp. 62, 107, 156–57; *Sixth Annual Report of the Philippine Commission, 1905* (Washington, D.C.: GPO, 1906), pt. 1, pp. 437, 447, 480, 560; "James Francis Case," "U.S. Passport Applications," and "New York Passenger Entry," http://www.ancestry.com.

Enrico Caviglia (4 May 1862–22 March 1945). Caviglia attended military schools in Milan and Turin and was appointed an officer in the Italian Army's Artillery Corps in 1883. He served in Italian campaigns in Africa and participated in the Italian defeat at Adowa in Ethiopia in 1897. In 1904 he was sent to Tokyo as an Italian military attaché to observe the Japanese in the Russo-Japanese War. He remained an Italian military attaché in Tokyo and also in Beijing until 1911. He then served in north Africa in 1912 and was appointed vice director of the Military Geographic Institute in Florence in 1913. When Italy entered the war in 1915, Caviglia was promoted to major general and commanded against Austro-Hungarian forces. He was promoted to lieutenant general in June 1917 and in August commanded the XXIV Corps in the victory over the Austro-Hungarians in the Eleventh Battle of the Isonzo. In 1918 he commanded the X Corps and Eighth Army in the defeat of the Austro-Hungarians at Vittorio Veneto. He was later minister of war in 1919. He was appointed marshal of Italy in June 1926, but was not a supporter of Benito Mussolini. "Enrico Caviglia," http://www.treccani.it/enciclopedia/enrico-caviglia_(Dizionario-Biografico)/.

Adna R. Chaffee (14 August 1842–1 November 1914). Chaffee enlisted in Company K of the Regular Army's 6th Cavalry in July 1861. He served as a private, sergeant, and first sergeant and saw action in the Peninsular campaign and at Antietam. In May 1863 he was commissioned and was wounded at Gettysburg. He remained in the army after the war and was promoted to captain in October 1867. He served mainly on the frontier with his regiment until 1888 and was involved in numerous skirmishes with Indians. Chaffee served under Nelson Miles during the campaign against the Cheyenne Indians in Indian Territory (1874–1875). While with the 6th Cavalry in Arizona Chaffee led a troop that accompanied Crook during his pursuit and capture of Geronimo in 1883. He was promoted to major and transferred to the 9th Cavalry in July 1888, leaving the 6th Cavalry for the first time since he enlisted in July 1861. He became commandant of the Cavalry School at Fort Riley, Kansas, in July 1897. With the coming of the Spanish-American War, he joined the 3d Cavalry and was then promoted to brigadier general, USV, in May 1898 and commanded the 3d Brigade, 2d Division, V Army Corps, under Henry Lawton in the United States and during the Santiago Campaign in Cuba. For his actions at El Caney (1 July 1898) he was promoted to major general, USV, effective 19 July. He then assumed command of the 2d Division (August–October 1898) upon its return to the United States and of the 1st Division, IV Army Corps (October–December 1898) before returning to Cuba to serve as chief of staff to Major General John R. Brooke, the military governor of Cuba (December 1898–December 1899) and then Major General Leonard Wood (December 1899–May 1900). Chaffee was discharged from the USV on 13 April 1899 and promoted to brigadier general, U.S. Army, the same day. He commanded the U.S. troops assigned to the international China Relief Expedition to reduce the Boxer Rebellion in China (June 1900–May 1901) and led U.S. troops in the relief of the foreign legations in Peking (14 August 1900). As a result of his leadership in China, Chaffee was promoted to major general, U.S. Army, in February 1901 and became governor and commander of U.S. forces in the Philippines (July 1901–September 1902). He left that post to take over as commander, Department of the East, at Governor's Island, New York. Early in October 1903, he became assistant chief of staff, War Department, in preparation for assuming the post of chief of staff on 9 January 1904 and receiving his promotion to lieutenant general. He retired at his own request on 1 February 1906. He relocated to Los Angeles, California, where he soon became president of the Board of Public Works and oversaw the construction of the aqueduct that was opened in November 1913 to supply the city with water from northern California. Chaffee's son, Adna R. Chaffee Jr. (23 September 1884–22 August 1941), graduated from the USMA in 1906 and was a pioneer in the use of tanks and armored vehicles in the U.S. Army. The younger Chaffee, known as the "father of the Armored Force," headed the Armored Force (later I Armored Corps) when it was created in July 1940 and died of cancer shortly after he was promoted to major general, U.S. Army, in August 1941. Major General William H. Carter, *The Life of Lieutenant General Chaffee* (Chicago: Univ. of Chicago Press, 1917), passim; TAGO, *OAR, 1897,* p. 255; TAGO, *OAR, 1901,* pp. 85, 353; Heitman, *Historical Register,* vol. 1, p. 177; "Adna R. Chaffee (1842–1914)" and "Adna R. Chaffee (1884–1941)," *Webster's American Military Biographies,* pp. 66–67; "Adna Romanza Chaffee (father and son)," *Who Was Who–The Military,* p. 89; "Adna R. Chaffee (Major 9th Cavalry)," in *Powell's Records,* pp. 122–23; "Adna Romanza Chaffee," in Gates, *Men of Mark,* vol. 1, pp. 210–12.

George C. Charlton (22 February 1871–27 March 1930). Charlton served as a private, corporal, sergeant, quartermaster sergeant, and first sergeant, in Company B, 22d Infantry Regiment, and then as a battalion sergeant major in the 22d Infantry (February 1893–March 1905). He was appointed a second lieutenant in the Philippine Scouts in March 1905, was promoted to first lieutenant in September 1908, and to captain in September 1911 and reappointed to that rank in September 1915. He retired from the Philippine Scouts in June 1918 but was recalled to active duty (July 1918–November 1920). He was then reappointed in the Regular Army as a captain in July 1920 and immediately promoted to major that month. He was promoted to lieutenant colonel in January 1929. No information has been found on his active duty assignments. "George C. Charlton," Department of Veterans' Affairs, Nationwide Gravesite Locator, http://gravelocator.cem.va.gov/j2ee/servlet/NGL_v1; TAGO, *OAR, 1920,* p. 1002; and TAGO, *OAR, 1930,* p. 112.

Sydney A. Cloman (10 October 1867–12 May 1923). Cloman graduated from the USMA in June 1889 and was commissioned in the 1st Infantry. He served in the field with the 1st Infantry during the Pine Ridge campaign against the Sioux Indians (December 1890–February 1891). He was then assigned to posts in California and New Mexico (1892–1897), after which he was professor of military science and tactics at the University of California, Berkeley, until May 1898. He was appointed major and chief commissary, USV, and assigned to the Philippine expedition in San Francisco and the Philippines (May–July 1898). He was promoted to captain, 23d Infantry, on 7 September 1899 and served with the regiment, which was stationed on Jolo Island in the Philippines, until October 1901. In 1899–1900, he was governor of Bongao and the Tawi-Tawi Islands in the Sulu Archipelago before becoming acting inspector general of the Department of Mindanao and Jolo under James Pettit and William Kobbé. After he retired, Cloman wrote a series of articles in *The World's Work* on his experiences with the Moros which was then published as *Myself and a Few Moros* (New York: Doubleday, Page, 1923). After serving at posts in New York, in August 1903 Cloman was detailed to the new General Staff as one of its initial members. He was at the Army War College and on the General Staff until April

1905, when he was appointed a military attaché with the Russian Army in Manchuria and accompanied Major General Thomas Barry on that mission. After returning from Manchuria, he was on the General Staff until December 1906, when he was assigned as military attaché at the U.S. embassy in London. After lengthy service as attaché until March 1911, he was promoted to major in the 26th Infantry. He then commanded the 23d Infantry at El Paso, Texas, and the 12th Infantry at Nogales, Arizona, during the Mexican border problems. He resigned from the army in January 1917 only to return to active duty as a lieutenant colonel in June. Appointed colonel of infantry, NA, in August, he organized and commanded the 320th Infantry Regiment, 80th Division, in the United States (September 1917–May 1918) and France (May–June 1918). After completing the General Staff College course at Langres in September, Cloman was assistant chief of staff, Operations, I Corps, during the St. Mihiel offensive (September 1918) and later chief of staff, 29th Division, in Alsace and during the Argonne campaign at Verdun to 11 November 1918. He returned to the United States in May 1919 and retired at his own request as a lieutenant colonel. "Sydney A. Cloman," *Fifty-Sixth Annual Report of the Association of Graduates of the United States Military Academy at West Point, New York, June 11, 1925* (Saginaw, Mich.: Seemann and Peters, Printers and Binders, 1925), pp. 108–10; "Report of the Lieutenant General Commanding the Army," 29 October 1900, in *ARWD, 1900,* vol. 1, pt. 3, pp. 16–17, 36; *ARWD, 1900,* vol. 1, pt. 3, p. 417; *ARWD, 1901,* vol. 1, pt. 2, pp. 138, 140; "Report of the Lieutenant General Commanding the Army," 1 October 1901, in *ARWD, 1901,* vol. 1, pt. 3, pp. 23–33; *ARWD, 1901,* vol. 1, pt. 3, pp. 358, 361, 416.

James L. Collins (10 December 1882–30 June 1963). Collins graduated from the USMA in June 1907 and was commissioned in the 8th Cavalry. In late 1910, he was sent to the Philippines, where he was stationed on Luzon until May 1912 and then at Jolo participating in operations against hostile Moros (May–October 1912). He was Pershing's aide-de-camp at Zamboanga (October 1912–July 1913) and was acting chief of staff for the Department of Mindanao during the Bud Bagsak operation on Jolo Island (11–15 June 1913). He then moved to Manila as the aide-de-camp to the governor-general of the Philippines (July–September 1912) before returning to Zamboanga as Pershing's aide until December 1913. He accompanied Pershing to the Presidio of San Francisco, where he was aide again until April 1914 and then at El Paso until December 1915. Pershing once again called Collins to be his aide during the Mexican Expedition (March 1916–February 1917). He remained with Pershing when the latter replaced Funston as commander of the Southern Department at Fort Sam Houston, Texas (February–May 1917). He was a member of Pershing's AEF headquarters, still as his aide (May–October 1917). He was promoted to major, field artillery, NA, in August 1917 and completed the Field Artillery School at Saumur (October–December 1917). He was once against Pershing's aide until May 1918, when he was appointed the secretary of the General Staff, AEF, and promoted to lieutenant colonel, NA (June 1918). He commanded the 7th Field Artillery, 1st Division, during the Meuse-Argonne offensive and in occupied Germany (October–December 1918). Collins returned to AEF headquarters as secretary of the General Staff (December 1918–July 1919). He was assigned to the War Department General Staff (1920–1924) and later served as the U.S. military attaché in Rome (1928–1932) before returning to Fort Sill, Oklahoma (1932–1934). He was assistant chief of staff,

G-4, Second Corps Area, at Governor's Island, New York (1934–1938). He commanded the 6th Field Artillery, 1st Field Artillery Brigade, and Fort Hoyle, Maryland (1938–1939), and was promoted to brigadier general early in 1939. He was then at Fort Sam Houston in command of the 2d Field Artillery Brigade, 2d Division, and later headed the division artillery until April 1940. He assumed command of the 2d Division in April 1940 and was promoted to major general in October. In April 1941, he was transferred to command of the Puerto Rican Department. In March 1943 he became Director of Administration for the War Department in Washington. His final active duty post was as commanding general, Fifth Service Command, in Columbus, Ohio (December 1943–February 1946). Two of Collins's sons graduated from the Military Academy: Brigadier General James L. Collins Jr. (USMA, 1939) and Major General (U.S. Air Force Reserve) Michael Collins (USMA, 1952), one of the first American astronauts. His brother, J. (Joseph) Lawton Collins, graduated from the USMA in April 1917 and during World War II commanded the VII Corps in the European Theater of Operations and later became the army chief of staff (1949–1953).

Henry C. Corbin (15 September 1842–8 September 1909). Corbin served as an officer in the 83d Ohio Infantry and then the 79th Ohio Infantry in 1862–1863. He later accepted a commission as a major in the 14th Infantry (U.S. Colored Troops) in November 1863. In May 1866 he was commissioned in the 17th U.S. Infantry, later transferring to the 24th Infantry in November 1869. After serving on the frontier since 1866, Corbin was detailed to the White House staff in March 1877 as aide to the new president, Rutherford B. Hayes, a fellow Ohioan. Once he assumed the post, he became acquainted with a number of influential Ohio Republican politicians, including James A. Garfield and William McKinley. He remained in the White House under President James A. Garfield. He was with Garfield when he was shot on 2 July 1881 and stayed with him until his death on 19 September. After Garfield's death, he served as adjutant general in the Department of the South until 1884 and at the Department of the Missouri in Omaha (1884–1891). He was in the Department of Arizona (1891–1892) before returning to the Office of the Adjutant General in Washington (1892–1895) and serving as adjutant general in the Department of the East (1895–1897). In February 1898 he became the army's adjutant general with the rank of brigadier general and held that post until April 1904. Because of the falling out that President William McKinley and his Secretary of War, Russell Alger, had with Lieutenant General Nelson A. Miles before the Spanish-American War and his personal friendships, Corbin emerged as the principle military advisor to McKinley and Alger during the war and had very significant influence on the shaping of the army's operations and organization. As a reward for his services during the Spanish-American War, the Congress increased the rank of the adjutant general's position to major general and Corbin was promoted in June 1900. When Elihu Root replaced Alger as Secretary of War, Corbin remained as indispensable as before. He was instrumental in pushing through the entire package of Root reforms in the War Department, including the army's reorganization in February 1901, the establishment of the Army War College, and the creation of the General Staff. After leaving as adjutant general, Corbin commanded the Atlantic Division (January–October 1904) and then the Philippine Division (November 1904–October 1905) before returning to the United States to replace John F. Weston as commander of the Northern Division (January–

September 1906). In a unique maneuver, Corbin was promoted to lieutenant general in April 1906 when Brigadier General J. Franklin Bell replaced Bates as chief of staff, allowing him to retire in that rank in September. Gates, *Men of Mark,* vol. 1, pp. 240-42; *Who Was Who–The Military,* p. 109; Heitman, *Historical Register,* vol. 1, p. 327; "Henry Clarke Corbin, Lieutenant General, United States Army," Arlington National Cemetery Website, http://arlingtoncemetery.net/hccorbin.htm; Graham A. Cosmas, *An Army for Empire: The United States Army in the Spanish-American War* (College Station: Texas A&M Univ. Press, 1998), pp. 57–59.

Charles Pierre René Corvisart (29 June 1857–7 May 1939). Corvisart graduated from the French military academy at St. Cyr and was commissioned in the French Army in 1877. He was the French military attaché in Tokyo (January 1900–July 1904) before being designated as a military observer attached to the Japanese armies in Manchuria. He was promoted to brigadier general in 1911 and at the start of the war was commanding the 11th Dragoon Brigade. He commanded the 9th and later the 123d Infantry Divisions before assuming command of the XVII Corps in April 1917. He later commanded the XVI and XV Corps and was especially prominent in operations around Verdun in 1918. For his wartime accomplishments and assistance to the AEF, the U.S. Army awarded Corvisart a Distinguished Service Medal in 1923. "Charles Pierre Corvisart," http://en.wikipedia.org/wiki/Charles_Pierre_Corvisart; TAGO, *American Decorations, 1862-1926,* p. 809.

Louis A. Craig (17 March 1851–22 March 1904). Craig graduated from the USMA in 1874 and was commissioned in the 9th Infantry, with his duty station at Fort Laramie, Wyoming. In May 1875 he transferred to the 6th Cavalry. He saw extensive duty against Apache and other Indian tribes while stationed at various posts in Arizona and New Mexico. At the outbreak of the Spanish-American War he was promoted to major and assigned as assistant adjutant general in the V Army Corps and then 1st Division, I Army Corps, of Major General James H. Wilson in the Puerto Rican Campaign (June–September 1898). Upon returning to the United States in October, he was adjutant general with 1st Division, IV Army Corps, under Chaffee. Craig was appointed colonel of the 32d U.S. Infantry in July 1899 and took the regiment to the Philippines in October. There he and the 32d Infantry saw extensive action in operations against the insurrectionists on Luzon. While in the Philippines, Craig became ill for several extended periods until he returned to the United States with the regiment in April 1901. He then served with the 15th Cavalry until he was retired on 23 March 1903 for disability in the line of duty. His two sons, General Malin Craig (USMA, 1898) and Major General Louis A. Craig (USMA, 1913), had distinguished careers in the U.S. Army. "Louis A. Craig," *Thirty-Sixth Annual Reunion of the Association of Graduates of the United States Military Academy at West Point, New York, June 13th, 1905* (Saginaw, Mich.: Seemann and Peters, Printers and Binders, 1905), pp. 36–39.

Malin Craig (5 August 1875–25 July 1945). Craig graduated from the USMA in April 1898, transferred to the 4th Cavalry in June, and served in the Santiago Campaign in Cuba before joining the 6th Cavalry in December. After service in the China Relief Expedition (June–September 1900), he moved to the Philippines for service with the

6th Cavalry during the insurrection. There he was aide-de-camp first to Thomas Barry, who was then chief of staff and adjutant general in the Division of the Philippines (1900–1901), and later to J. Franklin Bell, first in the Philippines (to December 1902) and then when Bell commanded the Army Service Schools at Fort Leavenworth, Kansas (to June 1903). Assigned to 1st Cavalry, he was the regimental quartermaster (1906–1909), was active in the army's relief work after the San Francisco earthquake (April 1906), and then served in the Philippines again (1907–1909). He attended and then taught at the Army War College (1909–1911) and was a member of the General Staff Corps with various duties to October 1912. Following duty with the 1st Cavalry, Craig was once again aide-de-camp to Major General Bell (January–June 1915), on duty with the 1st Cavalry (1915–1916), and an instructor at the Army Service Schools at Fort Leavenworth (1916–1917). With U.S. entrance into the war, Craig was detailed to the General Staff Corps once again and appointed chief of staff to Major General Hunter Liggett, commander, 41st Division. He moved with the division to France in 1917. In January 1918 he became chief of staff, I Corps, AEF, under Liggett, and was promoted to temporary brigadier general (June 1918). Except for a brief time when he also commanded the 166th Infantry Brigade, 83d Division (July–August 1918), Craig served as chief of staff during the I Corps' entire involvement in combat operations in France—during the Aisne-Marne, Chateau-Thierry, St. Mihiel, and Meuse-Argonne campaigns. After duty as chief of staff with the Third U.S. Army in occupied Germany (1918–1919), Craig became director of the Army War College (1919–1920). He was commander, District of Arizona, at Fort Douglas, and was promoted to brigadier general on 28 April 1921. While serving as commandant of the Cavalry School at Fort Riley (1921–1923), he was promoted to major general on 24 July 1924 and appointed as the U.S. Army's chief of cavalry (1924–1926). He was assistant chief of staff, organization and training (ACS, G-3), War Department General Staff (1926–1927) and then commander of the Fourth Corps Area in Atlanta (April–October 1927). After commanding the Panama Canal Division (1927–1928), Craig commanded the Panama Canal Department (1928–1930). He then moved to San Francisco, where he was commanding general, Ninth Corps Area (1930–1935) and also the Fourth U.S. Army (1933–1935). Following a brief tour as commandant of the U.S. Army War College (February–October 1935), Craig was promoted to chief of staff, War Department, with the rank of full general on 2 October 1935. Craig's tenure as chief of staff was critical to the rebuilding, reequipping, and modernization of the army and army Air Corps prior to World War II. He retired from active duty on 31 August 1939 and was recalled to active duty as chairman, War Department Personnel Board (1941–1945). "Malin Craig (1875–1945)," *Webster's American Military Biographies*, pp. 82–83; *The Army Almanac*, pp. 19, 92, 199; "Malin Craig," in Davis, *Generals in Khaki*, pp. 85–86.

George Crook (23 September 1823–21 March 1890). Crook graduated from the USMA in 1852 and was commissioned in the 4th Infantry. He served against the Indians in California, Oregon, and Washington. He was promoted to captain in May 1861 and involved in operations in western Virginia until September 1861, when he became commander of the 36th Ohio Volunteer Infantry Regiment. Crook established a fine reputation as a commander during the Civil War. In July 1866 he reverted to his permanent rank of lieutenant colonel with the 23d Infantry in

Idaho, where he successfully put down an uprising of Paiute Indians in Idaho, Oregon, and Nevada (1866–1868). He commanded the Department of the Columbia (1868–1870). With a strong reputation as the army's best Indian fighter, Crook then moved to the Arizona Territory as commander of the Department of Arizona in June 1871 with the job of pacifying the Apaches, who were on the warpath under Chief Cochise, Geronimo, and others. By 1873 Crook had succeeded in this mission and had returned the Apaches to peaceful pursuits through his honest and thoughtful approach and policies. He was rewarded with promotion to brigadier general in 1873 and then given command of the Department of the Platte in Omaha, Nebraska, in 1875. The discovery of gold in the Black Hills of South Dakota in 1874 brought an influx of whites into these lands of the Sioux and Cheyenne Indians that sparked heavy fighting. Crook commanded the campaign against the Sioux and Cheyenne during the summer of 1876 that resulted in significant reverses for the U.S. Army and Crook at Rosebud Creek (17 June) and for Custer at the Little Bighorn (25 June). Crook finally gained the upper hand in August–September 1876 and remained in the field with Miles until June 1877. In 1882 he was moved back to Arizona, to regain control of the Apache uprising under Geronimo, which he did in 1883. In 1885 he was once again called on to track Geronimo down, before Sheridan replaced him with Nelson Miles and returned him to his command of the Department of the Platte in April 1886. Crook regarded Miles's claims for credit in this campaign to be badly exaggerated, and the two generals had poor relations thereafter. In April 1888 he was promoted to major general and transferred to Chicago, Illinois, to command the Division of the Missouri. He was still in this post when he unexpectedly died from a heart attack on 21 March 1890. "George Crook," *Twenty-First Annual Reunion of the Association of Graduates of the United States Military Academy at West Point, New York, June 12, 1890* (Saginaw, Mich.: Evening News Printing and Binding House, 1890), pp. 40–43; "George Crook (1829–1890)," *Webster's American Military Biographies*, pp. 86–87; Odie B. Faulk, *The Geronimo Campaign* (New York: Oxford Univ. Press, 1969), passim; Thrapp, *The Conquest of Apacheria*, passim; Martin Schmitt, ed., *General George Crook: His Autobiography* (Norman: Univ. of Oklahoma Press, 1960), passim; Boatner, *The Civil War Dictionary*, p. 209; Heitman, *Historical Register*, vol. 1, p. 210.

Lorenzo Crounse (27 January 1834–13 May 1909). Born in New York, Crounse taught school and then studied law and was admitted to the practice of law in Fort Plain, New York, in 1857. In the Civil War, he raised Battery K, 1st Regiment, New York Light Artillery, and became its captain. He saw some fighting before he was wounded on the Rappahannock River in Virginia. As he recovered from his wounds, he resigned his commission and moved to Nebraska in 1864. He entered the territorial legislature as a Republican in 1864 and was appointed to its judiciary committee in 1866. He became a judge on the Nebraska Supreme Court when the state was admitted to the Union in March 1867 and served a six-year term. He was nominated as the Republican candidate for the House of Representatives in 1872 and won. He was reelected in 1874 but ran for the U.S. Senate in 1876 and lost. He returned to farming in Fort Calhoun until he became the collector of internal revenue (1879–1883). He was appointed assistant secretary of the Treasury (April 1891–October 1892) but resigned to run for governor in 1892. He was elected and served one term

(1893–1895) and refused to stand for reelection in 1894. He was elected to the state senate in 1900 and served one term, narrowly losing an appointment as U.S. senator in 1901. "Lorenzo Crounse (1834–1909)," *Biographical Directory of the United States Congress,* http://bioguide.congress.gov/scripts/biodisplay.pl?index=C000935; "Lorenzo Crounse," in J. Sterling Morton, Albert Watkins, and George R. Miller, *Illustrated History of Nebraska: A History of Nebraska from the Earliest Explorations of the Trans-Mississippi Region . . . ,* vol. 1 (Lincoln, Nebr.: Western Publishing and Engraving Company, 1911), pp. 631–34.

Waller H. Dade (?–26 December 1920). Dade received his medical degree from Jefferson Medical College in Philadelphia in the 1880s and later served as the prison physician at the Kentucky State Penitentiary in Frankfort. He was appointed a major and the chief surgeon in the 2d Kentucky Volunteer Infantry in 1898. He was a contract surgeon with the 16th Infantry in the Philippines (1899–1900). Dade was appointed a captain and assistant surgeon, USV, in March 1901 and was discharged in November 1902. He then was again a contract surgeon in the Army Medical Department, serving in the Philippines and the United States until 1908, when all contracts were terminated with the creation of the Medical Reserve Corps. After serving as *presidenté* of the Municipality of Davao, Mindanao, he was appointed director of the San Ramon Penal Farm at Zamboanga by Pershing and later was the director of the Bureau of Prisons, Insular Government (1914–1920). He left civil service in the Philippines in 1920 and returned to the United States, where he died of heart disease at Norfolk, Virginia, on 26 December 1920. Heitman, *Historical Register,* vol. 1, p. 350, and vol. 2, p. 274; *ARWD, 1915,* vol. 3, *Philippine Commission,* p. 274; telegram, P.A. Grimes to Newton D. Baker for General Pershing, 27 December 1920, LC/Pershing, Box 57, Folder: Waller H. Dade.

George W. Davis (26 July 1839–12 July 1918). Davis attended the State Normal School at New Britain, Connecticut, before joining the 11th Connecticut Infantry as a quartermaster sergeant in November 1861. In April 1862 he was commissioned in the 11th, and saw considerable action with it for the duration of the war. He was appointed captain in the 14th Infantry in January 1867 and served in Arizona, the Dakotas, Nebraska, Wyoming, Utah, and Texas until he was appointed assistant engineer for the Washington National Monument (1878–1885). After duty as aide-de-camp to Lieutenant General Sheridan in 1885, Davis returned to regimental duty with the 14th Infantry at Vancouver Barracks, Washington (1885–1887) and Fort Leavenworth (1887–1889). He was promoted to major in the 11th Infantry in 1894, transferred to the 9th Infantry in May 1897, and promoted to lieutenant colonel with the declaration of war with Spain in April 1898. Early in May he was appointed brigadier general, USV, and commanded the 2d Division, II Army Corps, in the United States until November 1898. He then moved to Cuba, where he was acting commander (1898–1899) and then commander of the Department of Pinar del Rio until he was mustered out of the Volunteers in April 1899. He was then assigned as the military governor of Puerto Rico and commander of the Department of Puerto Rico (1899–1900). Davis was colonel of the 23d Infantry Regiment (1899–1901) before he was transferred to the Philippines and promoted to brigadier general in February 1901. He served as provost marshal general of the Military Division of the Philippines (February–August 1901) before commanding the 7th Separate Brigade (Mindanao) and the Department of Mindanao and Jolo (August 1901–July 1902). He was promoted to major general in July 1902 and commanded the Department of Luzon until he succeeded Adna Chaffee as commander of the Division of the Philippines (October 1902–July 1903). He held this post until he retired on 26 July 1903. At the same time, he was involved in the development of a Nicaraguan canal company (1900–1903) and later served on special duty with the Secretary of War (1903–1906). Davis was appointed a member of Isthmian Canal Commission (1904–1905) and then served as the first governor of the Panama Canal Zone (1905–1906). TAGO, *OAR, 1901,* pp. 213, 357; TAGO, *OAR, 1916,* p. 532; "George Whitefield Davis," *Who Was Who–The Military,* p. 126; "George Whitefield Davis," in Gates, *Men of Mark,* vol. 1, pp. 277–79; Heitman, *Historical Register,* vol. 1, p. 358; "George W. Davis," *Powell's Records,* pp. 168–69.

Charles G. Dawes (27 August 1865–23 April 1951). The son of Rufus R. Dawes, a successful businessman and Union Civil War veteran (Brevet Brigadier General, USV) who had commanded the 6th Wisconsin Volunteer Infantry, Dawes was born in Ohio and completed Marietta College (1884) before receiving his law degree from Cincinnati Law School (1886). He moved to Lincoln, Nebraska, where he practiced law and built large local business holdings (1887–1894). After expanding his business holdings to include significant interests in a number of gas and electric companies in Wisconsin and Illinois, he moved to Evanston, Illinois, in 1894 and became involved in Republican politics. He supported William McKinley in the 1896 Republican Convention and was named comptroller of the currency (1898–1901). He tried for the Republican nomination as U.S. senator in 1901 but withdrew when McKinley was assassinated. Dawes then went into banking, establishing the Central Trust Company of Illinois in 1902. Except for brief periods, he remained involved with the bank and its successors thereafter. He was commissioned as a major of engineers in June 1917 and was sent to France in July 1917 with the 17th Engineer Regiment (Railway). At the end of August Pershing met with Dawes and ordered him to General Headquarters, AEF, to control procurement for the entire AEF. He was promoted to brigadier general, NA, in October 1918 and headed the liquidation of the AEF's assets through August 1919. In France, Dawes was one of Pershing's closest and most trusted advisors. Resuming his political career after the war, he was appointed the first director of the Bureau of the Budget under President Warren G. Harding (1921–1922). Appointed to the Allied Reparations Commission to oversee the fulfillment of the terms of the Versailles Treaty ending World War I, he developed the "Dawes Plan" that resolved Germany's problems in paying the enormous reparations levied on it and reorganized Germany's financial structure. Unfortunately, the Dawes Plan only temporarily prevented economic collapse in Europe. Dawes and Sir Austen Chamberlain, the British Foreign Secretary, shared the Nobel Peace Prize in 1925 for the achievement. Dawes ran as President Calvin Coolidge's vice presidential candidate in 1924 and served as vice president until March 1929. The new president, Herbert Hoover, appointed Dawes as ambassador to the United Kingdom (1929–1932), and he returned to the United States in 1932 at Hoover's request to run the Reconstruction Finance Corporation (RFC) that was trying to revive the American economy. He resigned that year to return to save his bank, then called the Central Republic

Bank and Trust Company, from financial collapse, which he did by creating the City National Bank and Trust Company and serving as it chairman until his death. He wrote a number of works, including *A Journal of the Great War* (1921), *Notes as Vice President, 1928-1929* (1935), *A Journal of Reparations* (1939), *Journal as Ambassador to Great Britain* (1939), and *A Journal of the McKinley Years* (1950). Charles G. Dawes, *A Journal of the Great War,* vol. 1 (Boston: Houghton Mifflin, 1921), pp. 4, 19–23; "Charles G. Dawes," Encyclopaedia Britannica Online, http://www.britannica.com/EBchecked/topic/152943/Charles-G-Dawes; "The Nobel Prize in Peace 1925: Sir Austen Chamberlain, Charles G. Dawes," Official Site of the Nobel Prize, http://nobelprize.org/nobel_prizes/peace/laureates/1925/dawes-bio.html; "Charles Gates Dawes (1865-1951)," Biographical Directory of the United States Congress, http://bioguide.congress.gov/scripts/biodisplay.pl?index=d000147; "Charles Gates Dawes," *Who Was Who–The Military,* p. 128.

George McC. Derby (1 November 1856–24 October 1948). The son of Captain George H. Derby (3 April 1823-15 May 1861) (USMA, 1846), an officer of the Corps of Topographical Engineers and an American humorist who wrote about California, Derby graduated from the USMA in June 1878 and was commissioned in the Corps of Engineers. After serving with the Engineer Battalion at Willet's Point, New York, he was involved in river and harbor work in New York City and New Jersey (1881–1888). He was assigned to the Military Academy as instructor in practical engineering and in command of the Engineer Company E (1888-1893). On 9 May 1898, he was appointed lieutenant colonel of volunteers and chief engineer, V Army Corps, in Tampa and was in the field throughout the Santiago Campaign. Derby was in charge of all engineering support for the V Army Corps, including reconnaissance of routes to attack the Spanish defenses and the heavily criticized use of an observation balloon on 1 July. Derby and the commander of the Signal Corps' balloon detachment, Lieutenant Colonel Joseph E. Maxfield, brought the balloon up to the front lines that day. Their tactical reconnaissance drew the attention and heavy fire of the Spanish defenders on the balloon (which was shot down but with no injuries to Derby and Maxfield) and on the American troops below, who were moving forward to attack the San Juan Heights. Although roundly criticized by those on the ground, such as Leonard Wood and Pershing, Derby and Maxfield located a previously unknown trail that allowed the advance of Kent's 1st Division. Upon his return to the United States, he was made chief engineer, II Army Corps (1898-1899). He was promoted to lieutenant colonel in May 1906 and retired on 7 June 1907 at his own request. Residing in New Orleans, Derby was recalled to active duty in April 1917 as commander of the New Orleans Engineer District. Cosmas, *An Army for Empire,* pp. 216-17; "Balloon Operations at Santiago, Cuba" and "George McClellan Derby (1846-1948)," in Berner, ed., *The Spanish-American War,* pp. 33-34, 104.

George H. Dern (8 September 1872–27 August 1936). Dern was born and raised in Nebraska. He completed the Nebraska State Normal School at Fremont and then attended the University of Nebraska (1893-1894), during which time he was captain of the football team and a member of the cadet battalion. He then moved to Utah with his family in 1894. There he became involved in gold mining and ore processing, and also developed processes for roasting ore and metal extraction (Holt-

Dern patents). He rose to the position of vice president and general manager of the Holt-Christenson Processing Company by 1913 and was involved in other business ventures. During this time he became involved in the Democratic Party and was elected to the Utah Senate in 1914, serving until 1923. He was elected governor in 1924, was reelected in 1928, but did not seek reelection in 1932. While chairman of the National Governors' Conference, he became acquainted with Franklin D. Roosevelt, then governor of New York. He strongly supported FDR's election in 1932. President Roosevelt rewarded his support with an appointment as the Secretary of War in March 1933. Dern guided the army through the Depression years, early New Deal projects, Civilian Conservation Corps (CCC), and initial steps towards modernization and the development of the army Air Corps. He served until his death on 27 August 1936. "George Henry Dern," *Who Was Who–The Military,* p. 134; Newell G. Bringhurst, "George Henry Dern," Utah History to Go, http://historytogo.utah .gov/people/georgehenrydern.html.

George D. Deshon (5 August 1864–24 June 1917). Deshon graduated from the USMA with Pershing in June 1886 and was commissioned in the 23d Infantry Regiment. In March 1890, he resigned his commissioned to attend medical school and obtained his M.D. from Bellevue Hospital Medical College, New York, in March 1890 and an M.D. from the University of Pennsylvania in 1893. He was appointed assistant surgeon (lieutenant) in the Army Medical Corps in May 1892 and served in Wyoming, at the Chicago World's Fair, in Colorado, and Utah (1892–1896). He was a staff surgeon at Washington Barracks, D.C. (May 1897–December 1898) and also an instructor at the Army Medical School. He was chief surgeon, 4th Infantry, in the United States and Philippines (1898–1899) and then with the 11th U.S. Volunteer Cavalry in the Philippines (1899–1900). He remained in the Philippines as executive officer of the hospital ship *Relief* (1900–1901) and then as chief surgeon, Department of Luzon (1901–1903). Deshon was surgeon at Fort Des Moines, Iowa (1904–1907), and commanding officer, Army and Navy General Hospital, Hot Springs, Arkansas (1907–1912). He commanded the Medical Supply Depot at San Francisco (1912–1914) before he was transferred to the Panama Canal Zone as superintendent of the Ancon Hospital (1914–1917). He returned to the United States in May 1917 to assume duty in Boston as the department surgeon, Northeastern Department, where he died on 24 June.

Jacob M. Dickinson (30 January 1851–13 December 1928). Dickinson received his A.B. at the University of Nashville (1871) and studied law at Columbia Law School in New York. He was admitted to the bar in Nashville, Tennessee, in 1874 and practiced law there (1874–1899). He was an assistant U.S. attorney general (1895–1897) and later served as the lawyer for the Illinois Central Railroad (1899–1909). He served as Secretary of War under President Taft (March 1909–May 1911). Dickinson's trip to the Philippines took place from his arrival in Manila on 24 July 1910 to his departure from Manila on 3 September 1910. His report and recommendations were submitted to President Taft on 23 November 1910 and published as House Document 1261, 61st Congress, 3d Session, in 1911. The War Department reprinted his report along with former Secretary of War Taft's report of 23 January 1908 to President Roosevelt in *Special Reports on the Philippines to the President* (Washington, D.C.: GPO, 1919), pp. 97–189. "Jacob McGavock Dickinson," *Who Was Who–The Military,* p. 136.

Robert Dickson (30 May 1864–18 August 1923). Dickson served as a private, corporal, sergeant, and first sergeant in Troop G, 5th Cavalry (February 1884–February 1894). He left the service and then returned as a private, corporal, sergeant, and first sergeant with Troop A, 3d Cavalry (March–June 1899) and as squadron sergeant major and command sergeant with the 5th Cavalry (June–July 1901). He was appointed to the Philippine Scouts as a second lieutenant in July 1901 and promoted to first lieutenant in December 1904. He was reappointed a first lieutenant in July 1905 and captain in September 1908 and reappointed in that rank in September 1912 and September 1916. He retired as a captain, Philippine Scouts, in September 1918 and then served as a major, U.S. Guards (September 1918–January 1919). TAGO, *OAR, 1920,* p. 1003, and TAGO, *OAR, 1924,* p. 788.

George A. Dodd (26 July 1852–28 June 1925). Dodd graduated from the USMA in June 1876 and was commissioned in the 3d Cavalry. He served in Wyoming, Nebraska, and the Dakotas against the Sioux, Nez Percé, northern Cheyennes, and Utes (1876–1881) before moving to Arizona, where he saw action against Geronimo's Apaches and other bands (1881–1885), and then to Texas for operations against the Kiowas (1885–1888). After two years on recruiting duty, he returned to garrison duty in Texas, Kansas, and Vermont (1891–1898), where he established a reputation for training cavalry troops. Dodd participated with the 3d Cavalry in the Santiago Campaign in Cuba and in the fighting for the San Juan Heights (1–3 July 1898), where he was wounded and left for dead on the battlefield. He returned to garrison duty in September 1898 and was sent to the Philippines with his regiment in August 1899. He was assigned to the Cavalry Brigade, 1st Division, VIII Army Corps, in the Philippines and saw extensive action in northern Luzon. Dodd was promoted to major in the 14th Cavalry in 1901 and returned to the United States in July, where he rejoined the 3d Cavalry in 1903. He was promoted to lieutenant colonel, 10th Cavalry, in July 1904 and served with the 10th in Nebraska and Wyoming (1906–1907) until he was assigned to the General Staff Corps and appointed chief of staff, Northern Division, in Chicago in April 1907 and then the Department of the Lakes (1907–1908). He was promoted to colonel, 12th Cavalry, in 1908 and commanded the regiment in the United States and the Philippines (1908–1911). He returned with the 12th Cavalry to Fort Robinson, Nebraska, and commanded Columbus Barracks, Ohio (1911–1915). He then commanded the 2d Cavalry Brigade at Fort Douglas, Arizona, patrolling the Mexican border from Columbus, New Mexico, to Nogales, Arizona (1915–1916). He led the brigade in a number of engagements against Villa's forces during the Mexican Expedition (March–July 1916). He was promoted to brigadier general on 3 July 1916 and retired from active service on 26 July due to age. "George Allen Dodd," *Fifty-Ninth Annual Report of the Association of Graduates of the United States Military Academy at West Point, New York, June 8, 1928,* pp. 49–53.

Edgar S. Dudley (14 June 1845–9 January 1911). After serving as lieutenant in the 1st New York Artillery in 1864, Dudley attended the USMA, graduating in 1870 with a commission in the 2d Artillery. While serving in Washington, North Carolina, and at Fort Monroe, Virginia (1870–1876), he took a leave of absence and completed his law degree at Albany Law School, Union University (1874–1875). In September 1876 he was assigned as professor of military science and tactics at the University of

Nebraska, Lincoln. After duty in Washington and Kentucky, during which he was acting judge advocate for the Department of the South (1882–1883), Dudley once again was at the University of Nebraska until September 1888. He was acting judge advocate, Department of Arizona, in Los Angeles (1891–1893). He was promoted to assistant quartermaster in December 1892 and was an assistant to the chief quartermaster, Department of Texas, San Antonio, and in charge of building construction at Fort Sam Houston (1893–1895) and then quartermaster in charge of construction at Columbus Barracks, Ohio (1895–1896). He served as the judge advocate for II Army Corps (June–September 1898) and then was on duty at the Judge Advocate General's Office in Washington until December. Dudley was assigned as judge advocate, Division (later Department) of Cuba, in Havana (1898–1901) and acted as legal advisor to the military governors of Cuba, John R. Brooke and Leonard Wood. He was appointed professor of law and history at the USMA in July 1901 and promoted to colonel, judge advocate, in November 1903. He retired 14 June 1909 and was promoted to brigadier general, U.S. Army retired, the same day. "Edgar S. Dudley," *Forty-Second Annual Reunion of the Association of Graduates of the United States Military Academy at West Point, New York, June 12, 1911,* pp. 129–30.

George B. Duncan (10 October 1861–15 March 1950). Duncan graduated from the USMA in June 1886 with Pershing and was commissioned in the 9th Infantry. He served on frontier duty in New Mexico and Arizona (1886–1892) and then on the staff of John Schofield, commanding general of the army (1892–1894), after which he returned to duty with the 4th Infantry Regiment in Idaho (1894–1896) and at Fort Sheridan, Illinois (1896–1898). After the 4th Infantry moved to Tampa, Florida, in readiness for deployment to Cuba, he was appointed captain, USV, serving as adjutant general for the several brigades of the IV, V, and VII Army Corps, and finally reached Cuba in late July with the Provisional Division. He returned to the United States late in 1898 and rejoined his regiment in January 1899, immediately sailing for the Philippines. He went straight into action as part of the 2d Division, VIII Army Corps, in Luzon. Duncan later commanded in the field against insurgents (1900–1901). He was reassigned to the Philippines again in the Department of Luzon (1903–1905), and was appointed major, Philippine Scouts, and rose to be acting chief, Philippine Scouts, on the Philippine Division staff (1905–1909). After some months on sick leave, he joined the 4th Infantry as commander of the 2d Battalion at Fort Leavenworth (1910–1911) and was then a student at the Army War College (1911–1912). He was assigned to the War Department General Staff (1914–1915) and then on the Mexican border with the 2d Infantry in 1915. He once again served on the General Staff (1916–1917) and was promoted to colonel in September 1916. In June 1917 he was relieved at his own request and assigned to command the 26th Infantry, 1st Division, as it left for France. He was appointed brigadier general, NA, in August 1917 and attached to the French 94th Division at Verdun in August. In September 1917 he was assigned to the 1st Brigade, 1st Division, and then commanded it in combat at the front (January–May 1918). Promoted to major general, NA, in May, he assumed command of the 77th Division, which he trained and commanded until October 1918, when he took over the 82d Division. Duncan commanded the 82d Division throughout its heavy fighting in the Meuse-Argonne offensive (October–November 1918) and until May 1919. He commanded the 21st Infantry in 1920 and then the 5th and 7th Infantry Brigades (1920–1922). He was commanding general of the Seventh Corps Area at Omaha, Nebraska (1922–1925). Promoted to major general in December 1922, he was retired on 10 October 1925. "George Brand Duncan," *Assembly* 9, no. 3 (October 1950), p. 44; Clay, *U.S. Army Order of Battle*, vol. 1, pp. 297, 298, 302, 379.

Edward Dworak (31 January 1874–17 June 1950). Dworak was born in Austria-Hungary and immigrated to the United States. He served as a private, corporal, and sergeant major in the 18th Infantry from February 1893 until July 1901, when he was commissioned in the Philippine Scouts. He was later promoted to first lieutenant (September 1902) and captain (September 1908) and served until he resigned from the Philippine Scouts in March 1912. Pershing appointed Dworak as the first civilian governor of Cotabato District, Moro Province, in August 1912. With the establishment of the civilian Department of Mindanao and Sulu in 1914, he became governor of the province of Cotabato, a post he held until November 1914. He was added to the army's retired list effective 24 June 1916 but returned to active duty for extended periods thereafter (1916–1918 and 1919–1921). In September 1921 he was commissioned a major of Infantry and transferred to the Finance Department from September 1924 until he retired in January 1929. No information has been found on his wife, Anna Dworak. TAGO, *OAR, 1931*, p. 805; TAGO, *OAR, 1951*, vol. 1, p. 860; Brigadier General John J. Pershing, *The Annual Report of the Governor of the Moro Province for the Fiscal Year Ended June 30, 1913* (Zamboanga, Philippines: Mindanao Herald Publishing Company, 1913) (hereafter Pershing, *AR, Moro Province*, and year), p. 82; U.S. War Department, *Report of the Philippine Commission to the Secretary of War, July 1, 1913 to December 31, 1914* (Washington, D.C.: GPO, 1915), p. 397.

Frank D. Eager (27 August 1872–3 September 1960). Eager graduated from the University of Nebraska in 1893 and was a member of the cadet battalion under Lieutenant John Pershing, being a captain in 1893. He studied law in Lincoln after graduating from the university and was admitted to the bar in 1896. In 1895 he purchased the *Lincoln Independent* and the *Wealth-Makers and Populist* newspapers, which he merged into the *Nebraska Independent*. He was elected to the state legislature in 1896. Eager joined the Nebraska National Guard after 1894, and in 1896 he became first lieutenant in Company D, 1st Regiment, Nebraska National Guard, and served as regimental adjutant. He was mustered into the 1st Nebraska in May 1898 and promoted to captain and commander of Company H. The 1st was sent to the Philippines in June 1898, where it saw extensive action in 1898–1899 on Luzon under Colonels John Bratt and then John Stotsenburg. Eager was promoted to major in April 1899 and lieutenant colonel in June. He was severely wounded on 25 April and received a citation for gallantry (later designated the Silver Star Medal). Eager returned to Nebraska with the regiment in August 1899 and later served as commandant of cadets at the university (1901–1902). He disposed of his newspaper holdings several years later and turned his personal attention to real estate and investments. He was particularly deeply involved in matters dealing with the continued development and expansion of the University of Nebraska in Lincoln, his alma mater. "Frank DeWitt Eager 1872-1960, Biographical Note," in "Manuscript Record, Frank DeWitt Eager Collection (MS2420)," Nebraska State Historical Society, Lincoln, Nebraska; Lieutenant Colonel Frank D. Eager, comp., *History of the Operations of the 1st Nebraska Infantry, U.S.V. in the Campaign in the Philippine Islands* (Lincoln, Nebr.: N.p., n.d.), p. 49; Morton and Watkins, *History of Nebraska*, rev. ed., pp. 690–91.

Martin Egan (18 June 1872–7 December 1938). Egan was admitted to the California bar in 1898 but opted to become a foreign correspondent for various American and Canadian newspapers and the Associated Press. As an AP correspondent, he was posted in New York, London, Tokyo, Beijing, and Manila and covered the Spanish-American War, Philippine-American War, Boxer Rebellion, and Russo-Japanese War. He then edited the *Manila Times* (1908–1914) and became a close friend of governor-generals and military personnel who served there, including later President William Howard Taft, Leonard Wood, and John Pershing. Egan returned to the United States to join the staff of J. P. Morgan and Company in New York City in 1914 and remained associated with the company until 1935. During World War I, he was personal assistant to the chairman of the American Red Cross (1917) and then General Pershing's top civilian assistant for public relations and propaganda (1918). "Martin Egan," *Who Was Who*, vol. 1, *1897-1942*, p. 362; "Martin Egan Papers," Archives of the Pierpont Morgan Library, New York, http://www.themorgan.org/research/FindingAids/archives/ARC1222-Egan.pdf.

Charles A. Elliot (6 March 1873–26 June 1939). Elliot was born in Lincoln, Nebraska, and attended the University of Nebraska, graduating in 1895. He was a cadet captain under Pershing as a senior. He completed his medical education at Northwestern University Medical School in Chicago, Illinois, receiving his M.D. in 1898. He practiced internal medicine in Chicago (1900–1919) and was then a professor of medicine at Northwestern University Medical School (1919–1939). "Charles Addison Elliott" [*sic*], *Who Was Who*, vol. 1, *1897-1942*, p. 366.

Charles B. Elliott (6 January 1861–18 September 1935). Elliott attended Marietta College in Ohio and received his law degrees from the University of Iowa (1881, 1895). He was the recipient of the first Ph.D. ever awarded by the University of Minnesota in 1888, and his dissertation was published as *The United States and Northeastern Fisheries* in 1887. He practiced law in Minneapolis and was appointed a judge at the levels of the municipal courts (1890–1893), district court (1893–1904), and state supreme court (1904–1909). He served as a justice on the Supreme Court of the Philippines (September 1909–February 1910) and then as a member of the Philippine Commission and as secretary of commerce and police (February 1910–December 1912). He taught law at the University of the Philippines (1911–1912) and later returned to Minneapolis, where he practiced law and authored a number of books, including *The Philippines to the End of the Military Régime: America Overseas* (1916) and *The Philippines to the End of the Commission Government: A Study in Tropical Democracy* (1917). Charles B. Elliott, *The Philippines to the End of the Commission Government* (Indianapolis: Bobbs-Merrill, 1917), pp. 395 n, 510, and passim; "Charles Burke Elliott," *Who Was Who*, vol. 1, *1897-1942*, p. 366.

Edward C. Elliott (21 December 1874–16 June 1960). Elliott grew up in North Platte, Nebraska, and attended the University of Nebraska (1891–1897). During his final year in the cadet battalion under Pershing, he was a cadet lieutenant. He received his bachelor's degree in science in 1895 and master of arts in 1897. He taught in high school at Leadville, Colorado (1897–1903), and then completed a doctorate at Columbia University's Teachers College in 1905. He served as a professor at the University of Wisconsin (1905–1916), chancellor of the University of Montana (1916–1922), and then as president of Purdue University in West Lafayette, Indiana (1922–1945). During his tenure as Purdue's president the university experienced a very significant increase in its enrollment, curriculum, and physical facilities. "Biographical Information," Inventory of the Edward C. Elliott Papers, Purdue University Libraries, http://www.lib.purdue.edu/spcol/fa/html/Elliot.

Hanson E. Ely (23 November 1867–28 April 1958). Ely graduated from the USMA in June 1891 and was commissioned in the 22d Infantry. He served in Montana, North Dakota, and Nebraska (1891–1897) and in the Philippines with his regiment (1899–1900), where he commanded Funston's mounted scouts (May–June 1900). He served in the Department of Northern Luzon (1900–1901) and later with the 26th Infantry at Fort Sam Houston, Texas (1903–1904). He returned to the Philippines with the 26th Infantry and joined the Philippine Scouts in December 1908 as a major, commanding the 11th Battalion on Samar until September 1909. He remained with the Scouts in various posts until September 1912, when he returned to the United States. He completed the Army War College (1915–1916) and then was stationed at El Paso as chief of the El Paso District (1916–1917). Ely was sent to France to observe British and French armies in the field (May–July 1917) and was then in Paris as provost marshal, AEF (July–August 1917). He was then chief of staff, 1st Division (September–December 1917). He commanded the 28th Infantry Regiment, 1st Division, at the front (December 1917–May 1918) and received acclaim for capturing Cantigny on 28 May 1918. In June he was promoted to brigadier general, NA, and assigned to command the 3d Infantry Brigade, 2d Division, which he did through the Chateau-Thierry fighting and Soissons (June–July 1918). He then commanded the brigade in the Meuse-Argonne offensive at Mont Blanc (2–8 October 1918) before taking command of the 5th Division at Montfaucon on 16 October. He was promoted to major general, NA, on 1 October and continued in command of the 5th Division in the occupation of southern Luxembourg and Trier, Germany, until April 1919. He attended the Army War College (1919–1920) and was promoted to brigadier general, Regular Army, in July 1920. He commanded the 3d Infantry Brigade (1920–1921) and then the General Service Schools at Fort Leavenworth (1921–1923). He was promoted to major general in February 1923 and served as president of the Army War College (1923–1927) before his final active duty assignment as commanding general, Second Corps Area, Governor's Island, New York (1927–1931). "Hanson Edward Ely," *Assembly* 18, no. 1 (spring 1959), pp. 83–84.

Oswald H. Ernst (27 June 1842–21 March 1926). Ernst graduated from the USMA in June 1864 and was commissioned in the Corps of Engineers. He served in the Army of the Tennessee during the Georgia campaign and at the battle and siege of Atlanta. From 1871 to 1878, he was an instructor at the USMA. He was then assigned to various river and harbor improvements and studies (1880–1889) before being placed in charge of Public Buildings and Grounds in Washington, D.C. He was appointed superintendent of the U.S. Military Academy on 1 April 1893. He was appointed brigadier general, USV, in May 1898 and placed in command of the 1st Brigade, 1st Division, I Army Corps, under Major General James H. Wilson (June–October 1898) in Chickamauga Park and in the Puerto Rico Expedition. He was assigned as inspector general, Military Division of Cuba (January–June 1899), and then appointed as a member of the Isthmian Canal Commission to select a route for a canal across Panama (1899–1900). He commanded the Baltimore Engineer District (1900–1901) and the North West Engineer Division at Chicago (1901–1905). He served as chairman of the Mississippi River Commission (1903–1906) and was again a member of the Isthmian Canal Commission (1905–1906). "Oswald Herbert Ernst," *Fifty-Seventh Annual Report of the Association of Graduates of the United States Military Academy at West Point, New York, June 11, 1926,* pp. 172–74.

Ellwood W. Evans (26 April 1866–24 July 1917). Evans graduated from the USMA in June 1887 and was commissioned in the 8th Cavalry. He served on the frontier in Texas and South Dakota (1887–1894). He was actively involved in the campaign against the Sioux Indians (1890–1891) at the Pine Ridge Agency. He was appointed major, 1st Maryland Volunteer Infantry, and served with the 1st Brigade, 1st Division, II Army Corps (May 1898–February 1899), but did not see service in active military operations. After duty at Puerto Principe, Cuba, with the 5th Cavalry (1899–1900), Evans was chief quartermaster and adjutant general for the District of Puerto Principe and then at Santiago and Guantánamo until April 1902. He later served with the 8th Cavalry in the Philippines until 1907, when he was assigned to Fort Robinson, Nebraska (1907–1909). He was with the 10th Cavalry and commanded troops on the Mexican border in Arizona (1913–1915). During the Mexican Expedition he commanded the 10th Cavalry's 1st Squadron (March–October 1916) and then the regiment following his promotion to colonel in July 1916. He was inspector general of cavalry for a National Guard division when he died in July 1917.

Ezra P. Ewers (13 April 1837–16 January 1912). Ewers enlisted in Company E, 1st Battalion, 19th Infantry, on 18 January 1862 and was commissioned in December 1863. He remained in the army after the war, serving in Nelson Miles's 5th Infantry after 1869. During these years he was closely associated with Miles and saw heavy action against various Native American tribes. Ewers played a prominent role in Miles's campaign against the Sioux in the winter of 1876–1877. He later moved to the 9th Infantry as a major in March 1893 and was promoted to lieutenant colonel in April 1897. During the Spanish-American War, the 9th Infantry formed part of the 3d Brigade, 1st Division, V Army Corps, under Major General William R. Shafter and landed in Cuba in June 1898. On 1 July 1898, the 3d Brigade attacked San Juan Hill and Colonel C. A. Wikoff, the brigade commander, was killed and his two successors wounded. Although he did not know of these losses and that he was now the senior regular office in the brigade and in command, Ewers pushed through to take the enemy's position at San Juan Hill. He was commissioned brigadier general, USV, in August 1898 and served in Cuba in the Department of Santiago as a brigade commander at San Luis until April 1899. In May 1899 he was promoted to colonel, U.S. Army, and became commander of the 10th Infantry, then stationed near Havana. Ewers retired on 13 April 1901 and was promoted to brigadier general, retired list, in

1904. TAGO, *OAR, 1901,* pp. 161, 357; Major James B. Ronan II, "Ezra P. Ewers: Lt. Col., Commanding Third Brigade, 1st Division, 5th Army Corps at Santiago, Cuba," The Spanish-American War Centennial Website, http://www.spanamwar.com/ewers.htm; Patrick McSherry, "The Ninth U.S. Infantry," The Spanish-American War Centennial Website, http://www.spanamwar.com/9thusinfantry.htm; "Report of the Major-General Commanding the Army," *ARWD 1899,* pt. 1, p. 301; "Ezra Philetus Ewers," *Who Was Who–The Military,* p. 163.

Lea Febiger (4 January 1858–2 October 1922). Febiger was commissioned in the 23d Infantry in August 1876 and was promoted to major with the 10th Infantry in February 1901. He was detailed to the Inspector General's Department in April 1903. While on this detail he was assigned to the Pacific Division at the Presidio of San Francisco when the earthquake ravaged the city on 18 April 1906. Febiger was soon appointed chief of the army-controlled Bureau of Consolidated Relief Stations (23 May–13 July), which were responsible for distributing 8 million relief food rations and supplies to the citizens of San Francisco as well as feeding many thousands more. He was promoted to lieutenant colonel, 3d Infantry, at the Presidio in May 1906. He transferred to the 6th Infantry, then serving in the Philippines, in 1909. He was assigned to the General Staff Corps (1910–1911) as chief of staff for the Philippines Division. Febiger was promoted to colonel in January 1911 and assumed command of the 6th Infantry Regiment then at Camp Keithley, Mindanao, in Pershing's Department of Mindanao. He retired in March 1914. TAGO, *OAR, 1916,* p. 498; TAGO, *OAR, 1920,* p. 871; TAGO, *OAR, 1922,* p. 1420; *ARWD, 1906,* vol. 3, pp. 127–30, 235–53 (Febiger's report on his duties following the earthquake); *ARWD, 1911,* vol. 3, p. 189.

John Park Finley (11 April 1854–24 November 1943). Finley was not the average Army officer of his time. He received his undergraduate education at the State Normal School (now Eastern Michigan University) in Ypsilanti, Michigan, in 1869 and then completed a B.S. (1873) at Michigan Agricultural and Mechanical College (today Michigan State University), concentrating on the climatological and meteorological effects on agriculture. After taking a law course at the University of Michigan (1874–1875) and spending several years on the family farm, he enlisted in the army Signal Corps in March 1877 and served as a private, corporal, and sergeant. During his years in the signal service's weather bureau, Finley became the American and world expert on tornadoes and severe weather prediction, contributing numerous papers on the subjects and laying the foundations for the development of these aspects of modern meteorology. Michigan A&M awarded him a master's degree in science in 1881 in recognition of his pioneering work in meteorology. In 1887 he published the first book in the United States on tornadoes. He was commissioned in the Signal Corps in July 1884 and directed most of the signal service's meteorological data collection and research. He became involved in a dispute with the Signal Corps' chief, Adolphus Greely, and was forced out as the signal service transferred its weather functions to the new U.S. Weather Bureau in October 1890. After some machinations, Finley was transferred to the 9th Infantry in 1891. He transferred to the 27th Infantry in Mindanao in August 1902 and was appointed military governor of the Zamboanga District. He was promoted to major in October 1907 and remained in that post until July 1913, doing much to bring the Moros under control. Finley left the Philippines in September for his new post with the 13th Infantry in the United States. He later served with the 4th Infantry on the Mexican border. He was promoted to colonel in July 1916, but his assignments are not known. He was retired from active duty on 11 April 1918 but was immediately recalled on 25 April and assigned as professor of military sciences and tactics at Columbia University in New York City. In retirement, he returned to his meteorological career, establishing the National Storm Insurance Bureau (later the National Storm and Aviation Insurance Bureau) in New York in 1920 to provide insurance underwriters with assessments of risks to property owners from severe weather. He moved his business back to Ann Arbor, Michigan, in 1932 and opened the National Weather and Aviation School to train people in weather forecasting, especially for the burgeoning field of aviation. TAGO, *OAR, 1916,* p. 318; TAGO, *OAR, 1931,* p. 813; Joseph G. Galway, "J. P. Finley: The First Severe Storms Forescaster [Part 1]," *Bulletin of the American Meteorological Society* 66, no. 11 (November 1985), pp. 1389–95; Joseph G. Galway, "J. P. Finley: The First Severe Storms Forecaster [Part 2]," *Bulletin of the American Meteorological Society* 66, no. 12 (December 1985), pp. 1506–10; Marlene Bradford, "Historical Roots of Modern Tornado Forecasts and Warnings," *Weather and Forecasting* 14, no. 8 (August 1999), pp. 485–88, all at American Meteorological Society, AMS Journals Online, http://journals.ametsoc.org.

Lawrence J. Fleming (18 January 1868–23 November 1923). Fleming graduated from the USMA in 1890 and was commissioned in the 10th Cavalry. He served in Arizona and New Mexico, then moved with the regiment to the Department of Dakota at Forts Keogh, Buford, and finally Assinniboine in Montana until August 1897. Fleming accompanied the 5th Cavalry to Puerto Rico (1898-1900). He later transferred to the 5th Cavalry (1901-1903) in the Philippines. After returning to the United States, he was detailed as quartermaster and assigned to Fort Sam Houston, Texas, as constructing quartermaster (1903-1910). He returned to the Philippines with the 14th Cavalry (1910-1911) and was once again detailed as quartermaster (1911-1912). He served on the Mexican border at Columbus, New Mexico, with the 5th Cavalry in the Mexican Expedition (1916-1917). In January 1918 Fleming was sent to France, where he was chief, Remount Service, AEF, and commander of trains, 2d Division (July–September 1918). He was then inspector, 42d Division, during the Meuse-Argonne offensive (September–November 1918) and commander of trains, 42d Division (1918-1919). He returned to the United States in March 1919 and commanded the 14th Cavalry at Fort Sam Houston until November, and then the 12th Cavalry to March 1920. He retired at his own request on 22 July 1920. "Lawrence Julian Fleming," *Sixty-Second Annual Report of the Association of Graduates of the United States Military Academy at West Point, New York, June 10, 1931,* pp. 263–64.

Allen S. Fletcher (31 December 1876–17 December 1929). Fletcher grew up in Maine and enlisted in Company G, 19th Infantry, in May 1899. He served as a private and corporal until April 1902. He reenlisted in Company D, 21st Infantry (April-June 1905) and was then commissioned a second lieutenant in the Philippine Scouts in June. He was promoted to first lieutenant in September 1908 and reappointed in September 1912. Fletcher acquired the reputation of being one of the finest field officers in the army during his numerous operations against outlaw Moros and was commended by Major General Thomas Barry in September 1914 for his heroism in action on Mindanao. He was promoted to captain in January 1913 and reappointed in January 1917. He was promoted to major in July 1920 and was assigned to the 45th Infantry Regiment (Philippine Scouts) when it was organized in 1921. Fletcher commanded Pettit Barracks, Zamboanga, Mindanao, from 1921 until 1929. He was promoted to lieutenant colonel in 1928. "Allen S. Fletcher, Lieutenant Colonel, United States Army," Arlington National Cemetery, http://www.arlingtoncemetery.net/asfletcher.htm; TAGO, *OAR, 1920,* p. 844; TAGO, *OAR, 1930,* p. 1108; "Scout Twice Commended," *New York Times,* 25 September 1914.

W. (William) Cameron Forbes (1870–December 1959). Forbes graduated from Harvard University in 1892. He was chief of the financial department of Stone and Webster, architects and engineers (1897–1902), and a partner in J. M. Forbes and Company, Boston (1899–1959). He was appointed secretary of commerce and police in the civilian government of the Philippines (1904–1908) and then vice governorgeneral under James Smith (June 1908–November 1909). With Smith's resignation, Forbes was appointed governor-general and served until 1 September 1913, when he resigned. He was later a member of the Wood-Forbes mission sent to the Philippines by President Harding in 1921. He was U.S. ambassador to Japan (1930–1932) and then chairman of the American economic mission to the Far East in 1935. "W(illiam) Cameron Forbes," *Who Was Who,* vol. 3, *1951–1960,* p. 291.

James W. Forsyth (26 August 1834–24 October 1906). Forsyth graduated from the USMA in 1856 with a commission in the 9th Infantry. He was on frontier duty in Washington from 1856 to 1861. During the Civil War he held a number of different staff posts and also served with his permanent regiment, the 18th Infantry, in the Tennessee campaign and at Chickamauga (September 1863) and Missionary Ridge, Chattanooga (November 1863). He was inspector general and then chief of staff of the Cavalry Corps, Army of the Potomac, under Major General Philip Sheridan (1864–1865). He rejoined Sheridan at the headquarters of the Division of the Missouri (1867–1869) and then as his aide-de-camp (1869–1874) and later military secretary (1873–1878). He was involved in various expeditions against the Plains Indians while serving with Sheridan. He served as inspector of cavalry, Division of the Missouri (1880–1885), under Sheridan until the latter moved to Washington to be commanding general of the army in November 1883. Forsyth was promoted to colonel and commander of the 7th Cavalry at Fort Meade, Dakota Territory, in 1886. He commanded the 7th in the campaign against the Sioux at the Pine Ridge Reservation and was in overall command of the troops during the Wounded Knee action on 29–30 December 1890. Major General Miles, commander of the Division of the Missouri and responsible for army operations at Pine Ridge Agency, had tried to resolve the problems peacefully and in his memoirs, *Serving the Republic,* called the outcome "a deplorable tragedy." Miles relieved Forsyth of his command, but a court of injury called by Miles exonerated him, and he returned to duty with the 7th Cavalry at Fort Riley. Forsyth was promoted to brigadier general, U.S. Army, in 1894 and assigned as commander of the Department of California. Promoted to major general on 11 May 1897, he retired three days later. TAGO, *OAR, 1901,* pp. 258, 347, 360; "General

James William Forsyth," *Forty-First Annual Reunion of the Association of Graduates of the United States Military Academy at West Point, New York, June 14th, 1910* (Saginaw, Mich.: Seemann and Peters, Printers and Binders, 1910), pp. 45–59; "James William Forsyth," *Powell's Records,* pp. 215–19; Robert M. Utley, *Frontier Regulars: The United States Army and the Indian, 1866-1891* (New York: Macmillan, 1973), pp. 406–7; Nelson A. Miles, *Serving the Republic: Memoirs of the Civil and Military Life of Nelson A. Miles, Lieutenant-General, United States Army* (New York: Harper and Brothers, 1911), pp. 235–47.

William D. Forsyth (28 March 1876–27 May 1934). Forsyth was appointed a first lieutenant in the 1st Ohio Cavalry on 9 May 1898 and discharged in September. He was appointed a second lieutenant in the 19th Infantry in Puerto Rico in September and transferred to the 5th Cavalry in October. He was promoted to first lieutenant in the 15th Cavalry in February 1901 during his service in the Philippines. He served with the 5th during the Mexican Expedition (1916–1917). In World War I, he was promoted to major in the 5th Cavalry in May 1917. In August 1917 he was transferred to the 324th Infantry Regiment, 81st Division, at Camp Jackson, South Carolina, and served there until March 1918, when he moved to Fort Bliss, Texas, as deputy commander of the 314th Cavalry Regiment, which was then being organized. He was promoted to colonel, NA, in August 1918 and assigned as chief of staff to the new 11th Division. The 11th had completed training and was partially deployed to England on its way to France when the Armistice went into effect in November 1918, terminating its movement. Forsyth remained chief of staff until the division demobilized in February 1919. He was promoted to lieutenant colonel, U.S. Army, in July 1920, and to colonel in August 1920. After the war, he completed the School of the Line (1920) and the General Staff School (1921) at Fort Leavenworth. He commanded the 5th Cavalry Regiment at Fort Clark, Texas (1921–1923), while also holding two other commands along the Texas-Mexican Border–Big Bend District/ Marfa Command (August–October 1921) and Eagle Pass District/Fort Clark Command (November 1921–October 1923). He then served as chief of staff, 103d Division, Organized Reserve (Colorado, Arizona, and New Mexico), from January 1924 until his retirement in October 1925. TAGO, *OAR, 1916,* p. 156; TAGO, *OAR, 1931,* p. 815; TAGO, *OAR, 1935,* p. 1021; Lieutenant Colonel Steven E. Clay, U.S. Army (ret.), *U.S. Army Order of Battle,* vol. 2, *The Arms: Cavalry, Field Artillery, and Coast Artillery, 1919-41* (Fort Leavenworth, Kans.: Combat Studies Institute Press, 2010) (hereafter cited as Clay, *U.S. Army Order of Battle,* vol. 2), p. 619, and vol. 4, *The Services: Quartermaster, Military Police, Signal Corps, Chemical Warfare, and Miscellaneous Organizations, 1919-41* (hereafter cited as Clay, *U.S. Army Order of Battle,* vol. 4), p. 2625; U.S. Army Center of Military History, *Order of Battle of the United States Land Forces in the World War,* vol. 3, pt. 2, *Zone of the Interior: Territorial Departments, Tactical Divisions Organized in 1918, Posts, Camps, and Stations* (Washington, D.C.: U.S. Army Center of Military History, 1988) (hereafter cited as CMH, *Order of Battle,* vol. 3, pt. 2), pp. 644–47; "Here to Start 314th Cavalry," *El Paso (Texas) Herald,* 28 March 1918; "William D. Forsyth," in "Ohio Soldiers in WWI, 1917–1918" and "U.S., Returns from Military Posts, 1806–1916," http://www.ancestry.com.

Benjamin D. Foulois (9 December 1879–25 April 1967). Foulois served as a corporal and sergeant in Company G, 1st U.S. Engineers (1898–1899), and then as a private, corporal, sergeant, quartermaster sergeant, and first sergeant in Company G, 19th Infantry, in the Philippines (1899–1901). He was commissioned in the infantry in 1901. He transferred to the Signal Corps in April 1908 and completed the Army Signal School that year. He became the first dirigible pilot in the Signal Corps and then taught himself to fly with instructions received by mail from Orville and Wilbur Wright. He flew with Orville Wright in 1909–1910 and set up the army's first flying unit and field at Fort Sam Houston, Texas, in 1910. He served in the Signal Corps Aviation School at San Diego (1914–1915) and was the first commander of the 1st Aero Squadron at Fort Sill and later Fort Sam Houston. He took the squadron to New Mexico and Arizona in support of Pershing's Mexican Expedition. In 1917 he moved to Washington for duty in the Signal Corps' Aviation Section and was promoted to major in June 1917 and jumped to brigadier general, NA, in August. He went to France in October 1917 in charge of all U.S. Army air services in France. He was made chief, Air Service, AEF, in November and in May 1918 took command of the First Army's air service at the front. He was assistant chief, Air Service, Zone of the Advance, AEF (August 1918–July 1919). Upon returning to the United States in July 1919, he served in the Office of the Director, Air Service. He completed the Command and General Staff School in 1925. Foulois was promoted to brigadier general in December 1927 when he was appointed assistant to the chief, Air Corps. He was in charge of the Air Corps' Materiel Division at Wright Field, Ohio (1929–1930). He returned to the Office of the Chief of the Air Corps in 1930 and was selected as chief, Air Corps, and promoted to major general in December 1931. He retired in December 1935. For a full account of Foulois's career and time as chief, U.S. Army Air Corps, see Colonel John F. Shiner, *Foulois and the U.S. Army Air Corps, 1931-1935* (Washington, D.C.: Office of Air Force History, 1983). Benjamin D. Foulois with Colonel C. V. Glines, *From the Wright Brothers to the Astronauts: The Memoirs of Major General Benjamin D. Foulois* (New York: McGraw-Hill, 1968), passim; TAGO, *OAR, 1938*, p. 919; Shiner, *Foulois*, pp. 1–42.

Samuel W. Fountain (13 December 1846–15 November 1930). Fountain enlisted at the age of seventeen in Company K, 140th Ohio Infantry, in May 1864 and was discharged in September. He entered the USMA in 1866 and graduated in June 1870 with a commission in the 8th Cavalry. He served at various posts in New Mexico and Texas (1870–1886) and participated in numerous campaigns against the Indians. The 8th Cavalry then moved north to Missouri, Dakota, and Montana (1886–1891). He commanded a troop of the 8th Cavalry in the winter Pine Ridge campaign against the Sioux Indians (December 1890–February 1891). The 8th Cavalry remained in the United States until October 1898, when six troops under Fountain moved to Huntsville, Alabama, and then Puerto Principe, Cuba (1898–1899). He commanded the 2d squadron in Cuba until December 1899, when he was assigned to duty at the War Department in Washington. He was promoted to major and detailed as assistant adjutant general in February 1901 and transferred to the Department of Mindanao and Jolo in the Philippines as the adjutant general (April 1901–September 1903). Returning to the United States with the 4th Cavalry in March 1904, he was assigned as the commandant of the Jefferson Guard at the St. Louis World's Fair (1904–1905). Fountain was promoted to brigadier general on 10 April 1905 and retired on the next day. "Samuel Warren Fountain," *Sixty-Fifth Annual Report of the Association of Gradu-*

ates of the United States Military Academy at West Point, New York, June 11, 1934 (New-burgh, N.Y.: Moore Printing Company, 1934), pp. 73–75; "Samuel W. Fountain," *Powell's Records*, p. 221.

Claude S. Fries (30 August 1870–February 1952). Fries completed the Pennsylvania Military College, and in July 1898 he was appointed captain in the 4th New Jersey Volunteer Infantry, mustering out in April 1899. He was appointed captain, 28th U.S. Volunteer Infantry, in July 1899 and served in the Philippines (1899–1901). He was commissioned in the 27th U.S. Infantry in July 1901. He served as a company commander with the 27th on Mindanao and then as the regimental adjutant, and also as adjutant to Pershing's command at Camp Vicars. He remained with the 27th Infantry and returned to the United States. Pershing chose Fries as his aide-de-camp when he was promoted to brigadier general in September 1906. Fries trans-ferred back to the 27th in 1910. He completed the Army School of the Line in 1912 and graduated from the Staff College in 1914. Little is known of his wartime assign-ments except for his time as chief of staff, 8th Division (March–May 1918) and ser-vice with the AEF in various capacities. He was appointed colonel, NA (1919–1920), and assigned as an inspector general (1919–1920). In August 1920 he was promoted to lieutenant colonel and assigned to the General Staff Corps with duty in the field (1920–1924). He was promoted to colonel in September 1926 and then commanded the 12th Infantry Regiment, Fort Howard, Maryland (1927–1930). He retired from active service on 31 August 1934. TAGO, *OAR, 1938*, p. 921; Clay, *U.S. Army Order of Battle*, vol. 1, p. 368; CMH, *Order of Battle*, vol. 2, *American Expeditionary Forces, Divi-sions*, p. 106.

Frederick Funston (9 November 1865–19 February 1917). Born in Ohio and raised in Kansas, Funston was the son of Republican congressman Edward H. Funston (16 September 1836–10 September 1911), who served in Congress from March 1884 to August 1894. Young Funston attended but never completed his studies at the University of Kansas (1885–1888) after failing to gain admission to the U.S. Mili-tary Academy in 1884 due to a poor admissions test and his short stature. With the outbreak of the Cuban insurrection against Spain in 1895, he volunteered for ser-vice with the rebel forces in Cuba and was commissioned a captain in the artillery with no qualifications whatsoever. He went to Cuba in 1896 and served there under rebel General Máximo Gómez, advancing to lieutenant colonel. Seriously ill from malaria, Funston returned to the United States early in 1898 and was appointed col-onel and commander of the 20th Kansas Volunteer Infantry Regiment in May 1898. The 20th Kansas saw no action in Cuba and was assigned to Merritt's expeditionary force but did not reach Manila until 30 November 1898. Funston and the 20th Kan-sas were assigned to the 1st Brigade of MacArthur's 2d Division, guarding Manila until fighting flared on 4–5 February 1899 with Aguinaldo's forces. Under Funston's driving leadership, the 20th Kansas was most active in combat operations against the insurgent forces on Luzon. He was an aggressive leader and always in the field against the Filipino insurgents. He distinguished himself at the Battle of Calumpit and crossing of the Rio Grande de la Pampanga River on 27 April 1899, for which he was awarded a Medal of Honor on 14 February 1900 and received promotion to brigadier general of volunteers on 1 May 1899. He returned to the United States with the 20th Kansas in September 1899, but the War Department sent him back to the Philippines. He took command of 3d Brigade, 2d Division, in November 1899 for continuing operations in Luzon and then moved to command the division's 1st Brigade. With the reorganization of April 1900, he become commander of the 4th District, Department of Northern Luzon, until he left the Philippines late in 1901. Earlier that year he was denied a commission in the Regular Army and was scheduled for discharge from the Volunteers. In March he learned the location of Emilio Aguinaldo's secret headquarters at Palanan, Luzon, and devised a dangerous ruse with Filipino collaborators that led to Aguinaldo's capture on 23 March 1901, largely breaking the back of the guerrilla war. Funston's daring accomplishment received tremendous attention in the United States, making him into a national hero, and he was immediately transferred to the Regular Army as a brigadier general on 1 April 1901 at the age of thirty-five. He later wrote *Memories of Two Wars: Cuban and Philippine Experiences* (New York: Charles Scribner's Sons, 1914) about these years. Upon returning to the United States, he commanded the Departments of Colorado (1902-1903), the Columbia (1903-1904), the Lakes (1904-1905), and California (1905-1908). While commanding the Department of California, he was in charge of the army's disaster relief and rescue work following the San Francisco earthquake on 18 April 1906 that was instrumental in saving much of San Francisco. He also briefly commanded the 1st Expeditionary Brigade that went to Cuba in October 1906. After California, he was commandant of the Army Service Schools at Fort Leavenworth (1908-1911) before he returned to the Philippines to command the Department of Luzon (1911-1913). He then commanded the Hawaiian Department (1913-1914) until he was recalled to command the 2d Division at Texas City, Texas, and the division's 5th Brigade in the occupation of Vera Cruz, Mexico. He was military governor of Vera Cruz until November. Promoted to major general in November 1914, Funston was given command of the Southern Department in San Antonio in February 1915 and of all U.S. troops and military operations along the Mexican border. He was in overall command of Brigadier General Pershing's operations along the border and in northern Mexico after Pancho Villa's raid on Columbus, New Mexico. With a possible American entrance into the war in Europe looming, Funston was apparently the choice of President Woodrow Wilson and Secretary of War Newton Baker to head the American forces in France. When he died of a massive heart attack in San Antonio, Texas, on 19 February 1917 at the age of fifty-one, the command of the AEF fell to John J. Pershing. Frederick Funston, *Memories of Two Wars: Cuban and Philippine Experiences* (New York: Charles Scribner's Sons, 1914), pp. 149-444, covers his Philippine years; "Frederick Funston (1865-1917)," in *Webster's American Military Biographies*, pp. 152-53; "Memorandum," in Thian, *Notes*, pp. 190-93; Donald Smythe, *Guerrilla Warrior: The Early Life of John J. Pershing* (New York: Charles Scribner's Sons, 1973), p. 280; Frederick Palmer, *With My Own Eyes: A Personal Story of Battle Years* (Indianapolis, Ind.: Bobbs-Merrill, 1933), pp. 292-93; Thomas W. Crouch, "Frederick Funston of Kansas: His Formative Years, 1865-1891," *Kansas Historical Quarterly* (summer 1974), at Boyhood Home and Museum of Maj. Gen. Frederick Funston, http://www.skyways.org/museums/funston/form.html; "Frederick Funston," *Who Was Who–The Military*, pp. 190-91; Colonel John B. B. Trussell, "Frederick Funston: The Man Destiny Just Missed," *Military Review* 56, no. 6 (June 1973), pp. 59-73; Heitman, *Historical Register*, vol. 1, p. 441; TAGO, *OAR, 1916*, p. 6.

Charles B. Gatewood (6 April 1853–20 May 1896). Gatewood graduated from the USMA in 1877 with a commission in the 6th Cavalry. He served with the 6th in Arizona and New Mexico through 1886 and saw extensive action against numerous hostile Indian tribes, most of the time in command of Indian scouts in the field. Gatewood was commended for his bravery in the field and for gaining the surrender of the Chiricahua Apaches to Major General Crook in 1883. He accompanied Henry Lawton on the expedition that tracked down Geronimo and his band (April–September 1886) and played a major role in Geronimo's surrender to Brigadier General Miles. Gatewood then served as aide-de-camp to Miles when he commanded the Department of Arizona (1886–1890). He was severely injured at Fort McKinney, Wyoming, on 18 May 1892, and on sick leave from November 1892. He died of stomach cancer at Fort Monroe, Virginia, on 20 May 1896. "Charles B. Gatewood," *Twenty-Seventh Annual Reunion of the Association of Graduates of the United States Military Academy at West Point, New York, June 11th, 1896* (Saginaw, Mich.: Seemann and Peters, Printers and Binders, 1896), pp. 169–71; "Charles Bare Gatewood," http://www.arlingtoncemetery.net/charlesb.htm; Faulk, *The Geronimo Campaign*, 38–40, 112–47, 176–84; Thrapp, *The Conquest of Apacheria*, pp. 353–60.

George G. Gatley (10 September 1868–8 January 1931). Gatley graduated from the USMA in June 1890 and was commissioned in the 3d Artillery and stationed at posts in San Francisco and Washington (1890–1896). During the Spanish-American War, he transferred to the 5th Artillery with Siege Battery K at Tampa, Florida, but never saw duty in Cuba. In January 1903 he took the 17th Battery, Field Artillery, a mountain artillery battery, to the Philippines for duty at Camp Vicars. Gatley and the 17th Battery participated in campaigns against the Moros on Jolo Island and Mindanao, with both Pershing and later Leonard Wood. He served in Cuba throughout the Cuban Pacification (1906–1909) and then served as an instructor in field artillery to the Cuban Army (1909–1913). He was assigned to the 13th Field Artillery in Texas (1913–1915). He was promoted to lieutenant colonel in June 1916, colonel in May 1917, and brigadier general, NA, in August 1917. He organized the 55th Field Artillery Brigade, 30th Division, at Camp Sevier, South Carolina (1917–1918), and took it to France (May–July 1918). He transferred to the 67th Field Artillery Brigade, 42d Division, in July 1918 and commanded the brigade through the remainder of the war and until it was demobilized in April 1919. Upon returning to the United States he commanded the 8th Field Artillery Brigade at Camp Knox, Kentucky (1919–1920). Gatley completed the Army War College (1920–1921). After several post and artillery commands, he commanded the Overseas Discharge and Replacement Depot at Fort McDowell, California (1924–1929), and then the 15th Artillery Brigade (February–October 1929). He was hospitalized at Walter Reed General Hospital and Johns Hopkins from December 1929 until he was transferred to Letterman General Hospital at the Presidio of San Francisco in April 1930. He died there on 8 January 1931. He was promoted to brigadier general, U.S. Army retired, upon his death by provision of the Act of 21 June 1930. "George Grant Gatley," *Sixty-Third Annual Report of the Association of Graduates of the United States Military Academy at West Point, New York, June 9, 1932* (Newburgh, N.Y.: Moore Printing Company, 1932), pp. 267–71.

Robert A. Gillmore (1 May 1879–6 October 1956). Gillmore served as a private, corporal, sergeant, and first sergeant in Company I, 21st Infantry, and then post quartermaster sergeant (October 1899–October 1908). He was appointed a second lieutenant in the Philippine Scouts in October 1908, a first lieutenant in April 1911, reappointed in that rank in April 1915, and made a captain in April 1918. He was promoted to major in July 1920, completed the Advanced Course at the Infantry School (1925-1926) and the Command and General Staff School (1926-1927). He retired from active duty in August 1930. He was recalled to active duty as a major on 4 January 1941, was promoted to lieutenant colonel in March 1942, and was retired again in November 1943. TAGO, *OAR, January 1, 1938,* p. 926; TAGO, *OAR, 1950,* vol. 1, p. 721; "Robert Addison Gillmore," Department of Veterans' Affairs, Nationwide Gravesite Locator, http://gravelocator.cem.va.gov/j2ee/servlet/NGL_v1.

William W. Gordon (22 November 1879–12 March 1959). Gordon was commissioned in the 2d Cavalry in July 1902. He served as secretary of the Sulu District, Moro Province, from August 1910 to November 1912 and was then the Sulu District governor until June 1913. It was during his tenure as district governor that the Bud Bagsak campaign took place. He was promoted to temporary major (1917–1918). He was a major and lieutenant colonel, NA (1917–1920). He was promoted to major, Regular Army, in July 1920. He completed the Advanced Course at the Cavalry School in 1924 and then graduated from the Command and General Staff School in June 1925. He was promoted to lieutenant colonel that September and then commanded the 11th Cavalry Regiment (July–September 1925). He completed the Tank School in 1931 and the Army War College in 1932. He commanded the 7th Cavalry Regiment, 1st Cavalry Division, at Fort Bliss, Texas (March–October 1933), and was promoted to colonel in September 1934. He succeeded Colonel George S. Patton Jr., as commander of the 3d Cavalry at Fort Myer, Virginia, in July 1940 and commanded it until September 1941. He retired in June 1942 and was recalled to active duty until 23 February 1944. TAGO, *OAR, 1938,* p. 280; *OAR, 1950,* p. 723; *U.S. Army Register, 1960,* vol. 1, p. 1340; Clay, *U.S. Army Order of Battle,* vol. 1, pp. 618, 621, 623; Pershing, *AR, Moro Province, 1913,* p. 83.

William B. Gracie (20 October 1867–26 October 1919). Gracie served in the New York National Guard's 10th Battalion, 3d Brigade, in Albany as an enlisted man (1884–1893) until he was commissioned in January 1893 and promoted to first lieutenant in May 1893. He was appointed a captain in the 1st New York Volunteer Infantry in May 1898 and commanded Company D in the United States and Hawaii until mustered out in February 1899. In July 1899, he was appointed captain, 27th U.S. Volunteer Infantry, and served in the Philippines (1899–1901). He was commissioned in the 27th U.S. Infantry in July 1901. He commanded Company M of the 27th in the Philippines and especially distinguished himself during Pershing's expeditions around Lake Lanao in September–October 1902 and April–May 1903. He was detailed as quartermaster (1912–1916) and transferred to the Quartermaster Corps in July 1917. Nothing is known of his assignments during World War I. He died in Boston on 26 October 1919. TAGO, *OAR, 1918,* pp. 14, 608; New York State Adjutant General, *New York in the Spanish-American War 1898,* vol. 1 (Albany, N.Y.: James B. Lyon, State Printer, 1900), pp. 331–39, 397; "Official Register of the Organized Land and Naval Forces of the State of New York, December 31, 1896," in New York State

Adjutant General, *Annual Report of the Adjutant-General of the State of New York for the Year 1896* (Albany, N.Y.: Wynkoop Hallenbeck Crawford, 1897), p. 68.

Frederick D. Grant (30 May 1850–11 April 1912). Son of General U. S. Grant, he graduated from the USMA in 1871 and was commissioned in the 4th Cavalry Regiment. He was an aide-de-camp to Lieutenant General Sheridan, commanding general, Division of the Missouri, with the rank of lieutenant colonel (1873–1881). He resigned his commission in October 1881 and entered the business world, becoming president of the American Wood Working Company in 1886 and then serving as U.S. minister to the Austro-Hungarian Empire (1889–1893). He served with Theodore Roosevelt and Avery Andrews as a police commissioner of New York City (1895–1897). At the beginning of the Spanish-American War, he was appointed colonel, 14th Infantry, New York National Guard, in April 1898. He commanded the 1st Brigade, 1st Division, III Army Corps, Chickamauga Park, Georgia (June–July 1898), and the 1st Brigade, 2d Division, and 3d Brigade, 1st Division, I Army Corps (July 1898), before being ordered to Puerto Rico, where he commanded the 2d Brigade, 1st Division, I Army Corps (August–October 1898). He was ordered to Manila, Philippines, in June 1899, where he commanded the 2d Brigade, 1st Division, VIII Army Corps, under Henry Lawton (July–October 1899). He transferred to the 2d Brigade, 2d Division, under Arthur MacArthur for operations in northern Luzon until January 1900 and then commanded the 5th District in northern Luzon and extended civilian control and government to this area (1900–1901). He was promoted to brigadier general in February 1901. Grant commanded the 4th Separate Brigade in southern Luzon (1901–1902) until he took command of the 6th Separate Brigade in the final pacification of Samar and Leyte Islands in the southern Philippines. He commanded the Department of Texas (1902–1904), then the Department of the Lakes in Chicago in 1904, and the Department of the East at Governor's Island, New York (1904–1908). He was promoted to major general in February 1906. He again commanded the Department of the Lakes at Chicago (1908–1910) and returned to Governor's Island to command the Department of the East (1910–1911), and then the Eastern Division, established on 1 July 1911, until January 1912, when he went on sick leave. He died on 11 April 1912 in New York City. "Frederick Dent Grant," *Forty-Sixth Annual Reunion of the Association of Graduates of the United States Military Academy at West Point, New York, June 11th, 1915* (Saginaw, Mich.: Seemann and Peters, Printers and Binders, 1915), pp. 149–52.

Adolphus W. Greely (27 March 1844–20 October 1935). Greely enlisted as a private in Company B, 19th Massachusetts Volunteer Infantry, in July 1861. He was promoted to first sergeant with the regiment before being commissioned in the 81st U.S. Infantry (Colored Troops) in March 1863. He was involved in major battles and seriously wounded three times. He was mustered out of the volunteer service in March 1867, then commissioned in the 36th Infantry, and assigned to the 5th Cavalry in July 1869. He was later detailed to the army signal service and constructed more than two thousand miles of telegraph lines connecting army posts in Texas, the Dakotas, and Montana (1876–1879). In 1881 he volunteered to take part in an army expedition to the Arctic for the first International Polar Year (1882–1883). In July 1881 Greely led a team that was to establish a meteorological station on Ellesmere

Island in Lady Franklin Bay, from which wide-ranging explorations where made. Supply ships failed to reach Greely's camp in 1882 and 1883. By the time U.S. Navy relief ships under Commodore Winfield S. Schley reached Greely's group in June 1884 only Greely and six men were left alive. Sensational accusations were later made in the press of misconduct and cannibalism, but they were never proven. Greely was promoted to captain and assistant to the chief signal officer in June 1886. President Cleveland appointed Greely as chief signal officer (also chief of the U.S. Army Signal Service and Signal Corps) in March 1887, which carried a positional promotion to brigadier general. As chief signal officer he expanded the army's extensive network of telegraph lines and then added underwater cables to army units in Puerto Rico, Cuba, the Philippines, Alaska, and Hawaii after 1898. He pushed the army's adoption of wireless telegraphy and radio and supported Samuel Langley's early experiments with flying machines. Since early in his career, Greely was an avid weather observer and reporter, and as chief signal officer was also the head of the U.S. Weather Service until 1891. In February 1906 he was promoted to major general and commanded the Pacific Division (April–August 1906), where he took an active role in the relief operations after the San Francisco earthquake of 18 April 1906. He then commanded the Northern Division (1906–1907), while also commanding the Department of the Missouri (October 1906, December 1906–May 1907), and finally the Department of the Columbia until his retirement for age in March 1908. Greely was a prolific writer throughout his career and published his memoirs, *Reminiscences of Adventure and Service,* in 1927. He was very belatedly awarded a Medal of Honor for his career accomplishments by Special Act of Congress on 21 March 1935. TAGO, *OAR, 1901,* pp. 52, 352; TAGO, *OAR, 1916,* p. 533; "Adolphus W. Greely (1844–1935)," *Webster's American Military Biography,* p. 151; "Adolphus Washington Greely," *Who Was Who–The Military,* p. 218; Rebecca R. Raines, *Getting the Message Through: A Branch History of the U.S. Army Signal Corps* (Washington, D.C.: U.S. Army Center of Military History, 1996), passim.

Benjamin E. Grey (24 November 1881–19 March 1956). Grey graduated from the USMA in June 1903 and was commissioned in the 29th Infantry. He served in the Philippines (1903–1904) and in Arizona and Utah (1904–1906). He was an instructor in the Department of Tactics at the Military Academy (1906–1910), after which he returned to the Philippines for duty as a company commander with the 21st Infantry in the Lake Lanao District, Mindanao (1910–1912). He was involved in numerous expeditions into the interior of Mindanao with the 21st and later the 8th Infantry Regiments through October 1913. Upon returning to the United States, he was assigned to the 21st Infantry at Texas City, Texas, and was an instructor with the Massachusetts National Guard (1916–1917). After duty at the Northeastern Department as an intelligence officer (June–September 1917), he was appointed temporary major (1917–1918) and commanded the 55th Infantry until July 1918. He was sent to France in late July and served in various capacities with the 7th Division (September–October 1918) before being assigned to the 56th Infantry, 7th Division (October 1918–May 1919). He returned to the United States in June 1919 and commanded the 64th Infantry until May 1920. He completed the School of the Line at Fort Leavenworth (1920–1921) and was assigned to the 84th Division, Organized Reserves, in Indianapolis (1921–1928). He commanded the 3d Battalion, 3d Infantry (1928–1929).

He then served as professor of military science and tactics at Culver Military Academy (Indiana) until May 1935. Grey was promoted to colonel in October 1934 and commanded the post at Fort Hayes, Ohio (1935–1936). He was the district recruiting officer at Salt Lake City (1937–1942) when he retired. "Benjamin Edwards Grey," *Assembly* 16, no. 1 (April 1957), pp. 54–55.

Hubert Grieger (5 January 1870–19 October 1946). Little is known about Dr. Grieger's life or medical and military careers. He served as a contract surgeon for the Army Medical Department, but it is not known when this was other than his service on Mindanao and at Camp Vicars. He later served as an army medical officer, reaching the rank of at least captain in the Medical Reserve Corps during World War I, and was a major in the Medical Corps, Organized Reserves, in Colorado in the early 1920s. Heitman, *Historical Register,* vol. 2, p. 273; "Medical Mobilization and the War," *JAMA* 70, no. 11 (16 March 1918), p. 786; "Dr. Hubert Grieger," Find a Grave Memorial, http://www.findagrave.com; "Hubert Grieger, Maj, MRC," *Official List of Officers of the Officers' Reserve Corps of the Army of the United States, Supplemental to Volume I, Alphabetical Index, September 1, 1919 to December 31, 1919* (Washington, D.C.: GPO, 1920), p. 26.

George S. Grimes (15 February 1846–9 August 1920). Born in England, Grimes enlisted in Company G, 116th New York Volunteer Infantry, as a private in August 1862. He later served in the 89th and 93d Infantry (U.S. Colored Troops) as sergeant major until March 1865 and saw action in Louisiana. He was later commissioned in the 39th Infantry, which was combined with the 40th Infantry as the 25th Infantry in 1869. He was assigned to the 2d Artillery in 1870, but he served with the U.S. Army Signal Service from 1870 to 1883, most of the time being spent building and operating military telegraph lines in Texas, the Dakotas, and Montana. After completing the Artillery School of Application at Fort Monroe, Virginia (1884–1886), he was finally assigned to the Light Battery A, 2d Artillery. With the coming of the Spanish-American War, Grimes and his Battery A, 2d Artillery (four 3.2-inch field guns), known as "Grimes' Battery," were assigned to the light artillery brigade that was attached to Wheeler's dismounted Cavalry Division during Shafter's Santiago Campaign. Grimes's guns were positioned near El Pozo and played a large part in the attacks on Kettle Hill by the divisions of Kent and Wheeler on 1 July 1898. Because his guns only had dated black powder shells and not modern smokeless powder, Battery A's positions were quickly located by Spanish rapid-fire guns, whose fire effectively silenced the American artillery for several hours. When they resumed fire to support the successful attack on Kettle Hill, they were joined by John Henry Parker's Gatling guns. The battery remained in Cuba until 1899. Grimes was eventually promoted to colonel in July 1903. When the army's artillery was reorganized in 1907, he opted for the field artillery and was assigned to the 3d Field Artillery in June. He retired in August 1907 and was promoted to brigadier general, U.S. Army, retired, by the law of 23 April 1904 that applied to wounded Civil War veterans. TAGO, *OAR, 1916,* p. 555; TAGO, *OAR, 1921,* p. 1389; "George Simon (Simeon) Grimes (1846–1920)," in Berner, ed., *The Spanish-American War,* p. 160; Boyd L. Dastrup, *King of Battle: A Branch History of the U.S. Army's Field Artillery* (Washington, D.C.: U.S. Army Center of Military History, 1993), pp. 138–43; Heitman, *Historical Register,* vol. 1, p. 480;

Powell's Records, p. 251; Cosmas, *An Army for Empire,* pp. 214–28; Patrick McSherry, "A Brief History of the 2nd U.S. Artillery, Battery A," The Spanish-American War Centennial Website, http://www.spanamwar.com/2ndusbatterya.htm.

Lloyd C. Griscom (4 November 1872–1959). Griscom graduated from the University of Pennsylvania in 1891 and then studied law at New York Law School. After serving as a deputy district attorney in New York, he was appointed captain, USV, during the war with Spain (1898–1899) and served as aide-de-camp to Major General James F. Wade, commander of III Army Corps, in the United States and Cuba until January 1899. Well connected in Republican political circles, he then embarked on his diplomatic career, which saw him in Constantinople (1900–1901) and as minister to Persia (1901–1902), Japan (1903–1905), ambassador to Brazil (1906–1907), and ambassador to Italy (1907–1909). He then became a member of a New York City law firm and continued to be very active in New York Republican politics. With America's entry into World War I, he was appointed major and adjutant of the 77th Division. He went to France with the division and there he was appointed as Pershing's personal representative for coordinating with the British Ministry of War in London in May 1918. After his public service career ended, he was a successful publisher of newspapers in Florida and on Long Island for many years. He published his memoirs as *Diplomatically Speaking* (1940). Heitman, *Historical Register,* vol. 1, p. 480; Lloyd C. Griscom, *Diplomatically Speaking* (Boston: Little, Brown, 1940), passim; Frank E. Vandiver, *Black Jack: The Life and Times of John J. Pershing,* 2 vols. (College Station: Texas A&M Univ. Press, 1977) (hereafter cited as *Black Jack* and volume number), vol. 1, pp. 346–47, 354, 382; vol. 2, pp. 691, 1019–21, 1026, 1028, 1032.

William S. Guignard (30 September 1872–21 August 1940). Guignard graduated from the College of South Carolina (now the University of South Carolina) in 1891 and entered the USMA in June 1892 as a member of the Class of 1896. He graduated from the Military Academy in June 1896 and was commissioned in the 4th Artillery. After garrison duty to May 1898, he served with the Light Battery, 4th Artillery, in Cuba and then Puerto Rico. He was an instructor in modern languages at the Military Academy (1901–1903), then attended the French Cavalry School at Saumur (1903–1904). After commanding a company at Fort Washington, Maryland (1904–1905), he was the U.S. military attaché at Paris (1905–1909). He commanded batteries of the 1st Field Artillery in the United States and the Philippines (1910) and with the 2d Field Artillery (1910–1911). He returned to the United States, where he commanded a battalion of the 6th Field Artillery (1912–1913) before transferring to the 1st Field Artillery. He commanded a battalion of the 1st Artillery and then the 9th Field Artillery at Schofield Barracks, Hawaii (1914–1916), and was promoted to colonel and commander, 21st Field Artillery, in May 1917. He returned to the United States and commanded the regiment until November 1917 but then went on extended sick leave with tuberculosis until September 1919, when he was retired for disability. "William Slann Guignard," *Seventy-Second Annual Report of the Association of Graduates of the United States Military Academy at West Point, New York, June 10, 1941* (Newburgh, N.Y.: Moore Printing Company, 1941), pp. 216–18.

Harry C. Hale (10 July 1861–21 March 1946). Hale graduated from the USMA in

1883 with a commission in the 12th Infantry. On frontier duty at Fort Bennett, South Dakota, until December 1890, he was given the difficult mission of trying to round up and bring in the remnants of Sitting Bull's band after the Wounded Knee Creek massacre. Despite the severe weather and challenges, he went alone in the middle of winter and accomplished that mission without additional bloodshed. Hale later served as aide-de-camp to Wesley Merritt when he commanded the Department of Dakota, the Divisions of the Missouri and East, and the VIII Army Corps on the expedition to the Philippines. He was appointed major, USV, commanding the 1st Battalion, 44th U.S. Volunteer Infantry, in August 1899, and served with it in the Negros and Bohol Islands to February 1901. He was a member of the initial General Staff Corps (1903–1906) and attended the Naval War College in 1906. He returned to the Philippines in command of the 2d Battalion, 13th Infantry, at Fort McKinley at Manila (1906–1907) and was transferred to command the post at Parang, Mindanao (July–September 1907). Hale was detailed as adjutant general, Department of Mindanao (1907–1909), then under Tasker Bliss. Assignments as adjutant general followed at the Department of California in 1909, Department of the Lakes (1909–1910), and Department of the Missouri (1910–1911). He later served on the Mexican border with the 17th Infantry and as commander (1914–1915), then was selected colonel and commander of the 20th Infantry at El Paso until November 1915. He took command of the 15th Infantry at Tientsin, China, in February 1916. He was promoted to brigadier general, U.S. Army, in May 1917 and major general, NA, in August when he returned from China. He commanded the 84th Division at Camp Zachary Taylor, Kentucky (1917–1918), before taking it to France in September 1918. He commanded the 84th to early November, but the division never saw combat and was broken up to provide reinforcements for the St. Mihiel and then Meuse-Argonne offensives. He took over the 26th Division early in November and commanded it through redeployment to the United States and demobilization at Camp Devens, Massachusetts, in 1919. He later commanded the 2d Brigade, American Forces in Germany (1920–1921). He was promoted to major general, U.S. Army, on 2 November 1921 and then commanded the 1st Division at Camp Dix (February–June 1922). Hale commanded the Sixth Corps Area, Chicago, from December 1922 to July 1925, when he retired. "Harry Clay Hale," *Assembly* 5, no. 2 (July 1946), "In Memory" insert, pp. 3–4; "Harry Clay Hale," in Davis, *Generals in Khaki*, pp. 157–58.

Charles H. Halliday (26 September 1878–30 September 1950). Halliday served as a contract surgeon in the U.S. Army Medical Department on Samar and Mindanao from 1906 to July 1908, when he was commissioned in the Medical Reserve Corps. He served at several posts in the United States from 1909 to early 1913, when he returned to Mindanao as post surgeon at Augur Barracks, Jolo. In June 1914 he moved to Camp Stotsenburg and then Camp Elbridge on Luzon. He remained on active duty until relieved in June 1915, after which he headed the Episcopal mission hospital for Moros at Zamboanga until 1918. While he remained in the Medical Reserve, there is no information on his wartime service, but he apparently served in France. He served with U.S. Typhus Commission in Russia and Poland after World War I and with the Minnesota, California, and Maryland State Boards of Health as an epidemiologist and public health officer into the 1940s. Although moving around the country during the 1920s and 1930s, he remained in the Medical Officers' Reserve Corps (MORC), serving as a lieutenant colonel and executive officer of the 3d Convalescent Hospital, Third Army, and later as commander of the 23d Evacuation Hospital in New York and Pennsylvania (1929–1938) and then as a colonel commanding the 305th Medical Regiment, 80th Division (1939–1941), in Virginia. He served in World War II, but his assignments are unknown. TAGO, *OAR, 1916*, p. 668; "M.O.R.C.," *California and Western Medicine* 24, no. 4 (April 1926), p. 534; Clay, *U.S. Army Order of Battle*, vol. 4, pt. 1, pp. 2238, 2299; various records at "Charles H. Halliday," http://www.ancestry.com.

John Hance (? 1838–26 January 1919). Hance was born in Tennessee and fought for the Confederacy during the Civil War. He gave himself the title "Captain," but he had actually been a private prior to his capture by Union forces. He moved to Arizona in the late 1860s and settled in Williams. Hance first visited the south rim of the Grand Canyon in 1883 and settled there as one of the first non–Native American residents. He built his cabin east of Grandview Point, near the head of an established trail leading to asbestos mines in the canyon itself. He improved this trail into what is now known as the "Old Hance Trail" and would go on to establish others to the canyon's bottom, including the "New Hance Trail" (Red Canyon Trail) in 1894. However, he soon turned to guiding tourists to the bottom of the canyon as a more lucrative undertaking. In 1906 the Fred Harvey Company, working with the Santa Fe Railway, whose tracks had reached the south rim in 1901, built the El Tovar Hotel (opened 1905) and convinced Hance to move to Grand Canyon Village to work with them as a guide and storyteller. He died in January 1919, the year the Grand Canyon became a National Park. "John Hance (1838-1919)," All Hikers, Historical Figures, http://www.allhikers.com/allhikers/History/Historical-Figures/John-Hance.htm; "New Hance Trail," National Park Service, Grand Canyon National Park, http://www.nps.gov/grca/planyourvisit/upload/New_Hance_Trail .pdf; "New Hance Trail," Grand Canyon Association, Nature, Culture and History at the Grand Canyon, http://grandcanyonhistory.clas.asu.edu/sites_ rimtoriverandinnercanyon_newhancetrail.html.

James G. Harbord (21 March 1866–20 August 1947). Harbord attended Kansas State Agricultural College (now Kansas State University) in Manhattan and received his B.A. in 1886 and M.A. in 1895. He enlisted in the 4th Infantry in 1889 and served as private, corporal, and quartermaster sergeant until he was commissioned in the 5th Cavalry in 1891. He served in the 2d U.S. Volunteer Cavalry in 1898. He joined the 10th Cavalry in 1898 and was promoted to captain, 11th Cavalry, in 1901. He then served as assistant chief of the Philippine Constabulary as a colonel (1903–1914). Harbord was assigned to the 1st Cavalry in January 1914. He was promoted to lieutenant colonel, General Staff, in May 1917 upon completing the Army War College. Pershing then selected him as AEF chief of staff (May 1917–May 1918), and he was appointed brigadier general, NA, in August 1917. After commanding the 4th Marine Brigade, 2d Division, at Chateau-Thierry (May–July 1918), he was promoted to major general, NA, in June 1918. Harbord commanded the 2d Division in the Soissons offensive in July and then became commanding general, Services of Supply, AEF, until May 1919. He was once again AEF chief of staff in May. He was promoted to major general, U.S. Army, in September 1919 and in November 1920 returned to the

United States to command the 2d Division at Fort Sam Houston, Texas (1920–1921). He then served as Pershing's deputy chief of staff until December 1922, when he retired as a major general. He was later promoted to lieutenant general, U.S. Army retired, in July 1942. After retiring, he was the president of the Radio Corporation of America (RCA) (1923–1930) and chairman of the board (1930–1947). In retirement, he published several volumes on his wartime experiences: *Leaves from a War Diary* (1925), *The American Expeditionary Forces: Its Organization and Accomplishments* (1929), and *The American Army in France, 1917-1919* (1936). "James G. Harbord (1899–1947)," *Webster's American Military Biographies*, pp. 162–63; "James Guthrie Harbord," *Who Was Who–The Military*, p. 235; "James Guthrie Harbord (1866-1947)," in Venzon, ed., *The United States in the First World War*, pp. 272–75.

Letcher Hardeman (30 April 1864–16 February 1937). Hardeman graduated from the USMA in 1886 with Pershing and was commissioned in the 4th Cavalry. He served in Arizona, Idaho, and Washington with the 4th (1886–1893) until he transferred to the 10th Cavalry at Fort Assinniboine, Montana. He served in the 2d Missouri Volunteer Infantry in 1898 before becoming colonel, 6th Missouri Volunteer Infantry, until May 1899. He rejoined the 10th Cavalry in Cuba in June 1899 and was later promoted to captain and regimental quartermaster (May 1901–May 1905) in the 11th Cavalry, serving in the Philippines (1902–1904). He was detailed to the Quartermaster's Department (1905–1909) and then commanded the Fort Reno Remount Depot (1908–1909). He was reassigned to the 10th Cavalry (1909–1911) and then promoted to major in March 1911 and assigned to the 4th Cavalry in December. He commanded the 3d Squadron, 4th Cavalry, at Fort Apache, Arizona (April–July 1912), and then Fort Douglas, Arizona, until January 1913 before moving to Schofield Barracks, Hawaii, with his unit (1913–1915). He retired as a major in January 1915 but was recalled to active service on recruiting duty (1915–1917) when he was assigned as chief, Remount Service, and principal assistant in the supply section of the Office of the Quartermaster General in Washington. Promoted to colonel (May 1918), Quartermaster Corps, NA, he was sent to France (July–September 1918) before he returned to Washington and resumed his former position until his final retirement in 1919. "Letcher Hardeman," *Sixty-Ninth Annual Report of the Association of Graduates of the United States Military Academy at West Point, New York, June 13, 1938* (Newburgh, N.Y.: Moore Printing Company, 1938), pp. 137–40.

Francis Burton Harrison (18 December 1873–21 November 1957). Harrison graduated from Yale University in 1895 and completed the New York Law School in 1897. He was admitted to the bar in New York in 1898. In the Spanish-American War, he enlisted in Troop A, New York Volunteer Cavalry (May–June 1898), and was then appointed captain and assistant adjutant general, USV (June 1898–January 1899). He was elected to Congress from New York as a Democrat in 1902 but did not seek reelection in 1904 because he tried unsuccessfully for the nomination for lieutenant governor of New York. He was reelected to Congress in 1906 and served in Congress until he resigned in September 1913 to accept President Wilson's offer of the post of Governor-General of the Philippine Islands. Harrison aggressively pushed "Filipinization" of the Insular Government and replacement of American civilian officials during his tenure as governor-general until Wilson left office in 1921, at which time he resigned. He lived in Scotland until 1934. He later served as advisor to the president of the Philippine Commonwealth in 1935 and 1942 and also advised the early presidents of the Republic of the Philippines after independence in 1946. "Francis Burton Harrison," *Who Was Who*, vol. 3: *1951-1960*, p. 374; "Francis Burton Harrison (1873-1957)," in Biographical Directory of the United States Congress, http://bioguide.congress.gov/scripts/biodisplay.pl?index=H000268; Fulton, *Moroland*, pp. 455-82.

Henry C. Hasbrouck (26 October 1839–17 December 1910). Hasbrouck graduated from the USMA in May 1861 with a commission in the artillery. He served with the 4th Artillery from First Bull Run (July 1861) until August 1863. He was at West Point as assistant professor of natural and experimental philosophy from September 1863 until February 1865, when he again saw action at Richmond, Virginia, and the siege of Petersburg. He remained with the 4th Artillery after the war, serving at various posts before being transferred to the Presidio of San Francisco (1872–1873). He was on the Modoc Expedition (April–June 1873), commanding actions at Sorass Lake and Van Bremer's Ranch (May 1873). In 1882 he was appointed commandant of cadets at the Military Academy and served until 1888. He was promoted to brigadier general, USV, in May 1898 and commanded the 2d Brigade, 2d Division, VII Army Corps, in the Spanish-American War to March 1899. After Cuba, he commanded the 4th Artillery and Fort Adams (1899–1903). In December 1902 he was promoted to brigadier general, U.S. Army, and retired at his request with forty years of service on 5 January 1903. "Henry C. Hasbrouck," *Forty-Third Annual Reunion, Association of Graduates of the United States Military Academy at West Point, New York, June 11, 1912* (Saginaw, Mich.: Seemann and Peters, Printers and Binders, 1912), pp. 120–22.

Valery Havard (18 February 1846–6 November 1927). Born and raised in France, Havard came to the United States and attended the medical school of the University of New York. He graduated in 1869 and was appointed an acting assistant surgeon in the Army Medical Department in 1871. He served in the field with the 7th Cavalry against the Sioux and Nez Percé Indians (1874–1877) and with the 1st Infantry in Texas (1881–1884) before being assigned to New York City (1884–1887). He was once again on the frontier and saw action at the Pine Ridge Agency in the winter of 1890–1891. During the Spanish-American War he was assigned as chief surgeon, Cavalry Division, and served with it in the field in June–July 1898 and at San Juan Hill on 1 July. He was chief surgeon for the Department of Santiago under Leonard Wood and remained with him when he took over command of the Division of Cuba. After Cuba, he was assigned to the Military Academy (1902–1904) and then was promoted to colonel and assigned as chief surgeon, Department of the East, at New York City. In November 1904, he was detailed as a military medical observer with the Russian Army in Manchuria. While on this duty, he was captured by the Japanese along with follow observer William V. Judson during the Battle of Mukden on 10 March 1905. He then directed the Army Medical Museum and Library in Washington in May 1906 while also serving as president of the Army Medical School. Havard served briefly as the chief surgeon of the expeditionary force in Cuba until January 1907, when he resumed his duties in Washington. He retired in February 1910. He was recalled to active duty in September 1917 and sent to Havana, Cuba, to advise the Cuban government on the reorganization of the army and navy medical departments and was only relieved of this duty in May 1923. He was an expert on venereal diseases, yellow fever, and military hygiene and author of the *Manual of Military Hygiene* that was published by the surgeon general in 1909 and issued in revised editions in 1916 and 1917 for distribution in the Army. Colonel James M. Phalen, "Valery Havard, Colonel, Medical Corps, U.S. Army," *Army Medical Bulletin,* no. 50 (October 1939), pp. 126–29; "Valery Havard," *Who Was Who–The Military,* p. 244.

Frank B. Hawkins (14 July 1874–6 December 1929). Hawkins graduated from Washington and Jefferson College, in Washington, Pennsylvania, in 1896. He was appointed an officer in the 10th Pennsylvania Volunteer Infantry in May 1898 and commanded Company D in the Philippines (1898–1899). Under provisions directed by President McKinley that one officer from each volunteer regiment who had distinguished himself in action be selected for accession to the Regular Army, Hawkins was commissioned in the 3d U.S. Infantry then in the Philippines in 1899. In 1901 he joined the 27th Infantry and saw action in Mindanao commanding Company C. He later served in the Cuban Pacification (1906–1909) and again served in the Philippines (1909–1910). In September 1915 he transferred to the 12th Infantry, serving on the Mexican border. In World War I he was assigned to the 353d Infantry Regiment, 89th Division, during training in the United States and in France until he was promoted to colonel, NA, in July 1918 and made commander of the 60th Infantry Regiment, 5th Division, in August 1918. He commanded the 60th Infantry through combat operations at St. Mihiel and the Meuse-Argonne and in the Army of Occupation until the division returned to the United States in 1919. Hawkins completed the Advanced Course, Infantry School, in 1923 and the Command and General Staff College in 1924. He was promoted to colonel in September 1924 and commanded the 33d Infantry Regiment, Panama Canal Department (1926–1929). He returned to the United States and died at Walter Reed General Hospital on 6 December 1929. GHQ, American Expeditionary Forces, Citation Orders No. 9, Washington, D.C., 1 August 1920, p. 20, in National Archives and Records Administration, Record Group 120, Records of the AEF, Entry 458, Box 5079; TAGO, *OAR, 1916,* p. 360; TAGO, *OAR, 1929,* p. 282; TAGO, *OAR, 1930,* p. 1108; "Appointments for Gallantry," *New York Times,* 2 May 1899; Clay, *U.S. Army Order of Battle,* vol. 1, pp. 384, 400; U.S. Army Center of Military History, *Order of Battle of the United States Land Forces in the World War,* vol. 1, *American Expeditionary Forces: General Headquarters, Armies, Army Corps, Services of Supply, Separate Forces* (Washington, D.C.: U.S. Army Center of Military History, 1988) (hereafter cited as CMH, *Order of Battle,* vol. 1), p. 106; Society of the Fifth Division, *The Official History of the Fifth Division, U.S.A.* (Washington, D.C.: Society of the Fifth Division, 1919), passim and p. 371; Captain Charles F. Dienst et al., *History of the 353d Infantry Regiment, 89th Division, September 1917-June 1919* (Wichita, Kans.: Regimental Society of the 353d Infantry Regiment, 1921), chapter 1, in The Kansas Collection, http://www.kancoll.org/books/dienst/353-chap1.html.

William H. Hayward (29 April 1877–13 October 1944). Born in Nebraska, Hayward was educated at the University of Nebraska and also studied in Munich, Germany (1896–1897). While at the university he was a member of Pershing's cadet battalion. After graduating in 1897 with a law degree, he practiced law in his hometown of Nebraska City (1897–1898). At the outbreak of the Spanish-American War he was appointed a captain in the 2d Nebraska Volunteer Infantry Regiment but was soon appointed colonel, 2d Infantry, Nebraska National Guard (1898–1901). In 1899 he was briefly private secretary to his father, Monroe L. Hayward, who died on 5 December 1899 only months after being elected as a U.S. senator in March of that year. He served as a county judge in Nebraska (1901–1902), chairman of the Republican State Central Committee (1907–1909), and as secretary to the Republican National Committee (1908–1912). He moved his law practice to New York City in 1910 and was assistant to District Attorney Charles Whitman (1913–1914). He managed Whitman's successful election campaign for governor of New York in 1914 and again in 1916. In 1915 he was counsel to Governor Whitman, who appointed him to a five-year term (1915–1920) as public service commissioner, 1st District of New York. Both Whitman and Hayward believed that African Americans made fine soldiers. With American involvement in the European war seen as inevitable, in June 1916 Whitman authorized the raising of the 15th Infantry, New York National Guard (Colored), with Hayward as its colonel. With American entry into World War I, Hayward had raised, organized, and trained the 15th New York so that it was ready to enter Federal service that summer. Despite many problems, Hayward had his regiment trained and ready so that the first elements of the 15th arrived in France on 1 January 1918. In March the 15th New York was redesignated as the 369th Infantry Regiment, nicknamed the "Harlem Hellfighters" or "Black Rattlers," in the newly organized 93d Division, which would never fight as an entire division. The 369th served under French command with the 157th Division throughout the war and logged 191 days in the line, more than any other American regiment. After the war, Hayward served as U.S. attorney for the Southern District of New York (1921–1925) and then returned to his legal practice and spent much of his time exploring and hunting around the world. "William Hayward," *Who Was Who*, vol. 2, *1943-1950*, pp. 243–44; "Monroe Leland Hayward," *Who Was Who*, vol. 1, *1897-1942*, p. 541; William Hayward, "Cut Up Pershing's Breeches," *Boston Daily Globe*, 5 August 1917; Frank E. Roberts, *The American Foreign Legion: Black Soldiers of the 93d in World War I* (Annapolis, Md.: Naval Institute Press, 2004), passim.

Lawrence J. Hearn (20 November 1856–11 December 1912). Hearn was commissioned a second lieutenant in the 21st Infantry Regiment in November 1880. He graduated from Infantry and Cavalry School in 1885. Hearn was promoted to first lieutenant in July 1888 and captain in April 1898. He was promoted to major in August 1903 and transferred to the 3d Infantry in December 1909. He was promoted to lieutenant colonel of the 3d Infantry in March 1911 and returned to the United States with the 3d Infantry and was stationed at the Presidio of San Francisco when he died. "Lawrence J. Hearn," Department of Veterans' Affairs, Nationwide Gravesite Locator, http://gravelocator.cem.va.gov/j2ee/servlet/NGL_v1; TAGO, *OAR, 1913,* p. 281; TAGO, *OAR, 1914,* p. 635.

Elvin R. Heiberg (12 April 1873–2 March 1917). Heiberg graduated from the USMA in June 1896 and was commissioned in the 3d Cavalry. Heiberg's Troop H served in Puerto Rico in 1898 before returning to the United States. He transferred to the 6th Cavalry in 1900 and was assigned to transport the 6th Cavalry's horses to China for the China Relief Expedition and thereafter remained in China until November 1900. He was transferred to the Philippines with the 6th Cavalry and served in Luzon (1900–1903). He returned to the Philippines and was stationed on Mindanao and at Jolo, Jolo Island (1907–1908). He was detailed as a major in the Philippine Scouts in November 1908 and stationed at Jolo until June 1909 and then at Cotabato, Mindanao, commanding the 5th Battalion, Philippine Scouts, until June 1911. In January 1912 he assumed command of the 11th Battalion, Philippine Scouts, at Cotabato until August 1912, when he returned to the United States. He commanded a troop of the 6th Cavalry at Fort Des Moines, Iowa, and Texas City, Texas (1912–1915), and was then hospitalized at Walter Reed General Hospital in Washington and on sick leave until late 1915. He was assigned to the chief of staff's office in Washington in March 1916 and then sent to Italy as a military observer in April. On 2 March 1917, he accidentally fell from his horse while touring the front and died at Udine, Italy, that day. His two sons, Colonel Harrison H. D. Heiberg (USMA, 1919) and Brigadier General Elvin R. Heiberg (USMA, 1926), had long careers in the army, and his five grandsons also graduated from West Point, Elvin R. Heiberg III (USMA, 1953) reaching the post of U.S. Army chief of engineers (1984–1988) and the rank of lieutenant general. "Elvin R. Heiberg," *Forty-Eighth Annual Report of the Association of Graduates of the United States Military Academy at West Point, New York, June 12, 1917,* pp. 106–8; *Register of Graduates 2000,* passim.

Otto L. Hein (1 May 1847–26 July 1933). Hein graduated from the USMA in 1870 and was commissioned in the 1st Cavalry Regiment. He was assigned to frontier duty in Nevada, California, and Arizona before returning to duty at the Military Academy as an assistant instructor in infantry tactics (1874–1879). He served in Washington, California, Montana, and Kansas before being sent to Vienna, Austria, as the military attaché at the U.S. legation (1889–1894). He served as commandant of cadets at the Military Academy from June 1897 to June 1901 and as acting superintendent (June–August 1898) during Colonel Ernst's absence. He was promoted to major, 3d Cavalry, in February 1901 and commanded a squadron in the Philippines (1901–1902) before returning to the 3d Cavalry for duty at the Presidio of San Francisco. Hein was appointed lieutenant colonel in the 10th Cavalry in August 1903. He was at Fort Robinson, Nebraska, with the 10th until December 1903 when he went on sick leave prior to retiring for disability in the line of duty on 28 July 1904. Well after he retired, Hein published his *Memories of Long Ago* (New York: G. P. Putnam's Sons, 1925) about his years in the U.S. Army. "Otto Louis Hein," *Sixty-Fifth Annual Report of the Association of Graduates of the United States Military Academy at West Point, New York, June 11, 1934,* pp. 43–44.

Frank P. Helm Jr. (23 March 1877–9 June 1954). Helm grew up in Covington, Kentucky, and entered the U.S. Naval Academy in 1895. He graduated in January 1899 and later served aboard the USS *Brooklyn,* USS *Callao* (gunboat), and USS *Monterey* (monitor) in the Philippines and at Zamboanga. He resigned from the navy in April 1902 and in March 1904 joined the Insular Government as superintendent of the Division of Vessels, Bureau of Coast Guard and Navigation, Secretary of Commerce and Police. In November 1905 he was appointed assistant director, Bureau of Navigation, and then became director in August 1906. He remained director until the

Bureau of Navigation was abolished in December 1913, after which he returned to the United States. However, he remained a close friend of Pershing's afterward and met him at Bakersfield, California, on his trip to San Francisco to arrange for the burial of his wife and three daughters in late August 1915. As of 1916, he was living in San Francisco. Little else is known of his activities. See Vandiver, *Black Jack*, vol. 1, pp. 595–97; U.S. Naval Academy Graduates' Association, *Register of Graduates, June 1916* (Annapolis, Md.: Advertiser-Republican, 1916), pp. 126, 127; *Register of Commissioned and Warrant Officers of the Navy of the United States and of the Marine Corps to January 1, 1900* (Washington, D.C.: GPO, 1900) (hereafter cited as *Register of Commissioned and Warrant Officers* and year), pp. 42, 149; *Register of Commissioned and Warrant Officers, 1901*, pp. 40, 147; *Register of Commissioned and Warrant Officers, 1902*, pp. 38, 149; *Register of Commissioned and Warrant Officers, 1903*, p. 152; U.S. War Department, Bureau of Insular Affairs, *Fifth Annual Report of the Philippine Commission, 1904* (Washington, D.C.: GPO, 1905), pt. 3, p. 127; U.S. War Department, Bureau of Insular Affairs, *Seventh Annual Report of the Philippine Commission, 1906* (Washington, D.C.: GPO, 1907), pt. 2, pp. 210, 384; *ARWD, 1915, Report of the Philippine Commission to the Secretary of War, July 1, 1913 to December 31, 1914* (Washington, D.C.: GPO, 1915), p. 121; "Frank Pinckney Helm," Department of Veterans' Affairs, Nationwide Grave Locator, http://gravelocator.cem.va.gov/j2ee/servlet/NGL_v1.

Eli A. Helmick (27 September 1863–13 January 1945). Helmick graduated from the USMA in June 1888 and was commissioned in the 4th Infantry. He served on frontier duty in Washington and Idaho (1888–1893) and was a professor of military science and tactics at Hillsdale College, Michigan (1894–1896) before transferring to the 10th Infantry in 1895. He was appointed regimental quartermaster in May 1898 and served in Cuba during the Santiago Campaign, where he saw action at San Juan Heights (1–3 July 1898). He was with the regiment at Santiago, Cuba (1900–1901), and then in the Philippines (1901–1903), serving at Cotabato, Mindanao (July 1902–August 1903), and in the field under Pershing commanding a provisional infantry battalion (September–November 1902) against the Lake Lanao Moros. He returned with the 10th Infantry to the United States, and he later served in Washington and Alaska (1906–1908) before being assigned to the Army School of the Line as a student (1908–1909). He then completed the Army War College (1909–1910) and was assigned as assistant to the inspector general, Central Division (later Department) in Chicago (1911–1914). He was inspector, 2d Division, at Texas City, Texas (April–August 1914), and then assigned to the 27th Infantry in September. In September 1916 he was assigned as an inspector general at the Southern Department at Fort Sam Houston, Texas. Helmick was promoted to colonel in May 1917 and was inspector general, Southeastern Department, at Charleston, South Carolina, until September 1917. He was assigned to the Office of the Inspector General in Washington in October 1917 and promoted to brigadier general, NA, in December. He was promoted to major general, NA, and commander, 8th Division (August–November 1918), and then commander of Base Section No. 5 at Brest, France (1918–1919). In September he assumed duty as chief of staff, Central Department, and later Sixth Corps Area in Chicago (1919–1921). He was promoted to brigadier general, U.S. Army, in March 1921 and was acting inspector general until November 1921. Helmick was appointed the inspector general on 7 November 1921 and promoted to major general. He was reappointed for a second term in November 1925 and retired on 27 September 1927. His son, Charles G. Helmick, graduated from the U.S. Naval Academy in 1913 but then transferred to the U.S. Army, in which he had a distinguished career before retiring as a major general in 1952. "Eli Alva Helmich," *Assembly* 5, no. 2 (July 1946), "In Memory" insert, pp. 4–5; "Eli Alva Helmick," in Davis, *Generals in Khaki*, pp. 173–74; "Charles Gardiner Helmick," in R. Manning Ancell, with Christine M. Miller, *The Biographical Dictionary of World War II Generals and Flag Officers: The U.S. Armed Forces* (Westport, Conn.: Greenwood Press, 1996), p. 143.

Guy Vernor Henry (9 March 1839–27 October 1899). Guy V. Henry, the son of Major William S. Henry (USMA, 1835) and grandson of Daniel D. Tompkins, governor of New York (1807–1817) and two-term vice president of the United States under James Monroe (1817–1825), was born at Fort Smith, Indian Territory. He entered the USMA in 1856 and completed its five-year course (only in effect for the Classes of 1859, 1860, and May 1861) in May 1861, when he was commissioned in the 1st Artillery. He was colonel and commander of the 40th Massachusetts Volunteers in November 1863 and commanded it through the Florida campaign of early 1864 and at Cold Harbor, Virginia, where he earned a Medal of Honor for gallantry on 1 June 1864. He was mustered out of volunteer service in June 1865 and returned to his permanent rank of captain, 1st Artillery. He transferred to the 3d Cavalry Regiment in 1870 and served in Arizona, Wyoming, and Nebraska until 1876. He was with the 3d Cavalry during the Big Horn and Yellowstone Expedition (18 May–17 June 1876) and was severely wounded in the face and lost his left eye at the Battle of Rosebud Creek on 17 June. Upon recovery, he returned to duty against the Sioux, Utes, and various other Indian tribes until September 1881, when he transferred to the 9th Cavalry and commanded the posts at Fort Stanton, New Mexico, and then Fort Sill, Indian Territory. He assumed command of elements of the 9th Cavalry at Fort McKinney, Wyoming (1889–1891), during which he served in the Pine Ridge campaign against the Sioux. Henry was promoted to colonel, 10th Cavalry, in 1897 and assumed command of the 10th Cavalry at Fort Assinniboine, Montana, in October. During the Spanish-American War he was at Chickamauga, Georgia, with the 10th Cavalry and appointed brigadier general, USV, on 4 May. He commanded a brigade and then the 1st Division, VII Army Corps, at Tampa, Florida, but did not reach Cuba until 12 July, just in time to participate in the closing of the Santiago Campaign. He served as a brigade commander under Nelson Miles in the Puerto Rican Campaign (July–September 1898), after which he commanded the District of Ponce, Puerto Rico, and then the Department of Puerto Rico until May 1899. Henry was promoted to brigadier general, U.S. Army, on 11 October 1898 and major general, USV, on 7 December 1898. Just prior to his death from pneumonia at his home in New York City on 27 October 1898, he was appointed to command the Department of the Missouri in Omaha. His son, Guy V. Henry Jr. (28 January 1875–26 November 1967), graduated from the USMA in 1898 and had a long and distinguished career in the army before retiring as a major general in January 1939. He was recalled to active duty during and after World War II and held a number of important posts. "Guy V. Henry," *Thirty-First Annual Reunion of the Association of Graduates of the United States Military Academy at West Point, New York, June 12, 1900* (Saginaw, Mich.: Seemann and Peters, Printers and Binders, 1900), pp. 76–79; "Daniel D. Tompkins (1774–1825),"

Biographical Directory of the United States Congress, http://bioguide.congress
.gov/scripts/biodisplay.pl?index=T000306; "Guy V. Henry (both father and son),"
Who Was Who–The Military, p. 251.

Carl Adolf Maximilian Hoffmann (25 January 1869–8 July 1927). Max Hoffmann
may have been the best of Germany's General Staff officers during World War I.
After troop duty (1888–1895), he attended the War Academy in Berlin and studied
in Russia for six months. He was then assigned to the General Staff in Berlin as its
Russian specialist until 1912, during which time he was a military observer with the
Japanese forces in Manchuria attached to Kuroki's First Army (1904–1905). He was
then an instructor at the War Academy in Berlin (1912–1913) before commanding an
infantry regiment until the outbreak of the war, when he was assigned to the General Staff of the Eighth Army in East Prussia as chief operations officer and pulled
together the plans that led to the great German victories at Gumbinnen, Tannen-
berg, and Masurian Lakes (August–September 1914). He remained at the Eighth
Army under the team of Hindenburg and Ludendorff and helped engineer many of
the victories of the German and Austro-Hungarian forces in the east. When Hindenburg and Ludendorff moved to the Western Front and took over the German war
effort in 1916, Hoffmann remained in the east as chief of staff to the commander-
in-chief, East, Prince Leopold of Bavaria, and really the *de facto* commander. He was
promoted to colonel and major general with this appointment in August 1916. His
concepts led to the destruction of the Russian and Romanian armies in 1916–1917,
and he knocked Kerensky's army out after the tsar was forced from power early in
1917. After the Bolsheviks seized power in Russia in November 1917, Hoffman used
military operations to force them into the Treaty of Brest-Litovsk in March 1918,
thus freeing German divisions to move to the Western Front for a series of offensives
under Ludendorff. "Max Hoffmann," The Prussian Machine, http://home.Comcast
.net/~jcviser/aka/hoffmann.htm; Karl F. Novak, "Introduction: General Hoffmann," in *War Diaries and Other Papers,* vol. 1, by Major General Max Hoffmann,
(Uckfield, Sussex, England: Naval and Military Press, 2004), pp. 9–32.

Josiah H. Holland (6 May 1880–25 August 1961). Holland graduated from the
George Washington University College of Medicine in 1905. He was commissioned
a first lieutenant in the Medical Reserve Corps in September 1909 and joined the
Regular Army Medical Corps in March 1911. Following his assignment to the Philippines, he resigned his commission on 1 March 1914 and settled in Evanston, Wyoming. He served in the Army Medical Department again in World War I. After the
war he returned to Evanston and resumed his medical practice, served as mayor for
nine terms, and was a surgeon with the Union Pacific Railroad. He retired in 1952.
TAGO, *OAR, 1915,* p. 655; *JAMA* 150, no, 13 (1952), pp. 1316–23; Barbara Allen Bog-
art and Uinta County Museum, *Images of America: Evanston [Wyoming]* (Chicago, Ill.:
Acadia Publishing Company, 2009), p. 115; "Obituary," *Rocky Mountain Medical Journal* 58 (1961), p. 13.

Robert L. Howze (22 August 1864–19 December 1926). Howze graduated from the
USMA in June 1888 and was commissioned in the 6th Cavalry. He served with Pershing at Fort Wingate, New Mexico (1888–1890), and then participated in the Sioux

campaign at Pine Ridge Agency (November 1890–February 1891). He was awarded a Medal of Honor on 25 July 1891 for his gallantry in action against hostile Sioux while commanding Company K, 6th Cavalry, at Little Grass Creek, White River, South Dakota, on 1 January 1891. He later participated in the Santiago Campaign in Cuba with the 1st Cavalry Brigade and distinguished himself at San Juan Heights. It was here that he became friends with later President Theodore Roosevelt. He remained with the Cavalry Division until September 1898, when he returned to the Military Academy as senior instructor in cavalry tactics until July 1899. He was appointed lieutenant colonel, USV, with the 34th U.S. Volunteer Infantry on 5 July 1899 and organized and trained the regiment until it left for the Philippines in August. He was active in field operations in Luzon and received significant notice for his leadership. Upon returning from the Philippines, he was appointed major, Puerto Rico Provisional Regiment of Infantry (1901–1904). Howze then served as commandant of cadets, USMA (1905–1909), before returning to the Puerto Rico Regiment as regimental commander (1909–1912). He completed the Army War College (1915–1916) and then joined the Mexican Expedition on 17 March. He was in the field against Villa until October 1916. He was then detailed to the General Staff and served as chief of staff first of the 10th Infantry Division and the 1st Provisional Cavalry Division at Fort Bliss, Texas (1916–1917), and then of the Northeastern Department in Boston (1917–1918). After his promotion to brigadier general, NA, in December 1917, he commanded the 2d Cavalry Brigade at El Paso (February–May 1918) and then the El Paso District (May–August 1918). He was promoted to major general, NA, and commanded the 38th Division, NA, in the United States and France (August–October 1918) and during the Meuse-Argonne operations (21–29 October). He then briefly commanded the 4th and 3d Divisions in France and during the occupation of the Coblenz bridgehead as part of the U.S. Army of Occupation (1918–1919). He returned to the United States in August 1919 and took command of the El Paso District again (1919–1921). Howze was promoted to brigadier general in March 1921 and major general in December 1922 and commanded the 1st Cavalry Division (1921–1925). He then commanded the Fifth Corps Area at Columbus, Ohio, until his death in September 1926. While serving in this command, he was chairman of the court-martial of Colonel (later Brigadier General) William "Billy" Mitchell (28 October–17 December 1925). Two of Howze's sons graduated from West Point and had significant careers in the U.S. Army: Robert Lee Howze Jr. (23 March 1903–14 April 1983), USMA 1925, became a major general, and Hamilton H. Howze (21 December 1908–8 December 1998), USMA 1930, rose to the rank of full general and was instrumental in the development of helicopter air assault doctrine, organization, and equipment in the army. "Robert Lee Howze," *Fifty-Eighth Annual Report of the Association of Graduates of the United States Military Academy at West Point, New York, June 13, 1927* (Saginaw, Mich.: Seemann and Peters, Printers and Binders, 1927), pp. 121–24; TAGO, *Medals of Honor to October 31, 1897,* p. 66; *Register of Graduates, 2000,* "Genealogical Succession," pp. 3–14, and "Biographies," pp. 4–132 (Robert L., Jr.) and 4–151 (Hamilton); General Hamilton H. Howze, *A Cavalryman's Story: Memoirs of a Twentieth-Century Army General* (Washington, D.C.: Smithsonian Institution Press, 1996); Isaac Don Levine, *Mitchell: Pioneer of Air Power* (New York: Duell, Sloan and Pearce, 1943), pp. 347–68; "Robert Lee Howze," in Davis, *Generals in Khaki,* pp. 189–90.

Leonard S. Hughes (31 December 1872–3 January 1935). Hughes received his B.S. and master's degrees from the College of Kentucky in 1894 and completed his medical education (M.D.) at the Medical College, University of Louisville, in 1897. After serving as a contract surgeon in the Army Medical Department (September 1898–July 1908), he was commissioned a first lieutenant in the Medical Reserve Corps in July 1908 and came on active duty that month. He was appointed a first lieutenant in the Army Medical Corps in February 1911 and graduated from the Army Medical School the same year. He was promoted to captain in March 1914 and major in May 1917. He was appointed lieutenant colonel, Medical Corps, NA, in January 1918 and discharged in February 1920. He retired from active duty on 30 October 1922. TAGO, *OAR, 1916,* p. 65; TAGO, *OAR, 1931,* p. 842; TAGO, *OAR, 1936,* p. 1043.

Evan H. Humphrey (5 March 1875–30 August 1963). After several years at the University of Nebraska, Humphrey entered the USMA in June 1895. He graduated from the USMA in February 1899 and was commissioned in the 7th Cavalry. He served with his regiment in Cuba in 1899 and as assistant to the chief quartermaster, Division of Cuba (1901–1902). He later served in the Philippines as assistant to the chief quartermaster, Department of Luzon (1905–1906). He returned to the 7th Cavalry as a troop commander in August 1910 at Fort Riley and commanded his troop at Fort McKinley in the Philippines (1911–1912). He was appointed a major in the Philippine Scouts in December 1912 and commanded units throughout the Philippines until August 1916, when he returned to the United States and was assigned to the 14th Cavalry at Fort McIntosh, Texas. In August 1917 he was assigned to the 346th Infantry Regiment, 87th Division, until July 1918, when he was promoted to colonel and appointed chief of staff, 10th Division, at Fort Riley, Kansas. The division was demobilized in February 1919 and Humphrey transferred to the Central Department in Chicago as its chief of staff, assistant chief of staff, and ACS, Operations, until August 1920. He completed the School of the Line at Fort Leavenworth (1920–1921) and the General Service School (1921–1922). He was promoted to colonel in 1921 and was an instructor (1922–1923) and then chief (1923–1924) of the Cavalry Section, General Service School. He completed the Army War College (1924–1925) and then remained there until 1929 as an instructor and director, Operations and Training Division, when he was made commanding officer of the 6th Cavalry in July. He commanded the 6th Cavalry at Fort Oglethorpe, Georgia (1929–1931), before moving to Fort Bliss, Texas, as chief of staff, 1st Cavalry Division (1931–1933). He was assistant commandant of the Army War College (1933–1935) and while in this post was promoted to brigadier general in February 1935. He commanded the 1st Cavalry Brigade at Fort Clark, Texas (1935–1936), and then the 23d Brigade, Philippine Scouts, at Fort McKinley (1936–1937) and Fort Stotsenburg (1937–1938). After commanding the New York Port of Embarkation at Brooklyn (1938–1939), he retired from active duty on 31 March 1939.

Caleb Huse (11 February 1831–11 March 1905). Huse attended the U.S. Military Academy, graduated in 1851, and was commissioned in the artillery. He was an assistant professor of chemistry, mineralogy, and geology at the USMA (1852–1859). While on a leave of absence serving as the commandant of cadets and professor of chemistry at the University of Alabama in 1860–1861, he resigned his commission in February 1861 and eventually joined the Confederate cause. Granted the rank of colonel in the Alabama State Militia and soon commissioned a major in the Confederate States Army, Huse was sent to Europe through the North in April–May 1861 to act as the Confederacy's major purchasing agent for weapons and military equipment. From 1861 through 1865, he spent more than $10 million for military supplies of all sorts, but especially for all varieties of arms and ammunition, that then had to be run through the Union naval blockade. The end of the war in 1865 left Huse with little future and no money. He accepted the amnesty when offered and returned to the United States in 1868, but with no profession or useful business skills. In 1876 he established a school to prepare candidates for the difficult testing for admission to the Military Academy. Located initially at Sing Sing, New York, and moved in 1879 to a location near the Military Academy at Highland Falls, Huse's preparatory school was called the Highland Falls Academy, or "The Rocks," and it remained there until his death (1879–1905). In 1904 he published a brief memoir on his wartime experiences entitled *The Supplies for the Confederate Army: How They Were Obtained in Europe and How Paid For* (Boston, Mass.: Press of T. R. Marvin and Son, 1904). "Caleb Huse," *Thirty-Seventh Annual Reunion of the Association of Graduates of the United States Military Academy at West Point, New York, June 11th, 1906* (Saginaw, Mich.: Seemann and Peters, 1906), pp. 30–32.

Merritte W. Ireland (1 May 1867–5 July 1952). Ireland completed the Detroit College of Medicine in 1890 and received his medical degree in 1891 after attending the Jefferson Medical College in Philadelphia. He was commissioned in the Army Medical Department in 1891. He later served at Fort Riley and later at various posts in the West until the outbreak of the Spanish-American War saw him ordered to Chickamauga Park, Georgia, with the 3d Field Artillery. He served under La Garde at the reserve division hospital at Siboney, Cuba, and then at Camp Wikoff, Montauk Point, as executive officer of the general hospital. Ireland served as regimental surgeon, 45th U.S. Volunteers, in the Philippines (1899–1900) and as medical purveyor, Division of Philippines (1900–1902). He served in various positions as executive officer and in charge of the personnel and supply divisions at the Office of the Surgeon General under Brigadier General Robert M. O'Reilly (1902–1909) and his successor, Brigadier General George H. Torney (1909–1913), until he returned to the Philippines in 1912 as brigade surgeon at Fort McKinley. He returned to the United States in August 1915 and was assigned to Fort Sam Houston, Texas, where he was sanitary inspector for the Southern Department and then surgeon of the Cavalry Division, post, and general hospital during the Mexican Expedition. During this time he renewed his earlier contacts with Pershing, who selected Ireland as chief surgeon for the AEF in May 1917. However, the surgeon general had already selected Brigadier General Alfred E. Bradley for that post, so Ireland accompanied the AEF headquarters to France and acted as deputy surgeon until Bradley was forced to return to the United States due to illness in April 1918. Ireland was promoted to colonel, Medical Corps, in May 1917 and brigadier general in May 1918. He was selected to replace the surgeon general, Major General William C. Gorgas, and was promoted to major general and returned to the United States in October 1918. Ireland became the surgeon general on 30 October 1918 and served in that capacity until 31 May 1931, when he was retired for age. Ireland was a very innovative leader who stressed medical care, equipment, and training for the battlefield. His many accomplishments contributed greatly to the success of the U.S. Army Medical Department during World War II. Colonel James M. Phalen, "Merritte Weber Ireland (May 31, 1867–July 5, 1952)," in "Chiefs of the Medical Department, U.S. Army, 1775–1940: Biographical Sketches," *Army Medical Bulletin,* no. 52 (April 1940), pp. 94–100; "Merritte Weber Ireland," *Who Was Who–The Military,* p. 282.

James A. Irons (21 February 1857–22 July 1921). Irons graduated from the USMA in June 1879 and was commissioned in the 20th Infantry. He served in Texas, the Indian Territory, and Montana and was then a student and instructor at the Infantry and Cavalry School of Application at Fort Leavenworth (1883–1885, 1887–1891). After duty at Fort Leavenworth with the 20th Infantry (1894–1898), he participated in the Santiago Campaign in Cuba (June–July 1898) and saw action at El Caney on 1 July and San Juan Heights, 1–3 July 1898. Mustered out of volunteer service in early 1899, he went to the Philippines with the 20th Infantry (1898–1901). He was appointed to the initial General Staff in August 1903 and was the assistant to the chief of staff, Northern Division, in St. Louis (1904–1905). He was relieved from the General Staff and assigned to the 16th Infantry in April 1905 and then promoted to lieutenant colonel, 14th Infantry, the same month. He was appointed U.S. military attaché in Tokyo, Japan (1907–1910). Irons was promoted to colonel and commander of the 20th Infantry in June 1909 and commanded the regiment in Manila and Fort Douglas, Utah (1910–1913). He then served once more as attaché in Tokyo (February 1914–March 1917). Returning to the United States, he commanded the 2d Infantry (April–July 1917), and he was promoted to brigadier general, NA, in August and accompanied the Imperial Japanese War Mission to the United States (August–September 1917). He then commanded the 5th Infantry Brigade (January–March 1918) and was discharged from the National Army in March 1918 and assigned to command the 49th Infantry and Camp Merritt, New Jersey (March–June 1918). He was then transferred to the 29th Infantry Regiment (July 1918–November 1918), while also commanding the 17th Division (September–November 1918). He retired as a colonel on 1 July 1920. "James Anderson Irons," *Fifty-Fifth Annual Report of the Association of Graduates of the United States Military Academy at West Point, New York, June 11, 1924* (Saginaw, Mich.: Seemann and Peters, Printers and Binders, 1924), pp. 59–61.

William V. Judson (16 February 1865–30 March 1923). After completing two years at Harvard, Judson graduated from the USMA in June 1888 and was commissioned in the Corps of Engineers. After completing the Engineer School of Application (1888–1891), he was assigned to river and harbor work on Lake Erie (1891–1893), on the upper Mississippi River (1893–1894), and at Galveston, Texas (1894–1897). He was chief engineer, Department of Puerto Rico (1899–1900), and then in charge of river, harbor, and coastal fortification work on the Gulf Coast and in Alabama and Georgia (1900–1901). Judson was assigned as a military attaché and observer with the Russian Army in Manchuria (March 1904–March 1905) during the Russo-Japanese War and captured by the Japanese along with Colonel Valery Havard at Mukden. He was then assigned as district engineer in Milwaukee, Wisconsin, in charge of improvement work on the western shore of Lake Michigan (1905–1909). He served as engineer commissioner of the District of Columbia (1909–1913) and as assistant division engineer of the Panama Canal (1913–1914) before being appointed as the district and division engineer at Chicago (1914–1916) and then district engineer at Baltimore (1916–1917). He was promoted to colonel in May 1917 and brigadier general, NA, in August. Judson was attached to Elihu Root's mission to Russia and then remained as military attaché at Petrograd and chief of the U.S. Military Mission (May 1917–January 1918). Returning to the United States, he commanded the 38th Division briefly before taking over as commander of the New York Port of Embarkation (September–December 1918). He was relieved of this duty due to heart problems and returned to his permanent grade of colonel in 1919. He returned to Chicago as division engineer and continued to serve intermittently thereafter due to his illness and finally retired for disability on 31 August 1922. "William Voorhees Judson," in *Fifty-Fifth Annual Report of the Association of Graduates of the United States Military Academy at West Point, New York, June 11, 1924* (Saginaw, Mich.: Seemann and Peters, Printers and Binders, 1926), pp. 74–83.

Henry M. Kendall (17 September 1839–2 October 1912). Little is known about Henry Kendall. According to army documents, he was born in Massachusetts and joined the 5th Independent Battery, Indiana Light Artillery, in September 1861, serving as a private and corporal until mustered out in January 1863. He was commissioned a second lieutenant in the 6th Cavalry in July 1867. He served with the unit in Texas, Kansas, Arizona, New Mexico, and the Dakotas through his retirement as a major on 31 May 1898 for disability due to wounds suffered in the line of duty. He was a professor of military tactics at Gonzaga College in Washington until 1901, and then was secretary and treasurer of the U.S. Soldiers' Home in Washington, D.C., from November 1901 on. TAGO, *OAR, 1901,* p. 288; TAGO, *OAR, 1912,* p. 508; *New York Times,* 12 November 1901, 21 March 1902; "Henry M. Kendall (Captain 6th Cav.)," in *Powell's Records,* p. 326; William A. Ganoe, *The History of the United States Army* (New York: D. Appleton-Century, 1942), p. 419.

Jacob Ford (J. Ford) Kent (14 September 1835–22 December 1918). Kent graduated from the USMA in May 1861 and was commissioned in the 3d Infantry. He participated in the Bull Run campaign and at the Battle of Bull Run (21 July 1861), where he was wounded three times. He later served in the Army of the Potomac in Maryland and northern Virginia, including at Fredericksburg (13 December 1862). He was on the staff of VI Corps until March 1865, during which time he was involved in all of the corps' major battles from Chancellorsville (May 1863) to the siege of Petersburg (December 1864–March 1865). After the war he served as assistant instructor of infantry at the Military Academy (1865–1869) and then on frontier duty in Colorado (1869–1874). He joined the 3d Infantry on frontier duty at Fort Shaw, Montana (1878–1885). Kent was acting inspector general, Department of Dakota, in St. Paul, Minnesota (1890–1894). He was promoted to colonel and commander of the 24th Infantry Regiment at Fort Bayard, New Mexico (1895–1896), and then Fort Douglas, Utah (1896–1898). With the coming of the Spanish-American War, he took the 24th Infantry to Tampa to prepare for the Cuban campaign. There he was appointed brigadier general, USV, on 4 May 1898 and given command of the 1st Division, V Army Corps, which he commanded through the ensuing Santiago Campaign and attacks at the San Juan Heights until 24 August. He was promoted to major general,

USV, on 8 July and brigadier general, U.S. Army, on 4 October 1898. He retired from the U.S. Army on 15 October 1898 and was discharged from his volunteer service on 30 November 1898. Kent was advanced to major general on the retired list on 4 March 1915. "Jacob Ford Kent," *Fiftieth Annual Report of the Association of Graduates of the United States Military Academy at West Point, New York, June 10th, 1919,* pp. 153–55; Heitman, *Historical Register,* vol. 1, p. 593; "Jacob Ford Kent," *Who Was Who– The Military,* pp. 302–3.

John B. Kerr (12 March 1847–27 February 1928). Kerr graduated from the USMA in 1870 with a commission in the 6th Cavalry. He served with the 6th on frontier duty in Texas, the Indian Territory, Kansas, Arizona, and New Mexico through 1890. At Fort Wingate, New Mexico, he commanded Troop K against Geronimo and his band (1885–1886) and in other actions. Kerr deployed to the Pine Ridge Reservation with the 6th in November 1890 and participated in the campaign against the Sioux. On 1 January 1890, Kerr led his Troop K against hostile Sioux attempting to break out to the Bad Lands and forced them back to the Pine Ridge Reservation. For his heroism this day Kerr was awarded a Medal of Honor. He was then assigned with his troop at various posts, the last being at Fort Leavenworth (1892–1898). He commanded the 2d Squadron, 6th Cavalry, during the Spanish-American War and participated in the Santiago Campaign in Shafter's V Corps. Kerr was wounded in the assault on San Juan Heights on 1 July and evacuated to Key West, Florida. Upon recovery he was assigned to duty at the Paris Exposition (1898–1900), was promoted to major in the 10th Cavalry (October 1898), and then appointed as military attaché at the U.S. embassy in Berlin until September 1902. He was promoted to colonel, 12th Cavalry, in March 1903 and selected as an initial member of the new General Staff Corps in April. He served as chief of staff, Division of the Philippines (1903–1904), and of the Division of the Atlantic (1904–1906). Kerr commanded the 12th Cavalry Regiment (1906–1908) and was promoted to brigadier general in April. He commanded Fort Riley and was commandant of the Mounted Service School from May 1908 until he retired in May 1909. TAGO, *OAR, 1901,* pp. 93, 387; "John B. Kerr," *Powell's Records,* pp. 328–39.

Henry P. Kingsbury (25 April 1850–1 February 1923). Kingsbury graduated from the USMA in June 1871 and was commissioned in the 6th Cavalry. He served with his regiment on the frontier in Kansas, in Mississippi, in Indian Territory, and in Texas (1871–1875) before the regiment was transferred to Arizona (1875–1884) and then New Mexico (1884–1890). He was on garrison duty with the 6th Cavalry at Fort Myer, Virginia (1895–1898), and then at Camp Thomas, Georgia, Tampa, and in Cuba for the Santiago Campaign. He commanded a cavalry squadron at the Battle of San Juan Heights (1–2 July) and during the siege of Santiago (3–17 July). Promoted to major with the 3d Cavalry in January 1900, he commanded the post and 1st Squadron at Fort Myer until September 1900, when he departed with his unit for service in the Philippines. He commanded the 1st and 3d Squadrons in the Philippines (1900–1902). Kingsbury returned to the United States and was stationed at the Presidio of San Francisco and then Fort Assinniboine, Montana (1902–1903). He was promoted to lieutenant colonel with the 8th Cavalry in February 1903 and assumed command of Fort Sill, Oklahoma (1903–1904). He took the 1st Squadron, 8th Cavalry, to the Philippines (1905-1907). He was promoted to colonel and commander, 8th Cavalry, in 1906 and returned to duty at Fort Robinson, Nebraska (1907-1910). He went back to the Philippines with the regiment (1910-1912), where he was detailed as acting inspector general (June-July 1912), and then returned to the United States to become inspector general, Central Department, in Chicago (1912-1914). He retired on 25 April 1914 but was recalled to active duty in World War I as the commander of the Recruit Depot at Fort Slocum, New York (September 1917-December 1919).

Henry Kirby (20 October 1851–13 June 1925). Kirby graduated from the USMA in June 1877 and was commissioned in the 12th Infantry. He served on frontier duty in Texas and New Mexico and saw action against hostile Indians in the field (1877-1884). He was an instructor in the Department of Tactics at the Military Academy (1884-1888) and returned to frontier duty in New Mexico and Arizona in the 10th Infantry (1889-1894). He then served in the Indian Territory (1894-1897). He was promoted to captain, 10th Infantry, in April 1898 and commanded the post at Cárdenas, Cuba, in 1899. He was regimental adjutant (1899-1903) in Cuba, Nebraska, and then on Mindanao. He was promoted to major, 18th Infantry, in February 1903 and joined the unit on Leyte. He was then assigned with the 18th Infantry on Mindanao (1907-1908). Upon returning to the United States he commanded the post and 1st Battalion, 18th Infantry, at Whipple Barracks, Arizona (1909-1910). He was promoted to lieutenant colonel, 6th Infantry, in January 1911 and colonel, 3d Infantry, in March. He commanded the regiment at Pettit Barracks, Zamboanga, Mindanao, and in the field (March 1911-March 1912). He returned with the regiment to the United States, where he commanded Madison Barracks, New York (1912-1914). He retired on 9 March 1915. "Henry Kirby," *Sixtieth Annual Report of the Association of Graduates of the United States Military Academy at West Point, New York, June 12, 1929,* p. 195.

George W. Kirkpatrick (22 November 1870–20 May 1947). Kirkpatrick graduated from the USMA in June 1892 and was commissioned in the 10th Infantry and then transferred to the 8th Cavalry. In January 1899 he was sent to Cuba with the 8th. He was promoted to captain, 15th Cavalry, in February 1901 and served in the Philippines (1901-1903), where he commanded Troop L in operations under Pershing around Lake Lanao. He was then at Fort Ethan Allen, Vermont, with the regiment until it was sent to Cuba for service in the Army of Cuban Pacification (1906-1909). Kirkpatrick was later assigned to the 15th Cavalry at Fort Myer, Virginia (1911-1913), and then Fort Bliss, Texas, on the Mexican border (1913-1916). He was promoted to lieutenant colonel in June 1917 and then appointed colonel, infantry, NA, in August. He commanded the 123d Infantry Regiment, 31st Division (1917-1918). He was transferred to command the 311th Cavalry (April-August 1918) and then the 41st Infantry Regiment (1918-1919). He retired as a colonel for disability in the line of duty on 22 June 1920.

Ferdinand W. Kobbé (22 July 1869–4 June 1936). There is not a lot of information on Ferdinand W. Kobbé, the son of General Kobbé. He was commissioned a second lieutenant in the 22d Infantry in October 1891 and transferred to the 23d Infantry in April 1892. He was promoted to first lieutenant in April 1898 and served with the 23d in the Philippines, where he was aide-de-camp to his father (1899–1901). He was promoted to captain in the 28th Infantry in February 1901 and rose to major in the 14th Infantry in April 1914. He completed the Army War College in 1915–1916 and was promoted to lieutenant colonel in May 1917. He was briefly a colonel in the National Army (August 1917–January 1918). He was with the 1st Division in France (1917–1918) and commanded the 307th Trains, 82d Division, later in the war. He was promoted to colonel in May 1920 and retired in November 1920. TAGO, *OAR, 1901,* p. 214; TAGO, *OAR, 1920,* p. 532; TAGO, *OAR, 1931,* p. 854; TAGO, *OAR, 1937,* p. 1055.

William A. Kobbé (10 May 1840–18 November 1931). Kobbé served as an enlisted man in New York State Volunteer regiments (1862–1863) and was commissioned in 1863. In March 1866 he was appointed second lieutenant in the 19th Infantry. In 1869 he transferred to the 3d Infantry, and then to the 3d Artillery in 1872. He completed the Artillery School (1872–1873) and then returned to the 3d Artillery, where he served as adjutant (1873–1877), followed by a series of artillery assignments until he returned to the Artillery School as instructor in law (1885–1888) and engineering and military science (1888–1896). In 1898 he was promoted to major of artillery, and in July he was sent to the Philippines as part of Merritt's expeditionary force as commander of four foot batteries (artillerymen from heavy artillery units serving as infantrymen) of the 3d Artillery (Batteries G, H, K, and L). He distinguished himself in action near Manila on 5 February 1899 and later at Tuliahan River, Luzon, on 25 March 1899, and earned a reputation as an excellent combat commander. Upon his return to the United States, he was selected to command the 35th U.S. Volunteer Infantry Regiment, which he trained and then took to the Philippines in November 1899. There he was appointed brigadier general, USV, in December 1899 and appointed military governor and commander of the Department of Mindanao and Jolo (March 1900–August 1901). In a meteoric rise, Kobbé was promoted to brigadier general on 2 February 1901, less than two years after his promotion to permanent major of artillery on 8 March 1898. He returned to the United States and commanded the Department of Dakota from 26 April 1902 until his promotion to major general on 19 January 1904 and retirement on the 20th. TAGO, *OAR, 1901,* pp. 105, 355; TAGO, *OAR, 1920,* p. 906; "William A. Kobbé," *Who Was Who–The Military,* p. 312; "William A. Kobbé," *Powell's Records,* p. 336; Linn, *The Philippine War,* passim.

Herman J. Koehler (14 December 1859–1 July 1927). Koehler was born and educated in Wisconsin, receiving his education at the Milwaukee Normal School of Physical Training, which he attended from 1879 until his graduation in 1882. Here he learned a distinctly German form of gymnastics called the *Turnverein* style that emphasized strength and agility. He joined the faculty at the U.S. Military Academy in 1885 as the civilian Master of the Sword. In the following years, he completely revised the entire physical training program at West Point. He introduced an entirely new program designed to improve the cadets' physical conditioning and development as well as their personal health and physiques through calisthenics, exercise, and participation in organized intramural and collegiate sports activities. He coached the army football teams from 1897 to 1900. After some years of effort, Koehler finally convinced the superintendent in 1905 to extend the compulsory physical training program to the entire Corps of Cadets. He was commissioned a first lieutenant in

1901 and transferred to the Department of Tactics as "instructor in military gymnastics and physical culture." He was then promoted through the ranks to lieutenant colonel in September 1918. During World War I, he expanded his physical training concepts to the entire U.S. Army to improve the physical conditioning and stamina of the soldiers. Lieutenant Colonel Koehler retired on 14 December 1923. He is known as "the father of physical education at West Point." "Headquarters United States Military Academy, General Orders No. 26, 11 July 1927 [Notice of Herman J. Koehler's death]," in *Fifty-Ninth Annual Report of the Association of Graduates of the United States Military Academy at West Point, New York, June 8, 1928*, pp. 33–34; TAGO, *OAR, 1927*, p. 758; U.S. Military Academy, *Official Register of the Officers and Cadets of the U.S. Military Academy, West Point, New York, June 1901* (West Point, N.Y.: USMA Press and Bindery, 1901), p. 5; Captain Michael J. Reagor, "Herman J. Koehler: The Father of West Point Physical Education, 1885–1923," U.S. Military Academy Library, Digital Library, http://digital-library.usma.edu/libmedia/archives/toep/herman_ koehler_father_wp_phys_ed_1885_1923.pdf; Captain David J. Yebra, "Colonel Herman J. Koehler: The Father of Physical Education at West Point," 23 November 1998, U.S. Military Academy Library, Digital Library, http://digital-library.usma .edu/libmedia/archives/toep/col_herman_koehler_father_phys_ed_wp.pdf.

Louis A. La Garde (15 April 1849–7 March 1920). La Garde was educated at the Louisiana Military Academy (1866–1868) and the Bellevue Hospital Medical College (1870–1872), from which he received his medical degree. He was appointed an acting assistant surgeon (contract surgeon) in the Army Medical Department in April 1874 and was commissioned as an assistant surgeon in June 1878. He served with the 4th Cavalry during the Sioux campaign (1876–1877). Promoted to captain (1883) and major (1896), he commanded the reserve division hospital (field hospital), V Army Corps, at Siboney, Cuba, during the Santiago Campaign and was in charge of the evacuation of the sick and wounded to hospitals in the United States. La Garde was promoted to lieutenant colonel (1906) and colonel (1910). During these years he served in the Panama Canal Zone and the Philippines. After serving as chief surgeon, Department of Colorado, in Denver, he commanded the Army Medical School in Washington, D.C. (1910–1913), before retiring. He was a pioneering researcher in wound ballistics, the physiological effect of gunshot wounds on the human body, and how to treat gunshot wounds. He wrote the basic medical work of the time on gunshot wounds, *Gunshot Injuries*, published in 1914. A second edition came out in 1916. He was recalled to active duty in the Office of the Surgeon General during World War I and spent much of his time lecturing at medical training camps on the treatment of gunshot wounds. "Louis Anatole La Garde," *Who Was Who—The Military*, p. 315; Colonel James M. Phelan, "Louis Anatole La Garde, Colonel, Medical Corps, U.S. Army," *Army Medical Bulletin* 49, no. 1 (July 1939), pp. 88–93; Francis A. Winter, "The Field Hospital at Siboney," in *The Santiago Campaign: Reminiscences of the Operations for the Capture of Santiago de Cuba in the Spanish-American War, June and July 1898*, ed. Charles D. Rhodes, pp. 239–45 (Richmond, Va.: Williams Printing Company, 1927).

William Lassiter (29 September 1867–29 March 1959). Lassiter graduated from the USMA in June 1889 and was commissioned in the 5th Artillery. He served with

Light Battery K, 1st Artillery, throughout the Santiago Campaign in Cuba and was involved in the siege and capture of Santiago itself. He then commanded the 7th Battery, Field Artillery, at Fort Riley, Kansas (1901–1903), before serving as recorder for the Field Artillery Board in Washington and Fort Riley (1903–1908). He went to the Philippines as inspector of field artillery units of the Department of the Visayas, and as assistant to the inspector general of the Philippine Department (1909–1910). He was later assigned as military attaché in London (1916–1917) and also commanded all U.S. Army troops in England as commander of Base Section No. 3 (September–October 1917). He was promoted to brigadier general, NA, in August 1917 and took command of the 51st Field Artillery Brigade in October 1917 before being ordered to Paris to work with General Pershing on the movement of U.S. troops to France until December. He returned to the 51st in December and led it into combat with the 26th Division (February–April 1918). He was appointed chief of artillery, I Corps, in May 1918 and directed corps artillery during the campaigns at Chateau-Thierry and the Aisne-Marne until August 1918. Promoted to major general on 8 August, he became chief of artillery, IV Corps, on 22 August 1918 and directed it during the St. Mihiel offensive to 13 September. He then served on the Toul sector until 13 October, when he became chief of artillery, Second U.S. Army. He took command of the 32d Division in November 1918 and commanded it during its march to the Rhine and duty as part of the Army of Occupation at Coblenz (1918–1919). When the 32d Division was sent home, Lassiter was assigned to the Superior Board of Officers, which prepared lessons gleaned from the AEF's World War I experience (April–August 1919). He returned to the United States in August 1919 and was assigned to the War Plans Division, War Department General Staff. He was promoted to brigadier general in July 1920 and commanded Camp Knox, Kentucky (1920–1921), before being assigned as assistant chief of staff, G-3, War Department General Staff (1921–1923) and being promoted to major general in December 1922. He commanded the Panama Canal Division (1923–1924) and the Panama Canal Department (1924–1926). He replaced Pershing as president of the Plebiscitary Commission Tacna-Arica Arbitration and was on duty with the commission during 1926. He next commanded the Sixth Corps Area in Chicago (1927–1928), the Philippine Department (1928), and the Eighth Corps Area at Fort Sam Houston before commanding the Hawaiian Department at Fort Shafter (1930–1931). He retired on 30 September 1931. "William Lassiter," *Assembly* 18, no. 3 (fall 1959), p. 71; "William Lassiter," in Davis, *Generals in Khaki,* pp. 223–24.

Henry W. Lawton (17 March 1843–19 December 1899). After the outbreak of the Civil War, Lawton served as first sergeant in Company E, 9th Volunteer Infantry (April–August 1861), during operations in western Virginia. He was commissioned a lieutenant in the 30th Indiana Volunteer Infantry and served with the unit in the western theater for nearly four years. Following the war, Lawton rejoined the army as a lieutenant and a regular officer in May 1867 in the 41st Infantry Regiment in Texas. He transferred to the 4th Cavalry in 1871 and was promoted to captain and took command of Company B (later Troop B) in 1879. He saw considerable action against Indians in the Southwest and on the Great Plains through 1884, when the 4th Cavalry moved to Fort Huachuca, Arizona, to participate in the pacification of the Apaches and recapture of Geronimo and his band. When Miles replaced Crook in April 1886, he determined to track down and capture Geronimo and put a final end to this recurring drama. He assigned Lawton and his troop, accompanied by elements of the 8th Infantry and Apache scouts under Captain Charles Gatewood and a new assistant surgeon, Leonard Wood, to track down and capture Geronimo. After a five-month pursuit, Geronimo met with and surrendered to Miles on 4 September 1886 after Gatewood had negotiated with the Apache chief. Controversy lingers even today about Miles's allotment of credit for the capture of Geronimo more to Lawton and Wood than to Gatewood. With powerful allies in high places (Miles became commanding general of the army in 1895), Lawton's career was now made—as was Wood's. He was appointed to the Inspector General's Department (1888–1898) and promotions followed through lieutenant colonel. When the war against Spain broke out in April 1898, Miles arranged for Lawton to be appointed brigadier general of volunteers in May and to command of the 2d Division of Major General William R. Shafter's V Corps for the invasion of Cuba. Lawton led the American landing at Daiquiri on 22 June 1898, occupied Siboney, and led the storming of the Spanish stronghold at El Caney, which his troops took after a hard and confused fight on 1 July 1898. Although in July he was promoted to major general of volunteers and colonel, Regular Army, for his actions, Lawton did not particularly distinguish himself in this operation. He remained in Cuba as governor of the military department at Santiago, but in October 1898 he was recalled from his post for repeated heavy drinking and bad behavior. Lawton was saved from humiliation and dismissal from the service only by his many influential friends. President William McKinley, also a friend, then assigned Lawton to command a division in the Philippines to rehabilitate his reputation and career. Lawton arrived in Manila in March 1899 just as the Philippine Insurrection erupted against the occupying U.S. forces. He took the 1st Division into the field against the insurrectionists in April and conducted an energetic and largely successful campaign in Luzon patterned on the tactics he had learned in his old Indian-fighting days. While personally conducting operations on the firing line near San Mateo, Luzon, on 19 December 1899, Lawton was killed by hostile gunfire. The best available biographical sketch of Henry W. Lawton is Steven L. Ossad, "Henry Ward Lawton: Flawed Giant and Hero of Four Wars," *Army History*, no. 63 (winter 2007), pp. 5–21. See also TAGO, *OAR, 1899*, p. 9; Heitman, *Historical Register*, vol. 1, p. 403; "Major General Henry Ware Lawton," http://www.culbertsonmansion.us/Lawton_Bio.html; "Henry Ware Lawton, Major General, United States Army," http://www.arlingtoncemetery.net/hwlawton.htm; Mark J. Denger, California Military Museum, California Center for Military History, "Major-General Henry Ware Lawton, U.S. Volunteers," http://www.militarymuseum.org/Lawton.html; Faulk, *The Geronimo Campaign*, pp. 105–29, 143–48, 193–96; Thrapp, *The Conquest of Apacheria*, pp. 352–60.

Ben Lear Jr. (12 May 1879–1 November 1966). Lear served as first sergeant in Company C, 1st Colorado Volunteer Infantry (1898–1899), and saw extensive service in the Philippines. He was appointed a second lieutenant in the 1st Colorado on 1 April 1899 and mustered out in July, after which he joined the 36th U.S. Volunteer Infantry as a lieutenant and again served in the Philippines until mustered out in June 1901. He was commissioned an officer in the 15th Cavalry in June 1901. He was with the 15th Cavalry on Mindanao and saw action during Pershing's Moro expeditions of 1903. During World War I, he was assigned to the General Staff Corps (1917–

1918). He completed the Army School of the Line in 1922, the General Staff School in 1923, and the Army War College in 1926. He was detailed to the Inspector General's Department (1927–1930) and commanded the 11th Cavalry Regiment (1931–1933) before another detail to the Inspector General's Department (1933–1934). Lear was promoted to brigadier general in May 1936 and commanded the I Cavalry Corps and 1st Cavalry Division (1936–1938). Promoted to major general in October 1938, he was sent to the Panama Canal Zone, where he commanded the Pacific Sector until early 1940 and then the Panama Mobile Force until September. He returned to the United States in October and commanded the Second U.S. Army until April 1943. He was promoted to lieutenant general and retired in May 1943 but was immediately recalled to active duty as a member of the War Department Personnel Board. With Lieutenant General Lesley J. McNair's death in France in July 1944, Lear became commanding general, Army Ground Forces, until he was assigned to the European Theater of Operations (ETO) as deputy commanding general (January–July 1945). He retired in December 1945 and was promoted to the rank of general, U.S. Army retired, in July 1954. Ancell, *Biographical Dictionary*, p. 184; Clay, *U.S. Army Order of Battle*, vol. 1, pp. 115, 141, 289; vol. 2, pp. 569, 623, 1031; Heitman, *Historical Register*, vol. 1, p. 621; TAGO, *OAR, 1916*, p. 170; TAGO, *OAR, 1941*, p. 497; "Ben Lear," *Who Was Who–The Military*, p. 322.

Jesse M. Lee (2 January 1843–26 March 1926). In the Civil War, Lee served as a private and commissary sergeant in Company B, 59th Indiana Infantry (1861–1862). He was commissioned an officer in the 59th in October 1863 and participated in numerous western campaigns and the Vicksburg, Atlanta, and Carolina campaigns. He was mustered out in July 1865 and was appointed a captain in the 38th U.S. Colored Troops in August 1865 and mustered out in January 1867. He was commissioned in 39th U.S. Infantry (a black regiment) in July 1866. He transferred to the 25th Infantry in 1869 during the army's reorganization. He then transferred to the 9th Infantry in 1871. During his many years on the frontier he participated in numerous operations against the Indians. On several occasions Lee even acted as an Indian agent, including at the Spotted Tail Indian Agency when Sioux leader Crazy Horse was killed on 5 September 1877. He was promoted to major in April 1898. In May 1898 he was appointed colonel, 10th U.S. Volunteer Infantry, a regiment of African-American soldiers known as "immunes" whom Lee recruited for service in Cuba because of their supposed immunity to yellow fever. He was promoted to colonel with the 30th Infantry in November 1901 and commanded it until he was promoted to brigadier general in June 1902. He briefly commanded the 6th Separate Brigade (Leyte) and the 3d Brigade (southern Luzon) (October 1902) until called to Manila to escort General Miles on his visit to the Philippines. He replaced Frank Baldwin as commander of the Department of the Visayas (Panay) (February–May 1903). Lee was commanding general of the Department of Texas (1904–1906) and returned to the Philippines to command the garrison at Camp Stotsenburg, Luzon, before assuming command of the Department of the Visayas again until January 1907. Lee was promoted to major general in September 1906 at the same time that Arthur MacArthur was advanced to lieutenant general upon Henry Corbin's retirement and John Pershing was promoted to brigadier general. J. Franklin Bell, the senior brigadier general and War Department chief of staff, waived his own promotion to major general to allow Lee to be promoted to the next highest rank for the remaining months of his career. Lee retired from active duty in January 1907. Heitman, *Historical Register,* vol. 1, pp. 130, 624; TAGO, *Official Army Register for 1916,* p. 533; "Jesse M. Lee," *Powell's Records,* p. 346; "Jesse Matlack Lee," *Who Was Who–The Military,* p. 324; "Resigns His Colonelcy," *New York Times,* 12 July 1898; "Gen. MacArthur Promoted," *New York Times,* 16 September 1906; *ARWD, 1903,* vol. 3, passim; *ARWD, 1904,* vol. 3, p. 225; *ARWD, 1906,* vol. 3, pp. 135, 250; *ARWD, 1907,* vol. 3, p. 265; "Memorandum," in Thian, *Notes,* pp. 194, 199.

Elmer Lindsley (13 November 1866–6 November 1936). Lindsley graduated from the USMA in June 1891 and was commissioned in the 6th Cavalry. He served in Wyoming and at Yellowstone National Park (1891–1898). He was transferred to the 1st Cavalry in June 1898 and served in Montana and again at Fort Yellowstone until August 1902. He then was assigned to duty in the Philippines (1902–1903) before returning to regimental duty in Texas (1903–1907), where he established a reputation for quality work while serving as the quartermaster of the 1st Cavalry. Lindsley was detailed to duty with the Quartermaster Department at the Philadelphia Depot (1907–1911). He was then assigned to command a troop of the 4th Cavalry on the Mexican border, first at El Paso, Texas (1911–1912), and then at Fort Huachuca, Arizona (1912–1913). He transferred to the 7th Cavalry in February 1913 and was assigned to the Philippines commanding a troop until December 1913, when he was detailed as assistant to the chief quartermaster, Philippine Division, and officer in charge of construction and repair to September 1914. In November 1915 he was assigned to the 13th Cavalry at Columbus, New Mexico. He commanded a squadron of the 13th Cavalry in Pershing's Mexican Expedition until June 1916, when he was returned sick to El Paso. He was again detailed to the Quartermaster Department at Philadelphia (1916–1918) and was promoted to lieutenant colonel in March 1917 and temporary colonel in August 1917. He then commanded the 153d Depot Brigade at Fort Dix, New Jersey (1918–1919), and was recruiting officer there during 1919. Lindsley served in Texas and commanded the post at Corozal, Panama Canal Zone, until he was promoted to colonel and retired in July 1920. "Elmer Lindsley," *Sixtieth-Eighth Annual Report of the Association of Graduates of the United States Military Academy at West Point, New York, June 11, 1937,* pp. 165–68.

James Lockett (31 October 1855–4 May 1933). Lockett graduated from the USMA in June 1879 and was commissioned in the 4th Cavalry. He served on frontier duty in Kansas, New Mexico, Colorado, and Arizona (1879–1889). He saw significant action against the Apache Indians and Geronimo during these years. He was promoted to captain in April 1894 and assigned to the Presidio of San Francisco (1894–1898), during which he also was on duty guarding Sequoia National Park in 1895 and 1896. He left San Francisco for the Philippines with initial elements of Wesley Merritt's VIII Army Corps on 15 July 1898. In the Philippines, he was assigned as inspector general, 2d Division, VIII Army Corps, under Arthur MacArthur (1898–1899) and then as aide-de-camp to MacArthur (February–August 1899). In August 1899 he was appointed colonel and commander of the 11th U.S. Volunteer Cavalry, which was raised in the Philippines. He organized and commanded the 11th Regiment and was involved in numerous operations on Luzon through March 1901, when the regiment was returned to the United States and mustered out of service. He then commanded troops of the 4th Cavalry at various posts in the United States. He later commanded the 3d Squadron, which he took to the Philippines for duty, mainly on Mindanao (1905–1907). After returning to the United States, Lockett commanded squadrons of the 4th Cavalry at posts in Nebraska and Wyoming (1908–1911). He was promoted to lieutenant colonel and became commandant of the Mounted Service School at Fort Riley, Kansas (1911–1913). He was promoted to colonel in August 1912 and assigned to the 11th Cavalry in March 1913. He later served with his regiment in the Mexican Expedition (March–June 1916). He was appointed inspector of National Guard cavalry units at El Paso (1916–1917). He commanded the 11th Cavalry and Fort Oglethorpe, Georgia (1917–1918), and then moved to Fort Myer, Virginia, in command of the 11th and the post until he retired on 30 June 1919. "James Lockett," *Sixty-Fifth Annual Report of the Association of Graduates of the United States Military Academy at West Point, New York, June 11, 1934,* pp. 95–97.

Sylvester Chouteau Loring (6 June 1869–19 June 1936). Son of Army surgeon Major Leonard Y. Loring (1 February 1844–1 April 1903) and Sophie Chouteau of St. Louis, he was a descendant of Auguste Chouteau and the founding family of St. Louis, Missouri. According to Chouteau family genealogy files, Sylvester Chouteau, who often went by Chouteau, was born on 6 June 1869 but, much like Pershing, his birthdate was changed and in Army records was listed as 6 June 1873. This alteration allowed him to meet the age requirements for admission to the Military Academy when he was appointed from California. Loring entered the USMA in June 1892 as a member of the Class of 1896. He was turned back to the Class of 1897 for deficiency in mathematics and finally left the Military Academy in January 1895. In November 1900 he enlisted in Troop H, 2d Cavalry, as a private, serving until April 1901. In May 1901 he was commissioned in the 27th U.S. Infantry. He served with the 27th in operations on Mindanao, commanding Company G in actions against the Moros in September–October 1902. For his heroism in attempting to storm one of the heavily defended Moro *cottas* on 1 October, he won Pershing's recommendation for a brevet promotion. After returning to the United States, he transferred to the 15th Infantry in November 1905. He retired from active duty in April 1910 for disability received in the line of duty. "Report of Capt. John J. Pershing, Fifteenth Cavalry, of an expedition against hostile Moros of Maciu, September 28–October 3, 1902," 15 October 1902, in "Appendix IV: Occupation of Lake Lanao Region, Annual Report of Maj. Gen. George W. Davis, commanding Division of the Philippines," in *ARWD, 1903,* vol. 3: *Reports of Department and Division Commanders* (Washington, D.C.: GPO, 1903), p. 340; Vandiver, *Black Jack,* vol. 1, p. 294.

Arthur MacArthur (2 June 1845–5 September 1912). MacArthur was appointed a first lieutenant in the 24th Wisconsin Volunteer Infantry at the age of seventeen. His distinguished Civil War career included service at Murfreesboro (Stones River) and at Missionary Ridge, for which he was awarded a Medal of Honor on 30 June 1890. He was mustered out of the Volunteers in June 1865 and joined the army in February 1866 as a lieutenant in the 17th Infantry. After the army reorganization of 1869, he was assigned to the 13th Infantry, with which he served on the frontier, mainly in the Southwest. In July 1889 he transferred to the Adjutant General's Department as a major (later serving as adjutant general, Department of Texas), and in May 1896 he was promoted to lieutenant colonel while serving as adjutant general in the Department of Dakota. In May 1898 he was appointed adjutant general, III Army Corps, but his appointment as brigadier general, USV, on 27 May changed his assignment to a brigade command in VIII Army Corps of Merritt's Philippine expedition. MacArthur commanded the 1st Brigade, 1st Division, during the capture of Manila on 13 August 1898, in which he was again cited for gallantry and received a promotion to major general, USV. Otis now placed MacArthur in command of the 2d Division, VIII Army Corps, which he commanded until March 1899, when it became the Department of Northern Luzon (April 1899–May 1900). MacArthur was promoted to brigadier general in January 1900 and succeeded Otis as military governor and commander of the Division of the Philippines on 5 May 1900. He was promoted to major general on 2 February 1901. MacArthur had a very contentious relationship with the newly appointed civilian governor of the Philippines, William Howard Taft, which led to his relief and replacement by Adna Chaffee on 4 July 1901 and affected his subsequent Army career. Upon his return to the United States, MacArthur held a number of departmental commands over the next four years: the Department of Colorado (1901–1902), the Department of the Lakes twice (March–July 1902, November 1902–March 1903), the Department of the East (July–November 1902), and then the Department of California (1903–1904). While in command of the Department of California until October 1904, he also commanded the newly organized Pacific Division (January 1904–January 1905). Early in 1905, he requested detail to Japan as a special War Department observer of the Russo-Japanese War. Upon his return he resumed command of the Pacific Division and was promoted to lieutenant general, U.S. Army, on 15 September 1906 and was the senior officer in the U.S. Army. Although a favorite of Congress, he was never selected as chief of staff despite his seniority due to his continuing conflict with Taft, who was Secretary of War (February 1904–June 1908) during these years, and with President Roosevelt. He remained in command of the Pacific Division (redesignated the Department of the Pacific in 1 July 1907) until April 1909. He retired on 2 June 1909 and died on 5 September 1912 of a heart attack while addressing a reunion of the 24th Wisconsin Infantry in Milwaukee. MacArthur had two sons. His first, Arthur MacArthur III (1 June 1876–2 December 1924), graduated from the U.S. Naval Academy in 1896 and rose to the rank of captain prior to his sudden death. His second son, Douglas MacArthur (26 January 1880–5 April 1964), graduated from the USMA in June 1903 and achieved military and political fame that far transcended that of his father. TAGO, *OAR, 1901,* pp. 6, 348, 385; TAGO, *OAR, 1911,* p. 441; "Arthur MacArthur (1845–1912)," in *Webster's American Military Biographies,* pp. 252–53; Heitman, *Historical Register,* vol. 1, p. 652; "Arthur MacArthur, Jr.," *Powell's Records,* p. 360; "Arthur MacArthur, Jr.," *Who Was Who—The Military,* p. 343; "Memorandum," in Thian, *Notes,* pp. 189, 190, 192, 197–98; "Arthur MacArthur, Jr., Lieutenant General, United States Army" and "Arthur MacArthur III, Captain, United States Navy," Arlington National Cemetery Website, http://www.arlingtoncemetery.net/amacar3.htm.

Charles E. Magoon (5 December 1861–14 January 1920). Magoon grew up in Minnesota and attended the University of Nebraska (1876–1879) but left to study law with a law firm. He was admitted to the bar in 1882 and practiced law in Lincoln,

Nebraska. When Pershing was commandant of cadets at the University of Nebraska, he enrolled in the law school in 1892 and later received his law degree in June 1893. This brought Pershing into personal contact with the legal community of Lincoln, which then included young lawyers such as Charles Magoon, George Meiklejohn, and Charles Dawes as well as the soon to be famous William Jennings Bryan. Magoon entered the Nebraska National Guard as a major and served as its judge advocate. In 1899 Meiklejohn and Pershing selected Magoon to leave Lincoln to serve as a lawyer for the War Department's Bureau of Insular Affairs. There he established many of the legal precedents and foundations underlying American annexation and civil administration of Puerto Rico and the Philippines. He was then appointed general counsel for the Isthmian Canal Commission (July 1904–April 1905) and a member of the Commission (1905–1906), and he served as the governor of the Panama Canal Zone and representative to Panama (May 1905–October 1906). He replaced William Howard Taft as the provisional governor of Cuba during the American occupation (October 1906–January 1909). "Charles E. Magoon," *Who Was Who*, vol. 1: *1897-1942*, p. 768.

Wiley P. Mangum Jr. (3 June 1878–21 November 1908). Mangum graduated from the USMA in February 1901. He was commissioned a second lieutenant and assigned to the 15th Cavalry in the Philippines. He served with the 15th on Mindanao and was active in command of Troop A in Pershing's campaigns against the Moros in September–October 1902 and April 1903. He was wounded on 10 April 1903, as Pershing has described. He returned to the United States in October 1903, later serving with the 6th Cavalry and then the 8th Cavalry at Yellowstone National Park. In June 1907 Mangum was hospitalized with severe aphasia and on 3 August 1908 was retired for disability incurred in the line of duty. He died on 21 November 1908. "Wiley P. Mangum, Jr.," *Fortieth Annual Reunion of the Association of Graduates of the United States Military Academy at West Point, New York, June 10, 1909* (Saginaw, Mich.: Seemann and Peters, Printers and Binders, 1909), pp. 87–88.

Daniel E. McCarthy (14 April 1859–2 September 1922). McCarthy, known as "Little Mac" in the army, graduated from the USMA in June 1881 and was commissioned in the 12th Infantry. He was assigned to frontier duty at Fort Bowie, Arizona (1881–1882), and then to garrison duty at Plattsburgh Barracks, New York (1882–1885). He attended the Infantry and Cavalry School of Application at Fort Leavenworth (1885–1887) and then returned to frontier duty at Forts Sully, Yates, and Bennett in the Dakotas. He commanded Indian scouts at Fort Bennett to October 1891 before participating in the Pine Ridge campaign of 1890–1891. At the beginning of the Spanish-American War, he became the depot quartermaster at Chickamauga Park, Georgia, from April 1898 to 1899, when he moved to Cuba as assistant to the chief quartermaster to December 1900. In 1901, the War Department published his *Manual for Quartermasters Serving in the Field*. From December 1900 to 1905, McCarthy was constructing quartermaster at Fort Leavenworth. He then was stationed in the Philippines as chief quartermaster, Department of Luzon (1905-1907), before returning to assume the post of chief quartermaster, Department of the Missouri, in Omaha, Nebraska, until February 1911. He was then chief quartermaster for the Provisional Division at Fort Sam Houston, Texas (1911), chief quartermaster of the

Central Department at Chicago (September 1911–February 1912), in the Quartermaster General's Office in Washington (February–September 1912), and back at Chicago as chief quartermaster, Central Department (1912–1913). He was chief quartermaster, 2d Division, at Texas City, from February 1913 to August 1914 and promoted to colonel, Quartermaster Corps, in March 1914. He was back in Chicago as chief quartermaster, Central Department (1914–1916). McCarthy completed the Army War College in Washington (1916–1917). He was appointed chief quartermaster, American Expeditionary Forces, under Pershing, on 18 May 1917. On 10 June 1917 he became the first member of Pershing's staff and the AEF to set foot on French soil when he landed at Boulogne. He remained chief quartermaster and responsible for conceiving and building the complete logistical infrastructure for the AEF until August, when he fell ill with neuritis and was eventually ordered to return to the United States in January 1918. He was chief quartermaster, Southern Department, at Fort Sam Houston (1918–1919) and held the same post at the Southeastern Department, Charleston, South Carolina (1919–1920). In October 1920 he was appointed quartermaster, Fourth Corps Area, at Fort McPherson, Georgia, and retired on 30 June 1921. "Daniel Edward McCarthy," *Fifty-Fourth Annual Report of the Association of Graduates of the United States Military Academy at West Point, New York, June 11th, 1924* (Saginaw, Mich.: Seemann and Peters, Printers and Binders, 1924), pp. 81–85.

Edward J. McClernand (29 December 1848–9 February 1926). The son of a six-term Illinois congressman (1843–1851, 1859–1861) and Civil War major general, John A. McClernand, USV (30 May 1812–20 September 1900), Edward J. McClernand graduated from the USMA in June 1870 and was commissioned in the 2d Cavalry. He was on frontier duty at Fort Ellis, Montana, from 1870 to 1878 and was intimately involved in operations against hostile Sioux in southern and southeastern Montana. He was attached to Colonel (later Brigadier General) John Gibbon's column of the 7th Infantry as acting engineer for the Sioux expedition and the District of Montana in 1876. He was in the field at the Little Bighorn at the time of Custer's destruction on 25 June 1876, and was one of those who rescued what was left of Custer's command and then surveyed the battlefield. He later spoke and published extensively about his experiences on the frontier and at the Little Bighorn. He also served in the Nez Percé expedition of 1877 under Nelson A. Miles. For his actions on 30 September 1877 at Bear Paw Mountain, Montana, during this expedition, he was awarded a brevet rank of first lieutenant in February 1890 and later also a Medal of Honor in November 1894, both awards largely made through Nelson Miles's efforts. McClernand was then assigned to the Military Academy as an assistant instructor of tactics (1879–1883). He returned to frontier duty in Montana before being transferred to the Presidio of San Francisco (1884–1885) and becoming aide-de-camp to Brigadier General John Gibbon, commander of the Department of the Columbia at Vancouver Barracks, Washington (1885–1890). He served with the 2d Cavalry in Arizona and New Mexico (1890–1893) and then was a member of the Columbian Guard at the Chicago World's Exhibition (1893–1894) along with Pershing. With the declaration of war in 1898, he took his troop of the 2d Cavalry to Chickamauga Park, Georgia, and was appointed lieutenant colonel and assistant adjutant general, USV, on 9 May. He was assigned to duty with I Army Corps until he became adjutant general, V Army Corps, under Shafter on 28 May. He remained the adjutant general and virtual chief of staff throughout the ensuing Santiago Campaign in Cuba, and Pershing considered him "the brains of the expeditionary headquarters." Due to his incapacity, Shafter sent McClernand forward to set up a command post at El Pozo to coordinate operations against the San Juan Heights, and its was McClernand who ordered the attack on El Caney. Upon his discharge from volunteer service, he was appointed commander, 44th U.S. Volunteer Infantry (1899–1901), and saw action in the Philippines. He was adjutant general, Department of the Missouri (1901–1903), and then appointed as a member of the first War Department General Staff, serving as chief of staff, Department of the Missouri (1903–1904) and of the Northern Division (1904–1905). In March 1905 he was promoted to lieutenant colonel, 1st Cavalry, and appointed as a military attaché and observer with the Imperial Japanese Army in Manchuria and Japan (May–December 1905) with Pershing. He commanded the 1st Cavalry at Fort Clark, Texas (1906–1908), was promoted to colonel in November 1908, and served in the Philippines until December 1909. Upon his return to the United States he became president of the Cavalry Equipment Board (1910–1912) and then commanded the 1st Cavalry at the Presidio of San Francisco until he retired as a brigadier general on 29 December 1912. In October 1917, he was recalled to active duty again, this time as commander, Presidio of San Francisco (1917–1919). He authored a number of articles, especially dealing with his experiences against the Sioux from 1870 to 1878, which were pulled together in the book *On Time for Disaster: The Rescue of Custer's Command.* "Edward John McClernand," *Fifty-Eighth Annual Report of the Association of Graduates of the United States Military Academy at West Point, New York, June 13, 1927,* pp. 111–13; Robert Wooster, *Nelson A. Miles and the Twilight of the Frontier Army* (Lincoln: Univ. of Nebraska Press, 1993), p. 103; Edgar I. Stewart, *Custer's Luck* (Norman: Univ. of Oklahoma Press, 1955), passim; Cosmas, *An Army for Empire,* pp. 214, 216–17; "John Alexander McClernand (1812–1900)," Biographical Directory of the United States Congress, http://bioguide.congress.gov/scripts/biodisplay .pl?index=M000337; TAGO, *OAR, 1901,* pp. 61, 254, 388; TAGO, *OAR, 1916,* p. 559; Edward J. McClernand, *On Time for Disaster: The Rescue of Custer's Command* (Lincoln: Univ. of Nebraska Press, 1969).

Alexander McDowell McCook (22 April 1831–12 June 1903). McCook graduated from the USMA in 1852 with a commission in the 3d Infantry. He served against the Indians in New Mexico through early 1858, when he was promoted to first lieutenant and appointed assistant instructor in tactics at West Point. In the Civil War he first served as colonel, 1st Ohio Volunteer Infantry, and saw action at First Bull Run (21 July 1861). He was appointed brigadier general, USV, in September 1861 and commanded brigades, divisions, and corps until late 1863. Rosecrans accused McCook of losing the Battle of Chickamauga and relieved him from command, but a court of inquiry subsequently found for McCook. He was appointed lieutenant colonel with the 26th Infantry in March 1867 and commanded the regiment in Texas. In March 1869 he transferred to the 10th Infantry, which he commanded at various posts in Texas until 1874. He later served as aide-de-camp to General Sherman, commanding general of the army (1875–1881). Appointed colonel, 6th Infantry, in December 1880, he commanded the regiment in Colorado and Utah to May 1886. McCook commanded Fort Leavenworth and the Infantry and Cavalry School of Application to July 1890, when he was promoted to brigadier general and made commander,

Department of Arizona (1890–1893). He was then commander of the Department of Colorado and was promoted to major general in November 1894 and retired for age in April 1895. "Alexander McDowell McCook," *Thirty-fifth Annual Reunion of the Association of Graduates of the United States Military Academy at West Point, New York, June 14th, 1904* (Saginaw, Mich.: Seemann and Peters, Printers and Binders, 1904), pp. 38–100; "Alexander McDowell McCook (1831–1903)," *Webster's American Military Biography*, pp. 259–60.

Frank McCoy (29 October 1874–4 June 1954). McCoy graduated from the USMA in June 1897 and was commissioned in the 8th Cavalry. He transferred to the 10th Cavalry on 4 May 1898 and served in the United States and Cuba. He was involved in the fighting at Las Guasimas (24 June) and then the San Juan Heights (1–2 July), where he was wounded. After evacuation and recovery from his wound, he rejoined the 10th Cavalry at Montauk Point and Texas. The regiment then returned to Cuba for duty (1899–1902). He was aide-de-camp to Major General Leonard Wood, former governor-general of Cuba (1902–1903), accompanying him to the Philippines and Mindanao when he became commander and governor of Moro Province (1903–1906). During this assignment McCoy participated in numerous operations against the Moros. When Wood became commander of the Philippine Department, McCoy remained his aide until June 1906, when he returned to Washington to became aide to President Roosevelt and then aide to William H. Taft, the Secretary of War and provisional governor of Cuba. McCoy completed the Army War College (1907–1908) before commanding the post and squadron of the 3d Cavalry at Fort Wingate, New Mexico (1908–1910), and serving as a member of the War Department General Staff (1910–1914). He once again became aide to Major General Wood, commanding the Department of the East (June–December 1914), and then rejoined the 3d Cavalry on the Mexican border (1915–1916), during which he commanded two engagements with Mexican bandits. In June 1917 he joined Pershing's General Staff in Paris and served as assistant to the chief of staff, Major General James Harbord, and secretary of the General Staff to May 1918. He then commanded the 165th Infantry Regiment (the designation in federal service of the famous New York National Guard "Fighting 69th"), 42d Division, and the 63d Infantry Brigade, 32d Division, during combat operations until the Armistice in November 1918. He served as director, Army Transport Service (November 1918–January 1919), and deputy director-general and then director-general of transportation, AEF (January–August 1919). Other assignments followed in Washington, Chicago, and Fort Sheridan at Sixth Corps Area headquarters before he returned to the Philippines (1921–1925) with Major General Wood, who became governor-general. McCoy was promoted to brigadier general in December 1922. Returning to the United States, he commanded the 3d Infantry Brigade at Fort Sam Houston, Texas (1926–1927), and then the 1st Field Artillery Brigade and post at Fort Hoyle, Maryland. McCoy was sent on diplomatic missions to Nicaragua, Bolivia, and Paraguay (1927–1929). He was promoted to major general on 4 September 1929 and took command of the Fourth Corps Area, Fort McPherson, Georgia (1929–1932). President Herbert Hoover appointed McCoy as the U.S. member of the Lytton Commission (the League of Nations' commission investigating the Japanese-Chinese border dispute in Manchuria). In March 1933 he assumed command of the 1st Cavalry Division and Fort Bliss, Texas, until October, when he became commander of the Seventh Corps Area in Omaha, Nebraska. He next moved to Chicago, where he commanded the Second Army and Sixth Corps Area (1935–1936). His final assignment on active duty was as commander of the Second Corps Area at Governor's Island, New York (1936–1938), and also commander, First Army, in 1938. McCoy retired in October 1938. He became president of the Foreign Policy Association in New York (1939–1945) and was frequently called upon by the U.S. government during the war period. He was a member of the commissions that investigated the Pearl Harbor attack and tried the Nazi saboteurs in 1942. He briefly was recalled to active duty in 1943 to head the War Department Procurement Review Board. President Harry Truman appointed him as the U.S. member on the Far East Commission (FEC) that oversaw the development of international policies for the military occupation of Japan (1945–1949), and he served as the FEC's first chairman. "Frank Ross McCoy," *Assembly* 14, no. 3 (October 1955), pp. 53–56. For a complete biography of Frank Ross McCoy, see Andrew J. Bacevich, *Diplomat in Khaki: Major General Frank Ross McCoy and American Foreign Policy, 1898-1949* (Lawrence: Univ. Press of Kansas, 1989).

Charles E. McCullough (1872–?). McCullough grew up in Wisconsin and served as a private and corporal in Troop A, 7th Cavalry (12 August 1893–11 November 1896). He returned to the army as first sergeant, Troop L, 1st Illinois Volunteer Cavalry, on 26 April 1898. He was appointed second lieutenant on 18 August and mustered out of service on 11 October. He once again enlisted in the army as a private in Troop A, 6th Cavalry, on 7 September 1899 and was appointed second lieutenant, 9th Cavalry, in October 1899. On 2 February 1901 he was promoted to first lieutenant and transferred to the 15th Cavalry, where he commanded Troop G. He saw service with the 15th on Mindanao during Pershing's campaigns of 1902–1903 around Lake Lanao. He returned to the United States with the 15th, serving at Fort Ethan Allen, Vermont, until it was shipped to Cuba as part of the Army of Cuban Pacification late in 1906. McCullough was reported missing in Havana on 27 January 1907 with suspicion that he was the victim of a robbery. However, that was not the case—he was court-martialed in Cuba and found guilty of writing worthless checks, duplicating his pay accounts, submitting false claims against the government, embezzling funds from the camp exchange and officers' mess, and desertion. He was sentenced to two years in prison at Fort Leavenworth and "dismissed with ignominy" from the army on 5 September 1907. Heitman, *Historical Register,* vol. 1, p. 661; TAGO, *OAR, 1904,* p. 162; TAGO, *OAR, 1908,* p. 538; "Lieut. McCullough Missing," *New York Times,* 28 January 1907; "Dismissed with Ignominy: President Approves Sentence of Lieut. Charles E. McCullough," *Washington Herald,* 4 September 1907.

Carl F. McKinney (20 September 1889–8 August 1954). McKinney graduated from the USMA in June 1911 and was commissioned in the 8th Infantry. He was sent to the Philippines and served on Jolo Island with the 8th Infantry, seeing action while in command of a mountain gun detachment against the Moros at Bud Bagsak, Jolo Island (11–15 June 1913). He was then stationed at Manila (1913–1915), then returned to the United States, where he was assigned to the 27th Infantry. He was assigned to the 82d Division (1917–1918) when he was sent to Italy as adjutant to the American Military Mission to the Italian Supreme Command. He was promoted to major in

January 1918 and remained in Italy until September 1918. He was often at the Italian front during critical operations (June–July 1918) and with the U.S. 332d Infantry Regiment (July–September 1918). He was transferred to France in September 1918 and assigned to the 307th Infantry, 77th Division. He then commanded the 3d Battalion, 307th Infantry, during the Argonne offensive (September–October 1918), and commanded the battalion during the relief of Major Whittlesey's "lost battalion" of the 308th Infantry on 3 October. He was returned to the United States early in November for assignment to a new division at Camp Dix, New Jersey. With the Armistice, McKinney was reassigned to the Port of Embarkation at Hoboken until July 1920. He attended and instructed at the Infantry School (1920–1922) and then completed the Command and General Staff College (1922–1923). McKinney completed the Army War College (1925–1926) and was assigned to the War Department General Staff (1926–1928). After a tour as professor of military science and tactics at Johns Hopkins University (1928–1934) he was assigned to the 9th Infantry Regiment at Fort Sam Houston (1934–1936). He completed a tour with the Organized Reserves in Elizabeth, New Jersey (1936–1939), before being assigned as professor of military science and tactics at Kansas State College (now Kansas State University) (1939–1941). He was promoted to colonel in May 1940. He commanded the 368th Infantry Regiment, 93d Infantry Division (1941–1942), before serving as director of plans and operations for the San Francisco Port of Embarkation (1942–1944). He was then director of plans and training and later deputy chief of staff for the Fifth Service Command in Columbus, Ohio (1944–1946). In August 1946 he became chief, Claims Section, U.S. Forces Austria, in Vienna, and he retired on 22 August 1949. "Carl Fish McKinney," *Assembly* 14, no. 2 (July 1955), pp. 85–86.

William S. McNair (18 September 1868–6 April 1936). McNair graduated from the USMA in June 1890 and was commissioned in the 3d Artillery. He completed the Artillery School at Fort Monroe, Virginia (1894–1896), and was assigned to the Presidio of San Francisco (1896–1900) when he was sent with the 3d Artillery to China as part of the China Relief Expedition. He then served in the Philippines with the 3d before he was assigned to the 25th Battery, Field Artillery, in Manila (July 1901–April 1902), which he organized as a mountain artillery battery. He then moved his battery to Mindanao, where he commanded it in the campaigns against the Moros at Lake Lanao (April 1902–April 1903) under Pershing. He returned to the United States with the 25th Battery and was stationed at the Presidio of San Francisco and then at Fort Riley, Kansas, as commander until he transferred to the 6th Regiment, Field Artillery, as commander of Battery C in June 1907. He completed the Army War College (1913–1914), after which he was assigned to the 2d Battalion, 6th Field Artillery, on the Mexican border. McNair was detailed as an inspector general (1914–1916) and promoted to colonel on 1 July 1916. On 7 July he was appointed brigadier general, New York National Guard, and commanded the New York Field Artillery Brigade at Brownsville, Texas, until January 1917 and then the Provisional Field Artillery Brigade through February. He then rejoined the 6th Field Artillery and took the regiment to France in August 1917 when he was appointed brigadier general, NA. He commanded the 1st Field Artillery Brigade, 1st Division (August–October 1917), when he was ordered back to the United States to command the 151st Field Artillery Brigade, 76th Division, but first survived the sinking of his transport by a

German submarine on 17 October. He commanded the 151st in the United States and France (1917–1918) and was promoted to major general, NA, in August 1918. He was involved in the Meuse-Argonne offensive while assigned to army artillery at First Army headquarters (24 September–24 October 1918) and then was chief of artillery, I Corps, First Army (25 October–19 November 1918) and chief of artillery, First Army, until April 1919. Returning to the United States, he commanded Camps Taylor and Knox, Kentucky (1919), and Camp Bragg, North Carolina (1919–1920). He served on the General Staff in Washington (1920–1922) and then as chief of staff, Panama Canal Department (1922–1924). After serving as executive of the Field Artillery Group (Organized Reserves), New York City (1924–1928), McNair commanded the 6th Field Artillery (1928–1931). He was promoted to brigadier general in December 1930 and assigned to command the 4th Coast Artillery District at Fort McPherson, Georgia (1931–1932). He retired on 30 September 1932 and was promoted to major general, retired, by the Act of 21 June 1930. "William Sharp McNair," *Sixty-Seventh Annual Report of the Association of Graduates of the United States Military Academy at West Point, New York, June 11, 1936* (Newburgh, N.Y.: Moore Printing Company, 1936), pp. 171–74; "William Sharp McNair," in Davis, *Generals in Khaki*, pp. 263–64.

George D. Meiklejohn (26 August 1857–19 April 1929). Meiklejohn was born in Wisconsin and received his law degree from the University of Michigan in 1880. He moved to Fullerton, Nance County, Nebraska, that year and began his law practice. He was prosecuting attorney for Nance County (1881–1884) before being elected to the state senate (1884–1888) and then serving as lieutenant governor (1889–1891). He was elected to the U.S. House of Representatives in 1892 and reelected in 1894, but did not seek reelection in 1896. McKinley appointed him Assistant Secretary of War in April 1897 and he served in that post during the Spanish-American War (1898) and the early years of the Philippine Insurrection (1899–March 1901). He unsuccessfully ran as a candidate for the U.S. Senate in 1901, after which he resumed his law practice in Omaha. He moved to Los Angeles, California, in 1918 and remained active in Republican Party politics and his legal career. "George de Rue Meiklejohn (1857–1929)," Biographical Directory of the United States Congress, http://bioguide .congress.gov/scripts/biodisplay.pl?index=M000634; "George De Rue Meiklejohn," *Who Was Who*, vol. 1, *1897-1942*, p. 828.

Wesley Merritt (16 June 1836–3 December 1910). Born in New York City and appointed from Illinois, Merritt graduated from the USMA in 1860 and was commissioned in the 2d Dragoons. During the Civil War he had a distinguished career in the Union Army's cavalry and rose rapidly, receiving six brevet promotions in the USV and Regular Army, including major general, Regular Army, and major general, Volunteers, in April 1865. He commanded cavalry divisions under Major General Philip Sheridan in Grant's campaign in northern Virginia in 1864 and later in the Shenandoah Valley in 1864–1865. Upon mustering out in February 1866, he reverted to his permanent rank of lieutenant colonel and served with the 9th Cavalry in Louisiana and Texas (1867–1869) before commanding the 9th Cavalry at various posts in Texas (1871–1874). With the outbreak of the Sioux uprising and organization of the Sioux campaign in 1876, Merritt was promoted to colonel and given command of the 5th Cavalry and the cavalry forces of the Big Horn and Yellowstone Expedition, which he led through the ensuing operations against the Sioux and northern Cheyenne Indians until November 1876. After commanding the Wind River (1877) and Ute (1879) expeditions, Merritt was appointed as superintendent of the Military Academy in September 1882 and served until June 1887. After his promotion to brigadier general in April 1887, he commanded the Departments of the Missouri (1887–1891) and then Dakota (1891–1895). In April 1895 he was promoted to major general and again commanded the Department of the Missouri in Chicago, until April 1897, when he was given command of the Department of the East at Governor's Island, New York. With the coming of the Spanish-American War in April 1898, he commanded the VIII Corps on the expedition to the Philippine Islands, which sailed from San Francisco in June. Arriving at Manila in July, Merritt's forces captured the city in August 1898. He left the Philippines in August to attend the Paris peace negotiations with Spain and then returned to command the Department of the East until he retired on 16 June 1900. "Wesley Merritt," *Forty-Second Annual Reunion, Association of Graduates of the United States Military Academy at West Point, New York, June 12, 1911,* pp. 107–17; "Wesley Merritt," *Webster's American Military Biographies,* pp. 281–82; "Merritt, Wesley (Brigadier General, Commanding Department)," in *Powell's Records,* pp. 395–97; "Wesley Merritt," *Who Was Who–The Military,* p. 381.

Nelson A. Miles (8 August 1839–15 May 1925). Miles joined the 22d Massachusetts Volunteer Infantry as a captain in September 1861. He was noted for conspicuous bravery during the Peninsular campaign, after which he was promoted to lieutenant colonel in the 61st New York Infantry in May 1862. He assumed command of the 61st New York during the fighting at Antietam (17 September 1862) and again distinguished himself at Fredericksburg (13 December 1862) and Chancellorsville (2–4 May 1863). For his actions at this battle, he was awarded the brevet rank of brigadier general in March 1867 and later a Medal of Honor on 23 July 1892. Miles established a brilliant record as a fearless combat leader during the war, but he also established an equal record as an unabashed publicity seeker who coveted promotion and often alienated his fellow officers. He was commandant of Fort Monroe, Virginia, in 1865–1866 and had former Confederate president Jefferson Davis as his guest. He was appointed a colonel, U.S. Army, in July 1866 in command of the African-American 40th Infantry Regiment and the District of North Carolina. On 30 June 1868 he married Mary Hoyt Sherman, the niece of Senator John Sherman (R-Ohio) and General William T. Sherman. In March 1869 he assumed command of the 5th Infantry in an army restructuring, with units posted in western Kansas and eastern Colorado. His service thereafter was almost exclusively on the frontier against various Indian tribes throughout the western United States until 1891. His campaigns against the Plains Indians in Texas (1874–1875) gained him renown as one of the army's great Indian fighters, and he later was a key participant in the campaigning against the Sioux in 1876–1877. He then went on to end the Nez Percé uprising and capture Chief Joseph in October 1877, to pacify the Bannocks in 1878, and to promotion to brigadier general in December 1880 and command of the Department of the Columbia. In 1885, he moved to the Department of the Missouri at Fort Leavenworth, replacing Brigadier General George Crook, who had been sent to the Department of Arizona to end the Chiricahua Apache uprising under Geronimo. He then replaced Crook in April 1886 and completed the capture of Geronimo in September. He commanded the

Division of the Pacific in San Francisco (1888–1890) and was promoted to major general in April 1890 and moved to command the Division of the Missouri in Chicago after Crook's death. He was soon called upon to put down the final uprising of the Sioux under Chief Sitting Bull in South Dakota in December 1890. The Wounded Knee massacre of 29 December 1890 somewhat sullied Miles's reputation, as did his role in the use of federal troops against strikers in the Pullman strike in Chicago in 1894. His actions following Wounded Knee also badly soured his relations with his military and political superiors. As the army's senior major general, he commanded the restructured Department of the Missouri to November 1894, when he moved to New York to assume command of the Division of the East. He became commanding general of the army on 5 October 1895. Miles led the War Department and U.S. Army through the Spanish-American War, but his real role in the war was minimized by President William McKinley. Miles commanded the expedition that seized Puerto Rico (July–August 1898). He was promoted to lieutenant general on 6 June 1900, but significant controversy and conflicts with the Secretary of War and other military leaders marked his last years in office. He consistently opposed Secretary of War Root's effort to reform the army after the Spanish-American War and fell out of favor with both Presidents McKinley and Roosevelt. He retired on 8 August 1903 as the last general officer to hold the position of commanding general of the army, a position which was abolished with the 1903 army reorganization and creation of the War Department General Staff and the new post of chief of staff, War Department, beginning with his successor, Lieutenant General Samuel B. M. Young. Miles published two major autobiographical accounts of his life, *Personal Recollections and Observations of General Nelson A. Miles Embracing a Brief View of the Civil War or From New England to the Golden Gate and the Story of His Indian Campaigns with Comments on the Exploration, Development, and Progress of our Great Western Empire* (1896) and *Serving the Republic: Memoirs of the Civil and Military Life of Nelson A. Miles, Lieutenant-General, United States Army* (1911). Recent accounts of the military career and life of Nelson A. Miles are: Peter R. Demontravel, *A Hero to His Fighting Men: Nelson A. Miles, 1839-1925* (Kent, Ohio: Kent State Univ. Press, 1998), and Wooster, *Nelson A. Miles and the Twilight of the Frontier Army*. "Nelson Appleton Miles," in William Gardner Bell, *Commanding Generals and Chiefs of Staff, 1775-2005: Portraits and Biographical Sketches of the United States Army's Senior Officer* (Washington, D.C.: U.S. Army Center of Military History, 2005), p. 92; TAGO, *OAR 1901*, pp. 3, 347, 348, 385; Miles, *Serving the Republic*, passim; Heitman, *Historical Register*, vol. 1, p. 465; Wooster, *Nelson A. Miles and the Twilight of the Frontier Army*, passim; "Nelson A. Miles (Major General, U.S.A.)," in *Powell's Records*, p. 400; *Officers of the Army and Navy (Regular)*, p. 275.

John D. Miley (19 August 1862–18 September 1899). Miley graduated from the USMA in June 1887 and was commissioned in the 5th Artillery. He served at coastal forts in New York (1887–1890) but took advantage of his assignment to attend Columbia Law School, from which he received his law degree in 1889, and was then admitted to the New York bar. He then was transferred to San Francisco, California, where he served at various posts and coastal defense batteries (1890–1897). He was appointed aide-de-camp to Brigadier General William R. Shafter, commanding general, Department of California, in May 1897 and accompanied him to Tampa, Florida, when the general was placed in command of the Cuban expeditionary force. During the Santiago

Campaign in Cuba, Miley played a critical role as Shafter's liaison officer, often carrying orders to subordinate commanders, coordinating attacks, and even directing operations based on his knowledge of Shafter's intentions. He was appointed major and adjutant general of volunteers on 12 July 1898 and remained with V Army Corps until it was disbanded in October. Miley played an important part in negotiating the surrender of the Spanish garrison at Santiago and the remaining Spanish forces in the Santiago area. He was then inspector general, Department of the East, under Shafter until he was ordered to Manila, Philippines, for duty on the staff of Brigadier General Henry Lawton commanding the 1st Division, VIII Army Corps. In September 1899 he was appointed collector of customs at Manila. During his time in Cuba, he had become ill with typhoid fever but had recovered sufficiently to continue his duties. In Manila, he was afflicted with cerebral meningitis resulting from his typhoid fever and died on 18 September 1899. That year Miley's memoir of his service with Shafter was published as *In Cuba with Shafter* (New York: Charles Scribner's Sons, 1899). Miley had married Sara Mordecai, daughter of Alfred Mordecai (USMA, 1823), and had two sons who graduated from the USMA and had long careers in the army—John D. Miley (USMA, 1916) (15 May 1893–18 November 1967), who retired as a colonel, and William M. Miley (USMA, June 1918) (26 December 1897–24 September 1997), who pioneered the training and use of parachute forces in the army after 1940, commanded the 17th Airborne Division in Europe (February 1943–September 1945), and retired a major general. He was the last living Army division commander from World War II when he died. "John D. Miley," *Thirty-First Annual Reunion of the Association of Graduates of the United States Military Academy at West Point, New York, June 12, 1900*, pp. 68–70; "John David Miley (1862–1899)," in Berner, ed., *The Spanish-American War*, pp. 241–42.

Albert L. Mills (7 May 1854–18 September 1916). Mills graduated from the USMA in June 1879 and was commissioned in the 1st Cavalry. He was on frontier duty in Washington, Idaho (1879–1883), and Montana (1884–1886, 1887–1892). During his time in Montana, he participated in the Sioux campaign at Pine Ridge Agency (December 1890–February 1891). After an assignment in Arizona (1892–1894), Mills was an assistant instructor at the Infantry and Cavalry School at Fort Leavenworth (1894–1898). He served in the Santiago Campaign as acting assistant adjutant general, brigade inspector, and brigade adjutant general for Brigadier General Young's cavalry brigade (later 2d Brigade, Cavalry Division). He was actively engaged at Las Guasimas on 24 June and then the San Juan Heights on 1 July, earning commendations for both and being seriously wounded in the latter. On 9 July 1902 he was awarded a Medal of Honor for his bravery on 1 July, when he continued his assignment on the battlefield after being shot through the head and temporarily losing his eyesight. He was appointed superintendent at the Military Academy (1898–1906) with the rank of colonel and promoted to brigadier general in January 1904. While at West Point, he developed and had approved by the War Department plans to significantly modernize and expand the school's facilities. He commanded the Department of the Visayas in the Philippines (1907–1908) and then the Department of Luzon (1908–1909). Returning to the United States, he was commanding general of the Department of the Gulf at Atlanta (1909–1912). He was then president of the Army War College until August, when he was appointed chief of the Division of

Militia Affairs and the Militia Bureau, War Department. Responsible for all National Guard matters (1912–1916) during the critical years when many National Guard units were mobilized for duty on the Mexican border, Mills played an important part in preparing the state National Guard units for the upcoming world war. He was promoted to major general on 14 July 1916 and died in Washington on 18 September. "Albert L. Mills," in *Forty-Eighth Annual Report of the Association of Graduates of the United States Military Academy at West Point, New York, June 12, 1917*, pp. 62–68; TAGO, *American Decorations, 1862-1926*, p. 73; Charles J. Gross, "Guard Roots: Maj. Gen. Albert L. Mills," *National Guard* 62, no. 2 (February 2011), pp. 34–37.

Samuel M. Mills (15 December 1843–8 September 1907). Mills graduated from the USMA and was commissioned in the 19th Infantry in June 1865. He served in Georgia and Arkansas before joining the 5th Artillery in Connecticut in May 1870. He was assigned to the USMA as an assistant instructor in tactics (1872–1879) and as quartermaster and commissary of cadets (1876–1879). Mills served in the headquarters of the Signal Corps (1882–1885), and then as an instructor at the Artillery School for Practice (1885–1892). He next was commandant of cadets at the USMA (1892–1897). During the Spanish-American War he joined the New Jersey Volunteers in command of an artillery battalion in Florida (May–August 1898), but never moved overseas. He briefly commanded Fort Monroe and the Artillery School in 1898 and then the 6th Artillery, which deployed to the Hawaiian Islands (1899–1900) before being ordered to the Philippines. En route, Mills was ordered to accompany Chaffee as an observer on the China Relief Expedition to Peking (Beijing). He also served Chaffee as judge advocate and acting chief ordnance officer. He was on duty at Fort Wadsworth, New York (1901–1902), when he was promoted to colonel in September. From September 1902 to June 1905, he commanded coast artillery districts in Florida, Maine, and Massachusetts. Mills was promoted to brigadier general and chief of artillery on 20 June 1905 and retired on 30 September 1906. "Samuel Myers Mills," *Thirty-Ninth Annual Reunion of the Association of Graduates of the United States Military Academy at West Point, New York, June 12, 1908* (Saginaw, Mich.: Seemann and Peters, Printers and Binders, 1908), pp. 127–32.

Lewis S. Morey (19 July 1875–15 April 1948). Morey graduated from the USMA in June 1900 and was commissioned in the 10th Cavalry, then transferred to the 12th Cavalry in February 1901. After serving as aide-de-camp to Brigadier General Frederick D. Grant (1902–1903), he returned to the 12th until August 1906, when he was assigned as a student at the Infantry and Cavalry School at Fort Leavenworth. He then completed the Army Staff College (1907–1908). He was an instructor in modern languages at USMA (1908–1912). He transferred to the 7th Cavalry in January 1914 and served in the Philippines until December 1915. He transferred to the 15th Cavalry and returned to the United States in March 1916 and was assigned to the 10th Cavalry at Namiquipa in Mexico (March–August 1916). Morey commanded Troop K on 21 June 1916 at Carrizal, where he was wounded. He was professor of military science and tactics at the Pennsylvania Military College (1916–1917). He was promoted to lieutenant colonel, NA, in August 1917, and served as assistant chief of staff, 39th Division (1917–1918), before going to join the AEF in France. He completed the AEF General Staff College in May 1918 and was then attached to the 42d Division as an observer (June 1918) before moving to the 77th Division as G-3, G-2, and commander of the 305th Infantry Regiment until December 1918. Upon returning to the United States, he was assigned to the Office of the Director of Finance, War Department, in 1920 and transferred to the Finance Department. He remained in Washington until sent to the MBA course at Harvard (1923-1925). He then completed the Army War College (1925-1926) and then was reassigned to the Chief of Finance Office until promoted to colonel in 1929. He was finance officer, Fourth Corps Area, in Atlanta (1929-1935). He once again was assigned to the Finance Office in Washington, where he served until his retirement in July 1939. Morey was recalled to active duty during World War II. "Lewis Sidney Morey," *Assembly* 8, no. 1 (April 1949), p. 12.

Albert P. Morrow (10 March 1842–20 January 1911). Morrow served in the 17th Pennsylvania Volunteer Infantry in 1861 and then enlisted in the 6th Pennsylvania Cavalry in September, rising through the enlisted ranks to sergeant major in March 1862. That month he was commissioned in the 6th and served with it for the remainder of the Civil War. When he was mustered out of service in August 1865, Morrow sought an appointment in the Regular Army's cavalry units and was appointed a captain in the 7th Cavalry in July 1866. He moved to the 9th Cavalry in Texas for a major's rank in March 1867 and served with the "Buffalo Soldiers" of the 9th in numerous campaigns against the Indians throughout the West and Southwest. Morrow was known for his involvement in the pursuit of Victorio's band of Apaches in southern New Mexico and northern Mexico in 1879-1880. He was appointed colonel and aide-de-camp to Lieutenant General Sherman, commanding general of the army (1881-1883). In December 1882 he transferred to the 6th Cavalry, which he joined at Fort Huachuca, Arizona, in July 1883. He remained with the 6th commanding battalions and posts in Arizona and New Mexico until he was selected as colonel, 3d Cavalry, in February 1891 at Fort McIntosh, Texas. He retired at his own request on 16 August 1892. TAGO, *OAR, 1901*, pp. 226, 366; TAGO, *OAR, 1911*, p. 482; TAGO, *OAR, 1912*, p. 595; Thrapp, *The Conquest of Apacheria*, pp. 182-202; "Colonel Albert P. Morrow, U.S.A.," *Officers of the Army and Navy (Regular)*, p. 285.

Jay J. Morrow (20 February 1870–16 April 1937). Morrow graduated from the USMA in June 1891 and was commissioned in the Corps of Engineers. He attended the Engineer School and was assigned to the Company of Engineers (1891-1894). He was assigned to the Military Academy (1898-1901) and then to command of Company G, 2d Battalion of Engineers, at Willets Point, New York (March–June 1901), and in the Philippines in Manila, Mindanao, and on the Lake Lanao expedition (1901-1903). During this time he was chief engineer for the Department of Mindanao and Jolo (September 1901-July 1902) and military governor, Zamboanga Province (November 1901-May 1902). After serving at army headquarters in Manila (July–September 1903), he was assistant to the engineer commissioner of the District of Columbia (1903-1907) and then the engineer commissioner (1907-1908). He commanded the Washington Engineer District (1908-1910) and the 1st Portland (Oregon) Engineer District (1910-1915). He was then assigned as assistant to the engineer of maintenance and the engineer, Panama Canal (1915-1917). He returned from Panama to take command of the 4th Engineer Regiment, 4th Division, in the United States and France (August 1917-June 1918). Morrow was promoted to brigadier general, NA, in

June 1918 and then served as chief engineer, First U.S. Army (June–October 1918), during operations at Chateau-Thierry, St. Mihiel, and the Meuse-Argonne. He was chief engineer, Third U.S. Army (October–November 1918), and deputy chief engineer, AEF (November–December 1918), before returning to the United States to command the post and Engineer School at Camp Humphreys (now Fort Belvoir), Virginia (January–May 1919). Morrow returned to the Panama Canal as engineer of maintenance (1919–1921) and was appointed governor, Panama Canal, in March 1921. He retired in August 1922 but continued to serve as governor until October 1924. He remained active in business and consulting engineering after his retirement from the service. He was promoted to brigadier general, U.S. Army, retired, by the Act of 21 June 1930. His younger brother, Dwight W. Morrow (11 January 1873–5 October 1931), had a distinguished career as a lawyer, banker, diplomat, and U.S. Senator (New Jersey) (November 1930–5 October 1931). His niece, Anne Morrow, married the flyer Charles Lindbergh and was a well-known author. "Jay Johnson Morrow," *Seventieth Annual Report of the Association of Graduates of the United States Military Academy at West Point, New York, June 10, 1939*, pp. 155–59; "Jay Johnson Morrow" and "Dwight Whitney Morrow," *Who Was Who*, vol. 1, *1897–1942*, pp. 869, 870; "Dwight Whitney Morrow (1873–1931)," Biographical Directory of the United States Congress, http://bioguide.congress.gov/scripts/biodisplay.pl?index=M001002.

Patrick Moylan (26 May 1862–21 June 1948). Moylan was born in Ireland and came to the United States, where he enlisted in the 2d Cavalry Regiment. He served as a private, corporal, and sergeant (March 1883–March 1888). He later reenlisted in Troop H, 2d Cavalry, and served as a private, corporal, and first sergeant (July 1892–September 1905). He was appointed a second lieutenant in the Philippine Scouts in September 1905, promoted to first lieutenant in September 1908, and reappointed in the same grade in September 1912. He was promoted to captain in January 1913 and reappointed in January 1917. He retired in January 1920 and died in Philadelphia. TAGO, *OAR, 1920*, p. 844, *OAR, 1925*, p. 763, and TAGO, *OAR, 1949*, p. 843.

Arthur Murray (29 April 1851–12 May 1925). Murray graduated from the USMA in 1874 and was commissioned in the 1st Artillery. He returned to West Point as an assistant professor of natural and experimental philosophy under Peter Michie (1881–1886). He also used his time to study law and was later (1895) admitted to the bar and completed a "Manual for Courts-Martial," which served as the basis for future editions. He was then acting judge advocate, Departments of Missouri and Dakota (1887–1891). After commanding Battery L, 1st Artillery (1891–1896), he became professor of military science and tactics at Yale University (1896–1898). During the Spanish-American War, he once again commanded a battery of the 1st Artillery, before becoming acting judge advocate, I Army Corps, and holding various military government assignments in Cuba in 1899. In August 1899 Murray was appointed colonel, 43d U.S. Volunteer Infantry, and commanded it in the Philippine Insurrection. He then commanded the School of Submarine (mine) Defense (1901–1906) prior to his appointment as brigadier general and chief of artillery, War Department (1906–1908). Murray played an instrumental role in developing the legislation that separated the artillery into distinct field and coast artillery branches. This reform led to the field artillery's reorganization into battalions and regiments within the army's developing divisional structure and its modernization for maneuver warfare. On 1 July 1908, Murray became the first chief, coast artillery, and held that post until he was promoted to major general in March 1911. He served as assistant to the chief of staff and as a member of the Board of Ordnance and Fortification in 1911. In these posts he was critical in obtaining army appropriations for the purchase of Wright Brothers' airplanes. His last active duty assignment was in San Francisco as commanding general, Western Department, and the 3d Division (1911–1915). After retiring in December 1915 he served as vice chairman of the American Red Cross until December 1916. During World War I he was recalled to active duty as commander, Western Department (1917–1918). "Arthur Murray," *Sixty-First Annual Report of the Association of Graduates of the United States Military Academy at West Point, New York, June 11, 1930*, pp. 115–17; *Who Was Who*, vol. 1, p. 883; *The Army Almanac: A Book of Facts Concerning the United States Army* (Harrisburg, Pa.: Stackpole, 1959), pp. 12, 15; Dastrup, *King of Battle*, pp. 158–59.

Taylor A. Nichols (9 July 1879–13 June 1913). Nichols served as a private, corporal, and sergeant in Company E, Signal Corps (July 1900–March 1905). He was appointed a second lieutenant in the Philippine Scouts in March 1905, a first lieutenant in September 1908, and a captain in March 1912. He was killed in action against the Moros on 13 June 1913 at Bud Bagsak, Jolo Island. TAGO, *OAR, 1913*, p. 428, and TAGO, *OAR, 1914*, p. 636.

John C. Oakes (29 October 1871–11 November 1950). Oakes graduated from the City College of New York in 1891 and then from the School of Architecture, Columbia University, in June 1893, one day prior to his admission to the USMA in the Class of 1897. Oakes graduated from the USMA in June 1897 and was commissioned in the Corps of Engineers. He served in the Philippines at Manila while also commanding Company B, Battalion of Engineers (1899–1901). He was engineer officer, 1st Division, VIII Army Corps (1899–1900), and chief engineer officer, Department of Southern Luzon (1900–1901). Returning to the United States, he was an instructor in civil and military engineering at the Military Academy (1901–1903) and then assigned to the War Department as a member of the initial General Staff (1903–1906). He served in the Military Information Division (1903–1904) and as assistant chief of staff and chief engineer officer, Southwestern Division (1904–1905). He next went to Galveston, Texas, as assistant (1906–1907) and then district engineer (1907–1910). He was district engineer at Cincinnati (1910–1912). After being district engineer at Louisville, Kentucky (1910–1916), he moved to Philadelphia in the same post until August 1917. He was promoted colonel, NA, in August 1917 when he became commander of the 113th Engineer Regiment and division engineer, 38th Division, until June 1918. Then he was assigned to command the 5th Engineer Regiment, 7th Division, and moved to France in August 1918. He commanded the regiment in front of Metz (October–November 1918) before being chief engineer, VI Corps, Second U.S. Army, until April 1919. Upon his return to the United States he was made district engineer at Norfolk, Virginia (1919–1922). Oakes was engineer for the Second Corps Area at Governor's Island, New York (1922–1924), and then division engineer, Southeastern Division, Charleston, South Carolina (1924–1927), and district engineer, Charleston (1925–1927). He retired from active duty on 18 September 1927 due to disability incurred in the line of duty. "John Calvin Oakes," *Assembly* 10, no. 3 (October 1951), pp. 38–39.

Elwell S. Otis (25 March 1838–21 October 1909). Otis graduated from the University of Rochester in 1858 and received his law degree from Harvard in 1861. In September 1862 he was appointed captain and company commander of the 140th New York Infantry, with which he served throughout the Civil War. Otis was appointed lieutenant colonel in the 22d Infantry in July 1866 and served on the frontier under Colonel (later Brigadier General) David S. Stanley until February 1880, when he was promoted to colonel and commander of the 20th Infantry. During these years, he was active in campaigns against various Indian tribes, including the Sioux campaign (1876–1877). In November 1881, Otis was given the task of establishing the School of Application for Infantry and Cavalry at Fort Leavenworth, Kansas. He remained there until June 1885 and successfully laid the foundations for the army's professional awakening and today's U.S. Army Command and General Staff College. After duty with the 20th Infantry in Montana (1885–1890), Otis directed the army's recruiting service prior to being promoted to brigadier general in November 1893. He commanded the Department of Columbia (1893–1896) and the Department of Colorado (1896–1898). In May 1898, he was appointed major general, USV, and assigned to San Francisco as Major General Wesley Merritt's deputy to assist in the mobilization and shipment of Merritt's Department of the Pacific and VIII Army Corps to the Philippine Islands. Otis left for Manila with reinforcements in July 1898 and succeeded Merritt as commanding general and military governor on 29 August 1898. In this post, Otis oversaw all of the U.S. military operations to consolidate control of the entire Philippines and to defeat the Philippine Insurrection. In April 1900, he reorganized U.S. forces in the Philippines and established the Military Division of the Philippines that replaced the former organization. On 5 May 1900, he turned over command to Major General Arthur MacArthur, USV, and returned to the United States. He was promoted to major general on 16 June 1900 and commanded the Department of the Lakes in Chicago until he retired in March 1902. TAGO, *OAR, 1901,* pp. 6 and 348; Heitman, *Historical Register,* vol. 1, p. 762; "Elwell Stephen Otis (1838–1909)," *Webster's American Military Biographies,* p. 304; "Elwell Stephen Otis," *Who Was Who–The Military,* p. 418; "Elwell Stephen Otis," *Powell's Records,* p. 438.

William H. Oury (3 September 1871–26 November 1962). Oury attended the University of Nebraska and was an officer in the cadet battalion commanding Company A and the new Pershing Rifles during his final year (1896–1897). He was a captain in the 1st Nebraska Volunteer Infantry under Stotsenburg in 1898 but did not accompany it to the Philippines because he was commissioned in the 12th Infantry in September. Little is known of his assignments except that he was promoted to captain in August 1903, completed the Infantry and Cavalry School in 1904, and served with the Signal Corps (1906–1910). He was detailed to the Quartermaster General Department (1914–1917) and then promoted to lieutenant colonel (August 1917) and colonel (May 1918–March 1920), NA. He commanded the 311th Machine Gun Battalion, 79th Division, and then the division's 314th Infantry Regiment in the United States and France until it was demobilized (13 April 1918–29 May 1919). During the difficult fighting in the Montfaucon area in the Argonne Forest from 26 September to 3 October 1918, Oury took command of the 157th Infantry Regiment while still commanding his own 314th Infantry. He was promoted to colonel, Regular Army, in July 1920 and commanded the 14th Infantry, Panama Canal Division (1920–1923). He completed the Army War College in 1926 and was assigned to the Pennsylvania National Guard in Philadelphia as the senior army instructor until 1930, when he was appointed commandant of cadets at the University of Nebraska, his alma mater. He retired from active duty in September 1935 and was recalled in his former position until he retired again on 30 June 1939. Clay, *U.S. Army Order of Battle*, vol. 1, pp. 370, 458; TAGO, *American Decorations, 1862-1926*, p. 749; TAGO, *OAR, 1938*, p. 1019; University of Nebraska Military Department, *History of the Military Department: University of Nebraska, 1876-1941* (Lincoln: University of Nebraska, 1942), pp. 25, 52–54; *U.S. Army Register, 1963*, vol. 1, p. 755.

Richard B. Paddock (2 December 1859–9 March 1901). Paddock was born in Illinois and appointed as a second lieutenant in the 13th Infantry in October 1883. He served with the 13th Infantry at Fort Cummings and later Fort Bayard, New Mexico, where he transferred to the 6th Cavalry in February 1885 and soon moved to Fort Stanton. He attended the Infantry and Cavalry School at Fort Leavenworth (1886–1887). Upon his return to Fort Stanton, he met Lieutenant John Pershing, and the two quickly became good friends. He met Pershing's sister, Grace, when she visited Fort Stanton. Lieutenant Paddock and Grace Pershing married on 5 June 1890 in Chicago. He participated in the Pine Ridge campaign against the Sioux in 1890–1891. With the coming of the Spanish-American War, Paddock served with the 6th Cavalry in the Santiago Campaign and distinguished himself at the Battle of San Juan Hill. He returned from Cuba sick with malaria and then went to the Philippines in 1900. However, the 6th Cavalry was diverted to form part of the U.S. force under Adna Chaffee that was gathered as the China Relief Expedition to put down the Boxer Rebellion. Paddock was again in the forefront of operations against the Boxers. Attacks of malaria continued to recur until Paddock was hospitalized with pneumonia and died in Tientsin on 9 March 1901. Grace Pershing Paddock became seriously ill in 1903 and died on 25 April 1904. John F. Pershing became the guardian of the Paddock children, May (1892–1918) and Richard B. Paddock Jr. (1891–1952), in Chicago until his death on 16 March 1906, when John J. and Frankie Pershing assumed many of these duties. TAGO, *OAR, 1901*, p. 78; Gene Smith, *Until the Last Trumpet Sounds: The Life of General of the Armies John J. Pershing* (New York: John Wiley and Sons, 1998), pp. 29, 40, 97, 265; "Richard B. Paddock," http://en.wikipedia.org/wiki/Richard_B._Paddock.

Frederick Palmer (29 January 1873–2 September 1958). Palmer completed Allegheny College in 1893 and in 1895 turned his considerable talents to working as a foreign and war correspondent for a variety of magazines and newspapers for the next half century. He was incredibly prolific as a correspondent and author, producing novels as well as numerous personal accounts of his own adventures in various conflicts, including the Spanish-American, Boxer uprising, Philippine Insurrection, Russo-Japanese War, Balkan Wars, and the World War (five volumes, 1915–1919, 1937). He published his autobiography, *With My Own Eyes: A Personal Story of Battle*

Years, in 1933. He also completed a number of biographies, including works on *Tasker Bliss* (1934), *Newton D. Baker* (1931), and *Pershing* (1948). It was in Manchuria that Palmer first met Jack Pershing, who was there as an observer. Palmer was in France when Pershing and the AEF arrived in June 1917. Pershing soon asked him to oversee the press who covered the AEF and to lay out regulations and procedures governing mail and press censorship and activities of the correspondents with the AEF. He was appointed a lieutenant colonel in the Signal Corps reserve in 1917 and eventually rose to full colonel. For his services he became the first war correspondent to receive a Distinguished Service Medal, in 1923. Palmer continued his globe-trotting correspondent's career after World War I and even saw frontline reporting duty during World War II. "Frederick Palmer," *Who Was Who–The Military,* pp. 421–22; TAGO, *American Decorations, 1862-1926,* p. 750; Palmer, *With My Own Eyes,* passim, and Frederick Palmer, *John J. Pershing, General of the Armies: A Biography* (Harrisburg, Pa.: Military Service Publishing Company, 1948), passim.

John Henry Parker (19 September 1866–12 October 1942). Parker graduated from the USMA in June 1892 and was commissioned in the 13th Infantry. He served with the 13th Infantry (1892–1897) and found time to pass the examination to be admitted to the Missouri bar in 1896. He attended the war-shortened Infantry and Cavalry School course at Fort Leavenworth (1897–1898). Promoted to first lieutenant in the 25th Infantry on 26 April, Parker joined the regiment at Tampa and immediately set about convincing Shafter to detach him to organize and command a Gatling Gun Detachment for the V Army Corps. He had already proposed to the War Department the adoption of mobile machine-gun detachments to support the infantry, but was ignored. He won over Shafter, and Parker commanded the detachment throughout the Santiago Campaign, during which it played a significant role, especially in the fighting for the San Juan Heights (1–2 July). In his 1899 book *The Rough Riders,* Teddy Roosevelt wrote of Parker's role: "In fact, I think Parker deserved rather more credit than any other one man in the entire campaign." In 1898 his detailed account of the operations of his detachment was published as *History of the Gatling Gun Detachment, Fifth Army Corps, at Santiago, with a Few Unvarnished Truths Concerning that Expedition* (Kansas City, Mo.: Hudson-Kimberley Publishing, 1898), and the next year the same publisher produced his *Tactical Organization and Use of Machine Guns in the Field.* Appointed a major, USV, Parker joined Bullard's 39th U.S. Volunteer Infantry Regiment in September 1899 and served on Luzon in the Philippines until March 1901. After returning to the United States, he transferred to the 28th Infantry. Parker was the regimental quartermaster from October 1906 to January 1908 during the Cuban Pacification. He was then detached to the 20th Infantry at Monterey, California, to organize the initial Provisional Machine Gun Company in the U.S. Army and develop tactical doctrine for use of machine guns (1908–1909). After duty with the 28th Infantry (1909–1910), Parker was the professor of military science and tactics at the Kemper Military School in Boonville, Missouri (1910–1913). He was on duty with the 28th Infantry in the Philippines (1913–1916). He joined the 24th Infantry on the Mexican border and organized the first use of trucks to transport infantry on a campaign (May–June 1916) and remained with the Mexican Expedition as judge advocate until February 1917. During the years before World War I, Parker wrote prolifically about military topics, and especially about the organization and use of machine guns in the army in both professional military journals and popular magazines. He was assigned to Fort Sam Houston, Texas, in April 1917 to organize and conduct a school for machine-gun instructors and to codify the doctrine for machine-gun use that later became the official training memo in the AEF. In May 1917 he was assigned to Pershing's staff and accompanied Pershing to England and France and accumulated all information on British and French use of machine guns so that he could developed an AEF course of instruction. He was promoted to colonel, NA, in August 1917 and was involved in developing training until he was appointed commander of the 102d Infantry Regiment, 26th Division (January–July 1918). He was later awarded a Distinguished Service Cross for his bravery in action at Seicheprey on 20 April and two Bronze Oak Leaf Clusters to the DSC for actions at Trugny on 21 July and at La Fere Wood on 25 July. He was assigned to the 90th Division and commanded the 362d Infantry in operations in the Argonne at Gesnes during which he was severely gassed and twice wounded on 29 September. For this action he was awarded his third Oak Leaf Cluster (his fourth DSC), becoming the only American soldier to receive four DSCs "for extraordinary heroism in action" during World War I or any war. Parker was in the hospital recovering until 2 January 1919. Appointed commander of a troop barracks in Paris, he initiated a vocational training program for the soldiers that was later adopted for the entire Army in 1919. He was promoted to colonel in July 1920 and commanded Jefferson Barracks, Missouri (March–November 1921), and was then chief of staff, VII Corps, Organized Reserves, in St. Louis (January–December 1922). He was on recruiting duty (1922–1924) when he retired. Under a provision in the 13 June 1940 National Defense Authorization Act, he was promoted to brigadier general, U.S. Army, retired, effective that date. TAGO, *OAR, 1916,* p. 415; *OAR, 1941,* p. 1163; Linn, *The Philippine War,* pp. 164, 211; Theodore Roosevelt, *The Rough Riders* (New York: Review of Reviews Company, 1904), p. 162.

Leroy Vernon Patch (14 October 1876–24 March 1965). Born in Iowa and raised in Omaha, Nebraska, Patch attended the University of Nebraska, played varsity football, and was a member of Pershing's cadet battalion. He received his B.A. in 1898 and taught in the university's horticulture department (1898–1900). During the Spanish-American War he was a recruiting officer and served as a lieutenant in Company A, Nebraska National Guard. He was then superintendent of schools in Bartley and Kearney, Nebraska (1900–1902), before moving to Payette, Idaho, in 1904. There he bought an orchard and was soon a successful farmer, breeder, canner, and businessman. After settling in Idaho, he became actively involved in the Idaho State Militia (National Guard), serving in ranks from captain to colonel. He served as the Idaho state adjutant general (1913–1914) in command of the state's militia and National Guard and as lieutenant colonel of the 2d Idaho Infantry Regiment, which saw duty on the Mexican Border in 1916. In World War I, he was called up to service as part of the 2d Idaho Infantry, which was combined with units from the New Mexico and Washington State National Guards to form the 146th Field Artillery Regiment. During the regiment's training, Patch was sent to the Army Field Artillery School at Fort Sill, Oklahoma, from which he graduated in January 1918 and was sent to France as a lieutenant colonel. After commanding the base depot at Blois, France, he was ordered to the 146th Field Artillery Regiment as interim commander (25

April–6 May) until Colonel Ernest D. Scott, another member of Pershing's cadet battalion but a Regular Army officer, assumed command. He then commanded the 2d Battalion, 146th Field Artillery, and the regiment itself during fighting throughout the summer of 1918 and the St. Mihiel and Meuse-Argonne offensives. In November 1918 he was promoted to colonel and transferred to the command of the 303d Field Artillery Regiment, 76th Division. He returned to Idaho after the war and was appointed as state adjutant general again and retired with the rank of brigadier general in the Organized Reserve Corps in November 1921. "Gen. Leroy V. Patch," in Hiram T. French, *History of Idaho* (Chicago: Lewis Publishing Company, 1914), http://files.usgwarchives.org/id/payette/bios/patch25nbs.txt; "Colonel Leroy Vernon Patch," in James H. Hawley, *History of Idaho: The Gem of the Mountains*, vol. 2 (Chicago: S. J. Clarke Publishing Company, 1920), pp. 184–88; U.S. Senate, *Congressional Record*, vol. 61, pt. 8, 1921, pp. 7718, 8063; "History of the 146th Field Artillery," *A History of the Sixty-Sixth Field Artillery Brigade, American Expeditionary Forces* (Denver, Colo.: Smith-Brooks, n.d.), pp. 87–148.

George T. Patterson (23 March 1872–21 August 1918). Patterson graduated from the USMA in June 1896 and was commissioned in the artillery. He served in the coast artillery in New York and San Francisco (1896–1898) before joining the 8th U.S. Volunteer Cavalry during the Spanish-American War (June–August 1898). Several coast artillery assignments followed before he completed the School of Submarine Defense (1903–1904). He commanded the U.S. Army Torpedo Planter *Ringgold* (1904–1907) and then attended the Army War College (1907–1908). He then served in coast artillery assignments in the Philippines, New York, and New Jersey (1908–1912). Patterson was detailed to the Adjutant General's Department in April 1912 and served in various posts in the United States and Philippines until August 1916, when he was promoted to lieutenant colonel and returned to the United States. He commanded the coast defenses at Fort Rosecrans, San Diego (1916–1917), but was seriously ill and hospitalized from May to September 1917, when he was made commander of Fort Constitution and the coast defenses of Portsmouth, New Hampshire. Stricken with a relapse of his incurable illness, he committed suicide on 21 August 1918. "George Thomas Patterson," *Fiftieth Annual Report of the Association of Graduates of the United States Military Academy at West Point, New York, June 10, 1919*, pp. 78–90.

Robert U. Patterson (16 June 1877–6 December 1950). Patterson was born of American parents in Montreal, Canada, but then lived in San Antonio, Texas, until he returned to Montreal for his medical training and degree from McGill University (1898). He entered the Army Medical Department in June 1901 with the rank of first lieutenant. He completed the Army Medical School in Washington (November 1901–April 1902) and was assigned to duty in the Philippines. After several months in Luzon, he was sent to Mindanao and assigned to duty at Camp Vicars in January 1903. He actively participated in Pershing's expeditions against the Moros and later received two Silver Star Citations (Medals) for his heroism in tending to the wounded during the fighting at Fort Bacolod (8 April 1903) and Fort Pitacus (4 May 1903). Returning to Zamboanga early in 1904, he was on sanitary duty and working in the post hospital. After a spell of illness and duty in Manila, Patterson returned to the United States in June 1906 and served at the Presidio of San Francisco and was then assigned to Cuba as part of the Army of Cuban Pacification (October 1906–April 1909). He then commanded Company C, Hospital Corps, at Walter Reed General Hospital, Washington, and served at several posts in New York and Massachusetts until June 1913. He served with the American Red Cross (June 1913–April 1917) and spent several months with American Red Cross hospitals in Europe after the war began in August 1914. He took one of the first U.S. Army hospitals (Base Hospital No. 5) to Europe in May 1917. He was appointed a member of the American Military Mission to Italy (February 1918) and then as AEF general medical inspector (May–June 1918) and was with the 2d Division during the fighting at Chateau-Thierry (June–July 1918). He was an instructor at the Army War College (1919–1920) and then assigned to the War Department General Staff and completed the Army War College in June 1921. He was assigned as medical director, U.S. Veterans' Bureau (1921–1924). He was made executive officer, Surgeon General's Office (1923–1925), and then commanded the Army and Navy General Hospital, in Hot Springs, Arkansas (1925–1930). In August 1930 he went to Hawaii as the chief surgeon, Hawaiian Department, at Fort Shafter. Patterson was appointed army surgeon general and promoted to major general on 1 June 1931. He served until 31 May 1935, and when he retired on 30 November 1935 he became dean of the University of Oklahoma Medical School in Oklahoma City. He was appointed dean of the University of Maryland School of Medicine in Baltimore in 1942 but stepped down several years later due to ill health. "Robert Urie Patterson," in Colonel James M. Phalen, "Chiefs of the Medical Department, U.S. Army, 1775–1940, Biographical Sketches," *Army Medical Bulletin,* no. 52 (April 1940), pp. 101–6; "Robert Urie Patterson," *Who Was Who–The Military,* p. 429.

Ernest D. Peek (19 November 1878–22 April 1950). Peek graduated from the USMA in February 1901 and commissioned in the Corps of Engineers. After service at the Engineer School of Application at Willet's Point, New York, Peek was sent to the Philippines, where he served until September 1903. He was engaged in mapping and road work on Mindanao after June 1901 but also served on Pershing's expeditions of April and May 1903 and a later expedition against Bacolod in September. He was in charge of improvements at Yellowstone National Park (1906–1908). He attended the Army School of the Line (1909–1910) before completing the Army Staff College (1910–1911). Peek was at Duluth, Minnesota, on river and harbor work (1912–1916) and also in charge of the St. Paul Engineer District. He was assigned to the Chief of Engineers Office in Washington (1916–1917) and promoted to colonel, NA, in August 1917. He commanded the 21st Engineer Regiment in the United States until December 1917 and was with the AEF in France through November 1918. He was actively involved in the St. Mihiel and Meuse-Argonne offensives as the Engineer of Railways and Roads, First U.S. Army. He was then chief engineer, First U.S. Army, and deputy director-general of transportation, AEF, until June 1919. Upon returning to the United States, he was once again assigned to the Chief of Engineers Office and completed the Army War College (1919–1920) and remained an instructor there until February 1921. He was assigned to the Panama Canal Department (1921–1924), then returned to Washington and served in the office of the Assistant Secretary of War (1924–1927), working on procurement issues. He was then a student at the Babson Institute near Boston (1928–1929) studying business methods.

He returned to river and harbor work in New York City (1929–1930) and was then detailed to the Inspector General's Department at the Second Corps Area, Governor's Island, New York (1930–1934). Peek commanded the Norfolk Engineer District, Norfolk, Virginia (1934–1936), and then the North Atlantic Engineer Division at New York (1936–1937). He was promoted to brigadier general on 1 July 1937 and assumed command of the 4th Infantry Brigade, 2d Division, and Fort Francis E. Warren, Wyoming (1937–1939). He was chief, Infantry Section, Headquarters, 3d Infantry Division (1939–1940), and then chief of staff, Ninth Corps Area, at the Presidio of San Francisco (April–November 1940) when he was promoted to major general. He was commanding general, Ninth Corps Area (1940–1941), but had to leave this post due to ill health and commanded the Presidio of San Francisco until he retired from active duty in October 1942. "Ernest Dichmann Peek," *Assembly* 9, no. 4 (January 1951), pp. 56–57.

Julius A. Penn Jr. (19 February 1865–13 May 1934). Penn graduated from the USMA in 1886 with Pershing and was commissioned in the 13th Infantry and stationed at Fort Stanton, New Mexico, with Pershing. He served with the 2d Infantry at Fort Omaha, Nebraska (1893–1896), and Fort Keogh, Montana (1896–1898). In the Spanish-American War he served as captain and quartermaster, U.S. Volunteers, at Tampa, Florida (May–July 1898), when he came down with typhoid fever. After recovering, he was an instructor in tactics at the USMA (1898–1899) until he joined the 34th U.S. Volunteer Infantry as commander of its 2d battalion. His battalion arrived in Manila, Philippines, in October 1899 and was soon involved in operations against the insurrectionists on Luzon in which Penn distinguished himself. After a short period of duty in the United States, Penn headed back to the Philippines for a brief time with the 7th Infantry in 1902 and returned again in October 1903 to serve as adjutant with the 7th Infantry in Manila. He was aide-de-camp (1904–1906) and military secretary in 1906 to Major General (later Lieutenant General, April 1906) Henry C. Corbin, commander of the Philippine Division (1904–1905) in Manila and then of the Northern Division until September 1906 in Chicago. He joined the 12th Infantry in the Philippines as a battalion commander in February 1910 and remained there until June 1912, when he was assigned to the 1st Infantry. He moved to Hawaii in October 1912 as a battalion commander until December 1915. Penn then saw duty commanding the 3d Infantry at Madison Barracks, New York (January–May 1916), and on the Mexican border (May–July 1916) before organizing the 37th Infantry at Fort Sam Houston, Texas (1916–1917). He was promoted to colonel in March 1917 and brigadier general, NA, in August 1917 and placed in command of the 170th Infantry Brigade, 85th Division, at Camp Custer, Michigan (1917–1918). The 85th Division was shipped to France and joined the AEF in August. Penn was then assigned to General Headquarters, AEF, in Chaumont as chief, Personnel Bureau, and responsible for personnel matters of all officers and enlisted men in the AEF (August–October). He was also detailed as an observer with the 2d Division in the Meuse-Argonne offensive and to command the 76th Infantry Brigade, 38th Division, V Corps, in the Argonne (25 October–3 November) before returning to GHQ to 1 December. Penn was detailed to the Adjutant General's Office (1919–1922). He was commandant, Atlantic Branch, U.S. Disciplinary Barracks at Governor's Island, New York (1922–1923), before going on sick leave until he retired for disability on 5

December 1924. He was promoted to brigadier general, U.S. Army, retired list, by the Act of 21 June 1930. "Julius Augustus Penn," *Sixty-Sixth Annual Report of the Association of Graduates of the United States Military Academy at West Point, New York, June 11, 1935* (Newburgh, N.Y.: Moore Printing Company, 1935), pp. 132–37.

Kelton L. Pepper (27 October 1874–1 August 1971). Pepper served as an enlisted man in the 23d U.S. Infantry (August 1897–August 1900) and then a second tour as a private (February–April 1901). He was appointed a first lieutenant in the 26th Infantry in February 1901 and was commissioned in May, after which he transferred to the 27th Infantry. He was second lieutenant in Company C under Frank B. Hawkins during Pershing's operations against the Lake Lanao Moros in September–October 1902. He later served with the 22d Infantry (1902–1903) and then the 27th again before transferring to the 23d Infantry in March 1906. After serving with the 15th Infantry (1912–1914) he retired for disability incurred in the line of duty. He was restored to the active list in March 1915 and promoted to captain in July 1916. He was appointed major with the U.S. Guards in August 1918 and discharged in August 1919. He was promoted to major in July 1920 and retired again with the rank of lieutenant colonel in June 1921, but was again recalled to active duty from June 1921 to July 1923. Little is known of his actual assignments. TAGO, *OAR, 1916,* p. 527; TAGO, *OAR, 1920,* p. 620; TAGO, *OAR, 1931,* p. 888.

Frederick Perkins (21 August 1857–25 April 1940). Perkins graduated from the USMA in June 1883 and was commissioned in the 5th Infantry. He served on frontier duty in Montana and Texas (1883–1891). He was with the 8th Infantry in the United States and Cuba in 1898. He served at Havana, Cuba (January–July 1900), and later in Alaska (1902–1904). After commanding at posts in New York, he went to the Philippines with the 8th Infantry (1905–1906), then transferred to the 13th Infantry. He served in the Philippines until July 1907 and returned to the United States to command the 1st Battalion at Fort Leavenworth (1907–1908). He once again was sent to the Philippines in November 1908, detailed as the adjutant general, Department of Mindanao (January–December 1910). He was then adjutant general, Department of the East (1911–1912), and promoted to lieutenant colonel, 20th Infantry, in March 1912. After duty with the 20th Infantry he was sent to El Paso, Texas, on border patrol (1913–1914) and at Fort Bliss, Texas (January–August 1914). He completed the Army War College (1914–1915) and was assigned to be in charge of militia affairs at the Western Department (1915–1916). He was promoted to colonel in July 1916 and remained in charge of militia affairs at the Western Department (1916–1917). Perkins was promoted to brigadier general, NA, in August 1917 and commanded the 166th Infantry Brigade, 83d Division, at Camp Sherman, Ohio (August 1917–March 1918). He was discharged from the NA in March 1918 and appointed to head militia affairs at the Eastern Department headquarters (March 1918–February 1919). He retired on 3 May 1919 and was promoted to brigadier general, U.S. Army, retired, on 21 June 1930. "Frederick Perkins," *Seventy-Second Annual Report of the Association of Graduates of the United States Military Academy at West Point, New York, June 10, 1941,* pp. 136–38; TAGO, *OAR, 1931,* p. 889; "Frederick Perkins," in Davis, *Generals in Khaki,* pp. 296–97.

Francis Warren Pershing (24 June 1909–1 June 1980). Francis Warren Pershing was the only Pershing child to survive the fire at the Presidio of San Francisco on 27 August 1915. After this tragedy, Warren spent much of his time with his grandfather, Senator Francis E. Warren, due to his father's assignments, especially in France. He graduated from Yale University in 1931 and went into business as a stock broker and financier on Wall Street. He started his own firm, Pershing and Company, in 1934, and remained chairman until his death. He served in World War II, primarily on General George C. Marshall's staff in Washington, and rose to the rank of colonel. After the war he returned to his Wall Street pursuits as head of his firm. He had two sons, John Warren Pershing III (21 January 1941–23 June 1999) and Richard Warren Pershing (25 October 1942–17 February 1968). Richard Warren was killed in action in Vietnam on 17 February 1968 while serving as a second lieutenant in the 502d Infantry, 101st Airborne Division. John Warren served on active duty and then in the U.S. Army Reserve until his death. "John Warren Pershing III, Colonel, United States Army," Arlington National Cemetery, http://www.arlingtoncemetery .net/jwpershing.htm; "Richard Warren Pershing," Arlington National Cemetery, http://www.arlingtoncemetery.net/richardw.htm; "Francis Warren Pershing," *Who Was Who,* vol. 7, *1977-1981,* p. 450.

Helen Frances "Frankie" Warren Pershing (16 August 1880–27 August 1915). The daughter of Senator Francis E. Warren (R-Wyoming), she was a graduate of Wellesley College (1903). She died along with her three daughters—Helen Elizabeth (b. 8 September 1906), Anne Orr (b. 25 March 1908), and Mary Margaret (b. 19 May 1912)—in a fire at the Pershing residence at the Presidio of San Francisco on the night of 26–27 August 1915. Only the Pershings' son, Francis Warren Pershing (24 June 1909-1 June 1980), survived. Vandiver, *Black Jack,* vol. 1, passim.

Ward B. Pershing (29 March 1874–28 August 1909). Pershing's brother, Ward, grew up in Missouri, Nebraska, and Illinois, and graduated from the University of Chicago in 1898. He was an enlisted member of the Illinois National Guard and was commissioned a second lieutenant in the 6th Artillery on 9 July 1898. He transferred to the 4th Cavalry in April 1899 and served with his Troop C as part of Lawton's division in northern Luzon and saw considerable combat action before he became seriously ill and was hospitalized in October–November 1899. He then participated in Brigadier General Schwan's Southern Luzon Expedition (January–February 1900) before going on extended sick leave in the United States (April–October). His sickness was apparently related to serving in the tropical climate of Luzon, but he later also came down with tuberculosis. He was promoted to first lieutenant in February 1901 and rejoined the 4th Cavalry at the Presidio of San Francisco. He completed the Infantry and Cavalry School at Fort Leavenworth (September 1902–July 1903). He was promoted to captain with the 10th Cavalry at Fort Robinson, Nebraska, on 6 March 1905 but was retired for disability incurred in the line of duty on 1 June 1907. He moved to Denver and spent much of 1907–1909 in a tuberculosis sanitarium. He died on 28 August 1909 in Denver. TAGO, *OAR, 1909,* p. 422; TAGO, *OAR, 1910,* p. 578; "New Blood in the Army," *New York Times,* 20 June 1898; Vandiver, *Black Jack,* vol. 1, pp. 6, 156, 242, 324, 388, 395; "Military Record of 1st Lieutenant Ward B. Pershing, Fourth U.S. Cavalry," 2 September 1909, LC/Pershing Papers, Box 159, Pershing, Ward B.

James S. Pettit (4 August 1856–4 September 1906). Pettit graduated from the USMA in June 1878 and was commissioned in the 1st Infantry. After frontier duty in the Dakotas and Texas (1878–1880) he was assigned to the USMA as an instructor (1880–1883) and then returned to the 1st Infantry in Arizona, New Mexico, and California (1883–1888). A tour as an assistant professor at the USMA followed (1888–1892), after which he was professor of military science and tactics at Yale University (1892–1896). Pettit then returned to regimental duty in California until the Spanish-American War, when he was appointed colonel, 4th U.S. Volunteer Infantry (May 1898–June 1899), and saw duty in Cuba (October 1898–June 1899). On 5 July 1899, he was made colonel, 31st U.S. Volunteer Infantry, which he then trained and took to the Philippines in November. Sent to Mindanao, Pettit commanded his regiment as well as the Department of Mindanao and Jolo (February–April 1900; July 1900–May 1901). He remained in Mindanao but reverted in his permanent rank of major in June 1901 when the 31st Regiment returned to the United States. He then commanded the department's 2d and 3d districts and was active in operations against the Moros in the field in 1902. He also held various staff positions, including duty as inspector general, 7th Separate Brigade (1901–1902). He returned to the United States in November 1902 and was assigned to the Inspector General's Office in Washington (January–June 1903) and then the Adjutant General's Office (1903–1905). He was military secretary (adjutant general), Southwestern Division (January–June 1904). While serving four years in the Philippines, Pettit had developed serious health problems that were diagnosed as fatal and was assigned to the District of Columbia Militia from 22 September 1905 until his death on 4 September 1906. "James Sumner Pettit," *Thirty-Ninth Annual Reunion of the Association of Graduates of the United States Military Academy at West Point, New York, June 12, 1908*, pp. 47–61.

Edward H. Plummer (24 September 1855–11 February 1927). Plummer graduated from the USMA in June 1877 and was commissioned in the 10th Infantry. He served in Texas (1877–1879) and then in Michigan (1879–1884) before moving to assignments in New Mexico (1884–1894). When the war with Spain began, Plummer was at Fort Sill, Oklahoma, with the 10th Infantry. He moved with the 10th Infantry to Tampa, Florida, and was appointed as quartermaster for his brigade (May–July) and then for V Army Corps (July–August). He was aide-de-camp to Major General Shafter in Cuba, New York City, and then San Francisco (August 1898–July 1899). He organized and commanded the 35th U.S. Volunteer Infantry Regiment and then the 39th Volunteers before taking the 35th to the Philippines, where it was assigned to Lawton's 1st Division, then operating in northern Luzon. Appointed colonel of volunteers in December 1899, Plummer commanded his regiment through March 1901, when it returned to the United States. He remained in San Francisco to serve as Shafter's aide again (May–June 1901). After several other assignments, he returned to Mindanao in the Philippines (1909–1910). He was promoted to colonel of the 28th Infantry in March 1911, serving with it at Fort Snelling, Minnesota, and then on the Mexican border and at Vera Cruz, Mexico (1911–1914). He was promoted to brigadier general on 1 July 1916 and commanded forces along the Mexican border (June 1916–April 1917). He was commanding general of the Panama Canal Department (April–August 1917) and then promoted to major general, NA, and commander of the 88th Division. He was assigned to duty with the AEF in France, surveying conditions at the front (November 1917–February 1918). Plummer was promoted to brigadier general in March 1918 and assigned to command Fort Sill, Oklahoma, the Artillery School, and all associated training. He then commanded Camp Grant, Illinois, until he retired in November 1918. Plummer was promoted to major general, U.S. Army, upon his death in 1927. "Edward Hinckley Plummer," *Fifty-Ninth Annual Report of the Association of Graduates of the United States Military Academy at West Point, New York, June 8, 1928*, pp. 131–33.

Samuel T. Polk (1883?–21 June 1943). Polk was born in England about 1883 and was appointed a third lieutenant in the Constabulary in 1902, a second lieutenant in 1903, first lieutenant in 1904, and captain in 1905. He served on Leyte in 1902–1903 and 1905 and Cebu in 1903–1904. He was awarded the Constabulary's Distinguished Service Star (DSS) for his participation in the fight against the outlaw Tabaal in 1903. He resigned in 1917, but rejoined the Constabulary as a third lieutenant in 1932 and served at Zamboanga in 1932 and Davao, Mindanao, in 1932–1933. He resigned again in 1933. He was killed by the Japanese at Borongan, Samar, on 21 June 1943 while trying to evade capture. No other information has been located on this officer of the Philippine Constabulary or his time out of service. See "Samuel T. Polk," in U.S. Army Forces, American Historical Collection, Ateneo de Manila University, http://rizal.lib.admu.edu.ph/ahc/guides/US_Army_Forces.pdf; "Captain Samuel Polk," in email, Waldette M. Cueto, Curator, American Historical Collection, Rizal Library, Ateneo de Manila University, Quezon City, to Dr. John T. Greenwood, 13 June 2011.

Ernest M. Pollard (15 April 1869–24 September 1939). Born and raised in Nebraska, Pollard attended the University of Nebraska, graduating with his B.A. in 1893. During his senior year he was cadet captain of Pershing's cadet battalion. He managed the Pollard Fruit Farm in Cass County (1894–1927). Pollard was elected to the state house of representatives in 1896 and served until 1899. Active in Republican Party circles, he was elected to fill the unexpired term of Elmer J. Burkett, who resigned in March 1905 to accept the post of U.S. Senator. He served until March 1909, not winning reelection in November 1908. Pollard remained active in state politics, later serving as secretary of the Nebraska Department of Welfare and Labor (January 1929–January 1931). "Ernest Mark Pollard (1869–1939)," Biographical Directory of the United States Congress, http://bioguide.congress.gov/scripts/biodisplay.pl?index=P000413.

Oscar Preuss. Preuss was one of a number of legendary foreigners and soldiers of fortune who served as officers and leaders in the Philippine Constabulary during its early years. A German who had served in the German Army Hussars and later commanded a company of African Askaris in the German African colonies, Preuss was basically a soldier of fortune. He participated in the German expeditionary force during the Boxer Rebellion in China (1900) and fought with the Boers against the British in South Africa. He enlisted in the U.S. Army in 1903 and his regiment was sent to the Philippines for duty. When discharged in 1906, he applied for a commission in the Philippine Constabulary and was commissioned a third lieutenant. Preuss was as fearless as he was ruthless, and soon had a well-deserved reputation as a "bullet eater" for his utter disregard for his own safety. His exploits soon made him a legend in the Constabulary. He was known for his relentless tenacity in tracking down and eliminating outlaws and bandits, especially on Mindanao, where he was district chief at Cotabato. He received the Constabulary's highest award for heroism, the Medal of Valor, for tracking down and killing the outlaw Mamintung at Mailag on Lake Lanao early in 1911. He was wounded in action in 1909 and 1911. He was promoted to second lieutenant in 1907, first lieutenant in 1909, and captain in 1913. With the outbreak of the war in Europe, he apparently returned to Germany and was reported as killed in action on the Galician front in July 1915. However, later reports by the AEF's G-2 in France listed him as an agent in Spain in 1917–1918. He was also reported to be in the United States in the 1920s. Fulton, *Moroland*, pp. 407–9, 432, 434, 477; "Oscar Preuss," U.S. Army Forces in the Philippines, American Historical Collection, Ateneo de Manila University, http://rizal.lib.admu.edu.ph/ahc/guides/US_Army_Forces.pdf; "Oscar Preuss," in email, Waldette M. Cueto, Curator, American Historical Collection, Rizal Library, Ateneo de Manila University, Quezon City, to Dr. John T. Greenwood, 13 June 2011.

Cecelia "Celia" Sherman Miles Reber (12 September 1869–10 September 1952). Cecelia "Celia" Miles was the daughter of Nelson A. Miles and his wife, Mary Hoyt Sherman (1842–1904), the niece of Senator John Sherman (R-Ohio) and his brother, General William T. Sherman. On 10 January 1900, she married Captain Samuel Reber (16 October 1864–16 April 1933), a classmate of Pershing's from the USMA class of 1886 and her second cousin, and had two sons with him—Miles Reber (27 March 1902–24 November 1976), who graduated from the USMA in 1923 and retired as a major general in the U.S. Army on 31 December 1955, and Samuel Reber III, who graduated from Havard and spent a career in the U.S. Foreign Service. "Miles Reber," *Sixty-Fifth Annual Report of the Association of Graduates of the United States Military Academy at West Point, New York, June 11, 1934,* pp. 150–52; "Cecilia Miles Reber, Military Daughter & Spouse," Arlington National Cemetery, http://www.arlingtoncemetery.net/cmreber.htm; "Samuel Reber, Colonel, United States Army," Arlington National Cemetery, http://www.arlingtoncemetery.net/sreber.htm; "Miles Reber, Major General, United States Army," Arlington National Cemetery, http://www.arlingtoncemetery.net/mreber.htm; Wooster, *Nelson A. Miles and the Twilight of the Frontier Army,* pp. 237–65.

William O. Reed (23 January 1870–14 October 1922). Reed served as a second lieutenant in the 1st Kentucky Volunteer Infantry during the Spanish-America War and was mustered out in February 1899. In July 1899 he was appointed a second lieutenant in the 31st U.S. Volunteer Infantry (July 1899–June 1901) under Colonel James S. Pettit and served on the island of Mindanao in the southern Philippines. He was appointed a second lieutenant in the 6th Cavalry in February 1901 and was commissioned in February 1902. He was secretary of the Sulu District (December 1909–May 1910) and was twice the Sulu District governor (May 1910–February 1911; March–November 1912). He served as provincial secretary of the Moro Province under Pershing (March 1911–November 1912) while also serving as Sulu governor (March–November 1912). He was promoted to captain in June 1911 and later served again as Pershing's aide before returning to the United States and duty with the 6th Cavalry on the Mexican border and in the Mexican Expedition. In World War I, Pershing took Reed to France with him as a member of his staff on board the SS *Baltic*. He was promoted to temporary lieutenant colonel (November 1917–June 1920). Nothing more is known about his wartime service or assignments. He was promoted to lieutenant colonel in July 1920. TAGO, *OAR, 1916*, p. 160; TAGO, *OAR 1922*, p. 407; TAGO, *OAR, 1923*, p. 1288; Pershing, *AR, Moro Province, 1913*, pp. 81, 83; James G. Harbord, *The American Army in France, 1917-1919* (Boston: Little, Brown, 1936), p. 579.

George D. Rice (23 February 1861–21 December 1936). A Unitarian minister, Rice was appointed chaplain for the 6th Massachusetts Volunteer Infantry in May 1898 and was mustered out in January 1899 after serving in the Puerto Rican Campaign (July–October 1898). He served as chaplain and first lieutenant in the 26th U.S. Volunteer Infantry in the Philippines. He was appointed chaplain in the Regular Army in February 1901 and was commissioned captain (chaplain) in May. He was chaplain with the 27th U.S. Infantry and was actively involved in Baldwin's campaigns against the Moros in 1902. At Fort Pandapatan on 2 May 1902 he was on the battlefield aiding the wounded under heavy fire. In 1925, the War Department awarded him a Distinguished Service Cross for his actions that day. He also participated in Pershing's expedition against Bacolod in early April 1903, assisting the surgeons in caring for the wounded. He later served in the Army of Cuban Pacification. He was promoted to major in May 1911. During World War I, he served as division chaplain with the 8th Division in the United States, but the 8th was never shipped to France. He was promoted to lieutenant colonel upon retirement on 4 June 1920 but was recalled to active duty the next day, serving until April 1921. TAGO, *OAR, 1920*, p. 157; TAGO, *OAR, 1931*, p. 896; TAGO, *OAR, 1937*, p. 1056; TAGO, *American Decorations, 1862-1926*, p. 521; U.S. Army Center of Military History, *Correspondence Relating to the War with Spain, Including the Insurrection in the Philippine Islands and the China Relief Expedition April 15, 1898 to July 30, 1902*, vol. 1 (Washington, D.C.: GPO, 1993) (hereafter cited as *Correspondence Relating to the War with Spain*), p. 597.

Charles Richard (10 November 1854–19 April 1940). Richard graduated from the College of the City of New York (CCNY) in 1874 and received his medical degree from New York University in 1876. He was appointed assistant surgeon (first lieutenant) in July 1879. He was promoted to captain in June 1888, major in November 1896, lieutenant colonel in July 1905, and colonel in February 1909. After his assignment in the Philippines he was commandant and professor of military surgery at the Army Medical School (1913-1915). During World War I he served as chief surgeon, Eastern Department, and as an assistant to the army surgeon general. He was appointed brigadier general, Medical Corps, NA (August–November 1918), and retired on 10 November 1918. He was promoted to brigadier general, U.S. Army, retired, by the Act of 21 June 1930. TAGO, *OAR, 1938*, p. 1039; "Charles Richard," *Who Was Who–The Military*, p. 473; "Charles Richard, M.D.," in Davis, *Generals in Khaki*, p. 309.

William C. Rivers (11 January 1866–10 July 1943). Rivers graduated from the USMA in June 1887 and was commissioned in the 1st Cavalry. Assigned to frontier duty, he served in Wyoming (1887–1889) and Montana, during which time he saw field service in the Pine Ridge expedition against the Sioux in 1890–1891. After serving at the Military Academy (1891–1893), he was with the 3d Cavalry in Arizona until he transferred back to the 1st Cavalry in November 1895. In Cuba he served with the 1st Cavalry in the dismounted Cavalry Division, V Army Corps, until 30 June 1898, when he was evacuated due to sickness. He was later sent to the Philippines with duty at the Military Information (Intelligence) Division in Manila (1903–1904). He then served with the Philippine Constabulary as adjutant general at Manila and Lucena in 1904 and inspector general (1904–1906). He was assistant chief, Philippine Constabulary, at Manila and Iloilo (1906–1912) with the temporary rank of colonel. He commanded the Philippine Constabulary, District of North Luzon (1912–1913), then replaced James G. Harbord as acting chief, Philippine Constabulary, in Manila in December 1913 before being promoted to temporary brigadier general and chief, Philippine Constabulary (January–March 1914). Reverting to his permanent rank of major, Rivers returned to the United States in April 1914 and served with the 1st Cavalry at the Presidio of San Francisco and the 2d Cavalry at Fort Ethan Allen, Vermont (1915–1917). During the World War he oversaw the conversion of the 18th Cavalry into the 76th Field Artillery Regiment at Camp Merritt, New Jersey (March–April 1918), and took the regiment to France as part of the 3d Artillery Brigade, 3d Division. Rivers commanded the 76th Field Artillery in France (May–September 1918) during the difficult battles on the Marne River at Chateau-Thierry and the Ourcq River that helped to stem the German offensives that summer. He commanded the 76th in the St. Mihiel and Meuse-Argonne offensives until he was promoted to brigadier general, NA, on 1 October 1918. He then assumed command of the 5th Artillery Brigade, 5th Division (October 1918–March 1919). In August 1919 he was assigned to command the 12th Cavalry and subdistrict of New Mexico (1919–1920). He then commanded the 3d Cavalry at Fort Myer, Virginia (1920–1923), and was detailed to the Inspector General's Department at Governor's Island, New York (1923–1927). Rivers served as inspector general, U.S. Army, with promotion to major general (September 1927–January 1930). *ARWD, 1915*, vol. 4, *Report of the Philippine Commission*, 1 July 1913 to 31 December 1914, pp. 20, 121, 123; "William Cannon Rivers," in Davis, *Generals in Khaki*, pp. 312–13.

Charles B. Robbins (6 November 1877–5 July 1943). Robbins was born and raised in Iowa but attended the University of Nebraska, from which he graduated with a bachelor's degree in 1898. While a student, he was a member of the cadet battalion. At the outbreak of the Spanish-American War he enlisted as a private in Company B, 1st Nebraska Infantry, and was soon promoted to sergeant. He served with the 1st Nebraska in the Philippines from July 1898 to June 1899 and was severely wounded on 27 March 1899 at Marilao. He was commissioned a second lieutenant in Company I in April 1899. For his service in the Philippines he was subsequently awarded a Silver Star and Purple Heart. Upon returning to Nebraska, he completed postgraduate work at the University of Nebraska and then moved to New York City, where he studied law at Columbia University's College of Law, receiving his degree in 1903. He returned to Iowa in 1903, joined a law practice in Cedar Rapids, and was admitted to the Iowa bar in October 1904. In July 1909 he was appointed a judge in the Superior Court and remained in this post until 1919. He joined the Iowa National Guard's Company D, 1st Infantry, in 1914. In 1916 Robbins was commissioned a major in the Adjutant General's Department of the Iowa

National Guard and served on the Mexican Border. During World War I, he was a major and adjutant in the 67th Infantry Brigade, 34th Division, and later the 69th Brigade, 35th Division, and saw extensive service in France with the AEF. After the war he remained in the Organized Reserves, rising from major in 1921 to colonel in 1926. In 1928 he was appointed Assistant Secretary of War and held that post until March 1929. During this time he promoted the procurement of tanks and trucks based on his own military experience. "Charles Burton Robbins," *Who Was Who–The Military*, p. 478; "Charles Burton Robbins," Iowa in the Great War, http://iagenweb .org/greatwar/histo/Robbins_CharlesBurton.htm.

Samuel D. Rockenbach (27 January 1869–16 May 1952). Rockenbach attended the Virginia Military Institute, graduating in 1889 with a degree in civil engineering. He was accepted for a commission as a second lieutenant in the 10th Cavalry in August 1891 and served at Fort Leavenworth and in Arizona, North Dakota, and Montana. In the Spanish-American War he served with the 10th Cavalry during the Santiago Campaign in Cuba as aide-de-camp to Brigadier General Guy V. Henry, commander of 1st Division, V Corps, and during the Puerto Rico Expedition (1898) before returning to the United States. During this time he served under Colonel Samuel Whitside with Lieutenants John J. Pershing, James G. Harbord, and Letcher Hardeman. He went to the Philippines with his regiment in August 1903 and was then detailed as a major in the Philippine Scouts in February 1905. He commanded various battalions of Philippine Scouts (February 1905–1911) as well as served as chief, Philippine Scouts, at headquarters, Philippines Division (1908–1909). While commanding his battalion of Scouts on Mindanao he also served as governor in the civil government in Cotabato District. He attended the Army War College (1911–1912) and then transferred to the 11th Cavalry in August 1912. With the outbreak of the war in Europe, he served as a military observer with the Imperial German Army until June 1915. He was detailed to the Quartermaster Corps in December 1915 and sent to Laredo, Texas, to take charge of the advance base for Pershing's Mexican Expedition. In March 1917 he was ordered to El Paso, Texas, as a quartermaster officer of the Cavalry Division until May 1917. With the American entry into World War I, Pershing was selected to command American forces in France and he chose then Major (later Major General) James G. Harbord as his chief of staff for the AEF. Harbord remembered Rockenbach from their service together in the 10th Cavalry. He and Pershing, who had also served with Rockenbach in the 10th, positively evaluated Rockenbach's current service as a quartermaster officer and selected him to accompany the new headquarters as a quartermaster officer when it sailed for England aboard the SS *Baltic* on 28 May 1917. When Rockenbach arrived in France, he was given command of Base Section No. 1 at St. Nazaire, the initial entry point for the AEF. In December 1917 Pershing appointed him commander of the AEF's Tank Service (Tanks Corps as of January 1918). He was responsible for building this tank corps from scratch, selecting and training its personnel, and developing its doctrine and equipment. In July 1918 he was made brigadier general, NA, and commanded the Tank Corps during offensive operations at St. Mihiel and Meuse-Argonne. One of his key subordinates was Lieutenant Colonel George S. Patton Jr. of World War II fame. Upon his return to the United States, Rockenbach commanded the Tank School at Camp Meade, Maryland, and it was here that Major Dwight D. Eisenhower worked under Rockenbach's direction. Rockenbach was chief of the Tank Corps from December 1917 to June 1920, when the Tank Corps was abolished and the Tank School was assigned to the chief of infantry. Rockenbach transferred to the infantry in October 1920 and was promoted to colonel, U.S. Army. He commanded the Tank School until January 1924, when he was promoted to brigadier general, U.S. Army, and commanded the U.S. Army's Military District of Washington until July 1927. He then commanded the 2d Cavalry Brigade at Fort Bliss, Texas (1927–1928), the 2d Field Artillery Brigade (1928–1929), and ended his career as commander of the 2d Division and Fort Sam Houston, Texas. He retired on 31 January 1933. Jeffrey A. Gunsburg, "Samuel Dickerson Rockenbach: Father of the Tank Corps," *Virginia Cavalcade* 26, no. 1 (summer 1976), pp. 38–47; "Samuel Dickerson Rockenbach," *Who Was Who—The Military*, p. 485; TAGO, *OAR, 1920*, p. 176; TAGO, *OAR, 1941*, p. 1186; TAGO, *OAR*, vol. 1, *United States Army, Active and Retired Lists, 1953*, p. 947; "Brigadier General Samuel D. Rockenbach of Virginia" and "Memorandum of the Service of Brigadier General S. D. Rockenbach," Virginia Military Institute Archives, Preston Library, Lexington, Virginia, http://www.vmi.edu/archives; Harbord, *The American Army in France*, pp. 60–62, 68–70,122–23, 579; "Samuel Dickerson Rockenbach," in Davis, *Generals in Khaki*, pp. 313–14.

Alexander Rodgers (23 September 1852–11 December 1938). The son of Rear Admiral C. R. P. Rodgers, he graduated from the USMA in June 1875 and was commissioned in the 4th Cavalry. He served on frontier duty in the Southwest (1875–1879) and later in Colorado and New Mexico (1880–1882), and then as aide-de-camp to Brigadier General Ranald Mackenzie (1882–1884). After a tour at the USMA (1884–1887), he once again was assigned to frontier duty in Arizona (1887–1890). Rodgers was on duty at the Presidio of San Francisco and also served at Yosemite National Park (1895–1898). He was military attaché at Paris (April–May 1898) and returned to the United States in May to accept appointment as major and inspector general, USV. He was inspector general, 1st Division, III Army Corps (May–June 1898), then discharged and appointed lieutenant colonel, 3d Connecticut Volunteer Infantry, on 3 July 1898. In September 1899 he was sent to the Philippines, where he served with the 6th Cavalry until transferring to the 4th Cavalry in January 1900. He was on Henry Lawton's staff and was with him when he was killed in action on 19 December 1899. He commanded the 1st Squadron, 4th Cavalry, and the Cavalry School at Fort Riley (1901–1902), after which he was promoted to lieutenant colonel, 15th Cavalry, and assigned to the Philippines at Camp Vicars, Mindanao (June–September 1903). He returned to the United States in November 1903 and commanded the 15th Cavalry at Fort Ethan Allen, Vermont (1903–1906). He was promoted to colonel and commander, 6th Cavalry, in March 1906, and then took the regiment to Mindanao, where he commanded the regiment and post of Jolo and was governor of the District of Jolo (1907–1909) and in the field against the Moros (February–June 1909). After returning to the United States in January 1910, he commanded the 6th Cavalry at Fort Des Moines, Iowa, and retired in January 1911. "Alexander Rodgers," *Seventieth Annual Report of the Association of Graduates of the United States Military Academy at West Point, New York, June 10, 1939*, pp. 106–10.

Walter H. Rodney (6 February 1879–16 April 1911). Rodney, the son of recently retired Brigadier General George H. Rodney, was commissioned in the 1st Cavalry in February 1901. He was just assigned to the post at Jolo, Jolo Island, as the machine-gun platoon leader, when a local killed him. Colonel Frank West, the regimental commander, who witnessed the attack, identified the assailant, who was then cornered and killed by soldiers of the guard when he attacked them. The recriminations for this act of *juramentado* were swift in coming from General Rodney as well as others, who blamed Pershing for being too soft on the Moros and not completely disarming them. Pershing then implemented his new disarmament campaign. TAGO, *OAR, 1911,* p. 125; TAGO, *OAR, 1912,* p. 596; Fulton, *Moroland,* pp. 413–29.

Elihu Root (15 February 1845–7 February 1937). Root received his bachelor's and master's degrees from Hamilton College (1864, 1867) and his law degree from New York University (1867). Admitted to the bar in New York City, he soon established his own law firm and became one of the major corporate lawyers in the country and was active in Republican politics. He served as U.S. district attorney, Southern District of New York (1883–1885). On 1 August 1899, McKinley appointed Root as Secretary of War replacing Russell Alger. As Secretary of War, Root oversaw the successful ending of the Philippine Insurrection (1899–1902), the reorganization of the War Department and U.S. Army based on the lessons of the Spanish-American War in 1901, the transition from military to civil government in Puerto Rico and the Philippines, the complete revision of the militia system and establishment of the National Guard in the Militia (Dick) Act (1903), and the creation of the War Department General Staff and the position of War Department chief of staff, the General Staff Corps, and Army War College (1903). Perhaps more than any one man, Root laid the foundations for a new U.S. Army that would fight in World War I. In July 1905, he was appointed Secretary of State by President Roosevelt and held that post until January 1909. He served as U.S. senator from New York (March 1909–March 1915). Root was president of the Carnegie Foundation for International Peace (1910–1925) and a member of numerous international commissions and courts. He was awarded the Nobel Peace Prize for 1912 for his work on the Hague Tribunal of Arbitration, the Root-Takahara Open Door Agreement (1908), and his role in resolving other international disputes. Among his publications was *Military and Colonial Policy of the United States* (1917). "Elihu Root," Encyclopaedia Britannica Online, http://www.britannica .com/EBchecked/topic/509465/Elihu-Root; "Elihu Root (1845–1937), Biographical Directory of the United States Congress, http://bioguide.congress.gov/scripts/ biodisplay.pl?index=R000430; "The Nobel Prize in Peace 1912: Elihu Root," Official Site of the Nobel Prize, http://nobelprize.org/nobel_prizes/peace/laureates/1912/ root-bio.html; "Elihu Root," *Webster's American Military Biographies,* pp. 360–61; Weigley, *History of the United States Army,* pp. 314–22; Morris, *Encyclopedia of American History,* 711; "Elihu Root," *Who Was Who–The Military,* pp. 490–91.

Francis A. Ruggles (1 March 1880–9 February 1955). Ruggles was the son of Brigadier General George D. Ruggles (11 September 1833–19 October 1904) (USMA, 1855), a career U.S. Army officer (adjutant general of the army, 1893–1897). Ruggles attended Yale University, graduating in 1900. He was commissioned in the 4th Cavalry in 1901 and transferred to the 9th Cavalry in June 1902. He served in the Philippines and on Mindanao during the Moro expeditions as second in command, Troop G, 15th Cavalry, under Charles McCullough. In World War I, he was promoted to colonel, NA (1918–1920). He commanded a battalion in the 7th Field Artillery Regiment, 1st Division, in France during the Aisne-Marne offensive (18–25 July 1918) and later commanded the regiment during the St. Mihiel and Meuse-Argonne offensives (September–November 1918) and until January 1920. He graduated from the Field Artillery School's Battery Commander's Course in 1920, the Army School of the Line in 1922, the General Staff School in 1923, and the Army War College in 1924. He was twice assigned to the General Staff Corps (1924–1928; 1931–1934). He briefly commanded the 15th Field Artillery Regiment, 2d Division, in 1928–1929. He was promoted to colonel in August 1933. Following his second General Staff assignment, he commanded the 24th Field Artillery (Philippine Scouts), Philippine Division, at Fort Stotsenburg, Luzon (1934–1937). He retired from active duty on 30 June 1942 and was then recalled to active service until 31 January 1944. TAGO, *OAR, 1916,* p. 177; TAGO, *OAR, 1938,* p. 639; TAGO, *OAR,* vol. 1, *United States Army Active and Retired Lists, 1950,* p. 826; TAGO, *OAR,* vol. 1, *United States Army Active and Retired Lists, 1956,* p. 1074; Clay, *U.S. Army Order of Battle,* vol. 2, pp. 762, 768, 774; "George David Ruggles, Brigadier General, United States Army," Arlington National Cemetery, http://www.arlingtoncemetery.net/gruggles.htm.

James A. Ryan (22 October 1867–14 January 1956). Ryan graduated from the USMA in June 1890 and was commissioned in the 10th Cavalry. He served in Arizona and Kansas before moving to Fort Assinniboine, Montana (1895–1897). He transferred to the 9th Cavalry in February 1897 and participated in the round-up of the Cree Indians and their return to Canada. He commanded Troop A, 9th Cavalry, during the Santiago Campaign (June–August 1898). He was assigned to the Philippines from August 1900 to November 1903, serving with the 9th Cavalry and then the 15th Cavalry. He served with Pershing at Lake Lanao in 1902–1903. He returned to the United States and served at Fort Myer and Fort Ethan Allen (1903–1905) before attending the Infantry and Cavalry School and Staff College (1905–1906). Duty with the Army of Cuban Pacification followed to February 1909, during which he was aide-de-camp to the provisional governor. He was then at Fort Sheridan, Illinois, commanding a troop (1909–1911). He was an associate professor of modern languages at USMA (1911–1914). Reassigned to the 13th Cavalry in September 1914, he was sent to duty on the Mexican border until March 1916 and then served as intelligence officer for Pershing's Mexican Expedition (March–May 1916). Promoted to lieutenant colonel with the 1st Cavalry in July 1916, he was inspector of cavalry, Department of the Lakes, Chicago, and then returned to regimental duty on the Mexican border (October 1916–January 1917). He was promoted to colonel in July 1917 and brigadier general, NA, in December 1917. He commanded the 1st Brigade, 15th Cavalry Division, at Fort Sam Houston, Texas (February–September 1918) and then the 17th Infantry Brigade, 9th Division, and Camp Sheridan, Alabama (September 1918–April 1919). He retired as a colonel on 1 April 1919 and joined Merrill, Lynch and Company in Chicago as a stockbroker in May. Thereafter he held a number of corporate positions, including general manager of Utilities Securities Corporation (1924–1932), president of the Public Health Institute (1920–1926), and president of Ryber, Inc. (1940–1941). "James Augustine Ryan," *Assembly* 15, no. 2 (July 1956), p. 77.

John T. Sayles (19 March 1877–15 March 1967). Sayles enlisted as a private in Company L, 3d New York Infantry, and private first class in the Signal Corps (May–November 1898). He later served as a private first class in the Signal Corps (1898–1899) and was on active duty as a private first class, sergeant, and sergeant first class (1899–1900). He was appointed a second lieutenant in the Signal Corps, New York National Guard (1900–1901), and commissioned in the 2d Cavalry in September 1901. He was promoted to first lieutenant in the 8th Cavalry in September 1904 and captain in June 1916. During the World War, he served in the National Army as a major (1917–1918) and lieutenant colonel (1918–1920). He was the ordnance officer in the 34th Division (National Guard). In July 1920 he was promoted to lieutenant colonel. He was detailed to the Texas National Guard as an instructor (1920–1922) and completed the Cavalry School Field Officers' Course in 1922. He commanded the 5th Cavalry Regiment, 1st Cavalry Division, at Fort Clark, Texas (1923–1924). Sayles retired in July 1929. TAGO, *OAR, 1931*, p. 903; "John T. Sayles," Department of Veterans' Affairs, Nationwide Gravesite Locator, http://gravelocator.cem.va.gov/j2ee/servlet/NGL_v1; Clay, *U.S. Army Order of Battle*, vol. 1, pp. 619; U.S. War Department, Militia Bureau, *Official National Guard Register for 1922* (Washington, D.C.: GPO, 1922), p. 6.

Theodore Schwan (9 July 1841–27 May 1926). Born in Germany, Schwan came to the United States in 1857. He joined Company K, 10th U.S. Infantry, in June 1857 and rose through the enlisted ranks to regimental quartermaster sergeant until November 1863, when he was appointed an officer. He served with the 10th Infantry throughout the war and saw action at Chancellorsville, Gettysburg, the Wilderness, Spotsylvania Court House, North Anna, Cold Harbor, and Petersburg. Schwan was awarded a Medal of Honor on 12 December 1898 for his heroism at Peeble's Farm, Virginia, on 1 October 1864. He transferred to the 11th Infantry in December 1869 and served on the frontier in Texas (1870–1873, 1874–1876) and then in the Dakotas at the end of the Sioux campaign and in Montana (1876–1880). During his time in Montana he was detailed as acting Indian agent for the Sioux at the Cheyenne River Indian Agency (1878–1880). Schwan was then an instructor in infantry tactics and other subjects at the Infantry and Cavalry School at Fort Leavenworth (1882–1886). He transferred to the Adjutant General's Department in July 1886 as a major with duty at the War Department until 1892. He was attached to the U.S. embassy in Berlin (1892–1893) on a special mission. Upon his return, he wrote a major study of the German Army and General Staff that was published as *Report on the Organization of the German Army* (1894). He was promoted in May 1898 to colonel as well as to brigadier general, USV. He commanded the 1st Division, VII Army Corps, and then the 1st Brigade, 2d Division, IV Army Corps (May–July 1898) before he commanded the Independent Regular Brigade in Nelson Miles's campaign in Puerto Rico (25 July–13 August 1898). After Puerto Rico, he returned to the War Department. He was reappointed in his volunteer rank and in June 1899 was ordered to the Philippines as chief of staff to Otis, arriving in early August 1899. He also commanded several brigades in the field, including a provisional brigade against Cavite in October) and Schwan's Expeditionary Brigade during its operations to clear the area of Cavite, Batangas, Laguna, and Tayabas in January–February 1900. He returned to the United States in April 1900. He was promoted to brigadier general, U.S. Army, on 2 February 1901 and retired on the 21st. Schwan was promoted to major general, retired, by the Act of 26 August 1916. TAGO, *OAR, 1901,* pp. 7, 348, 386; TAGO, *OAR, 1920,* p. 906; "Theodore Schwan," *Powell's Records,* pp. 531–32; "Theodore Schwan," in Gates, *Men of Mark,* vol. 2, pp. 286–88; "Puerto Rican Campaign" and "Theodore Schwan," in Berner, ed., *The Spanish-American War,* pp. 302, 342; "Theodore Schwan," *Who Was Who—The Military,* p. 513; "Theodore Schwan," in Rossiter Johnson, ed., *The Biographical Dictionary of America,* vol. 9, *Qua-Stearns* (Boston: American Biographical Society, 1906), [not paginated].

Ernest D. Scott (6 September 1872–12 May 1962). Scott was born and spent his childhood years in Ontario, Canada, until his family immigrated to the United States, settling in Nebraska in 1885. He was a member of Pershing's cadet battalion while attending the University of Nebraska for several years before entering the Military Academy in June 1894. He graduated from the USMA in April 1898 and was commissioned in the 6th Artillery. That September he was sent to the Philippines in Merritt's expedition and participated in the fighting around Manila on 5 February 1899 that marked the beginning of the Philippine Insurrection. He was actively involved in combat operations under Henry Lawton throughout 1899 and was appointed a captain in the 37th U.S. Volunteer Infantry in July. He remained in the Philippines, later commanding Battery A, 6th Artillery, and returned to the artillery in February 1901 upon his discharge from the USV. He returned to the United States and held a number of coast artillery company commands before returning to the Philippines in 1907. He entered the Army School of the Line (1908–1909) and then completed the Army Staff College (1909–1910). He was an instructor in the Army Service Schools (1914–1916) and upon promotion to major was sent to the Army War College, which he completed in May 1917. He then organized and commanded the 12th Field Artillery Regiment and was promoted to temporary colonel in August before leaving for France in September 1917. Scott commanded the 6th Field Artillery Regiment, 1st Division (October 1917–February 1918), in training and at the front and then briefly the 146th Field Artillery Regiment, 66th Field Artillery Brigade, 41st Division (6 May–5 June 1918), temporarily replacing another of Pershing's boys, Leroy V. Patch. Scott assumed command of the 66th Field Artillery Brigade on 6 June and held it through early November. When the 41st Division was broken up to provide replacements for other AEF divisions that spring, the 66th Field Artillery Brigade was formed from the 146th and 148th Field Artillery Regiments and operated as a corps unit that supported the AEF in its summer battles along the Marne and Aisne Rivers and in the St. Mihiel and Meuse-Argonne offensives. In early November, Scott became the heavy artillery commander, V Corps, and then chief of operations for First Army's artillery. He commanded the 57th Field Artillery Brigade, 32d Division, in 1919 and then the 10th Field Artillery Regiment, 3d Division, and the division's 3d Artillery Brigade in the occupation of the Rhineland. After returning to the United States he was appointed assistant inspector general (1919–1920) and then inspector general, Southern Department, and later Eighth Corps Area, at Fort Sam Houston, Texas (March–November 1920). After commanding the 82d Field Artillery at Fort Bliss (1920–1921), Scott completed the Army War College (1921–1922) and the Naval War College (1922–1923). He then returned to Fort Sam Houston as inspector general, Eighth Corps Area (1923–1927), before commanding the 15th Field Artillery at Schofield Barracks, Hawaii (1927–1928), and the 11th Field Artillery (1929–

1931). He was promoted to brigadier general on 1 December 1931 and commanded the 3d Field Artillery Brigade at Fort Lewis, Washington (1931–1932), before moving on to the 1st Field Artillery Brigade at Fort Hoyle, Maryland, from September 1932 until he retired on 30 September 1936. "Ernest Darius Scott Sr., Brigadier General, United States Army," Arlington National Cemetery, http://www.arlingtoncemetery .net/edscottsr.htm; *A History of the Sixty-Sixth Field Artillery Brigade, American Expeditionary Forces,* passim.

George L. Scott (24 November 1849–5 December 1926). Scott graduated from the USMA with a commission in the 6th Cavalry in 1875. He served with the 6th on frontier duty against Apache and other Indian tribes at various posts in the Arizona Territory through June 1884, when the 6th moved to Fort Stanton, New Mexico. He commanded the Indian scouts in the field pursuing Geronimo (May–September 1886) and then was at Fort Stanton until the 6th Cavalry was moved to South Dakota in December 1890 for the campaign against the Sioux at Pine Ridge Agency. During the Spanish-American War he commanded his troop of the 6th Cavalry, which acted as the headquarters guard for Brigadier General John Brooke, the military governor, during the Puerto Rico Expedition (July–November 1898) and was then at Fort Sill, Oklahoma (1898–1900). Scott was the Indian agent at the Chippewa Indian Reservation at Leech Lake Agency, Walker, Minnesota, from December 1901 until he retired in December 1905. He was recalled to active duty and placed in charge of Apache prisoners at Fort Sill (1910–1911), then served as professor of military science and tactics at the State Agricultural College of Colorado (today Colorado State University) at Fort Collins (1911–1915). Scott was assigned to Fort McDowell, Arizona (August 1916), and remained there until he retired from active duty in April 1919. "George Lawson Scott," *Fifty-Eighth Annual Report of the Association of Graduates of the United States Military Academy at West Point, New York, June 13, 1927,* pp. 120–21.

Hugh L. Scott (22 September 1853–20 April 1934). Scott spent several years at Princeton before attending the USMA and graduating in June 1876. He was on frontier duty with the 7th Cavalry in the 1876–1877 campaign against Sitting Bull and Crazy Horse and in the 1877 Nez Percé expedition. He remained on duty with the 7th Cavalry in Dakota and Montana (1877–1886) and began his personal study of Indian spoken and sign languages. He developed a great fluency in the languages of the Native American tribes, which put him very much in demand on the frontier, where his presence frequently prevented significant hostilities. He was later assigned to Fort Sill, Indian Territory (1889–1895), where he organized Troop L, 7th Cavalry, consisting of Kiowa, Comanche, and Apache Indians. He was in charge of Geronimo's band at Fort Sill (1894–1897) and then was detailed to the Adjutant General's Office to work on the languages of the Plains Indians for the Ethnological Bureau, Smithsonian Institution, until the Spanish-American War. He was appointed major and assistant adjutant general, USV, in May 1898 and served as adjutant general, 2d Division, I Army Corps. He was then sent to Cuba, where he was successively adjutant general of the Department of Havana (1899–1900), the Division of Cuba (May–November 1900), and then Department of Cuba (1900–1902) under Leonard Wood. Scott was sent to the Philippines as governor of the Sulu Archipelago and commander of Jolo Island (September 1903–July 1906). Here he was involved in skirmishes with the Moros and wounded in both hands, losing parts of his fingers. He replaced Albert Mills as superintendent of the Military Academy (1906-1910). In March 1913 he was promoted to brigadier general and placed in command of the 2d Cavalry Brigade at El Paso, Texas, with responsibility for controlling the Mexican border from Texas to California (1913-1914). Detailed to the General Staff in April 1914, he was assigned as assistant chief of staff until November, when he was appointed chief of staff. He was promoted to major general in April 1915 and organized the U.S. Army and National Guard for duty on the Mexican border, laying the basis for the Army's World War I mobilization. Scott went to Russia as a member of the Root Mission (May–August 1917) to try to keep Russia in the war and toured battlefields and training centers in France (August–December 1917). He was retired for age on 22 September 1917 and immediately recalled to active duty. After returning from France and England in December 1917, he was given command of the 78th Division, NA, in January 1918. He also commanded Fort Dix, New Jersey, until May 1918, when he was relieved from active duty. In retirement, he was chairman of the State Highway Commission in New Jersey (1923-1933). Scott published his memoirs, *Some Memories of a Soldier,* in 1928. "Hugh Lenox Scott," *Sixty-Eighth Annual Report of the Association of Graduates of the United States Military Academy at West Point, New York, June 11, 1937,* pp. 97-102; "Hugh Lenox Scott (1852-1934)," *Webster's American Military Biographies,* pp. 370-71.

William R. Shafter (16 October 1835–12 November 1906). Shafter was commissioned in Company I, 7th Michigan Infantry, in August 1861 and so distinguished himself in action on 31 May 1862 at Fair Oaks during the Peninsula campaign that he was awarded a Medal of Honor. In September he was appointed major, 19th Michigan Infantry. He saw action in Tennessee and was promoted to lieutenant colonel in June 1863. He became colonel and commander of the 17th Infantry (U.S. Colored Troops) in April 1864, then joined the Regular Army as a lieutenant colonel in the 41st Infantry in 1867. He transferred to the 24th Infantry at Fort Davis on the southwest Texas frontier in 1869 and often led his black infantrymen against Cheyenne, Comanche, and Kiowa Indians in west Texas and New Mexico along the Pecos River, earning him the nickname "Pecos Bill." He was promoted to colonel and commander of the 1st Infantry in 1879. In May 1897 he was promoted to brigadier general and appointed commander of the Department of California. With the declaration of war against Spain, Shafter was appointed major general of volunteers in May 1898 and sent to Tampa, Florida, to organize the expeditionary force as commander of the V Army Corps. Shafter was a surprising and still controversial choice because he was grossly overweight, sixty-three years old, ill with gout, and lacked significant command experience beyond the regimental level. While he commanded the V Army Corps in Cuba, his physical condition made it impossible for him actually to command in the field. Nonetheless, he led the corps to victory with the surrender of Santiago on 16 July and overcame great logistical obstacles in the process. The V Corps quickly deteriorated in the unhealthy conditions in Cuba and had to be evacuated to Camp Wikoff, Montauk, Long Island, New York, for recovery. Shafter was made commander of the Department of the East in October 1898 and then transferred to command the Departments of California and the Columbia. He retired from the Regular Army in October 1899 but retained his volunteer commission until his final retirement in June 1901. That July he was raised to major general, U.S. Army, retired. "William Rufus Shafter (1835–1906)," *Webster's American Military Biographies*, pp. 376–77; TAGO, *OAR, 1901*, pp. 265, 363, 385; Paul Carlson, *"Pecos Bill": A Military Biography of William R. Shafter* (College Station: Texas A&M Univ. Press, 1989), passim; Wooster, *Nelson A. Miles and the Twilight of the Frontier Army*, pp. 216–18.

George C. Shaw (6 March 1866–10 February 1960). Shaw was commissioned in the 1st District of Columbia Volunteer Infantry in May 1898 and mustered out in November. On 12 July 1899, he enlisted as a private in the 27th U.S. Volunteer Infantry and a week later was commissioned an officer. He served with the 27th in the Philippines until he was mustered out with the regiment in May 1901. He was then commissioned in the 13th Infantry in October 1901 and promoted to first lieutenant, 27th U.S. Infantry, in April 1902. He commanded Company C in both of Pershing's expeditions in April and May 1903 against the Moros around Lake Lanao. He played a prominent part in the assault on and taking of Fort Pitacus on 4 May 1903 and was later awarded a Medal of Honor on 9 June 1904. In December 1912 he was appointed temporary major in the Philippine Scouts and commanded the 5th Battalion on Mindanao until April 1915, and again saw action against the Moros under Pershing at Bud Bagsak in June 1913. He served as colonel, NA, from October 1918 to March 1920. He was detailed to the Inspector General's Department (1919–1922). He completed the Advanced Course at the Infantry School, Fort Benning, Georgia, in 1923 and then the Command and General Staff School at Fort Leavenworth in 1924. He briefly commanded the 13th Infantry, 9th Division, before being assigned as the director of the civilian marksmanship program at the War Department. In June 1929 Shaw was promoted to brigadier general and took command of the 6th Infantry Brigade, 3d Division, and Fort Rosecrans (San Diego), California (1929–1930). He retired from active duty on 6 March 1930. TAGO, *OAR, 1915*, pp. 450, 459–60; TAGO, *OAR, 1916*, p. 446; TAGO, *OAR, 1938*, p. 1054; Clay, *U.S. Army Order of Battle*, vol. 1, pp. 298, 369; "George Clymer Shaw, Brigadier General, United States Army," Arlington National Cemetery, http://www.arlingtoncemetery.net/georgecl.htm.

George L. Sheldon (31 May 1870–5 April 1960). Born and raised in Nebraska, Sheldon attended the University of Nebraska and was captain of the cadet battalion during Pershing's first year as commandant. He graduated with a bachelor of letters degree in 1892 and received his A.B. from Harvard in 1893. During the Spanish-American War he served as a captain in command of Company B in William Jennings Bryan's 3d Nebraska Volunteer Infantry Regiment. He was elected to the state senate in 1902 and reelected two years later. Nominated as governor on the reform Republican ticket in 1906, he became the first native Nebraskan and the youngest person at thirty-six to be governor of the state. He was defeated for reelection in 1908. After his defeat he relocated to Mississippi, where he managed a plantation he had acquired earlier. "George Lawson Sheldon: Biographical Data," in Archives Record, Nebraska State Historical Society, Lincoln, http://www.nebraskahistory .org; "George Lawson Sheldon," *Who Was Who–The Military*, p. 522.

Walter C. Short (2 April 1870–5 March 1952). Short was commissioned in the 6th Cavalry in October 1891 after graduating from the Michigan Military Academy.

He served with the 6th Cavalry in Cuba at the San Juan Heights on 1 July, where he was wounded. He transferred to the 10th Cavalry in September 1898. He was appointed major, 35th U.S. Volunteer Infantry, in July 1899 and served in the Philippines under Colonel Edward H. Plummer, and was mustered out of volunteer service in May 1901 and returned to the 10th Cavalry. Recognized as one of the army's leading equestrians, in 1903 he was sent to the Cavalry and Field Artillery School at Fort Riley to develop a course in equitation and horsemanship. He established and directed the School for Farriers and Horseshoers until October 1906 while at the same time being the senior instructor in equitation (1904–1907). He completed the French Cavalry School at Saumur (1907–1908) and then returned to his former duties (1908–10, March–September 1911). He also served as assistant commandant during part of this period. He was assigned to the 1st Cavalry in September 1911 at the Presidio of San Francisco and commanded troops at Yosemite National Park for part of this assignment. He transferred to the 4th Cavalry at Fort Shafter, Hawaii, in July 1913 and was assigned to the 16th Cavalry on the Mexican Border at Fort Ringgold, Texas. Promoted to colonel, NA, in August 1917, he organized and trained the 327th Infantry Regiment, 82d Division (August 1917–April 1918), and then commanded the 312th and 315th Cavalry Regiments (Organized Reserve) (April–August 1918), successfully converting them into the 71st and 72d Field Artillery Regiments. He then commanded the 8th Infantry Regiment, 8th Division (September–October 1918). The division reached France in November after the Armistice and was returned to the United States in January 1919. He completed the School of the Line at Fort Leavenworth in 1920 and then commanded the 16th Cavalry Regiment at Fort Sam Houston, Texas (1920–1921). He commanded 7th Cavalry Regiment, 2d Cavalry Brigade, 1st Cavalry Division, at Fort Bliss, Texas (1921–1923), while also commanding the 2d Brigade (1921–1922) and later the 1st Cavalry Brigade (May–October 1923) at Fort Clark, Texas. He then was assigned to duty with the Inspector General's Department (1923–1927). Short was promoted to brigadier general in October 1927 and again commanded the 2d Cavalry Brigade at Fort Bliss (1928–1933). After temporarily commanding the 1st Cavalry Division in December 1930, he commanded the division for two separate tours prior to his retirement on 30 April 1934 (1932–1933, 1933–1934). TAGO, Headquarters of the Army, General Orders No. 15, 13 February 1900, pp. 23–24; TAGO, *OAR, 1909*, pp. 110–11; TAGO, *OAR, 1911*, p. 115; TAGO, *OAR, 1920*, p. 176; TAGO, *OAR, 1938*, p. 1056; TAGO, *OAR, 1955*, vol. 1, *United States Army, Active and Retired Lists* (Washington, D.C.: GPO, 1955), p. 1024; Clay, *U.S. Army Order of Battle*, vol. 2, pp. 569, 597, 621, 626, 648; Heitman, *Historical Register*, vol. 1, p. 884; U.S. Army Mounted Service School, *The Rasp* [Yearbook] (Fort Riley, Kans.: 1912), pp. 15, 37, 113, 233, and *The Rasp* (1913), p. 140; *ARWD, 1907*, vol. 4, pp. 268, 272; *ARWD, 1908*, vol. 4, p. 121; "Walter Cowan Short," in Davis, *Generals in Khaki*, pp. 332–33.

Herbert J. Slocum (25 April 1855–29 March 1928). Slocum attended the Military Academy as a member of the Class of 1876 but was found deficient in engineering and dismissed on 22 June 1876, eight days after his class graduated. He was commissioned in the 25th Infantry in July 1876 and transferred to the 7th Cavalry. He participated in the Yellowstone expedition in 1876 and against the Nez Percé Indians in the summer of 1877. He served with the 7th Cavalry on the frontier until May 1897, when he was detailed to the District of Columbia National Guard. He was appointed major and inspector general, USV, in May 1898 and served with the 3d Division, I Army Corps, in the United States and then as inspector general for the Department of Matanzas, Cuba. In 1903 he was sent to the Philippines and remained there until 1906, when he was sent to Cuba in duty with the Provisional Government in Havana. He was in charge of the Cuban Rural Guard and planning for the Cuban armed force until the end of the U.S. intervention in April 1909. He was acting inspector general, Department of the East, at Governor's Island, New York, until September 1912, when he was sent back to Havana as U.S. military attaché. In 1914 he was assigned to duty at the U.S. Military Prison at Fort Leavenworth and in September he was appointed commander of the 13th Cavalry at Columbus, New Mexico. He commanded the 2d Cavalry Brigade on the border (October 1915–March 1916) and was actively involved in the Mexican Expedition under Pershing until July. He then commanded the 3d Brigade, Southern Department, at Laredo, Texas (July 1916–February 1917). He commanded the Officers' Training Camps at Fort Oglethorpe, Georgia (1917–1918), and then commanded Fort Sam Houston prior to his retirement in April 1919. "Herbert J. Slocum," *Sixty-Ninth Annual Report of the Association of Graduates of the United States Military Academy at West Point, New York, June 13, 1938,* pp. 97–99; TAGO, *OAR, 1901,* pp. 82, 354; TAGO, *OAR, 1920,* p. 955; U.S. Military Academy, *Official Register of the Officers and Cadets of the U.S. Military Academy, West Point, N.Y. June 1876* (West Point: U.S. Military Academy, 1876), pp. 10, 30.

Frank O. Smith (4 October 1881–29 January 1955). Smith served as a private and corporal in Company M, 3d Infantry (January 1899–January 1902), and as a private, corporal, sergeant, and first sergeant in Company G, 21st Infantry (January 1903–December 1905). He was appointed a second lieutenant in the Philippine Scouts in December 1905, a first lieutenant in September 1908, a captain in September 1914, and reappointed in September 1918. He retired as a captain in January 1920. TAGO, *OAR, 1931,* p. 910; TAGO, *OAR, 1956,* vol. 1, p. 1075.

James F. Smith (28 January 1858–29 June 1928). A graduate of Santa Clara College in 1878, Smith studied law at Hastings Law School and was admitted to the California Bar in 1881. In April 1898 he became colonel and commander of the 1st California Volunteer Infantry Regiment, which was among the first American troops to reach the Philippines in June 1898. He participated in the battles against Aguinaldo's forces around and in Manila before becoming deputy provost marshal in Manila (August 1898–October 1899). He commanded the 1st Brigade, 1st Division, VIII Army Corps (October 1898–March 1899), and then commanded the Island of Negros (March–April 1899). Promoted to brigadier general, USV, in April 1899, he command the Department of the Visayas (April 1899) and was military governor of Negros (April–July 1899). He was collector of customs at Manila (1900–1901) and was discharged from volunteer service in June 1901. Remaining in the Philippines, he was appointed an associated justice, Supreme Court of the Philippine Islands, in June 1901 and then a member of the Philippine Commission (1903–1906). Smith was appointed governor-general of the Philippines on 20 September 1906 and served until he resigned on 11 November 1909. He was appointed an associate judge, U.S. Court of Customs Appeals, in 1910. "James Francis Smith," *Who Was Who–The Military,* p. 537.

Frank Sperbeck (25 August 1869–30 June 1922). Sperbeck served as a private, corporal, and sergeant in the 1st Cavalry (January 1890–January 1898, June 1898–May 1900). He then served in the 7th Cavalry as a private, corporal, sergeant, and first sergeant (September 1900–February 1905, March–October 1908). He was appointed a second lieutenant in the Philippine Scouts in October 1908, was promoted to first lieutenant in January 1910, and was reappointed in August 1914. He was promoted to captain in the Scouts in August 1917. He was promoted to major in July 1920 and died in San Francisco. TAGO, *OAR, 1921*, p. 1153, and TAGO, *OAR, 1923*, p. 1299.

George P. Stallman (26 October 1876–21 June 1921). Stallman enlisted in Battery B, 6th Artillery (61st Company, Coast Artillery), in October 1898 and served as a private until July 1901. He completed his M.D. at Indiana Medical College (now University of Indiana Medical School) in 1906. Stallman was commissioned a first lieutenant in the Medical Reserve Corps in July 1908. He was called to active duty in April 1917 and was appointed a major in July 1917. He vacated his reserve commission in February 1918 to accept a commission as first lieutenant in the Medical Corps. His wartime assignments are not known. He was assigned to General Hospital No. 2 at Fort McHenry, Maryland, in 1920 and promoted to captain. TAGO, *OAR, 1920*, p. 86, and TAGO, *OAR, 1921*, p. 1390; "Army Orders," *New York Times*, 30 December 1919.

John M. Stotsenburg (24 November 1858–23 April 1899). Stotsenburg graduated from the USMA in 1881 and was commissioned in the 6th Cavalry. He served with the 6th in Arizona and New Mexico from 1881 to 1890, when the regiment was moved to South Dakota during the Pine Ridge expedition. He completed the Infantry and Cavalry School at Fort Leavenworth (1896–1897) and was stationed at Fort Leavenworth with the 6th Cavalry to December 1897, when he was appointed professor of military science and tactics at the University of Nebraska, Lincoln. On 1 May 1898 he was appointed a major in the 1st Nebraska Volunteer Infantry and later colonel and commander of the regiment in November. He sailed with the regiment for the Philippines in June 1898 and distinguished himself in organizing and leading his soldiers. Stotsenburg was involved in numerous combat actions against Filipino insurrectionists around Manila. He was in the field continuously with the 1st Nebraska on Luzon until he was killed in action on 23 April 1899 at Quinqua, Bulacan, leading a charge against Filipino positions. Fort Stotsenburg, Luzon, near Angeles City, some fifty miles north of Manila, which later included Clark Field and then became Clark Air Base, was named in his honor in 1903. "John M. Stotsenberg" [*sic*], *Thirtieth Annual Reunion of the Association of Graduates of the United States Military Academy at West Point, New York, June 7th, 1899*, pp. 162–66; "John M. Stotsenburg," http://www.arlingtoncemetery.net/jmstots.htm. "Fort Stotsenburg in Angeles City-Philippines," http://angelesboard.com/fort-stotsenburg.php; "Fort Stotsenburg," http://en.wikipedia.org/wiki/Fort_Stotsenburg.

Willard D. Straight (31 January 1880–30 November 1918). Straight received his architecture degree from Cornell University in 1901. He served in the Chinese Imperial Maritime Customs Service at Nanking and Beijing (1902–1904) before becoming a correspondent for the Reuter's Agency and Associated Press in Seoul, Korea, Tokyo, and Manchuria during the Russo-Japanese War. He served in the U.S. diplomatic service at Seoul and Havana, and was the American consul general at Mukden. Manchuria (1906–1908). He was acting chief of the U.S. State Department's Division of Far Eastern Affairs (November 1908–June 1909) before returning to China as the representative of J. P. Morgan and Company and several large American banks until 1912. He resigned from Morgan in 1915 and joined American International Corporation as a vice president. He joined the army as a major in the Adjutant General's Department in 1917 and was responsible for the organization and administration of the War Department's War Risk Bureau, which handled the insurance of all American soldiers in the United States and AEF. He was dispatched to France, where he served in the personnel section, First U.S. Army, and was charged with making preparations for the American delegations to the Paris Peace Conference. While in Paris he came down with influenza and died on 30 November 1918. "Willard Dickerman Straight," *Who Was Who*, vol. 1, *1897-1942*, p. 1196; "Willard Dickerman Straight," http://en.wikipedia.org/wiki/Willard_Dickerman_Straight; "Biography: Willard D. Straight and His Days in Korea," http://rmc.library.cornell.edu/Straight/; "Willard Straight," World War I Honor Roll, American Battle Monuments Commission, http://www.abmc.gov; TAGO, *American Decorations, 1862-1926*, p. 773.

Edwin V. Sumner (16 August 1835–24 August 1912). Son of Union Army major general Edwin V. Sumner (1797–1863) and brother of Major General Samuel S. Sumner, Sumner was appointed second lieutenant in the 1st Cavalry Regiment in August 1861. He served in a variety of posts during the war and was mustered out as a brigadier general, USV, in November 1865. Returning to the 1st Cavalry after the war, Sumner saw duty on the frontier. He was promoted to major and battalion commander, 5th Cavalry, in March 1879 under Colonel Wesley Merritt. In April 1890 he was promoted to lieutenant colonel, 8th Cavalry, at Fort Meade, Dakota Territory, and commanded its units at the Pine Ridge Reservation during the Sioux campaign of December 1890–January 1891. He was promoted to colonel in November 1894 and became commander of the 7th Cavalry at Fort Riley, replacing Colonel James W. Forsyth. During the Spanish-American War he was advanced to brigadier general, USV, in May and commanded the Departments of the Colorado and the Missouri, first at Denver (1898–1899) and then at Omaha (February–March 1899). He was discharged from the USV in February 1899. Promoted to brigadier general, U.S. Army, on 27 March 1899, he retired three days later. TAGO, *OAR, 1901*, pp. 264, 363; "Edwin V. Sumner," *Powell's Records*, p. 574; "Edwin Vose Sumner," *Who Was Who– The Military*, p. 569; "Report of the Major-General Commanding the Army," *ARWD, 1899*, pt. 1, pp. 14, 465.

Samuel S. Sumner (6 February 1842–26 July 1937). The younger son of Union Army major general Edwin V. Sumner (1797–1863) and younger brother of Brigadier General Edwin V. Sumner, Sumner was commissioned in the 5th Cavalry (June 1861–August 1862), serving as aide-de-camp to his father until his death on 21 March 1863 and then to Major General John Wool in New York City until May 1863. He was aide to Major General Ambrose Burnside, Army of the Ohio, and Major General Robert B. Potter, IX Corps, during the Vicksburg campaign and in Tennessee until November 1863, when he rejoined his regiment in the Army of the Potomac. He was an escort officer to General Grant from April to November 1865. He served in the South with the 5th Cavalry (1865–1869) until his regiment was assigned to duty in the Department of the Platte. He saw heavy action against hostile Cheyenne Indians at Summit Springs, Colorado (11 July 1869). He was on frontier duty with the 5th Cavalry in Arizona (1872–1875) and then in Kansas until May 1876, when he participated in the campaign against the Sioux and Cheyenne through November. He was promoted to major, 8th Cavalry, in April 1879 and commanded Fort McIntosh, Texas, and other posts. He was promoted to colonel and commander of the 6th Cavalry in May 1896. He was appointed brigadier general, USV, on 4 May 1898 and given command of the 1st Brigade, Cavalry Division, V Army Corps, consisting of his 6th Cavalry and the 3d and 9th Cavalry Regiments. Sumner commanded the brigade in Cuba and temporarily assumed command of the dismounted Cavalry Division for the critical operations against the San Juan Heights on the morning of 1 July when division commander Wheeler fell ill. He was promoted to major general of volunteers on 7 September 1898 and discharged from the volunteer service on 15 April 1899. He served as military attaché in London (1899–1900) and then commanded a brigade under Chaffee in the China Relief Expedition (June–November 1900). He was assigned to the Philippines, where he took command of the 1st Brigade, 2d Division (1900–1901), and then the 1st District, Department of Southern Luzon, until November 1901. Sumner was promoted to brigadier general in February 1901. After another reorganization of the Division of the Philippines, he commanded the 1st Separate Brigade, Department of North Philippines (1901–1902). In July 1902 he moved south to command the 7th Separate Brigade, Department of South Philippines, in Mindanao (July–October 1902), and then the new Department of Mindanao (October 1902–June 1903) when Pershing was commanding the Moro District at Camp Vicars on Lake Lanao. He was promoted to major general in July 1903 and returned to the United States to command the Department of the Missouri (1903–1904) before assuming command of the newly formed Southwestern Division in Oklahoma City (1904–1905). In May 1905 he moved to San Francisco to command the Division of the Pacific until he retired on 6 February 1906. TAGO, *OAR, 1901,* pp. 77, 355; TAGO, *OAR, 1931,* p. 916; TAGO, *OAR, 1938,* p. 1108; Cosmas, *An Army for Empire,* pp. 214–17; Linn, *The Philippine War,* passim; Boatner, *The Civil War Dictionary,* pp. 818–19; "Samuel Storrow Sumner, Major General, United States Army," Arlington National Cemetery Website, http://www.arlingtoncemetery.net/sssumner .htm; "Samuel S. Sumner (Major 8th Cav)," *Powell's Records,* p. 574; Heitman, *Historical Register,* vol. 1, pp. 936–37; "Samuel Storrow Sumner," *Who Was Who–The Military,* p. 569; "Memorandum," in Thian, *Notes,* pp. 189, 193, 197.

Innis Palmer Swift (7 February 1882–3 November 1953). Swift was the son of Major General Eben Swift (USMA, 1876). He graduated from the USMA in June 1904, was commissioned in the 1st Cavalry, and soon transferred to the 12th Cavalry. He went to the Philippines with his regiment (1909–1911) and was aide-de-camp to Pershing (1911–1912). During much of this time he was actively engaged in operations against hostile Moros on Jolo Island. Swift was with Troop C, 13th Cavalry, in the Mexican Expedition (April–July 1916) and then with the 16th Cavalry before returning to the Mounted Service School (1916–1917). Promoted to lieutenant colonel, NA, in September 1918, he was assigned to the 86th Division as division adjutant (1917–1918) and was assistant chief of staff, G-1 (Personnel), for the division in France to November 1918.

Swift completed the Command and General Staff School (1922-1923) and remained there until June 1929 as a detachment commander and instructor. He completed the Army War College (1929-1930) and then the Army Industrial College (now the Industrial College of the Armed Forces, ICAF) (1930-1931). Swift commanded the 8th Cavalry (1936-1939) before commanding the 2d Cavalry Brigade (1939-1941) and being promoted to brigadier general in October 1940. He was promoted to major general in April 1941 and assumed command of the 1st Cavalry Division, completed its transition into an infantry division, and took it to Australia in the summer of 1942. He commanded the 1st Cavalry Division under Douglas MacArthur in the Southwest Pacific Area (SWPA) Theater in combat operations through the reconquest of the Dutch New Guinea and the Admiralty Islands. In August 1944 he was made commanding general, I Corps, Sixth U.S. Army, and commanded it through the final campaigns on Luzon (January-July 1945) that cleared the Philippines and in the occupation of Japan until December 1945. He retired in February 1946. "Innis Palmer Swift," *Assembly* 13, no. 2 (July 1954), pp. 69-70.

Rudolf B. Teusler (25 February 1876–10 August 1934). Teusler received his M.D. from the Medical College of Virginia in 1894 and then practiced in Richmond, Virginia, while also teaching at the Medical College of Virginia. He then went to Japan as a medical missionary in 1900 and was the director of St. Luke's International Hospital in Tokyo until his death. He was a staff physician of the U.S. embassy in Tokyo for many years. He accompanied the U.S. intervention forces to Siberia (1918-1921) as a colonel in command of the American Red Cross effort to support the Czech Legion and American forces. He was also director of St. Barnabas's Hospital in Osaka (1925-1934). "Rudolf B. Teusler," *Who Was Who,* vol. 1, *1897-1943*, p. 1224.

John M. Thayer (24 January 1820–19 March 1906). Born in Massachusetts, Thayer graduated from Brown University in 1841, studied law, and established his practice at Worcester. He then moved to Omaha, Nebraska Territory, in 1854 and was admitted to the bar but took up farming rather than practice law. He aligned himself with the new Republican Party and became involved in politics. The territorial legislature appointed him a brigadier general and then major general in command of Nebraska territorial forces engaged in operations against the Pawnee Indians (1855-1861). He served in the Nebraska territorial legislature (1860-1861). With the coming of the Civil War, he raised the 1st Nebraska Volunteer Infantry and became its colonel in June 1861. He spent the war in the western theater and commanded brigades at Fort Donaldson and Shiloh (1862) before he was promoted to brigadier general, USV, in October 1862 and was reappointed in that rank in March 1863. He commanded the 1st Division, XV Army Corps, under U. S. Grant during the Vicksburg campaign. He then served in the Department of Arkansas and commanded the District and Army of the Frontier at Fort Smith, Arkansas. He was awarded the rank of brevet major general, USV, in March 1865 for his services during the war. Upon Nebraska's admission as a state in March 1867, he served as a senator to 1871. Not winning reelection in 1870, President Grant made him governor of Wyoming Territory (1875-1879), after which he resumed his law practice. Thayer was governor of Nebraska for two terms (1887-1891) and briefly from May 1891 to February 1892 during a disputed election. After this he retired from politics and resumed his law practice in Lincoln.

"John Milton Thayer (1820–1906)," in Biographical Directory of the United States Congress, http://bioguide.congress.gov/scripts/biodisplay.pl?index=T000148; biographical footnote on John Milton Thayer in Morton et al., *Illustrated History of Nebraska*, footnote, pp. 527–28; Heitman, *Historical Register,* vol. 1, p. 636.

John M. Thurston (21 August 1847–9 August 1916). Thurston was born in Vermont but grew up and was educated in Wisconsin. He studied law at Wayland University in Wisconsin and was admitted to the bar in May 1869, then moved to Omaha, Nebraska, in October to set up his law practice. After serving on the city council (1872–1874) and as city attorney (1874–1877), during which time he also served in the state house of representatives (1875–1877), he became assistant attorney for the Union Pacific Railroad Company in Omaha (1877–1888) and general counsel (1888–1895, 1901–1916). He was an unsuccessful candidate for the Republican nomination for U.S. Senate in 1893, but succeeded in being elected in March 1895. He served until March 1901 but did not seek reelection. He moved to Washington in 1901 and resumed his legal career, later returning to Omaha, where he practiced until his death. "John Mellon Thurston (1847–1916)," Biographical Directory of the United States Congress, http://bioguide.congress.gov/scripts/biodisplay.pl?index=T000256; "John Mellon Thurston," *Who Was Who,* vol. 1, *1897-1942*, p. 1238.

Samuel E. Tillman (2 October 1847–24 June 1942). Tillman graduated from the USMA in 1869. Commissioned in the artillery, he served on the frontier with his battery at Fort Riley, Kansas (September 1869–August 1870). He returned to West Point as an instructor in the Department of Chemistry, Mineralogy, and Geology (August 1870–September 1872) and then as a principal assistant professor (September 1872–August 1873). He transferred to the Corps of Engineers in June 1872. In August 1879 he returned to the Military Academy, as an assistant professor of chemistry, mineralogy, and geology. He was appointed full professor and later chairman (with the rank of colonel) of the department in December 1880 and served in that position until October 1911, when he retired. Tillman was recalled to active duty in June 1917 and assigned as the superintendent for the remainder of World War I. He was promoted to brigadier general on the retired list in March 1919 and released from active duty on 15 August 1919. "Samuel Escue Tillman," *Assembly* 1, no. 4 (January 1943), "In Memory" insert, pp. 3–5; TAGO, *OAR, 1941,* p. 1221.

Frank Tompkins (28 September 1868–21 December 1954). Tompkins was the son of Civil War Brevet Brigadier General Charles H. Tompkins (four brevet ranks and a Medal of Honor recipient during the war) (12 September 1830–15 January 1915), who served in the army Quartermaster General's Department from 1861 until his retirement in September 1894. Tompkins was commissioned in August 1891 and transferred to the 7th Cavalry in October. He served with the 7th Cavalry in Cuba during the Spanish-American War. He had a distinguished record during the Philippine-American War, where he served on Luzon under J. Franklin Bell. He then served the first of his three tours as professor of military science and tactics and commandant at Norwich University, Vermont (1910–1913). He was assigned to the 10th Cavalry in March 1913, and he served with the 10th on the Mexican border in December 1913. He was promoted to major in April 1915 and assumed command of the 3d Squadron,

13th Cavalry, in May 1915 at Columbus, New Mexico. He commanded the squadron at Columbus against Pancho Villa's attack on 9 March 1916 and then, although seriously wounded in the knee, pursued the bandits back into northern Mexico, inflicting significant losses on them. On 12 April 1916 he was involved in another major firefight against Villa and Mexican forces at Parral during the Mexican Expedition and was wounded once again. After these actions and recuperation from his wounds, he was assigned to Norwich again in June. A year later, in June 1917, he left Norwich and was ordered to the 18th Cavalry Regiment and then was promoted to colonel, NA (1917–1920). He was commander of the 301st Infantry Regiment, 76th Division, in the United States and France (1917–1918). The division was sent to France in July 1918 and designated the 3d Depot Division, a replacement division. With the 301st Infantry never slated to see combat as a unit, Tompkins transferred to the 28th Division and was assigned to command the 110th Infantry on the Vesle River line on 12 August. While in combat in the Aisne-Marne offensive on 7 September at Baslieux, near Fismes on the Visle, Tompkins suffered severe mustard gas burns that left him temporarily blinded and seriously wounded. He was evacuated to a hospital near Paris, where he remained a patient until November. Found unfit for further front-line duty, Tompkins was returned to the United States in December and assigned to Fort Myers, Virginia, until March, when he was once again assigned as commandant at Norwich (1919–1923). He retired as a colonel on 1 July 1920 for disability received in combat and was immediately recalled to active duty until September 1923 to finish his tour as commandant. He remained closely affiliated with Norwich University for the rest of his life. He published a personal account of his experiences in the Mexican Expedition as *Chasing Villa: The Story behind the Story of Pershing's Punitive Expedition*, which was reprinted in 1996. TAGO, *OAR, 1901*, pp. 21, 271, 367, 381; TAGO, *OAR, 1916*, p. 194, 667; TAGO, *OAR, 1939*, p. 1077; TAGO, *OAR, 1956*, vol. 1, p. 1074; "Chronology of Commandants," Norwich University Archives and Special Collections, http://library2.norwich.edu/catablog/commandant/commandant; "Return of Major Tompkins as Commandant," *Reveille* 46, no. 9 (November 1916), pp. 3–6; "Colonel Frank Tompkins U.S. Infantry," *War Whoop 1922* (Norwich Yearbook), p. 23; "Norwich Loses Colonel Tompkins," *Norwich University Record* 46, no 8 (February 1955), pp. 2–3; "The Author," in Tompkins, *Chasing Villa*, pp. vii–viii.

Charles B. Townsend (5 January 1876–24 March 1932). Townsend served as a sergeant in the 2d Alabama Volunteer Infantry (May–October 1898) and then as a private, corporal, battalion sergeant major, and sergeant major in the 18th Infantry Regiment (1899–1907). He was appointed a second lieutenant in the Philippine Scouts in December 1907, promoted to first lieutenant in September 1908, and to captain in May 1917. He retired as a captain in November 1919 but was recalled to active duty until October 1921, when he was promoted to major of infantry. TAGO, *OAR, 1920*, p. 1188; TAGO, *OAR, 1925*, p. 601; TAGO, *OAR, 1933*, p. 755.

Tullius C. Tupper (23 September 1838–1 September 1898). Tupper enlisted in the 6th Cavalry Regiment in July 1861 and rose to be the regiment's sergeant major by July 1862. He saw action during the Peninsular campaign (1862) and was promoted to second lieutenant in July 1862. He served as regimental adjutant (1863–1864) and was in a number of engagements with the Cavalry Corps, Army of the Potomac, including Chancellorsville, Gettysburg, and Brandy Station and Cedar Creek, Virginia. He was promoted to first lieutenant in September 1864. He moved with the 6th Cavalry to the southern plains for frontier duty and was promoted to captain in September 1867. Tupper was most active in scouting and mounted operations against hostile Indians in Texas and Kansas (1870–1874), later in Arizona, where he played a key role in defeating Victorio's uprising in 1876, and then in New Mexico against other Chiricahua Apaches in 1882. He was promoted to major in October 1887 and commanded two troops of the 6th Cavalry during the Sioux campaign of 1890–1891. He led the relief of Lieutenant Kerr's Troop K on 1 January 1890. He retired for disability received in the line of duty in July 1893. TAGO, *OAR, 1897,* pp. 184, 319; TAGO, *OAR, 1899,* p. 296; "Tullius C. Tupper (Major 6th Cav.)," *Powell's Records,* p. 605; "Major Tullius C. Tupper, U.S.A.," *Officers of the Army and Navy (Regular),* p. 434.

Thomas F. Van Natta Jr. (25 November 1880–30 April 1940). Van Natta graduated from the USMA in June 1903 and was commissioned in the 8th Cavalry. He served at Fort Sill (1903–1905) and then in the Philippines (1905–1907) and at Fort Robinson, Nebraska (1907–1910). After completing the Mounted Service School, he was sent to the Philippines, where he served on Luzon (September 1911–March 1912) and Jolo Island (May 1912–June 1913). He was actively engaged in operations against the Moros from December 1912 to June 1913 in command of a mountain gun detachment that provided critical fire support at Bud Bagsak. He transferred to the 6th Cavalry in July 1914 and was posted at Texas City, Texas (1914–1915), and in the field on the Mexican border and in the Mexican Expedition (1915–1916). He was promoted to captain in the 16th Cavalry in July 1916 and again saw duty on the Mexican border (February–September 1917). In August 1917 he was assigned as the U.S. military attaché in Havana (1917–1918). He was promoted to temporary lieutenant colonel in July 1918 and posted to Madrid as U.S. military attaché to Spain and Portugal (1918–1921). He returned to Washington in military intelligence and was with the Disarmament Conference (1921–1922). He completed the Command and General Staff College (1922–1923) and then was an instructor (1923–1927). He completed the Army War College (1927–1928), then was assigned to the 2d Cavalry (1928–1930) and 14th Cavalry (1930–1932), and then was at the Army War College when he went on sick leave and retired for disability incurred in the line of duty. "Thomas Fraley Van Natta, Jr.," *Seventy-second Annual Report of the Association of Graduates of the United States Military Academy at West Point, New York, June 10, 1941,* pp. 259–61.

Thomas A. Vicars (?–2 May 1902). Camp Vicars was named in honor of First Lieutenant Vicars. Little is known about Vicars. He was born in Canada but came to the United States and enlisted in the 21st Infantry, serving as a private, corporal, and quartermaster sergeant in Company A from September 1892 until he was commissioned a second lieutenant on 5 April 1899. He was commanding Company F, 2d Battalion, 27th Infantry, under Baldwin when he was killed in the attack against the Bayan Moros at their Fort Pandapatan, at Bayan, Cotabato, Mindanao, near Lake Lanao. On 4 May, Camp Vicars was established about one-half mile south of the fort. TAGO, *OAR 1901,* p. 207; *ARWD, 1902,* vol. 9, pp. 176–77, 485–89, 567–73 (Baldwin's report).

Charles D. Vielé (7 February 1841–6 October 1916). Vielé was appointed a lieutenant in the 1st U.S. Infantry on 24 October 1861. He served with the 1st Infantry in the Regular Division, Fifth Corps, Army of the Potomac, until June 1862, when the 1st Infantry was assigned to General U. S. Grant's command and participated in the Vicksburg campaign and the capture of Vicksburg on 4 July 1863. He remained in the army following the war. In January 1871 he was assigned to the 10th Cavalry and served with the 10th and 1st Cavalry on the frontier in the Indian Territory, Arizona, Montana, and Texas through 1895. With the 10th Cavalry, he was active in operations against the southern Plains Indians in the Red River campaign (1874–1875) and later against the Apaches and Chief Victorio in Arizona and northern Mexico in 1880 and Geronimo in 1886. He was promoted to major and command of the 2d Battalion, 1st Cavalry, at Fort Custer, Montana, in August 1889 and led it during the Pine Ridge expedition of 1890–1891. He later served with the 1st Cavalry at Forts Riley and Sheridan (1895–1898). He was promoted to lieutenant colonel in November 1897 and commanded the 1st Cavalry as part of the dismounted Cavalry Division during the Santiago Campaign. He led the 1st Cavalry in the fighting at the San Juan Heights and in the siege of the city of Santiago. He was appointed brigadier general, USV, in September 1898. He commanded the 1st Cavalry and Fort Riley until January 1899, when he assumed command of Fort Robinson, Nebraska. In September 1899 Vielé was transferred to Manila, Philippines, and promoted to colonel as commander of the 4th Cavalry, and was retired for disability on 23 January 1900. He was promoted to brigadier general, U.S. Army, retired, on 23 April 1904 in recognition of his Civil War service. TAGO, *OAR, 1901,* pp. 228, 370; TAGO, *OAR, 1916,* p. 538; "Charles Delevan Vielé," *Who Was Who–The Military,* p. 607; William H. Leckie, *The Buffalo Soldiers: A Narrative of the Negro Cavalry in the West* (Norman: Univ. of Oklahoma Press, 1967), passim; Thrapp, *The Conquest of Apacheria,* pp. 205–6; Faulk, *The Geronimo Campaign,* p. 68.

Günther Franz Hermann von Etzel (14 December 1862–21 January 1948). Von Etzel was a German Army cavalryman who served with troops (1881–1893) and the General Staff (1894–1895) before assignments as a General Staff officer to divisions. During the Boxer Rebellion in 1900, he was a member of the Army Command East Asia. After another General Staff assignment in Berlin, he was appointed German military attaché in Tokyo in May 1902 and remained there until December 1908. During the Russo-Japanese War he was a military observer with the Japanese Army in the field. He was the German Army's best expert on the Japanese Army. He became commander of the 33d Cavalry Brigade in Metz 1912. He was promoted to major general in April 1914 and commanded his brigade as part of the Crown Prince's Fifth Army in the opening months of the war (August–September 1914). He then commanded the Guards Cavalry Division (September–December 1914), the Hussar Brigade (December 1914–May 1915), the 3d Cavalry Division (May 1915–August 1916), the 2d Cavalry Division (August 1916–May 1917), and the 11th Infantry Division (May 1917–January 1918). Most of his time was spent on the Eastern Front, but he served in France and Belgium in 1917–1918. He was promoted to lieutenant general in January 1918 and commanded the XVII Army Corps (June–August 1918) and the XVIII Army Corps (August–November 1918). "Günther von Etzel," The Prussian Machine, http://home.Comcast.net/~jcviser/aka/etzel.htm; "Günther von Etzel," http://en.wikipedia.org/wiki/Gunther_von_Etzel.

Adalbert Dáni von Gyarmata und Magyar-Cséke (26 May 1868–14 April 1920). The Austro-Hungarian military attaché and observer with the Japanese Army, whom Pershing called Bela de Dani, was born in Budapest, the son of a judge on the Royal Hungarian High Court of Justice. He was commissioned in 1889 and served with troops until he went to Russia to study Russian (1899–1900). He was assigned to the General Staff of the 27th Infantry Division, handling intelligence on the Russian Army. Dani was fluent in German, Hungarian, Italian, Russian, French, and English and was sent to Japan to learn Japanese and was appointed military attaché in Tokyo in February 1904. He was in the field with the Japanese Army from May 1904 to the end of the war in September 1905 and remained in Tokyo until May 1906, when he moved to China as the military attaché. He then commanded the 65th Infantry Regiment (1910–1912) and served as chief of staff, IV Corps, in Budapest (1912–1914). He remained as chief of staff of IV Corps in the Balkans and on the Russian Front and then moved to Army Group Tersztyánsky in the Balkans from May to September 1915. He later became commander of the 4th Mountain Brigade and served on the Italian Front (1916–1917) and was promoted to major general in November 1916. He was assigned as a section chief at the War Ministry in Vienna until 30 August 1918, when he took over command of the 40th Hungarian Infantry Division. With the demise of the Austro-Hungarian Empire and Army in 1918, he was pensioned in January 1919 and was a *Feldmarschall-Leutnant* (lieutenant general) in the Hungarian Reserve until his death. "Adalbert Dáni von Gyarmata," in Stefan Kurz, "Die Wahrnehmung des russischen Offizierskorps durch k. u. k. Offiziere in den Jahren 1904–1906" (Imperial and Royal Officers' Perception of the Russian Officer Corps in the Years 1904–1906) (Master's thesis, University of Vienna, June 2009), pp. 124–26, at http://othes.univie.ac.at/5360.

Francis E. Warren (20 June 1844–24 November 1929). Born and raised in Massachusetts, Warren enlisted in Company C, 49th Massachusetts Volunteer Infantry, in 1862 and served as a private and noncommissioned officer, mustering out of service in 1863. (Thirty years later, on 22 September 1893, he was awarded a Medal of Honor for his actions in combat at Port Hudson, Louisiana, on 27 May 1863, where he was wounded.) He moved to Wyoming in 1868 and soon became a successful merchant, rancher, and businessman in Cheyenne and deeply involved in politics and the Republican Party. He was elected to the territorial senate (1873–1874, 1884–1885) and served as territorial treasurer (1876, 1879, 1882, and 1884). President Chester A. Arthur appointed Warren the governor of Wyoming in 1885, but he was removed by President Grover Cleveland, a Democrat, in 1886. President Harrison, a Republican, reappointed Warren territorial governor again in March 1889 and he served until Wyoming was admitted to the Union as a state in 1890. He was then elected the first governor in September 1890 but resigned on 24 November 1890 after he was appointed to the U.S. Senate (December 1890–March 1893). He briefly resumed his farming and ranching career (1893–1894) until he was reelected as senator in 1894. He was reelected in every election thereafter until he died in November 1929. Warren, an extremely influential and powerful senator, served as chairman of a number of important committees when the Republicans controlled that house, such as Appropriations (1911–1920) and Military Affairs (1905–1911). In 1930, President Hoover renamed Fort D. A. Russell (1867–1930) as Fort Francis E. Warren in honor of Senator Warren, and it became Francis E. Warren Air Force Base when it was turned over to the U.S. Air Force in 1947. "Francis Emory Warren (1844–1929)," in Biographical Dictionary of the United States Congress, http://bioguide.congress .gov/scripts/biodisplay.pl?index=W000164; "Francis Emory Warren," *Who Was Who–The Military*, p. 618; TAGO, *Medals of Honor to October 31, 1897*, p. 125; "Francis Emory Warren [Senator Warren Answers Last Call, *The Lusk Herald*, November 29, 1929]," Niobrara County Library (Lusk, Wyoming), http://niobraracountylibrary. org/obituaries/index.php?id=5503; "F.E. Warren History," F.E. Warren Air Force Base, http://www.warren.af.mil/library/factsheets/factsheet.asp?id=4696.

Frederick E. Warren (20 January 1884–26 May 1949). The son of Senator Francis E. Warren and Pershing's brother-in-law, Fred received his bachelor's and master's degrees from Harvard (1905, 1906). He went into the livestock business with his father's company, Warren Live Stock Company, in Cheyenne, Wyoming, in 1905. He managed it from 1914 to 1929, when he became president upon his father's death. At this time he also took over all of his father's other businesses. "Frederick Emory Warren," *Who Was Who*, vol. 2, *1943-1950*, p. 558.

Frank W. Weed (12 April 1881–20 September 1945). Weed received his medical education at the University of Maryland Medical College in Baltimore, graduating in 1903. He was commissioned in the Army Medical Corps in May 1904, completed the Army Medical School (1904–1905), and then served in the Philippines until 1907. After several assignments in the United States, during which he was promoted to captain in April 1908, he once again was sent to the Philippines, where he served on Mindanao under Pershing before going to Tientsin, China, with the 15th Infantry Regiment until January 1915. He was next at Letterman General Hospital, Presidio of San Francisco (1915–1916). During World War I, he was appointed temporary colonel (1919–1920). He was a sanitation specialist and established the organization and policies that governed quarantine of infectious disease patients in mobilization camps. He was assigned to the Hospital Division, Surgeon General's Office, as a general sanitary inspector (January–August 1918) and then was assigned to the chief surgeon's office, AEF, where he was in charge of the evacuation of sick and wounded soldiers from France to the United States (August 1918–July 1919). From 1921 to 1928 he was assistant editor and then editor in chief of the Medical Department's fifteen-volume official history, *The Medical Department of the United States Army in the World War* (1921–1929). He completed the Army War College (1928–1929) and was promoted to colonel in May 1930. He commanded Sternberg General Hospital in Manila and was Philippines Department surgeon (1933–1935) before becoming the post surgeon and professor of military hygiene at the Military Academy (1935–1939). He was then chief surgeon, Second Corps Area, at Governor's Island, New York, that later became the First U.S. Army (1939–1942). Weed was promoted to brigadier general in July 1942 and commanded the Letterman General Hospital at the Presidio of San Francisco until his retirement in 1945. TAGO, *OAR, 1945*, p. 983, and TAGO, *OAR, 1946*, p. 1099; "Frank Watkins Weed," *Who Was Who–The Military*, p. 624; "Frank Watkins Weed," *JAMA* 130, no. 2 (12 January 1946), p. 104; U.S. Military Academy, *Official Register of the Officers and Cadets, United States Military Academy for the Academic Year Ending June 30, 1936* (West Point, N.Y.: United States Military

Academy Printing Office, 1936), p. 14; U.S. Military Academy, *Official Register of the Officers and Cadets, United States Military Academy for the Academic Year Ending June 30, 1940* (West Point, N.Y.: United States Military Academy Printing Office, 1940), p. 15.

Charles W. Weeks (15 March 1876–14 September 1953). Weeks attended the University of Nebraska, graduating in 1898 with a B.S. in electrical engineering. During his student days he was a cadet officer and member of the Pershing Rifles. He served as a private and sergeant in Company F, 2d Nebraska Volunteer Infantry Regiment, during the Spanish-American War (May–October 1898), and remained at Lincoln as the cadet major in command of the cadet battalion in 1898–1899 when Colonel John Stotsenburg and other officers had joined state volunteer units. He was commissioned in the 16th Infantry in June 1899. After serving as commandant of the cadet battalion at the State University of Iowa, Iowa City (1907–1910), he completed the School of the Line in 1911 and the Army Staff College in 1912. He served with the 31st Infantry in the Philippines, and at the start of the World War he returned to the United States and was promoted to lieutenant colonel (August 1917) and colonel (1918–1919), NA. He was chief of staff, 85th Division, in 1917–1918 and was then selected as the first chief of the Historical Branch, War Plans Division, War Department General Staff, that later became the War Department Historical Division (1918–1919). He completed the Army War College in 1920. He commanded the 21st Infantry Regiment, Hawaiian Division (July–October 1924), and later the division's 35th Infantry Regiment (1926–1928) after his promotion to colonel, RA, in July 1926. From August 1928 to July 1932, Weeks commanded the 52d Infantry Regiment, 6th Division, Organized Reserves, in Illinois. He then served as assistant commandant at the Infantry School, in Fort Benning, Georgia, until July 1936, when he became the professor of military science and tactics and commandant of cadets at Clemson College (now Clemson University), Clemson, South Carolina. He retired from active duty in September 1939. Clay, *U.S. Army Order of Battle*, vol. 1, pp. 376, 386, 396; TAGO, *OAR, 1938*, p. 780; TAGO, *OAR, 1940*, p. 1237; TAGO, *OAR, 1954*, vol. 1, p. 949; "Clemson Commandant," *Evening Herald* (Rock Hill, S.C.), 9 July 1936, http://news.google.com/newspapers; State University of Iowa, Iowa City, *Twenty-Fifth Report of the Board of Regents to the Governor and Thirty-Second General Assembly, 1905-1906* (Des Moines: Emory H. English, State Printer, 1907), p. 9; *University of Iowa Yearbook, 1911*, p. 323, http://www.e-yearbook.com/yearbooks/University_Iowa_Hawkeye_Yearbook/1911; "Report of the Governor General of the Philippine Islands," 1 July 1917, in *ARWD, 1918*, vol. 3, p. 2.

Frank West (26 September 1850–26 August 1923). West graduated from the USMA in June 1872 and was commissioned in the 6th Cavalry. He served on garrison duty and on the frontier in Indian Territory and participated in numerous skirmishes and battles against the southern Plains Indians (1872–1875). He then served in Arizona (1875–1878) before commanding the Indian Scouts at Camp Verde (1878–1881). He led the scouts during the campaigns against Apaches into Mexico (1882–1884) and later against Geronimo (1885–1886). For his heroism in the fight against the Apaches at Big Dry Wash, Arizona, on 17 July 1882, he was awarded a Medal of Honor on 12 July 1892. He commanded Troop G, 6th Cavalry, in New Mexico (January–December 1890) and during the Pine Ridge campaign (December 1890–February 1891). In the Spanish-American War he saw extended action in the Santiago Campaign, being engaged in the fighting at the San Juan Heights (1–3 July 1898). He transferred to the 9th Cavalry in April 1900 and was assigned to the Presidio of San Francisco (1900–1901), during which time he was the acting superintendent of Sequoia National Park in California. He was shipped to the Philippines with his regiment and in command of the 2d Squadron in April 1901. He saw action against the insurgents in Batangas, Luzon (April–December 1901), then served as assistant to the inspector general, Department of the Philippines (1902–1906). He transferred to the 7th Cavalry in March 1906 and was stationed at Camp McGrath in the Philippines (April–October 1906) until he was promoted to colonel, 2d Cavalry, in October. He commanded the 2d Cavalry at Fort Des Moines, Iowa (January–November 1909), before taking the regiment to the Philippines, where it was stationed at Jolo and Mindanao (January 1910–May 1912). He commanded the 2d Cavalry at Fort Bliss, Texas (1912–1913), and then the 1st Cavalry Brigade (February–March 1913). His final active duty was as commander of the Recruit Depot at Fort Slocum, New York (1913–1914). He retired on 26 September 1914. "Frank West," *Fifty-Sixth Annual Report of the Association of Graduates of the United States Military Academy at West Point, New York, June 11, 1925*, pp. 88–91; TAGO, *Medals of Honor to October 31, 1897*, p. 127.

Parker W. West (21 August 1858–20 January 1947). West was the son of Louisiana Republican U.S. senator Joseph R. West (19 September 1822–31 October 1898), a brevet major general in the Union Army, who served in Congress from March 1871 to March 1877 but did not seek reelection. Parker West graduated from the USMA in June 1881 and was commissioned in the 3d Cavalry. He served on the frontier in Wyoming, Arizona, and Texas (1881–1891) and again in Texas and Oklahoma (1892–1897). He was promoted to captain, 8th Cavalry, in May 1898 and was acting chief commissary, Wheeler's Cavalry Division, V Army Corps, in Cuba during the Santiago Campaign (June–July 1898), and then chief quartermaster (July–September 1898). He went to the Philippines as assistant to the inspector general, Department of the Pacific and VIII Army Corps, in Manila (1899–1900), and inspector general, Department of Northern Luzon (1900–1901), when he was discharged from volunteer service. West transferred to the newly organized 11th U.S. Cavalry in the United States in August 1901. He again served in the Philippines with the 11th Cavalry (1902–1903) and returned to the United States to be aide-de-camp to Major General MacArthur at the Department of California and Pacific Division (1904–1905). He accompanied MacArthur as an observer with the Imperial Japanese Army in Japan and Manchuria during and after the Russo-Japanese War (February 1905–March 1906). He served as assistant to the inspector general of the army (1906–1909) until he retired for disability in the line of duty on 29 November 1909. In retirement, he was deputy governor of the U.S. Soldiers' Home in Washington, D.C. (1910–1933). "Parker Whitney West," *Assembly* 6, no. 4 (January 1948), "In Memory" insert, p. 3; "Joseph Rodman West (1822–1898)," Biographical Directory of the United States Congress, http://bioguide.congress.gov/scripts/biodisplay.pl?index=W000303.

William L. Westermann (15 September 1873–4 October 1954). Westermann was born in Illinois and attended the University of Nebraska, from which he received a bachelor's degree in 1894 and a master's degree in 1896. During these years he was a member of Pershing's cadet battalion and also taught Latin at the university (1894–1896). He then taught high school Latin in Decatur, Illinois (1896–1899), before going to Germany to study at the University of Berlin (Ph.D., 1902). Upon returning to the United States, he taught Latin and Greek at the University of Missouri (1902–1906) and history at the Universities of Minnesota (1906–1908) and Wisconsin (1908–1920). He was the principal advisor on Turkish, Greek, and west Asian affairs to the U.S. delegation to the Paris Peace Conference (1918–1919) and was involved in resolving important postwar border disputes. After this, he was appointed professor of ancient history at Cornell University (1920–1923) before moving to become professor of history at Columbia University (1923–1948). A respected authority on ancient and Middle Eastern history, Westermann was a well-published author and frequent consultant and lecturer throughout the world. "William Linn Westermann," *Who Was Who,* vol. 3, *1951-1960,* p. 905; John Allen, "Inventing the Middle East: UW Classicist William Westermann Led America's First Attempt to Re-Create the Middle East," *On Wisconsin* (winter 2004), pp. 36–39.

John F. Weston (13 November 1854–3 August 1917). "Jack" Weston was commissioned in the 4th Kentucky Cavalry in November 1861, and was promoted to captain in January 1863 and major in November 1864. On 9 April 1898 he was awarded a Medal of Honor for his actions at Wetumpka, Alabama, on 13 April 1865. He was commissioned in the 7th Cavalry in August 1867, graduated from the Artillery School in 1875, and was appointed a captain in the Commissary Department in November 1875. He remained in the Commissary Department and rose to major (August 1892) and lieutenant colonel (November 1897) before being appointed colonel and assistant commissary general in April 1898. He became commissary general of subsistence, U.S. Army, on 6 December 1900, replacing Charles P. Eagan. He remained commissary general of subsistence until he was promoted to major general on 8 October 1905. After briefly commanding the Northern Division (1905–1906), Weston went to the Philippines, where he served as the commander of the Department of Luzon (1906–1908) and the Philippine Division (March–December 1908). Upon returning to the United States, he was commander of the Department of California (January–August 1909) and retired due to illness on 13 November 1909. Heitman, *Historical Register,* vol. 1, p. 1021; "John Francis Weston," *Who Was Who–The Military,* p. 627; "Memorandum," in Thian, *Notes,* p. 189; *ARWD, 1906,* vol. 3, p. 249; *ARWD, 1908,* vol. 3, pp. 210, 239; *ARWD, 1909,* vol. 3, pp. 127, 153; *ARWD, 1910,* vol. 3, p. 133.

Joseph Wheeler (10 September 1836–25 January 1906). Wheeler graduated from the USMA in July 1859 and was commissioned in the dragoons. He resigned his commission in April 1861 and joined the Confederate States Army. During the Civil War he established a significant reputation as a daring and successful cavalry commander and was involved in numerous battles, earning the nickname "Fightin' Joe." He quickly rose through the ranks, reaching major general in January 1863 and lieutenant general in February 1865 at the age of twenty-eight. After the war he became a planter and lawyer in Wheeler, Alabama, and was elected to Congress in 1880, and again served from 1884–1898, during which time he rose to be the ranking Democrat in the House, before resigning his seat in April 1900. On the outbreak of the Spanish-American War, Wheeler offered his services and President McKinley appointed him major general, USV, on 4 May 1898. He assumed command of the dismounted Cavalry Division, V Corps, on 14 May. He landed his division at Daiquiri, Cuba, on 23 June and commanded it at Las Guasimas (24 June) and later Kettle and San Juan Hills (1–2 July). Wheeler was intimately involved in all combat operations during the Santiago Campaign and also in the surrender negotiations with the Spanish. He returned to Camp Wikoff, Montauk, and commanded the convalescent camp for various periods from 18 August to 27 September, then assumed command of the IV Corps at Huntsville, Alabama, until December. During this time he completed an account of his actions during the war that was published as *The Santiago Campaign 1898* (Boston: Lamson, Wolffe, and Company, 1898). In April 1899 he was discharged from his commission as major general and reappointed as a brigadier general, volunteers. He was dispatched to the Philippines in July 1899 and commanded the 1st Brigade, 2d Division, VIII Corps (September 1899–January 1900) and was involved in numerous engagements with the Filipino *insurrectos* on Luzon. He returned to the United States in February 1900. Wheeler resigned his volunteer commission upon being appointed a brigadier general, RA, on 16 June 1900. Wheeler assumed command of the Department of the Lakes in Chicago on 18 June and was retired on 10 September 1900 for age. He died of pneumonia in Brooklyn, New York, on 25 January 1906. "Joseph Wheeler," *Thirty-Seventh Annual Reunion of the Association of Graduates of the United States Military Academy at West Point, New York, June 11, 1906*, pp. 62–82; "Joseph Wheeler (1836–1906)," Biographical Directory of the United States Congress, http://bioguide.congress.gov/scripts/biodisplay .pl?index=W000338; "Joseph Wheeler (1836–1906)," *Webster's American Military Biographies*, p. 475; "Joseph Wheeler," *Who Was Who—The Military*, p. 629. Two solid biographies of Wheeler are: Edward G. Longacre, *A Soldier to the Last: Maj. Gen. Joseph Wheeler in Blue and Gray* (Washington, D.C.: Potomac Books, 2007), and John P. Dyer, *From Shiloh to San Juan: The Life of Fightin' Joe Wheeler* (Baton Rouge, La.: Louisiana State Univ. Press, 1961).

Henry H. Whitney (25 December 1866–2 April 1949). Whitney received his A.B. from Dickinson Seminary (now Lycoming College), Williamsport, Pennsylvania, in 1884 and entered the USMA in June 1888 as a member of the Class of 1892. He graduated from the USMA in June 1892 and was commissioned in the 4th Artillery. After two regimental assignments, he was assigned to the Military Information Division (military intelligence), Adjutant General's Office, in Washington in April 1896. He was sent on a dangerous, secret reconnaissance mission to Cuba and Puerto Rico in May 1898 to gain valuable military information that would assist American forces on future operations. (In 1922 he was awarded as DSC for this most important and hazardous mission.) He was then on Nelson Miles's staff at Santiago and in the Puerto Rican Campaign in 1898, after which he returned to Washington for duty with Miles at army headquarters (1898–1903), including acting as Miles's aide-de-camp (1900–1903). He was later detailed as adjutant general at Fort Riley (1910), the Department of Mindanao (1911–1913), under Pershing, and at the Western Department (1914). He was once again assigned to coastal artillery duty in the San Francisco area (1914–1916) and detailed back to adjutant general duties in July 1916. He served as adjutant general at the El Paso District, Texas (1916–1917), and the Western

Department (April–August 1917). Whitney was promoted to colonel in June 1917 and brigadier general, NA, in August when he was assigned to command the 63d Field Artillery Brigade and the 38th Division (1917–1918). He was discharged from the National Army in March and assumed command of the coast defense of Long Island Sound (March–September 1918). In September 1918 he was again detailed as adjutant general and sent to Paris as chief of staff, District of Paris (October 1918–September 1919), and then sent to Berne, Switzerland, as military attaché (1919–1920). He retired on 29 June 1920 and was promoted to brigadier general, U.S. Army, retired, on 21 June 1930. "Henry Howard Whitney," *Assembly* 9, no. 2 (July 1950), p. 58; TAGO, *OAR, 1931*, p. 933; "Henry Howard Whitney," in Davis, *Generals in Khaki,* pp. 378–79.

Samuel M. Whitside (9 January 1839–15 December 1904). Whitside was born in Ireland and later immigrated to Canada and then the United States. He enlisted in the 3d Cavalry Regiment in November 1858 (redesignated the 6th Cavalry Regiment in August 1861) and rose to regimental sergeant major before he was commissioned in Company K in November 1861. He remained assigned to the 6th throughout the Civil War but served as aide-de-camp to Major General George B. McClellan (1861–1862), Major General Nathaniel P. Banks (1862–1863), Major General John H. Martindale, and finally Major General Alfred Pleasanton, commander of the Cavalry Corps, Army of the Potomac, until March 1864. He finally returned to serve in Company A, 6th Cavalry, following the Civil War. Whitside saw service with the 6th in Texas, Kansas, and Arizona from 1867 to 1877. After sixteen years in command of Troop B, 6th Cavalry, he was promoted to major and transferred to the 7th Cavalry at Fort Meade, Dakota Territory, in March 1885 as commander of the 2d Battalion and then moved with the 7th to Fort Riley in 1887. He commanded elements of the 1st Battalion, 7th Cavalry, at the Pine Ridge Agency (November 1890–January 1891) who were engaged in the capture of Spotted Elk (Big Foot) and his band on 28 December, the fight at Wounded Knee Creek on the 29th, and another action at Drexel's Mission on the 30th. He replaced Colonel James W. Forsyth in command of the 7th Cavalry from January 1891 until the close of the campaign. Whitside commanded the 5th Cavalry during the Spanish-American War, but it never saw duty outside the United States. In October 1898 he was promoted to colonel and commander of the 10th Cavalry Regiment, which he took to Cuba in May 1899 before assuming command of the Department of Santiago and Puerto Principe (December 1899), redesignated the Department of Eastern Cuba in mid-1900, and then the District of Santiago until his retirement. He was promoted to brigadier general, USV, on 3 January 1901, and brigadier general, U.S. Army, on 29 May 1902, just before he retired on 9 June. The only detailed biography of Brigadier General Whitside, entitled "Selfless Service: The Cavalry Career of Brigadier General Samuel M. Whiteside from 1858 to 1902," was completed by his great-grandson, Major Samuel L. Miller, U.S. Army, as his thesis for the degree Master of Military Art and Science (MMAS), Military History, at the U.S. Army Command and General Staff College, Fort Leavenworth, Kansas, in 2002. See also "Samuel M. Whitside (Major 7th Cav.)," *Powell's Records,* pp. 641–42; "Major S. Marmaduke Whiteside [Whitside], U.S.A.," *Officers of the Army and Navy (Regular),* p. 455; "Samuel Marmaduke Whiteside," http://www.arlingtoncemetery.net/smwhit.htm; "Samuel Marmaduke Whiteside," *Who Was Who–The Military,* p. 634.

Wilber E. Wilder (16 August 1856–30 January 1952). Wilder graduated from the USMA in June 1877 and was commissioned in the 4th Cavalry. He served on the frontier in Indian Territory, Texas, New Mexico, and Arizona and was involved in several skirmishes with southern Cheyennes and Geronimo's Apache Indians (1877–1890). On 17 August 1896, he was awarded a Medal of Honor for his gallantry in action at Horse Shoe Canyon, New Mexico, on 23 April 1882. He was the adjutant at USMA (1895–1898) and was appointed colonel, USV, and commanding officer of the 14th New York Volunteer Infantry Regiment in 1898. He was appointed a lieutenant colonel of the 43d U.S. Volunteer Infantry Regiment in August 1899 under Arthur Murray. He went to the Philippines with the 43d but never served in the field because Major General Arthur MacArthur ordered him to organize and command the Macabebe Scouts (1899–1900), which later played a prominent role in capturing Emilio Aguinaldo. He was later on MacArthur's military government staff and was the superintendent of police in Manila (1900–1901) until February 1901, when he was detailed as an assistant adjutant general. He was adjutant general, Department of Dakota, in St. Paul (1901–1905). After his promotion to lieutenant colonel, 11th Cavalry, in September 1906, he was detailed to the Inspector General's Department. He was inspector general at the Northern Division (1906–1907) and then the Philippine Department (1907–1909) and the Department of Colorado (1909–1911). Wilder was promoted to colonel, 5th Cavalry, in January 1911 and served with the regiment at Schofield Barracks, Hawaii (1911–1913), on the Mexican border (1913), and then commanding at Fort Myer, Virginia (1913–1916). The 5th Cavalry was assigned to the Mexican Expedition under Wilder's command until he was moved to command the Southern California Border District (1916–1917). He was promoted to brigadier general, NA, in August 1917 and took command of Camp Zachery Taylor, Kentucky, and the 84th Division (August–October 1917). He then commanded the 168th Infantry Brigade, 84th Division (October–December 1917), and once again the 84th Division (December 1917–March 1918), before commanding the 168th Infantry Brigade again at Camp Sherman, Ohio (March–August 1918). Wilder took his brigade to France in September 1918, but he never saw action. He was promoted to brigadier general, U.S. Army, retired, by Act of Congress on 28 February 1927. "Wilber Elliott Wilder," *Assembly* 11, no. 1 (April 1952), p. 63; TAGO, *Medals of Honor to October 31, 1897,* p. 128; "Wilber Elliott Wilder," in Davis, *Generals in Khaki,* p. 380.

Theodore J. Wint (6 March 1845–21 March 1907). Wint enlisted in Company F, 6th Pennsylvania Cavalry Regiment, in October 1861 and served as a private, corporal, and sergeant until September 1864. In February 1865 he enlisted in the mounted service and served until he was commissioned in the 4th Cavalry in November 1865. He was promoted to captain in April 1872, but he was not promoted to major in the 10th Cavalry until May 1892. In the Spanish-American War he served with the 10th Cavalry during the Santiago Campaign and was seriously wounded at the San Juan Heights on 1 July 1898. He was appointed lieutenant colonel of the 6th Cavalry in April 1899 and was ordered to China with two squadrons (eight troops) of the regiment as part of the China Relief Expedition under Chaffee (June–December 1900). Wint distinguished himself throughout the campaign against the Boxers, including the relief of Beijing in August. He was promoted to colonel and commander of the 10th Cavalry (1901–1902) and to brigadier general in June 1902. Assigned to the Philippines, he commanded the Department of Visayas (1903-1904) before returning to the United States to command the Department of the Missouri in Omaha (1904-1906), during which time he also served as acting commander of the Northern Division (June-July, October 1905). On 31 December 1906 he replaced Major General J. Franklin Bell as commander of the Army of Cuban Pacification. However, he was soon relieved of this assignment on 16 February 1907 due to his recurrent heart problems and returned for treatment to Philadelphia, where he died on 21 March 1907. Heitman, *Historical Register,* vol. 1, pp. 70, 72, 1051; "Theodore Jonathan Wint," *Who Was Who–The Military,* p. 643; "Theodore Jonathan Wint, Brigadier General, United States Army," Arlington National Cemetery Website, http://www.arlingtoncemetery .net/tjwint.htm; "Memorandum," in Thian, *Notes,* pp. 189, 193, 199; *ARWD, 1907,* vol. 3, pp. 101, 313.

Francis A. Winter (30 June 1867–11 January 1931). Winter received his medical degree from St. Louis University's Medical College in 1889. He joined the Army Medical Department in March 1892. He served in the divisional reserve hospital at Siboney, Cuba, and was later surgeon with the 37th U.S. Volunteer Infantry in the United States and Philippines (July 1899-February 1901). He was promoted to major, Medical Corps, in August 1903 and lieutenant colonel in April 1912. With the American entry into the war, he was promoted to colonel in May 1917 and accompanied the AEF to France, where he became chief surgeon, Line of Communications (July 1917-March 1918), and responsible for all medical care and treatment in the AEF except for the armies at the front. He was then chief surgeon, AEF, in the United Kingdom (May-October 1918). He was promoted to brigadier general, Medical Corps, National Army, on 1 May 1918 and honorably discharged on 1 June 1919. Surgeon General Merritte Ireland appointed him the director of the Army Medical Library (1918-1919) and then commandant of the Army Medical School in Washington, D.C. (1919-1922). Winter retired in September 1922 and was promoted to brigadier general, retired, by the Act of 21 June 1930, which immediately promoted retired personnel to the highest rank they had held during World War I. "Francis Anderson Winter," *Who Was Who–The Military,* p. 643.

John P. Wisser (19 July 1852–19 January 1927). Wisser graduated from the USMA in June 1874 and was commissioned in the 1st Artillery. He was assigned to the Military Academy as an assistant professor of science (1878-1882) and then as an assistant instructor at the Artillery School for Practice (1882-1884). He went to Europe to attend schools and the French maneuvers (January-October 1884) and returned to garrison duty in California and Washington (1884-1886). He returned to the USMA as principal professor of chemistry, mineralogy, and geology (1886-1894) and then once again had garrison duty (1894-1895). He was later artillery inspector, Pacific Division (January-June 1904), and then inspector general (1904-1906), including during the period of the San Francisco earthquake. Wisser was assigned briefly to the Office of the Chief of Staff in Washington in 1906 and then sent to Berlin as the U.S. military attaché (1906-1909). He returned to the United States and commanded the artillery district of Savannah, Georgia (1909-1911), and then commanded the artillery district of San Francisco (1911-1913). He commanded the Pacific Coast artillery district (February-September 1913) and was promoted to brigadier general in May 1913. Wisser was assigned to Texas City, Texas, commanding the 4th Brigade, 2d Division (1913–1914), before returning to the Pacific Coast artillery district (1914–1915). He was next assigned to Fort Shafter, Hawaii, where he commanded the post and the 1st Hawaiian Brigade until November 1915 and then the Hawaiian Department (1915–1916). He returned to the United States in May 1916 and retired on 19 July. He was recalled to active duty during the war to command the Hawaiian Department (September 1917–May 1918). "John Philip Wisser," *Fifty-Eighth Annual Report of the Association of Graduates of the United States Military Academy at West Point, New York, June 13, 1927*, pp. 128–30.

Leonard Wood (9 October 1860–7 August 1927). Wood completed Harvard Medical School in 1880 and received his M.D. in 1884. He was appointed a contract surgeon in the Army Medical Department (1885) and then an assistant surgeon (first lieutenant) in January 1886. He was assigned to Arizona Territory and participated in then Captain Henry Lawton's expedition against Geronimo in 1886. In April 1898 he was awarded a Medal of Honor for his actions during the summer of 1886. Remaining in the medical service, he eventually was assigned to Washington as a White House surgeon to President Grover Cleveland and then to President William McKinley. In this post he came into close contact with a number of important Republican political leaders, and especially with Theodore Roosevelt, who was then assistant secretary of the navy. When Roosevelt resigned his post to raise his 1st U.S. Volunteer Cavalry ("Rough Riders") for the Spanish-American War, he asked for Wood to lead the regiment as a colonel of volunteers. Wood subsequently commanded the "Rough Riders" in Cuba at Las Guasimas on 24 June, then took over command of Young's 2d Brigade, Dismounted Cavalry Division, for the rest of the campaign against the San Juan Heights and Santiago. His performance during the Santiago Campaign won Wood promotion to brigadier general of volunteers on 8 July 1898 and appointment as military governor of the city of Santiago on the 19th. He quickly set about reforming sanitation, improving public health, and restoring order to the city. He became military governor of the Santiago province and commander of the Department of Santiago in October and was promoted to major general of volunteers that December. He was reappointed as a brigadier general of volunteers in April 1899 and promoted to major general of volunteers in December 1899, when he replaced Major General John Brooke in Havana as military governor of Cuba after undermining Brooke through his contacts in the press. Wood's great successes in reforming public health, sanitation, education, law enforcement, and virtually all facets of the Cuban economy and society as well as establishing a new constitution brought him significant fame and recognition. In February 1901, Wood was promoted to brigadier general, U.S. Army, and in May 1902 he left Cuba upon the election of a new Cuban president. In March 1903 he went to the Philippines and was appointed governor of the rebellious Moro Province in July. That August he was promoted to major general, U.S. Army, amid significant controversy and criticism from politicians and line officers of Wood's political connections to Roosevelt and the Republican Party. In April 1906 he assumed command of the entire Department of the Philippines. He returned to the United States in November 1908 to command the Department of the East and was appointed chief of staff of the army in April 1910 but only assumed the duties in July. Wood's years as chief of staff were marked by conflict with the powerful bureau chiefs within the War Department, especially Major General Fred C. Ainsworth, the adjutant general, who was eventually forced into retirement. In many respects, Wood was an unconventional thinker who introduced numerous innovations during his tenure, especially in the creation of the provisional maneuver division, and stressed preparing the army for war. Wood remained in the army upon completion of his tour as chief of staff in April 1914, assuming command of the Eastern Department. Wood was a vocal supporter of military preparedness and was instrumental in the preparedness movement in the years before America's entry into the war in April 1917. He played a major role in the "Plattsburgh movement" that provided basic training for citizen-soldiers. As a longtime associate of Roosevelt, another preparedness advocate, Wood often found himself at odds with the Democratic administration of President Woodrow Wilson and also with the War Department. When the United States entered the war, Wood was shunted aside despite being the senior serving officer in the army. He commanded the 89th Division in training and also prepared others for service in France, but he was never allowed to go overseas himself because of Pershing's opposition. He was appointed commanding general of the Central Department in January 1919. Once considered a leading candidate for the Republican nomination for president in 1920, he lost to Warren Harding. In 1921 now President Harding sent him to the Philippines on a special mission and then appointed him as governor-general, a position which he held until just before he died following surgery for a brain tumor in Boston on 7 August 1927. "Leonard Wood (1860–1927)," *Webster's American Military Biographies,* pp. 487–88; "Leonard Wood," Encyclopaedia Britannica Online, http://www.britannica.com/EBchecked/topic/647355/Leonard-Wood; Weigley, *History of the United States Army,* pp. 296–374; "Leonard Wood," *Who Was Who–The Military,* pp. 645–46; "Major General Leonard Wood," in *Biographical Sketches of Distinguished Officers of the Army and Navy* (New York: Hamersly, 1905), pp. 202–8; "Leonard Wood (1860–1927)," *Webster's American Military Biographies,* pp. 487–88; Colonel Wallis L. Craddock, "Leonard Wood: Surgeon, Soldier, Administrator," *Military Surgeon* 160, no. 1 (January 1995), pp. 32–36; Jack C. Lane, *Armed Progressive: General Leonard Wood* (San Rafael, Calif.: Presidio Press, 1978), passim.

Dean C. Worcester (1 October 1866–2 May 1924). Educated at the University of Michigan (A.B., 1889), he was a member of the Steere scientific expedition to the Philippines (1887–1888), an assistant in botany at Michigan (1889–1890), and went on another scientific expedition to the Philippines (1890–1893). He was appointed an assistant professor of zoology and curator of the Zoological Museum at Michigan (1893–1899). He was appointed to the First Philippine Commission in January 1899 and served until September 1901. He was then secretary of the Interior, Philippine Insular Government (1901–1913), after which he held executive positions with several companies in the Philippines. He authored several books on the Philippines, including *The Philippines and Their People* (1899) and *The Philippines Past and Present* (2 vols., 1913). "Dean Conant Worcester," *Who Was Who,* vol. 1, *1897-1942,* p. 1382.

George H. Wright (3 January 1877–5 May 1927). Wright served as a private in Company D, 8th New York Infantry (May–November 1898), and then as a private, corporal, sergeant, and first sergeant in Company K, 16th Infantry (1899–1906). He was appointed a second lieutenant in the Philippine Scouts in March 1906, promoted to first lieutenant in September 1908, and reappointed in September 1912 before being promoted to captain in October 1914 and reappointed to the same rank in October 1918. He was appointed as a temporary major (1918–1919) and then promoted to major, Philippine Scouts (1920–1923). TAGO, *OAR, 1920,* p. 845; TAGO, *OAR, 1925,* p. 810; and TAGO, *OAR, 1928,* p. 841.

William M. Wright (24 September 1863–14 August 1943). Wright was a cadet at the U.S. Military Academy from 1 July 1882 until 11 January 1883, when he resigned due to his deficiency in mathematics. He was commissioned a second lieutenant in the 2d Infantry in January 1885. He later served as an assistant adjutant general in the Spanish-American War (1898–1899) and remained in the Adjutant General Corps after the war. Wright was selected but not appointed to the initial General Staff Corps of 1903, but later served on the General Staff (1905–1908). He was promoted to brigadier general in May 1917 and to major general, NA, in August 1917. He commanded the 35th Division both in the United States and with the American Expeditionary Forces in France. After the division's arrival in France, he briefly commanded III Corps before taking over the 89th Division and leading it through the St. Mihiel and Meuse-Argonne operations. Upon returning to the United States, he served as the executive assistant (deputy chief of staff) to General Peyton C. March, the War Department's chief of staff, until June 1921. Wright was promoted to major general in April 1921 and commanded the Ninth Corps Area (1921–1922) and Philippine Department (February–September 1922) before retiring in December 1922. TAGO, *OAR, 1941,* p. 1253; U.S. Military Academy, *Official Register of the Officers and Cadets of the U.S. Military Academy, West Point, N.Y., June, 1883* (West Point, N.Y.: U.S. Military Academy, 1883), p. 28; "William Mason Wright," *Who Was Who–The Military,* p. 649; "William Mason Wright," in Davis, *Generals in Khaki,* pp. 394–95.

Halsey E. Yates (13 May 1876–19 March 1963). Yates completed one year (1894–1895) at the University of Nebraska before enrolling at the Military Academy in June 1895 along with Nebraska classmate Evan Humphrey. Yates graduated from the USMA in February 1899 and was commissioned in the 5th Infantry. He served with his regiment in Cuba (1899–1900) and then in the Philippines (September 1900–1902). He was an instructor in the Department of Law at the Military Academy (1902–1906) before being promoted to captain and serving in Cuba (1906–1909). He returned to the University of Nebraska in September 1909 as the commandant of cadets. In July 1912 he was assigned to the 30th Infantry at the Presidio of San Francisco and remained with the regiment until January 1916, when he became the U.S. military attaché to Romania through January 1920. Yates was in charge of American observers on the Russian-Romanian front in South Russia and Hungary during World War I. From August to December 1919 he directed the reorganization of the Hungarian police and gendarmerie. He commanded Fort Ontario, New York (1920–1921), and then was at the Infantry School, Fort Benning, Georgia, when he was promoted to colonel in October 1921. He commanded the 6th Infantry Regiment and the post at Jefferson Barracks, Missouri (1922–1923), and then the Atlantic Branch, U.S. Disciplinary Barracks, at Governor's Island, New York (1924–1930). He retired from active duty as a colonel in May 1940 but organized the Home Guard of Los Angeles (June–

December 1940) at the request of the adjutant general of the state of California. He was recalled to active duty in December 1940 as chief of the Southern California Reserve District until January 1942. From December 1945 to 1950 he was the disaster coordinator for the city of Los Angeles.

Samuel B. M. Young (9 January 1840–1 September 1924). Born in Pittsburgh, Young received his education at Jefferson College (now Washington and Jefferson College) at Washington, Pennsylvania. With the outbreak of the Civil War, he enlisted in Company K, 12th Pennsylvania Infantry, but was soon commissioned a captain in the 4th Pennsylvania Cavalry in September. He rose through the volunteer ranks to reach brigadier general, USV, on 9 April 1865. He joined the Regular Army as a second lieutenant in the 12th Infantry in May 1866 but soon took an appointment as captain in the 8th Cavalry that July. During his years on the frontier, Young saw extensive action against various Indian tribes. He transferred to the 3d Cavalry as a major in April 1883 and was appointed lieutenant colonel with the 4th Cavalry stationed at the Presidio of San Francisco in August 1892. As part of his duties with the 4th Cavalry he was acting superintendent of Yosemite Park (now Yosemite National Park), California, in 1896. He returned to the 3d Cavalry as colonel and commander in June 1897, and again one of his duties was to act as superintendent of a national park, this time Yellowstone Park (June–November 1897). At the opening of the Spanish-American War Young was commissioned as a brigadier general of volunteers and placed in command of the 2d Brigade of Joseph Wheeler's dismounted Cavalry Division at Chickamauga, Georgia, and Tampa, Florida. By the time the 2d Brigade departed Tampa for Cuba it consisted of the Regular Army's 1st and 10th Cavalry Regiments and the 1st U.S. Volunteer Cavalry, the "Rough Riders" under Leonard Wood and Theodore Roosevelt. Young commanded the brigade in Cuba during the early days of the Santiago Campaign and at the Battle of Las Guasimas on 24 June 1898. Young then fell ill, probably with yellow fever, and Leonard Wood replaced him in command of the 2d Brigade before the attack on Kettle Hill (1 July) and San Juan Hill (2 July). Young then moved to command of the 1st Division, II Army Corps, at Augusta, Georgia, until he assumed command of the corps itself from 2 November 1898 through its disbandment early in May 1899. Young was sent to the Philippines in July 1899, where he served as commander of the cavalry brigade in Henry Lawton's 1st Division, VIII Corps, during operations against Emilio Aguinaldo in northern Luzon. He then served as military governor of the 1st District, Department of Northern Luzon, and was promoted to brigadier general in January 1900 and to major general in February 1901. Upon his return to the United States that month, he took command of the Department of California and also served as president of the War College Board, the predecessor and planner of the new War Department General Staff (1901–1902) being formed as part of Secretary of War Elihu Root's reform program. From July 1902 to July 1903 he served as the first president of the newly established Army War College and as a member of the committee to select the members of the initial War Department General Staff. In July 1903 he was appointed to replace Nelson Miles as commanding general, U.S. Army, which he did early in August 1903 before becoming the first chief of staff, U.S. Army (15 August 1903–8 January 1904). After retirement, Young again served as superintendent at Yellowstone National Park (1907–1908) and as governor of the Soldiers' Home in Washington (1910–1920). "Samuel Baldwin Marks Young," *Webster's American Military Biographies,* pp. 494–95; "Samuel Baldwin Marks Young," *Who Was Who–The Military,* p. 651; TAGO, *OAR, 1901,* p. 348; TAGO, *OAR, 1916,* p. 531; "Samuel Baldwin Marks Young, Lieutenant General, United States Army," http://www.arlingtoncemetery.net/sbmyoung.htm; "Superintendents," Yellowstone National Park, http://www.secretyellowstone.com/basic-park-information/superintendents.

Acknowledgments

I wish to acknowledge all of the assistance and support that I have received during my years of work on this project. Above all, the encouragement and support of Dr. Roger Cirillo, director of the Association of the United States Army's Book Program, have been critical to my success from the very beginning. Linda Hein of the Nebraska State Historical Society in Lincoln was untiring in her efforts to answer my inquiries and supply information about Pershing's time at the University of Nebraska. Jennifer Payne, archives assistant at the Norwich University Archives and Special Collections in Northfield, Vermont, was most generous in providing information and materials on Colonel Frank Tompkins, who played a critical role in the Mexican Expedition. Waldette Cueto of the American Historical Collection at Rizal Library, Ateneo de Manila University, in Quezon City, Philippines, responded faithfully to my questions about American personnel in the Philippine Scouts and Constabulary. Over a number of years now, the staff members of the Manuscript Division of the Library of Congress have always been not only helpful but also completely understanding to my many requests for assistance. To them I offer my thanks for safeguarding what Jack Pershing has left to the American people. What they have done for Pershing's textual records, the staff at the Library of Congress's Prints and Photographs Division has done for his numerous images.

My special thanks go to Stephen Wrinn and his exceptional staff at the University Press of Kentucky for their infinite patience in working with me on this manuscript. As always, their editorial and publication production skills have made this manuscript into a fine book. I must also add Derik Shelor, my editor, whose fine eye fortunately caught many problems I overlooked. Most of all, I want to thank my wife, Mary Ann, who suffered through my numerous trips to the Library of Congress and my endless hours of working through the manuscript, for her perseverance, good cheer, and love during what must have seemed like a never-ending project.

Notes

Editor's Note

1. "Autobiography of General of the Armies John J. Pershing," in the Papers of General John J. Pershing, Manuscript Division, Library of Congress (hereafter cited as LC/Pershing Papers), Box 429. There are six duplicate copies of the "Autobiography," two in each of three boxes (429–431). As explained in the Introduction, the "Autobiography" was compiled at an unknown date from various drafts of chapters found in other boxes in Pershing's papers.

Introduction

1. See Frank E. Vandiver, *Black Jack: The Life and Times of John J. Pershing*, 2 vols. (College Station: Texas A&M Univ. Press, 1977) (hereafter cited as *Black Jack* and volume); Donald Smythe, *Guerrilla Warrior: The Early Life of John J. Pershing* (New York: Charles Scribner's Sons, 1973); Donald Smythe, *Pershing: General of the Armies* (Bloomington: Indiana Univ. Press, 2007); Gene Smith, *Until the Last Trumpet Sounds: The Life of General of the Armies John J. Pershing* (New York: John Wiley and Sons, 1998); Jim Lacey, *Pershing: A Biography* (New York: Palgrave Macmillan, 2008); Richard O'Connor, *Black Jack Pershing* (Garden City, N.Y.: Doubleday, 1961); and Richard Goldhurst, *Pipeclay and Drill: John J. Pershing, the Classic American Soldier* (New York: Reader's Digest Press, 1977). In addition to full biographies, numerous authors of more narrowly focused works, such as Herbert Molloy Mason Jr., in his *The Great Pursuit: General John J. Pershing's Punitive Expedition across the Rio Grande to Destroy the Mexican Bandit Pancho Villa* (New York: Random House, 1970), and James R. Arnold, *The Moro War: How America Battled Muslim Insurgency in the Philippine Jungle, 1902-1913* (New York: Bloomsbury Press, 2011), have utilized chapters of the unpublished manuscript.

2. See letters, Pershing to Charles B. Elliott, 26 October 1926, and Elliott to Pershing, 13 November 1926, LC/Pershing Papers, Box 70, Folder: Judge Charles B. Elliott; and letter, Elliott to Pershing, 17 November 1926, LC/Pershing Papers, Box 370, Folder: Governor of Moro Province (2).

3. George E. Adamson (20 March 1875–5 October 1957). Adamson served as Pershing's civilian army field clerk in Mexico and then France from 29 August 1916 to 21 December 1917, when he was commissioned a first lieutenant, Adjutant General Corps, in the National Army. He was promoted to captain in October 1918 and was converted to captain, Quartermaster Corps, in July 1920. In 1922 he was awarded a Distinguished Service Medal for his work as confidential secretary to General Pershing

in France during and after the war. He was subsequently discharged as a captain and reappointed as a first lieutenant in 1922 and captain in 1924. He remained on active duty as Pershing's secretary until 28 March 1939, when he was promoted to colonel and made military secretary to Pershing by an Act of Congress. He retired on 31 March and was recalled to active duty on 1 July 1939 and remained with Pershing until his death in July 1948, closing the general's office on 31 December 1949. U.S. War Department, The Adjutant General's Office (TAGO), *Official Army Register, January 1, 1941* (Washington, D.C.: GPO, 1941) (hereafter cited as TAGO, *OAR,* and year of publication), p. 958; TAGO, *OAR, 1 January 1950,* vol. 1, *United States Army Active and Retired Lists,* p. 641; TAGO, *American Decorations: A List of Awards of the Congressional Medal of Honor, the Distinguished Service Cross, and the Distinguished Service Medal Awarded under Authority of the Congress of the United States, 1862-1926* (Washington, D.C.: GPO, 1927) (hereafter cited as TAGO, *American Decorations, 1862-1926*), p. 669; "George Edwin Adamson," Department of Veterans' Affairs, Nationwide Gravesite Locator, http://gravelocator.cem.va.gov/j2ee/servlet/NGL_v1.

4. Ralph A. Curtin (22 February 1894-12 November 1972). Curtin enlisted in the U.S. Army in September 1917 and was later sent to France, where he joined Pershing's GHQ staff. He was later commissioned in the Adjutant General Corps. He remained on the staff until Pershing's death in July 1948 and thereafter worked as secretary of the U.S. District Court in Washington. He was promoted to colonel, U.S. Army Reserve, prior to his retirement in the 1960s. "Ralph Augustine Curtin," Ancestry.com, http://search.ancestry.com/.

5. Charles B. Shaw (1 October 1893-16 December 1971). Shaw was hired as an acting army field clerk when the country entered the war and accompanied Pershing to France. He spent the war years on Pershing's administrative staff at Chaumont and returned with him to the United States in 1919. He remained a civilian senior army field clerk with Pershing until April 1926, when all field clerks in the army were given commissions as warrant officers. He was on Pershing's personal office staff until the late 1930s, when he was commissioned in the Organized Reserves and moved over to work for Pershing at the Washington office of the American Battle Monuments Commission. He rose to be the head of the ABMC's Washington office and the comptroller. He retired from the Army Reserve as a colonel on 31 October 1954 and was recalled to active duty annually in his former rank and position until he retired from the ABMC in the late 1960s. TAGO, *OAR, 1960,* vol. 2-3, p. 505; "Charles Burnham Shaw," Department of Veterans' Affairs, Nationwide Gravesite Locator, http://gravelocator.cem.va.gov/j2ee/servlet/NGL_v1; interview, Dr. John T. Greenwood with Mr. Russell Shaw, 16 December 2011.

6. See Appendix A: "Personnel of the *Baltic* Party," in James G. Harbord, *The American Army in France, 1917-1919* (Boston: Little, Brown, 1936), p. 581.

7. *Army Times,* eds., *The Yanks Are Coming: The Story of General John J. Pershing* (New York: G. P. Putnam's Sons, 1961), p. 166.

8. For the routing slip used in processing the manuscript, see "My Experiences in the World War, draft Chapters 1–10," LC/Pershing Papers, Box 363.

9. An extensive draft written on the back of United States Lines' stationery can be found in LC/Pershing Papers, Box 374.

10. As an example of this, see especially Pershing to Shaw, January 1937, LC/Pershing Papers, Box 373, Folder: Miscellaneous Notes (1), and Shaw to Pershing,

8 February 1937, LC/Pershing Papers, Box 384, untitled folder on memoirs; and Memo, Pershing to Adamson and Shaw, n.d., and Shaw to Adamson, "General Pershing's Manuscript," n.d., LC/Pershing Papers, Box 384, untitled folder on memoirs. On the Funston messages, see LC/Pershing Papers, Box 372, Punitive Expedition Reports (1).

11. See Vandiver, *Black Jack,* vol. 1, p. 443 n 8; Frankie and John Pershing, "Notes on Leave 1908 up to Paris—Vladivostock, Moscow, & Berlin, Brussels, Paris," entry for 24 August 1908, p. 3, LC/Pershing Papers, Box 2.

12. Pershing, 1934 memo book, LC/Pershing Papers, Box 428.

13. Frederick Moore (17 November 1877–?). Moore was born in New Orleans and began working as a correspondent in Washington in 1900. He then worked as a foreign correspondent for the *New York Times, London Times,* Associated Press, and Reuter's in London, the Balkans, Morocco, Turkey, Moscow, and China. In 1917 he returned to New York and became the managing editor of *Asia* magazine. He attended the Paris Peace Conference in 1919 and the League of Nations Assembly in Geneva, Switzerland, in 1920. Moore was then foreign counselor at the Japanese Ministry of Foreign Affairs (1921–1926) and a member of the Japanese delegation at the League of Nations meeting on the Manchuria crisis (1932–1933). He then left the Japanese service and settled in Washington, where he worked briefly on Pershing's memoirs (1934–1935) and did freelance writing. He returned to work for the Japanese Foreign Ministry in Washington from sometime after 1935 until the U.S. entry into the war in December 1941. He authored a number of volumes based on his foreign work, including *The Balkan Trail* (1906), *Chaos in Europe* (1919), and *With Japan's Leaders* (1942). *Who Was Who in America,* vol. 5, *1969-1973,* p. 508; "Author Gets Tokio Post," *New York Times,* 27 May 1921; Robert G. Woolbert, Book Review: "*With Japan's Leaders," Foreign Affairs* (October 1942), http://www.foreignaffairs .com/articles/105241/frederick-moore/with-japans-leaders.

14. Moore's draft is in LC/Pershing Papers, Box 375.

15. George E. Adamson to Frederick Moore, 12 January 1935, LC/Pershing Papers, Box 138, Correspondence: Frederick Moore.

16. Adamson to Moore, 12 January 1935, and Adamson to Moore, 4 February 1935, LC/Pershing Papers, Box 138, Correspondence: Frederick Moore.

17. Moore to Pershing, 12 January 1935, LC/Pershing Papers, Box 138, Correspondence: Frederick Moore.

18. Pershing to Moore, 16 January 1935, LC/Pershing Papers, Box 138, Correspondence: Frederick Moore.

19. Charles B. Shaw to Pershing, 4 February 1935, LC/Pershing Papers, Box 379, Folder: Chapters 18, 19, 20.

20. Shaw to Pershing, 5 March 1935, LC/Pershing Papers, Box 384, untitled folder on memoirs.

21. Pershing to Shaw, 5 June 1935, LC/Pershing Papers, Box 384, untitled folder on memoirs. Emphases are in the original correspondence.

22. On 13 June 1934 George Adamson sent one such inquiry to then Lieutenant Colonel (later Major General) James L. Collins, who had served as Pershing's aide on four separate occasions in the Moro Province, the Mexican Expedition, and in France, asking for any stories or diaries he may have on the Mexican Expedition that he could share. Collins replied on 29 June with some experiences that he recalled

from his days with Pershing in Mexico. Letter, Adamson to Collins, 13 June 1934, LC/Pershing Papers, Box 49, Correspondence: James L. Collins, and Letter, Collins to Adamson, 29 June 1934, LC/Pershing Papers, Box 372, Punitive Expedition (2), pt. 1.

23. Adamson to Brigadier General Henry H. Whitney, 28 June and 5 July 1935; Adamson to Brigadier General James A. Ryan, 12 July 1935; Adamson to Brigadier General M. H. Barnum, 10 August 1935; Adamson to Colonel W. W. Gordon and Colonel James L. Collins, 12 July 1935, LC/Pershing Papers, Box 384, untitled folder on memoirs.

24. Whitney to Adamson, 2 July 1935, LC/Pershing Papers, Box 384, untitled folder on memoirs.

25. James A. Ryan to Adamson, 10 September 1935, LC/Pershing Papers, Box 384, untitled folder on memoirs.

26. Brigadier General Malvern Hill Barnum to Adamson, 16 August 1935, LC/Pershing Papers, Box 384, untitled folder on memoirs.

27. See draft chapter VIII, p. 7, "Autobiography," in LC/Pershing Papers, Box 429.

28. Gordon to Adamson, 12 October 1935, Collins to Pershing, 4 January 1936, and Collins to Adamson, 7 January 1936, LC/Pershing Papers, Box 384, untitled folder on memoirs.

29. Shaw to Pershing, 1 July 1935, LC/Pershing Papers, Box 379, Folder: Chapters 18, 19, 20. Emphasis is in the original correspondence.

30. Shaw to Pershing, 12 August 1935, LC/Pershing Papers, Box 379, Folder: Chapters 18, 19, 20.

31. Shaw to Pershing, 4 February and 1 July 1935, LC/Pershing Papers, Box 379, Folder: Chapters 18, 19, 20; various drafts of chapters, LC/Pershing Papers, Boxes 373–80.

32. Charles B. Shaw's comments on draft memoirs, LC/Pershing Papers, Box 374, Memoirs, pp. 122–73.

33. Shaw, Memo, n.d., LC/Pershing Papers, Box 384, untitled folder on memoirs.

34. Memo, Pershing to Adamson and Shaw, n.d., LC/Pershing Papers, Box 384, untitled folder on memoirs.

35. Shaw to Adamson, "General Pershing's Manuscript," n.d., LC/Pershing Papers, Box 384, untitled folder on memoirs. Emphasis is in the original correspondence.

36. Shaw to Adamson, "General Pershing's Manuscript," n.d., LC/Pershing Papers, Box 384, untitled folder on memoirs. On Shaw's memo Adamson annotated "Approved G. E. A."

37. Pershing to Shaw, January 1937, LC/Pershing Papers, Box 373, Folder: Miscellaneous Notes (1).

38. Shaw to Pershing, 8 February 1937, LC/Pershing Papers, Box 384, untitled folder on memoirs.

39. Comment on title page, Chapter 17, LC/Pershing Papers, Box 380.

40. Moore to Pershing, 5 November 1939, LC/Pershing Papers, Box 138, Correspondence: Frederick Moore.

41. Moore to Pershing, 5 November 1939, LC/Pershing Papers, Box 138, Correspondence: Frederick Moore.

42. Pershing to Moore, 6 December 1939, LC/Pershing Papers, Box 138, Correspondence: Frederick Moore.

43. See "Last Drafts," in LC/Pershing Papers, Box 385.

44. See Chapters 1–9 versus Chapter 10–23 and Epitome, in LC/Pershing Papers Box 385; Memo, Pershing to Adamson and Shaw, n.d., and Shaw to Adamson, "General Pershing's Manuscript," n.d., LC/Pershing Papers, Box 384, untitled folder on memoirs.

45. See the final paragraph of chapter 21, in "Corrected Drafts 1934–35," LC/Pershing Papers, Box 379.

1. Ancestry and Boyhood

1. Western Reserve. The Western Reserve was approximately six thousand square miles of territory on the south shore of Lake Erie in what is now northeastern Ohio, including the city and suburbs of Cleveland and as far south as Akron and Youngstown. The colony of Connecticut had a colonial claim dating from a 1662 Royal charter for a wide expansion of unsettled lands in the West. When the United States came into existence, all of the new states except Connecticut gave over their land charters and claims to the new federal government. Connecticut "reserved" part of its claim for future compensation of its citizens for losses during the Revolutionary War. In 1800 Connecticut agreed to the inclusion of the "Connecticut Western Reserve" within the Ohio Territory (State of Ohio, 1803). "Western Reserve," Encyclopaedia Britannica Online, http://www.britannica.com/EBchecked/topic/640785/Western-Reserve; "Connecticut Western Reserve," Ohio Historical Society, Ohio History Central, http://ohiohistorycentral.org/entry.php?rec=691.

2. For more details of the Pershing family and its genealogical history in America, see Edgar J. Pershing, *The Pershing Family in America: A Collection of Historical and Genealogical Data, Family Portraits, Traditions, Legends and Military Records* (Philadelphia: George S. Ferguson, 1924). For John J. Pershing's direct family, see pp. 211–13, 404–5.

3. Palatinate. The historical Rhenish Palatinate in Germany included the Lower (Rhenish) Palatinate (on both sides of the middle Rhine River, from the Main to the Necker River), with its capital at Heidelberg, and the Upper Palatinate in northern Bavaria stretching to Bohemia. The area was often conquered and divided among various German and foreign rulers, and the Rhenish areas had close ties to France and Lorraine and Alsace, which it bordered. Since World War II, the Land (state) of Rhineland-Palatinate (Rheinland-Pfalz, or simply the Pfalz), with its capital at Mainz, was established largely in the former Rhenish Palatinate on the western side of the Rhine and bordering France, Luxembourg, and Belgium. "Palatinate," Encyclopaedia Britannica Online, http://www.britannica.com/EBchecked/topic/439207/Palatinate, and "Rhineland-Palatinate," http://www.britannica.com/EBchecked/topic/501375/Rhineland-Palatinate.

4. In the original manuscript, the figure for St. Louis's population in 1857 was left blank, to be added later, which it was not. I could find no figure for St. Louis's population in 1857, but selected 1860 as the best possible date for an accurate figure. St. Louis's population expanded from 77,860 in 1850 to 160,733 in 1860 according to the Seventh (1850) and Eighth (1860) U.S. Censuses. See J. D. B. DeBow, *Statistical*

View of the United States . . . Being a Compendium of the Seventh Census . . . (Washington, D.C.: Beverley Tucker, 1854), p. 398; Joseph C. G. Kennedy, *Population in the United States in 1860; Compiled from the Original Returns of the Eighth Census under the Direction of the Secretary of the Interior* (Washington, D.C.: GPO, 1864), pp. xxxii and 297.

5. Even at this late date in his life, Pershing maintained that his date of birth was 13 September 1860 although Father Donald Smythe has provided other information that strongly suggests Pershing's actual date of birth was probably 13 January 1860. Smythe concluded from available evidence that Pershing himself altered his actual date of birth so that he would meet the age standard (no older than twenty-two years of age at the time of admission) for the U.S. Military Academy when he entered as a cadet in the summer of 1882. See Donald Smythe, "Pershing's Falsified Birthday," *Guerrilla Warrior: The Early Life of John J. Pershing* (New York: Charles Scribner's Sons, 1973), pp. 283–84.

6. John J. Pershing's surviving brothers and sisters were Mary Elizabeth (Pershing) Butler (10 June 1864–14 December 1928), Anna May Pershing (30 June 1867–1955?), Grace (Pershing) Paddock (29 March 1869–25 April 1904); James F. Pershing (18 January 1862–9 February 1933), and Ward B. Pershing (29 March 1874–28 August 1909). Twin sisters Ruth and Rose, born in 1872, died in infancy, as did a brother, Frederick, who was born and died in 1876. See Pershing, *The Pershing Family in America,* pp. 404–5.

7. Bleeding Kansas. During the 1850s, the bitter conflict between abolitionist free-staters and pro-slavery forces on the border of Missouri and the Kansas Territory turned extremely bloody as these groups clashed over the admission of a new State of Kansas as a free or slave state. In the wake of the Kansas-Nebraska Act of 1854, which permitted the citizens of the Kansas Territory to determine whether the future state would be free or slave, free-staters and abolitionists, including John Brown and his followers, pushed into northern Missouri and the Kansas Territory. Armed pro-slavery forces in Missouri, known as "Border Ruffians," opposed the armed free-staters, known as "Jayhawkers," who were against slavery in the proposed new state (see "Jayhawkers" and "Bushwhackers" below). Pro- and anti-slavery factions soon clashed violently and frequently. Pro-slavery guerrillas attacked and sacked Lawrence, Kansas, in 1856, and John Brown's abolitionist group killed pro-slavery neighbors in the Pottowatomie Massacre in retaliation. These attacks resulted in serious loss of life and destruction of property, hence the term "Bleeding Kansas" for this vicious "Border War." This bloody conflict continued at a fever pitch throughout much of the Civil War. Kansas entered the United States as the thirty-fourth state, a free state, in 1861. "Kansas," Encyclopaedia Britannica Online, http://www.britannica.com/EBchecked/topic/311297/Kansas, "Missouri," http://www.britannica.com/EBchecked/topic/385713/Missouri, and "Bleeding Kansas," http://www.britannica.com/EBchecked/topic/69220/Bleeding-Kansas; Richard B. Morris, ed., *Encyclopedia of American History* (New York: Harper and Brothers, 1953), pp. 218–22; "Border War," in Frank W. Blackmar, ed., *Kansas: A Cyclopedia of State History, Embracing Events, Institutions, Industries, Counties, Cities, Towns, Prominent Persons, Etc.,* vol. 1 (Chicago: Standard Publishing Company, 1912), pp. 207–12, available at http://archive.org/details/kansascyc01blac/.

8. Border Ruffians. During the period of "Bleeding Kansas" and "Border War" in the middle and late 1850s, pro-slavery guerrilla forces were formed in

Missouri known as "Border Ruffians." They fought the free-staters and the "Jay-hawkers" (see below) who were violently against slavery and settling in the Kansas Territory. "Kansas," Encyclopaedia Britannica Online, http://www.britannica .com/EBchecked/topic/311297/Kansas; "Missouri," http://www.britannica.com/ EBchecked/topic/385713/Missouri; "Bleeding Kansas," http://www.britannica .com/EBchecked/topic/69220/Bleeding-Kansas; Morris, *Encyclopedia of American History,* pp. 219, 220; "Border Ruffians," in Blackmar, ed., *Kansas,* vol. 1, p. 207, available at http://archive.org/details/kansascyc01blac/.

9. Jayhawkers. The exact origin of the term Jayhawkers remains uncertain. Originally derived from the time of "Bleeding Kansas" and the "Border War" in the 1850s, "Jayhawkers" referred to free-state, anti-slavery guerrilla fighters and bands from the Kansas Territory. These bands fought against pro-slavery groups of Border Ruffians from the neighboring slave state, Missouri, before and during the Civil War. During the Civil War, the 7th Kansas Regiment was known as the "Jayhawkers." The Jayhawk was a mythical bird supposed to be a cross between the blue jay and sparrow hawk and today is often used as a nickname for the State of Kansas, the University of Kansas athletic teams, and Kansas residents and products. "Jayhawkers," in Blackmar, ed., *Kansas,* vol. 2, pp. 21–22, available at http://archive.org/details/ kansascycloped02blac/.

10. Sutler. Sutlers were civilian merchants who supplied a wide variety of goods and services to U.S. soldiers, whom they supported from the Revolutionary War until the twentieth century. Classed among a large group of "camp followers," which included prostitutes but also the wives and families of soldiers, sutlers at military posts, camps, and stations provided food, clothing, tobacco, coffee, alcohol, laundry services, and other goods and services that the U.S. Army did not supply to individual officers and enlisted men. In the twentieth century, military post and base exchanges replaced these civilian sutlers. See Holly A. Mayer, "Camp Followers," in *The Oxford Guide to American Military History,* ed. John W. Chambers II, p. 100 (New York: Oxford Univ. Press, 1999); James T. Delisi, "From Sutlers and Canteens to Exchanges," *Army Logistician,* November–December 2007, at http://www.alu.army .mil/alog/issues/NovDec07/canteen2_exchange.html.

11. Bushwhackers. From 1862 to 1864, a vicious war was waged between Confederate (pro-slavery) and Union (abolitionist) guerrilla and irregular bands along the Missouri-Kansas border and in northern Missouri. While the Kansas irregular forces aligned with the Union were generally known as Jayhawkers, the Confederate bands became known as "bushwhackers" because they often ambushed and killed their opponents. Among the most notorious of the southern bushwhackers were William C. Quantrill, William "Bloody Bill" Anderson, Frank and Jesse James, the Younger brothers, and Clifton D. Holtzclaw. Some of these men, such as "Captain" Holtzclaw, claimed military rank, but none of them apparently had been commissioned officially in the Confederate States Army. After the Civil War, many of these men continued their violent ways as bandits, bank and train robbers, and murderers. "Bushwhackers" and "Guerrillas," in Blackmar, ed., *Kansas,* vol. 1, pp. 263 and 797–99, available at http://archive.org/details/kansascyc01blac/.

12. "Best bib and tucker." This phrase derived from two items of women's clothing of the seventeenth to nineteenth centuries. It originated in eighteenth-century France and really referred to wearing one's finest clothes on special occasions. See

The Phrase Finder, "Best bib and tucker," http://www.phrases.org.uk/meanings/best-bib-and-tucker.html.

13. McGuffey's Readers. William H. McGuffey (23 September 1800–4 May 1873) was the editor of one of the most widely used and read school textbooks in the history of American education. A Presbyterian minister, he was appointed professor of languages at Miami University, Oxford, Ohio, in 1826 and married the next year. The father of five children, he was a firm believer in Christian religious education, ethical behavior, and morality. Upon the recommendation of Harriet Beecher Stowe, a close friend, the Cincinnati, Ohio, publishing firm of Truman and Smith asked McGuffey to prepare a series of four graded "Eclectic Readers" in 1835. The first two and a primer were completed and published in 1836, and the third and fourth in 1837. McGuffey's brother Alexander completed a fifth volume in 1844, a spelling book appeared in 1846, and a sixth reader in 1857. Each of the illustrated readers contained stories, essays, poems, speeches, and excerpts from noted writers of the day for a special school learning level. After 1857 the books were entitled *McGuffey's Eclectic Readers,* or simply *McGuffey's Readers.* By this time McGuffey had held already several other important academic positions, including president of Cincinnati College (1836–1839) and Miami University (1839–1843), and had moved to the University of Virginia as chair of the Department of Moral Philosophy (1845 until his death). More than 60 million copies of the *Readers* were sold by 1879, and that total now numbers more than 130 million copies. Interestingly, all of *McGuffey's Readers* remain in print and available for purchase. Obviously, *McGuffey's Readers* made as significant an impression on young John J. Pershing as they did upon generations of American schoolchildren from 1836 through the 1920s. They helped to shape American morals and character and the nation itself during these years. See Ohio Historical Society, "William H. McGuffey," http://www.ohiohistorycentral.org/entry.php?rec=263; Miami University, "William Holmes McGuffey Museum," http://www.units.muohio.edu/mcguffeymuseum/learn_more/readers.html; McGuffey's Readers World, "History of McGuffey Readers," http://www.mcguffeyreaders.com/history.htm.

14. Beadle's dime novels. Erastus F. Beadle and Beadle & Adams, Publishers, began selling short, illustrated paperback novels with attention-grabbing, brightly colored covers emphasizing adventure, daring-do, and the "wild west" in 1860 as part of the "Beadle's Dime Novels" series. These short (one-hundred-page) adventure novels appeared frequently and cost a mere 10 cents. They especially appealed to adolescents. Beadle introduced a series of "Nickel Novels" as well as other series, and a number of publishers were soon producing hundreds of similar novels. The dime novels craze died out by the turn of the century, but the Library of Congress today has a collection of nearly forty thousand titles. For the most comprehensive treatment of Beadle's publications and dime novels, see Albert Johannsen, "The House of Beadle and Adams and Its Dime and Nickel Novels: The Story of a Vanished Literature," Northern Illinois University Libraries, at http://www.ulib.niu.edu/badndp/bibindex.html; Library of Congress, "Dime Novels," at http://www.loc.gov/exhibits/treasures/tri015.html.

2. Youth—Its Happy Days and Others

1. Pickaninies. An offensive, pejorative term often used to refer to Negro children. See *Webster's Encyclopedic Unabridged Dictionary of the English Language* (New York: Gramercy Books, 1989), p. 1089.

2. Quarter sections. After the Revolutionary War, the new federal government became responsible for the vast lands west of the Appalachian mountains that were claimed by the thirteen former colonies. Before the land could be distributed to veterans or sold, it had to be surveyed. The Land Ordinance of 1785 and the Northwest Ordinance of 1787 established a systematic survey of these lands based on a rectangular survey system that is today called the Public Land Survey System (PLSS). This system divided the land into six-square-mile townships, which were divided into 36 one-square-mile sections of 640 acres each. Each section was then divided again into quarter sections (160 acres), quarter-quarter sections (80 acres), and even smaller lots, and federal, state, and local government sections. The Homestead Act (20 May 1862) allowed citizens to claim 160 acres of surveyed and unclaimed public land in return for complying with provisions on residency, claims, deeds, and improvements. See U.S. National Archives and Records Administration, National Atlas of the United States, "The Public Land Survey System (PLSS)," http://www.nationalatlas.gov/articles/boundaries/a_plss.html; National Archives and Records Administration, "Teaching with Documents: The Homestead Act of 1862," http://www.archives.gov/education/lessons/homestead-act/.

3. Depression of 1873. Probably better known as the "Panic of 1873," this depression began with the failure of the banking firm of Jay Cooke and Company on 18 September 1873 due to its overextension to finance the construction of the Northern Pacific Railroad. Cooke's collapse soon pulled down the stock and bond markets and set off reverberations that quickly spread throughout the entire banking and financial system and the economy. Overexpansion and rampant speculation in western railroad construction, industry, and farming underlay this economic downturn that falling demand for American farm products in Europe greatly exaggerated. The resulting depression that lasted to 1878 produced significant business closures and high unemployment at a time when monetary policy and currency were also being hotly debated. Morris, *Encyclopedia of American History,* pp. 251, 431, 645–46; Robert E. Riegel, *The Story of the Western Railroads: From 1852 through the Reign of the Giants* (Lincoln: Univ. of Nebraska Press, 1964), pp. 126–30; William J. Schultz and M. R. Caine, *Financial Development of the United States* (New York: Prentice-Hall, 1937), pp. 367–77.

4. Doxology. The doxology in the Protestant tradition and church to which John Pershing then belonged would probably have been as follows: "Praise God, from whom all blessings flow; Praise him, all creatures here below; Praise him above, ye heavenly host; Praise Father, Son, and Holy Ghost. Amen." "Doxology," Encyclopaedia Britannica Online, http://www.britannica.com/EBchecked/topic/170553/doxology.

5. What Pershing does not mention here is that he first taught at the Laclede Negro School from August to November 1878 before applying for the position at Prairie Mound School, where he began teaching in November. See Smythe, *Guerrilla Warrior,* p. 6; Vandiver, *Black Jack,* vol. 1, pp. 13–14.

6. The normal school (teacher's college) at Kirksville underwent a series of official name changes as it grew and changed over the years after Dr. Joseph Baldwin founded it as a private school in 1867. It was first named the North Missouri Normal School and Commercial College (1867–1868), then North Missouri Normal School (1868–1870). After it came under state control, it was called Missouri State Normal School for the First District (or more commonly as First District Normal School) (1870–1919), Northeast Missouri State Teachers College (or unofficially Kirksville State Teachers College) (1919–1968), Northeast Missouri State College (1968–1972), Northeast Missouri State University (1972–1996), and finally Truman State University (1996–present). See Appendix A, "Institutional Names throughout the Years," and Appendix B, "Presidents," in David C. Nichols, *Founding the Future: A History of Truman State University* (Kirksville, Mo.: Truman State University, 2007), pp. 316, 317.

3. West Point—Its Grind and Its Pleasures

1. Greenback Party. The Greenback Party, also known as the Independent Party, the National Party, and the Greenback Labor Party, grew out of the "Greenback movement" of the late 1860s and early 1870s. It was active from 1874 to 1884 and mainly coalesced in 1874 as a reaction to the Panic of 1873. Its name was derived from the paper currency, called "greenbacks" because of their color, issued by the U.S. government without the backing of gold during and after the Civil War. Many of the "Greenbackers" were farmers who had been hard hit in the Panic of 1873 and were against shifting from paper money to species (silver or gold) as the basis for the monetary system. They wanted greater circulation of paper currency and unlimited silver coinage. They believed that this would improve prices for agricultural products and allow debtors, especially farmers, to pay off their debts. The Greenback Party elected fourteen members to Congress in 1878 and ran presidential tickets in 1876, 1880, and 1884. By 1884 the party was largely finished as a political force and elected but one member to Congress and then ran its last presidential candidate in 1888. Morris, *Encyclopedia of American History,* pp. 252, 254–55, 257; Schultz and Caine, *Financial Development of the United States,* pp. 367–77; "Greenback Movement," Encyclopaedia Britannica Online, http://www.britannica.com/EBchecked/topic/245131/Greenback-movement.

2. In the original manuscript Pershing added a footnote here: "As I remember it, this was the number, but a friend of one of the examiners has recently said that this member of the Board told him that seven boys took the examination." Vandiver, *Black Jack,* vol. 1, pp. 21–22 n 43, states that Pershing recalled sixteen in his unpublished memoir and then cited the above footnote as reporting a total of seventeen, which it clearly did not. He cites other sources as reporting the number at fifteen and eighteen. Pershing in his "Greeting to the Class" in a commemorative volume for the twenty-fifth anniversary of the Class of 1886 states that he won his appointment "in a competitive examination with seventeen competitors," which reconfirms his original statement. Avery D. Andrews, ed., *1886-1911: In Commemoration of the 25th Anniversary of Graduation of the Class of '86, U.S.M.A., West Point, June, 1911* (Philadelphia: Holmes Press, 1911), p. 6.

3. According to U.S. Military Academy reports, the Class of 1886 admitted on 1 July of that year numbered 104. An additional 25 cadets were admitted on 1 Septem-

ber 1886, bringing the total of the new cadets (not counting the seven turned back from the Class of 1885) to 129. Avery D. Andrews, a classmate of Pershing's, noted that candidates for admission to the Military Academy were examined upon arrival and those who passed were admitted to the new class. In his *My Friend and Classmate John J. Pershing*, he listed 141 candidates reporting for examination in June and 42 more in September. Of these 183, 104 were admitted from the June exams and 25 from September for a total Class of 1886 of 129. See U.S. Military Academy, *Official Register of the Officers and Cadets of the U.S. Military Academy at West Point, N.Y. June 1882* (West Point: U.S. Military Academy, June 1882), pp. 19–21; U.S. Military Academy, *Official Register of the Officers and Cadets of the U.S. Military Academy at West Point, N.Y. June 1883* (West Point: U.S. Military Academy, June 1883), p. 19; Avery DeLano Andrews, *My Friend and Classmate John J. Pershing with Notes from My War Diary* (Harrisburg, Pa.: Military Service Publishing Company, 1939), pp. 20–21.

4. Brevet. The U.S. Army's use of brevet ranks until the reorganization of the army in the early twentieth century often produces a considerable amount of confusion. At a time when awards for gallantry and meritorious service did not exist except for the Medal of Honor introduced in July 1862, brevet ranks were awarded both to Regular Army and U.S. Volunteer officers for distinguished gallantry and honorable service during wartime. While the usage of the insignia of brevet rank on uniforms, assignment, and formal address were discontinued after 1870, officers holding brevet ranks were normally addressed by those ranks and were treated accordingly within the army of the time. Thus, Pershing in chapter 4 calls his first commanding officer at the 6th Cavalry "Colonel Eugene A. Carr, Brevet Major General," using both his permanent rank (colonel) and brevet rank (major general). The brevet ranks were purely honorific and conveyed no increase in salary, thus they were a particularly effective and economical way of rewarding distinguished military performance. Paul Andrew Hutton provides a succinct explanation of brevet rank in his *Phil Sheridan and His Army* (Norman: Univ. of Oklahoma Press, 1999), pp. xv–xvi. For a much more detailed account by someone who was himself a brevet major general in the U.S. Army, see Colonel James B. Fry, *The History and Legal Effect of Brevets in the Armies of Great Britain and the United States from Their Origin in 1692 to the Present Time* (New York: D. Van Nostrand, 1877).

5. Cavalry School. Although an army cavalry school had existed at Carlisle Barracks, Pennsylvania, before, during, and after the Civil War (to 1871), the first permanent Army school for advanced training in cavalry organization, operations, and doctrine was established in 1881 when the School of Application for Infantry and Cavalry was opened at Fort Leavenworth, Kansas. The lieutenants assigned were to disseminate what they learned when they returned to their units. A new school specifically designated for training young cavalry officers and enlisted personnel in mounted warfare was authorized in 1887 but not funded and established until 1891–1892, when the School of Application for Cavalry and Light Artillery ("The Cavalry School") opened at Fort Riley, Kansas, which already had a long tradition as a "cavalry" post. Renamed the U.S. Army Mounted Service School in 1907, it reverted once again to the U.S. Army Cavalry School in 1919. The school never left Fort Riley and existed until 31 October 1946, when the U.S. Army did away with its horse cavalry and converted the school into the Ground General School (October 1946–January 1950).

6. Tactical officer or "Tac." At the U.S. Military Academy, there were then and remain today two distinct elements—the academic faculty and the military staff, the latter coming under the commandant of cadets. The commandant was responsible to the superintendent for military order and discipline of all military personnel on the post and in the command and for administrating punishment for breaches of military regulations. The commandant also headed the Department of Tactics, and the officers under him were responsible for tactical instruction in their respective branches of service as well as the maintenance of order and discipline while serving as commanders of a company of cadets. Naturally, these officers were called tactical officers, or "tacs," and retain that nickname today.

7. According to the USMA's *Official Register* for 1886, all but one member of the Class of 1886 graduated (received their diplomas) on 12 June, but none of them were commissioned in their chosen branches of the army until 1 July. That lone cadet was Arthur Johnson, who was awaiting a general court-martial, and the Academic Board refused to grant him his diploma until the trial was completed. Johnson later received his diploma and was commissioned on 28 August. Brevet Major General George W. Cullum, ed., *Biographical Register of the Officers and Graduates of the U.S. Military Academy at West Point N. Y., From Its Establishment, in 1802, to 1890*, 3d ed., revised and extended, vol. 3, *Nos. 2001 to 3384* (Boston: Houghton, Mifflin, 1891) (hereafter cited as Cullum, *Biographical Register 3*), lists everyone, including Johnson, as being cadets from their original entry dates in 1881 or 1882 "to July 1, 1886, when he was graduated and promoted in the Army to . . . ," but Johnson's promotion date to second lieutenant was listed as 28 August. So, there is a gap in time (and some resulting confusion) between graduation and commissioning dates for this class. Incidentally, Arthur Johnson served his entire career in the army before retiring as a colonel in 1925. He received a promotion to the rank of Brigadier General, U.S. Army, retired, in June 1930 in recognition of his holding that rank in the National Army in World War I. U.S. Military Academy, *Official Register of the Officers and Cadets of the U.S. Military Academy at West Point, N.Y., June 1886* (West Point: U.S. Military Academy, June 1886), pp. 10–12; "Class of 1886," Cullum, *Biographical Register 3*, pp. 392–405; "Arthur Johnson," in Captain W. H. Donaldson, ed., *Biographical Register of the Officers and Graduates of the U.S. Military Academy at West Point, New York, Since Its Establishment in 1802,* Supplement, vol. 7, *1920-1930* (Chicago: R. R. Donnelley and Sons, 1931) (hereafter cited as Donaldson, *Biographical Register 7*), pp. 244–45.

8. Brigadier General (Brevet Major General and Major General, USV, in the Civil War) John Gibbon, not General William T. Sherman, delivered the address to the graduating class at the U.S. Military Academy's commencement ceremonies on 12 June 1886. "Good-Bye to West Point: The Class of Eighty-Six Sent into the World. Advice and Memories from Gen. Gibbon," *New York Times*, 13 June 1886; John Gibbon, *Address to the Graduating Class at the U.S. Military Academy, June 12, 1886* (Vancouver Barracks, Washington, D.C.: Headquarters, Department of the Columbia, 1886).

9. Guidons. In the U.S. Army, guidons are small (20 by 27 inches), swallow-tailed military standards designating a variety of military organizations and headquarters, usually a company, battery, or smaller. It carries the unit's branch or corps insignia and colors (for example, Cavalry or Infantry), and identifies the specific subunit

(for example, Company A, 15th Infantry). The guidon is used to designate the unit commander and in the past was used as a rallying point for the unit's personnel in combat as well as other activities. "Guidon (United States)," www.en.wiki.org/wiki/ Guidon_(United_States).

4. The Army—With the Sixth Cavalry in New Mexico

1. Boxer Rebellion. In the late nineteenth century, a violent anti-foreign movement which was known as the "Boxers" (from their Chinese name, "Righteous and Harmonious Fists") began rebellions against the then-ruling Qing dynasty and ever-present foreigners. The ruling empress, Cixi, and powerful groups supported the Boxers in hopes of driving out the foreign powers who had taken control of much of China. Attacks against foreign missionaries and westerners escalated rapidly in 1899–1900, especially in the vicinity of the imperial capital at Peking (Beijing). In June 1900, the violence became so widespread and bloody that the foreign powers formed an international military force to intervene. That month, at Cixi's urging, the Boxers besieged the foreign legations in Beijing. When the international force entered the city on 14 August and freed the legations, the empress and her advisors fled. The Boxer Rebellion was then put down forcefully, and a final agreement was reached in September 1901 granting reparations to the foreign powers. "Boxer Rebellion," Encyclopaedia Britannica Online, http://www.britannica.com/ EBchecked/topic/76364/Boxer-Rebellion.

2. Heliograph. The heliograph was invented by British scientist Sir Henry Mance. It was a visual signaling device using two mirrors so arranged that the light from the sun could be reflected in any direction. A shutter was placed between the mirrors so that a trained operator could form Morse code dots and dashes to transmit messages. "Heliograph (signaling device)," Encyclopaedia Britannica Online, http://www.britannica.com/EBchecked/topic/260046/heliograph.

3. Atchison, Topeka & Santa Fe Railway (AT&SF). Better known as simply "the Santa Fe," the Atchison, Topeka & Santa Fe Railway (AT&SF) was originally established by Cyrus K. Holliday of Topeka, Kansas, as the Atchison & Topeka Railway in 1859. His grander idea was to build a railroad along the old Santa Fe trail linking Independence, Missouri, with Santa Fe, New Mexico, and eventually the Pacific Coast. The rail system grew with the program of federal land grants for railroad rights of way that began after 1862. The sale of these lands provided significant income for the railroad, which in turn used the funds for continued growth and development along its various rail lines and the entire system. Construction began at Topeka, Kansas, in the fall of 1868. By the early 1890s, operating lines extended to Colorado, New Mexico, Texas, Arizona, Illinois, Iowa, Missouri, Nebraska, Oklahoma, and California and had grown to nine thousand miles of track. The Santa Fe had also joined with Fred Harvey to provide resorts, hotels, and restaurants along the routes to attract tourists to places such as the Grand Canyon, which a Santa Fe subsidiary served for many years. By the mid-twentieth century, the system had rail lines and facilities in twelve states and was part of a larger corporation. The "Santa Fe Railway" was a widely recognized rail system that featured "Super Chief" streamliner passenger trains like the "El Capitan" from Chicago to Los Angeles with "domed" observation cars and a bold logo emblazoned with "Santa Fe." As

business shrank, the system contracted and by 1971 had sold its passenger business to Amtrak. In 1995 it merged with Burlington Northern to form the Burlington Northern Santa Fe (BNSF) rail system. Ironically, the "Santa Fe" main line reached Santa Fe only with a branch line due to terrain. Riegel, *The Story of the Western Railroads*, passim; "Atchison, Topeka and Santa Fe Railway Company," Encyclopaedia Britannica Online, http://www.britannica.com/EBchecked/topic/40482/Atchison-Topeka-and-Santa-Fe-Railway; "Railroads," in Blackmar, ed., *Kansas*, vol. 2, pp. 535–48, available at http://archive.org/details/kansascycloped02blac/; "Cyrus Kurtz Holliday," in Blackmar, ed., *Kansas*, vol. 3, pp. 40–44, available at http://archive.org/details/kansascyclopedia03blac/.

4. During this journey, John M. Stotsenburg kept a journal that was only discovered and published in *Arizona and the West* many years after his death in the Philippines on 23 April 1899. See William Swilling Wallace, ed., "Lieutenants Pershing and Stotsenberg [*sic*] Visit the Grand Canyon: 1887," *Arizona and the West* 3, no. 3 (autumn 1961), pp. 265–84.

5. The Sioux Campaign and Commanding Indian Scouts

1. Sibley stoves. Henry Hopkins Sibley (25 May 1816–23 August 1886) graduated from the USMA in 1838 and served in the U.S. Army on the frontier and in the Seminole and Mexican wars. In 1856 he patented a design for a conical tent that was quite similar to the lodges or teepees of the Plains Indians. The Army tested the "Sibley tent" during the Utah expeditions of the winter of 1857–58 and adopted it for use. The tent could accommodate twelve men and their equipment and was used extensively in the Union Army during the Civil War. Sibley also designed a conical sheet iron stove for use in the tents. The "Sibley tent stove" remained in use in the U.S. Army well into the twentieth century and replicas can still be purchased today. Sibley resigned from the U.S. Army in May 1861 and joined the Confederate cause, serving as a brigadier general in Texas and New Mexico without particular distinction. After the war, he served the Khedive of Egypt (1869–1874) before returning to the United States. "Henry H. Sibley," in Mark Mayo Boatner III, *The Civil War Dictionary*, rev. ed. (New York: Vintage Books, 1991), pp. 759–60; "Henry H. Sibley," *Eighteenth Annual Reunion of the Association of Graduates of the United States Military Academy at West Point, New York, June 9th, 1887* (East Saginaw, Mich.: Evening News Printing and Binding House, 1887), pp. 21–23; "Henry Hopkins Sibley," http://en.wikipedia.org/wiki/Henry_Hopkins_Sibley; "Sibley tent," http://en.wikipedia.org/wiki/Sibley_tent.

2. Fetterman massacre. Long remembered in the U.S. Army, the "Fetterman massacre" of 21 December 1866 was the bloodiest disaster for the army on the frontier and the most severe shock to the American public about the dangers of the western expansion until the annihilation of Lieutenant Colonel (Brevet Major General) George A. Custer's command at the Little Bighorn River on 25 June 1876. In the winter of 1865–1866, the 18th Infantry under its wartime regimental commander, Colonel (Brevet Brigadier General, USV) Henry B. Carrington, marched westward from Louisville, Kentucky, to Fort Kearney, Nebraska, and then in June moved on to Fort Laramie on the Platte River in Dakota Territory (present-day Wyoming) for frontier duty in the Department of the Platte, Division of the Missouri.

As the new commander of the Mountain District, encompassing the Powder River basin of northern Wyoming and southern Montana, Carrington was to keep the Montana Road, also known as the Bozeman Trail, clear of Indians all the way to the goldfields around Virginia City, Montana. Because the road cut directly across traditional Sioux hunting grounds in the Powder River basin and Big Horn mountains, Chief Red Cloud was already waging a stubborn and effective campaign against the army along the Bozeman Trail that had made any travel into Montana and beyond extremely hazardous, if not often impossible. Lieutenant General William T. Sherman, now commanding the Division of the Missouri, planned to restrict the hostile Sioux under Chief Red Cloud and other leaders to an area east of the Bozeman Trail, west of the Missouri River, and north of the Platte River. Carrington's expedition into the Powder River basin was a key part of this overall strategy because he was to build a string of new military posts (Forts Reno, Philip Kearny, and C. F. Smith) from Fort Laramie, Wyoming, to Virginia City. When built and garrisoned, these posts would allow the army to regain control of the Montana Road and thus gain better control of the hostile Indian tribes. With the 2d Battalion, 18th Infantry, and part of the 2d Cavalry, actually far too few troops for such a mission, Carrington set out in June 1866 to establish the new forts and a strong Army presence along the trail. The second of the three forts, Fort Phil Kearny, lay in today's north central Wyoming, near the Montana border, just off the Bozeman Trail and adjacent to the Big Piney and Little Piney creeks that flowed northeast into Clear Creek, a tributary of the Powder River. An experienced veteran of the Civil War, Captain William J. Fetterman, commanding Company A, 18th Infantry, had been at Fort Phil Kearny since the camp was set up in mid-July. He was a seasoned and experienced Civil War veteran but lacked any knowledge of the hostile Plains Indians. Commissioned a lieutenant in the 18th U.S. Infantry in May 1861, he was promoted to captain in October. He commanded a company from December 1861 to April 1863 and saw action at Corinth and later Murfreesboro. He commanded the 2d Battalion, 18th Infantry, to July 1864 and was involved in the Atlanta campaign. Fetterman received brevet commissions as major for Murfreesboro and later as lieutenant colonel for the Atlanta campaign. In September 1866 he was awaiting transfer in place to the new 27th Infantry Regiment, which would be formed in December from the 2d Battalion as the 18th Infantry was reorganized into three separate regiments to be posted in the Department of the Platte. Since the camp's initial establishment, the Sioux and their Cheyenne and Arapahoe allies had harassed wood trains carrying timber from cutting teams back to camp for the fort's construction. These attacks had often required relief parties to be sent out to drive them off. By mid-December 1866, Red Cloud and Crazy Horse, the Oglala Lakota (Sioux) war leader, had carefully developed a plan to lure part of Carrington's command into a trap using decoy attacks on a wood train. After several apparent attempts had failed, the decoy attack was tried again on 21 December. This time Carrington ordered Fetterman to lead the relief of the train, but not to pursue the attackers. Spoiling for some time for a fight with the Indians, the impetuous Fetterman led his entire party of eighty-one men from the 18th Infantry and 2d Cavalry—three officers, seventy-six soldiers, and two civilians—into an ill-advised pursuit of the attacking Indians and fell completely into the waiting trap. The entire Fetterman party was annihilated and then mutilated in what quickly became known as the "Fetterman massacre." This disastrous outcome prompted much criticism of the army's leadership for their policies against the Sioux, harmed the morale of the troops, and led to continued skirmishes with the Sioux the following year at the hayfield near Fort C. F. Smith (1 August 1867) and the wagon box (2 August 1867) near Fort Phil Kearny. In line with the administration's peace policy, the Treaty of Fort Laramie (1868) ended Red Cloud's War and resulted in the closure of the Bozeman Trail and of the three forts along it and the establishment of the Sioux reservations and hunting grounds. The best and most complete account of what happened at Fort Phil Kearny remains Dee Brown, *Fort Phil Kearny: An American Saga* (Lincoln: Univ. of Nebraska Press, 1962), which was used extensively for this note. See also "William Judd Fetterman," in Francis B. Heitman, *Historical Register and Dictionary of the United States Army from Its Organization, September 29, 1789, to March 2, 1903*, 2 vols. (Washington, D.C.: GPO, 1903), vol. 1, p. 264; Roy E. Appleman, "The Fetterman Fight," in *Great Western Indian Fights*, ed. B. W. Allred et al., pp. 116–31 (Lincoln: Univ. of Nebraska Press, 1960); Cyrus Townsend Brady, *Indian Fights and Fighters* (Lincoln: Univ. of Nebraska Press, 1971), pp. 3–39; Robert M. Utley, *Frontier Regulars: The United States Army and the Indian, 1866-1891* (New York: Macmillan, 1973), pp. 93–115; Edgar I. Stewart, *Custer's Luck* (Norman: Univ. of Oklahoma Press, 1955), pp. 32–51; Mark H. Brown, *The Plainsmen of the Yellowstone: A History of the Yellowstone Basin* (Lincoln: Univ. of Nebraska Press, 1961), pp. 152–76; Remi Nadeau, *Fort Laramie and the Sioux Indians* (Englewood Cliffs, N.J.: Prentice-Hall, 1967), passim; Brevet Brigadier General Theo. F. Rodenbough and Major William L. Haskin, eds., *The Army of the United States: Historical Sketches of Staff and Line with Portraits of Generals-in-Chief* (New York: Maynard, Merrill, 1896), p. 653; "Report of Lieutenant General W. T. Sherman," 5 November 1866, in "Report of General U.S. Grant, Commanding Army," 21 November 1866, in *Report of the Secretary of War* (Washington, D.C.: GPO, 1866), pp. 19, 23.

6. New Assignments, New Challenges, New Friends

1. At the time that Pershing wrote these lines in the 1930s, two years of military training was compulsory at land-grant as well as other public universities that came under the Morrill Act of 1862. Compulsory Reserve Officers' Training Corps (ROTC) programs ended at all public institutions after 1961. John Whiteclay Chambers II, "ROTC," in Chambers, *The Oxford Guide to American Military History*, p. 626.

2. Pershing Rifles. Building on the success of the cadet battalion's elite drill team, three members organized the Varsity Rifles in October 1894 to maintain contact among members of the university's military department and to support the university. Pershing agreed to be the drillmaster for the new organization, which strove to be the best. In 1895 the leaders of the Varsity Rifles changed the organization's name to the "Pershing Rifles" to honor Lieutenant Pershing, who had joined the 10th Cavalry in September 1895. Today the Pershing Rifles is a national society, with headquarters at the University of Nebraska since 1928. The Pershing Rifles is composed of U.S. Army, Air Force, Navy, and Marine Corps officer cadets in Reserve Officers' Training Corps (ROTC) units at universities and colleges around the country. University of Nebraska Military Department, *History of the Military Department: University of Nebraska, 1876-1941* (Lincoln: University of Nebraska, 1942), pp. 14–24; National Society of Pershing Rifles, http://pershingriflessociety.org/NSPR/about

.php; Charles A. Elliot, "The Early Days of the Pershing Rifles," *Pershing Rifleman* 4, no. 3 (May 1935), pp. 6–7.

3. Columbian Guard. The Chicago World's Fair, or World's Columbian Exposition, commemorated the four hundredth anniversary of Christopher Columbus's discovery of the New World in 1492. Because planners believed that the Chicago city police could not handle the large crowds and security aspects, the War Department furnished 2,000–2,500 serving officers and enlisted men under Colonel Edmund Rice, a Civil War veteran, to form the Columbian Guard. Specially uniformed and outfitted, the unit was to guard the exhibitions and provide overall security, including fire protection. The fair was dedicated on 21 October 1892 but did not open until 1 May 1893 and ran until 30 October 1893. "The Columbian Guard" and "The Book of the Fair, Chapter the Fifth," World's Columbian Exposition of 1893, http://columbus.iit.edu/dreamcity/00024044.html, and http://columbus.gl.iit.edu/bookfair/ch5.html; "World's Columbian Exposition," Encyclopaedia Britannica Online, http://www.britannica.com/EBchecked/topic/649070/Worlds-Columbian-Exposition.

4. Although Pershing says only one of his cadets later became a general officer, I have identified at least three: Ernest D. Scott and Evan H. Humphrey in the Regular Army and Leroy V. Patch in the Organized Reserves or National Guard.

5. The original manuscript has a penciled question mark at this point, indicating Pershing's dubiousness about this contention. He was correct, for Bryan won election to the House of Representatives by "the narrow margin" of only 140 votes. See Andrew J. Sawyer, ed. *Lincoln, the Capital City, and Lancaster County, Nebraska*, 2 vols. (Chicago: S. J. Clarke, 1916), p. 19.

6. Cross of Gold. On 8 July 1896, William Jennings Bryan gave what became known as the "Cross of Gold" speech during the debate on the platform at the Democratic National Convention in Chicago. Reviving the old "Greenback" Party and populist attack, he used his eloquence to hammer home the point that gold was not the only approach to underpinning the nation's currency—"You shall not press down on the brow of labor this crown of thorns, you shall not crucify mankind on a cross of gold." In so doing, at thirty-six years old he won the party's nomination for president to run against William McKinley. "Cross of Gold speech," Encyclopaedia Britannica Online, http://www.britannica.com/EBchecked/topic/144147/Cross-of-Gold-speech; Morris, *Encyclopedia of American History*, p. 265.

7. The 10th Cavalry was one of four regiments in the post–Civil War U.S. Army that was composed of African American enlisted men and noncommissioned officers and mainly white officers. During the Civil War, the Union had raised 120 infantry regiments, seven cavalry regiments, and some artillery units from among freed slaves and other African Americans in what was called the U.S. Colored Troops. The initial postwar reorganization of the army in 1866 into forty-five infantry, ten cavalry, and five artillery regiments included six African American regiments—the 9th and 10th Cavalry and the 38th, 39th, 40th, and 41st Infantry Regiments—largely drawn from soldiers of the former U.S. Colored Troops. In the 1869 reorganization of the army that cut the infantry regiments to twenty-five, the 38th–41st Regiments were consolidated into the new 24th and 25th Infantry Regiments (Colored) while the two cavalry regiments remained unchanged. These segregated regiments would continue to serve in the U.S. Army until the Korean War period. Russell Weigley, *His-*

tory of the United States Army (New York: Macmillan, 1967), pp. 212, 266–67; William A. Ganoe, *The History of the United States Army* (New York: D. Appleton-Century, 1942), pp. 306–7; Morris J. MacGregor Jr., *Integration of the Armed Forces 1940-1965* (Washington, D.C.: U.S. Army Center of Military History, 1981), passim; T. G. Steward, *The Colored Regulars in the United States Army* (Philadelphia: A. M. E. Book Concern, 1904), passim.

    8. Riel Rebellion. Louis Riel (22 October 1844–16 November 1885) actually led two uprisings against Canadian federal authorities. The first, known as the Red River Rebellion, took place in 1869–1870. The Métis, a large group of French-speaking people of mixed Indian and white blood, who had settled in the area of the Red and Assinniboine rivers in present-day Manitoba, believed their distinctive culture, livelihoods, and lands were threatened as a result of Canada's expansion into the Northwest Territory, which the Canadian government had purchased from the Hudson Bay Company in 1869. Riel, a Métis, led the opposition to the central government. After the uprising was put down, Riel fled to the United States and then returned to Canada in 1871. By 1884, the Métis' situation had deteriorated and Riel, who had gone to Montana and become an American citizen, was convinced to return to help his people. Moving to Batoche, Saskatchewan, he helped local Métis request relief and assistance from the central government in Ottawa, Ontario. Apparently suffering a mental illness, Riel then led another uprising that was known as the North-West Rebellion. Riel and his armed followers, along with Cree and Assinniboine Indian allies, formed a new provisional government at Batoche and prepared for war. They fought the North-West Mounted Police and Canadian militia forces, which quickly put down the uprising. Riel was charged with treason, tried and convicted, and hung on 16 November 1885. Because of the cross-border involvement with tribes of Plains Indians, the U.S. government was always concerned that such uprisings in Canada could cause similar problems among related Indians living south of the border. "Louis Riel," Dictionary of Canadian Biography Online, http://www.biographi.ca/009004-119.01-e.php?Biold=39918; "The Riel Rebellions," Canadiana, http://www.canadiana.org/citm/specifique/rielreb_e.pdf; "Red River Rebellion," The Canadian Encyclopedia, http://www.thecanadianencyclopedia.com/index.cfm?PgNm=TCE&Params=a1ARTA0006727; "North-West Rebellion," The Canadian Encyclopedia, http://www.thecanadianencyclopedia.com/index.cfm?PgNm=TCE&Params=a1ARTA0005802.

    9. *The Winning of the West.* G. P. Putnam's Sons published the four large volumes of *The Winning of the West* from 1889 to 1896. These works constitute perhaps Roosevelt's most extensive foray into the writing of American history. He covers the period from 1769 and the earliest westward expansion across the Allegheny Mountains to 1807 and the settling of the Northwest Territories and acquisition and exploration of the Louisiana Purchase. "Theodore Roosevelt," Encyclopaedia Britannica Online, http://www.britannica.com/EBchecked/topic/509347/Theodore-Roosevelt.

    10. 17th Amendment. When ratified by the states in 1913, the 17th Amendment to the U.S. Constitution provided for the direct election of U.S. senators by voters of the various states. The Constitution (Article 1, Section 3, Paragraph 1) as originally written and ratified provided for the appointment of senators by state legislatures. This change was a Progressive era reform designed to reduce corruption and the influence of special interests in the selection of U.S. senators. "Seventeenth Amend-

ment (United States Constitution)," Encyclopaedia Britannica Online, http://www
.britannica.com/EBchecked/topic/536623/Seventeenth-Amendment.

7. The Spanish-American War to the San Juan Heights

1. Pershing's account of the Spanish-American War in chapters 7 and 8 drew
heavily on a speech that he delivered on the evening of Sunday, 20 November 1898,
about his experiences with the 10th U.S. Cavalry in the Santiago Campaign. He
was then on sick leave and recovering at his parents' home in Hyde Park, Chicago.
He spoke at a patriotic Thanksgiving service at the Hyde Park Methodist Episcopal
Church that his parents attended. The original version with Pershing's hand-written
annotations is in Appendix A and comes from LC/Pershing Papers, Box 368, Early
Years, 1886–1898. An edited version of this speech, which was only slightly different, was published in 1899 as Chapter 13, "The Campaign of Santiago: Lieutenant
John J. Pershing Gives His View of the Great Campaign—What the Tenth Cavalry
and Other Negro Troops Accomplished," in *Under Fire with the Tenth U.S. Cavalry,*
by Herschel V. Cashin, Charles Alexander, William T. Anderson, Arthur M. Brown,
and Horace W. Bivins (New York: F. T. Neely), republished most recently by the University Press of Colorado in 1993 (see pp. 195–216 of this reprint). Pershing's biographers have all relied heavily on these two chapters of his unpublished memoirs to
tell the story of his time in Cuba, and Pershing relied heavily on this speech to tell
that story as well.

2. Even today, the exact reason for the explosion that sank the USS *Maine* in
Havana harbor on 15 February 1898 and catapulted the United States into the war
with Spain remains in dispute. Originally the destruction of the *Maine* was attributed to an underwater mine set by the Spanish that exploded powder charges stored
in the magazines in the forward part of the ship. A naval board of inquiry conducted in Havana in 1898 concluded that a mine caused the explosion and sinking,
but reached no conclusion as to who placed it. A second board of inquiry met when
the *Maine*'s wreckage was removed from Havana harbor in 1911. After examining the
dewatered remains, the board found bottom hull plates bent inward and concluded
that an external explosion under the reserve 6-inch magazine was the cause. At the
time of both inquiries, some naval experts thought that the explosion was caused
by the spontaneous combustion of coal dust in the coal bunker next to the reserve
6-inch magazine. Admiral Hyman G. Rickover, the father of the U.S. Navy's nuclear
power program, conducted another study using modern analytical techniques. He
published his results in *How the Battleship* Maine *Was Destroyed* (Washington, D.C.:
GPO, 1976), concluding that the most likely cause was spontaneous combustion of
coal dust in the bunker next to the magazine. However, this conclusion has also been
attacked. An article on the destruction of the USS *Maine* on the U.S. Naval Historical
Center's Website concluded: "Yet evidence of a mine remains thin and such theories
are based on conjecture. Despite the best efforts of experts and historians in investigating this complex and technical issue, a definitive explanation for the destruction of the *Maine* remains elusive." One thing that does not remain elusive is that
the sinking of the *Maine* led the United States directly into the war with Spain. "The
Destruction of the USS *Maine,*" http://www.history.navy.mil/faqs/faq71-1.htm;
"*Maine,*" "*Maine* Investigations," and "*Maine* Newspaper Coverage," in *The Spanish-*

American War: A Historical Dictionary, ed. Brad K. Berner, pp. 214–218 (Lanham, Md.: Scarecrow Press, 1998).

3. Pershing noted in a footnote in the original manuscript that Daniel E. McCarthy (14 April 1859–2 September 1922) was the first chief quartermaster of the American Expeditionary Forces in France in 1917.

4. 1st U.S. Volunteer Cavalry (1 May–15 September 1898). Officially designated the 1st U.S. Volunteer Cavalry, this unit was the brainchild of recently resigned Assistant Secretary of the Navy Theodore Roosevelt as a means to get himself into the Spanish-American War. The unit soon became famous as "Roosevelt's Rough Riders," or more simply, the "Rough Riders." Raised largely in Texas, New Mexico, and Oklahoma and briefly trained at San Antonio, the 1st was composed of an odd assortment of cowboys, Indian fighters, Texas Rangers and lawmen, ranchers, and farmers together with men from New York City and the East. At Roosevelt's request, Secretary of War Russell Alger placed a Regular Army officer, Leonard Wood, in command. Roosevelt's influence got the "Rough Riders" assigned to Young's 2d Brigade, Cavalry Division, and shipped to Cuba with the expeditionary force, but without their horses and half their men. The Rough Riders fought bravely at Las Guasimas on 24 June, losing eight killed and thirty-one wounded. When Wood replaced Young as commander of the 2d Brigade, Roosevelt assumed command of the Rough Riders and led the famous charge up Kettle Hill on 1 July that won them fame and secured Roosevelt's political future and eventually the presidency. The troops remained in Cuba, suffering heavily from disease, and finally were evacuated to Camp Wikoff, Montauk Point, Long Island, landing on 14 August. The Rough Riders had suffered serious casualties in Cuba, including twenty-six killed in action, 104 wounded, and twenty died of disease. The 1st U.S. Volunteer Cavalry was mustered out of service at Camp Wikoff on 15 September 1898. Theodore Roosevelt, *The Rough Riders* (New York: Review of Reviews Company, 1904), passim; "Theodore Roosevelt (1858–1919)" and "Rough Riders," in Berner, ed., *The Spanish-American War,* pp. 319–20, 321–22; Peggy Samuels and Harold Samuels, *Teddy Roosevelt at San Juan: The Making of a President* (College Station: Texas A&M Univ. Press, 1997), passim; Jack C. Lane, *Armed Progressive: General Leonard Wood* (San Rafael, Calif.: Presidio Press, 1978), pp. 25–54.

5. Although Pershing clearly states that his and the army's preference was for Nelson Miles to command the Santiago expeditionary force, the selection of William Shafter to command remains another unresolved historical issue. Robert Wooster in his *Nelson A. Miles and the Twilight of the Frontier Army* provides an interesting analysis of this issue, its permutations, and the available evidence. Wooster quotes Pershing's contention that "Miles might become too strong politically after the war." Pershing, a former aide to Miles, was stationed at the Military Academy at this time and not really privy to why this decision was made despite his political connections. Paul Carlson in his biography of William R. Shafter, *"Pecos Bill,"* provides the answer: "Shafter's selection was largely political. . . . Certainly the publicity-seeking Miles, who had presidential ambitions, wanted to lead the campaign or a larger one to Havana or Puerto Rico. But the Republican McKinley and his chief political advisor, Mark Hanna, suspected that the dashing and dramatic Miles was a Democrat. More concerned that the war might create political heroes than with the selection of a competent commander, they turned to Shafter, who represented a threat to neither

McKinley nor Miles. Shafter harbored no political ambitions, and the army considered him a vigorous, aggressive, and forceful old soldier." Moreover, even had Miles been nonpolitical, his personal relationships with President McKinley and Secretary of War Russell Alger were very poor at the time. Robert Wooster, *Nelson A. Miles and the Twilight of the Frontier Army* (Lincoln: Univ. of Nebraska Press, 1993), pp. 216–18; Paul Carlson, *"Pecos Bill": A Military Biography of William R. Shafter* (College Station: Texas A&M Univ. Press, 1989), p. 163; Graham A. Cosmas, *An Army for Empire: The United States Army in the Spanish-American War* (College Station: Texas A&M Univ. Press, 1998), passim.

6. The men who drowned were Corporal Edward F. Cobb and Trooper George English, both from Troop B, 10th Cavalry. Cashin et al., *Under Fire with the Tenth U.S. Cavalry*, pp. 78, 338; Anthony L. Powell, "10th Cavalry Regiment Roster Spanish American War 1898," The Spanish American War Centennial Website, http://www.spanamwar.com/10thcav.htm.

7. Hotchkiss guns. The terrain and conditions of campaigning on the frontier made it difficult to employ the army's existing field artillery in support of either infantry or cavalry formations. Numerous complaints from field commanders concerning the inadequacy of the army's standard field artillery pieces and requests for more mobile and effective mountain guns finally forced the War Department into action. In 1876 it purchased from the French weapons manufacturer Hotchkiss Ordnance several 1.65-inch (42mm) breech-loading, rifled guns that were lightweight and easily broken down for movement by pack mules. After effective use by Nelson Miles in the Nez Percé campaign in 1877, more Hotchkiss guns were purchased, and the weapon was soon the primary field artillery piece for use on the frontier. They were sturdy and easy to handle and operate. At Las Guasimas and then Kettle Hill and San Juan Hill, the 10th Cavalry's four Hotchkiss guns under First Lieutenant James B. Hughes, Troop B, were most active and successful in supporting the infantry attacks and then defending the gains against Spanish counterattacks. The Hotchkiss was also used effectively during the Philippine Insurrection (1899–1902). "1.65 Inch Hotchkiss Mountain Gun," The Spanish-American War Centennial Website, http://www.spanamwar.com/hotchkis165.htm; "Hotchkiss gun," http://en.wikipedia.org/wiki/Hotchkiss_gun; Boyd L. Dastrup, *King of Battle: A Branch History of the U.S. Army's Field Artillery* (Washington, D.C.: U.S. Army Center of Military History, 1993), pp. 132–33.

8. Gatling guns. The only "automatic gun" or machine gun the army possessed during the Spanish-American War was the Gatling gun. Richard J. Gatling of Indianapolis, Indiana, invented the Gatling gun in 1862 and patented it in 1865. The Army adopted the Gatling gun and used it on the frontier. The gun usually had six to ten .30 caliber barrels that revolved in a central cylindrical frame on a field gun wheeled caisson. As the barrels revolved, a mechanical device automatically inserted .30 caliber rounds that fed from a supply atop the gun. A hand crank and later a motor drive were used to move the barrels around the frame, and as they moved the gun was cocked, fired, the shell casing extracted, and a new round loaded, all in one movement. When hand-cranked, the later model guns could fire twelve hundred rounds per minute, and as much as three thousand rounds per minute when motor-driven. Obviously, such an enormous increase in the volume of fire could prove most useful on the battlefield. The original models had some mechanical problems that

were eventually resolved, and the army purchased eighteen improved Model 1895 Gatling guns for use in the Spanish-American War. Lieutenant John Henry Parker commanded the Gatling Gun Detachment of Shafter's Corps in the United States and Cuba. Although inadequately equipped and trained, Parker's detachment of three guns was employed at San Juan Hill with great effect against the Spanish defenders on 1 July. In the army's first use of such automatic weapons to support an attack on a fortified position, the three guns each fired six thousand rounds in less than nine minutes of action. The guns were also used in the Puerto Rican Campaign and the Philippines. John Henry Parker, *History of the Gatling Gun Detachment, Fifth Army Corps, at Santiago, with a Few Unvarnished Truths Concerning that Expedition* (Kansas City, Mo.: Hudson-Kimberley Publishing, 1898), passim; Patrick McSherry, "The Gatling Gun," The Spanish-American War Centennial Website, http://www.spanamwar.com/Gatling.htm; "Gatling Gun," in Berner, ed., *The Spanish-American War*, p. 150.

8. The Spanish-American War—Victory in Cuba and Its Consequences

1. "Americanized Cuban." Neither Pershing in any of his writings on the fighting on 1 July nor any of his biographers has identified this Army physician. Indeed, Pershing as early as his lecture at his parents' Hyde Park Methodist Episcopal Church in Chicago on 27 November 1898 says virtually the same thing as here: "A surgeon of our brigade, an Americanized Cuban, stood in the water behind the bank in a bend in the river supporting two wounded colored troopers to keep them from drowning." After a thorough review of available information, this surgeon could have been one of three men—Acting Assistant Surgeon (Contract Surgeon) Juan (John) Guitéras (4 January 1852–28 October 1925), who was attached to Shafter's headquarters as a yellow fever expert during the Santiago Campaign but was often at the front; Acting Assistant Surgeon José M. Delgado, who was an assistant surgeon with the 1st Cavalry Regiment, 2d Brigade; or Acting Assistant Surgeon Francisco E. Menocal, who was an assistant surgeon with the 6th Cavalry, 1st Brigade. Based on Pershing's description of him as "a surgeon of our brigade," the most likely person to have been the "Americanized Cuban" surgeon at what was called either "Bloody Ford" or "Bloody Bend" dressing station on the Aguadores River that day was Dr. Menocal. However, Colonel Valery Havard, surgeon of the Cavalry Division, wrote in "The Medical Corps at Santiago" in Charles D. Rhodes's book of reminiscences, *The Santiago Campaign* (1927), that he sent Drs. Delgado and Menocal forward to the river with Major George J. Newgarden, surgeon of the 3d Cavalry, on 1 July to operate the dressing station. Newgarden in his memoir, "The Bloody Ford: The Story of the Dressing Station," in Rhodes's volume mentions only Dr. Menocal as being there on 1 July. Newgarden's official report of his actions also mentions only Dr. Menocal as present until 2 July, when Colonel Havard ordered him back to the 6th Cavalry. Confirmation of this is found in War Department General Orders No. 15, 13 February 1900, which cited Menocal for "gallant and meritorious conduct during the battle of Santiago, Cuba, where, under fire, he cared for the sick and wounded" on 1 July. Dr. Delgado received a similar mention for his work on 24 June at Las Guasimas, and Dr. Guitéras was cited for 24 June and 1–3 July. Like many of the Cuban professionals who sought refuge from Spanish oppression in the United States, little

is known about Dr. Menocal except that he served with the 2d and 6th Cavalry, 1st Infantry, and Headquarters, V Corps, in the United States and Cuba and cared for Spanish prisoners at El Caney. He remained in Cuba after his service in 1898, later became the director of Cuba's immigration department, and was the nephew of later President of Cuba Mario Garcia Menocal (May 1913–May 1921). Heitman, *Historical Register*, vol. 2, p. 277; TAGO, Headquarters of the Army, General Orders No. 15, 13 February 1900, pp. 3, 20, in U.S. War Department, The Adjutant General's Office (TAGO), *General Orders and Circulars 1900* (Washington, D.C.: GPO, 1901); John J. Pershing, "The Campaign of Santiago," in Cashin et al., *Under Fire with the Tenth U.S. Cavalry*, pp. 195–216 (see p. 207 for the quote); Charles D. Rhodes, ed., *The Santiago Campaign: Reminiscences of the Operations for the Capture of Santiago de Cuba in the Spanish-American War, June and July 1898* (Richmond, Va.: Williams Printing Company, 1927), pp. 208, 214, 226–38; George J. Newgarden, "Report of Capt. George J. Newgarden, Assistant Surgeon, United States Army, of His Services at Santiago, Cuba, with the Third United States Cavalry," *Annual Report of the Surgeon General of the Army to the Secretary of War for the Fiscal Year ending June 30, 1898* (Washington, D.C.: GPO, 1898) (hereafter cited as *ARSG, 1898*), pp. 227–28; *ARSG, 1898*, pp. 201–2.

2. In the original manuscript, Pershing inserted a footnote here as follows: "Major Wint received a wound during the Civil War which left him with one leg shorter than the other. This wound was in the other leg in exactly the same place and left his two legs again equal in length and without any limp at all."

3. Round Robin Letter. By late July 1898 the V Army Corps at Santiago faced a seriously deteriorating health situation from malaria, typhoid, diarrheas, and dysentery while the deadly threat of a yellow fever epidemic loomed. Shafter warned the War Department and Secretary of War Russell Alger about the disease problems on 2 August but received a condescending reply from Alger to move to higher ground. On 3 August, at Shafter's request, his brigade and division commanders met and signed what became known as the "Round Robin Letter" and gave it to him. The letter warned: "This army must be moved at once, or it will perish as an army." It warned that should a yellow fever epidemic occur in the near future, the corps in its weakened condition would "be practically entirely destroyed." All of the army surgeons also signed an accompanying letter warning of the dangers, as did Lieutenant Colonel Teddy Roosevelt of the Rough Riders. These letters were then "leaked" to the Associated Press reporter at Shafter's headquarters and appeared as part of sensational headlines in most U.S. newspapers on 4 August. While seriously embarrassing to the McKinley administration, the Round Robin Letter apparently came after the War Department had already decided to remove Shafter's forces from Cuba to Camp Wikoff, Montauk Point, Long Island, New York. The formal orders were quickly issued that day to remove the corps from Cuba. The first ships left Siboney for Montauk Point on 7 August, although the convalescent camp was not yet ready. "Round Robin Letter (3 August 1898)," in Berner, ed., *The Spanish-American War,* pp. 322–23; Cosmas, *An Army for Empire*, pp. 259–66; Carlson, *"Pecos Bill,"* pp. 182–84; Roosevelt, *The Rough Riders*, pp. 295–300; for the perspective of Shafter's headquarters and copies of Shafter's letters and those of the army surgeons and the "Round Robin" itself, see John D. Miley, *In Cuba with Shafter* (New York: Charles Scribner's Sons, 1899), pp. 215–24.

4. Weihai (then called Weihaiwei) is a port city with a well-protected natural harbor and fortified naval base located at the eastern tip of the Shandong Peninsula in Shandong Province, China. During the Sino-Japanese War (1894–1895) the Japanese captured Weihaiwei from the land side and destroyed the Chinese fleet in January–February 1895. The Japanese occupied Weihaiwei until 1898, but Great Britain obtained a lease in 1898. Weihaiwei was the Royal Navy's main base in northern China across from Korea and the Kwantung Peninsula (Port Arthur), first occupied by Russia and then Japan after the Russo-Japanese War. Weihaiwei was a British treaty port and the summer station of the Royal Navy in Chinese waters until 1923. Britain returned Weihaiwei to China in 1930, and it was later occupied by the Japanese (1938–1945) during the war in China. After 1949, it became a major base for the Chinese Peoples' Navy. "Weihai," Encyclopaedia Britannica Online, http://www.britannica.com/EBchecked/topic/638888/Weihai; Denis and Peggy Warner, *The Tide at Sunrise: A History of the Russo-Japanese War, 1904-1905* (New York: Charterhouse, 1974), passim.

9. The Division of Customs and Insular Affairs and My First Assignment to the Philippines

1. Cuban Interventions. Pershing here refers to the armed intervention by the United States in Cuba from 6 October 1906 to 1 April 1909, during which the United States established the Army of Cuban Pacification and a provisional governor to restore peace and a functional government on the island following a period of political turmoil. In early 1907, the United States had sixty-six hundred officers and men of the U.S. Army, Navy, and Marine Corps posted throughout Cuba. The U.S. intervention was based on Senator Orville H. Platt's amendment to the U.S. Army appropriations bill of March 1901, known as the Platt Amendment, which set stringent conditions for the withdrawal of American occupation forces from Cuba after the Spanish-American War. The amendment ceded Guantánamo Bay Naval Base to the United States and forced the Cuban constitution to include provisions allowing the United States to intervene in Cuban affairs whenever its interests were threatened. A second, much shorter armed intervention occurred in 1912. President Franklin D. Roosevelt abolished the Platt Amendment's most offensive provisions in 1934 but did not return Guantánamo Naval Base to Cuba. "Platt Amendment," Encyclopaedia Britannica Online, http://www.britannica.com/EBchecked/topic/464267/Platt-Amendment; *Annual Reports of the War Department for the Fiscal Year Ending June 30, 1907* (Washington, D.C.: GPO, 1907) (hereafter cited as *ARWD*, year, volume, and part), vol. 3, pp. 313–58; *ARWD, 1908*, vol. 3, pp. 299–326; *ARWD, 1909*, vol. 3, pp. 231–70.

2. Boer War (11 October 1899–31 May 1902). The Boer War, also known as the South African or Anglo-Boer War, was fought between Great Britain and the two Boer republics (Afrikaners or Dutch settlers) of the South African Republic (Transvaal) and the Orange Free State. The exact origins of the conflict remain disputed, but in effect the British were trying to extend their control over the Boer states, which were well-endowed with rich gold mines. After an initial successful Boer offensive in October 1899, which startled the British, the Boers were thrown on the defensive due to British numbers and largely pursed a guerrilla war against the Brit-

ish forces after 1900. The British attacks forced Paul Kruger, president of the South African Republic, to flee to Europe. The British spent enormous sums on the war and poured in nearly a half million troops to confront less than one hundred thousand soldiers for the Boers. And yet the British were seriously hard-pressed for several years to gain the upper hand. Lords Horatio Herbert Kitchener and Frederick Sleigh Roberts led the British operations after 1900. Kitchener especially adopted a brutal policy of destroying the Boer farming areas and established squalid concentration camps to imprison Boers, many of whom died in them. The war ended in May 1902 with the Peace of Vereeniging, which ended the independence of the two Boer republics and brought all of the area under British control, eventually forming the Union of South Africa after 1910. The war's outcome also created the atmosphere of severe discrimination against the black Africans among both the British and Boer populations, although their own relations were often hostile for many years to come. "South African War," Encyclopaedia Britannica Online, http://www .britannica.com/EBchecked/topic/555806/South-African-War; Craig Wilcox and Hugh Bicheno, "Second Boer War (1899–1902)," in *The Oxford Companion to Military History,* ed. Richard Holmes, pp. 137–40 (London: Oxford Univ. Press, 2001).

3. Seven Dials. The Seven Dials refers to a road junction in the West End of London (Covent Garden) where seven roads converge. Originally, six streets were to meet and a circular area where they converged had a pillar with six (not seven) sundials on it. Once a London slum, the area was redeveloped. Charles Dickens wrote of the area in chapter 5, "Seven Dials," of his *Sketches by Boz: Illustrative of Every-Day Life and Every-Day People* (London: John Macrone, 1836). The original pillar was taken down in 1773 but preserved and in 1820 reerected in nearby Weybridge at Earlham and Mercer streets. "Seven Dials," at http://en.wikipedia.org/wiki/Seven_Dials.

4. Bersaglieri. The Bersaglieri were originally formed as a special corps of marksmen in the Piedmontese (later Royal Italian) Army in June 1836. They were basically light infantry and mostly used for highly mobile operations regardless of terrain. They were distinguished by their brimmed hats that sported long black feathers and their high esprit de corps. Mike Bennighof, "Italy's Elite Infantry: The Bersaglieri," http://www.avalanchepress.com/Bersaglieri.php.

10. Duty in the Philippines—Manila, Mindanao, and Iligan

1. U.S. Volunteer Regiments. Pershing was incorrect in this statement because all twenty-five regiments of U.S. Volunteers served in the Philippines and, except for the three raised in the Philippines, none of them arrived prior to the first elements of the 34th Regiment, which reached Manila on 11 October 1899. As the fighting in the Philippines intensified early in 1899 and the state volunteer units raised in 1898 for the war against Spain were mustered out of service in 1899, the army urgently required additional men. On 2 March 1899, Congress passed a makeshift act that authorized the president to increase the Regular Army to sixty-five thousand and to raise thirty-five thousand volunteers organized in twenty-four regiments of infantry and one of cavalry specifically for service in the Philippines. So as not to disrupt recruiting for the army, the president delayed the creation of these special, short-term U.S. Volunteer regiments (to be discharged no later than 1 July 1901) and authorized their organization in five separate actions: on 5 July 1899, the

26th–35th Infantry Regiments; on 18 July, the 36th and 37th Infantry Regiments, to be recruited in the Philippines; on 10 August, the 11th Cavalry Regiment, to be recruited in the Philippines; on 17 August, the 38th–47th Infantry Regiments; and on 2 September, the 48th and 49th Infantry Regiments to be raised with white field officers and African American company officers and enlisted men. The first regiment to depart the Philippines was the 37th, which left Manila on 10 January 1901 and mustered out in San Francisco on 20 February. All of the units were mustered out by 8 July. "U.S. Volunteers," in "Report of the Major General Commanding the Army," 17 October 1899, in *ARWD, 1899,* vol. 1, pt. 3, pp. 369–75; "United States Volunteers," in "Report of the Lieutenant General Commanding the Army," 29 October 1900, in *ARWD, 1900,* vol. 1, pt. 3, pp. 16–17, 36; "United States Volunteers," in "Report of the Lieutenant General Commanding the Army," 1 October 1901, in *ARWD, 1901,* vol. 1, pt. 3, pp. 23–33; Ganoe, *The History of the United States Army,* pp. 399–400; Brian McAllister Linn, *The Philippine War, 1899-1902* (Lawrence: Univ. Press of Kansas, 2000), p. 125.

2. Sydney A. Cloman tells the entire story of this bloody episode in his *Myself and a Few Moros* (New York: Doubleday, Page, 1923), pp. 117–37. His book provides an informative personal insight into the customs and traditions of the Moros as well as the difficult problems of dealing with them.

3. Army Reorganization Act of 2 February 1901. The U.S. Army's overall performance in the Spanish-American War was inept and less than stellar in most respects. In September 1898, President McKinley launched a major investigation under railroad builder and Civil War major general of volunteers Grenville M. Dodge (12 April 1831–3 January 1916). The War Investigating Committee, better known as the Dodge Commission, reported on 9 February 1900 and outlined serious deficiencies in the organization and administration of the War Department that required correction. By late 1900, little aside from the reorganization of the U.S. Volunteer regiments had been accomplished, but the new Secretary of War, Elihu Root, was already developing a series of reforms for the War Department. Also now pressing heavily on the administration and Congress was the upcoming expiration on 1 July 1901 of the term of service of the U.S. Volunteer regiments then serving in the Philippines. Action had to be taken before then to expand the army and reorganize it to maintain continuing operations in the Philippines. The Army Reorganization Act of 2 February 1901 was the opening act of Elihu Root's effort to reform and modernize the entire War Department and U.S. Army. The Act increased the existing strength of the army from 65,000 to a maximum of 100,619 officers and men. Of this strength, 12,000 were to be natives of the Philippines and Puerto Rico who could not serve outside of their islands and would be commanded by Regular Army majors and captains—thus forming the Philippine Scouts and Puerto Rico Regiment (later redesignated the 65th Infantry Regiment). An additional five regiments of infantry (26th–30th Infantry Regiments) and five of cavalry (11th–15th Cavalry Regiments) were authorized, and each regiment would consist of three battalions of four companies manned at varying strengths (65–146 in the infantry and 110–164 in the cavalry). The number of general officers was increased to one lieutenant general, six major generals, and fifteen brigadier generals. The expansion created 1,135 vacancies for new officers in the Regular Army, most of which went to outstanding officers in the USV regiments. Significant changes were made in the organization of the artillery,

more clearly differentiating between coast artillery and field artillery under a new artillery corps and chief, foreshadowing the major reorganization of January 1907. The time that officers could be assigned to staff departments was limited to four years, after which duty with troops was required. While this tardy legislation was only the beginning of Root's reforms, it was not in time to recruit, train, and transport sufficient new units and troops to offset Major General Arthur MacArthur's pending loss of the twenty-five USV regiments from his force of seventy thousand then serving in the Philippines. This act formed an important early part of what William Ganoe called "the Army's renaissance." Ganoe, *The History of the United States Army*, pp. 411–13, 428, 432; Weigley, *History of the United States Army*, pp. 317–18; James E. Hewes Jr., *From Root to McNamara: Army Organization and Its Administration, 1900-1963* (Washington, D.C.: U.S. Army Center of Military History, 1975), pp. 6–8; Cosmas, *An Army for Empire*, pp. 284–98; "Grenville M. Dodge," *Webster's American Military Biographies* (Springfield, Mass.: G. and C. Merriam, 1978), pp. 103–4; "Grenville Mellen Dodge (1831–1916)" and "Dodge Commission (26 September 1898–9 February 1899)," in Berner, ed., *The Spanish-American War*, pp. 110–11.

4. At the time that Pershing took over at Iligan, the Malanao Moros of the Lake Lanao region numbered approximately eighty thousand to one hundred thousand. They made up three basic but intermingled tribal groupings: the Bayabaos, occupying the northern part of the lake region; the Onayans, occupying the western and southern shores; and the Macius, occupying the eastern and southeastern. Hereditary sultans supposedly descended from the Prophet Muhammad headed individual *rancherias,* as the Spanish called the territory of the various tribal clans and their settlements, but exercised only a most general control over sizable groupings of individual *rancherias.* A local leader or general, called a *datto* (also spelled *dato* and *datu,* but Pershing's spelling of *datto* is retained throughout), ruled each of the various subordinate *rancherias* within the large main *rancherias.* Within each larger *rancherias,* a hierarchical governing structure extended down from the sultan, who governed according the Islamic laws based on the Koran. However, the sultans, *rancherias,* and *dattos* were in an almost constant state of conflict among themselves, with frequent raids on each other and Christian settlements, stealing of carabao and slaves, and armed attacks. Pershing reported that there were "some 400 *rancherias*" around Lake Lanao as of 1902–1903 and 150 sultans or *dattos.* In June 1902, however, Pershing counted 101 *rancherias* on the coast of Lake Lanao alone. In May 1903, he compiled a more extensive list of *rancherias,* sultans, and *dattos* in the Lake Lanao region and came up with 52 main *rancherias* and 318 more that were subordinate to them, each of the 370 having a sultan, *datto,* or some of kind of leader. *ARWD, 1903,* vol. 3, p. 323; "Lanao, Mindanao," in U.S. War Department, Bureau of Insular Affairs, *A Pronouncing Gazetteer and Geographical Dictionary of the Philippines Islands* (Washington, D.C.: GPO, 1902), pp. 578–79; Pershing, "Names of rancherias on the Coast of Lake Lanao, going north from Madumba," 10 June 1902, LC/Pershing Papers, Box 317, Camp Vicars (3); Pershing, "List of Rancherias about Lake Lanao with Principal Datto of Each," 15 May 1903, and [List of Moro Titles], LC/Pershing Papers, Box 317, Camp Vicars (4).

11. Dealing with the Hostile Moros around Lake Lanao

1. Lieutenant Forsyth's detachment of himself and seventeen men from Troop A, 15th Cavalry, eighteen horses, along with a packer and two mules and some friendly Moros, left Parang-parang (also called Paran-paran), Cotabato, Mindanao, on 12 March to explore trails through the jungles northward toward Lake Lanao. A large group of hostile Moros (estimated at fifty to two hundred) under Sultan Uali of Butig attacked the column in thick jungle on 15 March, and in the encounter that followed Private Charles Keller and eight Moros were killed. Forsyth and the remaining members of the detachment reached safety at Buldun after abandoning their horses, mules, and equipment but keeping their weapons and ammunition. *ARWD, 1902*, vol. 9, pp. 171–72, 568.

2. Pershing's actions in compliance with Chaffee's directive of 13 April 1902 were reported in "Captain Pershing's Report on Moro Affairs. May, 1902," in *ARWD, 1902*, vol. 9, pp. 556–59, which is reproduced in Appendix B. However, he provided a much more personal view of these events in a letter of 28 January 1903 to Charles E. Magoon, his old friend from Lincoln days who was then in the War Department's Bureau of Insular Affairs. He wrote of his actions in April 1902:

> In the latter part of April while I was still at Iligan as commanding officer, General Chaffee sent me, or suggested that I go, to the Laguna [Lake Lanao], if possible, and use my influence to hold the north lake Moros—many of whom I had met on previous visits I had made there accompanied by only an interpreter—as our friends and keep them from uniting with the South Lake Moros then opposing our forces coming up from the South coast. . . . There was nothing for it but to go there in person which I did but you can readily imagine that I felt at times more or less in doubt as to whether I should ever return. At Madaya I met at the market a large crowd of Moros from all parts of the lake and explained fully that we were sending troops into the south lake country to punish some Moros who had killed a soldier near Malabang and that they need have no fear we would molest any others. They were however in a great state of excitement and ready to do almost any foolish thing, even to turning out en masse on the war path.

Letter, Pershing to Magoon, 28 January 1903, LC/Pershing Papers, Box 369, Philippines: 1901–03, Folder 2.

3. For additional details on the battle, see "Report, Col. Frank D. Baldwin, Commanding, U.S. 27th Infantry, Camp Vicars, to Adjutant General, Seventh Separate Brigade, Zamboanga, Mindanao, 11 June 1902," in *ARWD, 1902*, vol. 9, pp. 567–73; Robert A. Fulton, *Moroland: The History of Uncle Sam and the Moros, 1899-1920* (Bend, Oreg.: Tumalo Creek Press, 2009), pp. 99–120. Two war correspondents from Manila, James Edgar Allen and John J. Reidy, spent the period of 17 April–30 December 1902 with the troops in the Lake Lanao region and witnessed all operations during that time from the Bayan fighting through Maciu. They published their observations in a small book, *The Battle of Bayan and Other Battles* (Manila, Philippines: E. C. McCullough, 1903). Allen's account of the Bayan fighting and aftermath are covered in pp. 13–52.

4. On 15 May 1902 at Malabang, Pershing received orders to report to Camp Vicars to command a squadron of the 15th Cavalry (Troops A, F, and H) and act as the

intelligence officer for Baldwin's Lake Lanao expedition. He arrived at Vicars the same day. LC/Pershing Papers, Box 1, Notebook for Lake Lanao Expedition, entry for 15 May 1902; Major James S. Pettit, Acting Adj. Gen, Headquarters, 7th Separate Brigade, In the Field, "Field Order No. V," Camp Vicars, Mindanao, to Captain J. J. Pershing, 15 May 1902, LC/Pershing Papers, Box 317, Camp Vicars (6).

5. Camp Vicars was named in honor of First Lieutenant Thomas A. Vicars (?–2 May 1902).

6. According to General George W. Davis's annual report as commanding general of the 7th Separate Brigade (Mindanao and Jolo), Chaffee went to the newly established Camp Vicars on 12 May to meet with friendly *dattos* from the area. He also summoned Pershing from Iligan on 8 May to meet him at Malabang. Pershing left Iligan by steamer on 9 May and apparently arrived at Malabang on the 13th. It was after that meeting on 13 May that Chaffee issued his orders to Davis through his chief of staff, Colonel Joseph P. Sanger. A copy of Chaffee's orders of 13 May 1902 to General Davis are in LC/Pershing Papers, Box 369, Philippines: 1901–03 (2). See also LC/Pershing Papers, Box 317, Philippines: Camp Vicars (6); *ARWD, 1902*, vol. 9, p. 491; Smythe, *Guerrilla Warrior,* pp. 77–78.

7. In his letter to Charles Magoon on 28 January 1903 (see note 11.2 above), Pershing also commented on General Davis's meeting with him at Malabang:

After the battle of Bayan General Davis ordered me here and placed me in charge of Moro affairs under the designation of "Intelligence Officer." The first question I asked him was, "General, what do you expect of me?" "Well," he said, "Pershing, you seem to know how to handle these Moros and I want you to make friends of them for us." Then he went on to say that it might be possible to visit many places around the lake by vinta and so on. In short peace and friendship without force was the watchword and it was in line with my own views as to how we should proceed.

Letter, Pershing to Magoon, 28 January 1903, LC/Pershing Papers, Box 369, Philippines, 1901–03, Folder 2.

George Davis spent considerable time studying the Moros and their history and traditions as well as previous Spanish Army operations against them. He completed a detailed analysis on 25 August 1902, which he appended to his annual report as commander of the 7th Separate Brigade. This study was later published as Appendix 9, "Notes on the Government of the Country Inhabited by Non-Christians in Mindanao and the Neighboring Islands," *ARWD 1902*, vol. 9, pp. 560–67.

8. Pershing maintained a complete record of events at Camp Vicars from 15 May through 14 September in his personal notebook and diary, which can be found in his papers at the Library of Congress. The original notebook is in Box 1, and a copy is in Box 369, Philippines, 1901–03 (5): Diary of the Lake Lanao Expedition. For additional details based on Pershing's reports, see *ARWD, 1902*, vol. 9, pp. 483, 492–93.

9. The quotation is from a letter: Baldwin to Davis, 17 June 1902, LC/Pershing Papers, Box 369, Philippines, 1901–03 (2). In the letter, Baldwin sought Davis's approval for another campaign against the Moros of Maciu and Bacolod, which was not forthcoming.

10. 7th Separate Brigade. The U.S. Army in the Philippines underwent a number of organizational changes in the years immediately following the initial occupation in July–August 1898. The commanders of the Division of the Philippines were

trying to balance the demands of active military operations against Aguinaldo and the Filipino insurgents with those of establishing a military government focused on turning over responsibility to civil authorities. On 8 October 1901, Major General Adna Chaffee, then commander of the Division, abolished the former organization of departments and districts throughout the islands effective 1 November and established seven "separate brigades" in their place. This gave greater authority to local commanders as the transition to civil government progressed after the military government was abolished on 4 July 1902. Military government remained only in the Moro Provinces due to the continuing violence and opposition. The 7th Separate Brigade assumed responsibility for Mindanao and Jolo when it replaced the former Department of Mindanao and Jolo on 31 November 1901. In a subsequent reorganization under Major General George W. Davis in September 1902, a new Department of Mindanao replaced the 7th Separate Brigade on 1 October 1902. *ARWD, 1902,* vol. 9, p. 187; *ARWD, 1903,* vol. 3, pp. 135, 297.

11. According to Pershing's notebook and diary, Davis and Sumner were at Malabang, where Pershing met them on Sunday, 7 July 1902. He spent the next two days with them there before escorting them to Camp Vicars on Tuesday, 9 July. They were then at Vicars until Thursday, 11 July, when they departed for Malabang. LC/Pershing Papers, Box 1, Notebook for Lake Lanao Expedition, entries 7–11 July 1902.

12. Pershing's appreciation of Davis's support was fully echoed by Davis's recognition of Pershing's accomplishments and soldierly qualities. On 9 March 1906, Secretary of War William H. Taft requested more information on Pershing's activities in the Philippines from Davis, probably during the course of selecting him for promotion to brigadier general. The next day Davis, now retired and chairman of the Board of Consulting Engineers to the Isthmian Canal Commission, sent a lengthy reply that included his highly favorable evaluation of Pershing:

It was desired to place in command of this remote station at the lake [Camp Vicars] an officer of prudence, good judgment and tact, one who would regard his duty as best performed when executed with the least force. I thought I had such a man in Captain Pershing and placed him in command of the troops, remaining at Camp Vicars. His command was equal to about a regiment.

I found that I had not been mistaken in my confidence as to his energy, ability and capacity, and he remained in command at Camp Vicars for about a year subsequent to July, 1902, and until his health failed. While holding this very important command he personally conducted four military explorations in the neighborhood of the lake—one of them involving the repelling of an attack by Moros and of an assault upon a very strongly fortified place in Bacolod. He also conducted an expedition that entirely circuited the lake—the first civilized force that had ever done this. . . .

On the 26th of June, 1903, as Division Commander I addressed the Adjutant-General of the Army in Washington as follows:

. . . This officer has just been detailed on the General Staff of the Army, a detail which commends itself to me as most wise. When the time comes for the Department to make selection of general officers for promotion from the grade of captain, I hope that Captain Pershing may be selected for brigadier-general. I have frequently brought his merits to the attention of the Department, in routine and in special communications, for gallantry, good judgment, and thorough efficiency in every branch of the soldier's profession. He is the equal of any and the superior of most.

One of the reasons why I was especially pleased with this officer's behavior was that he seemed to enter fully into the spirit of my instructions, that the smaller the loss and the sacrifice, not only of our own men but of the Moros, the greater would be his merit. He carried out those instructions to the letter and I was especially gratified.

Letters, William H. Taft, Secretary of War, to Major General (retired) George W. Davis, 9 March 1906, and George W. Davis to Secretary Taft, 10 March 1906, LC/Pershing Papers, Box 281, Folder 2: Personal Military Career of Capt. Pershing.

13. Major General George W. Davis, Commanding General, Division of the Philippines, to The Adj. Gen., 19 February 1903, LC/Pershing Papers, Box 281. Folder 2: Personal Military Career of Capt. Pershing.

14. In his letter to Charles Magoon on 28 January 1903 (see note 11.2 above), Pershing added a different perspective to his dealings with the sultan of Binidayan that also laid out his fundamental principle for governing the Moros:

As to government, they [the Moros] now have about the only sort of government they can understand and our policy should be to let it alone. It has been my endeavor to preserve their government in its integrity and in all instances to uphold the authority of the Sultan or Datto in his own rancheria. On the other hand in their relations with us they fully understand that we hold the Sultan or Datto responsible for the acts of his people, that is, he cannot be Sultan and receive our support and recognition of his authority and at the same time deny his responsibility for the acts of his people. It was on this theory that I arrested the Sultan of Binidayan last July because he refused to deliver one of his subordinate dattos, Tangul by name, who with a few associates attempted to kill two soldiers on the trail between here and the sea coast. The Sultan while a prisoner went "juramentado," that is, ran amuck pursuant to a vow to kill, and was himself killed by the guards. The arrest of this powerful old Sultan, which by the way was attended with considerable difficulty, fully demonstrated to the whole Laguna that there would be no variation from this principle and it has led to positive action on the part of many important dattos who have said to their people "See here, if any of you molest the Americans in any way, off comes my head, for we do not intend to be held responsible for your foolish acts." The Dutch in their colonies in this part of the world seem to have little trouble and they maintain the kind of government they found in existence. To close this paragraph I will say that, at any rate, we cannot afford to tear down their established form of government without giving them something better and I fear it will be a long time before this can be done.

Letter, Pershing to Magoon, 28 January 1903, LC/Pershing Papers, Box 369, Philippines: 1901–03 (2).

Pershing also kept Davis completely informed of his activities, with regular updates on events around Lake Lanao. On 28 August 1902 he informed Davis about his continuing efforts to reach some sort of formalized agreement with the Moros of the area, something that never happened, and the death of the sultan of Binidayan:

On the night of August 11th, a party of about twenty Moros from Bacolod and Cauayan, a rancheria south of Bucuyauan, attacked the outpost at the Q. M. Corral and killed the Sergeant and the sentinel on post and wounded the others. One Moro was killed. On the next night the Camp was fired into by a party of about thirty from Maciu, undoubtedly under Amai-Benening and Amai-Grar, and on the 13th the Sultan of Binidayan when juramentado, struck the Sergeant of the Guard and the Sentry over him with a bamboo club taken from his bunk, grabbed the Sentry's gun and tried to kill the Sentry with it. The Guard filled him with lead and he died about three hours later. I thought at first that possibly trouble would be at once precipitated but it did not seem to make much difference. I wrote to the Binidayan and Bayan people explaining that the Sultan had gone juramentado and told them that he had held the Americans blameless and that before he died he had said that he hoped the Moros and Americans would forever be at peace. Their replies indicate that they have no resentment toward the Americans. It is believed that the Sultan heard the Moros yell when they attacked the outpost and thought his sons had gone juramentado. Letter, Pershing to Davis, 28 August 1902, LC/Pershing Papers, Box 317, Camp Vicars (4).

15. LC/Pershing Papers, Box 1, Notebook for Lake Lanao Expedition, entries 12–16 August 1902.

12. Military Operations against the Lake Lanao Moros and the Routine of Governing

1. In chapters 12 and 13, much of the detailed narrative information in the notes is drawn from Pershing's various reports to the commander of the Department of Mindanao during the time of his expeditions against the Lake Lanao Moros in September–October 1902 and April–May 1903. These citations will not be repeated for each officer who is mentioned here. Because the actions recounted in these hard-to-find reports were critical in establishing Pershing's military reputation and securing his entire future career, they have been attached as Appendices C–G. Sources: John J. Pershing to Adj. Gen., Dept. of Mindanao, 15 May 1903 [report on the period 30 June 1902 to 15 May 1903], pp. 322–28 [Appendix C]; Pershing to Adj. Gen., Dept. of Mindanao, 15 October 1902 ["Report of Captain John J. Pershing, Fifteenth Cavalry, of an expedition to the southeast of Lake Lanao, September 18–22, 1902"], pp. 332–35 [Appendix D]; Pershing to Adj. Gen., Dept. of Mindanao, 15 October 1902 ["Report of Capt. John J. Pershing, Fifteenth Cavalry, of an expedition against hostile Moros of Maciu, September 28–October 3, 1902"], pp. 338–41 [Appendix E]; Pershing to Adj. Gen., Dept. of Mindanao, 15 May 1903 ["Report of Capt. John J. Pershing, Fifteenth Cavalry, of an exploring expedition from Camp Vicars to Marahui, along the west shore of Lake Lanao, April 5–16, 1903"], pp. 342–46 [Appendix F]; Pershing to Adj. Gen., Dept. of Mindanao, 15 May 1903 ["Report of Capt. John J. Pershing, Fifteenth Cavalry, of an exploring expedition around Lake Lanao, May 2 to 10, 1903"], pp. 348–52 [Appendix G], all in "Appendix IV: Occupation of Lake Lanao Region," "Annual Report of Maj. Gen. George W. Davis, commanding Division of the Philippines," in *ARWD, 1903*, vol. 3: *Reports of Department and Division Commanders.* Copies of these reports can also be found in LC/Pershing Papers, Box 369, Philippines, 1901–1903 (1).

2. For a detailed account, see Appendix D, "Pershing to Adj. Gen., Dept. of Min-

danao, 15 October 1902" ["Report of Captain John J. Pershing, Fifteenth Cavalry, of an expedition to the southeast of Lake Lanao, September 18–22, 1902"], in "Appendix IV: Occupation of Lake Lanao Region," "Annual Report of Maj. Gen. George W. Davis, commanding Division of the Philippines," in *ARWD, 1903*, vol. 3: *Reports of Department and Division Commanders*, pp. 332–35. See also Vandiver, *Black Jack*, vol. 1, pp. 274–88; Smythe, *Guerrilla Warrior*, pp. 87–90, and for another firsthand account, Allen and Reidy, *The Battle of Bayan and Other Battles*, pp. 58–78.

3. For a detailed account, see Appendix E, "Pershing to Adj. Gen., Dept. of Mindanao, 15 October 1902" ["Report of Capt. John J. Pershing, Fifteenth Cavalry, of an expedition against hostile Moros of Maciu, September 28–October 3, 1902"], in "Appendix IV: Occupation of Lake Lanao Region," "Annual Report of Maj. Gen. George W. Davis, commanding Division of the Philippines," in *ARWD, 1903*, vol. 3: *Reports of Department and Division* Commanders, pp. 338–41. See also Vandiver, *Black Jack*, vol. 1, pp. 288–97; Smythe, *Guerrilla Warrior*, pp. 90–91; and for another firsthand account, Allen and Reidy, *The Battle of Bayan and Other Battles*, pp. 80–100.

4. Pershing mentions this trip in general terms in his report of 15 May 1903 on the period of his command at Camp Vicars (30 June 1902–15 May 1903) (see Appendix C). Soon after his return to Camp Vicars, on 5 December 1902, he reported in detail on this trip and its results to the Adjutant General, Department of Mindanao, for Brigadier General Sumner's information. Pershing noted:

> This being the first time in the history of this island so far as I am able to ascertain that any body of white men has crossed from one side of the island to the other by way of Lake Lanao, it can but impress the Moro mind with the ability of the Americans to go where they please and when they please. . . . The reception accorded us along the route by Moros of friendly rancherias has demonstrated their desire to be at peace with us and an evident purpose on their part to prevent any of their people from involving them in war with us.

Letter, Pershing to Adj. Gen., Dept. of Mindanao, 5 December 1902, LC/Pershing Papers, Box 369, Philippines, 1901–1903 (2).

5. General Nelson Miles spoke to the troops at Camp Vicars on 15 November 1902 and made the following comments:

> I desire to say a few words to this command on this occasion. It is a long distance from the Capitol—a long distance from what was a few years ago the only territory of the United States. I find this command occupying the most remote station of any portion of the Army. It occupies the position of honor and of glory, and I am gratified to find it in such splendid condition. Yesterday we passed over this beautiful and picturesque country, and I was fortunate in having with me several officers who have been my companions for many years. First, there was the distinguished Department Commander [Brigadier General Samuel Sumner], and we recalled scenes and incidents that occurred as we rode together years ago when we were young men in the days of '61. I am gratified that this portion of the territory is under a Commanding General of such experience, judgement, and ability. We also had with us a distinguished general [Brigadier General Jesse Lee] who had a splendid record in the great Civil War and on the frontier, and who, by his sterling integrity and ability, defended the rights and interests of the red men by the tens of thousands against injustice and wrong. We also had with us another general officer [Brigadier General Frank Bald-

win] who served with distinction during the Civil War and on the frontier, and who on this field of his campaign and battle achieved success and victory in this remote country. I find here an officer in command who years ago I prophesied would make his mark in the future if he ever had an opportunity [Captain Pershing]. That was nearly twenty years ago in Arizona. He was then a young lieutenant. You are fortunate now in having a so intelligent, judicious and able commanding officer, and I desire in this presence to thank not only the skillful and gallant officers, but the soldiers who have made such a splendid campaign, and who have exhibited such bravery and fortitude and maintained the honor and glory and character of the American Army. I see also the evidences of the tremendous amount of work that you have accomplished in building this great military road that opens to civilization this remote and dark region of country. You have certainly shown all the characteristics of the American soldier—fortitude, gallantry, patience, endurance, tenacity, and great intelligence, and I desire on this occasion to thank you, each and everyone, officers and soldiers, for the splendid service you have performed. I hear no complaints; no reports of cruelty or injustice by this command, but only of intelligent, humane, and heroic service, the best that could be performed by our Army, or any other army on earth. I congratulate you upon your achievements, and I prophesy equal success and glory for you in the future." "General Miles' Address to the Troops at Camp Vicars. November 15, 1902," LC/Pershing Papers, Box 281, Folder 2: Personal Military Career of Capt. Pershing; "General Miles Praises Capt. Pershing for Conduct of Negotiations," *Manila Cablenews*, 17 November 1902, LC/Pershing Papers, Box 318, Philippines, 1901–1903 (3).

6. Rinderpest is a highly infectious viral disease that strikes cattle, sheep, and other farm animals, resulting in a high fever, diarrhea, and lesions of the skin and mucous membrane. It is usually fatal. The disease is also known as cattle plague. *Webster's Encyclopedic Unabridged Dictionary*, p. 1234.

7. Surra is a very fatal infectious disease that affects horses. It is caused by a protozoan parasite that infects their blood. *Webster's Encyclopedic Unabridged Dictionary*, p. 1432.

13. Finishing the Campaign against the Lake Lanao Moros

1. As in chapter 12, much of the detailed narrative information in the notes is drawn from Pershing's various reports to the commander of the Department of Mindanao during the time of his expeditions against the Lake Lanao Moros in September–October 1902 and April–May 1903. These citations will not be repeated for each officer who is noted here. Because the actions recounted in these hard-to-find reports were critical in establishing Pershing's military reputation and securing his entire future career, they have been attached as Appendices C–G. Sources: John J. Pershing to Adj. Gen., Dept. of Mindanao, 15 May 1903 [report on the period 30 June 1902 to 15 May 1903], pp. 322–28 [Appendix C]; Pershing to Adj. Gen., Dept. of Mindanao, 15 October 1902 ["Report of Captain John J. Pershing, Fifteenth Cavalry, of an expedition to the southeast of Lake Lanao, September 18–22, 1902"], pp. 332–35 [Appendix D]; Pershing to Adj. Gen., Dept. of Mindanao, 15 October 1902 ["Report of Capt. John J. Pershing, Fifteenth Cavalry, of an expedition against hos-

tile Moros of Maciu, September 28–October 3, 1902"], pp. 338-41 [Appendix E]; Pershing to Adj. Gen., Dept. of Mindanao, 15 May 1903 ["Report of Capt. John J. Pershing, Fifteenth Cavalry, of an exploring expedition from Camp Vicars to Marahui, along the west shore of Lake Lanao, April 5-16, 1903"], pp. 342-46 [Appendix F]; Pershing to Adj. Gen., Dept. of Mindanao, 15 May 1903 ["Report of Capt. John J. Pershing, Fifteenth Cavalry, of an exploring expedition around Lake Lanao, May 2 to 10, 1903"], pp. 348-52 [Appendix G]; all in "Appendix IV: Occupation of Lake Lanao Region," "Annual Report of Maj. Gen. George W. Davis, commanding Division of the Philippines," in *ARWD, 1903,* vol. 3: *Reports of Department and Division Commanders.* Copies of these reports can also be found in LC/Pershing Papers, Box 369, Philippines, 1901-1903 (1).

2. Pershing's command actually did fire some shots, perhaps a lot of them. This action was not at Gata, but as the column was returning to Camp Vicars at the crossing of the Malaig River, where some six to eight Moros fired on the column from their *cotta,* acting on the orders of Sultan Ganduali. Five Moros were killed and the *cotta* was destroyed. Pershing reported to Davis in a letter of 4 March that "They rather got the worst of it." See Pershing to Adj. Gen., Dept. of Mindanao, 15 May 1903 [report on the period 30 June 1902 to 15 May 1903], p. 326 [Appendix C]; Letter, Pershing to Davis, 4 March 1903, LC/Pershing Papers, Box 369, Philippines, 1901-1903 (2).

3. For additional information, see Appendix F, Pershing to Adj. Gen., Dept. of Mindanao, 15 May 1903 ["Report of Capt. John J. Pershing, Fifteenth Cavalry, of an exploring expedition from Camp Vicars to Marahui, along the west shore of Lake Lanao, April 5-16, 1903"], extracted from "Appendix IV: Occupation of Lake Lanao Region," "Annual Report of Maj. Gen. George W. Davis, commanding Division of the Philippines," in *ARWD, 1903,* vol. 3, *Reports of Department and Division Commanders,* pp. 342-46. See also Vandiver, *Black Jack,* vol. 1, pp. 303-11, and Smythe, *Guerrilla Warrior,* pp. 94-102.

4. Pershing's pessimistic view of the eventual outcome was very different than that which he had predicted to Davis in letters of 23 January and 4 March 1903, when he believed that he would be able to win over the more recalcitrant of the Moro leaders. In January he had written confidently:

The circuit of the lake once made we are in a position to better understand the needs of these people and to formulate some sort of simple form of government for them. Their comprehension of anything in this line beyond what they have always been accustomed to is very limited as I found after further discussing with them some of the points I wrote you in a former letter, in view of which an acknowledgement by them of our authority to govern them and the enforcement by us of peace between different rancherias are about all that we should expect for the present. After we have visited the various rancherias and I have met the leading Moros personally, it seems to me that we may then consider further trouble as highly improbable and we shall certainly be in a position to overcome any opposition or resistance to our authority in future. I shall make every effort to the end that this may be accomplished without bloodshed for I consider that one friend won by peaceful methods worth many so called friends won by force.

Letter, Pershing to Davis, 23 January 1903, LC/Pershing Papers, Box 369, Philippines, 1901–1903 (2).

5. See Telegram, Davis (Manila) to Sumner (Zamboanga), 30 March 1903, in "Appendix IV: Occupation of Lake Lanao Region," "Annual Report of Maj. Gen. George W. Davis, commanding Division of the Philippines," in *ARWD, 1903,* vol. 3, *Reports of Department and Division Commanders,* p. 347.

6. A. Henry Savage Landor, an English explorer and travelogue writer, accompanied Pershing's expedition with General Sumner's approval. He provided a colorful and detailed account of Pershing's activities and leadership in his *The Gems of the East: Sixteen Thousand Miles of Research Travel among Wild and Tame Tribes on Enchanting Islands* (New York: Harper and Brothers, 1904), pp. 280–319. Landor's account added an important outside perspective on the expedition and further enhanced Pershing's growing reputation in the army and among the American public. Landor applauded Pershing's careful planning and preparation before attacking Bacolod and commented that "it really showed sound military judgment and common-sense on the part of the American commander [Pershing]—who never lost sight for one moment of the principle of inflicting upon the enemy as much damage as possible with as little to his own side." Landor, *The Gems of the East,* pp. 294–95.

7. For additional information about the May expedition, see Appendix G, Pershing to Adj. Gen., Dept. of Mindanao, 15 May 1903 ["Report of Capt. John J. Pershing, Fifteenth Cavalry, of an exploring expedition around Lake Lanao, May 2 to 10, 1903"], extracted from "Appendix IV: Occupation of Lake Lanao Region," "Annual Report of Maj. Gen. George W. Davis, commanding Division of the Philippines," in *ARWD, 1903,* vol. 3, *Reports of Department and Division Commanders,* pp. 348–52. See also Vandiver, *Black Jack,* vol. 1, pp. 311–16, and Smythe, *Guerrilla Warrior,* pp. 102–8.

8. The original manuscript initially listed the following details of this force in the text and then crossed out the information and indicated that it should be placed in a footnote as follows:

The command was composed about as above: Companies C, D (First Lieutenant C. S. Eskridge), G, and M, and 38 men of Company F, all Twenty-seventh Infantry; Troops A (Lieutenant Mangum, commanding), E (Captain F. J. Koester and First Lieutenant R. B. Going), and G, Fifteenth Cavalry; the Seventeenth Battery, Field Artillery; Second Lieutenant V. S. Foster, Acting Adjutant; Second Lieutenant W. C. Gardenhire, Acting Quartermaster; Second Lieutenant D. H. Currie, Engineer Officer; Captain W. F. Lewis and First Lieutenant R. U. Patterson, Surgeons.

9. In his report at Appendix G, Pershing lists a total of ten casualties during this expedition: two enlisted men of the 27th Infantry were killed in action at the Taraca River on 4 May (Corporal Samuel A. Schwartz Jr., Company F, and Private Burton S. Frank, Company M), and eight wounded. The losses at the Taraca River, Fort Pitacus, on 4 May were two killed in action and five wounded, not the one killed and six wounded as claimed by Pershing. See "Casualties during the expedition around Lake Lanao, May 2 to 10, 1903, inclusive," in "Appendix IV: Occupation of Lake Lanao Region," "Annual Report of Maj. Gen. George W. Davis, commanding Division of the Philippines," in *ARWD, 1903,* vol. 3, *Reports of Department and Division Commanders,* p. 353.

10. Rodgers spent only the months from June to September 1903 at Camp Vic-

ars before he returned to the United States when the 15th Cavalry Regiment rotated back to Fort Ethan Allen, Vermont, where he commanded the regiment (December 1903–April 1906). In November 1903, Major Robert L. Bullard, who had commanded the 3d Battalion, 28th Infantry, at Iligan since October 1902, became the first governor of the Lanao District, which was established with the creation of the Moro Province (see note 13.11 below).

11. Moro Province. All areas of the Philippine Islands except the Moro and pagan (non-Christian) areas of Mindanao and the Sulu Archipelago were returned to civil government and local civilian control under the governor-general and Philippine Commission by 1 October 1902. Inhabited largely by hostile Moros and pagan tribes, these areas remained under the military government control of the commander, Department of Mindanao, because of the armed threat presented by the Moros. Following the recommendation of Major General Adna Chaffee, Philippine Division commander, in his final Annual Report of 30 September 1902, early in 1903 the Secretary of War recommended to Governor-General Taft that a military-civil government be adopted for the Moro and pagan areas of Mindanao and Sulu to enhance their social, political, and economic progress. After closely coordinating the legislation with Major General George Davis, now the Division commander and the former commander on Mindanao, who was very well versed in Moro affairs, Taft and the Philippine Commission authorized the organization of a military-civil government under a general officer for these areas and grouped most Moros into a new Moro Province on 1 June 1903 (effective 15 July). The new governor would be responsible to the governor-general for the province's civil administration and to the Philippine Division's commanding general for its military administration as commander of the military Department of Mindanao. This new Moro Province included the largest concentrations of Moros living in the Sulu Archipelago and in the Rio Grande del Mindanao Valley and the Lake Lanao districts of Mindanao. Administratively it was divided into five districts, each under a military governor and with a five-member legislative council (controlled by the army officers on them): Zamboanga (Captain John P. Finley), Sulu (Major Hugh L. Scott), Lanao (Major Robert L. Bullard), Cotabato (Captain Carl Reichmann), and Davao (First Lieutenant Edward C. Bolton). The first military governor appointed under this law was Brigadier General Leonard Wood, who became governor on 25 July 1903 and assumed command of the Department of Mindanao on 6 August. *ARWD, 1902,* vol. 9, *Report of the Lieutenant-General Commanding the Army and Department Commanders,* pp. 193–95; *ARWD, 1903,* vol. 3, *Reports of Department and Division Commanders,* pp. 149–56; *ARWD, 1904,* vol. 3, *Reports of Department and Division Commanders,* pp. 207–8, 261; U.S. War Department, Bureau of Insular Affairs, *Fourth Annual Report of the Philippine Commission, 1903* (Washington, D.C.: GPO, 1904), pt. 1, pp. 76–81; *Annual Report of the Governor of the Moro Province: September 1, 1903 to August 31, 1904* (Washington, D.C.: GPO, 1904), pp. 3–4; Fulton, *Moroland,* passim; Arnold, *The Moro War,* pp. 76–109; Lane, *Armed Progressive,* pp. 114–31; Garel A. Grunder and William E. Livezey, *The Philippines and the United States* (Norman: Univ. of Oklahoma Press, 1951), pp. 139–43.

12. Pershing and those who assisted him added the words in parentheses to the original quotation in the manuscript. The quotation is from Pershing to Adj. Gen., Dept. of Mindanao, 15 May 1903 [report on period 30 June 1902 to 15 May 1903], in "Appendix IV: Occupation of Lake Lanao Region," "Annual Report of Maj. Gen.

George W. Davis, commanding Division of the Philippines," in *ARWD, 1903*, vol. 3, *Reports of Department and Division Commanders*, pp. 327–28. For Pershing's complete report on his activities at Camp Vicars from 30 June 1902 to 15 May 1903, see Appendix C, extracted from *ARWD, 1903*, vol. 3, *Reports of Department and Division Commanders*, pp. 322–28. Also see a copy of this report in LC/Pershing Papers, Box 369, Philippines, 1901–1903 (1).

14. Return to the United States, Duty with the General Staff, and Romance and Marriage

1. Taiping Rebellion. The Taiping Rebellion stretched from 1850 to 1864, eventually affecting seventeen Chinese provinces and claiming 20 million lives. It began when Hong Xiuquan (1814–1864) came to believe himself to be the younger brother of Jesus Christ whom God sent to reform the Qing Dynasty. He proclaimed a new Chinese dynasty, his own, the *Taiping Tianguo* (Heavenly Kingdom of Great Peace) in January 1851. Many dissatisfied and downtrodden peasants and workers joined the movement, which preached the sharing of property in common. Soon Hong's followers formed an enormous army of 1 million and seized Nanjing, which was declared their capital. The movement eventually suffered internal conflicts and fractured. Chinese armies commanded by Major General Charles George "Chinese" Gordon and an American, Frederick Ward, stopped the Taiping armies. Chinese armies then laid siege to Nanjing in 1862, and the city finally fell in July 1864 and Hong Xiuquan committed suicide. The Taiping Rebellion seriously undermined the Qing Dynasty, which never recovered full control of China thereafter. The movement's primitive communism and land distribution schemes led both the Chinese Nationalists and Communists to claim it as their ancestor. "Taiping Rebellion," Encyclopaedia Britannica Online, http://www.britannica.com/EBchecked/topic/580815/Taiping-Rebellion.

2. "White man's burden." During the nineteenth century a number of European writers, but especially British writers Rudyard Kipling and Thomas Carlyle, espoused the superiority of the white, Aryan race over the inferior nonwhite races populating their colonial domains. They saw it as the "white man's burden" to bring the blessings of white European civilization to these less fortunate peoples through an enlightened and benevolent colonial control. Many American leaders held similar views of the American blacks who were recently freed from slavery after the Civil War and of other peoples who populated the recently gained overseas possessions, especially the Filipinos. "White Supremacy," Encyclopaedia Britannica Online, http://www.britannica.com/EBchecked/topic/642638/white-supremacy.

3. Pershing is referring to U.S. Navy commodore Matthew C. Perry's "opening of Japan" to western contacts and influence in 1853–1854. After a number of unsuccessful U.S. Navy attempts to establish relations with the reclusive and anti-foreign Tokugawa Shogunate that then ruled Japan, on 8 July 1853 Perry anchored his squadron of four ships at Uraga (today's Yokosuka) in Edo (Tokyo) Bay. Perry carried a letter from President Millard Fillmore to the emperor requesting a treaty and establishment of relations with the United States. To the Japanese onshore, the American ships were "black ships," a term used since the earliest western contacts with Japan that dated to the black-hulled Portuguese ships which first touched Japa-

nese shores in the mid-1500s. Thereafter, the Japanese referred to any foreign ships as "black ships." Such visits were not welcome in the years of the Tokugawa Shogunate, which sought to isolate the Japanese islands and people as much as possible from any dangerous foreign influences. The four American ships were also painted black, and two were steam-powered, which meant that they emitted large volumes of black smoke when steaming, further reinforcing the Japanese perspective on the evil nature of the visitors. In February 1854 Perry returned with nine ships, again anchoring at Uraga, and concluded the Treaty of Kanagawa on 31 March 1854, the first treaty between the United States and Japan. Perry's activities marked the first formal "opening" of Japan to more widespread European and American contacts. "Matthew C. Perry," Encyclopaedia Britannica Online, http://www.britannica .com/EBchecked/topic/452613/Matthew-C-Perry; "Commodore Perry and the Opening of Japan," Navy Department Library, Naval History and Heritage Command, http://www.history.navy.mil/library/special/perry_openjapan1.htm; "Black Ships," http://en.wikipedia.org/wiki/Black_Ships; G. B. Sansom, *The Western World and Japan: A Study in the Interaction of European and Asiatic Cultures* (New York: Knopf, 1970), pp. 105, 275–309; David F. Long, *Gold Braid and Foreign Relations: Diplomatic Activities of U.S. Naval Officers, 1798-1883* (Annapolis, Md.: Naval Institute Press, 1988), pp. 236–50, especially 242–48.

4. Washington Treaty. Apparently Pershing is referring to the treaty of 17 November 1880 with China that gave the U.S. government the authority "to regulate, limit, or suspend" the immigration of Chinese into the United States but not prohibit it. Morris, *Encyclopedia of American History*, pp. 281–82; "U.S. Concludes Treaty with China—November 17, 1880," Miller Center of Public Affairs, University of Virginia, American President, An Online Reference Resource, http://millercenter .org/president/events/11_17; Morris, *Encyclopedia of American History*, pp. 281–82.

5. Exclusion Act. Known as the "Chinese Exclusion Act," this measure was signed by President Chester A. Arthur on 6 May 1882 and restricted Chinese immigration into the United States for a period of ten years. It was the first law ever passed and signed that denied entry into the country based on race or ethnic origins. The law was extended for another ten years by the Geary Act in 1892, and the extension was made permanent in 1902. The law was finally completely repealed in 1943 when the Republic of China was an American ally in the war against Japan. Morris, *Encyclopedia of American History*, pp. 282; "Chinese Exclusion Act of 1882," The Free Dictionary, http://legal-dictionary.thefreedictionary.com/Chinese+Exclusion+Act+of+1882; "Chinese Exclusion Act (1882)," *Our Documents,* at http://www.ourdocuments.gov/ doc.php?flash=old&doc=47.

15. Off to See a Modern War as the Military Attaché in Tokyo and Observer with the Imperial Japanese Army

1. Prince Albert. The Prince Albert was a double-breasted frock coat with knee-length skirts that men wore as standard morning and daytime business and formal clothing in Great Britain, Europe, and the United States during the Victorian era, from about the 1840s to about 1900. It was named after Prince Albert (1819-1861), Queen Victoria's consort, who was thought to have popularized its wear in Great Britain. "Frock Coat," http://en.wikipedia.org/wiki/Frock_coat.

2. The original text has a footnote here reading: "T.R. had been a boxer since his ranching days and kept it up even after he entered the White House, where he lost one of his eyes through an unfortunate blow from his adversary." Apparently, Roosevelt began to suffer a continuing loss of sight in his left eye following a blow he received in a boxing match in the White House. Although the cause for his loss of sight might have occurred earlier, present-day analysis indicates that the probable cause for his loss of vision was an undiagnosed detached retina suffered from a blow to his head. Edmund Morris, *Theodore Rex* (New York: Random House, 2002), p. 376; "Museum of Vision Recognizes President's Day with an Inside Look into the Eyesight Challenges of U.S. Presidents," American Academy of Ophthalmology, http://www.aao.org/newsroom/release/20120213.cfm.

3. Battle of Mukden (19 February–10 March 1905). Mukden was the longest and largest battle of the war, pitting 270,000 Japanese attackers against 293,000 Russian defenders. The fighting at Mukden often resembled World War I in the extensive use of field fortifications, artillery, and machine guns, with heavy losses suffered on both sides. The battle was fought astride the South Manchurian Railway line that was the Russians' single line of communications from Harbin and northern Manchuria. Once Japanese flanking moves threatened the Russian rear and the railway line, the Russians withdrew to the north. Warner and Warner, *The Tide at Sunrise*, pp. 498–513; "Battle of Mukden," in Holmes, ed., *The Oxford Companion to Military History*, p. 607.

4. The stresses of the war in the Far East, combined with growing social and political unrest in European Russia, led to what was known as the Revolution of 1905. The revolution began when imperial troops fired on strikers in St. Petersburg during a peaceful protest march on Sunday, 9 January 1905 (Old Style). The deaths of 130 protesters and the wounding of another 333 on what became known as "Bloody Sunday" quickly sparked widespread unrest against the tsarist government throughout the empire. This mounting domestic trouble threatened the monarchy and government and seriously weakened their ability to carry on any extended fighting in the Far East. The continuing unrest resulted in significant reforms in the government later in 1905. Sidney Harcave, *The Russian Revolution of 1905* (London: Collier Books, 1970), passim.

5. All seventeen of the U.S. Army's official military observers who were sent to Manchuria were directed to submit reports of their observations to the War Department General Staff upon the completion of their assignments. Not all of them later submitted the requested reports in writing. Ten reports were published in 1906–1907 in the five-part series *Reports of Military Observers Attached to the Armies in Manchuria during the Russo-Japanese War.* Although Pershing collected a large amount of information on military operations during the war, he never completed or apparently submitted an official report to the War Department General Staff. A ninety-four-page draft report of his experiences and observations of the Imperial Japanese Army can be found in LC/Pershing, Box 370, Memoirs: Russo-Japanese War, 1905–1906.

6. *Genro.* The *genro* (elder statesmen) formed an "extraconstitutional oligarchy" that controlled the Japanese government from the Mejii Constitution (1889) to the 1930s. These were men who had played central parts in the restoration of Emperor Mejii in 1868, the establishment of the new government and Mejii Constitution, and the building of the Imperial Japanese armed forces. Their positions as counselors to the emperor allowed them to influence all aspects of the government

while remaining out of sight. Death eventually claimed them all, the last *genro* dying in 1940. "Genro," Encyclopaedia Britannica Online, http://www.britannica.com/EBchecked/topic/229299/genro.

7. Battle of Nanshan Hill (25–26 May 1904). Nanshan Hill was the key to the Russian defensive position across a small neck of land blocking Japanese access to the Kwantung Peninsula, the port of Dalny, and the fortress of Port Arthur. This battle between divisions of the Japanese Second Army and Russian East Siberian rifle regiments was savagely contested. While Russian troops fought well, the incompetent General Anatoly Mikhailovich Stoessel provided no reinforcements and withdrew prematurely, effectively isolating the fortress and Russian fleet. Warner and Warner, *The Tide at Sunrise*, pp. 306–19.

8. During the Russo-Japanese War, the U.S. War Department sent a total of seventeen officers for duty as military observers with Russian and Japanese armies in Manchuria—nine to the Japanese and eight to the Russians. They served for varying periods and were replaced on a regular basis so that their observations could be reported to the War Department. Colonel Valery Havard, Medical Corps, and Captain William V. Judson, Corps of Engineers, were captured early in March 1905 when the hasty Russian retreat left them stranded in Mukden, where Japanese forces captured them.

9. Battle of Liaoyang (24 August–4 September 1904). This battle was one of the longest and most continuous military battles in history to that time. Nearly 158,000 Russians with 609 guns opposed 125,000 Japanese with 170 guns for control of the strategic city of Liaoyang. Sitting on the South Manchurian Railway line, which ran south from Harbin to the port of Dalny and Port Arthur, Liaoyang was a key to Japanese strategy and to preventing the relief of Port Arthur. Although the Russians generally had the better of the fighting and inflicted heavier losses on the attacking Japanese (23,600 total Japanese casualties versus 17,912 Russian), the Russians retreated when the Japanese First Army of Kuroki threatened the Russian line of communications. Although the Russians had victory within their grasp during this pivotal battle, incompetent and bumbling leadership left the field to the Japanese, who claimed a crucial victory. Warner and Warner, *The Tide at Sunrise*, pp. 378–99.

10. Pershing visited Corvisart, then commanding the XVI Corps, at his command post on 20 August 1917 to observe the French Second Army's offensive against Le Mort Homme and Hill 304 west of Verdun. During the visit he and Corvisart discussed their time together as observers in Manchuria and reminisced about their former colleagues. Pershing asked about then Major von Etzel, who had been the senior German attaché with the Japanese Army. Pershing noted that Corvisart smiled, "pointed to the battlefield and said 'I have just beaten him to-day. He is commanding a division opposite me.'" See Pershing, *My Experiences in the World War* (New York: Frederick A. Stokes, 1931), vol. 1, pp. 139–40; Vandiver, *Black Jack*, vol. 2, p. 766.

11. For information on the "black ships," see note 14.3.

12. In the summer of 1905 (July–September), Theodore Roosevelt sent William H. Taft, former governor-general of the Philippines and Secretary of War since 1 February 1904, on a "goodwill tour" that visited Hawaii, Japan, the Philippines, Hong Kong, and Shanghai. The party accompanying Taft included some thirty members of Congress, numerous military and civilian officials and leaders, Roosevelt's

daughter, Alice, and her then boyfriend but husband to be, Representative Nicholas Longworth. With the death of Secretary of State John Hay on 1 July 1905, Roosevelt used Taft as his personal representative and "trouble-shooter" to conduct some of his then most critical diplomatic initiatives. This was especially so for the Japanese, with whom Roosevelt had just bartered an agreement for him to host a peace conference to settle the Russo-Japanese War. Taft's original mission was to show off American accomplishments in the Philippines and to convince the congressional leaders traveling with him that the Filipinos were on the proper path toward future independence. Roosevelt then added the visit to Japan as a first priority, so that Taft could meet with Prime Minister Katsura Taro about working out some sort of U.S.-Japanese arrangement in the Far East, especially concerning the future of an independent Korea. While these meetings apparently reached some agreement that Roosevelt approved, the exact nature of the consequences are widely debated even today. While Taft did not visit Korea, Alice Roosevelt did. The more controversial aspects of the Taft tour concerned American relations with Korea and exactly what Taft and Katsura agreed to. Morris, *Theodore Rex*, pp. 395–402; Howard K. Beale, *Theodore Roosevelt and the Rise of America to World Power* (Baltimore, Md.: Johns Hopkins Univ. Press, 1984), passim; Tyler Dennett, *Roosevelt and the Russo-Japanese War: A Critical Study of American Policy in Eastern Asia in 1902-5, Based Primarily upon the Private Papers of Theodore Roosevelt* (Gloucester, Mass.: Peter Smith, 1959), pp. 111–15; Henry F. Pringle, *The Life and Times of William Howard Taft: A Biography* (New York: Farrar and Rinehart, 1939), vol. 1, pp. 291–300; Ralph E. Minger, "Taft's Mission to Japan: A Study in Personal Diplomacy," *Pacific Historical Review* 30, no. 3 (August 1961), pp. 279–94. A recent volume on this adventure called it "The Imperial Cruise": see James Bradley, *The Imperial Cruise: A Secret History of Empire and War* (New York: Little, Brown, 2009).

13. Hokkaido. The island of Hokkaido is the northernmost of the Japanese Home Islands.

14. These men were either Scottish or Irish Presbyterian missionaries serving in Manchuria, primarily at the Union Theological Seminary and its medical mission in Mukden. Of them, only Dugald Christie (1855-1936) was actually a trained physician. Thomas C. Fulton (1855-1942), Frederick W. S. O'Neill (1855-1952), and John Ross (1842-1915) were missionaries who had served long years in China and Korea. Christie first came to Manchuria in 1882 and provided medical care and training for many years before establishing the Mukden Medical College in 1912. "Dugald Christie," "Thomas Cosby Fulton," "Frederick W.S. O'Neill," and "John Ross," *Biographical Dictionary of Chinese Christianity*, http://www.bdcconline.net/.

15. The article in the *Washington Herald* that raised Warren's hackles ("Moros Cause Alarm") appeared on 11 March 1910, and attacked Pershing for his "leniency" with the Moros. What excited Senator Warren most was the comment that Pershing's policies "are occasioning no little concern to certain officials of the War Department, who do not approve of the lenient policy being pursued by Brig. Gen. John J. Pershing, but who are reluctant to take any action, for fear of offending Senator Francis E. Warren, chairman of the Military Affairs Committee, who is a relative and the principal backer of Gen. Pershing." Much more partisan public attacks had appeared in the *Washington Herald*, the *Washington Times*, and the *National Tribune* in the months after the announcement of Pershing's September 1906 promotion and had been successfully refuted. Within days, the *Herald* published its amends

for the inaccurate story. "Moros Cause Alarm," *Washington Herald*, 11 March 1910, p. 2, and "Moros and Gen. Pershing," *Washington Herald*, 16 March 1910; Theodore Roosevelt to F. E. Warren, 10 November 1910, LC/Pershing Papers, Box 370, Folder: Promotion to Brigadier General, and Warren to Pershing, 12 March 1910 [sent 16 March], Box 394, Folder: Correspondence with F. E. Warren, 1911–1915.

16. Actually, Barry did not take command in Cuba until 26 February 1907, nearly four months later than Pershing has it. The initial commander of the 1st Expeditionary Brigade going to Cuba was Brigadier General Frederick Funston, the commanding general of the Department of California, who only commanded it for several days (10–12 October 1906). Brigadier General J. Franklin Bell, the recently appointed chief of staff of the army, succeeded Funston and commanded the brigade until 16 October, when it was redesignated the Army of Cuban Pacification. Bell remained until 31 December 1906, when Brigadier General Theodore J. Wint, then commanding the Department of the Missouri, assumed command. On 16 February 1907 Wint had to leave Cuba due to a heart illness that soon claimed his life. Brigadier General (later Major General) Thomas H. Barry, then assistant to the chief of staff and president of the Army War College, took command on 26 February. Barry remained in command until the occupation forces were removed and the Army of Cuban Pacification disbanded on 1 April 1909. Brigadier General Thomas H. Barry, "Report Army of Cuban Pacification," 31 August 1907, *ARWD, 1907*, vol. 3, p. 313; Major General Thomas H. Barry, "Report of the Army of Cuban Pacification," 1 April 1909, *ARWD, 1909*, vol. 3, pp. 229–34.

17. In addition to the discrepancies noted in note 15.16 above, Pershing provides some other confusing information in this paragraph. He left Japan on 4 October and arrived in Vancouver, Canada, on the 15th and San Francisco on the 20th. Upon his arrival the War Department informed him that he was to command the Department of California because Frederick Funston, who had commanded the department since April 1905, was then commanding the 1st Expeditionary Brigade, which became the Army of Cuban Pacification. Because Funston was replaced by J. Franklin Bell before Pershing even arrived in San Francisco and would eventually return as department commander, Pershing commanded the Department of California on an interim basis and only briefly (2–8 and 18–20 November), due to taking leave and then requesting duty in the Philippines commanding an infantry brigade at Fort McKinley. He departed San Francisco on 20 November bound for Yokohama, where he arrived early in December to complete the move of his family to Manila and his new assignment. Thus, Pershing was not sailing for Japan "ten days after my arrival in San Francisco" on 20 October, but a full month later after returning from the leave he took (probably 8–18 November) to visit his family in Denver, Lincoln, and Chicago. He was actually sailing only two days after returning to San Francisco from leave and resuming command of the department (18–20 November 1906). See Vandiver, *Black Jack*, vol. 1, pp. 392–95, 400; *ARWD, 1907*, vol. 3, p. 183.

16. Brigade Commander, Fort McKinley, Philippines

1. Philippine Scouts. As authorized by Congress in the army reorganization of February 1901, the U.S. Army could recruit as many as twelve thousand native scouts

into organized units in the U.S. Army in the Philippines. Recruitment for the Philippine Scouts began in September 1901. The native Filipino units were raised to offset manpower requirements and the burden on Regular and Volunteer Army units in the Philippines in the fight against Aguinaldo's independence movement. The Philippine Scout units were filled with native Filipino enlistees, many of them formerly with the Spanish military in the islands, and officered by Americans until sufficient Filipino officers became available to fill in the lower company officer grades. After World War I, these units were reorganized into units of Philippine Scouts (PS) in the 43d, 45th, and 57th Infantry Regiments, 24th and 25th Field Artillery Regiments, the 26th Cavalry Regiment, and miscellaneous other support and logistical organizations. The PS units were grouped with the 31st Infantry Regiment to form the Philippine Division. These units were always distinct from the units of the Philippine Army that were organized in the 1930s. The Philippine Scout units performed well during the Japanese invasion of the Philippines and suffered high casualties, especially in the POW camps, and during the guerrilla war from 1942–1945. The Philippine Scouts were disbanded in 1947. *ARWD, 1901,* vol. 3, p. 23; *ARWD, 1902,* vol. 9, pp. 203–4; Colonel John E. Olson, "The History of the Philippine Scouts" and Chris Schaefer, "The Philippine Scouts," Philippine Scouts Heritage Society, http://www .philippine-scouts.org; Charles B. Elliott, *The Philippines to the End of the Commission Government: A Study in Tropical Democracy* (Indianapolis, Ind.: Bobbs-Merrill, 1917), pp. 169–73; "Philippine Scouts," http://en.wikipedia.org/wiki/Philippine_Scouts.

　　2. The Philippine Constabulary was patterned on the French gendarmerie and established as a paramilitary force for the Philippine Islands in August 1901 to replace the former *Guardia Civil.* The Constabulary came under the civil governor-general and was designed to maintain law and order. American Army officers organized, trained, armed, and led the Philippine Constabulary for a number of years. While most of the officers came from volunteer units leaving the Philippines or from specially commissioned former noncommissioned officers and foreigners with military service, a good number were graduates of the USMA with significant military careers both behind and ahead of them (see note 16.3 below). Slowly, trained Filipinos were brought into the Constabulary, until in 1917 Rafael Cramé, a native Filipino, assumed the post of commander and superintendent. Philippine Constabulary units fought against the Japanese in World War II. After Philippine independence, the Constabulary was merged into the new Armed Forces of the Philippines. In 1991, the Philippine Constabulary was merged with the local police forces to form the Philippine National Police. U.S. War Department, Bureau of Insular Affairs, *Reports of the Philippine Commission, the Governor, and the Heads of the Executive Departments of the Civil Government of the Philippine Islands (1900-1903)* (Washington, D.C.: GPO, 1904), pp. 181–84, 312–15, 611–19; Dean C. Worcester, *The Philippines Past and Present* (New York: Macmillan, 1914), vol. 1, pp. 378–99; Elliott, *The Philippines to the End of the Commission Government,* pp. 173–80; "Philippine Constabulary," http:// en.wikipedia.org/wiki/Philippine_Constabulary. For a more personal look at the activities of officers and enlisted men of the Constabulary, see the reprint of Vic Hurley's *Jungle Patrol: The Story of the Philippine Constabulary, 1901-1936* (Salem, Oreg.: Cerberus Books, 2011).

　　3. Including Allen, Bandholtz, Harbord, Duncan, and Ely, at least twenty-six Army general officers (on the active duty or retired lists) served at one time or

another in the Philippine Scouts or Philippine Constabulary during their careers. A very cursory review only of USMA graduates reveals thirteen generals who served in the Constabulary (major generals: Henry T. Allen, Harry H. Bandholtz, George B. Duncan, Mark L. Hersey, Dennis E. Nolan, William C. Rivers, and Peter E. Traub; brigadier generals: John B. Bennet, Marcus Cronin, Alexander L. Dade, Herman Hall, James C. Rhea, and William S. Scott). Eighth generals were found to have served in the Scouts (major generals: Hanson E. Ely; brigadier generals: Thomas W. Darrach, Evan H. Humphrey, John W. Lang, Robert W. Mearns, Ephraim G. Peyton (also a major general in the National Guard), George C. Saffarans, and William R. Sample). Although no exhaustive examination has been made of non–USMA graduates, Lieutenant General James G. Harbord was a non–West Pointer, as was Major General Charles E. Kilbourne Jr., both of whom served in the Constabulary, while Lieutenant General George H. Brett, U.S. Army Air Corps and Air Force, began his military career as a second lieutenant in the Philippine Scouts in 1910 and Lieutenant General Daniel Van Voorhis served as a major in the Scouts (1911-1913), as did Brigadier General George C. Shaw (1912-1915). Braden, *Biographical Register 5;* Robinson, *Biographical Register 6A and 6B;* Donaldson, *Biographical Register 7*; Association of Graduates, USMA, *Register of Graduates and Former Cadets of the United States Military Academy, 2000* (West Point, N.Y.: Association of Graduates, 2000) (hereafter cited as *Register of Graduates, 2000*), passim; "George H. Brett," *Webster's Biographical Dictionary* (Springfield, Mass.: G. and C. Merriam, 1972), p. 191; "George Howard Brett," in R. Manning Ancell, with Christine M. Miller, *The Biographical Dictionary of World War II Generals and Flag Officers: The U.S. Armed Forces* (Westport, Conn.: Greenwood Press, 1996), p. 371; "Daniel Van Voorhis," in Ancell, *Biographical Dictionary*, pp. 330-31; TAGO, *OAR, 1912,* p. 405; TAGO, *OAR, January 1, 1938,* p. 1054; Henry Blaine Davis Jr., *Generals in Khaki* (Raleigh, N.C.: Pentland Press, 1998), pp. 5, 20, 32, 88, 115, 158, 160, 176, 214, 267, 312-13, 325-26.

4. Reinforced brigade. At this point, Pershing inserted the following note: "The Thirteenth and Sixteenth regiments of infantry were commanded respectively by Colonels Alfred D. Markley and Cornelius Gardner, the Eighth Cavalry by Colonel H. P. Kingsbury, and the Tenth, which took its place, was under Colonel J. A. Augur. Captain John L. Hayden commanded Battery 'F' of the Fifth Artillery, First Lieutenant Albert E. Waldron, the company of engineers, and Major William P. Kendall was surgeon. In addition there were detachments of the Signal Corps and the Quartermaster Department. My aides were Lieutenants Charles Burnett, Cavalry, and Claude S. Fries, Infantry."

Pershing mentions that his command was a brigade post, which was a relatively new organization in the army. As the army restructured after the Spanish-American War, it began building a modern organization, which required the closing of many of the smaller and costly-to-maintain posts and forts, especially in the old areas of the western frontier, and consolidating units into larger tactical fighting elements of full regiments, brigades, and divisions. The new *Field Service Regulations, United States Army,* published on 1 February 1905, set the largest permanent unit of the army as the regiment but authorized temporary or provisional brigades and divisions for field exercises or maneuvers. A brigade consisted of two or more regiments, with three as the normal organization. A reinforced brigade added field artillery, engineer, and other support as necessary. The plans for consolidation of units on brigade posts in the United States was paralleled with a similar consolidation in the Philippines Division, as many smaller unit posts were turned over to the Philippine Scouts and Philippine Constabulary. Of course, in the United States political pressures quickly formed to slow or prevent closures of small posts. However, in the Philippines Congressional pressures were less effective, and Fort McKinley became a brigade post sometime before Pershing assumed command in January 1907. U.S. War Department, Office of the Chief of Staff, *Field Service Regulations, United States Army,* 1 February 1905 (Washington, D.C.: GPO, 1905), pp. 11–12; *ARWD, 1906,* vol. 1, pp. 552–53; John B. Wilson, *Maneuver and Firepower: The Evolution of Divisions and Separate Brigades* (Washington, D.C.: U.S. Army Center of Military History, 1998), pp. 23–27.

5. Philippine Commission. In January 1899, President William McKinley appointed the First Philippine Commission (Schurman Commission) under Dr. Jacob Schurman, Cornell University president, to examine conditions in the Philippine Islands. The commission recommended the establishment of a civilian government to replace the military governor and a legislature. The Second Philippine Commission (Taft Commission) under William Howard Taft was appointed in March 1900 and had legislative and executive powers. It established the legal code, Supreme Court, and other instruments of government. Taft became civil governor-general in July 1901 and the Insular Government would administer the islands until 1935. The Roosevelt administration, led by Secretary of War William H. Taft, former governor-general (1902–1904), pushed for a greater role for the Filipinos in the government. A lower house of the Philippine legislature was to be popularly elected, while the upper house consisted of appointed American and Filipino members of the Philippine Commission. Formal elections were held on 30 July 1907 and the first sessions of the legislature began on 26 October. The Philippine Commission was formally abolished in 1916, and the elected Philippine Senate took its place as part of President Wilson's "Filipinization" program leading to eventual independence. Dean C. Worcester, *The Philippines Past and Present,* vol. 1, pp. 301–59; Worcester, *The Philippines Past and Present,* vol. 2 (New York: Macmillan, 1914), pp. 768–91; Charles Burke Elliott, *The Philippines to the End of the Military Régime: America Overseas* (Indianapolis, Ind.: Bobbs-Merrill, 1916), pp. 422–527, and Elliott, *The Philippines to the End of the Commission Government,* pp. 96–126; James H. Blount, *The American Occupation of the Philippines, 1898-1912* (New York: G. P. Putnam's Sons, 1912), pp. 282–570; Victoriano D. Diamonon, "The Development of Self-Government in the Philippine Islands" (Ph.D. diss., State University of Iowa, 1920), passim; Fulton, *Moroland,* pp. 469–84; Grunder and Livezey, *The Philippines and the United States,* passim.

6. For a complete review of Taft's trip, which lasted from 13 September to 20 December 1907, with the period from 15 October to 9 November spent in the Philippines, and a copy of his speech to the Philippine Assembly, see "Special Report of Wm. H. Taft, Secretary of War, to the President on the Philippines, January 23, 1908," in U.S. War Department, *Special Reports on the Philippines to the President by Wm. H. Taft, Secretary of War, January 23, 1908 and J.M. Dickinson, Secretary of War, November 23, 1910* (Washington, D.C.: GPO, 1919), pp. 9–91.

7. The Philippine Commission made Baguio the summer capital of the Philippines in June 1903 (which it remains to this day), and 535 acres were designated for a military reservation. Upon the death of Secretary of State John Hay this reserva-

tion was named Camp John Hay in his honor, but was only transferred to the army in October 1910 due to litigation. It became the main rest and recreation area for the U.S. Army in the Philippines. It was expanded in the 1920s to include companies of Philippine Scouts. During World War II, the Japanese used the camp as a prison for interned U.S. and British civilians. In 1945 it became the Japanese headquarters and was largely destroyed in the fighting to recapture Luzon. The Japanese surrender on Luzon took place at Camp John Hay on 3 September 1945. The camp was rebuilt after the war and later served as an air base as well as a recreation facility for American troops in the Philippines. The camp was turned over to the Philippine government on 1 July 1991 and is currently being developed as a vacation resort. For more information on Camp John Hay and Baguio City, see: "Camp John Hay," http://www.campjohnhay.com.ph/history_iframe.php; Worcester, *The Philippines Past and Present,* vol. 1, pp. 449–87.

8. Pershing submitted an extensive report on his trip to Japan and observations to the War Department on 15 February 1908. A copy is in the Library of Congress, Pershing Papers, Box 370, Folder 3: Japanese Army Maneuvers 1907.

17. A Long Journey Home, Taft's Inauguration, Sick Leave, New Orders, and a Son Arrives

1. The unique Cathedral of St. Basil the Blessed on Red Square in Moscow was apparently designed and built by Postnik Yakovlev, a Russian architect and builder from Pskov whose real name may have been Ivan Yakovlevich Barma, but this is not at all clear. St. Basil's was constructed between 1555 and 1561 to commemorate Ivan the Terrible's capture of the cities of Kazan and Astrakhan on the Volga River. Yakovlev later designed other churches in Moscovy, including the northeast chapel added to St. Basil's in 1588, after Ivan the Terrible's death. Most likely the blinding story is exactly what Pershing said it was, a story, and yet a believable one given Ivan's blood reign. "Saint Basil the Blessed," Encyclopaedia Britannica Online, http://www.britannica.com/EBchecked/topic/516839/Saint-Basil-the-Blessed; "St. Basil's Cathedral (Moscow)," http://en.wikipedia.org/wiki/Saint_Basil's_Cathedral; "Postnik Yakovlev," http://en.wikipedia.org/wiki/Postnik_Yakovlev.

2. Partitions of Poland. Russia, Prussia, and Austria staged three partitions of Poland in 1772, 1793, and 1795. Frederick II of Prussia concocted the First Partition (5 August 1772) that was forced on a divided and weak Kingdom of Poland, which lost one-half of its population and one-third of its territory, as a way of preventing war between Austria and Russia over Turkish territory. In 1792, Russia and Prussia divided an additional 115,000 square miles of Polish territory between them. From March to November 1794, Tadeusz Kościuszko, a hero of the American Revolution, led a national fight against the foreign occupiers, which Russia and Prussia forcefully suppressed. In an agreement of 24 October 1795, the three states divided the last remnants of the independent Polish state and Poland was eradicated. The exact divisions were readjusted in 1807 when Napoleon created the Grand Duchy of Warsaw from the central area of Prussian Poland, which then included Warsaw. The Congress of Vienna (1815) created the Congress Kingdom of Poland, but it remained under strict and often brutal Russian control. The Polish state was finally restored on 11 November 1918 as a result of the collapse of the Russian, German,

and Austro-Hungarian empires at the end of World War I. "Partitions of Poland (1772, 1793, 1795)," Encyclopaedia Britannica Online, http://www.britannica.com/EBchecked/topic/466910/Partitions-of-Poland.

3. Grand Place, Brussels. The Grand Place in the city of Brussels, Belgium, is the medieval marketplace in the middle of the Old Town surrounded with ornate commercial and government buildings. Even in Pershing's time, it was one of Brussels' premier tourist attractions. "Brussels," Encyclopaedia Britannica Online, http://www.britannica.com/EBchecked/topic/82364/Brussels.

4. This quotation is from the first stanza of "The Eve of Waterloo" by Lord George Gordon Byron (22 January 1788–19 April 1824), which is an extract from his much longer third canto of "Childe Harold's Pilgrimage" (1816). The poem describes Brussels, Belgium, on the eve of the Battle of Waterloo (18 June 1815), in which the British and Prussian forces under the Duke of Wellington defeated Napoleon Bonaparte and ended his "100 days" return to the continent. "George Gordon Byron," Encyclopaedia Britannica Online, http://www.britannica.com/EBchecked/topic/87071/George-Gordon-Byron-6th-Baron-Byron; "Arthur Wellesey, 1st Duke of Wellington," Encyclopaedia Britannica Online, http://www.britannica.com/EBchecked/topic/639392/Arthur-Wellesley-1st-duke-of-Wellington; "The Eve of Waterloo," Lord Byron, PoetryArchive, http://www.poetry-archive.com/b/the_eve_of_waterloo.html.

5. Entente Cordiale. This was a secret diplomatic understanding between France and Great Britain resolving many points of contention that was signed on 8 April 1904 and agreeing to cooperate against increasing German pressures and possible threats. This agreement did not commit Great Britain as a party to the French-Russian treaty of 1894 that committed the countries to act against Germany in case either country was attacked. However, it most certainly put Britain in a position where it would almost have to join France in any continental war begun by Germany. Russia, France, and Great Britain were often called the "Triple Entente," although there was no formal "Entente" between Russia and Britain. "Entente Cordial," Encyclopaedia Britannica Online, http://www.britannica.com/EBchecked/topic/188822/Entente-Cordiale.

6. Triple Alliance. The Triple Alliance was the diplomatic alliance of Germany, Austro-Hungary, and Italy formed in May 1882 and renewed thereafter. It was primarily aimed at France and Russia, but certain provisions allowed Italy to remain neutral in case of war between Austro-Hungary and Russia. Italy actually had more serious territorial disputes with Austro-Hungary, especially in the Trentino area, so Italy and France reached an agreement in 1902 that allowed each to remain neutral should the other be attacked. When the war began in August 1914, Italy opted out of the Triple Alliance and eventually entered the war against Germany and Austro-Hungary in May 1915. The Ottoman Empire joined Germany and Austro-Hungary, forming the "Central Powers," on 20 October 1914, and Bulgaria joined them on 14 October 1915. "Triple Alliance," Encyclopaedia Britannica Online, http://www.britannica.com/EBchecked/topic/605722/Triple-Alliance; "Central Powers," Encyclopaedia Britannica Online, http://www.britannica.com/EBchecked/topic/102591/Central-Powers.

7. Casablanca Affair. A number of serious diplomatic crises between France and Germany arose over the status of Morocco, beginning with French expansion of its

sphere of influence from Algeria to Morocco in 1903. The First Moroccan Crisis (1905–1906) was brought about by Kaiser Wilhelm II's visit to Tangiers on 31 March 1905 and his support for Moroccan independence. This quickly blew up into a major crisis that almost led to a war until the international conference at Algeciras resolved the issue but hardened French and British determination to plan for military action against future German threats. The "Casablanca Affair" took place on 25 September 1908 when the French seized three German deserters from the French Foreign Legion at Casablanca while they were being escorted to a ship by the German consul. This dispute was turned over to the Hague Tribunal for resolution. The Second Moroccan Crisis occurred in July 1911 when the German gunboat *Panther* visited Agadir in southern Morocco while the French were militarily consolidating their control over Morocco. Again war was averted through diplomacy, but this crisis took the major European powers another step toward the outbreak of World War I in 1914. "Moroccan Crises," Encyclopaedia Britannica Online, http://www.britannica .com/EBchecked/topic/392599/Moroccan-crises; "The Moroccan Crises: International Relations involving Morocco, 1903–1914," Early Twentieth Century Timelines, http://cnparm.home.texas.net/Wars/MorCrises.htm.

8. The first flight over mountains was completed by pioneer Peruvian aviator Georges Chavez (1887–1910) when he flew a Blériot from France over the Simplon Pass through the Alps to Domodossola, Italy, on 23 September 1910. Chavez was killed when the aircraft crashed on landing. David Mondey, ed., *The International Encyclopedia of Aviation* (New York: Crescent Books, 1988), pp. 426, 429.

9. Pershing's memory failed him in this paragraph, although he had known Walter C. Short since they met on the battlefield at San Juan Hill, Cuba, in early July 1898. Short indeed had attended the French Cavalry School at Saumur from October 1907 through July 1908, but I have found no evidence to prove that he was at Saumur or even in France when Pershing visited there from October through December 1908. Short is listed as graduating from Saumur in 1908 (probably late July) and returning to his post as senior instructor in equitation at the Mounted Service School at Fort Riley, Kansas, from September 1908 through October 1910. The *Official Army Register* for 1908 (printed in December 1907) carries no listing of him on the officers' roster for the Mounted Service School because he was in France, but the *Official Army Register* for 1909 (printed December 1908) lists him as senior instructor in equitation and in charge of packing instruction. The Mounted Service School's listing of officer graduates of Saumur indicates that Captain Fitzhugh Lee, 7th Cavalry, attended Saumur in the 1908–1909 academic year. Guy V. Henry Jr. was the first Army officer to attend the school at Saumur, from August 1906 to July 1907, after which he served as senior instructor in equitation at the Mounted Service School while Short attended the course at Saumur. When Short returned from France, Henry was transferred to the USMA as senior instructor in cavalry tactics and equitation (August 1908–September 1911). When Short was ordered back to troop duty with the 1st Cavalry, Henry once again became the senior instructor at the Mounted Service School (September 1911–December 1913). U.S. Army Mounted Service School, *The Rasp* [Yearbook] (Fort Riley, Kans.: 1912), pp. 37, 233, and *The Rasp* (1913), p. 140; TAGO, *OAR, 1908*, p. 95; TAGO, *OAR, 1909*, pp. 110–11; *ARWD, 1907*, vol. 4, p. 268, 272; *ARWD, 1908*, vol. 4, p. 121; "Guy V. Henry," in Braden, *Biographical Register 5*, pp. 608–9; "Guy V. Henry," in Rob-

inson, *Biographical Register 6A,* pp. 848–49; "Walter C. Short," in Davis, *Generals in Khaki,* pp. 332–33.

10. Pershing here does not tell the entire story associated with his stay under George Deshon's care at the Army and Navy General Hospital. Even before he had returned to Washington from Europe, a new assignment was arranged with Senator Warren's involvement that would send Pershing back to the Philippines as commander of the Department of Mindanao and governor of the Moro Province. There he would replace Brigadier General Tasker H. Bliss, who was then commanding the Philippines Division as well as still holding his former post as commander of the Mindanao Department and Moro Province's governor. The War Department issued General Orders No. 9 on 20 January 1909 that directed this new assignment and gave Pershing a reporting date on or about 1 May. At this point his deteriorating health required observation, rest, and recuperation before any such strenuous assignment. On 6 March, in War Department Special Orders No. 52, Pershing was granted a leave of absence for six months and his orders were deferred for six months. He was sent off to Watkins Glen, New York, for recuperation. On 24 May 1909 his leave of absence was rescinded and he was ordered to the Army and Navy General Hospital at Hot Springs, Arkansas, to recover his health. An additional three months' leave of absence was granted on 14 June (War Department, Special Orders No. 136), effective 20 June. While still on leave, Pershing received a long letter from Bliss dated 27 September 1909 that detailed his experiences as department commander and governor of the Moro Province. U.S. War Department General Orders No. 9, 20 January 1909; Special Orders No. 52, 6 March 1909; Special Orders No. 136, 14 June 1909, all in LC/Pershing, Box 278, Philippines, A–D, Adjutant General, U.S. Army. Letters, Benjamin Alvord, The Adj. Gen., to Pershing, 20 January 1909; Henry P. McCain, The Adj. Gen., to Pershing, 24 May 1909; Bliss to Pershing, 27 September 1909, all in LC/Pershing, Box 370, Governor of Moro Province (3). See also Vandiver, *Black Jack,* vol. 1, pp. 454–62.

18. My Return to Mindanao

1. The Doherty (or Dougherty) wagon was a four-wheeled U.S. Army wagon drawn by four to six mules that was used as a transport for seated personnel or wounded men on stretchers.

2. According to Frank Vandiver in *Black Jack,* Datto Mandi actually said: "If the American government does not want the Moro Province any more they should give it back to us. It is a Moro Province. It belongs to us." See, Vandiver, *Black Jack,* vol. 1, p. 495.

3. Vandiver also provided another version of Datto Sacaluran's comment: "I am an old man. I do not want any more trouble. But if it should come to that, that we shall be given over to the Filipinos, I still would fight." Vandiver, *Black Jack,* vol. 1, p. 495.

4. For a review of Dickinson's trip, which lasted from 28 June to 7 November 1908, with the period from 24 July to 3 September spent in the Philippines, see "Special Report of J. M. Dickinson, Secretary of War, to the President on the Philippines, November 23, 1910," in U.S. War Department, *Special Reports on the Philippines to the President,* pp. 93–189.

5. Young Turks. The Young Turks was the name for a coalition of reform groups that eventually led a revolution against Abdülhamid II's repressive authoritarian regime. Beginning in the late 1880s, various reformers and revolutionaries began working to overthrow the backward Ottoman regime and revive and modernize the empire to regain to its former greatness and stop foreign influences from destroying it. The Committee for Union and Progress (CUP) was one of the most important of the groups that formed, but it was young military officers from Salonika (the 3d Army Corps) who revolted against the local authorities in July 1908. The uprising spread quickly throughout the empire and Abdülhamid II soon abdicated. The Young Turks had overthrown the regime, but their own disagreements prevented an effective government from forming until 1913. The CUP under the leadership of Talat Pasha, Ahmed Cemal Pasha, and Enver Pasha took over and carried out reforms, including secularization and education. They cast their lot with the Central Powers in World War I and were defeated and fled to Germany in October 1918. After 1918, Mustafa Kemal Pasha (Atatürk) (1881–10 November 1938) eventually built the modern state of Turkey from the ruins of the Ottoman Empire. "Young Turks," Encyclopaedia Britannica Online, http://www.britannica.com/EBchecked/topic/654123/Young-Turks; "Mustafa Kemal Atatürk," Encyclopaedia Britannica Online, http://www.britannica.com/EBchecked/topic/40411/Kemal-Ataturk.

6. Vedic gods. The Vedic gods, such as Agni, Soma, Indra, Varuna, Shiva, and Vishnu, form a central part of the Vedic religion that was practiced historically in present-day India dating back to 1500 B.C. The religion was polytheistic with often complex sacrificial rites to the different gods that were responsible for creation and life. Over the centuries much of the Vedic religion was incorporated into modern Hinduism. "Vedic Religion," Encyclopaedia Britannica Online, http://www.britannica.com/EBchecked/topic/624479/Vedic-religion.

7. Strictly speaking, Pershing succeeded Colonel Charles A. Williams, 21st Infantry, as commander of the Department of Mindanao and Captain Charles B. Hagadorn, 23d Infantry and provincial secretary, as governor, and not Tasker Bliss in either post. Leonard Wood commanded the Department of Mindanao and was governor of the Moro Province from 25 July 1903 to 16 April 1906, although he was absent on medical leave in the United States for many of these months. Wood was supposed to turn over both of his posts to Tasker Bliss on 1 February 1906 when he assumed command of the Philippines Division. He did not do this, so that he could command the Bud Dajo expedition of March 1906 against the Moros on Jolo Island. Bliss only assumed the post of Department commander on 12 April 1906 and that of governor on 16 April. After Major General Jack Weston, who had replaced Wood as Division commander in February 1908, departed the Philippines in December 1908, Bliss commanded both the Philippines Division (23 December 1908–6 April 1909) and remained in command of the Department of Mindanao for much of the time and as governor of the Moro Province until 5 April 1909. Had his health not prevented Pershing from complying with his original orders to assume command on 1 May 1909, he would have succeeded Bliss on Mindanao. After Bliss left the Philippines early in April, Major General William P. Duvall assumed command of the Philippines Division on 23 April 1909. Colonel (Brigadier General in March 1910) Ralph W. Hoyt, 25th Infantry, commanded the Department of Mindanao for

extended periods after Bliss went to Manila (12–22 December 1908, 30 December 1908–20 January 1909) and then replaced him permanently (5 February–6 September 1909) due to Pershing's postponed arrival. After Bliss resigned on 5 April, Hoyt was appointed governor on 26 April 1909 and remained until he departed Mindanao on 6 September to return to the United States with his regiment. Hoyt was followed as Department commander by Colonel Thomas C. Woodbury, 3d Infantry (7 September–4 October), and then Colonel Charles A. Williams (5 October–10 November 1909) on an interim basis. Captain Charles B. Hagadorn, the provincial secretary, was acting governor until Pershing's arrival and appointment as governor on 9 November. Pershing did not formally assume both posts until 11 November 1909, well after Bliss had left command and the Philippines. *ARWD, 1906, vol. 3, Reports of Division and Department Commanders,* pp. 207, 276, 300; *ARWD, 1909,* vol. 3, *Division and Department Commanders,* pp. 153, 207, 227; *ARWD, 1910,* vol. 3, *Division and Department Commanders,* pp. 245, 268; *Annual Report of the Governor of the Moro Province: Major General Leonard Wood, U.S.A., July 1, 1905, to April 16, 1906; Brigadier General Tasker H. Bliss, U.S.A., April 16, 1906, to August 27, 1906* (Zamboanga, Philippines: n.p., August 27, 1906), p. 102; *Annual Report of Colonel Ralph W. Hoyt, 25th United States Infantry, Governor of the Moro Province, for the Fiscal Year ended June 30, 1909* (Zamboanga, Philippines: Mindanao Herald Publishing Company, 1909), p. 34; *Annual Report of Brigadier General John J. Pershing, U.S. Army, Governor of the Moro Province, for the Year Ending August 31, 1910* (Zamboanga, Philippines: Mindanao Herald Publishing Company, 1910), p. 22; Vandiver, *Black Jack,* vol. 1, pp. 454–68.

8. According to the *Annual Reports of the War Department,* on 31 May 1909 the army had 274 officers and 5,314 enlisted men of Regular Army regiments and the Philippine Scouts in the Department of Mindanao. On 30 June 1910 there were 290 officers and 5,335 enlisted men. See *ARWD, 1909,* vol. 3, *Division and Department Commanders,* p. 221; *ARWD, 1910,* vol. 3, *Division and Department Commanders,* p. 267.

9. Pershing inserted a footnote at this point: "The American troops serving in the Department at the time of my arrival were the Third Infantry, Colonel Thomas C. Woodbury; Twenty-first Infantry, Colonel Charles A. Williams; Twenty-third Infantry, Lt. Colonel Edwin F. Glenn, replaced in March by the Sixth Infantry, Colonel Joseph I. Duncan; Sixth Cavalry, Colonel Alexander Rodgers, replaced in January by the Second Cavalry, Colonel Frank West; Batteries D, E, and F, Second Field Artillery; and Company L, Signal Corps. First Lieutenants William O. Reed and Walter O. Boswell were my aides; Colonel William W. Gray, Chief Surgeon; Major Frederick Perkins, Adjutant General, later succeeded by Major H. H. Whitney; Major George H. Penrose, Quartermaster; Major Joseph T. Dickman, Inspector General; Major Charles E. Stanton, Paymaster; Captain Frank H. Lawton, Chief Commissary; Captain Allan J. Greer, Judge Advocate; Captain William R. Sample, in charge of athletics; and First Lieutenant William N. Hughes, Jr., Signal Officer. Colonel Mark L. Hersey commanded the Filipino Constabulary."

10. In this paragraph, Pershing refers obliquely to the adverse effects of the frequently harsh and unbending administration of Leonard Wood as governor of the Moro Province (25 July 1903–16 April 1906). During his early years of working with the Moros (1901–1903) on Mindanao, Pershing developed a deep knowledge and understanding of the Moros and their customs and traditions and tried to resolve problems amicably while holding the use of force as a final resort. When Wood

became governor of the Moro Province in July 1903, he largely reversed the policies of Davis and Pershing, who had just left Mindanao in May. Wood never attempted to understand the Moros but approached them as implacable enemies to be "thrashed" and destroyed like the native American Indians. The use of force was Wood's first response to any problem solving and not his final recourse. Critics of Wood and his approach over the years have contended that his lack of professional military credentials as an army officer of the line drove Wood's military exploits in Mindanao—an effort to establish his reputation as a "soldier." On the other hand, Bliss had assiduously pursued a more peaceful and much less aggressive policy in dealing with the Moros that was almost the opposite of Wood's approach. See Arnold, *The Moro War,* pp. 76–206; Fulton, *Moroland,* pp. 161–320; Lane, *Armed Progressive,* pp. 125–26.

11. This quotation is from an extract of Major Finley's report in Pershing's "Report of the Department of Mindanao," to the Philippines Division, 30 June 1910, in *ARWD, 1910,* vol. 3, *Division and Department Commanders,* pp. 260–61.

12. Pershing was very familiar with this incident on Sunday, 16 April, but does not mention the second attack which occurred on Jolo on the following Wednesday (19 April), in which two Moros killed a Sergeant Fergusson at the guard house. He visited Jolo on his annual inspection tour just several days later and on 22 April wrote an extended description of these events to Major General Bell, the commander of the Philippines Division. In his letter, Pershing broached the question of disarming the Moros but noted that all of his predecessors had decided "that it is next to impossible to do so without a war." For a variety of reasons, he also concluded that "the time has not yet come" for disarmament. On 23 May, Bell replied:

Your report of the affair is entirely satisfactory and I am in full accord with your views. In fact I had anticipated that the facts would be as you state them. Of course there is nothing to be done, but I understand it has long been a custom to bury juramentados with pigs when they kill Americans. I think this a good plan, for if anything will discourage the juramentado it is the prospect of going to hell instead of to heaven. You can rely on me to stand by you in maintaining this custom. It is the only possible thing we can do to discourage crazy fanatics.

Letters, Pershing to Bell, 22 April 1911, and Bell to Pershing, 23 May 1911, LC/Pershing Papers, Box 370, Governor of the Moro Province (6).

13. Pershing inserted a note here as follows: "This governor was Lieutenant William O. Reed, Sixth Cavalry. The other district governors then were Major Elvin R. Heiberg, Philippine Scouts, Cotabato; Major Henry Gilsheuser, Philippine Constabulary, Davao; Major Cornelius C. Smith, Philippine Scouts, Lanao; and Major John P. Finley, Twenty-eighth Infantry, Zamboanga."

19. Disarming and Taming the Moros

1. Letter, W. Cameron Forbes, Governor General, to Pershing, 4 February 1913, LC/Pershing Papers, Box 76, Correspondence: W. Cameron Forbes, Governor-General, 1912–13.

2. Pershing's report of 31 May 1912 to The Adjutant General, War Department, on the Bud Dajo operation is at Appendix H. See also Vandiver, *Black Jack,* vol. 1, pp. 516–40, Smythe, *Guerrilla Warrior,* pp. 161–74; Arnold, *The Moro War,* pp. 221–26; Fulton, *Moroland,* pp. 407–31.

3. The handwritten letters to Frankie can be found in Pershing's field notebook for the period of the Bud Dajo campaign. LC/Pershing Papers, Box 1, Field notebook, Jolo 1911.

4. Pershing to Frankie, 2 December 1911, LC/Pershing Papers, Box 1, Field notebook, Jolo 1911. Where Pershing writes that he had "stood this sort of thing for a year once," he is referring to his tense dealings with the Moros around Lake Lanao in 1902–1903, when he commanded Camp Vicars and was compelled to tolerate frequent provocations and attacks by Moros before he could gain approval to take action.

5. Pershing to Frankie, 5 December 1911. LC/Pershing Papers, Box 1, Field notebook, Jolo 1911.

6. Pershing, Governor of the Moro Province, to Moros Nakib-Amil, Sansaui, Sabdani, Japal, and other Moros, 6 December 1911, LC/Pershing Papers, Box 371, Governor of the Moro Province (5). Also quoted in Vandiver, *Black Jack*, vol. 1, p. 536; Smythe, *Guerrilla Warrior*, pp. 167–68.

7. Battle of Bud Dajo (6–8 March 1906). Also known as the "first battle of Bud Dajo," "the battle of the clouds," and the "Moro crater massacre," the Battle of Bud (Mount) Dajo on Jolo Island remains extremely controversial even today. Major General Leonard Wood, commander of the Philippines Division, orchestrated this operation without the required approval from Washington. Opposing American taxation policies implemented by Wood, approximately 900 Tausug Moro warriors and their families had established *cotta* strongholds on the 2,100-foot-high extinct volcano Bud Dajo. During three days of fighting, 350–400 U.S. forces and Moro Philippine Constabulary overwhelmed the Tausugs, killing perhaps 700–850 Moros, many being women and children, who traditionally accompanied the warriors to their *cottas*. These are merely estimates, because no firm number of Moro dead was ever established. American and Constabulary losses were twenty-one killed and seventy-three wounded. When word of the "massacre" was made public, considerable public criticism in the United States was aimed at Wood, the administration, and the army. On 15 March, the House and Senate demanded copies of all pertinent "communications between the War Department and the officials in the Philippines" reporting of events from the Secretary of War, William H. Taft, who dribbled out the requested documents over the next ten days. These were printed in Senate Documents 276 (19 March 1906), 278 (21 March 1906), and 289 (26 March 1906). However, the San Francisco earthquake of 18 April and a quiet cover-up made this less-than-glorious episode in army history and Wood's role in it largely disappear from public view. Wood's official report on his tenure as governor of the Moro Province for this period is a study in obfuscation of the facts. Pershing was very much concerned about the possible negative effects of any wholesale killing of Moro women and children on the scale of Wood's action in March 1906 and made a great effort not to repeat that slaughter. Fulton contends in his *Moroland* that Pershing's more pacific campaign strategy was actually forced on him by Acting Governor-General Newton Gilbert, who arrived at Jolo harbor on 11 December after prompting from Washington and discussed the grave negative political ramifications for Taft and his administration of any repeat of the first Battle of Bud Dajo (see pp. 424–25). Fulton, *Moroland*, pp. 255–96, 407–20; and "The Battle of Bud Dajo (March 6–8, 1906)," Uncle Sam, the Moros, and the Moro Campaigns, http://www.morolandhistory.com; Arnold, *The*

Moro War, pp. 139–68; Lane, *Armed Progressive,* pp. 127–31; O'Connor, *Black Jack Pershing,* pp. 99–101; Smythe, *Guerrilla Warrior,* pp. 168–73; Vandiver, *Black Jack,* vol. 1, p. 537; "Third Annual Report of Major General Leonard Wood, U.S. Army, Governor of the Moro Province. From July 1, 1905 to April 16, 1906," pp. 12–13, in Wood and Bliss, *AR, Moro Province, 1905-1906;* U.S. Senate, Document No. 276, 19 March 1906, Document No. 278, 21 March 1906, and Document No. 289, 26 March 1906, in 59th Cong., 1st Sess., *Senate Documents,* vol. 6 (Washington, D.C.: GPO, 1906).

8. Pershing to Frankie, 14 December 1911, LC/Pershing Papers, Box 1, Field notebook, Jolo 1911, emphasis in the original document.

9. Pershing's report of 15 October 1913 to the Adjutant General, U.S. Army, on the Bud Bagsak operation is at Appendix I. Lieutenant James L. Collins, Pershing's aide, provided his personal experiences during this expedition and additional details of the fighting in his "The Battle of Bud Bagsak and the Part Played by Mountain Guns Therein," *Field Artillery Journal* 15 (November–December 1925), pp. 559–70. Collins's article contains excellent sketches of the Bud Bagsak terrain done by Captain Frederick W. Lewis, 8th Infantry, during the operation. See also Vandiver, *Black Jack,* vol. 1, pp. 556–69, and Smythe, *Guerrilla Warrior,* pp. 186–204. Recent publications on the Bud Bagsak operations include Arnold, *The Moro War,* pp. 228–43, and Fulton, *Moroland,* pp. 431–52. For the account of a Moro who fought against Pershing's forces, see Hurley, *Jungle Patrol,* pp. 332–36.

10. Telegram, Forbes, Baguio, to Pershing, Zamboanga, 5:52 pm, 27 February 1913, LC/Pershing Papers, Box 76, Correspondence: W. Cameron Forbes, Governor-General, 1912-1913.

11. Letter, Pershing to Forbes, 28 February 1913, LC/Pershing Papers, Box 76, Correspondence: W. Cameron Forbes, Governor-General, 1912-1913.

12. Pershing was subjected to a nasty attack in the U.S. and Manila newspapers in July and August 1913 accusing him of slaughtering thousands of innocent Moro men, women, and children in the Bud Bagsak operation. As it turned out, the story originated with a former Army enlisted man and Quartermaster Department employee, one John McLean, who was not even on Jolo during the operation and who was soon thoroughly discredited. Smythe, *Guerrilla Warrior,* pp. 202–4; Fulton, *Moroland,* pp. 450–52; "The Battle of Bud Bagsak (June 11–15, 1913)," Uncle Sam, the Moros, and the Moro Campaigns, at http://www.morolandhistory.com.

13. In his memoirs, however, Pershing did not relate his own story, probably because of his own reticence and also because the final resolution did not occur until after this draft of the manuscript was completed. For his own personal courage in the fighting at Bud Bagsak on 15 June, several of Pershing's subordinates, including Philippine Scouts Captain George C. Charlton, recommended him for a Medal of Honor. Pershing himself wrote to the Adjutant General on 30 September 1913 that he was only doing his duty and his actions did not merit such an award. The War Department decorations board had already decided against any award to Pershing, so this matter went away until the early 1920s, when the War Department reviewed pre–World War I personal actions in battle for possible awards of the newly established (1918) Distinguished Service Cross (DSC). The board recommended Pershing for Bud Bagsak, but he was then chief of staff and vetoed any such award. In 1940 the War Department, now under General George C. Marshall, awarded a DSC to Pershing for his heroism at Bud Bagsak. President Franklin D. Roosevelt

presented it to Pershing at the White House on 13 September 1940, which was Pershing's eightieth birthday according to Army records but not according to actual facts (see note 1.5). Smythe, *Guerrilla Warrior,* pp. 203–4; Vandiver, *Black Jack,* vol. 1, pp. 570–72; DSC Citation, Brigadier General John J. Pershing, 13 September 1940, Home of Heroes, http://www.militarytimes.com/citations-medals-awards/citation .php?citation=9922.

20. The Last Military Governor of the Moro Province

1. Even before the Battle of Bud Bagsak in June 1913, Pershing had already made his case to Governor-General Forbes for a transition from the military governorship of the Moro Province to a civilian administration in a lengthy letter of 7 April 1913. On 19 June, immediately after Bud Bagsak, he refined an earlier recommendation to Major General Bell, the Philippines Division commander, that the time had come to consider withdrawing army units from Mindanao and concentrating them around Manila and on Luzon, leaving the Philippine Scouts to handle any military support required by the civilian governor along with the Constabulary. He wrote, "The disarmament of the Moros and other natives by the Army has resulted in such a peaceful state of affairs that serious disturbance in the future is improbable." Pershing again wrote to Bell on 1 November recommending the end of military government in Mindanao, which Bell approved on 4 November and sent to the new governor-general, Francis Burton Harrison. Pershing's final letter on the subject, recommending the abolishment of the military department of Mindanao, was sent to Bell on 4 November. See Pershing to Bell, "Concentration at large posts in the vicinity of Manila of white troops serving in the District of Mindanao and substitution thereof of Philippine Scouts," 19 June 1913, and "Abolishment of the District of Mindanao," 4 November 1913, LC/Pershing Papers, Box 278, Philippines A-D, Folder: Concentration of Troops in the Philippine Island; Pershing to Bell, "Civil Government for the Moro Province," 1 November 1913, LC/Pershing, Box 371, Governor of the Moro Province (4); 1st Indorsement, Bell to Governor-General, 20 November 1913, LC/ Pershing, Box 370, Governor of the Moro Province (3); Pershing to Forbes, 7 April 1913, LC/Pershing, Box 371, Folder: Governor of the Moro Province (5); Forbes to Pershing, 25 April 1913, LC/Pershing Papers, Box 76, Correspondence: W. Cameron Forbes, Governor-General, 1912–13.

2. *The Sultan of Sulu* was a popular comic opera written and staged in 1902 by playwright, satirist, humorist, and author George Ade (9 February 1860–16 May 1944). Ade received his bachelor's degree from Purdue University in 1887 and embarked on a career as a newspaper journalist with the *Chicago Morning News* (later *Record*) (1890–1900), where he soon became a popular columnist with his "Stories of the Streets and of the Town." He turned a number of his columns into successful books, such as *Artie* (1896) and *Pink Marsh* (1897), but he became nationally known with his *Fables in Slang* (1899) and *More Fables in Slang* (1900), and many more works that followed. The outbreak of the Philippine-American War in 1899 turned Ade's sarcasm to full force with his stories on "benevolent assimilation." After visiting the Philippines, he returned to the United States and wrote the musical comedy *The Sultan of Sulu: An Original Satire in Two Acts,* which opened in Chicago in March 1902 and was soon a resounding success on Broadway and with road shows traveling

throughout the country. The show was very loosely based on the situation facing the United States in the Moro areas of the Philippines, and especially the Island of Jolo and its exotic Moro inhabitants, and the sultan of Sulu, Jamalul-Kiram II. Ade went on to have a very successful career both as an author and as one of the most successful playwrights of his time. He also was a trustee of Purdue University (1908–1915) and raised funds in 1923–1924 along with David E. Ross to build Purdue's football stadium, which bears his name, the Ross-Ade Stadium. "George Ade," Encyclopaedia Britannica Online, http://www.britannica.com/EBchecked/topic/5565/George-Ade; "George Ade," *Who Was Who in America*, vol. 2, *1943-1950*, p. 18; Fulton, *Moroland*, pp. 141–46.

3. Pershing to Bell, "Civil Government for the Moro Province," 1 November 1913, with 1st Indorsement, Bell to Governor-General, 20 November 1913, LC/Pershing, Box 371, Governor of the Moro Province (4), and in LC/Pershing, Box 370, Governor of the Moro Province (3).

21. Diplomatic Missions, Our Return to the United States, and Commanding the Eighth Brigade at the Presidio of San Francisco

1. The Taft administration appointed Charles R. Crane (7 August 1858–15 February 1939), a wealthy Chicago manufacturer, as U.S. minister to China in July 1909. The State Department then decided that Mr. Crane made unacceptable remarks about the U.S. government's attitude concerning recent treaties between China and Japan on railroads and mines in Manchuria before a meeting of the American Asiatic Association in Chicago. These remarks were printed in a Chicago newspaper prior to Crane's departure for China. In early October Secretary of State Knox recalled Crane to Washington from San Francisco (where he was then waiting for his ship to the Far East) to meet with him. After meeting with Crane on 9 and 10 October, Knox removed him as minister-designate and was backed up by President Taft. Crane went on to have a significant career in foreign affairs. He later served President Wilson in a number of diplomatic posts during and after World War I, including as a member of the American delegation to the Paris Peace Conference, on the Inter-Allied Commission on Mandates in Turkey (the King-Crane Commission), and as U.S. minister to China (1920–1921). "Charles Richard Crane," *Who Was Who in America*, vol. 1, *1897-1942*, p. 272; "Crane Takes Post as Envoy to China," *New York Times*, 17 July 1909; "State Secrets Out; Crane Questioned," *New York Times*, 11 October 1909; "Mr. Charles R. Crane," *New York Times*, 13 October 1909; "Charles Richard Crane," http://en.wikipedia.org/wiki/Charles_Richard_Crane.

2. Most likely this was Charles Page Bryan (2 October 1856–12 March 1918), who served as U.S. ambassador from 22 November 1911 to 1 October 1912, when he retired from the diplomatic service. The death notice in the 14 March 1918 edition of the *New York Times* noted that his retirement was as a result of a misunderstanding between Secretary of State Knox and Mr. Bryan and came within weeks of the emperor's funeral and burial on 13 September 1912. "Charles Page Bryan," *Who Was Who in America*, vol. 1: *1897-1942*, p. 157; "Charles Page Bryan, Ex-Ambassador Dies," *New York Times*, 14 March 1918.

3. At no point in this entire manuscript does Pershing mention the death of his wife, Helen Frances "Frankie," and their three daughters at their home at the Presidio

of San Francisco on the night of 26–27 August 1915. In the 1934–1935 draft of chapter 21 that was based on Frederick Moore's version, this final paragraph reads as follows: "I was with the family in San Francisco only a few months, being ordered to the Mexican border in April, 1914. There, from month to month for over a year, it seemed that we were on the verge of a war with the neighbor state, and the family therefore remained in our Presidio home. Life seemed to be safer and better for them in San Francisco. But on the night of August 26, 1915, the house took fire and only our son was saved." Pershing struck out most of the paragraph, leaving only: "I was with the family in San Francisco only a short time, being ordered to the Mexican border in April, 1914, and the family, after remaining in our Presidio home for awhile, went to Cheyenne, Wyoming." He then apparently wrote some six lines in pencil, but these were then so thoroughly erased that very few words can be deciphered on the original page of the manuscript carrying his editorial changes. That is a measure of just how much the loss of his wife and daughters still hurt him twenty years later. See the final paragraph of chapter 21 in "Corrected Drafts 1934–35," LC/Pershing Papers, Box 379.

22. On the Mexican Border with the Eighth Brigade

1. Shortly after he arrived at El Paso, Pershing wrote a letter on 1 May 1914 to Brigadier General Tasker Bliss, commanding general, Southern Department, at Fort Sam Houston, outlining his plans to carry out Bliss's policies along the border. On 6 May, Bliss replied with a detailed nine-page letter laying out the situation on the Mexican border as he saw it and his plans. These letters began an exchange of information and views between Bliss and Pershing that continued until Bliss moved to the War Department as assistant chief of staff in February 1915. LC/Pershing Papers, Box 372, Punitive Expedition, Folders 2, Parts 1 and 2.

2. Caciques and Caciquism. In Spanish but derived from an Indian word, a *cacique* was a local chief (boss) who the Spanish conquerors in Central and South America retained to control an Indian tribe. Eventually the system of caciques employed to control the people came to be known as caciquism or "bossism." This evolved into the system of local or state "caciques" who ruled the countries of Latin America. "Caciquism," Encyclopaedia Britannica Online, http://www.britannica.com/EBchecked/topic/87819/caciquism.

3. In the original version of the manuscript, Pershing and his associates garbled Mayo's message of 9 April 1914 to General Morales Zaragoza, the local Mexican commander, to read "formal disavowal and apology, punishment of the officer in charge of the Mexican squad and salute to the American flag within twenty-four hours." Exactly what source they used for this quotation could not be located in the Pershing Papers. For the reader's benefit, I chose to insert here the relevant portions of Mayo's message to Zaragoza extracted from the Department of State, *Papers Relating to the Foreign Relations of the United States with the Address of the President to Congress, December 8, 1914* (Washington, D.C.: GPO, 1922) (hereafter cited as *FRUS 1914*), pp. 448–49.

4. Pershing here is referring to the serious incident at the port of Mazatlán, Sinaloa, on the Gulf of California on 18 June 1916. A landing party of two officers and three sailors from the gunboat USS *Annapolis* went to the wharf to meet with Mexican authorities and the U.S. consul, A. Gordon Brown, about taking on local

American citizens who wished to leave Mexico. Mexican troops detained and arrested two of the ship's officers and then opened fire on the three sailors in the launch. The crew in the launch returned fire and reportedly wounded three Mexicans. Boatswain's Mate 2d Class Luther M. Laughter was wounded during the exchange and died of his wounds on 19 June. Under direction of the Carranza government, the governor of the state of Sinaloa on 17 June had issued a false proclamation that war would be declared against the United States. In view of the existing state of U.S.-Mexican relations, the proclamation had greatly agitated the local population as well as the local military commander, General Manuel Mezta, and had sparked this incident. The *Annapolis* had been patrolling Mexico's western coast and the Gulf of California as part of the Pacific Fleet since 1913 when the civil war flared against Huerta. The Mexican patrol's mission was to protect American citizens and interests. Early in June 1916, the State Department requested that the navy place more ships on the western Mexican coast from Guaymas to Acapulco, in case American citizens should need their assistance. In response, the *Annapolis* was at Mazatlán to consult with the American consul about picking up any American citizens who wished to leave that area. Lieutenant Commander Arthur G. Kavanaugh, the *Annapolis's* captain, Mr. Brown, and a local Mexican colonel prevailed upon Mezta to release the two officers before they were harmed and the incident exploded. After the incident Admiral Cameron McRae Winslow informed the Navy Department that "The outrage was wholly unprovoked, and I believe it to be a far more serious affront than the Tampico affair. The self control and temperate action of Commander Kavanaugh prevented a situation which might have been the cause of an immediate war." Winslow quickly rushed additional ships to the area in case the situation further deteriorated. A much more serious fight at Carrizal took place on 21 June (see chapter 23), and within days Carranza and Wilson agreed to mediate all of the issues in a Joint American-Mexican Commission that lessened the tensions. Documents pertaining to the Mazatlán incident are in U.S. Department of State, *Papers Relating to the Foreign Relations of the United States with the Address of the President to Congress, December 5, 1916* (Washington, D.C.: GPO, 1925) (hereafter cited as *FRUS 1916*), see especially Consul Brown's report of 19 June 1916 (pp. 578–80), Admiral Winslow's reports of 19 June (p. 578) and undated (p. 602), and exchanges between the Department of the Navy and the State Department, pp. 669–70, 687; "Sailors in Fight with Mexicans" and "Rush Pacific Fleet to Mexican Waters," *New York Times*, 20 June 1916; Lieutenant Commander Kavanaugh's report in "Says Mexicans Began Fight at Mazatlan," *New York Times*, 23 June 1916; Arthur S. Link, *Woodrow Wilson and the Progressive Era, 1910-1917* (New York: Harper and Brothers, 1954), pp. 140-43.

5. For Wilson's complete statement of 2 June 1915, see Edgar E. Robinson and Victor J. West, *The Foreign Policy of Woodrow Wilson, 1913-1917* (New York: Macmillan, 1918), pp. 268-70.

6. Carranza's forces under Álvaro Obregón soundly defeated Villa's Division of the North in the two battles at Celaya (6–15 April 1915) and then won the long, drawn-out battle at León (29 April–5 June) and again at Aguascalientes (June). Throughout the summer Villa tried to recover from these serious losses and rebuild his army. Seeking to reverse his fortunes, in September 1915 Villa moved west from Chihuahua into the state of Sonora with the objective of destroying the *de facto* (see note 21.7 below) garrison under General Plutarco Elías Calles at Agua Prieta on the

U.S.-Mexican border just south of Douglas, Arizona. Unknown to Villa, after Wilson recognized Carranza as the *de facto* government of Mexico in October, he also allowed Carranza to move *de facto* troops, weapons, and ammunition along the railroads on the U.S. side of the border from Laredo, Texas, through El Paso, to Douglas, where they unloaded and marched to reinforce Calles at Agua Prieta. According to newspaper reports, forty-five hundred new *de facto* troops joined the three thousand already at Agua Prieta, which allowed Calles to strongly fortify the town with trenches, barbed wire, and machine guns. George Carothers, U.S. consul at Torreón, Chihuahua, and a close acquaintance of Villa's who often traveled with him and as a special agent reported directly to the State Department on Villa's activities, sent a telegram to the Secretary of State from Douglas on 31 October that Villa just learned about the recognition and troop movement from a correspondent that day. He reported: "Villa was very indignant and defiant and is reported to have stated that he was through with any dealings with the United States and would attack Agua Prieta and also Americans if necessary." Believing that Calles had only twelve hundred or so troops, Villa attacked in the early morning hours of 1 November. He repeatedly threw his forces against the dug-in defenders over the next several days, largely destroying what was left of his Division of the North, before he fled the battlefield. Because of the possibility that the fighting might spill across the U.S. border, Funston had positioned more than six thousand troops of his Southern Department at Douglas and taken command there himself. Calles was one of Obregón's ablest generals and closest collaborators. He became governor of Sonora in 1917, displacing José Maria Maytorena, later serving as foreign minister (1920) and minister of the interior (1920–1924) under Obregón's presidency. He was elected president in 1924 and served from December 1924 to November 1928. With Obregón's assassination after his victory in the 1928 elections, Calles assumed his mentor's control of Mexican politics. He ruled from behind the scenes for some years but was later forced into exile as his political fortunes shifted. See John S. D. Eisenhower, *Intervention! The United States and the Mexican Revolution, 1913-1917* (New York: Norton, 1993), pp. 175–210; Clarence C. Clendenen, *Blood on the Border: The United States Army and the Mexican Irregulars* (New York: Macmillan, 1969), pp. 183–89; Friedrich Katz, *The Life and Times of Pancho Villa* (Stanford, Calif.: Stanford Univ. Press, 1998), pp. 487–529; "Americans Dig in for Border Battle," *New York Times*, 31 October 1915; "The Test at Agua Prieta" and "Villa Plans Attack Defying Our Troops," *New York Times*, 1 November 1915; "Funston Asks Right to Cross Border," *New York Times*, 3 November 1915; "Villa in Retreat from Agua Prieta," *New York Times*, 4 November 1915; "Special Agent Carothers to Secretary of State, 31 October 1915," in U.S. Department of State, *Papers Relating to the Foreign Relations of the United States with the Address of the President to Congress, December 7, 1915* (Washington, D.C.: GPO, 1924) (hereafter cited as *FRUS 1915*), p. 775; "Plutarco Elías Calles," Encyclopaedia Britannica Online, http://www .britannica.com/EBchecked/topic/89869/Plutarco-Elias-Calles; and for a somewhat fanciful version of events at Agua Prieta, see Haldeen Braddy's account, Haldeen Braddy, *Cock of the Walk: Qui-qui-ri-qui! The Legend of Pancho Villa* (Albuquerque: Univ. of New Mexico Press, 1955), pp. 111–27.

    7. *De facto* authorities. When Pershing refers to the *de facto* or Constitutionalist authorities, army, or government in chapters 22 and 23, he is referring to the existing Mexican federal government and forces of Venustiano Carranza, which were

also known as the Carrancistas or Constitutionalists. Carranza had declared his movement the Constitutional government of Mexico when Huerta was overthrown because it adhered to the provisions of the Mexican Constitution of 1857, which Huerta did not. He termed his anti-Huerta and later anti-Villa program the "Constitutionalist movement," claiming legitimacy from that Constitution and his pledge to restore it. Joseph A. Stout Jr., *Border Conflict: Villistas, Carrancistas, and the Punitive Expedition, 1915-1920* (Fort Worth, Tex.: Texas Christian Univ. Press, 1999), pp. 7–8.

8. Pershing took this quotation from Secretary of State Robert Lansing's telegram of 10 March 1916 to U.S. consular officers in Mexico:

The following statement has just been given to the press by the President:

An adequate force will be sent at once in pursuit of Villa with the single object of capturing him and putting a stop to his forays. This can and will be done in entirely friendly aid of the constituted authorities in Mexico and with scrupulous respect for the sovereignty of that Republic.

Lansing to all American consular offices in Mexico, 6 p.m., 10 March 1916, *FRUS 1916*, p. 484.

9. Telegram, McCain, The Adjutant General, to Commanding General, Southern Department, Fort Sam Houston, Texas [Funston], Number 883, 1159 p [p.m.], 10 March 1916, LC/Pershing Papers, Box 372, Punitive Expedition (3).

10. Pershing invited Villa and Obregón, Carranza's minister of War and Navy, to visit him at Fort Bliss outside of El Paso, Texas, as they traveled together from Chihuahua to Nogales, Sonora, for a meeting with José Maria Maytorena, the governor of Sonora. The two Mexican generals were using the safe and more secure railroad on the American side of the border to travel from El Paso to Tucson. On 26 August, Pershing greeted the two Mexican generals and entertained them at Fort Bliss. The next morning the *El Paso Morning Times* ran a lengthy front page story on Pershing's meeting and reception for Villa and Obregón, complete with its iconic photograph of the three men posing together. From El Paso they went on to Tucson on a special Southern Pacific train escorted by Captain (Brigadier General in World War I) Robert W. Mearns and twelve men from the 12th Infantry and then to Nogales, just south of the U.S. border, to meet Maytorena to resolve lingering conflicts among them and the Carranza government. The so-called Nogales Conference resolved nothing because Maytorena refused to meet with Obregón. The two came back through El Paso on 1 September and again met with Pershing, who was present when the collector of customs, Z. L. Cobb, read a telegram from Secretary of State William Jennings Bryan to Villa thanking him and Obregón for "restoring order in Sonora." The telegram ended: "Your patient labors in this matter are greatly appreciated by the State Department and the President." Pershing, who also spoke at the event as a representative of the U.S. government, noted that "we appreciate the work that Gen. Villa and Gen. Obregon have done. Peace has its victories no less than war and I want to say to you that the work you have just done will accrue as much, if not more, to your renown as the battles you have won." Within weeks, relations between Villa and Obregón fell apart, and they were at each other as Carranza refused to accept any agreements they had made and completely broke with Villa. Soon the entire rickety structure of the *Convention Aguascalientes* collapsed, Carranza refused to leave the office of the presidency he had assumed, the Convention directed Villa to remove Carranza, and Obregón sided with Carranza and declared war on Villa

on 19 November. Eisenhower, *Intervention!* pp. 154–56; Katz, *Pancho Villa,* pp. 314–15, 364–73; "Warm Welcome by General Pershing for Villa and Obregon in El Paso," 27 August 1914, *El Paso Times:* Tales from the Morgue, http://elpasotimes.typepad .com/morgue/2012/03/1914-warm-welcome-by-general-pershing-for-villa-and-obregon-in-el-paso.html; "Villa and Obregon Guests of U.S. Army; Villa Keeps on His Hat at Fort Reception," *El Paso Herald,* 27 August 1913; "Bryan Thanks Gen. Villa," *New York Times,* 2 September 1914; "Bryan Praises Mexico Leaders," *El Paso Herald,* 2 September 1914.

23. The Expedition into Mexico

1. Sierra Madre expeditions. In the 1880s, Generals George Crook and Nelson Miles commanded expeditions that penetrated to the Sierra Madre mountains in the state of Chihuahua, Mexico, in pursuit of Apache leader Geronimo. Crook twice directed his troops into the Sierra Madre mountains after Geronimo, in 1883 and again in 1885–1886, and Miles directed the final campaign against Geronimo in 1886, which resulted in his surrender and exile. Dan L. Thrapp, *The Conquest of Apacheria* (Norman: Univ. of Oklahoma Press, 1967), pp. 283–367.

2. Much of Pershing's discussion of the Mexican Expedition is drawn from his official report on operations in Mexico from 11 March to 30 June 1916. See John J. Pershing, Commanding General, Punitive Expedition, U.S. Army, to Commanding General, Southern Department, "Report of Operations of the Punitive Expedition to June 30, 1916," 7 October 1916 (hereafter cited as Pershing, "Report of Operations," 7 October 1916), in LC/Pershing Papers, Box 372, Folder: Punitive Expedition Reports (1). This document actually has two different dates—the original document that Pershing sent to the Commanding General, Southern Department, was dated 7 October 1916, to which a cover (title) sheet was later added that was dated 10 October 1916. I have used the date of the original document, 7 October 1916, not the date on the subsequently added cover sheet. An online digital version of Pershing's report is at the U.S. Army Command and General Staff College, Combined Arms Research Library (CARL) Digital Library, at http://cgsc.contentdm.oclc.org/ cdm/singleitem/collection/p4013c0117/id/702/rec/2.

The best overall coverage of the U.S. Army's military operations, especially of the cavalry units, during the Mexican Expedition can be found in Frank Tompkins, *Chasing Villa: The Story behind the Story of Pershing's Expedition into Mexico* (Harrisburg, Pa.: Military Service Publishing Company, 1934), reprinted in 1996 as *Chasing Villa: The Last Campaign of the U.S. Cavalry* (Silver City, N.Mex.: High-Lonesome Books). Although he borrowed quite liberally from Pershing's "Report of Operations," Tompkins also provides extensive documentation to augment his own personal experiences with the 13th Cavalry—from Villa's raid on Columbus, New Mexico, after which he and his troopers pursued Villa's men well into Mexico, until he returned to the United States to recover from wounds suffered at the fight at Parral on 12 April.

Pershing's Mexican Expedition has been the subject of a number of works over the years. Robert S. Thomas and Inez V. Allen of the U.S. Army Office of the Chief of Military History completed an unpublished monograph entitled "The Mexican Punitive Expedition under Brigadier General John J. Pershing, United States Army, 1916–1917" that draws heavily on Pershing's "Report of Operations of the Punitive

Expedition to June 30, 1916" and provides a sound overview of operations. Herbert M. Mason's classic *The Great Pursuit* is still useful but aged. Clarence C. Clendenen's *Blood on the Border* covers the history of the armed clashes along the border, with the focus on the 1910–1917 period. He also published *The United States and Pancho Villa: A Study in Unconventional Diplomacy* (Ithaca, N.Y.: Cornell Univ. Press for the American Historical Association, 1961). Eisenhower's *Intervention!* looks at the story of American intervention in Mexico and not just the border area conflicts. Joseph A. Stout Jr. provides a general overview in his *Border Conflict*. More recent books include Eileen Welsome, *The General and the Jaguar: Pershing's Hunt for Pancho Villa, A True Story of Revolution and Revenge* (New York: Little, Brown, 2006), and James W. Hurst, *Pancho Villa and Black Jack Pershing: The Punitive Expedition in Mexico* (Westport, Conn.: Praeger Publishers, 2008).

3. One of the consistent shortcomings of Pershing's manuscript is that it does not provide adequate details of troop strength at critical times during the Mexican Expedition. At the beginning Pershing reported the strength of his two columns to the Southern Department as follows: Columbus (Eastern) Column, 133 officers, 3,175 men, and 2,288 animals; Culberson (Western) Column, 59 officers, 1,625 men, 1,887 animals. The first elements of the Mexican Expedition thus totaled 192 officers, 4,800 men, and 4,175 animals. Thomas and Allen, *The Mexican Punitive Expedition*, footnote 29, p. II-18.

4. Caliche. Derived from the Spanish word, caliche is a hardened, often impermeable, deposit of calcium carbonate that is combined with gravel, clay, sand, etc. It usually occurs in arid and semiarid areas and is found worldwide and in the western deserts of the United States and northern deserts of Mexico. It is also known as hardpan, calcrete, and curicrust. "Caliche," http://en.wikipedia.org/wiki/Caliche.

5. Telegram, Pershing to Funston, 25 March 1916, LC/Pershing Papers, Box 372, Punitive Expedition Reports (1).

6. On 13 March 1916, Obregón sent a telegram to Mexican military and civil authorities that read as follows:

Our government having entered into an agreement with that of the United States of the North, providing that the troops of either government may cross the border, in pursuit of bandits who are committing depredations along our frontier, I advise you of same in order that you may in turn advise all commanders along the border in order that you may make judicious use of these powers, taking care in each case to act in accord with the military authorities of the American Army in order that the pursuit of these bandits may give best results.

Pershing's report of 7 October reprinted this key telegram and stated:

A proclamation had been issued by General Obregon and published in several towns, copies of which our columns carried and displayed as evidence of an agreement between the two governments. This proclamation should have settled the mooted question in so far as the local inhabitants were concerned, but it did not change their views nor their intentions, although it probably did prevent active hostilities at the start.

Pershing, "Report of Operations," 7 October 1916, p. 10.

7. In 1915 the 1st Aero Squadron had received eight new Curtiss JN-3s (Jennys) that were supposed to be the latest in aeronautical design. They proved to be anything but reliable in operations in northern Mexico. Four new Curtiss N-8s, a

domestic version of the JN-4 that was then being exported to Europe, were received in April 1916, but flight testing proved them to be unacceptable for service in Mexico. In May twelve Curtiss R-2s arrived but were also found to be less than suitable for the operational conditions in Mexico. A variety of different aircraft types were eventually sent to the 1st Aero Squadron based at Columbus, New Mexico, and Colonia Dublán, Mexico, most of them delivered after August 1916. See Benjamin D. Foulois with Colonel C. V. Glines, *From the Wright Brothers to the Astronauts: The Memoirs of Major General Benjamin D. Foulois* (New York: McGraw-Hill, 1968), pp. 118–37; Juliette A. Hennessey, *The United States Army Air Arm, April 1861 to April 1917* (Maxwell AFB, Ala.: USAF Historical Division, 1958), pp. 167–74. See also the shortened version of Foulois's report, "Report of Operations of the First Aero Squadron, Signal Corps, with the Punitive Expedition, U.S.A., for Period March 15 to August 15, 1916," Appendix H, in Pershing, "Report of Operations," 7 October 1916, pp. 85–91, and the full version of his "Report of the Operations of the First Aero Squadron, Signal Corps, with the Mexican Punitive Expedition, for Period March 15 to August 15, 1916," Appendix B, in Tompkins, *Chasing Villa*, pp. 236–45; Roger G. Miller, *A Preliminary to War: The 1st Aero Squadron in the Mexican Punitive Expedition of 1916* (Washington, D.C.: Air Force History and Museums Program, 2003).

8. The ground and air officers who served with Foulois in the 1st Aero Squadron during the Mexican Expedition were: Bert M. Atkinson, T. S. Bowen, John B. Brooks, Roy S. Brown, John W. Butts, J. E. Carberry, C. G. Chapman, John F. Curry, Herbert A. Dargue, T. F. Dodd, P. I. Ferron, Harry Gantz, E. S. Gorrell, Millard F. Harmon, H. W. Harms, L. G. Heffernan, Davenport Johnson, Byron Q. Jones, Walter G. Kilner, Maxwell Kirby, George E. Lovell, H. S. Martin, Ira A. Rader, G. E. A. Reinberg, Ralph Royce, C. W. Russell, Carl Spatz (later Spaatz), J. D. von Holtzendorff, John C. Walker, S. H. Wheeler, and R. H. Willis Jr. Of these thirty-one officers, Brooks, Curry, Dargue, Johnson, and Royce were major generals in World War II, Harmon was a lieutenant general, and Carl Spaatz was a full general and first chief of staff of the U.S. Air Force (1947) after commanding U.S. strategic bombing operations in Europe and the Pacific (1942, 1944–1945). Hennessey, *The United States Army Air Arm, April 1861 to April 1917,* pp. 167–76; "John F. Curry," "John Bernard Brooks," "Millard F. Harmon," "Davenport Johnson," and "Carl Spaatz," U.S. Air Force Biographies, http://www.af.mil/information/bios; "Herbert Dargue," http://en.wikipedia.org/wiki/Herbert_Dargue; "Ralph_Royce," http://en.wikipedia.org/wiki/Ralph_Royce.

9. In his report to Pershing about his experiences with Colonel Cano at Oso Canyon (26–28 March), Brown stated: "Have just had a conference with Cano who could not produce the man who saw Villa's trail. I fear he simply lied to me." Pershing, "Report of Operations," p. 11; Tompkins, *Chasing Villa*, p. 100.

10. Extracts from Colonel Dodd's report of 29 March are in Pershing, "Report of Operations," pp. 14–15.

11. Pershing here is quoting directly from his own report of 7 October 1916 on the Mexican Expedition (p. 18). However, this quote and that in Frank Tompkins's book, *Chasing Villa* (p. 131), differ. According to Tompkins, the Cavazos note read as follows:

> On the third of April I telegraphed you, advising you that I thought it prudent to suspend the advance of your troops until we both receive orders on this

subject from the Citizen Military Commander of the State [Carranza]. As I have just received knowledge that your forces are advancing in accordance with the itinerary which I have, with those under my orders, I would esteem it very much if you would suspend your advance until you receive the order to which I refer, by which means there can be avoided a conflict which may occur by reason of your advance. As I do not doubt that you are aware of the reasons which move me to write this, I hope that we can arrive at an agreement, for which I sign myself.

> Your attentive and true servant
> General Jose Cavazos

12. Pablo López was one of Villa's most ruthless commanders. He was responsible for the attack on the train at Santa Isabel on 10 January 1916 and the brutal execution of eighteen out of nineteen Americans who were returning to the Cusihuiráchic Mining Company to restart operations. He was wounded in the Columbus raid. After evading Pershing's columns and recovering from his wounds, Carrancistas captured him. López was publically executed at Chihuahua City on 5 June. Frank Tompkins quotes Robert Howze as recording in his diary in early April that he had learned that Carrancistas had wounded Villa in the knee at Guerrero in late March and "that the seriously wounded man was Pablo Lopez, and that Lopez had just died in the Cuevos region, which suggested to Villa to announce his own death." While Villa was definitely thought to be faking his death and lying low to throw the American pursuers off his trail, it must have been some other unidentified leader's death which led to this subterfuge, because López was not executed until several months later. Katz, *Villa*, pp. 557–62, 572–73, 575–77; Tompkins, *Chasing Villa*, pp. 158–59.

13. Pershing submitted three estimates of the situation and plans for future operations to Funston in mid-April. The first was his seven-page "Report of General Situation," 14 April 1916, that assayed the current situation in Mexico with regard to the various factions, the pursuit of Villa, relations with the local population, the forces of the *de facto* government, the Mexican attack on Tompkins at Parral, and recommendations for future action. Pershing recommended strengthening his regiments to their legal maximums, adding another cavalry regiment, and the possible seizure of the Mexican railroads and occupation of Chihuahua. He followed this with Telegram No. 115, 16 April, which reiterated the points made in his 14 April memorandum, again recommending the capture of the State and City of Chihuahua and all railroads therein as "preliminary to further necessary military operations." On 18 April, Pershing pressed Funston for added men for his regiments, the development and training of a mobile force, and taking action. He concluded: "The tremendous advantage we now have in penetration into Mexico for 500 miles parallel to the main line of the railway south should not be lost. With this advantage a swift stroke now would paralyze Mexican opposition throughout northern tier of states and make complete occupation of entire Republic comparatively easy problem." Pershing to Commanding General, Southern Department, "Report of General Situation," 14 April 1916; Telegram No. 115, Pershing to Funston, 16 April 1916; and Telegram No. 121, Pershing to Funston, 18 April 1916, all in LC/Pershing Papers, Box 372, Folder: Punitive Expedition Reports (1).

14. Telegram No. 114, Bundy for Funston, Southern Department, to Pershing, 19

April 1916, in LC/Pershing Papers, Box 372, Punitive Expedition Reports (1). The full message read:

> Your No. 121 received [18 April 1916 recommending action]. General Scott, Chief of Staff, leaves Washington tonight expect to arrive here Friday evening, evidently coming for conference on Mexican situation. Pending his arrival there will undoubtedly be no action taken by War Department on any recommendation which you and I have taken. After consultation with him it is probable that more definite line of action can be defined.

15. The quoted section in the original draft of Pershing's memoirs ended at "offenders" with a period. However, the paragraph in the General Orders No. 28 did not end with a period but continued with the text that is in brackets. See General Orders No. 28, Headquarters, Punitive Expedition, U.S. Army, Lt. Col. De Rosey C. Cabell, 29 April 1916, in Pershing, "Report of Operations," p. 25.

16. Copies of the numerous telegrams that Scott and Funston sent to the Secretary of War reporting the results of their meetings with General Obregón are in *FRUS 1916*, pp. 530–47. The critical message that Scott and Funston sent was on 8 May (see pp. 543–44), when they reported that the Mexican government had rejected an agreement they had worked out with Obregón. They concluded that the Mexicans had dealt with them in "bad faith" and were stalling for time to position their forces for military action. They concluded:

> We expect many attacks along whole border similar to latest attack in Big Bend Rio Grande. . . . Our line is thin and weak everywhere and inadequate to protect border anywhere if attacked in force. . . . There [are] no adequate reserves. There are many calls for help on border which cannot be given and we think the border should at once be supported by at least 150,000 additional troops. . . . We have struggled for a different result with all our intelligence, patience and courtesy, hoping against hope for a peaceful solution but are now convinced that such solution can no longer be hoped for. . . . In order to give some added protection to border points exposed to raids it is recommended militia of Texas, New Mexico and Arizona be called out at once, final actions as to that of other States to be deferred until receipt by us of Obregon's proposal.

Scott provided some additional details of these meetings in his memoirs (Hugh L. Scott, *Some Memories of a Soldier* [New York: Century, 1928], pp. 525–28) and in his annual report of 30 September 1916 to the Secretary of War in which he commented about the results:

> While the Carranza Government would not agree to ratify the tentative agreement signed with Gen. Obregon, the conference furnished most beneficial results in materially relieving a very acute situation and in demonstrating to Gen. Obregon and other Carranza leaders the pacific intentions of our Government. . . . It had in every way been most emphatically impressed on Gen. Obregon that whenever the Mexican Government had demonstrated its capacity, and provided proper protection for our border, consideration would then be given to the withdrawal of our troops from Mexico.

Scott, "Report of the Chief of Staff," 30 September 1916, *ARWD 1916*, vol. 1, p. 188.

17. For a complete account of Patton's actions, largely in his own words, see Martin Blumenson, ed., *The Patton Papers: 1885-1940* (Boston: Houghton Mifflin, 1972), vol. 1, pp. 359–69.

18. In the original version of the manuscript, part of Pershing's message of 16 June was deleted. The entire message to Trevino has been included here for historical completeness. See "Message No. 1642, Funston to Secretary of War, 17 June 1916, 4 p.m.," with the Trevino telegram and Pershing's reply at *FRUS 1916*, p. 577.

19. Pershing's view that Captain Charles T. Boyd had not followed his orders and had "failed in prudence at Carrizal" (Smythe, *Guerrilla Warrior*, p. 260) has largely been accepted as the truth in this matter in most published accounts. Vandiver quotes Pershing's letter of 23 June 1916 to Colonel Henry T. Allen, the new commander of the 11th Cavalry, that this fight was caused "by the error of judgment on poor Boyd's part" and that "It is entirely inexplicable to me in view of the fact that I personally gave him instructions, and especially cautioned him against exactly what happened" (*Black Jack*, vol. 2, p. 654, and Letter, Pershing to Allen, 23 June 1916, in LC/Pershing, Box 9, Correspondence: Henry T. Allen). Both Smythe and Vandiver largely relegate to footnotes some serious questions about the verbal orders that Pershing gave to Boyd, for Pershing never gave a written order to Boyd for his mission although written orders were sent to Morey. In his article "The Affair at Carrizal," in *Montana: The Magazine of Western History* 18, no. 4 (autumn 1968), pp. 24–39, H. B. Wharfield raises some valid questions about exactly what Pershing ordered Boyd to do and why (see especially pp. 28–39). Chris Emmett in his *In the Path of Events with Colonel Martin Lalor Crimmons: Soldier, Naturalist, Historian* (Waco, Tex.: Jones and Morrison, 1959) also notes that Crimmons, who was then in Mexico at El Valle as a captain with the 16th Infantry, had similar questions to those raised by Whar-field (pp. 307–10). In an undated, signed memorandum commenting on Lieutenant Colonel George O. Cress's investigation of the Carrizal affair in the Pershing Papers at the Library of Congress [Box 372, Folder: Punitive Expedition Reports, (1)], Pershing wrote the following: "Arriving immediately in front of the Mexican position, his [Boyd's] own command in an open plain, with mounted Mexican troops on his flanks within close range, it was a serious error to start a fight at all, but especially was it fatal to dismount to fight on foot under such disadvantage. *Even though Captain Boyd had been directed to fight his way through to Ahumada,* he would not have been in any way justified in deploying at such close range and engaging such a vastly superior force occupying such a strong defensive position" (emphasis added). Whether Pershing meant to write "Even if" rather than "Even though," this sentence raises serious questions about just exactly what Pershing ordered Boyd to do that day at Carrizal. Perhaps as amazing is that Pershing refers to Boyd, whom he had known for some years, as "Captain William T. Boyd" and not Charles T. Boyd. This memo is at Appendix J. Of course, the basic problem in this matter is that everything is now speculation because the only two people who really knew what the orders were, Pershing and Boyd, are now dead. In addition, those on Pershing's staff who may have known more about what actually took place, especially after the incident, are also deceased. The unanswerable questions about Boyd's orders and Pershing's intentions are an important part of what led to the events at Carrizal on 21 June 1916.

20. This number was left blank in the original manuscript. No exact figure for the strength of the Mexican Expedition in May 1916 has been found. The *Annual Reports of the War Department* for 1916 and 1917 provided some overall figures which can be used to fill in this blank. The 1916 report stated that the force varied from

eight thousand to twelve thousand men and averaged ten thousand on a monthly basis (*ARWD, 1916,* vol. 1, p. 474). The 1917 report noted that the force in Mexico "during most of its service consisted of approximately 12,000 men" (*ARWD, 1917,* vol. 1, p. 349). Arthur Link in *Woodrow Wilson and the Progressive Era, 1910-1917* put the number at 385 officers and 11,250 men on 19 June—a total of 11,635 (p. 137 n 67). In an undated memorandum entitled "Report of the Quartermaster, Punitive Expedition into Mexico for the Period July 1, 1916 to February 5, 1917," Captain [later Major General and Chief of Cavalry, 1934–38] Leon B. Kromer, Quartermaster, Expeditionary Force, stated that the total number of troops and animals from 1 July 1916 to 24 January 1917 was 309 officers, 10,575 men, and 8,924 animals. These numbers apply to a period when the Mexican Expedition had transitioned into a relatively static operation with little or no military action. See LC/Pershing Papers, Box 372, Punitive Expedition Reports (1). It is assumed that the maximum strength Pershing mentioned here would have been about twelve thousand men after the Parral (April) and Carrizal (June) incidents.

Epilogue

1. The Frederick A. Stokes Company of New York published Pershing's autobiography of his years in France in two volumes in 1931 as *My Experiences in the World War.* For additional information on this work and its aftereffects, see Smythe, *Pershing: General of the Armies,* pp. 288–95.

2. Tacna-Arica dispute. As a result of the War of the Pacific (April 1879–October 1883) against Bolivia and Peru, Chile occupied the Peruvian provinces of Arica and Tacna. The Treaty of Ancón (20 October 1883) that ended the conflict allowed Chile to occupy the two provinces for ten years, after which a plebiscite would be held, with the results to determine their future allegiance. No agreement on the terms of the plebiscite could ever be reached, so no plebiscite was ever conducted, even after Pershing's involvement. The United States continued to mediate the dispute, which was finally resolved between the two countries in 1929 with Tacna returning to Peru and Arica remaining as a part of Chile, which also received a $6 million dollar indemnity. "War of the Pacific," Encyclopaedia Britannica Online, http://www.britannica.com/EBchecked/topic/437568/War-of-the-Pacific.

3. The American Battle Monuments Commission (ABMC) was established as a federal government organization by Congress in 1923 to plan and manage construction and maintenance of military monuments, cemeteries, and markers on foreign soil. The ABMC's primary responsibility at its establishment was the development of American military cemeteries in Europe, primarily in France, and the care of the remains of American servicemen who died during World War I and were buried in temporary military cemeteries. General Pershing was appointed to the first board by President Warren Harding, and he was elected chairman by its members. He held that post until his death in 1948. Pershing was personally involved in the operations of the ABMC and played a leading role in its evolution and the development of the battlefield cemeteries in France during the 1920s and 1930s. Today, the ABMC manages a worldwide system of twenty-four permanent burial grounds and twenty-five memorials, including three in the United States. See "History" and "Commission-

ers," American Battle Monuments Commission, http://www.abmc.gov/commission/ history.php.

4. The AEF's Service of Supply (SOS) provided the logistical support for the frontline combat units. The SOS included all transportation by sea or land, railroads, storage depots, food and water supplies, repair and services, construction and maintenance of all American bases and camps, engineering and construction functions, aircraft assembly and maintenance, security (military police and provost marshal functions), and medical support, including hospitals. Originally known as the Line of Communications, these critical logistical functions were later redesignated the Services of Supply, with headquarters at Tours with its own complete headquarters and staff separate from General Headquarters, AEF, at Chaumont. The number of soldiers assigned to the SOS eventually reached more than 552,000. Pershing put Major General James G. Harbord, his former chief of staff at General Headquarters and commander of the 2d Division, in charge of the SOS in July 1918 to make sure that it functioned smoothly and efficiently during the critical period of the American offensives beginning in September 1918. "United States Army: Services of Supply," in Anne Cipriano Venzon, ed. *The United States in the First World War: An Encyclopedia* (New York: Garland Publishing, 1995), pp. 721–23; Harbord, *The American Army in France*, pp. 119–575.

Appendix A

1. For background information on Pershing's speech, see note 7.1.

Appendix I

1. Louis C. Mosher was awarded a Medal of Honor on 4 March 1913.

Bibliography

Manuscript Collections

Manuscript Division, Library of Congress, Washington, D.C.
  Papers of General of the Armies John J. Pershing
Nebraska State Historical Society, Lincoln, Nebraska.
  Frank D. Eager Collection (MS 2420)
Norwich University Archives and Special Collections, Kreitzberg Library, Norwich University, Norwich, Vermont.
  Papers of Colonel Frank Tompkins

Published Sources

Allen, James Edgar, and John J. Reidy. *The Battle of Bayan and Other Battles.* Manila, Philippines: E. C. McCullough, 1903.

Allen, John. "Inventing the Middle East: UW Classicist William Westermann Led America's First Attempt to Re-Create the Middle East." *On Wisconsin* (winter 2004), pp. 36–39.

Allred, B. W., et al., eds. *Great Western Indian Fights.* Lincoln: Univ. of Nebraska Press, 1960.

Ancell, R. Manning, with Christine M. Miller. *The Biographical Dictionary of World War II Generals and Flag Officers: The U.S. Armed Forces.* Westport, Conn.: Greenwood Press, 1996.

Andrews, Avery D., ed. *1886-1911: In Commemoration of the 25th Anniversary of Graduation of the Class of '86, U.S.M.A., West Point, June, 1911.* Philadelphia: Holmes Press, 1911.

———. *My Friend and Classmate John J. Pershing with Notes from My War Diary.* Harrisburg, Pa.: Military Service Publishing Company, 1939.

Annual Report of the Governor of the Moro Province: September 1, 1903 to August 31, 1904. Washington, D.C.: GPO, 1904. The Annual Reports of the Governor of the Moro Province were also reprinted in the Annual Reports of the Philippine Commission to the Secretary of War from 1904 to 1907.

Second Annual Report of the Governor of the Province of Moro for Fiscal Year Ended June 30, 1905. Manila, Philippines: Bureau of Printing, 1905.

Annual Report of the Governor of the Moro Province: Major General Leonard Wood, U.S.A., July 1, 1905, to April 16, 1906; Brigadier General Tasker H. Bliss, U.S.A., April 16, 1906, to August 27, 1906. Zamboanga, Philippines: n.p., August 27, 1906.

Annual Report of the Governor of the Moro Province for the Fiscal Year Ended June 30, 1907. Manila, Philippines: Bureau of Printing, 1907.

Annual Report of the Governor of the Moro Province for the Fiscal Year Ended June 30, 1908. Zamboanga, Philippines: Mindanao Herald Publishing Company, 1908.

Annual Report of Colonel Ralph W. Hoyt, 25th United States Infantry, Governor of the Moro Province, for the Fiscal Year Ended June 30, 1909. Zamboanga, Philippines: Mindanao Herald Publishing Company, 1909.

Annual Report of Brigadier General John J. Pershing, U.S. Army, Governor of the Moro Province, for the Year Ending August 31, 1910. Zamboanga, Philippines: Mindanao Herald Publishing Company, 1910.

Annual Report of Brigadier General John J. Pershing, U.S. Army, Governor of the Moro Province, for the Year Ending June 30, 1911. Zamboanga, Philippines: Mindanao Herald Publishing Company, 1911.

Annual Report of the Governor of the Moro Province for the Year Ending June 30, 1913. Zamboanga, Philippines: Mindanao Herald Publishing Company, 1913.

The Army Almanac: A Book of Facts Concerning the United States Army. Harrisburg, Pa.: Stackpole, 1959.

Army Times, eds. *The Yanks Are Coming: The Story of General John J. Pershing.* New York: G. P. Putnam's Sons, 1961.

Arnold, James R. *The Moro War: How America Battled a Muslim Insurgency in the Philippine Jungle, 1902-1913.* New York: Bloomsbury Press, 2011.

Association of Graduates, U.S. Military Academy. *Annual Reports of the Association of Graduates of the United States Military Academy, West Point, New York.* [1917–1941]. In 1917, the *Annual Reports* replaced the previous *Annual Reunions* with no basic change in content. They were produced annually in numbered and dated issues until 1941 (numbers 47 through 72), when the Association of Graduates began publication of its new quarterly magazine, *Assembly.* (All are available online from the Archives, U.S. Military Academy, at http://www.library.usma.edu/index.cfm?TabID=6&LinkCategoryID=49.)

———. *Annual Reunions of the Association of Graduates, United States Military Academy, West Point, New York.* [1870–1916]. Each year from 1870 through 1916 the Association of Graduates held an annual reunion at the U.S. Military Academy for all graduated classes and printed a dated report of the reunion, including obituaries of recently decreased graduates. Each issue was numbered consecutively from 1 to 46. (All are available online from the Archives, U.S. Military Academy, at http://www.library.usma.edu/index.cfm?TabID=6&LinkCategoryID=49.)

———. *Assembly* (April 1942–present). (Issues from 1941 to 1993 are available online from the Archives, U.S. Military Academy, at http://www.library.usma.edu/index.cfm?TabID=6&LinkCategoryID=49.)

———. *Biographical Register of the Officers and Graduates of the U.S. Military Academy at West Point, N. Y., From Its Establishment, in 1802.* The individual volumes are listed in the Bibliography under their respective editors: Lieutenant Charles Braden, Colonel Charles N. Branham, Brevet Major General George W. Cullum, Captain W. H. Donaldson, Lieutenant Colonel E. E. Farman, Edward S. Holden, and Colonel Wirt Robinson.

———. *Register of Graduates and Former Cadets of the United States Military Academy, 2000.* West Point, N.Y.: Association of Graduates, 2000.

Auge, M. *Lives of the Eminent Dead and Biographical Notices of Prominent Living Citizens of Montgomery County, PA.* Norristown, Pa.: Published by the author, 1879.

Bacevich, Andrew J. *Diplomat in Khaki: Major General Frank Ross McCoy and American Foreign Policy, 1898-1949.* Lawrence: Univ. Press of Kansas, 1989.

Beale, Howard K. *Theodore Roosevelt and the Rise of America to World Power.* Baltimore, Md.: Johns Hopkins Univ. Press, 1984.

Bell, William Gardner. *Commanding Generals and Chiefs of Staff, 1775-2005: Portraits and Biographical Sketches of the United States Army's Senior Officer.* Washington, D.C.: U.S. Army Center of Military History, 2005.

Berner, Brad K., ed. *The Spanish-American War: A Historical Dictionary.* Lanham, Md.: Scarecrow Press, 1998.

Biographical Register of the Officers and Graduates of the U.S. Military Academy at West Point, N. Y., From Its Establishment, in 1802. The individual volumes are listed in the Bibliography under their respective editors: Lieutenant Charles Braden, Colonel Charles N. Branham, Brevet Major General George W. Cullum, Captain W. H. Donaldson, Lieutenant Colonel E. E. Farman, Edward S. Holden, and Colonel Wirt Robinson.

Biographical Sketches of Distinguished Officers of the Army and Navy. New York: Hamersly, 1905.

Blount, James H. *The American Occupation of the Philippines, 1898-1912.* New York: G. P. Putnam's Sons, 1912.

Blumenson, Martin, ed. *The Patton Papers: 1885-1940.* 2 vols. Boston: Houghton Mifflin, 1972.

Boatner, Mark Mayo, III. *The Civil War Dictionary,* rev. ed. New York: Vintage Books, 1991.

Bowman, John S., ed. *The Civil War Almanac.* New York: Gallery Books, 1983.

Braddy, Haldeen. *Cock of the Walk: Qui-qui-ri-qui! The Legend of Pancho Villa.* Albuquerque: Univ. of New Mexico Press, 1955.

Braden, Lieutenant Charles, ed. *Biographical Register of the Officers and Graduates of the U.S. Military Academy at West Point, New York, Since Its Establishment in 1802,* Supplement, vol. 5, *1900-1910.* Saginaw, Mich.: Seemann and Peters, Printers, 1910. (Also available online from Special Collections, U.S. Military Academy Library, at http://digital-library.usma.edu/libmedia/archives/cullum/volume_5_cullum .pdf.)

Bradford, Marlene. "Historical Roots of Modern Tornado Forecasts and Warnings." *Weather and Forecasting* 14, no. 8 (August 1999), pp. 485–88.

Bradley, James. *The Imperial Cruise: A Secret History of Empire and War.* New York: Little, Brown, 2009.

Brady, Cyrus Townsend. *Indian Fights and Fighters.* Lincoln: Univ. of Nebraska Press, 1971.

Branham, Colonel Charles N., ed. *Biographical Register of the Officers and Graduates of the U.S. Military Academy at West Point, New York, Since Its Establishment in 1802,* Supplement, vol. 9, *1940-1950.* West Point, N.Y.: Association of Graduates, 1955. (Also available online from Special Collections, U.S. Military Academy Library, at http://digital-library.usma.edu/libmedia/archives/cullum/volume_9_cullum .pdf.)

Brimlow, George F. *Cavalryman Out of the West: Life of General William Carey Brown.* Caldwell, Idaho: Caxton Printers, 1944.

Brockett, L. P. *Men of Our Day; or, Biographical Sketches of Patriots, Orators, Statesmen, Generals, Reformers, Financiers and Merchants. . . .* Philadelphia: Ziegler and McCurdy, 1872.

[Brown, Arthur W.]. "Cornellian Named Judge Advocate." *Cornell Alumni News* 36, no. 10 (30 November 1933), p. 112.

Brown, Dee. *Fort Phil Kearny: An American Saga.* Lincoln: Univ. of Nebraska Press, 1962.

Brown, Mark H. *The Plainsmen of the Yellowstone: A History of the Yellowstone Basin.* Lincoln: Univ. of Nebraska Press, 1961.

Bullard, Robert Lee. "Among the Savage Moros." *Metropolitan* 24, no. 3 (June 1906), pp. 263–79.

———. *Personalities and Reminiscences of the War.* Garden City, N.Y.: Doubleday, Page, 1925.

———. "Preparing our Moros for Government." *Atlantic Monthly* 97, no. 3 (March 1906), pp. 385–94.

———. "Road Building among the Moros." *Atlantic Monthly* 92, no. 6 (December 1903), pp. 818–26.

Canfield, Dorothy. "A General in the Making." *Red Cross Magazine* 14, no. 9 (September 1919), pp. 19–23, 66–68.

Carlson, Paul. *"Pecos Bill": A Military Biography of William R. Shafter.* College Station: Texas A&M Univ. Press, 1989.

Carter, Major General William H. The *Life of Lieutenant General Chaffee.* Chicago: Univ. of Chicago Press, 1917.

Cashin, Herschel V., Charles Alexander, William T. Anderson, Arthur M. Brown, and Horace W. Bivins. *Under Fire with the Tenth U.S. Cavalry.* New York: F. T. Neely, 1899. Reprint, Niwot, Colo.: Univ. Press of Colorado, 1993.

Chambers, John W., II, ed. *The Oxford Guide to American Military History.* New York: Oxford Univ. Press, 1999.

Clay, Lieutenant Colonel Steven E., U.S. Army (ret.). *U.S. Army Order of Battle 1919–1941.* 4 vols. Fort Leavenworth, Kans.: Combat Studies Institute Press, U.S. Army Combined Arms Center, 2010.

Clendenen, Clarence C. *Blood on the Border: The United States Army and the Mexican Irregulars.* New York: Macmillan, 1969.

Cloman, Sydney A. *Myself and a Few Moros.* New York: Doubleday, Page, 1923.

Cogar, William B. *Dictionary of Admirals of the U.S. Navy,* vol. 1, *1862-1900.* Annapolis, Md.: Naval Institute Press, 1989.

Collins, James L. "The Battle of Bud Bagsak and the Part Played by Mountain Guns Therein." *Field Artillery Journal* 15 (November–December 1925), pp. 559–70.

Conard, Howard L., ed. *Encyclopedia of the History of Missouri.* 3 vols. New York: Southern History Company, 1901.

Cosmas, Graham A. *An Army for Empire: The United States Army in the Spanish-American War.* College Station: Texas A&M Univ. Press, 1998.

Craddock, Colonel Wallis L. "Leonard Wood: Surgeon, Soldier, Administrator." *Military Surgeon* 160, no. 1 (January 1995), pp. 32–36.

Cullum, Brevet Major General George W., ed. *Biographical Register of the Officers and*

Graduates of the U.S. Military Academy, From 1802 to 1867. Revised edition, with a Supplement, vol. 2, *1841-1867.* New York: James Miller, 1879.

——, ed. *Biographical Register of the Officers and Graduates of the U.S. Military Academy, From 1802 to 1867. Revised edition, with a Supplement Continuing the Register of Graduates to January 1, 1879,* vol. 3, *Supplement.* New York: James Miller, 1879.

——, ed. *Biographical Register of the Officers and Graduates of the U.S. Military Academy at West Point N. Y., From Its Establishment, in 1802, to 1890,* 3d ed., revised and extended, vol. 1, *Nos. 1 to 1000.* Boston: Houghton, Mifflin, 1891. (Also available online from Special Collections, U.S. Military Academy Library, at http://digital-library.usma.edu/libmedia/archives/cullum/volume_1_cullum.pdf.)

——, ed. *Biographical Register of the Officers and Graduates of the U.S. Military Academy at West Point N. Y., From Its Establishment, in 1802, to 1890,* 3d ed., revised and extended, vol. 2, *Nos. 1001 to 2000.* Boston: Houghton, Mifflin and Company, 1891. (Also available online from Special Collections, U.S. Military Academy Library, at http://digital-library.usma.edu/libmedia/archives/cullum/volume_2_cullum.pdf.)

——, ed. *Biographical Register of the Officers and Graduates of the U.S. Military Academy at West Point N. Y., From Its Establishment, in 1802, to 1890,* 3d ed., revised and extended, vol. 3, *Nos. 2001 to 3384.* Boston: Houghton, Mifflin and Company, 1891. (Also available online from Special Collections, U.S. Military Academy Library, at http://digital-library.usma.edu/libmedia/archives/cullum/volume_3_cullum.pdf.)

Dann, W. F. "James Hulme Canfield, Chancellor of the University of Nebraska 1891–1895." In *Semi-Centennial Anniversary Book: The University of Nebraska, 1869-1919.* Lincoln: University of Nebraska, 1919.

Dastrup, Boyd L. *King of Battle: A Branch History of the U.S. Army's Field Artillery.* Washington, D.C.: U.S. Army Center of Military History, 1993.

Davis, Henry Blaine, Jr. *Generals in Khaki.* Raleigh, N.C.: Pentland Press, 1998.

DeBow, J. D. B. *Statistical View of the United States . . . Being a Compendium of the Seventh Census . . .* Washington, D.C.: Beverley Tucker, 1854.

Demontravel, Peter R. *A Hero to His Fighting Men: Nelson A. Miles, 1839-1925.* Kent, Ohio: Kent State Univ. Press, 1998.

Dennett, Tyler. *Roosevelt and the Russo-Japanese War: A Critical Study of American Policy in Eastern Asia in 1902-5, Based Primarily upon the Private Papers of Theodore Roosevelt.* Gloucester, Mass.: Peter Smith, 1959.

Diamonon, Victoriano D. "The Development of Self-Government in the Philippine Islands." Ph.D. diss, State University of Iowa, 1920.

Donaldson, Captain W. H., ed. *Biographical Register of the Officers and Graduates of the U.S. Military Academy at West Point, New York, Since Its Establishment in 1802,* Supplement, vol. 7, *1920-1930.* Chicago: R.R. Donnelley and Sons, 1931. (Also available online from Special Collections, U.S. Military Academy Library, at http://digital-library.usma.edu/libmedia/archives/cullum/volume_7_cullum.pdf.)

Dunn, Robert. "With Pershing's Cavalry." *Collier's* 58, no. 2 (23 September 1916), pp. 8-9, 25–26, 28.

DuPre, Colonel Flint O., USAFR. *U.S. Air Force Biographical Dictionary.* New York: Franklin Watts, 1965.

Eager, Lieutenant Colonel Frank D., comp. *History of the Operations of the 1st Nebraska*

Infantry, U.S.V. in the Campaign in the Philippine Islands. Lincoln, Nebr.: N.p., n.d.

Eisenhower, John S. D. *Intervention! The United States and the Mexican Revolution, 1913-1917.* New York: Norton, 1993.

Elliot, Charles A. "The Early Days of the Pershing Rifles." *Pershing Rifleman* 4, no. 3 (May 1935), pp. 6–7.

Elliott, Charles B. *The Philippines to the End of the Commission Government: A Study in Tropical Democracy.* Indianapolis, Ind.: Bobbs-Merrill, 1917.

———. *The Philippines to the End of the Military Régime: America Overseas.* Indianapolis, Ind.: Bobbs-Merrill, 1916.

Elser, Frank B. "General Pershing's Mexican Campaign." *Century* 99, no. 4 (February 1920), pp. 433–47.

Emmett, Chris. *In the Path of Events with Colonel Martin Lalor Crimmons: Soldier, Naturalist, Historian.* Waco, Tex.: Jones and Morrison, 1959.

Farman, Lieutenant Colonel E. E., ed. *Biographical Register of the Officers and Graduates of the U.S. Military Academy at West Point, New York, Since Its Establishment in 1802,* Supplement, vol. 8: *1930-1940.* Chicago: R.R. Donnelley and Sons, 1941. (Also available online from Special Collections, U.S. Military Academy Library, at http://digital-library.usma.edu/libmedia/archives/cullum/volume_8_cullum.pdf.)

Farwell, C. W. "The Biggest Man in the Philippines: Story of the Wonderful Work of Frank W. Carpenter as Department Governor of Mindanao and Sulu." *Current History* 13 (October 1920), pp. 20a–21.

Faulk, Odie B. *The Geronimo Campaign.* New York: Oxford Univ. Press, 1969.

Forbes, W. Cameron. "A Decade of American Rule in the Philippines." *Atlantic Monthly* 103, no. 3 (February 1909), pp. 200–209.

Forbes-Lindsay, C. H. *The Philippines under Spanish and American Rules.* Philadelphia: John C. Winston, 1906.

Foreman, John. *The Philippine Islands.* New York: Charles Scribner's Sons, 1906.

Foulois, Benjamin D., with Colonel C. V. Glines. *From the Wright Brothers to the Astronauts: The Memoirs of Major General Benjamin D. Foulois.* New York: McGraw-Hill, 1968.

Friedman, Lawrence M. *A History of American Law.* New York: Simon and Schuster, 2007.

Fry, Colonel James B. *The History and Legal Effect of Brevets in the Armies of Great Britain and the United States from Their Origin in 1692 to the Present Time.* New York: D. Van Nostrand, 1877.

Fulton, Robert A. *Moroland: The History of Uncle Sam and the Moros, 1899-1920.* Bend, Oreg.: Tumalo Creek Press, 2009.

Funston, Frederick. *Memories of Two Wars: Cuban and Philippine Experiences.* New York: Charles Scribner's Sons, 1914.

Galway, Joseph G. "J. P. Finley: The First Severe Storms Forescaster [Part 1]." *Bulletin of the American Meteorological Society* 66, no. 11 (November 1985), pp. 1389–95.

———. "J. P. Finley: The First Severe Storms Forecaster [Part 2]." *Bulletin of the American Meteorological Society* 66, no. 12 (December 1985), pp. 1506–10.

Ganoe, William A. *The History of the United States Army.* New York: D. Appleton-Century, 1942.

Gantenbein, Brigadier General C. U., ed. *The Official Records of the Oregon Volunteers in the Spanish War and Philippine Insurrection.* Salem, Oreg.: W. H. Leeds, State Printer, 1902.

Gardner, Lester D., ed. *Who's Who in American Aeronautics.* New York: Gardner, Moffat, 1922.

Gates, Merrill E., ed. *Men of Mark in America: Ideals of American Life Told in Biographies of Eminent Living Americans.* 2 vols. Washington, D.C.: Men of Mark Publishing, 1905.

Gibbon, John. *Address to the Graduating Class at the U.S. Military Academy, June 12, 1886.* Vancouver Barracks, Washington, D.C.: Headquarters, Department of the Columbia, 1886.

Gillette, Mary C. *The Army Medical Department, 1865-1917.* Washington, D.C.: U.S. Army Center of Military History, 1995.

Goldhurst, Richard. *Pipeclay and Drill: John J. Pershing, the Classic American Soldier.* New York: Reader's Digest Press, 1977.

Griscom, Lloyd C. *Diplomatically Speaking.* Boston: Little, Brown, 1940.

Gross, Charles J. "Guard Roots: Maj. Gen. Albert L. Mills." *National Guard* 62, no. 2 (February 2011), pp. 34–37.

Grunder, Garel A., and William E. Livezey. *The Philippines and the United States.* Norman: Univ. of Oklahoma Press, 1951.

Gunsburg, Jeffrey A. "Samuel Dickerson Rockenbach: Father of the Tank Corps." *Virginia Cavalcade* 26, no. 1 (summer 1976), pp. 38–47.

Harbord, James G. *The American Army in France, 1917-1919.* Boston: Little, Brown, 1936.

Harcave, Sidney. *The Russian Revolution of 1905.* London: Collier Books, 1970.

Harrison, Francis Burton. *The Corner-Stone of Philippine Independence: A Narrative of Seven Years.* New York: Century, 1922.

Hawley, James H. *History of Idaho: The Gem of the Mountains.* 2 vols. Chicago: S. J. Clarke Publishing Company, 1920.

Hayward, Colonel William. "Cut Up Pershing's Breeches." *Boston Globe,* 5 August 1917.

Heitman, Francis B. *Historical Register and Dictionary of the United States Army from Its Organization, September 29, 1789, to March 2, 1903.* 2 vols. Washington, D.C.: GPO, 1903.

Hennessey, Juliette A. *The United States Army Air Arm, April 1861 to April 1917.* Maxwell AFB, Ala.: USAF Historical Division, 1958.

Herwig, Holger H., and Neil M. Heyman. *Biographical Dictionary of World War I.* Westport, Conn.: Greenwood Press, 1982.

Hewes, James E., Jr. *From Root to McNamara: Army Organization and Its Administration, 1900-1963.* Washington, D.C.: U.S. Army Center of Military History, 1975.

The History of Linn County, Missouri: An Encyclopedia of Useful Information, and a Compendium of Actual Facts. Kansas City, Mo.: Birdsall and Dean, 1882.

A History of the Sixty-Sixth Field Artillery Brigade, American Expeditionary Forces. Denver, Colo.: Smith-Brooks, n.d.

Holden, Edward S., ed. *Biographical Register of the Officers and Graduates of the U.S. Military Academy at West Point, New York, Since Its Establishment in 1802.* Supplement, vol. 4, *1890-1900.* Cambridge, Mass.: Riverside Press, 1901. (Also available online from Special Collections, U.S. Military Academy Library, at http://digital-library.usma.edu/libmedia/archives/cullum/volume_4_cullum.pdf.)

Holmes, Richard, ed. *The Oxford Companion to Military History.* London: Oxford Univ. Press, 2001.

Howze, General Hamilton H. *A Cavalryman's Story: Memoirs of a Twentieth-Century Army General.* Washington, D.C.: Smithsonian Institution Press, 1996.

Hume, Edgar E. *The Golden Jubilee of the Association of Military Surgeons of the United States: A History of Its First Half-Century: 1891-1941.* Washington, D.C.: Association of Military Surgeons, 1941.

Hurley, Vic. *Jungle Patrol: The Story of the Philippine Constabulary, 1901-1936.* Salem, Oreg.: Cerberus Books, 2011.

Hurst, James W. *Pancho Villa and Black Jack Pershing: The Punitive Expedition in Mexico.* Westport, Conn.: Praeger Publishers, 2008.

Huse, Caleb. *The Supplies for the Confederate Army: How They Were Obtained in Europe and How Paid For.* Boston, Mass.: Press of T. R. Marvin and Son, 1904.

Hutton, Paul Andrew. *Phil Sheridan and His Army.* Norman: Univ. of Oklahoma Press, 1999.

"In Memoriam: Allen Wescott Field." In *Reports of Cases in the Supreme Court of Nebraska January and September Terms, 1915,* vol. 98. Columbia, Mo.: Press of E. W. Stephens Publishing Company, 1915.

Johnson, Rossiter, ed. *The Biographical Dictionary of America,* vol. 9, *Qua-Stearns.* Boston: American Biographical Society, 1906.

Jones, Colonel Harold W. "Brigadier General William H. Arthur (1856-1936)." *Army Medical Bulletin,* no. 68 (July 1943), pp. 218–26.

Juettner, Otto. "Lawrence C. Carr." In *Daniel Drake and His Followers: Historical and Biographical Sketches.* Cincinnati: Harvey Publishing Company, 1909.

Katz, Friedrich. *The Life and Times of Pancho Villa.* Stanford, Calif.: Stanford Univ. Press, 1998.

Kennedy, Joseph C. G. *Population in the United States in 1860; Compiled from the Original Returns of the Eighth Census under the Direction of the Secretary of the Interior.* Washington, D.C.: GPO, 1864.

King, James T. *War Eagle: A Life of General Eugene A. Carr.* Lincoln: Univ. of Nebraska Press, 1963.

Kurz, Stefan. "Die Wahrnehmung des russischen Offizierskorps durch k. u. k. Offiziere in den Jahren 1904-1906" (Imperial and Royal Officers' Perception of the Russian Officer Corps in the Years 1904-1906). Master's thesis, University of Vienna, June 2009. Available at http://othes.univie.ac.at/5360.

Lacey, Jim. *Pershing: A Biography.* New York: Palgrave Macmillan, 2008.

Landor, A. Henry Savage. *The Gems of the East: Sixteen Thousand Miles of Research Travel among Wild and Tame Tribes on Enchanting Islands.* New York: Harper and Brothers, 1904.

Lane, Jack C. *Armed Progressive: General Leonard Wood.* San Rafael, Calif.: Presidio Press, 1978.

Leckie, William H. *The Buffalo Soldiers: A Narrative of the Negro Cavalry in the West.* Norman: Univ. of Oklahoma Press, 1967.

Levine, Isaac Don. *Mitchell: Pioneer of Air Power.* New York: Duell, Sloan and Pearce, 1943.

Link, Arthur S. *Woodrow Wilson and the Progressive Era, 1910-1917*. New York: Harper and Brothers, 1954.

Linn, Brian McAllister. *The Philippine War, 1899-1902*. Lawrence: Univ. Press of Kansas, 2000.

Long, David F. *Gold Braid and Foreign Relations: Diplomatic Activities of U.S. Naval Officers, 1798-1883*. Annapolis, Md.: Naval Institute Press, 1988.

MacAdam, George. "The Life of General Pershing." 11-part series. *The World's Work*, 37, no. 1 (November 1918), pp. 45–56; no. 2 (December 1918), pp. 161–72; no. 3 (January 1919), pp. 282–93; no. 4 (February 1919), pp. 449–61; no. 5 (March 1919), pp. 540–46; no. 6 (April 1919), pp. 681–97; 38, no. 1 (May 1919), pp. 86–103; no. 2 (June 1919), pp. 148–58; no. 5 (September 1919), pp. 537–52; 39, no. 1(November 1919), pp. 66–71; no. 2 (December 1919), pp. 132–37.

MacGregor, Morris J., Jr. *Integration of the Armed Forces 1940-1965*. Washington, D.C.: U.S. Army Center of Military History, 1981.

Machoian, Ronald G. *William Harding Carter and the American Army: A Soldier's Story*. Norman: Univ. of Oklahoma Press, 2006.

Mason, Herbert Molloy, Jr. *The Great Pursuit: General John J. Pershing's Punitive Expedition across the Rio Grande to Destroy the Mexican Bandit Pancho Villa*. New York: Random House, 1970.

Mattes, Merrill J. *Indians, Infants and Infantry: Andrew and Elizabeth Burt on the Frontier*. Lincoln: Univ. of Nebraska Press, 1988.

Maurer, Maurer, ed. *The U.S. Air Service in World War I*. 4 vols. Washington, D.C.: Office of Air Force History, 1978.

McClernand, Edward J. *On Time for Disaster: The Rescue of Custer's Command*. Lincoln: Univ. of Nebraska Press, 1969.

Miles, Nelson A. *Personal Recollections and Observations of General Nelson A. Miles Embracing a Brief View of the Civil War or From New England to the Golden Gate and the Story of His Indian Campaigns with Comments on the Exploration, Development, and Progress of our Great Western Empire*. Chicago: Werner Company, 1896.

———. *Serving the Republic: Memoirs of the Civil and Military Life of Nelson A. Miles, Lieutenant-General, United States Army*. New York: Harper and Brothers, 1911.

Miley, John D. *In Cuba with Shafter*. New York: Charles Scribner's Sons, 1899.

Miller, Roger G. *A Preliminary to War: The 1st Aero Squadron in the Mexican Punitive Expedition of 1916*. Washington, D.C.: Air Force History and Museums Program, 2003.

Miller, Major Samuel L., U.S. Army. "Selfless Service: The Cavalry Career of Brigadier General Samuel M. Whiteside from 1858 to 1902." Thesis for the degree Master of Military Art and Science (MMAS), Military History, U.S. Army Command and General Staff College, Fort Leavenworth, Kans., 2002.

Millett, Allen R. *The General: Robert L. Bullard and Officership in the United States Army, 1881-1925*. Westport, Conn.: Greenwood Press, 1975.

Minger, Ralph E. "Taft's Mission to Japan: A Study in Personal Diplomacy." *Pacific Historical Review* 30, no. 3 (August 1961), pp. 279–94.

Mondey, David, ed. *The International Encyclopedia of Aviation*. New York: Crescent Books, 1988.

Morris, Edmund. *Theodore Rex*. New York: Random House, 2002.

Morris, Richard B., ed. *Encyclopedia of American History.* New York: Harper and Brothers, 1953.

Morton, J. Sterling, and Albert Watkins. *History of Nebraska: From the Earliest Explorations of the Trans-Mississippi Region.* A Revised Edition. Edited and revised by Augustus O. Thomas, James A. Beattie, and Arthur C. Wakeley. Lincoln, Nebr.: Western Publishing and Engraving Company, 1918.

Morton, J. Sterling, Albert Watkins, and George R. Miller. *Illustrated History of Nebraska: A History of Nebraska from the Earliest Explorations of the Trans-Mississippi Region.* . . . 2 vols. Lincoln, Nebr.: Western Publishing and Engraving Company, 1911.

Nadeau, Remi. *Fort Laramie and the Sioux Indians.* Englewood Cliffs, N.J.: Prentice-Hall, 1967.

The National Cyclopaedia of American Biography, vol. 14, Supplement 1. New York: James T. White, 1910.

Newgarden, George J. "Report of Capt. George J. Newgarden, Assistant Surgeon, United States Army, of His Services at Santiago, Cuba, with the Third United States Cavalry." *Annual Report of the Surgeon General of the Army to the Secretary of War for the Fiscal Year ending June 30, 1898* (Washington, D.C.: GPO, 1898), pp. 227–28.

New York State Adjutant General. *Annual Report of the Adjutant-General of the State of New York for the Year 1896.* Albany, N.Y.: Wynkoop Hallenbeck Crawford, 1897.

———. *New York in the Spanish-American War 1898: Part of the Report of the Adjutant General of the State for 1900.* 3 vols. Albany, N.Y.: James B. Lyon, State Printer, 1900.

Nichols, David C. *Founding the Future: A History of Truman State University.* Kirksville, Mo.: Truman State University, 2007.

Nofi, Albert A. *A Civil War Treasury: Being a Miscellany of Arms and Artillery, Facts and Figures, Legends and Lore, Muses and Minstrels, Personalities and People.* Edison, N.J.: Castle Books, 2006.

Norwich University Archives and Special Collections. "Colonel Frank Tompkins U.S. Infantry." *War Whoop 1922* (Norwich Yearbook), p. 23.

———. "Norwich Loses Colonel Tompkins." *Norwich Record* 46, no 8 (February 1955), pp. 2–3.

———. "Return of Major Tompkins as Commandant." *Reveille* 46, no. 9 (November 1916), pp. 3–6.

Novak, Karl F. "Introduction: General Hoffmann." In *War Diaries and Other Papers,* vol. 1, by Major General Max Hoffmann, pp. 9–32. Uckfield, Sussex, England: Naval and Military Press, 2004.

O'Connor, Richard. *Black Jack Pershing.* Garden City, N.Y.: Doubleday, 1961.

Ohles, John F., ed. *Biographical Dictionary of American Educators,* vol. 1. Westport, Conn.: Greenwood Press, 1978.

Ossad, Steven L. "Henry Ward Lawton: Flawed Giant and Hero of Four Wars." *Army History,* no. 63 (winter 2007), pp. 5–21.

Palmer, Frederick. *Bliss, Peacemaker: The Life and Letters of General Tasker H. Bliss.* New York: Dodd, Mead, 1934.

———. *John J. Pershing, General of the Armies: A Biography.* Harrisburg, Pa.: Military Service Publishing Company, 1948.

———. "John J. Pershing—Plower." *Collier's* 63, no. 18 (3 May 1919), pp. 5–6, 30, 34–37.

——. *With Kuroki in Manchuria.* New York: Charles Scribner's Sons, 1904.

——. *With My Own Eyes: A Personal Story of Battle Years.* Indianapolis, Ind.: Bobbs-Merrill, 1933.

Parker, John Henry. *History of the Gatling Gun Detachment, Fifth Army Corps, at Santiago, with a Few Unvarnished Truths Concerning that Expedition.* Kansas City, Mo.: Hudson-Kimberley Publishing, 1898.

Parker, John L. *Henry Wilson's Regiment: History of the Twenty-Second Massachusetts Infantry, the Second Company Sharpshooters, and the Third Light Battery, in the War of the Rebellion.* Boston, Mass.: Press of Rand Avery Company, 1887.

Pershing, Edgar J. *The Pershing Family in America: A Collection of Historical and Genealogical Data, Family Portraits, Traditions, Legends and Military Records.* Philadelphia: George S. Ferguson, 1924.

Pershing, John J. "The Campaign of Santiago." In *Under Fire with the Tenth U.S. Cavalry,* by Herschel V. Cashin et al., pp. 195–216. New York: F. T. Neely, 1899. Reprint, Niwot, Colo.: Univ. Press of Colorado, 1993.

——. *My Experiences in the World War.* 2 vols. New York: Frederick A. Stokes, 1931.

Phalen, Colonel James M. "Louis Anatole La Garde, Colonel, Medical Corps, U.S. Army." *Army Medical Bulletin* 49, no. 1 (July 1939), pp. 88–93.

——. "Merritte Weber Ireland (May 31, 1867–July 5, 1952)." In "Chiefs of the Medical Department, U.S. Army, 1775–1940: Biographical Sketches." *Army Medical Bulletin,* no. 52 (April 1940), pp. 94–100.

——. "Robert Urie Patterson." In "Chiefs of the Medical Department, U.S. Army, 1775–1940, Biographical Sketches." *Army Medical Bulletin,* no. 52 (April 1940), pp. 101–6.

——. "Valery Havard, Colonel, Medical Corps, U.S. Army." *Army Medical Bulletin,* no. 50 (October 1939), pp. 126–29.

Pier, Arthur S. *American Apostles in the Philippines.* Boston: Beacon Press, 1950.

Powell, William H., ed. *List of Officers of the Army of the United States from 1779 to 1900.* New York: L. R. Hamersly, 1900.

——. *Officers of the Army (Volunteer) Who Served in the Civil War.* Philadelphia: L. R. Hamersly, 1893.

——. *Powell's Records of Living Officers of the United States Army.* Philadelphia: L. R. Hamersly, 1890.

Powell, Major William H., and Medical Director Edward Shippen, eds. *Officers of the Army and Navy (Regular) Who Served in the Civil War.* Philadelphia: L. R. Hamersly, 1892.

Pringle, Henry F. *The Life and Times of William Howard Taft: A Biography.* 2 vols. New York: Farrar and Rinehart, 1939.

Raines, Rebecca R. *Getting the Message Through: A Branch History of the U.S. Army Signal Corps.* Washington, D.C.: U.S. Army Center of Military History, 1996.

Rhodes, Charles D., ed. *The Santiago Campaign: Reminiscences of the Operations for the Capture of Santiago de Cuba in the Spanish-American War, June and July 1898.* Richmond, Va.: Williams Printing Company, 1927.

Riegel, Robert E. *The Story of the Western Railroads: From 1852 through the Reign of the Giants.* Lincoln: Univ. of Nebraska Press, 1964.

Roberts, Frank E. *The American Foreign Legion: Black Soldiers of the 93d in World War I.* Annapolis, Md.: Naval Institute Press, 2004.

Robinson, Edgar E., and Victor J. West. *The Foreign Policy of Woodrow Wilson, 1913-1917*. New York: Macmillan, 1918.

Robinson, Colonel Wirt, ed. *Biographical Register of the Officers and Graduates of the U.S. Military Academy at West Point, New York, Since Its Establishment in 1802*, Supplement, vols. 6-A and 6-B, *1910-1920*. Saginaw, Mich.: Seemann and Peters, Printers, 1920. (Also available online from Special Collections, U.S. Military Academy Library, at http://digital-library.usma.edu/libmedia/archives/cullum /volume_6A_cullum.pdf, and http://digital-library.usma.edu/libmedia/archives/ cullum/volume_6B_cullum.pdf.)

Rodenbough, Brevet Brigadier General Theo. F., and Major William L. Haskin, eds. *The Army of the United States: Historical Sketches of Staff and Line with Portraits of Generals-in-Chief*. New York: Maynard, Merrill, 1896.

Roosevelt, Theodore. *The Rough Riders*. New York: Review of Reviews Company, 1904.

Saleeby, Najeeb M. *The History of Sulu*. Manila, Philippines: Bureau of Public Printing, 1908.

———. *The Moro Problem: An Academic Discussion of the History and Solution of the Problem of the Government of the Moros of the Philippine Islands*. Manila, Philippines, 1913.

———. *Studies in Moro History, Law, and Religion*. Manila, Philippines: Bureau of Public Printing, 1905.

Samuels, Peggy, and Harold Samuels. *Teddy Roosevelt at San Juan: The Making of a President*. College Station: Texas A&M Univ. Press, 1997.

Sansom, G. B. *The Western World and Japan: A Study in the Interaction of European and Asiatic Cultures*. New York: Knopf, 1970.

Sargent, Herbert H. *The Campaign of Santiago de Cuba*. 3 vols. Chicago: A. C. McClurg and Company, 1907.

Sawyer, Andrew J., ed. *Lincoln, the Capital City, and Lancaster County, Nebraska*. 2 vols. Chicago: S. J. Clarke, 1916.

Schmitt, Martin, ed. *General George Crook: His Autobiography*. Norman: Univ. of Oklahoma Press, 1960.

Schultz, William J., and M. R. Caine. *Financial Development of the United States*. New York: Prentice-Hall, 1937.

Scott, Hugh L. *Some Memories of a Soldier*. New York: Century, 1928.

Shiner, Colonel John F. *Foulois and the U.S. Army Air Corps, 1931-1935*. Washington, D.C.: Office of Air Force History, 1983.

Sides, Hampton. *Ghost Soldiers: The Epic Account of World War II's Greatest Rescue Mission*. New York: Anchor Books, 2002.

Smith, C. C. "The Mindanao Moro." *Journal of the U.S. Cavalry Association* 17, no. 62 (October 1906), pp. 287–308.

Smith, Gene. *Until the Last Trumpet Sounds: The Life of General of the Armies John J. Pershing*. New York: John Wiley and Sons, 1998.

Smythe, Donald. *Guerrilla Warrior: The Early Life of John J. Pershing*. New York: Charles Scribner's Sons, 1973.

———. "John J. Pershing at the University of Nebraska, 1891–1895." *Nebraska History* 43, no. 3 (September 1962), pp. 169–95.

———. *Pershing: General of the Armies*. Bloomington: Indiana Univ. Press, 2007.

Society of the Fifth Division. *The Official History of the Fifth Division, U.S.A.* Washington, D.C.: Society of the Fifth Division, 1919.

The State University of Iowa, Iowa City. *Twenty-Fifth Report of the Board of Regents to the Governor and Thirty-Second General Assembly, 1905-1906.* Des Moines: Emory H. English, State Printer, 1907.

Steinbach, Robert H. *A Long March: The Lives of Frank and Alice Baldwin.* Austin: Univ. of Texas Press, 1989.

Stevens, Walter B. *Centennial History of Missouri (The Center State): One Hundred Years in the Union, 1820-1921.* 3 vols. St. Louis, Mo.: S. J. Clarke, 1921.

Steward, T. G. *The Colored Regulars in the United States Army.* Philadelphia: A. M. E. Book Concern, 1904.

Stewart, Edgar I. *Custer's Luck.* Norman: Univ. of Oklahoma Press, 1955.

Stout, Joseph A., Jr. *Border Conflict: Villistas, Carrancistas, and the Punitive Expedition, 1915-1920.* Fort Worth, Tex.: Texas Christian Univ. Press, 1999.

Sweetser, Arthur. *The American Air Service: A Record of Its Problems, Its Difficulties, Its Failures, and Its Final Achievements.* New York: D. Appleton, 1919.

Thian, Raphael P. *Notes Illustrating the Military Geography of the United States, 1813-1880.* Austin: Univ. of Texas Press, 1979.

Thomas, Robert S., and Inez V. Allen. "The Mexican Punitive Expedition under Brigadier General John J. Pershing, United States Army, 1916–1917." Washington, D.C.: U.S. Army Office of the Chief of Military History, n.d.

Thrapp, Dan L. *The Conquest of Apacheria.* Norman: Univ. of Oklahoma Press, 1967.

Tompkins, Frank. *Chasing Villa: The Story behind the Story of Pershing's Expedition into Mexico.* Harrisburg, Pa.: Military Service Publishing Company, 1934.

Trussell, Colonel John B. B. "Frederick Funston: The Man Destiny Just Missed." *Military Review* 56, no. 6 (June 1973), pp. 59–73.

Twitchell, Heath, Jr. *Allen: The Biography of an Army Officer, 1859-1930.* New Brunswick, N.J.: Rutgers Univ. Press, 1974.

University of Nebraska Military Department. *History of the Military Department: University of Nebraska, 1876-1941.* Lincoln: Univ. of Nebraska, 1942.

U.S. Army Center of Military History. *Correspondence Relating to the War with Spain, Including the Insurrection in the Philippine Islands and the China Relief Expedition April 15, 1898 to July 30, 1902.* 2 vols. Washington, D.C.: GPO, 1993.

———. *Order of Battle of the United States Land Forces in the World War.* 3 vols. Washington, D.C.: U.S. Army Center of Military History, 1988.

U.S. Army Headquarters, Department of the Pacific and Eighth Army Corps, Adjutant General's Office. *Roster of Troops Serving in the Department of the Pacific and Eighth Army Corps.* Manila, Philippines, January 1899.

U.S. Army Mounted Service School. *The Rasp* [Yearbook, 1912, 1913]. Fort Riley, Kans.: 1912, 1913.

U.S. Congress, Senate. 59th Congress, 1st Session. *Congressional Record.* Vol. 61, pt. 8, 1921.

———. Document No. 276, 19 March 1906, Document No. 278, 21 March 1906, Document No. 289, 26 March 1906. *Senate Documents.* Vol. 6. Washington, D.C.: GPO, 1906.

U.S. Department of Commerce, Bureau of the Census. *Official Register of the United States, 1927.* Washington, D.C.: GPO, 1927.

U.S. Department of State. *Papers Relating to the Foreign Relations of the United States with the Address of the President to Congress, December 8, 1914.* Washington, D.C.:

GPO, 1922. Also available online at http://digital.library.wisc.edu/1711.dl/FRUS.FRUS1914.

———. *Papers Relating to the Foreign Relations of the United States with the Address of the President to Congress, December 7, 1915.* Washington, D.C.: GPO, 1924. Also available online at http://digital.library.wisc.edu/1711.dl/FRUS.FRUS1915.

———. *Papers Relating to the Foreign Relations of the United States with the Address of the President to Congress, December 5, 1916.* Washington, D.C.: GPO, 1925. Also available online at http://digital.library.wisc.edu/1711.dl/FRUS.FRUS1916.

———. (The University of Wisconsin Library has also placed 375 volumes of the *Foreign Relations of the United States* [1861–1960] online for researchers at http://uwdc.library.wisc.edu/collections/FRUS.)

U.S. Military Academy. *Official Register of the Officers and Cadets of the U.S. Military Academy at West Point, N.Y.* [published annually, June 1876–June 1940]. West Point: U.S. Military Academy, 1876–1940. All annual registers from 1818 to 1966 are available online from the Archives, U.S. Military Academy Library, at http://www.library.usma.edu/index.cfm?TabID=6&LinkCategoryID=49.

U. S. Naval Academy, Graduates' Association. *Register of Graduates, June 1916.* Annapolis, Md.: Advertiser-Republican, 1916.

U.S. Navy Department. *Register of Commissioned and Warrant Officers of the Navy of the United States and of the Marine Corps. . . .* [published annually, January 1900–January 1903]. Washington, D.C.: GPO, 1900–1903.

U.S. War Department. *Annual Reports of the War Department* [1898–1919]. Washington, D.C.: GPO, 1898–1919.

———. *Official Army Register of the Volunteer Force of the United States Army for the Years 1861, '62, '63, '64, '65. Part VII: Missouri, Wisconsin, Iowa, Minnesota, California, Kansas, Oregon, Nevada.* Washington, D.C.: War Department, 1867.

———. "Report of Lieutenant General W. T. Sherman," 5 November 1866, in "Report of General U.S. Grant, Commanding Army," 21 November 1866, in *Report of the Secretary of War.* Washington, D.C.: GPO, 1866.

———. *Reports of Military Observers Attached to the Armies in Manchuria during the Russo-Japanese War.* 5 vols. Washington, D.C.: GPO, 1906–1907.

———. *Special Reports on the Philippines to the President by Wm. H. Taft, Secretary of War, January 23, 1908 and J.M. Dickinson, Secretary of War, November 23, 1910.* Washington, D.C.: GPO, 1919.

U.S. War Department, The Adjutant General's Office (TAGO). *American Decorations: A List of Awards of the Congressional Medal of Honor, the Distinguished Service Cross, and the Distinguished Service Medal Awarded under Authority of the Congress of the United States, 1862-1926.* Washington, D.C.: GPO, 1927.

———. *General Orders and Circulars 1900.* Washington, D.C.: GPO, 1901.

———. *Medals of Honor Issued by the War Department up to and Including October 31, 1897.* Washington, D.C.: GPO, 1897.

———. *Officers of Volunteer Regiments Organized under the Act of March 2, 1899 Arranged According to Relative Rank.* Washington, D.C.: GPO, 15 November 1899.

———. *Official Army Register.* [published annually]. Washington, D.C.: GPO, 1897–1956.

———. *Official List of Officers of the Officers' Reserve Corps of the Army of the United States, Supplemental to Volume I, Alphabetical Index, September 1, 1919 to December 31, 1919.* Washington, D.C.: GPO, 1920.

———. *Official List of Officers of Volunteers in the Service of the United States Organized under the Act of March 2, 1899.* Washington, D.C.: GPO, 1 June 1900.

———. *Register of General Officers and Officers of the General Staff, U.S. Volunteers.* Washington, D.C.: GPO, 1 March 1899.

U.S. War Department, Bureau of Insular Affairs. *A Pronouncing Gazetteer and Geographical Dictionary of the Philippines Islands.* Washington, D.C.: GPO, 1902.

U.S. War Department, Bureau of Insular Affairs, Philippine Commission. *Annual Reports of the Philippine Commission to the Secretary of War* [1900–1916]. Washington, D.C.: GPO, 1900–1917.

———. "Department of Mindanao and Sulu," in *Report of the Philippine Commission to the Secretary of War, July 1, 1913 to December 31, 1914: Annual Reports of the War Department for Fiscal Year Ended June 30, 1915.* Vol. 4. Washington, D.C.: GPO, 1915.

———. *Fourth Annual Report of the Philippine Commission, 1903.* Washington, D.C.: GPO, 1904.

———. *Reports of the Philippine Commission, the Governor, and the Heads of the Executive Departments of the Civil Government of the Philippine Islands (1900-1903).* Washington, D.C.: GPO, 1904.

U.S. War Department, Militia Bureau. *Official National Guard Register for 1922.* Washington, D.C.: GPO, 1922.

U.S. War Department, Office of the Chief of Staff. *Field Service Regulations, United States Army,* 1 February 1905. Washington, D.C.: GPO, 1905.

Utley, Robert M. *Frontier Regulars: The United States Army and the Indian, 1866-1891.* New York: Macmillan, 1973.

Vandiver, Frank E. *Black Jack: The Life and Times of John J. Pershing.* 2 vols. College Station: Texas A&M Univ. Press, 1977.

Venzon, Anne Cipriano, ed. *The United States in the First World War: An Encyclopedia.* New York: Garland Publishing, 1995.

Wallace, William Swilling, ed. "Lieutenants Pershing and Stotsenberg [*sic*] Visit the Grand Canyon: 1887." *Arizona and the West* 3, no. 3 (autumn 1961), pp. 265–84.

Warner, Denis, and Peggy Warner. *The Tide at Sunrise: A History of the Russo-Japanese War, 1904-1905.* New York: Charterhouse, 1974.

Webster's American Military Biographies. Springfield, Mass.: G. and C. Merriam, 1978.

Webster's Biographical Dictionary. Springfield, Mass.: G. and C. Merriam, 1972.

Webster's Encyclopedic Unabridged Dictionary of the English Language. New York: Gramercy Books, 1989.

Weigley, Russell. *History of the United States Army.* New York: Macmillan, 1967.

Welsome, Eileen. *The General and the Jaguar: Pershing's Hunt for Pancho Villa, A True Story of Revolution and Revenge.* New York: Little, Brown, 2006.

Wharfield, H. B. "The Affair at Carrizal." *Montana: The Magazine of Western History* 18, no. 4 (autumn 1968), pp. 24–39.

Wheeler, Joseph. *The Santiago Campaign 1898.* Boston: Lamson, Wolffe, and Company, 1898.

"When Pershing Put Discipline into the 'Varsity Rifles.'" *Literary Digest* 61, no. 1 (5 April 1919), pp. 46, 48, 51.

Whitehorne, Joseph W. A. *The Inspectors General of the United States Army, 1903-1939.* Washington, D.C.: GPO, 1998.

Who Was Who in America: Historical Volume, 1607-1896. Chicago: A. N. Marquis, 1963.
Who Was Who in America, vol. 1, 1897-1942. Chicago: A. N. Marquis, 1942.
Who Was Who in America, vol. 2, 1943-1950. Chicago: A. N. Marquis, 1975.
Who Was Who in America, vol. 3, 1951-1960. Chicago: Marquis Who's Who, 1966.
Who Was Who in America, vol. 4, 1961-1968. Chicago: Marquis Who's Who, 1968.
Who Was Who in America, vol. 5, 1969-1973. Chicago: Marquis Who's Who, 1973.
Who Was Who in America, vol. 7, 1977-1981. Chicago: Marquis Who's Who, 1981.
Who Was Who in American History–The Military. Chicago: Marquis Who's Who, 1975.
Wilson, John B. Maneuver and Firepower: The Evolution of Divisions and Separate Brigades. Washington, D.C.: U.S. Army Center of Military History, 1998.
Wooster, Robert. Nelson A. Miles and the Twilight of the Frontier Army. Lincoln: Univ. of Nebraska Press, 1993.
Worcester, Dean C. The Philippines Past and Present. 2 vols. New York: Macmillan, 1914.

Internet Sources

"Alton in the Civil War: Alton Prison." Alton [Illinois] Historical Society. http://www.altonweb.com/history/civilwar/confed/.
American Battle Monuments Commission. http://www.abmc.gov/commission/history.php.
American Meteorological Society, AMS Journals Online. http://journals.ametsoc.org.
Ancestry.com. http://www.ancestry.com.
"Arlington's Ghost Soldier [Captain James Canfield Fisher]." Bennington (Vt.) Banner, 27 May 2006. http://www.benningtonbanner.com/ci_3871459.
Bennighof, Mike. "Italy's Elite Infantry: The Bersaglieri." http://www.avalanchepress.com/Bersaglieri.php.
Biographical Directory of the United States Congress. http://bioguide.congress.gov/.
"Biographies in Naval History." Naval Historical Center. http://www.history.navy.mil/bios/bios.htm.
Biographies United States Air Force. http://www.af.mil/information/bios/.
"Biography: Willard D. Straight and His Days in Korea." http://rmc.library.cornell.edu/Straight/.
Blackmar, Frank W., ed. Kansas: A Cyclopedia of State History, Embracing Events, Institutions, Industries, Counties, Cities, Towns, Prominent Persons, Etc. 3 vols. Chicago: Standard Publishing Company, 1912. Internet archive available at http://archive.org/.
[Boswell, Walter O.] "Banner Boswell Celebrates 40th Anniversary" and "History." Banner Boswell Medical Center. http://www.bannerhealth.com.
"Brigadier General Samuel D. Rockenbach of Virginia." Virginia Military Institute Archives, Preston Library, Lexington, Virginia. http://www.vmi.edu/archives.
Bringhurst, Newell G. "George Henry Dern." Utah History to Go. http://historytogo.utah.gov/people/georgehenrydern.html.
Byron, Lord. "The Eve of Waterloo." Poetry archive available at http://www.poetry-archive.com/b/the_eve_of_waterloo.html.
"Camp John Hay." Camp John Hay. http://www.campjohnhay.com.ph/history_iframe.php.

"Charles Bourlon de Rouvre (1850–1924)." Database of French MPs since 1789, National Assembly. http://www.assemblee-nationale.fr/sycomore/fiche.asp?num_dept=1100.

"Charles Burton Robbins." Iowa in the Great War. http://iagenweb.org/greatwar/histo/Robbins_CharlesBurton.htm.

"Charles G. Bickham, 1891." Dayton Metro Library. http://www.flickr.com/photos/dmlhistory/5393790037.

"Charles Raymond Cameron." The Political Graveyard. http://politicalgraveyard.com/geo/NY/phi-beta-kappa.html.

"Chinese Exclusion Act (1882)." Our Documents. http://www.ourdocuments.gov/doc.php?flash=old&doc=47.

"Chinese Exclusion Act of 1882." Free Dictionary. http://legal-dictionary.thefreedictionary.com/Chinese+Exclusion+Act+of+1882.

Ciruzzi, Canice G. "'Phoenix' Revisited: Another Look at George Horatio Derby." *Journal of San Diego History* 26, no. 2 (spring 1980). http://www.sandiegohistory.org/journal/80spring/derby.htm.

[Cody, William F.] "Buffalo Bill's Life." Buffalo Bill Museum and Grave. http://www.buffalobill.org/history.htm.

———. "Old West Legends: Buffalo Bill Cody—Trapper, Trader and Frontiersman." Legends of America. http://www.legendsofamerica.com/we-buffalobill.html.

———. "William F. 'Buffalo Bill' Cody." Iowa History, Iowa Medal of Honor Heroes. http://www.iowahistory.org/museum/exhibits/medal-of-honor/sf-03-cody-iw/index.html.

"Commodore Perry and the Opening of Japan." Navy Department Library, Naval History and Heritage Command. http://www.history.navy.mil/library/special/perry_openjapan1.htm.

Crouch, Thomas W. "Frederick Funston of Kansas: His Formative Years, 1865–1891." *Kansas Historical Quarterly* 40, no. 2 (summer 1974), pp. 177–211. Available at Boyhood Home and Museum of Major General Frederick Funston, http://www.skyways.org/museums/funston/form.html.

[Dawes, Charles G.] "The Nobel Prize in Peace 1925: Sir Austen Chamberlain, Charles G. Dawes." Official Site of the Nobel Prize. http://nobelprize.org/nobel_prizes/peace/laureates/1925/dawes-bio.html.

Delisi, James T. "From Sutlers and Canteens to Exchanges." *Army Logistician* (November–December 2007). http://www.alu.army.mil/alog/issues/NovDec07/canteen2_exchange.html.

Denger, Mark J. "Major-General Henry Ware Lawton, U.S. Volunteers." California Military Museum, California Center for Military History. http://www.militarymuseum.org/Lawton.html.

"The Destruction of the USS *Maine*." Naval History and Heritage Command, Frequently Asked Questions. http://www.history.navy.mil/faqs/faq71-1.htm.

Dienst, Captain Charles F., et al. *History of the 353d Infantry Regiment, 89th Division, September 1917–June 1919*. Wichita, Kans.: Regimental Society of the 353d Infantry Regiment, 1921. Available online at The Kansas Collection, http://www.kancoll.org/books/dienst/.

"Distinguished Service Cross Citation, Brigadier General John J. Pershing, 13

September 1940." Home of Heroes. http://www.militarytimes.com/citations-medals-awards/citation.php?citation=9922.

"Dr. Hubert Grieger." Find A Grave Memorial. http://www.findagrave.com.

"Dugald Christie." Biographical Dictionary of Chinese Christianity. http://www.bdcconline.net/.

[Elliott, Edward C.] "Biographical Sketch." A Guide to the Edward C. Elliott Papers, Purdue University Libraries, Archives and Special Collections. http://oldsite.lib.purdue.edu/spcol/fa/pdf/elliott.pdf.

Encyclopaedia Britannica (2010, 2011, 2012). Encyclopaedia Britannica Online. http://www.britannica.com/.

"Enrico Caviglia." http://www.treccani.it/enciclopedia/enrico-caviglia_(Dizionario-Biografico)/.

"Erich Friedrich Wilhelm Ludendorff (1865–1937)." The Prussian Machine. http://home.comcast.net/~jcviser/aok/ludendorff.htm.

"Father: Gov. Frank W. Carpenter." Nonlinearhistorynut's Blog. http://nonlinearhistorynut.wordpress.com/father-gov-frank-w-carpenter.

"F. E. Warren History." F. E. Warren Air Force Base. http://www.warren.af.mil/library/factsheets/factsheet.asp?id=4696.

"Francis Emory Warren [Senator Warren Answers Last Call, *The Lusk Herald*, November 29, 1929]." Niobrara County Library (Lusk, Wyoming). http://niobraracountylibrary.org/obituaries/index.php?id=5503.

"Frederic Remington Biography." Frederic Remington. http://www.frederic-remington.org/biography.html.

"Frederick W.S. O'Neill." Biographical Dictionary of Chinese Christianity. http://www.bdcconline.net/.

Fulton, Robert A. "Bates Mission 1899," "The Battle of Bud Dajo (March 6–8, 1906)," and "The Battle of Bud Bagsak (June 11–15, 1913)." Uncle Sam, the Moros, and the Moro Campaigns. http://www.morolandhistory.com.

"Gen. Leroy V. Patch." In Hiram T. French, *History of Idaho*. Chicago: Lewis Publishing, 1914. Available at http://files.usgwarchives.org/id/payette/bios/patch25nbs.txt.

"George Lawson Sheldon: Biographical Data." Archives Record, Nebraska State Historical Society, Lincoln, Nebraska. http://www.nebraskahistory.org.

"Günther von Etzel." The Prussian Machine. http://home.Comcast.net/~jcviser/aka/etzel.htm.

Hartmann, Rudolf. "Japanische Offiziere im Deutschen Kaiserreich 1870–1914" (Japanese Officers in the German Empire, 1870–1914). *Japonica Humboldtiana* 11 (2007), p. 101. http://edoc.hu-berlin.de/japonica-hu/11/hartmann-rudolf-93/PDF/hartmann.pdf.

"History." Royal House of Sulu. http://royalsultanateofsulu.org/#!history.

[Hobson, Richmond P.] "Hobson." Dictionary of American Naval Fighting Ships, Naval Historical Center. http://www.history.navy.mil/danfs/h7/hobson.htm.

[Hump, Chief]. "Etokeah: Chief Hump, Minniconjou Lakota (ca. 1848–1908)." Akta Lakota Museum and Cultural Center. http://www.aktalakota.org/index.cfm?ca=1&artid=49.

"James Canfield Fisher." Special Forces Roll of Honor. http://www.specialforcesroh.com/roll-4469.html.

"James Hulme Canfield (4th President)." Past Presidents, Ohio State University. http://president.osu.edu/past-presidents.php.

Japan. National Diet Library, Portraits of Modern Japanese Historical Figures. http://www.ndl.go.jp/portrait/.

Johannsen, Albert. "The House of Beadle and Adams and Its Dime and Nickel Novels: The Story of a Vanished Literature." Northern Illinois University Libraries. http://www.ulib.niu.edu/badndp/bibindex.html.

"John Coalter Bates." "Commanding General and Chiefs of Staff, 1775–2005." U.S. Army Center of Military History. http://www.history.army.mil/books/cg&csa/bates-jc.htm.

"John Hance (1838–1919)." All Hikers, Historical Figures. http://www.allhikers.com/allhikers/History/Historical-Figures/John-Hance.htm.

"John Ross." Biographical Dictionary of Chinese Christianity. http://www.bdcconline.net/.

"Lieutenant George Patrick Ahern and Glacier National Park." http://homepages.rootsweb.ancestry.com/~aherns/ahglac.htm.

"Louis Riel." Dictionary of Canadian Biography Online. http://www.biographi.ca/009004-119.01-e.php?Biold=39918.

"Major General Henry Ware Lawton." http://www.culbertsonmansion.us/Lawton_Bio.html.

"Major General Sir William Henry Birkbeck (1863–1929)." Liddell Hart Centre for Military Archives, King's College London. http://www.kcl.ac.uk/lhcma/locreg/BIRKBECK.shtml.

"Martin Egan Papers." Archives of the Pierpont Morgan Library, New York. http://www.themorgan.org/research/FindingAids/archives/ARC1222-Egan.pdf.

"Max Hoffmann." The Prussian Machine. http://home.Comcast.net/~jcviser/aka/hoffmann.htm.

McGuffey's Readers World. "History of McGuffey Readers." http://www.mcguffeyreaders.com/history.htm.

McSherry, Patrick. "A Brief History of the 2nd U.S. Artillery, Battery A." The Spanish-American War Centennial Website. http://www.spanamwar.com/2ndusbatterya.htm.

———. "The Gatling Gun." The Spanish-American War Centennial Website. http://www.spanamwar.com/Gatling.htm.

"Memorandum of the Service of Brigadier General S. D. Rockenbach." Virginia Military Institute Archives, Preston Library, Lexington, Virginia, at http://www.vmi.edu/archives.

"The Moroccan Crises: International Relations Involving Morocco, 1903–1914." Early Twentieth Century Timelines. http://cnparm.home.texas.net/Wars/MorCrises.htm.

"Museum of Vision Recognizes President's Day with an Inside Look into the Eyesight Challenges of U.S. Presidents." American Academy of Ophthalmology. http://www.aao.org/newsroom/release/20120213.cfm.

National Society of Pershing Rifles. http://pershingriflessociety.org/NSPR/history.php.

"New Hance Trail." National Park Service, Grand Canyon National Park. http://www.nps.gov/grca/planyourvisit/upload/New_Hance_Trail.pdf.

"New Hance Trail." Grand Canyon Association, Nature, Culture and History at the Grand Canyon. http://grandcanyonhistory.clas.asu.edu/sites_rimtoriverandinnercanyon_newhancetrail.html.

Nishida Hiroshi. "Yoshimatsu, Motaro." Imperial Japanese Navy, Graduates of Naval Academy Class 7th. http://homepage2.nifty.com/nishidah/e/px07.htm.

"The Nobel Prize in Peace 1912: Elihu Root." Official Site of the Nobel Prize. http://nobelprize.org/nobel_prizes/peace/laureates/1912/root-bio.html.

"North-West Rebellion." The Canadian Encyclopedia. http://www.thecanadianencyclopedia.com/index.cfm?PgNm=TCE&Params=a1ARTA0005802.

Ohio Historical Society. Ohio History Central. http://ohiohistorycentral.org/.

"Oscar Preuss." U.S. Army Forces in the Philippines, American Historical Collection, Ateneo de Manila University. http://rizal.lib.admu.edu.ph/ahc/guides/US_Army_Forces.pdf.

Pershing, John J. "Report of Operations of the Punitive Expedition to June 30, 1916," 7 October 1916. U.S. Army Command and General Staff College, Combined Arms Research Library (CARL) Digital Library. http://cgsc.contentdm.oclc.org/cdm/singleitem/collection/p4013c0117/id/702/rec/2.

Philippine Scouts Heritage Society. http://www.philippine-scouts.org.

The Phrase Finder. "Best bib and tucker." http://www.phrases.org.uk/meanings/best-bib-and-tucker.html.

"Ransford Stevens Miller, Jr." Find A Grave Memorial. http://www.findagrave.com.

Reagor, Captain Michael J. "Herman J. Koehler: The Father of West Point Physical Education, 1885–1923." U.S. Military Academy Library, Digital Library. http://digital-library.usma.edu/libmedia/archives/toep/herman_koehler_father_wp_phys_ed_1885_1923.pdf.

"Red River Rebellion." The Canadian Encyclopedia. http://www.thecanadianencyclopedia.com/index.cfm?PgNm=TCE&Params=a1ARTA0006727.

"The Riel Rebellions." Canadiana. http://www.canadiana.org/citm/specifique/rielreb_e.pdf.

"Samuel Baldwin Marks Young." Commanding Generals and Chiefs of Staff. http://www.history.army.mil/books/CG&CSA/Young-SBM.htm.

"Samuel T. Polk." U.S. Army Forces, American Historical Collection, Ateneo de Manila University. http://rizal.lib.admu.edu.ph/ahc/guides/US_Army_Forces.pdf.

"Schuyler Colfax, 17th Vice President (1869–1873)." http://www.senate.gov/artandhistory/history/common/generic/VP_Schuyler_Colfax.htm.

[Sims, William S.] "Sims." Dictionary of American Naval Fighting Ships, Naval Historical Center. http://www.history.navy.mil/danfs/s13/sims-iii.htm.

"The Spanish American War Centennial Website." http://www.spanamwar.com/.

"Thomas Cosby Fulton." Biographical Dictionary of Chinese Christianity. http://www.bdcconline.net/.

[Tompkins, Frank]. "Chronology of Commandants." Norwich University Archives and Special Collections. http://library2.norwich.edu/catablog/commandant/commandant.

"Two Obituaries for Sir Berkeley Vincent, K.B.E." Brig. General Sir Berkeley Vincent. http://www.sirberkeleyvincent.co.uk.

University of Iowa Yearbook, 1911, p. 323. http://www.e-yearbook.com/yearbooks/University_Iowa_Hawkeye_Yearbook/1911.

"U.S. Army Personnel Buried at Arlington National Cemetery." Arlington National Cemetery. http://www.arlingtoncemetery.net/.

"U.S. Concludes Treaty with China—November 17, 1880." Miller Center of Public Affairs, University of Virginia, American President, An Online Reference Resource. http://millercenter.org/president/events/11_17.

U.S. Congress. Senate. "Henry Wilson, 18th Vice President (1873–1875)." http://www.senate.gov/artandhistory/history/common/generic/VP_Henry_Wilson.htm.

U.S. Department of Veterans' Affairs. Nationwide Gravesite Locator. http://gravelocator.cem.va.gov/j2ee/servlet/NGL_v1.

U.S. Library of Congress. "Dime Novels." http://www.loc.gov/exhibits/treasures/tri015.html.

U.S. National Archives and Records Administration. National Atlas of the United States. "The Public Land Survey System (PLSS)." http://www.nationalatlas.gov/articles/boundaries/a_plss.html.

———. "Teaching with Documents: The Homestead Act of 1862." http://www.archives.gov/education/lessons/homestead-act/.

"Warm Welcome by General Pershing for Villa and Obregon in El Paso." *El Paso Times:* Tales from the Morgue, 27 August 1914. http://elpasotimes.typepad.com/morgue/2012/03/1914-warm-welcome-by-general-pershing-for-villa-and-obregon-in-el-paso.html.

[Weeks, Charles W.] "Clemson Commandant." *Evening Herald* (Rock Hill, S.C.), 9 July 1936. http://news.google.com/newspapers.

Wikipedia. http://en.wikipedia.org/wiki/Main_Page.

"William Holmes McGuffey Museum." Miami University. http://www.units.muohio.edu/mcguffeymuseum/learn_more/readers.html.

"William McKinley." The White House. http://whitehouse.gov/about/presidents/williammckinley.

"William McKinley, 25th President of the United States." McKinley Museum. http://www.mckinley.lib.oh.us/index.php/biography.

Woolbert, Robert G. Book Review: "*With Japan's Leaders.*" *Foreign Affairs* (October 1942). Available at http://www.foreignaffairs.com/articles/105241/frederick-moore/with-japans-leaders.

"The World of 1898: The Spanish-American War." Hispanic Division, Library of Congress. http://www.loc.gov/rr/hispanic/1898/.

World's Columbian Exposition of 1893. http://columbus.iit.edu/dreamcity/00024044.html, and http://columbus.gl.iit.edu/bookfair/ch5.html.

Yebra, Captain David J. "Colonel Herman J. Koehler: The Father of Physical Education at West Point." 23 November 1998. Archives, U.S. Military Academy Library, Digital Library. http://digital-library.usma.edu/libmedia/archives/toep/col_herman_koehler_father_phys_ed_wp.pdf.

[Young, Samuel Baldwin Marks]. "Superintendents." Yellowstone National Park. http://www.secretyellowstone.com/basic-park-information/superintendents.

Newspapers and Journals

American Medicine.
Boston Daily Globe.

California and Western Medicine.
El Paso (Texas) Herald.
Journal of the American Medical Association (JAMA).
New York Times.
Princeton Alumni Weekly 4, no. 2 (10 October 1903).
Washington Herald.

Emails

"Captain Samuel Polk." In email, Waldette M. Cueto, Curator, American Historical Collection, Rizal Library, Ateneo de Manila University, Quezon City, to Dr. John T. Greenwood, 13 June 2011.
"Oscar Preuss." In email, Waldette M. Cueto, Curator, American Historical Collection, Rizal Library, Ateneo de Manila University, Quezon City, to Dr. John T. Greenwood, 13 June 2011.

Interview

Shaw, Russell. About his father, Colonel Charles B. Shaw. 16 December 2011.

Index

Page references given in *italics* indicate illustrations or material contained in their captions.

Abdul Hamid (Abdülhamid II), 278
Acosta, Julio, 354
Adair, Lt. Henry R., 358, 462–63, 465–66
Adam, Maj. Emil, 74, 466
Adams, 1st Lt. Robert W., 298, 454, 466
Adamson, George E.: assistance to Pershing in writing *A Memoir,* 2, 3, 5–8; service with Pershing, 2, 611–12n3
"Address on the Campaign of Santiago, An" (Pershing), 367–81
Ade, George, 666n2
adjutant general: of the Department of Mindanao and Jolo, 144–46; of the Military District of Mindanao and Jolo, 140–44
adobe houses, 360
Adta of Paigoay, 163, 401
agriculture: improvements in Moro Province, 304–6
Agua Caliente (Mexico), 350
Agua Prieta, battle of, 669–70n6
Aguinaldo, Emilio, 140, 146, 250, 516
Ahern, Maj. George P., 185
Ahmai-Benaning, 181, 199, 437
Ahmai-Manibilang: correspondence with Pershing, 156–57, 387–90; at Marahui, 441; Pershing's efforts at Moro pacification and, 156–57, 159, 192, 399, 401; relations with Pershing, 150–54, 159, 181, 184, 201;

relation to the North Lake Moros, 384–85
Ahmai-Sangacala, 391
Ahmai-Tampugao, 239, 281–82
Ahumada (Mexico), 356–57, 359
Ainsworth, Gen. Fred C., 242, 466–67
Ainus people, 239
airplanes. *See* aviation
Aliudan, 442
Allen, Lt. Col. Henry T., 247, 348, 350, 467
Allen, Lt. John H., 187, 407, 415, 468
Amai-Buncurang, 400, 401
Amai-Pasandalan, 408, 443
American Battle Monuments Commission, 1, 3, 366, 678n3
American Expeditionary Forces (AEF), 363–65
American imperialism: emergence of following the Spanish-American War, 122–25; "manifest destiny" and, 123; Theodore Roosevelt and, 252
American Indians: Cree Indians and the Duck Lake conspiracy, 90–93; Ghost Dance, 71; impact of western settlement on, 53–54, 69–70; Wounded Knee uprising, 72–77, 512; Zuni Indians, 59–60, 64–65. *See also* Apache Indians; Sioux Indians
Amil, 295, 299, 453
Ampuan, 428
Ampuan-Agus, 181, 199–200, 201, 437, 439
Anderson, Larz, 268, 277
Andrews, Avery D., 94, 468–69

Andrews, George L., 49, 469
Annapolis (USS gunboat), 668–69n4
Antao, 427
Apache Indians: army campaigns
  against, 54, 56, 60, 339; army
  pursuit of Geronimo, 54, 56, 499,
  517, 542–43, 671n1
Army and Navy General Hospital, 269,
  659–60n10
Army of Cuban Pacification: formation
  of, 634n1, 652n15; officers serving
  with, 470, 474, 478, 484, 539, 551–52,
  567, 574, 579, 603
Army War College, 214–15, 498
Arthur, Maj. William H., 134, 469–70
artillery: Japanese use of, 255;
  mountain artillery, 175, 426, 517, 552
Asia: Pershing's reflections on, 135–36;
  Taft's "goodwill tour" of, 238–39,
  651–52n12; Western imperialism
  and, 123–25
Atas, 280, 313
Atchison, Topeka & Santa Fe Railway
  (AT&SF), 60, 623–24n3
Augur, Col. J. A., 655n4
Austria-Hungary, 266, 658n6
aviation: 1st Aero Squadron, 514,
  673n7, 673–74n8; first flight over
  mountains, 659n8; in the Mexican
  Punitive Expedition, 346–47, 673n7,
  673–74n8; Wilbur Wright in France,
  266–67
Ayacucho (Peru), 365
Ayers, Capt. William J., 288, 470

Bacolod (Moro fort), 195–96, 425–27
Bacolod, Sultan of, 164, 191, 388
Bacolod Moros: attacks on Camp
  Vicars, 397–98; Pershing's efforts at
  pacification, 183–97, 399–403, 424–
  27; Pershing's observations of, 396
Bagobos, 279, 313
Baguio (Philippines), 253–54, 656n4
Baker, Lt. Chauncey B., 68, 470
Baldwin, Col. Frank D.: biographical
  information, 470–71; Lake Lanao
  Expedition of 1902, 155, 159–60;

Moro pacification and, 160–61;
  promotion to brigadier general, 169;
  visit to Pershing at Camp Vicars,
  184–85
Baldwin, Col. Theodore A., 103, 114,
  471–72
Baltic (SS), 2, 364
Bandholtz, Harry H., 247, 472
Bansayan (Philippines), 437
Barker, Capt. John W., 291, 295, 472–73
Barnum, Maj. Gen. Malvern Hill, 6, 7,
  114, 118, 473–74
barong, 146–47
Barry, Thomas H., 140, 245, 474,
  652–53n15
Barton, Clara, 121, 379
baseball, 277
Bass, Col. Edgar Wales, 42, 474–75
Bates, Maj. Gen. John C., 117, 142, 144,
  475–76
"Bates Agreement," 475
Bayabao (Philippines), 176
Bayabao, Sultan of, 408
Bayabao Moros, 395, 396, 399, 429
Bayan, Battle of, 159–60
Bayan Moros, 192–93, 399–400
Beacom, Col. John H., 355, 476
"Beadle's dime novels," 20–21, 618n14
bear hunting, 67
"Beast Barracks," 39–42
Beibi, Sultan of, 162–63
Beijing (China), 239, 623n1
Belgium, 265–66
Bell, Gen. George, Jr., 359, 476–77
Bell, Gen. James Franklin: biographical
  information, 477–78; in Cuba, 652n15;
  in the Philippines, 276, 312, 315
Berlin, 264–65
Berry, Col. Lucien G., *345*
Bersaglieri, 132–33, 635n4
"best bib and tucker," 19, 617–18n12
Beveridge, Albert J., 217
Bickham, Lt. Charles G.: biographical
  information, 478–79; September
  18–22, 1902 Moro pacification
  expedition, 176, 407, 409–11;
  September–October 1902 Moro

pacification expedition, 179, 415, 416, 419, 421
Big Foot, 72, 74–75
Bigger, C. W., 36–37
Bilanos, 313
Bilimbing (Philippines), 148
Binidayan, Sultan of, 641–42n14
Bintong (Philippines), 441
Birkbeck, Col. William Henry, 223
Birkhimer, Col. William E., 145–46, 479
Bishop, Flora, *61*
Black Jack (Vandiver), 5
Black Sea mutiny, 265
blacksmithing, 34–35
Blanco y Erenas, Gen. Ramón, 119
Bleeding Kansas, 15, 616n7
Blériot, Louis, 267
Bliss, Gen. Tasker H.: biographical information, 479–80; on Mexican Border conditions in 1914, 327–28; Mexican Punitive Expedition and, 344; in the Philippines, 280, 480, 661n7
blizzards, 77–78
Boardman, Mabel, 361
Boburan uprising, 282–83
Boer War, 130, 634–35n2
Bongao (Philippines), 147–48
"Border Ruffians," 15, 616–17n8
Bosnia, 266
Boswell, Lt. Walter O., 256, 447, 480–81
Boxer Rebellion, 56, 124, 208, 493, 623n1
Boyd, Capt. Charles T.: biographical information, 481–82; Carrizal affair, 357, 358–59, 461–64, 676–77n19
Brent, Charles H., 295, 482
brevet rank, 621n4
Brewster, 2d Lt. Andre W., 60–61, 482
Broadwood, Lt. Gen. Sir Robert G., 250
Brooke, Gen. John R., 93, 128, 482–83
Brown, Lt. Arthur W.: accompanies Pershing across Lake Lanao, 181, 184; April 1903 Moro pacification expedition, 424, 425, 429; biographical information, 483–84; September 18–22, 1902 Moro

pacification expedition, 407; September–October 1902 Moro pacification expedition, 415–17
Brown, Benjamin Gratz, 29
Brown, 1st Lt. Earl I., 178, 484
Brown, 2d Lt. Thomas W., 194, 423, 484–85
Brown, Col. William C.: biographical information, 485; Mexican Punitive Expedition, 342, 344, 347, 349, 352
Brussels, 265, 657n3
Bryan, Charles Page, 667n2
Bryan, William Jennings, 86–87, 94, 627n6
Bud Bagsak operation: Lt. Collins's personal account of, 664n8; description of, 295–302, 453–60; newspaper attacks on, 665n11; Pershing's bravery in, 665n12
Bud Bunga (Philippines), 300–301, 458
Bud Dajo, Battle of (1906), 663–64n6
Bud Dajo campaign (1911), 289–95, 447–51
buffalo, 69–70
"Buffalo Bill." *See* Cody, Col. William F. ("Buffalo Bill")
Bugulung, 163
Bullard, Maj. Robert Lee, 59, 198, 201, 485–86, 647n10
Bun Bun (Philippines), 298, 299, 457
Bunga (Moro fort), 298, 300
Bureau of Indian Affairs, 69–70
Burnett, Lt. Charles, 655n4
Burrows, Joseph H., 36
Burt, Col. Andrew, 92, 486–87
Burtt, Capt. Wilson B., *345*
"bushwhackers," 16–17, 617n11
Butig, Sultan of, 171, 175, 396
Butig Moros, 399

Cabell, Col. De Rosey C., *345*, 346, 487–88
"Caciques," 331, 668n2
Cagayan (Philippines), 144–46
"Caingin" farming, 305
Calahui (Philippines), 198, 402–3, 428–29

caliche, 341, 673n4
Calles, Gen. Plutarco Elías, 669–70n6
Cameron, Charles R., 309, 488
Camp John Hay, 254, 656n7
Camp McGrath, 248
camp meetings, 25
Camp Stotsenburg, 248
Camp Vicars: attacks by hostile Moros, 170–73, 397–98; conditions at, 161–62; establishment of, 161; Fourth of July celebrations, 167–68; Hospital Corps detachment, 189; Nelson Miles's visit to, 184–85, 643–44n5; Pershing given command of, 169; Pershing relieved by Lt. Col. Rodgers, 202–3; Pershing's 1902–1903 report of activities at, 203–5, 393–406; Gifford Pinchot's visit to, 185–86; soldier named for, 161, 639n5; Gen. Sumner's visits to, 184–85, 191
Canfield, James H., 81–84
Canfield Fisher, Dorothy, 85
Capistrano, 145, 146
Capron, Capt. Allyn, 112, 373, 488–89
Caquim, Nurul, 399, 437
carabao, 146
Cárdenas, Col. Julio, 355
Carpenter, Frank W., 315, 489
Carr, Gen. Eugene A.: biographical information, 489–90; hunting in New Mexico, 67; response to the aftermath of Wounded Knee, 75; service in New Mexico, 56, 58–59, 64
Carr, Maj. Lawrence C., 181, 184, 415, 490–91
Carranza, Venustiano: aftermath of the Carrizal affair and, 360; American recognition of, 333; de facto forces and, 334, 335, 670n7; Mexican bandits and, 334, 335, 339; Mexican internal politics and, 331–33
Carrington, Col. Henry B., 624–26n2
Carrizal affair, 356–61, 461–64, 676–77n19
Carter, Maj. William H., 213, 491–92
Casablanca affair, 266, 658n7

Casas Grandes (Mexico), 342, 343, 345
Case, Maj. James F., 146, 492
Cathedral of St. Basil (Moscow), 261, 657n1
Cather, Willa, 85
Cavalry School, 46, 493, 621n5
Caviglia, Maj. Enrico, 229, 230, 250, 492–93
Cervantes, Candelario, 355–56
Cervera y Topete, Adm. Pascal, 108, 378
Ceylon, 135
Chaffee, Gen. Adna R.: biographical information, 493–94; as chief of staff, 56, 214; Samuel Mills and, 558; Moro pacification and, 173, 639n6; 1902 proclamation to the Moros, 155–57, 159, 383, 386–87; with the Sixth Cavalry, 56
Chamberlain, Lt. Col. John L., 424
Chapman, A. W., 37–38
Charlton, Capt. George C., 298, 300, 301, 454, 459, 494
Chateau Petrovsky, 262
Chavez, Georges, 659n8
Cheyenne Indians, 70–72
Chicago Tribune, 224
Chicago World's Fair of 1893, 85, 627n3
chief of staff, 56, 214, 364
Chile, 365–66, 678n2
China: Boxer Rebellion, 56, 124, 493, 623n1; Exclusion Act and, 211, 649n5; Pershing's diplomatic mission to Hong Kong, 317–18; Pershing's observations as a military observer in Manchuria, 223–33, 234–37; Pershing's 1903 visit to and reflections on, 206–9; Taft's visit to, 239; U.S. ambassadors, 666–67n1, 667n2; Washington Treaty and, 211, 649n4; Weihai, 123, 634n4; Western imperialism and, 123, 124
China Relief Expedition, 469, 474, 482, 487, 493, 529, 552, 563, 602
"Chinese Exclusion Act," 211, 649n5
Chinese: in Mindanao and Jolo, 143; Pershing's observations of in Manchuria, 223–33, 234–37
Choate, Joseph H., 130

cholera, 187, 189, 399
Christie, Dugald, 240, 652n14
Church of the Savior (Moscow), 262
Civil War, 14–17
Clarke, 1st Lt. H. B., 407, 411, 415
Clayton, Maj. Jere B., *345*
Cleveland, Frances Folsom, 95
Cleveland, Grover, 95
Cloman, Capt. Sydney A., 145, 147–48, 494–95
Cobb, Cpl. Edward F., 631n6
Cody, Col. William F. ("Buffalo Bill"), 63–64, 72, 325, 326
Cole, Lt. Otis R., 424
Collins, Col. James L.: biographical information, 495–96; Bud Bagsak operation, 297, 299, 301, 454–57, 664n8; reviews chapters of Pershing's memoirs, 6, 7; service with Pershing, 613–14n22
Colonia Dublán (Mexico), 339, 341–42, 346, 348, 355, 360–61
colored troops. *See* Tenth Cavalry Regiment
Columbian Guard, 85, 549, 627n3
Columbus, N.Mex., 335–36, 339, 591–92
commandant of cadets, University of Nebraska, 81–87
"Composite Regiment," 363
Comstock, 2d Lt. H. E., 408, 412, 415
Coolidge, Calvin, 365, 366
Corbin, Maj. Gen. Henry C., 117, 120, 122, 213, 496–97
coronation of King George V, 317–18
Cortelyou, George B., 217
Corvisart, Col. Charles Pierre, 229, 497, 651n10
Cotabato (Philippines), 144
Cotabato Moros, 305
cottas: description of, 157, 159. *See also specific Moro forts*
Craig, Lt. Louis A., 58–59, 497
Craig, Gen. Malin, 59, 497–98
Crane, Charles R., 666–67n1
Cree Indians, 90–93
Crook, Gen. George, 54, 56, 498–99, 671n1

Crounse, Lorenzo, 64, 499–500
Crowder, David, 16
Crowder, Sally, 21
Cruse, 1st Lt. Thomas, *61*
Cuba: American interventions, 245, 634n1 (*see also* Cuban Pacification); American military occupation, 127–28, 652–53n15; events prior to the Spanish-American War, 98–99 (*see also* Spanish-American War)
Cuban Junta, 98–99
Cuban Pacification, 484, 486, 517, 527, 564. *See also* Army of Cuban Pacification
Currie, Lt. D. H., 436
Curtin, Ralph A.: assistance to Pershing in writing *A Memoir*, 2–4, 7; service with Pershing, 2, 612n4
Cusihuiráchic (Mexico), 354
cutting weapons: of the Moros, 146–47

Dade, Waller H., 306, 500
Daiquiri (Cuba), 370
Dalny (Manchuria), 223–24
dancing: the Ghost Dance, 71; Pershing's fondness for, 216; the Sioux Indians and, 80
Dansalan, Sultan of, 388
dattos: Gen. Chaffee's proclamation of 1902 and, 155–57, 159; in the governing structure of Lake Lanao Moros, 143, 637n4; opposition to Philippine independence, 277; Pershing elected a *datto*, 193; Pershing's relationship with and pacification of, 150–54, 163–73 (*see also* Moro pacification)
Davis, Elizabeth, 12
Davis, Brig. Gen. George W.: assumes command in the Philippines, 149; biographical information, 500–501; concerns with Moro affairs and pacification, 149–50, 160, 168, 194, 199, 383–84, 433, 443–44; designates Pershing as "Intelligence Officer" of Moro affairs, 639n7; evaluation of Pershing, 640–41n12; gives

Davis, Brig. Gen. George W. *(cont.)*
Pershing command of the Lake
Lanao Region, 169; governance of
Moro Province and, 203; as governor
of Puerto Rico, 128; Lake Lanao
Expedition of 1902, 159; orders for
the Bacolod expedition of 1903, 194,
433; Pershing's march around Lake
Lanao and, 199, 202, 443–44
Dawes, Charles G., 86, 94, 501–2
Dayton, Adm. John H., 365
De Armond, Lt. E. H., 424
Deems, Lt. Charles, 407
Deems, Lt. Clarence, 424, 430
deer hunting, 88, 90
de facto Mexican forces, 334, 335, 670n7
Degraw house, 26–28
Delgado, José M., 632n1
Department of California, 245, 653n16
Department of Mindanao (Philippines):
American forces in, 662n8, 662n9;
commanders of, 661n7; Pershing
as commanding general of, 271,
277–82. *See also* Mindanao and Jolo
(Philippines)
Department of Mindanao and Jolo
(Philippines): Pershing as adjutant
general, 144–46. *See also* Jolo Island
(Philippines); Mindanao and Jolo
(Philippines)
depression of 1873, 30–33, 619n3
Derby, Maj. George McC., 114, 502
Dern, George H., 87, 502–3
Deshon, Col. George D., 269, 503
Díaz, José de la Cruz Porfirio, 329, 330
Dibabawans, 313
Dickinson, Jacob M., 277, 503
Dickson, Capt. Robert S., 298, 504
"dime novels," 20–21, 618n14
disarmament: of the Moros, 285–302,
453–60, 663n11
discipline, 91
Dismounted Cavalry Division, 106, 114,
472, 589, 600
Division of Customs and Insular
Affairs, 127–28
divorce. *See* marriage customs

Dodd, Col. George A., 341, 347–48, 353,
354, 504
Dodge Commission, 636n3
Doherty wagon, 276, 660n1
Domingues, Cruz, 354
Dow, Miss, *61*
doxology, 32, 619n4
duck hunting, 239, 276
Duck Lake conspiracy, 90–93
Dudley, Lt. Edgar S., 82, 504–5
Duncan, George B., 247, 505–6
Duvall, Maj. Gen. William P., 276,
661n7
Dworak, Anna, 309
Dworak, Edward, 309, 506

Eagan, Brig. Gen. Charles P., 121
Eager, Col. Frank D., 87, 506–7
earthquakes, 186–87, 394. *See also* San
Francisco earthquake
education. *See* schools and education
Egan, Martin, 203, 251, 507
Egypt, 134
Eighteenth Infantry Regiment, 78,
624–26n2
Eighth Brigade: Pershing's assigned
command of, 323, 325; pursuit of
Pancho Villa (*see* Mexican Punitive
Expedition); service on the Mexican
border, 327–29, 332, 334–35
Eighth Cavalry Regiment, 514, 655n4
Eighth Infantry Regiment, 454–59
El Caney (Cuba), 372–74, 377
Eleventh Cavalry Regiment, 348–50,
353, 354
Eleventh Infantry Regiment, 176
Elliot, Charles A., 87, 507
Elliott, Charles B., 102, 317, 318, 507
Elliott, Edward C., 87, 507–8
El Paso District, 363
El Pozo field hospital, 117–19
El Pozo Hill (Cuba), 372, 374
El Valle (Mexico), 360, 361
Ely, Hanson E., 247–48, 508
"embalmed" beef, 121
English, George, 631n6
Entente Cordiale, 266, 658n5

Ernst, Col. Oswald H., 96, 508-9
Erwin, Col. James B., 342
Eskridge, Lt. O. S., 436
Evans, Maj. Ellwood W., 342, 344, 347, 353, 509
Evans, Rear Adm. Robley D., *191*
Ewers, Capt. Ezra P., 74, 509-10
Exclusion Act, 211-12, 649n5

Farrar, Geraldine, 265
Febiger, Col. Lea, 288, 510
Fernandez, Leon, 152, 424, 436, 443
Fetterman, Capt. William J., 625-26n2
Fetterman massacre, 78, 624-26n2
Field, Allan W., 86
field hospitals, 117-19
Fifteenth Cavalry Regiment: April 1903 Moro pacification expedition, 195-99, 401-3, 423-33; Wiley Mangum and, 554; May 1903 Moro pacification expedition around Lake Lanao, 199-202, 435-45; Charles McCullough and, 551; Moro attack on Lt. Forsyth, 155; Pershing joins in the Philippines, 148-49; September 18-22, 1902 Moro pacification expedition, 175-78, 398, 407-14; September-October 1902 Moro pacification expedition, 178-81, 398, 415-22
Fifth Cavalry Regiment, 63, 353
Filipinos: American attitudes toward, 251; issue of independence and self-government, 251-52, 277; in Mindanao and Jolo, 142-44; in Moro Province, 280
Finley, Maj. John P., 282-83, 510-11
firearms. *See* guns
First Aero Squadron, 514, 673n7, 673-74n8
First Cavalry Regiment, 106-10, 115, 118, 370-71
First Infantry Division, 114, 116, 117
First Regular Infantry Regiment, 370
First Volunteer Cavalry Regiment ("Rough Riders"): battle of San Juan Heights, 115, 116, 118; commander of, 106, 604; history of, 630n4; Las Guasimas engagement, 109-10, 370-72; "Mr. Dooley's" account of, 109
Fisher, Dorothy Canfield, 85
Fleming, 2d Lt. Lawrence J., 92, 511
Fletcher, Col. Allen S., 288, 511-12
Fletcher, Henry P., 265
Florence (Italy), 133
foot races, 68
Forbes, W. Cameron: biographical information, 512; disarmament of the Moros and, 286, 287-88, 296; visits to Zamboanga, 276-77, 312; visit to Pershing at Fort McKinley, 250
Forsyth, Col. James W., 75, 512-13
Forsyth, Lt. William D., 155, 513, 638n1
Fort Assinniboine, 88-94
Fort Bacolod, 195-96, 425-27
Fort Bayard, 56-63
Fort Bliss, 327, 338
Fort del Pilar, 142
Fort Erlangshan, *232*
Fortieth Volunteer Infantry Regiment, 144, 145
Fort McKinley, 246-53, 256
Fort Myer, 216
Fort Niobrara, 77-78, 81
Fort Pitacus, 199-200, 403, 438-39
Fort Riley, 267
Fort Santiago, 137
Fort Wingate, 59, 64-65, 67-68
Foster, Lt. Victor S., 423, 435
Foulois, Capt. Benjamin D., 346, 513-14
Fountain, Col. Samuel W., 149, 514-15
Fourth Cavalry Regiment, 542-43
Fourth of July, 24-25, 167-68
France: the Balkan issue and, 266; Casablanca affair, 266, 658n7; Entente Cordiale, 266, 658n5; imperialism in the Far East, 123; Pershing family visit to, 266-68
Franco-Prussian War, 267-68
Frank, Pvt. Burton S., 646n9
Frear, Walter F., 323
Fries, 1st Lt. A. A., 408

Fries, Lt. Claude S.: April 1903 Moro pacification expedition, 194, 423; biographical information, 515; observation of Japanese Army maneuvers, 254; reinforced brigade, 655n4; September 18-22, 1902 Moro pacification expedition, 177, 407, 411, 412; September-October 1902 Moro pacification expedition, 415

Fujii Shigeta, Gen., 227

Fukushima (Japan), 240

Fulton, Thomas C., 240

Funston, Gen. Frederick: biographical information, 515-16; in Cuba, 652n15; death of, 363; entertains Pershing in Honolulu, 323; Mexican Punitive Expedition and, 336-37, 341, 353, 355, 517; Pershing's recommendations to in Mexico, 351-52; response to the Carrizal affair, 359

Ganassi, Sultan of, 191, 239, 401

Ganduali (Moro fort), 412-13

Ganduali, Sultan of, 179, 398, 412, 418, 645n2

Gardenhire, Lt. William C., 435

Gardner, Col. Cornelius, 655n4

Garfield, James A., 496

Gata Moros, 190, 199, 437

Gatewood, Lt. Charles B., 56, 517, 543

Gatley, Capt. George G., 200, 424, 428, 436, 443, 517

Gatling guns, 110, 631-32n8

Gauan (Philippines), 408

General Staff, 212-14

genro, 222, 650-51n6

George V, 317-18

Germany: the Balkan issue and, 266; Casablanca affair, 266, 658n7; imperialism in the Far East, 123; Pershing family visit to, 264-65; Triple Alliance, 266, 658n6

Geronimo, 54, 56, 499, 517, 542-43, 671n1

Ghost Dance, 71

Gibbon, Brig. Gen. John, 622n8

Gillmore, Lt. Robert A., 305, 517-18

Giza Pyramid, 134

Going, Lt. R. B., 435

Gómez, Gen. Felix, 358, 462

Gordon, Charles George, 208

Gordon, Col. William W.: biographical information, 518; Bud Bagsak operation, 298, 455, 458; reviews chapters of Pershing's memoirs, 6, 7; talks with the Bud Bagsak Moros, 295

Gracie, Lt. William B.: April 1903 Moro pacification expedition, 424, 426, 428, 431; biographical information, 518-19; May 1903 Moro pacification expedition around Lake Lanao, 200, 436, 438-39, 443; September 18-22, 1902 Moro pacification expedition, 177, 408, 410, 411; September-October 1902 Moro pacification expedition, 178, 179, 415

Grand Canyon, 65-67

Grande of Makadar, 164, 165, 401, 443

Grand Place (Brussels), 265, 657n3

Grant, Frederick D., 94, 519

Grant, Gen. Ulysses, 39

Great Britain: the Balkan issue and, 266; Boer War, 130, 634-35n2; Entente Cordiale, 266, 658n5; Hong Kong and, 206, 207; imperialism in the Far East, 123; Pershing's first visit to, 129-31; relations with Japan, 125, 210

Greely, Maj. Gen. Adolphus, 247, 519-20

Greenback Party, 36, 620n1

Grew, Joseph H., 265

Grey, Lt. Benjamin E., 289, 520-21

Grieger, Hubert, 194, 423, 521

Grimes, Capt. George S., 114, 521-22

"Grimes Battery," 521

Griscom, Lloyd C., 215, 221, 522

Guerrero (Mexico), 347-48

guerrilla warfare: in the Philippine War, 140

guidons, 622-23n9

Guignard, Capt. William S., 267, 522

Guimba, Sultan of, 388

Guitéras, Juan, 632n1
guns: Gatling guns, 110, 631–32n8; Hotchkiss guns, 110, 631n7; the Moros and, 146; Moro stealing of American rifles, 162–63, 169–70; in Pershing's youth, 25–26. *See also* machine guns

Hack, Capt. C. W., 407
Hacker, Theodore B., *141*
Hagadorn, Capt. Charles B., 661n7
Hale, Benjamin, 17
Hale, Lt. Harry C., 74, 522–23
Halliday, 1st Lt. Charles H., 298, 454, 523–24
Hampton Court (London), 131
Hance, John, 66–67, 524
Hance's Place, 66–67
Hanna, Mark, 94
Hannibal & St. Joseph Railroad, 13, 14
Harbord, James G., 247, 524–25
Hardeman, Lt. Letcher, 88, 90, 93, 525
Harrison, Francis Burton, 315, 525–26
Hasbrouck, Lt. Col. Henry C., 45, 526
Havard, Col. Valery, 224, 526–27, 651n8
Hawaiian Islands, 211, 212
Hawkins, Lt. Frank B., 176, 407, 409, 415, 527
Hay, John, 123
Hayama (Japan), 241
Hayden, Capt. John L., 655n4
Hayward, William H., 87, 527–28
head knife, 146–47
Hearn, Col. Lawrence J., 289, 448, 528
Hegardt, Capt. Peter J., *230*
Heiberg, Maj. Elvin R., 284, 528–29
Hein, Lt. Col. Otto H., 96, 529
heliographs, 58, 623n2
Helm, Frank P., Jr., 253, 436, 529–30
Helmick, Capt. Eli A., 176, 530–31
Hemphill, Adm. Joseph N., 250
Henley, Samuel A., 33
Henry, Col. Guy Vernor, 102, 267, 531–32
Hermitage, 263
Herrera, Gen. Luis, 350
Herron, Capt. Joseph S., 447–48
Herzegovina, 266

Hicks, Frederick C., 365
Hines, Maj. John L., *345*
Hobson, Lt. Richmond P., 119
Hoffmann, Capt. Carl Maximilian, 227, 229, *230, 231*, 532
Hokkaido (Japan), 239
holidays: Fourth of July celebration at Camp Vicars, 167–68; in Pershing's youth, 24–25
Holland, Josiah H., 310, 532
Holtzclaw, Clifton D., 16–17, 617n11
Hong Kong, 206–7, 317–18
Honolulu, Hawaii, 211, 323
Hoover, Herbert, 366
Hopi Indians, 65, 68
Hotchkiss guns, 110, 631n7
Hot Springs, Ark., 269
Houses of Parliament, 131
Howze, Maj. Robert L., 348, 349–50, 359, 532–33
Hoyt, Col. Ralph W., 661n7
Hualapai Indians, 67
Huerta, Victoriano, 330–31, 332
Hughes, 1st Lt. Leonard S., 298, 454, 534
Hugo, Victor, 265
Hulett, Pvt. George D., 356
Hump, Chief, 72, 74
Humphrey, Evan H., 85, 534, 627n4
hunting: bear hunting, 67; buffalo hunting, 69–70; deer hunting, 88, 90; duck hunting, 239, 276; with Gen. Miles at Fort Assinniboine, 93–94; in Pershing's youth, 25–26
Huse, Col. Caleb, 38, 534–35

Igacin Moros, 395
Iligan District, Mindanao (Philippines): Pershing's command of, 149–54; Pershing's meetings with Manibilang, 150–54
Imam, 410
imperialism: in the Far East, 122–25. *See also* American imperialism
Inaugural Ball Committee, 268
Indian service. *See* Bureau of Indian Affairs

Industrial Trading Stores, 307
Infanta, Jose, 157–58
Ireland, Capt. Merritte W., 118, 535–36
Irkutsk (Russia), 259
Irons, Col. James A., 254, 536
Italy: Pershing's first visit to, 132–33; Triple Alliance, 266, 658n6
"Itinerant Traders Law," 307

Jackson, Capt. William P., 448
Jacob (passenger ship), 12
Jamalul-Kiram II, 312
Jami, 300
Japan: *genro*, 222, 650–51n6; Pershing as military attaché to Tokyo (*see* military attaché to Tokyo); Pershing at the Emperor Meiji's funeral, 319–22; Pershing's 1903 visit to and reflections on, 209–11; Pershing's travels in, 239–41, 258; reaction to Western imperialism, 124–25; relations with Great Britain, 125, 210; relations with Russia prior to 1904, 209–10; the U.S. Exclusion Act and, 211–12. *See also* Russo-Japanese War
Japanese First Army: ceremony to the dead, 233; Pershing and other military observers with, 222–33, 227, 229, *230, 231, 234–37*
Japanese military: emperor's review of troops, 240–41; Pershing as military observer, 222–33, *234–37*, 254–55; Pershing's reflections on, 210, 233, 238
Jardine, Capt. George H., *230*
"Jayhawkers," 15, 616n7, 617n9
Jews of Poland, 263–64
Johnson, Arthur, 622n7
Johnson, Richard W., *141*
Joint American-Mexican Commission, 360, 669n4
Jolo Island (Philippines): disarmament of the Moros, 289–302, 453–60; 1906 Battle of Bud Dajo, 663–64n6; problems with Moro outlaws and *juramentado,* 284–85. *See also* Mindanao and Jolo (Philippines)

Jolo Moros, 312
Jones, John H., 16
Josanie, 54
Judson, Maj. William, 224, 536–37, 651n8
juramentado, 147–48, 284–85, 578

kampilan, 146–47
Kandy (Sri Lanka), 135
Kaneko Kentaro, Baron, 241
Kearns Canyon, 65, 68
Keller, Pvt. Charles, 638n1
Kendall, Capt. Henry M., 56, 64, 537
Kendall, Maj. William P., 655n4
Kent, Brig. Gen. Jacob Ford, 114, 116, 117, 373–74, 537–38
Kerr, Capt. John B., 75, 538
Kettle Hill (Cuba), 116
Kicking Bear, 72, 74, 75
Kilrain, Jake, 217–18
Kingsbury, Capt. Henry P., 116, 538–39, 655n4
Kirby, Col. Henry, 289, 448, 449, 539
Kirkpatrick, Capt. George W.: April 1903 Moro pacification expedition, 423, 426, 430, 431; biographical information, 539; September 18–22, 1902 Moro pacification expedition, 176, 407–11
Kirksville Normal School, 34–35, 620n6
knives: of the Moros, 146–47
Knox, Philander C., 319, 321
Kobbé, Lt. Ferdinand W., *141,* 145, 539–40
Kobbé, Brig. Gen. William A., *141,* 144, 145, 148, 149, 540
Koehler, Herman J., 96, 540–41
Koester, Capt. F. J., 435, 439
Koran, 147, 152, 193
Korea (ship), 221, 245
Kremlin, 261
kris, 146–47
Kuroki Tamemoto, Gen., 227, *228*
Kwantung Peninsula, 210

Laclede, Mo.: during the Civil War, 14–17; depression of 1873 and its aftermath, 30-33; holidays in, 24-25; the Pershing family farm and business, 28-30; Pershing's childhood and youth in, 14-33; the Pershings' Degraw house, 26-28

Laclede Negro School, 619n5

La Garde, Maj. Louis A., 118, 541

Lake Butig, 175-76, 408

Lake Lanao Expedition of 1902, 155-60, 638n2

Lake Lanao Moros: attacks on American forces, 155, 170-73, 397-98, 400-401, 638n1; *cottas*, 157, 159; disarmament, 288-89, 453-60; marriage customs, 152-53; pacification expeditions of 1902, 155-60, 175-81, 398, 407-22; pacification expeditions of 1903, 193-202, 401-3, 423-33, 435-45; Pershing elected a *datto* by Sajiduciaman, 193; Pershing's command of the Iligan District, 149-54; Pershing's observations of, 395-96, 404-6; Pershing's relationship with and attempts to pacify, 150-54, 160-73, 181-84, 190-93; Pershing's summary reports on, 203-5, 383-91, 393-406; polygamy and, 167; problems with outlaws and *juramentado*, 285; slavery and, 167; stealing of American rifles, 162-63, 169-70; tribal groupings and governing structure, 637n4

Lake Lanao region (Philippines): Pershing given command of, 169-70; Pershing relieved by Lt. Col. Rodgers, 202-3; Pershing's description of, 162; Pershing's march around, 199-202, 435-45; Pershing's return to in 1909, 281-82; Pershing's summary report on, 203-5; Pershing's trip across to visit friendly Moros, 181-84; Helen Pershing's visit to, 239; pests, diseases, and natural disasters in, 186-89. *See also* Lake Lanao Moros

Lanao Constabulary, 448

Lanckton, Pvt. Frank, 274

Landor, J. Henry Savage, 424, 646n6

Languasan (Philippines), 457, 458

Las Guasimas engagement, 109-10, 370-72

Lassiter, Gen. William, 366, 541-42

law studies, 85-86

Lawton, Gen. Henry W.: biographical information, 542-43; pursuit of Geronimo, 56, 542-43; in the Spanish-American War, 109, 112, 114, 116-17

Lear, Lt. Ben, Jr., 198, 426, 429, 431, 543-44

Lee, Jesse M., 184, 544-45

Le Mans, 266-67

Leona (troop transport), 107-8, 109

lepers, 311

Lesseps, Ferdinand Marie de, 100

Leviathan (USS), 363

Lewis, Capt. W. F., 435

Liaoyang (Manchuria), 225

Liaoyang, battle of, 225, 227, 233, 651n9

Linares y Pombo, Arsenio, 110, 378

Lincoln, N.Mex., 61-62

Lindsley, Maj. Elmer, 348-49, 545

Little, Richard H., 224

Little Bighorn, 548

Liverpool (Great Britain), 129-30

Lockett, Col. James, 353, 545-46

locust plagues, 186

Lodge, Henry Cabot, 123

Lomax, John, 16

London, 130-31, 635n3

Longworth, Alice Roosevelt, 238

López, Pablo, 350, 674-75n12

Loring, Lt. Sylvester Chouteau: April 1903 Moro pacification expedition, 424; biographical information, 546; May 1903 Moro pacification expedition around Lake Lanao, 200, 436; September 18-22, 1902 Moro pacification expedition, 407, 411; September-October 1902 Moro pacification expedition, 179, 180, 416, 419, 421

Lozano, Gen. Ismael, 351

Lugard, Frederick, 317

Lumbayanagne (Philippines), 410
Lusitania (RMS), 332
Luzon (Philippines), 248

Macabebe Scouts, 602
MacArthur, Gen. Arthur, 145, 212, 221, 222, 546-47
MacArthur, Douglas, 212, 547
Macasasa, 427
Macbeth, Pvt. R. G., 420
machine guns: Japanese use of, 255; in Manchuria, *237*; John Parker and, 564, 565; Pershing's comments on the importance of, 59
Maciricampo, 385, 389
Maciu, Sultan of, 180
Maciu Moros: attacks on American forces, 400-401; 1902 pacification expeditions, 175-81, 398, 410-13; Pershing's observations of, 395, 396
Madaya (Philippines), 181-82, 384, 385, 399
Madaya, Sultan of, 156, 387-88
Madero, Francisco, 329, 330
Madumba (Philippines), 195, 401, 424
Magoon, Charles E., 86, 128, 553-54
Maguindanaw, Princess of, 313
Maine (USS), 99, 629n2
"Major and Ordnance Officer of Volunteers," 126-27
Makadar (Philippines), 164
Malabang (Philippines), 402
Malanaos. *See* Lake Lanao Moros
malaria, 121, 126-27, 311
Maliuanac (Philippines), 399-400
Mamalampac, 163
Mambao, 397
Manchuria (steamship), 211
Manchuria: Pershing's observations as a military observer, 222-33, *234-37*
Mandayans, 279-80
Mandi, 143, 277, 314, 454, 660n2
Mangum, Lt. Wiley P.: April 1903 Moro pacification expedition, 429, 431; biographical information, 554; May 1903 Moro pacification expedition around Lake Lanao, 435; Moro

attack on, 198; September–October 1902 Moro pacification expedition, 415, 419, 420
Mangus, 56, 58
"manifest destiny," 123
Manila (Philippines), 137-38, 203, 250-51
Manila Bay, Battle of, 103
Manobos, 279, 283-84, 313
Mansakas, 313
Mansion House (London), 131
Marahui (Philippines), 182-84, 201, 399, 401, 441
Marahui, Rajamunda of, *183*, 184
Marantao, Sultan of, 388
markets: improvements in Moro Province, 306-7
Markley, Col. Alfred D., 655n4
Marksbury, Cpl. David, 356
marriage customs: of the Lake Lanao Moros, 152-53
Martin, 2d Lt. Isaac S., 407, 423
Matunkup (Moro fort), 298-300, 457, 458
Mayo, Adm. Henry T., 331
Mazatlán incident, 331-32, 668-69n4
McCarthy, Maj. Daniel E., 105, 547-48, 630n3
McClernand, Col. Edward J., 107, *230*, 231, 233, *234, 548-49*
McCook, Brig. Gen. Alexander McDowell, 68, 549-50
McCoy, 2d Lt. Frank, 115, 550-51
McCullough, Lt. Charles E., 200, 423, 435, 442, 443, 551-52
McGuffey, William H., 618n13
McGuffey's Readers, 20, 618n13
McKinley, William: American imperialism and, 123; Henry Corbin and, 496; formation of the General Staff and, 213; Nelson Miles and, 556; Theodore Roosevelt and, 126; Spanish-American War and, 99
McKinney, 2d Lt. Carl F., 298, 299, 455, 457, 552
McLean, John, 665n11
McNair, Capt. William S.: April 1903

Moro pacification expedition, 424, 426, 430; biographical information, 552–53; September 18–22, 1902 Moro pacification expedition, 177, 407, 409–11, 413; September–October 1902 Moro pacification expedition, 179, 415–18, 421

medicine: field hospitals, 117–19; improvements in Moro Province, 310–11; medical missionaries, 240, 652n14

Meiji (Japanese emperor), 319–22

Meiklejohn, George D., 95, 102, 126, 128, 554

Menocal, Francisco E., 115, 632–33n1

Merrimac (USS), 119

Merritt, Brevet Major Gen. Wesley, 45, 554–55

Mescalero Apache Indians, 60

Metz (France), 267

Mexican Punitive Expedition: airplanes and, 346–47, 673n7, 673–74n8; De Rosey Cabell and, 487; the Carrizal fight and its aftermath, 356–61, 461–64, 676–77n19; consolidation at Colonia Dublán, 354–56; George Dodd's attack on Guerrero, 347–48; Frederick Funston and, 336–37, 341, 353, 355, 516, 517; Elmer Lindsley and, 545; James Lockett and, 546; military training during, 360–61; operations leading to Parral, 348–51; Pershing assigned command of, 336–37; Pershing's recommendations to Gen. Funston, 351–52; problems in the pursuit of Pancho Villa, 339–47; retirement to San Antonio and deployment of regiments, 352–54; strength of American forces, 672n3, 677n20; studies of, 672n2; Frank Tompkins and, 592; withdrawal from Mexico, 361–62

Mexico: Constitutionalists or *de facto* authorities, 334, 335, 670n7; internal politics and American relations with, 327–36; Mazatlán incident, 331–32, 668–69n4; Pershing's

service on the Mexican border with the Eighth Brigade, 327–29, 332, 334–35; pursuit of Pancho Villa (*see* Mexican Punitive Expedition); Pancho Villa's raid on Columbus, New Mexico, 335–36, 591–92

Michie, Peter Smith, 48

Midel, Isodoro, 143

Milan, 132–33

Miles, Gen. Nelson A.: Frank Baldwin and, 470–71; biographical information, 555–56; campaign against the Sioux, 72, 74, 75, 512; daughter of, 573; Geronimo's surrender to, 543, 671n1; hunting at Fort Assinniboine, 93–94; Edward McClernand and, 548–49; military instruction in New Mexico, 62; Pershing as aide to, 94–96; Spanish-American War and, 106, 121, 213, 630–31n5; visit to Pershing at Camp Vicars, 184–85, 643–44n5; Henry Whitney and, 600; Wounded Knee massacre and, 556

Miley, Lt. John D., 114, 556–57

military attaché to Tokyo: Pershing on medical missionaries, 240; Pershing's arrival in Tokyo, 221–22; Pershing's assignment to, 215–16; Pershing's meeting with Roosevelt, 217–18; Pershing's observations on Port Arthur, 229, 231; Pershing's reflections on Japanese soldiery, 233, 238; Pershing's travels in Japan, 239–41; Pershing with the Japanese First Army in Manchuria, 222–33, *234-37*

military instruction: Cavalry School, 46, 621n5; compulsory, 626n1; Pershing as commandant of cadets, University of Nebraska, 81–87; Pershing institutes during the Mexican Punitive Expedition, 360–61; Pershing's development of at Fort McKinley, 248–50; Saumur cavalry school, 267, 585, 659n9; Supreme Court ruling on, 82 military observers: Pershing observes the 1907 Imperial Japanese Army maneuvers, 254–55; Pershing with the Japanese First Army in Manchuria, 222–33, *234-37*; of the Russo-Japanese War, 227, 229, *230, 231,* 650n5, 651n8

Miller, Lt. B. F., 424, 436

Miller, Ranford S., 321

Milliron, Christena, 12

Mills, Capt. Albert L., 244, 557–58

Mills, Lt. Col. Samuel M., Jr., 96, 558

Minamioji, 257

Mindanao and Jolo (Philippines): American forces in, 144; defeat of the insurrectionists under Capistrano, 145–46; Pershing as adjutant general of the Department of, 144–46; Pershing as adjutant general of the Military District of, 140–44; Pershing as commanding general of the Department of Mindanao, 271, 277–82; Pershing's command of the Iligan District, 149–54; Pershing's description of, 140–44; polygamy in, 167; slavery in, 167. *See also* Jolo Island (Philippines); Lake Lanao Moros

mission hospitals, 240

Missouri (hospital ship), 129, 134–35, 469

Montana: duty with the 10th Cavalry Regiment, 88–94

Moore, Frederick, 5–6, 9, 613n13

Moqui (Hopi) Indians, 65, 68

Moran, Lt. E. J., 424

Morey, Capt. Lewis S., 357–58, 359, 463, 558–59

Morgan, Thomas J., 68

Moro pacification: April 1903 expedition, 193–99, 401–3, 423–33; April–May 1902 Lake Lanao expedition, 155–60, 638n2; Boburan uprising, 282–83; Gen. Chaffee's 1902 proclamation to the Moros, 155–57, 159, 383, 386–87; disarmament program, 285–302,

453–60, 663n11; Manobos rampage, 283–84; May 1903 expedition, 199–202, 453–45; Pershing's accounts of and reports on, 161–75, 181–84, 190–93, 383–91, 393–406, 645–46n4; September 18–22, 1902 expedition, 175–78, 398, 407–14; September–October 1902 expedition, 178–81, 398, 415–22

Moro Province: agricultural developments, 304–6; conditions prior to the American presence, 303–4; disarmament of the Moros and non-Christians, 285–302, 453–60, 663n11; Executive Order No. 24, 288; formation and governance of, 280–81, 647n11, 661n7; improvements in medical and health care, 310–11; improvements in public works, 309–10; improvements in schools and education, 307–9; improvements in trade and markets, 306–7; improvements to the system of government, 314–15; Manobos rampage, 283–84; peoples of, 278–80; Pershing as military governor, 271, 277–306; Pershing recommends transition from military to civil government, 665–66n1; Pershing's initial inspection trip, 281–82; Pershing's personal and family life at Zamboanga, 271–77; problems with Moro outlaws and *juramentado,* 284–85; uprising at Boburan, 282–83; Gen. Wood as military governor, 203, 661n7, 662n10; Zamboanga Fair, 311–14

Moros: areas inhabited by, 280; disarmament, 285–302, 453–60, 663n11; in Mindanao and Jolo, 142–44; opposition to Philippine independence, 277; origins of, 278–79; Pershing on the lawlessness and behavior of, 146–48; Pershing's principle for governing, 641n4; Pershing's reports on, 203–5, 383–91, 393–406; problems with outlaws and *juramentado*, 284–85; uprising of the Subanos at Boburan and, 282. *See also* Lake Lanao Moros

Moro Scouts, 298, 454, 458–59

Morrison, J. N., *141*

Morrow, Lt. Col. Albert P., 60, 559

Morrow, Capt. Jay J., 161, 178, 415–17, 559–60

Moscow (Russia), 260–62, 657n1

Moseley, Pvt. Thomas, 459

Mosher, Lt. Louis C., 459

mountain artillery, 175, 426, 517, 552

Moylan, Capt. Patrick, 298, 300, 455, 458, 560

"Mr. Dooley," 109

Mukden (Manchuria), 225–26, *227*, *230*, 240

Mukden, battle of, 222, 650n3

Mullins, Alex, 35

Murata Tsuneyoshi, Gen., 222

Murray, Maj. Gen. Arthur, 323, 325, 560–61

My Experiences in the World War (Pershing), 2

Nachez, 56

Nagasaki (Japan), 209

Namiquipa (Mexico), 355

Nanshan Hill, battle of, 224, 651n7

Naples (Italy), 133

Napoleon Bonaparte, 100

Napoleon's Tomb, 132

Navajo Indians, 68

Nebraska: commandant of cadets at the University of Nebraska, 81–87; duty at Fort Niobrara, 77–78, 81

Negritos, 278

Negro troops. *See* Tenth Cavalry Regiment

New Mexico: army forts, 55; duty at Fort Bayard, 56–60; duty at Fort Stanton, 60–63; duty at Fort Wingate, 64–65, 67–68; Sixth Cavalry campaigns against the Apaches, 54, 56–58; Pancho Villa's raid on Columbus, 335–36, 339, 591–92

Nichols, Capt. Taylor A., 298, 300, 454, 457, 459, 561

Nogales Conference, 337–38, 670–71n10

Nogi Maresuke, 322

Nolan, Pvt. James, 419, 421

Nuzca, 201, 403, 429, 441

Oakes, Capt. John C., 214, 561–62

Oato Moros, 198

Obregón, Álvaro: battle of Agua Prieta, 669n6; El Paso conference with Gens. Funston and Scott, 354; message to cooperate with American forces, 344–45, 673n6; Nogales Conference with Pershing, 337–38, 670–71n10; relations with Carranza, 332

observation balloons, 114, 374, 502

Ogallala Indian Scouts, 78–80

Ojos Azules (Mexico), 354

"Old Red" (Pershing nickname), 91

Onayan Moros, 395–96, 400–401

O'Neill, Frederick W. S., 240, 652n14

opium runners, 208

Organic Act (Philippines), 280

Orr, Anne, 256

Otis, Maj. Gen. Elwell S., 128, 138, 562

Oury, William H., 87, 562–63

Oyama Iwao, Field Marshal Prince, 226, 241

Paddock, 2d Lt. Richard B., 60, *61*, 563

Palatinate, 12, 615n3

Palmer, Frederick, 225, 563–64

Pandapatan, battle of, 159–60

Pandi-in, *172*

pandita schools, 308

Panglima Unga, 449

"Panic of 1873," 30–33, 619n3

Pantauan (Philippines), 408

Paris: Pershing family visit to, 266–68; Pershing's first visit to, 131–32

Parker, Lt. John Henry, 115, 564–65, 632n8

Parral (Mexico), 351, 352

Patch, Leroy Vernon, 87, 565–66, 627n4

Patterson, George T., 85, 566

Patterson, 1st Lt. Robert U., 194, 200, 423, 431, 435, 566–67

Patton, Lt. George S., Jr., *345*, 355
Pedro of Oato, 436, 437
Peek, 1st Lt. Ernest D., 194, 423, 426, 431, 567–68
Peking. *See* Beijing (China)
Penn, 2d Lt. Julius A., Jr., 60, *61*, 568–69
Pepper, Lt. Kelton L.: biographical information, 569; September 18–22, 1902 Moro pacification expedition, 177, 407, 409, 412; September–October 1902 Moro pacification expedition, 178, 415
Perkins, Maj. Frederick, 277–78, 569–70
Pershing, Anne Elizabeth (née Thompson): death of, 212; family history, 13–14; fondness for reading, 20; life in Laclede, Missouri, 15, 16, 18–19, 28; Pershing's correspondence with during the Moro disarmament, 289, 291, 293; response to John's interest in West Point, 38
Pershing, Anne Orr (daughter): birth of, 256; death of, *324*, 570, 667n3; dysentery, 322; at Zamboanga, *275*, 276
Pershing, Daniel, 12
Pershing, Elizabeth, 35
Pershing, Francis Warren: biographical information, 570; birth of, 270; saved from the Presidio fire, *324*, 570; at Zamboanga, *275*, 276
Pershing, Frederick, 11–12
Pershing, Grace, 60, 563
Pershing, Helen Elizabeth (daughter), 241, *275*, *324*, 570, 667n3
Pershing, Helen Frances (née Warren): biographical information, 570; birth of children, 241, 256, 270, 322; death of, 10, *325*, 570, 667n3; departure from the Philippines, 323; engagement and marriage to Pershing, *215*, 216; family life at Zamboanga, 271–77; in Japan with Pershing, 239–41; at the Presidio of San Francisco, *324*, 325–26; travel

across Russia and Europe, 1908–1909, 257–68; visit to the Philippines and China, 238–39
Pershing, Jim, 25, 30, 32, 34
Pershing, John Fletcher: advice to John, 23; depression of 1873, 30–33; family farm and business, 28–30; fondness for reading, 20; life in Laclede, Missouri, 15–19; marriage to Anne Elizabeth Thompson, 13; youth and early manhood, 12–13
Pershing, Gen. John J.: as aide to Gen. Miles, 94–96; ancestry, 11–14; appointments to South America, 365–66; appointment to the General Staff, 212–14; at the Army War College, 214–15; birth of, 616n5; birth of children, 241, 256, 270, 322; brothers and sisters, 616n6; chairman of the American Battle Monuments Commission, 1, 3, 366, 678n3; as chief of staff, 364; childhood and youth, 14–33; as commandant of cadets, University of Nebraska, 81–87; command of the Department of California, 245, 653n16; commands following the Mexican Punitive Expedition, 363; Gen. Davis's evaluation of, 640–41n12; Charles Dawes and, 501; death of wife and daughters, 10, *325*, 570, 667n3; diplomatic missions, 317–22; on discipline in the army, 91; with the Division of Customs and Insular Affairs, 127–28; drafts of *A Memoir*, 9–10; with the Eighth Brigade (*see* Eighth Brigade); engagement and marriage to Helen Frances Warren, *215*, 216; farewell message to the Army, 364–65; on the Franco-Prussian War, 267–68; as guardian of the Paddock children, 563; journey to the Grand Canyon, 65–67; at Kirksville Normal School, 34–35; law studies, 85–86; "Major and Ordnance Officer of Volunteers," 126–27; malaria

and, 121, 126–27; marksmanship of, 59, 164; 1914 meeting with Pancho Villa, 337–38; meeting with Roosevelt in 1905, 217–18; Mexican Punitive Expedition (*see* Mexican Punitive Expedition); military attaché to Tokyo (*see* military attaché to Tokyo); nicknames, 91; on Philippine independence, 315–16; in the Philippines (*see* Camp Vicars; Lake Lanao Moros; Lake Lanao region [Philippines]; Mindanao and Jolo [Philippines]; Moro pacification; Philippines); politics and, 95; on the popular vote and the Seventeenth Amendment, 95–96; at the Presidio in San Francisco, 323, 325–26; promotions, 148, 242–44; reflections on Asia, 135–36; repatriation of the A.E.F., 363; return from Europe in 1919, 363–64; Theodore Roosevelt and, 94; on the settlement of the western United States, 53–54; sick leave at the Army and Navy General Hospital, 269, 659–60n10; with the Sixth Cavalry Regiment, 51–52 (*see also* Sixth Cavalry Regiment); in the Spanish-American War (*see* Spanish-American War); Tacna-Arica mission, 1, 365–66, 678n2; Taft's inaugural ball and, 268–69; teaching career, 33–34, 619n5; with the Tenth Cavalry Regiment, 88–94 (*see also* Tenth Cavalry Regiment); transfer to the Fifteenth Cavalry, 148–49; travel across Russia and Europe, 1908–1909, 257–68; 1903 visit to and reflections on China, 206–9; at West Point (*see* West Point); writing of *A Memoir*, 1–10

Pershing, John Warren, III, 570
Pershing, Joseph, 12
Pershing, Mary Margaret, 322, *324*, 570, 667n3
Pershing, May, 60
Pershing, Richard Warren, 570

Pershing, Lt. Ward B., 135, 570
Pershing Rifles, 626n2
Peru, 365, 366, 678n2
Pettit, Col. James S., 142, 143, 408, 571
Peyton, Maj. E. G., 450
Philippine Assembly, 251, 252, 277
Philippine Commission, 252, 280, 489, 586, 647n11, 655–56n5
Philippine Constabulary: function of, 247; history of, 654n2; in Moro disarmament, 288, 289; in Moro Province, 281
Philippine Constabulary, American officers in, 654–55n3; Henry Allen, 467; Harry Bandholtz, 472; James Harbord, 524; Samuel Polk, 572; Oscar Preuss, 572–73; William Rivers, 575. *See also individual officers*
Philippines: American acquisition of, 122–23; American imperialism and, 123–24, 252; Baguio resort, 253–54, 656n4; Battle of Manila Bay, 103; Camp John Hay, 254, 656n7; Fifteenth Cavalry assigned to, 148–49; issue of self-government, 251–52; military governor, 128; native constabulary, 247; Pershing as brigade commander at Fort McKinley, 246–53, 256; Pershing compares to Hawaii, 211; Pershing on independence, 315–16; Pershing on the problem of, 207; Pershing's command of the Iligan District, Mindanao, 149–54; Pershing's departure from, 322–23; Pershing's description of Manila, 137–38; Pershing seeks assignment to, 128–29; Pershing's first assignment and trip to, 129, 134–36; Pershing's personal and family life at Zamboanga, 271–77; Pershing's promotion to captain, 148; Pershing's reassignment to in 1906, 245; Pershing's return voyage to the United States in 1903, 206–12; Helen Pershing's visit to, 238–39; pests, diseases, and natural disasters,

Philippines *(cont.)*
186–89; Philippine War, 138, 140;
reinforced brigade, 248, 655n4;
Spanish impact on, 138; Innis Swift
and, 589; Taft's visits to, 250–53;
Gen. Wood in, 203, 246–48, 604. *See
also* Jolo Island (Philippines); Lake
Lanao Moros; Lake Lanao region
(Philippines); Mindanao and Jolo
(Philippines); Moro pacification;
Moro Province; Moros
Philippines, Americans serving in:
Frank Baldwin, 471; John Barker,
472; Thomas Barry, 474; John Bates,
475; John Beacom, 476; George
Bell, 477; J. Franklin Bell, 477–78;
Charles Bickham, 478–79; William
Birkhimer, 479; Tasker Bliss, 280,
480, 661n7; Robert Bullard, 486;
Charles Cameron, 488; Frank
Carpenter, 489; James Cases, 492;
Sydney Cloman, 494; James Collins,
495; Malin Craig, 497–98; Waller
Dade, 500; George Davis, 500–
501; George Deshon, 503; George
Duncan, 505; Edward Dworak, 506;
Hanson Ely, 508; Lea Febiger, 510;
W. Forbes, 512; Claude Fries, 515;
Frederick Funston, 515–16; William
Gracie, 518; Frederick Grant, 519;
Harry Hale, 523; Frances Harrison,
535, 536; Robert Howze, 533;
Evan Humphrey, 534; Merritte
Ireland, 535; Henry Kingsbury, 538,
539; William Kobbé, 540; Henry
Lawton, 543; Ben Lear, 543; Jesse
Lee, 544; Elmer Lindsley, 545;
James Lockett, 545–46; Sylvester
Loring, 546; Arthur MacArthur,
547; Wiley Mangum, 554; Frank
McCoy, 550; Charles McCullough,
551; Carl McKinney, 552; William
McNair, 552–53; Wesley Merritt,
555; Jay Morrow, 559; John Oakes,
561; Elwell Otis, 562; John Parker,
510–11, 564; Robert Patterson, 566;
Ernest Peek, 567; Julius Penn,

568; Frederick Perkins, 569; James
Pettit, 571; Edward Plummer, 571;
William Reed, 573; George Rice,
574; Alexander Rodgers, 577; James
Ryan, 578–79; Theodore Schwan,
580; Ernest Scott, 581; Hugh Scott,
582–83; George Shaw, 584; James
Smith, 586; John Stotsenburg, 587;
Samuel Sumner, 589; Thomas Van
Natta, 593; Frank Weed, 596; Frank
West, 598; Parker West, 598; Joseph
Wheeler, 600; Wilber Wilder,
602; Samuel Young, 607. *See also
individual officers*
Philippine Scouts: Bud Bagsak
campaign, 298–302, 455–60; Bud
Dajo operation, 448, 450–51;
function of, 247; history of, 653–
54n1; in Moro disarmament, 289; in
Moro Province, 281; response to the
Manobos rampage, 284
Philippine Scouts, American officers in,
247–48, 654–55n3; William Ayers,
470; Charles Boyd, 481; George
Charlton, 494; Robert Dickson,
504; George Duncan, 505; Edward
Dworak, 506; Hanson Ely, 508; Allen
Fletcher, 511–12; Robert Gillmore,
518; Elvin Heiberg, 529; Evan
Humphrey, 534; Patrick Moylan,
560; Taylor Nichols, 561; Samuel
Rockenbach, 576; George Shaw, 584;
Frank Smith, 586; Frank Sperbeck,
587; Charles Townsend, 592; George
Wright, 606. *See also individual
officers*
Philippine War (Philippine
Insurrection), 138, 140, 250
Phillips, Capt. J. W. L., 415, 417–21
physical training, 540–41
Piang, 313, 314
Pinchot, Gifford, 185–86, 217
Pitacus, Sultan of, 200
Pitacus (Moro fort), 200, 403, 438–39
plagues: on the Philippines, 186
Platt Amendment, 634n1
Plummer, Capt. Edward H., 118, 571–72

poker, 59
Poland, 263-64, 657n2
Polk, Lt. Samuel T., 289, 572
Pollard, Ernest M., 87, 572
polygamy, 167
Port Arthur (China): Japanese capture during the Russo-Japanese War, 220; under Japanese control, 210; Pershing's observations of, 229, 231; Gen. Stoessel's surrender at, 263; wire entanglements, 232
Portsmouth conference, 218, 220
Potemkin (Russian battleship), 265
prairie chicken hunting, 94
Prairie Mound School, 33-34, 619n5
Presidio of San Francisco, 323-26, 667n3
Preuss, Lt. Oscar, 288, 572-73
Price, Gen. Sterling, 17
Prince Albert coat, 217, 649n1
prison camps, 222
Pryor, Charles A., 183
public baths, 209
public works: improvements in Moro Province, 309-10
Pueblo Indians. See Zuni Indians
Puerto Rico, 98, 106, 122, 128, 531, 600
Pujagan (Moro fort), 298, 300, 457, 458
Punilumabao, 437
Puyacabao (Moro fort), 298-99, 457-58
Pyramids, 134

quartermasters, 470, 548; Pershing as, 8, 102-6, 118
quarter sections, 28, 619n2

Rackley, Lt. Edwin H., 457, 459
Ragayan (Philippines), 201, 441
Rajamunda of Marahui, 183-84
rancherias, 637n4
Randolph, Ben H., 141
Reade, Cpl. Claude D., 198
Reber, Cecelia Sherman Miles, 95, 573
Reber, Capt. Samuel, 573
Red Cloud, Chief, 78-79, 625n2
Red Cross, 121, 361
Red Square (Moscow), 261
Reed, Capt. William O., 291, 350, 573-74

reinforced brigade, 248, 655n4
Remayn, Sultan of, 441
Remington, Frederic, 93
Reynolds, Adm. Alfred, 321
Rice, Col. Edmund, 627n3
Rice, George D., 195, 415, 423, 431, 574
rice colony, 305
Richard, Col. Charles, 310, 574
Riel Rebellion, 91, 628n8
rinderpest, 186, 644n6
Rivers, Lt. William C., 109, 574-75
roads: improvements in Moro Province, 309-10
Robbins, Charles B., 87, 575-76
Roberts, Elmer, 265
Robinson, Martha, 28
Rochester (U.S. cruiser), 366
Rockenbach, Samuel D., 88, 90, 247, 576-77
Rodgers, Lt. Col. Alexander, 202-3, 577, 646-47n10
Rodney, Lt. Walter H., 284, 577-78
Rogers, Miss B., 61
Rogers, Virginia, 61
Rome, 133
Roosevelt, Alice, 238
Roosevelt, Theodore: American imperialism and, 123; Avery Andrews and, 468; boxing and, 650n2; colonial expansion and, 252; first meeting with Pershing, 94; Henry Fletcher and, 265; Robert Howze and, 533; hunting trip to Africa, 268; William McKinley and, 126; meeting with Pershing in 1905, 217-18; "Mr. Dooley's" portrayal of during the Spanish-American War, 109; orders an attack on the Spanish fleet in Manila Bay, 103; Pershing's promotion to brigadier general and, 242, 244; Pershing's wedding and, 216; "Rough Riders" and, 109, 118, 630n4; Russo-Japanese War and, 218, 220; Adm. Sims and, 132; William Taft's "goodwill tour" of Asia and, 651-52n12; The Winning of the West, 94, 628n9; Leonard Wood and, 604

Root, Elihu: army reorganization and, 636–37n3; biographical information, 578; congratulates Pershing on the march around Lake Lanao, 202; Henry Corbin and, 496; formation of the General Staff and, 213–14; Charles Magoon and, 128; William Taft and, 253

Rosecrans, Gen. William S., 48

Ross, John, 240, 652n14

"Rough Riders." See First Volunteer Cavalry Regiment ("Rough Riders")

Round Robin letter, 122, 633n3

Rozhdestvensky, Adm. Zinovy Petrovich, 220

Ruggles, Lt. Francis A., 201, 423, 435, 442, 579

Russia: the Balkan issue and, 266; imperialism in the Far East, 123, 125; Pershing family travel across, 257–63; Pershing's reflections on the Russian military, 220–21; Pershing's visit to Sakhalin, 239–40; relations with Japan prior to 1904, 209–10; Revolution of 1905, 650n4

Russo-Japanese War: battle of Liaoyang, 225, 227, 233, 651n9; battle of Mukden, 222, 650n3; battle of Nanshan Hill, 224, 651n7; Pershing and other military observers of, 222–33, 227, 229, 230, 231, 234–37, 650n5, 651n8; Pershing's reflections on, 218, 220–21; Portsmouth conference and, 218, 220; theater of operations, 219

Ryan, Brig. Gen. James A.: biographical information, 578–79; in the Philippines, 183, 184, 201, 441; reviews chapters of Pershing's memoirs, 6, 7

Sacaluran, 277, 660n3

Saghalien (Russia), 239–40

Sajiduciaman, 192–93, 400

Sakhalin (Russia), 239–40

Sampson, Adm. William T., 107, 108

Samurai, 209

San Antonio, Tex., 352–53, 355

San Borja (Mexico), 349

San Francisco, Calif., 212, 323–26

San Francisco de Borja (Mexico), 349

San Francisco earthquake, 498, 510, 516, 520

San Juan Heights, battle for, 112–19, 374–78

San Miguel de Babícora (Mexico), 342, 344

San Ramon Farm (Philippines), 305–6, 500

Santa Cruz de Villegas (Mexico), 351

Santa Domingo, 100

Santa Fe Railway, 60, 623–24n3

Santiago (Cuba): siege and surrender of, 119–21, 378–80

Santo Domingo ranch (Mexico), 357, 358, 462

Sauir (Philippines), 177, 410, 411, 416, 420, 436

Saumur cavalry school (France), 267, 585, 659n9

Sayles, 1st Lt. John T., 298, 455, 579–80

Schallenberger, Lt. Martin C., 345

Schley, Adm. Winfield S., 108

schools and education: improvements in Moro Province, 307–9; pandita schools, 308; schools where Pershing taught, 33–34, 619n5

Schurz, Carl, 29

Schwan, Gen. Theodore, 140, 580–81

Schwartz, Cpl. Samuel A., Jr., 646n9

Scotland Yard, 131

Scott, Ernest D., 85, 581–82, 627n4

Scott, 1st Lt. George L., 62, 63, 582

Scott, Maj. Gen. Hugh L., 247, 582–83

Second Army of Intervention in Cuba, 245

Second Cavalry Regiment, 284, 447–50

Second Division, V Corps, 109, 112, 114, 116–17

Selim (horse), 24, 28

Services of Supply (S.O.S.), 366, 678n4

Seven Dials (London), 131, 635n3

Seventeenth Amendment, 95–96, 628–29n10

Seventh Cavalry Regiment: Thomas Barry and, 474; J. Franklin Bell and, 477; James Forsyth and, 512; Mexican Punitive Expedition, 341, 342, 347–48, 353, 354; Hugh Scott and, 582; Herbert Slocum and, 585; Frank Tompkins and, 591; Samuel Whitside and, 601

Seventh Infantry Regiment, 377, 454–59, 568

Seventh Separate Brigade, 168, 639–40n10, 639n6

Shafter, Maj. Gen. William R.: biographical information, 583–84; Round Robin letter, 122, 633n3; Spanish-American War and, 106, 108, 110–11, 117, 119, 120, 122, 380, 630–31n5

Shanghai (China), 207–9

Shaw, Charles B.: assistance to Pershing in writing *A Memoir*, 2–4, 7–9; service with Pershing, 2, 612n5

Shaw, Maj. George C.: April 1903 Moro pacification expedition, 424, 426, 431; battle of the Taraca River, 200; biographical information, 584; Bud Bagsak operation, 298–300, 455, 457, 458; May 1903 Moro pacification expedition around Lake Lanao, 436, 438, 443

Sheldon, George L., 87, 584

Sherman (U.S. transport ship), 323

Sherman, Gen. William Tecumseh, 45, 51, 625n2

Short, Lt. Walter C., 116, 267, 584–85, 659n9

Short Bull, 72, 74, 75

Siberia, 258–60

Sibley stoves, 624n177

Siboney (Cuba), 109, 118, 371

Sierra Madre expeditions, 339, 671n1

Signal Corps, 502, 514, 520, 580

Signal Service, 520

Sims, Adm. William S., 132

Sioux Indians: army scouts, 78–80; dancing and, 80; Fetterman massacre, 78, 624–26n2; Ghost

Dance, 71; origins of the 1890s uprising, 70–72; Wounded Knee uprising, 72–77, 512

Sitting Bull, Chief, 71, 72, 74

Sixteenth Infantry Regiment, 327, 341, 655n4

Sixth Cavalry Regiment: campaigns against the Apaches, 54, 56, 517; Adna Chaffee and, 493; Louis Craig and, 497; at Fort Bayard, 56–60; at Fort Niobrara, 77–78, 81; at Fort Stanton, 60–63; at Fort Wingate, 64–65, 67–68; Charles Gatewood and, 517; Robert Howze and, 532–33; John Kerr and, 538; Henry Kingsbury and, 538; Albert Morrow and, 559; Richard Paddock and, 563; Pershing joins, 51–52; Pershing's command of Sioux Indian Scouts, 78–80; San Juan Heights, 116; George Scott and, 582; John Stotsenburg and, 587; Tullius Tupper and, 593; Thomas Van Natta and, 593; war record of, 51–52; Samuel Whitside and, 601; Wounded Knee campaign, 72–77

Sixth Field Artillery, 341

Sixth Infantry Regiment, 327, 341

slavery: American Civil War and, 14–15, 616n7; Moros and, 151, 167; John Fletcher Pershing's opposition to, 15; in Shanghai, 208

Slingerland, Dan and Jake, 32

Slocum, Col. Herbert J., 265, 353, 585–86

Smith, Lt. Frank O., 289, 586

Smith, Col. James F., 250, 586

South America, 365–66

Southern Department, 363

Southwestern Division, 214

Spanish-American War: battle for San Juan Heights, 112–19, 374–78; Battle of Manila Bay, 103; Allyn Capron and, 488–89; William Carter and, 491; Adna Chaffee and, 493; George Derby and, 502; destruction of the Spanish fleet, 119; deteriorating

Spanish-American War *(cont.)*
health and return of American
forces, 121–22; George Dodd and,
504; emergence of American
international power, 122–25;
engagement at Las Guasimas, 109–
10, 370–72; events leading to, 98–99;
Ezra Ewers and, 509; field hospitals,
117–19; Jacob Ford and, 537; Gatling
guns, 110, 631–32n8; George Grimes
and, 521; Valery Havard and, 526;
Robert Howze and, 533; John Kerr
and, 538; Henry Kingsbury and,
538; landing and initial operations,
108–11, 369–70; Henry Lawton and,
543; Edward McClernand and, 549;
Frank McCoy and, 550; Nelson Miles
and, 556; John Miley and, 556–57;
military occupation of acquisitions
following, 127–28; Albert Mills
and, 557; outbreak of, 99–102;
Richard Paddock and, 563; John
Parker and, 564; Pershing rejoins
the 10th Cavalry, 102–3; Pershing's
"An Address on the Campaign of
Santiago," 367–81; preparations for
and movement to Cuba, 103, 105–8,
367–69; Round Robin letter, 122,
633n3; William Shafter and, 583;
siege and surrender of Santiago,
119–21, 378–80; sinking of the
Maine, 99, 629n2; Spanish forces
at Santiago, 108; strength of the
Spanish Army, 102; strength of the
U.S. Army, 101; Samuel Sumner and,
589; Charles Vielé and, 594; Frank
West and, 598; Joseph Wheeler and,
600; Theodore Wint and, 117, 602;
Samuel Young and, 607
Spanish armor, 185–86
Sparrow Hills (Moscow), 262
Sperbeck, 1st Lt. Frank, 298, 455, 587
St. Louis, Mo., 13, 615n4
St. Louis Globe-Democrat, 267
St. Petersburg (Russia), 262–63
Stallman, Lt. George P., 298, 454, 587
Stanton, Charles E., *141*

Stoessel, Anatoly Mikhailovich, 220, 263
Stone, F. P., 436
Stotsenburg, Col. John M., 65–67, 87,
587, 624n4
Straight, William, 226, 587–88
Strauss, Richard, 265
Strong, Mary, 323
Suárez, José María Pino, 330
Subanos (Subanon people), 279, 282–83
Sucre, Gen. Antonio de, 365
Sullivan, John L., 217–18
Sultan of Sulu, The (Ade), 666n2
sultans: in the governing structure
of Lake Lanao Moros, 637n4;
Pershing's relationship with and
pacification of, 163–67 (*see also* Moro
pacification)
Sulu, Sultan of, 454
Sulu Archipelago (Philippines), 141–44
Sulu Moros, 295–302
Sumner, Col. Edwin V., 74, 588
Sumner, Brig. Gen. Samuel S.:
command of the Southwestern
Division, 214; in London, 130; Moro
pacification and, 168, 169, 173, 175,
178, 194, 403, 407, 441; orders for
the April 1903 Moro pacification
expedition, 431–32; orders for
the May 1903 Moro pacification
expedition around Lake Lanao,
444–45; orders for the September
18–22, 1902 Moro pacification
expedition, 413–14; orders for the
September–October 1902 Moro
pacification expedition, 421–22; in
the Spanish-American War, 115,
117, 372; visits to Pershing at Camp
Vicars, 184–85, *191*
Sunderland, 1st Lt. A. H., 407, 408, 415
surra, 186, 644n7
sutlers, 16, 617n10
Swift, Lt. Innis Palmer, 317, 447, 589–90
Swobe, Thomas, *141*

Tacna-Arica mission, 1, 365–66, 678n2
tactical officers, 48, 50, 622n6; Pershing
as, 96–97

Taft, William Howard: Baguio resort and, 253; elected president, 268; Emperor Meiji's funeral, 319; "goodwill tour" of Asia, 238–39, 651–52n12; as the governor-general of the Philippines, 128, 647n11; Inaugural Ball, 268–69; Arthur MacArthur and, 547; Frank McCoy and, 550; Pershing's assignment as the military attaché to Tokyo and, 215; policy toward Mexico, 330; presidential aspirations, 252–53; selects Charles Magoon as the governor-general of Cuba, 128; visits to the Philippines, 238, 250–53

Taglibi Moros, 289–95

Taiping rebellion, 208

Talub (Philippines), 416, 420

Tampico (Mexico), 331, 332

Tampogao of Tuburan, 443

Tanandundan, 164

Tanculan (Philippines), 276–77

Tangul, 169–70, 396–97

Taraca (Moro fort), 403, 437–40

Taraca Moros, 181, 199–202

Taraca River, battle of, 199–201, 403, 437–40, 646n9

Tauagan (Moro fort), 412–13

Tauagan, Sultan of, 179, 398, 412, 418

Tawi-Tawi Island (Philippines), 148

Tenth Cavalry Regiment: Henry Adair's service with, 465; Theodore Baldwin and, 471–72; Malvern Barnum and, 473; battle of San Juan Heights, 112–19, 374–78; William Brown and, 485; George Dodd and, 504; duty in Montana, 88–94; Ellwood Evans and, 509; Letcher Hardeman and, 525; health conditions in Cuba and return to the United States, 121, 122; Guy Henry and, 531; history of, 627–28n7; Las Guasimas engagement, 110, 370–72; Mexican Punitive Expedition, 341, 342, 344, 353, 357–59, 461–64; movement to Cuba, 103, 105–8; Pershing rejoins at the beginning of the Spanish-American War, 102–3, *104*; Walter Short and, 585; Frank Tompkins and, 591; Theodore Wint and, 602

Tenth Infantry Regiment, 176, 530

Tenth Volunteer Infantry, 544

Terauchi Masatake, Gen., 222

Teusler, Rudolf B., 241, 590

Thackara, Alexander M., 265

Thayer, John M., 64, 590–91

Third Cavalry Regiment, 116

Third Infantry Regiment, 284, 448–50

Thirteenth Cavalry Regiment: Mexican Punitive Expedition, 341, 348–49, 351, 353; Pancho Villa's attack on, 335–36

Thirteenth Infantry Regiment, 56, 60, 117, 655n4

Thirty-first Volunteer Infantry Regiment, 144

Thompson, Anne Elizabeth, 13–14. *See also* Pershing, Anne Elizabeth (née Thompson)

Thompson, L. A., 14

Thunder Bull, 78

Thurston, John M., 95, 591

Tiehling (Manchuria), *237*

Tillman, Samuel E., 48, 591

Tirurais, 280, 313

Tokyo (Japan), 319–22

Tomochic (Mexico), 354

Tompkins, Maj. Frank, 335, 348, 349, 351, 591–92

Toral y Velázquez, Gen. José, 119, 120, 380

Toros, Sultan of, 388

Torres, Tomas, 408, 424, 436, 443

Tours (France), 266–67, 366

Tower of London, 131

Townsend, 1st Lt. Charles B., 298, 455, 592

Treaty of Ancón, 366, 678n2

Trevino, Gen. J. B., 356–57

Triple Alliance, 266, 658n6

Trotsky, Leon, 264

Tsushima, Battle of, 220

Tuba City, Ariz., 65

Tugayan Moros, 198

Tulawie, Arolas (Maas Arola Tulawi), 285
Tundia, 427
Tupper, Maj. Tullius C., 75, 77, 592–93
Twain, Mark, 49
Twelfth Infantry Regiment, 327, 377
Twenty-eighth Volunteer Infantry Regiment, 145–46, 198
Twenty-seventh Infantry Regiment: operations against the Lake Lanao Moros in 1902, 155, 159–60, 175–81; operations against the Lake Lanao Moros in 1903, 194–202, 646n9
Twenty-third Infantry Regiment, 144
typhoid epidemics, 106
typhoons, 187

Uali, 171, 396–98, 408
Umezawa Brigade, 233
Umezawa Michiharu, Gen., 233
United States Army: brevet rank, 621n4; failure to adopt the airplane, 267; Fetterman massacre, 78, 624–26n2; General Staff, 212–14; guidons, 622–23n9; military occupation of acquisitions following the Spanish-American War, 127–28; Pershing on discipline in the army, 91; reorganization and modernization, 214, 496, 636–37n3; state prior to the Spanish-American War, 100–101 (see also Spanish-American War); strength in the 1890s, 85, 100; sutlers, 16, 617n10; Volunteer Regiments, 635–36n1 (see also Volunteer Regiments)
University of Nebraska, 81–87
Utah (U.S. battleship), 365

Vandiver, Frank, 5
Van Natta, 1st Lt. Thomas F., Jr.: biographical information, 593; Bud Bagsak operation, 298–300, 301, 455, 457–59
Vedic gods, 279, 661n6
Venice (Italy), 133
Vera Cruz (Mexico), 331

Vicars, Lt. Thomas A., 161, 593, 639n5
Vielé, Lt. Col. Charles D., 106, 594
Villa, Francisco "Pancho": attack on Gen. Calles at Agua Prieta, 669–70n6; Pablo López and, 350, 674–75n12; in Mexican politics, 331; Nogales meeting with Pershing, 337–38, 670–71n10; Pershing's Mexican expedition in pursuit of (see Mexican Punitive Expedition); raid on Columbus, New Mexico, 335–36, 339, 591–92; turns against America, 333–34
Vincent, Capt. Berkeley, 223
vintas, 153, 181–82
Volunteer Regiments: in the Philippines, 144–46, 635–36n1; in the Spanish-American War, 106, 368. See also First Volunteer Cavalry Regiment ("Rough Riders")
von Etzel, Maj. Günther, 227, 230, 594, 651n10
von Gyarmata, Maj. Adalbert Dáni, 229, 595

Wagner, Richard, 265
Walapai (Hualapai) Indians, 67
Waldron, Lt. Albert E., 655n4
War College, 214–15
Warren, Francis E., 216, 239, 244, 323, 595–96
Warren, Frederick E., 239, 596
Warren, Helen Frances. See Pershing, Helen Frances (née Warren)
Warsaw (Poland), 263–64
Washington, George, 132
Washington Herald, 244
Washington Treaty, 211, 649n4
water buffalo, 146
Waterloo battlefield, 265–66
Weed, Capt. Frank W., 311, 596–97
Weeks, Charles W., 87, 597
Weihai (China), 123, 634n4
West, Col. Frank, 284, 289, 447, 578, 597–98
West, Capt. Parker, 221, 598
Westermann, William L., 87, 598–99

Western Reserve, 11, 615n1
Westminster Abbey, 131
Weston, Maj. Gen. John F., 118, 246–47, 599
West Point: George Andrews and, 469; Edgar Bass and, 474–75; First Year class, 48–51; Fourth Class year, 39–44; Graduation Day, 51, 622n8; Herman Koehler and, 540; Wesley Merritt and, 555; Albert Mills and, 557; number of cadets admitted in 1886, 620–21n3; organization of, 622n6; Pershing as an instructor in tactics and tactical officer, 96–97; Pershing on the importance of, 50–51; Pershing's choice of the Sixth Cavalry, 51–52; Pershing's pursuit of an appointment to, 36–39; portrait of Pershing as a cadet, 47; Second Class year, 46, 48; Third Class year, 44–46; Samuel Tillman and, 591
Weygandt, Maria Elizabeth, 12
Weyler y Nicolau, Gen. Valeriano, 98–99
Wheeler, Maj. Gen. Joseph, 106, 109, 115, 371, 374, 599–600
Whitney, Brig. Gen. Henry H., 6–7, 277–78, 600–601
Whitside, Maj. Samuel M., 75, 601
wild boar, 164
Wilder, Col. Wilbur E., 353, 602
Wild West Show, 63, 325, 326
Williams, Col. Charles A., 661n7
Wilson, Woodrow: in Europe after the Armistice, 363; policy toward Mexico, 329, 330, 332–33, 354, 360; recommends Philippine independence, 316
Winning of the West, The (Roosevelt), 94, 628n9
Wint, Maj. Theodore J., 117, 602–3, 652–53n15
Winter, Capt. Francis A., 118, 603
Winter Palace (St. Petersburg), 263
wire entanglements, 232
Wisser, Col. John, 264–65, 603–4
Wood, Gen. Leonard: Fred Ainsworth

and, 467; John Brooke and, 483; career and biographical information, 246, 604–5; Frank McCoy and, 550; military governor of Cuba, 128; Pershing and, 246; in the Philippines, 203, 246–48, 280, 661n7, 662n10, 663–64n6; promotion to brigadier general, 244; in the Spanish-American War, 106, 110, 114, 116, 117; John Weston and, 247
Woodbury, Col. Thomas C., 661n7
Worcester, Dean, 277, 605
World's Fair of 1893, 85
Wounded Knee campaign, 72–77, 512, 556
Wright, 1st Lt. George H., 298, 454–55, 605–6
Wright, Wilbur, 266–67
Wright, William M., 43, 606
Wright (U.S. transport ship), 297–98, 454, 455

Yakans, 280
Yamagata Aritomo, Field Marshal, 222
Yates, Halsey E., 85, 606–7
Yoquivo (Mexico), 354
Yoshimatsu Motaro, Rear Admiral, 250
Young, Brig. Gen. Samuel B. M., 106–10, 607–8
Young Turks, 278, 660n5

Zamboanga: disarmament of the Moros, 289; Fifteenth Cavalry at, 148–49; improvements in medical and health care, 311; improvements in public works, 310; improvements in trade and markets, 307; Pershing's departure from, 323; Pershing's description of, 140–43; Pershing's personal and family life at, 271–77; Thirty-first Volunteer Infantry at, 144
Zamboanga Fair, 311–14
Zapata, Emiliano, 331–32
Zuni Indians, 59–60, 64–65